Cases and Materials on Criminal Law

Cases and Materials on
Criminal Law

Sixth Edition

Janet Dine
Professor of Law, Queen Mary, University of London

James Gobert
Professor of Criminal Law, University of Essex

William Wilson
Professor of Criminal Law, Queen Mary, University of London

OXFORD
UNIVERSITY PRESS

OXFORD

UNIVERSITY PRESS

Great Clarendon Street, Oxford OX2 6DP

Oxford University Press is a department of the University of Oxford.
It furthers the University's objective of excellence in research, scholarship,
and education by publishing worldwide in

Oxford New York

Auckland Cape Town Dar es Salaam Hong Kong Karachi
Kuala Lumpur Madrid Melbourne Mexico City Nairobi
New Delhi Shanghai Taipei Toronto

With offices in

Argentina Austria Brazil Chile Czech Republic France Greece
Guatemala Hungary Italy Japan Poland Portugal Singapore
South Korea Switzerland Thailand Turkey Ukraine Vietnam

Oxford is a registered trade mark of Oxford University Press
in the UK and in certain other countries

Published in the United States
by Oxford University Press Inc., New York

© J. Dine, J. Gobert, and W. Wilson, 2011

Third edition, 2000
Fourth edition, 2003
Fifth edition, 2006

British Library Cataloguing in Publication Data
Data available

Library of Congress Cataloging in Publication Data
Data available

Typeset by Newgen Imaging Systems (P) Ltd, Chennai, India

Printed in Great Britain by Bell & Bain Ltd, Glasgow

ISBN 978-0-19-954198-0

5 7 9 10 8 6 4

OUTLINE CONTENTS

DETAILED CONTENTS

PREFACE

This sixth edition of *Cases and Materials on Criminal Law* has been written during a period of significant political and legal ferment in the UK. The Human Rights Act 1998, which came into force on 2 October 2000, is having an ever increasing influence, primarily in regard to criminal procedure but also in respect of the substantive criminal law. So too have treaties and directives of the EU, and cases decided by the European Court of Justice. In addition, there is the now-to-be-expected annual deluge of new legislation from Parliament and cases of note from the judiciary.

Although the substantive materials contained in this volume have changed to reflect new and pending legislation, as well as cases decided since publication of the previous edition, our philosophical approach to the teaching of criminal law has not changed. As we explained in the preface to the first edition, our goal is both to impart substantive knowledge and to teach the skills needed to be a successful lawyer or judge.

Most of the criminal law (with a few notable exceptions) is contained in statutes. Ambiguities can arise both because of the inherent indeterminacy of language and because it is impossible for Parliament, in drafting criminal statutes, to envisage the myriad factual guises of future cases. The successful lawyer needs to be able to read a statute with a critical eye, break the statute down into its component elements, and understand what each element requires in the way of proof.

In addition to statutory analysis skills, the successful lawyer needs to be able to identify the legal issues raised by a factual situation. This requires a careful sifting through the facts, a determination of which facts have legal significance, and an identification of the legal issues raised by these facts. For these reasons we have strived to include as many of the facts of each case as possible, although space limitations have somewhat impaired our ability to do so. (Space limitations have also precluded exploration of the many fascinating questions of procedure and evidence which permeate the criminal law.)

The purpose of the Notes and Questions that appear throughout the book is to raise issues and stimulate the student's thinking. The questions are of a type that would be considered by solicitors, barristers and judges, and thus form a part of the process of 'learning to think like a lawyer'. One should not accept uncritically judicial assumptions and pronouncements; judicial reasoning is not above criticism. In the Notes and Questions we seek to call attention to issues that may have been left unaddressed in a court's decision or which may have been inadequately answered by the court. Such issues are likely to arise in future cases. We also attempt to probe the not always obvious implications of judicial decisions. It should be observed that the Notes and Questions presented are not intended to be exhaustive but rather designed to spur the student's own critical thinking about the law.

The book is divided into four Parts. Part I seeks to identify and present fundamental principles of criminal liability and to introduce the student to basic criminal law concepts. While Chapter 1 might strike some as more appropriate to a course in philosophy or criminology, we believe that an appreciation of issues relating to such matters as criminalisation, human rights, grading of offences and theories of punishment is critically important. At the heart of the criminal law are fundamental questions about the values of a society, and the balance which that society has struck between individual freedom and social control.

In Part II we examine specific offences, primarily those against persons (murder, manslaughter, assault, battery, and rape) and property (theft, offences of deception, and related offences). It is impossible in a basic Criminal Law text to examine the tens of thousands of crimes now on the statute books, but the crimes we have selected are generally considered to be the most serious. Further, we anticipate that the skills used in analysing these crimes should be generalisable and transferable to other offences, including those which have yet to be enacted.

In Part III we examine various doctrines and defences that allow defendants to escape from the net of criminal liability. Lastly, in Part IV we examine how the law has been extended backwards in time to criminalise pre-crime actions (encouragement, assistance, conspiracy and attempt) and expanded outward in scope to ensnare persons other than the actor who commits the actual offence.

We wish to acknowledge, among others, the permissions received from Oxford University Press, Sweet & Maxwell, Butterworths, and the Incorporated Council for Law Reporting for England and Wales. We also wish to express our appreciation to the many readers of the previous editions who took the time to offer constructive comments. We have attempted to take account of these comments in the preparation of the present volume. We are indebted to the excellent research assistance of Annette Abanulo and Marios Kotsias. We are also grateful to our colleagues, Fernne Brennan and Sabine Michalowski, for their contributions to our analysis of, respectively, racially aggravated crimes and necessity.

Janet Dine, James Gobert and William Wilson
15 May 2010

ACKNOWLEDEGMENTS

The authors and publishers would like to thank the following for permission to reproduce copyright material:

Crown Copyright material is reproduced under Class Licence Number C2006010631 with the permission of OPSI and the Queen's Printer for Scotland.

The Incorporated Council of Law Reporting for England and Wales for extracts from the following Reports: *Appeal Cases* (AC), *Kings Bench Reports* (KB), *Queen's Bench Reports* (QB) and *Weekly Law Reports* (WLR).

Jordons for extracts from *Family Law Reports* (FLR).

Oxford University Press for extracts from N. Walker: *Crime and Criminology* (1987), A Ashworth: *Principles of Criminal Law* 2e (1995) and Grant Lamond *What is a Crime?* (2007) Oxford Journal of Legal Studies.

Reed Elsevier (UK) Limited trading as LexisNexis for extracts from *All England Law Reports* (All ER) and *Butterworths Company Law Cases* (BCLC)

Sweet and Maxwell Ltd for extracts from *European Human Rights Reports* (EHRR), *Common Market Law Reports* (CMLR) *Criminal Appeal Reports* (Cr App R), *Criminal Law Review* (CrimLR) and *Road Traffic Reports* (RTR)

University of Pennsylvania Law Review for extracts from J Andreas *The General Preventative Effects of Punishment* (1966)

The British Academy for extracts from the 1960 Maccabean Lecture by The Hon. Sir Patrick Devlin: *The Enforcement of Morals* published in *Proceedings of the British Academy, Volume ILV* (1959)

Every effort has been made to trace and contact copyright holders but this has not been possible in all cases. If notified, the publisher will undertake to rectify any errors or omissions at the earliest opportunity.

TABLE OF CASES

Page references in **bold** indicate extract material

TABLE OF STATUTES

Page references in **bold** indicate extract material

International Legislation

Canada

France

Hong Kong

India

Italy

Singapore

Table of European Union Secondary Legislation

Directives

Decisions

■ NOTES AND QUESTIONS

1. Crime is often said to be on the increase, but what does this mean? To some extent an increase in crime merely reflects an increase in the number of criminal laws. In theory we could 'solve' the 'crime problem' by doing away with all criminal laws. But this is not suggested seriously (although Marxist philosophy did envisage an ultimate utopia in which criminal law would be unnecessary). Why not? If criminal laws were to be eliminated, with what might they be replaced in order to protect the citizenry from harm?

2. Is it better to err on the side of over- or under-inclusiveness when it comes to criminalisation? If too broad a spectrum of human behaviour is made illegal, the inevitable result will be that many citizens will find themselves ensnared in the net of the criminal law, with the concomitant stigma of a criminal conviction. Is this desirable? The criminal law is a last, rather than a first, resort, to be employed only when all other means of addressing the social problem at issue have been exhausted. See D. Husak (2007).

3. Is a practical solution to over-criminalisation to have a large number of criminal offences on the books but to enforce only the most important of them? The law on the books would stand as a statement of the principles and values for which the society stands, and as a safety net to allow prosecutions in egregious cases. The decision not to prosecute would protect citizens who commit technical offences but who are not morally blameworthy. The prosecutor could be given discretion to proceed with formal charges only in those cases where the defendant's blameworthiness was manifest. What are the merits and demerits of such an approach?

If the criminalisation process is to become more rational and less haphazard, the challenge facing law-makers is to develop general criteria and principles which can be employed in determining whether or not to make conduct criminal. Legislators are not necessarily averse to a principled approach. In response to a question from Lord Dholakia, Lord Williams of Mostyn, the then Minister of State at the Home Office, indicated that it was the Labour Government's policy that offences 'should be created only when absolutely necessary', and that:

> In considering whether new offences should be created, factors taken into account include whether:
> — the behaviour in question is sufficiently serious to warrant intervention by the criminal law;
> — the mischief could be dealt with under existing legislation or by using other remedies;
> — the proposed offence is enforceable in practice;
> — the proposed offence is tightly drawn and legally sound; and
> — the proposed penalty is commensurate with the seriousness of the offence.
>
> The Government also takes into account the need to ensure, as far as practicable, that there is consistency across the sentencing framework.
>
> (HL Deb, vol. 602, WA 57 (18 June, 1999) quoted in Ashworth, 'Is the Criminal Law a Lost Cause' (2000) 116 LQR 225 at p. 229, who questions whether these criteria are followed in practice.)

What are arguably needed are general principles of inclusion and exclusion, i.e., principles which would advise the law-maker as to what should be made criminal (e.g., actions which cause or threaten physical harm to others should be made criminal) and principles that counsel against criminalisation (e.g., it is inadvisable to criminalise conduct which is approved of and engaged in by the vast majority of the citizenry). The following is an attempt by one noted criminologist to identify such principles:

N. Walker, *Crime and Criminology*

(1987)

(i) Objectives of the criminal law

Is it possible to discuss the proper content of the criminal law in general terms? If the contents of criminal codes are examined with a sociological eye, no fewer than fourteen different objectives can be discerned:

    (a) the protection of human persons (and to some extent animals also) against intentional violence, cruelty, or unwelcome sexual approaches;

    (b) the protection of people against some forms of unintended harm (for example from traffic, poisons, infections, radiation);

    (c) the protection of easily persuadable classes of people (that is, the young or the weak-minded) against the abuse of their persons or property (for example by sexual intercourse or hire-purchase);

    (d) the prevention of acts which, even if the participants are adult and willing, are regarded as 'unnatural' (for example incest, sodomy, bestiality, drug 'trips');

    (e) the prevention of acts which, though not included under any of the previous headings, are performed so publicly as to shock other people (for example public nakedness, obscene language, or heterosexual copulation between consenting adults);

    (f) the discouragement of behaviour which might provoke disorder (such as insulting words at a public meeting);

    (g) the protection of property against theft, fraud, or damage;

    (h) the prevention of inconvenience (for example the obstruction of roads by vehicles);

    (i) the collection of revenue (for example keeping a motor car or television set without a licence);

    (j) the defence of the State (for example espionage or—in some countries—political criticism);

    (k) the enforcement of compulsory benevolence (for example the offence of failing to send one's children to school);

    (l) the protection of social institutions, such as marriage or religious worship (for example by prohibiting bigamy or blasphemy);

    (m) the prevention of unreasonable discrimination (for example against ethnic groups, religions, the female sex);

    (n) the enforcement of the processes regarded as essential to these other purposes (for example offences connected with arrest, assisting offenders to escape conviction, and testimony at trials).

(ii) Moral limits

Now and again there have been attempts to formulate what might be called 'limiting principles', which declare that the criminal law should *not* be used for certain purposes, or in certain circumstances.

The oldest seems to be

    (A) Prohibitions should not be included in the criminal law for the sole purpose of ensuring that breaches of them are visited with retributive punishment.

and exploitation; the law must protect also the institutions and the community of ideas, political and moral, without which people cannot live together. Society cannot ignore the morality of the individual any more than it can his loyalty; it flourishes on both and without either it dies....

I return now to the main thread of my argument and summarise it. Society cannot live without morals. Its morals are those standards of conduct which the reasonable man approves. A rational man, who is also a good man, may have other standards. If he has no standards at all he is not a good man and need not be further considered. If he has standards, they may be very different; he may, for example, not disapprove of homosexuality or abortion. In that case he will not share in the common morality; but that should not make him deny that it is a social necessity. A rebel may be rational in thinking that he is right but he is irrational if he thinks that society can leave him free to rebel.

A man who concedes that morality is necessary to society must support the use of those instruments without which morality cannot be maintained. The two instruments are those of teaching, which is doctrine, and of enforcement, which is the law. If morals could be taught simply on the basis that they are necessary to society, there would be no social need for religion; it could be left as a purely personal affair. But morality cannot be taught in that way. Loyalty is not taught in that way either. No society has yet solved the problem of how to teach morality without religion. So the law must base itself on Christian morals and to the limit of its ability enforce them, not simply because they are the morals of most of us, nor simply because they are the morals which are taught by the established Church—on these points the law recognises the right to dissent—but for the compelling reason that without the help of Christian teaching the law will fail.

H. L. A. Hart, *Law, Liberty, and Morality*
(1963)

Both in England and in America the criminal law still contains rules which can only be explained as attempts to enforce morality as such: to suppress practices condemned as immoral by positive morality though they involve nothing that would ordinarily be thought of as harm to other persons....

I shall start with an example stressed by Lord Devlin. He points out that, subject to certain exceptions such as rape, the criminal law has never admitted the consent of the victim as a defence. It is not a defence to a charge of murder or a deliberate assault, and this is why euthanasia or mercy killing terminating a man's life at his own request is still murder. This is a rule of criminal law which many now would wish to retain, though they would also wish to object to the legal punishment of offences against positive morality which harm no one. Lord Devlin thinks that these attitudes are inconsistent, for he asserts of the rule under discussion, 'There is only one explanation,' and this is that 'there are certain standards of behaviour or moral principles which society requires to be observed'....

But this argument is not really cogent, for Lord Devlin's statement that 'there is only one explanation' is simply not true. The rules excluding the victim's consent as a defence to charges of murder or assault may perfectly well be explained as a piece of paternalism, designed to protect individuals against themselves.... [P]aternalism—the protection of people against themselves—is a perfectly coherent policy. Indeed, it seems very strange in mid-twentieth century to insist upon this, for the wane of laissez faire since Mill's day is one of the commonplaces of social history, and instances of paternalism now abound in our law, criminal and civil. The supply of drugs or narcotics, even to adults, except under medical prescription is punishable by the criminal law, and it would seem very dogmatic to say of the law creating this offence that 'there is only one explanation,' namely, that the law was concerned not with the protection of the would-be purchasers against themselves, but only with the punishment of the seller for his immorality. If, as seems obvious, paternalism is a possible explanation of such laws, it is also possible in the case of the rule excluding the consent of the victim as a defence to a charge of assault. In neither case are we forced to conclude with Lord Devlin that the law's 'function' is 'to enforce a moral principle and nothing else'....

According to the moderate thesis, a shared morality is the cement of society; without it there would be aggregates of individuals but no society. 'A recognised morality' is, in Lord Devlin's words, 'as necessary to society's existence as a recognised government,' and though a particular act of immorality may not harm or endanger or corrupt others nor, when done in private, either shock or give offence to others, this does not conclude the matter. For we must not view conduct in isolation from its effect on the moral code: if we remember this, we can see that one who is 'no menace to others' nonetheless may by his immoral conduct 'threaten one of the great moral principles on which society is based.' In this sense the breach of moral principle is an offence 'against society as a whole,' and society may use the law to preserve its morality as it uses it to safeguard anything else essential to its existence. This is why 'the suppression of vice is as much the law's business as the suppression of subversive activities'....

Lord Devlin appears to defend the moderate thesis. I say 'appears' because, though he says that society has the right to enforce a morality as such on the ground that a shared morality is essential to society's existence, it is not at all clear that for him the statement that immorality jeopardises or weakens society is a statement of empirical fact. It seems sometimes to be an *a priori* assumption, and sometimes a necessary truth and a very odd one. The most important indication that this is so is that, apart from one vague reference to 'history' showing that 'the loosening of moral bonds is often the first stage of disintegration,' no evidence is produced to show that deviation from accepted sexual morality, even by adults in private, is something which, like treason, threatens the existence of society. No reputable historian has maintained this thesis, and there is indeed much evidence against it. As a proposition of fact it is entitled to no more respect than the Emperor Justinian's statement that homosexuality was the cause of earthquakes. Lord Devlin's belief in it, and his apparent indifference to the question of evidence, are at points traceable to an undiscussed assumption. This is that all morality—sexual morality together with the morality that forbids acts injurious to others such as killing, stealing, and dishonesty—forms a single seamless web, so that those who deviate from any part are likely or perhaps bound to deviate from the whole. It is of course clear (and one of the oldest insights of political theory) that society could not exist without a morality which mirrored and supplemented the law's proscription of conduct injurious to others. But there is again no evidence to support, and much to refute, the theory that those who deviate from conventional sexual morality are in other ways hostile to society.

There seems, however, to be central to Lord Devlin's thought something more interesting, though no more convincing, than the conception of social morality as a seamless web. For he appears to move from the acceptable proposition that *some* shared morality is essential to the existence of any society to the unacceptable proposition that a society is identical with its morality as that is at any given moment of its history, so that a change in its morality is tantamount to the destruction of a society. The former proposition might be even accepted as a necessary rather than an empirical truth depending on a quite plausible definition of society as a body of men who hold certain moral views in common. But the latter proposition is absurd. Taken strictly, it would prevent us saying that the morality of a given society had changed, and would compel us instead to say that one society had disappeared and another one taken its place. But it is only on this absurd criterion of what it is for the same society to continue to exist that it could be asserted without evidence that any deviation from a society's shared morality threatens its existence.

It is clear that only this tacit identification of a society with its shared morality supports Lord Devlin's denial that there could be such a thing as private immorality and his comparison of sexual immorality, even when it takes place 'in private,' with treason. No doubt it is true that if deviations from conventional sexual morality are tolerated by the law and come to be known, the conventional morality might change in a permissive direction, though this does not seem to be the case with homosexuality in those European countries where it is not punishable by law. But even if the conventional morality did so change, the society in question would not have been destroyed or 'subverted'. We should compare such a development not to the violent overthrow of government but to a peaceful constitutional change in its form, consistent not only with the preservation of a society but with its advance.

...A very great difference is apparent between inducing persons through fear of punishment to abstain from actions which are harmful to others, and inducing them to abstain from actions which deviate from accepted morality but harm no one. The value attached to the first is easy to understand; for the protection of human beings from murder or violence or other forms of injury remains good whatever the motives are by which others are induced to abstain from these crimes. But where there is no harm to be prevented and no potential victim to be protected, as is often the case where conventional sexual morality is disregarded, it is difficult to understand the assertion that conformity, even if motivated merely by fear of the law's punishment, is a value worth pursuing, notwithstanding the misery and sacrifice of freedom which it involves...Lord Devlin assumes that the society to which his doctrine is to apply is marked by a considerable degree of moral solidarity, and is deeply disturbed by infringements of its moral code. Just as for Lord Devlin the morality to be enforced by law must be 'public', in the sense that it is generally shared and identifiable by the triple marks of 'intolerance, indignation, and disgust,' so for Stephen 'you cannot punish anything which public opinion as expressed in the common practice of society does not strenuously and unequivocally condemn...To be able to punish a moral majority must be overwhelming'. It is possible that in mid-Victorian England these conditions were satisfied in relation to 'that considerable number of acts' which according to Stephen were treated as crimes merely because they were regarded as grossly immoral. Perhaps an 'overwhelming moral majority' then actually did harbour the healthy desire for revenge of which he speaks and which is to be gratified by the punishment of the guilty. But it would be sociologically naïve to assume that these conditions obtain in contemporary England at least as far as sexual morality is concerned. The fact that there is lip service to an official sexual morality should not lead us to neglect the possibility that in sexual, as in other matters, there may be a number of mutually tolerant moralities, and that even where there is some homogeneity of practice and belief, offenders may be viewed not with hatred or resentment but with amused contempt or pity.

In a sense, therefore, Stephen's doctrine, and much of Lord Devlin's, may seem to hover in the air above the *terra firma* of contemporary social reality; it may be a well-articulated construction, interesting because it reveals the outlook characteristic of the English judiciary but lacking application to contemporary society....

■ NOTES AND QUESTIONS

1. Is Hart correct when he asserts that there is no such thing as a moral consensus? Are moral judgements like tastes in food, there being no right or wrong but only personal preferences?

2. If society does have a common morality, how is its content to be ascertained? What is Devlin's answer? Of what relevance might be an opinion poll? What if it turns out that popular opinion is based on stereotypes?

3. Is the State not entitled to show moral leadership such that, irrespective of the views of the majority, certain values are appropriately underpinned through coercive law? See Wilson (2011) 2.2.

4. Of what relevance are the practical problems that might arise from trying to enforce a law? For example, may not the law as a practical matter be powerless to enforce a prohibition against homosexual conduct? The conduct typically occurs in private, the participants are not about to report their activities to the police, the authorities may be unwilling to spare the resources necessary to conduct an investigation on the ground that there are more pressing offences to be investigated, and there is something terribly unseemly about, for example, spying on a men's toilet in order to catch violators. Should such considerations be taken into account in making the criminalisation decision? If the government decides to prohibit an activity, does it thereby commit itself to whatever resources may be necessary to enforce its law?

SECTION 2: WHAT IS A CRIME?

A: Relevant considerations

How can one tell whether or not one is dealing with a 'crime'? This is a critical question because it will determine not only the potential consequences of failing to abide by the relevant law, but also the procedures which will be followed if there is to be a trial. Indeed, the latter point was given prominence by Glanville Williams in his conception of a crime as an act capable of being followed by criminal proceedings (Williams, 'The Definition of Crime' [1955] *Current Legal Problems* 107). A more subtle analysis is given by Lamont:

G. Lamont
(2007) Oxford Journal of Legal Studies 609

There are many answers to the question 'what is a crime?' To a practising lawyer, a crime is anything prohibited under the criminal law—the criminal law being that branch of law dealing with state punishment. Yet, as many legal commentators point out, not all state punishments are part of the criminal law—civil penalties and civil contempt of court are just two examples. A more accurate test of the scope of the criminal law lies in its adjectival incidents, i.e. in the distinctive ways in which criminal *proceedings* differ from civil proceedings. Briefly put, a legal prohibition is a criminal prohibition when it is subject to criminal proceedings. What characterizes proceedings as criminal are such things as the type of bodies having jurisdiction over the matter (the Crown Court, magistrates courts), the manner in which the proceeding can be commenced (charge, information), the rules of evidence employed (standard of proof, rules on admissibility), and the types of outcome to which the proceeding may give rise (conviction, sentence). The scope of the criminal law can only be set in adjectival terms because there is simply too much variety in the content of those things subject to criminal prohibition. Almost anything can be prohibited under the criminal law, and so there is no substantive unity of the kind found, for example, in contract law.

Another answer to 'What is a crime?' is provided by criminologists. They emphasize the need for a broader, social context. Crimes are not simply artificial creations of the law, like a *cestui que trust*, or a negative covenant. Instead, criminal law has a crucial social dimension. A successful prosecution does not simply result in a defendant being held liable for the breach of a legal prohibition—instead she is *convicted* of committing a *crime*—she is found *guilty* of the *charge* against her. These are socially expressive terms. The criminal law serves an important condemnatory function in social life—it marks out some behaviour as specially reprehensible, so that the machinery of the state needs to be mobilized against it. An account of crime that restricted its attention to the doctrinal analysis of lawyers, then, would miss out on a crucial dimension that helps to explain both the social significance of liability and the use made by the state of criminal liability.

Under the jurisprudence of the European Court of Human Rights (ECtHR) (whose decisions must be taken into account by national courts under the HRA 1998), one must determine whether an offence or charge is criminal in order to determine what procedures will be applied. In making this determination, a court is not bound by the label or characterisation placed on the misconduct by Parliament. (See below, Chapter 11)

Benham v United Kingdom
(1996) 22 EHRR 293, ECtHR

On 1 April 1990 Mr Benham became liable to pay a community charge of £325. Since he did not pay it, on 21 August 1990 the Poole Magistrates' Court ordered the issue of a liability order, entitling Poole Borough Council ('the charging authority') to commence enforcement proceedings against him.

Mr Benham did not pay the amount owed, and bailiffs visited his parents' house (where he was living), but were told that he had no goods of any value there or elsewhere which could be seized by them and sold in order to pay the debt.

Under Regulation 41 of the Community Charge (Administration and Enforcement) Regulations 1989 if a person is found to have insufficient goods on which to levy outstanding community charge the charging authority may apply to a magistrates' court for an order committing him to prison. On such an application being made, the court must inquire in the presence of the debtor as to his present means and also whether his failure to pay which led to the liability order being made was due to wilful refusal or culpable neglect.

The charging authority applied for such an order, and on 25 March 1991 Mr Benham appeared at the Poole Magistrates' Court for the inquiry required by the Regulations.

He was not assisted or represented by a lawyer, although he was eligible for 'Green Form' legal advice and assistance before the hearing, and the magistrates could have made an order for Assistance by Way of Representation ('ABWOR') if they had thought it necessary.

The magistrates found that Mr Benham, who had 9 '0' level General Certificates of Secondary Education, had started a Government Employment Training Scheme in September 1989, but had left it in March 1990 and had not worked since. He had applied for income support, but had been turned down because it is not payable to those who are voluntarily unemployed, and he had no personal assets or income.

On the basis of this evidence, the magistrates concluded that his failure to pay the community charge was due to his culpable neglect, 'as he clearly had the potential to earn money to discharge his obligation to pay'. Accordingly, they decided that he ought to be sent to prison for thirty days unless he paid what was owing.

Mr Benham was taken to Dorchester prison on the same day.

. . .

The applicant, with whom the Commission agreed, argued that the proceedings before the magistrates involved the determination of a criminal charge for the purposes of Article 6(3)(c). He referred to the facts that what was in issue was not a dispute between individuals but rather liability to pay a tax to a public authority, and that the proceedings had many 'criminal' features, such as the safeguards available to defendants aged under 21, the severity of the applicable penalty and the requirement of a finding of culpability before a term of imprisonment could be imposed. Furthermore, it was by no means clear that the proceedings were classified as civil rather than criminal under the domestic law.

The Government argued that Article 6(3)(c) did not apply because the proceedings before the magistrates were civil rather than criminal in nature, as was borne out by the weight of the English case-law. The purpose of the detention was to coerce the applicant into paying the tax owed, rather than to punish him for not having paid it.

The case-law of the Court establishes that there are three criteria to be taken into account when deciding whether a person was 'charged with a criminal offence' for the purposes of Article 6. These are the classification of the proceedings under national law, the nature of the proceedings and the nature and degree of severity of the penalty.

As to the first of these criteria, the Court agrees with the Government that the weight of the domestic authority indicates that, under English law, the proceedings in question are regarded as civil rather than criminal in nature. However, this factor is of relative weight and serves only as a starting-point.

The second criterion, the nature of the proceedings, carries more weight. In this connection, the Court notes that the law concerning liability to pay the community charge and the procedure upon non-payment was of general application to all citizens, and that the proceedings in question were brought by a public authority under statutory powers of enforcement. In addition, the proceedings had some punitive elements. For example, the magistrates could only exercise their power of committal to prison on a finding of wilful refusal to pay or of culpable neglect.

Finally, it is to be recalled that the applicant faced a relatively severe maximum penalty of three months' imprisonment and was in fact ordered to be detained for thirty days.

Having regard to these factors, the Court concludes that Mr Benham was 'charged with a criminal offence' for the purposes of Article 6(1) and (3). Accordingly, these two paragraphs of Article 6 are applicable....

■ NOTES AND QUESTIONS

1. Of the three criteria identified in *Benham* as bearing on whether there is a criminal offence at issue, why is the characterisation of the offence by Parliament not given more weight? Why is the penalty accorded so much weight? In respect of the penalty, should the critical factor be the potential penalty to which the defendant could have been subjected or the actual penalty imposed in the case?

2. The importance that attaches from a determination that a defendant has been charged with a *criminal* offence is that the fair trial provisions of Article 6 of the ECHR must be observed. The criminal defendant is entitled to the presumption of innocence, prompt notice of the charges, adequate time and facilities for the preparation of a defence, legal assistance and the right to an interpreter if needed, the right to compel the attendance of witnesses and to cross-examine witnesses, and the right to be tried by an independent and impartial tribunal at a public hearing held within a reasonable time of the offence. Included in the right to legal assistance is the right to a free lawyer if required by the defendant's financial circumstances and the interests of justice.

B: Civil v criminal law

What are the differences between a civil suit and a criminal prosecution? Bearing in mind that the same facts can give rise to criminal liability, civil liability or both, let us examine the differences that typically will follow depending on whether a criminal prosecution or a civil action is brought.

Example

An absent-minded professor, while driving his automobile out of the university parking lot, hits a student. The student suffers serious injuries. There is, however, some question whether either the student or the professor was paying close attention to what the other was doing.

(i) Generally

Civil law is concerned with private rights; criminal law is concerned with public wrongs. Civil law is also primarily concerned with compensating the injured victim; criminal law is concerned with condemning and punishing the guilty

	Civil	*Criminal*
Initiator of suit	student	DPP, CPS
Victim	student	State
Title of case	Student v Professor	R v Professor
Fault standard	negligence	recklessness
Damage	harm to claimant	harm to State
Burden of proof	balance of probabilities	beyond reasonable doubt
Procedures	no jury; differing rules of evidence	jury possibility in serious cases
Remedies/sanctions	damages	fine/imprisonment/community service
Goal	compensate victim	punish offender

offender, and deterring others who would commit the offence. Both aim to redress past harms and shape future behaviour.

(ii) Who decides to bring the action?

In civil cases, it is for the victim to decide whether or not to bring suit. No State authority can force the victim to do so. In our example, a decision by Student to curry favour with Professor by not suing him might be considered crass but it would nonetheless be legally permissible. In criminal law, on the other hand, the decision to proceed is made by the State in its various guises. The police will decide whether to investigate, and thereafter whether to arrest or caution the offender or take no further action. The prosecutor, either the Director of Public Prosecutions (DPP) or, more typically, the Crown Prosecution Service (CPS), will decide whether formal charges should be brought. Technically, the desires of the victim are irrelevant to this decision, although often they may be taken into account as a practical matter.

(iii) Title of case

A criminal case is brought in the name of the Crown (*R* v *Defendant*), while a civil case is brought in the name of the injured party (*Claimant* v *Defendant*). The title of the case illustrates an important theoretical point about who is considered to be the aggrieved party. In our example it is Student who has been injured, but the titular victim in a criminal case is the State. Because the victim in the civil suit is the claimant, his negligence may be a relevant legal consideration. But in the criminal case the victim is the State; the contributory negligence of the person injured is irrelevant (although where the victim is largely at fault, the defendant may be able to argue that the victim's negligence was the *legal cause* of the injury).

(iv) Fault

Criminal law is primarily, although not exclusively, concerned with moral fault and blameworthiness. Civil law is more concerned with victim compensation. One consequence is that the legal system makes it easier for a civil claimant to recover than it does for the Crown to obtain a criminal conviction. In our example, Student will succeed in his civil suit if he can establish that Professor was negligent. To secure a conviction in a criminal court, the Crown will have to establish more than mere negligence, probably reckless or intentional misconduct.

(v) Damage

The goal of civil law is to provide compensation to an injured victim; in our example, if Student had not been injured, either physically or psychologically, there would be little point in a civil suit. In criminal law, however, it is not necessary that any person be injured. In our example Professor could be prosecuted for dangerous or careless driving even if he was fortunate enough to avoid hitting anybody. If he had intentionally tried to run down Student but failed, he could be charged with attempted murder.

(vi) Burden of proof

Another manifestation of the greater rigour demanded in criminal law is the higher burden of proof placed on the Crown. In order to secure a criminal conviction, the prosecution must establish its case by proof beyond reasonable doubt. In order to prevail in his civil case, Student would need only to establish his case by a balance of probabilities. Thus if a court or jury were to conclude that a defendant had probably committed the wrongful act alleged, but still had some reasonable doubts, it could return a verdict for a claimant in the civil case but would have to acquit in the criminal prosecution. Before imposing the stigma and sanctions (including imprisonment) of a criminal conviction, society wants to be sure that it is doing the right thing.

(vii) Difference in procedures

Beside the burden of proof, procedures are generally stricter in criminal cases than in civil cases. Again, the concern with the consequences of getting it wrong inclines the law to err on the side of caution in criminal cases. Rules of evidence differ, with the rules in criminal trials on the whole being more stringent. Furthermore, the defendant facing a serious criminal charge has the right to a jury trial. Jury trials are permitted in only a very small category of civil cases, and as a practical matter are extremely rare. In addition, the right of the State to appeal against a jury acquittal in a criminal case is more restricted than is the right of an unsuccessful civil claimant to appeal.

(viii) Remedies and sanctions

One of the key features which distinguishes criminal from civil law is the penalty attached to a verdict against the defendant. The criminal defendant can be sent to jail. In a civil case, the defendant will usually only have to pay money damages; the defendant's liberty is not in jeopardy. The amount of damages in a civil case is determined by the extent of the harm to the victim. The harm to the victim is not necessarily a critical variable in determining the length of sentence imposed on the convicted criminal defendant. Note that while one of the primary goals of both systems is to deter future would-be wrongdoers, civil damages may not be a sufficient deterrent to wealthy defendants. In these cases criminal sanctions may have greater effect. On the other hand, for many crimes the penalty is a relatively minor fine, but civil damages can run high if the victim has suffered serious injuries. In cases where corporate fault has resulted in, for example, an aeroplane crash, the civil penalty may be far in excess of the criminal fine. The two sets of remedies, in any event, are not mutually exclusive. In our example Professor can be made to pay damages in civil court and be sent to prison if convicted in a criminal trial. A feature of contemporary coercive law is the development of civil/criminal hybrid procedures such as ASBOs.

C: The sources of the criminal law

(i) The common law

Originally, the criminal law was developed by the courts. The courts set out general principles of criminal liability, established the specific elements of offences, and determined what defences should be permitted. This so-called 'common law' was not contained in any code or statute book but had to be distilled from the opinions of the courts. Today the common law of crimes has been largely, but not completely, displaced by statute. *But*:

(a) Certain crimes, most notably murder and manslaughter, have never been defined in statute. One needs to look at common law decisions in order to determine the elements of these crimes. Likewise, many defences have never been reduced to statute and retain their common law meaning.

(b) Often Parliament will use a term in a statute without defining it. There is, interestingly, no statutory definition of even such basic criminal law terms as 'intent' or 'recklessness'. On the other hand, there may be a well-settled meaning of the term in judicial decisions. It may have been Parliament's intent to preserve that meaning, in which case the judicial decisions will need to be consulted in order to determine that meaning. In the case of terms that are not given specific definition by Parliament, judges may resort to common law cases for guidance or may utilise techniques of interpretation embodied in common law decisions.

(c) Some common law crimes may still be in force:

Shaw v *Director of Public Prosecutions*
[1962] AC 220, House of Lords

The appellant published a booklet, the Ladies' Directory, of some 28 pages, most of which were taken up with the names and addresses of prostitutes; the matter published left no doubt that the advertisers could be got in touch with at the telephone numbers given and were offering their services for sexual intercourse and, in some cases, for the practice of sexual perversions. The appellant's avowed purpose in publication was to assist prostitutes to ply their trade when, as a result of the Street Offences Act 1959, they were no longer able to solicit in the street. The prostitutes paid for the advertisements and the appellant derived a profit from the publication. The appellant pleaded not guilty to an indictment charging him with (1) conspiracy to corrupt public morals in that he conspired with the advertisers and other persons by means of the Ladies' Directory and the advertisements to debauch and corrupt the morals of youth and other subjects of the Queen; (2) living on the earnings of prostitution contrary to s. 30 of the Sexual Offences Act 1956; and (3) publishing an obscene article contrary to s. 2 of the Obscene Publications Act 1959.

At the trial evidence was given by prostitutes that they had paid for the advertisements out of their earnings, that the advertisements were good at bringing clients in, and as to the ages of the persons resorting to them and the meaning of abbreviations and expressions in the advertisements; they also gave evidence of the practices in which they indulged and there was evidence by the police as to objects found at their addresses. The summing-up gave no direction to the jury as to the relevance of the appellant's honesty of purpose. The jury convicted the appellant. He appealed, on the ground, *inter alia*, that there was no such offence at common law as the conspiracy alleged.

VISCOUNT SIMONDS: My Lords, . . . the first count in the indictment is 'Conspiracy to corrupt public morals,' and the particulars of offence will have sufficiently appeared. I am concerned only to assert what was vigorously denied by counsel for the appellant, that such an offence is known to the common law, and that it was open to the jury to find on the facts of this case that the appellant was guilty of such an offence. I must say categorically that, if it were not so, Her Majesty's courts would strangely have failed in their duty as servants and guardians of the common law. Need I say, my Lords, that I am no advocate of the right of the judges to create new criminal offences? I will repeat well-known words:

> Amongst many other points of happiness and freedom which your Majesty's subjects have enjoyed there is none which they have accounted more dear and precious than this, to be guided and governed by certain rules of law which giveth both to the head and members that which of right belongeth to them and not by any arbitrary or uncertain form of government.

These words are as true today as they were in the seventeenth century and command the allegiance of us all. But I am at a loss to understand how it can be said either that the law does not recognise a conspiracy to corrupt public morals or that, though there may not be an exact precedent for such a conspiracy as this case reveals, it does not fall fairly within the general words by which it is described. . . . The fallacy in the argument that was addressed to us lay in the attempt to exclude from the scope of general words acts well calculated to corrupt public morals just because they had not been committed or had not been brought to the notice of the court before. It is not thus that the common law has developed. We are perhaps more accustomed to hear this matter discussed upon the question whether such and such a transaction is contrary to public policy. At once the controversy arises. On the one hand it is said that it is not possible in the twentieth century for the court to create a new head of public policy, on the other it is said that this is but a new example of a well-established head. In the sphere of criminal law I entertain no doubt that there remains in the courts of law a residual power to enforce the supreme and fundamental purpose of the law, to conserve not only the safety and order but also the moral welfare of the State and that it is their duty to guard it against attacks which may be the more insidious because they are novel and unprepared for . . . .

■ **NOTES AND QUESTIONS**

1. May only the courts repeal a common law crime which they created? Or should Parliament be able to do so? If Parliament fails to do so, should its inaction be taken as implicit approval of the common law crime?

2. After *Shaw* the question that remained was whether courts could create new common law crimes. The issue was addressed in *Knuller* v *Director of Public Prosecutions* [1973] AC 435, where the House of Lords purported to limit the judiciary's power to create new common law crimes. One might question whether it really matters, however, given the breadth of many of these offences. Take, for instance, the common law crime of 'outraging public decency', considered in the next case.

R v *Gibson and Another*

[1991] 1 All ER 439, Court of Appeal

The first defendant exhibited at an exhibition in a commercial art gallery run by the second defendant a model's head to which were attached earrings made out of freeze-dried human foetuses. The exhibit was entitled 'Human Earrings'. The gallery was open to, and was visited by, members of the public. The defendants were charged with, and convicted of, outraging public decency contrary to common law.

LORD LANE CJ: The article in question was one of 41 items which had been selected for display out of a much larger number by Sylveire. It was exhibit number 9, and was described in the catalogue as 'Human Earrings'.

Although it was not suggested that Sylveire had taken active steps to publicise this particular exhibit, there was no doubt that the more people who attended the gallery, the better pleased Sylveire would be, and the greater would be the likelihood of selling exhibits.

Now by leave of this court these two men appeal against their convictions.

...

The first ground is that the prosecution were precluded from proceeding on count 1, on which the appellants were eventually convicted, by s. 2(4) of the Obscene Publications Act 1959. That subsection reads as follows:

A person publishing an article shall not be proceeded against for an offence at common law consisting of the publication of any matter contained or embodied in the article where it is of the essence of the offence that the matter is obscene.

The first question to decide then is whether there is an offence at common law of outraging public decency. The answer to that question is to be found in the speech of Lord Simon of Glaisdale in the well-known case of *Knuller (Publishing Printing and Promotions) Ltd* v *DPP* [1972] 2 All ER 898 at 935:

Fourthly, my noble and learned friend, Lord Morris of Borth-y-Gest, in [*Shaw* v *DPP*] [1961] 2 All ER 446 at 467, where, though there was no count of conspiracy to outrage public decency, most of the cases were reviewed, said: 'The cases afford examples of the conduct of individuals which has been punished because it outraged public decency...' And my noble and learned friend, Lord Reid, though dissenting on the main issue, said ([1961] 2 All ER 446 at 460): 'I think that they [the authorities] establish that it is an indictable offence to say or do or exhibit anything in public which outrages public decency, whether or not it also tends to corrupt and deprave those who see or hear it.'

...Mr Worsley points out, and points out correctly, that the object of the common law offence is to protect the public from suffering feelings of outrage by such exhibition. Thus, if a defendant intentionally does an act which in fact outrages public decency, the public will suffer outrage whatever the defendant's state of mind may be. If the defendant's state of mind is a critical factor, then, he submits, a man could escape liability by the very baseness of his own standards.

...The authorities on the question of exhibition outraging public decency are few and far between. One of the very few which it has been possible to trace is *R* v *Crumden* (1809) 2 Camp 89. That was a case where a gentleman was bathing in the nude at Brighton. It is a brief report, and M'Donald CB said (2 Camp 89 at 90):

I can entertain no doubt that the defendant, by exposing his naked person on the occasion alluded to, was guilty of a misdemeanour. The law will not tolerate such an exhibition. Whatever his intention might be, the necessary tendency of his conduct was to outrage decency, and to corrupt the public morals. Nor is it any justification that bathing at this spot might a few years ago be innocent. For any thing that I know, a man might a few years ago have harmlessly danced naked in the fields beyond Montague house; but it will scarcely be said by the learned counsel for the defendant, that any one might now do so with impunity in Russell Square. Whatever place becomes the habitation of civilized men, there the laws of decency must be enforced.

The defendant was found guilty; and when he was brought up for judgment, the Court of KB expressed a clear opinion, that the offence imputed to him was a misdemeanour, and that he had been properly convicted.

The result, in our judgment, seems to be this. First of all the requirements with regard to *mens rea* should be the same in this offence as they are in the cognate offence of obscene libel. That is borne out by what Lord Scarman said in *R v Lemon* [1979] 1 All ER 898. If that is so, then the decision of the House of Lords in *R v Lemon*, albeit by a majority, indicates that the submissions of the prosecution in this case are to be preferred to those of the appellants'.

One turns then to examine in a little more detail the speeches of their Lordships in that case. They are most conveniently summarised by Lord Russell of Killowen, where he said, in his usual trenchant and felicitous language ([1979] 1 All ER 898 at 921):

> So I return to the question of intent. The authorities embrace an abundance of apparently contradictory or ambivalent comments. There is no authority in your Lordships' House on the point. The question is open for decision. I do not, with all respect to the speech of my noble and learned friend, Lord Diplock, consider that the question is whether this is an offence of strict liability. It is necessary that the editor or publisher should be aware of that which he publishes. Indeed that was the function of Lord Campbell's Act (Libel Act 1843), which assumed the law to be that an intention in the accused to blaspheme was not an ingredient of the offence, since it removed by statute a vicarious liability for an act of publication done by another without authority. Why then should this House, faced with a deliberate publication of that which a jury with every justification has held to be a blasphemous libel, consider that it should be for the prosecution to prove, presumably beyond reasonable doubt, that the accused recognised and intended it to be such or regarded it as immaterial whether it was? I see no ground for that. It does not to my mind make sense: and I consider that sense should retain a function in our criminal law. The reason why the law considers that the publication of a blasphemous libel is an offence is that the law considers that such publication should not take place. And if it takes place, and the publication is deliberate, I see no justification for holding that there is no offence when the publisher is incapable for some reason particular to himself of agreeing with a jury on the true nature of the publication.

Moreover, *R v Lemon*, as will have been clear from the passages which we have cited, was an allegation of an outrage on the public on a religious basis rather than a general basis, which is the case in the instant appeal. But outrage it certainly was, and the same considerations in logic should apply to this case as applied to the religious outrage in *R v Lemon*. That is the submission to us this morning of Mr Worsley, and we find that a cogent argument.

The result is this. Those passages, and the argument of Mr Worsley to which I have just made reference, lead us to the conclusion that, where the charge is one of outraging public decency, there is no requirement that the prosecution should prove an intention to outrage or such recklessness as is submitted by Mr Robertson. If the publication takes place, and if it is deliberate, there is, in the words of Lord Russell—no justification for holding that there is no offence when the publisher is incapable for some reason particular to himself of agreeing with the jury on the true nature of the publication.

...

■ NOTES AND QUESTIONS

1. It is said that hard cases make bad law. What does this mean? Do *Shaw* and *Gibson* illustrate the point? Do common law crimes provide judges (who have been described as middle-aged, middle-class and middle-minded) a means of punishing conduct of which they personally disapprove?

2. Some would argue that common law crimes serve as a safety net in which to catch those individuals who violate society's norms but not its statutory criminal law. What are the dangers in having this safety net?

3. For individuals to obey the State's criminal law, they must first know what it is that the law forbids. Do common law crimes such as conspiring to corrupt public morals or outrage public decency provide 'fair notice' to ordinary citizens of what is legal and what is illegal?

Article 7 of the ECHR provides that no one shall be convicted of a criminal offence which was not an offence at the time of its commission. Do common law crimes violate Article 7? See Chapter 11.

Gay News Ltd and Lemon v *United Kingdom*
(1982) 5 EHRR 123, European Court of Human Rights

The applicants, who are respectively the publisher and the responsible editor of a journal for homosexuals, were found guilty of the common law offence of blasphemous libel in connection with the publication of a certain poem. They complain that this conviction amounted to an unjustified interference with their freedom of expression as guaranteed by Article 10 of the Convention. They further claim that the publication of the poem amounted to an exercise of their right to freedom of thought and religion within the meaning of Article 9 of the Convention, and that the interference with this right was likewise unjustified. Apart from the argument that the restriction imposed on them was not necessary in a democratic society for any of the legitimate purposes enumerated in the above two Convention Articles, the applicants submit in particular that their conviction was based on legal principles which had not existed, or at least had not been defined with sufficient clarity, at the time of the commission of the offence. In this respect they claim that the restriction was not 'prescribed by law' as required under paragraph (2) of Articles 9 and 10, and they allege in addition a violation of Article 7 of the Convention. The applicants finally complain that they have been discriminated against, contrary to Article 14 of the Convention, in the exercise of their freedom under Articles 9 and 10 of the Convention.
...
   In the present case, the parties are first of all in disagreement as to whether the criminal offence of blasphemous libel was defined with sufficient certainty in the common law principles which were applied by the courts. The existence of the offence, i.e. the fact that it has not fallen in *desuetudo*, is apparently no longer challenged even by the applicants themselves. But they contend that essential elements of the offence, in particular the principle of strict liability (i.e. the necessity to prove only the intent to publish but not the intent to blaspheme), had not been laid down in pre-existing rules of law but were developed by the courts only in the course of the proceedings in their own case. In this connection it is alleged that even the majority of the House of Lords itself recognised the law-making function of its decision when it took up this particular issue. The Government, on the other hand, denies that the courts, including the House of Lords, created new law in this case when they applied a standard of strict liability. They merely clarified the existing law and in doing so based themselves on established case law without departing from the views expressed in recent leading textbooks.
   The Commission first observes that not only written statutes but also rules of common or other customary law may provide a sufficient legal basis both for restrictions of fundamental rights subject to exception clauses such as the one contained in Article 10(2) of the Convention, and for the criminal convictions envisaged in Article 7 of the Convention. The problem in the present case therefore does not reside in the fact that the offence of blasphemous libel was not a statutory, but a common law offence.
   The crucial point is rather one of the certainty of the law, and the functions of the courts in clarifying or developing vague legal provisions or concepts. This problem was also considered in the *Sunday Times* case both by the Commission and the Court (see European Court of Human Rights A30 (1979)). In paragraph 49 of its judgment, the Court said the following:

   In the Court's opinion, the following are two of the requirements that flow from the expression 'prescribed by law'. Firstly, the law must be adequately accessible: the citizen must be able to have an indication that is adequate in the circumstances of the legal rules applicable to a given case. Secondly, a norm cannot be regarded as a 'law' unless it is formulated with sufficient precision to enable the citizen to regulate his conduct: he must be able—if need be with appropriate advice—to foresee, to a degree that is reasonable in the circumstances, the consequences which a given action may entail. Those consequences need not be foreseeable with absolute certainty: experience shows this to be unattainable. Again, whilst certainty is highly desirable, it may bring in its train excessive rigidity and the law must be able to keep pace with changing circumstances. Accordingly, many laws are inevitably couched in terms which, to a greater or lesser extent, are vague and whose interpretation and application are questions of practice.

...

The Commission considers that the same principles also apply to the interpretation and application of the common law. While this branch of the law presents certain particularities for the very reason that it is by definition law developed by the courts, it is nevertheless subject to the rule that the law-making function of the courts must remain within reasonable limits. In particular in the area of the criminal law it is excluded, by virtue of Article 7(1) of the Convention, that any acts not previously punishable should be held by the courts to entail criminal liability, or that existing offences should be extended to cover facts which previously clearly did not constitute a criminal offence. This implies that constituent elements of an offence such as, e.g. the particular form of culpability required for its completion may not be essentially changed, at least not to the detriment of the accused, by the case law of the courts. On the other hand it is not objectionable that the existing elements of the offence are clarified and adapted to new circumstances which can reasonably be brought under the original concept of the offence.

The Commission notes that the Law Commission has criticised the state of the law of blasphemous libel in particular with regard to its lacking clarity, but it nevertheless considers that the courts in the present case in fact did not go beyond the limits of a reasonable interpretation of the existing law. The House of Lords in particular was aware of the limits of its law-making functions in the area of the criminal law which had been circumscribed in the practice statement of 1966 and put into operation in the case of *Knuller* v *DPP* [1973] AC 435. The courts of all degrees confirmed the continued existence of the offence of blasphemous libel. There was only one point which was not clear, namely the particular requirements as to the *mens rea* of a person who commits this offence. This question was answered in the same way by each of the courts. Despite the admission by the Court of Appeal and the majority of the House of Lords that a point of principle was involved in the determination of this question which required clarification, it is equally clear that the application of a test of strict liability and the exclusion of evidence as to the publisher's and editor's intention to blaspheme did not amount to the creation of new law in the sense that earlier case law clearly denying such strict liability and admitting evidence as to the blasphemous intentions was overruled. By stating that the *mens rea* in this offence did only relate to the intention to publish, the courts therefore did not overstep the limits of what can still be regarded as an acceptable clarification of the law. The Commission further considers that the law was also accessible to the applicants and that its interpretation in this way was reasonably foreseeable for them with the assistance of appropriate legal advice. In conclusion therefore the Commission finds that there is no appearance of a violation of Article 7(1) of the Convention in this case, and the applicants' complaint in this respect must accordingly be rejected as being manifestly ill-founded within the meaning of Article 27(2) of the Convention. From that it follows that the requirement under Article 10(2) of the Convention that any restriction on the freedom of expression must be 'prescribed by law' has also been complied with.

■ **NOTES AND QUESTIONS**

1. In *R* v *Goldstein* [2003] EWCA Crim 3450, the Court of Appeal recognised the common law offence of public nuisance, rejecting an Article 7 challenge.
2. In most European countries there are neither common law crimes nor statutes but written codes. Unlike statutes, which are adopted piecemeal over time, a code constitutes a comprehensive and integrated expression of the whole of a country's law. Greater consistency in terminology can be achieved than in

SECTION 3: **THE RELEVANCE OF THE EUROPEAN CONVENTION FOR THE PROTECTION OF HUMAN RIGHTS AND FUNDAMENTAL FREEDOMS**

Following World War II, the Council of Europe promulgated the 'European Convention for the Protection of Human Rights and Fundamental Freedoms' (often referred to, more simply, as the European Convention on Human Rights or by the acronym ECHR). The UK played a key role in the drafting of the Convention and was the first country to ratify it (March 1951). The Convention sets out the basic human rights to which all persons are entitled. It also created a European Commission (since abolished) and a European Court of Human Rights to enforce these rights.

While the UK ratified the European Convention early, it did not incorporate it into its domestic law, as did most other European States. The most significant ramification of the UK approach was that the rights set out in the Convention could not be enforced in a court in England or Wales. Thus, in order to vindicate their rights, aggrieved individuals had to take their case against the government to Strasbourg (the home of the Commission and Court). Unfortunately, this was often an expensive and time-consuming process.

A: The Human Rights Act 1998

In 1998 Parliament enacted the HRA 1998. The Act came into force on 2 October 2000. It has implications for Parliament's authority to create crimes, and may alter the historic balance between the judiciary and Parliament (although it is still too soon to offer a judgement on how great the effects will be). Most significantly, the Act allows individuals who believe that their human rights have been violated by the government to have their claims heard in a domestic court.

Section 1 of the Act specifies the Articles and Protocols of the Convention which are to be incorporated into domestic law (see below for specific provisions). Section 2 instructs courts and tribunals that they *must*, in determining issues which raise questions of rights under the Convention, take into account the relevant judgments, decisions, declarations and advisory opinions of the European Commission, the European Court of Human Rights and the Committee of Ministers of the Council of Europe. In this regard it should be noted that the UK does not have to have been a party to the original decision for its courts to have to take account of it. Section 3 provides that all primary and subordinate legislation must, as far as possible, be interpreted in a way that is compatible with the Convention. Section 4 permits the courts to make a 'declaration of incompatibility' when the law in question fails to comply with the requirements of the Convention. The effect of a 'declaration of incompatibility' is not to invalidate primary legislation (the courts will, however, be able to strike down secondary legislation) but to alert Parliament of the need to amend the law so that it will be compatible. The White Paper accompanying the Bill confidently predicted that prompt Parliamentary action to redress any incompatibility would be forthcoming but to heighten the likelihood of this prediction coming true, the Act provides for a 'fast-track' procedure which allows a government Minister to take immediate steps to change the law with prompt subsequent submission of the Minister's order to Parliament for approval (s. 10). Judicial proceedings to enforce the Convention may be brought by any individual whose rights under the Convention have been, or threaten to be, violated by a public authority (s. 7) and reliance on Convention rights may be had in any legal proceeding. (For full coverage and discussion of the European dimension see Chapter 11.)

SECTION 4: GRADING AND PUNISHMENT

Once the decision to criminalise has been made, there is a still a grading issue to be considered. Not all crimes engender the same degree of concern, or cause the same amount of harm. Few would disagree that murder and rape are more serious offences than criminal damage and tax evasion. All may need to be made criminal, but the same punishment should not be attached to each. The sanction that is attached to an offence reflects the grading of the offence by Parliament.

A: The grading of offences

There are issues of both absolute ranking (which is the most serious crime, the second most serious, etc.) and relative ranking (*how much* more serious is one crime than another).

A. Ashworth, *Principles of Criminal Law*
2nd ed. (1995)

... In essence, then, we may distinguish five stages in the calculation of offence-seriousness that von Hirsch and Jareborg [A. von Hirsch and N. Jareborg, 'Gauging Criminal Harms: A Living Standard Analysis' [1991] OJLS 1] propose:

1. the interests violated by the offence are identified;
2. the effect on a typical victim's living standard is quantified on the scale ranging from offences that merely affect significant enhancement to those that affect subsistence;
3. the culpability of the offender is taken into account;
4. the level of seriousness may be reduced to reflect the remoteness of the offence from the actual harm; and
5. transfer this assessment on to a scale that in some way quantifies the degree of seriousness.

It would be possible to devise an elaborate 100-point scale for this, but von Hirsch and Jareborg say that this would give the impression of a 'misleading sense of precision', and their preference is for a scale with five broad bands. This both allows further adjustment within each band and signifies that it remains a rather approximate enterprise.

Inexact it may be, but the enterprise is essential. Judgments of relative seriousness are made frequently in all walks of life—not just by legislators when deciding whether to criminalize and what maximum penalty to assign to an offence, but also by judges and magistrates when sentencing, and also by lay people in commenting on whether the official response is proportionate. The value of the von Hirsch-Jareborg approach is that it identifies the stages of thought through which it is desirable to pass when making these judgments. In practice many of the judgments are made impressionistically, often on the basis of traditional assumptions about the ranking of offences. The von Hirsch-Jareborg approach urges one to dig deeper, and to look more closely at the interests affected. However, their approach is confined to harms with individual victims. It awaits development to deal with the myriad other forms of conduct that modern systems of criminal law tend to criminalize.... We must enquire...not only whether the behaviour is serious enough to be made into a criminal offence, but also, if it is an offence, how serious it is when compared with other crimes.

It is not difficult to see some toeholds for the assessment of relative seriousness. There is a widely held view that, in general, offences of violence are more serious than property offences. Thus Lord Lane CJ, assessing the relative seriousness of frauds on the social security system, remarked that 'it must be remembered that they are non-violent nonsexual and non-frightening crimes'. However, the very breadth of modern systems of criminal law means that this point is no more than a toehold. It is not difficult to think of circumstances in which an offence against property (say, stealing £1 million) might be thought more serious than a particular offence of violence (such as one person pushing another while queuing). Thus it is necessary to press the enquiry further by examining those values or interests which are protected by the offence, and those elements which distinguished it from other similar offences. This task soon reveals a bewildering number of separate factors. When passing sentence, the courts have to range the different crimes along a single scale of relative gravity (represented by imprisonment, fines, and other non-custodial sentences). Is it possible to range the various offences along a single scale of social seriousness?

There are some who would argue that, academically interesting though this enquiry might be, it is quite unnecessary in practice, because most people in most countries agree on the relative gravity of harms. Research by the criminologists Sellin and Wolfgang purported to find considerable agreement in ranking criminal offences, whether amongst people from different countries or from different social groups in one country. However, the questions asked in this research were relatively unsophisticated for the purpose of the criminal law, and its findings cannot sustain the argument that it is unnecessary to think further about the grading of crimes as more or less serious....

■ NOTES AND QUESTIONS

1. Issues of both inter-crime and intra-crime grading can arise. Intra-crime grading relates to offences which address a related subject matter, while inter-crime grading involves unrelated and dissimilar offences.

2. Consider the following inter-crime grading problem. Rank the following offences on a 'most serious' to 'least serious' scale, identifying the reasons for each ranking.

   • aggressive begging
   • assault
   • assault with a deadly weapon
   • burglary
   • reckless driving
   • murder
   • rape
   • theft
   • vagrancy

Let us now examine a problem of intra-crime grading. In the following statutes Parliament has purported to draw a distinction between a number of similar but distinguishable vehicular-related offences:

ROAD TRAFFIC ACT 1991

1. Causing death by dangerous driving

A person who causes the death of another person by driving a mechanically propelled vehicle dangerously on a road or other public place is guilty of an offence.

2. Dangerous driving

A person who drives a mechanically propelled vehicle dangerously on a road or other public place is guilty of an offence.

3. Careless, and inconsiderate, driving

If a person drives a mechanically propelled vehicle on a road or other public place without due care and attention, or without reasonable consideration for other persons using the road or place, he is guilty of an offence.

3A. Causing death by careless driving when under influence of drink or drugs

(1) If a person causes the death of another person by driving a mechanically propelled vehicle on a road or other public place without due care and attention, or without reasonable consideration for other persons using the road or place, and—

  (a) he is, at the time when he is driving, unfit to drive through drink or drugs, or
  (b) he has consumed so much alcohol that the proportion of it in his breath, blood or urine at that time exceeds the prescribed limit, or
  (c) he is, within 18 hours after that time, required to provide a specimen in pursuance of section 7 of this Act, but without reasonable excuse fails to provide it, he is guilty of an offence.

...

22A. Causing danger to road-users

(1) A person is guilty of an offence if he intentionally and without lawful authority or reasonable cause—

  (a) causes anything to be on or over a road, or
  (b) interferes with a motor vehicle, trailer or cycle, or
  (c) interferes (directly or indirectly) with traffic equipment, in such circumstances that it would be obvious to a reasonable person that to do so would be dangerous.

...

28. Dangerous cycling

(1) A person who rides a cycle on a road dangerously is guilty of an offence.

AGGRAVATED VEHICLE TAKING ACT 1992

12A. Aggravated vehicle-taking

(1) Subject to subsection (3) below, a person is guilty of aggravated taking of a vehicle if—

  (a) he commits an offence under section 12(1) above (in this section referred to as a 'basic offence') in relation to a mechanically propelled vehicle; and
  (b) it is proved that, at any time after the vehicle was unlawfully taken (whether by him or another) and before it was recovered, the vehicle was driven, or injury or damage was caused, in one or more of the circumstances set out in paragraphs (a) to (d) of subsection(2) below.

(2) The circumstances referred to in subsection (1)(b) above are—

  (a) that the vehicle was driven dangerously on a road or other public place;
  (b) that, owing to the driving of the vehicle, an accident occurred by which injury was caused to any person;

(c) that, owing to the driving of the vehicle, an accident occurred by which damage was caused to any property, other than the vehicle;

(d) that damage was caused to the vehicle.

■ NOTES AND QUESTIONS

1. What penalties should be attached to each of these offences? The penalties under the Road Traffic Act 1991 can be found in the schedules attached to the statute. The penalty for violation of the Aggravated Vehicle Taking Act 1992 is contained in s. 4 of the relevant statute.

2. One factor which often serves as the basis for attaching greater penalties to one crime rather than another is that the offence results in death. Thus, causing death by dangerous driving attracts a greater penalty than dangerous driving. But is the difference between the two offences simply a matter of chance, one of the drivers being unlucky enough to have a victim cross the road while he is engaged in his act of dangerous driving? In cases such as this, should the penalties for the offence be based on the risk of death that has been created rather than on the fact that a death actually occurs? See generally Gobert, 'The Fortuity of Consequences' (1993) 4 Criminal Law Forum 1; J.C. Smith, 'The Element of Chance in Criminal Liability' [1971] Crim LR 63.

B: Punishment

One critical effect of having been convicted of a criminal offence is that sanctions may be imposed on the offender in the name of the State. But what purpose is sought to be achieved through this punishment? Over the years many answers have been offered to this question. Probably the four most commonly given follow.

(i) Retribution

Retribution is the oldest of the rationales for punishment, tracing its roots to the Bible:

LEVITICUS 24:17–22, THE NEW ENGLISH BIBLE

When one man strikes another and kills him, he shall be put to death. Whoever strikes a beast and kills it shall make restitution, life for life. When one man injures and disfigures his fellow-countryman, it shall be done to him as he has done; fracture for fracture, eye for eye, tooth for tooth; the injury and disfigurement that he has inflicted upon another shall in turn be inflicted upon him.

Retribution is often assimilated to revenge, but a public rather than a private revenge. Sir James Stephen put it this way: 'The sentence of the law is to the moral sentiment of the public in relation to any offence what a seal is to wax' (Stephen, *A History of the Criminal Law in England*, II (1883), p. 81). Indeed, one of the arguments for a retributive theory of punishment is that it forestalls the need for private revenge. Implicit in retribution is the condemnation or denunciation of both the offender and the offending behaviour. Retribution, however, is not in kind – society does not rape rapists or steal from thieves (although in some countries the death penalty is exacted for murder). Instead, the law imposes a sentence (typically a fine, imprisonment or term of community service) which is proportional to the harm caused. In this regard it might be observed that retribution, with its emphasis on proportional punishment, provides a basis for grading offences.

Retribution as a justification for punishment has been criticised as backwards-looking and vindictive. As retribution has fallen into disfavour, however, there has been a rise in interest in the concept of 'just deserts'. Both retribution and 'just deserts' theory boil down to the idea that criminals are punished because they deserve to be. The State is right to denounce criminals and to punish them for their crimes. In the following extract Grant Lamont gives his account of how the specific elements of a crime are an expression of the State's duty to express, through punishment, condemnation for the disrespect shown by the accused for a social value, be that value the sanctity of life, the autonomy of the individual, or the sovereignty of property. He makes clear that whatever purposes, deterrence, restraint, rehabilitation and so on, punishment can have only one justification, namely that it is deserved.

Grant Lamond, What is a Crime?

(2007) *Oxford Journal of Legal Studies* 609

There is a better way to understand crimes as public wrongs, viz., not as wrongs *to* the public but as wrongs that the community is *responsible* for punishing, i.e. whose prosecution is appropriately a case for the community rather than the individual victim. It is not that the community is the victim, but that the community is the appropriate body to bring proceedings and impose punishment. This raises a new question—which wrongs are the state responsible for punishing? There are, in fact, two questions here: which wrongs merit punishment, and which merit state punishment. To get to the bottom of this, it is best to deal with them in that order.

The first question is which wrongs merit punishment. A number of preliminary points are relatively straightforward. Punishment, I take it, is the deliberate imposition of a burdensome liability on an individual for some blameworthy conduct in order to censure that conduct. Punishment, then, presupposes blameworthy conduct. What makes conduct blameworthy? There are a number of features. The first is that the conduct in question is wrongful.... The second feature is that the wrongdoer is a responsible agent who acted without either justification or excuse.... The fact that someone is blameworthy, however, still falls short of showing that they deserve to be punished. It establishes only that they are liable to be blamed or criticized for what they have done, and that there are grounds for such censure...

Punishment goes beyond criticism and blame. Not every act of wrongdoing merits punishment—many wrongs are just not serious enough. But what makes some wrongdoing 'serious enough' to call for punishment? The fundamental answer to this is that it is the type of blameworthy conduct that manifests a *disrespect* for the interest or value that has been violated. What does this mean? To respect a value is to treat it in the way appropriate to its nature. Some values can be promoted, whereas others can only be upheld (or honoured), and others still can be both promoted and upheld. Whatever is the case, a failure to respect a value goes beyond the mere failure to be guided by it, i.e. it goes beyond simply violating the value. What marks out the failure to be guided as particularly reprehensible, and thus eligible for punishment, is an *unwillingness* to be guided by the value in the appropriate way. This is most obvious in the case of intentional wrongs, where the wrongdoer deliberately violates some value. But it is also true of cases where the wrongdoer knows that they are violating some value, and those where the wrongdoer is aware that they are taking an unjustified risk of doing so...

That a wrong manifests an attitude of disrespect for some value, then, marks out the wrong as punishable. But, as in the case of blame, it only marks out the wrongdoer as *liable* for punishment and provides *a* reason in favour of doing so. The strength of the reason in favour of punishment will depend upon the overall gravity of the wrong, which depends in turn on the importance of the interest or value at stake, the degree of violation (or risk of violation) that the wrong created, and the kind of disrespect shown by the wrongdoer. Punishment is a form of censure that goes beyond simply bringing the wrongdoing to the attention of the offender and confronting them with it. But there is an enormous range of punishments, from public condemnation to forfeiture of life. Hence the 'seriousness' of the wrongdoing (the aspect that renders it liable to punishment) is merely one dimension of the ultimate 'gravity' of the wrong (how deserving of punishment it is). And even in the case of grave wrongs, there is always the question of whether the wrongdoer should be punished all things considered, since there may be extenuating circumstances militating against punishment.

What of the second issue raised earlier? Which wrongs not only merit punishment, but merit punishment by the *state*? . . . In principle, any serious violation of a value that the state is responsible for supporting is a candidate for criminal punishment. The broader the range of values and activities that are properly the responsibility of the state, the broader the scope for the criminal law. Thus, if all values are supportable by public action then all forms of serious immorality are potentially within the criminal law, whereas if a more limited range of values are the responsibility of the state the criminal law will be similarly circumscribed. Of course, it might be wondered whether state punishment really does extend (even potentially) to *every* value it may support. Surely, for instance, there is a distinction between those values that a state is *required* to support, and those that it is merely at liberty to support. If the state is required to support some value, then it would be wrong to fail to do so, whereas it is not wrong to fail to support a value that it is simply at liberty to promote. Hence, it might be thought, only serious violations of mandatory values (those the state is required to support) could ground punishment. The state is not *responsible* for supporting merely permissible values, so how can it be responsible for punishing their violation? Appealing as this line of argument might seem, the conclusion does not follow from its premisses. If the state is permitted to support a value, then there is nothing in the argument to establish that it may not do so by punishing serious violations of that value. What is needed is not an argument that some values are mandatory and others merely permissive, but that some values (possibly including mandatory ones) may not be supported by *coercive* means, whereas others may. . . .

It is not enough to say that a wrong is a *candidate* for such punishment, i.e. that it lies within the scope of the state's responsibility—it must also be the case that it is the type of wrong that *ought* to be punished by the state. The only wrongs that should be criminalized are those that are reasonably grave, i.e. that involve the violation of an important value. Why is this? State punishment, by its very nature, is imposed in the name of the whole community, not merely in the name of some other institution of civil society. The condemnatory force of that judgment is correspondingly greater, and given that expressive power the wrong must be sufficiently grave to warrant such condemnation. Regardless of what other consequences follow, to be found to have committed a crime involves being convicted by a court, i.e. being adjudged to have been *guilty* of committing a crime. Conviction is an authoritative judgment on behalf of the community that the defendant has committed such a serious violation of some value that it calls for punishment *by* the community. The defendant is being held to account in the face of the whole community, and consequently this must not be a disproportionate response to the gravity of the wrongdoing. The force of such public conviction means that in the case of many wrongs it would be manifestly excessive to impose it, because it would be too severe or too blunt an instrument of censure. So punishment by the state must be necessary to bring home to the perpetrator and the wider community the gravity of the wrongdoing. By its very nature it is inappropriate for dealing with wrongs that are not grave enough to merit such public condemnation.[45] . . .

The key to the nature of crime, then, lies in understanding that they are public wrongs not because they are wrongs *to* the public, but because they are wrongs that the public is responsible for punishing. There is a public interest in crimes not because the public's interests are necessarily affected, but because the public is the appropriate body to bring proceedings and punish them. Crimes are a sub-set of the wrongs that generally merit punishment. That larger class is composed of those blameworthy wrongs that manifest a disrespect for the value violated, because they evince an unwillingness to be guided appropriately by the value at the time the wrongdoer acted. The state, however, is only concerned with the graver cases of such wrongdoing, because of the condemnatory force of conviction in the name of the community as a whole.

(ii) Restraint

Restraint theory has a more pragmatic focus. The theory here is that criminals need to be separated from the rest of society in order to protect ordinary persons from their predatory behaviour. The implicit premise is that, if not incarcerated, the offender will continue in his criminal ways. Whether this is true as an empirical proposition is not entirely clear. Even if true, the corollary question arises for how long the offender should be confined. A plausible answer is until he or she is no longer a threat to society. This answer is troublesome, however, for it can lead to lengthy imprisonment for some who commit minor offences but who are likely to do so again (e.g., shoplifters and anti-war protesters who violate public order laws) and minimal imprisonment for some who commit serious offences but who are unlikely to do so ever again (e.g., a bank robber who is rendered paraplegic as a consequence of a shoot-out with police).

(iii) Rehabilitation

The other side of the restraint coin is rehabilitation. If dangerous offenders need to be isolated until no longer dangerous, it behoves the State to rehabilitate such offenders so that they can be released. This makes sense both from the altruistic perspective of helping the offender and from the pragmatic perspective of not burdening the State with the costs of maintaining an offender in prison any longer than is necessary. But being in favour of rehabilitation is one thing and knowing how to rehabilitate criminals is quite another. Innumerable rehabilitation programmes have been essayed over the years but often with limited success, at least as measured by recidivism figures, and sometimes unpredictable results. It may well be that our hopes for rehabilitation exceed our knowledge of why people commit crimes. Despite what seemed at one time to be promising advances in the fields of psychology and sociology, professionals in these disciplines still find the scientific control of criminal behaviour to be largely beyond their capability.

(iv) Deterrence

Whereas restraint and rehabilitation theory focus on the individual offender, general deterrence is concerned with other would-be offenders. The idea is to make an example of actual offenders so that others will not be tempted into similar criminal activity. In like vein, the offenders themselves should also be deterred from future criminal activities as a result of the punishment. Society will be protected if deterrence works as envisaged. Whether or not it in fact does is difficult to prove, for success can only be measured by the incidence of those who do not commit crimes. And how is one to measure this negative? Moreover, the process by which deterrence works, assuming it does, is not at all clear. Consider the views of the respected criminologist Johannes Andenaes:

Johannes Andenaes, 'The General Preventive Effects of Punishment'

(1966) 114 *University of Pennsylvania Law Review* 949

In continental theories of criminal law, a basic distinction is made between the effects of punishment on the man being punished—individual prevention or special prevention—and the effects of punishment upon the members of society in general—general prevention. The characteristics of special prevention are termed 'deterrence,' 'reformation' and 'incapacitation,' and these terms have meanings similar to their meanings in the English speaking world. General prevention, on the other hand, may be described as the *restraining influences emanating from the criminal law and the legal machinery.*

By means of the criminal law, and by means of specific applications of this law, 'messages' are sent to members of a society. The criminal law lists those actions which are liable to prosecution, and it specifies the penalties involved. The decisions of the courts and actions by the police and prison officials transmit knowledge about the law, underlining the fact that criminal laws are not mere empty threats, and providing detailed information as to what kind of penalty might be expected for violations of specific laws. To the extent that these stimuli restrain citizens from socially undesired actions which they might otherwise have committed, a general preventive effect is secured.

... While the effects of special prevention depend upon how the law is implemented in each individual case, general prevention occurs as a result of an interplay between the provisions of the law and its enforcement in specific cases. In former times, emphasis was often placed on the physical exhibition of punishment as a deterrent influence, for example, by performing executions in public. Today it is customary to emphasize the *threat* of punishment as such. From this point of view the significance of the individual sentence and the execution of it lies in the support that these actions give to the law....

The effect of the criminal law and its enforcement may be *mere deterrence.* Because of the hazards involved, a person who contemplates a punishable offense might not act. But it is not correct to regard general prevention and deterrence as one and the same thing. The concept of general prevention also includes the *moral* or *sociopedagogical* influence of punishment. The 'messages' sent by law and the legal processes contain factual information about what would be risked by disobedience, but they also contain proclamations specifying that it is *wrong* to disobey....

The moral influence of the criminal law may take various forms. It seems to be quite generally accepted among the members of society that the law should be obeyed even though one is dissatisfied with it and wants it changed. If this is true, we may conclude that the law as an institution itself to some extent creates conformity. But more important than this formal respect for the law is respect for the values which the law seeks to protect. It may be said that from law and the legal machinery there emanates a flow of propaganda which favors such respect. Punishment is a means of expressing social disapproval. In this way the criminal law and its enforcement supplement and enhance the moral influence acquired through education and other non-legal processes. Stated negatively, the penalty neutralizes the demoralizing consequences that arise when people witness crimes being perpetrated.

Deterrence and moral influence may both operate on the conscious level. The potential criminal may deliberate about the hazards involved, or he may be influenced by a conscious desire to behave lawfully. However, with fear or moral influence as an intermediate link, it is possible to create unconscious inhibitions against crime, and perhaps to establish a condition of habitual lawfulness. In this case, illegal actions will not present themselves consciously as real alternatives to conformity, even in situations where the potential criminal would run no risk whatsoever of being caught.

General preventive effects do not occur only among those who have been informed about penal provisions and their applications. Through a process of learning and social imitation, norms and taboos may be transmitted to persons who have no idea about their origins—in much the way that innovations in Parisian fashions appear in the clothing of country girls who have never heard of Dior or Lanvin.

There is an interesting interplay between moral reprobation and legal implementation. At least three conditions combine to prevent an individual from perpetrating a punishable act he is tempted to perform: his moral inhibitions, his fear of the censure of his associates and his fear of punishment. The latter two elements are interwoven in many ways. A law violation may become known to the criminal's family, friends and neighbors even if there is no arrest or prosecution. However, it is frequently the process of arrest, prosecution and trial which brings the affair into the open and exposes the criminal to the censure of his associates. If the criminal can be sure that there will be no police action, he can generally rest assured that there will be no social reprobation. The legal machinery, therefore, is in itself the most effective means of mobilizing that kind of social control which emanates from community condemnation.

■ NOTES AND QUESTIONS

1. The theories of punishment which have been discussed are not mutually exclusive. Imprisoning an offender may serve both retributive and deterrent functions, while at the same time restraining the offender for the duration of the sentence and offering the opportunity for rehabilitation.

2. To what extent under each theory will punishment fit (a) the crime, (b) the criminal?

3. Consider the task of a Parliament which has decided to make careless driving a criminal offence. What penalties should be imposed if the goal is (a) restraint, (b) rehabilitation, (c) deterrence, (d) retribution?

4. To what extent are the various theories based on different theories of human nature? Which of the theories is premised on an assumption of 'free will'? What would be the implications if one were to accept a determinist philosophy that events are predetermined by forces beyond the control of individuals?

5. While we have set out the most frequently discussed theories of punishment, there are others that also deserve mention. Some penologists see a major function of punishment as denunciation (or, as it tends to be known colloquially, 'naming and shaming'). John Braithwaite, who has written extensively on the topic, would combine 'shaming' with reintegration into the community. See Braithwaite, *Crime, Shame and Reintegration* (1989). A strategy of 'naming and shaming' may be particularly effective in the case of companies which violate the law. A company obviously cannot be imprisoned and can usually afford to pay any fine that might realistically be levied against it (often passing the fine on to its customers). However, the potential loss of custom resulting from a well-publicised criminal conviction may have significant effects.

Other penologists have noted the educative potential of punishment. This function may take prominence in areas of law where the criminality of the conduct in question is not clear or disputed (e.g., insider dealing and gambling). It is also useful in respect of crimes that have long gone unprosecuted.

In recent years there has been a growing interest in restorative justice. (See von Hirsch, Roberts, Bottoms, Roach and Schiff, *Restorative Justice and Criminal Justice* (2003).) In restorative justice the goal is to have the offender make amends to the victim for the harm that the latter has suffered as a result of the offence. This might include compensating the victim, or rectifying the damage caused to the victim (in the case of a violation of the Criminal Damage Act, for instance). Some restorative justice proponents see a role for allowing a victim to confront the offender, enabling a reconciliation to be made between restoration and retribution.

Sometimes a philosophy of punishment is implicit in legislation.

CRIMINAL JUSTICE ACT 1991

1. Restrictions on imposing custodial sentences

(1) This section applies where a person is convicted of an offence punishable with a custodial sentence other than one fixed by law.

(2) Subject to subsection (3) below, the court shall not pass a custodial sentence on the offender unless it is of the opinion—

(a) that the offence, or the combination of the offence and one other offence associated with it, was so serious that only such a sentence can be justified for the offence; or

(b) where the offence is a violent or sexual offence, that only such a sentence would be adequate to protect the public from serious harm from him.

(3) Nothing in subsection (2) above shall prevent the court from passing a custodial sentence on the offender if he refuses to give his consent to a community sentence which is proposed by the court and requires that consent.

(4) Where a court passes a custodial sentence, it shall be its duty—

(a) in a case not falling within subsection (3) above, to state in open court that it is of the opinion that either or both of paragraphs (a) and (b) of subsection (2) above apply and why it is of that opinion; and

(b) in any case, to explain to the offender in open court and in ordinary language why it is passing a custodial sentence on him.

(5) A magistrates' court shall cause a reason stated by it under subsection (4) above to be specified in the warrant of commitment and to be entered in the register.

2. Length of custodial sentences

(1) This section applies where a court passes a custodial sentence other than one fixed by law.

(2) The custodial sentence shall be—

(a) for such term (not exceeding the permitted maximum) as in the opinion of the court is commensurate with the seriousness of the offence, or the combination of the offence and other offences associated with it; or

(b) where the offence is a violent or sexual offence, for such longer term (not exceeding that maximum) as in the opinion of the court is necessary to protect the public from serious harm from the offender.

(3) Where the court passes a custodial sentence for a term longer than is commensurate with the seriousness of the offence, or the combination of the offence and other offences associated with it, the court shall—

(a) state in open court that it is of the opinion that subsection (2)(b) above applies and why it is of that opinion; and

(b) explain to the offender in open court and in ordinary language why the sentence is for such a term.

(4) A custodial sentence for an indeterminate period shall be regarded for the purposes of subsections (2) and (3) above as a custodial sentence for a term longer than any actual term.

...

29. Effect of previous convictions etc.

(1) An offence shall not be regarded as more serious for the purposes of any provision of this Part by reason of any previous convictions of the offender or any failure of his to respond to previous sentences.

(2) Where any aggravating factors of an offence are disclosed by the circumstances of other offences committed by the offender, nothing in this Part shall prevent the court from taking those factors into account for the purpose of forming an opinion as to the seriousness of the offence.

■ NOTES AND QUESTIONS

1. What theory of punishment underlies ss. 1(2)(a) and 2(2)(a) of the 1991 Act? Sections 1(2)(b) and 2(2)(b)? Section 29?

2. It has been claimed that the Criminal Justice Act 1991 should lead to proportionate sentences. Proportionate to what?

3. The White Paper preceding the Act (*Crime, Justice, and Protecting the Public* (Cmd. 965, 1990) made some telling observations about the value of deterrent sentences:

> [M]uch crime is committed on impulse, given the opportunity presented by an open window or unlocked door, and it is committed by offenders who live from moment to moment; their crimes are as impulsive as the rest of their feckless, sad or pathetic lives. It is unrealistic to construct sentencing arrangements on the assumption that most offenders will weigh up the possibilities in advance and base their conduct on rational calculation. Often they do not.

In contrast to the Criminal Justice Act 1991, the Criminal Justice Act 2003 is more 'up front' and specific about what it views as the proper purposes of sentencing:

CRIMINAL JUSTICE ACT 2003

142. Purposes of sentencing

(1) Any court dealing with an offender in respect of his offence must have regard to the following purposes of sentencing—
  (a) the punishment of offenders,
  (b) the reduction of crime (including its reduction by deterrence),
  (c) the reform and rehabilitation of offenders,
  (d) the protection of the public, and
  (e) the making of reparation by offenders to persons affected by their offences.
(2) Subsection (1) does not apply—
  (a) in relation to an offender who is aged under 18 at the time of conviction,
  (b) to an offence the sentence for which is fixed by law,
  (c) to an offence the sentence for which falls to be imposed under section 51A(2) of the Firearms Act 1968 (c. 27) (minimum sentence for certain firearms offences), under subsection (2) of section 110 or 111 of the Sentencing Act (required custodial sentences) or under any of sections 225 to 228 of this Act (dangerous offenders), or
  (d) in relation to the making under Part 3 of the Mental Health Act 1983 (c. 20) of a hospital order (with or without a restriction order), an interim hospital order, a hospital direction or a limitation direction.

■ NOTES AND QUESTIONS

1. Does the Criminal Justice Act 2003, when compared with the Criminal Justice Act 2001 (see also the Crime (Sentences) Act 1997) suggest that theories of punishment, like fashions in clothes, are subject to constant change? What explanations may underlie shifts in penal philosophy?

2. How helpful in practice are the list of sentencing purposes in s. 142(1) of the Criminal Justice Act 2003 likely to be? They do not provide guidance to the judge on what the priorities should be if the purposes of sentencing conflict. Even when they do not conflict, the list does not indicate what weight should be attached to each of the respective purposes.

3. The Criminal Justice Act 2003 also provides for the establishment of a Sentencing Guidelines Council, whose pronouncements and elucidations should help to promote consistency in sentencing. One function of the Council might be to give guidance on the issues raised in the preceding question.

C: Sentencing: the implementation of the theories in practice

Every time a defendant is convicted, the trial court must pass sentence. This may require the judge to consider the purposes of punishment. Sentences may also be appealed by both dissatisfied defendants and the prosecution. Again, theories of punishment may need to be considered by the appellate court:

R v Sargeant
(1974) 60 Cr App R 74, Court of Appeal

LAWTON LJ: On May 20, 1974, at the Central Criminal Court, the appellant pleaded guilty to a charge of affray at the end of the prosecution's case. On May 24, 1974, he was sentenced by His Honour Judge Argyle to two years' imprisonment. He now appeals against that sentence.

During the evening of October 26, 1973, the appellant was on duty at a discotheque at Crown Hill at Croydon, together with three other doormen. Their job in colloquial language was to act as 'bouncers.' The appellant had no criminal record. The other bouncers had. One of them had a bad criminal record. There was another man on the staff of this discotheque who was taking part in what the prosecution alleged was the affray. He too had a bad criminal record.

. . . [The] appellant has had no previous convictions. He is 26 years of age, and a skilled green-keeper in the golfing world. He started acting as an assistant green-keeper in his adolescence. He has acquired a good deal of expertise. He has had jobs as green-keeper with a number of distinguished and well-known golf clubs. The tragedy of his case is that the very day on which he appeared at the Central Criminal Court he should have been starting work as head green-keeper with one of the best known golf clubs in the south of England. His conviction has inevitably meant that that job is no longer available to him, and it also means that there is a strong possibility that no golf club will ever employ him again. By his stupidity on this occasion he has deprived himself of a career in the golfing world, and all because he lost his temper when trouble started. The very fact that he has lost his career is of course a severe penalty for him.

The problem for this Court is whether the sentence was wrong in principle. It is necessary for this Court to analyse the facts of this case. We have come to the conclusion that, if the trial judge did analyse them, he analysed them incorrectly. What really was the case against this appellant? His job was to help to keep order. He was inexperienced in that job. It is clear from his record that he is inclined to be headstrong. I say that, because despite his skill as a green-keeper, he has had some difficulty in keeping jobs, because he cannot always see eye to eye with golf clubs' secretaries. He had had something to drink whilst he was on duty that night, though there was nothing to suggest that he had had too much to drink. If he had followed the instructions of his employers, he would not have had anything to drink. He was faced with a situation in which a young man had been misbehaving. He took the view, wrongly with hindsight, that the best way of dealing with the potential difficulties which that young man might cause, if he resumed misbehaving, was to use some force on him. He used no weapon. What he did do was to butt the young man, which can be very painful for the victim. If he had thought for a moment, he would have appreciated the nature and extent of the chain of events which he was starting. It is almost certain that he did not think. Young men who act in this kind of physical way seldom do think of which the consequences are going to be. The evidence establishes that very soon after he did what he did he was put out of action and took no further part in the appalling violence which followed.

What ought the proper penalty to be? We have thought it necessary not only to analyse the facts, but to apply to those facts the classical principles of sentencing. Those classical principles are summed up in four words: retribution, deterrence, prevention and rehabilitation. Any judge who comes to sentence ought always to have those four classical principles in mind and to apply them to the facts of the case to see which of them has the greatest importance in the case with which he is dealing.

I will start with retribution. The Old Testament concept of an eye for an eye and tooth for tooth no longer plays any part in our criminal law. There is, however, another aspect of retribution which is frequently overlooked; it is that society, through the courts, must show its abhorrence of particular types of crime, and the only way in which the courts can show this is by the sentences they pass. The courts do not have to reflect public opinion. On the other hand courts must not disregard it. Perhaps the main duty of the court is to lead public opinion. Anyone who surveys the criminal scene at the present time must be alive to the appalling problem of violence. Society, we are satisfied, expects the courts to deal with violence. The weapons which the courts have at their disposal for doing so are few. We are satisfied that in most cases fines are not sufficient punishment for senseless violence. The time has come, in the opinion of this Court, when those who indulge in the kind of violence with which we are concerned in this case must expect custodial sentences.

But we are also satisfied that, although society expects the courts to impose punishment for violence which really hurts, it does not expect the courts to go on hurting for a long time, which is what this sentence is likely to do. We agree with the trial judge that the kind of violence which occurred in this case called for a custodial sentence. This young man has had a custodial sentence. Despite his good character, despite the excellent background from which he comes, very deservedly he has had the humiliation of hearing prison gates closing behind him. We take the view that for men of good character the very fact that prison gates have closed is the main punishment. It does not necessarily follow that they should remain closed for a long time.

I turn now to the element of deterrence, because it seems to us the trial judge probably passed this sentence as a deterrent one. There are two aspects of deterrence: deterrence of the offender and deterrence of likely offenders. Experience has shown over the years that deterrence of the offender is not a very useful approach, because those who have their wits about them usually find the closing of prison gates an experience which they do not want again. If they do not learn that lesson, there is likely to be a high degree of recidivism anyway. So far as deterrence of others is concerned, it is the experience of the courts that deterrent sentences are of little value in respect of offences which are committed on the spur of the moment, either in hot blood or in drink or both. Deterrent sentences may very well be of considerable value where crime is premeditated. Burglars, robbers and users of firearms and weapons may very well be put off by deterrent sentences. We think it unlikely that deterrence would be of any value in this case.

We come now to the element of prevention. Unfortunately it is one of the facts of life that there are some offenders for whom neither deterrence nor rehabilitation works. They will go on committing crimes as long as they are able to do so. In those cases the only protection which the public has is that such persons should be locked up for a long period. This case does not call for a preventive sentence.

Finally, there is the principle of rehabilitation. Some 20 to 25 years ago there was a view abroad, held by many people in executive authority, that short sentences were of little value, because there was not enough time to give in prison the benefit of training. That view is no longer held as firmly as it was. This young man does not want prison training. It is not going to do him any good. It is his memory of the clanging of prison gates which is likely to keep him from crime in the future.

In the light of that analysis of the classical principles to be applied in sentencing, what is the result on the facts of this case? The answer is that this sentence is much too long. It was submitted that a suspended sentence should have been passed. For the reasons I have already given, we do not agree. But we are satisfied, having regard to the facts of this case and the social inquiry and prison reports which the Court has been given that we can deal with this case by substituting for the sentence which was passed such a sentence as will enable him to be discharged today. To that extent the appeal is allowed.

■ **NOTES AND QUESTIONS**

1. Is the matter of the appropriate theory (theories) of punishment for the legislature or the judiciary to decide?

2. The court in *Sargeant* states its view that 'for men of good character the very fact that the prison gates have closed is the main punishment'. Should punishments

be based on a defendant's acts or the defendant's 'character'? Would sentencing based on 'character' (whatever might be embraced within this term) be potentially discriminatory and in violation of Article 14 of the ECHR?

3. Who should be responsible for sentencing in a particular case? The judge who presided over the trial? A different judge? A panel of experts (what expertise is needed?)? The jury which has found the defendant guilty? A different jury? A sentencing council (composed of whom?)? What are the advantages and disadvantages of these respective potential sentencers? In the UK, sentencing is the responsibility of the trial court, although, as can be seen in *Sargeant*, sentences may be appealed and reviewed by the Court of Appeal.

4. Should Parliament avoid issues like those contained in the previous question by imposing fixed sentences for crimes (as opposed to allowing sentencing within a range of sentences)? What are the advantages and disadvantages?

Increasingly, one can expect punishments authorised by statute to be challenged as violative of the HRA 1998.

R v Lichniak

[2001] 4 All ER 934, Queen's Bench Division, Divisional Court and Court of
Appeal (Criminal Division)

KENNEDY LJ: [1] Each of these claimants seeks judicial review of a decision to impose a mandatory sentence of life imprisonment following their separate convictions for murder. They contend that s 1 of the Murder (Abolition of Death Penalty) Act 1965 is incompatible with arts 3 and 5 of the European Convention for the Protection of Human Rights and Fundamental Freedoms (Rome, 4 November 1950; TS 71 (1953); Cmd 8969) (as set out in Sch 1 to the Human Rights Act 1998). Section 1(1) of the 1965 Act so far as material provides that 'a person convicted of murder shall...be sentenced to imprisonment for life'. Article 3 of the convention reads: 'No one shall be subjected to torture or to inhuman or degrading treatment or punishment.'

Article 5 so far as material reads:

'1. Everyone has the right to liberty and security of person. No one shall be deprived of his liberty save in the following cases and in accordance with a procedure prescribed by law: (a) the lawful detention of a person after conviction by a competent court...'

Permission to apply for judicial review was granted by Scott Baker J on 23 January 2001 when he also ordered that this court sit both as a Divisional Court and as the Court of Appeal (Criminal Division), which we have done.

...

The basic submission

Mr Fitzgerald's basic submission is that now that all mandatory life sentences are recognised to fall into two parts, namely first a penal element to meet the requirements of retribution and general deterrence (fixed by the Home Secretary after considering the views of the trial judge and the Lord Chief Justice) and, secondly, a subsequent period of detention justified on preventive grounds, life sentences should not be imposed where at the time of sentencing there is no foreseeable risk of the defendant being a danger to the public after he or she has served the penal element of the sentence. Referring to the convention, Mr Fitzgerald argues that the mandatory life sentence has no clear penological objective. It violates art 5 because it is arbitrary, and art 3 because it is disproportionate. Before we turn to look at these submissions in more detail we must say something about the jurisdiction of this court.

...

General approach

Mr Fitzgerald submits that under art 5 of the convention the basic principle is that no one should be deprived of their liberty in an arbitrary fashion, and that if a life sentence is imposed where there is no objective justification for that sentence then the sentence is both arbitrary and disproportionate. Under art 3 a sentence which is manifestly disproportionate can be an 'inhuman and degrading' punishment.

For the defendant Mr Pannick's response is that these issues have been addressed by the European Court of Human Rights in *V* v *UK*, *T* v *UK* (1999) 30 EHRR 121, where the appellants had been sentenced to be detained during Her Majesty's pleasure. That too is a sentence which is automatically imposed where a defendant of the prescribed age is convicted of murder. It is imposed irrespective of the circumstances of the offence and of the offender. Some offenders may present no risk of future offending, and may have committed an offence less grave than other offences which do not require a mandatory indeterminate sentence from which the offender will only be released after serving a tariff period, when it is considered that he may safely be released, and on the basis that thereafter he will be at risk of recall for the rest of his life. In other words, Mr Pannick submits, for present purposes the cases of *T* and *V* are indistinguishable on their facts, and this court is required by s 2(1) of the 1998 Act to take into account the decisions of the European Court. Mr Fitzgerald submits that in *V* v *UK*, *T* v *UK* there was an important distinction, in that the two boys could not be regarded as presenting no danger if released at the end of their tariff period, and that is something which we must examine more closely in due course.

Mr Pannick goes on to submit that there was a very good reason why the European Court decided *V* v *UK*, *T* v *UK* as it did—namely because an indeterminate sentence (whether it be mandatory life imprisonment or detention during Her Majesty's pleasure) allows for and involves in practice an individualised assessment of tariff, risk and recall, so that it is neither degrading nor arbitrary. It may be that an assessment should not be made by the executive, but that is not something for consideration in this case.

...

Mr Pannick further submits that there are three principles established under the convention to which we must have regard. First, the relevant provisions of the convention require a balance between the interests of the applicant and those of the community. In *Soering* v *UK* (1989) 11 EHRR 439 a West German national was seeking to avoid extradition to Virginia to face a charge of capital murder, and in its judgment the court said (at 468 (para 89)):

'... inherent in the whole of the Convention is a search for a fair balance between the demands of the general interest of the community and the requirements of the protection of the individual's fundamental rights.'

Secondly, the European Court in its approach to the convention does not concentrate on formal procedures, but looks at the realities. In *Van Droogenbroeck* v *Belgium* (1982) 4 EHRR 443, a case concerned with detention of a recidivist, the court said (at 456 (para 38)) 'one must look beyond the appearances and the language used and concentrate on the realities of the situation'. Here, Mr Pannick submits, the claimants are putting too much weight on the language used when a judge sentences a defendant to life imprisonment, and not concentrating on the realities of the situation.

Thirdly, Mr Pannick reminds us that in *Brown* v *Stott* (*Procurator Fiscal, Dunfermline*) [2001] 2 All ER 97 at 114, [2001] 2 WLR 817 at 834 Lord Bingham of Cornhill said:

'Judicial recognition and assertion of the human rights defined in the convention is not a substitute for the processes of democratic government but a complement to them. While a national court does not accord the margin of appreciation recognised by the European Court as a supranational court, it will give weight to the decisions of a representative legislature and a democratic government within the discretionary area of judgment accorded to those bodies.'

Other members of the Privy Council made observations to the same effect. That, he submits, is of particular relevance to a controversial issue of policy which has been the subject of repeated consideration by Parliament. In his reply Mr Fitzgerald reminded us of an additional principle, that decisions of the European Court and Commission are made on their particular facts rather than reviewing national law in abstracto (see *Håkansson and Sturesson* v *Sweden* (1990) 13 EHRR 1 at 11 (para 46)). Decisions need to be read with that in mind.

Previous litigation

Mr Pannick submits that this case is the latest in a series of cases in England and in Strasbourg which have challenged various aspects of the requirement that a life sentence be imposed after a conviction for murder. Each challenge has failed because on each occasion the courts have said that Parliament is entitled to maintain its statutory requirement.

Article 3

In *Costello-Roberts* v *UK* (1993) 19 EHRR 112, a case about corporal punishment in a school, the European Court stated (at 133 (para 30)):

> '...in order for punishment to be "degrading" and in breach of Article 3, the humiliation or debasement involved must attain a particular level of severity and must in any event be other than that usual element of humiliation inherent in any punishment. Indeed Article 3, by expressly prohibiting "inhuman" and "degrading" punishment, implies that there is a distinction between such punishment and punishment more generally. The assessment of this minimal level of severity depends on all the circumstances of the case. Factors such as the nature and context of the punishment, the manner and method of its execution, its duration, its physical and mental effects and, in some instances, the sex, age and state of health of the victim must all be taken into account.'

In *V* v *UK*, *T* v *UK* (1999) 30 EHRR 121 the European Court considered whether that article could be invoked in relation to the sentence of detention during Her Majesty's pleasure passed on the two boys. It recorded the Commission's acceptance of the case for the government, saying (at 182 (para 95)):

> '[The Commission] referred to [*Hussain* v *UK* (1996) 22 EHRR 1] where the Court held that the sentence of detention during Her Majesty's pleasure was primarily preventative, attracting the guarantees of Article 5(4). It could not, therefore, be said that the applicant had forfeited his liberty for life or that his detention gave rise to a violation of Article 3.'

Mr Fitzgerald submits that the reference to *Hussain's* case is significant because in that case, which also concerned a sentence of detention during Her Majesty's pleasure, the court had said (at 24 (para 53)):

> '...an indeterminate term of detention for a convicted young person, which may be as long as that person's life, can only be justified by considerations based on the need to protect the public.'

The same point was repeated by the court in *V* v *UK*, *T* v *UK* (1999) 30 EHRR 121 at 183 (para 96). Thus the context, submits Mr Fitzgerald, is an indeterminate sentence for which the only justification is preventive.

In *V* v *UK*, *T* v *UK* the court expressed its conclusion in relation to art 3, saying (at 183 (para 98)):

> 'The Court recalls that States have a duty under the Convention to take measures for the protection of the public from violent crime. It does not consider that the punitive element inherent in the tariff approach itself gives rise to a breach of Article 3, or that the Convention prohibits States from subjecting a child or young person convicted of a serious crime to an indeterminate sentence allowing for the offenders continued detention or recall to detention following release where necessary for the protection of the public.'

As Mr Pannick points out, there is nothing there to suggest that the sentence will only be legitimate if at the time of sentencing it is envisaged that the offender will present an ongoing risk. Indeed para 99 (at 183) begins:

> 'The applicant has not yet reached the stage in his sentence where he is able to have the continued lawfulness of his detention reviewed with regard to the question of dangerousness...'

That would tend to suggest that so far as the European Court was concerned any assessment of dangerousness that may or may not have been made at the time of sentence was of no significance. Overall, the court's conclusions are expressed in terms that indicate no objection under art 3 to a mandatory indeterminate sentence for murder.

The only other decision to which we need refer in relation to art 3 is the decision on admissibility of the European Commission in *Bromfield* v *UK* (1 July 1998, unreported). There the applicant, aged 20, had been sentenced to custody for life after being convicted of murder. Dealing with his complaint in relation to art 3, para 2 of the decision states:

> 'The Commission recalls that there is no incompatibility with the convention in the imposition of a life sentence as a security or retributive measure in a particular case or in a decision to keep a recidivist or habitual offender at the disposal of the government (*Weeks* v *UK* (1987) 10 EHRR 293). While in the cases concerning detention during Her Majesty's pleasure, the court commented that a sentence pursuant to which young persons forfeited their liberty for the rest of their lives might raise issues under art 3 of the convention (see eg *Hussain* v *UK* (1996) 22 EHRR 1), the Commission considers that these remarks apply to sentences of life imprisonment imposed on children under the age of 18 to whom special considerations apply. It does not find that the imposition of a mandatory sentence of life imprisonment in respect of the offence of murder committed by young adults between the ages of 18 and 21 discloses treatment or punishment prohibited by art 3 of the convention.'

In our judgment the weight of the jurisprudence is overwhelming. Whatever one may think about the desirability of a change of policy, it cannot be accepted that a mandatory sentence of life imprisonment for murder is incompatible with art 3. In reality, as Mr Pannick points out, the sentence is an indeterminate one—rarely will there be imprisonment for life. In other cases the penal element having been decided upon at a earlier stage, when that element has been served the Secretary of State may, if recommended to do so by the Parole Board, after consultation with the Lord Chief Justice and the trial judge if available, release the prisoner on licence (see s 29 of the Crime (Sentences) Act 1997). In practice the Secretary of State does refer cases to the Parole Board for consideration, and if a prisoner has been released on licence and is recalled he will have the opportunity to have his recall considered by the Parole Board (see s 31 of the 1997 Act). That is all part of what is involved in the mandatory life sentence, and in reality such a sentence, which includes the policy applied in relation to it, cannot be labelled inhuman or degrading. There is sufficient individualised consideration of the offender's case within the context of the sentence. Thus it is open to Parliament, acting within its discretionary area of judgment, to retain the sentence without violating art 3.

Article 5

We turn now to the complaint in relation to art 5. Mr Fitzgerald submits that to have an indeterminate sentence for all murders is arbitrary. In some cases a lesser determinate sentence would suffice because culpability and the needs of retribution and deterrence can be evaluated at the end of the trial, and there is no discernible risk to warrant an indeterminate sentence. Furthermore, as such a sentence is at least in theory the most severe sentence available to an English judge it should not be imposed as a matter of course for murders where the gravity of the offence is less than the gravity of other crimes. It is arbitrary to impose a sentence that can neither be justified on preventive grounds nor justified on the basis of retributive proportionality.

...

In so far as Mr Fitzgerald submits that where there is not a discernible risk of re-offending it is wrong to impose an indeterminate sentence, Mr Pannick responds by saying that such a submission falls outside the scope of art 5. In *Weeks* v *UK* (1987) 10 EHRR 293, a case concerned with the lawfulness of detention after recall, the European Court said (at 312 (para 50)) that 'it is not for the Court, within the context of Article 5, to review the appropriateness of the original sentence'. Even if that be wrong, Mr Pannick submits, and we accept, that a sentence cannot be arbitrary for an adult when an equivalent sentence has been found not to be so in the case of a young offender, and when in each case the application of the sentence is individualised, and everyone knows that it will be individualised from the moment it is imposed. Although, as Mr Fitzgerald pointed out, decisions of the European Court are related to their own particular facts, the process of reasoning displayed by the European Court is of assistance, as illustrated by both counsel during the course of this case. The reasoning in the decided cases tells strongly against the claimant's case on art 5.

...

Conclusion

The arguments put forward by Mr Fitzgerald are persuasive in favour of a change of policy, and may carry weight in a political debate, but in our judgment, as the law now stands, they do not enable this court to allow these appeals against sentence on the basis that the mandatory sentences imposed were incompatible with the convention. We therefore dismiss these appeals.

Appeals dismissed.

Matthew Barry, James Offen
[2001] 1 Cr App R 24, Court of Appeal ...

LORD WOOLF CJ: This judgment relates to five appeals. In each case where leave is required to appeal against sentence, we give leave. The five appeals all involve section 2 of the Crime (Sentences) Act 1997 'the 1997 Act'. (This is now section 109 Powers of the Criminal Courts (Sentencing) Act 2000. In this judgment we will refer to section 2 in the 1997 Act.) The application of section 2 has already given rise to a number of decisions by this Court. They illustrate the problems which can arise in practice in applying statutory provisions which require the courts to impose an automatic life sentence on certain offenders.

The policy of Parliament for establishing the automatic life sentences emerges clearly from the then Government's White Paper, *Protecting the Public, the Government's Strategy on Crime in England and Wales* (1996). In Cm 3190, paragraph 10.11 the White Paper states:

'Too often in the past, those who had shown a propensity to commit serious, violent or sex offences have served their sentences and been released only to offend again. In many such cases the danger of releasing the offender has been plain for all to see—but nothing could be done, because once the offender has completed the sentence imposed, he or she has to be released. Too often, victims have paid the price when the offender has repeated the same offences. The Government is determined that the public should receive proper protection from persistent violent or sex offenders. That means requiring the courts to impose an automatic indeterminate sentence, and releasing the offender if and only if it is safe to do so.'

In *Buckland* [2000] 1 Cr.App.R.471; [2000] 1 W.L.R. 1262 Lord Bingham of Cornhill C.J. described the rationale of section 2 in these terms, at pages 478 and 1268:

'The section is founded on an assumption that those who have been convicted of two qualifying serious offences present such a serious and continuing danger to the safety of the public that they should be liable to indefinite incarceration and, if released should be liable indefinitely to recall to prison. In any case where, on all the evidence, it appears that such a danger does or may exist, it is hard to see how the court can consider itself justified in not imposing the statutory penalty, even if exceptional circumstances are found to exist. But if exceptional circumstances are found, and the evidence suggests that an offender does not present a serious and continuing danger to the safety of the public, the court may be justified in imposing a lesser penalty.'

The reason why we have heard these appeals together is because in each case it is contended that either the interpretation of section 2 of the 1997 Act is affected by section 3 of the Human Rights Act 1998 ('the 1998 Act'), or that section 2 is incompatible with a Convention right so that the appellants are entitled to a declaration of incompatibility. The impact of the 1998 Act on the interpretation of legislation arises under section 3 of the Act, which provides:

'3.—(1) So far as it is possible to do so, primary legislation and subordinate legislation must be read and given effect in a way which is compatible with the Convention rights.'

The legislation

Section 2 of the 1997 Act, so far as relevant, is in the following terms:

...

'(1) This section applies where—
  (a) a person is convicted of a serious offence committed after the commencement of this section; and
  (b) at the time when that offence was committed, he was 18 or over and had been convicted in any part of the United Kingdom of another serious offence.
(2) The court shall impose a life sentence, that is to say—
  (a) where the person is 21 or over, a sentence of imprisonment for life;
  (b) where he is under 21, a sentence of custody for life under section (2) of the Criminal Justice Act 1982 ("the 1982 Act"),

unless the court is of the opinion that there are *exceptional circumstances relating to either of the offences or to the offender which justify its not doing so*. [Emphasis added.]

(6) Where the court does not impose a life sentence, it shall state in open court that it is of that opinion and what the exceptional circumstances are.
(7) An offence the sentence for which is imposed under sub-section (2) above shall not be regarded as an offence the sentence for which is fixed by law.
(8) An offence committed in England and Wales is a serious offence for the purposes of this section if it is any of the following, namely—
  (a) an attempt to commit murder, a conspiracy to commit murder or an incitement to murder;
  (b) an offence under section 4 of the Offences against the Person Act 1861 (soliciting murder);
  (c) manslaughter;
  (d) an offence under section 18 of the Offences against the Person Act 1861 (wounding, or causing grievous bodily harm, with intent);
  (e) rape or an attempt to commit rape;
  (f) an offence under section 5 of the Sexual Offences Act 1956 (intercourse with a girl under 13);
  (g) an offence under section 16 (possession of a firearm with intent to injure), section 17 (use of a firearm to resist arrest) or section 18 (carrying a firearm with criminal intent) of the Firearms Act 1968; and
  (h) robbery where, at some time during the commission of the offence, the offender had in his possession a firearm or imitation firearm within the meaning of that Act.'

The following features of the section will be noted:

(i) It refers to two offences having been committed by the offender.
(ii) It is only the second offence (the 'trigger offence') which has to have been committed after the commencement of the section. The earlier offence may have been committed at any time.
(iii) When the second offence is committed the offender is required to be over 18, but there is no age requirement in relation to the first offence.
(iv) The proviso of 'exceptional circumstances' applies to both offences. The 'exceptional circumstances' can relate either to the offences or to the offender but what constitutes exceptional circumstances is not otherwise defined by the section.
(v) All offences identified as serious offences are offences for which life imprisonment could be imposed quite apart from section 2.

...

The Human Rights Act 1998

The appellants contend that as previously applied, section 2 of the 1997 Act is incompatible with Articles 3, 5, 7 and 8 of the Convention.

Article 7

As the argument as to Article 7 is discrete, it is convenient to start with that Article. It is Article 7.1 which is relevant. It provides:

> 'No one shall be held guilty of any criminal offence on account of any actual omission which did not constitute a criminal offence under national or international law at the time it was committed. Nor shall a heavier penalty be imposed than one that was applicable at the time the criminal offence was committed.'

...

Mr Fitzgerald advances the argument, which is adopted by all appellants, that there is a contravention. He submits that the argument has two aspects. Both involve changing the consequences of a conviction of the first serious offence after the date of the offence and after the sentence for which it was imposed. It is submitted that after a punishment for the first serious offence had been imposed, the subsequent coming into force of section 2 increased the penalty for the initial offence since the offender then became liable, if he committed a further serious offence, to be automatically sentenced to life imprisonment. It is also submitted that section 2 itself increased the penalty for the first serious offence since on conviction of the second serious offence a life sentence would be imposed, in reality, in respect of both offences.

Mr Fitzgerald's argument was well illustrated by the practice in Association Football of sending off a player who is shown two yellow cards. If the rule which brings this about was to be imposed after one yellow card had been shown this would give greater significance to the first yellow card than was the case when it was shown. It could adversely affect a player, since if a player knew he would be sent off if he had two yellow cards, he would make greater efforts to avoid being shown even the first yellow card.

This attractive argument depends upon treating the life sentence as being imposed at least in part or both offences. This is not, however, the manner in which, in our judgment, section 2 works. Section 2 imposes the penalty of the automatic life sentence for the second offence alone. The imposition of the automatic life sentence is, however, subject to certain conditions. Those are that the offender was 18 or over and that he had been previously convicted of another serious offence. The language of section 2(1) makes this clear. The sentence is not being imposed in relation to the earlier offence.

Articles 3 and 5

The relevant provisions of Article 3 and Article 5 are as follows:

> 'Article 3: Prohibition of torture
>
> No one shall be subjected to torture or to inhuman or degrading treatment or punishment.'

> 'Article 5: Right to Liberty and Security
>
> 1 Everyone has the right to liberty and security of person. No one shall be deprived of his liberty save in the following cases and in accordance with a procedure prescribed by law:
>   (a) the lawful detention of a person after conviction by a competent court.
>   ...
>   (4) Everyone who is deprived of his liberty by arrest or detention shall be entitled to take proceedings by which the lawfulness of his detention shall be decided speedily by a court and his release ordered if the detention is not lawful.'

In approaching these articles, it is important to recognise that the 1998 Act is a constitutional instrument introducing into domestic law the relevant articles of the Convention. The consequence of section 3 is that legislation which affects human rights is required to be construed in a manner which conforms with the Convention wherever this is possible.

...

The problem arises because of the restrictive approach which has so far been adopted to the interpretation of exceptional circumstances in section 2. If exceptional circumstances are construed in a manner which accords with the policy of Parliament in passing section 2, the problem disappears.

Section 2 establishes a norm. The norm is that those who commit two serious offences are a danger or risk to the public. If in fact, taking into account all the circumstances relating to a particular offender, he does not create an unacceptable risk to the public, he is an exception to this norm. If the offences are of a different kind, or if there is a long period which elapses between the offences during which the offender has not committed other offences, that may be a very relevant indicator as to the degree of risk to the public that he constitutes. Construing section 2 in accordance with the duty imposed upon us by section 3 of the 1998 Act, and taking into account the rationale of the section as identified by Lord Bingham gives content to exceptional circumstances. In our judgment, section 2 will not contravene Convention rights if courts apply the section so that it does not result in offenders being sentenced to life imprisonment when they do not constitute a significant risk to the public. Whether there is significant risk will depend on the evidence which is before the court. If the offender is a significant risk, the court can impose a life sentence under section 2 without contravening the Convention. Either there will be no exceptional circumstances, or despite the exceptional circumstances the facts will justify imposing a life sentence.

Under section 2 it will be part of the responsibility of judges to assess the risk to the public that offenders constitute. In many cases the degree of risk that an offender constitutes will be established by his record, with or without the assistance of assessments made in reports which are available to the court. If a court needs further assistance, they can call for it. The courts have traditionally had to make a similar assessment when deciding whether a discretionary life sentence should be imposed. There should be no undue difficulty in making a similar assessment when considering whether the court is required to impose an automatic life sentence, although the task will not be straightforward, because of the lack of information as to the first serious offence which will sometimes exist because of the passage of time.

This does not mean that we are approaching the passing of an automatic life sentence as though it is no different from the imposition of a discretionary life sentence. Notwithstanding the interpretation resulting from the application of section 3(1) of the 1998 Act suggested, section 2 will still give effect to the intention of Parliament. It will do so, however, in a more just, less arbitrary and more proportionate manner. Section 2 will still mean that a judge is obliged to pass a life sentence in accordance with its terms unless, in all the circumstances, the offender poses no significant risk to the public. There is no such obligation in cases where section 2 does not apply. In addition, if the judge decides not to impose a life sentence under section 2, he will have to give reasons as required by section 2(3). Furthermore, the issue of dangerousness will have to be addressed in every case and a decision made as to whether or not to impose a life sentence.

The objective of the legislature will be achieved, because it will be mandatory to impose a life sentence in situations where the offender constitutes a significant risk to the public. Section 2 therefore provides a good example of how the 1998 Act can have a beneficial effect on the administration of justice, without defeating the policy which Parliament was seeking to implement.

In view of our conclusions as to the impact of Articles 3 and 5, it is not necessary to consider Article 8.

■ NOTES AND QUESTIONS

1. One gets the impression that courts are generally reluctant to find punishments at odds with either the HRA 1998 or the ECHR. What might account for this reluctance?

2. Some punishments may run afoul of Article 3's prohibition of inhuman or degrading punishment. See, e.g., *Tyrer* v *UK* (1978) 2 EHRR 1 (ECtHR) (element of humiliation in corporal punishment inflicted on a schoolboy was 'degrading' in violation of Article 3).

3. In *Soering* v *United Kingdom* (1989) 11 EHRR 439, the ECtHR considered the extradition of a German national to the US State of Virginia, which intended to put

him on trial for murder. Had he been convicted, he was potentially subject to the death penalty. The European Court, while 'declining' to find the death penalty *per se* violative of Article 3, was of the opinion that the extended period on death-row which US prisoners often had to endure before their execution could amount to torture or inhuman or degrading treatment in violation of Article 3. See also the decision of the European Commission in *Altum* v *Germany* (1983) 36 DR 209.

SECTION 5: **ANALYSING A CRIME**

It is important for students and practitioners alike to appreciate what must be established in order to warrant a conviction of a criminal defendant. This entails being able to identify the elements of the offence charged. The prosecution must do so because it has to prove each and every element of the crime beyond reasonable doubt. Without a knowledge of the elements, the prosecution will not know what it needs to prove. Defence counsel, on the other hand, will want to identify the elements of the crime because if counsel can establish a reasonable doubt as to *any* of the elements, the jury must acquit (for the prosecution will not have carried its burden of proof).

Below we present two approaches for analysing the elements of a crime. The two approaches are not mutually exclusive, and conscientious lawyers – and students – will use the two in tandem.

A: A conceptual model

It is possible to look at a crime as consisting of a number of building blocks. These building blocks draw our attention not only to the common elements of the typical offence, but also to how the elements relate to one another. In addition, they provide a benchmark against which any crime might be critically evaluated, and thereby further our understanding of the nature of the criminal law. That said, there is no legal requirement that each of the elements must be present in every offence, and the fact that an element may be omitted from the definition of a particular crime does not serve to invalidate the relevant statute.

The elements themselves can be schematically subdivided. There are two formal preconditions to a crime – the existence of a law that makes conduct criminal and the attachment of a potential sanction to a violation of that law. In order to be subject to the criminal law, an individual must also be deemed to have the legal capacity to commit a crime. The courts recognise certain categories of individuals, such as children and the insane, as not having this capacity and exempt them from the law.

In terms of the crime itself, there are two core elements – *actus reus* and *mens rea*. The former refers to the conduct element of the crime and the latter to the mental element. The relationship that needs to exist between *actus reus* and *mens rea* is, somewhat inaccurately described as one of 'concurrence' implying a simultaneity that is not essential. Offences that are defined in terms of a result (murder and manslaughter, for example, require that a person be killed) envisage a certain relationship between *actus reus* and result, which is referred to, again somewhat inaccurately, as 'causation'. Lastly, there are circumstances that justify or excuse what would otherwise be a crime.

(i) Preconditions to criminal liability

(a) Law
The existence of a law forbidding the conduct in question is an absolute prerequisite to the imposition of criminal liability (*nullum crimen sine lege*). One cannot be prosecuted for an offence that was not in existence at the time it was committed. See Article 7 of the ECHR. The law need not necessarily be written in a statute book, as we saw in the case of common law crimes, but it must exist. Those subject to the law have a right to know what it proscribes, in order that they may conform their conduct to the law's requirements.

(b) Punishment
A second prerequisite is that the law in question must prescribe punishment for its violation. Without prescribed punishment the law is not a criminal law. The punishment is inflicted in the name of the State for the violation of its law, and exists separate and independent of whether the defendant is required to pay damages in a civil suit and of any disgrace that the defendant might suffer as a result of the attendant publicity.

(ii) Capacity

The working assumption of the criminal law is that human beings are autonomous individuals with free will and the ability to choose between good and evil. Although biological, psychological, social and economic forces may impinge on the exercise of free will, the law generally chooses to ignore these factors in assessing a defendant's criminality (considerations such as these are more likely to be taken into account at the sentencing stage). Nonetheless, there are instances where the courts are prepared to recognise that certain individuals may not have the requisite capacity to choose between legal and illegal conduct. Young children, for example, often do not understand the wrongfulness of their mischief. Individuals who suffer from mental illness likewise may be incapable of appreciating when they are doing something wrong. Such persons may not be morally responsible for their actions, and the law, recognising this incapacity, does not seek to hold them criminally responsible. The rationale behind this allowance, however, does not apply to individuals who are responsible for their own lack of capacity, such as by becoming voluntarily intoxicated and thereafter committing an offence that they would not have committed had they been sober, and the law takes a less indulgent view in these circumstances.

The incapacity of the mentally ill and children is a mental incapacity – they lack the ability to understand the nature of their actions. Sometimes, however, individuals have the requisite understanding but are unable to prevent themselves from committing the criminal action. When a defendant acts involuntarily against his will, and there is no fault on the defendant's part in being unable to control his conduct, the law again is prepared to make an exception from a general rule of liability. Such individuals are permitted a defence of automatism. Technically this defence turns on the involuntary nature of the defendant's acts, but in recent times the courts have drawn a distinction between insane and non-insane automatism, thereby confusing issues of mental incapacity and physical incapacity. Both automatism and insanity, as well as incapacity based on age, will be examined in Chapter 9.

(iii) *Actus reus* and *mens rea*

Actus reus and *mens rea* are the two most critical components of a crime. *Actus reus* refers to the conduct component, and *mens rea* to the mental component. At common law it was said that '*actus non facit reum nisi mens sit rea*', which literally means that an act is not wrongful unless accompanied by a wrongful state of mind. However, the maxim has typically been construed to mean that before criminal liability can attach, at least for serious offences, the Crown must prove both *actus reus* and *mens rea*.

(a) Actus reus

While literally translated as a wrongful act, the term *actus reus* may actually encompass three distinct dimensions. There is first the conduct which one must engage in before one can be held criminally liable, although it is also important to note that in some instances a failure to act or omission may satisfy the requirement of *actus reus*. The second dimension arises in respect of a crime defined in terms of a specified result (murder requires the killing of a human being, and criminal damage the destruction of or damage to property) and embodies the relationship between the defendant's act and the result. If no person has died, the defendant cannot be convicted of murder; and if no property has been damaged, there is no crime of criminal damage. The final dimension to *actus reus* consists of the attendant circumstances that lend colour to what might otherwise appear to be a neutral act. The attendant circumstance that converts sexual relations with an adult woman into rape is the absence of consent on the part of the woman, and that which converts an ordinary marriage into bigamy is the fact that the defendant is already married to another at the time. Thus *actus reus*, like *mens rea*, although on the one hand a seemingly out-moded Latin term of art, conveys a commonly understood (at least among the legal community) constellation of ideas and concepts that facilitate analysis. *Actus reus*, along with causation, will be examined in Chapter 2.

(b) Mens rea

Just as one cannot be punished for bad thoughts alone, one generally cannot be punished for acts which are not accompanied by a guilty mind. The term *mens rea* refers to the wrongful state of mind required to be proven by the prosecutor in order to secure a conviction. Usually the type of *mens rea* which will suffice for a conviction will be specified by statute or case law. In some instances the prosecutor will have to prove that the defendant acted intentionally; in others only that the defendant acted recklessly; and in still others simply that the defendant acted negligently or carelessly. A sliding scale of mental fault exists which varies depending on the crime charged. At the far end of this scale can be found statutes which do away with *mens rea* altogether and impose strict liability. *Mens rea*, along with concurrence, will be examined in Chapter 3.

(iv) Critical relationships

(a) Concurrence
Concurrence refers to the temporal relationship between *mens rea* and *actus reus*. Usually they will coincide at the point of the *actus reus*, but in crimes of intention it may be a more accurate description of the relationship to say that the *mens rea* was the precipitating factor in the defendant's decision to commit the crime.

(b) Causation
Some crimes are defined in terms of the occurrence of a particular result, of which murder is the clearest example. The defendant's acts must be the cause of that result. As we will see, problems arise when the results are other than those intended or occur in a way other than intended.

(v) Defences

If the Crown has established each and every element of the crime charged by proof beyond a reasonable doubt, it would seem to follow that the defendant will be convicted. However, this is not necessarily so. Sometimes the defendant is prepared to concede that he has violated the law, but argues that he was justified in doing so or should be excused despite having done so. The courts have recognised a number of *general defences* that will in effect negate the defendant's liability.

Conceptually, *defences* can be divided into justifications and excuses, although the practical effect is the same – they both lead to a verdict of not guilty. To say that the defendant's conduct was justified is to say that the defendant was right to have acted as he did. Acting in self-defence or to prevent a crime are examples of justifications. In contrast, criminal conduct which is excusable is still wrong, but the law is prepared to relieve the defendant of the normal consequences of a conviction. A defendant who claims that he committed a crime under duress, for instance, is seeking to be excused.

While both justifications and excuses result in the defendant not being subjected to penal sanction, there are some technical differences that emanate from the fact that the defendant is raising one or the other. For example, some cases suggest that a defendant charged with aiding and abetting cannot be convicted if the principal's conduct is found to have been justified but conviction is possible if the conduct is only excusable. Interestingly, it is not the defendant's burden to prove a justification or excuse, but rather the Crown's obligation to negate the claim by proof beyond reasonable doubt, at least once the defendant has introduced sufficient evidence in support of the defence to raise a reasonable doubt as to guilt.

Specific defences will be examined in Chapter 10.

B: Parsing a statute

The conceptual model of a criminal offence is useful in indicating the criminological basis of legal liability and how the elements of a crime fit together. However, the model holds the danger of leading astray anybody who takes it too literally. Some crimes, for example, impose strict liability, and any attempt to identify the *mens rea* of the crime would be impossible; there is no *mens rea*. Similarly, issues of causation arise only in respect of crimes which are defined in terms of a particular result. Where the offence consists of simply an act, such as driving a motor vehicle in excess of the speed limit, any effort to identify a causation relationship would be doomed to failure.

The conceptual model can also be frustrating, for it fails to accord with the way that criminal laws are written in practice. No statute declares that the *actus reus* of an offence is X and the *mens rea* is Y. Statutes are drafted in ordinary English and not Latin. Nor do statutes generally speak in terms of concurrence or causation; these are relationships which are implicit within the law. In many statutes, moreover, there may be multiple mental and conduct elements which have more complex interrelationships than the simple statement of the conceptual model might suggest.

Finally, the conceptual model, because of its abstract nature, can be misleading. *Actus reus* and *mens rea* do not exist in a vacuum, as the model might seem to intimate. They come to life only within the context of a specific criminal offence. Each crime has its own *actus reus* and its own *mens rea*, and, although the terminology of *actus reus* and *mens rea* may remain constant, their specific content will differ from statute to statute. One must examine each crime on an individual basis in order to determine its particular *actus reus* and *mens rea*. Thus one needs to dissect a statute in the same way as a student of English might parse the subject, verb, object, etc. of a sentence. In criminal law it is necessary to identify each element of the crime. In a criminal case a prosecutor will go through this exercise in order to ensure that no element is overlooked (as noted previously, the Crown must prove each and every element of the offence beyond reasonable doubt or its case fails); and a defence lawyer will go through the same exercise in order to hold the prosecution to its legal burden of proof. It is helpful at this stage of your career to get into the habit of identifying the elements of a crime and determining how each of the elements is satisfied in a particular case.

It may be useful to illustrate both the conceptual and element-by-element approaches to understanding a crime in respect of a specific statute. Consider s. 1 of the Criminal Damage Act 1971:

CRIMINAL DAMAGE ACT 1971

1. Destroying or damaging property

(1) A person who without lawful excuse destroys or damages any property belonging to another intending to destroy or damage any such property or being reckless as to whether any such property would be destroyed or damaged shall be guilty of an offence.

If one were to dissect this provision, element by element, one could identify six distinct elements that would have to be proved by the prosecutor in a given case: that (i) a person; (ii) without lawful excuse; (iii) destroyed or damaged; (iv) property; (v) belonging to another; (vi) with the intent to destroy or damage that property or being reckless as to whether any such property would be destroyed or damaged. In respect of each of these elements, one might also perceive a number of issues which would need to be clarified before the element could be fully understood. For purposes of illustration, let us attempt to flag the relevant elements and some (but by no means all) of the possible issues:

(a) *'A person'*. It might not be readily apparent when 'personhood' might become an issue. We have already alluded to the problem of whether a company can be charged with criminal damage for polluting a river. Is the company a person? What about when someone's pet dog fouled another's property – can the dog be guilty of criminal damage? The dog's owner?

(b) *'without lawful excuse'*. This provision raises the question of what constitutes a 'lawful excuse'. Part of the answer is provided in a separate section of the statute (see s. 5).

(c) *'destroys or damages'*. Note that the Crown can succeed by proving either that the defendant has destroyed or has damaged property. But how much must one alter the state of property before it can be said to be sufficiently damaged to come within the criminal law? One might also wonder why the two terms are used and whether it is possible to destroy property without damaging it.

(d) *'property'*. What constitutes 'property'? Are both personal and real property included? Can one destroy or damage intangible property? Are there some things that within normal parlance we may refer to as property but which are not considered such for the purposes of the law (an issue which will be explored in Chapter 7 on Theft)?

(e) *'belonging to another'*. Note that a defendant cannot be convicted for destroying or damaging his or her own property. But what if the defendant has possession of the property pursuant to a rental agreement, or has simply been left in charge of property?

(f) *'intending to destroy or damage . . . property or being reckless as to whether any such property would be destroyed or damaged'*. Note again that the Crown has alternative methods of establishing its case. It can prove that the defendant acted either intentionally *or* recklessly. The question of what constitutes 'recklessness' has been one that has proved extremely problematic and controversial. The issue will be examined in Chapter 3.

If one were to take a conceptual approach to this same provision of the Criminal Damage Act 1971, our analysis would look a bit different:

(a) The preconditions of law and punishment are established. Section 1 establishes the offence and a subsequent section (s. 4) establishes the maximum penalty following a conviction.

(b) The law says nothing about capacity other than its reference to 'person'. But this would be misleading if it were taken to imply, for example, that a child under the age of 10 – who undoubtedly is a person – can be convicted of criminal damage. As we shall see in Chapter 9, a child so young is not capable of being convicted of any crime. Criminal statutes tend not to indicate that children, the mentally ill, and those who act in a state of automatism are not subject to its provisions, for the repetition of such a provision in every statute would become tedious. On the other hand, this omission illustrates how looking at a statute in terms of its expressed elements might cause one to overlook critical issues.

(c) The *actus reus* of the offence consists of destroying or damaging property belonging to another.

(d) The crime is defined in terms of a result – damaging or destroying property. This automatically raises the question of whether the defendant's conduct caused the result. Again this is a 'hidden' issue in the sense that there is no specific reference to causation on the face of the statute.

(e) The *mens rea of* the offence is '*intending* to destroy or damage...property or *being reckless* as to whether any such property would be destroyed or damaged'.

(f) The statute, rather oddly, specifies that the defendant's conduct must be 'without lawful excuse'. This would seem otiose because a 'lawful excuse' would in any event render non-criminal what would otherwise be criminal. Moreover, even more oddly in light of this reference to excuses, the Act is silent on justifications. Yet, criminal damage can clearly be justifiable, as, for example, when the victim of an attack breaks a chair over the head of the attacker.

While one can effectively use either the conceptual approach or an element-by-element approach to analysing a statute, the conscientious student and lawyer will employ both. Using both approaches may allow one to see issues that might be overlooked if either approach were to be used by itself.

FURTHER READING

Wilson, *Criminal Law: Doctrine and Theory* (2010) Chapters 1–3

Arden, 'Criminal Law at the Cross-roads: The Impact of Human Rights from the Law Commission's Perspective and the Need for a Code' [1999] Criminal Law Review 439

Ashworth, 'Is the Criminal Law a Lost Cause?' (2000) 116 Law Quarterly Review 225

Ashworth, 'The European Convention and Criminal Law' in *The Human Rights Act and the Criminal and Regulatory Process* (1999)

Buxton, 'The Human Rights Act and Substantive Criminal Law' [2000] Criminal Law Review 33

Cross, Bell & Engle, *Statutory Interpretation* (3rd ed. 1995)

Dine, 'European Community Criminal Law' [1993] Criminal Law Review 246

Duff, 'Choice, Character and Criminal Responsibility' [1993] Law and Philosophy 345

Hirsch & Roberts, 'Legislating Sentencing Principles: the Provisions of the Criminal Justice Act 2003 Relating to Sentencing Purposes and the Role of Previous Convictions' [2004] Criminal Law Review 639

Husak, 'The Criminal Law as Last Resort' (2004) 24 Oxford Journal of Legal Studies 207

Husak, *Overcriminalisation: The Limits of the Criminal Law* (2007) (Oxford University Press)

Lamont, 'What is a Crime?' (2007) 27 Oxford Journal of Legal Studies 609–63

Marshall and Duff, 'Criminalization and Sharing Wrongs' (1998) 11 Canadian Journal of Law and Jurisprudence 7

Packer, *The Limits of the Criminal Sanction* (1968)

2

The Conduct Component of Crime: *Actus Reus*

A common law maxim held that *actus non facit reum nisi mens sit rea*. The maxim drew attention to the two most critical elements of a crime: *actus reus* and *mens rea*. Literally translated, the maxim stated that an act is not wrongful unless accompanied by a wrongful state of mind. However, it has generally been interpreted to require the prosecutor to prove both a wrongful act *and* a wrongful state of mind on the part of the accused.

At its most basic, the *actus reus* or act requirement means that one cannot be convicted for mere criminal thoughts. One must normally do something towards bringing those thoughts to fruition. This approach to criminal liability is justified by three primary considerations:

(a) the difficulty in proving what a person is thinking;

(b) the difficulty in distinguishing between persons with a genuine criminal purpose and those who may simply be engaged in idle fantasy; and

(c) perhaps most importantly, to exclude from criminal liability those whose criminality does not extend beyond the daydreaming stage. The rationales that we examined for imposing punishment do not apply to such individuals. They are neither dangerous nor in need of restraint or rehabilitation. They have caused no harm and do not pose a threat to the public.

The act requirement does not mean that action *per se* on the part of the accused must be established in order for the prosecution to secure a conviction. Some crimes are defined in such a way that the failure to act constitutes the *actus reus* of the offence; and in others an omission to act when there is a legal duty to act is treated as if it were the equivalent of a positive act. A parent can murder an infant by starvation as much as by smothering the child to death. Further, in respect of some offences, the *actus reus* is a state of affairs, as, for example, being drunk in charge of a vehicle, or being in possession of an illegal substance or dangerous item. Finally, it should be noted that there are situations in which it is not necessary for the offender to have acted personally: the act of another person will satisfy the *actus reus* requirement.

While one might be tempted to conclude that *actus reus* is an artificial construct which has no significance in and of itself, it nevertheless provides a useful and shorthand way of referring to that part of the crime concerned with the conduct prohibited by the law. As such, it is a useful mechanism for distinguishing between (criminal) conduct and guilty mind.

The value of utilising *actus reus* and *mens rea* as analytical tools is not without its critics, however. In *R v Miller* [1983] 1 All ER 978, House of Lords, Lord Diplock observed:

> My Lords, it would I think be conducive to clarity of analysis of the ingredients of a crime that is created by statute, as are the great majority of criminal offences today, if we were to avoid bad Latin and instead to think and speak . . . about the conduct of the accused and his state of mind at the time of that conduct, instead of speaking of *actus reus* and *mens rea*.

Whether or not Lord Diplock is correct, he draws our attention to two important points. First, a coherent code of criminal law could easily be constructed without ever mentioning the terms *actus reus* or *mens rea*. Parliament does not use these terms in its criminal law enactments, nor did the Law Commission in its Draft Criminal Code Bill (1989) (preferring 'fault' to *mens rea* and 'act' to *actus reus*). Secondly, the concepts of *actus reus* and *mens rea* are intended to aid analysis. If they have the opposite effect, then there is little point in stubbornly pursuing the search for them as such. It is sufficient to be clear about the elements of the crime as spelled out in the relevant statute.

To the extent that it remains useful to speak of an *actus reus*, and courts and commentators alike do continue to use the term, it is best understood to refer to the prohibited conduct (or omission) component of a crime, as opposed to its mental component. As commonly used in practice, the term may also encompass the results of the defendant's conduct and/or the attendant circumstances which convert what might otherwise be an innocent or neutral act into one that is criminal. While it may be no crime to fire a gun in a deserted area, it is attempted murder if the gun is aimed at another human being; and if the bullet finds its human target, the defendant may be guilty of either murder or manslaughter.

Some respected theorists, such as Glanville Williams, have suggested that *actus reus* should be conceived of as including the absence of excuse or justification. We believe, however, that it will promote clarity of analysis to discuss excuse and justification in the context of defences (see Chapter 10) rather than as part of *actus reus*. This is the more usual approach adopted.

The relationship between the mind and physical acts is complex. Acts, by their very nature, may involve a mental component. A person who blacks out while driving a car may still be behind the wheel but this is not the same as saying that he or she is 'driving' the car. Courts have long accepted that a defendant whose acts are not the product of the defendant's will has not committed an *actus reus*. While if starting afresh one might include this so-called requirement of voluntariness within the rubric of *mens rea*, the judicial tradition has been to view it as part of the *actus reus*.

More broadly, the mental state accompanying an act will often determine whether the act is wrongful or not. A person does not commit theft simply by picking up an object; she does so only if she intends to keep it. Many acts are ambiguous, and *mens rea* can thus help to determine whether the act is wrongful (*reus*). In *R v Court* [1988] 2 All ER 221, a defendant who smacked a 12-year-old girl on her buttocks was charged with indecent assault. To determine whether the assault was indecent, the court looked at the defendant's state of mind. See also *R v Marcus* [1981] 2 All ER 833 (whether sleeping pills are a 'noxious thing' within the meaning of a statute depends in part on the intent with which they are administered).

Conversely, a defendant's acts can assist the jury in determining whether the defendant had the *mens rea* required for a crime. If an accused shot her victim in the heart from close range, the jury may infer an intent to kill. This, however, must be understood only as a *logical inference* for a jury to draw; it is not a conclusion that they can be required to reach (as we will see in the next chapter).

SECTION 2: LIABILITY FOR FAILURE TO ACT

A: Crimes defined in terms of a failure to act

Some statutory offences are defined in terms of a failure to act.

ROAD TRAFFIC ACT 1988

6. Breath tests

(1) Where a constable in uniform has reasonable cause to suspect—
   (a) that a person driving or attempting to drive or in charge of a motor vehicle on a road or other public place has alcohol in his body or has committed a traffic offence whilst the vehicle was in motion, or
   (b) that a person has been driving or attempting to drive or been in charge of a motor vehicle on a road or other public place with alcohol in his body and that that person still has alcohol in his body, or
   (c) that a person has been driving or attempting to drive or been in charge of a motor vehicle on a road or other public place and has committed a traffic offence whilst the vehicle was in motion,

he may, subject to section 9 of this Act, require him to provide a specimen of breath for a breath test.

...

(4) A person who, without reasonable excuse, fails to provide a specimen of breath when required to do so in pursuance of this section is guilty of an offence.

R v Mavji
[1987] 2 All ER 758, Court of Appeal

MICHAEL DAVIES J: . . . [I]t was alleged by the prosecution that . . . the appellant was trading in gold on a large scale at prices which would have inevitably produced a loss but for the fact that the appellant pocketed value added tax moneys which he charged but for which he did not account. The appellant was a director of a company called Princeve Ltd which traded from a shop with work-shop and flat attached in North Wembley . . . .

'Cheating' is, as counsel for the appellant correctly submitted, a common law offence. As such, it was abolished by s. 32(1)(a) of the Theft Act 1968 'except as regards offences relating to the public revenue'. Punishment for cheating the revenue at common law remains at large . . . To establish cheating, so it was submitted, there must be an actual deceit, a positive act such as a false representation and not merely an omission such as a failure to make a value added tax return, even if the purpose of the omission is to avoid the payment of value added tax lawfully due. No such deceit or misrepresentation or other positive act was alleged in this indictment or in the prosecution's evidence or argument at the trials.

...In our judgment, 'cheating the revenue' can take place without any positive act of deceit or, to adopt and respectfully indorse the words of Drake J when ruling on this matter in the appellant's first trial:

> The common law offence of cheating does not necessarily require a false representation, either by words or conduct. Cheating can include any form of fraudulent conduct which results in diverting money from the revenue and in depriving the revenue of money to which it is entitled.

The appellant was in circumstances in which he had a statutory duty to make value added tax returns and to pay over to the Crown the value added tax due. He dishonestly failed to do either. Accordingly, he was guilty of cheating HM The Queen and the public revenue. No further act or omission required to be alleged or proved.

Appeal dismissed.

Although most of the offences where a failure to act will satisfy the requirement of the *actus reus* are statutory, the issue may arise with respect to common law crimes as well.

R v Dytham

[1979] 3 All ER 641, Court of Appeal

LORD WIDGERY CJ: The appellant was a police constable in Lancashire. On 17th March 1977 at about one o'clock in the morning he was on duty in uniform and was standing by a hot dog stall in Duke Street, St Helens. A Mr Wincke was inside the stall and a Mr Sothern was by it. Some thirty yards away was the entrance to Cindy's Club. A man named Stubbs was ejected from the club by a bouncer. A fight ensued in which a number of men joined. There arose cries and screams and other indications of great violence. Mr Stubbs became the object of a murderous assault. He was beaten and kicked to death in the gutter outside the club. All this was audible and visible to the three men at the hot dog stall. At no stage did the appellant make any move to intervene or any attempt to quell the disturbance or to stop the attack on the victim. When the hubbub had died down he adjusted his helmet and drove away ....

His conduct was brought to the notice of the police authority. As a result he appeared on 10th October 1978 in the Crown Court at Liverpool to answer an indictment which was in these terms:

> ...the charge against you is one of misconduct of an officer of justice, in that you...miscon-ducted yourself whilst acting as an officer of justice in that you being present and a witness to a criminal offence namely a violent assault upon one...Stubbs by three others deliberately failed to carry out your duty as a police constable by wilfully omitting to take any steps to preserve the Queen's Peace or to protect the person of the said...Stubbs or to arrest or otherwise bring to justice [his] assailants.

[After conceding that a police constable was a public officer and that there did exist at common law an offence of misconduct in office, counsel for the appellant argued] that not every failure to discharge a duty which devolved on a person as the holder of a public office gave rise to the com-mon law offence of misconduct in that office. As counsel for the appellant put it, non-feasance was not enough. There must be a malfeasance or at least a misfeasance involving an element of corruption. In support of this contention a number of cases were cited from 18th and 19th century reports. It is the fact that in nearly all of them the misconduct asserted involved some corrupt taint; but this appears to have been an accident of circumstance and not a necessary incident of the offence....

In the present case it was not suggested that the appellant could not have summoned or sought assistance to help the victim or to arrest his assailants. The charge as framed left this answer open to him. Not surprisingly he did not seek to avail himself of it, for the facts spoke strongly against any such answer. The allegation made was not of mere non-feasance but of deliberate failure and wilful neglect. This involves an element of culpability which is not restricted to corruption or dishonesty but which must be of such a degree that the misconduct impugned is calculated to injure the public interest so as to call for condemnation and punishment. Whether such a situation is revealed by the evidence is a matter that a jury has to decide . . .

The appeal is dismissed . . . .

■ NOTES AND QUESTIONS

1. The court in *Dytham* distinguishes between failing to do what one ought to do (nonfeasance) and deliberate and wilful neglect (misfeasance). Is this a useful or meaningful distinction, or rather simply a way of characterising those cases where the accused's inaction has deviated so far from what would generally be deemed acceptable that a court has no compunction in imposing criminal liability?

2. To anticipate an issue which will be addressed later in this chapter, if Dytham could have prevented the victim's death by acting as his duty required, has he not caused the victim's death for the purpose of liability for manslaughter?

3. Is there a difference in *moral* culpability between the infliction of harm and the failure to prevent harm; between one whose inaction causes death and one whose actions cause death? If so, should this difference be reflected in the criminal law? For discussion of this question see Wilson, *Criminal Law* (4th edition, Chapter 4).

B: Crimes of omission

In the preceding section we saw instances where the failure to act was itself a crime. These cases pose little problem other than semantic – can an omission be deemed an act? The problem is caused by the tradition of using the term *actus reus*, which seems to imply affirmative action, to include inaction. Once it is recognised that the envisaged illegality consists of the failure to act itself, the problem disappears.

A somewhat different situation occurs where the definition of the crime appears to require affirmative conduct leading to a particular result, but the defendant is tried for a failure to act that would have prevented that result. The issue has arisen most often in cases of homicide, where the victim would have lived if the defendant had taken appropriate action. Two issues should be addressed. The first is how to distinguish acts and omissions. There are significant difficulties attending their analytical separation. For example, if C begins to rescue D but then, on realising it is his enemy, releases his grip so as to let D drown is it C's act – releasing his grip – or his omission – failing to complete the mission – which causes D's death?[1] It is clearly of central importance, given that liability for murder may depend upon it, to know whether given conduct constitutes one rather than the other. This was the central question in *Airedale AHA* v *Bland* (see below) in which the House of Lords were asked to decide whether a doctor turning off a patient's life support machine when there was no prospect of recovery was 'acting' (the

---

1 M Moore, op cit 27.

bodily movement involved in flicking a switch) or omitting to act (omitting to provide the patient with the nutritional resources needed to live). If it was the former the doctor would be acting unlawfully which could mean he/she would be guilty of murder. If it was the latter he/she may be acting lawfully depending upon the answer to the second question which is when a failure to act warrants criminal liability?

As a starting point, we might note that in the UK there is no legal (as opposed to moral) duty to help others. There is thus no obligation to shout a warning to a blind man about to walk off a cliff or to summon aid when he in fact falls over the cliff. Whether such duties *should* be imposed by law is an issue worthy of debate, but is a matter for Parliament to decide. In many European countries there is a statutory duty to help a person in peril if the actor can do so without personal risk or risk to others. For example, Article 63(2) of the French Penal Code provides:

> Any person who voluntarily fails to render assistance to a person in peril, which he or she could have given either personally or by calling for help, without personal danger or danger to others, is guilty of an offence and may be punished by imprisonment from three months to five years or by a fine of 360 francs to 20,000 francs or both.

In England and Wales, what we are concerned with is situations where there is a legal, and not simply a moral, duty to help another, where the failure to help will lead to criminal liability for the **consequences** of that failure. The situations where such liability can arise are discussed below.

(i) Duties created by contract or office

A professional swimmer who happens to be standing by the pool in which a child is drowning has no legal duty to rescue the child. But is the same true for the lifeguard employed to watch the children in the pool? The lifeguard is under a *contractual* duty to prevent harms of precisely this type. The lifeguard who sits idly by while a child drowns is in breach of contract, but is he also criminally liable for the child's death?

R v Pittwood
(1902) 19 TLR 37, Taunton Assizes

Philip Pittwood was charged with manslaughter. It appeared that the prisoner occupied a hut as a gate-keeper on the Somerset and Dorset Railway near Glastonbury. His duties were to keep the gate shut whenever a train was passing along the line, which was a single line, and not many trains used to pass during the day. His hours of duty were from 7 in the morning till 7 p.m. On 18 July, at about 2.45 in the afternoon, White was in a hay cart crossing the line with several others, when a train came up and hit the cart, White being struck and killed. Another man was also seriously injured, while the three remaining men by jumping out of the cart saved their lives.

MR JUSTICE WRIGHT: without calling upon the prosecution, gave judgment. He said he was clearly of opinion that in this case there was gross and criminal negligence, as the man was paid to keep the gate shut and protect the public. In his opinion:—(1) There might be cases of misfeasance and cases of mere non-feasance. Here it was quite clear there was evidence of misfeasance as the prisoner directly contributed to the accident. (2) A man might incur criminal liability from a duty arising out of contract.

■ NOTES AND QUESTIONS

1. Compare *Pittwood* with *Dytham*, above. Dytham was convicted of misconduct in office; Pittwood of manslaughter. Which is more appropriate – to charge defendants such as Pittwood and Dytham with crimes based on their failure to act, without regard to the consequences of their inaction, or to charge them with a crime that reflects the resulting harm? It can be argued that harm often is a matter of bad luck. If no person had been crossing the railroad tracks, or if the conductor of the train had been able to bring it to a timely stop, there would have been no death in *Pittwood*. Should liability hang on such an accident of fate? A contemporary variant on *Dytham* involves social workers who fail to respond to a manifest risk to a child in the custody of brutal parents. Should they/could they be prosecuted for manslaughter?

2. Pittwood's liability would seem to turn on the fact that there was a clause in his contract that could be made the basis for imposing liability. Yet the contract was between Pittwood and his employer. Pittwood's contractual duty was owed to his employer, not to members of the general public. Is it possible (desirable) to find an implied contractual duty to the public in regard to all occupations where the failure to perform competently can give rise to harm? Consider the situation of prison officials or warders in an institution. Should they be held criminally responsible if one of their charges were to escape and commit a crime? See *Dorset Yacht Co.* v *Home Office* [1970] AC 1004. Reconsider *Dytham*.

(ii) Duties arising from the voluntary assumption of care

Similar and yet distinguishable from cases of duties arising out of the obligation of office (e.g., *Dytham*) and duties arising out of the obligation of contract (e.g., *Pittwood*) are cases where a duty of care has been voluntarily undertaken. In these cases the person has undertaken a duty but, unlike in the other two categories, there is no legal consideration for the undertaking. Can there nonetheless be criminal liability?

R v Instan
[1893] 1 QB 450, Queen's Bench Division

DAY J: Kate Instan . . . who is between thirty and forty years of age and unmarried, had no occupation and no means of her own of living. She was a niece of the deceased.

At the time of the committal of the alleged offence, and for some time previous thereto, she had been living with and had been maintained by the deceased. Deceased was a woman of some seventy-three years of age, and until a few weeks before her death was healthy and able to take care of herself. . . .

The deceased shortly before her death suffered from gangrene in the leg, which rendered her during the last ten days of her life quite unable to attend to herself or to move about or to do anything to procure assistance. No one but the prisoner had previous to the death any knowledge of the condition in which her aunt thus was. The prisoner continued to live in the house at the cost of the deceased, and took in the food supplied by the tradespeople; but does not appear to have given any to the deceased, and she certainly did not give or procure any medical or nursing attendance to or for her, or give notice to any neighbour of her condition or wants, although she had abundant opportunity and occasion to do so.

The body of the deceased was on August 2, while the prisoner was still living in the house, found much decomposed, partially dressed in her day clothes, and lying partly on the ground and partly prone upon the bed. The death probably occurred from four to seven days before August 3, the date of the post-mortem examination of the body. The cause of death was exhaustion caused by the gangrene, but substantially accelerated by neglect, want of food, of nursing, and of medical attendance during several days previous to the death....

LORD COLERIDGE CJ: We are all of opinion that this conviction must be affirmed. It would not be correct to say that every moral obligation involves a legal duty; but every legal duty is founded on a moral obligation. A legal common law duty is nothing else than the enforcing by law of that which is a moral obligation without legal enforcement. There can be no question in this case that it was the clear duty of the prisoner to impart to the deceased so much as was necessary to sustain life of the food which she from time to time took in, and which was paid for by the deceased's own money for the purpose of the maintenance of herself and the prisoner; it was only through the instrumentality of the prisoner that the deceased could get the food. There was, therefore, a common law duty imposed upon the prisoner which she did not discharge.

Nor can there be any question that the failure of the prisoner to discharge her legal duty at least accelerated the death of the deceased, if it did not actually cause it. There is no case directly in point; but it would be a slur upon and a discredit to the administration of justice in this country if there were any doubt as to the legal principle, or as to the present case being within it. The prisoner was under a moral obligation to the deceased from which arose a legal duty towards her; that legal duty the prisoner has wilfully and deliberately left unperformed, with the consequence that there has been an acceleration of the death of the deceased owing to the non-performance of that legal duty. It is unnecessary to say more than that upon the evidence this conviction was most properly arrived at.

R v Stone; R v Dobinson
[1977] 2 All ER 341, Court of Appeal

GEOFFREY LANE LJ:...In 1972, at 75 Broadwater, Bolton-on-Dearne in Yorkshire, there lived three people. Stone, an ex-miner now aged 67, widowed for ten years, who is partially deaf, almost totally blind and has no appreciable sense of smell; Gwendoline Dobinson, now aged 43, who had been his housekeeper and mistress for some eight years, and Stone's son called Cyril, aged 34, who is mentally subnormal. Stone is of low average intelligence. Dobinson is described as ineffectual and somewhat inadequate.

...Stone had a younger sister called Fanny, about 61 at the date of her death. She had been living with another sister called Rosy. For some reason, probably because Rosy could not tolerate her any longer, she had decided to leave. She came to live at no. 75, where she occupied a small front room. She was in receipt of a pension of £11.60 per week and gave her brother £1.50 towards the rent. She was eccentric in many ways. She was morbidly and unnecessarily anxious about putting on weight and so denied herself proper meals. She would take to her room for days. She would often stay in her room all day until the two appellants went to the public house in the evening, when she would creep down and make herself a meal.

In early spring 1975 the police called at the house. Fanny had been found wandering about in the street by herself without apparently knowing where she was. This caused the appellants to try and find Fanny's doctor. They tried to trace him through Rosy, but having walked a very considerable distance in their search they failed.... Fanny herself refused to tell them the doctor's name. She thought she would be 'put away' if she did. Nothing more was done to enlist outside professional aid.

In the light of what happened subsequently there can be no doubt that Fanny's condition over the succeeding weeks and months must have deteriorated rapidly. By July 1975 she was, it seems, unable or unwilling to leave her bed...

...It seems that some efforts were made to get a local doctor, but the neighbour who volunteered to do the telephoning (the appellants being incapable of managing the instrument themselves) was unsuccessful.

On 2nd August 1975 Fanny was found by Dobinson to be dead in her bed....

[The] contention was advanced by counsel...that the evidence which the judge had suggested to the jury might support the assumption of a duty by the appellants did not, when examined, succeed in doing so. He suggested that the situation here was unlike any reported case. Fanny came to this house as a lodger. Largely, if not entirely due to her own eccentricity and failure to look after herself or feed herself properly, she became increasingly infirm and immobile and eventually unable to look after herself. Is it to be said, asks counsel for the appellants rhetorically, that by the mere fact of becoming infirm and helpless in these circumstances, she casts a duty on her brother and Mrs Dobinson to take steps to have her looked after or taken to hospital? The suggestion is that, heartless though it may seem, this is one of those situations where the appellants were entitled to do nothing; where no duty was cast on them to help, any more than it is cast on a man to rescue a stranger from drowning, however easy such a rescue might be.

This court rejects that proposition. Whether Fanny was a lodger or not she was a blood relation of the appellant Stone; she was occupying a room in his house; Mrs Dobinson had undertaken the duty of trying to wash her, of taking such food to her as she required. There was ample evidence that each appellant was aware of the poor condition she was in by mid-July. It was not disputed that no effort was made to summon an ambulance or the social services or the police despite the entreaties of Mrs Wilson and Mrs West. A social worker used to visit Cyril. No word was spoken to him. All these were matters which the jury were entitled to take into account when considering whether the necessary assumption of a duty to care for Fanny had been proved.

This was *not* a situation analagous to the drowning stranger. They *did* make efforts to care. They tried to get a doctor; they tried to discover the previous doctor. Mrs Dobinson helped with the washing and the provision of food. All these matters were put before the jury in terms which we find it impossible to fault. The jury were entitled to find that the duty had been assumed. They were entitled to conclude that once Fanny became helplessly infirm, as she had by 19th July, the appellants were, in the circumstances, obliged either to summon help or else to care for Fanny themselves....

The duty which a defendant has undertaken is a duty of caring for the health and welfare of the infirm person. What the Crown has to prove is a breach of that duty in such circumstances that the jury feel convinced that the defendant's conduct can properly be described as reckless. That is to say a reckless disregard of danger to the health and welfare of the infirm person. Mere inadvertence is not enough. The defendant must be proved to have been indifferent to an obvious risk of injury to health, or actually to have foreseen the risk but to have determined nevertheless to run it.

The direction given by the judge was wholly in accord with these principles. If any criticism is to be made it would be that the direction was unduly favourable to the defence. The appeals against conviction therefore fail.

Appeals against conviction dismissed.

■ **NOTES AND QUESTIONS**

1. Is the decision in *Stone and Dobinson* a logical extension of *Instan*? In what ways are the two cases distinguishable?

2. Both Stone and Dobinson left something to be desired in terms of competence— Stone was described as deaf, blind, and of low intelligence; his mistress Dobinson as ineffectual and inadequate. Was it fair to impose a duty on them to care for Fanny when they could barely care for themselves, not to mention Stone's mentally subnormal son? The Court of Appeal did not seem at all troubled by their general inadequacy, let alone their inability to cope with the extraordinary situation in which they found themselves, one which may well have taxed persons of far greater competence.

3. What was the legal basis for imposing a duty on Stone and Dobinson? Of what relevance was:

   (a) The fact that Fanny was a blood relation? (In the case, Stone, the victim's brother, initially received almost twice the sentence of Dobinson, who was not a blood relative. The sentence, however, was modified on appeal because of Stone's handicapped condition.)

   (b) The fact that Fanny paid £1.50 per week towards the rent? Did this create a contractual obligation? Are landlords generally responsible for the welfare of their tenants?

   (c) The fact that Stone and Dobinson had taken Fanny into their home and provided her with shelter? From a legal point of view, would they have been better advised to have been more cold-hearted and turned Fanny away at the door? What if she had refused to leave?

   (d) The fact that if Stone and Dobinson had not undertaken the care of Fanny, some social agency might have discovered her plight and provided the necessary care? Indeed, a social worker regularly visited Stone and Dobinson because of their disabled child, yet they failed to take advantage of the opportunity to alert the social worker of Fanny's condition. In a sense, Stone and Dobinson isolated Fanny and prevented her from receiving help from others.

   (e) The fact that at the end Fanny was totally helpless. See *R v Smith* [1979] Crim LR 251.

4. What of the responsibility of Fanny, an adult, to care for herself? She refused to cooperate in the search for a doctor and also refused to eat properly. Did Stone and Dobinson incur as a result an obligation to force feed her? Would to do so have constituted an assault (see Chapter 5 and consider *Bland*, below)?

5. Should there be a general duty to help others in distress? What are the arguments for and against such a duty? Should a duty to help others be seen as part of one's obligation of citizenship? Or should that obligation be limited to not causing harm to others? What practical problems of proof might be posed if a law such as that in France (above, p. 65) were to be enacted?

If Stone and Dobinson – ordinary persons – can incur a duty to care for a third party, what of professional carers, such as nurses and doctors (who also may be under a professional duty, a contractual duty and an ethical duty to provide care for their patients)? If such a duty exists, when, if ever, does it come to an end?

Airedale NHS Trust v Bland
[1993] 1 All ER 821, House of Lords

LORD KEITH OF KINKEL : My Lords, as a result of injuries sustained in the Hillsborough disaster, Anthony Bland has for over three years been in the condition known as persistent vegetative state (PVS). It is unnecessary to go into all the details about the manifestations of this state, which are fully set out in the judgments of the courts below. It is sufficient to say that it arises from the destruction, through prolonged deprivation of oxygen, of the cerebral cortex, which has resolved into a watery mass. The cortex is that part of the brain which is the seat of cognitive function and sensory capacity. Anthony Bland cannot see, hear or feel anything. He cannot communicate in any way.

The consciousness which is the essential feature of individual personality has departed for ever. On the other hand the brain stem, which controls the reflexive functions of the body, in particular heartbeat, breathing and digestion, continues to operate. In the eyes of the medical world and of the law a person is not clinically dead so long as the brain stem retains its function. In order to maintain Anthony Bland in his present condition, feeding and hydration are achieved artificially by means of a nasogastric tube and excretionary functions are regulated by a catheter and by enemas. The catheter from time to time gives rise to infections which have to be dealt with by appropriate medical treatment. The undisputed consensus of eminent medical opinion is that there is no prospect whatever that Anthony Bland will ever make any recovery from his present condition, but that there is every likelihood that he will maintain his present state of existence for many years to come, provided that the medical care which he is now receiving is continued.

In that state of affairs the medical men in charge of Anthony Bland's case formed the view, which was supported by his parents, that no useful purpose was to be served by continuing that medical care and that it was appropriate to stop the artificial feeding and other measures aimed at prolonging his existence. Since, however, there were doubts as to whether this course might not constitute a criminal offence, the responsible hospital authority, the Airedale NHS Trust, sought in the High Court of Justice declarations designed to resolve these doubts. In the result declarations on the lines asked for were granted by judgment of Sir Stephen Brown P on 19 November 1992. That judgment was affirmed by the Court of Appeal (Sir Thomas Bingham MR, Butler-Sloss and Hoffmann LJJ) on 9 December 1992. The declarations are in these terms:

> . . . that despite the inability of [the defendant] to consent thereto the Plaintiffs and the responsible attending physicians: (1) may lawfully discontinue all life-sustaining treatment and medical support measures designed to keep [the defendant] alive in his existing persistent vegetative state including the termination of ventilation nutrition and hydration by artificial means; and (2) may lawfully discontinue and thereafter need not furnish medical treatment to [the defendant] except for the sole purpose of enabling [him] to end his life and die peacefully with the greatest dignity and the least of pain suffering and distress . . .

Anthony Bland, by the Official Solicitor as his guardian ad litem, now appeals, with leave given in the Court of Appeal, to your Lordships' House. At the hearing of the appeal your Lordships were assisted by submissions made by Mr Anthony Lester QC as amicus curiae instructed by the Treasury Solicitor.

The broad issue raised by the appeal is stated by the parties to be: 'In what circumstances, if ever, can those having a duty to feed an invalid lawfully stop doing so?' The immediate issue, however, is whether in the particular circumstances of Anthony Bland's case those in charge of it would be acting lawfully if they discontinued the particular measures, including feeding by nasogastric tube, which are now being used to maintain Anthony Bland in his existing condition.

. . .

Where one individual has assumed responsibility for the care of another who cannot look after himself or herself, whether as a medical practitioner or otherwise, that responsibility cannot lawfully be shed unless arrangements are made for the responsibility to be taken over by someone else. Thus a person having charge of a baby who fails to feed it, so that it dies, will be guilty at least of manslaughter. The same is true of one having charge of an adult who is frail and cannot look after herself: see *R* v *Stone* [1977] 2 All ER 341, [1977] QB 354. It was argued for the guardian ad litem, by analogy with that case, that here the doctors in charge of Anthony Bland had a continuing duty to feed him by means of the nasogastric tube and that if they failed to carry out that duty they were guilty of manslaughter, if not murder. This was coupled with the argument that feeding by means of the nasogastric tube was not medical treatment at all, but simply feeding indistinguishable from feeding by normal means. As regards this latter argument, I am of opinion that regard should be had to the whole regime, including the artificial feeding, which at present keeps Anthony Bland alive. That regime amounts to medical treatment and care, and it is incorrect to direct attention exclusively to the fact that nourishment is being provided. In any event, the administration of nourishment by the means adopted involves the application of a medical technique. But it is, of course, true that in general it would not be lawful for a medical practitioner who assumed responsibility for the care of an unconscious patient simply to give up treatment in circumstances where continuance of it would confer some benefit on the patient. On the other hand a medical practitioner is under no duty to continue to treat such a patient where a large body of informed and responsible medical opinion is to the effect that no benefit at all would be conferred by continuance. Existence in a vegetative state with no prospect of recovery is by that opinion regarded as not being a benefit, and that, if not unarguably correct, at least forms a proper basis for the decision to discontinue treatment and care: see *Bolam* v *Friern Hospital Management Committee* [1957] 2 All ER 118, [1957] 1 WLR 582.

Given that existence in the persistent vegetative state is not a benefit to the patient, it remains to consider whether the principle of the sanctity of life, which it is the concern of the state, and the judiciary as one of the arms of the state, to maintain, requires this House to hold that the judgment of the Court of Appeal was incorrect. In my opinion it does not. The principle is not an absolute one. It does not compel a medical practitioner on pain of criminal sanctions to treat a patient, who will die if he does not, contrary to the express wishes of the patient. It does not authorise forcible feeding of prisoners on hunger strike. It does not compel the temporary keeping alive of patients who are terminally ill where to do so would merely prolong their suffering. On the other hand it forbids the taking of active measures to cut short the life of a terminally ill patient. In my judgment it does no violence to the principle to hold that it is lawful to cease to give medical treatment and care to a PVS patient who has been in that state for over three years, considering that to do so involves invasive manipulation of the patient's body to which he has not consented and which confers no benefit upon him.

LORD GOFF OF CHIEVELEY: . . . I start with the simple fact that, in law, Anthony is still alive. It is true that his condition is such that it can be described as a living death; but he is nevertheless still alive.

This is because, as a result of developments in modern medical technology, doctors no longer associate death exclusively with breathing and heart beat, and it has come to be accepted that death occurs when the brain, and in particular the brain stem, has been destroyed (see Professor Ian Kennedy's paper entitled 'Switching off life support machines: the legal implications' reprinted in *Treat Me Right, Essays in Medical Law and Ethics* (1988) esp at 351–352 and the material there cited). There has been no dispute on this point in the present case, and it is unnecessary for me to consider it further. The evidence is that Anthony's brain stem is still alive and functioning and it follows that, in the present state of medical science, he is still alive and should be so regarded as a matter of law.

It is on this basis that I turn to the applicable principles of law. Here, the fundamental principle is the principle of the sanctity of human life—a principle long recognised not only in our own society but also in most, if not all, civilised societies throughout the modern world, as is indeed evidenced by its recognition both in art 2 of the European Convention on Human Rights (Convention for the Protection of Human Rights and Fundamental Freedoms (Rome, 4 November 1950; TS 71 (1953); Cmd 8969)) and in art 6 of the International Covenant on Civil and Political Rights (New York, 19 December 1966; TS 6 (1977); Cmnd 6702).

But this principle, fundamental though it is, is not absolute. Indeed there are circumstances in which it is lawful to take another man's life, for example by a lawful act of self-defence, or (in the days when capital punishment was acceptable in our society) by lawful execution. We are not however concerned with cases such as these. We are concerned with circumstances in which it may be lawful to withhold from a patient medical treatment or care by means of which his life may be prolonged. But here too there is no absolute rule that the patient's life must be prolonged by such treatment or care, if available, regardless of the circumstances.

First, it is established that the principle of self-determination requires that respect must be given to the wishes of the patient, so that, if an adult patient of sound mind refuses, however unreasonably, to consent to treatment or care by which his life would or might be prolonged, the doctors responsible for his care must give effect to his wishes, even though they do not consider it to be in his best interests to do so (see *Schloendorff* v *Society of New York Hospital* (1914) 211 NY 125 at 129–130 per Cardozo J, *S* v *S, W* v *Official Solicitor* [1970] 3 All ER 107 at 111, [1972] AC 24 at 43 per Lord Reid and *Sidaway* v *Bethlem Royal Hospital Governors* [1985] 1 All ER 643 at 649, [1985] AC 871 at 882 per Lord Scarman). To this extent, the principle of the sanctity of human life must yield to the principle of self-determination (see p 851 ante, per Hoffmann LJ), and, for present purposes perhaps more important, the doctor's duty to act in the best interests of his patient must likewise be qualified. On this basis, it has been held that a patient of sound mind may, if properly informed, require that life support should be discontinued: see *Nancy B* v *Hôtel-Dieu de Québec* (1992) 86 DLR (4th) 385. Moreover the same principle applies where the patient's refusal to give his consent has been expressed at an earlier date, before he became unconscious or otherwise incapable of communicating it; though in such circumstances especial care may be necessary to ensure that the prior refusal of consent is still properly to be regarded as applicable in the circumstances which have subsequently occurred (see e.g. *Re T (adult: refusal of medical treatment), Re* [1992] 4 All ER 649, [1992] 3 WLR 782). I wish to add that, in cases of this kind, there is no question of the patient having committed suicide, nor therefore of the doctor having aided or abetted him in doing so. It is simply that the patient has, as he is entitled to do, declined to consent to treatment which might or would have the effect of prolonging his life, and the doctor has, in accordance with his duty, complied with his patient's wishes.

But in many cases not only may the patient be in no condition to be able to say whether or not he consents to the relevant treatment or care, but also he may have given no prior indication of his wishes with regard to it. In the case of a child who is a ward of court, the court itself will decide whether medical treatment should be provided in the child's best interests, taking into account medical opinion. But the court cannot give its consent on behalf of an adult patient who is incapable of himself deciding whether or not to consent to treatment. I am of the opinion that there is nevertheless no absolute obligation upon the doctor who has the patient in his care to prolong his life, regardless of the circumstances . . . .

I must however stress, at this point, that the law draws a crucial distinction between cases in which a doctor decides not to provide, or to continue to provide, for his patient treatment or care which could or might prolong his life and those in which he decides, for example by administering a lethal drug, actively to bring his patient's life to an end. As I have already indicated, the former may be lawful, either because the doctor is giving effect to his patient's wishes by withholding the treatment or care, or even in certain circumstances in which (on principles which I shall describe) the patient is incapacitated from stating whether or not he gives his consent. But it is not lawful for a doctor to administer a drug to his patient to bring about his death, even though that course is prompted by a humanitarian desire to end his suffering, however great that suffering may be.

. . .

At the heart of this distinction lies a theoretical question. Why is it that the doctor who gives his patient a lethal injection which kills him commits an unlawful act and indeed is guilty of murder, whereas a doctor who, by discontinuing life support, allows his patient to die may not act unlawfully and will not do so if he commits no breach of duty to his patient? Professor Glanville Williams has suggested (see *Textbook of Criminal Law* (2nd edn, 1983) p 282) that the reason is that what the doctor does when he switches off a life support machine 'is in substance not an act but an omission to struggle' and that 'the omission is not a breach of duty by the doctor, because he is not obliged to continue in a hopeless case'.

I agree that the doctor's conduct in discontinuing life support can properly be categorised as an omission. It is true that it may be difficult to describe what the doctor actually does as an omission, for example where he takes some positive step to bring the life support to an end. But discontinuation of life support is, for present purposes, no different from not initiating life support in the first place. In each case, the doctor is simply allowing his patient to die in the sense that he is desisting from taking a step which might, in certain circumstances, prevent his patient from dying as a result of his pre-existing condition; and as a matter of general principle an omission such as this will not be unlawful unless it constitutes a breach of duty to the patient. I also agree that the doctor's conduct is to be differentiated from that of, for example, an interloper who maliciously switches off a life support machine because, although the interloper may perform exactly the same act as the doctor who discontinues life support, his doing so constitutes interference with the life-prolonging treatment then being administered by the doctor. Accordingly, whereas the doctor, in discontinuing life support, is simply allowing his patient to die of his pre-existing condition, the interloper is actively intervening to stop the doctor from prolonging the patient's life, and such conduct cannot possibly be categorised as an omission.

The distinction appears, therefore, to be useful in the present context in that it can be invoked to explain how discontinuance of life support can be differentiated from ending a patient's life by a lethal injection. But in the end the reason for that difference is that, whereas the law considers that discontinuance of life support may be consistent with the doctor's duty to care for his patient, it does not, for reasons of policy, consider that it forms any part of his duty to give his patient a lethal injection to put him out of his agony.

...

It is of course the development of modern medical technology, and in particular the development of life support systems, which has rendered cases such as the present so much more relevant than in the past. Even so, where, for example, a patient is brought into hospital in such a condition that, without the benefit of a life support system, he will not continue to live, the decision has to be made whether or not to give him that benefit, if available. That decision can only be made in the best interests of the patient. No doubt, his best interests will ordinarily require that he should be placed on a life support system as soon as necessary, if only to make an accurate assessment of his condition and a prognosis for the future. But, if he neither recovers sufficiently to be taken off it nor dies, the question will ultimately arise whether he should be kept on it indefinitely. As I see it, that question (assuming the continued availability of the system) can only be answered by reference to the best interests of the patient himself having regard to established medical practice. Indeed, if the justification for treating a patient who lacks the capacity to consent lies in the fact that the treatment is provided in his best interests, it must follow that the treatment may, and indeed ultimately should, be discontinued where it is no longer in his best interests to provide it. The question which lies at the heart of the present case is, as I see it, whether on that principle the doctors responsible for the treatment and care of Anthony Bland can justifiably discontinue the process of artificial feeding upon which the prolongation of his life depends.

It is crucial for the understanding of this question that the question itself should be correctly formulated. The question is not whether the doctor should take a course which will kill his patient, or even take a course which has the effect of accelerating his death. The question is whether the doctor should or should not continue to provide his patient with medical treatment or care which, if continued, will prolong his patient's life. The question is sometimes put in striking or emotional terms, which can be misleading. For example, in the case of a life support system, it is sometimes asked: should a doctor be entitled to switch it off, or to pull the plug? And then it is asked: can it be in the best interests of the patient that a doctor should be able to switch the life support system off, when this will inevitably result in the patient's death? Such an approach has rightly been criticised as misleading, for example by Professor Ian Kennedy (in his paper in *Treat Me Right, Essays in Medical Law and Ethics* (1988)), and by Thomas J in *Auckland Area Health Board* v A-G [1993] 1 NZLR 235 at 247. This is because the question is not whether it is in the best interests of the patient that he should die. The question is whether it is in the best interests of the patient that his life should be prolonged by the continuance of this form of medical treatment or care.

The correct formulation of the question is of particular importance in a case such as the present, where the patient is totally unconscious and where there is no hope whatsoever of any amelioration of his condition. In circumstances such as these, it may be difficult to say that it is in his best interests that the treatment should be ended. But, if the question is asked, as in my opinion it should be, whether it is in his best interests that treatment which has the effect of artificially prolonging his life should be continued, that question can sensibly be answered to the effect that it is not in his best interests to do so.

■ NOTES AND QUESTIONS

1. In *Re A (Conjoined Twins: Medical Treatment)* [2001] 1 FLR 1 (for facts and holding see p. 504) the duty to provide care for one conjoined twin conflicted with the duty not to kill the other. Reflecting on the decision in *Bland,* Brooke LJ stated:

   I turn now to the world 'kills' in the definition of murder. In the Tony Bland case (*Airedale NHS Trust* v *Bland* [1993] AC 789) the House of Lords was much exercised with the question whether the cessation of medical treatment and care to a patient who had been in a persistent vegetative state for three years constituted an intentional killing of that patient for the purposes of the law of murder. Lord Goff identified what he described as a crucial distinction in these terms at p 865:

   'I must however stress, at this point, that the law draws a crucial distinction between cases in which a doctor decides not to provide, or to continue to provide, for his patient treatment or care which could or might prolong his life, and those in which he decides, for example by administering a lethal drug, actively to bring his patient's life to an end. As I have already indicated, the former may be lawful, either because the doctor is giving effect to his patient's wishes by withholding the treatment or care or even in certain circumstances in which (on principles which I shall describe) the patient is incapacitated from stating whether or not he gives his consent. But it is not lawful for a doctor to administer a drug to his patient to bring about his death, even though that course is prompted by a humanitarian desire to end his suffering, however great that suffering may be: see *Reg* v *Cox* (unreported), 18 September 1992. So to act is to cross the Rubicon which runs between on the one hand the care of the living patient and on the other hand euthanasia—actively causing his death to avoid or to end his suffering. Euthanasia is not lawful at common law.'

In the Tony Bland case the House of Lords was satisfied that the cessation of life-prolonging treatment or care could not be categorised as a positive act for the purposes of the law of murder, and since on the facts of that case the doctors owed no duty to the patient to prolong his life (since that course, the House of Lords held, would not be in their patient's best interests), they could not be found guilty of a culpable omission to act, either.

It was this distinction between acts and omissions which the judge had in mind when he held that it would be lawful to perform the proposed operation. He explained his thinking in the long passage which Ward LJ has recited fully in his judgment. He believed, in short, that the proposed operation was not unlawful because it did not represent a positive act but merely the withdrawal of Mary's blood supply.

On the hearing of the appeal only Mr Whitfield QC sought to persuade us to uphold the judge's approach. I am satisfied that the judge's approach was wrong. The proposed operation would involve a number of invasions of Mary's body, in the process of identifying which organ belonged to which child, before the positive step was taken of clamping the aorta and bringing about Mary's death. These acts would bear no resemblance to the discontinuance of artificial feeding sanctioned by the House of Lords in the Tony Bland case. They would be positive acts, and they would directly cause Mary's death.

2. Should specific laws be enacted to protect doctors and other medical staff who find themselves in situations such as arose in *Bland* and *Re A*? Should the protection extend to persons such as Stone and Dobinson? What is the difference in their situation?

3. It can be argued that the ultimate issue in cases such as *Bland* and *Re A*, where the potential victim is unable to express an opinion as to whether he or she wishes for life sustaining treatment to be terminated or continued, devolves into the question of 'Who decides?' – the family, the doctors or the courts. Are there sound reasons for preferring one of these potential decision-makers to another? What about leaving the decision to a jury of ordinary citizens?

4. If, while still competent and able to express an opinion, a patient states that he wishes for life sustaining treatment to be continued should he enter into a permanent vegetative state, should the patient be legally entitled to have his views honoured? See *R (on the application of Burke)* v *General Medical Council* [2005] EWCA Civ 1003, [2005] All ER (D) 445.

(iii) Duties arising from a close familial relationship

We said previously that an experienced swimmer would not be criminally liable for failing to rescue a drowning child in a pool, but that a lifeguard under a contractual duty to safeguard the welfare of those in the pool would be liable. What of the parents of the child? Are they under a legal duty to save their drowning child?

R v Gibbins and Proctor
(1919) 13 Cr App R 134, Court of Criminal Appeal

DARLING J: The two appellants were indicted and tried together for the wilful murder of Nelly Gibbins, the daughter of Gibbins. The facts were that Gibbins's wife had left him, and he was living in adultery with Proctor. There were several children, one of whom was the child of Proctor, in the house. He earned good wages, which he brought home and gave to Proctor to maintain the house and those in it. There is no evidence that there was not enough to keep them all in health. And all were looked after except one, namely Nelly, who was starved to death. Her organs were healthy, and there was no reason why she should have died if she had been supplied with food.

. . .

. . . It is sufficient to refer to *Bubb and Hook* [(1850) 4 Cox CC 457], where Williams J said:

> It remains for me to explain to what extent she is responsible. If the omission or neglect to perform the duty was malicious, then the indictment would be supported, and the crime of murder would be made out against the prisoner; but if the omission or neglect were simply culpable, but not arising from a malicious motive on the part of the prisoner, then, though it would be your duty to find her guilty, it should be of manslaughter only. And here it becomes necessary to explain what is meant by the expression malicious, which is thus used. If the omission to provide necessary food or raiment was accompanied with an intention to cause the death of the child, or to cause some serious bodily injury to it, then it would be malicious in the sense imputed by this indictment, and in a case of this kind it is difficult, if not impossible, to understand how a person who contemplated doing serious bodily injury to the child by the deprivation of food, could have meditated anything else than causing its death.

The word used is 'contemplated,' but what has to be proved is an intention to do grievous bodily injury. In our opinion the judge left the question correctly to the jury, and there is no ground for interfering with the convictions for those reasons.

It has been said that there ought not to have been a finding of guilty of murder against Gibbins. The Court agrees that the evidence was less against Gibbins than Proctor, Gibbins gave her money, and as far as we can see it was sufficient to provide for the wants of themselves and all the children. But he lived in the house and the child was his own, a little girl of seven, and he grossly neglected the child. . . .

The case of Proctor is plainer. She had charge of the child. She was under no obligation to do so or to live with Gibbins, but she did so, and receiving money, as it is admitted she did, for the purpose of supplying food, her duty was to see that the child was properly fed and looked after, and to see that she had medical attention if necessary. We agree with what Lord Coleridge CJ said in *Instan* [1893] 1 QB 450. 'There is no case directly in point, but it would be a slur upon, and a discredit to the administration of, justice in this country if there were any doubt as to the legal principle, or as to the present case being within it. The prisoner was under a moral obligation to the deceased from which arose a legal duty towards her; that legal duty the prisoner has wilfully and deliberately left unperformed, with the consequence that there has been an acceleration of the death of the deceased owing to the non-performance of that legal duty.' Here Proctor took upon herself the moral obligation of looking after the children; she was *de facto*, though not *de jure*, the wife of Gibbins and had excluded the child's own mother. She neglected the child undoubtedly, and the evidence shews that as a result the child died. So a verdict of manslaughter at least was inevitable.

Appeals dismissed.

R v Lowe
[1973] 1 QB 702, Court of Appeal

On 20 July 1972, at Nottingham Crown Court (May J), the defendant, Robert Lowe, was charged jointly with Patricia Marshall, with whom he was living, on two counts in an indictment. The first count charged him with manslaughter, in that between

4 October 1971, and 5 November 1971, he unlawfully caused the death of Amanda Marshall. The second count charged him with cruelty to a child, contrary to s. 1(1) of the Children and Young Persons Act 1933, in that he, being a person who had attained the age of 16 years and who had the custody, charge or care of Amanda Marshall, a child under the age of 16 years, wilfully neglected Amanda Marshall in a manner likely to cause her unnecessary suffering or injury to health. The defendant submitted that he had done all that he could have been expected to do and that it was possible that the child's critical condition had arisen only in the last few days prior to 5 November 1971, when he assumed that Patricia Marshall had taken the child to the doctor. By their verdict the jury exonerated the defendant of gross negligence or recklessness but found him guilty of wilful neglect.

PHILLIMORE LJ: . . . In the present case the jury negatived recklessness. How then can mere neglect, albeit wilful, amount to manslaughter? This court feels that there is something inherently unattractive in a theory of constructive manslaughter. It seems strange that an omission which is wilful solely in the sense that it is not inadvertent and the consequences of which are not in fact foreseen by the person who is neglectful should, if death results, automatically give rise to an indeterminate sentence instead of the maximum of two years which would otherwise be the limit imposed.

We think that there is a clear distinction between an act of omission and an act of commission likely to cause harm. Whatever may be the position with regard to the latter it does not follow that the same is true of the former. In other words, if I strike a child in a manner likely to cause harm it is right that, if the child dies, I may be charged with manslaughter. If, however, I omit to do something with the result that it suffers injury to health which results in its death, we think that a charge of manslaughter should not be an inevitable consequence, even if the omission is deliberate.

■ NOTES AND QUESTIONS

1. In *Gibbons and Proctor*, is the rationale for imposing criminal liability on Gibbons (the father) and Proctor (his unmarried partner) the same? Does the court treat Proctor as if she was Gibbons's wife and/or the victim's mother, when in fact she was neither?

2. Which decision – that in *Lowe* or that in *Gibbons and Proctor* – do you find the more persuasive? Which is more likely to promote the welfare of young children? Should this be a relevant consideration?

3. Where a legal duty is imposed as a result of contract or voluntary agreement, the scope and extent of the duty are determined by the terms of the contract or agreement. Where a legal duty arises as a result of a relationship, however, no contractual terms exist. Are there logical limits on the scope and extent of the duty? In the drowning child situation, for example, would a parent who could not swim be liable for failing to jump into the water to attempt to save his or her child? A parent who was a weak swimmer? Discussion of this and related problems is to be found in A. Smart, 'Criminal Liability for Failing to do the Impossible' [1987] 103 LQR 532 and see Wilson (2011) 4.5.

4. What if the parents in the preceding question were unaware of the plight of their child – that the child, for example, has jumped into a neighbour's swimming pool? Is there a duty to be aware of what is happening to one's child? In this context one must carefully distinguish between unawareness of a legal duty, which is generally not a defence (ignorance of the law will not excuse), and unawareness of facts which give rise to a legal duty, which may be a defence.

5. Is there a geographical limitation on liability? Is a parent responsible for his or her child when the child is visiting a friend? When the child is living with one's ex-spouse in another country? Does the duty extend only to members of one's household?

6. If a parent has a duty to his or her child, does an adult child have a duty to his or her parents? Do spouses have duties to one another? See *R v Smith* [1979] Crim LR 251. Do siblings?

7. The Domestic Violence, Crime and Victims Act 2004, s. 5, creates an offence where (a) a child or vulnerable adult dies as a result of the unlawful act of a person who was a member of the same household as the victim and had frequent contact with him; (b) the defendant was such a person at the time of the act; (c) there was a significant risk of serious physical harm being caused to the victim by the unlawful act of such a person; and (d) either the defendant was the person whose act caused the victim's death, or the defendant was, or ought to have been aware of the risk mentioned in (c), failed to take such steps as he could reasonably have been expected to take to protect the victim from the risk, and the act occurred in circumstances of the kind that the defendant foresaw or ought to have foreseen. Would this Act address the problem raised in *Lowe*? In *Stone and Dobinson*?

(iv) Duties arising by virtue of the creation of danger

Consider the person whose actions or inactions are responsible for creating a situation of peril. By virtue of those actions or inactions, does a legal duty arise which did not previously exist?

R v Miller
[1983] 1 All ER 978, House of Lords

LORD DIPLOCK: My Lords, the facts which give rise to this appeal are sufficiently narrated in the written statement made to the police by the appellant Miller. That statement, subject to two minor orthographical corrections, reads:

> Last night I went out for a few drinks and at closing time I went back to the house where I have been kipping for a couple of weeks. I went upstairs into the back bedroom where I've been sleeping. I lay on my mattress and lit a cigarette. I must have fell to sleep because I woke up to find the mattress on fire. I just got up and went into the next room and went back to sleep. Then the next thing I remember was the police and fire people arriving. I hadn't got anything to put the fire out with so I just left it.

He was charged on indictment with the offence of 'arson contrary to section 1(1) and (3) of the Criminal Damage Act, 1971'....

Since arson is a result-crime the period may be considerable, and during it the conduct of the accused that is causative of the result may consist not only of his doing physical acts which cause the fire to start or spread but also of his failing to take measures that lie within his power to counteract the danger that he has himself created. And if his conduct, active or passive, varies in the course of the period, so may his state of mind at the time of each piece of conduct. If, at the time of any particular piece of conduct by the accused that is causative of the result, the state of mind that actuates his conduct falls within the description of one or other of the states of mind that are made a necessary ingredient of the offence of arson by s. 1(1) of the Criminal Damage Act 1971 (i.e. intending to damage property belonging to another or being reckless whether such property would be damaged), I know of no principle of English criminal law that would prevent his being guilty of the offence created by that subsection. Likewise I see no rational ground for excluding from conduct capable of giving rise to criminal liability conduct which consists of failing to take measures that lie within one's power to counteract a danger that one has oneself created, if at the time of such conduct one's state of mind is such as constitutes a necessary ingredient of the offence. I venture to think that the habit of lawyers to talk of 'actus reus', suggestive as it is of action rather than inaction, is responsible for any erroneous notion that failure to act cannot give rise to criminal liability in English law.

No one has been bold enough to suggest that if, in the instant case, the accused had been aware at the time that he dropped the cigarette that it would probably set fire to his mattress and yet had taken no steps to extinguish it he would not have been guilty of the offence of arson, since he would have damaged property of another being reckless whether any such property would be damaged.

I cannot see any good reason why, so far as liability under criminal law is concerned, it should matter at what point of time before the resultant damage is complete a person becomes aware that he has done a physical act which, whether or not he appreciated that it would at the time when he did it, does in fact create a risk that property of another will be damaged, provided that, at the moment of awareness, it lies within his power to take steps, either himself or by calling for the assistance of the fire brigade if this be necessary, to prevent or minimise the damage to the property at risk.

...

My Lords, in the instant case the prosecution did not rely on the state of mind of the accused as being reckless during that part of his conduct that consisted of his lighting and smoking a cigarette while lying on his mattress and falling asleep without extinguishing it. So the jury were not invited to make any finding as to this. What the prosecution did rely on as being reckless was his state of mind during that part of his conduct after he awoke to find that he had set his mattress on fire and that it was smouldering, but did not then take any steps either to try to extinguish it himself or to send for the fire brigade, but simply went into the other room to resume his slumbers, leaving the fire from the already smouldering mattress to spread and to damage that part of the house in which the mattress was.

The recorder, in his lucid summing up to the jury (they took 22 minutes only to reach their verdict), told them that the accused, having by his own act started a fire in the mattress which, when he became aware of its existence, presented an obvious risk of damaging the house, became under a duty to take some action to put it out. The Court of Appeal upheld the conviction, but its ratio decidendi appears to be somewhat different from that of the recorder. As I understand the judgment, in effect it treats the whole course of conduct of the accused, from the moment at which he fell asleep and dropped the cigarette onto the mattress until the time the damage to the house by fire was complete, as a continuous act of the accused, and holds that it is sufficient to constitute the statutory offence of arson if at any stage in that course of conduct the state of mind of the accused, when he fails to try to prevent or minimise the damage which will result from his initial act, although it lies within his power to do so, is that of being reckless whether property belonging to another would be damaged.

My Lords, these alternative ways of analysing the legal theory that justifies a decision which has received nothing but commendation for its accord with common sense and justice have, since the publication of the judgment of the Court of Appeal in the instant case, provoked academic controversy. Each theory has distinguished support. Professor J C Smith espouses the 'duty theory' (see [1982] Crim LR 526 at 528); Professor Glanville Williams who, after the decision of the Divisional Court in *Fagan* v *Metropolitan Police Comr* [1968] 3 All ER 442, [1969] 1 QB 439 appears to have been attracted by the duty theory, now prefers that of the continuous act (see [1982] Crim LR 773). When applied to cases where a person has unknowingly done an act which sets in train events that, when he becomes aware of them, present an obvious risk that property belonging to another will be damaged, both theories lead to an identical result and, since what your Lordships are concerned with is to give guidance to trial judges in their task of summing up to juries, I would for this purpose adopt the duty theory as being the easier to explain to a jury; though I would commend the use of the word 'responsibility', rather than 'duty' which is more appropriate to civil than to criminal law since it suggests an obligation owed to another person, i.e. the person to whom the endangered property belongs, whereas a criminal statute defines combinations of conduct and state of mind which render a person liable to punishment by the state itself.

While, in the general run of cases of destruction or damage to property belonging to another by fire (or other means) where the prosecution relies on the recklessness of the accused, the direction recommended by this House in *R* v *Caldwell* [1982] AC 341 is appropriate, in the exceptional case (which is most likely to be one of arson and of which the instant appeal affords a striking example), where the accused is initially unaware that he has done an act that in fact sets in train events which, by the time the accused becomes aware of them, would make it obvious to anyone who troubled to give his mind to them that they present a risk that property belonging to another would be damaged, a suitable direction to the jury would be that the accused is guilty of the offence under s. 1(1) of the 1971 Act if, when he does become aware that the events in question have happened as a result of his own act, he does not try to prevent or reduce the risk of damage by his own efforts or if necessary by sending for help from the fire brigade and the reason why he does not is either because he has not given any thought to the possibility of there being any such risk or because having recognised that there was some risk involved he has decided not to try to prevent or reduce it.

Appeal dismissed. Certified question answered in the affirmative.

R v Evans
(2009) EWCA 650

The 24-year-old appellant gave C, her 16-year-old half-sister, some heroin. C self-injected the heroin and then developed and complained of symptoms which the appellant recognised as being consistent with a heroin overdose. The appellant and her mother believed that they were responsible for the care of C but they decided not to seek medical assistance because they feared that they, and possibly C, would get into trouble. Instead they put C to bed, hoping that she would recover spontaneously. They remained at the house, checking on C at intervals and then sleeping in the same room as her. The following morning the appellant was woken by her mother who told her that C was dead. The cause of death was heroin poisoning. The appellant was charged with manslaughter. At the end of the prosecution case, the appellant submitted that there was no case to answer as the prosecution had failed to adduce evidence capable of establishing that she had owed C a duty of care. The judge ruled that the appellant was capable of owing a duty of care to C and that the jury should consider whether she did in fact owe such a duty on the basis that she had supplied her with the heroin. In summing up, the judge emphasised that the prosecution case was based solely on the appellant's omission to summon medical help, that before they could convict of manslaughter by omission there had to be a pre-existing duty to act, that it was for the jury to decide whether the appellant owed C a duty of care and that, in the circumstances, the only matter which was capable of giving rise to such a duty was if the appellant had supplied C with the heroin. The appellant was convicted.

On appeal against conviction—

LORD JUDGE CJ: The question in this appeal is not whether the appellant may be guilty of manslaughter for having been concerned in the supply of the heroin which caused the deceased's death. It is whether, notwithstanding that their relationship lacked the features of familial duty or responsibility which marked her mother's relationship with the deceased, she was under a duty to take reasonable steps for the safety of the deceased once she appreciated that the heroin she procured for her was having a potentially fatal impact on her health.

21. When omission or failure to act are in issue two aspects of manslaughter are engaged. Both are governed by decisions of the House of Lords. The first is manslaughter arising from the defendant's gross negligence: *R v Adomako* [1995] 1 AC 171. The second arises when the defendant has created a dangerous situation and when, notwithstanding his appreciation of the consequent risks, he fails to take any reasonable preventative steps: *R v Miller* [1983] 2 AC 161. Gross negligence manslaughter and unlawful act manslaughter are not necessarily mutually exclusive: *R v Willoughby* [2005] 1 WLR 1880. The same applies to the aspects of manslaughter presently under consideration. Indeed care needs to be taken to avoid the risk of allowing the convenience of addressing the different circumstances in which manslaughter may arise to be converted into a compartmentalised, mutually isolated series of offences each inconveniently described by the same word, 'manslaughter'.

22. Miller's duty to act arose after he fell asleep in a squat while holding a lighted cigarette. He woke up and found that his mattress was smouldering. He left the room in which he had been asleep and went back to sleep in an adjoining room. He wholly ignored the smouldering mattress. The house caught fire. He was convicted of arson. In the House of Lords argument ranged over whether his omission to act engaged what was described as the 'duty theory' espoused by Professor J C Smith or whether his reckless omission to rectify the consequences of his earlier unintended act attracted the 'continuing act theory' supported by Professor Glanville Williams. It was submitted that there was no liability in criminal law for an omission unless there was a legal duty to act imposed by common law or by statute, and that no statutory provision imposed a duty neglect of which involved criminal liability, and no common law duty to extinguish an accidental fire or fire innocently started had previously been 'declared'.

23. The decision of the House of Lords was expressed in the single opinion of Lord Diplock. Both theories, he said, led to an identical result. The 'continuing act' basis for liability was not disavowed, but the duty theory was adopted only on the basis that it was easier to explain to a jury, provided the word 'responsibility' rather than 'duty' was used. In fact, the issue has continued to be addressed in the context of 'duty' rather than responsibility, and we shall continue to do so. More important, however, Lord Diplock observed, at p 176, that he could see

> no rational ground for excluding from conduct capable of giving rise to criminal liability, conduct which consists of failing to take measures that lie within one's power to counteract a danger that one has oneself created, if at the time of such conduct one's state of mind is such as constitutes a necessary ingredient of the offence ... I cannot see any good reason why, so far as liability under criminal law is concerned, it should matter at what point of time before the resultant damage is complete a person becomes aware that he has done a physical act which, whether or not he appreciated that it would at the time when he did it, does in fact create a risk that property of another will be damaged; provided that, at the moment of awareness, it lies within his power to take steps, either himself or by calling for the assistance of the fire brigade if this be necessary, to prevent or minimise the damage to the property at risk.

24. The mens rea necessary for arson was, and thereafter the analysis focussed on, recklessness. But the reasoning in the decision does not exclude liability where a different mens rea is required. And if, for example, the result of the fire in *R v Miller* had included the death of a fellow squatter, it appears to us that Miller would properly have been convicted of manslaughter by gross negligence as well as arson: *R v Willoughby* [2005] 1 WLR 1880.

25. Adomako was an anaesthetist and the deceased was his patient. He plainly owed him a duty of care. Lord Mackay of Clashfern LC in the only speech, expressed the opinion that [1995] 1 AC 171, 187: 'the ordinary principles of the law of negligence apply to ascertain whether or not the defendant has been in breach of a duty of care towards the victim who has died.' He answered the certified question, at p 188: 'In cases of manslaughter by criminal negligence involving a breach of duty, it is a sufficient direction to the jury to adopt the gross negligence test set out by the Court of Appeal in the present case ...'

26. Our attention was drawn to a number of subsequent authorities. In *R v Khan (Rungzabe)* [1998] Crim LR 830 a young woman was supplied by the appellants with heroin. This was probably the first occasion on which she had used heroin. She took ten times the recommended therapeutic

dosage and twice the amount likely to be taken even by an experienced user of heroin. She became 'obviously very ill'. She needed medical attention. The appellants, who were drug dealers, left her where she was and did nothing to assist. On the next day they returned and found that she was dead. If she had received medical attention she would probably have survived.

27. The jury was directed that they could consider a manslaughter verdict on the basis of omission. This could arise only if the appellants had set in train 'a chain of events' which gave rise to a risk of harm to the deceased. The relevant act was the supply of heroin to her. The second necessary ingredient was knowledge or awareness of the obvious risk that, having taken the heroin, the deceased would or might be harmed, and that they deliberately took no steps to rectify it. The effect of the direction was 'to extend the duty to summon medical assistance to a drug dealer who supplies heroin to a person who subsequently dies'. This court held that that might be correct (sed quaere today, in the light of *R* v *Kennedy (No 2)* [2008] AC 269), but the issue needed to be closely addressed with the jury. The summing up in relation to manslaughter by omission was flawed. The convictions were quashed. The issue which arises in the present appeal was not directly addressed, although impliedly at any rate it appears that the court would not have rejected criminal liability on this basis.

28. *R* v *Sinclair, Johnson and Smith* (1998) 148 NLJ 1353 raised similar issues. For these purposes the detailed facts need no narrative. Johnson's conviction for manslaughter was quashed on the basis that his conduct had not demonstrated a 'voluntary assumption of a legal duty of care'. What he had done was rather 'a desultory attempt to be of assistance'. The facts were not capable of giving rise to a legal duty of care in his case. Sinclair, however, was in a different position. He was a close friend of the deceased. They lived together, almost like brothers. Sinclair paid for and supplied the deceased with the first dose of methadone and helped him to obtain the second dose. He knew that the deceased was not an addict. He remained with the deceased throughout the period of his unconsciousness. For a long time he was the only person who was with him. On this basis there was material on which the jury, properly directed, could have found that Sinclair owed the deceased a legal duty of care. That accords with the present case.

29. In *R* v *Willoughby* [2005] 1 WLR 1880 the appellant was convicted of manslaughter on the basis of arson. He owned some premises which he decided to destroy by fire. He recruited a man called Drury to help him set fire to the premises. In an explosion the premises collapsed and Mr Drury died. The court accepted that a duty to look after the deceased did not arise merely because the appellant owned the premises which collapsed and in which he was killed. But that fact, taken together with the additional facts that the destruction of the premises was for his financial benefit, that he enlisted the deceased to take part, and that his role was to spread petrol inside the premises, were sufficient, 'in conjunction' to be capable of giving rise to a duty of care: para 20.

30. In *R* v *Wacker* [2003] QB 1207 the appellant's convictions for manslaughter arose from the horrific deaths of 58 illegal immigrants hiding in a container loaded on to a trailer. The appellant was the lorry driver. It was suggested that he owed no duty of care to any of the deceased because they were parties to the same illegal purpose. The court, at para 38, had 'no difficulty in concluding that . . . the [appellant] did voluntarily assume the duty of care [for those in the container]', and he was aware that 'no one's actions other than his own could realistically prevent [them] from suffocating to death'. The appeal was dismissed on the basis that, once the jury decided that the appellant knew about those travelling in the container, it was a very plain case of gross negligence manslaughter.

31. These authorities are consistent with our analysis. None involved what could sensibly be described as manslaughter by mere omission and in each it was an essential requirement of any potential basis for conviction that the defendant should have failed to act when he was under a duty to do so. The duty necessary to found gross negligence manslaughter is plainly not confined to cases of a familial or professional relationship between the defendant and the deceased. In our judgment, consistently with *R* v *Adomako* [1995] 1 AC 171 and the link between civil and criminal liability for negligence, for the purposes of gross negligence manslaughter, when a person has created or contributed to the creation of a state of affairs which he knows, or ought reasonably to know, has become life threatening, a consequent duty on him to act by taking reasonable steps to save the other's life will normally arise.

The directions to the jury

The ingredients of the offence

32. When directing the jury as to the constituents of manslaughter by gross negligence, the judge prepared a detailed note for the jury. He summarised the propositions in four questions:

(1) Has the prosecution made you sure that that defendant . . . owed Carly Townsend a duty of care? (2) If so, has the prosecution made you sure that that defendant was in breach of that duty of care? (3) If so, has the prosecution made you sure that the defendant's breach of that duty of care caused the death of Carly Townsend? (4) If so, has the prosecution made you sure that that defendant's breach of that duty of care was such gross negligence as to amount to the crime of manslaughter?

33. In his summing up the judge emphasised that the prosecution case against the appellant was based 'solely' on her omission 'to summon medical help when Carly . . . was suffering from a heroin overdose', and that the negligence alleged by the prosecution was not any positive act but omission, taking this form. He directed the jury that before they could convict on manslaughter by omission, 'there must be a pre-existing duty to act'.

34. The judge told the jury that he would direct them 'as to the circumstances in which such a duty can arise as a matter of law' but it would be for the jury to decide whether, on the facts they found, either or each of the defendants owed such a duty towards the deceased. In the case of the appellant he directed the jury that as a matter of law the blood relationship between the appellant and her half-sister, who was a minor, did not 'of itself' give rise to a duty of care. He then directed the jury that they had heard that the appellant

did perform some acts to assist Carly during the evening of 2 May, in particular she and her mother placed Carly in the recovery position and they took turns to look to see if she was alright. However, I direct you that as a matter of law there is nothing in that course of conduct which is capable of amounting to an acceptance or an assumption by Gemma Evans of responsibility for Carly so as to give rise to a duty of care. In the present case, the only matter which in law is capable of giving rise to a duty of care owed by Gemma Evans to Carly Townsend would be if Gemma Evans did, on this occasion, as the prosecution allege, act as an intermediary, giving the drugs to Carly herself having first obtained them from Andrew Taylor. If the prosecution have made you sure that Gemma Evans did on this occasion act as an intermediary, giving the drugs to Carly herself, having first obtained them from Andrew Taylor, that is a matter which in law is capable of giving rise to a duty of care. It is for you to decide whether the prosecution has made you sure that such a duty of care has arisen on the facts found by you . . . if the prosecution has not made you sure that Gemma Evans did, on this occasion, act as an intermediary, giving the drugs to Carly herself having first obtained them from Andrew Taylor, then she cannot have owed a duty of care to Carly Townsend and you must find Gemma Evans not guilty. It is for you to decide, having regard to all the circumstances of this case as you find them to be, whether each defendant owed a duty of care towards Carly Townsend.

35. In relation to the circumstances in which a duty of care might arise in this case, these observations must be seen in their context, which is that the only issue of fact which the jury had to decide was the supply issue. Unless the jury was sure of this fact, the remaining undisputed areas of the appellant's involvement (summarised at para 12) would, on the judge's directions, have been insufficient for the purposes of gross negligence manslaughter. Without her involvement in the supply of heroin, the jury was directed that there was no duty on the appellant to act even after she became aware of the serious adverse effect of the drug taking on Carly. If on the other hand she was so involved, that fact, taken with the other undisputed facts would, and on our analysis of the relevant principles did, give rise to a duty on the appellant to act. In law the judge's directions about the ingredients of gross negligence manslaughter, as applied to this case, were correct.

36. We would merely record that the judge's direction that a duty to act did not arise from a voluntary assumption of risk by the appellant may have been appropriate in this case, but it would not

be of universal application where, for example, a voluntary assumption of risk by the defendant had led the victim, or others, to become dependent on him to act.

■ NOTES AND QUESTIONS

1. What was Miller's *actus reus* – the setting of the fire, or the failure to take steps to extinguish the fire after he became aware of it? The problem with finding the *actus reus* in the former is that at that time Miller did not have the mental state required by the statute; indeed, at that time he was asleep. In conceptual terms, there may have been an *actus reus* but there was no *mens rea*. After awakening and discovering the fire, however, Miller took no steps to cause it to be extinguished. Now there was arguably a *mens rea* (recklessness) but no act. The problem is one of 'concurrence' – the requirement that the *actus reus* and the *mens rea* concur, or, stated perhaps more accurately, that the *actus reus* be the product of the *mens rea*. Lord Diplock surmounted the difficulty by finding that Miller's failure to act when he had a legal duty to do so constituted the *actus reus*. An alternative approach would have been to regard the entire series of events as one transaction, with the concurrence element satisfied if there was the requisite *mens rea* at any time during the course of the transaction. See, e.g., *Attorney-General's Reference (No. 4 of 1980)* [1981] 1 WLR 705; *Fagan* v *Metropolitan Police Commissioner* [1968] 3 All ER 442; *R* v *Thabo Meli* [1954] 1 WLR 228. Issues of concurrence will be discussed further in the next chapter.

2. What if the fire had been accidentally set by a visiting friend who had since departed or caused by a faulty lighting circuit? Would Miller still be liable for failing to take steps to extinguish it? If so, on what basis could a duty to act be said to arise? Wilson suggests that a new duty situation could be created out of the responsibilities owed by the occupiers of premises to those who might be affected if hazards arise on the premises and are not remedied. See Wilson, *Criminal Law* (2011) 4.5.

3. In Evans who created the dangerous situation. The respondent or the deceased? Does it matter?

(v) Duties arising by virtue of a duty to control

In some instances persons who have the power to control other persons or animals can be held criminally responsible for harm caused by those other entities. An owner of a dangerous animal, for example, may be liable if the animal escapes and attacks another:

DANGEROUS DOGS ACT 1991

3. Keeping dogs under proper control

　(1) If a dog is dangerously out of control in a public place—
　　(a) the owner; and
　　(b) if different, the person for the time being in charge of the dog, is guilty of an offence, or, if the dog while so out of control injures any person, an aggravated offence, under this subsection.

　　. . .

　(3) If the owner or, if different, the person for the time being in charge of a dog allows it to enter a place which is not a public place but where it is not permitted to be and while it is there—
　　(a) it injures any person; or

(b) there are grounds for reasonable apprehension that it will do so, he is guilty of an offence, or, if the dog injures any person, an aggravated offence, under this subsection.

Where one's power to control relates to another person, there may also be potential criminal liability. Often the crime charged will be one of aiding and abetting (see generally Chapter 13), but the *actus reus* will consist of the failure to prevent the other's actions.

Du Cros v Lambourne
[1907] 1 KB 40, King's Bench Division

LORD ALVERSTONE CJ: . . . We have to consider the facts found in this case. The case states that the appellant must have known that the speed of the car was dangerous; that if Miss Godwin was driving, she was doing so with the consent and approval of the appellant, who was in control of the car, and that he could, and ought to, have prevented her from driving at this excessive and dangerous speed, but that he allowed her to do so and did not interfere in any way. I will not attempt to lay down any general rule or principle, but having regard to these findings of fact, it is, in my opinion, impossible to say that there was in this case no evidence of aiding and abetting on the part of the appellant. . . .

DARLING J: I am of the same opinion. I think that there was ample evidence on which the appellant could be convicted of aiding and abetting Miss Godwin in driving the car at a speed dangerous to the public. The appellant was the owner of the car and in control of it, and he was therefore the person to say who should drive it. The case finds that he *allowed* (I emphasise that) Miss Godwin to do so; that he knew that the speed was dangerous, and that he could and ought to have prevented it. Now, does it affect the validity of the conviction that the appellant was not charged with aiding and abetting but with having driven the car himself? I do not think that it does. . . .

Appeal dismissed.

■ NOTES AND QUESTIONS

1. The idea of holding a defendant liable for failing to prevent the crime of another may make particularly good sense in the corporate crime field. A company is a fictitious, inanimate entity. To say it has committed an *actus reus* or has a *mens rea* may call for considerable stretching of legal doctrines designed originally to apply to natural persons. Might it not make more sense to hold the company liable for failing to prevent a crime by one of its employees or agents? See Gobert and Punch, *Rethinking Corporate Crime* (2003).

2. Would the defendant in *Du Cros* v *Lambourne* have been liable if he had not been present in the car, if he had simply loaned the car to Miss Godwin? If she had borrowed it without permission?

C: Vicarious liability

Similar to cases involving a duty to control are cases in which an individual has the right to supervise the actions of others. If a person under one's supervision commits an offence, is the person in charge also liable for the offence? In such cases there usually has been a positive *actus reus* committed, but not by the supervisor. The cases generally arise in the employment context, and, when liability is imposed, it is generally characterised as 'vicarious'. Vicarious liability has a long history in tort law, but there its purpose is largely to provide compensation for the injured victim. In the criminal law field, vicarious liability is more controversial. The general rule is said to be that one individual is not liable for the criminal acts of another, but there are many exceptions, sometimes created by statute. Consider, for example, the following statute (since amended).

LICENSING ACT 1964

59. Prohibition of sale, etc. of intoxicating liquor outside permitted hours

(1) Subject to the provisions of this Act, no person shall, except during the permitted hours—

(a) himself or by his servant or agent sell or supply to any person in licensed premises or in premises in respect of which a club is registered any intoxicating liquor, whether to be consumed on or off the premises;

...

■ NOTES AND QUESTIONS

1. What considerations might prompt Parliament to enact a statute imposing vicarious liability? What are the pros and cons of such liability?

2. A publican instructs her employees that under no circumstances is any of them to sell liquor to customers outside permitted hours. The publican maintains a constant supervision of the employees. One day, however, the publican is ill, and stays at home so as not to infect her customers. On that day her employee sells liquor during a time when such sales are prohibited. Is the publican liable under the above statute? See *Lindsay* v *Vickers Ltd* [1978] Crim LR 55; *Anderton* v *Rodgers and Others* [1981] Crim LR 404.

3. What if the publican's employee, unbeknownst to her, sells stolen radios to customers in the pub? Assume that the employee is guilty of handling stolen goods. Would the publican also be vicariously liable? Is this situation different from the previous hypothetical? How so?

4. In the United States, vicarious liability serves as the basis for holding companies liable for criminal offences, at least in federal courts but also in many state courts. The company is liable for an offence committed by an employee if the employee was acting within the scope of employment and with the intent to benefit the company at the time of the commission of the offence. The seminal decision is that of the United States Supreme Court in *New York Central & H.R.R.R.* v *United States*, 212 US 481 (1909). In the UK, on the other hand, the judges have been less enamoured by vicarious liability in the corporate crime context. See *Seaboard Offshore Ltd.* v *Secretary of State for Transport* [1994] 1 WLR 541. Because most of the major developments relating to the criminal liability of companies in the UK have occurred in cases involving prosecutions for manslaughter, the discussion of corporate criminal liability (an arguable form of vicarious liability) will be deferred to Chapter 4 on homicide.

In some situations vicarious liability is contemplated by Parliament and the statute is clear on this point. In other cases, the statute does not on its face impose vicarious liability. If vicarious liability is to be imposed, it will be as a result of the court's interpretation of the statutory language.

Mousell Brothers Ltd v *London and North-Western Railway Company*

[1917] 2 KB 836, King's Bench Division

VISCOUNT READING CJ: In this case Foss, whose duty it was as manager to fill up or direct the filling up of the consignment notes from his principals, the appellants, to the respondents, wrongly described the goods with intent to avoid the payment of the rate payable in respect of the right classification of the goods. The question of law is whether the appellants, a limited liability company, can be convicted for this offence. It was not suggested that the directors of the appellant company were themselves parties to this false description. But it is suggested that they can be made criminally responsible for the act of their servant entrusted with the performance of this class of acts, and therefore acting within the scope of his employment. The magistrate convicted the appellants and stated a case for this Court....

The first thing to consider is the language of the statute. Section 98 imposes upon every person being the owner or having the care of goods the obligation to give an exact account in writing of the number or quantity of goods liable to each of the tolls. Then by s. 99: 'If any such owner or other such person fail to give such account, or to produce his way-bill or bill of lading to such... servant of the company demanding the same'—then comes these important words—'or if he give a false account... with intent to avoid the payment of any tolls payable in respect thereof, he shall for every such offence forfeit to the company a sum not exceeding ten pounds for every ton of goods,... and such penalty shall be in addition to the toll to which such goods may be liable.' By s. 2 of the Interpretation Act 1899, it is provided that 'In the construction of every enactment relating to an offence punishable on indictment or on summary conviction, whether contained in an Act passed before or after the commencement of this Act, the expression "person" shall, unless the contrary intention appears, include a body corporate.' In order to determine whether or not the contrary intention does appear, we must consider the broad question under what circumstances can a principal be made criminally responsible for the act of his servant. And then the narrower question, does this section, which imposes the penalty upon the owner, make the principal liable for the act of his servant done within the scope of his employment, but without the knowledge or the instructions of the principal?

The true principle of law is laid down in the case of *Pearks, Gunston & Tee* v *Ward* [1902] 2 KB 1. The passage to which I particularly wish to refer is in the judgment of Channell J:

> By the general principles of the criminal law, if a matter is made a criminal offence, it is essential that there should be something in the nature of mens rea, and, therefore, in ordinary cases a corporation cannot be guilty of a criminal offence, nor can a master be liable criminally for an offence committed by his servant. But there are exceptions to this rule in the case of quasi-criminal offences, as they may be termed, that is to say, where certain acts are forbidden by law under a penalty, possibly even under a personal penalty, such as imprisonment, at any rate in default of payment of a fine.

> ...

Prima facie, then, a master is not to be made criminally responsible for the acts of his servant to which the master is not a party. But it may be the intention of the Legislature, in order to guard against the happening of the forbidden thing, to impose a liability upon a principal even though he does not know of, and is not party to, the forbidden act done by his servant. Many statutes are passed with this object. Acts done by the servant of the licensed holder of licensed premises render the licensed holder in some instances liable, even though the act was done by his servant without the knowledge of the master. Under the Food and Drugs Acts there are again instances well known in these Courts where the master is made responsible, even though he knows nothing of the act done by his servant, and he may be fined or rendered amenable to the penalty enjoined by the law. In those cases the Legislature absolutely forbids the act and makes the principal liable without a mens rea.

> ...

Coming now to the present case, in my view the Legislature must be taken to have known that the forbidden acts were of a kind which, even in the year 1845, would in most cases be done by servants; and yet the penalty is imposed upon 'every person being the owner or having the care of any carriage or goods passing or being upon the railway.' It may be that the words 'person having the care of any carriage or goods,' etc., are wide enough to cover a person who occupied the position of Foss. I am by no means convinced of it. I am inclined to think they mean the bailee who is entrusted with the goods for carriage and who is not the owner. They would clearly not include a servant merely entrusted with the duty of filling up a consignment note. But the forbidden acts are such as would be performed by a servant. The object of the statute was, in my opinion, to forbid the giving of a false description of goods carried by the railway and so protect the railway company from being cheated into carrying goods at less than the due rate. I think, looking at the language and the purpose of this Act, that the Legislature intended to fix responsibility for this quasi-criminal act upon the principal if the forbidden acts were done by his servant within the scope of his employment. If that is the true view, there is nothing to distinguish a limited company from any other principal, and the defendants are properly made liable for the acts of Foss. The magistrate was right and this appeal fails.

ATKIN J: I agree, but I should like to add a few words in view of the argument of Mr Atkinson. I think that the authorities cited by my Lord make it plain that while prima facie a principal is not to be made criminally responsible for the acts of his servants, yet the Legislature may prohibit an act or enforce a duty in such words as to make the prohibition or the duty absolute; in which case the principal is liable if the act is in fact done by his servants. To ascertain whether a particular Act of Parliament has that effect or not regard must be had to the object of the statute, the words used, the nature of the duty laid down, the person upon whom it is imposed, the person by whom it would in ordinary circumstances be performed, and the person upon whom the penalty is imposed....

■ NOTES AND QUESTIONS

1. Vicarious liability is not limited to the employer–employee context. See *Quality Dairies (York) Ltd* v *Pedley* [1952] 1 KB 275 (liability for acts of sub-contractor); *Linnet* v *Metropolitan Police Commissioner* [1946] 1 All ER 380 (liability for acts of co-licensee); *Clode* v *Barnes* [1974] 1 All ER 1166 (liability for acts of partner); *Anderton* v *Rodgers* [1981] Crim LR 404 (liability of committee members of club for illegal sales of barman).

2. Crimes imposing vicarious liability need to be distinguished from those imposing strict liability (to be discussed in Chapter 3). With respect to crimes imposing strict liability, Parliament has dispensed with the need for the prosecution to prove *mens rea*. With respect to crimes imposing vicarious liability, it is the requirement of a personal *actus reus* which has been dispensed with. Often crimes which impose strict liability are construed to allow vicarious liability as well. This coupling is not mere coincidence. *Mens rea* cannot as easily be attributed to another as *actus reus*, so if strict liability could not be imposed, there would be no vicarious liability where such was intended by Parliament. On the other hand, where a statute requires proof of a mental element, the courts will usually hold that that there cannot be vicarious liability. See, e.g., *James & Son Ltd.* v *Smee* [1955] 1 QB 78. Why should the courts be willing to impute an employee's *actus reus* to an employer but not the employee's *mens rea*?

In addition to vicarious liability, the courts have been willing to hold employers liable for crimes committed by a person to whom they have 'delegated' responsibility.

Allen v *Whitehead*

[1930] 1 KB 211

LORD HEWART CJ: This is a case stated by one of the Metropolitan Police magistrates and it raises a question under s. 44 of the Metropolitan Police Act, 1839. The respondent was summoned to answer an information, laid by the appellant, which charged that the respondent on a day in February, 1929, being the keeper of certain premises where refreshments were sold or consumed, did knowingly suffer prostitutes to meet together and remain therein contrary to s. 44 of the statute. [His Lordship having read the material words of the section, continued:] The magistrate, having heard the evidence, came to the conclusion that the charge was not proved, and the question for this Court is whether he came to a correct determination in point of law in dismissing the case.

The facts of the case are simple enough. It is found as a fact that the respondent, who was the occupier and licensee of a refreshment house, which was open day and night, did not himself manage the premises. He received the profits of the business, but for the purpose of the conduct of the business he chose to employ a manager. In these circumstances it was proved that on a certain day in February, and on each of the seven days following, a number of women, known to the respondent's manager to be prostitutes, resorted to the refreshment house, meeting there together with a number of men and remaining therein between the hours of 8 P.M. and 4 A.M., and using obscene language. There are other findings of fact of a similar character. Before the happening of those events—namely, on September 1, 1928—the respondent had been warned by the police about harbouring prostitutes at this refreshment house. Having received that warning, he gave instructions to the manager that no prostitute should be allowed to congregate in the premises, and, more than that, a notice was displayed forbidding them to enter the refreshment house after midnight. So far as the respondent's own acts are concerned, the case finds that he visited the premises about once or twice a week.

Now what is the fair meaning of those facts, if it be not this, that the respondent was to all intents and purposes an absentee who had told his manager to use the discretion which, if he had been upon the premises, he must have used himself?

...

Now here, upon the facts of the case, it is abundantly plain that there was knowledge on the part of the manager. The question is whether upon the proper construction of s. 44 of the Metropolitan Police Act, 1839, that knowledge in the servant is to be imputed to the employer so as to make the employer liable. In my opinion, the answer to that question is in the affirmative. The principle seems to me to be that which was explained, for example, in *Mousell Brothers* v *London and North Western Ry* (1), where Atkin J. (as he then was) said (2): 'I think that the authorities cited by my Lord make it plain that while prima facie a principal is not to be made criminally responsible for the acts of his servants, yet the Legislature may prohibit an act or enforce a duty in such words as to make the prohibition or the duty absolute; in which case the principal is liable if the act is in fact done by his servants. To ascertain whether a particular Act of Parliament has that effect or not regard must be had to the object of the statute, the words used, the nature of the duty laid down, the person upon whom it is imposed, the person by whom it would in ordinary circumstances be performed, and the person upon whom the penalty is imposed.' Applying that canon to the present case, I think that this provision in this statute would be rendered nugatory if the contention raised on behalf of this respondent were held to prevail. That contention was this, that as the respondent did not himself manage the refreshment house and had no personal knowledge that prostitutes met together and remained therein, and had not been negligent in failing to notice these facts, and had not wilfully closed his eyes to them, he could not in law be held responsible. There is a whole chain of cases on the lines of the passage which I have just read from *Mousell Brothers* v *London and North Western Ry*. (1) Reference has been made to *Mullins* v *Collins* (3); *Coppen* v *Moore* (No. 2) (4); and *Bond* v *Evans* (5) and other cases. This seems to me to be a case where the proprietor, the keeper of the house, had delegated his duty to a manager, so far as the conduct of the house was concerned. He had transferred to the manager the exercise of discretion in the conduct of the business, and it seems to me that the only reasonable conclusion is, regard being had to the purposes of this Act, that the knowledge of the manager was the knowledge of the keeper of the house. I think, therefore, that this case ought to go back to the learned magistrate with a direction to convict.

■ NOTES AND QUESTIONS

1. What is the rationale behind the 'delegation' principle? When is there sufficient 'delegation' to hold an employer liable for a crime of an employee? Does *Allen* v *Whitehead* answer these questions?

2. In order to avoid criminal liability, must employers personally supervise all of their employees? Is this practical in a large company? Is it fair to the employer?

3. In *Vane* v *Yiannopoullos* [1965] AC 486 a waitress, contrary to instructions, sold liquor to unauthorised persons. The House of Lords held that the licensee had not committed the offence of knowingly selling liquor to unauthorised persons. Interestingly, the licensee in the case was on the premises at the time, but on a different floor. Why should the licensee in *Allen* v *Whitehead*, who was away from the premises, be held criminally liable, while the licensee in *Vane* v *Yiannopoullos*, who was on the premises, was not? Can the two decisions be reconciled?

4. In order for the 'delegation' principle to apply, the delegation must be 'complete' (whatever that might mean). See *R* v *Winson* [1969] 1 QB 371.

D: Situational liability

On rare occasions, one's circumstances, status or situation may be enough to satisfy the *actus reus* requirement of an offence. As in cases of a failure to act, the defendant has not performed any act. In the failure to act cases, however, the defendant has omitted to do something which he or she should have done. In respect of status or situational offences, it is often not clear what, if anything, the defendant could have done to avoid prosecution.

R v Larsonneur
(1933) 149 LT 542, Court of Criminal Appeal

The appellant who was a French subject, landed in the United Kingdom on the 14 March 1933 with a French passport, which was endorsed with conditions prohibiting her employment in the United Kingdom. On the 22 March 1933 these conditions were varied by a condition requiring her to leave the United Kingdom on that date. She went ... to the Irish Free State, and an order for her deportation therefrom was subsequently made by the executive of that country. On the 20 April she was brought to Holyhead in the custody of the Irish Free State police, who there handed her over to the police of the United Kingdom, and she was kept in custody until her trial. She was convicted of a charge that she 'being an alien to whom leave to land in the United Kingdom had been refused was found in the United Kingdom' contrary to arts 1(3) and 18(1)(b) of the Aliens Order 1920, as amended.

LORD HEWART C J: ... The fact is, as the evidence shows, that the appellant is an alien. She has a French passport, which bears this statement under the date the 14th March 1933, 'Leave to land granted at Folkestone this day on condition that the holder does not enter any employment, paid or unpaid, while in the United Kingdom,' but on the 22nd March that condition was varied and one finds these words: 'The condition attached to the grant of leave to land is hereby varied so as to require departure from the United Kingdom not later than the 22nd March 1933.' Then follows the signature of an Under-Secretary of State. In fact, the appellant went to the Irish Free State and afterwards, in circumstances which are perfectly immaterial, so far as this appeal is concerned, came back to Holyhead. She was at Holyhead on the 21st April 1933, a day after the day limited by the condition on her passport.

In these circumstances, it seems to be quite clear that art. 1(4) of the Aliens Order 1920 (as varied by the Orders of the 12th March 1923 and the 11th Aug. 1931) applies. The article is in the following terms:

> An immigration officer, in accordance with general or special directions of the Secretary of State, may, by general order or notice or otherwise, attach such conditions as he may think fit to the grant of leave to land, and the Secretary of State may at any time vary such conditions in such manner as he thinks fit, and the alien shall comply with the conditions so attached or varied. An alien who fails to comply with any conditions so attached or varied, and an alien who is found in the United Kingdom at any time after the expiration of the period limited by any such condition, shall for the purposes of this Order be deemed to be an alien to whom leave to land has been refused.

The appellant was, therefore, on the 21st April 1933, in the position in which she would have been if she had been prohibited from landing by the Secretary of State and, that being so, there is no reason to interfere with the finding of the jury. She was found here and was, therefore, deemed to be in the class of persons whose landing had been prohibited by the Secretary of State, by reason of the fact that she had violated the condition on her passport. The appeal, therefore, is dismissed and the recommendation for deportation remains.

Appeal dismissed.

■ **NOTES AND QUESTIONS**

1. Lord Hewart CJ, says that the circumstances by which Ms Larsonneur found herself in England were 'perfectly immaterial'. Is the fact that she was returned involuntarily by the police entitled to no weight? Might it have made a difference if she had been forcibly brought back to England by kidnappers?

2. The importance of identifying precisely the elements of the crime charged was stressed in Chapter 1. Part of the explanation for the result in *Larsonneur* may lie in how the offence was defined – 'being found' in England. The *actus reus* was mere physical presence in a particular place; and the statute contained no *mens rea*.

3. In *Winzar* v *Chief Constable of Kent* (1983) *The Times*, 28 March 1983, the defendant was brought to a hospital in a state of intoxication. He was subsequently removed by the police to a public highway, where he was arrested and charged with being found drunk in the highway. His conviction was affirmed on appeal. A contrary result was reached in the American case of *Martin* v *State* (1944) 31 Ala App 334, 17 So 2d 427, where the court said that 'an accusation of drunkenness in a designated public place cannot be established by proof that the accused, while in an intoxicated condition, was involuntarily and forcibly carried to that place by the arresting officer'. Which result, that in *Winzar* or that in *Martin*, do you think is better reasoned? Why?

The potentially harsh results which can flow from situational liability can sometimes be avoided by resourceful statutory interpretation on the part of the court.

Lim Chin Aik v R
[1963] 1 All ER 223, Judicial Committee of the Privy Council

LORD EVERSHED: The appellant Lim Chin Aik (who appears to have been known by several other names but to whom their Lordships will hereafter refer as 'the appellant') has appealed to the Board by special leave from the dismissal on Feb. 24, 1960, by the High Court of Singapore of his appeal against conviction by a magistrate on Aug. 27, 1959, for an offence under s. 6 of the Immigration Ordinance, (1), of the State of Singapore (as later amended) and the sentence then imposed of a fine of $1,250 or three months' imprisonment. The relevant facts fall within a small compass but the point involved in the appeal is one, their Lordships think, of no little importance.

... This charge was in the following terms:

> ... you ... having entered Singapore from the Federation of Malaya in May, 1959, did remain therein whilst prohibited by an order made by the minister under s. 9 prohibiting you from entering Singapore and have thereby contravened s. 6(2) of the Immigration Ordinance, an offence under s. 6(3) punishable under s. 57 thereof.

It is not in dispute that . . . the Minister of Labour and Welfare did make, on May 28, 1959, an order prohibiting the appellant from entering Singapore.

At the trial (which as already stated took place on Aug. 17, 1959) it was proved by the Deputy Assistant Controller of Immigration that the minister's order was received by him on the day on which it was made; but there was no evidence of what was done with the order thereafter and no evidence of any step having been taken by way of publication or otherwise so as to bring the order to the attention of the appellant—or indeed of anyone else. The appellant at his trial did not personally give any evidence at all.

It follows from the foregoing recital of facts that there was at the trial no evidence at all from which it could be properly inferred that the order had in fact come to the notice or attention of the appellant. It was therefore said on the appellant's behalf before the magistrate that, since there was no evidence of guilty intent on his part and that since such a guilty intent on general principles must be an ingredient of any criminal offence, it therefore followed that no offence had been proved against the appellant under the ordinance. This plea was rejected by the magistrate who, basing himself on the terms of the relevant section of the ordinance, held that there was in this case no need for any evidence of *mens rea*. The appellant then appealed to the High Court of Singapore but that court dismissed his appeal without stating any reasons for the dismissal . . . .

Where the subject-matter of the statute is the regulation for the public welfare of a particular activity—statutes regulating the sale of food and drink are to be found among the earliest examples—it can be and frequently has been inferred that the legislature intended that such activities should be carried out under conditions of strict liability. The presumption is that the statute or statutory instrument can be effectively enforced only if those in charge of the relevant activities are made responsible for seeing that they are complied with. When such a presumption is to be inferred, it displaces the ordinary presumption of *mens rea* . . . .

But it is not enough in their Lordships' opinion merely to label the statute as one dealing with a grave social evil and from that to infer that strict liability was intended. It is pertinent also to inquire whether putting the defendant under strict liability will assist in the enforcement of the regulations. That means that there must be something he can do, directly or indirectly, by supervision or inspection, by improvement of his business methods or by exhorting those whom he may be expected to influence or control, which will promote the observance of the regulations. Unless this is so, there is no reason in penalising him, and it cannot be inferred that the legislature imposed strict liability merely in order to find a luckless victim . . . .

. . . Counsel for the respondent was unable to point to anything that the appellant could possibly have done so as to ensure that he complied with the regulations. It was not, for example, suggested that it would be practicable for him to make continuous inquiry to see whether an order had been made against him. Clearly one of the objects of the ordinance is the expulsion of prohibited persons from Singapore, but there is nothing that a man can do about it if, before the commission of the offence, there is no practical or sensible way in which he can ascertain whether he is a prohibited person or not.

Counsel for the respondent, therefore, relied chiefly on the text of the ordinance and their Lordships return, accordingly, to the language of the two material sections. It is to be observed that the Board is here concerned with one who is said (within the terms of s. 6(3)) to have 'contravened' the subsection by 'remaining' in Singapore (after having entered) when he had been 'prohibited' from entering by an 'order' made by the ministry containing such prohibition. It seems to their Lordships that, where a man is said to have contravened an order or an order of prohibition, the common sense of the language presumes that he was aware of the order before he can be said to have contravened it. Their Lordships realise that this statement is something of an oversimplification when applied to the present case: for the 'contravention' alleged is of the unlawful act, prescribed by sub s. (2) of the section, of remaining in Singapore after the date of the order of prohibition. None the less it is their Lordships' view that, applying the test of ordinary sense to the language used, the notion of contravention here alleged is more consistent with the assumption that the person charged had knowledge of the order than the converse. But such a conclusion is in their Lordships' view much reinforced by the use of the word 'remains' in its context. It is to be observed that if the respondent is right a man could lawfully enter Singapore and could thereafter lawfully remain in Singapore until the moment when an order of prohibition against his entering was made; that then, instanter, his purely passive conduct in remaining—that is, the mere continuance, quite unchanged, of his previous behaviour, hitherto perfectly lawful—would become criminal. These considerations bring their Lordships clearly to the conclusion that the sense of the language here in question requires for the commission of a crime thereunder *mens rea* as a constituent of such crime; or at least that there is nothing in the language used which suffices to exclude the ordinary presumption. Their Lordships do not forget the emphasis placed by counsel for the respondent on the fact that the word 'knowingly' or the phrases 'without reasonable cause' or 'without reasonable excuse' are found in various sections of the ordinance (as amended) but find no place in the section now under consideration—see for example s. 16(4), s. 18(4), s. 19(2), s. 29, s. 31(2), s. 41(2) and s. 56(d) and (e) of the ordinance. In their Lordships' view the absence of such a word or phrase in the relevant section is not sufficient in the present case to prevail against the conclusion which the language as a whole suggests. In the first place, it is to be noted that to have inserted such words as 'knowingly' or 'without lawful excuse' in the relevant part of s. 6(3) of the Immigration Ordinance would in any case not have been sensible. Further, in all the various instances where the word or phrase is used in the other sections of the ordinance before-mentioned the use is with reference to the doing of some specific act or the failure to do some specific act as distinct from the more passive continuance of behaviour theretofore perfectly lawful....

■ **NOTES AND QUESTIONS**

1. In which case, *Larsonneur* or *Lim Chin Aik*, was the court more faithful to legislative intent? Note that, unlike Mrs Larsonneur, Lim Chin Aik could, at least in theory, have avoided violating the law if he had known of its existence.

2. Crimes of 'possession' can also be interpreted to require 'knowing' possession. See, e.g., *Lockyer* v *Gibb* [1967] 2 QB 243. Problems can be avoided if care is taken in drafting the statute in the first place. In *Warner* v *Metropolitan Police Commissioner* [1969] 2 AC 256 Lord Pearce suggested:

   It would, I think, be an improvement of a difficult position if Parliament were to enact that when a person has ownership or physical possession of drugs he shall be guilty unless he proves on a balance of probabilities that he was unaware of their nature or had reasonable excuse for their possession.

SECTION 3: CAUSATION

Some crimes are defined such that the offence consists of wrongful conduct accompanied by a wrongful state of mind. No harm need occur. Examples include perjury (neither the judge nor the jury has to believe the perjurer's lies) and dangerous driving (no damage to another vehicle or injury to a person has to result from defendant's driving). Other crimes, however, have as a requirement that a certain result occur. Examples include murder and manslaughter, where a human being has to have died, and criminal damage, where there must have been some damage to property. In crimes defined in terms of results, the prosecution must prove that the defendant's acts *caused* the harmful result.

The term 'causation' may be an unfortunate one. The criminal law is not really concerned with causation at all but with whether it is fair, proper and just to hold a particular defendant responsible for a particular result. Sometimes the answer to this question is 'yes' – because the defendant caused the result – but sometimes the answer is 'yes' although we cannot really say in any strictly logical sense that the defendant caused the result.

The issue most commonly arises in cases of homicide. Where a person has set out to cause death, and the intended victim has died, the issue of causation might seem a formality. However, even here the matter may not be so simple. Sometimes the analysis can be complicated by intervening events. For example, X shoots Y, who is destined to die as a result of the bullet wound. But say that before Y's death from the bullet wound occurs, an ambulance is summoned to transport Y to a hospital. The ambulance is then struck by a car which is being recklessly driven by Z. All in the ambulance, including Y, are instantly killed. Who caused Y's death – X, but for whose assault Y would not have been in the ambulance in the first place, or Z? Or what if the ambulance arrives safely at the hospital, but an incompetent doctor botches a simple operation which would have saved Y's life? Or what if the operation is successful, but Y subsequently contracts pneumonia due to a combination of his weakened condition and his own failure to take adequate care of himself? Or what if the hospital is the target of a terrorist bomb and Y dies in the explosion?

The question of causation can become even more complex when the *actus reus* is an omission. Say that a lifeguard fails to rescue a child in waters which are under the lifeguard's control. We have already noted that the lifeguard is under a legal, and not just a moral, duty to save the child. This supports the view that causation is but one way in which the criminal law makes the determination that it is fair to hold the defendant to account for the consequence. It is fair because he could have prevented it and was under a duty to do so. Why would it be wrong to hold him responsible? Let us examine this hypothetical situation more closely, for it points out several features of causation:

(a) The coroner's report will read 'death by drowning'. The doctor who performs an autopsy will not be able to say whose acts caused that death. The point is that medical cause should not be confused with legal cause – medical cause is concerned with *what* caused the death; legal cause is concerned with *who* caused the death.

(b) There are frequently multiple causes of a result. One cause of the child's death was the child's inability to swim. Another was the lifeguard's failure to rescue the child. If others were present who could have saved the child, they too may be considered as part of the cause of the child's death. The death may further be traced back to the parent's decision to allow the child to go to the pool unaccompanied, knowing that the child was a poor swimmer. Which of these multiple contributors to the child's death should be held legally responsible? Or should they all be held responsible?

(c) To hold a defendant criminally liable for a death one must at a minimum be able to say that 'but for' that person's action or inaction, the death would not have resulted. However, 'but for' or *sine qua non* causation, while *necessary* to justify criminal liability, is not *sufficient* to justify criminal liability. There may be, as we have just seen, an infinite number of 'but for' causes – but for the lifeguard's inaction, the child would not have drowned; but for the parents' decision to allow the child to go to the pool unaccompanied, the child would not have drowned; but for an earlier decision not to provide the child with swimming lessons, but for the parents' decision to conceive the child, etc., etc. The list seems endless and clearly a line must be drawn somewhere. Equally clearly many of the 'but for' causes we have just mentioned are unlikely to be deemed to be legally relevant. *Sine qua non* or 'but for' causation is a *necessary but not a sufficient condition* of criminal liability. It would be improper to convict somebody of a result crime if we cannot say that but for that person's actions the result would have occurred; but the fact that we can say that but for defendant's actions the result would not have occurred is not enough to justify a conviction.

The cause beyond 'but for' cause that is necessary for criminal liability is sometimes called legal or proximate cause. The term 'legal', however, seems otiose, and the term 'proximate' may be misleading. If A sends a letter bomb through the post to B, the fact that it does not arrive until two months later will not break the chain of causation. Nor will the postman who delivers the letter be held liable for the death, even though his acts are most proximate to it. The real issue may be seen as one of imputability or attribution – is it fair and just to attribute the bad result to a particular defendant's act or failure to act, as the case may be? Recognition that this is the real issue in one sense advances our inquiry and in one sense does not. It advances our inquiry in that it directs our attention to questions other than the narrow one of simply whether the defendant's acts caused the result in question. It does not, however, tell us when it would be fair and just to attribute the bad result to the defendant. The student should be aware that a statement that a defendant caused a harmful result may be nothing more than a shorthand way of stating a conclusion rather than providing an explanation. The law clothes the decision with a legal and 'rational' framework which may simply be concealing the moral judgment which deems someone to be responsible for whatever has happened.

There are two questions which must be answered in the affirmative before a defendant can be said to have caused a harmful result:

(a) But for the defendant's action or inaction, would the harmful result have occurred?

(b) Is the defendant's action the legal cause of the result?

A: 'But for' causation

'But for' or *sine qua non* cause (sometimes also referred to as cause in fact) is, as we have said, a necessary but not sufficient condition of liability. So, in a case of a homicide, if it can be shown that the defendant's acts made no difference to the outcome and did not accelerate the time of the deceased's death, then the defendant cannot be convicted of murder, even where he had the intent to kill. In *R v White* [1910] 2 KB 124, for example, the defendant put poison in his mother's drink over a period of time. He was acquitted of murder on the basis of medical evidence that she had died of a heart attack. A conviction for murder would only have been appropriate if the poison had caused the heart attack, which it did not. However, the defendant would be liable for conviction for attempted murder. It is only the result crime that is affected by the failure to establish causation.

Even if a result would not have occurred but for a defendant's acts, it is appropriate to ask to what extent the defendant's acts contributed to the result. An old Latin maxim holds that *de minimis non curat lex* (the law does not care about trifles). The critical question then becomes, how much must a defendant's acts have contributed to the harmful result before the law will take cognisance?

R v Cato and Others

[1976] 1 All ER 260, Court of Appeal

LORD WIDGERY CJ: . . . The victim was a young man called Anthony Farmer. The events leading up to his death occurred on 25th July 1974. On that day Cato and Farmer had been in each other's company for most of the day. (During the day Cato injected Farmer with heroin)

. . . The method, was that each would take his own syringe. He would fill it to his own taste with whatever mixture of powder and water he thought proper. He would then give his syringe to the other half of his pair—in this case Farmer would give his syringe to Cato—and the other half of the pair would conduct the actual act of injection. It is important to notice that the strength of the mixture to be used was entirely dictated by the person who was to receive it because he prepared his own syringe; but it is also to be noticed that the actual act of injection was done by the other half of the pair, which of course has a very important influence on this case when one comes to causation.

. . . The first question was: was there sufficient evidence on which the jury could conclude, as they must have concluded, that adequate causation was present?

When one looks at the evidence it is important to realise that no other cause of Farmer's death was supplied.

Of course behind this whole question of the sufficiency of evidence of causation is the fact that it was not necessary for the prosecution to prove that the heroin was the only cause. As a matter of law, it was sufficient if the prosecution could establish that it was *a* cause, provided it was a cause outside the de minimis range, and effectively bearing on the acceleration of the moment of the victim's death.

When one has that in mind it is, we think, really possible to say that if the jury had been directed to look for heroin as a cause, not de minimis but a cause of substance, and they came back with a verdict of not guilty, the verdict could really be described as a perverse one. The whole background of the evidence was the other way and there certainly was ample evidence, given a proper direction, on which a charge of manslaughter could be supported.

The fact that a victim is near death will not affect the defendant's liability if the defendant's acts hasten or accelerate the death. In a ghoulish sense, every homicide is but a hastening of the inevitable. Thus a mercy killing may still constitute murder or manslaughter. The legal position was set out by Devlin J in the trial of Dr Adams for murder:

Henry Palmer, 'Dr Adams' Trial for Murder'
[1957] Crim LR 365

Devlin J, summing-up to the jury, said murder was an act or series of acts, done by the prisoner, which were intended to kill, and did in fact kill. It did not matter whether Mrs Morrell's death was inevitable and that her days were numbered. If her life were cut short by weeks or months it was just as much murder as if it was cut short by years. There had been a good deal of discussion as to the circumstances in which doctors might be justified in administering drugs which would shorten life. Cases of severe pain were suggested and also cases of helpless misery. The law knew of no special defence in this category, but that did not mean that a doctor who was aiding the sick and dying had to calculate in minutes or even hours, perhaps not in days or weeks, the effect on a patient's life of the medicines which he would administer. If the first purpose of medicine—the restoration of health—could no longer be achieved, there was still much for the doctor to do, and he was entitled to do all that was proper and necessary to relieve pain and suffering even if the measures he took might incidentally shorten life by hours or perhaps even longer. The doctor who decided whether or not to administer the drug could not do his job if he were thinking in terms of hours or months of life. The defence in the present case was that the treatment given by Dr Adams was designed to promote comfort, and if it was the right and proper treatment, the fact that it shortened life did not convict him of murder.

■ NOTES AND QUESTIONS

1. Raising similar issues to *Adams* is the case involving Dr Cox reported in (1992) 12 BMLR 38. See generally Price, 'Euthanasia, Pain Relief and Double Effect' 17 *Legal Studies* 323 and J. C. Smith, 'A Comment on Moor's Case' [2000] Crim LR 41. The relevant themes will be returned to in Chapter 4 on Homicide. Consider also *Re A (Conjoined Twins: Medical Treatment)* [2001] 1 FLR 1 (discussed in Ch. 10).

2. Review the decision in *Bland*. Does the decision in *Adams* provide a more persuasive rationale than that offered in *Bland* for allowing doctors freedom to exercise their best clinical judgment without having to worry about potential homicide charges?

B: Legal or proximate cause

Once the Crown has established 'but for' cause, the issue becomes whether the defendant's acts were the legal or proximate cause of the result. The most difficult cases involve intervening acts by the victim or a third party.

(i) Intervening acts of the victim

There are two types of cases which have frequently arisen. In the first, the victim of a serious but not fatal attack fails to take proper care to treat his or her wounds, with the result that the wounds become infected and the victim dies. Is the individual who inflicted the initial wounds liable for the death? The second type of case occurs where the victim is injured or killed while attempting to escape from an assault. Is the would-be assailant liable for injuries or death stemming from the escape attempt?

(a) Failure to treat one's wounds

R v Dear

[1996] Crim LR 595, Court of Appeal

The appellant appealed against his conviction of murder. The prosecution case was that, following allegations by the appellant's 12-year-old daughter that the deceased had sexually interfered with her, the appellant had slashed the deceased repeatedly with a Stanley knife, and that he had died two days later as a result of the wounds inflicted. The appellant's case was that he had been provoked, but that in any event the chain of causation had been broken between his actions and the death because the deceased had committed suicide either by reopening his wounds or, the wounds having reopened themselves, by failing to take steps to staunch the consequent blood flow. It was argued on the appeal that the suicide of the deceased would have been a *novus actus interveniens* and that the judge had misdirected the jury on the issue of causation.

Held, dismissing the appeal, that the real question in the case was, as the judge had correctly directed the jury, whether the injuries inflicted by the appellant were an operating and significant cause of the death. That had been enunciated as the correct approach in *R v Smith* [1959] 2 QB 35; *R v Blaue* [1975] 1 WLR 1411; *R v Malcherek* [1981] 1 WLR 690; *R v Cheshire* (1991) 93 Cr App R 251, and Smith & Hogan's *Criminal Law* (7th ed.). It would not be helpful to juries if the law required them to decide causation in a case such as the present by embarking on an analysis of whether a victim had treated himself with mere negligence or gross neglect, the latter breaking but the former not breaking the chain of causation between the defendant's wrongful act and the victim's death. It would be a retrograde step if the niceties of apportionment of fault and causation in the civil law, and the roles which the concepts of *novus actus interveniens* and foreseeability did or should play in causation, were to invade the criminal law. In the present case the cause of the deceased's death was bleeding from the artery which the defendant had severed. Whether or not the resumption or continuation of that bleeding was deliberately caused by the deceased, the jury were entitled to find that the appellant's conduct made an operative and significant contribution to the death.

R v Dhaliwal

[2006] EWCA Crim 1139 Court of Appeal, Criminal Division

The facts appear in the judgment of SIR IGOR JUDGE P:

1. On the evening of 22 February 2005, D's wife committed suicide by hanging herself in an outhouse at the back of the matrimonial home. D was indicted with manslaughter of his wife, and inflicting grievous bodily harm on her. On 7 March 2006, at the Central Criminal Court, His Honour Judge Roberts QC ruled that the case should not proceed to trial. There was no basis on which a reasonable jury, properly directed in law, could convict D of either offence. This is an application by the prosecution under section 58 of the Criminal Justice Act 2003 for leave to appeal this terminating ruling.

...

6. On the evening on which she committed suicide there was an argument between Mr and Mrs D, in the course of which, as he admitted later, he struck her on the forehead. The bangle he was wearing at the time cut her skin at the point where his blow landed. It seems likely that this assault operated as the immediate trigger which precipitated her suicide. Psychiatric evidence suggested that the 'overwhelming primary cause' for the suicide 'was the experience of being physically abused by her husband in the context of experiencing many such episodes over a very prolonged period of time'.

7. In the context of this assault, Judge Roberts suggested that, where 'a decision to commit suicide has been triggered by a physical assault which represents the culmination of a course of abusive conduct,' it would be possible for the Crown 'to argue that that final assault played a significant part in causing the victim's death'. That, however, was an argument which the prosecution expressly "disavowed" before him. He went on, 'they preferred the section 20 route, I suspect

because they felt it presented less difficulty when it came to the question of causation. But I do not see any reason in principle why the final assault which triggered the suicide should be looked at in isolation. If a defendant by his previous conduct has reduced the victim to a psychological state in which the "last straw which broke the camel's back" is liable to tip her (or him) over the edge, I would have thought there was some force in the argument that the "last straw" played a significant part in causing the death.'

8. The Crown maintained the same position before us. We were not invited to consider the correctness, or otherwise, of the views expressed on this subject by Judge Roberts. We should however record that, subject to evidence and argument on the critical issue of causation, unlawful violence on an individual with a fragile and vulnerable personality, which is proved to be a material cause of death (even if the result of suicide) would at least arguably, be capable of amounting to manslaughter.

■ NOTES AND QUESTIONS

1. If V chose to commit suicide, albeit under extreme provocation, how could D be said to have caused her death? If I give you an ice-cream, knowing you are on a diet but knowing you love ice creams, and you eat it, have I caused you to eat it?

2. What, if any, is the justification for treating differently two otherwise similarly situated defendants, each of whom stabs his victim, where one victim takes proper care of himself and recovers from his wounds while the other does not and dies?

3. What if the victim in *Dear* had committed suicide, not two days but two years later, because of feelings of guilt – would the defendant still have been responsible? What if, instead of feelings of guilt, the main reasons for the victim's suicide was the pain that was caused by the wounds inflicted in the original assault? Is the foreseeability of suicide a relevant consideration?

4. *Dear* involved a case where the victim could be said to have acted in a contributorily negligent manner. Although a relevant consideration in tort cases, contributory negligence is not generally recognised as a defence in criminal cases. Why should this be so?

What if the defendant's victim refuses all life-saving treatment. Should this fact affect the defendant's liability?

R v Blaue

[1975] 1 WLR 1411, Court of Appeal

LAWTON LJ: . . . The victim was aged 18. She was a Jehovah's Witness. She professed the tenets of that sect and lived her life by them. During the late afternoon of May 3, 1974, the defendant came into her house and asked her for sexual intercourse. She refused. He then attacked her with a knife inflicting four serious wounds. One pierced her lung. The defendant ran away. She staggered out into the road. She collapsed outside a neighbour's house. An ambulance took her to hospital, where she arrived at about 7.30 p.m. Soon after she was admitted to the intensive care ward. At about 8.30 p.m. she was examined by the surgical registrar who quickly decided that serious injury had been caused which would require surgery. As she had lost a lot of blood, before there could be an operation there would have to be a blood transfusion. As soon as the girl appreciated that the surgeon was thinking of organising a blood transfusion for her, she said that she should not be given one and that she would not have one. To have one, she said, would be contrary to her religious beliefs as a Jehovah's Witness. She was told that if she did not have a blood transfusion she would die. She said that she did not care if she did die. She was asked to acknowledge in writing that she had refused to have a blood transfusion under any circumstances. She did so. The prosecution admitted at the trial that had she had a blood transfusion when advised to have one she would not have died. She did so at 12.45 a.m. the next day. The evidence called by the prosecution proved that at all relevant times she was conscious and decided as she did deliberately, and knowing what the consequences of her decision would be. In his final speech to the jury, Mr Herrod for the prosecution accepted that her refusal to have a blood transfusion was *a* cause of her death....

As was pointed out to Mr Comyn in the course of argument, two cases, each raising the same issue of reasonableness because of religious beliefs, could produce different verdicts depending on where the cases were tried. A jury drawn from Preston, sometimes said to be the most Catholic town in England, might have different views about martyrdom to one drawn from the inner suburbs of London. Mr Comyn accepted that this might be so: it was, he said, inherent in trial by jury. It is not inherent in the common law as expounded by Sir Matthew Hale and Maule J. It has long been the policy of the law that those who use violence on other people must take their victims as they find them. This in our judgment means the whole man, not just the physical man. It does not lie in the mouth of the assailant to say that his victim's religious beliefs which inhibited him from accepting certain kinds of treatment were unreasonable. The question for decision is what caused her death. The answer is the stab wound. The fact that the victim refused to stop this end coming about did not break the causal connection between the act and death.

If a victim's personal representatives claim compensation for his death the concept of foreseeability can operate in favour of the wrong-doer in the assessment of such compensation: the wrong-doer is entitled to expect his victim to mitigate his damage by accepting treatment of a normal kind: see *Steele* v *R. George & Co. (1937) Ltd* [1942] AC 497. As Mr Herrod pointed out, the criminal law is concerned with the maintenance of law and order and the protection of the public generally. A policy of the common law applicable to the settlement of tortious liability between subjects may not be, and in our judgment is not, appropriate for the criminal law.

The issue of the cause of death in a trial for either murder or manslaughter is one of fact for the jury to decide. But if, as in this case, there is no conflict of evidence and all the jury has to do is to apply the law to the admitted facts, the judge is entitled to tell the jury what the result of that application will be. In this case the judge would have been entitled to have told the jury that the defendant's stab wound was an operative cause of death. The appeal fails.

■ NOTES AND QUESTIONS

1. For what proposition of law does *Blaue* stand? That one must take one's victim as one finds her, even if she is not a reasonable person? That the victim, a Jehovah's Witness, was not unreasonable in her refusal to accept a blood transfusion, even though it would cost her her life? That whether or not the victim's refusal was unreasonable, it did not 'break the chain of causation'? That the contributory acts of a victim are not (or rarely) relevant to the issue of causation?

2. The doctrine that one must take the victim as one finds him is usually applied in cases of victims who have a physical disability, such as a so-called 'eggshell skull' or haemophilia, and who die from wounds which would not have proved fatal to a 'normal' person. Is *Blaue* distinguishable? In what way?

3. How foreseeable is it that one will prefer to keep faith with the tenets of one's religion rather than receive life-saving treatment? Is this fact relevant? Should it be? Should it matter whether the defendant was aware of the victim's religiosity?

4. What if a victim, elderly and in frail health prior to being assaulted, refuses treatment because she wants her assailant subjected to the maximum legal penalty possible?

5. Note finally that the issue in *Blaue* is not whether the defendant will escape criminal liability. He still has committed a very serious form of assault. Rather,

the issue is whether he is liable for a crime of homicide that entails proof that he caused the victim's death.

(b) Injuries suffered in attempting to escape

The second type of case where it is alleged that the chain of causation has been broken occurs where the victim is injured or killed while trying to escape from an attacker. As a general proposition, this will not affect the defendant's criminal liability, for escape in the face of danger is foreseeable. But does there come a point where the victim's response to the assailant's attack is so unforeseeable and bizarre as to break the chain of causation?

R v Roberts
(1971) 56 Cr App Rep 95, Court of Appeal

The girl's story was that on the evening of May 1 she went to a base camp for troops in Lancashire, being at that time engaged to be married to an American service-man who had gone to Vietnam. She was friendly with many of the people at that base, and from there she went on to a party where she met the appellant, for the first time. She left that party at about 3 a.m., having agreed to travel with the appellant in his car to what he said was another party in Warrington. After they had driven out of Warrington in the direction of Liverpool, she asked the appel-lant where the party was, and he said that they were going to Runcorn. They took a curious route to Runcorn, and eventually, she said, they stopped on what seemed like a big cinder-track. The time by then was apparently about 4 a.m. Then, she said, 'He just jumped on me. He put his hands up my clothes and tried to take my tights off. I started to fight him off, but the door of the car was locked and I could not find the catch. Suddenly he grabbed me and then he drove off and I started to cry and asked him to take me home. He told me to take my clothes off and, if I did not take my clothes off, he would let me walk home, so I asked him to let me do that. He said, if he did, he would beat me up before he let me go. He said that he had done this before and had got away with it and he started to pull my coat off. He was using foul language.' And then she said that she told him, 'I am not like this,' and he said something like, 'You are all like that.' Then he drove on. 'Again,' said the girl, 'he tried to get my coat off, so I got hold of my handbag and I jumped out of the car. When I opened the door he said something and revved the car up and I jumped out....'

STEPHENSON LJ: We have been helpfully referred to a number of reported cases, some well over a century old, of women jumping out of windows, or jumping or throwing themselves into a river, as a consequence of threats of violence or actual violence. The most recent case is the case of *R v Lewis* [1970] Crim LR 647. An earlier case is that of *R v Beech* (1912) 7 Cr App R 197, which was a case of a woman jumping out of a window and injuring herself, and of a man who had friendly relations with her, whom she knew and might have had reason to be afraid of, being prosecuted for inflicting grievous bodily harm upon her, contrary to section 20 of the Offences against the Person Act. In that case the Court of Criminal Appeal (at p. 200) approved the direction given by the trial judge in these terms: 'Will you say whether the conduct of the prisoner amounted to a threat of causing injury to this young woman, was the act of jumping the natural consequence of the conduct of the prisoner, and was the grievous bodily harm the result of the conduct of the prisoner?' That, said the Court, was a proper direction as far as the law went, and they were satisfied that there was evi-dence before the jury of the prisoner causing actual bodily harm to the woman. 'No-one could say,' said Darling J when giving the judgment of the Court, 'that if she jumped from the window it was not a natural consequence of the prisoner's conduct. It was a very likely thing for a woman to do as the result of the threats of a man who was conducting himself as this man indisputably was.'

This Court thinks that that correctly states the law, and that Mr Carus was wrong in submitting to this Court that the jury must be sure that a defendant, who is charged either with inflicting grievous bodily harm or assault occasioning actual bodily harm, must foresee the actions of the victim which result in the grievous bodily harm, or the actual bodily harm. That, in the view of this Court, is not the test. The test is: Was it the natural result of what the alleged assailant said and did, in the sense that it was something that could reasonably have been foreseen as the consequence of what he was saying or doing? As it was put in one of the old cases, it had got to be shown to be his act, and if of course the victim does something so 'daft,' in the words of the appellant in this case, or so unexpected, not that this particular assailant did not actually foresee it but that no reasonable man could be expected to foresee it, then it is only in a very remote and unreal sense a consequence of his assault, it is really occasioned by a voluntary act on the part of the victim which could not reasonably be foreseen and which breaks the chain of causation between the assault and the harm or injury.

■ **NOTES AND QUESTIONS**

1. Should it matter whether V's action was reasonable or reasonably foreseeable if it was nevertheless triggered by D's unlawful act? See *Cheshire* below.

2. In *R v Williams and another* [1992] 2 All ER 182, a hitchhiker was picked up in a car driven by Williams in which the two co-defendants were passengers. The prosecution's case was that the defendants intended to rob the hitch-hiker. However, before they could execute their plan, the hitchhiker, perhaps sensing danger, jumped from the car and was killed. Commenting on the issue of causation, the Court of Appeal stated that the jury should be told to consider two questions: 'first, whether it was reasonably foreseeable that some harm, albeit not serious harm, was likely to result from the threat itself; and, secondly, whether the deceased's reaction in jumping from the moving car was within the range of responses which might be expected from a victim placed in the situation which he was.' What result should the jury have reached?

(c) Self-administration of drugs following unlawful supply
Cases involving defendants who have supplied drugs to a victim who self-injected the drugs and then died as a result, present a problem because of uncertainty as to which test of causation to apply. The *Roberts* test convicts the supplier, as self injection is foreseeable, but why should the supplier be accountable for the fatal consequence of the free deliberate and informed choice of the victim? After years of confusion this is now the position reached by the House of Lords:

R v Kennedy
[2007] UKHL 38, The Appellate Committee

2. The question certified by the Court of Appeal Criminal Division for the opinion of the House neatly encapsulates the question raised by this appeal:

When is it appropriate to find someone guilty of manslaughter where that person has been involved in the supply of a class A controlled drug, which is then freely and voluntarily self-administered by the person to whom it was supplied, and the administration of the drug then causes his death?

3. The agreed facts are clear and simple. The appellant lived in a hostel in which Marco Bosque and Andrew Cody, who shared a room, also lived. On 10 September 1996 the appellant visited the

room which Bosque and Cody shared. Bosque was drinking with Cody. According to Cody, Bosque told the appellant that he wanted 'a bit to make him sleep' and the appellant told Bosque to take care that he did not go to sleep permanently. The appellant prepared a dose of heroin for the deceased and gave him a syringe ready for injection. The deceased then injected himself and returned the empty syringe to the appellant, who left the room. Bosque then appeared to stop breathing. An ambulance was called and he was taken to hospital, where he was pronounced dead. The cause of death was inhalation of gastric contents while acutely intoxicated by opiates and alcohol.

4. The appellant was tried at the Central Criminal Court on an indictment containing two counts: an unparticularised count of manslaughter; and a count of supplying a class A drug (heroin) to another in contravention of section 4(1) of the Misuse of Drugs Act 1971. The appellant pleaded not guilty to both counts.

5. He was convicted of manslaughter. His appeal was dismissed by the Court of Appeal Criminal Division. Prompted by doubts as to the soundness of the Court of Appeal's grounds for dismissing the appellant's first appeal and the safety of his conviction, the Criminal Cases Review Commission on 24 February 2004 exercised its power under section 9 of the Criminal Appeal Act 1995 to refer the appellant's manslaughter conviction back to the Court of Appeal, for reasons which it set out in considerable detail. The reference therefore fell to be treated as an appeal, which the Court of Appeal (Lord Woolf CJ, Davis and Field JJ) heard on 31 January and dismissed on 17 March 2005: [2005] EWCA Crim 685, [2005] 1 WLR 2159. This is the decision which the appellant now challenges.

Manslaughter

6. It is well-established and not in any way controversial that a charge of manslaughter may be founded either on the unlawful act of the defendant ("unlawful act manslaughter") or on the gross negligence of the defendant. This appeal is concerned only with unlawful act manslaughter and nothing in this opinion should be understood as applying to manslaughter caused by gross negligence.

7. To establish the crime of unlawful act manslaughter it must be shown, among other things not relevant to this appeal,

(1) that the defendant committed an unlawful act;
(2) that such unlawful act was a crime (*R v Franklin* (1883) 15 Cox CC 163; *R v Lamb* [1967] 2 QB 981, 988; *R v Dias* [2001] EWCA Crim 2986, [2002] 2 Cr App R 96, para 9); and
(3) that the defendant's unlawful act was a significant cause of the death of the deceased (*R v Cato* [1976] 1 WLR 110, 116–117).

There is now, as already noted, no doubt but that the appellant committed an unlawful (and criminal) act by supplying the heroin to the deceased. But the act of supplying, without more, could not harm the deceased in any physical way, let alone cause his death. As the Court of Appeal observed in *R v Dalby* [1982] 1 WLR 425, 429, 'the supply of drugs would itself have caused no harm unless the deceased had subsequently used the drugs in a form and quantity which was dangerous'. So, as the parties agree, the charge of unlawful act manslaughter cannot be founded on the act of supplying the heroin alone.

8. The parties are further agreed that an unlawful act of the appellant on the present facts must be found, if at all, in a breach of section 23 of the Offences against the Person Act 1861. Although the death of the deceased was the tragic outcome of the injection on 10 September 1996 the death is legally irrelevant to the criminality of the appellant's conduct under the section: he either was or was not guilty of an offence under section 23 irrespective of the death.

9. As it now effectively reads, section 23 of the 1861 Act provides:

Maliciously administering poison, etc, so as to endanger life or inflict grievous bodily harm

Whosoever shall unlawfully and maliciously administer to or cause to be administered to or taken by any other person any poison or other destructive or noxious thing, so as thereby to endanger the life of such person, or so as thereby to inflict upon such person any grievous bodily harm, shall be guilty of [an offence] and being convicted thereof shall be liable . . . to [imprisonment] for any term not exceeding ten years . . . .

The opening and closing words of the section raise no question relevant to this appeal. The substance of the section creates three distinct offences: (1) administering a noxious thing to any other person; (2) causing a noxious thing to be administered to any other person; and (3) causing a noxious thing to be taken by any other person. It is not in doubt that heroin is a noxious thing, and the contrary was not contended.

The factual situations covered by (1), (2) and (3) are clear. Offence (1) is committed where D administers the noxious thing directly to V, as by injecting V with the noxious thing, holding a glass containing the noxious thing to V's lips, or (as in *R v Gillard* (1988) 87 Cr App R 189) spraying the noxious thing in V's face.

Offence (2) is typically committed where D does not directly administer the noxious thing to V but causes an innocent third party TP to administer it to V. If D, knowing a syringe to be filled with poison instructs TP to inject V, TP believing the syringe to contain a legitimate therapeutic substance, D would commit this offence.

Offence (3) covers the situation where the noxious thing is not administered to V but taken by him, provided D causes the noxious thing to be taken by V and V does not make a voluntary and informed decision to take it. If D puts a noxious thing in food which V is about to eat and V, ignorant of the presence of the noxious thing, eats it, D commits offence (3).

The House of Lords stated the agreed basis for a conviction for manslaughter, namely that K had committed an unlawful act which caused V's death.

In the course of his accurate and well-judged submissions on behalf of the crown, Mr David Perry QC accepted that if he could not show that the appellant had committed offence (1) as the unlawful act necessary to found the count of manslaughter he could not hope to show the commission of offences (2) or (3). This concession was rightly made, but the committee heard considerable argument addressed to the concept of causation, which has been misapplied in some of the authorities, and it is desirable that it should be clear why the concession is rightly made.

The criminal law generally assumes the existence of free will. The law recognises certain exceptions, in the case of the young, those who for any reason are not fully responsible for their actions, and the vulnerable, and it acknowledges situations of duress and necessity, as also of deception and mistake. But, generally speaking, informed adults of sound mind are treated as autonomous beings able to make their own decisions how they will act, and none of the exceptions is relied on as possibly applicable in this case. Thus D is not to be treated as causing V to act in a certain way if V makes a voluntary and informed decision to act in that way rather than another. There are many classic statements to this effect. In his article *"Finis for Novus Actus?"* (1989) 48(3) CLJ 391, 392, Professor Glanville Williams wrote:

> I may suggest reasons to you for doing something; I may urge you to do it, tell you it will pay you to do it, tell you it is your duty to do it. My efforts may perhaps make it very much more likely that you will do it. But they do not cause you to do it, in the sense in which one causes a kettle of water to boil by putting it on the stove. Your volitional act is regarded (within the doctrine of responsibility) as setting a new 'chain of causation' going, irrespective of what has happened before.

In chapter XII of *Causation in the Law*, 2nd ed (1985), p 326, Hart and Honoré wrote:

> The free, deliberate, and informed intervention of a second person, who intends to exploit the situation created by the first, but is not acting in concert with him, is normally held to relieve the first actor of criminal responsibility.

This statement was cited by the House with approval in *R v Latif* [1996] 1 WLR 104, 115. The principle is fundamental and not controversial.

15. Questions of causation frequently arise in many areas of the law, but causation is not a single, unvarying concept to be mechanically applied without regard to the context in which the question arises. That was the point which Lord Hoffmann, with the express concurrence of three other members of the House, was at pains to make in *Environment Agency (formerly National Rivers Authority) v Empress Car Co (Abertillery) Ltd* [1999] 2 AC 22. The House was not in that decision purporting to lay down general rules governing causation in criminal law. It was construing, with reference to the facts of the case before it, a statutory provision imposing strict criminal liability on those

who cause pollution of controlled waters. Lord Hoffmann made clear that (p 29E–F) common sense answers to questions of causation will differ according to the purpose for which the question is asked; that (p 31E) one cannot give a common sense answer to a question of causation for the purpose of attributing responsibility under some rule without knowing the purpose and scope of the rule; that (p 32B) strict liability was imposed in the interests of protecting controlled waters; and that (p 36A) in the situation under consideration the act of the defendant could properly be held to have caused the pollution even though an ordinary act of a third party was the immediate cause of the diesel oil flowing into the river. It is worth underlining that the relevant question was the cause of the pollution, not the cause of the third party's act.

16.   The committee would not wish to throw any doubt on the correctness of *Empress Car*. But the reasoning in that case cannot be applied to the wholly different context of causing a noxious thing to be administered to or taken by another person contrary to section 23 of the 1861 Act. In *R v Finlay* [2003] EWCA Crim 3868 (8 December 2003) V was injected with heroin and died. D was tried on two counts of manslaughter, one on the basis that he had himself injected V, the second on the basis that he had prepared a syringe and handed it to V who had injected herself. The jury could not agree on the first count but convicted on the second. When rejecting an application to remove the second count from the indictment, the trial judge ruled, relying on *Empress Car*, that D had produced a situation in which V could inject herself, in which her self-injection was entirely foreseeable and in which self-injection could not be regarded as something extraordinary. He directed the jury along those lines. The Court of Appeal upheld the judge's analysis and dismissed the appeal. It was wrong to do so. Its decision conflicted with the rules on personal autonomy and informed voluntary choice to which reference has been made above. In the decision under appeal the Court of Appeal did not follow *R v Finlay* in seeking to apply *Empress Car*, and it was right not to do so.

17.   In his article already cited Professor Glanville Williams pointed out (at p 398) that the doctrine of secondary liability was developed precisely because an informed voluntary choice was ordinarily regarded as a *novus actus interveniens* breaking the chain of causation:

> Principals cause, accomplices encourage (or otherwise influence) or help. If the instigator were regarded as causing the result he would be a principal, and the conceptual division between principals (or, as I prefer to call them, perpetrators) and accessories would vanish. Indeed, it was because the instigator was not regarded as causing the crime that the notion of accessories had to be developed. This is the irrefragable argument for recognising the *novus actus* principle as one of the bases of our criminal law. The final act is done by the perpetrator, and his guilt pushes the accessories, conceptually speaking, into the background. Accessorial liability is, in the traditional theory, 'derivative' from that of the perpetrator.

18.   This is a matter of some significance since, contrary to the view of the Court of Appeal when dismissing the appellant's first appeal, the deceased committed no offence when injecting himself with the fatal dose of heroin. It was so held by the Court of Appeal in *R v Dias* [2002] 2 Cr App R 96, paras 21–24, and in *R v Rogers* [2003] EWCA Crim 945, [2003] 1 WLR 1374 and is now accepted. If the conduct of the deceased was not criminal he was not a principal offender, and it of course follows that the appellant cannot be liable as a secondary party. It also follows that there is no meaningful legal sense in which the appellant can be said to have been a principal jointly with the deceased, or to have been acting in concert. The finding that the deceased freely and voluntarily administered the injection to himself, knowing what it was, is fatal to any contention that the appellant caused the heroin to be administered to the deceased or taken by him.

The sole argument open to the crown was, therefore, that the appellant administered the injection to the deceased. It was argued that the term 'administer' should not be narrowly interpreted. Reliance was placed on the steps taken by the appellant to facilitate the injection and on the trial judge's direction to the jury that they had to be satisfied that the appellant handed the syringe to the deceased 'for immediate injection'. But section 23 draws a very clear contrast between a noxious thing administered to another person and a noxious thing taken by another person. It cannot ordinarily be both. In this case the heroin is described as 'freely and voluntarily self-administered' by the deceased. This, on the facts, is an inevitable finding. The appellant supplied the heroin and prepared the syringe. But the deceased had a choice whether to inject himself or not. He chose to do so, knowing what he was doing. It was his act.

In resisting this conclusion Mr Perry relied on *R* v *Rogers* [2003] 1 WLR 1374. In that case the defendant pleaded guilty, following a legal ruling, to a count of administering poison contrary to section 23 of the 1861 Act and a count of manslaughter. The relevant finding was that the defendant physically assisted the deceased by holding his belt round the deceased's arm as a tourniquet, so as to raise a vein in which the deceased could insert a syringe, while the deceased injected himself. It was argued in support of his appeal to the Court of Appeal that the defendant had committed no unlawful act for purposes of either count. This contention was rejected. The court held (para 7) that it was unreal and artificial to separate the tourniquet from the injection. By applying and holding the tourniquet the defendant had played a part in the mechanics of the injection which had caused the death. There is, clearly, a difficult borderline between contributory acts which may properly be regarded as administering a noxious thing and acts which may not. But the crucial question is not whether the defendant facilitated or contributed to administration of the noxious thing but whether he went further and administered it. What matters, in a case such as *R* v *Rogers* and the present, is whether the injection itself was the result of a voluntary and informed decision by the person injecting himself. In *R* v *Rogers*, as in the present case, it was. That case was, therefore, wrongly decided.

It is unnecessary to review the case law on this subject in any detail. In *R* v *Cato* [1976] 1 WLR 110 the defendant had injected the deceased with heroin and the present problem did not arise. In *R* v *Dalby* [1982] 1 WLR 425 the deceased had died following the consumption of drugs which the defendant had supplied but the deceased had injected. There was apparently no discussion of section 23, but it was held that the supply could not support a conviction of manslaughter...

In *R* v *Dias* [2002] 2 Cr App R 96 the defendant had been convicted of manslaughter. He had prepared a syringe charged with heroin which he had handed to the deceased, who had injected himself. The court recognised that the chain of causation had probably been broken by the free and informed decision of the deceased, and noted the error in the decision on the appellant's first appeal as to the unlawfulness of the deceased's injection of himself.

In rejecting the appellant's second appeal in the decision now challenged, the Court of Appeal reviewed the history of the case and the authorities in some detail. The court expressed its conclusion in these paragraphs:

51 In view of the conclusions that we have come to as a result of our examination of the authorities, it appears to us that it was open to the jury to convict the appellant of manslaughter. To convict, the jury had to be satisfied that, when the heroin was handed to the deceased 'for immediate injection', he and the deceased were both engaged in the one activity of administering the heroin. These were not necessarily to be regarded as two separate activities; and the question that remains is whether the jury were satisfied that this was the situation. If the jury were satisfied of this then the appellant was responsible for taking the action in concert with the deceased to enable the deceased to inject himself with the syringe of heroin which had been made ready for his immediate use.

52 In our view, the jury would have been entitled to find (and indeed it is an appropriate finding) that in these circumstances the appellant and the deceased were jointly engaged in administering the heroin. This was the conclusion of this court on the first appeal, as we understand Waller LJ's judgment, and we do not feel it necessary to take a different view, though we do accept that the issue could have been left by the trial judge to the jury in more clear terms than it was.

53 The point in this case is that the appellant and the deceased were carrying out a 'combined operation' for which they were jointly responsible. Their actions were similar to what happens frequently when carrying out lawful injections: one nurse may carry out certain preparatory actions (including preparing the syringe) and hand it to a colleague who inserts the needle and administers the injection, after which the other nurse may apply a plaster. In such a situation, both nurses can be regarded as administering the drug. They are working as a team. Both their actions are necessary. They are interlinked but separate parts in the overall process

of administering the drug. In these circumstances, as Waller LJ stated on the first appeal, they 'can be said to be jointly responsible for the carrying out of that act'.

54 Whether the necessary linkage existed between the actions of the appellant and the deceased was very much a matter for the jury to determine. The question then arises as to whether the trial judge in the summing up expressed the issue in sufficiently clear terms for the jury? As to this, we share similar reservations to those expressed by Waller LJ in his judgment on the first appeal. There was no need for the jury to find the encouragement that Waller LJ thought was necessary. However, the jury did have to find that the appellant and the deceased were acting in concert in administering the heroin.

The court went on in the next paragraph to refer to the deceased and the appellant acting in concert in administering the heroin. Thus the essential ratio of the decision is that the administration of the injection was a joint activity of the appellant and the deceased acting together.

It is possible to imagine factual scenarios in which two people could properly be regarded as acting together to administer an injection. But nothing of the kind was the case here. As in *R* v *Dalby* and *R* v *Dias* the appellant supplied the drug to the deceased, who then had a choice, knowing the facts, whether to inject himself or not. The heroin was, as the certified question correctly recognises, self-administered, not jointly administered. The appellant did not administer the drug. Nor, for reasons already given, did the appellant cause the drug to be administered to or taken by the deceased.

The answer to the certified question is: 'In the case of a fully-informed and responsible adult, never'. The appeal must be allowed and the appellant's conviction for manslaughter quashed. The appellant must have his costs, here and below, out of central funds.

Much of the difficulty and doubt which have dogged the present question has flowed from a failure, at the outset, to identify the unlawful act on which the manslaughter count is founded. It matters little whether the act is identified by a separate count or counts under section 23, or by particularisation of the manslaughter count itself. But it would focus attention on the correct question, and promote accurate analysis of the real issues, if those who formulate, defend and rule on serious charges of this kind were obliged to consider how exactly, in law, the accusation is put.

■ **NOTES AND QUESTIONS**

1. The Draft Criminal Code 1989 would have provided:

17.—(1) Subject to subsections (2) and (3), a person causes a result which is an element of an offence when—

    (a) he does an act which makes a more than negligible contribution to its occurrence; or

    (b) he omits to do an act which might prevent its occurrence and which he is under a duty to do according to the law relating to the offence.

(2) A person does not cause a result where, after he does such an act or makes such an omission, an act or event occurs—

    (a) which is the immediate and sufficient cause of the result,

    (b) which he did not foresee, and

    (c) which could not in the circumstances reasonably have been foreseen.

(3) A person who procures, assists or encourages another to cause a result that is an element of an offence does not himself cause that result so as to be guilty of the offence as a principal except when—

    (a) section 26(1)(c) applies; or

    (b) the offence itself consists in the procuring, assisting or encouraging another to cause the result.

If the Code were implemented would this make any difference to the decision in *Kennedy*?

(ii) Intervening acts of third parties

As a general proposition, one is legally responsible only for one's own acts. If Smith invites Jones to dinner at her house and Jones is assaulted and robbed en route,

Smith is not legally liable, even if she was well aware that she lived in a high crime area where an assault was foreseeable. The mere fact that that Smith's invitation caused Jones to be in a particular place at a particular time when Jones became the victim of a crime will not provide a basis for Smith's liability. On the other hand, Smith would be liable if the robbers had acted on her directions, she having 'set up' Jones for the robbery. In this case the intervening acts of the third party were an integral part of the criminal plan.

Between the case of the innocent act which sets the stage for the commission of a crime and the not-so-innocent act which is part and parcel of the criminal scheme, lie the more troublesome cases where the initial act is wrongful but a subsequent act neither intended nor foreseen by the original actor causes fatal results. Of particular significance in this regard are those cases where there is a joint enterprise between two or more parties to injure V, one of the parties, D, withdraws from that enterprise and the others carry on to kill V. The rules governing this situation are complex and will be covered in Chapter 13. At this stage it suffices to say that in certain circumstances D will remain liable for the death on the basis of his initial participation in a fatal attack but if the killing bears no relation to what D originally signed up for he may escape liability on the basis of the intervening acts of his co-attackers.

Rafferty

[2007] EWCA Crim 1846

The defendant was a party to a brutal attack on V on a Swansea beach involving punches and kicks. D then withdrew from the attack and left the scene. His co-attackers eventually stripped V naked, dragged him into the sea and drowned him.

LORD JUSTICE HOOPER:

39. Mr Spencer helpfully took us through various academic writings and in particular the work of Professor Glanville Williams. Mr Spencer relied upon a passage from the Professor's article *Finis for Novus Actus?* [1989] Cambridge Law Journal 391, at page 396:

If D murderously attacks a victim and leaves him for dead, when in fact he is not dead or even fatally injured, and if X then comes along and, acting quite independently from D, dispatches the victim, the killing will be X's act, not D's, and D would be completely innocent of it. It makes no difference that [D's] act reduced the victim to a condition of helplessness so that he could not defend himself against [X]. (D would, however, be guilty of attempted murder). The analysis is not changed if D was aware of the possibility or even probability of X's intervention, provided that he was not acting in complicity with X . . . (emphasis supplied).

Mr Spencer cited the following passage from Hart and Honore, *Causation in the Law* (2nd edn., 1985), Chapter 12, Criminal Law: Causing Harm at p. 326, a passage which was approved by the Court of Appeal in *Pagett* (1983) 76 Cr.App.R.279.

The free deliberate and informed intervention of a second person, who intends to exploit the situation created by the first, but is not acting in concert with him, is normally held to relieve the first actor of criminal responsibility. (Emphasis added)

Mr Spencer submitted that Rafferty's co-defendants were not acting independently from Rafferty and that Rafferty was acting in complicity with or in concert with them. He submits:

. . . the appellant had undoubtedly been part of a joint enterprise to assault the deceased, and some degree of joint enterprise was still running . . . in that the appellant had agreed to meet up with the other defendants at the scene upon his return from the cash point. This can only have been with a view to sharing the proceeds, or endeavouring to obtain the correct pin number. (Emphasis added)

We do not agree. If Rafferty had withdrawn from the joint enterprise to assault the deceased then, it seems to us, there was no 'degree of [relevant] joint enterprise ... still running'. These passages do not, in our view, therefore help Mr Spencer on the facts of this case.

As we have seen, the judge gave the following direction on *novus actus interveniens*:

Thirdly, that the drowning of Ben Bellamy by Taylor and Thomas was not such a new and intervening act in the chain of events, which was so completely different from the injuries for which Rafferty was responsible, that it overwhelmed those injuries and destroyed any causal connection between them and the death of Ben Bellamy.

44. We have reached the conclusion that no jury could properly conclude that the drowning of Ben Bellamy by Taylor and Thomas was other than a new and intervening act in the chain of events.

If the cause of death is clearly foreseeable, such as the victim who is left unconscious by the ocean's edge and is drowned when the tide comes in, the defendant will be held liable. When the cause of death is less clearly foreseeable, however, the courts have experienced difficulties.

This situation has often arisen in cases of medical malpractice where an injured victim is rushed to a hospital, and a doctor botches an operation that would have saved the victim's life. Is it the original assailant's wound or the doctor's (gross) negligence, or both, which has caused the death? The original assailant would still be liable, of course, for assault, but the question is whether he is liable for a crime of homicide.

These cases have proved troublesome both in theory and practice. In part the problem is that, perhaps more clearly than in other causation cases, the actions of several individuals have contributed to the resulting death, yet the Crown has chosen to single out one (usually the most morally culpable of the actors) for prosecution. The confusion is in no way lessened by the invocation of the Latin phrase *novus actus interveniens* to describe the rationale for holding that the second act prevents the original actor's conviction. Compare the following cases:

R v Jordan

(1956) 40 Cr App R 152, Court of Criminal Appeal

HALLETT J: The facts of the case, so far as I need refer to them, are as follows. The appellant, together with three other men, all serving airmen of the United States Forces, were charged with the murder of a man named Beaumont as the result of a disturbance which arose in a café at Hull. Beaumont was stabbed with a knife. There was no evidence that any one of the other three men used a knife on Beaumont or was acting in concert with the man who did use the knife, and accordingly Byrne J, who tried the case, directed the acquittal of those three men. With regard to the appellant it was ultimately conceded by Mr Veale, who appeared for him in the court below and in this court, that he did use the knife and stab Beaumont. Beaumont was admitted to hospital very promptly and the wound was stitched up, but none the less he died not many days after. In those circumstances the appellant was tried for murder. Various defences were raised, accident, self-defence, provocation and stabbing in the course of a quarrel. On all of those defences the direction of the learned judge is not in any way challenged and the jury rejected them.

... The further evidence is said to show that death was not, to use the words of Byrne J, 'consequent upon the wound inflicted.' On the contrary, both the doctors called are of opinion that, from the medical point of view, it cannot be described as caused by the wound at all. Whether from the legal point of view it could be described as caused by the wound is a more doubtful question.... First, as to the requirements allowing fresh evidence to be called; in the present case it seems clear to us that the fresh evidence was not in any true sense available at the trial. It did not occur to the prosecution, the defence, the judge, or the jury that there could be any doubt but that the stab caused death. The trial proceeded upon that basis. In those circumstances we thought it right to take the view that this was a case where the evidence sought to be given had not been in any true sense available at the trial....

As to the second requisite, namely, that the evidence proposed to be tendered is such that, if the jury had heard that evidence, they might very likely, and indeed probably would, have come to a different verdict, we feel that, if the jury had heard two doctors of the standing of Dr Keith Simpson and Mr Blackburn give evidence that in their judgment death was not due to the stab wound but to something else, the jury might certainly have hesitated very long before saying that they were satisfied that death was due to the stab wound. The jury, of course, would not be bound by medical opinion, but flying in the face of it, particularly in a capital case, is a thing any jury would hesitate to do.... There were two things other than the wound which were stated by these two medical witnesses to have brought about death. The stab wound had penetrated the intestine in two places, but it was mainly healed at the time of death. With a view to preventing infection it was thought right to administer an antibiotic, terramycin.

It was agreed by the two additional witnesses that that was the proper course to take, and a proper dose was administered. Some people, however, are intolerant to terramycin, and Beaumont was one of those people. After the initial doses he developed diarrhoea, which was only properly attributable, in the opinion of those doctors, to the fact that the patient was intolerant to terramycin. Thereupon the administration of terramycin was stopped, but unfortunately the very next day the resumption of such administration was ordered by another doctor and it was recommenced the following day. The two doctors both take the same view about it. Dr Simpson said that to introduce a poisonous substance after the intolerance of the patient was shown was palpably wrong. Mr Blackburn agreed.

Other steps were taken which were also regarded by the doctors as wrong – namely, the intravenous introduction of wholly abnormal quantities of liquid far exceeding the output. As a result the lungs became waterlogged and pulmonary oedema was discovered. Mr Blackburn said that he was not surprised to see that condition after the introduction of so much liquid, and that pulmonary oedema leads to broncho-pneumonia as an inevitable sequel, and it was from broncho-pneumonia that Beaumont died.

We are disposed to accept it as the law that death resulting from any normal treatment employed to deal with a felonious injury may be regarded as caused by the felonious injury, but we do not think it necessary to examine the cases in detail or to formulate for the assistance of those who have to deal with such matters in the future the correct test which ought to be laid down with regard to what is necessary to be proved in order to establish causal connection between the death and the felonious injury. It is sufficient to point out here that this was not normal treatment. Not only one feature, but two separate and independent features, of treatment were, in the opinion of the doctors, palpably wrong and these produced the symptoms discovered at the post-mortem examination which were the direct and immediate cause of death, namely, the pneumonia resulting from the condition of oedema which was found.

The question then is whether it can be said that, if that evidence had been before the jury, it ought not to have, and in all probability would not have, affected their decision. We recognise that the learned judge, if this matter had been before him, would have had to direct the jury correctly on how far such supervening matters could be regarded as interrupting the chain of causation; but we feel that in the end it would have been a question of fact for the jury depending on what evidence they accepted as correct and the view they took on that evidence. We feel no uncertainty at all that, whatever direction had been given to the jury and however correct it had been, the jury would have felt precluded from saying that they were satisfied that death was caused by the stab wound.

For these reasons we come to the conclusion that the appeal must be allowed and the conviction set aside.

R v Smith

[1959] 2 QB 35, Courts-Martial Appeal Court

LORD PARKER CJ: ... The deceased man in fact received two bayonet wounds, one in the arm and one in the back. The one in the back, unknown to anybody, had pierced the lung and caused haemorrhage. There followed a series of unfortunate occurrences. A fellow-member of his company tried to carry him to the medical reception station. On the way he tripped over a wire and dropped the deceased man. He picked him up again, went a little farther, and fell apparently a second time, causing the deceased man to be dropped onto the ground. Thereafter he did not try a third time but went for help, and ultimately the deceased man was brought into the reception station. There, the medical officer, Captain Millward, and his orderly were trying to cope with a number of other cases, two serious stabbings and some minor injuries, and it is clear that they did not appreciate the seriousness of the deceased man's condition or exactly what had happened. A transfusion of saline solution was attempted and failed. When his breathing seemed impaired he was given oxygen and artificial respiration was applied, and in fact he died after he had been in the station about an hour, which was about two hours after the original stabbing. It is now known that having regard to the injuries which the man had in fact suffered, his lung being pierced, the treatment that he was given was thoroughly bad and might well have affected his chances of recovery. There was evidence that there is a tendency for a wound of this sort to heal and for the haemorrhage to stop. No doubt his being dropped on the ground and having artificial respiration applied would halt or at any rate impede the chances of healing. Further, there were no facilities whatsoever for blood transfusion, which would have been the best possible treatment. There was evidence that if he had received immediate and different treatment, he might not have died. Indeed, had facilities for blood transfusion been available and been administered, Dr Camps, who gave evidence for the defence, said that his chances of recovery were as high as 75 per cent.

In these circumstances Mr Bowen urges that not only was a careful summing-up required but that a correct direction to the court would have been that they must be satisfied that the death of Private Creed was a natural consequence and the sole consequence of the wound sustained by him and flowed directly from it. If there was, says Mr Bowen, any other cause, whether resulting from negligence or not, if, as he contends here, something happened which impeded the chance of the deceased recovering, then the death did not result from the wound. The court is quite unable to accept that contention. It seems to the court that if at the time of death the original wound is still an operating cause and a substantial cause, then the death can properly be said to be the result of the wound, albeit that some other cause of death is also operating. Only if it can be said that the original wounding is merely the setting in which another cause operates can it be said that the death does not result from the wound. Putting it in another way, only if the second cause is so overwhelming as to make the original wound merely part of the history can it be said that the death does not flow from the wound.

...

In the present case it is true that the judge-advocate did not in his summing-up go into the refinements of causation. Indeed, in the opinion of this court he was probably wise to refrain from doing so. He did leave the broad question to the court whether they were satisfied that the wound had caused the death in the sense that the death flowed from the wound, albeit that the treatment he received was in the light of after-knowledge a bad thing. In the opinion of this court that was on the facts of the case a perfectly adequate summing-up on causation; I say 'on the facts of the case' because, in the opinion of the court, they can only lead to one conclusion: a man is stabbed in the back, his lung is pierced and haemorrhage results; two hours later he dies of haemorrhage from that wound; in the interval there is no time for a careful examination, and the treatment given turns out in the light of subsequent knowledge to have been inappropriate and, indeed, harmful. In those circumstances no reasonable jury or court could, properly directed, in our view possibly come to any other conclusion than that the death resulted from the original wound. Accordingly, the court dismisses this appeal.

R v Cheshire

[1991] 3 All ER 670, Court of Appeal

In the course of an argument in a fish and chip shop the appellant shot the deceased in the leg and stomach seriously wounding him. The deceased was taken to hospital where he was operated on and placed in intensive care. While in hospital he developed respiratory problems and a tracheotomy tube was placed in his windpipe to assist his breathing. The tube remained in place for four weeks. The deceased suffered further chest infections and other complications and complained of difficulty in breathing. More than two months after the shooting, while still in hospital, the deceased died of cardio-respiratory arrest because his windpipe had become obstructed due to narrowing where the tracheotomy had been performed, such a condition being a rare but not unknown complication arising out of a tracheotomy. The appellant was charged with murder. At his trial evidence for the defence was given by a consultant surgeon that the deceased's leg and stomach wounds no longer threatened his life at the time of his death and that his death was caused by the negligent failure of the medical staff at the hospital to diagnose and treat the deceased's respiratory condition. The trial judge directed the jury that the appellant was responsible for the deceased's death even if the treatment given by the hospital medical staff was incompetent and negligent and it was only if they had been reckless in their treatment of the deceased that he was entitled to be acquitted. The appellant was convicted. He appealed.

BELDAM LJ: . . . [W]hat we think does emerge from . . . the . . . cases is that when the victim of a criminal attack is treated for wounds or injuries by doctors or other medical staff attempting to repair the harm done, it will only be in the most extraordinary and unusual case that such treatment can be said to be so independent of the acts of the accused that it could be regarded in law as the cause of the victim's death to the exclusion of the accused's acts.

Where the law requires proof of the relationship between an act and its consequences as an element of responsibility, a simple and sufficient explanation of the basis of such relationship has proved notoriously elusive.

In a case in which the jury have to consider whether negligence in the treatment of injuries inflicted by the accused was the cause of death we think it is sufficient for the judge to tell the jury that they must be satisfied that the Crown have proved that the acts of the accused caused the death of the deceased, adding that the accused's acts need not be the sole cause or even the main cause of his death, it being sufficient that his acts contributed significantly to that result. Even though negligence in the treatment of the victim was the immediate cause of his death, the jury should not regard it as excluding the responsibility of the accused unless the negligent treatment was so independent of his acts, and in itself so potent in causing death, that they regard the contribution made by his acts as insignificant.

It is not the function of the jury to evaluate competing causes or to choose which is dominant provided they are satisfied that the accused's acts can fairly be said to have made a significant contribution to the victim's death. We think the word 'significant' conveys the necessary substance of a contribution made to the death which is more than negligible.

In the present case the passage in the summing up complained of has to be set in the context of the remainder of the direction given by the judge on the issue of causation. He directed the jury that they had to decide whether the two bullets fired into the deceased on 10 December caused his death on 15 February following. Or, he said, put in another way, did the injuries caused cease to operate as a cause of death because something else intervened? He told them that the prosecution did not have to prove that the bullets were the only cause of death but they had to prove that they were one operative and substantial cause of death. He was thus following the words used in *R v Smith*.

The judge then gave several examples for the jury to consider before reverting to a paraphrase of the alternative formulation used by Lord Parker CJ in *R v Smith*. Finally, he reminded the jury of the evidence which they had heard on this issue. We would remark that on several occasions during this evidence the jury had passed notes to the judge asking for clarification of expressions used by the medical witnesses, which showed that they were following closely the factual issues they had to consider. If the passage to which exception has been taken had not been included, no possible criticism could have been levelled at the summing up. Although for reasons we have stated we think that the judge erred when he invited the jury to consider the degree of fault in the medical treatment rather than its consequences, we consider that no miscarriage of justice has actually occurred. Even if more experienced doctors than those who attended the deceased would have recognised the rare complication in time to have prevented the deceased's death, that complication was a direct consequence of the appellant's acts, which remained a significant cause of his death. We cannot conceive that, on the evidence given, any jury would have found otherwise.

Accordingly, we dismiss the appeal.

■ NOTES AND QUESTIONS

1. When analysing a question involving a death caused through a combination of an unlawful attack by D and medical negligence by M it is important to separate two questions. The first is whether the actions of the medics break the chain of causation. The second is whether the medics' actions are so bad that they deserve punishment for homicide. Only reasons of policy prevent a prosecution of both parties where the chain of causation is not broken but the actions of the medics are nevertheless a substantial cause of death.

2. Should medical incompetence simply be a risk that a defendant has to accept, just as the defendant must take the victim as she finds him?

3. In *R v Malcherek and Steel* [1981] 2 All ER 422, it was claimed that the treating physicians had switched off the victim's life support machines prematurely, thereby causing the victim's death. At the time there was a legitimate medical debate as to when a person should be deemed to have died. The court held that the fact that the doctors in the case had adopted a definition of death with which other doctors might disagree would not break the chain of causation. Whatever might be said about the doctors' treatment, the wound inflicted by the accused was one of the operative causes of death. Stepping back from a strict legal perspective, courts may well be reluctant to expose doctors, trying to do their best in an often difficult situation, to either criminal liability or the civil liability which might follow if any legal responsibility were to be attributed to their actions in the trial of the original assailant.

R v Pagett
(1983) 76 Cr App R 279, Court of Appeal

The defendant, who was armed with a shotgun, used his pregnant girlfriend (Ms Kinchen) as a shield to prevent his arrest by armed police. He fired at the police, who returned his shots. One of the bullets fired by the police killed the girlfriend.

ROBERT GOFF LJ: ... [I]t was pressed upon us by Lord Gifford that there either was, or should be, a...rule of English law, whereby, as a matter of policy, no man should be convicted of homicide (or, we imagine, any crime of violence to another person) unless he himself, or another person acting in concert with him, fired the shot (or, we imagine, struck the blow) which was the immediate cause of the victim's death (or injury).

No English authority was cited to us in support of any such proposition, and we know of none. So far as we are aware, there is no such rule in English law; and, in the absence of any doctrine of constructive malice, we can see no basis in principle for any such rule in English law. Lord Gifford urged upon us that, in a case where the accused did not, for example, fire the shot which was the immediate cause of the victim's death, he will inevitably have committed some lesser crime, and that it would be sufficient that he should be convicted of that lesser crime. So, on the facts of the present case, it would be enough that the appellant was convicted of the crime of attempted murder of the two police officers, D.S. Sartain and D.C. Richards. We see no force in this submission. In point of fact, it is not difficult to imagine circumstances in which it would manifestly be inadequate for the accused merely to be convicted of a lesser offence; for example, a man besieged by armed terrorists in a house might attempt to make his escape by forcing some other person to act as a shield, knowing full well that that person would in all probability be shot, and possibly killed, in consequence. For that man merely to be convicted of an assault would, if the person he used as a shield were to be shot and killed, surely be inadequate in the circumstances; we can see no reason why he should not be convicted at least of manslaughter. But in any event there is, so far as we can discern, no basis of legal principle for Lord Gifford's submission. We are therefore unable to accept it.

In our judgment, the question whether an accused person can be held guilty of homicide, either murder or manslaughter, of a victim the immediate cause of whose death is the act of another person must be determined on the ordinary principles of causation, uninhibited by any such rule of policy as that for which Lord Gifford has contended. We therefore reject the second ground of appeal.

We turn to the first ground of appeal, which is that the learned judge erred in directing the jury that it was for him to decide *as a matter of law* whether by his unlawful and deliberate acts the appellant caused or was a cause of Gail Kinchen's death . . . .

In cases of homicide, it is rarely necessary to give the jury any direction on causation as such. Of course, a necessary ingredient of the crimes of murder and manslaughter is that the accused has by his act caused the victim's death. But how the victim came by his death is usually not in dispute. What is in dispute is more likely to be some other matter: for example, the identity of the person who committed the act which indisputably caused the victim's death; or whether the accused had the necessary intent; or whether the accused acted in self-defence, or was provoked. Even where it is necessary to direct the jury's minds to the question of causation, it is usually enough to direct them simply that in law the accused's act need not be the sole cause, or even the main cause, of the victim's death, it being enough that his act contributed significantly to that result. It is right to observe in passing, however, that even this simple direction is a direction of law relating to causation, on the basis of which the jury are bound to act in concluding whether the prosecution has established, as a matter of fact, that the accused's act did in this sense cause the victim's death. Occasionally, however, a specific issue of causation may arise. One such case is where, although an act of the accused constitutes a *causa sine qua non* of (or necessary condition for) the death of the victim, nevertheless the intervention of a third person may be regarded as the sole cause of the victim's death, thereby relieving the accused of criminal responsibility. Such intervention, if it has such an effect, has often been described by lawyers as a *novus actus interveniens*. We are aware that this time-honoured Latin term has been the subject of criticism. We are also aware that attempts have been made to translate it into English; though no simple translation has proved satisfactory, really because the Latin term has become a term of art which conveys to lawyers the crucial feature that there has not merely been an intervening act of another person, but that that act was so independent of the act of the accused that it should be regarded in law as the cause of the victim's death, to the exclusion of the act of the accused. At the risk of scholarly criticism, we shall for the purposes of this judgment continue to use the Latin term.

Now the whole subject of causation in the law has been the subject of a well-known and most distinguished treatise by Professors Hart and Honoré, *Causation in the Law*. Passages from this book were cited to the learned judge, and were plainly relied upon by him; we, too, wish to express our indebtedness to it. It would be quite wrong for us to consider in this judgment the wider issues discussed in that work. But, for present purposes, the passage which is of most immediate relevance is to be found in Chapter XII, in which the learned authors consider the circumstances in which the intervention of a third person, not acting in concert with the accused, may have the effect of relieving the accused of criminal responsibility. The criterion which they suggest should be applied in such circumstances is whether the intervention is voluntary i.e. whether it is 'free, deliberate and informed.' We resist the temptation of expressing the judicial opinion whether we find ourselves in complete agreement with that definition; though we certainly consider it to be broadly correct and supported by authority. Among the examples which the authors give of non-voluntary conduct, which is not effective to relieve the accused of responsibility, are two which are germane to the present case, *viz*, a reasonable act performed for the purpose of self-preservation, and an act done in performance of a legal duty.

There can, we consider, be no doubt that a reasonable act performed for the purpose of self-preservation, being of course itself an act caused by the accused's own act, does not operate as a *novus actus interveniens*.... if a reasonable act of self-defence against the act of the accused causes the death of a third party, we can see no reason in principle why the act of self-defence, being an involuntary act caused by the act of the accused, should relieve the accused from criminal responsibility for the death of the third party. Of course, it does not necessarily follow that the accused will be guilty of the murder, or even of the manslaughter, of the third party; though in the majority of cases he is likely to be guilty at least of manslaughter. Whether he is guilty of murder or manslaughter will depend upon the question whether all the ingredients of the relevant offence have been proved; in particular, on a charge of murder, it will be necessary that the accused had the necessary intent....

No English authority was cited to us, nor we think to the learned judge, in support of the proposition that an act done in the execution of a legal duty, again of course being an act itself caused by the act of the accused, does not operate as a *novus actus interveniens*.... We agree with the learned judge that the proposition is sound in law, because as a matter of principle such an act cannot be regarded as a voluntary act independent of the wrongful act of the accused. A parallel may be drawn with the so-called 'rescue' cases in the law of negligence, where a wrongdoer may be held liable in negligence to a third party who suffers injury in going to the rescue of a person who has been put in danger by the defendant's negligent act. Where, for example, a police officer in the execution of his duty acts to prevent a crime, or to apprehend a person suspected of a crime, the case is surely *a fortiori*. Of course, it is inherent in the requirement that the police officer, or other person, must be acting in the execution of his duty that his act should be reasonable in all the circumstances: see section 3 of the Criminal Law Act 1967. Furthermore, once again we are only considering the issue of causation. If intervention by a third party in the execution of a legal duty, caused by the act of the accused, results in the death of the victim, the question whether the accused is guilty of the murder or manslaughter of the victim must depend on whether the necessary ingredients of the relevant offence have been proved against the accused, including in particular, in the case of murder, whether the accused had the necessary intent.

The principles which we have stated are principles of law. This is plain from, for example, the case of *Pitts* (1842) C & M 284, to which we have already referred. It follows that where, in any particular case, there is an issue concerned with what we have for convenience called *novus actus interveniens*, it will be appropriate for the judge to direct the jury in accordance with these principles. It does not however follow that it is accurate to state broadly that causation is a question of law. On the contrary, generally speaking causation is a question of fact for the jury.... But that does not mean that there are no principles of law relating to causation, so that no directions on law are ever to be given to a jury on the question of causation. On the contrary, we have already pointed out one familiar direction which is given on causation, which is that the accused's act need not be the sole, or even the main, cause of the victim's death for his act to be held to have caused the death.... [I]n cases where there is an issue whether the act of the victim or of a third party constituted a *novus actus interveniens*, breaking the causal connection between the act of the accused and the death of the victim, it would be appropriate for the judge to direct the jury, of course in the most simple terms, in accordance with the legal principles which they have to apply. It would then fall to the jury to decide the relevant factual issues which, identified with reference to those legal principles, will lead to the conclusion whether or not the prosecution have established the guilt of the accused of the crime of which he is charged.

...

There is however one further aspect of the present case to which we must advert. On the evidence, Gail Kinchen was not just an innocent bystander killed by a shot fired from the gun of a police officer who, acting in reasonable self-defence, fired his gun in response to a lethal attack by the appellant: though on those facts alone it would, in our opinion, have been open to the jury to convict the appellant of murder or manslaughter. But if, as the jury must have found to have occurred in the present case, the appellant used Gail Kinchen by force and against her will as a shield to protect him from any shots fired by the police, the effect is that he committed not one but two unlawful acts, both of which were dangerous – the act of firing at the police, and the act of holding Gail Kinchen as a shield in front of him when the police might well fire shots in his direction in self-defence. Either act could in our judgment, if on the principles we have stated it was held to cause the death of Gail Kinchen, constitute the *actus reus* of the manslaughter or, if the necessary intent were established, murder of Gail Kinchen by the appellant, even though the shot was fired not by the appellant but by a police officer.

■ NOTES AND QUESTIONS

1. What is the test of causation that the court uses in *Pagett*?

2. The shots that killed the victim in *Pagett* were fired by the police. Why should Pagett be held responsible for their actions? Were the actions of the police foreseeable? Reasonable? Daft? Should it matter? It is understandable that the courts would not, under the circumstances, have wanted to hold the police liable, but does it follow that Pagett should have been held liable? Is the unstated but implicit premise that *somebody* has to be held legally responsible for the death? Is the same premise implicit in the medical malpractice cases?

3. Consider the case where the police aim is faulty and a third party, not Pagett or his hostage, is killed. Is this a stronger or weaker case for Pagett's liability? For liability on the part of the officer who fired the fatal shot?

4. Did the decision in *Pagett* turn on the fact that the actions of the police were justifiable? If the judge had ruled at the trial that the police should have held their fire and were wrong not to do so, would (should) it have made any difference to Pagett's liability? Could it be argued that the police acted irresponsibly in exposing the hostage to the risk of harm?

5. In April 1993, in Waco, Texas, a religious sect known as the Branch Davidians set their compound on fire rather than submit to arrest by federal officers. The latter had laid siege to the compound for 51 days following the killing of several of their number in the initial attempt to arrest the Branch Davidians for firearms violations. Eighty-six members of the cult were killed in the blaze. Did the FBI 'cause' the deaths?

In *Pagett*, the police arguably were acting pursuant to their legal duty to arrest the defendant, or perhaps in self-defence. But what if the acts of the third party are themselves clearly criminal?

Environment Agency (Formerly National Rivers Authority) v Empress Car Co. (Abertillery) Ltd.

[1999] 2 AC 22, House of Lords

LORD HOFFMANN: My Lords, Empress Car Co. (Abertillery) Ltd. ('the company') was convicted at the Crown Court sitting at Newport, Gwent (Judge Crowther Q.C. and two justices) of 'causing poisonous, noxious or polluting matter or solid waste to enter controlled waters' contrary to section 85(1) of the Water Resources Act 1991.

...

The facts as found in the case stated may be summarised as follows. The company maintained a diesel tank in a yard which was drained directly into the river. The tank was surrounded by a bund to contain spillage, but the company had overridden this protection by fixing an extension pipe to the outlet of the tank so as to connect it to a drum standing outside the bund. It appears to have been more convenient to draw oil from the drum than directly from the tank. The outlet from the tank was governed by a tap which had no lock. On 20 March 1995 the tap was opened by a person unknown and the entire contents of the tank ran into the drum, overflowed into the yard and passed down the drain into the river.

...

Before your Lordships, Mr. Philpott for the company repeated his submission that the cause of the escape was not the keeping of the oil by the company but the opening of the tap by the stranger. He also said that 'causing' for the purposes of section 85(1) required some positive act and that the escape could not be said to have been caused by any such act by the company. All it had done was to create a state of affairs in which someone else could cause the oil to escape. There are accordingly two issues in the case. The first is whether there has to have been some 'positive act' by the company and, if so, whether the company did such an act. The second is whether what it did 'caused' the oil to enter the river.

...

The first point to emphasise is that common sense answers to questions of causation will differ according to the purpose for which the question is asked. Questions of causation often arise for the purpose of attributing responsibility to someone, for example, so as to blame him for something which has happened or to make him guilty of an offence or liable in damages. In such cases, the answer will depend upon the rule by which responsibility is being attributed. Take, for example, the case of the man who forgets to take the radio out of his car and during the night someone breaks the quarterlight, enters the car and steals it. What caused the damage? If the thief is on trial, so that the question is whether he is criminally responsible, then obviously the answer is that he caused the damage. It is no answer for him to say that it was caused by the owner carelessly leaving the radio inside. On the other hand, the owner's wife, irritated at the third such occurrence in a year, might well say that it was his fault. In the context of an inquiry into the owner's blameworthiness under a non-legal, common sense duty to take reasonable care of one's own possessions, one would say that his carelessness caused the loss of the radio.

I turn next to the question of third parties and natural forces. In answering questions of causation for the purposes of holding someone responsible, both the law and common sense normally attach great significance to deliberate human acts and extraordinary natural events. A factory owner carelessly leaves a drum containing highly inflammable vapour in a place where it could easily be accidentally ignited. If a workman, thinking it is only an empty drum, throws in a cigarette butt and causes an explosion, one would have no difficulty in saying that the negligence of the owner caused the explosion. On the other hand, if the workman, knowing exactly what the drum contains, lights a match and ignites it, one would have equally little difficulty in saying that he had caused the explosion and that the carelessness of the owner had merely provided him with an occasion for what he did. One would probably say the same if the drum was struck by lightning. In both cases one would say that although the vapour-filled drum was a necessary condition for the explosion to happen, it was not caused by the owner's negligence. One might add by way of further explanation that the presence of an arsonist workman or lightning happening to strike at that time and place was a coincidence.

On the other hand, there are cases in which the duty imposed by the rule is to take precautions to prevent loss being caused by third parties or natural events. One example has already been given; the common sense rule (not legally enforceable, but neglect of which may expose one to blame from one's wife) which requires one to remove the car radio at night.

. . .

These examples show that one cannot give a common sense answer to a question of causation for the purpose of attributing responsibility under some rule without knowing the purpose and scope of the rule. Does the rule impose a duty which requires one to guard against, or makes one responsible for, the deliberate acts of third persons? If so, it will be correct to say, when loss is caused by the act of such a third person, that it was caused by the breach of duty.

. . .

Before answering questions about causation, it is therefore first necessary to identify the scope of the relevant rule. This is not a question of common sense fact; it is a question of law. In *Stansbie v Troman* the law imposed a duty which included having to take precautions against burglars. Therefore breach of that duty caused the loss of the property stolen. In the example of the vapour-filled drum, the duty does not extend to taking precautions against arsonists. In other contexts there might be such a duty (compare *The Fiona* [1994] 2 Lloyd's Rep. 506, 522) but the law of negligence would not impose one.

. . .

Clearly, therefore, the fact that a deliberate act of a third party caused the pollution does not in itself mean that the defendant's creation of a situation in which the third party could so act did not also cause the pollution for the purposes of section 85(1).

. . .

In the sense in which the concept of foreseeability is normally used, namely as an ingredient in the tort of negligence, in the form of the question: ought the defendant reasonably to have foreseen what happened, I do not think that it is relevant. Liability under section 85(1) is not based on negligence; it is strict.

The true common sense distinction is, in my view, between acts and events which, although not necessarily foreseeable in the particular case are in the generality a normal and familiar fact of life, and acts or events which are abnormal and extraordinary. Of course an act or event which is in general terms a normal fact of life may also have been foreseeable in the circumstances of the particular case, but the latter is not necessary for the purposes of liability. There is nothing extraordinary or abnormal about leaky pipes or lagoons as such: these things happen, even if the particular defendant could not reasonably have foreseen that it would happen to him. There is nothing unusual about people putting unlawful substances into the sewage system and the same, regrettably, is true about ordinary vandalism. So when these things happen, one does not say: that was an extraordinary coincidence, which negatived the causal connection between the original act of accumulating the polluting substance and its escape. In the context of section 85(1), the defendant's accumulation has still caused the pollution. On the other hand, the example I gave of the terrorist attack would be something so unusual that one would not regard the defendant's conduct as having caused the escape at all.

. . .

I shall try to summarise the effect of this discussion.

(1) Justices dealing with prosecutions for 'causing' pollution under section 85(1) should first require the prosecution to identify what it says the defendant did to cause the pollution. If the defendant cannot be said to have done anything at all, the prosecution must fail: the defendant may have 'knowingly permitted' pollution but cannot have caused it.

(2) The prosecution need not prove that the defendant did something which was the immediate cause of the pollution: maintaining tanks, lagoons or sewage systems full of noxious liquid is doing something, even if the immediate cause of the pollution was lack of maintenance, a natural event or the act of a third party.

(3) When the prosecution has identified something which the defendant did, the justices must decide whether it caused the pollution. They should not be diverted by questions like 'What was the cause of the pollution' or 'Did something else cause the pollution' because to say that

something else caused the pollution (like brambles clogging the pumps or vandalism by third parties) is not inconsistent with the defendant having caused it as well.

(4) If the defendant did something which produced a situation in which the polluting matter could escape but a necessary condition of the actual escape which happened was also the act of a third party or a natural event, the justices should consider whether that act or event should be regarded as a normal fact of life or something extraordinary. If it was in the general run of things a matter of ordinary occurrence, it will not negative the causal effect of the defendant's acts, even if it was not foreseeable that it would happen to that particular defendant or take that particular form. If it can be regarded as something extraordinary, it will be open to the justices to hold that the defendant did not cause the pollution.

(5) The distinction between ordinary and extraordinary is one of fact and degree to which the justices must apply their common sense and knowledge of what happens in the area.

Applying these principles, it seems to me that there was ample evidence on which the Crown Court was entitled to find that the company had caused the pollution. I would therefore dismiss the appeal.

Appeal dismissed.

■ NOTES AND QUESTIONS

1. Does the House of Lords in *Empress Car* confuse the creation of a condition necessary to the commission of a crime with its causation? Does it confuse the effect of voluntary human interventions and natural events?

2. Were the acts of vandalism in *Empress Car* foreseeable in some sense other than that any and all crimes are foreseeable? Consider the homeowner who fails to install a burglar alarm. Can the homeowner be said to be the cause of her own losses following a burglary because it was foreseeable that any home could be the target of a burglary? Has the homeowner, or Empress Car Co., done anything more than provide the setting for the offence?

3. Is the ordinary–extraordinary distinction drawn by Lord Hoffmann in *Empress Car* meaningful? Helpful?

4. Recall that in *Kennedy* the House of Lords held that the victim's voluntary act of injecting himself with heroin broke the chain of causation begun when the defendant had supplied heroin to the victim. Are the decisions in *Kennedy* and *Empress Car* compatible?

5. Did the House of Lords in *Empress Car* decide the causation issue as it did in order to encourage companies to do their utmost to prevent pollution?

C: Reflections on causation

Cases which raise causation issues can, as we have seen, be problematic. Fortunately for the courts, they arise infrequently. When they do, however, they expose a certain fortuity inherent in the criminal law – two offenders who do the identical act with the identical state of mind may wind up with quite different punishments because of the results that their actions produce. Fair enough, one might say – offenders should have to bear the risk of the consequences of their evil acts. But is it fair to treat as a murderer the defendant whose victim neglects his wound with the result that gangrene sets in with fatal effect, while the defendant whose victim takes proper care of himself is convicted only of assault? Is it fair that whether a defendant receives a mandatory life sentence for murder turns on whether, unbeknownst to the defendant, the victim is a religious fundamentalist who refuses all medical treatment, preferring to place her faith in God? Although, if convicted of attempted murder, the defendant in such a case could receive the same life sentence as a murderer, this does not automatically follow as it does after a conviction for murder. Indeed, in practice the attempted murderer is likely to receive a significantly lesser sentence. The point is that in some instances focusing on results allows an offender to receive less in the way of punishment than would have been predicted if one had looked at the situation as of the time the defendant committed the *actus reus*; while in other instances it leads to an offender facing charges far more serious than would have been predicted as of the same time.

Faced with the sometimes almost random results of legal principles of causation, and understandably reluctant to allow malefactors to escape their just deserts because of the intervening acts of a victim, third party or simply fate, courts seem to stretch legal principle to achieve equitable results. They are not content with simply finding a defendant liable for the way he has behaved, but strive to hold him liable for the results that follow from his actions. To a large extent this desire to hold a defendant liable for the full effects of his conduct may be traceable to the retributive philosophy that a defendant's punishment should be proportionate to the harm which the defendant's acts have produced.

The problem is that the perspective of a criminal trial is always backwards-looking. The jurors know what results have occurred, and they ask themselves whether such results were foreseeable. The fact that they in fact have occurred may skew the enquiry, while casting the defendant's character in a more sinister light than it might otherwise have appeared had the results of the defendant's conduct been more benign.

Might it be argued that the proper focal point for evaluating a defendant's fault is at the moment of the defendant's acts. What results were likely to be produced by the defendant's misconduct? What results were foreseen (or foreseeable?) as of that moment? If one accepts this proposition, it would follow that actual results should be irrelevant to a defendant's liability. Crimes could then be defined in terms of *actus reus, mens rea* and the results that a type of conduct *threatens* to produce, as opposed to the results the conduct in fact produces, which may be completely fortuitous. In other words, a defendant should be punished not for the harm that he or she actually causes, but for the harm that he or she sets out to cause or recklessly risks causing, at least in the absence of excuse or justification. In this connection, consider the merits of the following proposed statute (NZ):

ENDANGERING

130. Endangering with intent to cause serious bodily harm

(1) Every person is liable to imprisonment for 14 years who—

    (a) Does any act, or omits without lawful excuse to perform or observe any legal duty, with intent to cause serious bodily harm to any other person; or

    (b) With reckless disregard for the safety of others, does any act or omits without lawful excuse to perform or observe any legal duty, knowing that the act or omission is likely to cause serious bodily harm to any other person.

(2) This section applies whether or not the act or omission results in death or bodily harm to any other person.

...132. Endangering with intent to injure, etc.

(1) Every person is liable to imprisonment for five years who—

(a) Does any act, or omits without lawful excuse to perform or observe any legal duty, with intent to injure any other person; or

(b) With reckless disregard for the safety of others, or heedlessly, does any act or omits without lawful excuse to perform or observe any legal duty, the act or omission being likely to cause injury to any other person or to endanger the safety or health of any other person.

(2) Every person is liable to imprisonment for two years who negligently does any or omits without lawful excuse to perform or observe any legal duty, the act or omission being likely to cause injury.

■ NOTES AND QUESTIONS

1. Does the proposed legislation go too far? Should negligent endangerment be criminal? What constitutes heedlessness?

2. Late to catch her train, Maria dashes down the street. Rounding the corner, she collides with Greg, who is knocked over and injured. Has Maria violated the New Zealand statute? Should her conduct be criminal?

3. The issues raised by the fortuity of consequences have been well explored in the legal literature. See, e.g., Ashworth, 'Criminal Attempts and the Role of Resulting Harm under the Code and in the Common Law' 19 Rutgers LJ 725 (1988); Ashworth, 'Belief, Intent, and Criminal Liability' in Eekelar and Bell (eds.), *Oxford Essays in Jurisprudence* 1 (1987); Gobert, 'The Fortuity of Consequence' (1993) 4 Crim Law Forum 1; J.C. Smith, 'The Element of Chance in Criminal Liability' [1971] Crim LR 63.

FURTHER READING

Wilson, *Criminal Law: Doctrine and Theory* (2011), Chapter 4

Alexander, 'Criminal Liability for Omissions' in Shute and Simester eds., *Criminal Law Theory: Doctrines of the General Part* (2001), p. 121

Ashworth, 'The Scope of Criminal Liability for Omissions' (1989) 105 Law Quarterly Review 424

Elliott and de Than, 'Prosecuting the Drug Dealer When a Drug User Dies' (2006) 69 Modern Law Review 986–995

Finnis, '*Bland*: Crossing the Rubicon?' (1993) 109 Law Quarterly Review 329

Glanville Williams, 'What Should the Code do about Omissions?' (1987) Legal Studies 92

Glazebrook, 'Situational Liability' in Glazebrook (ed.), *Reshaping the Criminal Law* (1978)

Hart and Honore, *Causation in the Law* (2nd ed. 1985)

Jones, 'Causation, Homicide and the Supply of Drugs' (2006) 26 Legal Studies 139

Keown, 'Restoring the Sanctity of Life' [2006] Legal Studies109

Lanham, '*Larsonneur* Revisited' [1976] Criminal Law Review 276

Moore, *Act and Crime* (1993) at p. 27

Nagel, 'Mortal Questions' in *Moral Luck*, (1979) pp. 24–38

Norrie, 'A Critique of Criminal Causation' (2006) 54 Modern Law Review 685

Ormerod and Fortson, 'Drug Suppliers as Manslaughterers (Again)' [2005] Criminal Law Review 819

Price, 'My View of the sanctity of Life' [2007] Legal Studies 549

Simester, 'Why Omissions are Special' (1995) 1 Legal Theory 311

Smith, J.C. 'Liability for Omissions in the Criminal Law' [1984] Legal Studies 88

Williams, 'Moral Luck' in *Moral Luck* (1982), pp. 20–39

Williams, 'Criminal Omissions: The Conventional View' (1991) 107 Law Quarterly Review

Williams [2005] Current Law Journal 66

Williams, 'Gross Negligence Manslaughter and Duty of Care in "Drugs" Cases: R v Evans' [2009] Criminal Law Review 631

Weinrib, 'The Case for a Duty to Rescue' (1980) 90 Yale Law Journal 247

Wilson, 'Dealing with Drug Induced Homicide' in Clarkson and Cunningham eds, *Criminal Liability for Non-Aggressive Deaths* (2008), pp. 176–198

Wilson, *Central Issues in Criminal Theory* (2002), chapters 3, 6

Wilson, 'Murder by Omission: Some Observations on a Mismatch between the General and Special Parts' (2010) New Criminal Law Review 1

3

The Mental Component of Crime: *Mens Rea*

Mens rea is the generic term which refers to the mental element of a crime. It is misleading, however, to talk of *mens rea* in the abstract. In regard to any specific crime, the statutory or common law definition of the crime must be consulted in order to determine the *mens rea* of the crime in question. In addition, many crimes have more than one mental element, and different types of *mens rea* may be applicable to different elements of the crime.

Mens rea is more elusive than *actus reus*. An act is observable, and provable through objective evidence. Witnesses can and will testify to what a defendant did. But who can testify as to what the defendant was thinking? State of mind often can only be inferred from actions. If X stands immediately in front of Y with a loaded gun and shoots Y, a jury might infer that X intended to kill Y. But what if X testifies that she was only intending to wound Y or to scare him? What if X says that she did not know that the gun was loaded, or that she thought Y was a cardboard dummy and not a real person. What if she claims that she thought that Y intended to kill her and fired in self-defence? Implausible, you might say; but how does one know for sure? Unless a defendant confesses (and sometimes not even then: there are many documented cases of false confessions, for reasons ranging from improper police pressure to guilt on the part of the confessor for some unrelated incident), there will always remain doubt about what was going on in the defendant's mind at the time of the offence.

Notwithstanding the problems relating to proof, *mens rea* is perhaps the most critical concept in criminal law. Mental state will often be the determining factor as to whether one who causes another's death will receive a life sentence, a term of years in prison short of life, or no legal sanction whatsoever. For example, driving through the High Street D hits a child who subsequently dies from the injuries: if D intended to kill the child, he is guilty of murder; if he did not intend to kill but was driving extremely recklessly, he would likely be convicted of manslaughter or causing death by dangerous driving; and if the child jumped in front of his car and the accident was unavoidable, he will have committed no offence. The same act, the same result, but entirely different legal consequences because of D's state of mind.

A: Motive

Before examining specific cases, there are several preliminary points worth making. The first relates to motive – the reason why a defendant acted as he did. Generally speaking, the law is not concerned with motive. A praiseworthy motive will not alter what would otherwise be a crime, and a blameworthy motive will not justify the conviction of a defendant who lacks *mens rea*. For example, if D robs Barclay's Bank, it does not matter, for legal purposes, whether she planned to give the money to charity or to spend it on herself.

The reason motive is said to be irrelevant is not only that motive is so difficult to prove (so is intent), nor that it is so easy to fabricate ('Of course I was going to give the proceeds from the bank robbery to charity'), but that we do not want to get into the messy business of evaluating individual motives and saying whether or not they justify criminal conduct. What if our bank robber wanted to give the money to the Labour Party? The leader of the Labour Party might find this an honourable motive, but would jurors who belonged to the Conservative or Liberal Democrat Parties?

While motive is not relevant to guilt, it may be relevant at other stages of the criminal process. First, it may affect the decision to bring formal charges. Prosecutors often have considerable discretion in this matter, both so that the Crown's limited resources are not wasted in frivolous actions, and so that defendants who are not truly blameworthy are not subjected to the emotional trauma and legal expense of a criminal prosecution, despite a technical violation of the law. The defendant's motive may have some bearing at this point. Secondly, at trial the prosecution may want to introduce evidence of motive, although it is not required to do so, because it supports the State's contention that the defendant was the one who committed the crime (e.g., the fact that the defendant was the sole beneficiary under the terms of the will of the wealthy victim provides a motive for the killing; if nobody else had a motive, it makes it more likely that the defendant was the murderer). Motive may also influence a jury's uncontrollable discretion to acquit – either the absence of motive may lead them to conclude that the defendant did not commit the crime; or an honourable motive, as in the case of a mercy killing, may lead them to acquit despite the belief that the defendant was technically guilty. Lastly, a judge may take motive into account in sentencing (except in cases of murder where the imposition of a life sentence is required by law).

To say that motive is legally irrelevant may also be a bit misleading. Motive may have legal significance in some instances. If D's motive in striking V is to prevent him from attacking her, that motive may lead to a viable claim of self-defence. Similarly, if D's motive for driving the car of the bank robbers was that they had kidnapped her children and were threatening to kill them if she did not cooperate, that motive may lead to a successful defence of duress. Whether it is semantically correct to use motive in the context of defences is debatable, but clearly we are talking about the reasons why the defendant acted as he or she did.

B: Subjective and objective *mens rea*

A distinction that is worth bearing in mind is that between subjective and objective states of mind. Subjective states of mind are concerned with what a defendant was actually thinking; objective states of mind refer to what a reasonable person in the position of the defendant would have been thinking. Where *mens rea* is objective, a defendant's fault consists of failing to appreciate a risk that would have been appreciated by a reasonable person. Crimes which involve subjective fault require that the prosecution prove that the defendant actually had the state of mind required for the crime. Crimes that involve objective fault do not require that the prosecution prove that the defendant actually had a particular state of mind but only that the defendant failed to meet a certain standard of conduct, usually determined by what would have been expected of a reasonable person. For example, if D drives his car on the High Street at a pedestrian, intending to run him over, his subjective state of mind is to kill the pedestrian. But if D is simply paying insufficient attention to what he is doing, his subjective state of mind is not to run anybody over, although a reasonable person would have seen that there was a clear risk that this might occur. As a general proposition (although not always), persons who commit crimes with subjective *mens rea* are considered to be more morally blameworthy, and therefore deserving of greater punishment, than persons whose *mens rea* is objective.

To determine whether a statute requires proof of objective or subjective *mens rea* one needs to look at the statute, the words it uses, and how those words have been interpreted by the courts. Listed below are examples of words which are generally held to connote subjective or objective fault.

Subjective Fault	*Objective Fault*
purposely	
recklessly	
knowingly	negligently
intentionally	carelessly
wilfully	
deliberately	
with intent to…	without due care and attention

Until recently, 'recklessly' would have been included on both sides of our ledger, the courts having recognised both a subjective and an objective strain of recklessness. However, as we shall see, the House of Lords has now signalled its disapproval of objective recklessness and its continuing viability is consequently subject to doubt. Nevertheless, examples of statutes where objective recklessness may satisfy the *mens rea* element of the offence remain in the law and it is always possible that in the future this fault state may be resurrected by the courts

In addition to objective and subjective *mens rea*, sometimes statutes appear to contain no *mens rea*. The statute defines the crime only in terms of the *actus reus* without any express reference to mental state, imposing what is referred to as strict liability. This category of strict liability crimes is obviously an exception to the Latin maxim *actus non facit reum nisi mens sit rea*. Problems arise, however, because Parliament does not always say what it means, or so the courts believe. Thus statutes which contain no mental element on their face may be interpreted by a court so as to require proof of some sort of *mens rea*.

In creating a new offence, Parliament can draft the statute to require proof of either subjective or objective *mens rea*, or can make the offence one of strict liability. Which path it chooses will be reflected in the wording of the statute. Say, for instance, Parliament decides to make the handling of stolen goods a crime. It can make an element of the offence 'knowing the goods to be stolen', thus requiring subjective *mens rea* in the form of proof that the defendant actually knew the goods were stolen. Or it can write the statute in terms of 'having reason to believe' that the goods were stolen, thus requiring only objective *mens rea* and proof that a reasonable person would have appreciated that the goods were most likely stolen. Or it can make the crime into one of strict liability, mentioning nothing about knowing or having reason to believe that the goods were stolen, but simply making criminal the handling of goods that are in fact stolen. In the latter instance a court might nonetheless choose to read into such a statute a *mens rea* element but if Parliament really wanted to, it could expressly declare that proof that a defendant knew or had reason to know that the goods were stolen is not required for conviction.

Whenever you analyse the *mens rea* of a statute, you should ask yourself whether the statute requires a subjective or objective *mens rea*, or whether the statute imposes no requirement of proof of *mens rea*. If *mens rea* is an element of a crime and the prosecution does not prove it, or if the defence raises a reasonable doubt about the presence of *mens rea*, the defendant cannot be convicted, even though he may have committed the *actus reus* of the crime and brought about the proscribed consequences.

While courts will often draw a sharp distinction in theory between objective and subjective states of mind, in practice the distinction is frequently blurred. The reason is this: the question of whether the defendant possessed the subjective *mens rea* required for a particular crime is a question of fact for the jury. Suppose that after pumping six bullets into her victim's heart from close range, a defendant claims that she did not intend to kill but simply intended to frighten the victim. The jury is likely to decide that the defendant's denial is not credible. Why? – because if they were in the defendant's shoes, they would have realised that the bullets from the gun would kill the victim. They would have realised it because they are reasonable persons, and any reasonable person would have so realised. By projecting on to the defendant the thought processes which they themselves would have gone through the jurors reason that the defendant in all probability lied, and in fact had the requisite subjective intent to kill. But what has happened is that, as a result of an objective exercise in logical deduction, the jurors will have *inferred* a subjective state of mind on the part of the defendant.

C: *Mens rea* in respect of what?

Often a crime can contain more than one *mens rea* element. Different elements of a crime may have attached to them different *mens rea* requirements. It is therefore always important to ask what it is that the particular *mens rea* element or elements refer to:

Mens rea can refer to:

(a) acts (but where the defendant's act is not the product of his will, as we saw in Chapter 2, the practice of the courts is to categorise this absence of intentionality as an involuntary *actus reus* rather than a lack of *mens rea*);

(b) circumstances (as, in theft, where one of the elements of the offence is the defendant's knowledge that the property he is taking belongs to another);

(c) results (as, in homicide, the intended death of the victim).

CRIMINAL DAMAGE ACT 1971

1. Destroying or damaging property

(1) A person who without lawful excuse destroys or damages any property belonging to another intending to destroy or damage any such property or being reckless as to whether any such property would be destroyed or damaged shall be guilty of an offence.

(2) A person who without lawful excuse destroys or damages any property, whether belonging to himself or another—

(a) intending to destroy or damage any property or being reckless as to whether any property would be destroyed or damaged; and

(b) intending by the destruction or damage to endanger the life of another or being reckless as to whether the life of another would be thereby endangered;

shall be guilty of an offence.

(3) An offence committed under this section by destroying or damaging property by fire shall be charged as arson.

■ NOTES AND QUESTIONS

1. What are the *mens rea* elements of s. 1(2)? To what does each of the elements refer?

2. Note in s. 1(2) the conjunction 'and' which joins paras. (a) and (b). This means that the *mens rea* elements in each paragraph must be proved. Had the conjunction *'or'* been substituted for *'and'* (as it is in s. 1(1) [intending...or being reckless] between the sub-clauses of s. 1(2), the prosecution could satisfy their burden of proof by establishing either the *mens rea* of para. (a) or (b).

3. Sometimes a *mens rea* may be implicit rather than explicit, although the parties may not know this until there has been a judicial interpretation to this effect. Is part of the *mens rea* of criminal damage in s. 1(1) a requirement that the defendant must *know* or have reason to know that the property which is damaged 'belongs to another'? The issue might arise where the defendant claimed that he thought that it was his own property that he was destroying.

D: Proof of *mens rea*

We noted previously the difficulty of establishing what is going on in a defendant's mind at the time of the crime. How, then, is the Crown supposed to prove *mens rea*?

R v Steane
[1947] KB 997, Court of Criminal Appeal

The appellant, a British subject, entered the service of the German broadcasting system, and on several occasions broadcast through that system. The evidence called by the prosecution was that of one witness who proved that the appellant did, in fact, so broadcast and said that he had seen a telegram, in the appellant's possession, signed Emmie Goering, which stated that he could expect to be released and be home very shortly. The principal evidence against him was a statement taken from him by an officer of the British Intelligence Service in October, 1945, purporting to give an account of his activities in the German broadcasting service, concluding with the words: 'I have read this statement over and to the best of my knowledge and belief it is all true, and must request it to be used in conjunction with my written report dated July 5, 1945 to the American C.I.C. in Augsburg.' This earlier report was not produced in evidence. Before the war, the appellant was employed in Germany as a film actor and was so engaged when the war broke out. His wife and two sons were living in Germany. On the outbreak of war the appellant was at once arrested, but his wife and two sons remained in Oberammergau.

The only other evidence was that of the appellant. He said that on his arrest he was questioned and that the interview ended with the order: 'Say Heil Hitler, you dirty swine.' He refused and was thereupon knocked down losing several teeth, and he was interned on September 11, 1939. Just before Christmas of that year he was sent for by Goebbels, who asked him to broadcast. He refused. He was thereupon warned that he was in an enemy country and that they had methods of making people do things. A week later an official named von Bockman saw him and dropped hints as to German methods of persuasion. A professor named Kossuth also warned him that these people could be dangerous to those who gave trouble. In consequence he submitted to a voice test, trying to perform as badly as he could. The next day he was ordered to read news three times a day, and did so until April, 1940. In that month he refused to do any more broadcasting. Two Gestapo men called on him. They said: 'If you don't obey, your wife and children will be put in a concentration camp.' In May three Gestapo men saw him and he was badly beaten up, one ear being partly torn off. He agreed to work for his old employers, helping to produce films. There was no evidence that the films he helped to produce were or could be of any assistance to the Germans or at all harmful to this country. He swore that he was in continual fear for his wife and children. He asserted, and said he had asserted, in his report of July 5, 1945, that he never had the slightest idea or intention of assisting the enemy, and that what he did was done to save his wife and children and that what he did could not have assisted the enemy except in a very technical sense. There was no record of the actual broadcasts made by the appellant.

LORD GODDARD: . . . In the opinion of the court, there was undoubtedly evidence from which a jury could infer that the acts done by the appellant were acts likely to assist the enemy.

The far more difficult question that arises, however, is in connexion with the direction to the jury with regard to whether these acts were done with the intention of assisting the enemy. The case as opened, and indeed, as put by the learned judge appears to this court to be this: A man is taken to intend the natural consequences of his acts; if, therefore, he does an act which is likely to assist the enemy, it must be assumed that he did it with the intention of assisting the enemy. Now, the first thing which the court would observe is that, where the essence of an offence or a necessary constituent of an offence is a particular intent, that intent must be proved by the Crown just as much as any other fact necessary to constitute the offence.

The wording of the regulation itself shows that it is not enough merely to charge a prisoner with doing an act likely to assist the enemy; he must do it with the particular intent specified in the regulation. While no doubt the motive of a man's act and his intention in doing the act are, in law, different things, it is, none the less, true that in many offences a specific intention is a necessary ingredient and the jury have to be satisfied that a particular act was done with that specific intent, although the natural consequences of the act might, if nothing else were proved, be said to show the intent for which it was done. . . .

. . . No doubt, if the prosecution prove an act the natural consequence of which would be a certain result and no evidence or explanation is given, then a jury may, on a proper direction, find that the prisoner is guilty of doing the act with the intent alleged, but if on the totality of the evidence there is room for more than one view as to the intent of the prisoner, the jury should be directed that it is for the prosecution to prove the intent to the jury's satisfaction, and if, on a review of the whole evidence, they either think that the intent did not exist or they are left in doubt as to the intent, the prisoner is entitled to be acquitted....

Now, another matter which is of considerable importance in the case, but does not seem to have been brought directly to the attention of the jury, is that very different considerations may apply where the accused at the time he did the acts is in subjection to an enemy power and where he is not. British soldiers who were set to work on the Burma road or, if invasion had unhappily taken place, British subjects who might have been set to work by the enemy digging trenches would undoubtedly be doing acts likely to assist the enemy. It would be unnecessary surely in their cases to consider, any of the niceties of the law relating to duress, because no jury would find that merely by doing this work they were intending to assist the enemy. In our opinion it is impossible to say that where an act was done by a person in subjection to the power of others, especially if that other be a brutal enemy, an inference that he intended the natural consequences of his act must be drawn merely from the fact that he did it. The guilty intent cannot be presumed and must be proved. The proper direction to the jury in this case would have been that it was for the prosecution to prove the criminal intent, and that while the jury would be entitled to presume that intent if they thought that the act was done as the result of the free uncontrolled action of the accused, they would not be entitled to presume it, if the circumstances showed that the act was done in subjection to the power of the enemy, or was as consistent with an innocent intent as with a criminal intent, for example, the innocent intent of a desire to save his wife and children from a concentration camp. They should only convict if satisfied by the evidence that the act complained of was in fact done to assist the enemy, and if there was doubt about the matter, the prisoner was entitled to be acquitted.

■ NOTES AND QUESTIONS

1. What was Steane's intent? His motive? Does the court confuse the two?

2. Given its logical force, why does the court reject the proposition that a defendant should be held to have intended the natural and probable consequences of his acts?

3. If the *mens rea* refers to acts which Steane *knows* will help the enemy, he may or may not have been guilty but if it refers to acts which Steane *should know* will help the enemy, he would most likely have been convicted. The actual statutory language was '*with intent to assist the enemy*'. Did Steane have this intent?

4. What if Steane did his broadcasts in order to establish his reputation as an announcer but without any thought as to whether his acts would help the enemy? In such a case, as in the original, there may be no intent to assist the cause of the enemy, but might not a jury have less sympathy for Steane? If *Steane* had been analysed in terms of whether he had a valid defence of duress (he committed the crime in order to avoid the greater evil of death to his family), as perhaps it should have been, there would have been a sounder basis for distinguishing the original case from our example.

5. Alan Norrie in 'After Woollin' [1999] Crim LR 532 argues that where good motives are involved (as in *Steane*), a moral threshold should have to be passed before an outcome seen as virtually certain can be regarded as intended. Is this a better explanation of *Steane*? See also Simester and Shute, 'Letter to the Editor' [2000] Crim LR 204.

6. In respect to the motive/intent distinction you should review the medical cases, p. 129, where doctors hastened death.

Parliament has now enacted the following statute which addresses the issue dealt with in *Steane*:

CRIMINAL JUSTICE ACT 1967

8. A court or jury, in determining whether a person has committed an offence—
   (a) shall not be bound in law to infer that he intended or foresaw a result of his actions by reason only of its being a natural and probable consequence of those actions; but
   (b) shall decide whether he did intend or foresee that result by reference to all the evidence, drawing such inferences from the evidence as appear proper in the circumstances.

SECTION 2: VARIETIES OF *MENS REA*

It is difficult to generalise about *mens rea*, for there is a great variety of states of mind that can be found in the statute books. The following list, which contains the most common types, is by no means exclusive:

- intention
- knowledge
- recklessness
- gross negligence
- negligence
- strict liability

In the sections which follow, an attempt will be made to analyse each of these states of mind in turn.

A: Intention

(i) Intention and foresight of consequences

What does it mean to say that a defendant acted intentionally? The paradigmatic situation is where the defendant brings about the very result which it was the defendant's purpose to bring about. More troublesome has been the situation where results are virtually certain to follow from the defendant's acts and which the defendant knew (or should have known?) would follow from his acts as a virtual certainty. Is it fair to say under the latter circumstances that the defendant intended the consequences? This was one of the issues raised by *Steane* (above): If Steane knew that his acts would help the enemy, can it be said that he intended to help the enemy?

On 7 July 2005, four suicide bombers set off explosives on three London Underground trains and a bus. Fifty-six persons were killed, including the bombers. On 21 July, a second series of similar attacks was unsuccessful. Four suspects were subsequently arrested. Assume, for the sake of argument, that the suspects wished only to make a political/religious statement but were aware (on the basis of the previous incident) that, if the bombs had exploded in accord with their plans, train and bus passengers inevitably would have been killed. Could it be said that the bombers 'intended' to cause death?

From a criminalisation perspective, perhaps the more important question is whether it should matter? If not, then Parliament could draft the statute accordingly. A murder statute, for example, could be written so that the mental element was either intending to cause death or engaging in conduct which the actor is aware is virtually certain to cause death. This is in fact the approach taken by the drafters of the Model Penal Code in America. In England, however, murder retains its common law definition, which requires proof of malice aforethought (which the courts define as either an intent to kill or an intent to inflict grievous bodily harm). This definition has forced the courts to wrestle with the question of whether engaging in acts 'knowing' that death or GBH is virtually certain to follow amounts to an intent to kill.

R v Nedrick
[1986] 3 All ER 1, Court of Appeal

LORD LANE CJ:...The case for the Crown was that the appellant had a grudge against a woman called Viola Foreshaw, as a result of which, after threats that he would 'burn her out', he went to her house in the early hours of 15 July 1984, poured paraffin through the letter box and onto the front door and set it alight. He gave no warning. The house was burnt down and one of Viola Foreshaw's children, a boy aged 12 called Lloyd, died of asphyxiation and burns.

After a number of interviews during which he denied any responsibility, the appellant eventually confessed to the police that he had started the fire in the manner described, adding, 'I didn't want anyone to die, I am not a murderer; please tell the judge; God knows I am not a murderer.' When asked why he did it, he replied. 'Just to wake her up and frighten her.'

We have endeavoured to crystallise the effect of their Lordships' speeches in *R* v *Moloney* and *R* v *Hancock* in a way which we hope may be helpful to judges who have to handle this type of case.

It may be advisable first of all to explain to the jury that a man may intend to a certain result whilst at the same time not desiring it to come about. In *R* v *Moloney* [1985] 1 All ER 1025 at 1037, [1985] AC 905 at 926 Lord Bridge gave an illustration of the distinction:

> A man who, at London Airport, boards a plane which he knows to be bound for Manchester, clearly intends to travel to Manchester, even though Manchester is the last place he wants to be and his motive for boarding the plane is simply to escape pursuit.

The man who knowingly boards the Manchester aircraft wants to go there in the sense that boarding it is a voluntary act. His desire to leave London predominates over his desire not to go to Manchester. When he decides to board the aircraft, if not before, he forms the intention to travel to Manchester.

In *R* v *Hancock* the House decided that the *R* v *Moloney* guidelines require a reference to probability. Lord Scarman said ([1986] 1 All ER 641 at 651, [1986] AC 455 at 473):

> They also require an explanation that the greater the probability of a consequence the more likely it is that the consequence was foreseen and that if that consequence was foreseen the greater the probability is that that consequence was also intended.

When determining whether the defendant had the necessary intent, it may therefore be helpful for a jury to ask themselves two questions. (1) How probable was the consequence which resulted from the defendant's voluntary act? (2) Did he foresee that consequence?

If he did not appreciate that death or serious harm was likely to result from his act, he cannot have intended to bring it about. If he did, but thought that the risk to which he was exposing the person killed was only slight, then it may be easy for the jury to conclude that he did not intend to bring about that result. On the other hand, if the jury are satisfied that at the material time the defendant recognised that death or serious harm would be virtually certain (barring some unforeseen intervention) to result from his voluntary act, then that is a fact from which they may find it easy to infer that he intended to kill or do serious bodily harm, even though he may not have had any desire to achieve that result.

As Lord Bridge said in *R v Moloney* [1985] 1 All ER 1025 at 1036, [1985] AC 905 at 925:

> ...the probability of the consequence taken to have been foreseen must be little short of overwhelming before it will suffice to establish the necessary intent.

Later he uses the expression 'moral certainty' (see [1985] 1 All ER 1025 at 1037, [1985] AC 905 at 926) and says, 'will lead to a certain consequence unless something unexpected supervenes to prevent it' (see [1985] 1 All ER 1025 at 1039, [1985] AC 905 at 929).

Where the charge is murder and in the rare cases where the simple direction is not enough, the jury should be directed that they are not entitled to infer the necessary intention unless they feel sure that death or serious bodily harm was a virtual certainty (barring some unforeseen intervention) as a result of the defendant's actions and that the defendant appreciated that such was the case.

Where a man realises that it is for all practical purposes inevitable that his actions will result in death or serious harm, the inference may be irresistible that he intended that result, however little he may have desired or wished it to happen. The decision is one for the jury to be reached on a consideration of all the evidence.

R v Woollin

[1998] 3 WLR 382, House of Lords

[The defendant threw his 3-month-old son four or five feet across a room in the direction of his pram, causing him to suffer a fractured skull, from which he died.]

LORD STEYN: The Court of Appeal certified the following questions as of general importance:

1. In murder, where there is no direct evidence that the purpose of a defendant was to kill or to inflict serious injury on the victim, is it necessary to direct the jury that they may only infer an intent to do serious injury if they are satisfied (a) that serious bodily harm was a virtually certain consequence of the defendant's voluntary act and (b) that the defendant appreciated that fact?

2. If the answer to question 1 is 'Yes,' is such a direction necessary in all cases or is it only necessary in cases where the sole evidence of the defendant's intention is to be found in his actions and their consequence to the victim?

On appeal to your Lordships' House the terrain of the debate covered the correctness in law of the direction recommended by Lord Lane CJ in *Nedrick* and, if that direction is sound, whether it should be used only in the limited category of cases envisaged by the Court of Appeal. And counsel for the appellant renewed his submission that by directing the jury in terms of substantial risk the judge illegitimately widened the mental element of murder.

...

The Crown did not argue that as a matter of policy foresight of a virtual certainty is too narrow a test in murder. Subject to minor qualifications, the decision in *Nedrick* was widely welcomed by distinguished academic writers: see Professor J.C. Smith QC's commentary on *Nedrick* [1986] Crim LR 742, 743–744; Glanville Williams, 'The *Mens Rea* for Murder: Leave it Alone' (1989) 105 LQR 387; J.R. Spencer, 'Murder in the Dark: A Glimmer of Light?' [1986] CLJ 366–367; Ashworth, *Principles of Criminal Law*, 2nd ed. (1995), p. 172. It is also of interest that it is very similar to the threshold of being aware 'that it *will* occur in the ordinary course of events' in the Law Commission's draft Criminal Code (see Criminal Law: Legislating the Criminal Code: Offences against the Person and General Principles, Law Com. No. 218 (1993) (Cm. 2370), Appendix A (Draft Criminal Law Bill with Explanatory Notes), pp. 90–91): compare also Professor J.C. Smith QC, 'A Note on "Intention"' [1990] Crim LR 85, 86. Moreover, over a period of 12 years since *Nedrick* the test of foresight of virtual certainty has apparently caused no practical difficulties. It is simple and clear. It is true that it may exclude a conviction of murder in the often cited terrorist example where a member of the bomb disposal team is killed. In such a case it may realistically be said that the terrorist did not foresee the killing of a member of the bomb disposal team as a virtual certainty. That may be a consequence of not framing the principle in terms of risk-taking. Such cases ought to cause no substantial difficulty since immediately below murder there is available a verdict of manslaughter which may attract in the discretion of the court a life sentence. In any event, as Lord Lane CJ eloquently argued in a debate in the House of Lords, to frame a principle for particular difficulties regarding terrorism 'would produce corresponding injustices which would be very hard to eradicate:' Hansard (H.L. Debates), 6 November 1989. col. 480. I am satisfied that the *Nedrick* test, which was squarely based on the decision of the House in *Moloney*, is pitched at the right level of foresight.

The status of *Nedrick*

In my view Lord Lane CJ's judgment in *Nedrick* provided valuable assistance to trial judges. The model direction is by now a tried-and-tested formula. Trial judges ought to continue to use it. On matters of detail I have three observations, which can best be understood if I set out again the relevant part of Lord Lane's judgment. It was:

(A) When determining whether the defendant had the necessary intent, it may therefore be helpful for a jury to ask themselves two questions. (1) How probable was the consequence which resulted from the defendant's voluntary act? (2) Did he foresee that consequence? If he did not appreciate that death or serious harm was likely to result from his act, he cannot have intended to bring it about. If he did, but thought that the risk to which he was exposing the person killed was only slight, then it may be easy for the jury to conclude that he did not intend to bring about that result. On the other hand, if the jury are satisfied that at the material time the defendant recognised that death or serious harm would be virtually certain (barring some unforeseen intervention) to result from his voluntary act, then that is a fact from which they may find it easy to infer that he intended to kill or do serious bodily harm, even though he may not have had any desire to achieve that result . . .

(B) Where the charge is murder and in the rare cases where the simple direction is not enough, the jury should be directed that they are not entitled to infer the necessary intention, unless they feel sure that death or serious bodily harm was a virtual certainty (barring some unforeseen intervention) as a result of the defendant's actions and that the defendant appreciated that such was the case.

(C) Where a man realises that it is for all practical purposes inevitable that his actions will result in death or serious harm, the inference may be irresistible that he intended that result, however little he may have desired or wished it to happen. The decision is one for the jury to be reached upon a consideration of all the evidence. (Lettering added)

First, I am persuaded by the speech of my noble and learned friend, Lord Hope of Craighead, that it is unlikely, if ever, to be helpful to direct the jury in terms of the two questions set out in (A). I agree that these questions may detract from the clarity of the critical direction in (B). Secondly, in their writings previously cited Glanville Williams, Professor Smith and Andrew Ashworth observed that the use of the words 'to infer' in (B) may detract from the clarity of the model direction. I agree. I would substitute the words 'to find'. Thirdly, the first sentence of (C) does not form part of the model direction. But it would always be right for the judge to say, as Lord Lane CJ put it, that the decision is for the jury upon a consideration of all the evidence in the case.

The certified questions

Given my conclusions the certified questions fall away.

LORD HOPE OF CRAIGHEAD: My Lords, I have had the advantage of reading in draft the speech which has been prepared by my noble and learned friend, Lord Steyn. I agree with it, and I wish to add only these brief comments.

I attach great importance to the search for a direction which is both clear and simple. It should be expressed in as few words as possible. That is essential if it is to be intelligible. A jury cannot be expected to absorb and apply a direction which attempts to deal with every situation which might conceivably arise. I think that the *Nedrick* direction, which is (B) in Lord Steyn's analysis, fulfils this requirement admirably. But the substitution of the word 'find' for 'infer' is an improvement, in the interests of clarity, and I also would make this change to it. However I regard the questions in (A), which are derived from Lord Scarman's speech in *R v Hancock* [1986] AC 455, 473, as detracting from the clarity of the critical direction. I would prefer to say therefore that it is unlikely, if ever, to be helpful to tell the jury that they should ask themselves these questions. I think that it would be better to give them the critical direction, and then to tell them that the decision was theirs upon a consideration of all the evidence.

As for the terrorist example. I think that Lord Mustill's observations in *Attorney-General's Reference (No. 3 of 1994)* [1998] AC 245, 261 are also relevant. In that passage he gave as an example of 'indiscriminate malice', which belongs to the category of deliberate murder where the defendant consciously intended to kill the victim, the example of the terrorist who hides a bomb in an aircraft. As he explained, the intention is aimed at the class of potential victims of which the actual victim forms part, even although the identity of the ultimate victim is not yet fixed at the start when the intent is combined with the *actus reus* which ultimately causes the explosion. The answer to the question whether those who attempt to dispose of the bomb are within that class will depend on the circumstances. All that needs to be said is that it may not be necessary in every such case to rely on the alternative verdict of manslaughter.

Appeal allowed.
Conviction of murder quashed.
Conviction of manslaughter substituted.

■ NOTES AND QUESTIONS

1. If a defendant foresees death or serious injury as a virtual certainty, should it matter whether the defendant intended to cause death? Is not that defendant as morally culpable as the defendant who intended to cause death? Indeed, can it not be said that the defendant's callousness to the obvious risk of death is even more reprehensible?

2. The Law Commission in their 2006 Report on Murder and Mansalughhter recommend that the existing law governing the meaning of intention is codified as follows:

   (1) A person should be taken to intend a result if he or she acts in order to bring it about.

   (2) In cases where the judge believes that justice may not be done unless an expanded understanding of intention is given, the jury should be directed as follows: an intention to bring about a result may be found if it is shown that the defendant thought that the result was a virtually certain consequence of his or her action.

3. The use of the word 'may be found' creates an ambiguity. The judge does not direct the jury that they must find intention, only that they may. A jury in the conjoined twins case (see Ch. 10) may have to ask the judge for guidance. For example 'We are convinced the doctors knew for certain that the death of Mary was cetain if they performed the separation operation'. Do we have to find that they intended it? Can you help please.' How should the judge respond?

4. In *R v Stringer* [2008] EWCA Crim 1222 the Court of Appeal stated that if the consequence of what the defendant did (death or serious injury) was objectively certain the inference that the defendant foresaw the consequence as certain was inescapable.

Lord Justice Toulson: 'Applying the judge's written direction on intent, if the jury were satisfied (as they must have been) that Matthew started the fire after putting accelerant at the foot of the stairs, that he watched it take hold and then walked away, there could be only one answer to the question whether in fact it was a virtual certainty that somebody in the house would suffer really serious harm or death from Matthew's actions. It would be wholly unrealistic to imagine all the occupants escaping from the house by jumping from the upstairs windows without any of them suffering any serious harm. This must have been obvious to any ordinary person at the time. Even taking account of Matthew's age and the fact that his IQ was low/average, the inference that he must have appreciated it on that morning was also overwhelming. On the facts as the jury must have found them, the conclusion that Matthew had the necessary intent was bound to follow'.

Is the Court correct?

5. In addition to this 'oblique' intent, the courts have at times distinguished between so-called 'basic' and 'specific' intent. As with oblique intent, it is not clear whether the distinction between basic and specific intent is helpful for analytic purposes. The distinction is most commonly drawn in respect of crimes committed while the defendant was intoxicated and the issue will be deferred to the discussion of that topic. See Chapter 10.

(ii) Transferred intent

Must *mens rea* be directed towards a specific goal, or, in cases of homicide, a particular person? Suppose that X shoots at Y, intending to kill him. His aim is off, and the bullet hits Z with fatal results. Alternatively, Y moves at the critical moment and the bullet hits Z, who is directly behind him, again with fatal results. Is X, who had no intent to kill Z, guilty of Z's murder?

R v Saunders and Archer
(1573) 2 Plowden 473

John Saunders had a wife whom he intended to kill, in order that he might marry another woman with whom he was in love, and he opened his design to the said Alexander Archer, and desired his assistance and advice in the execution of it, who advised him to put an end to her life by poison. With this intent the said Archer bought the poison, viz. arsenick and roseacre, and delivered it to the said John Saunders to give it to his wife, who accordingly gave it to her, being sick, in a roasted apple, and she eat a small part of it, and gave the rest to the said Eleanor Saunders, an infant, about three years of age, who was the daughter of her and the said John Saunders her husband. And the said John Saunders seeing it, blamed his wife for it, and said that apples were not good for such infants; to which his wife replied that they were better for such infants than for herself: and the daughter eat the poisoned apple, and the said John Saunders, her father, saw her eat it, and did not offer to take it from her lest he should be suspected, and afterwards the wife recovered, and the daughter died of the said poison.

And whether or no this was murder in John Saunders, the father, was somewhat doubted, for he had no intent to poison his daughter, nor had he any malice against her, but on the contrary he had a great affection for her, and he did not give her the poison, but his wife ignorantly gave it her, and although he might have taken it from the daughter, and so have preserved her life, yet the not taking it from her did not make it felony, for it was all one whether he had been present or absent, as to this point, inasmuch as he had no malice against the daughter, nor any inclination to do her any harm. But at last the said justices, upon consideration of the matter, and with the assent of Saunders, Chief Baron, who had the examination of the said John Saunders before, and who had signified his opinion to the said justices (as he afterwards said to me) were of opinion that the said offence was murder in the said John Saunders. And the reason thereof (as the said justices and the Chief Baron told me) was, because the said John Saunders gave the poison with an intent to kill a person, and in the giving of it he intended that death should follow. And when death followed from his act, although it happened in another person than her whose death he directly meditated, yet it shall be murder in him, for he was the original cause of the death, and if such death should not be punished in him, it would go unpunished; for here the wife, who gave the poisoned apple to her daughter, cannot be guilty of any offence, because she was ignorant of any poison contained in it, and she innocently gave it to the infant by way of necessary food, and therefore it is reasonable to adjudge her innocent in this case, and to charge the death of the infant, by which the Queen has lost a subject, upon him who was the cause of it, and who intended death in the act which occasioned the death here. (a) But if a man prepares poison, and lays it in several parts of his house, with an intent to kill rats and such sort of vermin, and a person comes and eats it, and dies of it, this is not felony in him who prepared and laid it there, because he had no intent to kill any reasonable creature. (b) But when he lays the poison with an intent to kill some reasonable creature, and another reasonable creature, whom he does not intend to kill, is poisoned by it, such death shall not be dispunishable, but he who prepared the poison shall be punished for it, because his intent was evil. And therefore it is every man's business to foresee what wrong or mischief may happen from that which he does with an ill intention, and it shall be no excuse for him to say that he intended to kill another, and not the person killed. (c) For if a man of malice prepense shoots an arrow at another with an intent to kill him, and a person to whom he bore no malice is killed by it, this shall be murder in him, for when he shot the arrow he intended to kill, and inasmuch as he directed his instrument of death at one, and thereby has killed another, it shall be the same offence in him as if he had killed the person he aimed at, for the end of the act shall be construed by the beginning of it, and the last part shall taste of the first, and as the beginning of the act had malice prepense in it, and consequently imported murder, so the end of the act, viz. the killing of another, shall be in the same degree, and therefore it shall be murder, and not homicide only. (d) For if one lies in wait in a certain place to kill a person, and another comes by the place, and he who lies in wait kills him out of mistake, thinking that he is the very person whom he waited for, this offence is murder in him, and not homicide only, for the killing was founded upon malice prepense. So in the principal case, when John Saunders of malice prepense gave to his wife the instrument of death, viz. the poisoned apple, and this upon a subsequent accident killed his daughter, whom he had no intention to kill, this is the same offence in him as if his act had met with the intended effect, and his intention in doing the act was to commit murder, wherefore the event of it shall be murder. And so the justices declared their opinion, to the jurors, whereupon they found both the prisoners guilty, and John Saunders had his judgment, and was hanged.

Attorney-General's Reference (No. 3 of 1994)
[1997] 3 All ER 936, House of Lords

LORD MUSTILL: . . . As will appear, the events which founder the appeal were never conclusively proved at the trial, but are assumed to have been as follows. At the time in question a young woman M was pregnant, with between 22 and 24 weeks of gestation. According to the present state of medical knowledge if her baby had been born after 22 weeks it would not have had any significant prospect of survival. Two further weeks would have increased the chance to about 10 per cent. The pregnancy was, however, proceeding normally, and the risk that it would fail to continue to full term and be followed by an uneventful birth was very small indeed. Sadly, however, the natural father B quarrelled with M and stabbed her in the face, back and abdomen with a long-bladed kitchen knife in circumstances raising a prima facie inference that he intended to do her grievous bodily harm. M was admitted to hospital for surgical treatment and was later discharged in an apparently satisfactory state, still carrying the baby. Unfortunately, some 17 days after the incident M went into premature labour. The baby, named S, was born alive. The birth was still grossly premature, although by that time the chance that the baby would survive had increased to 50 per cent. Thereafter S lived for 121 days, when she succumbed to broncho-pulmonary dysplasia from the effects of premature birth. After her birth it was discovered that one of the knife cuts had penetrated her lower abdomen. The wound needed surgical repair, but it is agreed that this 'made no provable contribution to her death'.

The case for the Crown at the trial of B was that the wounding of M by B had set in train the events which caused the premature birth of S and hence her failure to achieve the normal prospect of survival which she would have had if the pregnancy had proceeded to full term. In this sense, therefore, we must assume that the wounding of M, at a time when S was a barely viable foetus, was the reason why she later died when she did.

... The point of law referred was as follows:

1.1 Subject to the proof by the prosecution of the requisite intent in either case: whether the crimes of murder or manslaughter can be committed where unlawful injury is deliberately inflicted:

(i) to a child in utero
(ii) to a mother carrying a child in utero where the child is subsequently born alive, enjoys an existence independent of the mother, thereafter dies and the injuries inflicted while in utero either caused or made a substantial contribution to the death.

1.2 Whether the fact that the death of the child is caused solely as a consequence of injury to the mother rather than as a consequence of direct injury to the foetus can negative any liability for murder or manslaughter in the circumstances set out in question 1.1.

...

I turn to the second rule, of 'transferred malice.' For present purposes this is more important and more difficult. Again, one must look at its origins to see whether they provide a theme which can be applied today. Three of them are familiar. Taking Lord Coke's example of the glancing arrow we have seen how one explanation of the poacher's responsibility founded on the notion of risk. The person who committed a crime took the chance that the outcome would be worse than he expected. Amongst many sources one can find the idea in *Russell on Crime*, 4th ed. (1845), p. 739:

If an action, unlawful in itself, be done deliberately, and with the intention of mischief or great bodily harm to particular individuals, or of mischief indiscriminately, fall where it may, and death ensue or beside the original intention of the party, it will be murder.

In a later edition (1855: p. 759) this was exemplified by cases of particular malice to one individual failing by mistake upon another. In support are cited *R v Saunders* (1573) 2 Plowd 473 (a poisoned apple intended for the mother but given to the child) and *Gore 9* Co Rep 81 (medicine poisoned by the wife to kill her husband and consumed by the apothecary to prove his innocence); also 1 Hawkins P.C., c. 31, 545 and 1 Hale 436. As already suggested, this doctrine does survive in some small degree today, but as the foundation of a modern doctrine of transferred malice broad enough to encompass the present case it seems to me quite unsupportable.

Secondly, there is the reversed burden of proof whereby the causing of death is prima facie murder, unless it falls within one of the extenuating categories recognised by the institutional writers. Again, this concept is long out-of-date. Nobody could seriously think of using it to make new law.

Third, there was the idea of 'general malice', of an evil disposition existing in the general and manifesting itself in the particular, uniting the aim of the offender and the result which his deeds actually produced. According to this theory, there was no need to 'transfer' the wrongful intent from the intended to the actual victim; for since the offender was (in the words of *Blackstone*, supra, pp. 198–200) 'an enemy to all mankind in general', the actual victim was the direct object of the offender's enmity. Plainly, this will no longer do, for the last vestiges of the idea disappeared with the abolition of the murder/felony doctrine.

... [H]arking back to a concept of general malice, which amounts to no more than this, that a wrongful act displays a malevolence which can be attached to any adverse consequence, has long been out of date. And to speak of a particular malice which is 'transferred' simply disguises the problem by idiomatic language. The defendant's malice is directed at one objective, and when after the event the court treats it as directed at another object it is not recognising a 'transfer' but creating a new malice which never existed before. As Dr Glanville Williams pointed out (*Criminal Law*, the General Part 2nd Ed. (1961), p. 184) the doctrine is 'rather an arbitrary exception to general principles.' Like many of its kind this is useful enough to yield rough justice, in particular cases, and it can sensibly be retained notwithstanding its lack of any sound intellectual basis. But it is another matter to build a new rule upon it.

I pause to distinguish the case of indiscriminate malice from those already discussed, although even now it is sometimes confused with them. The terrorist who hides a bomb in an aircraft provides an example. This is not a case of 'general malice' where under the old law any wrongful act sufficed to prove the evil disposition which was taken to supply the necessary intent for homicide. Nor is it transferred malice, for there is no need of a transfer. The intention is already aimed directly at the class of potential victims of which the actual victim forms part. The intent and the actus reus completed by the explosion are joined from the start, even though the identity of the ultimate victim is not yet fixed. So also with the shots fired indiscriminately into a crowd. No ancient fictions are needed to make these cases of murder.

My Lords, the purpose of this enquiry has been to see whether the existing rules are based on principles sound enough to justify their extension to a case where the defendant acts without an intent to injure either the foetus or the child which it will become. In my opinion they are not. To give an affirmative answer requires a double 'transfer' of intent: first from the mother to the foetus and then from the foetus to the child as yet unborn. Then one would have to deploy the fiction (or at least the doctrine) which converts an intention to commit serious harm into the mens rea of murder. For me, this is too much. If one could find any logic in the rules I would follow it from one fiction to another, but whatever grounds there may once have been have long since disappeared. I am willing to follow old laws until they are overturned, but not to make a new law on a basis for which there is no principle.

Moreover, even on a narrower approach the argument breaks down. The effect of transferred malice, as I understand it, is that the intended victim and the actual victim are treated as if they were one, so that what was intended to happen to the first person (but did not happen) is added to what actually did happen to the second person (but was not intended to happen), with the result that what was intended and what happened are married to make a notionally intended and actually consummated crime. The cases are treated as if the actual victim had been the intended victim from the start. To make any sense of this process there must, as it seems to me, be some compatibility between the original intention and the actual occurrence, and this is, indeed, what one finds in the cases. There is no such compatibility here. The defendant intended to commit and did commit an immediate crime of violence to the mother. He committed no relevant violence to the foetus, which was not a person, either at the time or in the future, and intended no harm to the foetus or to the human person which it would become. If fictions are useful, as they can be, they are only damaged by straining them beyond their limits. I would not overstrain the idea of transferred malice by trying to make it fit the present case.

Accordingly, I would . . . hold that on the presumed facts the judge was right to direct an acquittal on the count of murder.

■ NOTES AND QUESTIONS

1. Does it make sense to charge a defendant like Saunders with a crime that he did not intend to commit (murder of the child) rather than with the crime that he did intend to commit (attempted murder of his wife)?

2. In *Saunders and Archer* and in *Attorney-General's Reference (No. 3 of 1994)* the crime charged was of the same type (homicide) as was intended. All that changed was the victim. In such circumstances the courts have had little difficulty concluding that an accused who has the intent to kill, who acts pursuant to that intent, and whose acts result in death, is liable for that death. Another way of stating this is that the identity of the victim is not relevant for legal purposes. An even clearer example would occur where D, intending to kill V, mistook T for V and killed T. D would still be liable for murder. These are cases of what we might call

intra-crime transferred intent. More troublesome analytically are cases of inter-crime transferred intent (see *Pembliton*, below).

3. In *Woollin* Lord Hope referred to a category of 'indiscriminate malice' and the concept is again alluded to in *Attorney-General's Reference (No. 3 of 1994)*. To what does it refer? Would it apply to those killed by a terrorist's bomb if the terrorist intended only to make a political statement? What about a bomb disposal expert who accidentally killed himself while attempting to dismantle the bomb? Would this be a case of transferred indiscriminate malice?

R v Pembliton

[1874–80] All ER 1163, Court for Consideration of Crown Cases Reserved

At the quarter sessions of the peace held at Wolverhampton on Jan. 8, 1874, Henry Pembliton was indicted for that he 'unlawfully and maliciously did commit damage, injury, and spoil upon a window in the house of Henry Kirkham,' contrary to s. 51 of the Malicious Damage Act 1861.

On the night of Dec. 6, 1873, the prisoner was drinking with others at a public house called 'The Grand Turk' kept by the prosecutor. At about eleven o'clock p.m. the whole party were turned out of the house for being disorderly, and they then began to fight in the street and near the prosecutor's window, where a crowd of from 40 to 50 persons collected. The prisoner, after fighting some time with persons in the crowd, separated himself from them, and removed to the other side of the street, where he picked up a large stone, and threw it at the persons he had been fighting with. The stone passed over the heads of those persons, and struck a large plate glass window in the prosecutor's house, and broke it, thereby doing damage to the extent of £7 12s. 9d. The jury, after hearing evidence on both sides, found that the prisoner threw the stone which broke the window, but that he threw it at the people he had been fighting with, intending to strike one or more of them with it, but not intending to break the window. They returned a verdict of 'guilty.' The recorder respited the sentence, and admitted the prisoner to bail, and prayed the judgment of the Court for Crown Cases Reserved, whether, on the facts stated, and the finding of the jury, the prisoner was rightly convicted or not.

LORD COLERIDGE CJ: I am of opinion that this conviction must be quashed. [His Lordship stated the facts, and continued:] The question is whether, under an indictment for unlawfully and maliciously committing an injury to the window in the house of the prosecutor, the proof of these facts alone coupled with the finding of the jury will do. I think that is not enough. The indictment is framed under the Malicious Damage Act 1861, s. 51, which relates to malicious injuries to property, and the section enacts that whosoever shall unlawfully and maliciously commit any damage, etc., to or upon any real or personal property whatsoever either of a public or a private nature shall be guilty of a misdemeanour. Section 58 also deserves attention. That enacts:

Every punishment and forfeiture by this Act imposed on any person maliciously committing any offence, whether the same be punishable upon indictment or upon summary conviction, shall equally apply and be enforced, whether the offence shall be committed from malice conceived against the owner of the property in respect of which it shall be committed, or otherwise.

It seems to me that, in both these sections, what was intended to be provided against by the Act is the wilfully doing an unlawful act, and that that act must be wilfully and intentionally done on the part of the person doing it to render him liable to be convicted. Without saying that, on these facts, if the jury had found that the prisoner had been guilty of throwing the stone recklessly, knowing that there was a window near which it might probably hit, I should have been disposed to interfere with the conviction, yet, as they have found that he threw the stone at the people he had been fighting with intending to strike them and not intending to break the window, I think that the conviction must be quashed. I do not intend to throw any doubt on the cases which have been cited and which show what is sufficient to constitute malice in the case of murder. They rest on the principles of the common law, and have no application to a statutory offence.

Conviction quashed.

■ NOTES AND QUESTIONS

1. In principle, what is the problem with mixing and matching the *actus reus* of one crime with the *mens rea* of another, particularly when the defendant might otherwise escape liability for both crimes? At a minimum, why not permit inter-crime transferred intent when the crime actually committed is less serious than the crime intended?

2. Usually there will be little difficulty in holding an accused such as Pembliton criminally liable. Either he could be charged with an attempt to commit the crime he intended, or, alternatively, he could be charged with a crime of reck-lessness if that would be appropriate. For example, under the Criminal Damage Act 1971, Pembliton could have been convicted because his arguably reckless acts caused the damage and recklessness is, as we have seen, a sufficient *mens rea* for criminal damage.

3. The issues raised by the transferred intent cases will be revisited when we dis-cuss concurrence and correspondence in the final section of this chapter.

B: Knowledge

We have seen that, in cases of homicide where death is virtually certain to fol-low from the defendant's acts, the defendant's knowledge of the outcome can be equated with an intention to cause that outcome. Does the term 'knowingly' have an independent meaning in other contexts?

Roper v Taylor's Central Garage (Exeter) Ltd
[1951] 2 TLR 284, King's Bench Division

DEVLIN J.: . . . All that the word 'knowingly' does is to say expressly what is normally implied, and if the presumption that the statute requires *mens rea* is not rebutted I find difficulty in seeing how it can be said that the omission of the word 'knowingly' has, as a matter of construction the effect of shifting the burden of proof from the prosecution to the defence . . . it seems to me to be very important, in cases of this sort, that the prosecution, where the burden lies on the prosecution, should explain to lay justices, who are not necessarily very skilled in the handling of evidence and in the drawing of distinctions which the law requires to be drawn, exactly what sort of knowledge the prosecution desires to be found. There are, I think, three degrees of knowledge which it may be relevant to consider in cases of this kind. The first is actual knowledge, which the justices may find because they infer it from the nature of the act done, for no man can prove the state of another man's mind; and they may find it even if the defendant gives evidence to the contrary. They may say, 'We do not believe him; we think that that was his state of mind.' They may feel that the evidence falls short of that, and if they do they have then to consider what might be described as knowledge of the second degree; whether the defendant was, as it has been called, shutting his eyes to an obvious means of knowledge. Various expressions have been used to describe that state of mind. I do not think it necessary to look further, certainly not in cases of this type, than the phrase which Lord Hewart, CJ, used in a case under this section, *Evans* v *Dell* ((1937) 53 *The Times* LR 310), where he said (at p. 313): '…the respondent deliberately refrained from making inquiries the results of which he might not care to have.'…

The third kind of knowledge is what is generally known in the law as constructive knowledge: it is what is encompassed by the words 'ought to have known' in the phrase 'knew or ought to have known.' It does not mean actual knowledge at all; it means that the defendant had in effect the means of knowledge. When, therefore, the case of the prosecution is that the defendant fails to make what they think were reasonable inquiries it is, I think, incumbent on them to make it plain which of the two things they are saying. There is a vast distinction between a state of mind which consists of deliberately refraining from making inquiries, the result of which the person does not care to have, and a state of mind which is merely neglecting to make such inquiries as a reasonable and prudent person would make. If that distinction is kept well in mind I think that justices will have less difficulty than this case appears to show they have had in determining what is the true position. The case of shutting the eyes is actual knowledge in the eyes of the law; the case of merely neglecting to make inquiries is not knowledge at all—it comes within the legal conception of constructive knowledge, a conception which, generally speaking, has no place in the criminal law.

■ NOTES AND QUESTIONS

1. What does it mean to 'know' something? If Eve believes that a particular result is 70 per cent likely to follow from her acts, does she 'know' that the result will follow? What if the result is 90 per cent likely? Must she be 100 per cent certain? Is there ever such a thing as 100 per cent certainty?

2. Is Devlin J correct in stating that 'knowingly' only says expressly what is implied? If so, why would Parliament bother including 'knowingly' as part of the definition of the crime?

3. Devlin J's second category of knowledge is sometimes referred to as 'wilful blindness'. It occurs where the reason why a defendant does not have the requisite knowledge of consequences is because he chooses to turn a blind eye to them. Is it appropriate to equate wilful blindness and knowledge? Why?

Does 'knowingly' imply a subjective standard? If a reasonable person, albeit not the defendant, 'knows' what results will occur as a result of particular acts, should the defendant also be deemed to have this knowledge?

PROTECTION FROM HARASSMENT ACT 1997

1. Prohibition of harassment

(1) A person must not pursue a course of conduct—
   (a) which amounts to harassment of another, and
   (b) which he knows or ought to know amounts to harassment of the other.

(2) For the purposes of this section, the person whose course of conduct is in question ought to know that it amounts to harassment of another if a reasonable person in possession of the same information would think the course of conduct amounted to harassment of the other.

(3) Subsection (1) does not apply to a course of conduct if the person who pursued it shows—
   (a) that it was pursued for the purpose of preventing or detecting crime,
   (b) that it was pursued under any enactment or rule of law or to comply with any condition or requirement imposed by any person under any enactment, or
   (c) that in the particular circumstances the pursuit of the course of conduct was reasonable.

■ **NOTES AND QUESTIONS**

1. Does the Protection from Harassment Act 1997, s. 1, contain a subjective or objective standard of knowledge? Or what Devlin J in *Roper* referred to as 'constructive knowledge'? What language in s. 1 might suggest the latter interpretation?

2. The history leading up to passage of the Protection from Harassment Act 1997 indicates that its aim was to address the then highly publicised social problem of 'stalking'. If so, was the test of knowledge adopted in the Act necessary to achieve that aim?

The term 'knowingly' in a statute may, and frequently does, refer to knowledge of the existence of circumstances.

R v Taaffe

[1984] AC 539, House of Lords

On his arraignment on a charge of having been knowingly concerned in the fraudulent evasion of the prohibition on the importation of cannabis resin, contrary to section 170(2) of the Customs and Excise Management Act 1979 and the Misuse of Drugs Act 1971, the defendant pleaded not guilty. No evidence having been called, the recorder was asked to rule on the question whether the defendant's version of events, if accepted by the jury, would entitle him to be acquitted. That version was: (a) the defendant had been enlisted by a third party in Holland to import a substance from that country into England in fraudulent evasion of the prohibition on its importation and had so imported it; (b) that substance had in fact been cannabis, importation of which was prohibited by the Act of 1971; (c) the defendant had mistakenly believed the substance to be currency; (d) currency was not subject to any such prohibition; (e) the defendant had believed that it was. The recorder ruled that he would be obliged, even on the defendant's version of events, to direct the jury to convict. Thereupon, the defendant pleaded guilty and was sentenced. The Court of Appeal (Criminal Division) allowed his appeal against conviction.

LORD SCARMAN:....Lord Lane CJ construed the subsection under which the respondent was charged as creating not an offence of absolute liability but an offence of which an essential ingredient is a guilty mind. To be 'knowingly concerned' meant, in his judgment, knowledge not only of the existence of a smuggling operation but also that the substance being smuggled into the country was one the importation of which was prohibited by statute. The respondent thought he was concerned in a smuggling operation but believed that the substance was currency. The importation of currency is not subject to any prohibition. Lord Lane CJ concluded, at p. 631:

> [The respondent] is to be judged against the facts that he believed them to be. Had this indeed been currency and not cannabis, no offence would have been committed.

Lord Lane CJ went on to ask this question:

> Does it make any difference that the [respondent] thought wrongly that by clandestinely importing currency he was committing an offence?

The Crown submitted that it does. The court rejected the submission: the respondent's mistake of law could not convert the importation of currency into a criminal offence: and importing currency is what it had to be assumed that the respondent believed he was doing.

My Lords, I find the reasoning of the Lord Chief Justice compelling. I agree with his construction of section 170(2) of the Act of 1979: and the principle that a man must be judged upon the facts as he believes them to be is an accepted principle of the criminal law when the state of a man's mind and his knowledge are ingredients of the offence with which he is charged.

■ NOTES AND QUESTIONS

1. The Draft Criminal Code Bill 1989 provides as follows:

DRAFT CRIMINAL CODE BILL 1989

18. For the purposes of this Act and of any offence other than a pre-Code offence as defined in section 6 (to which section 2(3) applies) a person acts—
  (a) 'Knowingly' with respect to a circumstance not only when he is aware that it exists or will exist, but also when he avoids taking steps that might confirm his belief that it exists or will exist;
  ...

Does the Draft Bill adopt a subjective or an objective test of 'knowingly'?

2. In *R v Leeson* [2000] Cr App R 233, the Court of Appeal held that it was irrelevant that the defendant did not know that the drug in his possession was cocaine but believed it to be amphetamine since the drug belonged to the same category of prohibited drugs. See also *R v McNamara* (1988) 87 Cr App R 246; *R v Ellis, Street and Smith* (1987) 84 Cr App R 235. Should knowing that one of a number of conditions (X, Y or Z), but not all three, exist, be sufficient to satisfy a 'knowledge' requirement in a statute?

C: Recklessness

When the law refers to intent in relation to results, it is concerned with results which it was the actor's purpose to bring about or knows are virtually certain to follow. When it speaks in terms of knowledge, it is concerned with results that the actor has good reason to believe will come about. When the reference is to subjective recklessness, in contrast, the courts are concerned not with results which the actor intends to bring about or knows will come about, but rather with results of which the actor may be aware will come about but in regard to which he is ambivalent. In respect of objective recklessness, the actor may be ignorant of the potential results of his conduct.

Recklessness may exist in respect of:

  (a) acts;
  (b) circumstances; or
  (c) consequences.

For many modern statutory crimes (e.g., the Criminal Damage Act 1971), the prosecution may satisfy its burden of proof by establishing either that the defendant acted intentionally or that he was reckless. Unfortunately the term 'recklessness' is not always defined in the statute; indeed, the term may not even appear in the statute.

R v Cunningham

[1957] 2 QB 396, Court of Criminal Appeal

BYRNE J:...The facts were that the appellant was engaged to be married and his prospective mother-in-law was the tenant of a house, No. 7A, Bakes Street, Bradford, which was unoccupied, but which was to be occupied by the appellant after his marriage. Mrs Wade and her husband, an elderly couple, lived in the house next door. At one time the two houses had been one, but when the building was converted into two houses a wall had been erected to divide the cellars of the two houses, and that wall was composed of rubble loosely cemented.

On the evening of January 17, 1957, the appellant went to the cellar of No. 7A, Bakes Street, wrenched the gas meter from the gas pipes and stole it, together with its contents, and in a second indictment he was charged with the larceny of the gas meter and its contents. To that indictment he pleaded guilty and was sentenced to six months' imprisonment. In respect of that matter he does not appeal.

The facts were not really in dispute, and in a statement to a police officer the appellant said: 'All right, I will tell you. I was short of money, I had been off work for three days, I got eight shillings from the gas meter. I tore it off the wall and threw it away.' Although there was a stop tap within two feet of the meter the appellant did not turn off the gas, with the result that a very considerable volume of gas escaped, some of which seeped through the wall of the cellar and partially asphyxiated Mrs Wade, who was asleep in her bedroom next door, with the result that her life was endangered.

...

The act of the appellant was clearly unlawful and therefore the real question for the jury was whether it was also malicious within the meaning of section 23 of the Offences against the Person Act, 1861.

Before this court Mr Brodie has taken three points, all dependent upon the construction of that section. Section 23 provides: 'Whosoever shall unlawfully and maliciously administer to or cause to be administered to or taken by any other person any poison or other destructive or noxious thing, so as thereby to endanger the life of such person, or so as thereby to inflict upon such person any grievous bodily harm, shall be guilty of felony...'

Mr Brodie argued, first, that *mens rea* of some kind is necessary. Secondly, that the nature of the *mens rea* required is that the appellant must intend to do the particular kind of harm that was done, or, alternatively, that he must foresee that that harm may occur yet nevertheless continue recklessly to do the act....

...[W]e have...considered,..., the following principle which was propounded by the late Professor C. S. Kenny in the first edition of his Outlines of Criminal Law published in 1902 and repeated at p. 186 of the 16th edition edited by Mr J. W. Cecil Turner and published in 1952:

> In any statutory definition of a crime, malice must be taken not in the old vague sense of wickedness in general but as requiring either (1) An actual intention to do the particular kind of harm that in fact was done; or (2) recklessness as to whether such harm should occur or not (i.e., the accused has foreseen that the particular kind of harm might be done and yet has gone on to take the risk of it). It is neither limited to nor does it indeed require any ill will towards the person injured.

The same principle is repeated by Mr Turner in his 10th edition of Russell on Crime at p. 1592.

We think that this is an accurate statement of the law. It derives some support from the judgments of Lord Coleridge CJ and Blackburn J in *Pembliton's* case [1874–80] All ER 1163. In our opinion the word 'maliciously' in a statutory crime postulates foresight of consequence.

■ NOTES AND QUESTIONS

1. The trial judge in *Cunningham* had instructed the jury that 'maliciously' could be equated with wickedly, and this was an error. The Court of Appeal did not have to go any further to decide the case, but nonetheless chose to seize the opportunity to explain what it deemed to constitute recklessness.

2. Which of the following facts would the prosecution have had to have established in order to prove that Cunningham was reckless?

   (a) that he knew that coal gas could cause asphyxiation;
   (b) that he foresaw that coal gas would escape as a result of his removal of the meter;
   (c) that he knew that coal gas would remain in its lethal form after being exposed to air;
   (d) that he foresaw that the coal gas could and would seep through the wall connecting the basements of two houses;
   (e) that he foresaw that the coal gas could and would seriously harm the occupant of the house next door;
   (f) that a reasonable person would have foreseen or known all of the above.

3. How would the Crown go about satisfying a jury of each of the above elements that needed to be proved?

For many years the courts distinguished between subjective and objective recklessness. Subjective (or *Cunningham*) recklessness referred to situations where the actor was aware of the risks that might be brought about by his conduct, yet proceeded to take the risks. Objective recklessness, in contrast, referred to risks of which the actor was unaware, but which the actor would have appreciated had he given the matter any thought, or, perhaps risks of which a reasonable person would have been aware. It should be noted that neither the subjectively nor objectively reckless actor necessarily desired to cause harm.

The leading decision on objective recklessness was *R* v *Caldwell* [1982] AC 341. In this case the defendant, while drunk, set fire to a hotel. He pleaded guilty to destroying or damaging property (a violation of s. 1(1) of the Criminal Damage Act 1971) but not guilty to the more serious charge of destroying or damaging property *intending to endanger the life of another or being reckless as to whether the life of another would be endangered* (s. 1(2) of the Criminal Damage Act 1971 (emphasis added)). Caldwell claimed that, because of his drunkenness, he did not appreciate that there might be people in the hotel who would be put at risk by his actions. While the case probably could have been decided on the basis that in such circumstances drunkenness is not a valid defence, the House of Lords seized the opportunity to expand the definition of recklessness. According to Lord Diplock:

> In my opinion, a person charged with an offence under section 1(1) of the Criminal Damage Act 1971 is 'reckless as to whether any such property would be destroyed or damaged' if (1) he does an act which in fact creates an obvious risk that property will be destroyed or damaged and (2) when he does the act he either has not given any thought to the possibility of there being any such risk or has recognised that there was some risk involved and has nonetheless gone on to do it.

In *Caldwell* Lord Diplock indicated that a defendant would be liable for risks which he (the defendant) would have appreciated if he had given the matter any thought. In a companion case, *R* v *Lawrence* [1982] AC 510, where the charge was causing death by reckless driving, Lord Diplock stated that it 'is for the jury to decide whether the risk created by the manner in which the vehicle was being driven was both obvious and serious and, in deciding this, they may apply the standard of the ordinary prudent motorist as represented by themselves.' Thus, under *Lawrence*, a defendant is responsible for risks that would have been obvious to the reasonable person, regardless of whether the risks would have been appreciated by the particular defendant had he given the matter consideration.

The difference between the *Caldwell* and *Lawrence* tests can be seen in *Elliott* v *C* [1983] 1 WLR 939. In this case, an overtired 14-year-old schoolgirl, of low intelligence and in remedial education, poured white spirit on to a carpet in a shed and set the carpet alight. The shed was destroyed and the girl charged with criminal damage. The magistrates acquitted, interpreting the reference to 'obvious risk' as referring to a risk that would have been obvious to the defendant. On appeal, the Divisional Court directed the magistrates to convict, holding that the risk only had to be obvious to the reasonable person. Although expressing serious reservations about the result, Goff LJ (as he then was) felt constrained to reach it because of Lord Diplock's pronouncements in *Lawrence*.

For two decades *Caldwell* recklessness, as it came to be known, was the subject of intense criticism by academics, practitioners and judges. Lord Diplock's observation in *Caldwell* that there was little difference in terms of blameworthiness between the defendant who ignores a risk of which he is conscious and the defendant who gives no thought to the potential risk was found unpersuasive: a person who is aware of a risk and proceeds to ignore it has made a choice, and may be held responsible for the consequences of that choice; the person who is unaware of an obvious risk may be lazy, absent-minded, mentally handicapped or just plain stupid, but has not made a conscious choice to expose others to danger.

Lord Diplock in *Caldwell* had also observed that the distinction between the defendant who ignored a risk of which he is aware and the defendant who gives no thought to a potential risk was not a practicable one. Perhaps so, but it seemed that such a distinction was necessary in order to be able to distinguish between recklessness and negligence (see below). Furthermore, in some instances the distinction might not be that difficult to apply. Arguably this was the case in *Elliot* v *C*. Similarly, in *R* v *Stephenson* [1979] 1 QB 695, a schizophrenic had set fire to a haystack in order to keep himself warm. His conviction was quashed by the Court of Appeal (after *Caldwell*, *Stephenson* was no longer good law).

In *Caldwell* Lord Diplock had asserted that the ordinary meaning of recklessness included both a subjective and objective dimension. This pronouncement ignored the history of the Criminal Damage Act. The Law Commission, which had drafted the Act, had taken the view that recklessness should be understood in its subjective sense and Parliament had apparently agreed. Far from being a term which should be given its 'ordinary meaning', recklessness was arguably intended to be given a *legal* meaning. Some commentators also pointed out a 'lacuna' in *Caldwell*, in that it failed to deal with the defendant who stopped to consider the possibility of risk but who concluded incorrectly that there was none present.

Several attempts to ameliorate the potential harshness of *Caldwell* proved unsuccessful. We have noted already the interpretation advanced by the magistrates in *Elliot* v *C*, subsequently rejected by the Divisional Court, that an obvious risk should be construed as one that is obvious to the particular defendant. Another effort to circumvent *Caldwell* was advanced in *R* v *Stephen Malcolm R* (1984) 79 Cr App R 334, where it was argued that the reasonable person should be imbued with the salient characteristics of the defendant. This, as we shall see in the next chapter, is an approach that has commended itself to the House of Lords in other contexts. However, the Court of Appeal in *Stephen Malcolm R* rejected the argument as not being consistent with *Caldwell*.

In *R* v *Reid* [1992] 3 All ER 673, the House of Lords suggested that the model direction set out by Lord Diplock in *Lawrence* need not be strictly followed. Whether or not this statement could have provided the springboard for developing a less stringent interpretation of *Caldwell* recklessness became a moot point when the House of Lords abruptly changed direction in *R* v *G* [2003] UKHL 50.

R v *G and another*

[2003] UKHL 50, House of Lords

LORD BINGHAM OF CORNHILL :

My Lords,

The point of law of general public importance certified by the Court of Appeal to be involved in its decision in the present case is expressed in this way:

Can a defendant properly be convicted under section 1 of the Criminal Damage Act 1971 on the basis that he was reckless as to whether property was destroyed or damaged when he gave no thought to the risk but, by reason of his age and/or personal characteristics the risk would not have been obvious to him, even if he had thought about it?

The appeal turns on the meaning of 'reckless' in that section. This is a question on which the House ruled in *R* v *Caldwell* [1982] AC 341, a ruling affirmed by the House in later decisions. The House is again asked to reconsider that ruling.

The agreed facts of the case are very simple. On the night of 21–22 August 2000 the appellants, then aged 11 and 12 respectively, went camping without their parents' permission. In the early hours of 22 August they entered the back yard of the Co-op shop in Newport Pagnell. They found bundles of newspapers which they opened up to read. The boys then lit some of the newspapers with a lighter they had with them. Each of them threw some lit newspaper under a large plastic wheelie-bin, between which and the wall of the Co-op there was another similar wheelie-bin. The boys left the yard without putting out the burning papers. The newspapers set fire to the first wheelie-bin and the fire spread from it to the wheelie-bin next to the shop wall. From the second bin the fire spread up under the overhanging eave, to the guttering and the fascia and then up into the roof space of the shop until eventually the roof of the shop and the adjoining buildings caught fire. The roof collapsed. Approximately £ 1 m worth of damage was caused. The appellants' case at trial was that they expected the newspaper fires to extinguish themselves on the concrete floor of the yard. It is accepted that neither of them appreciated that there was any risk whatsoever of the fire spreading in the way that it eventually did.

. . .

The task confronting the House in this appeal is, first of all, one of statutory construction: what did Parliament mean when it used the word 'reckless' in section 1(1) and (2) of the 1971 Act? In so expressing the question I mean to make it as plain as I can that I am not addressing the meaning of 'reckless' in any other statutory or common law context. . . .

Since a statute is always speaking, the context or application of a statutory expression may change over time, but the meaning of the expression itself cannot change. So the starting point is to ascertain what Parliament meant by 'reckless' in 1971. As noted above in paragraph 13, section 1 as enacted followed, subject to an immaterial addition, the draft proposed by the Law Commission. It cannot be supposed that by 'reckless' Parliament meant anything different from the Law Commission. The Law Commission's meaning was made plain both in its Report (Law Com No 29) and in Working Paper No 23 which preceded it. These materials (not, it would seem, placed before the House in *R* v *Caldwell*) reveal a very plain intention to replace the old-fashioned and misleading expression 'maliciously' by the more familiar expression 'reckless' but to give the latter expression the meaning which *R* v *Cunningham* [1957] 2 QB 396 and Professor Kenny had given to the former. In treating this authority as irrelevant to the construction of 'reckless' the majority fell into understandable but clearly demonstrable error. No relevant change in the mens rea necessary for proof of the offence was intended, and in holding otherwise the majority misconstrued section 1 of the Act.

That conclusion is by no means determinative of this appeal. For the decision in *R v Caldwell* was made more than 20 years ago. Its essential reasoning was unanimously approved by the House in *R v Lawrence* [1982] AC 510. Invitations to reconsider that reasoning have been rejected. The principles laid down have been applied on many occasions, by Crown Court judges and, even more frequently, by justices. In the submission of the Crown, the ruling of the House works well and causes no injustice in practice. If Parliament had wished to give effect to the intention of the Law Commission it has had many opportunities, which it has not taken, to do so. Despite its power under Practice Statement (Judicial Precedent) [1966] 1 WLR 1234 to depart from its earlier decisions, the House should be very slow to do so, not least in a context such as this.

These are formidable arguments, deployed by Mr Perry with his habitual skill and erudition. But I am persuaded by Mr Newman QC for the appellants that they should be rejected. I reach this conclusion for four reasons, taken together.

First, it is a salutary principle that conviction of serious crime should depend on proof not simply that the defendant caused (by act or omission) an injurious result to another but that his state of mind when so acting was culpable. This, after all, is the meaning of the familiar rule actus non facit reum nisi mens sit rea. The most obviously culpable state of mind is no doubt an intention to cause the injurious result, but knowing disregard of an appreciated and unacceptable risk of causing an injurious result or a deliberate closing of the mind to such risk would be readily accepted as culpable also. It is clearly blameworthy to take an obvious and significant risk of causing injury to another. But it is not clearly blameworthy to do something involving a risk of injury to another if (for reasons other than self-induced intoxication: *R v Majewski* [1977] AC 443) one genuinely does not perceive the risk. Such a person may fairly be accused of stupidity or lack of imagination, but neither of those failings should expose him to conviction of serious crime or the risk of punishment.

Secondly, the present case shows, more clearly than any other reported case since *R v Caldwell*, that the model direction formulated by Lord Diplock . . . is capable of leading to obvious unfairness. . . . , [t]he trial judge regretted the direction he (quite rightly) felt compelled to give, and it is evident that this direction offended the jury's sense of fairness. The sense of fairness of 12 representative citizens sitting as a jury (or of a smaller group of lay justices sitting as a bench of magistrates) is the bedrock on which the administration of criminal justice in this country is built. A law which runs counter to that sense must cause concern. Here, the appellants could have been charged under section 1(1) with recklessly damaging one or both of the wheelie-bins, and they would have had little defence. As it was, the jury might have inferred that boys of the appellants' age would have appreciated the risk to the building of what they did, but it seems clear that such was not their conclusion (nor, it would appear, the judge's either). On that basis the jury thought it unfair to convict them. I share their sense of unease. It is neither moral nor just to convict a defendant (least of all a child) on the strength of what someone else would have apprehended if the defendant himself had no such apprehension. Nor, the defendant having been convicted, is the problem cured by imposition of a nominal penalty.

Thirdly, I do not think the criticism of *R v Caldwell* expressed by academics, judges and practitioners should be ignored. A decision is not, of course, to be overruled or departed from simply because it meets with disfavour in the learned journals. But a decision which attracts reasoned and outspoken criticism by the leading scholars of the day, respected as authorities in the field, must command attention . . . .

Fourthly, the majority's interpretation of 'recklessly' in section 1 of the 1971 Act was, as already shown, a misinterpretation. If it were a misinterpretation that offended no principle and gave rise to no injustice there would be strong grounds for adhering to the misinterpretation and leaving Parliament to correct it if it chose. But this misinterpretation is offensive to principle and is apt to cause injustice. That being so, the need to correct the misinterpretation is compelling.

In the course of argument before the House it was suggested that the rule in *R v Caldwell* might be modified, in cases involving children, by requiring comparison not with normal reasonable adults but with normal reasonable children of the same age. This is a suggestion with some attractions but it is open to four compelling objections. First, even this modification would offend the principle that conviction should depend on proving the state of mind of the individual defendant to be culpable. Second, if the rule were modified in relation to children on grounds of their immaturity it would be anomalous if it were not also modified in relation to the mentally handicapped on grounds of their limited understanding. Third, any modification along these lines would open the door to difficult and contentious argument concerning the qualities and characteristics to be taken into account for purposes of the comparison. Fourth, to adopt this modification would be to substitute one mis-interpretation of section 1 for another. There is no warrant in the Act or in the travaux préparatoires which preceded it for such an interpretation.

A further refinement, advanced by Professor Glanville Williams in his article 'Recklessness Redefined' (1981) 40 CLJ 252, 270–271, adopted by the justices in *Elliott* v *C* [1983] 1 WLR 939 and commented upon by Robert Goff LJ in that case is that a defendant should only be regarded as hav-ing acted recklessly by virtue of his failure to give any thought to an obvious risk that property would be destroyed or damaged, where such risk would have been obvious to him if he had given any thought to the matter. This refinement also has attractions, although it does not meet the objection of principle and does not represent a correct interpretation of the section. It is, in my opinion, open to the further objection of over-complicating the task of the jury (or bench of justices). It is one thing to decide whether a defendant can be believed when he says that the thought of a given risk never crossed his mind. It is another, and much more speculative, task to decide whether the risk would have been obvious to him if the thought had crossed his mind. The simpler the jury's task, the more likely is its verdict to be reliable.

...

For the reasons I have given I would allow this appeal and quash the appellants' convictions. I would answer the certified question obliquely, basing myself on clause 18(c) of the Criminal Code Bill annexed by the Law Commission to its Report 'A Criminal Code for England and Wales Volume 1: Report and Draft Criminal Code Bill' (Law Com No 177, April 1989):

> A person acts recklessly within the meaning of section 1 of the Criminal Damage Act 1971 with respect to—
> (i) a circumstance when he is aware of a risk that it exists or will exist;
> (ii) a result when he is aware of a risk that it will occur; and it is, in the circumstances known to him, unreasonable to take the risk.

LORD BROWNE-WILKINSON:

> My Lords,
>
> I agree with the reasons given by Lord Bingham of Cornhill. I would allow the appeal and answer the certified question as he proposes.

LORD STEYN:

> ...
>
> Ignoring the special position of children in the criminal justice system is not acceptable in a mod-ern civil society. In 1990 the United Kingdom ratified the Convention on the Rights of the Child which entered into force September 1990. Article 40.1 provides:
>
> > States Parties recognise the right of every child alleged as, accused of, or recognised as having infringed the penal law to be treated in a manner consistent with the promotion of the child's sense of dignity and worth, which reinforces the child's respect for the human rights and funda-mental freedoms of others and which takes into account the child's age and the desirability of promoting the child's reintegration and the child's assuming a constructive role in society.
>
> > ... This provision imposes both procedural and substantive obligations on state parties to protect the special position of children in the criminal justice system. For example, it would plainly be contrary to article 40.1 for a state to set the age of criminal responsibility of children at, say, five years. Similarly, it is contrary to article 40.1 to ignore in a crime punishable by life imprisonment, or detention during Her Majesty's pleasure, the age of a child in judging whether the mental element has been satisfied. It is true that the Convention became binding on the

United Kingdom after Caldwell was decided. But the House cannot ignore the norm created by the Convention. This factor on its own justified a reappraisal of Caldwell.

If it is wrong to ignore the special characteristics of children in the context of recklessness under section 1 of the 1971 Act, an adult who suffers from a lack of mental capacity or a relevant personality disorder may be entitled to the same standard of justice. Recognising the special characteristics of children and mentally disabled people goes some way towards reducing the scope of section 1 of the 1971 Act for producing unjust results which are inherent in the objective mould into which the Caldwell analysis forced recklessness. It does not, however, restore the correct interpretation of section 1 of the 1971 Act. The accepted meaning of recklessness involved foresight of consequences. This subjective state of mind is to be inferred 'by reference to all the evidence, drawing such inferences from the evidence as appear proper in the circumstances': see Lord Edmund-Davies, citing section 8 of the Criminal Justice Act 1967; at 358E. That is what Parliament intended by implementing the Law Commission proposals.

This interpretation of section 1 of the 1971 Act would fit in with the general tendency in modern times of our criminal law. The shift is towards adopting a subjective approach. It is generally necessary to look at the matter in the light of how it would have appeared to the defendant.

. . .

The surest test of a new legal rule is not whether it satisfies a team of logicians but how it performs in the real world. With the benefit of hindsight the verdict must be that the rule laid down by the majority in Caldwell failed this test. It was severely criticized by academic lawyers of distinction. It did not command respect among practitioners and judges. Jurors found it difficult to understand: it also sometimes offended their sense of justice. Experience suggests that in Caldwell the law took a wrong turn.

That brings me to the question whether the subjective interpretation of recklessness might allow wrongdoers who ought to be convicted of serious crime to escape conviction. Experience before Caldwell did not warrant such a conclusion. In any event, as Lord Edmund-Davies explained, if a defendant closes his mind to a risk he must realise that there is a risk and, on the evidence, that will usually be decisive . . . One can trust the realism of trial judges, who direct juries, to guide juries to sensible verdicts and juries can in turn be relied on to apply robust common sense to the evaluation of ridiculous defences. Moreover, the endorsement by Parliament of the Law Commission proposals could not seriously have been regarded as a charter for the acquittal of wrongdoers.

In my view the case for departing from Caldwell has been shown to be irresistible.

■ NOTES AND QUESTIONS

1. Which test of recklessness – subjective or objective – is more likely to cause persons to think before they act? Is this something with which the law should be concerned? Or is the issue more one of moral fault?

2. While the decision in *R* v *G* is limited to the meaning of 'recklessness' in the Criminal Damage Act, it is difficult to see how, in light of their reasoning, the House of Lords could accept an objective test of recklessness in other contexts. Nonetheless, their Lordships consciously and perhaps prudently chose to leave open the possibility.

3. When a defendant denies subjective awareness of a risk, how is a jury to determine whether the defendant is telling the truth? Will not the jurors ask themselves whether, in the same circumstances, they would have been aware of the risk? If so, and as presumably jurors are reasonable persons, will not an objective test of recklessness slip in through the back door? It is only in the exceptional cases involving, for instance, children (e.g., *R* v *G*; *Elliot* v *C*) and the mentally handicapped (e.g., *R* v *Stephenson*), where jurors may reach a different conclusion. But then why did their Lordships not more simply create an exception from *Caldwell* to cover such cases?

4. One area where an objective test of recklessness may still make sense is in relation to allegedly reckless harm-causing acts perpetrated by a company. A company is a fictional entity with no 'brain' as such. For it to be deemed to have been subjectively reckless requires that some individual's mind be equated with that of the company. As will be seen in Chapter 4, this in fact is how the courts have chosen to deal with the problem. However, this solution is unsatisfactory because of the difficulty of deciding whose mind should count as that of the company. Far better, perhaps, to consider whether the company has been objectively reckless in comparison to other companies. See Gobert and Punch, *Rethinking Corporate Crime* (2003) pp. 90–92.

D: Gross and ordinary negligence

(i) Gross negligence

While, following *R* v *G*, cases involving recklessness are likely to be defined in subjective terms, echoes of an objective test of liability can still be seen in crimes where the fault element is negligence or gross negligence. In respect of serious offences, probably the foremost example of basing liability on gross negligence occurs in the field of manslaughter.

R v Adomako
[1995] 1 AC 171, House of Lords

LORD MACKAY OF CLASHFERN LC:... The conviction arose out of the conduct of an eye operation carried out at the Mayday Hospital, Croydon on 4 January 1987. The appellant was, during the latter part of that operation, the anaesthetist in charge of the patient.

The operation was carried out by two surgeons supported by a team of five nurses and a theatre sister. Anaesthesia commenced at about 9.45 am. The patient was paralysed by injection of a drug and an endotracheal tube was inserted to enable the patient to breathe by mechanical means. At the start of the operation the anaesthetist was Dr Said, a registrar. An operating department assistant was also present to help him. At about 10.30 am there was a changeover of anaesthetists. The appellant was called to attend and take Dr Said's place following which both Dr Said and his assistant departed to deal with another operation elsewhere in the hospital. Another assistant was called to attend but did not arrive until later.

At approximately 11.05 am a disconnection occurred at the endotracheal tube connection. The supply of oxygen to the patient ceased and this led to cardiac arrest at 11.14 am. During this period the appellant failed to notice or remedy the disconnection.

...

The jury convicted the appellant of manslaughter by a majority of 11 to 1. The Court of Appeal, Criminal Division dismissed the appellant's appeal against conviction but certified that a point of law of general public importance was involved in the decision to dismiss the appeal, namely:

In cases of manslaughter by criminal negligence not involving driving but involving a breach of duty is it a sufficient direction to the jury to adopt the gross negligence test set out by the Court of Appeal in the present case following *R* v *Bateman* (1925) 19 Cr App R 8 and *Andrews* v *DPP* [1937] 2 All ER 552, [1937] AC 576 without reference to the test of recklessness as defined in *R* v *Lawrence* [1981] 1 All ER 974, [1982] AC 510 or as adapted to the circumstances of the case?

In opening his very cogent argument for the appellant before your Lordships, counsel submitted that the law in this area should have the characteristics of clarity, certainty, intellectual coherence and general applicability and acceptability. For these reasons he said the law applying to involuntary manslaughter generally should involve a universal test and that test should be the test already applied in this House to motor manslaughter. He criticised the concept of gross negligence which was the basis of the judgment of the Court of Appeal submitting that its formulation involved circularity, the jury being told in effect to convict of a crime if they thought a crime had been committed and that accordingly using gross negligence as the conceptual basis for the crime of involuntary manslaughter was unsatisfactory and the court should apply the law laid down in *R v Seymour* [1983] 2 All ER 1058, [1983] 2 AC 493 generally to all cases of involuntary manslaughter or at least use this as the basis for providing general applicability and acceptability.

Like the Court of Appeal your Lordships were treated to a considerable review of authority. I begin with *R v Bateman* (1925) 19 Cr App R 8 and the opinion of Lord Hewart CJ, where he said (at 12–13):

> If a person holds himself out as possessing special skill and knowledge and he is consulted, as possessing such skill and knowledge, by or on behalf of a patient, he owes a duty to the patient to use due caution in undertaking the treatment. If he accepts the responsibility and undertakes the treatment and the patient submits to his direction and treatment accordingly, he owes a duty to the patient to use diligence, care, knowledge, skill and caution in administering the treatment. No contractual relation is necessary, nor is it necessary that the service be rendered for reward. It is for the judge to direct the jury what standard to apply and for the jury to say whether that standard has been reached. The jury should not exact the highest, or a very high, standard, nor should they be content with a very low standard. The law requires a fair and reasonable standard of care and competence . . . be reached in all the matters above mentioned . . . .

Next I turn to *Andrews v DPP* [1937] 2 All ER 552, [1937] AC 576 which was a case of manslaughter through the dangerous driving of a motor car. In a speech with which all the other members of this House who sat agreed, Lord Atkin said ([1937] 2 All ER 552 at 554–555, [1937] AC 576 at 581–582):

> . . . of all crimes manslaughter appears to afford most difficulties of definition, for it concerns homicide in so many and so varying conditions. From the early days, when any homicide involved penalty, the law has gradually evolved 'through successive differentiations and integrations' until it recognises murder on the one hand, based mainly, though not exclusively, on an intention to kill, and manslaughter on the other hand, based mainly, though not exclusively, on the absence of intention to kill, but with the presence of an element of 'unlawfulness' which is the elusive factor. In the present case it is necessary to consider manslaughter only from the point of view of an unintentional killing caused by negligence, i.e., the omission of a duty to take care. I do not propose to discuss the development of this branch of the subject as treated in the successive treatises of Coke, Hale, Foster and East, and in the judgments of the courts to be found either in directions to juries by individual judges, or in the more considered pronouncements of the body of judges which preceded the formal Court of Crown Cases Reserved. Expressions will be found which indicate that to cause death by any lack of due care will amount to manslaughter; but, as manners softened and the law became more humane, a narrower criterion appeared. After all, manslaughter is a felony, and was capital, and men shrank from attaching the serious consequences of a conviction for felony to results produced by mere inadvertence. The stricter view became apparent in prosecutions of medical men, or men who professed medical or surgical skill, for manslaughter by reason of negligence. As an instance I will cite *R v Williamson* ((1807) 3 C & P 635, 172 ER 579) where a man who practised as an accoucheur, owing to a mistake in his observation of the actual symptoms, inflicted on a patient terrible injuries from which she died. Lord Ellenborough said: 'To substantiate that charge [of manslaughter] the prisoner must have been guilty of criminal misconduct, arising either from the grossest ignorance or the most criminal inattention.' The word 'criminal' in any attempt to define a crime is perhaps not the most helpful, but it is plain that Lord Ellenborough meant to indicate to the jury a high degree of negligence. So at a much later date in *R v Bateman* (1925) 19 Cr App R 8) a charge of manslaughter was made against a qualified medical practitioner in similar circumstances to those of *Williamson's* case.

Lord Atkin then refers to the judgment of Lord Hewart CJ from which I have already quoted and goes on:

> The principle to be observed is that cases of manslaughter in driving motor cars are but instances of a general rule applicable to all charges of homicide by negligence. Simple lack of care such as will constitute civil liability is not enough. For purposes of the criminal law there are degrees of negligence, and a very high degree of negligence is required to be proved before the felony is established. Probably of all the epithets that can be applied 'reckless' most nearly covers the case. It is difficult to visualise a case of death caused by 'reckless' driving, in the connotation of that term in ordinary speech, which would not justify a conviction for manslaughter, but it is probably not all-embracing, for 'reckless' suggests an indifference to risk, whereas the accused may have appreciated the risk, and intended to avoid it, and yet shown in the means adopted to avoid the risk, such a high degree of negligence as would justify a conviction. If the principle of *Bateman's* case ((1925) 19 Cr App R 8) is observed, it will appear that the law of manslaughter has not changed by the introduction of motor vehicles on the road. Death caused by their negligent driving, though unhappily much more frequent, is to be treated in law as death caused by any other form of negligence, and juries should be directed accordingly.

In my opinion the law as stated in these two authorities is satisfactory as providing a proper basis for describing the crime of involuntary manslaughter. Since the decision in *Andrews* v *DPP* [1937] 2 All ER 552, [1937] AC 576 was a decision of your Lordships' House, it remains the most authoritative statement of the present law which I have been able to find and although its relationship to *R* v *Seymour* [1983] 2 All ER 1058, [1983] 2 AC 493 is a matter to which I shall have to return, it is a decision which has not been departed from. On this basis in my opinion the ordinary principles of the law of negligence apply to ascertain whether or not the defendant has been in breach of a duty of care towards the victim who has died. If such breach of duty is established the next question is whether that breach of duty caused the death of the victim. If so, the jury must go on to consider whether that breach of duty should be characterised as gross negligence and therefore as a crime. This will depend on the seriousness of the breach of duty committed by the defendant in all the circumstances in which the defendant was placed when it occurred. The jury will have to consider whether the extent to which the defendant's conduct departed from the proper standard of care incumbent upon him, involving as it must have done a risk of death to the patient, was such that it should be judged criminal.

...

My Lords in my view the law as stated in *R* v *Seymour* [1983] 2 All ER 1058, [1983] 2 AC 493 should no longer apply since the underlying statutory provisions on which it rested have now been repealed by the Road Traffic Act 1991. It may be that cases of involuntary motor manslaughter will as a result become rare but I consider it unsatisfactory that there should be any exception to the generality of the statement which I have made, since such exception, in my view, gives rise to unnecessary complexity....

In my opinion it is quite unnecessary in the context of gross negligence to give the detailed directions with regard to the meaning of the word 'reckless' associated with *R* v *Lawrence* [1981] 1 All ER 974, [1982] AC 510. The decision of the Court of Appeal, Criminal Division in the other cases with which they were concerned at the same time as they heard the appeal in this case indicates that the circumstances in which involuntary manslaughter has to be considered may make the somewhat elaborate and rather rigid directions inappropriate. I entirely agree with the view that the circumstances to which a charge of involuntary manslaughter may apply are so various that it is unwise to attempt to categorise or detail specimen directions. For my part I would not wish to go beyond the description of the basis in law which I have already given.

■ **NOTES AND QUESTIONS**

1. Is the concept of gross negligence in tension with the decision in *R* v *G*? Is a concept such as gross negligence necessary to catch offenders who are not aware

of serious risks (but where the risk is not a virtual certainty) although capable of appreciating them?

2. In *Adomako* it was argued that the court's definition of gross negligence provided juries with little in the way of guidance. Lord MacKay responded:

> It is true that to a certain extent this involves an element of circularity, but in this branch of the law I do not believe that is fatal to its being correct as a test of how far conduct must depart from accepted standards to be characterised as criminal. This is necessarily a question of degree and an attempt to specify that degree more closely is I think likely to achieve only a spurious precision. The essence of the matter, which is supremely a jury question, is whether, having regard to the risk of death involved, the conduct of the defendant was so bad in all the circumstances as to amount in their judgment to a criminal act or omission.

Was this a satisfactory answer?

3. Is it appropriate to characterise gross negligence as a state of mind or *mens rea*? In *Attorney-General's Reference* (*No. 2 of 1999*) [2000] QB 796 the Court of Appeal said that 'evidence of…state of mind is not a prerequisite to a conviction for manslaughter by gross negligence'. The court added, however, that 'there may be cases where the defendant's state of mind is relevant to the jury's consideration when assessing the grossness and criminality of his conduct'.

4. In *R v Misra and Srivastava* [2004] EWCA Crim 2375 (discussed in Ch. 4), the Court of Appeal rejected a challenge to *Adomako* that claimed that the ambiguity of the test of gross negligence articulated by Lord MacKay violated the European Convention on Human Rights.

(ii) Negligence

One of the criticisms of *Caldwell* recklessness was that it seemed to blur the traditional line between recklessness and negligence, negligence (the failure to do what a reasonable person would have done in the circumstances) being a standard employed more commonly in civil rather than criminal cases. While *Caldwell* recklessness may no longer survive, there remain on the statute books crimes defined in terms of negligence, such as driving without due care and attention (see Road Traffic Act 1991, s. 2). Logically, negligence entails a lesser degree of fault than does gross negligence, although how much less may not always be clear. Often the distinction between gross and ordinary negligence becomes visible only within the context of a statutory scheme that has graded offences based on the two concepts. So, for instance, the Road Traffic Act 1991 contains both an offence of driving dangerously (arguably a form of gross negligence) and an offence of careless and inconsiderate driving (arguably a form of negligence).

As indicated above, negligence is measured by an objective standard, the failure to do what the reasonable person would have done in the circumstances. This failure can embrace not foreseeing a possible risk, foreseeing but miscalculating the extent of the risk, or acting in a manner that falls below what would be expected of the reasonable person. The common thread is that the reasonable person would not have behaved as did the defendant. Negligence, because it is linked to the reasonable person, is a standard that does not vary with the individual characteristics and competencies of the defendant on trial, whether specially skilled (*R v Bannister* [2009] EWCA Crim 1571), or otherwise.

McCrone v *Riding*

[1938] 1 All ER 157, King's Bench Division

The respondent was charged with driving a private motor vehicle without due care and attention contrary to the Road Traffic Act 1930, s. 12. The justices dismissed the charge, on the ground that the respondent 'was exercising all the skill and attention to be expected from a person with his short experience'.

> LORD HEWART LCJ: . . . That standard is an objective standard, impersonal and universal, fixed in relation to the safety of other users of the highway. It is in no way related to the degree of proficiency or degree of experience attained by the individual driver. I think that it is made quite plain that the justices held the notion that two standards could be entertained, because they say in their findings ultimately that they were of opinion that, 'had the respondent been an ordinary driver, we would have convicted him on the information.' They add, however:
>
> > Though he failed to display such skill as would be expected from an ordinary driver under the circumstances and drove into the said pedestrian, such failure being due to his inexperience and lack of skill did not constitute such want of care and attention [as amounted to an offence].
>
> I think, therefore, that the proper course is that the appeal should be allowed, and that the case should go back to the justices with the direction that regard must be had to the words of this statute 'without due care and attention,' and that it is wrong to assume that the word 'skill' is synonymous with the word 'care,' and that it is wrong to assume that there can be one standard for an ordinary driver and another standard for somebody else . . . .

■ NOTES AND QUESTIONS

1. The court in *McCrone* does not ask whether the defendant exercised the due care and caution that it would be reasonable to expect from a learner driver. Why is this not the relevant standard? What purposes are served by applying an objective standard to all?

2. Is the reasoning of the court in *McCrone* consistent with that in *R* v *G*? May *R* v *G* portend the death of liability based on negligence?

3. In tort law, where negligence is a common basis of liability, the defendant faces only money damages. Having to pay money damages is generally regarded as a less serious interference with liberty than is imprisonment. That said, most offences where negligence will serve as the basis of criminal liability are relatively minor and, if convicted, the defendant will usually only have to pay a fine. That fine, moreover, could be far less than the damages that might be awarded in a civil suit.

4. Recall the discussion from Chapter 1 of the purposes of punishment. What purposes support punishing a defendant who has been negligent?

E: Strict liability

The final group of crimes which needs to be examined consists of those which, at least on their face, appear to have no *mens rea*. These are referred to as offences of strict or (less accurately) absolute liability. Looks can be deceiving, however. While the crimes in question may appear on their face to have no *mens rea* requirement, courts have been known to interpret the statute in a way which introduces a *mens rea* requirement.

(i) Common law crimes

Strict liability offences are generally the product of statute, but some common law offences have been construed to impose strict liability. The clear implication of the common law maxim *'actus non facit reum nisi mens sit rea'* is that *mens rea* is required for all crimes. The law, however, was never this stringent, and the most that could be said is that crimes without *mens rea* were the exception (with libel and public nuisance being the most prominent examples).

Curiously, there seems to have been a revival of prosecutions for common law crimes, in regard to which the courts have found no *mens rea* requirement.

R v Lemon, R v Gay News Ltd
[1979] 1 All ER 898, House of Lords

LORD DIPLOCK (dissenting): My Lords, the appellants are the editor and publishers of a newspaper called Gay News. As its name suggests its readership consists mainly of homosexuals though it is on sale to the general public at some bookstalls. In an issue of Gay News published in June 1976 there appeared a poem by a Professor James Kirkup entitled 'The Love that Dares to Speak its Name' and accompanied by a drawing illustrating its subject-matter. The poem purports to describe in explicit detail acts of sodomy and fellatio with the body of Christ immediately after His death and to ascribe to Him during His lifetime promiscuous homosexual practices with the Apostles and with other men.

The issue in this appeal is not whether the words and drawing are blasphemous. The jury, though only by a majority of ten to two, have found them to be so. As expressed in the charge against them they 'vilify Christ in His life and His crucifixion', and do so in terms that are likely to arouse a sense of outrage among those who believe in or respect the Christian faith and are not homosexuals and probably among many of them that are. The only question in this appeal is whether in 1976 the mental element or mens rea in the common law offence of blasphemy is satisfied by proof only of an intention to publish material which in the opinion of the jury is likely to shock and arouse resentment among believing Christians or whether the prosecution must go further and prove that the accused in publishing the material in fact intended to produce that effect on believers, or (what comes to the same thing in criminal law) although aware of the likelihood that such effect might be produced, did not care whether it was or not, so long as the publication achieved some other purpose that constituted his motive for publishing it. Wherever I speak hereafter of 'intention' I use the expression as a term of art in that extended sense....

My Lords, if your Lordships were to hold that Lord Coleridge CJ and those judges who preceded and followed him in directing juries that the accused's intention to shock and arouse resentment among believing Christians was a necessary element in the offence of blasphemous libel were wrong in doing so, this would effectively exclude that particular offence from the benefit of Parliament's general substitution of the subjective for the objective test in applying the presumption that a man intends the natural consequences of his acts; and blasphemous libel would revert to the exceptional category of crimes of strict liability from which, on what is, to say the least, a plausible analysis of the contemporary authorities, it appeared to have escaped nearly a century ago. This would, in my view, be a retrograde step which could not be justified by any considerations of public policy.

The usual justification for creating by statute a criminal offence of strict liability, in which the prosecution need not prove mens rea as to one of the elements of the actus reus, is the threat that the actus reus of the offence poses to public health, public safety, public morals or public order. The very fact that there have been no prosecutions for blasphemous libel for more than fifty years is sufficient to dispose of any suggestion that in modern times a judicial decision to include this common law offence in this exceptional class of offences of strict liability could be justified on grounds of public morals or public order....

VISCOUNT DILHORNE: In the light of the authorities to which I have referred and for the reasons I have stated, I am unable to reach the conclusion that the ingredients of the offence of publishing a blasphemous libel have changed since 1792. Indeed, it would, I think, be surprising if they had. If it be accepted, as I think it must, that that which it is sought to prevent is the publication of blasphemous libels, the harm is done by their intentional publication, whether or not the publisher intended to blaspheme. To hold that it must be proved that he had that intent appears to me to be going some way to making the accused judge in his own cause. If Mr Lemon had testified that he did not regard the poem and drawing as blasphemous, that he had no intention to blaspheme, and it might be, that his intention was to promote the love and affection of some homosexuals for Our Lord, the jury properly directed would surely have been told that unless satisfied beyond reasonable doubt that he intended to blaspheme they should acquit, no matter how blasphemous they thought the publication. Whether or not they would have done so on such evidence is a matter of speculation on which views may differ.

The question we have to decide is a pure question of law and my conclusions thereon do not, I hope, evince any distrust of juries. The question here is what is the proper direction to give to them, not how they might act on such a direction; and distrust, which I do not have, of the way a jury might act, does not enter into it.

My Lords, for the reasons I have stated in my opinion the question certified should be answered in the affirmative. Guilt of the offence of publishing a blasphemous libel does not depend on the accused having an intent to blaspheme but on proof that the publication was intentional (or, in the case of a bookseller, negligent (Lord Campbell's Libel Act 1843)) and that the matter published was blasphemous.

I would dismiss these appeals.

Appeals dismissed.

■ NOTES AND QUESTIONS
1. Does having a strict liability common law offence compound the 'fair notice' problems already inherent in common law offences and discussed in Chapter 1?
2. The defendants in *Lemon* pursued their arguments before the European Court of Human Rights. The decision of the Court (1982) 5 EHRR 123 was presented in Chapter 1, p. 25.

(ii) Statutory offences

Most crimes which impose strict liability are the product of statute. Some of these statutes are quite clear in their intent to impose strict liability:

CONTEMPT OF COURT ACT 1981

1. The strict liability rule
In this Act 'the strict liability rule' means the rule of law whereby conduct may be treated as a contempt of court as tending to interfere with the course of justice in particular legal proceedings regardless of intent to do so.

2. Limitation of scope of strict liability
(1) The strict liability rule applies only in relation to publications, and for this purpose 'publication' includes any speech, writing, broadcast or other communication in whatever form, which is addressed to the public at large or any section of the public.
(2) The strict liability rule applies only to a publication which creates a substantial risk that the course of justice in the proceedings in question will be seriously impeded or prejudiced.
(3) The strict liability rule applies to a publication only if the proceedings in question are active within the meaning of this section at the time of the publication.

On the other hand, Parliament is not always as clear as to its intent. The fact that the legislation is silent as to whether strict liability is intended leaves the issue up in the air. The question which then confronts the courts is whether to read a *mens rea* requirement into a statute when none appears on its face.

The relevant judicial decisions are noteworthy for their lack of a coherent and consistent rationale. In some cases the judicial analysis begins and ends with the words of the statute; but in others the courts take a less literal and more functional approach, looking at the purpose to be served by the statute. It is also not uncommon to find courts claiming that they are merely implementing Parliamentary intent, but until the decision in *Pepper* v *Hart* [1992] 3 WLR 1032 the courts would not allow themselves to examine the relevant Parliamentary debates, White Papers or other official reports to determine Parliamentary intent. As well as the general conflict between a literal and a functional approach to statutory interpretation, one can observe conflicts relating to specific interpretative guides. The evil to be eradicated is often cited as a factor in imposing strict liability, with the implication that the greater the evil, the more likely the statute will be found to impose strict liability. This rationale was used to justify strict liability for offences involving drugs (see *Yeandel* v *Fisher* [1966] 1 QB 440). But in other cases the courts have reasoned that, because strict liability offences are not 'true crimes' and carry little stigma, it is not necessary to put the Crown to the inconvenience and expense of proving *mens rea*. Thus, the seriousness of the offence can cut both ways. In construing a statute to require *mens rea*, the courts may point to the fact that there was nothing more that the defendant could have done to avoid liability; but when they want liability to be strict they say that such considerations are irrelevant. Sometimes the courts will compare the wording of a specific provision of a statute with other parts of the same statute or comparable statutes; but at other times they will simply brush aside any striking change of expression as being entitled to no weight.

If a statute contains words expressive of a *mens rea* element – such as 'intentionally', 'recklessly', or 'knowingly' – the courts will not construe the statute to be one of strict liability. While a court will not abrogate a *mens rea* element where Parliament has clearly included one, the converse is not true. The courts may read in a mental element although the wording of the statute contains none on its face. Indeed, it is often stated, that there is a presumption of *mens rea*. The leading modern case is *Sweet* v *Parsley*:

Sweet v Parsley

[1970] AC 132, House of Lords

By section 5 of the Dangerous Drugs Act, 1965:

> If a person—(a) being the occupier of any premises, permits those premises to be used for the purpose of smoking...cannabis resin...or (b) is concerned in the management of any premises used for any such purpose as aforesaid; he shall be guilty of an offence against this Act.

The appellant, the sub-tenant of a farmhouse, let out several rooms to tenants who shared the use of the kitchen. She herself retained and occupied a bedroom. Later she gave up living there, though she came occasionally to collect letters and rent. On June 11, 1967, quantities of drugs, including cannabis resin, were found in the farmhouse and the appellant was charged with being concerned in the management of premises used for the purpose of smoking cannabis resin, contrary to section 5(b) of this Act. The appellant conceded that the premises had been so used. The prosecutor conceded that she did not know this. She was convicted of the offence.

LORD REID: . . . My Lords, a Divisional Court dismissed her appeal, holding that she had been concerned in the management of those premises. The reasons given for holding that she was managing the property were that she was in a position to choose her tenants: that she could put them under as long or as short a tenancy as she desired: and that she could make it a term of any letting that smoking of cannabis was not to take place. All these reasons would apply to every occupier who lets out parts of his house or takes in lodgers or paying guests. But this was held to be an absolute offence, following the earlier decision in *Yeandel v Fisher* [1966] 1 QB 440.

How has it come about that the Divisional Court has felt bound to reach such an obviously unjust result? It has in effect held that it was carrying out the will of Parliament because Parliament has chosen to make this an absolute offence. And, of course, if Parliament has so chosen the courts must carry out its will, and they cannot be blamed for any unjust consequences. But has Parliament so chosen?

. . .

Our first duty is to consider the words of the Act: if they show a clear intention to create an absolute offence that is an end of the matter. But such cases are very rare. Sometimes the words of the section which creates a particular offence make it clear that *mens rea* is required in one form or another. Such cases are quite frequent. But in a very large number of cases there is no clear indication either way. In such cases there has for centuries been a presumption that Parliament did not intend to make criminals of persons who were in no way blameworthy in what they did. That means that whenever a section is silent as to *mens rea* there is a presumption that, in order to give effect to the will of Parliament, we must read in words appropriate to require *mens rea*.

. . .

It is also firmly established that the fact that other sections of the Act expressly require *mens rea*, for example because they contain the word 'knowingly', is not in itself sufficient to justify a decision that a section which is silent as to *mens rea* creates an absolute offence. In the absence of a clear indication in the Act that an offence is intended to be an absolute offence, it is necessary to go outside the Act and examine all relevant circumstances in order to establish that this must have been the intention of Parliament. I say 'must have been' because it is a universal principle that if a penal provision is reasonably capable of two interpretations, that interpretation which is most favourable to the accused must be adopted.

What, then, are the circumstances which it is proper to take into account? In the well known case of *Sherras v De Rutzen* [1895] 1 QB 918 Wright J only mentioned the subject matter with which the Act deals. But he was there dealing with something which was one of a class of acts which 'are not criminal in any real sense, but are acts which in the public interest are prohibited under a penalty' (p. 922). It does not in the least follow that when one is dealing with a truly criminal act it is sufficient merely to have regard to the subject matter of the enactment. One must put oneself in the position of a legislator. It has long been the practice to recognise absolute offences in this class of quasi-criminal acts, and one can safely assume that, when Parliament is passing new legislation dealing with this class of offences, its silence as to *mens rea* means that the old practice is to apply. But when one comes to acts of a truly criminal character, it appears to me that there are at least two other factors which any reasonable legislator would have in mind. In the first place a stigma still attaches to any person convicted of a truly criminal offence, and the more serious or more disgraceful the offence the greater the stigma. So he would have to consider whether, in a case of this gravity, the public interest really requires that an innocent person should be prevented from proving his innocence in order that fewer guilty men may escape. And equally important is the fact that fortunately the Press in this country are vigilant to expose injustice and every manifestly unjust conviction made known to the public tends to injure the body politic by undermining public confidence in the justice of the law and of its administration. But I regret to observe that, in some recent cases where serious offences have been held to be absolute offences, the court has taken into account no more than the wording of the Act and the character and seriousness of the mischief which constitutes the offence.

The choice would be much more difficult if there were no other way open than either *mens rea* in the full sense or an absolute offence; for there are many kinds of case where putting on the prosecutor the full burden of proving *mens rea* creates great difficulties and may lead to many unjust acquittals. But there are at least two other possibilities. Parliament has not infrequently transferred the onus as regards *mens rea* to the accused, so that, once the necessary facts are proved, he must convince the jury that on balance of probabilities he is innocent of any criminal intention. I find it a little surprising that more use has not been made of this method: but one of the bad effects of the decision of this House in *Woolmington* v *Director of Public Prosecutions* [1935] AC 462 may have been to discourage its use. The other method would be in effect to substitute in appropriate classes of cases gross negligence for *mens rea* in the full sense as the mental element necessary to constitute the crime. It would often be much easier to infer that Parliament must have meant that gross negligence should be the necessary mental element than to infer that Parliament intended to create an absolute offence. A variant of this would be to accept the view of Cave J in *R* v *Tolson* (1889) 23 QBD 168, 181. This appears to have been done in Australia where authority appears to support what Dixon J said in *Proudman* v *Dayman* (1941) 67 CLR 536, 540:

> As a general rule an honest and reasonable belief in a state of facts which, if they existed, would make the defendant's act innocent affords an excuse for doing what would otherwise be an offence.

It may be that none of these methods is wholly satisfactory but at least the public scandal of convicting on a serious charge persons who are in no way blameworthy would be avoided.

If this section means what the Divisional Court have held that it means, then hundreds of thousands of people who sublet part of their premises or take in lodgers or are concerned in the management of residential premises or institutions are daily incurring a risk of being convicted of a serious offence in circumstances where they are in no way to blame. For the greatest vigilance cannot prevent tenants, lodgers or inmates or guests whom they bring in from smoking cannabis cigarettes in their own rooms. It was suggested in argument that this appellant brought this conviction on herself because it is found as a fact that when the police searched the premises there were people there of the 'beatnik fraternity'. But surely it would be going a very long way to say that persons managing premises of any kind ought to safeguard themselves by refusing accommodation to all who are of slovenly or exotic appearance, or who bring in guests of that kind. And unfortunately drug taking is by no means confined to those of unusual appearance.

■ NOTES AND QUESTIONS

1. Lord Reid says that if a statute contains no *mens rea* on its face, the presumption should be that proof of *mens rea* is intended. Why should a court engage in this presumption rather than the opposite one – that Parliament did not intend to require the Crown to be put to the proof of *mens rea*? After all, if Parliament did not include words of *mens rea*, is it not reasonable to assume that it did not intend that there should be a *mens rea*? In *B (a minor* v *DPP)* [2000] AC 428 Lord Steyn explained why courts are not prepared to accept this analysis:

   > [T]he principle of legality means that Parliament must squarely confront what it is doing and accept the political cost. Fundamental rights cannot be overridden by general or ambiguous words. This is because there is too great a risk that the full implications of their unqualified meaning may have passed unnoticed in the democratic process. In the absence of express language or necessary implication to the contrary, the courts therefore presume that even the most general words were intended to be subject to the basic rights of the individual.

   > This passage admirably captures, if I may say so, the rationale of the principle of legality. In successive editions of his classic work, Professor Sir Rupert Cross cited as the paradigm of the principle the 'presumption' that *mens rea* is required in the case of statutory crimes.

2. If a court decides to presume *mens rea* when a statute is silent, what *mens rea* should it presume – intent, knowledge of circumstances, recklessness, negligence? Since the statute is silent, how is the court to choose? Interestingly, the House of Lords in *Sweet* was not prepared to adopt a negligence standard, deeming the choice to lie between no *mens rea* or some form of traditional *mens rea*. Why?

3. The reluctance of the House of Lords to adopt a negligence standard makes even less sense when placed against the assertions of several of their Lordships that Ms Sweet had taken appropriate steps to inform herself of the true state of affairs, and that it would be unfair to punish her when there had been no showing that she had been anything but diligent. Is this not another way of saying that she had not been negligent? Had it been proved that she had been negligent, on the other hand, in, say, ignoring the strange and sweet-smelling aroma which was emanating from the farmhouse and which was making her giddy, would their Lordships have strained so to avoid holding her liable?

4. Lord Reid draws a distinction between truly criminal acts and those which are illegal only because the public welfare so demands. Is this a viable distinction? How is a court to determine whether an offence falls into the true crime or the public welfare category? Into which camp did Ms Sweet's offence fall? How do we know?

Despite the decision by the House of Lords in *Sweet*, there have been subsequent cases where the House of Lords has upheld strict liability offences, notably where the statute contains implications that this was intended. See *R v G* (2008) UKHL 37, at page 334 *supra*.

Pharmaceutical Society of Great Britain v *Storkwain*
[1986] 2 All ER 635, House of Lords

LORD GOFF OF CHIEVELEY: My Lords, this appeal is concerned with a question of construction of s. 58 of the Medicines Act 1968. Section 58(2)(a) of that Act provides as follows:

> Subject to the following provisions of this section—(a) no person shall sell by retail, or supply in circumstances corresponding to retail sale, a medicinal product of a description, or falling within a class, specified in an order under this section except in accordance with a prescription given by an appropriate practitioner . . . .

By s. 67(2) of the 1968 Act it is provided that any person who contravenes, inter alia, s. 58 shall be guilty of an offence. The question which has arisen for decision in the present case is whether, in accordance with the well-recognised presumption, there are to be read into s. 58(2)(a) words appropriate to require mens rea, on the principle stated in *R v Tolson* (1889) 23 QBD 168, [1886–90] All ER Rep 26 and *Sweet v Parsley* [1969] 1 All ER 347, [1970] AC 132.

The matter has arisen in the following way. On 2 February 1984 informations were preferred by the respondents, the Pharmaceutical Society of Great Britain, against the appellants, Storkwain Ltd, alleging that the appellants had on 14 December 1982 . . . unlawfully sold by retail, to a person purporting to be Linda Largey, 200 Physeptone tablets and 50 Ritalin tablets, and further that they unlawfully sold by retail, to a person purporting to be Thomas J. Paterson, 50 ampoules of Physeptone and 30 Valium tablets. All these medicines are substances controlled under art. 3(1)(b) of the Medicines (Prescription Only) Order 1980, SI 1980/1921; and the informations alleged in each case that the sale was not in accordance with a prescription issued by an appropriate practitioner, contrary to ss. 58(2) and 67(2) of the 1968 Act. Before the magistrate, the evidence (which was all agreed) was to the effect that the medicines were supplied under documents which purported to be prescriptions signed by a doctor, Dr Irani, of Queensdale Road, London, but that subsequent inquiries revealed that the prescriptions were both forgeries. It was submitted on behalf of the appellants that the presumption of mens rea applied to the prohibition in s. 58(2)(a) of the 1968 Act and that, the medicines having been supplied by the appellants on the basis of prescriptions which they believed in good faith and on reasonable grounds to be valid prescriptions, the informations should be dismissed. The magistrate accepted that submission and accordingly dismissed the informations: but he stated a case for the opinion of the High Court, the question for the opinion of the court being whether or not mens rea was required in the case of a prosecution under ss. 58(2) and 67(2) of the 1968 Act. On 2 May 1985 a Divisional Court (Farquharson and Tudor Price JJ) ([1985] 3 All ER 4) answered the question in the negative, and accordingly allowed the appeal of the respondents and directed that the case should be remitted to the magistrate with a direction to convict. The Divisional Court certified the following point of law as being of general public importance:

> Whether the prosecution have to prove mens rea where an information is laid under Section 58(2)(a) of the Medicines Act 1968 where the allegation is that the supply of 'prescription only' drugs was made by the [defendant] in accordance with a forged prescription and without fault on [his] part.

From that decision, the appellants now appeal with leave of your Lordships' House, the Divisional Court having refused leave.

For the appellants, counsel submitted that there must, in accordance with the well-recognised presumption, be read into s. 58(2)(a) words appropriate to require mens rea in accordance with *R v Tolson* (1889) 23 QBD 168, [1886–90] All ER Rep 26; in other words, to adopt the language of Lord Diplock in *Sweet* v *Parsley* [1969] 1 All ER 347 at 361, [1970] AC 132 at 163, the subsection must be read subject to the implication that a necessary element in the prohibition (and hence in the offence created by the subsection together with s. 67(2) of the 1968 Act) is the absence of belief, held honestly and on reasonable grounds, in the existence of facts which, if true, would make the act innocent. He further submitted, with reference to the speech of Lord Reid in *Sweet* v *Parsley* [1969] 1 All ER 347 at 350, [1970] AC 132 at 149, that the offence created by ss. 58(2(a) and 67(2) of the 1968 Act was not to be classified as merely an offence of a quasi-criminal character in which the presumption of mens rea might more readily be rebutted, because in his submission the offence was one which would result in a stigma attaching to a person who was convicted of it, especially as Parliament had regarded it as sufficiently serious to provide that it should be triable on indictment, and that the maximum penalty should be two years' imprisonment. He also submitted that, if Parliament had considered that a pharmacist who dispensed under a forged prescription in good faith and without fault should be convicted of the offence, it would surely have made express provision to that effect: and that the imposition of so strict a liability could not be justified on the basis that it would tend towards greater efficiency on the part of pharmacists in detecting forged prescriptions. Finally, he referred your Lordships to the Misuse of Drugs Act 1971. Under s. 4(1) and (3) of that Act it is an offence to supply a controlled drug to another: but it is provided in s. 28 that subject to an immaterial exception) it shall be a defence for the accused to prove that he neither knew of nor suspected nor had reason to suspect the existence of some fact alleged by the prosecution which it is necessary for the prosecution to prove if he is to be convicted of the offence charged. Counsel for the appellants submitted that it would be anomalous if such a defence were available in the case of the more serious offence of supplying a controlled drug to another, but that the presumption of mens rea should be held inapplicable in the case of the offence created by ss. 58(2)(a) and 67(2) of the 1968 Act.

I am unable to accept counsel's submission, for the simple reason that it is, in my opinion, clear from the 1968 Act that Parliament must have intended that the presumption of mens rea should be inapplicable to s. 58(2)(a). First of all, it appears from the 1968 Act that, where Parliament wished to recognise that mens rea should be an ingredient of an offence created by the Act, it has expressly so provided. Thus, taking first of all offences created under provisions of Pt II of the 1968 Act, express requirements of mens rea are to be found both in s. 45(2) and in s. 46(1), (2) and (3) of the Act. More particularly, in relation to offences created by Pt III and Pts V and VI of the 1968 Act, s. 121 makes detailed provision for a requirement of mens rea in respect of certain specified sections of the act, including ss. 63 to 65 (which are contained in Pt III), but significantly not s. 58, nor indeed ss. 52 and 53. I have already set out the full text of s. 121 and need not repeat it. It is very difficult to avoid the conclusion that, by omitting s. 58 from those sections to which s. 121 is expressly made applicable, Parliament intended that there should be no implication of a requirement of mens rea in s. 58(2)(a). This view is fortified by sub-ss. (4) and (5) of s. 58 itself. Subsection (4)(a) provides that any order made by the appropriate ministers for the purposes of s. 58 may provide that s. 58(2)(a) or (b), or both, shall have effect subject to such exemptions as may be specified in the order. From this subsection alone it follows that the ministers, if they think it right, can provide for exemption where there is no mens rea on the part of the accused. Subsection (5) provides that any exemption conferred by an order in accordance with sub-s. (4)(a) may be conferred subject to such conditions or limitations as may be specified in the order. From this it follows that, if the ministers, acting under sub-s. (4), were to confer an exemption relating to sales where the vendor lacked the requisite mens rea, they may nevertheless circumscribe their exemption with conditions and limitations which render the exemption far narrower than the implication for which counsel for the appellants contends should be read into the statute itself. I find this to be very difficult to reconcile with the proposed implication.

It comes as no surprise to me, therefore, to discover that the relevant order in force at that time, the Medicines (Prescriptions Only) Order 1980, is drawn entirely in conformity with the construction of the statute which I favour. It is unnecessary, in the present case, to consider whether the relevant articles of the order may be taken into account in construing s. 58 of the 1968 Act; it is enough, for present purposes, that I am able to draw support from the fact that the ministers, in making the order, plainly did not read s. 58 as subject to the implication proposed by counsel for the appellants....

■ NOTES AND QUESTIONS

1. When a statute is aimed at those in a particular trade, business or profession, there may be a greater willingness to construe a criminal statute to impose strict liability. Those in the trade can be presumed to have made a conscious choice to enter it. If they do not like the idea of strict liability, they can earn their living in some other way. Those who choose to continue in the trade, business or profession are expected to be fully conversant with the statutes which affect them, and how those statutes are interpreted by the courts. That said, what can a pharmacist do, as a practical matter, to avoid a criminal prosecution? What advice would you give to your pharmacist client?

2. The maximum sentence to which the defendant in *Storkwain* could have been subjected was two years. Should the severity of the sanction have strengthened – or weakened – the argument in favour of strict liability?

3. Under the Draft Criminal Code Bill 1989, *mens rea* is presumed and strict liability can be imposed only if Parliament expressly or impliedly so provides. See Commentary on Draft Criminal Code Bill, Clause 20.

4. What policies support the imposition of strict liability? Are these policy considerations counter-balanced by the risk that morally blameless individuals may be subjected to criminal liability?

5. In *Crime and the Criminal Law* (1963) Baroness Wooten argues that all crimes should be defined in 'strict liability' mode, with *mens rea* becoming relevant only at the sentencing stage. What are the advantages and disadvantages to such an approach to criminal liability?

In *Sweet*, several of their Lordships suggested a middle position between requiring proof of traditional *mens rea* and imposing strict liability. This middle position would allow the Crown to establish its case without proof of *mens rea*, but permit the defendant to raise a defence of 'due diligence'. Many statutes, such as the Trade Descriptions Act 1968, s. 24(1), the Weights and Measures Act 1985, s. 34, the Consumer Protection Act 1987, s. 39, the Food Safety Act 1991, s. 21 and the Licensing Act 2003, s.139, contain a due diligence defence. A due diligence defence was also judicially approved by the Canadian Supreme Court in *R* v *City of Sault Ste Marie* (1978) 85 DLR (3d) 161. But how much 'diligence' is 'due' for the defence to succeed?

Rotherham Metropolitan Borough Council v Raysun (UK) Ltd

[1988] BTLC 292, 153 JP 37, 8 Tr L 6, [1989] CCLR 1, Queen's Bench Division

WOOLF LJ: This is an appeal by case stated by South Yorkshire Justices in respect of a decision of the justices when sitting at the magistrates' court at Rotherham in relation to two informations, which had been preferred on 16 April 1987 and heard on 8 October 1987.

The informations were preferred against the respondent company, Raysun (UK) Ltd, who are large-scale importers into this country of items manufactured in the Far East, and the offences alleged in the informations arose out of the same facts. The offences were charged as follows:

'The commission of an offence on 30th October 1986 by one Stuart Bray whereby he had sold children's wax crayons to which were applied a false trade description (namely the word poison-less) when the black crayon contained excessive amounts of toxic material contrary to s 1(1)(b) Trade Descriptions Act 1968 was due to the act or default of the said respondent whereby the said respondent is guilty of the offence by virtue of s 23 Trade Descriptions Act 1968.'

The second offence was in similar terms to the first offence, except that it alleged that, by selling a box of children's wax crayons, the black crayon contained 1,200 parts of soluble lead per million parts of crayon, contrary to s 2(1) of the Consumer Protection Acts 1961 and 1971. In this case the offence was alleged to have been committed by virtue of s 12(6) of the Consumer Safety (Amendment) Act 1986.

. . .

The defence which is available to a person against whom proceedings are brought either under s 1

(1) or under s 23 is contained in s 24, which, so far as relevant, provides: '(1) In any proceedings for an offence under this Act it shall, subject to subsection (2) of this section, be a defence for the person charged to prove—(a) that the commission of the offence was due to . . . the act or default of another person . . . and (b) that he took all reasonable precautions and exercised all due diligence to avoid the commission of such an offence by himself or any person under his control.'

. . .

The Consumer Safety (Amendment) Act 1986 contains a similar defence. In this case it is contained in s 12(2) of that Act. That subsection provides:

'Subject to the following provisions of this section, in proceedings against any person for an offence to which this section applies it shall be a defence for that person to show that he took all reasonable steps and exercised all due diligence to avoid committing the offence.'

There is no dispute on the facts found by the justices that the respondent company did take precautions in this case and did exercise diligence to avoid the commission of the offences by them and, equally, it is not disputed that the commission of the offence was due to the act or default of another person, namely the manufacturers of those who supplied the crayons from abroad. What is in issue is whether they took all reasonable precautions and exercised due diligence to avoid the commission of the offence.

. . .

The appellant council contended before the justices that they did not. However, the justices came to the conclusion that the defence which is available in s 24 of the Trade Descriptions Act 1968 and s 12(2) of the Consumer Safety (Amendment) Act 1986 had been made out. Before this court it is contended that the justices were not entitled to come to that conclusion on the evidence which was before them.

In his succinct and helpful submissions before this court, counsel for the appellants accepts that there is no case to which he can refer in which this court had intervened where the respondent has taken steps of the type which were in fact taken by these respondents to avoid the commission of the offence. None the less, he submits that, when the facts found by the justices are examined, the only proper conclusion that one can come to is that the necessary factual basis for the decision of the justices is not present. It is therefore important to consider the facts found by the justices as set out in the case.

Having dealt with the purchase of the crayons which led to the laying of the charge—the justices go on to say:

> 'D. The defendant company was a concern employing eighteen full-time staff with a 1986 turnover of £4 million arising from the importation of 13.3 million items. It dealt with the manufacture through agents based in Hong Kong. The duties of the agents included checking the quality of the crayons by visiting the factory and submitting samples for analysis by a "Government Analyst" in Hong Kong. The directors of the defendant company had visited the factory in 1984, they had some direct dealings with the manufacturer and, on an on-going basis, the company had agents in Hong Kong who monitored the quality of the crayons. E. The defendant company had provided the manufacturer with the legal requirements relating to the production of crayons, although the crayons were a proprietory brand not manufactured to the specification of the defendant company. F. Only adverse reports by the Hong Kong analyst were expected to be conveyed to the defendant company and no such adverse reports had been received. G. The crayons were imported once a year in a single batch, each batch containing between 7,000 and 10,000 dozen packets, each containing 12 crayons, and had been so imported since 1982. The 1986 consignment had consisted of 10,800 dozen of such packets. H. From each batch of crayons imported a single packet had been selected at random as a sample analysis by a public analyst in Manchester. I. All the samples analysed, ie those in 1983, 1984 and 1985 and in particular the one from the 1986 consignment which contained the crayon which was the subject of the charge, were found to comply with the requirements of the Pencils and Graphic Instruments (Safety) Regulations 1974 [SI 1974/226]. J. The defendant company had been given no reason to suspect the quality of the crayons either from analyses carried out in Hong Kong and this country or from the Toy Importers' Association of which it was a member and which would have notified any difficulties encountered by other importers in relation to the same type of crayons.'

...

First of all, with regard to what happened in Hong Kong, it is right to note that in this case there was some contact between the respondent company and the manufacturer in Hong Kong. It is also right, on the findings of fact, to take into account that the manufacturers were being supervised, or should have been supervised, to some extent by the agents of the respondents in Hong Kong. What is more, those Hong Kong agents should have carried out sampling and had the samples checked by analysis by the Government Analyst in Hong Kong. However, I would also point out that because of the method adopted of reporting to the respondents, there was no check which the respondents apparently made that that analysis was taking place at the instigation of their agents. The respondents relied on a system where, if the analysis was adverse, they would be informed, but, if it was favourable, they would not be informed. As the case makes clear, the respondent company merely assumed, because they had not heard of any adverse analysis, that in fact the analyses were taking place in Hong Kong and were proving favourable. Furthermore, there was no material before the justices to indicate the basis on which the sampling was being carried out by their agents. They were not told what percentage of the goods imported were being sampled or should have been sampled, and how those samples were being chosen.

With regard to the sampling which took place in this country, the selection of one packet of crayons in respect of an importation of a batch of 10,000 dozen crayons, as counsel for the appellants points out, is a very modest sample indeed. By itself, in my view, certainly in relation to offences of this sort, it does not indicate the taking of the standard of care required by the relevant statutory provisions. I recognise that, if the sampling had been supported by evidence that indicated that the standard throughout a large consignment such as 10,000 dozen packets could be expected to be the same, then it is conceivable that to choose one sample in relation to such a large batch might suffice. But, in the absence of any supporting evidence of that sort, in the absence of any evidence indicating why the respondents had selected only one packet of crayons out of a batch of 10,000 dozen crayons, this does not appear to me to be the sort of proportion which would comply with the standards laid down in the relevant statutory provisions.

As for their reliance on the Toy Importers' Association, I apprehend that is also not the sort of matter which can assist someone seeking to rely on the statutory defence. By itself, it does not assist the justices other than to a very marginal degree. The justices would not know the extent to which the Toy Importers' Association in fact monitor difficulties of importation of this particular product. Indeed, there is no evidence before the justices that any of these crayons were being imported by anyone other than the respondent company. Unless there was a proper factual foundation to show that the absence of any notification by the Toy Importers' Association was something to which the respondent company could reasonably attach attention, it was (if I may say so) merely window-dressing, which the justices should have ignored.

This case boils down to this. This respondent company were relying on their agents to do what should be done in Hong Kong to provide precautions. In addition, they were carrying out a very sparse sampling exercise in this country. Apart from that, they were really taking no action in order to fulfil the statutory obligations which are placed on them under the respective Acts, to which I have made reference.

In my view, albeit that this was a standard of conduct which was higher than that indicated in previous cases which have come before this court, it is not sufficient to justify the justices coming to the conclusion to which they did in this case. I understand that the justices, not having been referred to any authority which precisely covered the facts of this case, cannot be criticised for coming to the decision which they did. None the less, I take the view that, having regard to the statutory language, this was one of those cases where the justices came to a conclusion which they were not entitled to and indeed to that extent their decision must be regarded as being perverse.

Accordingly, I would allow this appeal and, subject to hearing any submissions which counsel for the appellant has to make in this regard, I would direct that the case be remitted to the justices with the direction that they should convict the respondents of both of these offences. In relation to the question which the justices stated for the opinion of this court, which was in these terms:

'Whether it was open to us on the facts as found to conclude that the [respondents] had taken all reasonable precautions and exercised all due diligence to avoid the commission of an offence'.

I would give the answer No.

Appeal allowed. Case remitted to justices with direction to convict.

■ NOTES AND QUESTIONS

1. Does a due diligence defence in effect convert a crime of strict liability into one of negligence, but with the burden of proving non-negligence resting on the defendant (albeit usually by a balance of probabilities rather than by proof beyond reasonable doubt)? Does imposing such a burden on the defendant violate the presumption of innocence contained in Art. 6 of the ECHR?

2. The use of strict liability offences with due diligence defences may make particularly good sense in respect of crimes committed by companies. The difficulty of attributing a *mens rea* to a company argues in favour of strict liability offences but the harshness of imposing strict liability when there may have been no fault on the part of the company argues in favour of allowing a due

diligence defence. If such a test were to be adopted in this context, should due diligence be measured by what similarly situated companies are doing? Would such an approach encourage companies to adopt a 'lowest common denominator' approach to their legal obligations?

3. Should issues of corporate due diligence be left for the jury to decide? What do ordinary persons from the community know about what it is reasonable to expect from companies in respect of their legal obligations?

SECTION 3: RELATIONSHIP BETWEEN *ACTUS REUS* AND *MENS REA*: COINCIDENCE, CONCURRENCE AND CORRESPONDENCE

In discharging its burden of proof, it is not enough for the prosecution simply to establish that the *actus reus* and *mens rea* of the offence were both present, or even present at the same time. Rather, the prosecution must establish that all the elements 'line up' in a fashion which justifies the conclusion that the accused is properly held responsible for the occurrence of the relevant harm.

> Jack leaves a party with Jill, his lover and Adam's wife. Adam sees them go and follows them in his car. Jack notices Adam following and increases speed as he goes round a very dangerous bend in the road above a cliff. Attempting to stay close, Adam spins off the road and over the cliff. Jack gets out of the car and hears Adam calling for help. Although Jack realises that if he does not help, Adam will die, he decides to do nothing. Adam dies within the hour.

Here there is a death but would it be proper to attribute that death to Jack's conduct? To answer this question all the elements of the crime of murder or manslaughter must concur. If we add up all the information so far learned about the elements in crime we know that the *actus reus* is an act or, exceptionally, an omission in breach of duty; that the *mens rea* is the state of mind which accompanies the act or omission and justifies the conclusion that the actor is blameworthy and therefore deserving of punishment; and that, for crimes defined in terms of result, such as homicide, the act must cause the result. Further problems arise in respect of our example, however:

1. Was Jack's act of increasing speed while rounding a dangerous bend *accompanied at the time he performed it* by a state of mind (intent to kill or foresight of certain death) which would warrant a conviction for murder? There is little that can be inferred regarding Jack's state of mind before the 'accident'. The stronger evidence of his mental state is that which appears afterwards (Jack's awareness of Adam's virtually certain death). This, however, is insufficient. Jack's *actus reus* (speeding up) and *mens rea* (knowledge of certain death) do not coincide in point of time.

2. Might there be any other way of lining up the factual ingredients of this scenario to establish a case of culpable homicide? If we ignore Jack's act of speeding up and concentrate on his refusal to lend assistance after the 'accident' we may be in more promising territory. Jack's failure to help may be argued to satisfy the *actus reus* requirement as there are grounds for asserting that

Jack was under a legal duty to prevent the risk of harm created by his previous conduct (recall the decision in *Miller*, p. 77). This omission was accompanied by *mens rea* (knowledge of certain death). This *mens rea* coincides in point of time with the *actus reus* (the failure to help), which arguably was a substantial contributing factor (i.e., cause) of Adam's death.

The key point to be drawn from our example is that the coincidence of *actus reus* and *mens rea* will not necessarily lead to criminal liability. There is the additional requirement that the *actus reus* and *mens rea* be related in a particular way. Coincidence in time may be only the starting point.

A: Temporal coincidence

Say that Eve, speeding home from work, is contemplating how best to kill her husband, Adam, whom she hates. She decides to kill him by running him over in the car in such a way as to make it look like an accident. While she is engaged in this line of thinking, Adam leaps in front of her car, bent on committing suicide. Adam dies.

Is Eve guilty of murder? Although her speeding may have been the cause of Adam's death, and although Eve wanted to kill Adam at the critical moment, and her mind may have been full of homicidal thoughts, that would not be enough to warrant a conviction of murder. The prosecution must further show that Eve was of a mind to kill Adam by the act which caused Adam's death. Stated another way, Eve's evil thoughts must have been the activating reason for her evil deeds. This is what the courts have in mind when they speak of concurrence or the requirement that *mens rea* and *actus reus* should coincide. The criminal law does not prohibit evil thoughts. How could it? It prohibits (and punishes) only acts based on evil thoughts.

Problems arise in situations where the defendant's *mens rea* is formed only after the *actus reus* is completed, as in our first example involving Jack. In such a case, liability may depend upon the prosecution being able to convince the court of an alternative *actus reus*, namely an omission in breach of duty. In the converse case where a crime is complete, a subsequent change of heart is irrelevant. Thus, if Oliver, a pickpocket, changes his mind upon realising the victim is his friend, Jack, and returns the wallet immediately, Oliver will still be guilty of theft. His *actus reus* of appropriating the wallet was accompanied *at the time it occurred* by the *mens rea* of a dishonest intent to keep it. All the elements of the crime of theft were satisfied at that split second. This is correct in principle but perhaps not always sensible in terms of policy since it leaves Oliver with no incentive to undo his wrong. Courts are no doubt suspicious when a putative criminal who has been apprehended says, 'Well, the fact is that I had already changed my mind.'

R v Jakeman
(1982) 76 Cr App R 223, Court of Appeal

The applicant travelled by air to Accra in Ghana. She took with her two suitcases. There she booked a return flight to Rome two days later and a day after that a further flight from there to London. When she checked in at Accra for the return flight with her two suitcases, she booked them through to London. They contained 21.44 kilogrammes of cannabis, a controlled drug pursuant to section 2(1) of, and Part II of Schedule 2 to, the Misuse of Drugs Act 1971, and the importation of which to the United Kingdom was prohibited by section 3(1) of that Act. The flight to Rome was cancelled and the next day the passengers, including the applicant, were flown to Paris, where she took a flight to Rome, leaving her luggage in Paris, and then on to London. The customs officials in Paris assumed that the applicant's luggage there had been mis-routed and sent it on to London where customs officers on examination found the aforesaid amount of cannabis. They interviewed the applicant who eventually admitted that the two suitcases were hers and that she knew they contained cannabis. She was charged with being knowingly concerned in the fraudulent evasion of a prohibition in relation to goods contrary to section 170(2) of the Customs and Excise Management Act 1979, 'goods' in that subsection under paragraphs 1 and 3 of Schedule 1 to that Act including cannabis. At her trial she contended that she had been persuaded by two unknown men to take the drugs to London for £500; but that upon leaving Accra she had decided to have nothing further to do with the fraudulent enterprise and so had not collected the suitcases in Paris and had torn up her baggage tags. Her counsel then asked the trial judge whether in his view the intention to abandon her part in the importation, if accepted by the jury, provided a defence. The judge indicated that he thought that it did not and that he would so direct the jury. The applicant thereupon changed her plea to one of guilty. On an application for leave to appeal against conviction on the ground that the judge's ruling was wrong it was argued that for the offence under section 170(2) the participation of the applicant and her *mens rea* must continue throughout the offence, i.e. until the aircraft touched down at London Airport.

WOOD J: ... We will deal first with the application for leave to appeal against conviction. Mr Mansfield first submits that the learned judge was wrong in the ruling which he gave. He submits that for the offence under section 170(2) of the 1979 Act, the participation of the applicant and her *mens rea* must continue throughout the offence—in this case at least until the wheels of the aircraft touched down at Heathrow Airport.

...

In developing his submission on the first ground of appeal, Mr Mansfield relied upon the applicant's assertion that she had changed her mind immediately on leaving Accra and on the facts that she did not collect her suitcases in Paris, that she tore up the baggage tags on arrival at Heathrow and that she did not seek to claim her suitcases. He submitted that whether one referred to 'withdrawal' or 'abandonment' or 'lack of *mens rea*' as the necessary ingredient of the defence, assistance was to be obtained from such cases as *R v Croft* (1944) 29 Cr App R 169 and *R v Becerra and Cooper* (1975) 62 Cr App R 212. These cases are concerned with accomplices and secondary parties to crime, not to the principal offender, and in the view of this court are not of assistance to test the submission which is made. It is our view that the correct approach is to analyse the offence itself, but before turning to consider the wording of the section as a whole, it is valuable to look at decided cases and to see what assistance can be derived from them.

The following propositions are supported by decisions of this court. First, that the importation takes place when the aircraft bringing the goods lands at an airport in this country, see *R v Smith (Donald)* (1973) 57 Cr App R 737, 748. Secondly, acts done abroad in order to further the fraudulent evasion of a restriction on importation into this country are punishable under this section, see *R v Wall (Geoffrey)* (1974) 59 Cr App R 58, 61.

For guilt to be established the importation must, of course, result as a consequence, if only in part, of the activity of the accused. If, for example, in the present case the applicant had taken her two suitcases off the carousel at Charles de Gaulle airport in Paris, removed all the luggage tags, placed the suitcases in a left luggage compartment and thrown the key of that compartment into the Seine, and then subsequently, in a general emergency, all left luggage compartments had been opened, a well-known English travel label had been found on her suitcase and those suitcases had been sent to the Travel Agents' agency, care of Customs and Excise at Heathrow, then that undoubted importation would not be the relevant one for the purposes of a charge against the applicant.

We have already set out the wording of the relevant section and where the allegation concerns cannabis, the offence is, to be knowingly concerned in the fraudulent evasion (or attempt at evasion) of the prohibition on the importation of cannabis. Put more shortly, it is to be knowingly concerned in the fraudulent importation (or attempt at importation) of cannabis.

Although the importation takes place at one precise moment—when the aircraft lands—a person who is concerned in the importation may play his part before or after that moment. Commonly, the person responsible for despatching the prohibited drugs to England acts fraudulently and so does the person who removes them from the airport at which they have arrived. Each is guilty. *Wall* (*supra*) is an example of the former and *R* v *Green* (1975) 62 Cr App R 74 of the latter.

There is no doubt, that, putting aside the question of duress, as we have done, the applicant had a guilty mind when at Accra she booked her luggage to London. By that act, she brought about the importation through the instrumentation of innocent agents. In this way, she caused the airline to label it to London, and the labels were responsible for the authorities in Paris sending it on to London.

What is suggested is that she should not be convicted unless her guilty state of mind subsisted at the time of importation. We see no reason to construe the Act in this way. If a guilty mind at the time of importation is an essential, the man recruited to collect the package which has already arrived and which he knows contains prohibited drugs commits no offence. What matters is the state of mind at the time the relevant acts are done, i.e. at the time the defendant is concerned in bringing about the importation. This accords with the general principles of common law. To stab a victim in a rage with the necessary intent for murder or manslaughter leads to criminal responsibility for the resulting death regardless of any repentance between the act of stabbing and the time of death, which may be hours or days later. This is so even if, within seconds of the stabbing, the criminal comes to his senses and does everything possible to assist his victim. Only the victim's survival will save him from conviction for murder or manslaughter.

The applicant alleged that she repented as soon as she boarded the aircraft; that she deliberately failed to claim her luggage in Paris, that she tore up the baggage tags attached to her ticket and so on, but none of this could have saved her from being held criminally responsible for the importation which she had brought about by deliberate actions committed with guilty intent. Thus, the learned judge was right in the ruling he made.

Appeal dismissed.

(i) Qualifying the requirement of temporal coincidence: the supposed corpse cases

The more troublesome cases, at least intellectually, involve the defendant who commits a series of acts: the original acts are done with intent to bring about a result but are ineffectual; the subsequent acts are not done with any criminal intent but bring about the originally desired result:

Thabo Meli and Others v *R*

[1954] 1 WLR 228, Privy Council

LORD REID: The four appellants in this case were convicted of murder after a trial before Sir Walter Harragin, judge of the High Court of Basutoland, in March, 1953. The appeal which has been heard by this Board dealt with two matters: first, whether the conclusions of the learned judge on questions of fact were warranted: and, secondly, whether, on a point of law, the accused are entitled to have the verdict quashed.

On the first matter, there really is no ground for criticising the learned judge's treatment of the facts. It is established by evidence, which was believed and which is apparently credible, that there was a preconceived plot on the part of the four accused to bring the deceased man to a hut and there to kill him, and then to fake an accident, so that the accused should escape the penalty for their act. The deceased man was brought to the hut. He was there treated to beer and was at least partially intoxicated; and he was then struck over the head in accordance with the plan of the accused. Witnesses say that while the deceased was seated and bending forward he was struck a heavy blow on the back of the head with a piece of iron like the instrument produced at the trial. But a postmortem examination showed that his skull had not been fractured and medical evidence was to the effect that a blow such as the witnesses described would have produced more severe injuries than those found at the post-mortem examination. There is at least doubt whether the weapon which was produced as being like the weapon which was used could have produced the injuries that were found, but it may be that this weapon is not exactly similar to the one which was used, or it may be that the blow was a glancing blow and produced less severe injuries than those which one might expect. In any event, the man was unconscious after receiving the blow, but he was not then dead. There is no evidence that the accused then believed that he was dead, but their Lordships are prepared to assume from their subsequent conduct that they did so believe; and it is only on that assumption that any statable case can be made for this appeal. The accused took out the body, rolled it over a low krantz or cliff, and dressed up the scene to make it look like an accident. Obviously, they believed at that time that the man was dead, but it appears from the medical evidence that the injuries which he received in the hut were not sufficient to cause the death and that the final cause of his death was exposure when he was left unconscious at the foot of the krantz.

The point of law which was raised in this case can be simply stated. It is said that two acts were done:—first, the attack in the hut; and, secondly, the placing of the body outside after-wards—and that they were separate acts. It is said that, while the first act was accompanied by *mens rea*, it was not the cause of death; but that the second act, while it was the cause of death, was not accompanied by *mens rea*; and on that ground, it is said that the accused are not guilty of murder, though they may have been guilty of culpable homicide. It is said that the *mens rea* necessary to establish murder is an intention to kill, and that there could be no intention to kill when the accused thought that the man was already dead, so their original intention to kill had ceased before they did the act which caused the man's death. It appears to their Lordships impossible to divide up what was really one series of acts in this way. There is no doubt that the accused set out to do all these acts in order to achieve their plan, and as parts of their plan; and it is much too refined a ground of judgment to say that, because they were under a misapprehension at one stage and thought that their guilty purpose had been achieved before, in fact, it was achieved, therefore they are to escape the penalties of the law. Their Lordships do not think that this is a matter which is susceptible of elaboration. There appears to be no case, either in South Africa or England, or for that matter elsewhere, which resembles the present. Their Lordships can find no difference relevant to the present case between the law of South Africa and the law of England; and they are of opinion that by both laws there can be no separation such as that for which the accused contend. Their crime is not reduced from murder to a lesser crime merely because the accused were under some misapprehension for a time during the completion of their criminal plot.

Their Lordships must, therefore, humbly advise Her Majesty that this appeal should be dismissed.

■ NOTES AND QUESTIONS

1. In *Thabo Meli* the defendants' acts were performed with a guilty mind and pursuant to a plan to cause death. Why, then, did the court make such heavy weather of finding them guilty?

2. Glanville Williams suggests that an alternative way of dealing with cases such as *Thabo Meli* is to say that 'If a killing by the first act would have been murder/manslaughter, a later destruction of the supposed corpse should also be murder/manslaughter.' Another solution would have been to charge the defendants with attempted murder (see Chapter 12) based on the initial attack.

(ii) A single transaction

Another approach to cases like *Thabo Meli* is to consider the entire sequence of events as a single transaction:

R v Le Brun
[1991] 4 All ER 673, Court of Appeal

LORD LANE CJ: On 31 March 1990 in the Crown Court at Plymouth before Hutchison J and a jury the appellant, John Le Brun, was convicted on a majority verdict of manslaughter. He was found not guilty of murder, with which he had originally been charged. He was sentenced to four years' imprisonment. He now appeals against conviction by leave of the single judge.

The facts giving rise to the charge were these. In September 1989 the appellant, who was then serving in the Royal Navy, was living at an address in Plymouth with his wife, who was the victim in the present case. They went out for the evening to some friends, the Cartwrights, on 23 September 1989. They left the house of the friends in the early hours at about 2 am. They did not have very far to go to their own home. They had been drinking. They were both described as merry, but neither, it was said, was drunk.

It was only two or three minutes' walk to get to their own home. But during that short journey it is quite plain that a heated argument developed between the two of them. To come to the end of the story, after a short interval, which was really only sufficient for the friends whose house they had visited to have tidied up the house, taken the dog for a walk and prepared for bed, the appellant returned to the Cartwrights, banged on the door and shouted, 'It's Joannie...she's collapsed. There's blood everywhere. Get an ambulance.'

In fact the wife (as I shall call her now) was lying near the top of some steps leading from the pathway to their home. She had sustained two wounds to the back of her head: a fracture to the back of the skull and a severe injury to her chin, which had produced what might be described as a star-shaped wound. That wound had broken the jaw and caused bleeding into the joints on each side. She had sustained also a bruise on the outer edge of the lip on the left, a fracture to both wings of the hyoid bone at the top of the neck. As can be seen from the photographs, there was a good deal of blood at the scene and—a matter of some importance—some hair which had plainly been pulled by the roots out of her scalp was lying at the scene.

The cause of death was bruising to the brain, which in its turn had been caused by the fracture to the back of the skull.

...

The main thrust of [defendant's] argument is to be found in ground 3 of the notice of appeal, which I will now read:

'The learned judge erred in law in directing the jury that they could convict the appellant of murder or manslaughter (depending on the intention with which he had previously assaulted the victim) if they were sure that, having committed the assault with no serious injury resulting, the appellant had accidentally dropped the victim causing her death whilst either: (a) attempting to move her to her home against her wishes, including any wishes she may have expressed prior to the previous assault, and/or (b) attempting to dispose of her body or otherwise cover up the previous assault.'

Problems of causation and remoteness of damage are never easy of solution. We have had helpful arguments from both counsel on this point, the point in the present case being, to put it in summary before coming to deal with it in more detail, that the intention of the appellant to harm his wife one way or another may have been separated by a period of time from the act which in fact caused the death, namely the fact of her falling to the ground and fracturing her skull. That second incident may have taken place without any guilty mind on the part of the appellant.

...

The question can be perhaps framed in this way. There was here an initial unlawful blow to the chin delivered by the appellant. That, again on what must have been the jury's finding, was not delivered with the intention of doing really serious harm to the wife. The guilty intent accompanying that blow was sufficient to have rendered the appellant guilty of manslaughter, but not murder, had it caused death. But it did not cause death. What caused death was the later impact when the wife's head hit the pavement. At the moment of impact the appellant's intention was to remove her, probably unconscious, body to avoid detection. To that extent the impact may have been pro tanto accidental. May the earlier guilty intent be joined with the later non-guilty blow which caused death to produce in the conglomerate a proper verdict of manslaughter?

...

It will be observed that the present case is different from the facts of those two cases [*Thabo Meli* and *R. v. Moore and Dorn* [1975] Crim L. R. 229] in that death here was not the result of a preconceived plan which went wrong, as was the case in those two decisions which we have cited. Here the death, again assuming the jury's finding to be such as it must have been, was the result of an initial unlawful blow, not intended to cause serious harm, in its turn causing the appellant to take steps possibly to evade the consequences of his unlawful act. During the taking of those steps he commits the actus reus but without the mens rea necessary for murder or manslaughter. Therefore the mens rea is contained in the initial unlawful assault, but the actus reus is the eventual dropping of the head on the ground.

Normally the actus reus and the mens rea coincide in point of time. What is the situation when they do not? Is it permissible, as the Crown contends here, to combine them to produce a conviction for manslaughter?

The answer is perhaps to be found in the next case to which we were referred, and that was *R v Church* [1965] 2 All ER 72, [1966] 1 QB 59. In that case the defendant was charged with the murder of a woman whose body was found in a river. The cause of death was drowning. The defendant had it seemed attacked the woman and rendered her semi-conscious. He thought she was dead and in his panic he threw her into the river. He was acquitted of murder but convicted of manslaughter. Edmund Davies J, giving the judgment of the court, said ([1965] 2 All ER 72 at 76, [1966] 1 QB 59 at 70):

'...the conclusion of this court is that an unlawful act causing the death of another cannot, simply because it is an unlawful act, render a manslaughter verdict inevitable. For such a verdict inexorably to follow, the unlawful act must be such as all sober and reasonable people would inevitably recognise must subject the other person to, at least, the risk of some harm resulting therefrom, albeit not serious harm...In the light of *Thabo Meli* v. *R.* ([1954]) 1 All ER 373, [1954] 1 WLR 228), it is conceded on behalf of the appellant that, on the murder charge, the trial judge was perfectly entitled to direct the jury, as he did: "Unless you find that something happened in the course of this evening between the infliction of the injuries and the decision to throw the body into the water, you may undoubtedly treat the whole course of conduct of the [appellant] as one." For some reason, however, which is not clear to this court, counsel for the appellant denies that such an approach is possible when one is considering a charge of manslaughter. We fail to see why. We adopt as sound Dr. Glanville Williams' view in [*Criminal Law: The General Part* (2nd edn, 1961) p 174] that, "If a killing by the first act would be manslaughter, a later destruction of the supposed corpse should also be manslaughter." Had Mrs. Nott [the victim] died of her initial injuries, a manslaughter verdict might quite conceivably have been returned on the basis that the appellant inflicted them under the influence of provocation or that the jury were not convinced that they were inflicted with murderous intent. All that was lacking in the direction given in this was that, when the judge turned to consider manslaughter, he did not again tell the jury that they were entitled (if they thought fit) to regard the conduct of the appellant in relation to Mrs. Nott as constituting throughout a series of acts which culminated in her death, and that, if that was how they regarded the appellant's behaviour, it mattered not whether he believed her to be alive or dead when he threw her in the river.'

It seems to us that where the unlawful application of force and the eventual act causing death are parts of the same sequence of events, the same transaction, the fact that there is an appreciable interval of time between the two does not serve to exonerate the defendant from liability. That is certainly so where the appellant's subsequent actions which caused death, after the initial unlawful blow, are designed to conceal his commission of the original unlawful assault.

It would be possible to express the problem as one of causation. The original unlawful blow to the chin was a causa sine qua non of the later actus reus. It was the opening event in a series which was to culminate in death: the first link in the chain of causation, to use another metaphor. It cannot be said that the actions of the appellant in dragging the victim away with the intention of evading liability broke the chain which linked the initial blow with the death.

In short, in circumstances such as the present, which is the only concern of this court, the act which causes death and the necessary mental state to constitute manslaughter need not coincide in point of time.

Appeal dismissed

■ NOTES AND QUESTIONS

1. Reconsider *R* v *Miller* (Ch. 2). Might liability in *LeBrun* and *Thabo Meli* have been premised on the failure to assist a victim in peril, where the defendant was the creator of the peril?

2. Say that Le Brun's wife had collapsed in the middle of the road after he had punched her and dropped her there, and she had then been run over by a car. Would an unsuccessful attempt on his part to rescue her from the path of oncoming cars have served as a basis for escaping liability for manslaughter?

3. Should *Le Brun* be considered as a case of concurrence or causation? Does it matter?

B: The concurrence principle

So far we have examined the requirement that *actus reus* and *mens rea* should coincide in point of time in a way so as to justify the conclusion that it was by the accused's culpable act that the victim suffered the relevant harm and so is deserving of punishment for bringing about that harm. *Thabo Meli* and *Le Brun* are not truly exceptions to that rule since the defendants caused the relevant harm albeit in a roundabout way by acts performed with an accompanying guilty mind. A related principle is what might be called the concurrence principle. It requires that the defendant's mental state should concur definitionally with the harm addressed by the definition of the offence. A few examples may serve to make this more clear.

> Adam, wishing to kill Eve, shoots a gun in her direction. In fact, he was mistaken. The image was a reflection in a mirror. The mirror is destroyed and Adam is charged with criminal damage.

Adam is obviously not guilty of a crime of homicide since no death has occurred. But what about criminal damage for destruction of the mirror? This runs into a different problem. Adam's *mens rea* (an intention to kill Eve) is not related to the *actus reus* of the offence charged (destroying or damaging property). Only if it could be found that Adam was reckless as to damaging the mirror would Adam be guilty of criminal damage. This is unlikely under a subjective test of recklessness (see *R v G*, Ch. 3) if he was unaware of the risk to the mirror. Adam is guilty only of the crime for which his *mens rea* concurs with his *actus reus*, in this situation attempted murder. He has taken more than merely preparatory steps towards killing Eve with the required intent to kill.

> Adam, for target practice, shoots at a scarecrow in a field. In fact it is Eve who lacks taste in clothing. Eve is killed.

This is the converse case to our previous example. Adam cannot be charged with murder or manslaughter since he intended no harm to Eve. On the other hand, as Adam did intend to damage the scarecrow, if he did cause such damage, he can be convicted of criminal damage.

This discussion can be related back to the cases that we examined previously in which the doctrine of transferred malice was applied. It can now be seen that cases like *Saunders and Archer* and *Pembliton* conflict with the principle of concurrence. In *Saunders and Archer* the correct charge should have been attempted murder of the wife rather than actual murder of the child. Similarly in *Pembliton* the defendant should probably have been charged with some form of assault and battery or an attempt to commit grievous bodily harm as opposed to criminal damage. This, however, is not the way that the courts have necessarily approached these issues.

C: The correspondence principle

Related to, or perhaps a subcategory of, the concurrence principle is the principle of correspondence. It is widely thought that, as a matter of basic criminal justice, a person should be held responsible for the commission of a crime only to the extent of his *mens rea*. The correspondence principle holds that defendant's *mens rea* should relate to the prescribed harm envisaged in the crime charged (see A. Ashworth, *Principles of Criminal Law* p. 81 (76, 6th ed. 2009). What this means is that, for example, if the harm envisaged is one of causing death, then it would have to be shown under the principle of correspondence that the defendant had the intent to cause death or, perhaps, acted recklessly in respect of causing death. When the defendant's intent was only to cause serious injury, he should not be held liable for a crime that envisages causing death. As we have seen, however, this principle of correspondence is not reflected in the current law in England and Wales relating to homicide. It is submitted that when the harm occurring is different from or more serious than that intended or envisaged, the defendant should not be convicted simply for having been at fault in contributing to its occurrence. Liability should be linked to what the defendant intended or foresaw.

R v Powell and another, R v English
(1997) 4 All ER 545

The appellants engaged in a joint enterprise to purchase drugs from a drug dealer. They went to purchase drugs from a drug dealer, but having gone to his house for that purpose, the drug dealer was shot dead when he came to the door. The Crown was unable to prove which of three men fired the gun which killed the drug dealer, but it was the Crown case that if the third man fired the gun, the two appellants were guilty of murder because they knew that the third man was armed with a gun and realised that he might use it to kill or cause really serious injury to the drug dealer. P and D appealed against their convictions to the House of Lords who dismissed their appeals.

LORD STEYN: . . . That brings me to the qualification which I have foreshadowed. In English law a defendant may be convicted of murder who is in no ordinary sense a murderer. It is sufficient if it is established that the defendant had an intent to cause really serious bodily injury. This rule turns murder into a constructive crime. The fault element does not correspond to the conduct leading to the charge, i.e. the causing of death. A person is liable to conviction for a more serious crime than he foresaw or contemplated: see *Glanville Williams, Textbook of Criminal Law*, 2nd ed. (1983), pp. 250–251; *Ashworth, Principles of Criminal Law*, 2nd ed. pp. 85 and 261; *Card, Cross and Jones, Criminal Law*, 12th ed. (1992), pp. 203–204. This is a point of considerable importance. The Home Office records show that in the last three years for which statistics are available mandatory life sentences for murder were imposed in 192 cases in 1994; in 214 cases in 1995; and in 257 cases in 1996. Lord Windlesham, writing with great Home Office experience, has said that *a minority* of defendants convicted of murder have been convicted on the basis that they had an intent to kill: 'Responses to Crime', vol. 3 (1996), at 342, n. 29. That assessment does not surprise me. What is the justification for this position? There is an argument that, given the unpredictability whether a serious injury will result in death, an offender who intended to cause serious bodily injury cannot complain of a conviction of murder in the event of a death. But this argument is outweighed by the practical consideration that immediately below murder there is the crime of manslaughter for which the court may impose a discretionary life sentence or a very long period of imprisonment. Accepting the need for a mandatory life sentence for murder, the problem is one of classification. The present definition of the mental element of murder results in defendants being classified as murderers who are not in truth murderers. It happens both in cases where only one offender is involved and in cases resulting from joint criminal enterprises. It results in the imposition of mandatory life sentences when neither justice nor the needs of society require the classification of the case as murder and the imposition of a mandatory life sentence.

The observations which I have made about the mental element required for murder were not directly in issue in the appeals under consideration. But in the context of murder the application of the accessory principle, and the definition of murder, are inextricably linked. For that reason I have felt at liberty to mention a problem which was not addressed in argument. That counsel did not embark on such an argument is not altogether surprising. After all, in *Reg. v. Cunningham* [1982] A.C. 566 the House of Lords declined to rationalise and modernise the law on this point. Only Lord Edmund-Davies expressed the hope that the legislature would undertake reform: see p. 583B–C. In my view the problem ought to be addressed. There is available a precise and sensible solution, namely, that a killing should be classified as murder if there is an intention to kill or an intention to cause really serious bodily harm coupled with awareness of the risk of death: 14th Report of the Law Revision Committee, (1980), para. 31, adopted in the Criminal Code, for England and Wales, (Law Com. No. 177), (1986), clause 54(1). This solution was supported by the House of Lords Select Committee on Murder and Life Imprisonment, HL Paper 78–1, 1989, par 68.

■ NOTES AND QUESTIONS

1. Until 1957 a person could be guilty of murder, although lacking the intention to kill or any foresight of death, simply for being involved in a serious crime (e.g., robbery) in which a death occurred. This was known as constructive malice. The concept was abolished by the Homicide Act 1957. After the Act, to convict a defendant of murder the prosecution had to prove the *mens rea* for murder; that is, an intent to kill or cause GBH. Nothing less would do, however reprehensible the accused's conduct.

2. It should be pointed out that pure correspondence between *mens rea* and *actus reus* is the exception rather than the norm for most crimes of violence. As we shall see in Chapter 4, for neither murder nor manslaughter is it necessary to show an intention to kill or even foresight of death. For assault occasioning actual bodily harm, it is not necessary to show that actual bodily harm was intended or foreseen. For maliciously inflicting grievous bodily harm, it is necessary to show that bodily harm was intended or foreseen but not grievous bodily harm. What justifies this state of affairs?

FURTHER READING

Wilson, *Criminal Law: Doctrine and Theory* (2011), Ch. 6–8

Ashworth, 'A Change of Normative Position' NCLR 2008, 232

Duff, 'The Politics of Intention: A Response to Norrie' [1990] Criminal Law Review 637

Goff, 'The Mental Element in the Crime of Murder' (1988) 104 Law Quarterly Review 30

Griew 'States of Mind, Presumptions and Inferences' in P. Smith (ed.) *Criminal Law: Essays in Honour of J.C. Smith* (1987)

Horder, 'A Critique of the Correspondence Principle' [1995] Criminal Law Review 759

Horder, 'Strict Liability, Statutory Construction and the Spirit of Liberty' (2002) 118 Law Quarterly Review 458

Lacey, 'A Clear Concept of Intention: Elusive or Illusory' (1993) 56 Modern Law Review 621

Mitchell, 'In Defence of the Correspondence Principle' [1999] Criminal Law Review 195

Norrie, 'Oblique Intention and Legal Politics' [1989] Criminal Law Review 793

Simester, 'Can Negligence be Culpable' in J. Horder (ed.) *Oxford Essays in Jurisprudence* (2000)

J.C. Smith, 'A Note on Intention' [1990] Criminal Law Review 85

Wells, 'Swatting the Subjectivist Bug' [1982] Criminal Law Review 209

Williams, 'Oblique Intention' (1987) 46 Cambridge Law Journal 417

Wilson, *Central Issues in Criminal Theory* (2002) chapter 5

PART II

Substantive Offences

4

Homicide

SECTION 1: **INTRODUCTION**

In the course of our examination of the foundational principles of Criminal Law we have already learned much about the law relating to homicide. We saw in cases like *Pittwood, Stone and Dobinson*, and *Gibbins and Proctor* that the *actus reus* for a homicide can be an omission or failure to act. In respect of causation, we discovered that intervening acts of third parties, including those of negligent doctors and even the victim herself, will not necessarily break the chain of causation between the *actus reus* and the resulting death. And we learned in the chapter on *mens rea* that the *mens rea* of murder is the intention to kill or cause serious bodily harm; but that where death or serious bodily harm would follow from the defendant's acts as a virtual certainty, and the defendant appreciated this fact, a jury could also find the requisite intention. In this chapter we continue our examination of these issues but in an exclusively homicide context. Although there are other offences involving death (e.g., infanticide, causing death by dangerous driving, and causing death by careless driving while under the influence of drink or drugs), our attention will be directed primarily to the two most serious homicide offences, murder and manslaughter.

The unjustified killing of another human being has traditionally – and rightly – been regarded as the most serious offence known to the law. It is for this reason that the most severe sentences are reserved for homicide offences. In the case of a defendant convicted of murder, the judge must impose a mandatory life sentence (which is not to say that the defendant will be required to spend the rest of his life in jail). For manslaughter a life sentence is also possible, although not obligatory. The judge has the discretion to impose a lesser sentence. Because murder and manslaughter are so severely punished, the border between a killing which falls into these categories and one that is either justifiable or excusable has been the subject of numerous closely reasoned decisions.

The offences of murder and manslaughter have a common *actus reus*, which is the unlawful killing of another human being. Killing in the context of homicide refers to any acceleration of death (out of recognition that all human beings eventually die). Because of this common element of an unlawful killing, the discussion of the *actus reus* of murder which follows will be equally applicable when the offence of manslaughter is under consideration.

SECTION 2: MURDER

Murder is a common law offence. There is no statutory definition of the crime. The usual starting point for consideration of the elements of murder is the definition put forward by Coke:

> Murder is when a man of sound memory, and of the age of discretion, unlawfully killeth within any county of the realm any reasonable creature *in rerum natura* under the king's peace, with malice aforethought, either expressed by the party or implied by law, so as the party wounded, or hurt etc. die of the wound or hurt, etc. within a year and a day after the same. (3 Inst 47) [The year and a day requirement has now been abolished.]

At common law the sentence for murder was death, the extreme example of retributive theory in practice. The death penalty has now been abolished, but the judge, as already noted, must impose a sentence of life imprisonment. This mandatory life sentence has been the subject of much criticism, as it leaves no room for consideration by the sentencing judge of mitigating circumstances. Perhaps, as a consequence, several partial 'defences' have been created which will reduce murder to manslaughter, the most important of which are diminished responsibility (abnormality of mind) and provocation (loss of self-control). If the defendant's crime is reduced to manslaughter, the sentencing judge can impose any sentence permitted by law, including a discharge.

A: The killer and the victim

The term 'man' in Coke's definition is not to be taken literally. Any person may be guilty of murder, provided that he or she has legal capacity (see Chapter 9) and satisfies the general principles of criminal responsibility.

Any human being can be the victim of murder. The two problems that can be encountered relate to when life begins for the purposes of being a victim and when life ends such that one can no longer be a victim. Under the view taken by the judges, the commencement of life requires full extrusion from the birth canal but not necessarily that respiration should have commenced:

R v Poulton

(1832) 5 C & P 329, Central Criminal Court

The prisoner was indicted for wilful murder. The indictment stated, in substance, that the prisoner, on a certain day, was delivered of a female bastard child, which was born alive; and that she afterwards, to wit, on the same day, a certain string of no value, around the neck of the said female bastard child, did bind, tie, and fasten, and by such binding, etc., the said child feloniously and wilfully, of her malice aforethought, did choke and strangle, etc.

LITTLEDALE J: . . . With respect to the birth, the being born must mean that the whole body is brought into the world; and it is not sufficient that the child respires in the progress of the birth. Whether the child was born alive or not depends mainly upon the evidence of the medical men. None of them say that the child was born alive; they only say that it had breathed: and if there is all this uncertainty among these medical men, perhaps you would think it too much for you to say that you are satisfied that the child was born alive.

R v Brain

(1834) 6 C & P 350, Oxford Assizes

The prisoner was indicted for the murder of her male bastard child. It appeared that the prisoner had been delivered of a child at Sandford Ferry; and that the body of the child was afterwards found in the water, about fifteen feet from the lock gate, near the ferry-house; but it was proved by two surgeons, Mr Box and Mr Hester, that the child had never breathed.

PARK J: A child must be actually wholly in the world in a living state to be the subject of a charge of murder; but if it has been wholly born, and is alive, it is not essential that it should have breathed at the time it was killed; as many children are born alive, and yet do not breathe for some time after their birth. But you must be satisfied that the child was wholly born into the world at the time it was killed, or you ought not to find the prisoner guilty of murder. This is not only my opinion, but the law was so laid down in a case as strong as this, by a very learned Judge (Mr Justice Littledale) at the Old Bailey. (His Lordship read the case of *R v Poulton*.)

Verdict—Not guilty of murder, but guilty of concealment.

While a child must be born alive in order for it to be a victim of homicide, the act which caused the death, such as an attack on the mother or a grossly negligent delivery by a midwife, can take place before the birth.

Attorney-General's Reference (No. 3 of 1994)

[1997] 3 All ER 936

■ NOTES AND QUESTIONS

1. The point at which a human entity is capable of being killed is an issue with both legal and moral dimensions. Some people believe that human life begins at conception, and that therefore abortion is murder. English law does not accept this view, although in appropriate circumstances both abortion and the destruction of a child capable of being born alive can be criminal.

2. When the initial assault is directed at the mother and, as a result the child is born prematurely and as a result of the premature birth dies, is the defendant guilty of homicide? Or is it necessary that the fatal blow be directed at the foetus?

3. The killing of an infant under 12 months old by its mother may constitute the crime of infanticide rather than murder (Infanticide Act 1938) if the mother establishes that her mind was disturbed by virtue of her not having fully recovered from the effect of giving birth or by reason of lactation consequent on the birth. The medical underpinnings of this crime (breast feeding adversely affects the mother's mental state) are no longer regarded as valid. If so, are there other justifications for preserving the offence? Should it be extended to fathers (given that its aim is to allow a distraught parent who has killed a baby to be prosecuted for a less serious crime than murder)? The Ministry of Justice has recently made proposals for reform of this and other areas of homicide. (http://www.justice.gov.uk/docs/murder-manslaughter-infanticide-consultation.pdf)

Another problem concerns the attributes of what might be called human-being-hood. The purpose of having crimes of homicide is to protect human beings from potentially fatal attacks on their person. But what if the individual concerned lacks the normal physical or mental attributes associated with being human?

Re A (Conjoined Twins: Medical Treatment)
[2001] 1 FLR 1

For the facts see p. 504.

LORD JUSTICE BROOKE:

12. Is Mary a reasonable creature?

For the reasons given by Ward LJ and Robert Walker LJ, with which I agree, I am satisfied that Mary's life is a human life that falls to be protected by the law of murder. Although she has for all practical purposes a useless brain, a useless heart and useless lungs, she is alive, and it would in my judgment be an act of murder if someone deliberately acted so as to extinguish that life unless a justification or excuse could be shown which English law is willing to recognise.

In recent editions of Archbold, including the 2000 Edition, the editors have suggested that the word 'reasonable' in Coke's definition (which they wrongly ascribe to Lord Hale in para 19.1) related to the appearance rather than the mental capacity of the victim and was apt to exclude 'monstrous births'. Spurred on by this suggestion, and because the present case broke so much novel ground, we explored with counsel some of the thinking of seventeenth century English philosophers in an effort to ascertain what Coke may have meant when he used the expression 'any reasonable creature' as part of his definition. We had in mind their absorbing interest in the nature of 'strange and deformed births' and 'monstrous births' (see Thomas Hobbes, Elements of Law, II. 10.8, and John Locke, An Essay Concerning Human Understanding, III.III.17, III.VI.15 and 26 and III.XI.20).

In Attorney-General's Reference (No. 3 of 1994) [1998] AC 245 Lord Mustill referred at p 254F to another statement in Coke's Institutes, not mentioned in that passage in Archbold, where after referring to prenatal injuries which lead to the delivery of a dead child, Coke writes (Co Inst Pt III, Ch. 7, p 50):

> 'if the childe be born alive, and dieth of the potion, battery, or other cause, this is murder; for in law it is accounted a reasonable creature, in rerum natura, when it is born alive'.

In these circumstances I have no hesitation in accepting the submission by Miss Davies QC (whose assistance, as the friend of the court, was of the greatest value), which was in these terms:

'In "The Sanctity of Life and the Criminal Law" (1958), Professor Glanville Williams stated at p 31:

> "There is, indeed some kind of legal argument that a 'monster' is not protected even under the existing law. This argument depends upon the very old legal writers, because the matter has not been considered in any modern work or in any court judgment."

After discussing the meaning of the word 'monster' (which might originally have connoted animal paternity) he states at pp 33–34:

> "Locked (Siamese) twins present a special case, though they are treated in medical works as a species of monster. Here the recent medical practice is to attempt a severance, notwithstanding the risks involved. Either the twins are successfully unlocked, or they die" (emphasis added).

It is implicit in this analysis that the author is of the view that 'Siamese' twins are capable of being murdered and the amicus curiae supports this view.

Advances in medical treatment of deformed neonates suggest that the criminal law's protection should be as wide as possible and a conclusion that a creature in being was not reasonable would be confined only to the most extreme cases, of which this is not an example. Whatever might have been thought of as 'monstrous' by Bracton, Coke, Blackstone, Locke and Hobbes, different considerations would clearly apply today. This proposition might be tested in this way: suppose an intruder broke into the hospital and stabbed twin M causing her death. Clearly it could not be said that his actions would be outside the ambit of the law of homicide.'

■ NOTES AND QUESTIONS

1. It is noteworthy that the judgment in *Re A* does not address the wider question as to whether the law of murder should have any role to play in cases where no discernible interests are served by affording the affected individual the protection of the criminal law. Already a distinction is drawn between acts and omissions. A doctor owes no duty to keep alive a person whose interests cannot be advanced by treatment. It remains the case, however, that this does not entitle a doctor, or anyone else, to take active steps to terminate the life of such a person. See *Bland* and *Pretty*, below.

2. If it is true that the protection of the criminal law attaches to human-being-hood then wider questions of what counts as a human being must be considered. If the genome project indicates, for example, that the genetic differences between human beings and higher primates are no greater than differences between humans themselves, as some experts believe, then what justifies the different treatment in the law of homicide accorded human beings and higher primates? Is it intelligence, speech, or some other factor which accounts for the fact that higher primates do not receive the same protection as human beings?

Problems have also been encountered with identifying when life ends. For example, consider the case of a victim of a serious assault who is placed on a life support system. Such systems are capable of supporting breathing and heart function after a patient has no functioning of the central nervous system and is so-called 'brain dead'. Is it open to the perpetrator of the assault to argue that the doctors who turn off the life support system of a victim deemed to be 'brain dead' are the cause of the victim's death?

R v *Malcherek and Steel*
[1981] 1 WLR 690, Court of Appeal

LORD LANE CJ:...This is not the occasion for any decision as to what constitutes death. Modern techniques have undoubtedly resulted in the blurring of many of the conventional and traditional concepts of death. A person's heart can now be removed altogether without death supervening; machines can keep the blood circulating through the vessels of the body until a new heart can be implanted in the patient, and even though a person is no longer able to breathe spontaneously a ventilating machine can, so to speak, do his breathing for him, as is demonstrated in the two cases before us. There is, it seems, a body of opinion in the medical profession that there is only one true test of death and that is the irreversible death of the brain stem, which controls the basic functions of the body such as breathing. When that occurs it is said the body has died, even though by mechanical means the lungs are being caused to operate and some circulation of blood is taking place.

Airedale NHS Trust v *Bland*
[1993] 1 All ER 821, House of Lords

A hot topic is whether, in the case of serious degenerative illness, a person can help the sufferer to die when that person lacks the physical means to end their own life.

R (on the application of Pretty) v Director of Public Prosecutions
[2002] 1 All ER 1, House of Lords

LORD BINGHAM OF CORNHILL: . . . Mrs Pretty bases her case on the convention. But it is worthy of note that her argument is inconsistent with two principles deeply embedded in English law. The first is a distinction between the taking of one's own life by one's own act and the taking of life through the intervention or with the help of a third party. The former has been permissible since suicide ceased to be a crime in 1961. The latter has continued to be proscribed. The distinction was very clearly expressed by Hoffmann LJ in *Airedale NHS Trust* v *Bland* [1993] 1 All ER 821 at 855, [1993] AC 789 at 831:

> 'No one in this case is suggesting that Anthony Bland should be given a lethal injection. But there is concern about ceasing to supply food as against, for example, ceasing to treat an infection with antibiotics. Is there any real distinction? In order to come to terms with our intuitive feelings about whether there is a distinction, I must start by considering why most of us would be appalled if he was given a lethal injection. It is, I think, connected with our view that the sanctity of life entails its inviolability by an outsider. Subject to exceptions like self-defence, human life is inviolate even if the person in question has consented to its violation. That is why although suicide is not a crime, assisting someone to commit suicide is. It follows that, even if we think Anthony Bland would have consented, we would not be entitled to end his life by a lethal injection.'

The second distinction is between the cessation of life-saving or life-prolonging treatment on the one hand and the taking of action lacking medical, therapeutic or palliative justification but intended solely to terminate life on the other. This distinction provided the rationale of the decisions in *Bland*'s case. It was very succinctly expressed in the Court of Appeal in *Re J* (*a minor*) (*wardship: medical treatment*) [1990] 3 All ER 930, [1991] Fam 33, in which Lord Donaldson of Lymington MR said:

> 'What doctors and the court have to decide is whether, in the best interests of the child patient, a particular decision as to medical treatment should be taken which *as a side effect* will render death more or less likely. This is not a matter of semantics. It is fundamental. At the other end of the age spectrum, the use of drugs to reduce pain will often be fully justified, notwithstanding that this will hasten the moment of death. What can never be justified is the use of drugs or surgical procedures with the primary purpose of doing so.' (See [1990] 3 All ER 930 at 938, [1991] Fam 33 at 46.)

Similar observations were made by Balcombe and Taylor LJJ ([1990] 3 All ER 930 at 941–942, 943, [1991] Fam 33 at 51, 53 respectively). While these distinctions are in no way binding on the European Court of Human Rights there is nothing to suggest that they are inconsistent with the jurisprudence which has grown up around the convention. It is not enough for Mrs Pretty to show that the United Kingdom would not be acting inconsistently with the convention if it were to permit assisted suicide; she must go further and establish that the United Kingdom is in breach of the convention by failing to permit it or would be in breach of the convention if it did not permit it. Such a contention is in my opinion untenable, as the Divisional Court rightly held.

In the later case of *Purdy* the House of Lords departed from the decision in *R (Pretty) v Director of Public Prosecutions (Secretary of State for the Home Department intervening)* [2002] 1 AC 800 holding that the DPP's refusal to publish guidelines might be in breach of the claimant's human rights under Art. 8(1)

The claimant suffered from primary progressive multiple sclerosis for which there was no known cure. She expected that there would come a time when she would regard her continuing existence as unbearable and she would want to end her life while still physically able to do so. By that stage, however, she would be unable to do so without assistance, so she would want to travel to a country where assisted suicide was lawful. Her husband was willing to help her to make the journey, but she was concerned that he might be prosecuted for an offence under s. 2(1) of the Suicide Act 1961[1] if he did so. She sought information from the Director of Public Prosecutions as to the factors which he would take into consideration in deciding under s. 2(4) whether a prosecution should be brought, but he declined that information. She sought judicial review of his refusal to publish details of his policy as to the circumstances in which a prosecution would be brought for complicity in a suicide contrary to s. 2(1) and/or of his failure to promulgate such a policy, relying on her right to respect for her private life under Art. 8(1) of the European Convention for the Protection of Human Rights and Fundamental Freedoms, as scheduled to the Human Rights Act 1998[2]. The Divisional Court of the Queen's Bench Division dismissed her claim and the Court of Appeal dismissed her appeal.

BARONESS HALE OF RICHMOND:

57. My Lords, as I begin to write this opinion, the House of Lords in its legislative capacity (Hansard (HL Debates) 7 July 2009, cols 595–634) has just been debating an amendment to the Coroners and Justice Bill which might have made it unnecessary for the House in its judicial capacity to decide this case. Lord Falconer's amendment was designed to take one type of assistance out of the scope of the offence of assisting or encouraging suicide. This was 'enabling or assisting [another adult] to travel to a country or territory in which assisted dying is lawful' (clause 49(1)(a)) but only if two conditions were satisfied. Two doctors would have to certify that the person to be helped was terminally ill and that she had the capacity to make the required declaration. She would have to make a written declaration, independently witnessed, that she knew the contents of the medical certificates and had decided to travel to a country where assisted dying was lawful for the purpose of obtaining that assistance.

58. After three hours of anxious, thoughtful and well-informed debate the House rejected the amendment by 194 votes to 141. In his closing speech, Lord Falconer commented (col 633) that 'Although huge passions were expressed during the debate, I never detected at any stage that anybody in the Committee wanted to prosecute the well intentioned person who went with their loved one to help them in their assisted dying'. Many who opposed the amendment were concerned that, as Baroness O'Neill of Bengarve put it (col 609), 'we have to take account not merely of compassionate assistance but of interested assistance and it is extraordinarily difficult to imagine any drafting that would do that'. Another former Lord Chancellor, Lord Mackay of Clashfern, explained (cols 599–600) that

> 'The main reason why I feel that this amendment is not justified is that the present law, with and on the assumption that what is involved is a criminal offence, permits the circumstances to be looked at by the criminal prosecuting authority . . . The fact that they felt that there was no obligation to raise a prosecution [in recent cases] showed that the circumstances in their view made that a proper decision.'

59. Thus there would appear to be a general feeling that, while there are cases in which a prosecution would not be appropriate, it is necessary to retain the offence, with its current wide ambit, in order to cater for the cases in which prosecution would be appropriate. But a major objective of the criminal law is to warn people that if they behave in a way which it prohibits they are liable to prosecution and punishment. People need and are entitled to be warned in advance so that, if they are of a law-abiding persuasion, they can behave accordingly. Hence the problem faced by Ms Purdy, her husband and other people who feel as she does:

> 'I want to avoid the situation where I am too unwell to terminate my life. I want to retain as much autonomy as possible. I want to make a choice about when the quality of my life is no longer adequate and to die a dignified death. The decision is of my own making. Nobody has suggested this to me or pressured me to reach this view. It is a decision that I have come to of my own free will.'

60. In *Pretty v United Kingdom* 35 EHRR 1, the European Court of Human Rights considered that 'the notion of personal autonomy is an important principle underlying the interpretation' of the right to respect for private and family life, home and correspondence, guaranteed by article 8 of the Convention: para 61. It went on to point out that

> 'the ability to conduct one's life in a manner of one's own choosing may also include the opportunity to pursue activities perceived to be of a physically or morally harmful or dangerous nature for the individual concerned': para 62.

The fact that death was not usually the intended consequence of such activities could not be decisive. Imposing medical treatment without consent would 'interfere with a person's physical integrity in a manner capable of engaging the rights protected under article 8(1) ': para 63. Domestic law recognised that a person may exercise a choice to die by refusing consent to life-prolonging treatment. Mrs Pretty also wished to exercise a choice to end her life. 'As stated by Lord Hope, the way she chooses to pass the closing moments of her life is part of the act of living, and she has a right to ask that this too must be respected': para 64, referring to *R (Pretty) v Director of Public Prosecutions (Secretary of State for the Home Department intervening)* [2002] 1 AC 800, para 100.

61. After this reasoning, it is scarcely surprising that the court took the view, most clearly articulated in relation to the claim that the law discriminated against people who were too disabled to take their own lives, that Mrs Pretty's rights under article 8 were engaged (para 87); and that it was not prepared to exclude that the law, which prevented her from exercising her choice to avoid an undignified and distressing end to her life, constituted an interference with her right to respect for her private life (para 67); and therefore went on to consider whether such interference could be justified under article 8(2) : paras 68–78.

62. In those circumstances, and despite the skilful and obviously sincerely believed argument to the contrary on behalf of the intervener, the Director was in my view correct to concede that the right to respect for private life was engaged and that the potential for interference had to be justified under article 8(2). In *Pretty v United Kingdom*, it was common ground that the restriction on assisted suicide was 'in accordance with the law' and in pursuit of the legitimate aim of safeguarding life and thereby protecting the rights of others. The only issue was whether it was 'necessary in a democratic society': para 69. The applicant argued that it was disproportionate to impose a "blanket ban" which applied both to those who did and to those who did not need the protection of the law. In view of the seriousness of the harm involved and the clear risks of abuse, the court did not consider that the blanket nature of the ban was disproportionate: para 76.

63. However, the court went on to take account of the flexibility in the law produced both by the requirement that the Director of Public Prosecutions consent to any prosecution and by the wide range of permissible sentences. Thus, at para 76:

> 'It does not appear to be arbitrary to the court for the law to reflect the importance of the right to life, by prohibiting assisted suicide while providing for a system of enforcement and adjudication which allows due regard to be given in each particular case to the public interest in bringing a prosecution, as well as to the fair and proper requirements of retribution and deterrence.'

Both sides have understandably gained comfort from that passage. For the Director of Public Prosecutions, it justifies a blanket ban coupled with flexible enforcement. For Ms Purdy, it contemplates that there will be individual cases in which the deterrent effect of a prosecution would be a disproportionate interference with the autonomy of the person who wishes to end her life. Moreover, in an argument which was not raised in *Pretty v United Kingdom*, if the justification for a blanket ban depends upon the flexibility of its operation, it cannot be 'in accordance with the law' unless there is greater clarity about the factors which the Director of Public Prosecutions and his subordinates will take into account in making their decisions.

64. My Lords, I accept that argument on Ms Purdy's behalf. Ms Dinah Rose QC, on behalf of the Director of Public Prosecutions, made a valiant attempt to suggest that all the factors which the Director of Public Prosecutions was likely to take into account in these cases could be gleaned from the current Code for Crown Prosecutors. But the way in which the Director of Public Prosecutions had to explain his decision in the case of Daniel James ('Decision on Prosecution—The Death by Suicide of Daniel James', 9 December 2008) shows that some of the listed factors have to be turned

on their head and other unlisted factors introduced in order to cater for these difficult decisions. Furthermore, as it seems to me, the object of the exercise should be to focus, not upon a generalised concept of 'the public interest', but upon the features which will distinguish those cases in which deterrence will be disproportionate from those cases in which it will not. The exercise will be important, not only in guiding the small number of Crown prosecutors who decide the small number of cases which are actually referred to them by the police, but also in guiding the police and thus the general public about the factors to be taken into account in deciding whether a prosecution will or will not be in the public interest.

65. I do not underestimate the difficulty of the task. Clearly, the prime object must be to protect people who are vulnerable to all sorts of pressures, both subtle and not so subtle, to consider their own lives a worthless burden to others. These were the pressures about which the members of this House were most concerned. But at the same time, the object must be to protect the right to exercise a genuinely autonomous choice. The factors which tell for and against such a genuine exercise of autonomy free from pressure will be the most important.

66. But I have also been concerned about whether account should be taken of the reasons why a person might wish to die. Take the example of Lord Falconer's amendment, which would have restricted the right to exercise choice to those who were terminally ill. If we are serious about protecting autonomy we have to accept that autonomous individuals have different views about what makes their lives worth living. There are many, many people who can live with terminal illness; there are many, many people who can live with a permanent disability at least as grave as that which afflicted Daniel James; but those same people might find it impossible to live with the loss of a much-loved partner or child, or with permanent disgrace, or even with financial ruin. Yet in attitudinal surveys the British public have consistently supported assisted dying for people with a painful or unbearable incurable disease from which they will die, if they request it, while rejecting it for people with other reasons for wanting to die: National Centre for Social Research, *British Social Attitudes—Perspectives on a changing Society*, 23rd Report (2007), chapter 2.

67. Here we are, of course, concerned about people who are unable or unwilling to end their own lives without assistance. The need for more precise guidelines governing the prosecution of those who may help them stems from the right to respect for their private lives protected by article 8. So I come back to what the European Court said about that right in *Pretty v United Kingdom* 35 EHRR 1, in the well known passage, at para 65:

> 'The very essence of the Convention is respect for human dignity and human freedom. Without in any way negating the principle of sanctity of life protected under the Convention, the court considers that it is under article 8 that notions of the quality of life take on significance. In an era of growing medical sophistication combined with longer life expectancies, many people are concerned that they should not be forced to linger on in old age or in states of advanced physical or mental decrepitude which conflict with strongly held ideas of self and personal identity.'

68. It is not for society to tell people what to value about their own lives. But it may be justifiable for society to insist that we value their lives even if they do not. In considering the factors for and against prosecution in the *Daniel James* case, the Director of Public Prosecutions did not focus upon the reasons why Daniel wished to die. Rather, he focussed upon the fact that he was 'a mature, intelligent and fiercely independent young man with full capacity to make decisions about his medical treatment' (paragraph 32), who had tried to commit suicide before, and whose parents had tried relentlessly to persuade him not to do so; also, far from gaining any advantage from his death, it had caused his parents profound distress. These are obviously among the most important factors, although no doubt there are many more. But among them, I would hope that some attention would be paid to the reasons why the person (whose Convention rights are engaged) wished to be helped to end his or her life. The House, when debating Lord Falconer's amendment, was clearly concerned that some of the people who had made use of the services of Dignitas in Switzerland were not suffering from terminal or seriously debilitating diseases. If it is the Convention which is leading us to ask the Director for greater clarity, a relevant question must be in what circumstances the law is justified in interfering with a genuinely autonomous choice.

69. For all those reasons, in addition to those given by your Lordships, I too would allow this appeal and make the order proposed by my noble and learned friend, Lord Hope of Craighead. However, I

do not think it necessary to decide whether section 2(1) of the 1961 Act covers acts here which aid and abet a suicide which is to be assisted in another jurisdiction where such acts are lawful. The question has not yet been decided here and the risk that it might be decided adversely to Ms Purdy and her husband is sufficient to raise the main issue which is before us now.

■ NOTES AND QUESTIONS

1. Since 1976, the medical profession has accepted the brain 'death test' for determining when a patient is dead.

2. In other areas of the law, such as in respect of the legal definition of insanity (see Chapter 9), legal doctrine does not necessarily accord with medical doctrine. Should it in respect to questions relating to when life begins and when it ends? Why?

3. As a result of the House of Lords decision in *Purdy* the DPP engaged in a consulation exercise with the public and produced guidelines to be taken into account when deciding whether to prosecute someone for assisted suicide. A CPS circular summarises the policy and guidelines as follows:

> The policy is now more focused on the motivation of the suspect rather than the characteristics of the victim. The policy does not change the law on assisted suicide. It does not open the door for euthanasia. It does not override the will of Parliament. What it does is to provide a clear framework for prosecutors to decide which cases should proceed to court and which should not.
>
> Assessing whether a case should go to court is not simply a question of adding up the public interest factors for and against prosecution and seeing which has the greater number. It is not a tick-box exercise. Each case has to be considered on its own facts and merits.
>
> As a result of the consultation exercise there have been changes to the policy. But that does not mean prosecutions are more or less likely. The policy has not been relaxed or tightened but there has been a change of focus.

The sixteen public interest factors in favour of prosecution are:

- The victim was under 18 years of age.
- The victim did not have the capacity (as defined by the Mental Capacity Act 2005) to reach an informed decision to commit suicide.
- The victim had not reached a voluntary, clear, settled and informed decision to commit suicide.
- The victim had not clearly and unequivocally communicated his or her decision to commit suicide to the suspect.
- The victim did not seek the encouragement or assistance of the suspect personally or on his or her own initiative.
- The suspect was not wholly motivated by compassion; for example, the suspect was motivated by the prospect that he or she or a person closely connected to him or her stood to gain in some way from the death of the victim.
- The suspect pressured the victim to commit suicide.
- The suspect did not take reasonable steps to ensure that any other person had not pressured the victim to commit suicide.
- The suspect had a history of violence or abuse against the victim.
- The victim was physically able to undertake the act that constituted the assistance himself or herself.
- The suspect was unknown to the victim and encouraged or assisted the victim to commit or attempt to commit suicide by providing specific information via, for example, a website or publication.

- The suspect gave encouragement or assistance to more than one victim who were not known to each other.
- The suspect was paid by the victim or those close to the victim for his or her encouragement or assistance.
- The suspect was acting in his or her capacity as a medical doctor, nurse, other healthcare professional, a professional carer (whether for payment or not), or as a person in authority, such as a prison officer, and the victim was in his or her care.
- The suspect was aware that the victim intended to commit suicide in a public place where it was reasonable to think that members of the public may be present.
- The suspect was acting in his or her capacity as a person involved in the management or as an employee (whether for payment or not) of an organisation or group, a purpose of which is to provide a physical environment (whether for payment or not) in which to allow another to commit suicide.

The six public interest factors against prosecution are:

- The victim had reached a voluntary, clear, settled and informed decision to commit suicide.
- The suspect was wholly motivated by compassion.
- The actions of the suspect, although sufficient to come within the definition of the crime, were of only minor encouragement or assistance.
- The suspect had sought to dissuade the victim from taking the course of action which resulted in his or her suicide.
- The actions of the suspect may be characterised as reluctant encouragement or assistance in the face of a determined wish on the part of the victim to commit suicide.
- The suspect reported the victim's suicide to the police and fully assisted them in their enquiries into the circumstances of the suicide or the attempt and his or her part in providing encouragement or assistance.

How easy will it be to apply these guidelines? What should a prosecutor do when some of the guidelines point in one direction and others in a different direction?

4. Will this policy statement be useful to people such as Debbie Purdy?

B: Causation

(i) Death within a year and a day

In the case of both murder and manslaughter the common law rule was that death had to occur within a year and a day of the infliction of injury. The original rationale for this rule lay in the difficulty in proving a causal connection between old injuries and a subsequent death. This rationale became increasingly tenuous with scientific advances and the rule has now been abolished by statute (Law Reform (Year and a Day Rule) Act 1996). However, prosecutions brought more than three years after the *actus reus* was committed, or where the defendant has already been convicted of an offence in connection with the death, require the consent of the Attorney-General (Law Reform (Year and a Day Rule) Act 1996, s. 2).

To cause death means, it will be remembered, to advance the time that a person's death would otherwise have occurred. Say that Eve happens upon Adam who is trapped in a blazing car. He pleads with her to shoot him dead to avoid the dreadful pain of death by burning. She does so. In law Eve has caused Adam's death. This conclusion is not affected by the fact that Adam was going to die soon anyway. In cases of medical treatment the courts treat this principle with a degree of flexibility, however, as we saw in the case of Dr. Adams (Ch. 2).

(ii) Contributing causes

The problems involved in determining causation were examined in Chapter 2. As was seen then, causation does not turn solely on a test that asks whether 'but for' the defendant's conduct the victim would be dead. In the context of homicide the courts also ask whether the defendant's acts were the legal or proximate cause, sometimes expressed in the cases as the 'substantial and operating' cause, of the death. As a practical matter, the starting point for determining the cause of death is the death itself. The investigating police officers will not concern themselves with philosophical questions as to why a person died. Rather they will seek to trace the death to a wrongful action which brought it about. At that point the inquiry will usually stop although other people and events also may have contributed to the death. If we re-examine the case of *Smith* (Ch. 2), for example, the investigating officers would have been anxious to trace the victim's death to the person who stabbed the victim with a bayonet. Although a few eyebrows may have been raised by the incompetent medical treatment and the sloppy attempt at care provided by the victim's fellow officers, the police will be looking for a person to hold to account. Who better than the person who did the stabbing? This is not to say that the fellow officers and the medics were not also contributors to, and in that sense causes of, the death but they are not pertinent to the practical penological question as to whom to hold responsible. No doubt they would be, however, if the victim's initial injuries had been the result of natural causes. For similar reasons the investigating officers, and the criminal law, will not normally be particularly interested in the contributions of the victim or others prior to the stabbing unless they afford evidence of a possible defence or they cause or propel the perpetrator to act as he did.

In the cases that follow, we will examine instances where the defendant's act combined with other factors to bring about the death of the victim. In each case death would not have occurred except for the occurrence of an unforeseen event or the negligent or deliberate acts of others (including the victim). As we shall see, it is only rarely that such acts or events prevent the attribution of cause to the culpable initiator of a causal sequence leading to the death of the victim.

R v Pagett

(1983) 76 Cr App R 279, Court of Appeal

For facts and holding, see p. 112.

. . .

There is however one further aspect of the present case to which we must advert. On the evidence, Gail Kinchen was not just an innocent bystander killed by a shot fired from the gun of a police officer who, acting in reasonable self-defence, fired his gun in response to a lethal attack by the appellant: though on those facts alone it would, in our opinion, have been open to the jury to convict the appellant of murder or manslaughter. But if, as the jury must have found to have occurred in the present case, the appellant used Gail Kinchen by force and against her will as a shield to protect him from any shots fired by the police, the effect is that he committed not one but two unlawful acts, both of which were dangerous—the act of firing at the police, and the act of holding Gail Kinchen as a shield in front of him when the police might well fire shots in his direction in self-defence. Either act could in our judgment, if on the principles we have stated it was held to cause the death of Gail Kinchen, constitute the *actus reus* of the manslaughter or, if the necessary intent were established, murder of Gail Kinchen by the appellant, even though the shot was fired not by the appellant but by a police officer.

(a) Acts of the victim

The victim's contribution to his own death is generally deemed to be irrelevant.

R v Benge

(1865) 4 F & F 504, Maidstone Crown Court

The prosecution arose out of a fatal railway accident, which occurred on the South Eastern Railway at a place called Staplehurst, where there was a bridge, about two miles in the direction towards London from a station called Headcorn....

Piggott, B, said, that assuming culpable negligence on the part of the prisoner which materially contributed to the accident, it would not be material that others also by their negligence contributed to cause it. Therefore he must leave it to the jury whether there was negligence of the prisoner which had been the substantial cause of the accident. In summing up the case to the jury, he said, their verdict must depend upon whether the death was mainly caused by the culpable negligence of the prisoner. Was the accident mainly caused by the taking up of the rails at a time when an express train was about to arrive, was that the act of the prisoner, and was it owing to culpable negligence on his part? His counsel had urged that it was not so, because the flagman and engine-driver had been guilty of negligence, which had contributed to cause the catastrophe; but they, in their turn, might make the same excuse, and so, if it was valid, no one could be criminally responsible at all. This would be an absurd and unreasonable conclusion, and showed that the contention of the prisoner's counsel could not be sound. Such was not the right view of the law—that of the negligence of several persons at different times and places contributed to cause an accident, any one of them could set up that his was not the sole cause of it. It was enough against any one of them that his negligence was the substantial cause of it. Now, here the primary cause was certainly the taking up of the rails at a time when the train was about to arrive, and when it would be impossible to replace them in time to avoid the accident. And this the prisoner admitted was owing to his own mistake. Was that mistake culpable negligence, and did it mainly or substantially cause the accident? The book was clearly and plainly printed, and must have been read carelessly to admit of such a mistake.

Was it not the duty of the prisoner who knew the fearful consequences of a mistake to take reasonable care to be correct? And had he taken such care? Then as to its being the main cause of the accident, it was true that the company had provided other precautions to avoid any impending catastrophe, and that these were not observed upon this occasion; but was it not owing to the prisoner's culpable negligence that the accident was impending, and, if so, did his negligence the less cause it, because if other persons had not been negligent it might possibly have been avoided?

Verdict—Guilty.

R v Swindall and Osborne

(1846) 2 Car & Kir 230, Nisi Prius

Manslaughter.—The prisoners were indicted for the manslaughter of one James Durose. The second count of the indictment charged the prisoners with inciting each other to drive their carts and horses at a furious and dangerous rate along a public road, and with driving their carts and horses over the deceased at such furious and dangerous rate, and thereby killing him.

...

Pollock, CB (in summing up).—The prisoners are charged with contributing to the death of the deceased, by their negligence and improper conduct, and, if they did so, it matters not whether he was deaf, or drunk, or negligent, or in part contributed to his own death . . .

As we have seen in Chapter 2, courts generally take the view that one must take one's victim as one finds him. Normally the rule applies to physical frailties such as the haemophilia or eggshell skull of the victim but, as we saw in *R* v *Blaue* (p. 83), the rule can extend to the religious convictions or psychological predilections of the victim. Two other situations can also be considered where the actions of the victim do not break the chain of causation:

(a) where the cause of the death is pressure exerted by threats; and
(b) where the victim is frightened into taking his own life.

R v Hayward

(1908) 21 Cox CC 692, Maidstone Autumn Assizes

It appeared from the evidence of neighbours that on the night in question the prisoner came home before his wife. He was in a condition of violent excitement, and was overheard to express a determination of 'giving his wife something' when she came in. When the woman did come home there were at once sounds of an altercation, and shortly afterwards the woman was seen by several witnesses to rush from the house into the road closely pursued by the prisoner, who was at the same time using violent threats towards her. She was then seen to fall into the roadway, and lying there she was kicked on the left forearm by the prisoner. When picked up she was found to be dead.

The medical evidence showed that the bruise on her arm, due to the kick, could not have been the cause of death. The post-mortem examination showed that the deceased, whose organs were otherwise in a perfectly healthy condition, was suffering from a persistent thymus gland, two inches wide and weighing one and three-quarter ounces, lying at the base of the heart. Such a state of affairs was proved to be quite abnormal at the deceased's age—22. The cause of death was given as cardiac inhibition, and the medical evidence was to the effect that in a person the subject of persistent thymus gland, such as the deceased, any combination of physical exertion and fright or strong emotion might occasion death in such a fashion.

...

Ridley, J, in summing up, directed the jury that if they believed the witnesses there was a sufficient chain of evidence to support a conviction of manslaughter. He pointed out that no proof of actual physical violence was necessary, but that death from fright alone, caused by an illegal act, such as threats of violence, would be sufficient. The abnormal state of the deceased's health did not affect the question whether the prisoner knew or did not know of it if it were proved to the satisfaction of the jury that the death was accelerated by the prisoner's illegal act.

The prisoner was convicted and sentenced to three months' imprisonment with hard labour.

R v Halliday

(1889) 61 LT 701, Court of Appeal

LORD COLERIDGE CJ: . . . Here the woman came by her mischief by getting out of the window—I use a vague word on purpose—and in her fall broke her leg. Now that might have been caused by an act which was done accidentally or deliberately, in which case the prisoner would not have been guilty. It appears from the case, however, that the prisoner had threatened his wife more than once, and that on this occasion he came home drunk, and used words which amounted to a threat against her life saying, 'I'll make you so that you can't go to bed;' that she rushing to the window got half out of the window when she was restrained by her daughter. The prisoner threatened the daughter, who let go, and her mother fell. It is suggested to me by my learned brother that, supposing the prisoner had struck his daughter's arm without hurting her but sufficiently to cause her to let go and she had let her mother fall, could anyone doubt but that that would be the same thing as if he had pushed her out himself? If a man creates in another man's mind an immediate sense of danger which causes such person to try to escape, and in so doing he injures himself, the person who creates such a state of mind is responsible for the injuries which result. I think that in this case there was abundant evidence that there was a sense of immediate danger in the mind of the woman caused by the acts of the prisoner, and that her injuries resulted from what such sense of danger caused her to do. I am therefore of opinion that the prisoner was rightly convicted, and that this conviction must be affirmed.

A defendant who has the *mens rea* for murder or manslaughter but whose actions do not materially affect the outcome cannot be liable for the substantive crime (although there could be liability for attempted murder).

R v White

[1910] 2 KB 124, Court of Criminal Appeal

BRAY J: In this case the appellant was indicted for the murder of his mother and was convicted of an attempt to murder her and sentenced to penal servitude for life. He appeals from this conviction on several grounds, which we will deal with one by one. First it is said that there was no reasonable evidence on which he could be convicted, or, as it is put in s. 4 of the Criminal Appeal Act, that the verdict cannot be supported having regard to the evidence.

The evidence put shortly was this. On January 9 last the mother was found dead in a sitting posture on a sofa in a sitting-room in her house. There was a round table standing two feet from the sofa, on the further side of which was a wine glass three parts filled with a liquid made up of a drink called nectar and, as was afterwards shewn, containing two grains of cyanide of potassium. There were also on the table a nectar bottle, two lumps of sugar, and a spoon. There was no evidence to shew that she had taken any of this liquid, and the result of the post-mortem examination and of the analysis of the contents of the stomach and of the contents of the wine glass was to shew that she had not died from poisoning by cyanide of potassium, but that death was most probably caused by syncope or heart failure, due to fright or some other external cause.

Appeal dismissed.

A defendant is only responsible for those consequences which are attributable to his/her *wrongful* action. If the death would have occurred whether or not the defendant had behaved improperly, the defendant will not be deemed the legal cause of death.

R v Dalloway

(1847) 2 Cox CC 273, Stafford Crown Court

The prisoner was indicted for the manslaughter of one Henry Clarke, by reason of his negligence as driver of a cart.

It appeared that the prisoner was standing up in a spring-cart, and having the conduct of it along a public thoroughfare. The cart was drawn by one horse. The reins were not in the hands of the prisoner, but loose on the horse's back. While the cart was so proceeding down the slope of a hill, the horse trotting at the time, the deceased child, who was about three years of age, ran across the road before the horse, at the distance of a few yards, and one of the wheels of the cart knocking it down and passing over it, caused its death. It did not appear that the prisoner saw the child in the road before the accident.

Erle, J, in summing up to the jury, directed them that a party neglecting ordinary caution, and, by reason of that neglect, causing the death of another, is guilty of manslaughter; that if the prisoner had reins, and by using the reins could have saved the child, he was guilty of manslaughter; but that if they thought he could not have saved the child by pulling the reins, or otherwise by their assistance, they must acquit him.

The jury acquitted the prisoner.

■ NOTES AND QUESTIONS

1. Dalloway clearly caused the death of the child. On what basis, then, did he escape criminal liability?

2. Must the threat to the defendant be a physical one before the defendant can be said to have 'caused' the death in circumstances where the immediate cause is the victim's action? How immediate must it be?

3. What if the victim perceived a threat that was not intended? Or, perhaps, would not have been so perceived by a resonable person? If the victim then takes evasive actions that result in her death is the defendant liable?

(b) Acts of third parties

The action or inaction of third parties is often claimed to be the cause of death, rather than the acts of the defendant. It should be remembered that the chain of causation will rarely be broken where the third party reacts to the wrongdoing of the defendant and in so doing contributes to the occurrence of death. This will be most usual in cases of (inappropriate) medical intervention as discussed in Chapter 2. It extends beyond this situation, however, to others where there is a duty of intervention, as occurred in *Pagett*, involving the death of a 'human shield'. In principle, however, it is not limited to the case of persons acting under a duty.

Where the death occurs in the manner intended by the original assailant, the unwitting intervention of a third party is generally held to be irrelevant.

R v Michael
(1840) 9 C & P 356, Central Criminal Court

It appeared that the deceased was a child between nine and ten months old, and that the prisoner was its mother, and was a single woman living in service as wet nurse at Mrs Kelly's, in Hunter Street, Brunswick Square. The child was taken care of by a woman named Stevens, living at Paddington, who received five shillings a week from the prisoner for its support. A few days before its death the prisoner told Mrs Stevens that she had an old frock for the child, and a bottle of medicine, which she gave her, telling her it would do the baby's bowels good. Mrs Stevens said the baby was very well, and did not want medicine; but the prisoner said it had done her mistress's baby good, and it would do her baby good, and desired Mrs Stevens to give it one tea-spoonful every night. Mrs Stevens did not open the bottle, or give the child any of its contents, but put the bottle on the mantel-piece, where it remained till Tuesday, the 31st of March, on which day, about half-past four in the afternoon, Mrs Stevens went out, leaving the prisoner's child playing on the floor with her children, one of whom, about five years of age, during the absence for about ten minutes of his elder sister, gave the prisoner's child about half the contents of the bottle, which made it extremely ill, and in the course of a few hours it died. The bottle was found to contain laudanum.

Alderson B, in his summing up, told the jury, that if the prisoner delivered the laudanum to Sarah Stevens with the intention that she should administer it to the child, and thereby produce its death, and the quantity so directed to be administered was sufficient to cause death, and while the prisoner's original intention continued, the laudanum was administered by an unconscious agent, the death of the child, under such circumstances, would sustain the charge of murder against the prisoner. His Lordship added, that if the tea-spoonful of laudanum was sufficient to produce death, the administration by the little boy of a much larger quantity would make no difference.

The jury found the prisoner guilty . . . .

At a subsequent Session, Mr Baron Alderson, in passing sentence upon the prisoner, said, that the Judges were of opinion that the administering of the poison by the child of Mrs Stevens, was, under the circumstances of the case, as much, in point of law, an administering by the prisoner as if the prisoner had actually administered it with her own hand. They therefore held that she was rightly convicted.

C: *Mens rea*

Under Coke's definition of murder (see above), the prosecution must establish *malice aforethought*. The meaning of this concept must be gleaned from judicial pronouncements in decided cases as there is no statutory definition of the term. The courts have now settled that malice aforethought means an intention to kill or cause grievous (serious) bodily harm to any person. As explained in Chapter 3 there are two alternate forms of intention: direct intention – the intention of desire – and indirect intention – the intention of knowledge of a virtually certain result. Either the prosecution proves direct intention (which is the usual type and will normally, as in a shooting, be clear). The probability of death or serious injury resulting from the actions of the defendant are not relevant where the defendant desires the death (see *Michael*, above). Say that Adam, wishing to kill Eve, and having no other means of doing so, points a rifle in her direction and fires although he knows, from the fact she is so far away, that the rifle is untrustworthy, and that he is an appalling shot, that hitting her would be 'a chance in a million'. Nonetheless, Adam intends to kill Eve. He has a direct intention to kill. That his chances of success are slim does not affect this. In R.A. Duff's words Adam intends to kill as he would treat his actions as a failure if the death did not occur.

Even if there is no evidence of a (direct) intention to kill or cause serious harm the jury may be directed that they may nevertheless find that the *mens rea* element has been satisfied if the accused knew that death or serious bodily harm would, barring unforeseen circumstances, be virtually certain to occur or would be if things went according to plan. Suppose Adam, having raped Eve, throws her into a raging torrent. He does not do so in order to kill her but to eradicate any DNA evidence that he was the rapist. He knows, from the fact that Eve is a poor swimmer and that the current is strong, that it would be a miracle if Eve survived. The jury would be entitled to conclude that Adam intended to kill Eve, although this was not his purpose. Remember the jury is only entitled to reach this conclusion if death was virtually certain and Adam knew this. If the jurors conclude only that he knew it was highly probable only a manslaughter conviction will lie (see *Woollin*, p. 131, Ch. 3). The relevant cases were presented in Chapter 3 and should be reviewed at this point. As Matthews indicates, proving that the defendant foresaw death as a certainty does not mean he intended death as a matter of law but it will (usually) provide irresistible **evidence** that it was intended.

The alternative *mens rea* which will justify a conviction for murder is an intent to cause 'grievous bodily harm'. This is the 'implied malice' referred to in Coke's definition. See *Cunningham* [1982] AC 566. In *Director of Public Prosecutions* v *Smith* [1961] AC 290, 'grievous bodily harm' was explained as 'really serious harm'. Whether this clarification adds much to our understanding of the concept is debatable. The basic policy question presented is whether one who does not have the intent to kill should be subject to a conviction for murder.

Matthews and Alleyne
[2003] 2 Cr App R, Court of Appeal

The appellants were convicted, *inter alia*, of murder. The victim had been thrown into a river from a bridge. The trial judge gave a direction to the jury, in relation to intent to kill, in the following terms:

'With regard to proving an *intent to kill*, the prosecution will only succeed in proving this intent *either*:

(i) by making you sure that this specific intention was actually in the mind/s of the defendants, *or*

(ii)

    (a) by making you sure that [the deceased's] death was a virtual certainty (barring some attempts to save him), and

    (b) the defendant whose case you are considering appreciated at the time [the deceased] was thrown off the bridge that this was the case, *and* he *then* had no intention of saving him, and knew or realised that the others did not intend to save him either.'

The appellants contended, *inter alia*, that that was a misdirection because the alternative (ii) was put as a substantive rule of law rather than as a rule of evidence.

LORD JUSTICE RIX :

. . .

43. In our judgment…the law has not yet reached a *definition* of intent in murder in terms of appreciation of a virtual certainty. Lord Lane was speaking not of what was decided in Nedrick (or in the other cases which preceded it) nor of what was thereafter to be decided in Woollin, but of what the law in his opinion should be, as represented by the clause 18(b) definition…[We] do not regard Woollin as yet reaching or laying down a substantive rule of law. On the contrary, it is clear from the discussion in Woollin as a whole that Nedrick was derived from the existing law, at that time ending in Moloney and Hancock, and that the critical direction in Nedrick was approved, subject to the change of one word.

. . .

45. Having said that, however, we think that, once what is required is an appreciation of virtual certainty of death, and not some lesser foresight of merely probable consequences, there is very little to choose between a rule of evidence and one of substantive law. It is probably this thought that led Lord Steyn to say that a result foreseen as virtually certain is an intended result. Lord Bridge had reflected the same thought when he had said, in Moloney at 920C, that if the defendant there had had present to his mind, when he pulled the trigger, that his gun was pointing at his stepfather's head at a distance of six feet and 'its inevitable consequence', then 'the inference was inescapable, using words in their ordinary, everyday meaning, that he intended to kill his stepfather.'
Lord Lane had also spoken in Nedrick of an irresistible inference.

. . .

Appeals dismissed.

R v MD
[2004] EWCA Crim 1391, Court of Appeal

LORD JUSTICE HOOPER:

. . .

3. The appellant is the mother of MD who was aged 7 years old at the time of his death and also of KD who is two years older.

. . .

14. Some four days before the close of the prosecution case, the Crown abandoned the count of murder. The reasons for that decision are to be found in the same ruling. The judge said:

'What happened and what has caused the prosecution to take the view they have, rightly, of the count of murder is not that anything has changed in relation to those facts both as to her actions in the ambulance nor as to her intention when she carried out the actions in the ambulance is the prosecution's acceptance that they cannot prove that those actions caused or contributed to the death of M. The highest that they can put their case, which is what Dr Firmin said in his evidence yesterday, is he thought it probable that there had been a second aspiration into M's lungs in the ambulance, but he was unable to be certain that there was. In the absence of any certainty as to a second aspiration there could be no certainty that the actions of the defendant in the ambulance caused or contributed to M's death.'

. . .

20. The judge then gave the jury this direction on the law:

'To establish count 10 the prosecution must also prove that she did that act intending to kill M. You can only find that she had that necessary intention if you are sure that death was, on the situation as she believed it to be, a virtual certainty, barring some unforeseen intervention, as a result of what she was doing, and that she appreciated that death was a virtual certainty on the situation as she believed it to be. If you are not sure of that she would be not guilty of count 10. Putting it in factual terms, you may agree with Mr Holroyde that it means in this case that you must be sure that she believed the nasogastric tube to be misplaced, not in his stomach but up towards the entrance to his lungs so that she believed that it was virtual certainty that fluid would enter his lungs because, as Mr Holroyde says, if the fluid goes into his stomach then it does not do any harm, as indeed events proved. So you may find that the factual issue which you have to grapple with, importantly in relation to that count and other, is that you must be sure she believed the nasogastric tube to be misplaced in such a way that she also believed that it was a virtual certainty that fluid would enter his lungs.'

. . .

26. It follows that the jury could not properly be sure, on the judge's direction, that the appellant, when in the ambulance passing fluid via the tube, had the necessary intention to kill because they could not be sure:

'that death was, on the situation as she believed it to be, a virtual certainty, barring some unforeseen intervention, as a result of what she was doing, and that she appreciated that death was a virtual certainly on the situation as she believed it to be.
   Nor could the jury properly be sure that "she believed that it was a virtual certainty that fluid would enter his lungs".'

. . .

28. In Woolin, as in a number of cases considered in Woolin, the House of Lords was concerned with 'what state of mind, apart from the case where a defendant acts with the purpose of killing or causing serious injury, may be sufficient to constitute the necessary intention' (page 90), 'in the rare cases where the simple direction is not enough' (page 93).

   11. The question which the learned judge had to pose, in relation to the question of intent, was this: could a jury, properly directed, infer from all of the relevant evidence that her intention was to kill? In answering this question, it must be borne in mind that the jury was entitled to consider all of the relevant evidence, not merely the events of the morning in question, as the wider context was relevant for them to decide what her intent was.

   12. Thus, the jury would be entitled to take her repeated predictions of M's death (at a time when she was the architect of his condition) into account just as it would have been entitled to take a threat to kill into account. Although the Appellant argues that these were evidence of a general wish for his death, it was a matter for the jury to decide what weight to attach to these assertions: it was open to a reasonable jury to conclude that they reflected the Appellant's intentions. Similarly, properly directed (as it was) as to lies, the jury was entitled to take her lies on that subject into

account (her denials), just as it was entitled to take her changing story of the events of the morning of his final admission into account.

13. There was thus a number of sources from which the jury was entitled to make the appropriate inference as to the Appellant's intention. The learned judge was correct to leave the count to the jury.

■ NOTES AND QUESTIONS

1. What is the justification for equating an intent to cause grievous bodily harm with an intent to cause death? Is there a moral distinction between the defendant who intends to cause grievous bodily harm and the defendant who intends to cause death?

2. The Law Commission (Law Com No. 304, 'Murder, Manslaughter and Infanticide', 28 November 2006) (below) has proposed a radical new structure of homicide which neatly sidesteps much of the malign influence of the mandatory sentence and the problems posed by the GBH murder rule by dividing murder into two degrees of gravity. First degree murder, which continues to carry the mandatory sentence, encompasses (a) intentional killing; or (b) killing with an intention to cause serious injury, in the awareness that there is a serious risk of causing death. Simple GBH murder is retained but is relegated to second-degree murder where the mandatory sentence will not bite. Would such a change make a difference as a matter of theory? As a matter of practice?

3. An alternative approach is adopted in the Indian Criminal Code, s. 300, where the fault element is 'the intention of causing bodily injury to any person and the bodily injury intended to be inflicted is sufficient in the ordinary course of nature to cause death'. There is no requirement that the defendant be aware that the injury he intends is mortal. Is this alternative superior to the Law Commission's proposals? How so?

4. The Law Commission also includes within second-degree murder an intention to cause some injury, or the fear of some injury or a risk of some injury, whilst being aware of a serious risk of causing death. Such a mental attitude would have the felicitous effect of acquitting most dangerous drivers who kill but would cover cases where, as in *Hyam* v *DPP* [1974] 2 All ER 41, the intention to kill or cause serious injury could not be proved but the defendant was nevertheless reckless as to the prospect of causing death. It would also cover cases such as killing in the course of torture where an intention to cause serious injury could not be proven so long as there is awareness that there is a serious risk of causing death.

5. Successfully prosecuted cases of murder by omission are extremely rare. This suggests that prosecuting authorities are unwilling to prosecute killings by omission as murder unless persuaded that the evidence showed that the killing was purposive? In practice, if not theory, therefore the *mens rea* for murder may differ depending upon whether the *actus reus* relied upon is an act or an omission. See W. Wilson, 'Murder by Omission' (2010) New Crim LR 1.

D: Jurisdiction

The normal territorial jurisdiction of the English courts has been extended for the offences of murder and manslaughter:

(a) A killing by a British citizen can found a conviction for murder or manslaughter whether the killing takes place in England or Wales or abroad (i.e., outside the normal territorial limits of the court's jurisdiction) (Offences Against the Person Act 1861, s. 9, and British Nationality Act 1948, s. 3). The defendant may also be subject to the jurisdiction of the courts in the territory where the killing takes place. Interestingly, this provision does not apply to cases of corporate manslaughter.

(b) Murder or manslaughter committed on a British ship or aircraft is triable in England or Wales whether the killing is committed by a British citizen or not.

(c) Murder *of* a British citizen committed abroad is *not* triable in England or Wales merely because of the nationality of the victim.

Where the crime is committed outside the jurisdiction of the UK courts and the offender is arrested where the crime is committed, it will be necessary to extradite the defendant if he or she is to stand trial in the United Kingdom. Although most countries will allow extradition for murder or manslaughter, it is not automatic. If the courts of the foreign jurisdiction conclude that the defendant will not receive a fair trial in the United Kingdom, they may refuse to order extradition. The relevance of the European Convention on Human Rights in this context is examined in *Soering* v *United Kingdom* (1989) 11 EHRR 439, where a German national sought to block the UK from extraditing him to the United States.

E: Reform of the law of murder

The law relating to murder seems almost a quaint oddity in modern times. In an era where the definitions of virtually all crimes can be found in statute, it is anomalous that one must search ancient tomes to find the definition of the most serious crime known to the law. The task of reform was originally entrusted to the Criminal Law Revision Committee, whose efforts were reflected in the Draft Criminal Code Bill 1989. As we know, the Draft Bill never found its way on to the statute books. In 2005 the Law Commission revisited the issues, publishing 'A New Homicide Act for England and Wales' (Consultation Paper No. 177). The Consultation Paper made numerous far-reaching proposals for reform of the law of murder. This was followed by the final report in November 2006.

Law Commission
Law Com No. 304, 'Murder, Manslaughter and Infanticide', 28 November 2006

OVERVIEW

1.63 We recommend that there should be a new Homicide Act for England and Wales. The new Act should replace the Homicide Act 1957. The new Act should, for the first time, provide clear and comprehensive definitions of the homicide offences and the partial defences. In addition, the new Act should extend the full defence of duress to the offences of first degree and second degree murder and attempted murder, and improve the procedure for dealing with infanticide cases.

In structuring the general homicide offences we have been guided by a key principle: the 'ladder' principle. Individual offences of homicide should exist within a graduated system or hierarchy of offences. This system or hierarchy should reflect the offence's degree of seriousness, without too much overlap between individual offences. The main reason for adopting the 'ladder' principle is as Lord Bingham has recently put it (in a slightly different context):

> The interests of justice are not served if a defendant who has committed a lesser offence is either convicted of a greater offence, exposing him to greater punishment than his crime deserves, or acquitted altogether, enabling him to escape the measure of punishment which his crime deserves. The objective must be that defendants are neither over-convicted nor under-convicted....

1.65 The 'ladder' principle also applies to sentencing. The mandatory life sentence should be confined to the most serious kinds of killing. A discretionary life sentence should be available for less serious (but still highly blameworthy) killings.

1.66 Partial defences currently only affect the verdict of murder. This is because a verdict of murder carries a mandatory sentence. That sentence is not appropriate where there are exceptional mitigating circumstances of the kind involved in the partial defences. These mitigating circumstances necessitate a greater degree of judicial discretion in sentencing. The law creates this discretion by means of the partial defences which reduce what would otherwise be a verdict of murder, which carries a mandatory sentence, to manslaughter, which does not. Therefore, our recommended scheme does not extend the application of the partial defences to second degree murder or manslaughter. These offences would permit the trial judge discretion in sentencing and they therefore lack the primary justification for having partial defences.

The structure of offences

1.67 We believe that the following structure would make the law of homicide more coherent and comprehensible, whilst respecting the principles just set out above:

(1) **First degree murder** (mandatory life penalty)
  (a) Killing intentionally.
  (b) Killing where there was an intention to do serious injury, coupled with an awareness of a serious risk of causing death.
(2) **Second degree murder** (discretionary life maximum penalty)
  (a) Killing where the offender intended to do serious injury.
  (b) Killing where the offender intended to cause some injury or a fear or risk of injury, and was aware of a serious risk of causing death.
  (c) Killing in which there is a partial defence to what would otherwise be first degree murder.
(3) **Manslaughter** (discretionary life maximum penalty)
  (a) Killing through gross negligence as to a risk of causing death.
  (b) Killing through a criminal act:
    (i) intended to cause injury; or
    (ii) where there was an awareness that the act involved a serious risk of causing injury.
  (c) Participating in a joint criminal venture in the course of which another participant commits first or second degree murder, in circumstances where it should have been obvious that first or second degree murder might be committed by another participant.

Partial Defences reducing first degree murder to second degree murder

1.68 The following partial defences would reduce first degree murder to second degree murder:

(1) provocation (gross provocation or fear of serious violence);
(2) diminished responsibility;
(3) participation in a suicide pact.

Other specific homicide offences

1.69 There will remain a number of specific homicide offences, such as infanticide, assisting suicide and causing death by dangerous driving.

■ **NOTES AND QUESTIONS**

1. The Law Commission's proposals for reforming the law of homicide have been partly implemented, namely those in relation to the partial defences of

diminished responsibility, infanticide and provocation (loss of self control). There is a deafening silence on the proposal to restructure homicide itself. This is a great pity as the proposals were largely sound, and, moreover, were conceived as a package with the partial defences. For comment see Ashworth, 'Principles, Pragmatism and the Law Commission's Recommendations on Homicide Law Reform' [2007] Crim LR 333; W. Wilson, The Structure of Criminal Homicide (2005) Crim LR 471; W. Wilson, 'What's Wrong with Murder? [2006] Criminal Law and Philosophy 151.

2. Is the framework proposed by the Law Commission for separating the law of murder into first and second degree murder an improvement on the current law? How so? Would abolishing the mandatory life sentence for murder in the current law be a more straightforward and simpler way of achieving the same ends?

3. The Commission's proposals for duress to act as a partial defence to murder will be considered in Chapter 10.

4. A more radical reform would be to abolish murder (and manslaughter), crimes which are defined in terms of result (the death of the victim), and substitute crimes of endangering life. Should a defendant who intends to kill be guilty of murder while his counterpart who commits the identical *actus reus* with the identical intent to kill but whose victim manages to survive, be guilty of a non-homicide offence? As we noted in Chapter 2, whether or not death follows from an attack may be a matter of fortuity, such as the thickness of the victim's skull or a weapon that misfires. On the other hand, would the failure to label as a murderer a defendant who intentionally causes an innocent person's death be acceptable to the public, not to mention the victim's family?

F: Partial Defences to Murder

The Homicide Act 1957 established three murder-specific defences which had the effect of reducing murder to manslaughter, namely provocation, diminished responsibility and suicide pact. All of the general defences discussed in Chapter 10 are also available to a defendant charged with murder, and if they succeed the defendant will be acquitted. In contrast, a successful defence of provocation, diminished responsibility or suicide pact will not lead to an acquittal, but only to a reduction in the severity of the offence from murder to manslaughter. Following the Law Commission reports on Murder and Partial Defences to Murder the Ministry of Justice published, in 2007, a consultation paper 'Murder, Manslaughter and Infanticide: proposals for reform of the law'. Having considered the responses to this consultation the Government decided to proceed with reforms to the partial defences to murder of provocation and diminished responsibility and reform of the law on infanticide. See Coroners and Justice Act 2009, 55, 52–56.

These reforms become law in October 2010. Both provocation, now termed loss of self control, and diminished responsibility have been significantly restricted in their application. Under the previous law diminished responsibility was a rather vaguely defined defence which vagueness had the beneficial consequence, given the mandatory sentence, of enabling juries, where they were so disposed, to prefer a manslaughter verdict over the more natural murder verdict in cases where the defendant, although not suffering a clinically recognised mental disorder, nevertheless killed while suffering from substantial emotional or mental disturbance. Defendants who killed following cumulative domestic violence and those who performed 'mercy killngs' were typical beneficiaries of such 'jury equity' in addition to its core coverage which was recognised mental abnormality. Diminished responsibility thus dovetailed quite effectively with provocation in providing mitigation for killngs where the defendant had lost self control due to the operation of an external trigger (provocation) or an internal trigger (diminished responsibility). *Ahluwalia* (below) exemplifies this pragmatic approach. The 2009 Act removes this ambiguity restricting the defence to cases involving a medically identified mental disorder which accounts for the killing.

Provocation is replaced by a partial defence of loss of self control. It mimics provocation in that it requires an external trigger which caused the defendant to lose self control (*Acott* ([1997] 1 All ER 706, House of Lords) under circumstances where ordinary people with normal powers of restraint and self control but otherwise sharing the same characteristics as the defendant might have reacted in a similar way (See *Director of Public Prosecutions* v *Camplin* [1978] AC 705 HL). It differs in a number of important respects, however. In particular it loses its erstwhile character as a partial excuse for killings manifesting everyday human frailty. Thus it specifies that sexual jealousy does not qualify as a trigger capable of grounding the defence. This was a core provocation scenario. More generally, the external triggers resulting in loss of self control must be such as to create a partial justification for the killing rather than a partial excuse. One trigger is the fear of serious violence from the deceased. A typical scenario covered by this trigger is the person who, after a period of cumulative violence, snaps and kills her tormentor (see *Ahluwalia*, below). The other trigger are acts or words which constitute circumstances of an extremely grave character such that they cause the defendant to have a justified sense of being seriously wronged. No other external trigger is acceptable. It does not apply to those who 'snap' under understandable but not (partly) justified conditions of mental or emotional stress. Thus it is no longer available to parents who 'lose it' and kill their screaming baby as happened in *Doughty* (1986) 83 Cr App R 319.

SECTION 3: MANSLAUGHTER

There are two categories of manslaughter, voluntary and involuntary. A killing which would otherwise be murder may be reduced to *voluntary manslaughter* if the jury decide that the defendant is entitled to rely on one of three statutory defences specific to murder. *Involuntary manslaughter* consists of all other killings which do not amount to murder, but for which a defendant is criminally liable. Unlike for murder, there is no mandatory sentence of life imprisonment for manslaughter, although a life sentence can be imposed at the discretion of the judge.

A: Voluntary manslaughter

(i) Diminished responsibility

The defence of diminished responsibility was established in the Homicide Act 1957, s. 2 whose provisions are now substituted by s. 52 of the The Coroners and Justice Act 2009 as follows:

"(1) A person ("D") who kills or is a party to the killing of another is not to be convicted of murder if D was suffering from an abnormality of mental functioning which—
  (a) arose from a recognised medical condition,
  (b) substantially impaired D's ability to do one or more of the things mentioned in subsection (1A), and
  (c) provides an explanation for D's acts and omissions in doing or being a party to the killing.

(1A) Those things are—
  (a) to understand the nature of D's conduct;
  (b) to form a rational judgment;
  (c) to exercise self-control.

(1B) For the purposes of subsection (1)(c), an abnormality of mental functioning provides an explanation for D's conduct if it causes, or is a significant contributory factor in causing, D to carry out that conduct."

(2) In section 6 of the Criminal Procedure (Insanity) Act 1964 (c. 84) (evidence by prosecution of insanity or diminished responsibility), in paragraph (b) for "mind" substitute "mental functioning".

The burden of proving diminished responsibility rests on the defendant. The standard of proof required is a balance of probabilities (*Dunbar* [1958] 1 QB 1). Unlike in the case of insanity, the issue of diminished responsibility may not be raised by the prosecution; and, indeed, the judge cannot instruct the jury on the issue without the defendant's consent. See *Campbell* (1986) 84 Cr App R 255. The defence must be supported by medical or other scientific evidence.

R v Dix

(1982) 74 Cr App R 306, Court of Appeal

SHAW LJ: ... [Counsel] pointed out that there have been cases in which medical evidence was tendered by both defence and prosecution supporting a plea of diminished responsibility, but the jury rejected that evidence and convicted of murder. The history and circumstances of the offence were treated by the jury as having greater significance than the scientific evidence. If, so Mr Hamilton contended, a jury was entitled to act in that way and to convict of murder, why are they not entitled to come to a conclusion, one way or the other, as to diminished responsibility when there is no medical evidence at all?

The logic of this argument might be stronger if there was no onus on the defence to prove diminished responsibility. Having regard to that onus the argument must fail. In any case, it is inseparable from the proposition that the part of section 2(1) in parenthesis is descriptive of all forms of abnormality of the mind so that no proof is required that an accused's asserted abnormality of mind falls within the categories described within the brackets. Mr Hamilton's argument to this effect was cogent and almost persuasive but the judgment of the Court of Criminal Appeal in *Byrne* (1960) 44 Cr App R 246; [1960] 2 QB 396 is conclusive against his proposition. Giving the judgment of the Court, Lord Parker CJ said at p. 252 and p. 402 respectively: 'It is against that background of the existing law that section 2(1) of the Homicide Act 1957 falls to be construed. To satisfy the requirements of the subsection the accused must show: (a) that he was suffering from an abnormality of mind; and (b) that such abnormality of mind (i) arose from a condition of arrested or retarded development of mind or any inherent causes or was induced by disease or injury; and (ii) was such as substantially impaired his mental responsibility for his acts in doing or being a party to the killing.'

This analysis of the subsection has not been doubted or criticised. Notwithstanding Mr Hamilton's attractive argument, this Court sees no reason to qualify it in any way whatsoever. What emerges from Lord Parker's statement is that scientific evidence of a medical kind is essential to establish what is referred to in (b)(i) and (b)(ii). Thus while the subsection does not in terms require that medical evidence be adduced in support of a defence of diminished responsibility, it makes it a practical necessity if that defence is to begin to run at all. In the result, Griffith J's ruling was in substance a correct one. The appeal accordingly fails and is dismissed.

■ NOTES AND QUESTIONS

1. Why should the law require medical or other scientific evidence? Why should not the testimony of ordinary persons who observed the defendant at the time of the killing suffice?

2. One problem with a medical examination is that it may not occur until arrest, which may be some time after the killing and after arrest. The examining doctor must make an informed guess at the defendant's mental state at a previous point in time based on this later examination. A further complicating factor is that the killing itself may have had an effect on the defendant's mental state. Guilt about the killing may have exacerbated the defendant's condition, or conversely, the killing may have relieved the mental stress which gave rise to the urge to kill. In either case the doctor will not see the same person that he or she would have seen had the examination taken place prior to the killing. This same problem can occur, it might be observed, in respect of insanity.

Three major problems have been encountered in respect of the defence of diminished responsibility:

(a) What is meant by *abnormality of mind*?

(b) What is the relationship between the abnormality and the defendant's responsibility for the killing?

(c) What is the relationship between diminished responsibility and other defences?

(a) Abnormality of Mental functioning

This phrase replaces 'abnormality of mind', a phrase which was not susceptible to any cogent medical diagnosis. The new phrase makes clear that whether or not a person is suffering from such abnormality is to be determined symptomatically (s. 52(1)A). Was the defendant's ability to (a) understand what she was doing, (b) form a rational judgment, that is, order her conduct according to reason, (c) exercise self-control substantially impaired so that it would be unfair to treat her as fully responsible? If that impairment was due to a recognised medical condition, the defence is available.

(b) The relationship between abnormality of mental functioning and impaired responsibility for the killing

Mere proof of abnormality of mental functioning is not enough to establish the defence of diminished responsibility. The abnormality must provide an explanation for the defendant's acts and omissions in doing or being a party to the killing. In other words the mere fact that the defendant suffers from a medically recognised condition will not be sufficient to ground the defence. It must form part of the story as to why this killing took place. His mind was not working properly at the time of the killing, his self control was lacking and so on. This was not a requirement under the previous law. A psychopath is unlikely to be able to avail himself of this defence. In theory, at least, this was possible before 2010 (see *Byrne* [1960] 2 QB 396, CCA).

(c) The relationship between diminished responsibility and other defences

In addition to any overlap between diminished responsibility and insanity (see above), the question often arises as to the relationship between diminished responsibility and some other defence. What happens when there are multiple causes of the defendant's abnormal behaviour, one of which is outside those listed in the Homicide Act 1957, s. 2? The most common situation involves intoxication.

R v Dietschmann

[2003] 1 AC 1209, Court of Appeal

The defendant killed his victim by repeatedly punching him and kicking him in the head. At his trial for murder the defendant admitted the killing and his only defence was that of diminished responsibility pursuant to section 2(1) of the Homicide Act 1957. The evidence was that at the time of the killing the defendant was suffering from a mental abnormality caused by a grief reaction to the recent death of his aunt with whom he had had a physical relationship and also that he had consumed alcohol and was heavily intoxicated. The judge in his summing up directed the jury that the questions they should ask themselves were, whether the defence had satisfied them on a balance of probabilities first, that if the defendant had not taken drink he would have killed, and second, whether he would have been under diminished responsibility when he did so, and that the defence of diminished responsibility was available to the defendant only if the jury could answer 'Yes' to both those questions. The jury convicted the defendant of murder and he appealed on the ground that the judge had misdirected the jury. The Court of Appeal dismissed the appeal.

. . .

The Court of Appeal certified the following question of general public importance:

'(1) Does a defendant seeking to prove a defence of diminished responsibility under section 2(1) of the Homicide Act 1957 in a case where he had taken drink prior to killing the victim, have to show that if he had not taken drink (a) he would have killed as in fact he did; and (b) he would have been under diminished responsibility when he did so? (2) If not, what direction ought to be given to a jury as to the approach to be taken to self-induced intoxication which was present at the material time in conjunction with an abnormality of mind which falls within section 2(1) of the 1957 Act?'

LORD HUTTON:

. . .

18. In a case where the defendant suffered from an abnormality of mind of the nature described in section 2(1) and had also taken alcohol before the killing and where (as the Court of Appeal held in this case) there was no evidence capable of establishing alcohol dependence syndrome as being an abnormality of mind within the subsection, the meaning to be given to the subsection would appear on first consideration to be reasonably clear. I would read the subsection to mean that if the defendant satisfies the jury that, notwithstanding the alcohol he had consumed and its effect on him, his abnormality of mind substantially impaired his mental responsibility for his acts in doing the killing, the jury should find him not guilty of murder but (under subsection (3)) guilty of manslaughter. I take this view because I think that in referring to substantial impairment of mental responsibility the

subsection does not require the abnormality of mind to be the sole cause of the defendant's acts in doing the killing. In my opinion, even if the defendant would not have killed if he had not taken drink, the causative effect of the drink does not necessarily prevent an abnormality of mind suffered by the defendant from substantially impairing his mental responsibility for his fatal acts.

...

Conclusion

41. ... I would answer the first part of the certified question in the negative. As regards the second part of the question, without attempting to lay down a precise form of words as the judge's directions are bound to depend to some extent on the facts of the case before him, I consider that the jury should be directed along the following lines:

> Assuming that the defence have established that the defendant was suffering from mental abnormality as described in section 2, the important question is: did that abnormality substantially impair his mental responsibility for his acts in doing the killing? You know that before he carried out the killing the defendant had had a lot to drink. Drink cannot be taken into account as something which contributed to his mental abnormality and to any impairment of mental responsibility arising from that abnormality. But you may take the view that both the defendant's mental abnormality and drink played a part in impairing his mental responsibility for the killing and that he might not have killed if he had not taken drink. If you take that view, then the question for you to decide is this: has the defendant satisfied you that, despite the drink, his mental abnormality substantially impaired his mental responsibility for his fatal acts, or has he failed to satisfy you of that? If he has satisfied you of that, you will find him not guilty of murder but you may find him guilty of manslaughter. If he has not satisfied you of that, the defence of diminished responsibility is not available to him.

Although Dietschman may now fall outside the coverage of the 2009 Act, unless his grief resulted in a clinically recognised mental disorder, such as depression, the principle remains sound. So long as the abnormality of mental functioning provides part of the explanation for the killing the defence is available.

A related question concerns the status of alcoholism. A person who kills another under the influence of alcohol cannot avail themselves of the defence of diminished responsibility as his/her mental abnormality is not due to a medically recognised condition. If he suffers from chronic alcoholism, however, and the intoxication was attributable to this condition would this count as an explanation for the defendant's loss of self control, disordered rationality, etc? Under the previous law the alcoholism could be relied upon to ground a finding that the mental abnormality was due to disease or inherent causes. It may be that a similar conclusion would follow under the new provisions.

R v Wood

[2008] EWCA Crim 1305

PRESIDENT OF THE QUEEN'S BENCH DIVISION:

1. This is an appeal by Clive Wood against his conviction for murder before Mitting J and a jury at Wolverhampton Crown Court on 11 October 2006.

2. In the early hours of 21 July the appellant mounted a frenzied attack on Francis Ryan with murderous intent. The deceased was struck 37 times with a meat cleaver and a lump hammer was also used in the attack. It was agreed between the Crown and the defence that at the time of the killing the appellant suffered from alcohol dependency syndrome. The single issue in this appeal concerns the accuracy, or otherwise, of the judge's directions on diminished responsibility in the context of the appellant's undoubted alcoholism.

> 'It is common ground that the defendant was suffering from alcohol dependency syndrome. That is not the same as drunkenness. Except where drunkenness is produced by the involuntary

consumption of alcohol, the law requires you to disregard it in assessing a man's mental responsibility for killing. What would otherwise be murder is not reduced to manslaughter by reason of bad judgment or loss of self-control caused only by drunkenness'.

Pausing there, no complaint is made by Mr Malcolm Bishop QC on behalf of the appellant about the impact of this direction on the issue of drink and intent. At this stage in the summing up Mitting J was plainly directing the jury in the context of drunkenness and diminished responsibility. He continued:

'it is accepted by all four psychiatrists that alcohol dependency syndrome can produce changes in the brain which may impair judgment or cause loss of self control ... If you are satisfied that it was more likely than not, by reason of alcohol dependency syndrome and its effect on this defendant's brain, he was suffering from an abnormality of mind and that in consequence his mental responsibility for killing Francis Ryan was substantially reduced, your verdict would be ... guilty of manslaughter.'

17. This direction addressed the possible relevance of brain damage consequent on alcoholism, and the judge later summarised the differences of opinion between the psychiatrists on the question whether there were changes in the brain which would have impaired the appellant's judgment. We shall describe this as the first limb of the direction.

18. Mitting J then continued, in a passage which has been subjected to analysis in the course of the submissions before us:

'Where a man becomes so drunk that he suffers, temporarily, from an abnormality of mind, he may also be acquitted of murder but convicted of manslaughter by reason of diminished responsibility applying the same tests that I have outlined, but that verdict would only be open to you if you found it more likely than not that his consumption of alcohol was truly involuntary. A man's act is involuntary if, and only if, he could not have acted otherwise. Giving in to a craving is not an involuntary act, even if it is very difficult to do otherwise. An alcoholic not suffering from severe withdrawal symptoms, who tops up his overnight level or who later chooses to accept a drink after he's reached his normal quota, is not drinking involuntarily.'

This will be described as the second limb of the direction ... The concern in this appeal is the accuracy of the second limb direction, on which we shall now focus.

22. Section 2(1) of the Homicide Act 1957 provides:

'Where a person kills or is a party to the killing of another he shall not be convicted of murder if he was suffering from such abnormality of mind (whether arising from a condition of arrested or retarded development of mind or any inherent causes or induced by disease or injury) as substantially impaired his mental responsibility for his acts and omissions in doing or being a party to the killing.'

23. Dealing with the point very broadly, the consumption of alcohol before a defendant acts with murderous intent and kills cannot, without more, bring his actions within the concept of diminished responsibility. On its own, voluntary intoxication falls outside the ambit of the defence. This is consistent with the general approach of the law that, save in the context of offences of specific intent, and proof of that intent, criminal acts committed under the influence of self induced intoxication are not for that reason excused. Public policy proceeds on the basis that a defendant who voluntarily takes alcohol and behaves in a way which he might not have behaved when sober is not normally entitled to be excused from the consequences of his actions. (See, for example, Law Commission *Legislating the criminal code: intoxication and criminal liability: No 220 [1995]*).

24. In the context of diminished responsibility, alcoholism has now been recognised as a disease which may fall within the ambit of section 2 of the 1957 Act. The principle was summarised in the Court of Appeal in *Dietschmann* by Rose LJ [2001] EWCA Crim 2052:

'The general rule that drink does not give rise to an abnormality of mind due to inherent causes was authoritatively established in R v Fenton [1975] 61 CAR 261 and confirmed in R v Gittens [1984] 79 CAR 272 [1984] QB 698. In line with those authorities, R v Tandy [1989] 1 All ER 267 established that drink is only capable of giving rise to a defence under section 2 if it either causes damage to the brain or produces an irresistible craving so that consumption is involuntary.'

It seems clear that Mitting J had this passage in mind when he was structuring his directions to the jury. In order to analyse Mr Bishop's submissions, we must attempt to establish the basis for Rose LJ's summary, noting that in *Dietschmann*, in the House of Lords, the issue of its correctness or otherwise did not arise for consideration.

30 *Tandy* established that for the purposes of section 2 'chronic alcoholism' could amount to an abnormality of mind, but it simultaneously imposed very strict limits indeed on the circumstances in which the defence might be available to those suffering from the condition. Either the 'repeated insult from intoxicants' must have physically damaged the defendant's brain thus leading to 'gross impairment' of her judgment and emotional responses, or if the brain was not so damaged, her alcoholism should have reached the stage where her drinking had become 'involuntary'. To be regarded as 'involuntary' for this purpose, the defendant should have 'no immediate control over the consumption of alcohol'. This analysis therefore encompassed the defendant who could not resist the impulse to drink but did not extend to the defendant who could have resisted it, but 'simply' chose not to do so. Thus even in the context of an established 'craving' for alcohol, the craving had to be of such a nature that the defendant's drinking was rendered 'involuntary', but this rather begged the question whether, and when a 'craving' was properly to be described as irresistible. The court's determination to control the possible extension of defences based on self induced intoxication as a defence is evident not only in *Tandy* but in subsequent decisions such as *Atkinson* [1985] Crim LR 314, and *Egan* [1992] 95 CAR 278. . . .

36. The present appeal illustrates something of the problems created by the literal application of *Tandy*. Assuming that the jury rejected a defence arising out of the first limb of the direction (identifiable brain damage caused by alcoholism) the second limb arose for consideration in a case in which, to put it neutrally, the unanimous view of the experts was that the appellant suffered from a condition which encompassed very serious problems with drink control. One of the Crown's experts, whose evidence was otherwise adverse to the appellant, accepted that he could not resist the compulsion to take the first drink of the day, but the expert rejected diminished responsibility on the basis that the appellant had a choice over the amount of alcohol he took later in the day, that is, at the end of a lengthy drinking session. The jury in the present case had to address a further complication, which was that when the killing occurred the appellant had stopped drinking and fallen asleep, and then woke up to find the deceased making unwanted sexual advances.

37. As a matter of practical reality the bar the defendant is required to surmount before diminished responsibility can be established in the context of chronic addiction to alcohol may have been set too high. In our judgment neither *Tandy* nor *Inseal* establishes that it is a pre-requisite to the availability of diminished responsibility to a defendant suffering from alcohol dependency syndrome that he never does anything other than drink alcohol. Even a true alcoholic stops drinking sometimes. He will get dressed, or wash, or perform everyday functions without necessarily keeping a glass or bottle to his lips. He will stop drinking and go to bed. In one sense these actions all represent a deliberate choice not to drink, and if so, that implies that the defendant makes a further choice about when he will resume drinking. Yet the defence does not require proof that the alcohol dependent defendant is subject to or acting under some form of automatism, either when he is drinking or when he is behaving violently. That might provide a different defence. The issue of automatism was not addressed at any stage in the evidence in the present case, nor indeed on the appeal, and it would be inappropriate for us to seek to address it now.

38. We do however emphasise that nothing in section 2 itself suggests that alcohol dependency syndrome is excluded from consideration as a possible source of abnormality of mind. Indeed, as we come to *Dietschmann* in the House of Lords, it is perhaps important to highlight Lord Hutton's observation that in the context of diminished responsibility, as a defence to murder, (rather than any other defence based on intoxication) and addressing the asserted public policy of the law to maintain close limits on the consumption of alcohol as a defence, 'the policy of the criminal law in respect of persons suffering from mental abnormality is to be found in the words of s 2'.

39. *Dietschmann* was concerned with a defendant suffering from an abnormality of mind other than alcohol dependency syndrome, who had voluntarily taken alcohol at the time of the killing. The question addressed by the House of Lords was:

'...Does a defendant seeking to prove a defence of diminished responsibility... in a case where he had taken drink prior to killing the victim, have to show that if he had not taken drink

(a) he would have killed as he in fact did; and

(b) he would have been under diminished responsibility when he did so?...'

The answer was negative. Diminished responsibility could be established if the defendant satisfied the jury that notwithstanding the consumption of alcohol and its effects, his

'...abnormality of mind substantially impaired his mental responsibility... in referring to substantial impairment of mental responsibility the subsection does not require the abnormality of mind to be the sole cause of the defendant's acts in doing the killing. In my opinion, even if the defendant would not have killed if he had not taken drink, the causative effect of the drink does not necessarily prevent an abnormality of mind suffered by the defendant from substantially impairing his mental responsibility for his fatal acts.' (per Lord Hutton in the only reasoned speech)

The observations in a number of earlier decisions such as *Egan* [1992] 95 CAR 278, which in effect suggested that the defendant's voluntary consumption of alcohol closed the door to the diminished responsibility defence were overruled.

40. *Dietschmann* did not alter the principle that, *on its own*, the voluntary consumption of alcohol, however excessive, does not constitute an abnormality of mind. It did however establish that, the defence of diminished responsibility within section 2 is not precluded by the mere fact that the defendant consumed alcohol voluntarily before committing the fatal act. Therefore the question which arises is whether *Dietschmann* produced some dilution in the rigid principles laid down in *Tandy*, at any rate, where they are applied in shorthand form, or whether, what Lord Lane in *Gittens* and Rose LJ in *Dietschmann* explained was the 'general rule', (ie that alcohol consumption does not give rise to an abnormality of mind due to inherent causes) may not have been applied over-prescriptively in the context of current understanding of alcoholism and alcohol dependency syndrome.

41. In our judgment *Dietschmann* requires a re-assessment of the way in which *Tandy* is applied in the context of alcohol dependency syndrome where observable brain damage has not occurred. The sharp effect of the distinction drawn in *Tandy* between cases where brain damage has occurred as a result of alcohol dependency syndrome and those where it has not, is no longer appropriate. Naturally, where brain damage has occurred the jury may be more likely to conclude that the defendant suffers from an abnormality of mind induced by disease or illness, but whether it has occurred or not, logically consistent with *Dietschmann*, the same question (i.e. whether it has been established that the defendant's syndrome is of such an extent and nature that it constitutes an abnormality of mind induced by disease or illness) arises for decision. That is for the jury. If the syndrome does not constitute such an abnormality of mind, diminished responsibility based on the consumption of alcohol will fail. If, on the other hand, it does, the jury must then be directed to address the question whether the defendant's mental responsibility for his actions at the time of the killing was substantially impaired as a result of the syndrome. In deciding that question the jury should focus exclusively on the effect of alcohol consumed by the defendant as a direct result of his illness or disease and ignore the effect of any alcohol consumed voluntarily. Assuming that the jury has decided that the syndrome constitutes an abnormality of mind induced by disease or illness, its possible impact and significance in the individual case must be addressed. The resolution of this issue embraces questions such as whether the defendant's craving for alcohol was or was not irresistible, and whether his consumption of alcohol in the period leading up to the killing was voluntary (and if so, to what extent) or was not voluntary, and leads to the ultimate decision, which is whether the defendant's mental responsibility for his actions when killing the deceased was substantially impaired as a result of the alcohol consumed under the baneful influence of the syndrome.

42. The problem with Mitting J's second limb direction is that whether the appellant was suffering from alcohol induced brain damage or not, the experts agreed that the alcohol was consumed by a man suffering from alcohol dependency syndrome. When he directed the jury that 'giving in to a craving is not an involuntary act, even if it is very difficult to do otherwise', he was implying that there was no such thing as an irresistible craving and the observation might well have been

regarded as a direction to conclude that any consumption of alcohol by the appellant as a result of a craving did not or could not give rise to the defence. When Mitting J added that a defendant 'later choosing to accept a drink after he has reached his normal quota, is not drinking involuntarily', he was in effect directing the jury to accept that such a choice was voluntary even when made by an alcoholic. Taken together, these observations implied that unless every drink consumed that day by the appellant was involuntary, his alcohol dependency syndrome was to be disregarded. In our judgment they are inconsistent with the analysis of the relevant principles consequent on the decision of the House of Lords in *Dietschmann* as we have endeavoured to explain them.

43. In our judgment this appeal must be allowed and the conviction for murder quashed. We shall invite submissions whether a new trial should be ordered, or whether a conviction for manslaughter on the grounds of diminished responsibility should be entered.

Considerable overlap existed between diminished responsibility and provocation, although this overlap is now reduced. Indeed, for some time it has been unclear whether the essential difference between them is simply the aetiology of the reduced responsibility, so that if responsibility is reduced due to internal factors it amounts to diminished responsibility, but provocation if due to an external trigger. This caused particular problems in cases where loss of self-control may be attributable to a reduced capacity to withstand external provocation due to mental abnormality.

R v Kiranjit Ahluwalia
[1993] 96 Cr App R 133, Court of Appeal

In 1989 the appellant, after enduring many years of violence and humiliation from her husband, threw petrol in his bedroom and set it alight. Her husband sustained terrible burns and after lingering for six days he died. She was charged with his murder. At her trial she did not give evidence and no medical evidence was adduced on her behalf. The defence case was that she did not intend seriously to harm her husband, only to inflict some pain. Provocation was a second line of defence, reliance being placed upon the whole history of ill-treatment throughout the marriage, especially on the night in question. The defence sought a verdict of manslaughter, but the jury returned one of murder. On the defence of provocation the judge had directed the jury in accordance with the classic definition of provocation in Duffy [1949] 1 All E.R. 932 as conduct 'which would cause in any reasonable person and actually causes in the accused, a sudden and temporary loss of self-control.' She was convicted of murder and appealed on the ground, *inter alia*, that following the enactment of section 3 of the Homicide Act 1957 as explained in D.P.P. v. Camplin (1978) 67 Cr.App.R. 14, the Duffy direction was now wrong. Alternatively, that the defence of diminished responsibility, albeit not put forward at the trial, was open to the appellant on the facts of the case.

Held, (1) that the words 'sudden and temporary loss of control' encapsulated an essential ingredient of the defence of provocation in a clear and readily understandable phrase. It served to underline that the defence was concerned with the actions of an individual who was not, at the moment when he or she acted violently, master of his or her own mind. However, the longer the delayed reaction to the provocation and the stronger the evidence of deliberation on the part of the defendant, the more likely it would be that the prosecution would negative provocation.

(2) In the instant case, despite the delay after the last provocative act or words of the deceased, and despite the appellant's deliberation in seeking and lighting the petrol, the trial judge nevertheless left the issue of provocation to the jury. His references to 'sudden and temporary loss of self-control' were correct and in accordance with well established law. Accordingly, that ground of appeal failed.

(3) On the ground of diminished responsibility, there was a medical report available before the appellant's trial in which was expressed the opinion that she was suffering from endogenous

depression at the material time, which in the opinion of some experts would be termed 'a major depressive disorder', which report came to be overlooked or was not further perused at the time of the trial; nor was the appellant consulted about it or about the possibility of investigating it further. The court, considering it expedient to admit that fresh evidence under section 23(1) of the Criminal Appeal Act 1968 at the hearing of the appeal, did so, and thereby in the wholly exceptional circumstances of the present case, regarded the verdict of the jury as unsafe and unsatisfactory. The appeal would be allowed and the conviction of murder quashed and a re-trial ordered.

■ NOTES AND QUESTIONS

1. The Law Commission suggests that the effect of a successful defence of diminished responsibility should be to reduce first degree murder to second degree murder, but not second degree murder to manslaughter. Why? Is it appropriate to label as a murderer (albeit in the second degree) one whose killing is attributable to diminished responsibility?

2. Is the new definition of diminished responsibility an improvement over the previous law? If so, in what ways? Would it make more sense to abolish the crime of murder and replace it with an offence of criminal or culpable homicide, with the judge then being able to take account of such factors as provocation and diminished responsibility in determining the appropriate sentence? See Blom-Cooper and Morris, *With Malice Aforethought: A Study of the Crime and Punishment for Homicide* (2004). If adopted, this approach would also obviate the need to distinguish between first and second degree murder.

(ii) Loss of Self Control

Provocation will continue to be a defence for those committing murder before October 2010. The new partial defence of loss of self control follows the same defence structure as provocation. The defendant must lose his self control. This must be the result of an external trigger. His reaction must be consistent with that of people with normal powers of self control but otherwise sharing those of his characteristics which made him respond as he did to the trigger.

---

54 Partial defence to murder: loss of control

(1) Where a person ('D') kills or is a party to the killing of another ('V'), D is not to be convicted of murder if—
  (a) D's acts and omissions in doing or being a party to the killing resulted from D's loss of self-control,
  (b) the loss of self-control had a qualifying trigger, and
  (c) a person of D's sex and age, with a normal degree of tolerance and self-restraint and in the circumstances of D, might have reacted in the same or in a similar way to D.

(2) For the purposes of subsection (1)(a), it does not matter whether or not the loss of control was sudden.

(3) In subsection (1)(c) the reference to "the circumstances of D" is a reference to all of D's circumstances other than those whose only relevance to D's conduct is that they bear on D's general capacity for tolerance or self-restraint.

(4) Subsection (1) does not apply if, in doing or being a party to the killing, D acted in a considered desire for revenge.

(5) On a charge of murder, if sufficient evidence is adduced to raise an issue with respect to the defence under subsection (1), the jury must assume that the defence is satisfied unless the prosecution proves beyond reasonable doubt that it is not.

(6) For the purposes of subsection (5), sufficient evidence is adduced to raise an issue with respect to the defence if evidence is adduced on which, in the opinion of the trial judge, a jury, properly directed, could reasonably conclude that the defence might apply.

(7) A person who, but for this section, would be liable to be convicted of murder is liable instead to be convicted of manslaughter.

(8) The fact that one party to a killing is by virtue of this section not liable to be convicted of murder does not affect the question whether the killing amounted to murder in the case of any other party to it.

55   Meaning of "qualifying trigger"

(1) This section applies for the purposes of section 54.

(2) A loss of self-control had a qualifying trigger if subsection (3), (4) or (5) applies.

(3) This subsection applies if D's loss of self-control was attributable to D's fear of serious violence from V against D or another identified person.

(4) This subsection applies if D's loss of self-control was attributable to a thing or things done or said (or both) which—

   (a) constituted circumstances of an extremely grave character, and

   (b) caused D to have a justifiable sense of being seriously wronged.

(5) This subsection applies if D's loss of self-control was attributable to a combination of the matters mentioned in subsections (3) and (4).

(6) In determining whether a loss of self-control had a qualifying trigger—

   (a) D's fear of serious violence is to be disregarded to the extent that it was caused by a thing which D incited to be done or said for the purpose of providing an excuse to use violence;

   (b) a sense of being seriously wronged by a thing done or said is not justifiable if D incited the thing to be done or said for the purpose of providing an excuse to use violence;

   (c) the fact that a thing done or said constituted sexual infidelity is to be disregarded.

(7) In this section references to 'D' and 'V' are to be construed in accordance with section 54.

56   Abolition of common law defence of provocation

(1) The common law defence of provocation is abolished and replaced by sections 54 and 55.

(2) Accordingly, the following provisions cease to have effect—

   (a) section 3 of the Homicide Act 1957 (c. 11) (questions of provocation to be left to the jury);

   (b) section 7 of the Criminal Justice Act (Northern Ireland) 1966 (c. 20) (questions of provocation to be left to the jury).

There are several points to note about these provisions. First, there must be a loss of self control caused by an external trigger, what used to be termed an act of provocation. Second, both acts and omissions are covered. Third, the defence is not available unless there is a qualifying trigger. Not all triggers are sufficient. Fourth, the loss of self control does not have to be sudden. If it is not, however, it may be evidence that there was no loss of self control.

Unlike diminished responsibility, provocation was a recognised defence at common law. However, the test of provocation was in several respects a matter of controversy. The defence was only available where the loss of self control was sudden. As illustrated by *Ahluwalia*, this was disadvantageous to women, whose psychological make up, unlike men, does not typically react with immediate violence to a provocative act or event. Another taxing problem was whether the defendant could rely on personal characteristics which made him particularly susceptible to provocation. By the time the 2009 Act was passed the position was finally made clear. The killer could rely on characteristics if those characteristics were pertinent to why the actions or deeds of the other were provocative to him. He could not rely on those characteristics if they simply reduced his powers of self control. So an alcoholic could rely on his alcoholism if he killed in response to a taunt that he was an alcoholic. Such a taunt, for people with that condition, is likely to be wounding and provocative. If, however, he killed in response to an accusation of theft, because his powers of self control were reduced having just consumed a bottle of whisky, he would not be able to rely on his alcoholism as an explanation for his loss of self control (*see R v Camplin* [1978] AC 705, *R v Smith (Morgan)* [2000] 3 WLR 654, House of Lords, *Attorney-General for Jersey v Holley* [2005] 2 AC 580, Privy Council, *Luc Thiet Thuan v The Queen* [1997] AC 131). Another problem concerned the relative function of judge and jury. Could the judge withdraw provocation from the jury on the ground that 'reasonable people' would never be provoked to kill under these circumstances. Until 1957 this was possible. The Homicide Act 1957, s. 3 left the question 'whether the provocation was enough to make a reasonable man do as he did...to be determined by the jury; and in determining that question the jury shall take into account everything both done and said according to the effect which, in their opinion, it would have on a reasonable man.'

Like diminished responsibility, loss of self control is *only* a partial defence and *only* a defence to a charge of murder. It is not a defence to lesser crimes, even attempted murder. The effect of a successful defence is to reduce the defendant's crime from murder to manslaughter. Unlike in respect of diminished responsibility, the defendant needs only introduce some evidence of loss of self control to force the prosecution to prove beyond reasonable doubt that the elements of the defence are absent.

■ NOTES AND QUESTIONS

1. Note that defendants who raise the issue of loss of control are not saying that they did not have an intent to kill or cause grievous bodily harm. Rather they are saying that they did so in a situation where they were induced to lose self-control due to a qualifying trigger.

2. Why should not the burden of persuading the jury of the defence of loss of self control be on the defendant?

The line between self-defence and provocation was often murky (see *Johnson* below). The effect of the new law is to ensure that those who overreact and kill as a result of fearing serious violence have their crime and sentence mitigated.

R v Johnson

[1989] 1 WLR 740, Court of Appeal

WATKINS LJ:...The deceased died during the night of 18/19 May 1987 in a night club in Sheffield when the appellant stabbed him in the chest with a knife. The blade of the knife, 3.8 inches long, penetrated the chest to the heart. The wound, there was but one, travelled from the deceased's left to right parallel with the ground. There were no defensive wounds on the deceased.

During the evening both the appellant and the deceased had been drinking at the night club. The appellant was carrying a knife. It was a flick or 'swish' knife. The deceased was unarmed. A tense atmosphere developed in the club when the appellant started to behave in an unpleasant way. Threats of violence were made by him to a female friend of the deceased and then to the deceased himself. This woman and the deceased became extremely annoyed. A struggle developed between the two men during the course of which the stabbing occurred.

...

It was accepted before us by counsel for the Crown that the evidence before the jury included the following. Before the stabbing incident the appellant had been taunted by a woman who called him a 'white nigger'. Apparently, although a white man himself, he affected at times a West Indian accent. He reacted to that abuse. It upset him. It made him angry. There were high words between him and others, the deceased included. Seemingly to leave the club or that part of it, the appellant walked away towards the exit. The deceased however followed him and poured beer over him. The deceased then removed his jacket. The appellant did not. The deceased by placing his arm across the appellant's chest or throat seized hold of the appellant and pinned him against a wall. While he was thus pinned against the wall the woman, who had described him as a 'white nigger,' attacked him by punching his head and pulling his hair. There were shouts from some of the others present that the deceased should drop the glass which he held in his hand. He did so. Until this moment the appellant had not retaliated. But his attitude to being held captive suddenly changed. He somehow bent down and produced the knife and lunged at the deceased with it. He lunged again, so it was said, but failed to make contact. He was restrained by one of his friends. His explanation for his conduct was, as has been stated, a fear of being 'glassed'. He did not, as has also been stated, claim that he had lost his self-control.

Nevertheless, if the jury rejected, as they did, his account that he was acting in self-defence they might, in our judgment, very well have inferred from all that evidence that there had indeed been a sudden loss of self-control.

That evidence may not have been powerfully suggestive of provocation. But it was, in our view, rather more than tenuous. It is easily conceivable, we think, that the jury, if directed on the issue, would have come to the conclusion that the appellant was so provoked as to reduce murder to manslaughter. Therefore, subject only to the question of self-induced provocation referred to by the judge, in our judgment this defence should have been left to the jury.

... In view of the express wording of section 3, as interpreted in *R v Camplin* [1978] AC 705 which was decided after *Edwards v The Queen* [1973] AC 648, we find it impossible to accept that the mere fact that a defendant caused a reaction in others, which in turn led him to lose his self-control, should result in the issue of provocation being kept outside a jury's consideration. Section 3 clearly provides that the question is whether things done or said or both provoked the defendant to lose his self-control. If there is any evidence that it may have done, the issue must be left to the jury. The jury would then have to consider all the circumstances of the incident, including all the relevant behaviour of the defendant, in deciding (a) whether he was in fact provoked and (b) whether the provocation was enough to make a reasonable man do what the defendant did.

Accordingly, whether or not there were elements in the appellant's conduct which justified the conclusion that he had started the trouble and induced others, including the deceased, to react in the way they did, we are firmly of the view that the defence of provocation should have been left to the jury.

Since it is not possible for us to infer from their verdict that the jury inevitably would have concluded that provocation as well as self-defence had been disproved the verdict of murder will be set aside. A conviction for manslaughter on the basis of provocation will be substituted.

(a) Elements of the defence

Like provocation, the defence of loss of self control contains both a subjective and an objective component. To succeed the defendant must introduce some evidence that:

(a) he lost his self-control (subjective)

(b) there was a qualifying trigger (objective) for the loss of self control

(c) a person of D's sex and age, with a normal degree of tolerance and self-restraint and in the circumstances of D, might have reacted in the same or in a similar way to D (objective).

The subjective element should not be overlooked. If a person of a normal degree of tolerance and self-restraint and in the circumstances of D would have been driven wild with rage by the provoking act, but the defendant was not, the defence will not succeed. This point is accentuated by section 55(6)(a) and (b).

(b) The Qualifying Trigger

Even under the old law it was not enough to ground the defence simply to give evidence of loss of self control. There had to be evidence of specific words or deeds which caused that loss. People may easily lose their self control in the course of an argument but this does not mean that they are provoked to, lose their self control (*R v Acott* [1997] 1 All ER 706, House of Lords). However, the jury alone had the task of deciding whether the trigger was operative and whether it may have triggered a similar reaction in other people. Even a crying baby could be a sufficient trigger (*Doughty* (1986) 83 Cr App R 319).

The new defence creates a fundamental change here. There are only two qualifying triggers. These are (i) a fear of serious violence; and (ii) words or conduct of an extremely grave character which caused the defendant to have a justifiable sense of being seriously wronged. In neither case is there a requirement for loss of self-control to be 'sudden', although clearly the longer the delay between trigger and response the less likely it is that the response was premeditated. In this connection the Act specifies that a killing undertaken in a considered desire for revenge will not ground the defence. This reflects the previous common law position.

More generally the provision makes clear that there must be objective grounds capable of justifying the defendant's reaction. Under neither limb will trivial wrongdoing be a qualifying trigger. Under the first limb D or a specified other must be threatened with **serious** violence. Under the second limb D must be subjected to words or deeds of an extremely grave character and they must be of a nature to cause the defendant to have a justifiable sense of being seriously wronged. This means for, example, that a serious allegation made against D could count as a qualifying trigger only if it was untrue. It would mean that D's own sense of what counts as being 'seriously wronged' will be ignored if the sense is not justifiable.

The Act specifies, presumably in case the jury were minded to disagree, that sexual infidelity is not a qualifying trigger. It also provides that the 'fear of serious violence' limb should succeed only where the victim is the source of the violence feared by the defendant and the threat is targeted at the defendant or specified others. Killing the threatener's messenger would not afford a defence. There is no such restriction with regard to the second limb, however. So if A kills B, a member of C's paedophile ring, having heard from B that C has abused A's child, the trigger is a qualifying trigger.

(c) The objective prong

The two limbs of s. 55 only apply if a person of the defendant's sex and age, with a normal degree of tolerance and self-restraint and in the circumstances of the defendant, might have reacted in the same or in a similar way. Unlike under the common law, the judge should not leave either of these defences to the jury unless there is evidence on which a reasonable jury, properly directed, could conclude that they might apply.

Subjection (3) confirms the common law position that circumstances and characteristics of the defendant which bear on the reasonabless of the loss of self control are to be taken into account but not characteristics or circumstances which bear upon D's ability to control himself. In subsection (1)(c) the reference to 'the circumstances of D' is a reference to all of D's circumstances other than those whose only relevance to D's conduct is that they bear on D's general capacity for tolerance or self-restraint.

In other words, to succeed with the defence requires the defendant's reaction to be a manifestation of his humanity rather than of a dangerous disposition. The court must distinguish, then between characteristics and circumstances which affect the gravity or seriousness of the words or deeds to which D was subjected (e.g. alleging wrongdoing, or taunting someone because of some supposed defect of appearance, weakness of character, race, religion, and characteristics which affect the defendant's ability to maintain self-control (e.g. drunkenness, mental illness, short temper). The jury may clearly take into account the former, but not the latter.

■ NOTES AND QUESTIONS

1. Do you agree with the major change wrought by the 2009 Act, namely that the partial defence should only be available where the defendant's reaction is partially justified. Given the mandatory sentence is there no place for mercy in a one-off instance where the defendant inexcusably loses his control as a result of some external trigger?

2. Is it appropriate for sexual infidelity to have been singled out for special treatment? Consider the phenomenon of 'honour killings' when a family member or her lover is killed for having besmirched the family's honour. Is there any reason why this should potentially be a qualifying trigger if sexual infidelity is not?

3. Under the Law Commission's proposals loss of self control would remain a partial defence, but rather than reducing murder to manslaughter, it would reduce first degree murder to second degree murder. The enacted position is to reduce murder to manslaughter.

4. The defence is only available where the relevant provocation was of a nature to justify the defendant's conclusion that he has been 'seriously wronged' or to inspire fear of serious violence to himself or another. Is this too demanding an approach?

5. Under these proposals, would the jury's role be reduced? Is this advisable given the oft-expressed view that provocation is a concession to human weakness?

6. When we considered the proposals on diminished responsibility, we raised the question of whether it might not be better to simply have a single offence of criminal or culpable homicide, leaving such factors as diminished responsibility and provocation to be taken into account at the sentencing stage. That question might again be considered in respect of the loss of self control defence.

7. The Law Commission's proposal for the defence omitted a requirement of loss of self control. It emphasised rather the two triggers and the reaction thereto – fear of serious violence and justifiable sense of being seriously wronged. What does loss of self control add to this which makes the reaction any more understandable or excusable? Indeed it may well only serve to confuse the jury. What if, in cases such as *Ahluwalia*, the jury are convinced of the terror and misery to which she was subject but believe her reaction was not because she 'snapped' but the result of her not knowing what else to do and having no-one to support her? Should that make a difference?

(iv) Suicide pact

We conclude our examination of voluntary manslaughter by looking at the partial defence of suicide pact. In contrast with provocation and diminished responsibility, this defence is rarely invoked.

HOMICIDE ACT 1957

...

4.—(1) It shall be manslaughter, and shall not be murder, for a person acting in pursuance of a suicide pact between him and another to kill the other or be a party to the other killing himself or being killed by a third person.

(2) Where it is shown that a person charged with the murder of another killed the other or was a party to his killing himself or being killed, it shall be for the defence to prove that the person charged was acting in pursuance of a suicide pact between him and the other.

(3) For the purposes of this section 'suicide pact' means a common agreement between two or more persons having for its object the death of all of them, whether or not each is to take his own life, but nothing done by a person who enters into a suicide pact shall be treated as done by him in pursuance of the pact unless it is done while he has the settled intention of dying in pursuance of the pact.

■ NOTES AND QUESTIONS

1. The burden of proving a suicide pact rests on the defendant, but only by a 'balance of probabilities' standard (as opposed to 'beyond reasonable doubt').

2. At common law suicide was a crime. Although the individual who was successful could obviously not be tried, his estate was forfeited to the Crown. Today, when suicide is no longer a crime, should the killing of a partner in the course of a suicide pact also cease to attract criminal sanctions? Is the issue of consent to one's own death a relevant consideration here? If so, should euthanasia (or mercy killing) be decriminalised?

3. The Law Commission in its 2005 Consultation Paper recommended abolition of the suicide pact defence and its incorporation, where appropriate, within diminished responsibility:

Focusing on depression and not on consent

5.91 Under the current law, the depressed killer who kills pursuant to a suicide pact is at an advantage. The law assumes that he or she is severely depressed. By contrast, the severely depressed killer who is not a party to a suicide pact has to prove diminished responsibility. This, at least in theory, should be difficult because reactive depression does not arise from a condition of 'arrested or retarded development of mind or any inherent causes or induced by disease or injury'. The problem has to some extent been overcome by pretending that the problem does not exist.

5.92 We believe that the current partial defence of killing after entering into a suicide pact is unsatisfactory . . . and are provisionally proposing that it should be abolished.

5.93 Instead, we envisage that deserving cases that currently come within the suicide pact defence, and also deserving cases that the defence does not currently cater for, should be accommodated by the partial defence of diminished responsibility. Conversely, undeserving defendants . . . who currently are able to take advantage of the suicide pact defence should in the future be guilty of 'first degree murder'.

B: Involuntary manslaughter

This category of homicide includes all killings which are regarded as criminally unlawful but where the defendant does not have the *mens rea* of murder. The term 'involuntary manslaughter' is, however, a misnomer, for the killings involved are not involuntary as that term has traditionally been used in the context of *actus reus*. It is used only to distinguish this class of homicide from murder and voluntary manslaughter. In struggling to define the boundaries of involuntary manslaughter the courts have encountered considerable difficulties and the resulting muddle is not a credit to English jurisprudence. There are at least two categories, but some killings could fit into both, and there may also be some less clearly defined categories. The two categories are:

(a) constructive manslaughter;
(b) gross negligence manslaughter.

(i) Constructive manslaughter

It is manslaughter when the defendant performs an unlawful and dangerous act likely to cause physical harm and death results. This is a 'constructed' offence in that it is 'built upon' another, i.e., the death is an incidental result of the unlawful act. For that reason there has been some confusion as to whether the usual causation rules apply. The issue has appeared in the case law as a question as to whether the defendant's act must be 'aimed or directed' at the victim (see extracts below).

(a) An unlawful act

The essence of constructive manslaughter is an unlawful act which causes death. The import seems to be that an omission cannot form the basis of this form of manslaughter. If so, a parent who strikes his child resulting in that child's death is guilty of constructive manslaughter. If, on the other hand, a child dies because his parent omits to do something, say calling a doctor for a poorly child, which results in death – constructive manslaughter would not be a viable charge. Either the charge is wilful neglect (See *Lowe* [1973] QB 702) or, if the neglect is of a very high degree it may be gross negligence manslaughter.

R v Lowe

[1973] 1 QB 702, Court of Appeal

The defendant, who was of low average intelligence, knew that his infant child was sick but did not call a doctor. The child died from dehydration and gross emaciation. The defendant was indicted on counts of manslaughter of the child and of wilfully neglecting it so as to cause unnecessary suffering or injury to health, contrary to s. 1(1) of the Children and Young Persons Act 1933. The jury, in convicting the defendant on both counts, negatived reckless behaviour by him as being the cause of death and emphasised that the conviction of manslaughter was solely due to the direction of the judge that a finding of manslaughter must follow a conviction of wilful neglect if that neglect was the cause of death.

PHILLIMORE LJ: . . . Now in the present case the jury negatived recklessness. How then can mere neglect, albeit wilful, amount to manslaughter? This court feels that there is something inherently unattractive in a theory of constructive manslaughter. It seems strange that an omission which is wilful solely in the sense that it is not inadvertent and the consequences of which are not in fact foreseen by the person who is neglectful should, if death results, automatically give rise to an indeterminate sentence instead of the maximum of two years which would otherwise be the limit imposed.

We think that there is a clear distinction between an act of omission and an act of commission likely to cause harm. Whatever may be the position with regard to the latter it does not follow that the same is true of the former. In other words, if I strike a child in a manner likely to cause harm it is right that, if the child dies, I may be charged with manslaughter. If, however, I omit to do something with the result that it suffers injury to health which results in its death, we think that a charge of manslaughter should not be an inevitable consequence, even if the omission is deliberate.

Appeal against conviction of manslaughter allowed.

■ NOTES AND QUESTIONS

1. The reference to a 'deliberate' omission in *Lowe* might best be understood in relation to the particular facts of the case. It seems clear that the defendant neglected the child 'deliberately' in the sense that he decided not to call the doctor. However, the defendant was not aware of the probable consequences of his failure. It is therefore likely that the problems which commentators have with regard to the concept of 'deliberate' neglect are unfounded as the word was used in a rather idiosyncratic fashion in the case. If that is so, however, what is the purpose of drawing a distinction between omissions and actions?

2. *Lowe* reflects a class of case where a vulnerable victim (usually a child), for whom two carers (usually parents) are responsible, dies. At trial each of the carers accuses the other of causing the death (what is known as a 'cutthroat defence'). One of the defendants is no doubt guilty of homicide but the prosecutor may find it difficult to prove which one beyond reasonable doubt if neither of the defendants admits to the killing. The Domestic Violence, Crime and Victims Act 2004, s. 5, addresses this situation by creating an offence where (a) a child or vulnerable adult dies as a result of the unlawful act of a person who was a member of the same household as the victim and had frequent contact with him; (b) the defendant was such a person at the time of the act; (c) there was a significant risk of serious physical harm being caused to the victim by the unlawful act of such a person; and (d) either the defendant was the person whose act caused the victim's death, or the defendant was, or ought to have been aware of the risk mentioned in (c), failed to take such steps as he could reasonably have been expected to take to protect the victim from the risk, and the act occurred in circumstances of the kind that the defendant foresaw or ought to have foreseen. If in force, would this Act have changed the result in *Lowe*?

(b) The act must be unlawful in the sense that it is criminal

A tortious act causing death is not enough to sustain liability for constructive manslaughter. It must be an act unlawful on the ground that it is a criminal offence. Moreover, it must be an act unlawful in itself. It must not be a lawful act which is unlawful only because it is performed dangerously (e.g. driving offences). However, such acts may form the basis of a conviction for gross negligence manslaughter if the actor's performance was particularly reprehensible.

Andrews v *Director of Public Prosecutions*
[1937] AC 576, House of Lords

LORD ATKIN: ... There is an obvious difference in the law of manslaughter between doing an unlawful act and doing a lawful act with a degree of carelessness which the Legislature makes criminal. If it were otherwise a man who killed another while driving without due care and attention would ex necessitate commit manslaughter ....

■ NOTES AND QUESTIONS

1. What Lord Atkin means is that to be guilty of manslaughter the prosecution must prove that the act performed by D was unlawful in itself (e.g. an assault). If it is unlawful only because it is performed carelessly then the proper charge is manslaughter by gross negligence which will not succeed unless the jury are satisfied the carelessness was extreme. Is this a cogent distinction? Consider:

   A. A drives his car at B hoping to frighten him. By mistake the car hits B killing him. Is it appropriate to charge unlawful act manslaughter. What is the unlawful act?

   B. A overtakes C on a dangerous bend. He crashes into B, a cyclist, who is coming from the opposite direction. Should the fact that A is guilty of careless driving or dangerous driving is not relevant in this context. Driving, unlike assault, is not unlawful in itself. The only possible charge is, therefore, gross negligence manslaughter. To be guilty of this form of manslaughter the jury must be convinced that A's carelessness is of such a high degree that he deserves to be held accountable for the death.

2. An act is not 'unlawful' if it is justified, as it might be if the defendant struck a fatal blow to the victim in self-defence. In *Slingsby* [1995] Crim LR 570 the accused managed to inflict some serious internal injuries on the deceased with a signet ring in the course of violent but entirely consensual sexual activity. She died later of septicaemia consequent upon the injuries. The Crown Court judge ruled that since the injuries were not deliberately inflicted and were an accidental by-product of consensual conduct there was no assault upon which to support a conviction for manslaughter. Was the outcome correct? Would it matter if the defendant was aware of the potential dangerousness of the ring?

3. Whether the defendant has committed an unlawful act is a jury question and the court may not decide the issue on its own authority. See *R* v *Jennings* [1990] Crim LR 588.

Both the *mens rea* and the *actus reus* of the unlawful act must be proved:

R v Lamb
[1967] 2 QB 981, Court of Appeal

SACHS LJ: . . . The defendant, Terence Walter Lamb, aged 25, had become possessed of a Smith & Wesson revolver. It was a revolver in the literal old-fashioned sense, having a five-chambered cylinder which rotated clockwise each time the trigger was pulled. The defendant, in jest, with no intention to do any harm pointed the revolver at the deceased, his best friend, when it had two bullets in the chambers, but neither bullet was in the chamber opposite the barrel. His friend was similarly treating the incident as a joke. The defendant then pulled the trigger and thus killed his friend, still having no intention to fire the revolver. The reason why the pulling of the trigger produced that fatal result was that its pulling rotated the cylinder and so placed a bullet opposite the barrel so that it was struck by the striking pin or hammer.

The defendant's defence was that, as neither bullet was opposite the barrel, he thought they were in such chambers that the striking pin could not hit them; that he was unaware that the pulling of the trigger would bring one bullet into the firing position opposite the barrel; and that the killing was thus an accident. There was not only no dispute that that was what he in fact thought, but the mistake he made was one which three experts agreed was natural for somebody who was not aware of the way the revolver mechanism worked . . . . The trial judge took the view that the pointing of the revolver and the pulling of the trigger was something which could of itself be unlawful even if there was no attempt to alarm or intent to injure . . . .

[Prosecution counsel] had at all times put forward the correct view that for the act to be unlawful it must constitute at least what he then termed 'a technical assault.' In this court moreover he rightly conceded that there was no evidence to go to the jury of any assault of any kind. Nor did he feel able to submit that the acts of the defendant were on any other ground unlawful in the criminal sense of that word. Indeed no such submission could in law be made: if, for instance, the pulling of the trigger had had no effect because the striking mechanism or the ammunition had been defective no offence would have been committed by the defendant.

Another way of putting it is that *mens rea*, being now an essential ingredient in manslaughter...that could not in the present case be established in relation to the first ground except by proving that element of intent without which there can be no assault.

Appeal allowed.

■ NOTES AND QUESTIONS

1. Is the decision in *Lamb* based on the fact that the victim was not put in fear (a requirement of the crime of assault), or the fact that there was no assault because the defendant lacked the *mens rea* of that crime?

(c) A dangerous act

Not all unlawful acts support a conviction for manslaughter. The act must also pose a danger of harm.

R v Church

[1965] 2 All ER 72, Court of Criminal Appeal

EDMUND DAVIES J: ... The facts may be shortly stated. On Sunday, May 31, 1964, the dead body of Mrs Nott was found in the River Ouse within a few yards of the appellant's van which stood near the bank. The corpse bore the marks of grave injuries. The face had been battered, the hyoid bone had been broken and there had been some degree of manual strangulation. These injuries were likely to have caused unconsciousness and eventually death, but they were inflicted a half-hour or an hour before death supervened and did not in fact cause it. According to the medical evidence, her injuries were inflicted not long before Mrs Nott was thrown into the river, but she was alive when that was done, she continued to breathe for an appreciable time afterwards, and the eventual cause of death was drowning. When the appellant was first interviewed about the matter he lied, but ultimately signed a statement admitting complicity in the death. He then said that he had taken Mrs Nott to his van for sexual purposes, that he was unable to satisfy her and she then reproached him and slapped his face; that they then had a fight during which he knocked her out and thereafter she only moaned. The statement continued:

'I was shaking her to wake her for about half-an-hour, but she didn't wake up, so I panicked and dragged her out of the van and put her in the river.'

He repeated this account at his trial and then said for the first time, 'I thought she was dead'.
...

(c) *An unlawful act causing death.* Two passages in the summing up are here material. They are these:

(i)—If, by an unlawful act of violence done deliberately to the person of another, that other is killed, the killing is manslaughter even though the accused never intended either death or grievous bodily harm to result. If [the deceased] was alive, as she was, when he threw her in the river, what he did was a deliberate act of throwing a living body into the river. That is an unlawful killing and it does not matter whether he believed she was dead, or not, and that is my direction to you.

and (ii)—

I would suggest to you, though, of course, it is for you to approach your task as you think fit, that a convenient way of approaching it would be to say: What do we think about this defence that he honestly believed the [deceased] to be dead? If you think that it is true, why then, as I have told you, your proper verdict would be one of manslaughter, not murder.

Such a direction is not lacking in authority...Nevertheless, in the judgment of this court [that] was a misdirection. It amounted to telling the jury that, whenever any unlawful act is committed in relation to a human being which resulted in death there must be, at least, a conviction for manslaughter. This might at one time have been regarded as good law. It appears to this court, however, that the passage of years has achieved a transformation in this branch of the law and, even in relation to manslaughter, a degree of mens rea has become recognised as essential. To define it is a difficult task, and in *Andrews* v *Director of Public Prosecutions* [1937] AC 576 Lord Atkin spoke of 'the element of "unlawfulness" which is the elusive factor'. Stressing that we are here leaving entirely out of account those ingredients of homicide which might justify a verdict of manslaughter on the grounds of (a) criminal negligence, or (b) provocation or (c) diminished responsibility, the conclusion of this court is that an unlawful act causing the death of another cannot, simply because it is an unlawful act, render a manslaughter verdict inevitable. For such a verdict inexorably to follow, the unlawful act must be such as all sober and reasonable people would inevitably recognise must subject the other person to, at least, the risk of some harm resulting therefrom, albeit not serious harm. See, for example, *R* v *Franklin* (1883) 15 Cox CC 163, *R* v *Senior* [1899] 1 QB 283.

If such be the test, as we adjudge it to be, then it follows that, in our view, it was a misdirection to tell the jury simpliciter that it mattered nothing for manslaughter whether or not the appellant believed Mrs Nott to be dead when he threw her into the river ....

■ NOTES AND QUESTIONS

1. According to the court, the unlawful act has to be such that 'all sober and reasonable people would inevitably recognise [it as an act which] must subject the other person to, at least, the risk of some harm resulting therefrom, albeit not serious harm'. In *Attorney-General's Reference (No. 3 of 1994)*, Lord Hope of Craighead stated: 'Dangerousness in this context is not a high standard. All it requires is that it was an act which was likely to injure another person.' The test is an objective one; actual foresight by the defendant of danger to others is not required; what is critical is the perception of the reasonable man. If so, why did the court in *Church* deem it a misdirection for the trial judge to have told the jury that the defendant's belief as to whether the victim was dead at the time that he threw her into the river mattered nothing?

2. What if it could be shown that the defendant was not a reasonable man; that, for example, he was mentally retarded? Is it just to hold a defendant to the standard of the reasonable man if the defendant is incapable through no fault of his own of achieving such a standard?

The harm which the reasonable person must be able to foresee is physical harm, but shock which produces physical injury may suffice if the other elements of the offence are present.

R v Dawson

(1985) 81 Cr App R 150, Court of Appeal

After midnight one night two masked men, one carrying a pickaxe handle and another armed with a replica gun, while a third kept watch, demanded money from a 60-year-old petrol filling station attendant who, unknown to them, suffered from heart disease. The attendant pressed the alarm button and the three men fled. Shortly after the police arrived, the attendant collapsed and died from a heart attack.

WATKINS LJ: ... It has, in our experience, been generally understood that the harm referred to in the second element of the offence of manslaughter, namely, the unlawful act, must be one that all sober and reasonable people would realise was likely to cause some, albeit not serious, harm, means physical harm....

However, there seems to us to be no sensible reason why shock produced by fright should not come within the definition of harm in this context. From time to time one hears the expression 'frightened to death' without thinking that the possibility of such event occurring would be an affront to reason or medical knowledge. Shock can produce devastating and lasting effects, for instance upon the nervous system. That is surely harm, i.e. injury to the person. Why not harm in this context?

...[The judge] directed the jury that a definition of harm was 'emotional disturbance which is detrimental produced by terror'. He had, as we have seen from a transcript of discussion between him and counsel, intended to direct the jury that a definition of harm for present purposes was emotional *and* physical disturbance produced by terror. We think it was unfortunate that the judge, probably through inadvertence, used the disjunctive 'or.' As it was, the jury were left with a choice. Which they chose and acted upon we cannot tell. If they acted upon the basis that emotional disturbance was enough to constitute harm then, in our judgment, they would have done so upon a misdirection. Emotional disturbance does not occur to us as sensibly descriptive of injury or harm to the person through the operation of shock produced by terror or fright; morever, we do not think the word 'deterimental' assists to clarify whatever the expression 'emotional disturbance' is meant to convey. The further phrase used, namely, 'some such disturbance which would be bad for him' is likewise not helpful.

In his endeavours to give the jury appropriate guidance upon the meaning of harm within the facts of this case the judge was sailing uncharted seas. We have every sympathy with him. Unfortunately we think that what he said, other than the use of the phrase 'physical disturbance which is detrimental' (this was, we think, by itself, though easier to understand, inadequate) could have led the jury to contemplate merely a disturbance of the emotions as harm sufficient for the purpose of the second element when clearly, in our view, it is not.

In our judgment, a proper direction would have been that the requisite harm is caused if the unlawful act so shocks the victim to cause him physical injury.

■ NOTES AND QUESTIONS

1. The reasonable person is taken to know facts known to the defendant or which would be evident to the reasonable bystander. In *Dawson* Watkins LJ stated:

   We look finally at the direction, 'That is to say all reasonable people who knew the facts that you know.' What the jury knew included, of course, the undisputed fact that the deceased had a very bad heart which at any moment could have ceased to function. It may be the judge did not intend that this fact should be included in the phrase 'the facts that you know.' If that was so, it is regrettable that he did not make it clear. By saying as he did, it is argued 'including the fact that the gun was a replica' and so on, the jury must have taken him to be telling them that all facts known to them, including the heart condition, should be taken into account in performing what is undoubtedly an objective test. We think there was a grave danger of that.

   This test can only be undertaken upon the basis of the knowledge gained by a sober and reasonable man as though he were present at the scene of and watched the unlawful act being performed and who knows that, as in the present case, an unloaded replica gun was in use, but that the victim may have thought it was a loaded gun in working order. In other words, he has the same knowledge as the man attempting to rob and no more. It was never suggested that any of these appellants knew that their victim had a bad heart. They knew nothing about him.

   A jury must be informed by the judge when trying the offence of manslaughter what facts they may and those which they may not use for the purpose of performing the test in the second element of this offence....

2. Is there tension between the decision in *Dawson* and the general rule that one must take one's victim as one finds her?

3. In *R v Watson* [1989] 2 All ER 865, the Court of Appeal stated that the jury could take into account facts acquired by a defendant during the course of the crime. In *Watson* the defendants, two burglars, discovered that the resident of the house which they were burgling was an old and frail lady. An hour and a half after the crime she died of a heart attack. The Court of Appeal held that the defendants should be credited with knowledge of the victim's condition, even though they became aware of it only after the break-in.

4. In *R v Carey and Ors* [2006] EWCA Crim 17, the Court of Appeal indicated that, in respect of a charge of unlawful act manslaughter, the attributes of the victim could be relevant in assessing whether the unlawful act was dangerous.

(d) The effect of intoxication

Where intoxication would not prevent a conviction of the defendant for the alleged unlawful act, it follows that he or she may also be convicted of manslaughter if death ensues.

R v Lipman
[1970] 1 QB 152, Court of Appeal

WIDGERY LJ:...Both the defendant and the victim were addicted to drugs, and on the evening of September 16, 1967, both took a quantity of a drug known as LSD. Early on the morning of September 18, the defendant, who is a United States citizen, hurriedly booked out of his hotel and left the country. On the following day, September 19, the victim's landlord found her dead in her room. She had suffered two blows on the head causing haemorrhage of the brain, but she had died of asphyxia as a result of some eight inches of sheet having been crammed into her mouth.

The defendant was returned to this country by extradition proceedings, and at the trial he gave evidence of having gone with the victim to her room and there experienced what he described as an LSD 'trip'. He explained how he had the illusion of descending to the centre of the earth and being attacked by snakes, with which he had fought. It was not seriously disputed that he had killed the victim in the course of this experience, but he said he had no knowledge of what he was doing and no intention to harm her. He was charged with murder, but the jury evidently accepted that he lacked the necessary intention to kill or to do grievous bodily harm.

...

It was pointed out in this court that [in *R v Lamb* [1967] 2 QB 981] no unlawful act on the part of the prisoner had been proved in the absence of the necessary intent to constitute an assault. But this is intention of a different kind. Even if intent has to be proved to constitute the unlawful act, no specific further intent is required to turn that act into manslaughter. Manslaughter remains a most difficult offence to define because it arises in so many different ways and, as the mental element (if any) required to establish it varies so widely, any general reference to mens rea is apt to mislead.

We can dispose of the present application by reiterating that when the killing results from an unlawful act of the prisoner no specific intent has to be proved to convict of manslaughter, and self-induced intoxication is accordingly no defence. Since in the present case the acts complained of were obviously likely to cause harm to the victim (and did, in fact, kill her) no acquittal was possible and the verdict of manslaughter, at the least, was inevitable.

If and so far as this matter raises a point of law on which the defendant was entitled to appeal without leave, such appeal is dismissed.

■ NOTES AND QUESTIONS

1. What was the unlawful act in *Lipman*? What was the *mens rea* of that crime?

2. Is *Lipman* distinguishable from *Lamb*? How so? See also *O'Driscoll* (1977) 65 Cr App R 50.

(e) Causation – must the act be directed at the victim?

Because constructive manslaughter requires proof of the *mens rea* and *actus reus* of the 'unlawful act', it might be thought that if death follows from the unlawful act, however tenuous the causal link, then the offence would be made out. However, the courts have been reluctant to go this far, which would have meant abandoning general well-established principles of causation.

Attorney-General's Reference (No. 3 of 1994)
[1997] 3 All ER 936, House of Lords

For facts and holding, see p. 157.

LORD HOPE OF CRAIGHEAD: . . . [I]t is enough that the original unlawful and dangerous act, to which the required mental state is related, and the eventual death of the victim are both part of the same sequence of events.

Nor is it necessary, in order to constitute manslaughter, that the death resulted from an unlawful and dangerous act which was done with the intention to cause the victim to sustain harm. This is because it is clear from the authorities that, although the accused must be proved to have intended to do what he did, it is not necessary to prove that he knew that his act was unlawful or dangerous. So it must follow that it is unnecessary to prove that he knew that his act was likely to injure the person who died as a result of it. All that need be proved is that he intentionally did what he did, that the death was caused by it and that, applying an objective test, all sober and reasonable people would recognise the risk that some harm would result. The case of *R v Mitchell* [1983] QB 741 is a good example of this point. During an altercation in a queue at a busy post office the appellant hit a man who fell against an old lady, causing her to fall to the ground. Her leg was broken, with the result that she died later as a result of a pulmonary embolism. The Court of Appeal held that he was rightly convicted of manslaughter, although he had aimed no blow at the lady and had had no other physical contact with her . . . .

In *R v Dalby* [1982] 1 WLR 425, 428H Waller LJ said that, in all the cases of manslaughter by an unlawful and dangerous act, the researches of counsel had failed to find any case where the act which led to the death of the victim was not a direct act. In that case the appellant had supplied to the deceased a number of tablets of a class A controlled drug. A substantial cause of his death was the intravenous consumption of the drug with which he had injected himself on receipt of it from the appellant. The appellant's conviction of manslaughter was quashed on the ground that, where a charge of manslaughter was based on an unlawful and dangerous act, the act must be directed at the victim and likely to cause immediate injury, however slight. In the judgment of the court, the unlawful act of supplying drugs was not an act directed to the person of the deceased, and the supply did not cause any direct injury to him. Waller LJ summarised the effect of the cases to which the court was referred in this way at p. 429C:

> The kind of harm envisaged in all the reported cases of involuntary manslaughter was physical injury of some kind as an immediate and inevitable result of the unlawful act, e.g. a blow on the chin which knocks the victim against a wall causing a fractured skull and death, or threatening with a loaded gun which accidentally fires, or dropping a large stone on a train (*Director of Public Prosecutions v Newbury* [1977] AC 500) or threatening another with an open razor and stumbling with death resulting: *R v Larkin*, 29 Cr App R 18.

But none of the examples which were discussed in *R v Dalby*, which raised a different issue in view of the nature of the unlawful act of supplying the controlled drug, was concerned with the problem which arises here. In each of the cases which were cited as examples of an unlawful and dangerous act causing death which was held to be manslaughter the act was directed at the person who died as a result of it. In *R v Church* [1966] 1 QB 59 the victim was a woman whom the appellant believed to be already dead when, after knocking her semi-conscious, he threw her into a river when she was still alive. In *Director of Public Prosecutions v Newbury* [1977] AC 500 the victim was a train guard who was sitting next to the driver in the front cab when the appellants pushed a paving stone over the parapet of a bridge in the path of the oncoming train. It is important to notice that it was not suggested in that case that it was an essential element, in finding the appellants guilty of manslaughter, that their act was directed at the train guard in particular. It was enough that their act was dangerous because it was likely to injure some person on the train. This can be seen from the words used by the trial judge, Watkins J, who said at p. 502D:

> If that is your conclusion you then proceed to consider whether the next ingredient, as it is called, of this offence of manslaughter has been established. It is this: that the unlawful act was such as all sober and reasonable people would be bound to realise must expose someone such as the guard on this train or, . . . the driver on this train to, at least, the risk of some harm although not serious.

Lord Salmon, in rejecting the argument that the trial judge should have told the jury that they should acquit unless they were satisfied that the appellants had foreseen that they might cause harm to someone by pushing the paving stone off the parapet into the path of the train, said at p. 506G that his direction was completely in accordance with established law. He went on to add this, at p. 506H:

In *R v Larkin* (1942) 29 Cr App R 18, Humphreys J said, at p. 23:

> 'Where the act which a person is engaged in performing is unlawful, then if at the same time it is a dangerous act, that is, an act which is likely to injure another person, and quite inadvertently the doer of the act causes the death of that other person by that act, then he is guilty of manslaughter.'

I agree entirely with Lawton LJ that that is an admirably clear statement of the law which has been applied many times. It makes it plain (a) that an accused is guilty of manslaughter if it is proved that he intentionally did an act which was unlawful and dangerous and that that act inadvertently caused death and (b) that it is unnecessary to prove that the accused knew that the act was unlawful or dangerous.

Although the passage which Lord Salmon quoted from what was said by Humphreys J might be taken as suggesting that the accused's act must have been directed against the other person who dies as a result of it, the circumstances of that case and Lord Salmon's own statement of the law both show that this is not an essential element of the offence. The only questions which need to be addressed are (1) whether the act was done intentionally, (2) whether it was unlawful, (3) whether it was also dangerous because it was likely to cause harm to somebody and (4) whether that unlawful and dangerous act caused the death.

I think, then, that the position can be summarised in this way. The intention which must be discovered is an intention to do an act which is unlawful and dangerous. In this case the act which had to be shown to be an unlawful and dangerous act was the stabbing of the child's mother. There can be no doubt that all sober and reasonable people would regard that act, within the appropriate meaning of this term, as dangerous. It is plain that it was unlawful as it was done with the intention of causing her injury. As the defendant intended to commit that act, all the ingredients necessary for *mens rea* in regard to the crime of manslaughter were established, irrespective of who was the ultimate victim of it. The fact that the child whom the mother was carrying at the time was born alive and then died as a result of the stabbing is all that was needed for the offence of manslaughter when *actus reus*, for that crime was completed by the child's death. The question, once all the other elements are satisfied, is simply one of causation. The defendant must accept all the consequences of his act, so long as the jury are satisfied that he did what he did intentionally, that what he did was unlawful and that, applying the correct test, it was also dangerous. The death of the child was unintentional, but the nature and quality of the act which caused it was such that it was criminal and therefore punishable. In my opinion that is sufficient for the offence of manslaughter. There is no need to look to the doctrine of transferred malice for a solution to the problem raised by this case so far as manslaughter is concerned.

■ NOTES AND QUESTIONS

1. Is the concept of constructive manslaughter misconceived? What justifies convicting a defendant of a homicide offence when the defendant did not intend to kill and was not even reckless in endangering life? Often the death is due to a

fortuity. Would it not make more sense to convict the defendant of the underlying crime, taking into account where appropriate at sentencing the fact that a death resulted? See the discussion on causation in Chapter 2.

2. What does Lord Hope mean when he says that *Dalby* 'raised a different issue in view of the nature of the unlawful act of supplying the controlled drug'?

3. The self-injection cases, where the person on trial for manslaughter supplied the drugs to the victim, who injected himself with fatal results, were considered in Chapter 2 and, more particularly in *R* v *Kennedy*, which discusses the line of cases involving this troublesome fact situation.

(ii) Gross negligence manslaughter

This form of manslaughter is constituted upon proof of a gross breach of a duty of care resulting in death. The elements therefore are as follows:

1. The defendant owed the victim a duty of care.
2. The defendant breached the duty.
3. The breach of duty caused death.
4. The breach of duty was gross.

The classic account of this category of manslaughter is to be found in *R* v *Bateman*:

R v *Bateman*
(1925) 19 Cr App R 8, Court of Criminal Appeal

LORD HEWART LCJ: ... In explaining to juries the test which they should apply to determine whether the negligence, in the particular case, amounted or did not amount to a crime, judges have used many epithets, such as 'culpable,' 'criminal,' 'gross,' 'wicked,' 'clear,' 'complete.' But, whatever epithet be used and whether an epithet be used or not, in order to establish criminal liability the facts must be such that, in the opinion of the jury, the negligence of the accused went beyond a mere matter of compensation between subjects and showed such disregard for the life and safety of others as to amount to a crime against the State and conduct deserving punishment.

R v *Adomako*
[1995] 1 AC 171, House of Lords

LORD MACKAY OF CLASHFERN LC: ... The conviction arose out of the conduct of an eye operation carried out at the Mayday Hospital, Croydon on 4 January 1987. The appellant was, during the latter part of that operation, the anaesthetist in charge of the patient.

The operation was carried out by two surgeons supported by a team of five nurses and a theatre sister. Anaesthesia commenced at about 9.45 a.m. The patient was paralysed by injection of a drug and an endotracheal tube was inserted to enable the patient to breathe by mechanical means. At the start of the operation the anaesthetist was Dr Said, a registrar. An operating department assistant was also present to help him. At about 10.30 a.m. there was a changeover of anaesthetists. The appellant was called to attend and take Dr Said's place following which both Dr Said and his assistant departed to deal with another operation elsewhere in the hospital. Another assistant was called to attend but did not arrive until later.

At approximately 11.05 a.m. a disconnection occurred at the endotracheal tube connection. The supply of oxygen to the patient ceased and this led to cardiac arrest at 11.14 a.m. During this period the appellant failed to notice or remedy the disconnection.

The appellant first became aware that something was amiss when an alarm sounded on the Dinamap machine, which monitors the patient's blood pressure. From the evidence it appears that some 4½ minutes would have elapsed between the disconnection and the sounding of this alarm. When this alarm sounded the appellant responded in various ways by checking the equipment and by administering atropine to raise the patient's pulse. But at no stage before the cardiac arrest did he check the integrity of the endotracheal tube connection. The disconnection itself was not discovered until after resuscitation measures had been commenced.

For the prosecution it was alleged that the appellant was guilty of gross negligence in failing to notice or respond appropriately to obvious signs that a disconnection had occurred and that the patient had ceased to breathe. In particular the prosecution alleged that the appellant had failed to notice at various stages during the period after disconnection and before the arrest either occurred or became inevitable that the patient's chest was not moving, the dials on the mechanical ventilating machine were not operating, the disconnection in the endotracheal tube, that the alarm on the ventilator was not switched on and that the patient was becoming progressively blue. Further the prosecution alleged that the appellant had noticed but failed to understand the correct significance of the fact that during this period the patient's pulse had dropped and the patient's blood pressure had dropped.

...

The jury convicted the appellant of manslaughter by a majority of 11 to 1. The Court of Appeal (Criminal Division) dismissed the appellant's appeal against conviction but certified that a point of law of general public importance was involved in the decision to dismiss the appeal, namely:

> in cases of manslaughter by criminal negligence not involving driving but involving a breach of duty is it a sufficient direction to the jury to adopt the gross negligence test set out by the Court of Appeal in the present case following *Rex* v *Bateman* (1925) 19 Cr App R 8 and *Andrews* v *Director of Public Prosecutions* [1937] AC 576, without reference to the test of recklessness as defined in *Reg* v *Lawrence (Stephen)* [1982] AC 510 or as adapted to the circumstances of the case?

...

The decision of the Court of Appeal is reported sub nom. *R* v *Prentice* [1994] QB 302 along with a number of other cases involving similar questions of law. The Court of Appeal held that except in cases of motor manslaughter the ingredients which had to be proved to establish an offence of involuntary manslaughter by breach of duty were the existence of the duty, a breach of the duty which had caused death and the jury considered to justify a criminal conviction; the jury might properly find gross negligence on proof of indifference to an obvious risk of injury to health or of actual foresight of the risk coupled either with a determination nevertheless to run it or with an intention to avoid it but involving such a high degree of negligence in the attempted avoidance as the jury considered justified conviction or of inattention or failure to advert to a serious risk going beyond mere inadvertence in respect of an obvious and important matter which the defendant's duty demanded he should address; and that, in the circumstances, the appeals of the two junior doctors and the electrician would be allowed and the appeal of the anaesthetist, namely Dr Adomako, would be dismissed. The reason that the Court of Appeal excepted the cases of motor manslaughter and their formulation of the law was the decision of this House in *R* v *Seymour (Edward)* [1983] 2 AC 493 in which it was held that where manslaughter was charged and the circumstances were that the victim was killed as a result of the reckless driving of the defendant on a public highway, the trial judge should give the jury the direction which had been suggested in *R* v *Lawrence (Stephen)* [1982] AC 510 but that it was appropriate also to point out that in order to constitute the offence of manslaughter the risk of death being caused by the manner of the defendant's driving must be very high.

... in my opinion the ordinary principles of the law of negligence apply to ascertain whether or not the defendant has been in breach of a duty of care towards the victim who has died. If such breach of duty is established the next question is whether that breach of duty caused the death of the victim. If so, the jury must go on to consider whether that breach of duty should be characterised as gross negligence and therefore as a crime. This will depend on the seriousness of the breach of duty committed by the defendant in all the circumstances in which the defendant was placed when it occurred. The jury will have to consider whether the extent to which the defendant's conduct departed from the proper standard of care incumbent upon him, involving as it must have done a risk of death to the patient, was such that it should be judged criminal.

It is true that to a certain extent this involves an element of circularity, but in this branch of the law I do not believe that is fatal to its being correct as a test of how far conduct must depart from accepted standards to be characterised as criminal. This is necessarily a question of degree and an attempt to specify that degree more closely is I think likely to achieve only a spurious precision. The essence of the matter which is supremely a jury question is whether having regard to the risk of death involved, the conduct of the defendant was so bad in all the circumstances as to amount in their judgment to a criminal act or omission.

My Lords, the view which I have stated of the correct basis in law for the crime of involuntary manslaughter accords I consider with the criteria stated by counsel although I have not reached the degree of precision in definition which he required, but in my opinion it has been reached so far as practicable and with a result which leaves the matter properly stated for a jury's determination.

My Lords, in my view the law as stated in *R* v *Seymour* [1983] 2 AC 493 should no longer apply since the underlying statutory provisions on which it rested have now been repealed by the Road Traffic Act 1991. It may be that cases of involuntary motor manslaughter will as a result become rare but I consider it unsatisfactory that there should be any exception to the generality of the statement which I have made, since such exception, in my view, gives rise to unnecessary complexity. For example in *Kong Cheuk Kwan* v *The Queen* (1985) 82 Cr App R 18 it would give rise to unnecessary differences between the law applicable to those navigating vessels and the lookouts on the vessels.

I consider it perfectly appropriate that the word 'reckless' should be used in cases of involuntary manslaughter, but as Lord Atkin put it 'in the ordinary connotation of that word.' Examples in which this was done, to my mind, with complete accuracy are *R* v *Stone* [1977] QB 354 and *R* v *West London Coroner, Ex parte Gray* [1988] QB 467.

In my opinion it is quite unnecessary in the context of gross negligence to give the detailed directions with regard to the meaning of the word 'reckless' associated with *R* v *Lawrence* [1982] AC 510. The decision of the Court of Appeal (Criminal Division) in the other cases with which they were concerned at the same time as they heard the appeal in this case indicates that the circumstances in which involuntary manslaughter has to be considered may make the somewhat elaborate and rather rigid directions inappropriate. I entirely agree with the view that the circumstances to which a charge of involuntary manslaughter may apply are so various that it is unwise to attempt to categorise or detail specimen directions. For my part I would not wish to go beyond the description of the basis in law which I have already given.

For these reasons I am of the opinion that this appeal should be dismissed and that the certified question should be answered by saying:

> In cases of manslaughter by criminal negligence involving a breach of duty, it is a sufficient direction to the jury to adopt the gross negligence test set out by the Court of Appeal in the present case following *R* v *Bateman*, 19 Cr App R 8 and *Andrews* v *Director of Public Prosecutions* [1937] AC 576 and that it is not necessary to refer to the definition of recklessness in *R* v *Lawrence* [1982] AC 510, although it is perfectly open to the trial judge to use the word 'reckless' in its ordinary meaning as part of his exposition of the law if he deems it appropriate in the circumstances of the particular case.

Who decides whether a duty of care is owed, judge or jury?

R v Evans

(2009) EWCA 650

For facts see p. 79.

LORD JUDGE CJ . . .

The responsibilities of the judge and jury

37. The authorities in relation to this question have been compendiously collected in an illuminating analysis by Jonathan Herring and Elaine Palser entitled 'The Duty of Care in Gross Negligence Manslaughter' [2007] Crim LR 24. We shall not recite them in this judgment. The thesis is that the current law is unclear. The authors suggest that there are three possible solutions to the question

whether the judge or the jury is responsible in an individual case for deciding whether the defendant owed a duty of care to the deceased: p 25. They are:

"View 1. It is for the judge to decide when in law a duty of care arises. But it is for the jury to decide what the facts are . . . View 2. The jury are to decide not only what the facts are, but also the meaning of duty of care and whether there is a duty of care on those facts. View 3. The definition of the duty of care is shared between a judge and a jury. The judge can decide whether in law there *could* be a duty of care, but if there could it is for the jury to decide whether or not there is . . ."

38. We agree that there is an inconsistency between the authorities, and the court as presently constituted must address and resolve them.

39. The starting point is to reflect on first principles. Subject to any statutory exceptions, in the criminal trial decisions of fact are the exclusive responsibility of the jury and questions of law are for the judge. In principle therefore the existence, or otherwise, of a duty of care or, we would add, a duty to act, is a stark question of law: the question whether the facts establish the existence of the duty is for the jury.

40. In *R* v *Adomako* [1995] 1 AC 171 the essential question related to gross negligence in the context of the professional care of an anaesthetist for his patient during the course of an operation. The duty was plain on ordinary principles of law. It was argued on behalf of the appellant that the jury should have been directed that they had to be satisfied that the defendant owed a duty of care to the deceased. That submission is not directly addressed in the opinion of Lord Mackay of Clashfern LC who observed, at p 187:

'the ordinary principles of the law of negligence apply to ascertain whether or not the defendant has been in breach of a duty of care towards the victim who has died. If such breach of duty is established the next question is whether that breach of duty caused the death of the victim. If so, the jury must go on to consider whether that breach of duty should be characterised as gross negligence . . .'

41. Following *R* v *Adomako*, the existence or otherwise of a duty of care, and its nature, was closely addressed in *R* v *Wacker* [2003] QB 1207, where it was argued that the application of the 'ordinary principles of the law of negligence' in their full rigour extinguished the duty relationship which would otherwise have been owed by the driver of the lorry to those travelling within the container. The court was unimpressed with the submission that all the wider manifestations of tortious liability for negligence should apply to gross negligence manslaughter, but *R* v *Wacker* confirmed, if authority were needed for this purpose, the plain fact that in the context of the existence of a duty of care or duty to act there is, for the reasons given earlier in this judgment, a close correlation between the civil and criminal law, and that in relation to the question whether a duty of care or duty to act is owed by one individual to another, the question is a question of law.

42. In *R* v *Willoughby* [2005] 1 WLR 1880 the court directly addressed what was said to be a 'conflict' between the authorities on the question whether the judge or jury should decide whether such a duty existed. It was held, after examining the words used by Lord Mackay LC in *R* v *Adomako* [1995] 1 AC 171, that this issue, as well as the issues of breach of duty and assessment of criminality, were matters for the jury.

43. We are troubled by this conclusion. It depends on the view that this was indeed the effect of Lord Mackay LC's observations in *R* v *Adomako*. We are unable to agree that this interpretation is correct. It was suggested in *R* v *Willoughby* that Lord Mackay's use of the words 'the jury must go on' carried the clear implication that the existence or otherwise of a duty of care would usually be a matter for the jury. However it is plain that Lord Mackay was anxious to avoid over elaboration, and we find it difficult to agree that his use of colloquial language ('the jury must go on') was intended to bear the weight laid upon it by *R* v *Willoughby*. Our view is reinforced by Lord Mackay's later observation [1995] 1 AC 171, 189 that "The task of trial judges in setting out for the jury the issues of fact and the relevant law in cases of this class is a difficult and demanding one".

44. In our view if Lord Mackay LC had been intending to depart from what we have described as first principles he would have said so and explained why. Moreover, although we agree that before a conviction can be returned the jury must indeed be sure that the defendant owed the necessary duty of care, this begs the question whether the conclusions of the jury should follow on the basis of their findings of fact or whether the jury is required or indeed entitled to make a decision of law. Notwithstanding the terms of the judgment, in his valuable commentary on *R v Willoughby* [2005] Crim LR 389, 392, Professor Ormerod suggests that 'The present decision does not relegate the duty question to one of fact. It remains a question of law, and the jury are to be directed on what the law is—ie whether a duty exists—if they find certain facts to be established.' His reasoning is persuasive, and consistent with principle.

45. In some cases, such as those arising from a doctor/patient relationship where the existence of the duty is not in dispute, the judge may well direct the jury that a duty of care exists. Such a direction would be proper. But if, for example, the doctor were on holiday at the material time, and the deceased asked a casual question over a drink, it may very well be that the question whether a doctor/patient relationship existed, and accordingly whether a duty of care arose, would be in dispute. In any cases where the issue is in dispute, and therefore in more complex cases, and assuming that the judge has found that it would be open to the jury to find that there was a duty of care, or a duty to act, the jury should be directed that if facts a + b and/or c or d are established, then in law a duty will arise, but if facts x or y or z were present, the duty would be negatived. In this sense, of course, the jury is deciding whether the duty situation has been established. In our judgment this is the way in which *R v Willoughby* should be understood and, understood in this way, no potential problems arising from article 6 and article 7 of the Convention are engaged.

46. This conclusion seems to us to accord with the principles which would obtain if, in the extremely unlikely event of an order for trial by jury, the issues arose in a civil action. The current edition of *Halsbury's Laws of England*, 4th ed reissue, vol 33 (1997), 'Negligence', para 685 addresses the functions of judge and jury in stark terms:

> "In those rare cases where there is still a jury in an action of negligence the respective functions of judge and jury are as follows: the judge decides whether the defendant owed a duty to the plaintiff, directs the jury on the standard of care required, decides whether there is any evidence on which a jury may infer that that standard has not been attained, instructs the jury on causation and remoteness, and lays down the principles for assessing damages. The jury decides whether the conduct of the parties fell below the standard of care as laid down by the judge, decides issues of causation and assesses the damages."

47. We also note for present purposes the provisions of the Corporate Manslaughter and Corporate Homicide Act 2007 which are concerned with gross breaches of a 'relevant duty of care' owed to the deceased. Section 2(5) provides: 'For the purposes of this Act, whether a particular organisation owes a duty of care to a particular individual is a question of law. The judge must make any findings of fact necessary to decide that question.' In the context of the criminal law, the proposition that the trial judge should decide disputed questions of fact and then apply them to the relevant questions of law is, to put it no higher, unusual. However for present purposes it would, we believe, be remarkable if appropriate statutory provisions would not have been made in relation to questions of law if it was in the faintest degree possible that Parliament believed that the jury might decide a question of law after findings of fact made by the judge. The silence of section 2(5) on this point must be deliberate. Its effect in this statute is that the judge must make the necessary findings of fact and also decide the relevant question of law. This provision, and its very enactment, is, we suggest, entirely consistent with our understanding of first principles.

48. In our judgment the jury should not have been left to decide the question whether the appellant owed a duty of care to the deceased. The judge is not to be criticised for doing so. He was following *R v Willoughby* [2005] 1 WLR 1880 as it was commonly understood.

49. The important question however is whether his direction renders the conviction unsafe. It does not. On our analysis there was a plain case to answer. On the facts actually found by the jury

on the supply issue, and the undisputed facts, in our judgment the appellant was under a plain and obvious duty to take reasonable steps to assist or provide assistance for Carly. The jury were sure, both in law and in fact on this point: so, as a matter of law, are we. The fact that the jury was sure as a matter of law may help to reinforce our conclusion, but in the ultimate analysis is irrelevant to it. The remaining ingredients of the offence were proved. Accordingly this appeal against conviction will be dismissed.

■ NOTES AND QUESTIONS

1. At one time the courts recognised a separate category of 'reckless' manslaughter which incorporated an 'objective' test of recklessness (see *R* v *Seymour* [1983] 2 AC 493). It is unclear whether the crime of reckless manslaughter survives the decision in *Adomako*, but if it does, it would now (in light of the decision in *R* v *G*, (Ch. 3) presumably require a subjective awareness of the risk of death or grievous bodily harm in order for the defendant to be convicted. In most cases such a killing would amount to unlawful act manslaughter. Procedurally, however, it might be easier for a jury to convict a defendant of reckless manslaughter in cases where they were convinced the defendant foresaw the risk of death or grievous bodily harm.

   In *Attorney-General's Reference (No. 2 of 1999)* [2000] QB 796, the Court of Appeal stated that 'evidence of . . . state of mind is not a pre-requisite to conviction for manslaughter by gross negligence'. The Court added, however, that 'there may be cases where the defendant's state of mind is relevant to the jury's consideration when assessing the grossness and criminality of his conduct'.

In *R* v *Misra and Srivastava* [2004] EWCA Crim 2375 the test of gross negligence manslaughter as articulated in *Adomako* was challenged as being in breach of the European Convention on Human Rights.

R v *Misra and Srivastava*
[2004] EWCA Crim 2375, Court of Appeal

The victim was Sean Phillips. He underwent unremarkable surgery to repair his patella tendon at Southampton General Hospital on 23 June 2000. Unfortunately he became infected with staphylococcus aureus. The condition was untreated. There was a gradual build up of poison within his body, which culminated in toxic shock syndrome (TSST1) from which he died on 27 June. The appellants were senior house officers involved in the post-operative care of the deceased during the period beginning on the evening of 23 June until the afternoon of 25 June. It was alleged that each was grossly negligent in respect of the medical treatment he provided to the deceased and that these failures caused the death. Each was convicted of manslaughter by gross negligence. . . .

It is convenient now to address the argument that the decision in *R* v *G and Another* should lead us to reassess whether gross negligence manslaughter should now be replaced by and confined to reckless manslaughter. As we have shown, precisely this argument by Lord Williams of Mostyn was rejected in *Adomako*. We also note, first, that Parliament has not given effect to possible reforms on this topic discussed by the Law Commission and, second, notwithstanding that *Adomako* was cited in argument in *R* v *G and Another*, it was not subjected to any reservations or criticisms. Indeed in his speech Lord Bingham of Cornhill emphasised that in *R* v *G* he was not addressing the meaning of 'reckless' in any other statutory or common law context than section 1(1) and (2) of the Criminal Damage Act 1971. In these circumstances, although we gave leave to Mr Gledhill to amend his grounds of appeal to enable him to deploy the argument, we reject it.

We can now reflect on Mr Gledhill's associated contention that if recklessness is not a necessary ingredient of this offence, the decision in *Attorney General's Reference (No. 2 of 1999)* [2000] QB 796 led to the unacceptable conclusion that manslaughter by gross negligence did not require proof of any specific state of mind, and that the defendant's state of mind was irrelevant. In our judgment the submission is based on a narrow reading of the decision that a defendant may properly be convicted of gross negligence manslaughter in the absence of evidence as to his state of mind. However when it is available, such evidence is not irrelevant to the issue of gross negligence. It will often be a critical factor in the decision (see *R (Rowley)* v *DPP* [2003] EWHC 693). In *Adomako* itself, Lord Mackay directed attention to 'all' of the circumstances in which the defendant was placed: he did not adopt, or endorse, or attempt to redefine the list of states of mind to which Lord Taylor CJ referred in *Prentice*, which was not in any event 'exhaustive' of possible relevant states of mind. It is therefore clear that the defendant is not to be convicted without fair consideration of all the relevant circumstances in which his breach of duty occurred. In each case, of course, the circumstances are fact-specific.

Mr Gledhill nevertheless contended that even so, the problem of mens rea remains. This, he argued was a necessary, but absent ingredient of the offence. We have reflected, of course, that if the defendant intends death or really serious harm, and acts in such a way to cause either, and death results, he would be guilty of murder. If he intends limited injury, and causes death, he would be guilty of manslaughter in any event. We are here concerned with the defendant who does not intend injury, but who in all the contemporaneous circumstances is grossly negligent. As a matter of strict language, 'mens rea' is concerned with an individual defendant's state of mind. Speaking generally, negligence is concerned with his failure to behave in accordance with the standards required of the reasonable man. Looked at in this way, the two concepts are distinct. However the term 'mens rea' is also used to describe the ingredient of fault or culpability required before criminal liability for the defendant's actions may be established. In *Sweet* v *Parsley* [1970] AC 132, Lord Reid explained that there were occasions when gross negligence provided the 'necessary mental element' for a serious crime. Manslaughter by gross negligence is not an absolute offence. The requirement for gross negligence provides the necessary element of culpability.

We can now return to the argument based on circularity and uncertainty, and the application of Articles 6 and 7 of the ECHR. The most important passages in the speech of Lord Mackay on the issue of circularity read:

> '... The jury must go on to consider whether that breach of duty should be characterised as gross negligence and therefore as a crime. This will depend on the seriousness of the breach of duty committed by the defendant in all the circumstances in which the defendant was placed when it occurred. The jury will have to consider whether the extent to which the defendant's conduct departed from the proper standard of care incumbent upon him, involving as it must have done a risk of death to the patient, was such that it should be judged criminal.
>
> It is true that, to a certain extent, this involves an element of circularity, but in this branch of the law I do not believe that is fatal to its being correct as a test of how far conduct must depart from accepted standards to be characterised as criminal ... The essence of the matter which is supremely a jury question is whether, having regard to the risk of death involved, the conduct of the defendant was so bad in all the circumstances as to amount in their judgment to a criminal act or omission.'

Mr Gledhill suggested that this passage demonstrated that an additional specific ingredient of this offence was that the jury had to decide whether the defendant's conduct amounted to a crime. If the jury could, or was required to, define the offence for itself, and accordingly might do so on some unaccountable or unprincipled or unexplained basis, to adopt Bacon, the sound given by the law would indeed be uncertain, and would then strike without warning. Mr Gledhill's argument then would be compelling.

Looking at the authorities since *Bateman*, the purpose of referring to the differences between civil and criminal liability, whether in the passage in Lord Mackay's speech to which we have just referred, or in directions to the jury, is to highlight that the burden on the prosecution goes beyond proof of negligence for which compensation would be payable. Negligence of that degree could not lead to a conviction for manslaughter. The negligence must be so bad, 'gross', that if all the other ingredients of the offence are proved, then it amounts to a crime and is punishable as such.

This point was addressed by Lord Atkin in *Andrews* at p. 582, when he referred to *Williamson* (1807) 3 C&P 635:

'.... where a man who practiced as an accoucheur, owing to a mistake in his observation of the actual symptoms, inflicted on a patient terrible injuries from which she died.' To substantiate that charge—namely, manslaughter—Lord Ellenborough said, 'The prisoner must have been guilty of criminal misconduct, arising either from the grossest ignorance or the most criminal inattention.' The word 'criminal' in any attempt to define a crime is perhaps not the most helpful: but it is plain that the Lord Chief Justice meant to indicate to the jury a high degree of negligence. So at a much later date in *Bateman* [1925] 18 Cr. App. R 8 a charge of manslaughter was made against a qualified medical practitioner in similar circumstances to those of Williamson's case.... I think with respect that the expressions used are not, indeed they were probably not intended to be, a precise definition of the crime.'

Accordingly, the value of references to the criminal law in this context is that they avoid the danger that the jury may equate what we may describe as 'simple' negligence, which in relation to manslaughter would not be a crime at all, with negligence which involves a criminal offence. In short, by bringing home to the jury the extent of the burden on the prosecution, they ensure that the defendant whose negligence does not fall within the ambit of the criminal law is not convicted of a crime. They do not alter the essential ingredients of this offence. A conviction cannot be returned if the negligent conduct is or may be less than gross. If however the defendant is found by the jury to have been grossly negligent, then, if the jury is to act in accordance with its duty, he must be convicted. This is precisely what Lord Mackay indicated when, in the passage already cited, he said, '... The jury must go on to consider whether that breach of duty should be characterised as gross negligence and *therefore* as a crime' (our emphasis). The decision whether the conduct was criminal is described not as 'the' test, but as 'a' test as to how far the conduct in question must depart from accepted standards to be 'characterised as criminal'. On proper analysis, therefore, the jury is not deciding whether the particular defendant ought to be convicted on some unprincipled basis. The question for the jury is not whether the defendant's negligence was gross, and whether, *additionally*, it was a crime, but whether his behaviour was grossly negligent and *consequently* criminal. This is not a question of law, but one of fact, for decision in the individual case.

On examination, this represents one example, among many, of problems which juries are expected to address on a daily basis. They include equally difficult questions, such as whether a defendant has acted dishonestly, by reference to contemporary standards, or whether he has acted in reasonable self-defence, or, when charged with causing death by dangerous driving, whether the standards of his driving fell far below what should be expected of a competent and careful driver. These examples represent the commonplace for juries. Each of these questions could be said to be vague and uncertain. If he made enquiries in advance, at most an individual would be told the principle of law which the jury would be directed to apply: he could not be advised what a jury would think of the individual case, and how it would be decided. That involves an element of uncertainty about the outcome of the decision-making process, but not unacceptable uncertainty about the offence itself.

In our judgment the law is clear. The ingredients of the offence have been clearly defined, and the principles decided in the House of Lords in *Adomako*. They involve no uncertainty. The hypothetical citizen, seeking to know his position, would be advised that, assuming he owed a duty of care to the deceased which he had negligently broken, and that death resulted, he would be liable to conviction for manslaughter if, on the available evidence, the jury was satisfied that his negligence was gross. A doctor would be told that grossly negligent treatment of a patient which exposed him or her to the risk of death, and caused it, would constitute manslaughter.

After Lord Williams' sustained criticism of the offence of manslaughter by gross negligence, the House of Lords in *Adomako* clarified the relevant principles and the ingredients of this offence. Although, to a limited extent, Lord Mackay accepted that there was an element of circularity in the process by which the jury would arrive at its verdict, the element of circularity which he identified did not then and does not now result in uncertainty which offends against Article 7, nor if we may say so, any principle of common law. Gross negligence manslaughter is not incompatible with the ECHR. Accordingly the appeal arising from the question certified by the trial judge must be dismissed.

■ **NOTES AND QUESTIONS**

1. In the course of its opinion in *Misra and Srivastava* the Court of Appeal clarified an issue about which there had been some confusion after *Adomako*; namely whether, for gross negligence manslaughter, the prosecution needed to prove that the risk created by the defendant was that of death, or simply of serious injury. The Court of Appeal indicated that only a risk of death will suffice. In light of the fact that an intent to cause really serious injury will satisfy the *mens rea* of murder, why should it be necessary to prove that there was a risk of death for purposes of establishing the lesser offence of gross negligent manslaughter?

(iii) Reform of the law of manslaughter

In 2000, the government published a consultation paper on reforming the law of involuntary manslaughter which drew on a 1996 Law Commission Report (No. 239) on the same topic. The government proposed the creation of two separate offences of unintentional killing – 'reckless killing' and 'killing by gross carelessness'. That Consultation paper did not lead to a formal bill. In 2005, the Law Commission reconsidered the topic in Law Commission Consultation Paper No. 177. Its proposals in a slightly modified form were adopted in its final report on homicide (LC 304):

9.9 We recommend that manslaughter should encompass:

    (1) killing another person through gross negligence ("gross negligence manslaughter"); or

    (2) killing another person:

        (a) through the commission of a criminal act intended by the defendant to cause injury, or

        (b) through the commission of a criminal act that the defendant was aware involved a serious risk of causing some injury ("criminal act manslaughter"). (Paragraph 2.163)

9.11 We recommend that 'awareness' of risk should be understood to involve consciously adverting to a risk. (Paragraph 3.35)

9.12 We recommend that a risk should be regarded as 'serious' if it is more than insignificant or remote. (Paragraph 3.40)

9.13 We recommend the adoption of the definition of causing death by gross negligence given in our earlier report on manslaughter:

    (1) a person by his or her conduct causes the death of another;

    (2) a risk that his or her conduct will cause death would be obvious to a reasonable person in his or her position;

    (3) he or she is capable of appreciating that risk at the material time; and

    (4) his or her conduct falls far below what can reasonably be expected of him or her in the circumstances. (Paragraph 3. 60)

■ **NOTES AND QUESTIONS**

1. How, if at all, do the Law Commission's proposals for reform change the present law of manslaughter.

2. Consider a hypothetical case given in Wilson, CLDT (2008).

As a joke, A removes a ladder leaning against a first floor balcony on which W, a window cleaner, is working. He knows the window cleaner will not be able to get down to the ground without jumping, and that he may break a leg trying to do so, but the height is not enough to alert him nor a reasonable person in his position to a significant risk of death. W makes the jump and dies as a result of breaking his back.

Consider A's liability for manslaughter under (a) the present law, (b) under the law as recommended by the Law Commission. Would it make any difference if A acted without thinking of the risk that V might break his leg?

SECTION 4: CORPORATE MANSLAUGHTER

Many deaths occur in the workplace. The victims may be employees or members of the public (as where a train crashes, killing passengers). Even where the deaths in question are attributable to the company's arguable gross negligence, the company is typically charged with a violation of the Health and Safety at Work etc. Act 1974. See, e.g., *R v British Steel Ltd* [1995] ICR 586. Part of the reluctance to charge the company with manslaughter has been the absence of a coherent theory whereby a company, a fictitious entity, can be held to have committed this crime. Whether a company could be guilty of manslaughter remained an unanswered question as recently as 1990. The capsize of the Herald of Free Enterprise outside of Zeebrugge, with a death toll of nearly 200 passengers and crew, caused much public outcry and gave rise to a prosecution for manslaughter against the ship's parent company, P&O. The Sheen Committee, which had investigated the disaster, concluded that the company was 'infected with sloppiness' from top to bottom. But would this be enough to warrant a prosecution for gross negligence manslaughter? And if so, could a company be convicted of this offence?

P&O European Ferries (Dover) Ltd
(1991) 93 Cr App R 72, Central Criminal Court

TURNER J: . . . The main thrust of the argument for the company in support of the submission that the four counts of manslaughter in this indictment should be quashed was not merely that English law does not recognise the offence of corporate manslaughter but that, as a matter of positive English Law, manslaughter can only be committed when one natural person kills another natural person. Hence it was no accident that there is no record of any corporation or non-natural person having been successfully prosecuted for manslaughter in any English Court. It was, however, accepted that there is no conceptual difficulty in attributing a criminal state of mind to a corporation. The broad argument advanced on behalf of the prosecution was that, there being no all embracing statutory definition of murder or manslaughter, there is, in principle, no reason why a corporation, or other non-natural person, cannot be found guilty of most offences in the criminal calendar. The exceptions to such a broad proposition could be found either in the form of punishment, which would be inappropriate for a corporation, or in the very personal nature of individual crimes or categories of crime such as offences under the Sexual Offences Act, bigamy and, arguably, perjury. It was further argued that the definitions of homicide to be found in the works of such as *Coke, Hale, Blackstone* and *Stephen* and which were strongly relied upon by the company, were and were not intended to be exclusive, but reflected the historical fact that, at the dates when these definitions originated, the concept of criminal liability of a corporation, just as their very existence, was not within the contemplation of the courts or the writers of the legal treatises referred to. Before the days when corporate crime was in contemplation, it can be a matter of no surprise to find that the definition of homicide did not include the possibility of a corporation committing such a crime. As recently as 1701 Sir John Holt, CJ is reported as having said: 'A corporation is not indictable but the particular members of it are.' Reported in 12 Mod 559. History does not, however, relate what was the subject matter of the litigation which provoked the above *dictum*.

The prosecution advanced an alternative argument to the effect that, if it were necessary that the death be, in fact, caused by a human being, then given the modern doctrine of 'identification,' as to which see below, if the perpetrator of the act who was a human being which caused death could be treated as the embodiment of the corporation, then to that extent the test would be satisfied. It is obvious however, that this alternative argument detracts from the force of the main argument.

Since the nineteenth century there has been a huge increase in the numbers and activities of corporations whether nationalised, municipal or commercial, which enter the private lives of all or most of 'men and subjects' in a diversity of ways. A clear case can be made for imputing to such corporations social duties including the duty not to offend all relevant parts of the criminal law. By tracing the history of the cases decided by the English Courts over the period of the last 150 years, it can be seen how first tentatively and, finally confidently the Courts have been able to ascribe to corporations a 'mind' which is generally one of the essential ingredients of common law and statutory offences. Indeed, it can be seen that in many Acts of Parliament the same concept has been embraced. The parliamentary approach is, perhaps, exemplified by section 18 of the Theft Act, 1968 which provides for directors and managers of a limited company to be rendered liable to conviction if an offence under section 15, 16 or 17 of the Act is proved to have been committed—and I quote: 'with the consent, connivance of any director, manager, secretary...purporting to act in such capacity, then such director, manager or secretary shall be guilty of the offence.' Once a state of mind could be effectively attributed to a corporation, all that remained was to determine the means by which that state of mind could be ascertained and imputed to a non-natural person. That done, the obstacle to the acceptance of general criminal liability of a corporation was overcome. *Cessante ratione legis, cessat ipsa lex.* As some of the decisions in other common law countries indicate, there is nothing essentially incongruous in the notion that a corporation should be guilty of an offence of unlawful killing. I find unpersuasive the argument of the company that the old definitions of homicide positively exclude the liability of a non-natural person to conviction of an offence of manslaughter. Any crime, in order to be justiciable must have been committed by or through the agency of a human being. Consequently, the inclusion in the definition of the expression 'human being' as the author of the killing was either tautologous or, as I think more probable, intended to differentiate those cases of death in which a human being played no direct part and which would have led to forfeiture of the inanimate, or if animate non-human object which caused the death (*deodand*) from those in which the cause of death was initiated by human activity albeit the instrument of death was inanimate or if animate non-human. I am confident that the expression 'human being' in the definition of homicide was not intended to have the effect of words of limitation as might have been the case had it been found in some Act of Parliament or legal deed. It is not for me to attempt to set the limits of corporate liability for criminal offences in English Law. Examples of other crimes which may or may not be committed by corporations will, no doubt, be decided on a case by case basis in conformity with the manner in which the common law has adapted itself in the past. Suffice it that where a corporation, through the controlling mind of one of its agents, does an act which fulfils the prerequisites of the crime of manslaughter, it is properly indictable for the crime of manslaughter.

In arriving at this decision, which may be thought by some to have increased the scope of English criminal law, but which I believe merely reflects the extent of developments which have already occurred, I have borne fully in mind the warning shot put across my bows by Mr Kentridge when he referred me to the passage in *Withers v Director of Public Prosecutions* (1974) 60 Cr App R 85, [1975] AC 842, in the course of which Lord Simon of Glaisdale, p. 95 and at p. 863, had said: 'The first principle is that it is not open to the courts nowadays either to create new offences or so to widen existing offences as to make punishable conduct of a type hitherto not subject to punishment (*Newland*

(1953) 37 Cr App R 154, 153, [1954] 1 QB 158, 167; *Shaw v Director of Public Prosecutions* (1961) 45 Cr App R 113, 157, [1962] AC 220, 267; *R v Knuller (Publishing, Printing and Promotions) Limited* (1972) 56 Cr App R 633, [1973] AC 435).'

As it seemed to me, however, the decision that manslaughter is an offence which may be committed by corporations involves neither the widening of any existing offence nor the making punishable conduct of a type hitherto not subject to punishment. Counsel for the Crown, in his admirable reply, reminded me of the second of Lord Simon's principles in *Withers* case which is that 'the courts cannot refuse to apply a legal rule deducible from an authoritative decision to circumstances analogous to those inherent in such decision.' In support of which Lord Simon referred to *Mirehouse v Rennell* (1833) 1 Cl & F 527. 546, which was approved in *Shaw v Director of Public Prosecutions* and *Knuller,* already referred to. My decision in the present case is, I believe, in accord with the second rather than the first of these principles.

The charges against P&O were dismissed after Turner, J ruled that P&O's directors had not been 'reckless' in failing to appreciate the risks of an open bow sailing. Under the 'identification' test of a company's criminal liability, which was (and remains) the test of corporate criminal liability, a company could only be convicted of a crime committed by a person 'identified' with the company; that is, a person who was part of the company's 'directing mind and will' (usually a director, executive officer or senior manager). As it could not be proved that the directors of P&O were guilty of reckless manslaughter, the company also could not be convicted of that crime.

In 2000 the government issued a consultation paper on involuntary manslaughter which proposed a crime of 'corporate killing' based on a proposal of the Law Commission made some four years previously. Under that proposal a company would have been subject to prosecution for 'corporate killing' if:

(a) a management failure by the corporation is the cause or one of the causes of a person's death; and

(b) that failure constitutes conduct falling far below what can reasonably be expected of the corporation in the circumstances.

Management failure was defined in the following way:

(a) there is a management failure by a corporation if the way in which its activities are managed or organised fails to ensure the health and safety of persons employed in or affected by those activities; and

(b) such a failure may be regarded as a cause of a person's death notwithstanding that the immediate cause is the act or omission of an individual.

In 2005, having completed its various consultation exercises (several times over), the government proposed a draft bill. It was followed in 2007 by the Corporate Manslaughter and Corporate Homicide Act 2007(CMCHA). In some ways the Act is an advance on the common law as represented by the *P&O Ferries* Case. In particular it applies to a wider range of organisations, including public sector organsations, charities, the police and prison services, and charities. If the intended effect is to rid the relevant law of the identification doctrine the Act is not entirely successful. This is because the organisation can be held accountable for death only where a substantial element in the breach is attributable to the defaults of **senior management**. (In this context section 3 of the Act states that (c) 'senior management', in relation to an organisation, means the persons who play significant roles in—

(i) the making of decisions about how the whole or a substantial part of its activities are to be managed or organised, or

(ii) the actual managing or organising of the whole or a substantial part of those activities.

This restriction has been criticised as a weakness in the new Act. Although the prosecution of companies will become easier to mount they will remain procedurally complex and less likely to be useful in the very cases where they are most needed, namely cases of gross organisational failure. Particularly in large companies and organisations, it may be impossible to define, let alone identify, those senior people whose conduct was responsible for the death. Moreover, given the Act's focus on the defaults of senior managers, it is surprising to say the least that the Act does not allow those identified as substantially to blame for the outcome to be convicted of the offence, as accessories to the organisation's crime. CMCHA s. 18. See, generally Gobert, 'The Corporate Manslaughter and Corporate Homicide Act 2007 – Thirteen years in the making but was it worth the wait?' 171 Modern Law Review 413.

(i) The Duty of Care

Although matters relating to the constitution of the duty of care are not spelt out in the new Act it seems likely that the existence of a duty of care will be treated as a matter of law and will not go beyond the common law as developed since *Adomako*. By ss. 3–7 the duty of care of public bodies is circumscribed to ensure these bodies are not liable for, say, matters of public policy in relation to public authorities, or operational activities in relation to the police, emergency services or military. More broadly, the civil law of negligence, which takes into account matters such as the claimant's own relative moral and legal fault in determining his worthiness for compensation, may well be inappropriate in the criminal law where public interests in setting standards of carefulness are paramount. The Act provides that the organisation must owe a 'relevant duty of care' under the law of negligence in relation to duties:

(a) owed to its employees or others working for the organisation or performing services for it;

(b) owed as occupier of premises;

(c) owed in connection with (i) the supply of goods or services, (ii) the carrying on of construction or maintenance operations, (iii) the carrying on of any other activity on a commercial basis, (iv) or the use or keeping of any plant or vehicle;

(d) owed to a person, such as a person subject to criminal or medical detention or other custodial status, by reason of being a person for whose safety the organisation is responsible.

(ii) The Standard of Care

Corporate manslaughter is dependent upon showing of a gross breach of duty resulting in death. Such a breach occurs when an organisation's conduct falls far below what can reasonably be expected of it in the circumstances. It is for the jury to determine whether a breach of duty is a 'gross breach'. To guide this decision the Act provides a number of statutory criteria to which the jury should or may have regard. These include the organisation's obligations under health and safety legislation, the extent to which the organisation was in breach of these and the risk to life posed by the breach. Section 8 also permits the jury to have regards to the defendant's 'corporate culture', consisting of its attitude, policies, systems and accepted practices and the extent to which they encouraged the breach of duty. However, 'corporate culture' is only relevant in the context of a health and safety violation.

The restricted scope of the offence, the way in which it tends to favour large organisations with less transparent managerial systems, the opaque nature of the duty of care, and the imprecision of 'gross' in relation to the standard of care renders the CMCHA both less likely to affect corporate behaviour and address irresponsible corporate practices than other solutions on offer. One alternative solution may have been to create an offence of corporate killing, whose elements require a death caused as a result of a statutory duty, howsoever arising. This would make a clear linkage between statutory obligations designed to ensure health and safety and corporate responsibility for fatal outcomes.

FURTHER READING

Wilson, *Criminal Law: Doctrine and Theory* (2011), Chapter 13

Ashworth, 'A Change of Normative Position' (2008) NCLR 232

Ashworth, 'Reforming the Law of Murder' [1990] Criminal Law Review 75

Ashworth and Mitchell (eds.), *Rethinking English Homicide Law* (2000)

Blom-Cooper and Morris, *With Malice Aforethought: A Study of the Crime and Punishment for Homicide* (2004)

Clarkson, 'Corporate Manslaughter: Yet More Government Proposals' [2005] Criminal Law Review 677

Clarkson, 'Corporate Manslaughter: Need for a Special Offence?' in C Clarkson and S Cunningham eds., *Criminal Liability for Non-Aggressive Death* (2008)

Gardner and Macklem, 'No Provocation without Responsibility: A Reply to Mackay and Mitchell' [2004] Criminal Law Review 213

Gobert and Punch, *Rethinking Corporate Crime* (2003)

Gobert, 'The Corporate Manslaughther and Corporate Homicide Act 2007 – Thirteen years in the making but was it worth the wait?' (2008) Modern Law Review 413

Ormerod and Taylor, The Corporate Manslaughter and Corporate Homicide Act 2007 [2008] Criminal Law Review 589

Goff, 'The Mental Element in Murder' (1988) 104 Law Quarterly Review 30

Griew, 'The Future of Diminished Responsibility' [1988] Criminal Law Review 75

Mackay and Mitchell, 'But is this Provocation? Some Thoughts on the Law Commission's Report on Partial Defences to Murder' [2005] Criminal Law Review 44

Mackay and Mitchell, 'Provoking Diminished Responsibility: Two Pleas Merging into One' [2003] Criminal Law Review 745

Mitchell, 'More Thoughts About Unlawful Act Manslaughter and the One Punch Killer' [2009] Criminal Law Review 502

Mitchell, 'Minding the Gap in Unlawful and Dangerous Act Manslaughter; A Moral Defence of One Punch Killers' [2009] Criminal Law Review 502

Wells, *Corporations and Criminal Responsibility* (2nd ed. 2001)

Wilson, 'Murder and the Structure of Homicide' in Ashworth and Mitchell (eds.), *Rethinking English Homicide Law* (2000)

Wilson, 'The Structure of Criminal Homicide' [2006] Criminal Law Review 471 5

Wilson, 'Murder by Omission' (2010) New Criminal Law Review 1

5

Non-fatal Offences Against the Person

SECTION 1: **INTRODUCTION**

This chapter deals with attacks on the personal integrity of a victim. The criminal law in this area is hardly a model of clarity. The basic offences, of common law origin, have been replaced by a number of statutory offences. The principal statute, the Offences Against the Person Act 1861, contains much antiquated language and many anachronisms. It covers several aggravated offences, which require proof of a common law assault as a prerequisite to conviction of a more serious, aggravated offence under the statute.

It would require a separate book to examine all the offences contained in the 1861 Act, and many of them are rarely charged. However, a student would be well advised to look at the whole statute in order to acquire the flavour of the legislation. In this chapter the common law offences and the main aggravated assaults are covered.

Anyone studying the topic of assault needs to be sensitive to the value judgments, which have to be made; for instance, the age at which people may consent to various activities or the purposes for which consent may be given. The answer to such questions may vary as society's attitudes change over time.

SECTION 2: ASSAULT

Confusion is often caused by the court's use of the term 'assault' to cover two distinct offences:

(a) assault; and

(b) battery.

This is perhaps because typically a defendant commits both offences at the same time. However, the two offences are not identical and each will be examined separately. It should be noted that this, as well as many of the other common law distinctions, will lose its importance if the Government's 1998 proposals for reform (set out later in the chapter) are enacted into law.

An assault (or 'common assault', as it is sometimes called) is committed when the accused intentionally or recklessly causes the victim to apprehend the application of immediate and unlawful physical force to his or her person. The essence of the offence is the inducing of fear. No touching, nor indeed physical harm, is necessary.

A: *Actus reus*

The victim must anticipate the immediate unlawful application of force to his or her person. No force need actually be applied (if it is, the defendant is guilty of battery). The victim has only to be in fear of a battery which 'need not necessarily be hostile, rude or aggressive' according to Lord Lane in *Faulkner* v *Talbot* [1981] 3 All ER 468, at p. 471.

It should be noted that the force which must be apprehended is *unlawful* force. If there is evidence that the victim consented or that the force was in any other way lawful (see defences, below) it will be for the prosecution to establish beyond reasonable doubt that the force was unlawful. If the victim did not apprehend the application of force no offence is committed, even if the victim was tragically wrong, as in *R* v *Lamb* [1967] 2 QB 981 (Ch. 4).

The victim must apprehend the *immediate* application of force. However, in recent years the courts have interpreted the immediacy requirement with a degree of flexibility and in a manner that takes into account the victim's state of mind. In particular, the cases require no physical confrontation between defendant and victim. They also raise (and resolve) the issue whether silence and, by implication, words can form the basis of a charge of assault, and whether harm includes psychological harm.

Smith v *Chief Superintendent of Woking Police Station*
(1983) 76 Cr App R 234, Divisional Court

KERR LJ: . . . The justices found the following facts. On the evening of September 8, 1982, the defendant entered the grounds of Milford House and looked through the windows of Miss Mooney's bed-sitting room, and that the grounds form part of an enclosed garden. Then they found that Miss Mooney saw the defendant through the windows and recognised him and, 'she was absolutely terrified, to the extent that she was very nervous and jumpy for a few days afterwards.' Finally, they found that the defendant intended to frighten the person in that room.

In view of the question of law I must also refer shortly to the evidence on the basis of which the justices convicted. The incident happened at about 11 p.m., when Miss Mooney was in her room wearing a pink, knee-length nightie. There was a bay window and a side window. The curtains were drawn but they left a gap. She saw the defendant peering in and stated that he was right up against the window. She said: 'I instantly recognised him. I was very scared, very shocked. He was there about three or four seconds. I walked backwards and could no longer see him. I turned and he was at the other window, again right against the glass. I just stood and stared at him, didn't know what to do. He was just standing there, didn't seem he was going to go away. I jumped across the bed towards the window and screamed. I was terrified, absolutely terrified. He must have seen me look at him. He moved away when I went across the bed. I looked at him for about 20 seconds at the side window. . . .'

. . .

Ultimately, as it seems to me, the only point taken by Mr Denny which requires some consideration is whether there was a sufficient apprehension, within the definition which I have read, of immediate and unlawful violence. He takes the point that there is no finding here that what Miss Mooney was terrified of was some violence, and indeed some violence which can be described as immediate. However, as it seems to me, Mr Greenbourne is right when he submits, really in the form of a question: 'What else, other than some form of immediate violence, could Miss Mooney have been terrified about?'

When one is in a state of terror one is very often unable to analyse precisely what one is frightened of as likely to happen next. When I say that, I am speaking of a situation such as the present, where the person who causes one to be terrified is immediately adjacent, albeit on the other side of a window. Mr Denny relied on a sentence in Smith and Hogan's *Criminal Law* (4th ed.), p. 351, where an illustration is given as follows: 'There can be no assault if it is obvious to P'—the complainant—'that D'—the defendant—'is unable to carry out his threat, as where D shakes his fist at P who is safely locked inside his car.' That may be so, but those are not the facts of the present case.

In the present case the defendant intended to frighten Miss Mooney and Miss Mooney was frightened. As it seems to me, there is no need for a finding that what she was frightened of, which she probably could not analyse at that moment, was some innominate terror of some potential violence. It was clearly a situation where the basis of the fear which was instilled in her was that she did not know what the defendant was going to do next, but that, whatever he might be going to do next, and sufficiently immediately for the purposes of the offence, was something of a violent nature. In effect, as it seems to me, it was wholly open to the justices to infer that her state of mind was not only that of terror, which they did find, but terror of some immediate violence. In those circumstances, it seems to me that they were perfectly entitled to convict the defendant who had gone there, as they found, with the intention of frightening her and causing her to fear some act of immediate violence, and therefore with the intention of committing an assault upon her. Accordingly, I would dismiss this appeal.

R v Constanza

[1997] Crim LR 576, Court of Appeal

The appellant was convicted of occasioning actual bodily harm. The victim was a female ex-colleague. Between October 1993 and June 1995 he followed her home from work, made numerous silent telephone calls, sent over 800 letters, repeatedly drove past her home, visited against her expressed wish, and on three occasions wrote offensive words on her front door. In June of 1995 the victim received two further letters which she interpreted as clear threats. She believed that he had 'flipped' and that he might do something to her at any time. On July 27, 1995 she was diagnosed as suffering from clinical depression and anxiety. It was the doctor's view that the appellant's actions had caused this harm.

The defence conceded that the appellant's behaviour had occasioned actual bodily harm but submitted that what the appellant had done could not amount in law to an assault and that the judge should have allowed a submission of no case to answer.

Held, dismissing the appeal, the issue before the Court was whether it was enough if the Crown have proved a fear of violence at some time not excluding the immediate future. In the Court's view it was. It was an important factor that the appellant lived near the victim and she thought that something could happen at any time. The judge was entitled to leave to the jury the question whether or not she had a fear of immediate violence, and the jury were entitled to find that she did. The Court rejected the defence submission that a person cannot have a fear of immediate violence unless they can see the potential perpetrator. It rejected a further submission that an assault could not be committed by words alone without a physical action. The indictment made it clear that the assault relied on was that constituted by the last letter. The Court certified a point of general public importance but refused leave to appeal to the House of Lords.

R v Ireland, R v Burstow

[1997] 3 WLR 534, House of Lords

LORD STEYN: My Lords, it is easy to understand the terrifying effect of a campaign of telephone calls at night by a silent caller to a woman living on her own. It would be natural for the victim to regard the calls as menacing. What may heighten her fear is that she will not know what the caller may do next. The spectre of the caller arriving at her doorstep bent on inflicting personal violence on her may come to dominate her thinking. After all, as a matter of common sense, what else would she be terrified about? The victim may suffer psychiatric illness such as anxiety neurosis or acute depression. Harassment of women by repeated silent telephone calls, accompanied on occasions by heavy breathing, is apparently a significant social problem. That the criminal law should be able to deal with this problem, and so far as is practicable, afford effective protection to victims is self-evident.

From the point of view, however, of the general policy of our law towards the imposition of criminal responsibility, three specific features of the problem must be faced squarely. First, the medium used by the caller is the telephone: arguably it differs qualitatively from a face to face offer of violence to a sufficient extent to make a difference. Secondly, ex hypothesi the caller remains silent: arguably a caller may avoid the reach of the criminal law by remaining silent however menacing the context may be. Thirdly, it is arguable that the criminal law does not take into account 'mere' psychiatric illnesses.

The two appeals before the House

There are two appeals before the House. In *R* v *Ireland* appellant was convicted on his plea of guilty of three offences of assault occasioning actual bodily harm, contrary to section 47 of the Act of 1861. The judgment of the Court of Appeal dismissing his appeal is reported [1997] QB 114. The case against Ireland was that during a period of three months in 1994 covered by the indictment he harassed three women by making repeated telephone calls to them during which he remained silent. Sometimes, he resorted to heavy breathing. The calls were mostly made at night. The case against him, which was accepted by the judge and the Court of Appeal, was that he caused his victim to suffer psychiatric illness. Ireland had a substantial record of making offensive telephone calls to women. The judge sentenced him to a total of three years' imprisonment.

Before the Court of Appeal there were two principal issues. The first was whether psychiatric illness may amount to bodily harm within the meaning of section 47 of the Act of 1861. Relying on a decision of the Court of Appeal in *R* v *Chan-Fook* [1994] 1 WLR 689 the Court of Appeal in *Ireland's* case concluded that psychiatric injury may amount to bodily harm under section 47 of the Act of 1861. The second issue was whether Ireland's conduct was capable of amounting to an assault. In giving the judgment of the court in Ireland's case Swinton Thomas LJ said at p. 119:

> It has been recognised for many centuries that putting a person in fear may amount to an assault. The early cases predate the invention of the telephone. We must apply the law to conditions as they are in the 20th century.

The court concluded that repeated telephone calls of a menacing nature may cause victims to apprehend immediate and unlawful violence. Given these conclusions of law, and Ireland's guilty plea, the Court of Appeal dismissed the appeal. The Court of Appeal certified the following question as being of general public importance, namely 'As to whether the making of a series of silent telephone calls can amount in law to an assault'. But it will also be necessary to consider the question whether psychiatric illness may in law amount to bodily harm under section 47 of the Act of 1861. Those are the issues of law before the House in the appeal of *R* v *Ireland*.

In *R* v *Burstow* the appellant was indicted on one count of unlawfully and maliciously inflicting grievous bodily harm, contrary to section 20 of the Act of 1861. The facts are fully set out in the reported judgment of the Court of Appeal [1997] 1 Cr App R 144. I can therefore describe the facts shortly. Burstow had a social relationship with a woman. She broke it off. He could not accept her decision. He proceeded to harass her in various ways over a lengthy period. His conduct led to several convictions and periods of imprisonment. During an eight-month period in 1995 covered by the indictment he continued his campaign of harassment. He made some silent telephone calls to her. He also made abusive calls to her. He distributed offensive cards in the street where she lived. He was frequently, and unnecessarily, at her home and place of work. He surreptitiously took photographs of the victim and her family. He sent her a note which was intended to be menacing, and was so understood. The victim was badly affected by this campaign of harassment. It preyed on her mind. She was fearful of personal violence. A consultant psychiatrist stated that she was suffering from a severe depressive illness. In the Crown Court counsel asked for a ruling whether an offence of unlawfully and maliciously inflicting grievous bodily harm contrary to section 20 may be committed where no physical violence has been applied directly or indirectly to the body of the victim. The judge answered this question in the affirmative. Burstow thereupon changed his plea to guilty. The judge sentenced him to three years' imprisonment. Burstow applied for leave to appeal against conviction. The Court of Appeal heard full oral argument on the application, and granted the application for leave to appeal but dismissed the appeal. Two questions of law were canvassed before the Court of Appeal. First, there was the question whether psychiatric injury may amount to bodily harm under section 20. The Court of Appeal regarded itself as bound by the affirmative decision in *R v Chan-Fook* [1994] 1 WLR 689. The second issue was whether in the absence of physical violence applied directly or indirectly to the body of the victim an offence under section 20 may be committed. The Court of Appeal concluded that this question must be answered in the affirmative. The concluding observations of Lord Bingham of Cornhill CJ were, at p. 149:

> It is not straining language to speak of one person inflicting psychiatric injury on another. It would in our judgment be an affront to common sense to distinguish between section 18 and section 20 in the way contended for by the applicant. It would also, we think, introduce extreme and undesirable artificiality into what should be a very practical area of the law if we were to hold that, although grievous bodily harm includes psychiatric injury, no offence against section 20 is committed unless such psychiatric injury is the result of physical violence applied directly or indirectly to the body of the victim. The decision in *Chan-Fook* is in our view fatal to the applicant's submission.

In the result the Court of Appeal dismissed the appeal against conviction. The court certified the following point as of general importance, namely:

> Whether an offence of inflicting grievous bodily harm under section 20 of the offences against the Person Act 1861 can be committed where no physical violence is applied directly or indirectly to the body of the victim.

It will be noted that in neither appeal is there an issue on *mens rea*: the appeals focus on questions of law regarding the *actus reus*.

The common question: Can psychiatric illness amount to bodily harm?

It will now be convenient to consider the question which is common to the two appeals, namely, whether psychiatric illness is capable of amounting to bodily harm in terms of sections 18, 20 and 47 of the Act of 1861. The answer must be the same for the three sections.

The only abiding thing about the processes of the human mind, and the causes of its disorders and disturbances, is that there will never be a complete explanation. Psychiatry is and will always remain an imperfectly understood branch of medical science. This idea is explained by Vallar's psychiatrist in Iris Murdoch's *The Message to the Planet*:

> Our knowledge of the soul, if I may use that unclinical but essential word, encounters certain seemingly impassable limits, set there perhaps by the gods, if I may refer to them, in order to preserve their privacy, and beyond which it may be not only futile but lethal to attempt to pass and though it is our duty to seek for knowledge, it is also incumbent on us to realise when it is denied us, and not to prefer a fake solution to no solution at all.

But there has been progress since 1861. And courts of law can only act on the best scientific understanding of the day. Some elementary distinctions can be made. The appeals under consideration do not involve structural injuries to the brain such as might require the intervention of a neurologist. One is also not considering either psychotic illness or personality disorders. The victims in the two appeals suffered from no such conditions. As a result of the behaviour of the appellants they did not develop psychotic or psychoneurotic conditions. The case was that they developed mental disturbances of a lesser order, namely neurotic disorders. For present purposes the relevant forms of neurosis are anxiety disorders and depressive disorders. Neuroses must be distinguished from simple states of fear, or problems in coping with everyday life. Where the line is to be drawn must be a matter of psychiatric judgment. But for present purposes it is important to note that modern psychiatry treats neuroses as recognisable psychiatric illnesses: see 'Liability for Psychiatric Injury', Law Commission Consultation paper No. 137 (1995) Part III (The Medical Background); *Mullany and*

Hanford, Tort Liability for Psychiatric Damages (1993), discussion on 'The Medical Perspective', at pp. 24–42, and particularly at p. 30, footnote 88. Moreover, it is essential to bear in mind that neurotic illnesses affect the central nervous system of the body, because emotions such as fear and anxiety are brain functions.

The civil law has for a long time taken account of the fact that there is no rigid distinction between body and mind. In *Bourhill* v *Young* [1943] AC 92, 103 Lord Macmillan said:

> The crude view that the law should take cognisance only of physical injury resulting from actual impact has been discarded, and it is now well recognised that an action will lie for injury by shock sustained through the medium of the eye or the ear without direct contact. The distinction between mental shock and bodily injury was never a scientific one.

This idea underlies the subsequent decisions of the House of Lords regarding post-traumatic stress disorder in *McLoughlin* v *O'Brian* [1983] 1 AC 410, 418, *per* Lord Wilberforce; and *Page* v *Smith* [1996] AC 155, 181A–D, *per* Lord Browne-Wilkinson. So far as such cases are concerned with the precise boundaries of tort liability they are not relevant. But so far as those decisions are based on the principle that the claimant must be able to prove that he suffered a recognisable psychiatric illness or condition they are by analogy relevant. The decisions of the House of Lords on post traumatic stress disorder hold that where the line is to be drawn is a matter for expert psychiatric evidence. By analogy those decisions suggest a possible principled approach to the question whether psychiatric injury may amount to bodily harm in terms of the Act of 1861.

The criminal law has been slow to follow this path. But in *R* v *Chan-Fook* [1994] 1 WLR 689 the Court of Appeal squarely addressed the question whether psychiatric injury may amount to bodily harm under section 47 of the Act of 1861. The issue arose in a case where the defendant had aggressively questioned and locked in a suspected thief. There was a dispute as to whether the defendant had physically assaulted the victim. But the prosecution also alleged that even if the victim had suffered no physical injury, he had been reduced to a mental state which amounted to actual bodily harm under section 47. No psychiatric evidence was given. The judge directed the jury that an assault which caused an hysterical and nervous condition was an assault occasioning actual bodily harm. The defendant was convicted. Upon appeal the conviction was quashed on the ground of misdirections in the summing up and the absence of psychiatric evidence to support the prosecution's alternative case. The interest of the decision lies in the reasoning on psychiatric injury in the context of section 47. In a detailed and careful judgment given on behalf of the court Hobhouse LJ said, at p. 695:

> The first question on the present appeal is whether the inclusion of the word 'bodily' in the phrase 'actual bodily harm' limits harm to harm to the skin, flesh and bones of the victim . . . . The body of the victim includes all parts of his body, including his organs, his nervous system and his brain. Bodily injury therefore may include injury to any of those parts of his body responsible for his mental and at faculties.

In concluding that 'actual bodily harm' is capable of including psychiatric injury Hobhouse LJ emphasised, at p. 696:

> it does not include mere emotions such as fear or distress nor panic nor does it include, as such, states of mind that are not themselves evidence of some identifiable clinical condition.

He observed that in the absence of psychiatric evidence a question whether or not an assault occasioned psychiatric injury should not be left to the jury.

The Court of Appeal, as differently constituted in *R* v *Ireland* and *R* v *Burstow*, was bound by the decision in *R* v *Chan-Fook*. The House is not so bound. Counsel for the appellants in both appeals submitted that bodily harm in Victorian legislation cannot include psychiatric injury. For this reason they argued that *R* v *Chan-Fook* was wrongly decided. They relied on the following observation of Lord Bingham of Cornhill CJ in *R* v *Burstow* [1997] 1 Cr App R 144 148–149:

> Were the question free from authority we should entertain some doubt whether the Victorian draftsman of the 1861 Act intended to embrace psychiatric injury within the expressions 'grievous bodily harm' and 'actual bodily harm'.

Nevertheless, Lord Bingham CJ observed that it is now accepted that in the relevant context the distinction between physical and mental injury is no means clear cut. He welcomed the ruling in *R v Chan-Fook* at p. 149B. I respectfully agree. But I would go further and point out that, although out of considerations of piety we frequently refer to the actual intention of the draftsman, the correct approach is simply to consider whether the words of the Act of 1861 considered in the light of contemporary knowledge cover a recognisable psychiatric injury. It is undoubtedly true that there are statutes where the correct approach is to construe the legislation 'as if one were interpreting it the day after it was passed': *The Longford* (1889) 14 PD 34. Thus in *The Longford* the word 'action' in a statute was held not to be apt to cover an Admiralty action in rem since when it was passed the Admiralty Court 'was not one of His Majesty's Courts of Law': see pp. 37, 38. Bearing in mind that statutes are usually intended to operate for many years it would be most inconvenient if courts could never rely in difficult cases on the current meaning of statutes. Recognising the problem Lord Thring, the great Victorian draftsman of the second half of the last century, exhorted draftsmen to draft so that 'An Act of Parliament should be deemed to be 'always speaking': *Practical Legislation* (1902), p. 83; see also Cross, *Statutory Interpretation*, 3rd ed. (1995), p. 51; Pearce and Geddes, *Statutory Interpretation in Australia*, 4th ed. (1996), pp. 90–93. In cases where the problem arises it is a matter of interpretation whether a court must search for the historical or original meaning of a statute or whether it is free to apply the current meaning of the statute to present day conditions. Statutes dealing with a particular grievance or problem may sometimes require to be historically interpreted. But the drafting technique of Lord Thring and his successors have brought about the situation that statutes will generally be found to be of the 'always speaking' variety: see *Royal College of Nursing of the United Kingdom* v *Department of Health and Social Security* [1981] AC 800 for an example of an 'always speaking' construction in the House of Lords.

The proposition that the Victorian legislator when enacting sections 18, 20 and 47 of the Act 1861, would not have had in mind psychiatric illness is no doubt correct. Psychiatry was in its infancy in 1861. But the subjective intention of the draftsman is immaterial. The only relevant inquiry is as to the sense of the words in the context in which they are used. Moreover the Act of 1861 is a statute of the 'always speaking' type: the statute must be interpreted in the light of the best current scientific appreciation of the link between the body and psychiatric injury.

For these reasons I would, therefore, reject the challenge to the correctness of *R v Chan-Fook* [1994] 1 WLR 689. In my view the ruling in that case was based on principled and cogent reasoning and it marked a sound and essential clarification of the law. I would hold that 'bodily harm' in sections 18, 20 and 47 must be interpreted so as to include recognisable psychiatric illness.

. . .

For the reasons I have given I would answer the certified question in *R v Burstow* in the affirmative.

R v Ireland: was there an assault?

It is now necessary to consider whether the making of silent telephone calls causing psychiatric injury is capable of constituting an assault under section 47. The Court of Appeal, as constituted in *R v Ireland* case, answered that question in the affirmative. There has been substantial academic criticism of the conclusion and reasoning in *R v Ireland*; see *Archbold News*, Issue 6, 12 July 1996; *Archbold's Criminal Pleading, Evidence & Practice*, Supplement No. 4 (1996), pp. 345–347; *Smith and Hogan, Criminal Law*, 8th ed. (1996), 413; 'Assault by Telephone' by Jonathan Herring [1997] CLJ 11; 'Assault' [1997] Crim LR 434, 435–436. Counsel's arguments, broadly speaking, challenged the decision in *R v Ireland* on very similar lines. Having carefully considered the literature and counsel's arguments, I have come to the conclusion that the appeal ought to be dismissed.

The starting point must be that an assault is an ingredient of the offence under section 47. It is necessary to consider the two forms which an assault may take. The first is battery, which involves the unlawful application of force by the defendant upon the victim. Usually, section 47 is used to prosecute in cases of this kind. The second form of assault is an act causing the victim to apprehend an imminent application of force upon her: see *Fagan v Metropolitan Police Commissioner* [1969] 1 QB 439, 444D–E.

One point can be disposed of, quite briefly. The Court of Appeal was not asked to consider whether silent telephone calls resulting in psychiatric injury is capable of constituting a battery. But encouraged by some academic comment it was raised before your Lordships' House. Counsel for Ireland was most economical in his argument on the point. I will to match his economy of words. In my view it is not feasible to enlarge the generally accepted legal meaning of what is a battery to include the circumstances of a silent caller who causes psychiatric injury.

It is to assault in the form of an act causing the victim to fear an immediate application of force to her that I must turn. Counsel argued that as a matter of law an assault can never be committed by words alone and therefore it cannot be committed by silence. The premise depends on the slenderest authority, namely, an observation by Holroyd J to a jury that 'no words or singing are equivalent to an assault': *R* v *Meade and Belt* (1823) 1 Lew 184. The proposition that a gesture may amount to an assault, but that words can never suffice, is unrealistic and indefensible. A thing said is also a thing done. There is no reason why something said should be incapable of causing an apprehension of immediate personal violence, e.g. a man accosting a woman in a dark alley saying, 'Come with me or I will stab you'. I would, therefore, reject the proposition that an assault can never be committed by words.

That brings me to the critical question whether a silent caller may be guilty of an assault. The answer to this question seems to me to be 'Yes depending on the facts.'

It involves questions of fact within the province of the jury. After all, there is no reason why a telephone caller who says to a woman in a menacing way 'I will be at your door in a minute or two' may not be guilty of an assault if he causes his victim to apprehend immediate personal violence. Take now the case of the silent caller. He intends by his silence to cause fear and he is so understood. The victim is assailed by uncertainty about his intentions. Fear may dominate her emotions, and it may be the fear that the caller's arrival at her door may be imminent. She may fear the *possibility* of immediate personal violence. As a matter of law the caller may be guilty of an assault: whether he is or not will depend on the circumstance and in particular on the impact of the caller's potentially menacing call or calls on the victim. Such a prosecution case under section 47 may be fit to leave to the jury. And a trial judge may, depending on the circumstances, put a common sense consideration before the jury, namely what, if not the possibility of imminent personal violence, was the victim terrified about? I conclude that an assault may be committed in the particular factual circumstances which I have envisaged. For this reason I reject the submission that as a matter of law a silent telephone caller cannot ever be guilty of an offence under section 47. In these circumstances no useful purpose would be served by answering the vague certified question in *R* v *Ireland*.

Having concluded that the legal arguments advanced on behalf of Ireland on section 47 must fail, I nevertheless accept that the concept of an assault involving immediate personal violence as an ingredient of the section 47 offence is a considerable complicating factor in bringing prosecutions under it in respect of silent telephone callers and stalkers. That the least serious of the ladder of offences is difficult to apply in such cases is unfortunate. At the hearing of the appeal of *R* v *Ireland* attention was drawn to the Bill which is annexed to Law Commission report, 'Legislating the Criminal Code: Offences Against the Person and General Principles,' (Law Com. No. 218) (1993) (Cm. 2370). Clause 4 of that Bill is intended to replace section 47. Clause 4 provides that 'A person is guilty of an offence if he intentionally or recklessly causes injury to another'. This simple and readily comprehensible provision would eliminate the problems inherent in section 47. In expressing this view I do not, however, wish to comment on the appropriateness of the definition of 'injury' in clause 18 of the Bill, and in particular the provision that 'injury' means 'impairment of a person's mental health'.

The disposal of the appeals

The legal arguments advanced on behalf of Burstow have failed. The appeal must be dismissed.

The legal arguments advanced on behalf of Ireland have also failed. But counsel for the appellant submitted that the appeal should be allowed because on an examination of the statements there was no prima facie case against him. I reject this submission. The prosecution case was never fully deployed because Ireland pleaded guilty. The fact of his plea demonstrated his *mens rea*. It was said, however, that the ingredient of psychiatric injury was not established on the statements. It is true that the statement from the psychiatrist is vague. But I would not accept that read in context it was insufficient to allow the case to go before a jury. It would be an exceptional course, in the face of an unequivocal and deliberate plea of guilty, to entertain an appeal directed exclusively to the sufficiency of evidence. Such a course is not warranted in the present case. I would therefore dismiss the appeal of Ireland.

■ NOTES AND QUESTIONS

1. Do *Ireland* and *Constanza* eliminate the immediacy requirement altogether? The Court of Appeal in *Ireland* referred to *Smith* v *Chief Superintendent of Woking Police Station* (above) on this point. Are the two cases in fact distinguishable?

2. The psychological symptoms experienced by the victims in *Ireland* and *Constanza* developed gradually over time. This being so, at what point did the actions of the defendants become an assault?

3. The type of behaviour (stalking) involved in these cases is now dealt with by the Protection from Harassment Act 1997. If the facts of the cases were to arise again, the prosecution would presumably be brought under this statute. Thus, the precedential effect of the two decisions may be limited and the door remains open for the restoration of an immediacy requirement in other cases of assault.

While words may constitute an assault, they may also serve to nullify what would otherwise be a threat of immediate harm.

Turberville v *Savage*
(1669) 1 Mod Rep 3, King's Bench Division

Action of *assault, battery*, and *wounding*. The evidence to prove a provocation was, that the plaintiff put his hand upon his sword and said, '*If it were not assize-time, I would not take such language from you.*'—The question was, if that were an assault?—The Court agreed that it was not; for the declaration of the plaintiff was, that he would not assault him, the Judges being in town; and *the intention* as well as *the act* makes an assault. Therefore if one strike another upon the hand, or arm, or breast in discourse, it is no assault, there being no *intention* to assault; but if one, intending to assault, strike *at* another and miss him, this is an assault: so if he hold up his hand against another in a threatening manner and say nothing, it is an assault.—In the principal case the plaintiff had judgment.

B: *Mens rea*

The *mens rea* of assault is the same as the *mens rea* for assault occasioning actual bodily harm. There is no requirement that A foresaw harm.

R v *Savage, Director of Public Prosecutions* v *Parmenter*
[1991] 3 WLR 914, House of Lords

LORD ACKNER: My Lords, these two appeals have been heard together, because they each raise the issue of the mental element which the prosecution have to establish in relation to offences under two sections of the Offences against the Person Act 1861, viz. section 20, unlawfully and maliciously wounding or inflicting grievous bodily harm and section 47, assault occasioning actual bodily harm.

It will be observed that some of the certified questions in *Parmenter* overlap with those in *Savage*. My Lords, I will now seek to deal with the issues raised by these appeals seriatim.

...

2. *Can a verdict of assault occasioning actual bodily harm be returned upon proof of an assault together with proof of the fact that actual bodily harm was occasioned by the assault, or must the prosecution also prove that the defendant intended to cause some actual bodily harm or was reckless as to whether such harm would be caused?*

Your Lordships are concerned with the mental element of a particular kind of assault, an assault 'occasioning actual bodily harm'. It is common ground that the mental element of assault is an intention to cause the victim to apprehend immediate and unlawful violence or recklessness whether such apprehension be caused: see *R* v *Venna* [1976] QB 421. It is of course common ground that Mrs Savage committed an assault upon Miss Beal when she threw the contents of her glass of beer over her. It is also common ground that however the glass came to be broken and Miss Beal's wrist thereby cut, it was, on the finding of the jury, Mrs Savage's handling of the glass which caused Miss Beal 'actual bodily harm.' Was the offence thus established or is there a further mental state that has to be established in relation to the bodily harm element of the offence? Clearly the section, by its terms, expressly imposes no such a requirement. Does it do so by necessary implication? It neither uses the word 'intentionally' or 'maliciously'. The words 'occasioning actual bodily harm' are descriptive of the word 'assault', by reference to a particular kind of consequence.

In neither *Savage*, nor *Spratt*, nor in *Parmenter* was the court's attention invited to the decision of the Court of Appeal in *R* v *Roberts* (1971) 56 Cr App R 95. [In that case the Court of Appeal used the following test:]

> Was it [the action of the victim which resulted in actual bodily harm] the natural result of what the alleged assailant said and did, in the sense that it was something that could reasonably have been foreseen as the consequence of what he was saying or doing? As it was put in one of the old cases, it had got to be shown to be his act, and if of course the victim does something so 'daft', in the words of the appellant in this case, or so unexpected, not that this particular assailant did not actually foresee it but that no reasonable man could be expected to foresee it, then it is only in a very remote and unreal sense a consequence of his assault, it is really occasioned by a voluntary act on the part of the victim which could not reasonably be foreseen and which breaks the chain of causation between the assault and the harm or injury.

Accordingly no fault was found in the following direction of the chairman to the jury, at p. 103:

> If you accept the evidence of the girl in preference to that of the man, that means that there was an assault occasioning actual bodily harm, that means that she did jump out as a direct result of what he was threatening her with, and what he was doing to her, holding her coat, telling her he had beaten up girls who had refused his advances, and that means that through his acts he was in law and in fact responsible for the injuries which were caused to her by her decision, if it can be called that, to get away from his violence, his threats, by jumping out of the car.

Thus once the assault was established, the only remaining question was whether the victim's conduct was the natural consequence of that assault. The words 'occasioning' raised solely a question of causation, an objective question which does not involve inquiring into the accused's state of mind.... The decision in *Roberts*' case, (1971) 56 Cr App R 95 was correct. The verdict of assault occasioning actual bodily harm may be returned upon proof of an assault together with proof of the fact that actual bodily harm was occasioned by the assault. The prosecution are not obliged to prove that the defendant intended to cause some actual bodily harm or was reckless as to whether such harm would be caused.

■ **NOTES AND QUESTIONS**

1. Eve hits Adam intentionally, not foreseeing any actual bodily harm, but he (reasonably foreseeably) trips, falls and fractures his skull. Is Eve guilty of a s. 47

offence? What would be the position if Adam died (in answering this question you may wish to review the materials on unlawful act manslaughter presented in Chapter 4)?

2. If the Government's proposals for reform (presented below) are enacted, they will go a long way towards clarifying the *mens rea* of assault.

SECTION 3: BATTERY

A: *Actus reus*

The *actus reus* of battery is the application of unlawful physical force against the person of the victim. An assault is not necessary – there need be no apprehension of an attack by the victim. Thus, if the victim is struck from behind, unaware of the presence of her assailant, that will be a battery, although it will not have been preceded by an assault. Further, it is not of the essence of a battery that some physical harm is caused.

(i) May a battery be based on a failure to act?

Fagan v Metropolitan Police Commissioner
[1969] 1 QB 439, Queen's Bench Division

JAMES J: . . . On August 31, 1967, the appellant was reversing a motor car in Fortunegate Road, London, N.W.10, when Police Constable Morris directed him to drive the car forwards to the kerbside and standing in front of the car pointed out a suitable place in which to park. At first the appellant stopped the car too far from the kerb for the officer's liking. Morris asked him to park closer and indicated a precise spot. The appellant drove forward towards him and stopped it with the offside wheel on Morris's left foot. 'Get off, you are on my foot,' said the officer. 'Fuck you, you can wait,' said the appellant. The engine of the car stopped running. Morris repeated several times 'Get off my foot.' The appellant said reluctantly 'Okay man, okay,' and then slowly turned on the ignition of the vehicle and reversed it off the officer's foot. The appellant had either turned the ignition off to stop the engine or turned it off after the engine had stopped running.

. . . An assault is any act which intentionally—or possibly recklessly—causes another person to apprehend immediate and unlawful personal violence. Although 'assault' is an independent crime and is to be treated as such, for practical purposes today 'assault' is generally synonymous with the term 'battery' and is a term used to mean the actual intended use of unlawful force to another person without his consent. On the facts of the present case the 'assault' alleged involved a 'battery' Where an assault involves a battery, it matters not, in our judgement, whether the battery is inflicted directly by the body of the offender or through the medium of some weapon or instrument controlled by the action of the offender. An assault may be committed by the laying of a hand upon another, and the action does not cease to be an assault if it is a stick held in the hand and not the hand itself which is laid on the person of the victim. So for our part we see no difference in principle between the action of stepping on to a person's toe and maintaining that position and the action of driving a car on to a person's foot and sitting in the car whilst its position on the foot is maintained . . .

To constitute the offence some intentional act must have been performed: a mere omission to act cannot amount to an assault. . . .

Appeal dismissed.

■ **NOTES AND QUESTIONS**

1. James J in his opinion in *Fagan* v *MPC* stated that 'a *mere* omission to act cannot amount to an assault'. Does the thrust of the opinion contradict this statement?

2. *Fagan* v *MPC* was decided prior to *R* v *Miller* (for facts and holding, see Ch. 2) and the court's reasoning was based on the series of events constituting a single transaction. *Miller* would now provide an alternative rationale for reaching the same result. Compare *Santa-Bermudez*, below.

(ii) When is an application of force unlawful?

The problems of analysis are compounded by the fact that a battery may consist of anything from a slight touching to a severe beating. Is it possible in this regard for the law to recognise the types of distinctions that ordinary people make in their everyday lives?

Collins v *Wilcock*
[1984] 3 All ER 374, Queen's Bench Division

ROBERT GOFF LJ: There is before the court an appeal by way of a case stated by a metropolitan stipendiary magistrate sitting at Marylebone, under which the appellant, Alexis Collins, appeals against her conviction on 20 January 1983, of assaulting the respondent, Tracey Wilcock, a constable of the Metropolitan Police Force, in the execution of her duty at Craven Road, London W2, on 22 July 1982, contrary to s. 51(1) of the Police Act 1964. The magistrate found the following facts. (a) On 22 July 1982 the respondent and Police Sgt Benjamen were on duty in a police vehicle and saw two women walking along the street; one of the two was a known prostitute, the other was the appellant. (b) The officers observed the two women, both of whom appeared to them to be soliciting men in the street. (c) The officers, without alighting from their vehicle, asked the two women to get into the police car so that they could have a word with them. One woman got into the car, the appellant refused to do so. (d) The officers repeated their request to the appellant, who again refused and walked away, followed by the police car which then pulled up alongside her. She again walked away. (e) The respondent got out of the car and followed the appellant on foot, asking her why she didn't want to talk to the police, and also for her name and address. The appellant again started to walk away. The respondent told her that she had not finished talking to her and the appellant replied, 'Fuck off', and started to walk away yet again. (f) The respondent took hold of the appellant by the left arm to restrain her and the appellant shouted, 'Just fuck off, Copper' and scratched the respondent's right forearm with her fingernails. (g) The appellant was then arrested for assaulting a police officer in the execution of her duty.

Before the magistrate, the contentions of the parties were as follows. For the appellant, it was contended that the respondent was not acting in the execution of her duty at the time when the assault (if any) took place, having gone beyond the scope of her duty in detaining the appellant in circumstances short of arresting her. It was contended by the respondent, on the other hand, that there was on the evidence good ground for her to make inquiries and administer a caution under the Street Offences Act 1959, and that she was therefore acting in the execution of her duty at the time when the assault took place.

...[W]e think it right to consider whether, on the facts found in the case, the magistrate could properly hold that the respondent was acting in the execution of her duty. In order to consider this question, it is desirable that we should expose the underlying principles.

The law draws a distinction, in terms more easily understood by philologists than by ordinary citizens, between an assault and a battery. An assault is an act which causes another person to apprehend the infliction of immediate, unlawful, force on his person; a battery is the actual infliction of unlawful force on another person. Both assault and battery are forms of trespass to the person.

...

We are here concerned primarily with battery. The fundamental principle, plain and incontestable, is that every person's body is inviolate. It has long been established that any touching of another person, however slight, may amount to a battery. So Holt CJ held in 1704 that 'the least touching of another in anger is a battery': see *Cole* v *Turner* (1704) 6 Mod Rep 149, 90 ER 958. The breadth of the principle reflects the fundamental nature of the interest so protected; as Blackstone wrote in his Commentaries, 'the law cannot draw the line between different degrees of violence, and therefore totally prohibits the first and lowest stage of it; every man's person being sacred, and no other having a right to meddle with it, in any the slightest manner' (see 3 Bl Com 120). The effect is that everybody is protected not only against physical injury but against any form of physical molestation.

But so widely drawn a principle must inevitably be subject to exceptions. For example, children may be subjected to reasonable punishment; people may be subjected to the lawful exercise of the power of arrest; and reasonable force may be used in self-defence or for the prevention of crime. But, apart from these special instances where the control or constraint is lawful, a broader exception has been created to allow for the exigencies of everyday life. Generally speaking, consent is a defence to battery; and most of the physical contacts of ordinary life are not actionable because they are impliedly consented to by all who move in society and so expose themselves to the risk of bodily contact. So nobody can complain of the jostling which is inevitable from his presence in, for example, a supermarket, an underground station or a busy street; nor can a person who attends a party complain if his hand is seized in friendship, or even if his back is (within reason) slapped (see *Tuberville* v *Savage* (1669) 1 Mod Rep 3, 86 ER 684). Although such cases are regarded as examples of implied consent, it is more common nowadays to treat them as falling within a general exception embracing all physical contact which is generally acceptable in the ordinary conduct of daily life. We observe that, although in the past it has sometimes been stated that a battery is only committed where the action is 'angry, or revengeful, or rude, or insolent' (see 1 Hawk PC c. 62, s. 2), we think that nowadays it is more realistic, and indeed more accurate, to state the broad underlying principle, subject to the broad exception.

Among such forms of conduct, long held to be acceptable, is touching a person for the purpose of engaging his attention, though of course using no greater degree of physical contact than is reasonably necessary in the circumstances for that purpose. So, for example, it was held by the Court of Common Pleas in 1807 that a touch by a constable's staff on the shoulder of a man who had climbed on a gentleman's railing to gain a better view of a mad ox, the touch being only to engage the man's attention, did not amount to a battery (see *Wiffin* v *Kincard* (1807) 2 Bos & PNR 471, 127 ER 713; for another example, see *Coward* v *Baddeley* (1859) 4 H & N 478, 157 ER 927). But a distinction is drawn between a touch to draw a man's attention, which is generally acceptable, and a physical restraint, which is not. So we find Parke B observing in *Rawlings* v *Till* (1837) 3 M & W 28 at 29, 150 ER 1042, with reference to *Wiffin* v *Kincard*, that 'There the touch was merely to engage a man's attention, not to put a restraint on his person.' Furthermore, persistent touching to gain attention in the face of obvious disregard may transcend the norms of acceptable behaviour, and so be outside the exception. We do not say that more than one touch is never permitted; for example, the lost or distressed may surely be permitted a second touch, or possibly even more, on a reluctant or impervious sleeve or shoulder, as may a person who is acting reasonably in the exercise of a duty. In each case, the test must be whether the physical contact so persisted in has in the circumstances gone beyond generally acceptable standards of conduct; and the answer to that question will depend on the facts of the particular case.

The distinction drawn by Parke B in *Rawlings* v *Till* is of importance in the case of police officers. Of course, a police officer may subject another to restraint when he lawfully exercises his power of arrest; and he has other statutory powers, for example, his power to stop, search and detain persons under s. 66 of the Metropolitan Police Act 1839, with which we are not concerned. But, putting such cases aside, police officers have for present purposes no greater rights than ordinary citizens. It follows that, subject to such cases, physical contact by a police officer with another person may be unlawful as a battery, just as it might be if he was an ordinary member of the public. But a police officer has his rights as a citizen, as well as his duties as a policeman. A police officer may wish to engage a man's attention, for example if he wishes to question him. If he lays his hand on the man's sleeve or taps his shoulder for that purpose, he commits no wrong. He may even do so more than once; for he is under a duty to prevent and investigate crime, and so his seeking further, in the exercise of that duty, to engage a man's attention in order to speak to him may in the circumstances be regarded as acceptable (see *Donnelly* v *Jackman* [1970] 1 All ER 987, [1970] 1 WLR 562). But if, taking into account the nature of his duty, his use of physical contact in the face of non-co-operation persists beyond generally acceptable standards of conduct, his action will become unlawful; and if a police officer restrains a man, for example by gripping his arm or his shoulder, then his action will also be unlawful, unless he is lawfully exercising his power of arrest. A police officer has no power to require a man to answer him, though he has the advantage of authority, enhanced as it is by the uniform which the state provides and requires him to wear, in seeking a response to his inquiry. What is not permitted, however, is the unlawful use of force or the unlawful threat (actual or implicit) to use force; and, excepting the lawful exercise of his power of arrest, the lawfulness of a police officer's conduct is judged by the same criteria as are applied to the conduct of any ordinary citizen of this country.

... The fact is that the respondent took hold of the appellant by the left arm to restrain her. In so acting, she was not proceeding to arrest the appellant; and since her action went beyond the generally acceptable conduct of touching a person to engage his or her attention, it must follow, in our judgement, that her action constituted a battery on the appellant, and was therefore unlawful. It follows that the appellant's appeal must be allowed, and her conviction quashed.

■ NOTES AND QUESTIONS

1. What should the officer have done? Was she required to permit the defendant to walk away?

2. The court creates an exception for 'all' physical contact which is generally acceptable in the ordinary conduct of daily life. Who decides? Is this (should this be) a question of law or fact? If in a given community it is customary to punch a friend in the ribs as a greeting, would this be a battery elsewhere?

3. Does the 'implied consent' theory really explain the lawfulness of pushing and jostling? Is the true rationale for 'implied consent' that such contacts are unavoidable and that criminalising them would make normal social interaction difficult if not impossible? For discussion see Wilson, chapter 11. See (iii) below for another possibility.

(iii) Must the touching be hostile?

Wilson v *Pringle*
[1986] 2 All ER 440, Court of Appeal

The plaintiff and the defendant were two schoolboys involved in an incident in a school corridor as the result of which the plaintiff fell and suffered injuries. The plaintiff issued a writ claiming damages and alleging that the defendant had committed a trespass to the person of the plaintiff. In his defence the defendant admitted that he had indulged in horseplay with the plaintiff.

CROOM-JOHNSON LJ: ... Nevertheless, it still remains to indicate what is to be proved by a plaintiff who brings an action for battery. Robert Goff LJ's judgment [in *Collins* v *Wilcock* [1984] 3 All ER 374] is illustrative of the considerations which underlie such an action, but it is not practicable to define a battery as 'physical contact which is not generally acceptable in the ordinary conduct of daily life'.

In our view, the authorities lead one to the conclusion that in a battery there must be an intentional touching or contact in one form or another of the plaintiff by the defendant. That touching must be proved to be a hostile touching. That still leaves unanswered the question, when is a touching to be called hostile? Hostility cannot be equated with ill-will or malevolence. It cannot be governed by the obvious intention shown in acts like punching, stabbing or shooting. It cannot be solely governed by an expressed intention, although that may be strong evidence. But the element of hostility, in the sense in which it is now to be considered, must be a question of fact for the tribunal of fact. It may be imported from the circumstances. Take the example of the police officer in *Collins* v *Wilcock*. She touched the woman deliberately, but without an intention to do more than restrain her temporarily. Nevertheless, she was acting unlawfully and in that way was acting with hostility. She was acting contrary to the woman's legal right not to be physically restrained ....

■ NOTES AND QUESTIONS

1. Is 'hostility' as defined in *Wilson* v *Pringle* a helpful concept? Does it add anything to the notion of unlawfulness as set out in *Collins* v *Wilcock?*

2. Can an action be hostile but not unlawful? Unlawful but not hostile?

3. In *F* v *West Berkshire Health Authority* [1989] 2 All ER 545, at pp. 563–564, Lord Goff doubted the correctness of a requirement that the touching be hostile.

4. It is generally assumed that a battery requires a positive action on the part of the defendant (see *Innes* v *Wylie* (1844) 1 Car & Kir 257), although it may be seen that an accidental application of force followed by a refusal to desist may be a battery (see *Fagan* v *MPC*, above). The court in *Fagan* held that there was a continuing act, not a mere omission. In *DPP* v *K* [1990] 1 All ER 331 Parker LJ stated (at p. 333) that he had no doubt that if the defendant in the case had placed acid in a hand drier, which ejected onto the next user, an assault or battery would have been committed.

(iv) Can force be applied indirectly?

Haystead v Chief Constable of Derbyshire
[2000] 3 All ER 890, Queen's Bench Division

Appeal by way of case stated against the appellant's conviction of an offence of assault upon a child.

...

11. (ii) Did the facts disclose a battery properly so called? It is to this question that the appeal is directed. It is accepted that the meaning of battery is correctly given in the current edition of *Archbold's Criminal Pleading, Evidence and Practice* (2000 edn), para 19–166a: '... an act by which a person intentionally or recklessly applies unlawful force to the complainant...'

12. The crucial question is, what is meant by the application of force in the context of the offence of battery?

13. The case stated makes it plain that the magistrates heard only exiguous argument on this issue.

This is what they said in conclusion: 'To be guilty of a reckless battery it was necessary to establish in this case that unlawful force was applied by the appellant to the child and that the appellant saw that possibility. The appellant's use of force on this occasion was unlawful. He punched Angela Wright twice and in such a way that the child fell from her hands and was injured. It is plain to us that the application of the force to Miss Wright is indistinguishable from the application of force to the child. The fact that the unlawful force caused the child to fall is in our view the same as applying the force directly to the person of the child. The situation was entirely foreseeable. The force applied to Miss Wright was the same force which caused the child to fall, and it was unlawful force. If the appellant had swung a punch at the child and missed it is likely that no "assault" would have taken place because the child would not have apprehended immediate violence. If he had swung a punch at Miss Wright and missed but hit the child he would have been guilty of a reckless assault by beating. There is no suggestion that the child jumped—he fell as a direct consequence of the application of force to the person that was holding him. Accordingly, to suggest that by swinging a punch at Miss Wright, connecting and directly caus-ing the child to fall thereby suffering an injury, no offence is committed in respect of the child, we believe to be absurd. The single act of unlawful violence by the appellant was a battery to both Angela Wright and the child.'

14. The question for this court is put in this way:

'The question for the opinion of the High Court is whether on the facts found in this case the defendant could be said to have assaulted the child Matthew Wright by beating.'

15. I should add, perhaps it is plain already, that in putting forward the question in that way the magistrates were not, as I understand it, proposing that this court should examine their finding as to recklessness. I have already said there is no challenge to that. The case is concerned entirely with the proper meaning of 'battery' within the context here of a common assault by beating.

16. The appellant's submission is summarised by Mr Head in para 9 of his skeleton argument:

'It is submitted that a direct application of force requires the assailant to have had direct physi-cal contact with the complainant either through his body eg a punch or through a medium controlled by his actions eg a weapon.'

...

32. Here the movement of Miss Wright whereby she lost hold of the child was entirely and imme-diately the result of the appellant's action in punching her. There is no difference in logic or good sense between the facts of this case and one where the defendant might have used a weapon to fell the child to the floor, save only that this is a case of reckless and not intentional battery.

33. In a case such as the present, it seems to me plain that it is right that the offence of assault by beating should be available for the criminal condemnation of the defendant's conduct.

34. Mr King for the respondent prosecutor put in a short skeleton argument submitting that on the facts this was a case of transferred malice. With respect to him, I greatly doubt whether that is the case; but I would uphold this conviction and dismiss the appeal on the grounds I have set out. If my Lord were to agree, then any question of transferred malice does not arise.

35. I would answer the question posed by the magistrates in the affirmative.

SILBER J: I agree.

Appeal dismissed. Permission to appeal to the House of Lords refused, but court certifying that a point of law of general public importance was involved in its decision, namely whether the actus reus of the offence of battery required that there be direct physical contact between defendant and complainant (whether by the body or by a medium controlled by the defendant such as a weapon).

R v Martin

(1881) 8 QBD 54, Divisional Court

Shortly before the conclusion of a performance at a theatre, M, with the intention and with the result of causing terror in the minds of persons leaving the theatre, put out the gaslights on a stair-case which a large number of such persons had to descend in order to leave the theatre, and he also, with the intention and with the result of obstructing the exit, placed an iron bar across a door-way through which they had in leaving to pass.

Upon the lights being thus extinguished a panic seized a large portion of the audience, and they rushed in fright down the staircase forcing those in front against the iron bar. By reason of the pres-sure and struggling of the crowd thus created on the staircase, several of the audience were thrown down or otherwise severely injured, and amongst them A and B.

On proof of these facts the jury convicted M of unlawfully and maliciously inflicting grievous bod-ily harm upon A and B:—

Held, by the Court (Lord Coleridge, CJ, Field, Hawkins, Stephen, and Cave, JJ), that M was rightly convicted.

DPP v Santa-Bermudez

(2003) EWHC 2908 (admin)

MR JUSTICE MAURICE KAY: This is a prosecutor's appeal by way of case stated from a decision of the Crown Court sitting at Middlesex Guildhall on 6 December 2001 . . . On the hearing of the appeal PC Hill gave evidence that at about 5.45 pm on 3 June 2001 she and other officers had been called to Stockwell Underground Station where ticket touts were operating. She was in full uniform. She saw the respondent by the ticket machines and apparently acting as a tout. She approached him and after a brief conversation she asked him to accompany her to the station supervisor's office, which he did. In the office PC Hill informed the respondent that she intended to carry out a full body search pursuant to section 1 of the Police and Criminal Evidence Act 1984. She first asked him to turn out all his pockets and to place the contents on a table. The respondent did so. The items placed on the table included one or more syringes without needles. PC Hill also asked the respondent to pull out the linings of the pockets of the leather jacket which he was wearing, and this he did with the exception of two small breast pockets, one on either side, at the top of the jacket. The linings of these pockets could not be pulled out.

3. There was then a short conversation. The officer asked the respondent 'Is that everything', to which he replied 'Yes'. She then asked 'Are you sure', and he again replied 'Yes'. She then asked 'Are you sure that you do not have any needles or sharps on you?', and the respondent replied 'No'. Following this conversation PC Hill commenced the search, and in the course of so doing put two fingers of her left hand into one of the small pockets. She felt a stinging sensation to her middle finger, and on withdrawing her fingers from the pocket she saw that her middle finger had been pierced by a hypodermic needle which was still hanging from her fingertip. She removed the needle and saw that her finger was bleeding. She noticed that the respondent had a smirk on his face. He also immediately took another needle from a small pocket at the top of his trousers. PC Hill said 'I thought you didn't have any sharps on you', at which the respondent merely shrugged his shoulders and again smirked. . . .

4. At the end of the prosecution case a submission was made on behalf of the respondent that he had no case to answer on the charge of assault occasioning actual bodily harm. The submission was to the effect that an omission to act cannot amount to an assault or battery and that there was no evidence of any act on the part of the respondent capable of amounting to an assault. The court came to the reluctant conclusion that this submission was well founded. The decision is summarised in these paragraphs:

> '10. We came to the conclusion that the submission advanced on behalf of the Respondent was well founded and correct in law. We were prepared to assume for the purposes of the submission that the Respondent's smirking was evidence from which it could be inferred that the way in which matters developed was neither unforeseen by him nor unwelcome to him. Nevertheless the evidence did not disclose any positive act committed by him and his untruthful answers to questions did not convert a (negative) omission to act into a (positive) act. We accepted that an omission to act cannot in law amount to an assault.
>
> 11. We did not consider the analogy sought to be drawn with cases where the harm actually sustained by the victim is the indirect consequence of something done by the defendant (in the sense that while it is the victim's own act or course of conduct which is the immediate cause of the injury, nevertheless the victim's actions are themselves caused or provoked by the defendant's act) . . . to be a valid one in the circumstances of this case. In truth the Respondent did not do anything to cause PC Hill to take the actions she did take. What he did was permissively to stand back and allow her to do as she did. The fact that he did not warn her of the risks that she thereby ran could not turn his conduct, reprehensible as it otherwise was, into an assault. Had we been of the opinion that his conduct was capable in law of amounting to an assault, we would have been willing to conclude that there was evidence capable of establishing causation of the harm. But in short we concluded that the prosecution had not produced any evidence of any (positive) act on the part of the defendant capable of amounting to the *actus reus* of the offence of assault.

12. For these reasons we came to the conclusion that there was no case to answer and that the defendant was entitled to be acquitted. We therefore allowed the appeal and quashed the conviction.' (The emphases appear in the case stated)

5. The question posed for the opinion of this court is simply whether the Crown Court was correct in law in reaching these conclusions...

8. Miss Lawrence has referred us to a number of authorities over and above Roberts. She places particular reliance on *Director of Public Prosecutions* v *K* (1990) 91 Cr App R 23. The facts of that case were set out as follows in the headnote:

'The defendant, a schoolboy aged 15, was attending a chemistry class at his school. Pupils were provided at the outset with an instruction sheet emphasising the need of great care with carrying out experiments and were orally warned of the dangers of working with acid. The lesson included observations of the effects of putting concentrated sulphuric acid into chlorine, water and ammonia. During the lesson the defendant obtained permission to visit the lavatory to wash some acid off his hand and, unknown to the master in charge, took with him a boiling tube of concentrated acid. He went into a cubicle to test the reaction of the acid with toilet paper and, upon hearing footsteps outside, panicked and poured the rest of the acid into the upturned nozzle of an air hand-face drying machine. When the footsteps receded, he returned to his class discarding the empty tube on the way. He intended to return and deal with the acid in the dryer later. In the meanwhile another pupil went to the lavatory to wash his hands and turned on the dryer with the result that the acid was ejected onto his face, leaving a permanent scar. The defendant was charged with assault causing actual bodily harm contrary to section 47 of the Offences Against the Persons Act 1861. The justices dismissed the charge finding that the defendant panicked on hearing the footsteps approaching the lavatory but his motive was only to conceal the acid and his omission to warn others did not constitute an assault for the purposes of section 47.'

The Divisional Court allowed the prosecutor's appeal holding that, on the justices' findings of fact, 'it was clear that the Defendant knew full well that he had created a dangerous situation and the inescapable inference was that he decided to take the risk of someone using the machine before he could get back and render it harmless or gave no thought to that risk.' In his judgment Parker LJ referred to the case of Clarence (1888) 22 QBD 23 in which Stephen J said (at page 45):

'If a man laid a trap for another into which he fell after an interval the man who laid it would during the interval be guilty of an attempt to assault and of an actual assault as soon as the man fell in.'

Parker LJ concluded (at page 27):

'In the same way a Defendant, who pours a dangerous substance into a machine, just as truly assaults the next user of the machine as if he had himself switched the machine on. So, too, in my judgment would he be guilty of an assault if he was guilty of relevant recklessness.'

9. Of the other authorities referred to by Miss Lawrence, it is appropriate to refer to *Regina* v *Miller* [1983] 2 AC 161. That was a case of arson rather than assault but, apparently speaking in terms of general principle, Lord Diplock said (at page 176D):

'... I see no rational ground for excluding from conduct capable of giving rise to criminal liability, conduct which consists of failing to take measures that lie within one's power to counteract a danger that one has oneself created, if at the time of such conduct one's state of mind is such as constitutes a necessary ingredient of the offence. I venture to think that the habit of lawyers to talk of *actus reus* , suggestive as it is of action rather than inaction, is responsible for any erroneous notion that failures to act cannot give rise to criminal liability in English Law.'

In the present case, the relevant state of mind would be one of recklessness rather than intention.

10. A great deal of undesirable complexity has bedevilled our criminal law as a result of quasi theological distinctions between acts and omissions. Some of the illogicality is identified in Smith and Hogan, *Criminal Law*, 10th Edition, pages 46 to 52. In my judgment, and without the need to

express oneself in the language of universal principle, the authorities of *Roberts* , *K* and *Miller* support the following proposition: where someone (by act or word or a combination of the two) creates a danger and thereby exposes another to a reasonably foreseeable risk of injury which materialises, there is an evidential basis for the *actus reus* of an assault occasioning actual bodily harm. It remains necessary for the prosecution to prove an intention to assault or appropriate recklessness.

11. In the present case, if (as the court implicitly found) the respondent, by giving PC Hill a dishonest assurance about the contents of his pockets, thereby exposed her to a reasonably foreseeable risk of an injury which materialised, it was erroneous of the court to conclude that there was no evidential basis for the *actus reus* of assault occasioning actual bodily harm. For my part I would answer the question posed in the negative — the court was not correct to accede to the submission of no case to answer. I would therefore allow the appeal but without further order.

■ NOTES AND QUESTIONS

1. What was the *actus reus* of the offence of battery in this case? Is it central to the decision in *Santa-Bermudez* that a false assurance was given? Should it not be enough that the defendant had effectively set a trap for the unwary? Would a conviction have been proper if the defendant had at all times refused to answer the police officer's questions?

2. Consider the case of *DPP* v *K* referred to in the course of Maurice Kay's judgment. What was the actus reus in this case?

B: *Mens rea*

The *mens rea* of battery is an intention to apply unlawful force, or subjective recklessness as to whether such force will be applied. See *R* v *Savage* and *DPP* v *Parmenter*, above.

SECTION 4: DEFENCES TO ASSAULT AND BATTERY

A: In general

The defences which may defeat a charge of assault and/or battery are also relevant to the more serious (aggravated) assaults discussed later in this chapter. This is because some of the latter require proof of an assault or battery before a conviction for the more serious offence can be made out.

Any of the general defences discussed in Chapter 10 may also be relevant, although self-defence is the most commonly pleaded. It must be noted that provocation is not a defence to either assault or battery; it is a defence only in the sense that it will reduce a charge of murder to manslaughter. Provocation may be relevant to reduce the sentence of the court following a conviction for assault and battery, but it will not prevent the defendant from being convicted in the first place.

B: Consent

A defence often raised in cases of assault and battery is that of consent. We have already examined that aspect of consent which operates to prevent a conviction for battery when a touching is 'generally acceptable in the ordinary conduct of daily life' (*Collins* v *Wilcock*, above). Ordinary citizens are deemed to have given an implied consent to such touching. Whether absence of consent is an element of the crime (to be proved by the prosecution beyond reasonable doubt regardless of whether the accused introduces any evidence on the issue), or a defence (such that the accused has the burden of introducing some relevant evidence, with the prosecution then having to rebut the defence by proof beyond reasonable doubt) has been a matter of dispute. If absence of consent is an element of the offence, it would mean, for example, that if A kissed B and was prosecuted for assault and battery, there would be no case to answer unless the prosecution could establish that the kiss was not consented to (typically proved through the testimony of the victim). If consent is a defence, the accused would have to introduce evidence that B consented to the kiss (typically satisfied through the testimony of the defendant), with the prosecution thereafter having to negative the defence by proof beyond reasonable doubt.

Where actual bodily harm or worse results matters are more complicated. As a general proposition, to which there are a number of exceptions, absence of consent is not an element in crimes involving death or personal injury. This is why duelling to the death and so-called euthanasia are illegal and chargeable as murder. However, consent may be relevant if, as in medical surgery, the State deems the conduct resulting in the injury to be in the public interest, or where, as where an adult chooses to have a tattoo, criminalising the activity would be considered an unjustified interference with individual freedom and autonomy. There are many problematic issues in this area, not least the meaning of consent itself and the age and/or mental capacity necessary before 'real' consent can be given. Further, where the behaviour carries a hidden risk (such as a risk of AIDS), there is the additional question of whether true consent can be given by a person who is unaware of the hidden risk.

The issues raised may be broken down into the following questions, although they overlap to a degree:

(i)   What limits will the State place on the ability of a victim to consent to conduct which would be criminal in the absence of consent?

(ii)   When will the State imply or impose consent on a victim?

(iii)   What constitutes valid consent?

(i) State limitations on effective consent

Consent is not a defence to a charge of murder or manslaughter. This is the case even if a victim begs to be killed because he or she is in intolerable pain.

Further down the 'harm' table, the courts seek to balance the benefit that the behaviour may bring, either to the public or to the individual, against the degree of harm that is inflicted upon the victim. Thus, even quite serious injury may be consented to where the perception of a useful outcome is high. This is the case in consent to surgery. Conversely, where the harm inflicted is slight but there is no benefit, the courts are less willing to recognise consent as a defence. As a general proposition, the more serious the harm inflicted, the less likely consent is to be effective, even where the behaviour takes place in private and the only persons directly affected are the participants. The factors to consider are:

(a)   the possible benefits to individuals or to the public;

(b) the degree of harm inflicted on the victim;

(c) the extent to which the law is prepared to interfere with private behaviour.

The delicate balancing required will often result in decisions which are extremely controversial.

R v Brown

[1993] 2 All ER 75, House of Lords

The appellants, a group of sado-masochistics, willingly and enthusiastically participated in the commission of acts of violence against each other for the sexual pleasure it engendered in the giving and receiving of pain. They pleaded guilty on arraignment to counts charging various offences under ss. 20 and 47 of the Offences against the Person Act 1861, relating to the infliction of wounds or actual bodily harm on genital and other areas of the body of the consenting victim. On a ruling by the trial judge that, in the particular circumstances, the prosecution did not have to prove lack of consent by the victim, the appellants were re-arraigned, pleaded guilty, some to offences under s. 20 and all to offences under s. 47 and they were convicted. They appealed against conviction on the ground that the judge had erred in his rulings, in that the willing and enthusiastic consent of the victim to the acts on him prevented the prosecution from proving an essential element of the offence, whether charged under s. 20 or s. 47.

LORD TEMPLEMAN: ... In some circumstances violence is not punishable under the criminal law. When no actual bodily harm is caused, the consent of the person affected precludes him from complaining. There can be no conviction for the summary offence of common assault if the victim has consented to the assault. Even when violence is intentionally inflicted and results in actual bodily harm, wounding or serious bodily harm the accused is entitled to be acquitted if the injury was a foreseeable incident of a lawful activity in which the person injured was participating. Surgery involves intentional violence resulting in actual or sometimes serious bodily harm but surgery is a lawful activity. Other activities carried on with consent by or on behalf of the injured person have been accepted as lawful notwithstanding that they involve actual bodily harm or may cause serious bodily harm. Ritual circumcision, tattooing, ear-piercing and violent sports including boxing are lawful activities.

In earlier days some other forms of violence were lawful and when they ceased to be lawful they were tolerated until well into the 19th century. Duelling and fighting were at first lawful and then tolerated provided the protagonists were voluntary participants. But where the results of these activities was the maiming of one of the participants, the defence of consent never availed the aggressor; see *Hawkins' Pleas of the Crown*, 8th ed. (1824), vol. 1, ch. 15. A maim was bodily harm whereby a man was deprived of the use of any member of his body which he needed to use in order to fight but a bodily injury was not a maim merely because it was a disfigurement. The act of maim was unlawful because the King was deprived of the services of an able-bodied citizen for the defence of the realm. Violence which maimed was unlawful despite consent to the activity which produced the maiming. In these days there is no difference between maiming on the one hand and wounding or causing grievous bodily harm on the other hand except with regard to sentence.

When duelling became unlawful, juries remained unwilling to convict but the judges insisted that persons guilty of causing death or bodily injury should be convicted despite the consent of the victim.

Similarly, in the old days, fighting was lawful provided the protagonists consented because it was thought that fighting inculcated bravery and skill and physical fitness. The brutality of knuckle fighting however caused the courts to declare that such fights were unlawful even if the protagonists consented. Rightly or wrongly the courts accepted that boxing is a lawful activity.

...

The question whether the defence of consent should be extended to the consequences of sado-masochistic encounters can only be decided by consideration of policy and public interest. Parliament can call on the advice of doctors, psychiatrists, criminologists, sociologists and other experts and can also sound and take into account public opinion. But the question must at this stage be decided by this House in its judicial capacity in order to determine whether the convictions of the appellants should be upheld or quashed.

Counsel for some of the appellants argued that the defence of consent should be extended to the offence of occasioning actual bodily harm under section 47 of the Act of 1861 but should not be available to charges of serious wounding and the infliction of serious bodily harm under section 20. I do not consider that this solution is practicable. Sado-masochistic participants have no way of foretelling the degree of bodily harm which will result from their encounters. The differences between actual bodily harm and serious bodily harm cannot be satisfactorily applied by a jury in order to determine acquittal or conviction.

Counsel for the appellants argued that consent should provide a defence to charges under both section 20 and section 47 because, it was said, every person has a right to deal with his body as he pleases. I do not consider that this slogan provides a sufficient guide to the policy decision which must now be made. It is an offence for a person to abuse his own body and mind by taking drugs. Although the law is often broken, the criminal law restrains a practice which is regarded as dangerous and injurious to individuals and which if allowed and extended is harmful to society generally. In any event the appellants in this case did not mutilate their own bodies. They inflicted bodily harm on willing victims. Suicide is no longer an offence but a person who assists another to commit suicide is guilty of murder or manslaughter.

The assertion was made on behalf of the appellants that the sexual appetites of sadists and masochists can only be satisfied by the infliction of bodily harm and that the law should not punish the consensual achievement of sexual satisfaction. There was no evidence to support the assertion that sado-masochist activities are essential to the happiness of the appellants or any other participants but the argument would be acceptable if sado-masochism were only concerned with sex, as the appellants contend. In my opinion sado-masochism is not only concerned with sex. Sado-masochism is also concerned with violence. The evidence discloses that the practices of the appellants were unpredictably dangerous and degrading to body and mind and were developed with increasing barbarity and taught to persons whose consents were dubious or worthless.

A sadist draws pleasure from inflicting or watching cruelty. A masochist derives pleasure from his own pain or humiliation. The appellants are middle-aged men. The victims were youths some of whom were introduced to sado-masochism before they attained the age of 21. In his judgment in the Court of Appeal, Lord Lane CJ said that two members of the group of which the appellants formed part, namely one Cadman and the appellant Laskey:

> were responsible in part for the corruption of a youth K . . . It is some comfort at least to be told, as we were, that K has now it seems settled into a normal heterosexual relationship. Cadman had befriended K when the boy was 15 years old. He met him in a cafeteria and, so he says, found out that the boy was interested in homosexual activities. He introduced and encouraged K in 'bondage affairs'. He was interested in viewing and recording on videotape K and other teenage boys in homosexual scenes . . . One cannot overlook the danger that the gravity of the assaults and injuries in this type of case may escalate to even more unacceptable heights.

The evidence disclosed that drink and drugs were employed to obtain consent and increase enthusiasm. The victim was usually manacled so that the sadist could enjoy the thrill of power and the victim could enjoy the thrill of helplessness. The victim had no control over the harm which the sadist, also stimulated by drink and drugs might inflict. In one case a victim was branded twice on the thigh and there was some doubt as to whether he consented to or protested against the second branding. The dangers involved in administering violence must have been appreciated by the appellants because, so it was said by their counsel, each victim was given a code word which he could pronounce when excessive harm or pain was caused. The efficiency of this precaution, when taken, depends on the circumstances and on the personalities involved. No one can feel the pain of another. The charges against the appellants were based on genital torture and violence to the buttocks, anus, penis, testicles and nipples. The victims were degraded and humiliated, sometimes beaten, sometimes wounded with instruments and sometimes branded. Bloodletting and the smearing of human blood produced excitement. There were obvious dangers of serious personal injury and blood infection. Prosecuting counsel informed the trial judge against the protests of defence counsel, that although the appellants had not contracted Aids, two members of the group had died from Aids and one other had contracted an H.I.V. infection although not necessarily from the practices of the group. Some activities involved excrement. The assertion that the instruments employed by the sadists were clean and sterilised could not have removed the danger of infection, and the assertion that care was taken demonstrates the possibility of infection. Cruelty to human beings was on occasions supplemented by cruelty to animals in the form of bestiality. It is fortunate that there were no permanent injuries to a victim though no one knows the extent of harm inflicted in other cases. It is not surprising that a victim does not complain to the police when the complaint would involve him in giving details of acts in which he participated. Doctors of course are subject to a code of confidentiality.

In principle there is a difference between violence which is incidental and violence which is inflicted for the indulgence of cruelty. The violence of sado-masochistic encounters involves the indulgence of cruelty by sadists and the degradation of victims. Such violence is injurious to the participants and unpredictably dangerous. I am not prepared to invent a defence of consent for sado-masochistic encounters which breed and glorify cruelty and result in offences under sections 47 and 20 of the Act of 1861.

Society is entitled and bound to protect itself against a cult of violence. Pleasure derived from the infliction of pain is an evil thing. Cruelty is uncivilised. I would answer the certified question in the negative and dismiss the appeals of the appellants against conviction.

LORD MUSTILL (dissenting) . . .

I: THE DECIDED CASES

Throughout the argument of the appeal I was attracted by an analysis on the following lines. First, one would construct a continuous spectrum of the infliction of bodily harm, with killing at one end and a trifling touch at the other. Next, with the help of reported cases one would identify the point on this spectrum at which consent ordinarily ceases to be an answer to a prosecution for inflicting harm. This could be called 'the critical level'. It would soon become plain however that this analysis is too simple and that there are certain types of special situation to which the general rule does not apply. Thus, for example, surgical treatment which requires a degree of bodily invasion well on the upper side of the critical level will nevertheless be legitimate if performed in accordance with good medical practice and with the consent of the patient. Conversely, there will be cases in which even a moderate degree of harm cannot be legitimated by consent. Accordingly, the next stage in the analysis will be to identify those situations which have been identified as special by the decided cases, and to examine them to see whether the instant case either falls within one of them or is sufficiently close for an analogy to be valid. If the answer is negative, then the court will have to decide whether simply to apply the general law simply by deciding whether the bodily harm in the case under review is above or below the critical level, or to break new ground by recognising a new special situation to which the general law does not apply.

For all the intellectual neatness of this method I must recognise that it will not do, for it imposes on the reported cases and on the diversities of human life an order which they do not possess. Thus, when one comes to map out the spectrum of ordinary consensual physical harm, to which the special situations form exceptions, it is found that the task is almost impossible, since people do not ordinarily consent to the infliction of harm. In effect, either all or almost all the instances of the consensual infliction of violence are special. They have been in the past, and will continue to be in the future, the subject of special treatment by the law.

There are other objections to a general theory of consent and violence. Thus, for example, it is too simple to speak only of consent, for it comes in various sorts. Of these, four spring immediately to mind. First, there is an express agreement to the infliction of the injury which was in the event inflicted. Next, there is express agreement to the infliction of some harm, but not to that harm which in the event was actually caused. These two categories are matched by two more, in which the recipient expressly consents not to the infliction of harm, but to engagement in an activity which creates a risk of harm; again, either the harm which actually results, or to something less. These examples do not exhaust the categories, for corresponding with each are situations of frequent occurrence in practice where the consent is not express but implied. These numerous categories are not the fruit of academic over-elaboration, but are a reflection of real life. Yet they are scarcely touched on in the cases, which just do not bear the weight of any general theory of violence and consent.

...'Contact' sports

Some sports, such as the various codes of football, have deliberate bodily contact as an essential element. They lie at a mid-point between fighting, where the participant knows that his opponent will try to harm him, and the milder sports where there is at most an acknowledgement that someone may be accidentally hurt. In the contact sports each player knows and by taking part agrees that an opponent may from time to time inflict upon his body (for example by a rugby tackle) what would otherwise be a painful battery. By taking part he also assumes the risk that the deliberate contact may have unintended effects, conceivably of sufficient severity to amount to grievous bodily harm. But he does not agree that this more serious kind of injury may be inflicted deliberately. This simple analysis conceals a number of difficult problems, which are discussed in a series of Canadian decisions, culminating in *R* v *Ciccarelli* (1989) 54 CCC (3d) 121, on the subject of ice hockey, a sport in which an ethos of physical contact is deeply entrenched. The courts appear to have started with the proposition that some level of violence is lawful if the recipient agrees to it, and have dealt with the question of excessive violence by enquiring whether the recipient could really have tacitly accepted a risk of violence at the level which actually occurred. These decisions do not help us in the present appeal, where the consent of the recipients was express, and where it is known that they gladly agreed, not simply to some degree of harm but to everything that was done. What we need to know is whether, notwithstanding the recipient's implied consent, there comes a point at which it is too severe for the law to tolerate. Whilst common sense suggests that this must be so, and that the law will not license brutality under the name of sport, one of the very few reported indications of the point at which tolerable harm becomes intolerable violence is in the direction to the jury given by Bramwell LJ in *R* v *Bradshaw* (1878) 14 Cox CC 83 that the act (in this case a charge at football) would be unlawful if intended to cause 'serious hurt'. This accords with my own instinct, but I must recognise that a direction at nisi prius, even by a great judge, cannot be given the same weight as a judgment on appeal, consequent upon full argument and reflection. The same comment may be made about *R* v *Moore* (1898) 14 TLR 229.

5. Surgery

Many of the acts done by surgeons would be very serious crimes if done by anyone else, and yet the surgeons incur no liability. Actual consent, or the substitute for consent deemed by the law to exist where an emergency creates a need for action, is an essential element in this immunity; but it cannot be a direct explanation for it, since much of the bodily invasion involved in surgery lies well above any point at which consent could even arguably be regarded as furnishing a defence. Why is this so? The answer must in my opinion be that proper medical treatment, for which actual or deemed consent is a prerequisite, is in a category of its own.

6. Lawful correction

It is probably still the position at common law, as distinct from statute, that a parent or someone to whom the parent has delegated authority may inflict physical hurt on his or her child, provided that it does not go too far and is for the purpose of correction and not the gratification of passion or rage: see *R* v *Conner* (1836) 7 C & P 438; *R* v *Cheeseman* (1836) 7 C & P 455; *R* v *Hopley* (1860) 2 F & F 202; *R* v *Griffin* (1869) 11 Cox CC 402. These cases have nothing to do with consent, and are useful only as another demonstration that specially exempt situations can exist and that they can involve an upper limit of tolerable harm. [Lord Mustill went on to consider the arguments against consent being a defence.]

...I ask myself, not whether as a result of the decision in this appeal, activities such as those of the appellants should *cease* to be criminal, but rather whether the Act of 1861 (a statute which I venture to repeat once again was clearly intended to penalise conduct of a quite different nature) should in this new situation be interpreted so as to *make* it criminal. Why should this step be taken? Leaving aside repugnance and moral objection, both of which are entirely natural but neither of which are in my opinion grounds upon which the court could properly create a new crime, I can visualise only the following reasons. (1) Some of the practices obviously created a risk of genitourinary infection, and others of septicaemia. These might indeed have been grave in former times, but the risk of serious harm must surely have been greatly reduced by modern medical science.

(2) The possibility that matters might get out of hand, with grave results. It has been acknowledged throughout the present proceedings that the appellants' activities were performed as a prearranged ritual, which at the same time enhanced their excitement and minimised the risk that the infliction of injury would go too far. Of course things might go wrong and really serious injury or death might ensue. If this happened, those responsible would be punished according to the ordinary law, in the same way as those who kill or injure in the course of more ordinary sexual activities are regularly punished. But to penalise the appellants' conduct even if the extreme consequences do not ensue, just because they might have done so would require an assessment of the degree of risk, and the balancing of this risk against the interests of individual freedom. Such a balancing is in my opinion for Parliament, not the courts; and even if your Lordships' House were to embark upon it the attempt must in my opinion fail at the outset for there is no evidence at all of the seriousness of the hazards to which sado-masochistic conduct of this kind gives rise. This is not surprising, since the impressive argument of Mr Purnell for the respondents did not seek to persuade your Lordships' to bring the matter within the Act of 1861 on the ground of special risks, but rather to establish that the appellants are liable *under the general law* because the level of harm exceeded the critical level marking off criminal from non-criminal consensual violence which he invited your Lordships to endorse.

(3) I would give the same answer to the suggestion that these activities involved a risk of accelerating the spread of auto-immune deficiency syndrome, and that they should be brought within the Act of 1861 in the interests of public health. The consequence would be strange, since what is currently the principal cause for the transmission of this scourge, namely consenting buggery between males, is now legal. Nevertheless, I would have been compelled to give this proposition the most anxious consideration if there had been any evidence to support it. But there is none, since the case for the respondent was advanced on an entirely different ground.

(4) There remains an argument to which I have given much greater weight. As the evidence in the present case has shown, there is a risk that strangers (and especially young strangers) may be drawn into these activities at an early age and will then become established in them for life. This is indeed a disturbing prospect, but I have come to the conclusion that it is not a sufficient ground for declaring these activities to be criminal under the Act of 1861. The element of the corruption of youth is already catered for by the existing legislation; and if there is a gap in it which needs to be filled the remedy surely lies in the hands of Parliament, not in the application of a statute which is aimed at other forms of wrongdoing. As regards proselytisation for adult sado-masochism the argument appears to me circular. For if the activity is not itself so much against the public interest that it ought to be declared criminal under the Act of 1861 then the risk that others will be induced to join in cannot be a ground for making it criminal.

Leaving aside the logic of this answer, which seems to me impregnable, plain humanity demands that a court addressing the criminality of conduct such as that of the present should recognise and respond to the profound dismay which all members of the community share about the apparent increase of cruel and senseless crimes against the defenceless. Whilst doing so I must repeat for the last time that in the answer which I propose I do not advocate the decriminalisation of conduct which has hitherto been a crime; nor do I rebut a submission that a new crime should be created, penalising this conduct, for Mr Purnell has rightly not invited the House to take this course. The only question is whether these consensual private acts are offences against the existing law of violence. To this question I return a negative response.

Appeal dismissed.

The defendants proceeded to take their claims to the European Court of Human Rights:

Laskey, Jaggard and Brown v United Kingdom
(1997) 24 EHRR 39, European Court of Human Rights

Alleged violation of Article 8 of the Convention

The applicants contended that their prosecution and convictions for assault and wounding in the course of consensual sado-masochistic activities between adults was in breach of Article 8 of the Convention which provides:

1. Everyone has the right to respect for his private and family life, his home and correspondence.
2. There shall be no interference by a public authority with the exercise of this right except such as is in accordance with the law and is necessary in a democratic society in the interests of national security, public safety or the economic well-being of the country, for the prevention of disorder or crime, for the protection of health or morals, or for the protection of the rights and freedoms of others.

It was common ground among those appearing before the Court that the criminal proceedings against the applicants which resulted in their conviction constituted an 'interference by a public authority' with the applicants' right to respect for their private life. It was similarly undisputed that the interference had been 'in accordance with the law'. Furthermore, the Commission and the applicants accepted the Government's assertion that the interference pursued the legitimate aim of the 'protection of health or morals', within the meaning of the second paragraph of Article 8.

The Court observes that not every sexual activity carried out behind closed doors necessarily falls within the scope of Article 8. In the present case, the applicants were involved in consensual sado-masochistic activities for purposes of sexual gratification. There can be no doubt that sexual orientation and activity concern an intimate aspect of private life. However, a considerable number of people were involved in the activities in question which included, *inter alia*, the recruitment of new 'Members', the provision of several specially-equipped 'chambers', and the shooting of many videotapes which were distributed among the 'Members'. It may thus be open to question whether the sexual activities of the applicants fell entirely within the notion of 'private life' in the particular circumstances of the case.

However, since this point has not been disputed by those appearing before it, the Court sees no reason to examine it of its own motion in the present case. Assuming, therefore, that the prosecution and conviction of the applicants amounted to an interference with their private life, the question arises whether such an interference was 'necessary in a democratic society' within the meaning of the second paragraph of Article 8.

'Necessary in a democratic society'

The applicants maintained that the interference at issue could not be regarded as 'necessary in a democratic society'. This submission was contested by the Government and by a majority of the Commission.

In support of their submission, the applicants alleged that all those involved in the sadomasochistic encounters were willing adult participants; that participation in the acts complained of was carefully restricted and controlled and was limited to persons with like-minded sado-masochistic proclivities; that the acts were not witnessed by the public at large and that there was no danger or likelihood that they would ever be so witnessed; that no serious or permanent injury had been sustained, no infection had been caused to the wounds, and that no medical treatment had been required. Furthermore, no complaint was ever made to the police—who learnt about the applicants' activities by chance....

The applicants submitted that their case should be viewed as one involving matters of sexual expression, rather than violence. With due regard to this consideration, the line beyond which consent is no defence to physical injury should only be drawn at the level of intentional or reckless causing of serious disabling injury.

For the Government. The State was entitled to punish acts of violence, such as those for which the applicants were convicted, that could not be considered of a trifling or transient nature, irrespective of the consent of the victim. In fact, in the present case, some of these acts could well be compared to 'genital torture' and a Contracting State could not be said to have an obligation to tolerate acts of torture because they are committed in the context of a consenting sexual relationship. The State was moreover entitled to prohibit activities because of their potential danger.

The Government further contended that the criminal law should seek to deter certain forms of behaviour on public health grounds but also for broader moral reasons. In this respect, acts of torture—such as those at issue in the present case—may be banned also on the ground that they undermine the respect which human beings should confer upon each other. In any event, the whole issue of the role of consent in the criminal law is of great complexity and the contracting States should enjoy a wide margin of appreciation to consider all the public policy options.

The Commission noted that the injuries that were or could be caused by the applicants' activities were of a significant nature and degree, and that the conduct in question was, on any view, of an extreme character. The State authorities therefore acted within their margin of appreciation in order to protect its citizens from real risk of serious physical harm or injury.

According to the Court's established case law, the notion of necessity implies that the interference corresponds to a pressing social need and, in particular, that it is proportionate to the legitimate aim pursued; in determining whether an interference is 'necessary in a democratic society', the Court will take into account that a margin of appreciation is left to the national authorities, whose decision remains subject to review by the Court for conformity with the requirements of the Convention.

The scope of this margin of appreciation is not identical in each case but will vary according to the context. Relevant factors include the nature of the Convention right in issue, its importance for the individual and the nature of the activities concerned.

The Court considers that one of the roles which the State is unquestionably entitled to undertake is to seek to regulate, through the operation of the criminal law, activities which involve the infliction of physical harm. This is so whether the activities in question occur in the course of sexual conduct or otherwise.

The determination of the level of harm that should be tolerated by the law in situations where the victim consents is in the first instance a matter for the State concerned since what is at stake is related, on the one hand, to the public health considerations and to the general deterrent effect of the criminal law, and, on the other, to the personal autonomy of the individual.

The applicants have contended that, in the circumstances of the case, the behaviour in question formed part of private morality which is not the State's business to regulate. In their submission the matters for which they were prosecuted and convicted concerned only private sexual behaviour.

The Court is not persuaded by this submission. It is evident from the facts established by the national courts that the applicants' sado-masochistic activities involved a significant degree of injury or wounding which could not be characterised as trifling or transient. This, in itself, suffices to distinguish the present case from those applications which have previously been examined by the Court concerning consensual homosexual behaviour in private between adults where no such feature was present.

Nor does the Court accept the applicants' submission that no prosecution should have been brought against them since their injuries were not severe and since no medical treatment had been required.

In deciding whether or not to prosecute, the State authorities were entitled to have regard not only to the actual seriousness of the harm caused—which as noted above was considered to be significant—but also as stated by Lord Jauncey of Tullichettle, to the potential for harm inherent in the acts in question. In this respect it is recalled that the activities were considered by Lord Templeman to be 'unpredictably dangerous'.

The applicants have further submitted that they were singled out partly because of the authorities' bias against homosexuals. They referred to the recent judgment in the *Wilson* case, where, in their view, similar behaviour in the context of a heterosexual couple was not considered to deserve criminal punishment.

The Court finds no evidence in support of the applicants' allegations in either the conduct of the proceedings against them or the judgment of the House of Lords. In this respect it recalls the remark of the trial judge when passing sentence that 'the unlawful conduct now before the court would be dealt with equally in the prosecution of heterosexuals or bisexuals if carried out by them'.

Moreover, it is clear from the judgment of the House of Lords that the opinions of the majority were based on the extreme nature of the practices involved and not the sexual proclivities of the applicants.

R v Wilson

[1996] 3 WLR 125, Court of Appeal

At his wife's instigation the appellant branded his initials on her buttocks with a hot knife. He was charged with assault occasioning actual bodily harm contrary to section 47 of the Offences Against the Person Act 1861. At the close of the prosecution case, on a submission of no case to answer, the judge ruled that despite the wife's consent he was bound by authority to direct the jury to convict. In the light of that ruling the appellant was not called to give evidence and defence counsel did not make any submissions to the jury. The appellant was convicted. On appeal against conviction:

RUSSELL LJ: . . . We are abundantly satisfied that there is no factual comparison to be made between the instant case and the facts of either R v Donovan [1934] 2 KB 498 or R v Brown [1994] 1 AC 212: Mrs Wilson not only consented to that which the appellant did, she instigated it. There was no aggressive intent on the part of the appellant. On the contrary, far from wishing to cause injury to his wife, the appellant's desire was to assist her in what she regarded as the acquisition of a desirable piece of personal adornment, perhaps in this day and age no less understandable than the piercing of nostrils or even tongues for the purposes of inserting decorative jewellery.

In our judgment R v Brown is not authority for the proposition that consent is no defence to a charge under section 47 of the Act of 1861, in all circumstances where actual bodily harm is deliberately inflicted. It is to be observed that the question certified for their Lordships in R v Brown related only to a 'sado-masochistic encounter.' . . .

Does public policy or the public interest demand that the appellant's activity should be visited by the sanctions of the criminal law? The majority in R v Brown clearly took the view that such considerations were relevant. If that is so, then we are firmly of the opinion that it is not in the public interest that activities such as the appellant's in this appeal should amount to criminal behaviour. Consensual activity between husband and wife, in the privacy of the matrimonial home, is not, in our judgment, normally a proper matter for criminal investigation, let alone criminal prosecution. Accordingly we take the view that the judge failed to have full regard to the facts of this case and misdirected himself in saying that R v Donovan [1934] 2 KB 498 and R v Brown [1994] 1 AC 212 constrained him to rule that consent was no defence.

In this field, in our judgment, the law should develop upon a case basis rather than upon general propositions to which, in the changing times in which we live, exceptions may arise from time to time not expressly covered by authority.

We shall allow the appeal and quash the conviction . . . .

In *R v Emmett* [1999] EWCA 1710 Crim the defendant relied on *Wilson* in a case involving consensual sado-masochistic acts between a male and his consenting female partner. The acts included the infliction of burns to the woman's chest and haemorrhaging to the eyes caused by the tightening of a ligature to the woman's neck in the course of oral sex designed to enhance the sexual experience.

The appellant, understandably, relies strongly upon these passages (in *Wilson* above), but we have come to the clear conclusion that the evidence in the instant case, in striking contrast to that in *Wilson*, made it plain that the actual or potential damage to which the appellant's partner was exposed in this case, plainly went far beyond that which was established by the evidence in *Wilson*.

The lady suffered a serious, and what must have been, an excruciating painful burn which became infected, and the appellant himself recognised that it required medical attention. As to the process of partial asphyxiation, to which she was subjected on the earlier occasion, while it may be now fairly well known that the restriction of oxygen to the brain is capable of heightening sexual sensation, it is also, or should be, equally well known that such a practice contains within itself a grave danger of brain damage or even death. There have been, in recent years, a number of tragic cases of persons who have taken this practice too far, with fatal consequences.

As the interview made plain, the appellant was plainly aware of that danger. In the course of argument, counsel was asked what the situation would have been if, in the present case, the process had gone just a little further and the appellant's partner had died. No satisfactory answer, unsurprisingly, as we think could be given to that question.

Accordingly, whether the line beyond which consent becomes immaterial is drawn at the point suggested by Lord Jauncey and Lord Lowry, the point at which common assault becomes assault occasioning actual bodily harm, or at some higher level, where the evidence looked at objectively reveals a realistic risk of a more than transient or trivial injury, it is plain, in our judgment, that the activities involved in by this appellant and his partner went well beyond that line. The learned judge, in giving his ruling said:

> 'In this case, the degree of actual and potential harm was such and also the degree of unpredictability as to injury was such as to make it a proper cause from the criminal law to intervene. This was not tattooing, it was not something which absented pain or dangerousness and the agreed medical evidence is in each case, certainly on the first occasion, there was a very considerable degree of danger to life; on the second, there was a degree of injury to the body.'

With that conclusion, this Court entirely agrees. The learned judge was right to rule that these matters should be left to the jury, on the basis that consent could not amount to a defence.

■ **NOTES AND QUESTIONS**

1. Is *Wilson* distinguishable from *Brown*? In his commentary on *Wilson*, Prof J.C. Smith observed ([1996] Crim LR 573):

> It is not at all surprising that the trial judge reluctantly took the view that he was bound by *Brown* to direct the jury to convict. Thus Lord Jauncey, one of the majority in *Brown* stated ([1993] 2 All ER 75 at 90):
>
> > In my view the line properly falls to be drawn between assault at common law and the offence of assault occasioning actual bodily harm created by section 47 of the 1861 Act, with the result that consent of the victim is no answer to anyone charged with the latter offence or with a contravention of section 20 unless the circumstances fall within one of the well-known exceptions such as organised sporting contests and games, parental chastisement or reasonable surgery.
>
> Who was to know that marital bottom-branding was to be added to the list of exceptions? What reasons can be discerned in the present judgment for the distinction?
>
> (i) Mrs W did not only consent to the branding but 'instigated' it. Would the House in *Brown* have taken a different view of a particular activity if it had been shown to have been instigated by the 'victim'? It seems highly unlikely. It was said, for example (p. 83), that the victim was usually manacled so that he 'could enjoy the thrill of helplessness.' He wanted to be manacled. (ii) There was in the present case 'no aggressive intent.' But the goings-on in *Brown* could hardly have been more friendly. Everyone was having a jolly good time. (iii) W had no wish to cause injury to his wife. If the branding had been done without consent, the court would not have had the slightest hesitation in describing it as 'injury;' and W intended to cause it. (iv) This was consensual activity between husband and wife in the privacy of the matrimonial home. It can hardly be supposed, in these days, that the decision is limited to marital activity. 'Partners' and adult girl or boy friends could hardly be treated differently. But group branding sessions might fall foul of the next point. (v) *Brown* was a case involving 'sadomasochism of the grossest kind.' This is perhaps the substantial reason. W, unlike the defendants in *Brown*, apparently derived no sexual satisfaction from what he did, any more than a surgeon or professional tattooist. It was not essentially different from the lawful practice of tattooing. This seems to be the only basis on which *Donovan* (the court says '[Donovan's] act had about it an aggressive element') can realistically be distinguished. What if the Wilsons had admitted that the operation gave them a thrill?
>
> The approach of the majority in *Brown* was to ask, does public policy require us to create a new defence to sections 47 and 20, so as to exempt these revolting sadomasochists? The

answer, inevitably, was no. The approach of the present court was to ask, does the public interest require that this activity be condemned as criminal? It is not surprising that the answer to that question too should be in the negative. This is more in tune with the approach of the minority in *Brown*; and it is submitted that it is to be preferred. The decision leaves the law in an uncertain state; and it is noteworthy that the court thought that the law should be left to develop on a case by case basis. Contrast the effort made by the Law Commission to introduce principle into the law – with a second, large, Consultation Paper (No. 139).

2. Is the court in *Brown* being unduly paternalistic? Does the State and/or the judiciary have an obligation to enforce the prevailing moral values of the community? How does one determine what those values are? Recall the Hart – Devlin debate presented in Chapter 1.

3. In *Dudgeon* v *United Kingdom* (1981) 4 EHRR 149, the European Court of Human Rights ruled that Northern Ireland laws which criminalised homosexual activities between consenting adults committed in private infringed the right to respect for private life contained in Article 8 of the European Convention on Human Rights. In what sense is *Brown* distinguishable?

4. *Brown* and *Wilson* involve cases where the defendant committed an act of violence for reasons of sexual gratification. The principle that a person cannot consent to such acts does not apply where an act is not intended to cause harm and harm occurs as a by-product of that act. This was made clear in *Dica* (see below) in which it was acknowledged that informed consent to intercourse with a person suffering HIV is effective. If consent is not informed the defendant may be convicted of an offence against the person, although not rape.

(ii) When will the State infer consent?

We have already seen in *Collins* v *Wilcock* that the law implies consent to physical contact which is generally acceptable in the ordinary conduct of daily life. Similarly, the courts will not, for example, allow the absence of formal consent by an unconscious patient to convert a beneficial medical procedure into a battery. Thus, if a paramedic comes upon an unconscious victim of a car accident and gives a blood transfusion it will not amount to a battery, even though the recipient is a Jehovah's Witness who would have refused such treatment on religious grounds had she been conscious. Medical treatment of a person incapable of consent because of mental incapacity will also not amount to assault or battery (see *In re F (Mental Patient: Sterilisation)* [1990] 2 AC 1). In the case of an emergency, a doctor should do no more than is reasonably required in the best interests of the patient. Where the incapacity is more permanent, treatment is justified to save the life of the victim, or to ensure improvement or prevent a deterioration of the victim's physical or mental health'.

It has also long been thought that participants in a sporting event consent to the injuries associated with the sport. The position was expressed by Lord Lane in *Attorney General's Reference (No. 6 of 1980)* [1981] QB 715, a case which arose from an impromptu fight between two young men in a street. The court held that 'it is not in the public interest that people should try to cause, or should cause, each other actual bodily harm for no good reason'. The participants' consent to the fight was rejected as a defence. Lord Lane then went on to say:

> Nothing which we have said is intended to cast doubt on the accepted legality of properly conducted games and sports...

This obiter notwithstanding, a prosecution for battery may occur where the force used exceeds the legitimate parameters of the rules of the game.

Regina v Barnes

[2005] 1 WLR 910, Court of Appeal

The appellant was playing in an amateur football match when he tackled a player on the opposing team and caused him a serious injury to his right leg. He was charged with inflicting grievous bodily harm, contrary to section 20 of the Offences against the Person Act 1861, the allegation being that the tackle which caused the injury was crushing, late, unnecessary, reckless and high. The appellant claimed that the tackle was a fair, if hard, challenge and that any injury caused was accidental. In summing up, the judge directed the jury that the appellant could only be convicted if the prosecution had proved that what he had done had not been done by way of legitimate sport. The appellant was convicted.

On appeal against conviction—

Held, allowing the appeal, that most organised sports had their own disciplinary procedures for enforcing their particular rules and standards of conduct and therefore, in the majority of situations, there was no need for, and it was undesirable that there should be, any criminal proceedings when a player injured another player in the course of a sporting event; that criminal proceedings should only be brought in such a situation if a player's conduct was sufficiently grave to be properly categorised as criminal; that, if criminal proceedings were justified, the consent of the victim to the possibility of injury would only be a defence if what had occurred had not gone beyond what a player could reasonably be regarded as having accepted by taking part in the sport; that in highly competitive sports conduct outside the rules could be expected to occur in the heat of the moment which, even if it justified a warning or a sending off, still might not reach the threshold required for it to be criminal; that whether conduct reached that required threshold would depend on all the circumstances, including the type of sport, the level at which it was played, the nature of the act, the degree of force used, the extent of the risk of injury and the defendant's state of mind; that in borderline cases the jury would need to ask themselves, among other questions, whether the contact was so obviously late and/or violent that it could not be regarded as an instinctive reaction, error or misjudgment in the heat of the game; that whilst the concept of 'legitimate sport' in itself was not unhelpful, an explanation should have been given to the jury as to how they should identify what was and was not legitimate in the context of the relevant sport; and that, accordingly, since the judge had not provided such an explanation, the summing up was inadequate and the conviction was unsafe.

. . .

12. The fact that the participants in, for example, a football match, implicitly consent to take part in a game, assists in identifying the limits of the defence. If what occurs goes beyond what a player can reasonably be regarded as having accepted by taking part in the sport, this indicates that the conduct will not be covered by the defence. What is implicitly accepted in one sport will not necessarily be covered by the defence in another sport. In *R* v *Cey* (1989) 48 CCC (3d) 480, the Saskatchewan Court of Appeal was concerned with ice hockey which is a very physical game. Despite the nature of ice hockey, in giving the majority judgment, Gerwing JA (Cameron JA concurring), made it clear, at p 490, that even in ice hockey:

'some forms of bodily contact carry with them such a high risk of injury and such a distinct probability of serious harm as to be beyond what, in fact, the players commonly consent to, or what, in law, they are capable of consenting to.'

13. The general position as to contact sports was helpfully considered by the Law Commission in its consultation paper Consent and Offences against the Person (1993) (Consultation Paper No 134). The Commission indicated, at para 10.12, its approval of the approach adopted by the

Criminal Injuries Compensation Board which we would also approve. This is that

'in a sport in which bodily contact is a commonplace part of the game, the players consent to such contact even if, through unfortunate accident, injury, perhaps of a serious nature, may result. However, such players do not consent to being deliberately punched or kicked and such actions constitute an assault for which the board would award compensation.'

14. Subject to what we have to say hereafter we would in general accept the view of the Commission, at para 10.18, that:

'the present broad rules for sports and games appear to be: (i) the intentional infliction of injury enjoys no immunity; (ii) a decision as to whether the reckless infliction of injury is criminal is likely to be strongly influenced by whether the injury occurred during actual play, or in a moment of temper or over-excitement when play has ceased, or "off the ball"; (iii) although there is little authority on the point, principle demands that even during play injury that results from risk-taking by a player that is unreasonable, in the light of the conduct necessary to play the game properly, should also be criminal.'

...

28. We appreciate the difficulty that the judge had summing up this case because of the state of the authorities. The concept of 'legitimate sport' in itself is not unhelpful. However, it required an explanation of how the jury should identify what is and what is not 'legitimate' in the context of the relevant sport. The case called out for the jury to be given help as to the approach they should adopt in determining what is or is not 'legitimate sport'. The judge should have given the jury a direction to determine for themselves what actually happened at the critical time when the injury was inflicted. Broadly speaking, were they satisfied that the case for the prosecution was correct? They should have been told that if they were not, and they thought that the appellant's description of what occurred might be correct, then that was in all probability the end of the case. It should have been pointed out to the jury that even if the offending contact was a foul, it was still necessary for them to determine whether it could be anticipated in a normal game of football or was it something quite outside what could be expected to occur in the course of a football game. The summing up should also have made it clear that even if a tackle results in a player being sent off, it may still not reach the necessary threshold to constitute criminal conduct.

29. The jury were not given any examples of conduct which could be regarded as 'legitimate sport' and those which were not 'legitimate sport' for the purposes of determining whether they were criminal. The jury did not need copies of the rules, but they did need to be told why it was important to determine where the ball was at the time the tackle took place. They should have been told the importance of the distinction between the appellant going for the ball, albeit late, and his 'going for' the victim.

30. Having carefully considered the summing up as a whole, we can well understand why the jury felt they needed further assistance after they retired. The further direction they received did not give them that assistance. Without it, it is difficult to determine what they thought they had to decide in order to find the appellant guilty. This being the position, we are forced to come to the conclusion that the summing up was inadequate, and that as a result the conviction is unsafe. Accordingly the appeal will be allowed and the orders made set aside.

Appeal allowed.

■ **NOTES AND QUESTIONS**

1. Should distinctions be drawn between amateur and professional events? Between pick-up games and organised games? Between different sports?

2. In some sports, such as boxing, the aim is to injure one's opponent. In *R v Coney* (1882) 8 QBD 534 a prosecution was brought against the spectators at a public prize fight. The court held that the activity in question was against public policy and illegal. Yet, to the consternation of many, boxing remains legal. Why? In what way is *Coney* distinguishable?

(iii) What constitutes valid consent

(a) Consent and age

If a victim is unable to comprehend the nature of the act to which he or she apparently consented, the consent will be invalid.

Burrell v Harmer

[1965] 3 All ER 684, Divisional Court

The defendant tattooed devices on the arms of two boys aged respectively 12 and 13. The marks subsequently became inflamed and he was charged with, and convicted of, causing the boys actual bodily harm.

Held, dismissing his appeal, that if a child of the age of understanding was unable to appreciate the nature of an act, apparent consent to it was no consent at all.

R v D

[1984] 1 AC 778, House of Lords

LORD BRANDON OF OAKBROOK: . . . I must now deal with two matters to which I said that I would return later. One of those matters is whether the doctrine laid down by the Irish Supreme Court in *Edge's* case [1943] IR 115 that the person the absence of whose consent is an essential ingredient of the common law offence of kidnapping is that of the child if it has reached an age of discretion fixed by law, but that of its father or other guardian if it has not, applies also under English law.

In my opinion, to accept that doctrine as applicable under English law would not be consistent with the formulation of the third ingredient of the common law offence of kidnapping which I made earlier on the basis of the wide body of authority to which your Lordships were referred. That third ingredient, as I formulated it earlier, consists of the absence of consent on the part of the person taken or carried away. I see no good reason why, in relation to the kidnapping of a child, it should not in all cases be the absence of the child's consent which is material, whatever its age may be. In the case of a very young child, it would not have the understanding or the intelligence to give its consent, so that absence of consent would be a necessary inference from its age. In the case of an older child, however, it must, I think be a question of fact for a jury whether the child concerned has sufficient understanding and intelligence to give its consent; if, but only if, the jury considers that a child has these qualities, it must then go on to consider whether it has been proved that the child did not give its consent. While the matter will always be for the jury alone to decide, I should not expect a jury to find at all frequently that a child under 14 had sufficient understanding and intelligence to give its consent.

■ NOTES AND QUESTIONS

1. In *Burrell* v *Harmer*, is the court's position that the boys did not appreciate what it meant to be tattooed; or that even if they did know, they were not legally capable of giving consent? Would the result have been different if the boys had been 15? 18? Tattooing of minors below the age of 16 is now illegal under the Tattooing of Minors Act 1969.

2. Should the defendant's honest and reasonable belief in the consent of the victim be a defence? In the case of a very young child, absence of consent will be implied from the child's age. See, e.g., *R* v *Howard* [1965] 3 All ER 684 (child of six unable to comprehend sexual intercourse and so unable to consent). In other cases the jury must decide whether there was a valid consent.

(b) Consent, Fraud, and Non Disclosure

An apparent consent, which is the product of a threat, will not be valid. What then of consent induced by fraud or which is not fully informed?

R v Tabassum
[2000] Crim LR 686, Court of Appeal

Three women, all of whom knew the defendant, made complaints of indecent assault against him. The first took a computer course on which he was a lecturer. He told her that he had worked at Christies, a well-known cancer hospital is Manchester, and was a breast cancer specialist. She thought that he was a doctor. He said that he was doing a study on breast cancer, and she agreed to take part. There was a meeting at which she filled in a questionnaire and signed a consent form, then she removed her bra at his request and he showed her how to examine her breasts. A little later, after asking her some questions, he asked her to take off her top again, but she declined and asked him to leave, which he did. Her evidence was that he showed no sign of sexual excitement, but she would not have allowed him to touch her if she had known that he had no relevant qualifications.

The second complainant said that the defendant came to her house, and told her he was doing a survey on breast cancer. He seemed very knowledgeable and she agreed to take part. He returned at a later date. She filled in the questionnaire and the consent form and he examined her breasts. She would not have allowed him to do so if she had known that he had no relevant qualifications, which he had led her to believe he had. The third complainant knew the defendant through his lectures. She filled in the form and he visited her at her home by appointment. He checked her blood pressure, pulse and heart. She asked him if he was a doctor, and he said he was not but had done a lot of work for Christies cancer hospital. She refused to let him examine her breasts, though he put his stethoscope under her bra.

She would not have let him touch her if she had known that he did not work at Christies hospital, where she thought he had been training.

At the trial evidence was adduced that the defendant had worked for several years as a hospital representative, who called on doctors to tell them about drugs. He had received training on drugs and diseases.

In evidence, the defendant said that he had no convictions, and had postgraduate degrees in science and business administration. In his work as a hospital representative he had gained knowledge about breast cancer and seen the need for a database. He had prepared a leaflet to guide women in examining their breasts. The complainants had given their consent to what he did. He agreed that he had no medical qualifications but felt entitled to say that he had medical training. He accepted that he had not been trained to examine for breast cancer. At the time of his arrest he had not started his database, because he did not have enough details.

The defendant was convicted of three offences of indecent assault and appealed against his conviction. Counsel submitted that: (1) consent could be negatived only where the victim was deceived or mistaken about the identity of the perpetrator of the act, or where the nature and quality of the act was different from that for which consent was given. Consent was not negatived merely because the victim would not have consented if she had known all the facts. (2) The judge failed to direct the jury to the reasonableness of the defendant's belief in the complainants' consent.

Held, dismissing the appeal, that (1) the victims had consented to the nature of the defendant's acts, but not their quality, since they believed he was medically qualified or had trained at Christies, and that the touching was for a medical purpose; and that, accordingly, there was no true consent. (2) The only issues were consent and whether the defendant may have believed that the complainants were consenting. On these issues the judge's directions were entirely adequate.

Bolduc and Bird v R
(1967) 63 DLR (2d) 82, Supreme Court of Canada

A physician, about to conduct a vaginal examination and, if necessary, perform a medical procedure in the area to be examined, falsely introduced a lay friend of his to the patient as a medical intern and asked if the friend, who, in fact, was present for his own gratification, might observe the examination. The patient consented to the friend's presence and the physician proceeded with the examination during which he touched the patient's private parts and inserted an instrument therein for the purposes of the examination while the friend looked on but at no time touched the patient. Both the physician and his friend were convicted of indecent assault on the patient and their conviction was affirmed by the Court of Appeal but on their further appeal from conviction, *held*, Spence, J, dissenting, the appeals should be allowed and the convictions quashed.

Per Hall, J, Cartwright, Fauteux and Ritchie, JJ, concurring: It cannot be said that the fraud practised on the patient vitiated her consent to what the physician was supposed to do and to what, in fact, he did do and, accordingly, the consent of the patient was not obtained by false and fraudulent representations as to the nature and quality of the act. The fraud related rather to the friend's identity as a medical intern and his presence, having regard for the fact that he did not touch the patient, was not an assault.

Per Spence, J, dissenting: Under s. 230 of the *Criminal Code*, the application of force, however slight, is an assault when it is 'without the consent of another person or with consent, where it is obtained by fraud.' The patient's consent to the touching of her person by the physician was a consent to such touching in the presence of a doctor and not a mere layman. The indecent assault upon her was not, then, the act to which she consented and, hence, even without recourse to the provisions of s. 141(2), the accused physician's conduct amounted to the offence of indecent assault to which the co-accused was a party by virtue of the provisions of s. 21 of the *Code*.

■ NOTES AND QUESTIONS

1. What is the rationale of the above decisions? Would it have been relevant whether the woman would have consented to the examination if she had known the true state of affairs?

2. A doctor indicates that he intends to perform a vaginal examination. The patient consents and the doctor proceeds (in a highly unprofessional manner) to engage in conduct, which in law would amount to an indecent assault. Would consent be a defence to the ensuing charge? How does this case differ from *Bolduc and Bird*? See *R* v *Williams* [1980] Crim LR 589. For further discussion of this and related issues see *Kumar* v *The Queen* [2006] EWCA Crim 1946, and Chapter 6 generally.

3. In *R* v *Richardson* [1998] 3 WLR 1292, it was held that a dentist who had been suspended from her profession was not guilty of assault merely because she was no longer qualified to carry out dental procedures. Her patients had consented to dental treatment and were not deceived about her identity, only about her continuing qualification to practice.

When can it be said that a fraud has occurred?

R v Dica

[2004] EWCA Crim 1103, Court of Appeal

The defendant, knowing he was infected with HIV, had intercourse with two women who were unaware of his condition and who subsequently became infected. He was convicted of maliciously inflicting grievous harm. The trial withdrew the issue of consent from the jury, on the basis of *Brown*. On appeal on this issue:

...

41. As a general rule, unless the activity is lawful, the consent of the victim to the deliberate infliction of serious bodily injury on him or her does not provide the perpetrator with any defence. Different categories of activity are regarded as lawful. Thus no-one doubts that necessary major surgery with the patient's consent, even if likely to result in severe disability (e.g. an amputation) would be lawful. However the categories of activity regarded as lawful are not closed, and equally, they are not immutable. Thus, prize fighting and street fighting by consenting participants are

unlawful: although some would have it banned, boxing for sport is not. Coming closer to this case, in *Bravery* v *Bravery* [1954] 3 All ER 59, Denning LJ condemned in the strongest terms, and as criminal, the conduct of a young husband who, with the consent of his wife, underwent a sterilisation operation, not so as to avoid the risk of transmitting a hereditary disease, or something similar, but to enable him to 'have the pleasure of sexual intercourse without shouldering the responsibilities attaching to it'. He thought that such an operation, for that reason, was plainly 'injurious to the public interest'. This approach sounds dated, as indeed it is. Denning LJ's colleagues expressly and unequivocally dissociated themselves from it. However, judges from earlier generations, reflecting their own contemporary society, might have agreed with him. We have sufficiently illustrated the impermanence of public policy in the context of establishing which activities involving violence may or may not be lawful.

42. The present policy of the law is that, whether or not the violent activity takes place in private, and even if the victim agrees to it, serious violence is not lawful merely because it enables the perpetrator (or the victim) to achieve sexual gratification. Judge Philpot was impressed with the conclusions to be drawn from the well-known decision in *R* v *Brown* [1994] 1 AC 212. Sadomasochistic activity of an extreme, indeed horrific kind, which caused grievous bodily harm, was held to be unlawful, notwithstanding that those who suffered the cruelty positively welcomed it. This decision of the House of Lords was supported in the ECtHR on the basis that although the prosecution may have constituted an interference with the private lives of those involved, it was justified for the protection of public health (*Laskey* v *United Kingdom* [1997] 24 EHRR 34).

43. The same policy can be seen in operation in *R* v *Donovan* [1934] 2 KB 498, where the violence was less extreme and the consent of the victim, although real, was far removed from the enthusiastic co-operation of the victims in *Brown*.

44. *R* v *Boyea* [1992] 156 JPR 505 represents another example of the application of the principle in *Donovan*. If she consented to injury by allowing the defendant to put his hand into her vagina and twist it, causing, among other injuries, internal and external injuries to her vagina and bruising on her pubis, the woman's consent (if any) would have been irrelevant. Recognising that social attitudes to sexual matters had changed over the years, a contemporaneous approach to these matters was appropriate. However, 'the extent of the violence inflicted went far beyond the risk of minor injury to which, if she did consent, her consent would have been a defence'. On close analysis, however, this case was decided on the basis that the victim did not in fact consent.

45. In *R* v *Emmett* (unreported, 18th June 1999), as part of their consensual sexual activity, the woman agreed to allow her partner to cover her head with a plastic bag, tying it tightly at the neck. On a different occasion, she agreed that he could pour fuel from a lighter onto her breasts and set fire to the fuel. On the first occasion, she was at risk of death, and lost consciousness. On the second, she suffered burns, which became infected. This Court did not directly answer the question posed by the trial judge in his certificate, but concluded that *Brown* demonstrated that the woman's consent to these events did not provide a defence for her partner.

46. These authorities demonstrate that violent conduct involving the deliberate and intentional infliction of bodily harm is and remains unlawful notwithstanding that its purpose is the sexual gratification of one or both participants. Notwithstanding their sexual overtones, these cases were concerned with violent crime, and the sexual overtones did not alter the fact that both parties were consenting to the deliberate infliction of serious harm or bodily injury on one participant by the other. To date, as a matter of public policy, it has not been thought appropriate for such violent conduct to be excused merely because there is a private consensual sexual element to it. The same public policy reason would prohibit the deliberate spreading of disease, including sexual disease.

47. In our judgement the impact of the authorities dealing with sexual gratification can too readily be misunderstood. It does not follow from them, and they do not suggest, that consensual acts of sexual intercourse are unlawful merely because there may be a known risk to the health of one or other participant. These participants are not intent on spreading or becoming infected with disease through sexual intercourse. They are not indulging in serious violence for the purposes of sexual gratification. They are simply prepared, knowingly, to run the risk, not the certainty, of infection, as well as all the other risks inherent in and possible consequences of sexual intercourse, such as, and despite the most careful precautions, an unintended pregnancy. At one extreme there is casual sex

between complete strangers, sometimes protected, sometimes not, when the attendant risks are known to be higher, and at the other, there is sexual intercourse between couples in a long-term and loving, and trusting relationship, which may from time to time also carry risks.

48. The first of these categories is self-explanatory and needs no amplification. By way of illustration we shall provide two examples of cases which would fall within the second.

49. In the first, one of a couple suffers from HIV. It may be the man: it may be the woman. The circumstances in which HIV was contracted are irrelevant. They could result from a contaminated blood transfusion, or an earlier relationship with a previous sexual partner, who unknown to the sufferer with whom we are concerned, was himself or herself infected with HIV. The parties are Roman Catholics. They are conscientiously unable to use artificial contraception. They both know of the risk that the healthy partner may become infected with HIV. Our second example is that of a young couple, desperate for a family, who are advised that if the wife were to become pregnant and give birth, her long-term health, indeed her life itself, would be at risk. Together the couple decide to run that risk, and she becomes pregnant. She may be advised that the foetus should be aborted, on the grounds of her health, yet, nevertheless, decide to bring her baby to term. If she does, and suffers ill health, is the male partner to be criminally liable for having sexual intercourse with her, notwithstanding that he knew of the risk to her health? If he is liable to be prosecuted, was she not a party to whatever crime was committed? And should the law interfere with the Roman Catholic couple, and require them, at the peril of criminal sanctions, to choose between bringing their sexual relationship to an end or violating their consciences by using contraception?

50. These, and similar risks, have always been taken by adults consenting to sexual intercourse. Different situations, no less potentially fraught, have to be addressed by them. Modern society has not thought to criminalise those who have willingly accepted the risks, and we know of no cases where one or other of the consenting adults has been prosecuted, let alone convicted, for the consequences of doing so.

51. The problems of *criminalising* the consensual taking of risks like these include the sheer impracticability of enforcement and the haphazard nature of its impact. The process would undermine the general understanding of the community that sexual relationships are pre-eminently private and essentially personal to the individuals involved in them. And if adults were to be liable to prosecution for the consequences of taking known risks with their health, it would seem odd that this should be confined to risks taken in the context of sexual intercourse, while they are nevertheless permitted to take the risks inherent in so many other aspects of everyday life, including, again for example, the mother or father of a child suffering a serious contagious illness, who holds the child's hand, and comforts or kisses him or her goodnight.

52. In our judgement, interference of this kind with personal autonomy, and its level and extent, may only be made by Parliament.

...

54. We have taken note of the various points made by the interested organisations. These include the complexity of bedroom and sex negotiations, and the lack of realism if the law were to expect people to be paragons of sexual behaviour at such a time, or to set about informing each other in advance of the risks or to counsel the use of condoms. It is also suggested that there are significant negative consequences of disclosure of HIV, and that the imposition of criminal liability could have an adverse impact on public health because those who ought to take advice, might be discouraged from doing so. If the criminal law was to become involved at all, this should be confined to cases where the offender deliberately inflicted others with a serious disease.

55. In addition to this material our attention has been drawn to the decisions in *R v Mwai* [1995] 3 NZLR 149, a decision of the Court of Appeal in New Zealand, and *R v Cuerrier* [1998] 27 CCC (3d) 1, in the Supreme Court of Canada. Both cases arose out of legislative provisions different to our own. Nevertheless, if we may say so, the judgments were illuminating, not least in the context of the views expressed in *Cuerrier*, which were inconsistent with some of the arguments put to us by the interested organisations. We also notice Professor Spencer's illuminating conclusion on the question of recklessness. 'To infect an unsuspecting person with a grave disease you know you have, or may have, by behaviour that you know involves a risk of transmission, and that you know you could

easily modify to reduce or eliminate the risk, is to harm another in a way that is both needless and callous. For that reason, criminal liability is justified unless there are strong countervailing reasons. In my view there are not.'

56. Although we have considered these judgments, and the remaining material to which our attention was drawn, in this Court we are concerned only to decide what the law is now, and in this jurisdiction. Having done so, it is for Parliament if it sees fit, to amend the law as we find it to be.

Conclusion

58. We repeat that the Crown did not allege, and we therefore are not considering the deliberate infection, or spreading of HIV with intent to cause grievous bodily harm. In such circumstances, the application of what we may describe as the principle in Brown means that the agreement of the participants would provide no defence to a charge under s. 18 of the 1861 Act.

59. The effect of this judgment in relation to s.20 is to remove some of the outdated restrictions against the successful prosecution of those who, knowing that they are suffering HIV or some other serious sexual disease, recklessly transmit it through consensual sexual intercourse, and inflict grievous bodily harm on a person from whom the risk is concealed and who is not consenting to it. In this context, *Clarence* has no continuing relevance. Moreover, to the extent that *Clarence* suggested that consensual sexual intercourse of itself was to be regarded as consent to the risk of consequent disease, again, it is no longer authoritative. If however, the victim consents to the risk, this continues to provide a defence under s.20. Although the two are inevitably linked, the ultimate question is not knowledge, but consent. We shall confine ourselves to reflecting that unless you are prepared to take whatever risk of sexually transmitted infection there may be, it is unlikely that you would consent to a risk of major consequent illness if you were ignorant of it. That said, in every case where these issues arise, the question whether the defendant was or was not reckless, and whether the victim did or did not consent to the risk of a sexually transmitted disease is one of fact, and case specific.

60. In view of our conclusion that the trial judge should not have withdrawn the issue of consent from the jury, the appeal is allowed. Notwithstanding the arguments to the contrary, we unhesitatingly order a retrial, which should take place at the earliest possible date.

■ NOTES AND QUESTIONS

1. Was there fraud in *Dica* or simply non-disclosure? Is there a difference? Does it matter? Given that *Brown* renders conduct creating the risk of harm unlawful, consent notwithstanding, how does one reconcile *Dica* and *Brown?*

2. In *R v Konzani* [2005] EWCA Crim 706, a post-*Dica* decision, the defendant had failed to disclose his known HIV status to his sexual partners. The Court of Appeal held that his failure to inform the victims of his status prevented their consenting. The appellant had admitted that he was aware of the risk of transmitting HIV to his partners and the court ruled that he had been reckless in not revealing this information. *Konzani* appears to require consent to be fully informed to constitute true consent.

3. In a much criticised nineteenth century decision, *R v Clarence* (1888) 22 QBD 23, the defendant had intercourse with his wife but failed to inform her that he had a venereal disease. She contracted the disease and he was prosecuted for assault. The court held that his concealment of his condition was *not* a sufficient fraud as to the nature and quality of act so as to prevent the victim's consent from being a valid consent. In *R v Dica*, it was held that *Clarence* was no longer good law.

4. The Court of Appeal In *Dica* makes reference to the case of *Boyea*. In *Meachen* the victim's consent to injury to the anus was ruled effective where the perpetrator neither intended nor foresaw harm ([2006] EWCA Crim 2414). Are the two decisions compatible?

C: Human rights limits on defences

Some defences traditionally permitted under the common law may be in conflict with the rights guaranteed by the European Convention on Human Rights. It has often been stated obiter that parents may use reasonable force for the purpose of lawful chastisement of a child. Whether it was ever really accurate to say that the child 'consented' to such force was questionable. In any event, the limits of this doctrine have now been considered by the European Court of Human Rights.

A v *United Kingdom*
(1999) 27 EHRR 611, European Court of Human Rights

On 5 February 1993 the applicant was examined by a consultant paediatrician, who found the following marks on his body, *inter alia*: (1) a fresh red linear bruise on the back of the right thigh, consistent with a blow from a garden cane, probably within the preceding twenty-four hours; (2) a double linear bruise on the back of the left calf, consistent with two separate blows given some time before the first injury; (3) two lines on the back of the left thigh, probably caused by two blows inflicted one or two days previously; (4) three linear bruises on the right bottom, consistent with three blows, possibly given at different times and up to one week old; (5) a fading linear bruise, probably several days old.

The paediatrician considered that the bruising was consistent with the use of a garden cane applied with considerable force on more than one occasion.

The stepfather was charged with assault occasioning actual bodily harm and tried in February 1994. It was not disputed by the defence that the stepfather had caned the boy on a number of occasions, but it was argued that this had been necessary and reasonable since A was a difficult boy who did not respond to parental or school discipline.

In summing up, the judge advised the jury on the law as follows:

> ...What is it the prosecution must prove? If a man deliberately and unjustifiably hits another and causes some bodily injury, bruising or swelling will do, he is guilty of actual bodily harm. What does 'unjustifiably' mean in the context of this case? It is a perfectly good defence that the alleged assault was merely the correcting of a child by its parent, in this case the stepfather, provided that the correction be moderate in the manner, the instrument and the quantity of it. Or, put another way, reasonable. It is not for the defendant to prove it was lawful correction. It is for the prosecution to prove it was not.
>
> This case is not about whether you should punish a very difficult boy. It is about whether what was done here was reasonable or not and you must judge that...

The jury found by a majority verdict that the applicant's stepfather was not guilty of assault occasioning actual bodily harm.

In criminal proceedings for the assault of a child, the burden of proof is on the prosecution to satisfy the jury, beyond a reasonable doubt, *inter alia*, that the assault did not constitute lawful punishment.

Parents or other persons *in loco parentis* are protected by the law if they administer punishment which is moderate and reasonable in the circumstances. The concept of 'reasonableness' permits the courts to apply standards prevailing in contemporary society with regard to the physical punishment of children.

Corporal punishment of a child by a teacher cannot be justified if the punishment is inhuman or degrading. In determining whether punishment is inhuman or degrading, regard is to be had to 'all the circumstances of the case, including the reason for giving it, how soon after the event it is given, its nature, the manner and circumstances in which it is given, the persons involved and its mental and physical effects' (section 47(1)(a) and (b) of the Education (No. 2) Act 1986, as amended by section 293 of the Education Act 1993).

The Court recalls that ill-treatment must attain a minimum level of severity if it is to fall within the scope of Article 3. The assessment of this minimum is relative: it depends on all the circumstances of the case, such as the nature and context of the treatment, its duration, its physical and mental effects and, in some instances, the sex, age and state of health of the victim (see the *Costello-Roberts* v *The United Kingdom*, 25 March 1993, Series A No. 247-C, p. 59, H 30).

The Court recalls that the applicant, who was then nine years old, was found by the consultant paediatrician who examined him to have been beaten with a garden cane which had been applied with considerable force on more than one occasion.

The Court considers that treatment of this kind reaches the level of severity prohibited by Article 3.

It remains to be determined whether the State should be held responsible, under Article 3, for the beating of the applicant by his stepfather.

The Court considers that the obligation on the High Contracting Parties under Article 1 of the Convention to secure to everyone within their jurisdiction the rights and freedoms defined in the Convention, taken together with Article 3, requires States to take measures designed to ensure that individuals within their jurisdiction are not subjected to torture or inhuman or degrading treatment or punishment, including such ill-treatment administered by private individuals (see, *mutatis mutandis, HLR* v *France*, 29 April 1997, *Reports* 1997-III, p. 758, n 40). Children and other vulnerable individuals, in particular, are entitled to State protection in the form of effective deterrence, against such serious breaches of personal integrity.

The Court recalls that under English law it is a defence to a charge of assault on a child that the treatment in question amounted to 'reasonable chastisement'. The burden of proof is on the prosecution to establish beyond reasonable doubt that the assault went beyond the limits of lawful punishment. In the present case, despite the fact that the applicant had been subjected to treatment of sufficient severity to fall within the scope of Article 3, the jury acquitted his stepfather, who had administered the treatment.

In the Court's view, the law did not provide adequate protection to the applicant against treatment or punishment contrary to Article 3. Indeed, the Government have accepted that this law currently fails to provide adequate protection to children and should be amended.

In the circumstances of the present case, the failure to provide adequate protection constitutes a violation of Article 3 of the Convention....

■ NOTES AND QUESTIONS

1. Human rights can sometimes be in conflict. Is the disciplining of a child by a parent a matter of 'private life' protected by Article 8 of the European Convention? Even if not, is it a family matter in which the State should not, as a matter of policy, become involved?

2. Opinion polls in the UK show general public support for a parent's right to 'smack' a child. Does the European Court's decision preclude 'smacking'? In *Costello-Roberts* v *United Kingdom* (1993) 19 EHRR 112, the Court held that there had not been a violation of Article 3 where a school master had 'whacked' a seven-year-old boy three times on his clothed buttocks with a slipper for repeated violations of school rules. On the other hand, in several European countries – but not in England – child 'smacking' is illegal.

3. Note that in both *A* and *Costello-Roberts* it is the UK's failure to protect its citizens from Article 3 violations which is at issue, not the criminal liability of the perpetrator of the assaults.

SECTION 5: AGGRAVATED ASSAULTS

The Offences Against the Person Act 1861 and other statutes contain many offences, which are regarded as more serious than assault and battery because of aggravating factors. The most commonly charged are examined here. In most of these offences the *actus reus* and *mens rea* of assault or battery must be proved as well as the aggravating factor.

A: Assault occasioning actual bodily harm

OFFENCES AGAINST THE PERSON ACT 1861

47. Whosoever shall be convicted upon an indictment of any assault occasioning actual bodily harm shall be liable ... to be kept in penal servitude ...; and whosoever shall be convicted upon an indictment for a common assault shall be liable, at the discretion of the court, to be imprisoned for any term not exceeding one year, with or without hard labour.

'Actual bodily harm' was defined in the following case:

R v Miller

[1954] 2 QB 282, Queen's Bench Division

LYNSKEY J: ... The point has been taken that there is no evidence of bodily harm. The bodily harm alleged is said to be the result of the prisoner's actions, and that is, if the jury accept the evidence, that he threw the wife down three times. There is evidence that afterwards she was in a hysterical and nervous condition, but it is said by counsel that that is not actual bodily harm. Actual bodily harm, according to Archbold, 32nd ed., p. 959, includes 'any hurt or injury calculated to interfere with the health or comfort of the victim.' There was a time when shock was not regarded as bodily hurt, but the day has gone by when that could be said. It seems to me now that if a person is caused hurt or injury resulting, not in any physical injury, but in an injury to her state of mind for the time being, that is within the definition of actual bodily harm, and on that point I would leave the case to the jury.

■ NOTES

1. In *R v Ireland* [1997] 3 WLR 534, and *R v Constanza* [1997] Crim LR 576, it was held that telephone calls causing significant psychological symptoms were capable of constituting assault occasioning actual bodily harm. However, where psychological rather than physical injury is the harm alleged, expert testimony may be required. See *R v Chan-Fook* [1994] 1 WLR 689.

2. There was some doubt as to the *mens rea* for this offence, in particular the extent to which the defendant must foresee the degree of harm which would result. This controversy was settled by the opinion of the House of Lords in *R v Savage* and *DPP v Parmenter*.

B: Wounding and inflicting grievous bodily harm

OFFENCES AGAINST THE PERSON ACT 1861

18. Whosoever shall unlawfully and maliciously by any means whatsoever wound or cause any grievous bodily harm to any person, or shoot at any person, or, by drawing a trigger or in any other manner attempt to discharge any kind of loaded arms at any person, with intent, in any of the cases aforesaid, to maim, disfigure, or disable any person, or with intent to resist or prevent the lawful apprehension or detainer of any person, shall be guilty of felony, and being convicted thereof shall be liable ... to be kept in penal servitude for life ...

20. Whosoever shall unlawfully and maliciously wound or inflict any grievous bodily harm upon any other person, either with or without any weapon or instrument, shall be guilty of a misdemeanour, and being convicted thereof shall be liable ... to be kept in penal servitude ...

(i) *Actus reus*

The *actus reus* of a s. 20 offence is an unlawful wounding *or* the unlawful infliction of grievous bodily harm. In contrast, a s. 18 offence requires proof of an unlawful wounding or the causing of grievous bodily harm. The courts had in the past drawn a distinction between infliction and causing, but this distinction was rejected in *R* v *Burstow* [1997] 1 Cr App R 144. There is also a difference in the *mens rea* requirements for the two sections which is explored below.

The reasons for treating wounding and infliction of GBH as equivalent are historical, since when the Act was passed even a small breaking of the skin was liable to lead to infection and death.

A wound is a breaking of the skin:

Moriarty v Brooks
(1834) 6 C & P 684, Court of Appeal

LORD LYNDHURST CB: The definition of a wound in criminal cases is an injury to the person, by which the skin is broken. If the skin is broken, and there was a bleeding, that is a wound.

His Lordship (in summing up) said—If the violence which occurred took place in an endeavour by the defendant to turn the plaintiff out of the house, the third plea is proved. However, this plea does not profess to justify any wounding; therefore, if there was a wound, the plaintiff is entitled to recover for that. It is proved that the plaintiff was cut under the eye, and that it bled; and I am of opinion that that is a wound. ...

R v McLoughlin
(1838) 8 C & P 635, Central Criminal Court

A surgeon, named Hore, was called as a witness, and said, – 'About eleven o'clock on the night of the 14th of July, I was called on to attend the prosecutor; I examined his head and found an abrasion of the skin, with blood issuing from it; he had received a violent blow on the left temple, there was great tumefaction; I could not ascertain at the time whether the bone was fractured; he lost the sight of his left eye, and it rendered him deaf on the left ear; he had great difficulty of speech; he could scarcely answer questions put to him, not being able to articulate; and on moving the bandage off his head, he shortly became insensible; I have seen the fragments of the bottle; it was such a wound as might have been inflicted with a bottle; I have attended him ever since, frequently twice a-day; I considered him in a dangerous state for several weeks; he is not yet recovered.' On his cross-examination, *inter alia*, he said – 'The skin was broken on the left temple, that would not be visible now, nor the cicatrix, from its having healed; I never said the skin was not broken; I have said it was a sort of injury which a medical man would hardly consider a wound, but it was in the eye of the law a wound; there were signs of it visible four days after.'

COLERIDGE J: . . . It is essential for you to be quite clear that a wound was inflicted. I am inclined to understand, and my learned brothers are of the same opinion, that, if it is necessary to constitute a wound, that the skin should be broken, it must be the whole skin, and it is not sufficient to shew a separation of the cuticle only. You will, therefore, have to say on the first three counts, whether there was a wounding in the sense in which I have stated it, viz. was there a wound—a separation of the whole skin? If you think there was not, you will find the prisoner not guilty upon these counts. Then, as to the fourth count, which charges an intent to murder, you will, perhaps, think, that under all the circumstances of this case, there is not sufficient evidence of that malice aforethought which is necessary to constitute such an intent. But you may on either of the counts find the prisoner guilty of an assault.

C (a minor) v Eisenhower

[1984] 1 QB 331, Queen's Bench Division

The defendant, aged 15, was involved in an incident in which C was hit by an air gun pellet near his eye. The defendant was charged with unlawfully and maliciously wounding C, contrary to section 20 of the Offences against the Person Act 1861. The justices held that the abnormal presence of red blood cells in the fluid of the eye, indicating at least the rupture of one or more internal blood vessels, was sufficient to constitute a wound for the purposes of section 20.

On appeal by the defendant:—

Held, allowing the appeal, that on the authorities, the word 'wound' meant a break in the continuity of the whole skin; that, accordingly, the rupture of internal blood vessels was not sufficient to constitute a wound for the purposes of section 20 of the Act of 1861; and that, therefore, the defendant had not committed an offence under the section . . .

■ **NOTES AND QUESTIONS**

1. 'Grievous bodily harm' was defined as 'really serious harm' in *Director of Public Prosecutions* v *Smith* [1961] AC 290. Is this redefinition any more enlightening?

2. Who should decide whether grievous bodily harm has occurred? Is this a question that should be reserved for medical personnel? Is a jury capable of deciding it? Of what relevance is the victim's opinion – if the victim believes that she has suffered grievous injury, has she?

3. A defendant charged under s. 18 can be convicted under s. 20 or s. 47. See *R* v *Mandair* [1995] 1 AC 208.

(ii) 'Inflict' and 'wound'

In respect of *actus reus*, what are the differences between the aggravated offences? The precise differences have been the subject of some confusion in the case law, but basically:

(a) s. 47 requires an assault or a battery;

(b) s. 20 requires *infliction* of GBH or a *'wounding'*;

(c) s. 18 requires the *causing* of GBH.

In a series of cases it was held that 'inflict' and 'wound' required proof of an assault. See *R* v *Taylor* (1869) LR 1 CCR 194, *R* v *Clarence* (1888) 22 QBD 23. However, in a poorly reasoned judgment in *R* v *Wilson* [1984] AC 242, the House of Lords held that the word 'inflict' did not necessarily imply an assault. This ruling was considered and better explained in *R* v *Ireland, R* v *Burstow*.

R v Ireland, R v Burstow
[1997] 3 WLR 534, House of Lords

For facts, see p. 284.

LORD HOPE OF CRAIGHEAD: ...

R v Burstow: 'inflict'
In this case the appellant changed his plea to guilty after a ruling by the trial judge that the offence of unlawfully and maliciously inflicting grievous bodily harm contrary to section 20 of the Act of 1861 may be committed where no physical violence has been applied directly or indirectly to the body of the victim. Counsel for the appellant accepted that if *R v Chan-Fook* [1994] 1 WLR 689 was correctly decided, with the result that 'actual bodily harm' in section 47 is capable of including psychiatric injury, the victim in this case had suffered grievous bodily harm within the meaning of section 20. But he submitted that no offence against section 20 had been committed in this case because, although the appellant might be said to have 'caused' the victim to sustain grievous bodily harm, he had not 'inflicted' that harm on her because he had not used any personal violence against her.

Counsel based his submission on the decision in *R v Clarence* 22 QBD 23. In that case it was held that some form of direct personal violence was required for a conviction under section 20. The use of the word 'inflict' in the section was said to imply that some form of battery was involved in the assault. The conviction was quashed because although the venereal infection from which the victim was suffering was the result of direct physical contact, there had been no violence used and thus there was no element of battery. It seems to me however that there are three reasons for regarding that case as an uncertain guide to the question which arises where the bodily harm which has resulted from the defendant's conduct consists of psychiatric injury.

The first is that the judges in *R v Clarence* were concerned with a case of physical, not psychiatric, injury. They did not have to consider the problem which arises where the grievous bodily harm is of a kind which may result without any form of physical contact. The second is that the intercourse had taken place with consent, as the defendant's wife was ignorant of his venereal disease. So there was no question in that case of an assault having been committed, if there was no element of violence or battery. Also, as Lord Roskill pointed out in *R v Wilson (Clarence)* [1984] AC 242, 260c the judgments of the judges who formed the majority are not wholly consistent with each other. This casts some doubt on the weight which should be attached to the judgment when the facts are entirely different, as they are in the present case.

In *R v Wilson*, Lord Roskill referred, at pp. 259E–260B, with approval to the judgment of the Supreme Court of Victoria in *R v Salisbury* [1976] VR 452, in which the following passage appears, at p. 461:

> although the word 'inflicts'...does not have as wide a meaning as the word 'causes'...the word 'inflicts' does have a wider meaning than it would have if it were construed so that inflicting grievous bodily harm always involved assaulting the victim.

Lord Roskill said [1984] AC 242, 260H that he was content to accept, as was the full court in *R v Salisbury*, that there can be an infliction of grievous bodily harm contrary to section 20 without an assault being committed. But these observations do not wholly resolve the issue which arises in this case, in the context of grievous bodily harm which consists only of psychiatric injury.

The question is whether there is any difference in meaning, in this context, between the word 'cause' and the word 'inflict'. The fact that the word 'caused' is used in section 18, whereas the word used in section 20 is 'inflict', might be taken at first sight to indicate that there is a difference. But for all practical purposes there is, in my opinion, no difference between these two words. In *R v Mandair* [1995] 1 AC 208, 215B Lord Mackay of Clashfern LC said that the word 'cause' is wider or at least not narrower than the word 'inflict'. I respectfully agree with that observation. But I would add that there is this difference, that the word 'inflict' implies that the consequence of the act is something which the victim is likely to find unpleasant or harmful. The relationship between cause and effect, when the word 'cause' is used, is neutral. It may embrace pleasure as well as pain. The relationship when the word 'inflict' is used is more precise, because it invariably implies detriment to the victim of some kind.

In the context of a criminal act therefore the words 'cause' and 'inflict' may be taken to be inter-changeable. As the Supreme Court of Victoria held in *R* v *Salisbury* [1976] VR 452, it is not a neces-sary ingredient of the word 'inflict' that whatever causes the harm must be applied directly to the victim. It may be applied indirectly, so long as the result is that the harm is caused by what has been done. In my opinion it is entirely consistent with the ordinary use of the word 'inflict' in the English language to say that the appellant's actions 'inflicted' the psychiatric harm from which the victim has admittedly suffered in this case. The issues which remain are issues of fact and, as the appellant pled guilty to the offence, I would dismiss his appeal.

The House of Lords in *Wilson* and *Burstow* did not deal with whether 'wound' implied an assault, but in *R* v *Savage* [1991] 3 WLR 418, Glidewell LJ was of the opin-ion that wounding did require an assault. This question was dealt with on appeal to the House of Lords in *R* v *Savage* and *DPP* v *Parmenter*.

The disapproving comments made regarding *Clarence* in *Burstow* has led to its effective repudiation as an authority, both as regards the meaning of inflict and as regards the relevance of informed consent to the lawfulness of transmitting a sexually transmitted disease.

R v *Dica*
For facts see p. 276.

JUDGE LJ:

Inflicting and Causing GBH

In *Ireland and Burstow* , much argument also centred around the difference between the concept of inflicting grievous bodily harm in s.20 and causing it in s.18. Lord Steyn recognised that the two words, 'inflict' and 'cause', are not synonymous. In relation to *Clarence* , he acknowledged that the possibility of inflicting or causing psychiatric injury would not then have been in contemplation, whereas nowadays it is. In his view the infliction of psychiatric injury without violence could fall within the ambit of s.20. Lord Steyn described *Clarence* as a 'troublesome authority', and in the specific context of the meaning of 'inflict' in s.20 said expressly that *Clarence* 'no longer assists'. Lord Hope similarly examined the consequences of the use of the word 'inflict' in s.20 and 'cause' in s.18. He concluded that for practical purposes, and in the context of a criminal act, the words might be regarded as interchangeable, provided it was understood that 'inflict' implies that the conse-quence to the victim involved something detrimental or adverse.

30. Such differences as may be discerned in the language used by Lord Steyn and Lord Hope respectively do not obscure the fact that this decision confirmed that even when no physical vio-lence has been applied, directly or indirectly to the victim's body, an offence under s.20 may be committed. Putting it another way, if the remaining ingredients of s.20 are established, the charge is not answered simply because the grievous bodily harm suffered by the victim did not result from direct or indirect physical violence. Whether the consequences suffered by the victim are physical injuries or psychiatric injuries, or a combination of the two, the ingredients of the offence prescribed by s.20 are identical. If psychiatric injury can be inflicted without direct or indirect violence, or an assault, for the purposes of s.20 physical injury may be similarly inflicted. It is no longer possible to discern the critical difference identified by the majority in *Clarence* , and encapsulated by Stephen J. in his judgment, between an 'immediate and necessary connection' between the relevant blow and the consequent injury, and the 'uncertain and delayed' effect of the act which led to the eventual development of infection. The erosion process is now complete.

31. In our judgment, the reasoning which led the majority in *Clarence* to decide that the conviction under s.20 should be quashed has no continuing application. If that case were decided today, the conviction under s.20 would be upheld. Clarence knew, but his wife did not know, and he knew that she did not know he was suffering from gonorrhoea. Nevertheless he had sexual intercourse

with her, not intending deliberately to infect her, but reckless whether she might become infected, and thus suffer grievous bodily harm. Accordingly we agree with Judge Philpot's first ruling, that notwithstanding the decision in Clarence , it was open to the jury to convict the appellant of the offences alleged in the indictment.

R v Savage, Director of Public Prosecutions v Parmenter
[1991] 3 WLR 914, House of Lords

For facts and holding, see p. 250.

LORD ACKNER: . . . 1. *Is a verdict of guilty of assault occasioning actual bodily harm a permissible alternative verdict on a count alleging unlawful wounding contrary to section 20 of the Act?*
    . . . The allegation of inflicting grievous bodily harm or for that matter wounding, as was observed by Glidewell LJ, giving the judgment of the court in the *Savage* case [1991] 3 WLR 418, 421, inevitably imports or includes an allegation of assault, unless there are some quite extraordinary facts.
    The critical question remained—do the allegations in a section 20 charge 'include either expressly or by implication' allegations of assault occasioning actual bodily harm. As to this, Lord Roskill concluded [1984] AC 247, 261:

> If 'inflicting' can, as the cases show, include 'inflicting by assault', then even though such a charge may not necessarily do so, I do not for myself see why on a fair reading of section 6(3) these allegations do not at least impliedly *include* 'inflicting by assault.' That is sufficient for present purposes though I also regard it as also a possible view that those former allegations *expressly* include the other allegations.

I respectfully agree with this reasoning and accordingly reject the submission that *R v Wilson* was wrongly decided. I would therefore answer the first of the certified questions in the *Savage* case in the affirmative. A verdict of guilty of assault occasioning actual bodily harm is a permissible alternative verdict on a count alleging unlawful wounding contrary to section 20 of the Offences against the Person Act 1861.

(iii) *Mens rea*

The wounding or infliction of GBH must be done 'maliciously'. Must the defendant actually foresee the possibility of harm, and, if so, what degree of harm must be foreseen?

R v Mowatt
[1968] 1 QB 421, Court of Appeal

DIPLOCK LJ: . . . In the offence under section 20, and in the alternative verdict which may be given on a charge under section 18, for neither of which is any specific intent required, the word 'maliciously' does import upon the part of the person who unlawfully inflicts the wound or other grievous bodily harm an awareness that his act may have the consequence of causing some physical harm to some other person. That is what is meant by 'the particular kind of harm' in the citation from Professor Kenny. It is quite unnecessary that the accused should have foreseen that his unlawful act might cause physical harm of the gravity described in the section, i.e., a wound or serious physical injury. It is enough that he should have foreseen that some physical harm to some person, albeit of a minor character, might result.

    3. *In order to establish an offence under section 20 of the Act, must the prosecution prove that the defendant actually foresaw that his act would cause harm, or is it sufficient to prove that he ought so to have foreseen?*
    . . . [I]n order to establish an offence under section 20 the prosecution must prove either the defendant intended or that he actually foresaw that his act would cause harm.

    4. *In order to establish an offence under section 20 is it sufficient to prove that the defendant intended or foresaw the risk of some physical harm or must he intend or foresee either wounding or grievous bodily harm?*

...Professor Glanville Williams and ... Professor J. C. Smith in their text books and in articles [and] commentaries ... argue that a person should not be criminally liable for consequences of his conduct unless he foresaw a consequence falling into the same legal category as that set out in the indictment.

Such a general principle runs contrary to the decision in *Roberts'* case, 56 Cr App R 95 which I have already stated to be, in my opinion, correct. The contention is apparently based on the proposition that as the actus reus of a section 20 offence is the wounding or the infliction of grievous bodily harm, the mens rea must consist of foreseeing such wounding or grievous bodily harm. But there is no such hard and fast principle. To take but two examples, the actus reus of murder is the killing of the victim, but foresight of grievous bodily harm is sufficient and indeed, such bodily harm, need not be such as to be dangerous to life. Again, in the case of manslaughter, death is frequently the unforeseen consequence of the violence used.

The argument that as section 20 and section 47 have both the same penalty, this somehow supports the proposition that the foreseen consequences must coincide with the harm actually done, overlooks the often repeated statement that this is the irrational result of this piece-meal legislation.

If section 20 was to be limited to cases where the accused does not desire but does foresee wounding or grievous bodily harm, it would have a very limited scope. The mens rea in a section 20 crime is comprised in the word 'maliciously'. As was pointed out by Lord Lane CJ, giving the judgment of the Court of Appeal in *R v Sullivan* on 27 October 1980 (unreported save in [1981] Crim LR 46) the 'particular kind of harm' in the citation from Professor Kenny was directed to 'harm to the person' as opposed to 'harm to property.' Thus it was not concerned with the degree of the harm foreseen. It is accordingly in my judgment wrong to look upon the decision in *Mowatt* [1968] 1 QB 421 as being in any way inconsistent with the decision in *Cunningham* [1957] 2 QB 396.

My Lords, I am satisfied that the decision in *Mowatt* was correct and that it is quite unnecessary that the accused should either have intended or have foreseen that his unlawful act might cause physical harm of the gravity described in section 20, i.e. a wound or serious physical injury. It is enough that he should have foreseen that some physical harm to some person, albeit of a minor character, might result.

■ **NOTES AND QUESTIONS**

1. In requiring that the defendant actually foresees that his act would cause harm, the House of Lords apparently adopts a subjective approach to recklessness. But in requiring that the defendant should have to see only *some* harm, rather than the type of harm, which occurred, the court seems to qualify this test. One issue in the case was whether a defendant could be convicted of inflicting *grievous* bodily harm if he foresaw only *some* harm.

2. The s. 18 offence requires proof of an ulterior intention specified in the section – an intent to do GBH, or an intent to prevent the lawful apprehension or detention of any person. Proof of recklessness is not enough. An intention simply to wound the victim is not enough. In the following case a useful explanation is given of the relationship between s. 20 and s. 18 where the conduct element relied up is a wound. As Lord Justice Thomas points out it seems that counsel for the defence were not entirely clear about this.

R v Taylor

[2009] EWCA Crim 544

LORD JUSTICE THOMAS:

On 18th July 2007 the appellant was convicted of unlawful wounding with intent contrary to section 18 of the Offences Against the Person Act 1861 and subsequently sentenced to imprisonment for public protection with a minimum term of three years, less time on remand. Counsel who then appeared for the appellant, and who is not counsel who appears today, sought leave to appeal on various grounds. The judge who tried this matter, His Honour Judge Gilbart QC, said:

'The prosecution must prove that the defendant intended to cause grievous bodily harm or to cause a wound to Brown [Brown being the complainant]. Grievous bodily harm means really serious harm. A wound, of course, is as I have described it.'

A few sentences earlier he had described a wound as 'a wound means a break in the continuity of the skin.' He continued:

'Now, if you are sure that Taylor (the appellant) attacked Brown, that the result of the attack was that Brown was wounded and that Taylor intended to cause grievous bodily harm or to cause a wound, then the elements of the offence are made out and if you are sure of those elements you must convict. If you are not sure you must acquit.'

After giving the usual direction as to what a defendant intended, the judge continued:

'Patently, if you are not sure that any attack took place, you do not have to get as far as intention. The question does not arise. If you are sure that an attack took place then you have to consider intention but no one has suggested that someone who attacks someone else with a knife is not intending to cause them a wound. You may think that if you found that the attack took place and that it was an attack with a knife, that finding an intention to cause a wound is not going to take you very long.

Again, I remind you that you must not convict of this charge unless you are sure that the defendant intended to cause grievous bodily harm or to cause a wound.'

Counsel who appears for the Crown today and who also appeared for the Crown at the trial concedes, as it seems to us was inevitable in the light of the authorities, that there was a misdirection in relation to the intent required; an intent to wound is insufficient. There must be an intent to cause really serious bodily injury. It is not necessary for us to set out why that was so because the statutory language is clear.

However, it is argued on behalf of the Crown that the conviction is nonetheless safe in all the circumstances. Before considering that argument we should point out that it is unfortunate that when counsel for the Crown was asked by the judge whether there was any direction of law which either he had not given or had given that the Crown considered should be corrected, no correction was made. We should also point out that we are told there was some discussion as to whether an alternative count under section 20 or an alternative verdict should be left to the jury. It was agreed none should be. That to an extent is relied on by the Crown but we cannot attach weight to it. The defence may have taken the view that it was better that it should be an all or nothing case on section 18, rather than having an alternative verdict left. Secondly, we cannot be sure and certainly we would have doubts as to whether counsel then representing the appellant had actually understood the difference in the offences under section 18 and under section 20. It is a comment we regret that we have to make, but in the light of the fact that nothing was said by defence counsel in relation to the summing-up, bearing in mind the seriousness of the conviction under section 18, we feel nonetheless compelled to make it.

We turn to consider safety and to consider the evidence relied on to prove the intent to cause really serious bodily injury. When we enquired first of all what was relied on, we were told that there were two matters: (a) what had happened in the flat and in particular the evidence of the complainant Mr Brown and (b) the medical evidence.

We turn first to the medical evidence. We need not set out the medical evidence in any detail because it is now accepted that the medical evidence helps not one iota in relation to whether there was an intention to cause really serious bodily injury. That is because the medical report does not set out the depth of the wound; it is also quite impossible for us to divine from the report whether any internal or other injuries were caused. There is certainly nothing on the face of the report that shows that. There is one passage about a CT thorax but that, on examination of the report, is inconclusive. In our judgment counsel for the Crown was right to accept that there was nothing in the medical evidence that assists an iota in relation to intention.

We therefore turn to look at the issue of intention by reference to the objective evidence of the knife. We have a photograph of the knife, but unfortunately at this stage there are no visible dimensions of the knife marked on it. No-one measured the knife. It is therefore impossible for us to work out from the information we have any possible extent of the depth of the wound from the width of the knife.

...

[His Lordship considered other evidence including the testimony of the victim and concluded . . .] The difficulty that we face is, first, the fact the jury were told to treat his evidence with caution; secondly, the fact that the jury plainly did do so; thirdly, the evidence that we have set out is equivocal as to whether there was an intention to cause really serious bodily injury. It has been submitted ably on behalf of the appellant that as there were lots of knives in the kitchen, if the appellant had really intended really serious bodily injury he would have come back with a knife and not with a fork and done something more than merely scratched the face. The real difficulty that in the end we face in this case in looking at all the pieces of evidence, is whether there is something upon which we could say the jury would have been satisfied there was an intention to cause really serious bodily injury. But as we have endeavoured to explain, there is no medical evidence that provides evidence of such an intention, the evidence in relation to the knife is inconclusive and, as is apparent from the passage in the evidence of the complainant which we have set out, bearing in mind the caution the jury were directed to place on that evidence, we cannot say that the jury would have been sure on that evidence of the requisite intent. They may have been, but on the other hand they may not. It seems to us therefore that we cannot conclude that the conviction under section 18 was safe in the light of the clear and accepted misdirection to the jury. For those reasons this appeal is allowed.

What of an intention merely to frighten the victim?

R v Sullivan
[1981] Crim LR 46, Court of Appeal

The victim's evidence was that the appellant and a companion were undoubtedly drunk and, while the victim was in a street only eight feet wide with a narrow pavement, the appellant drove his car through the street at 25 to 30 miles per hour, mounted the pavement and injured the victim. The appellant, who had made a written statement to the police denying that he was the driver, did not give evidence and, in an unsworn statement from the dock, said that he could add nothing to the written statement he had given to the police. The sole defence was that the appellant was not driving, but during counsel's closing speech for the defence he suggested that all that the appellant had been intending to do was to frighten the victim and no more and that was insufficient mens rea.

Held . . . [M]ere intention to frighten without more was insufficient; the person charged must be proved to have been aware that probable consequences of his voluntary act would be to cause some injury to the victim, but not necessarily grievous bodily harm.

C: Racially aggravated crimes

The Crime and Disorder Act 1998 (CDA) provided for the imposition of greater sentences for existing crimes where they have been 'racially motivated'. This was followed by the Anti-terrorism, Crime and Security Act 2001 (s. 39 of this more recent act amended s. 29 of CDA), which added the possibility of longer sentences for crimes motivated by religious hostility. The crimes affected are assault, including ss. 47 and 20 of the Offences Against the Person Act 1861, criminal damage, public order offences such as causing fear of violence (Public Order Act 1986, s. 4) and causing harassment, alarm or distress (Public Order Act 1986, s. 5) and harassment and putting people in fear of violence (Protection from Harassment Act 1997, ss. 2 and 4).

The definitions of the offences remain the same; the only change is the maximum permissible penalty. The crucial provisions are: s. 28 of the Crime and Disorder Act 1998 (as amended by the Anti-terrorism, Crime and Security Act 2001). The penalty is raised if:

> at the time of committing the offence, or immediately before or after having done so, the offender demonstrates towards the victim of the offence hostility based on the victim's membership (or presumed membership) of a racial or religious group, or the offence is motivated (wholly or partly) by racial or religious hostility towards members of a racial or religious group based on their membership of that group. [s. 28(1)]

When is an offence 'racially motivated'? The following case was the first reported appeal dealing with an application of s. 29.

Director of Public Prosecutions v *Pal*
[2000] Crim LR 756, Divisional Court

E, a man in his 60s of Asian appearance was a caretaker at a community centre. In accordance with his duties, he asked four youths, two white and two of Asian appearance, to leave the premises. Three of the youths left, but the respondent, one of the two Asians, remained. He assaulted E and called him a 'white man's arse licker' and a 'brown Englishman'. E did not retaliate, he again asked the respondent to leave which he then did. The respondent was charged with an offence of racially aggravated common assault contrary to section 29(1)(c) and (3) of the Crime and Disorder Act 1998. The justices concluded that the phrases used by the respondent were not motivated by any racial hostility in accordance with section 28(1) of the 1998 Act, but that he had used those particular phrases because he was aggrieved at being asked to leave the premises rather than intentionally engaging in racial hostility. They accordingly acquitted the respondent. The prosecution appealed by way of case stated.

Held, dismissing the appeal, an offence of racially aggravated common assault might be made out if, for example, one white man were to assault another white man and to make a grossly offensive remark, such as 'nigger lover' to that man upon seeing his victim rejoin a group of black friends, but that was not what had occurred in the present case. It would always be necessary for the prosecution to prove the demonstration of racial hostility, but the use of racially abusive insults would ordinarily be found sufficient for that purpose. Moreover, section 28(1) would have application to a street argument when insults were thrown without thought being given to whether the same were racially abusive. In the present case, but for E being an Asian, the respondent would not have used the words he had used as they would have had no meaning, however, that *sine qua non* was not a sufficient basis for concluding that the respondent's hostility towards E was in any material sense based on E's membership of the Asian race. What he was demonstrating was not hostility towards Asians, but hostility towards E's conduct that night. It followed that the justices were correct to be satisfied that the use of the phrases 'white man's arse licker' and 'brown Englishman' which accompanied the assault did not make the offence racially aggravated within the meaning of section 28.

■ NOTES AND QUESTIONS

1. The restricted approach taken in *DPP* v *Pal* within the statutory definition of racial aggravation has expanded in subsequent cases. Racial aggravation has been deemed to exist with the use of racist language. For example, in *DPP* v *Woods* on appeal by the prosecution, the appeal was allowed because, according to the court, the insult itself was, 'a demonstration of hostility based on the victim's membership of a racial group.' (See also *DPP* v *Green* [2004] All ER (D) 70 (May); *DPP* v *McFarlane* [2002] EWHC Admin 485); *DPP* v *M* [2004] EWHC 1453, [2005] Crim LR 392).

2. Prior to the Crime and Disorder Act 1998, the issue of what constitutes a racial group was examined in *Mandla* v *Dowell-Lee* [1983] 2 AC 548.

DPP v Woods

[2002] EWHC Admin 85, Queen's Bench Division

MR JUSTICE MAURICE KAY:

1. This is a prosecutor's appeal by case stated. On 6th August 2001 Craig Leslie Woods appeared before the Kingston upon Hull Justices for trial. The charge he faced was that 'on 27/04/01 at the City of Kingston upon Hull assaulted Sunny Efosa Ogbevoen by beating him and the offence was racially aggravated contrary to s 29 of the Crime and Disorder Act 1998'.

2. The respondent had previously pleaded guilty to an offence of common assault based on the same facts, absent the elements which the prosecution contended made the offence a racially aggravated one. The case stated lists a number of undisputed facts that arose from the evidence. They were as follows:

'(a) Mr Ogbevoen was on duty as a door supervisor at the Circus Circus On-licensed premises, Kingston upon Hull on the night of 27th April 2001.

(b) At approximately 10.30 pm the Respondent and two other young men approached the entrance door to the premises.

(c) The Respondent and his companions had consumed alcohol during the course of the evening.

(d) Upon Mr Ogbevoen refusing to allow one of the Respondent's companions entry into the premises an altercation took place. Shortly thereafter, Mr Ogbevoen was assaulted.

(e) The respondent assaulted Mr Ogbevoen by punching him to the head.

(f) Mr Ogbevoen restrained the Respondent who was detained at the scene until the police arrived.

(g) The Respondent admitted the assault during interview and subsequently pleaded guilty to a charge of common assault.'

3. What was disputed by the respondent was that he had ever uttered the words 'you black bastard' immediately prior to the assault and that he had demonstrated hostility towards Mr Ogbevoen based upon his membership of a racial group.

4. In evidence Mr Ogbevoen described the use of the words 'you black bastard' but said that he was not bothered by such comments which were often made in that type of situation '...so long as they don't touch me.' The respondent gave evidence in the course of which he denied the use of the disputed words.

5. The Justices found that the respondent had assaulted Mr Ogbevoen and had uttered the words 'you black bastard' a few moments before the assault. In retirement the Justices sought the advice of their clerk and were advised by reference to the decision of the Divisional Court in *Director of Public Prosecutions v Pal*, 3rd February 2000. It seems that the advice they received from the clerk was that whilst the use of racially abusive insults would ordinarily be found sufficient for the purposes of the section, it was possible that such words could be spoken and yet the offence be not proved.

6. The conclusions of the Justices are set out in these paragraphs from the case stated:

'16. We took into account how the victim assaulted perceived the comments. In his evidence Mr Ogbevoen made no play (at any stage) of the words being racially offensive and said he was not bothered by such comments "...so long as they don't touch me".

17. We found the Respondent's hostility to be borne out of his frustration and annoyance as a result of his companion being denied entry to the premises, and whilst he may have intended to cause offence by the words, this was not "hostility based on the victims membership (or presumed membership) of a racial group". We believed that the Respondent's frame of mind was such that he would have abused any person standing in Mr Ogbevoen's shoes by reference to an obvious physical characteristic had that individual happened to possess one.'

7. The case stated poses the single question: 'Did we err in law in concluding that, in all the circumstances of this case, the words "you black bastard" uttered a few moments before the assault were not such to prove that the Respondent had demonstrated hostility towards the victim based upon his membership of a racial group?'

15. In my judgment, the conclusions that I have reached in this case are entirely consistent with the judgment of Simon Brown LJ in *Pal*.

16. Accordingly, to the question posed in the case stated, I answer with the single word, 'Yes'. I shall remit the matter to the Justices with a direction to convict.

May a racially aggravated offence occur when both the defendant and the victim are of the same race?

R v White

[2001] WLR 1352, Court of Appeal

The defendant, who had been born in the West Indies and viewed himself as being African, was a passenger on a bus. The conductress, who originally came from Sierra Leone, believed that she saw him putting his hand into the handbag of another passenger and challenged him. She alleged that he, on leaving the bus, was aggressive and abusive towards her, called her an 'African bitch' and a 'stupid bitch, stupid fool' and threatened to kill her. He was tried on an indictment charging him with using racially aggravated threatening, abusive or insulting words or behaviour, contrary to section 4 of the Public Order Act 1986 [FN1] and section 31 of the Crime and Disorder Act 1998. At the close of the prosecution case the defendant, who admitted calling the complainant a 'stupid African bitch', submitted that there was no case to answer since that expression was not capable of demonstrating hostility towards her based on her membership or presumed membership of a racial group within the meaning of section 28 of the 1998 Act since the term 'African' was not a reference to race, colour, nationality or ethnic or national origin or any of them. The judge rejected the submission and ruled that the word 'African' would fall within 'race' or 'ethnic' for the purposes of section 28. The defendant was convicted.

FN1 Public Order Act 1986, s. 4(1): 'A person is guilty of an offence if he—(a) uses towards another person threatening, abusive or insulting words or behaviour . . . with intent to cause that person to believe that immediate unlawful violence will be used against him . . . or whereby that person is likely to believe that such violence will be used . . .'

FN2 Public Order Act 1986, s. 4(1): 'A person is guilty of an offence if he—(a) uses towards another person threatening, abusive or insulting words or behaviour . . . with intent to cause that person to believe that immediate unlawful violence will be used against him . . . or whereby that person is likely to believe that such violence will be used . . .' Crime and Disorder Act 1998, s. 28.

On appeal by the defendant—

Held, dismissing the appeal, that the word 'African' as generally used in ordinary speech in England and Wales, although not referring to a group of persons defined by reference to nationality or ethnic or national origins, described a 'racial group' defined by reference to race in that it denoted a person characteristic of the blacks of Africa who were a limited group of people regarded as of common stock and as one of the major divisions of humankind having in common distinct physical features; that the use of the expression 'African bitch' was therefore capable of demonstrating towards the complainant hostility based on her membership or presumed membership of a racial group within the meaning of section 28 of the Crime and Disorder Act 1998 and thus rendering an offence under section 4 of the Public Order Act 1986 racially aggravated for the purpose of section 31(1) of the 1998 Act; that even if the defendant were a member of the same racial group as the complainant that did not as a matter of law make it impossible for him to demonstrate hostility towards her based on her membership of that group, although it might in those circumstances be more difficult to prove that the hostility was so based; and that, accordingly, the judge had been entitled to leave the case to the jury.

Johnson v DPP

[2008] EWHC 509 (Admin)

J appealed against the trial judge's decision in the Crown Court to uphold his conviction for a racially aggravated public order offence. J was a black man who had
an angry confrontation with two white traffic wardens on the basis that he was
being picked on. Amongst other things, J said that they did not 'belong here', that
'this is our patch not yours' and 'why don't you [go an deal with] your white uncles
and aunties'. J was convicted of the racially aggravated form of s. 5 of the Public
Order Act 1986. On appeal against conviction J argued that these statements did
not express racial hostility. The Divisional Court disagreed:

> Turning to questions (iii) and (iv), Ms Mushtaq's essential submission is that the mere fact that refer-
> ence was made to the colour of the parking attendants and an indication given that they should
> leave the black community alone and that this was an area predominantly inhabited by the black
> community, was not sufficient to found a conviction. It is said that the words are simply not capable
> of demonstrating racial hostility. I for my part have no hesitation in rejecting those submissions.
> 11. The circumstances were such, in my judgment, as to make it reasonably open to the Crown
> Court to find that the appellant demonstrated racial hostility (to use a shorthand). The language used
> and the court's findings as to the meaning of the words used make clear that the appellant was pre-
> senting the matter in racial terms by reference to colour. He was telling the parking attendants to
> leave the black community alone, to get out of the black area where they were and to go to white
> areas, and he was telling all this as a black person addressing two white people. The words were
> capable of demonstrating racial hostility. Whether the appellant was in fact demonstrating racial hos-
> tility by the use of those words, rather than simply demonstrating hostility towards the two parking
> attendants based on their job as parking attendants, was a question of fact for the Crown Court. But
> there was an entirely adequate evidential basis for the finding that was made as to racial hostility.
> 12. It does not matter whether the appellant's hostility was partly racial and partly hostility
> towards parking attendants generally or by reason of their duties as parking attendants. The effect
> of section 28(3) the 1998 Act is that it is sufficient if the hostility is based in part on the victim's mem-
> bership or presumed membership of a racial group. There may of course be cases where the words
> used are capable of demonstrating racial hostility, but it is found as a fact that there was no racial
> hostility demonstrated at all: see for example *Director of Public Prosecutions* v *Howard*, a decision
> of the Divisional Court presided over by Moses LJ on 7 February 2008 (for which a neutral citation
> does not yet appear to be available).
> 13. In the present case, however, the Crown Court must have found that the appellant's hostility
> was, at least in part, racial hostility, and there was, as I have said, a proper evidential basis for that
> finding.

■ NOTES AND QUESTIONS

1. In his commentary on *Pal* Professor Sir John Smith observes:

   > It is a very great pity that our already over-complex law of offences against the person
   > should have been further complicated by these elaborate provisions. If it was necessary to
   > do anything at all, surely a Practice Direction requiring courts and judges to give full weight
   > to racially aggravating features of offences would have been enough. Maxima were high
   > enough already.

2. Is the basic philosophy underlying the 1998 law ill-conceived? Should victims
   of crimes be treated as victims in their own right or as victims belonging to an
   identifiable group?

3. What should be the aggravating factor – the offender's motivation, the victim's
   discriminatory treatment, or the victim's special vulnerability to racist violence
   and discrimination?

4. A major reason for the 1998 Act was the relative vulnerability to attack of ethnic minorities. In fact it is often used against such minorities as *Johnson* illustrates. Given that the racial context only aggravates what is already a criminal offence should the coverage of the Act be restricted to such vulnerable minority groups?

SECTION 6: REFORM OF THE LAW

The law of non-fatal offences has been heavily criticised. It is not just that it is archaic, but, more importantly, that it lacks coherence, uses confusing terminology, and fails to provide useful guidance both to citizens who are expected to obey it and to courts who are required to implement it. The Criminal Law Revision Commission proposed its overhaul, and the Law Commission subsequently produced a draft statute, which was incorporated into its Draft Criminal Code Bill 1989. That draft in turn formed the basis for a proposed Bill that was brought forth by the Labour Government in 1998 but which was never enacted. The Bill consisted of 28 clauses, the most significant of which are set out below:

VIOLENCE: REFORMING OFFENCES AGAINST THE PERSON: DRAFT BILL

1.—(1) A person is guilty of an offence if he intentionally causes serious injury to another.

(2) A person is guilty of an offence if he omits to do an act which he has a duty to do at common law, the omission results in serious injury to another, and he intends the omission to have that result.

2.—(1) A person is guilty of an offence if he recklessly causes serious injury to another.

3.—(1) A person is guilty of an offence if he intentionally or recklessly causes injury to another.

4.—(1) A person is guilty of an offence if—

   (a) he intentionally or recklessly applies force to or causes an impact on the body of another, or

   (b) he intentionally or recklessly causes the other to believe that any such force or impact is imminent.

(2) No such offence is committed if the force or impact, not being intended or likely to cause injury, is in the circumstances such as is generally acceptable in the ordinary conduct of daily life and the defendant does not know or believe that it is in fact unacceptable to the other person.

   ...

6.—(1) A person is guilty of an offence under this section if he causes serious injury to another intending to resist, prevent or terminate the lawful arrest or detention of himself or a third person.

(2) The question whether the defendant believes the arrest or detention is lawful must be determined according to the circumstances as he believes them to be.

7.—(1) A person is guilty of an offence if he assaults another intending to resist, prevent or terminate the lawful arrest or detention of himself or a third person.

(2) The question whether the defendant believes the arrest or detention is lawful must be determined according to the circumstances as he believes them to be.

8.—(1) A person is guilty of an offence if he acts as mentioned in subsection (2) and—

   (a) he intends to cause serious injury, or

   (b) he is reckless whether serious injury is caused.

(2) A person acts as mentioned in this subsection if he—

   (a) causes an explosive substance to explode,

   (b) places a dangerous substance in any place,

      (c) delivers or sends a dangerous substance to a person,

      (d) throws a dangerous substance at or near a person, or

      (e) applies a dangerous substance to a person.

...

10.—(1) A person is guilty of an offence if he makes to another a threat to cause the death of, or serious injury to, that other or a third person, intending that other to believe that it will be carried out.

...

12.—(1) A person is guilty of an offence if he intentionally inflicts severe pain or suffering on another and he does the act—

      (a) in the performance or purported performance of his official duties as a public official, or

      (b) at the instigation or with the consent or acquiescence of a public official who is performing or purporting to perform his official duties.

  (2) A person is guilty of an offence if—

      (a) he omits to do an act which he has a duty to do at common law,

      (b) he makes the omission as mentioned in subsection (1)(a) or (b),

      (c) the omission results in the infliction of severe pain, or suffering on another, and

      (d) he intends the omission to have that result.

  (3) The following are immaterial—

      (a) the nationality of the persons concerned,

      (b) whether anything occurs in the United Kingdom or elsewhere,

      (c) whether the pain or suffering is physical or mental.

...

Meaning of fault terms and of injury

14.—(1) A person acts intentionally with respect to a result if—

      (a) it is his purpose to cause it, or

      (b) although it is not his purpose to cause it, he knows that it would occur in the ordinary course of events if he were to succeed in his purpose of causing some other result.

  (2) A person acts recklessly with respect to a result if he is aware of a risk that it will occur and it is unreasonable to take that risk having regard to the circumstances as he knows or believes them to be.

  (3) A person intends an omission to have a result if—

      (a) it is his purpose that the result will occur, or

      (b) although it is not his purpose that the result will occur, he knows that it would occur in the ordinary course of events if he were to succeed in his purpose that some other result will occur.

  (4) A person is reckless whether an omission will have a result if he is aware of a risk that the result will occur and it is unreasonable to take that risk having regard to the circumstances as he knows or believes them to be.

  (5) Related expressions must be construed accordingly.

  (6) This section has effect for the purposes of this Act.

15.—(1) In this Act 'injury' means—

      (a) physical injury, or

      (b) mental injury.

Matters affecting liability

16.—(1) Where it is an offence under this Act to be at fault in causing a result by an act and a person lacks the fault required when he does an act that may cause or does cause the result, he nevertheless commits the offence if—

      (a) being aware that he has done the act and that the result may occur or (as the case may be) has occurred and may continue, and

    (b) with the fault required, he fails to take reasonable steps to prevent the result occurring or continuing and it does occur or continue.

  (2) Where it is an offence under this Act to be at fault in causing a result by an omission and a person lacks the fault required when he makes an omission that may cause or does cause the result, he nevertheless commits the offence if—

    (a) being aware that he has made the omission and that the result may occur or (as the case may be) has occurred and may continue, and

    (b) with the fault required, he fails to take reasonable steps to prevent the result occurring or continuing and it does occur or continue.

  (3) For the purposes of this section fault is intention or recklessness, and references to a person being at fault must be construed accordingly.

  (4) Common law rules relating to matters provided for in this section do not apply to offences under this Act.

17.—(1) This section applies in determining whether a person is guilty of an offence under this Act.

  (2) A person's intention, or awareness of a risk, that his act will cause a result in relation to a person capable of being the victim of the offence must be treated as an intention or (as the case may be) awareness of a risk that his act will cause that result in relation to any other person affected by his act.

  (3) A person's intention, or awareness of a risk, that his omission will have a result in relation to a person capable of being the victim of the offence must be treated as an intention or (as the case may be) awareness of a risk that his omission will have that result in relation to any other person affected as a result of his omission.

  (4) Common law rules relating to matters provided for in this section do not apply to offences under this Act.

   . . .

19.—(1) For the purposes of this Act a person who was voluntarily intoxicated at any material time must be treated—

    (a) as having been aware of any risk of which he would have been aware had he not been intoxicated, and

    (b) as having known or believed in any circumstances which he would have known or believed in had he not been intoxicated.

  (2) Whether a person is voluntarily intoxicated for this purpose must be determined in accordance with the following provisions.

  (3) A person is voluntarily intoxicated if—

    (a) he takes an intoxicant otherwise than properly for a medicinal purpose,

    (b) he is aware that it is or may be an intoxicant, and

    (c) he takes it in such a quantity as impairs his awareness or understanding.

  (4) An intoxicant, although taken for a medicinal purpose, is not properly so taken if—

    (a) the intoxicant is not taken on medical advice, and the taker is aware that the taking may result in his doing an act or making an omission capable of constituting an offence of the kind in question, or

    (b) the intoxicant is taken on medical advice, but the taker fails then or afterwards to comply with any condition forming part of the advice and he is aware that the failure may result in his doing an act or making an omission capable of constituting an offence of the kind in question.

  (5) Intoxication must be presumed to have been voluntary unless there is adduced such evidence as might lead the court or jury to conclude that there is a reasonable possibility that the intoxication was involuntary.

  (6) An intoxicant is any alcohol, drug or other thing which, when taken into the body, may impair the awareness or understanding of the person taking it.

  (7) A person must be treated as taking an intoxicant if he permits it to be administered to him.

■ NOTES AND QUESTIONS

1. Compare the proposals, above with the law as contained in the Offences Against the Person Act 1861. What are the major differences?

2. Notice that the proposed Act not only sets out the various substantive terms of offences, but also defines such fault terms as 'intentional' and 'reckless'. In what way do these definitions differ from those developed by the courts (discussed in Chapter 3)? Should these definitions be adopted across the board?

3. Notice also that the proposed Act addresses the question of when liability should be based on an omission. In what way does it differ from the existing law developed by the courts (discussed in Chapter 2)? Should the proposed approach be adopted across the board?

4. In some instances acts of physical and mental violence, including acts of rape, may be so extreme as to constitute torture and cause a State to be in violation of Article 3 of the European Convention on Human Rights. See, e.g., *Aydin* v *Turkey* (1997) 25 EHRR 251.

FURTHER READING

Wilson, *Criminal Law: Doctrine and Theory* (2011), Chapter 11

Bell and Harrison, 'R v *Savage*, DPP v *Parmenter* and the Law of Assault' (1993) 56 Modern Law Review 83

Brennan, 'Racially Motivated Crime: the Response of the Criminal Justice System' [1999] Criminal Law Review 17

Burney, 'Using the Law on Racially Aggravated Offences' [2003] Criminal Law Review 28

Danner, 'Bias Crimes and Crimes Against Humanity: Culpability in Context' (2002) 6 Buffalo Criminal Law Review 389

Elliott and de Than, 'Restructuring the Homicide Offences to Tackle Violence, Discrimination and Drugs in a Modern Society' (2009) 20 KLJ 69

Elliot and de Than, 'A Case for Rational Reconstruction of Consent in Criminal Law' (2007) 70 Modern Law Review 225

Gardner, 'Rationality and the Rule of Law in Offences against the Person' (1994) 53 Cambridge Law Journal 502

Harel and Parchomovsky, 'On Hate and Equality' 109 Yale LJ 507 (1994)

Horder, 'Rethinking Non-fatal Offences against the Person' (1994) 14 Oxford Journal of Legal Studies 335

Roberts, 'The Philosophical Foundations of Consent in the Criminal Law' (1997) 17 Oxford Journal of Legal Studies 389

Rogers, 'A Criminal Lawyer's Response to Chastisement in the European Court of Human Rights' [2002] Criminal Law Review 98

Weait, 'Criminal Law and the Sexual Transmission of HIV: *R* v *Dica*' (2005) 68 Modern Law Review 121

Weait, 'Knowledge, Autonomy and Consent: *R* v *Konzani*' [2005] Criminal Law Review 763

Wilson, 'Is Hurting People Wrong?' (1992) JSWFL 388

6

Sexual Offences

The law relating to sexual offences underwent a major transformation as a result of the Sexual Offences Act 2003 (hereafter cited as SOA 2003). In the White Paper that preceded the Act, the Home Secretary described the law as it then stood as 'archaic, incoherent and discriminatory'. One of the main aims of the SOA 2003 was to address these deficiencies and to provide a modern, coherent and clear account of the law. Under the SOA 2003 sexual offences are not so much crimes of violence as they are offences against the victim's sexual autonomy. In a further attempt to modernise the law, the drafters, wherever possible, have removed all vestiges of sexual stereotyping and substituted gender-neutral categories and language. Ultimately, the goal of the new legislation is to provide better protection and fairer treatment for victims, with the hope that this will encourage increased reporting of offences, while at the same time avoiding potential unfairness to defendants on trial for one of the most serious crimes known to the law.

As it pertains to adult victims, whom the SOA 2003 designates by the letter B (which approach will be adopted in this chapter), there are four prime offences:

(1) Rape

(2) Assault by penetration

(3) Sexual assault

(4) Causing a person to engage in sexual activity without consent

In addition to the above offences, there are specific offences relating to victims under the age of 13, and others relating to victims over 13 but under 16. The discussion of these offences in this chapter will concentrate on the distinctive elements that distinguish them from the comparable offences against adults.

For the sake of completeness, it should be noted that the SOA 2003 also addresses child sex offences within the family, sexual offences against persons with mental disorders, sexual offences by care workers and those in a position of trust, the abuse of children through prostitution and pornography, the trafficking of children for sexual exploitation, and such varied and specific topics as exposure, voyeurism, intercourse with an animal, intercourse with a corpse and sexual activity in a public lavatory. And this list does not exhaust the coverage of the Act. Under the SOA 2003, the number of sexual offences that may be committed has multiplied significantly, often with more severe penalties than was formerly the case.

Because of the recent enactment of the SOA 2003, there has been relatively little time for a body of case law to develop. On the other hand, the continuing viability of pre-2003 decisions has been cast in doubt by the Act. As a result, this chapter will contain far fewer cases than in other chapters. Nonetheless, study of the Act itself will prove rewarding as it illustrates an attempt by Parliament to create an integrated, structured and comprehensive scheme of graded offences to deal with a complicated topic.

SECTION 2: SEXUAL OFFENCES AGAINST ADULT VICTIMS

In referring to crimes against 'adult' victims, we do not mean to suggest that the crimes to be discussed may not be committed against a child. A child under 16 may be, for example, the victim of a rape. Rather, our aim is to differentiate the four main offences, all of which are not age-specific, from the separate set of restricted offences relating to victims under the age of 16 (and, more specifically, under the age of 13), which will be examined in Section 3 of this chapter.

A: Rape

Prior to passage of the SOA 2003, rape was defined as sexual intercourse (whether vaginal or anal) with a person who did not consent to the intercourse, where the offender knew that the victim did not consent or was reckless as to whether or not she consented. (See Sexual Offences Act 1956 (SOA 1956)(as amended).) Under SOA 2003, rape is now defined as follows:

SEXUAL OFFENCES ACT 2003

1. Rape

(1) A person (A) commits an offence if—
 (a) he intentionally penetrates the vagina, anus or mouth of another person (B) with his penis,
 (b) B does not consent to the penetration, and
 (c) A does not reasonably believe that B consents.
(2) Whether a belief is reasonable is to be determined having regard to all the circumstances, including any steps A has taken to ascertain whether B consents.
(3) Sections 75 and 76 apply to an offence under this section.
(4) A person guilty of an offence under this section is liable, on conviction on indictment, to imprisonment for life.

To secure a conviction under this section, the prosecutor will have to prove:

(1) that the defendant (A) intentionally penetrated the vagina, anus or mouth of another person (B) with his penis;
(2) that B did not consent to the penetration; and
(3) that A did not reasonably believe that B consented.

In contrast with the previous law, the SOA 2003 explicitly includes oral sex, as well as vaginal and anal sex, within the definition of rape. While the victim of a rape may be either male or female, the offender (because of the reference to a penis) has to be male (although this includes a person who has had a female-to-male sex change operation and has an artificial penis).

(i) Penetration

Any penetration, no matter how slight, will be sufficient for the offence. This interpretation of 'penetration' accords with the former law (see *R* v *Hughes* (1841) 9 C & P 752, Court of Appeal). The penetration must also be intentional. Under s. 79(2), penetration is defined as a continuing act from entry to removal. The significance of defining penetration as a 'continuing act' is that even if A has B's consent when he first effects penetration, he may still commit rape if, during the intercourse, B changes her mind and withdraws consent. To avoid criminal liability, B would now need to terminate the penetration. This too accords with the approach taken under the previous law (see *R* v *Kaitamaki* [1985] AC 147, Privy Council).

(ii) Absence of consent

Consent has been, and remains, the critical feature which distinguishes a rape from an act of love-making. Rape, like assault and battery, is a crime which protects autonomy generally rather than prohibits harmful acts specifically. While previously courts provided little in the way of guidance as to the meaning of consent except to draw the jury's attention to the distinction between 'consent' and 'submission' (see *R* v *Olugboja* [1982] QB 320, Court of Appeal), the SOA 2003 provides not only a general statutory definition of consent (s. 74), but also two conclusive presumptions (s. 76) and numerous evidential presumptions (s. 75) relating to consent (see generally, J. Temkin and A. Ashworth, 'Rape, Sexual Assault and the Problems of Consent' [2004] Crim LR 328):

74. 'Consent'

For the purposes of this Part, a person consents if he agrees by choice, and has the freedom and capacity to make that choice.

75. Evidential presumptions about consent

    (1) If in proceedings for an offence to which this section applies it is proved—

        (a) that the defendant did the relevant act,

        (b) that any of the circumstances specified in subsection (2) existed, and

        (c) that the defendant knew that those circumstances existed,

the complainant is to be taken not to have consented to the relevant act unless sufficient evidence is adduced to raise an issue as to whether he consented, and the defendant is to be taken not to have reasonably believed that the complainant consented unless sufficient evidence is adduced to raise an issue as to whether he reasonably believed it.

    (2) The circumstances are that—

        (a) any person was, at the time of the relevant act or immediately before it began, using violence against the complainant or causing the complainant to fear that immediate violence would be used against him;

        (b) any person was, at the time of the relevant act or immediately before it began, causing the complainant to fear that violence was being used, or that immediate violence would be used, against another person;

        (c) the complainant was, and the defendant was not, unlawfully detained at the time of the relevant act;

        (d) the complainant was asleep or otherwise unconscious at the time of the relevant act;

(e) because of the complainant's physical disability, the complainant would not have been able at the time of the relevant act to communicate to the defendant whether the complainant consented;

(f) any person had administered to or caused to be taken by the complainant, without the complainant's consent, a substance which, having regard to when it was administered or taken, was capable of causing or enabling the complainant to be stupefied or overpowered at the time of the relevant act.

(3) In subsection (2)(a) and (b), the reference to the time immediately before the relevant act began is, in the case of an act which is one of a continuous series of sexual activities, a reference to the time immediately before the first sexual activity began.

76. Conclusive presumptions about consent

(1) If in proceedings for an offence to which this section applies it is proved that the defendant did the relevant act and that any of the circumstances specified in subsection (2) existed, it is to be conclusively presumed—

(a) that the complainant did not consent to the relevant act, and

(b) that the defendant did not believe that the complainant consented to the relevant act.

(2) The circumstances are that—

(a) the defendant intentionally deceived the complainant as to the nature or purpose of the relevant act;

(b) the defendant intentionally induced the complainant to consent to the relevant act by impersonating a person known personally to the complainant.

As can be deduced from the above sections, a prosecutor may seek to establish non-consent in any of three ways. First, the prosecutor may rely on the *general definition* of consent. Secondly, the prosecutor may seek to bring the facts of the case within one or more of the *evidential* presumptions. And finally, the prosecutor may seek to establish one of the *conclusive* presumptions.

From a prosecutor's perspective, the easiest way to prove non-consent would lie in establishing one of the two conclusive presumptions. The advantage is that once the facts giving rise to the presumption have been proved, there is no evidence that the defendant can introduce to rebut the presumption. It is irrebuttable. Section 76(2) creates a conclusive presumption of non-consent in two instances: where A intentionally deceives B as to the nature or purpose of the relevant act; and when A intentionally induces B to consent by impersonating a person known personally to B. Note that under s. 76(2)(a) the deception may relate to either the *nature* or the *purpose* of the act. Nature and purpose may not be mutually exclusive. In the pre-Act case of *R* v *Williams* [1923] 1 KB 340 where a singing instructor persuaded one of his students that having sexual intercourse with him would improve her singing voice, there arguably was deception about both the nature and purpose of the act. Section 76(2)(b), which refers to an impersonation of a person known to B, has in mind an individual known *personally* to B (such as a partner or close friend) as opposed to a person known by reputation (such as a movie star or well-known sports personality).

If unable to fit the circumstances of the case within a conclusive presumption, a prosecutor may try to take advantage of one or more of the evidential presumptions created by s. 75. If the prosecution establishes any of these, and the defendant fails to introduce any evidence to rebut the presumption, non-consent will be deemed to have been established. On the other hand, unlike in respect of a conclusive presumption, the defendant may prevail by introducing evidence of consent. Thus the practical effect of the presumption is to shift to the defendant the burden of introducing evidence of consent. The presumptions created by s. 75 arise in the following circumstances:

(a) where a person, at the time of the relevant act or immediately before it began, used violence against the victim or caused the victim to fear that immediate violence would be used against him or her;

(b) where a person, at the time of the relevant act or immediately before it began, used violence against the victim or caused the victim to fear that immediate violence would be used against another person;

(c) where the victim was, and the defendant was not, unlawfully detained;

(d) where the victim was asleep or otherwise unconscious at the time;

(e) where, because of the victim's physical disability, the victim would not have been able at the time of the relevant act to communicate to the defendant whether or not she consented;

(f) where any person has administered to or caused to be taken by the victim, without the victim's consent, a substance which, having regard to when it was administered or taken, was capable of causing or enabling the victim to be stupefied or overpowered at the time of the relevant act.

If the prosecution is unable to fit the circumstances of the case within either one of the conclusive presumptions of s. 76 or any of the evidential presumptions of s. 75, it will need to rely on the general definition of consent under s. 74. This section provides that 'a person consents if he agrees by choice, and has the freedom and capacity to make that choice.'

Such an eventuality occurred in:

Jheeta

[2007] 2 Cr App R 34

V acquiesced in intercourse with D, believing due to letters he had sent her but purporting to come from the police, that if she did not do she would be prosecuted.

SIR IGOR JUDGE P: The starting point in our analysis is to acknowledge that in most cases, the absence of consent, and the appropriate state of the defendant's mind, will be proved without reference to evidential or conclusive presumptions. When they do apply, section 75 and section 76 are directed to the process of proving the absence of consent to whichever sexual act is alleged. They are concerned with presumptions about rather than the definition of consent The evidential presumptions in section 75 continue to require the prosecution to disprove consent if, in the circumstances defined in the section, there is sufficient evidence to raise the issue. These presumptions are not conclusive, merely evidential. However section 76 raises presumptions conclusive of the issue of consent, and thus where intercourse is proved, conclusive of guilt. They therefore require the most stringent scrutiny.

24. In our judgment the ambit of section 76 is limited to the 'act' to which it is said to apply. In rape cases the 'act' is vaginal, anal or oral intercourse. Provided this consideration is constantly borne in mind, it will be seen that section 76(2)(a) is relevant only to the comparatively rare cases where the defendant deliberately deceives the complainant about the *nature or purpose* of one or other form of intercourse. No conclusive presumptions arise merely because the complainant was deceived in some way or other by disingenuous blandishments of or common or garden lies by the defendant.

These may well be deceptive and persuasive, but they will rarely go to the nature or purpose of intercourse. Beyond this limited type of case, and assuming that, as here, section 75 has no application, the issue of consent must be addressed in the context of section 74.

25. It may be helpful to reinforce these observations by reference to a number of cases at common law which provide examples of deceptions as to the nature or purpose of the act of intercourse. As to the nature of the relevant act, in *R v Flattery* [1877] 2QBD 410 the Court of Crown Cases Reserved upheld a conviction for rape where intercourse took place after the complainant, a girl of 19, was persuaded that the defendant was performing a surgical operation which would break 'nature's string' and provide a remedy for the fits to which she was subject. In *R v Williams* [1923] 1 KB 340 the conviction for rape was upheld where the defendant deceived a girl of 16 into having sexual intercourse with him to cure a problem with her breathing which prevented her from singing properly. The judge summed up the legal principles in terms approved by the Court of Criminal Appeal:

> 'The law has laid it down that where a girl's consent is procured by the means which the girl says this prisoner adopted, that is to say, where she is persuaded that what was being done to her is not the ordinary act of sexual intercourse but is some medical or surgical operation in order to give her relief from some disability from which she is suffering, then that is rape although the actual thing that was done was with her consent, because she never consented to the act of sexual intercourse. She was persuaded to consent to what he did because she thought it was not sexual intercourse and because she thought it was a surgical operation.'

26. Deception as to purpose is sometimes said to be exemplified in *R v Tabassum* [2000] 2 CAR 328, a decision described by the late Professor Sir John Smith as a 'doubtful case'. A number of women agreed to participate in a breast cancer research programme at the behest of the appellant when, as a result of what he said or did, or both, they wrongly believed that he was medically qualified or trained. They consented to a medical examination, not to sexual touching by a stranger. 'There was consent to the nature of the act, but not to its quality'. However section 76(2)(a) does not address the 'quality' of the act, but confines itself to its 'purpose'. In the latest edition of *Smith and Hogan Criminal Law*, (11th edition) Professor David Ormerod identifies a better example, *R v Green* [2002] EWCA Crim 1501. Bogus medical examinations of young men were carried out by a qualified doctor, in the course of which they were wired up to monitors while they masturbated. The purported object was to assess their potential for impotence. Although the experiment did not involve any form of intercourse, it illustrates the practice of a deception as to the 'purpose' of the physical act.

27. These examples demonstrate the likely rarity of occasions when the conclusive presumption in section 76(2)(a) will apply. For example, *R v Linekar* [1995] 2 CAR 49 would not fall within its ambit. The appellant promised to pay a prostitute £25 if she had intercourse with him. It was a promise he never intended to keep. On this aspect of the case, that is, that the defendant tricked the prostitute into having intercourse with him, the judge left it to the jury to consider whether his fraud vitiated her consent which was given on the basis that he would pay. The conviction was quashed. The consent given by the complainant was a real consent, which was not destroyed by the appellant's false pretence. If anything, he was guilty of an offence under section 3 of the 1956 Act, that is an offence identical to the offence alleged in counts one and two of the present indictment. *Linekar* deceived the prostitute about his intentions. He undoubtedly lied to her. However she was undeceived about either the nature or the purpose of the act, that is intercourse. Accordingly the conclusive presumptions in section 76 would have no application.

28. With these considerations in mind, we must return to the present case. On the written basis of plea the appellant undoubtedly deceived the complainant. He created a bizarre and fictitious fantasy which, because it was real enough to her, pressurised her to have intercourse with him more frequently than she otherwise would have done. She was not deceived as to the nature or purpose of intercourse, but deceived as to the situation in which she found herself. In our judgment the conclusive presumption in section 76(2)(a) had no application, and counsel for the appellant below were wrong to advise on the basis that it did. However that is not an end of the matter.

We are being asked to examine the safety of convictions for rape where the appellant pleaded guilty. He did so on the basis of plea which accepted the accuracy of his admissions in interview with the police, and in particular did not question his unequivocal admission that there were occasions when sexual intercourse took place when the complainant was not truly consenting. This is entirely consistent with his acknowledgement that he persuaded the complainant to have intercourse with him more frequently than otherwise, and the persuasion took the form of the pressures imposed on her by the complicated and unpleasant scheme which he had fabricated. This was not a free choice, or consent for the purposes of the Act. In these circumstances we entertain no reservations that on some occasions at least the complainant was not consenting to intercourse for the purposes of section 74, and that the appellant was perfectly well aware of it. His guilty plea reflected these undisputed facts. Accordingly the appeal against conviction is dismissed.

It can be expected that what constitutes 'freedom' and 'capacity' will be vigorously contested in future cases, as these terms raise not only legal but also philosophical issues. What does it mean to be 'free to choose'? (On this see J. Herring, 'Mistaken Sex' [2005] Crim LR 311; contra Hyman Gross [2005] Crim LR 220). Does, for instance, an illegal immigrant who is poor and unable to feed her children, and who fears arrest, have the 'freedom' to resist an offer of money for sex? What of an aspiring actress who, desperate for a particular role, is told that she can have the role if she consents to having sex with the producer? Is there a difference between 'I will give you the role if...' and 'I will not give you the role unless.'? And is 'freedom' to be measured from the perspective of the victim or that of a reasonable person? On the issue of 'capacity', there are separate offences dealing with sexual offences against both children and the mentally disordered, one might wonder what is left for s. 74.

The relevance of mental disorder to the question of consent

A person who has intercourse with a person suffering a mental disorder may be guilty of rape by virtue of s. 1 and also the offence of sexual activity with a person with a mental disorder impeding choice (s. 30 SOA 2003). In *R v C*, below the defendant was charged with this offence although, as it will appear at the end of the extract, he could also have been charged and convicted of rape on the basis that consent to penetrative sex was lacking due to incapacity. The facts appear in the opinion of Baroness Hale which begins with a helpful historical and philosophical introduction to the issue of sexual relations and the mentally disordered.

R v C
[2009] UKHL 42

BARONESS HALE:
8. The second half of the twentieth century saw a revolution in the law's attitudes towards people with a mental disorder or disability. Previously they had been segregated from the rest of society, detained in large institutions on the outskirts of town or deep in the countryside, and denied the benefits of close personal relationships. The Mental Health Act 1959 introduced a new policy. As much as possible, people with mental disorders and disabilities should be integrated into society, treated as much like anyone else as it was possible to do and enjoying the same rights as other people.
9. One of the rights which other people take for granted is the right to have sexual relationships with the partners of their choice. But the 1959 Act (and its successor, the Mental Health Act 1983) did not change the old attitudes in one respect. Section 7 of the Sexual Offences Act 1956 made it an offence for any man to have extra-marital sexual intercourse with a 'defective', defined as any woman who suffered from 'a state of arrested or incomplete development of mind which includes

severe impairment of intelligence and social functioning' (1956 Act, s 45, as substituted by s 127(1) of the 1959 Act). Nor could such a woman or such a man give a valid consent to an indecent assault (1956 Act, ss 14(4) and (15(3)). It was also an offence for a man to commit homosexual acts with a severely impaired man (Sexual Offences Act 1967, s 1(3) and (4)).

10. This approach was both under- and over-inclusive. It included some severely handicapped women and men who might be quite capable of making a genuine choice about their sexual partners and would not be harmed by their sexual relationships. It denied them the sexual fulfilment which most people take for granted these days, simply on the basis of a status or diagnosis. On the other hand, it did not include people with other mental disorders which might well mean that they lacked the capacity to make a genuine choice about their sexual relationships.

11. This problem formed a small part of two separate law reform projects which gathered momentum during the 1990s. In 1989, the Law Commission began a project on decision-making on behalf of people who lacked the capacity to make decisions for themselves. This culminated in their Report on Mental Incapacity (1995, Law Com No 231). The proposals in that Report were taken forward by the Government in a Consultation Paper, *Who Decides?* (1997, Cm 3803) and their Report, *Making Decisions* (1999, Cm 4465). After further pre-legislative scrutiny of a draft Bill, the Mental Capacity Act was passed in 2005 and came into force in 2007.

12. Nothing in that Act, of course, allows a decision about sexual relations to be taken on behalf of anyone else (s 27(1)(b)). That is a decision which only the person concerned can take. But the project was important because it discussed the essential ingredients of the capacity to make a decision for oneself. Three broad approaches could be discerned in the existing law and literature: the 'status', the 'outcome' and the 'functional' approaches. The status approach excluded all people with a particular characteristic from a particular decision, irrespective of their actual capacity to make it at the time: this, of course, was the approach of the Sexual Offences Act 1956 to sexual relations with mental 'defectives'. The Commission pointed out that 'the status approach is quite out of tune with the policy aim of enabling and encouraging people to take for themselves any decision which they have capacity to take' (Law Com No 231, para 3.3).

13. The 'outcome' approach focused on the final content of the decision: a decision which is inconsistent with conventional values or with which the assessor disagreed might be classified as incompetent. This approach 'penalises individuality and demands conformity at the expense of personal autonomy' (Law Com No 231, para 3.4). The Commission therefore recommended the functional approach: this asked whether, at the time the decision had to be made, the person could understand its nature and effects. 'Importantly, both partial and fluctuating capacity can be recognised' (Law Com No 231, para 3.5). However, the Commission went on to accept that understanding might not be enough. There were cases where people could understand the nature and effects of the decision to be made but the effects of their mental disability prevented them from using that information in the decision-making process. The examples given were an anorexic who always decides not to eat or a person whose mental disability meant that he or she was 'unable to exert their will against some stronger person who wishes to influence their decisions or against some *force majeure* of circumstances' (Law Com No 231, para 3.17).

14. In 1999, the Home Office embarked upon a Review of Sex Offences. The meaning of consent and capacity to consent were obviously important parts of that. The Law Commission had already done a considerable amount of work on Consent in the Criminal Law ((1995) Consultation Paper No 139) and was asked for its help. The resulting Report on Consent in Sex Offences was published as an Appendix to the Home Office Report, Setting the Boundaries: Reforming the Law on Sex Offences (Home Office, 2000).

15. This adopted essentially the same 'functional' approach as had the earlier Report on Mental Incapacity, but using simplified language 'more apt to describe the process of deciding to consent to sexual activity, as opposed to deciding upon a course of conduct with civil legal consequences. Essentially this is because it is perceived to be a visceral, rather than a cerebral, process of decision-making' (para 4.59). Quite so. But the same two elements remained – inability to understand or inability to decide (para 4.84). The Commission also stressed that their proposed test 'would require assessment of capacity on the material occasion' (para 4.48). Their whole concern was to protect sexual autonomy, which 'includes a right to refuse unwanted sexual attention (a negative

aspect of this concept) as well as the right to choose to engage in sexual activity (a positive aspect)' (para 4.69). Any particular choice to engage in sexual activity is, of course, both person-specific and occasion-specific: with you here and now, or not with you, (although possibly with someone else), or not here, or not now.

16. The Sexual Offences Act 2003 provides a number of offences against persons 'with a mental disorder impeding choice' in sections 30 to 33, and a number of offences involving inducements, threats or deception to procure sexual activity with a person with a mental disorder, in sections 34 to 37. Relevant for our purposes is the offence in section 30:

"(1) A person (A) commits an offence if—
    (a) he intentionally touches another person (B),
    (b) the touching is sexual,
    (c) B is unable to refuse because of or for a reason related to a mental disorder, and
    (d) A knows or could reasonably be expected to know that B has a mental disorder and that because of it or for a reason related to it B is likely to be unable to refuse.
(2) B is unable to refuse if—
    (a) he lacks the capacity to choose whether to agree to the touching (whether because he lacks sufficient understanding of the nature or reasonably foreseeable consequences of what is being done, or for any other reason), or
    (b) he is unable to communicate such a choice to A."

(3) and (4) deal with penalties, distinguishing between penetration of anus or vagina and penetration of mouth with penis, which carry up to life imprisonment, and other sexual touchings, which carry up to 14 years' imprisonment on indictment but may be tried summarily.

The Facts:

... The complainant was a 28 year old woman with an established diagnosis of schizo-affective disorder, an emotionally unstable personality disorder, an IQ of less than 75, and a history of harmful use of alcohol. Schizo-affective disorder is a mental illness, the effects of which may come and go. When unwell, a sufferer may experience delusions, hallucinations and severe disturbances of mood. An emotionally unstable personality disorder is an intrinsic abnormality of mood, ability to interact with other people, thought processes and thinking style. A sufferer has a tendency to become upset without rational cause, act impulsively, develop unstable relationships and repeatedly self-harm...

18. The complainant had had at least four admissions to hospital, including three periods of detention under the Mental Health Act 1983. She was discharged to a hostel in Croydon on 13 June 2006. On 27 June 2006 she visited the community mental health team resource centre where she saw her care co-ordinator, Mrs Hannan, who was concerned because she kept on repeating that she wanted to leave Croydon, people were after her and she did not want to die. She was seen by a consultant forensic psychiatrist, Dr Picchoni, but walked out of the interview dramatically in a distressed and agitated state. He completed a form recommending her compulsory admission to hospital. Later that day, the complainant met the defendant (also a user of the mental health resource centre) in the car park outside the centre. She told him that she had been in hospital for 9 years and had recently left. She said that she wanted to leave Croydon because she believed that people were after her. The defendant offered to help. She went with him to his friend's house. He sold her a mobile telephone and bicycle and gave her crack. She went to the bathroom but the defendant came in and asked her to give him a 'blow job'. Her evidence was that she was really panicky and afraid and wanted to get out of there. She was saying to herself 'these crack heads ... they do worse to you'. She did not want to die so she just stayed there and just took it all.

19. Dr Picchoni assessed the complainant again two days later. He said that it was likely that her symptoms had persisted after the morning of 27 June. Her capacity was likely to be affected by her relapsed mental state, because of her diminished ability to take in information and weigh it up to make a decision. The complainant's treating psychiatrist, Dr Harty, gave evidence that given the deterioration in her mental state before the alleged events, her presentation during the interview with Dr Picchoni, her learning disability and impaired intellectual functioning, and highly aroused

state, she would not have had the ability to consent to sexual contact at the time of the alleged offence.

20. After the alleged offence, the complainant made a 999 call and around midnight she was found by police officers running about the street, screaming and saying 'they're going to kill me. They're going to kill me.' They thought she might have mental health problems and discovered that she was missing from the hostel. She was taken back there, although she kept saying that she did not want to go back. The next day social workers from the centre visited and found her distressed and withdrawn, lying on the bed in a foetal position. She told them something of what had happened and the police were called.

21. The only passage in the judge's summing up which was directed towards the complainant's capacity was this:

> "Now [the complainant] would be unable to refuse if she lacked the capacity to choose whether to agree to the touching, in other words the sexual activity, for any reason, for example, an irrational fear arising from her mental disorder or such confusion of mind arising from her mental disorder, that she felt that she was unable to refuse any request the defendants made for sex. Alternatively, [she] would be unable to refuse if through her mental disorder she was unable to communicate such a choice to the defendants even though she was physically able to communicate with them."

22. The defendant was convicted but his conviction was set aside on appeal. The Court of Appeal [2008] EWCA Crim 1155 ; [2009] 1 Cr App R 211 relied heavily upon the observations of Munby J when exercising the inherent jurisdiction of the High Court in *Re MAB* [2006] EWHC (Fam) 168 and *Re MM* [2007] EWHC (Fam) 2003, both decided before the Mental Capacity Act 2005 came into force. He expressed the view that the test for capacity to consent to sexual relations must be the same in its essentials as the test in the criminal law; more importantly 'a woman either has capacity, for example, to consent to "normal" penetrative vaginal intercourse, or she does not...Put shortly, capacity to consent to sexual relations is issue specific; it is not person (partner) specific' (*MM*, para 87). The Court of Appeal agreed: 'Irrational fear that prevents the exercise of choice cannot be equated with lack of capacity to choose. We agree with Munby J's conclusion that a lack of capacity to choose to agree to sexual activity cannot be "person specific" or, we would add, "situation specific"' (para 53). They also disagreed with the judge's direction that if the complainant were unable to say no because of an irrational fear, this was capable of amounting to an inability to communicate her choice (paras 54, 55). Hence the judge's directions about inability to communicate and irrational fear were inadequate (paras 61, 62); his direction about 'confusion of mind' came closer to an adequate direction but 'the problem with it was that it was "person specific"' (para 63). Hence the conviction was unsafe.

23. The questions certified for us by the Court of Appeal have been summarised for us by the parties as follows:

> "Whether the decision of the Court of Appeal...has unduly limited the scope of section 30(1) of the Sexual Offences Act beyond that which Parliament intended. Specifically
> (a) in holding that a lack of capacity to choose cannot be person or situation specific
> (b) in holding that an irrational fear that prevents the exercise of choice cannot be equated with a lack of capacity to choose
> (c) in holding that to fall within section 30(2)(b) a complainant must be physically unable to communicate by reason of his mental disorder."

24. My Lords, I have no doubt that the answer to questions (a) and (b) is 'yes'. The Court of Appeal acknowledged that this was a difficult area and they were, in my view, unduly influenced by the views of Munby J in another context. I am far from persuaded that those views were correct, because the case law on capacity has for some time recognised that, to be able to make a decision, the person concerned must not only be able to understand the information relevant to making it but also be able to 'weigh [that information] in the balance to arrive at [a] choice': see *Re C (Adult: Refusal of Treatment)* [1994] 1 WLR 290, 295, approved in *Re MB (Medical Treatment)* [1997] 2 FLR 426. In *Re C*, the patient's persecutory delusions might have prevented him from weighing the information relevant to having his leg amputated because of gangrene, which he

was perfectly capable of understanding, but they did not. But in *NHS Trust v T (adult patient: refusal of medical treatment)* [2004] EWHC 1279 (Fam), [2005] 1 All ER 387, the patient had a history of self harming leading to dangerously low haemoglobin levels. She knew that if she refused a blood transfusion she might die; nevertheless she believed that her blood was evil and that the healthy blood given her in a transfusion became contaminated and thus increased the volume of evil blood in her body and 'likewise the danger of my committing acts of evil'. Charles J concluded that she was unable to use and weigh the relevant information, and thus the competing factors, in the process of arriving at her decision to refuse a transfusion (para 63). In the same way, a person's delusions that she was being commanded by God to have sexual intercourse, an act which she was perfectly capable of understanding, might make her incapable of exercising an autonomous choice in the matter.

25. However, it is not for us to decide whether Munby J was right or wrong about the common law. The 2003 Act puts the matter beyond doubt. A person is unable to refuse if he lacks the capacity to choose whether to agree to the touching 'whether because he lacks sufficient understanding of the nature or reasonably foreseeable consequences of what is being done, or for any other reason' (s 30(2)(a)). Provided that the inability to refuse is 'because of or for a reason related to a mental disorder' (s 30(1)(c)), and the other ingredients of the offence are made out, the perpetrator is guilty. The words 'for any other reason' are clearly capable of encompassing a wide range of circumstances in which a person's mental disorder may rob them of the ability to make an autonomous choice, even though they may have sufficient understanding of the information relevant to making it. These could include the kind of compulsion which drives a person with anorexia to refuse food, the delusions which drive a person with schizophrenia to believe that she must do something, or the phobia (or irrational fear) which drives a person to refuse a life-saving injection (as in *Re MB*) or a blood transfusion (as in *NHS Trust v T*).

26. The 2003 Act also makes it clear that the question is whether the complainant has the capacity to choose whether to agree to 'the touching', that is, the specific act of sexual touching of which the defendant is accused. It is, perhaps, easier to understand how the test of capacity might be 'act specific' but not 'person specific' or 'situation specific' if intellectual understanding were all that was required. The complainant here did know what a 'blow job' was. Even then, it is well accepted that capacity can fluctuate, so that a person may have the required degree of understanding one day but not another. But that is because of a fluctuation in the mental disorder rather than a fluctuation in the circumstances. Once it is accepted that choice is an exercise of free will, and that mental disorder may rob a person of free will in a number of different ways and in a number of different situations, then a mentally disordered person may be quite capable of exercising choice in one situation but not in another. The complainant here, even in her agitated and aroused state, might have been quite capable of deciding whether or not to have sexual intercourse with a person who had not put her in the vulnerable and terrifying situation in which she found herself on 27 June 2007. The question is whether, in the state that she was in that day, she was capable of choosing whether to agree to the touching demanded of her by the defendant.

27. My Lords, it is difficult to think of an activity which is more person and situation specific than sexual relations. One does not consent to sex in general. One consents to this act of sex with this person at this time and in this place. Autonomy entails the freedom and the capacity to make a choice of whether or not to do so. This is entirely consistent with the respect for autonomy in matters of private life which is guaranteed by article 8 of the European Convention on Human Rights. The object of the 2003 Act was to get away from the previous 'status' based approach which assumed that all 'defectives' lacked capacity, and thus denied them the possibility of making autonomous choices, while failing to protect those whose mental disorder deprived them of autonomy in other ways.

28. My Lords, I believe that the Court of Appeal were led astray by their understandable reliance upon the contrary view, that capacity could not be situation specific, and it was for this reason that they found the matter so difficult. Mr Richard Wormald, for the defendant, has not seriously tried to uphold their reasoning on the questions which we have been asked. He accepts that an irrational fear plainly is *capable* of depriving a person of capacity. The question is whether it does. He has, understandably, pointed to all the features in the evidence which suggest that the complainant was indeed exercising a choice, a choice reluctantly to go along with what was being asked of

her because of her fear of the consequences if she did not. But if the judge's direction on lack of capacity is upheld, as I consider it should be, it is difficult to suggest that the jury were not entitled to reach the verdict they did on the evidence they heard.

29. Alison Foster QC, for the Crown, does not place so much reliance on the inability to communicate the choice to refuse. But in my opinion the judge was also correct on this point. Indeed. Mr Wormald accepts that it may be that the complainant's description of herself was closer in kind to an inability to communicate than to any lack of understanding. There is a significant difference between the approaches of the 2003 and 2005 Acts on this subject. The Mental Capacity Act 2005 provides that 'a person lacks capacity in relation to a matter if at the material time he is unable to make a decision for himself in relation to the matter because of an impairment of, or disturbance in the functioning of, the mind or brain' (s 2(1)). For this purpose, a person is unable to make a decision for himself if he is unable, *inter alia*, 'to communicate his decision (whether by talking, using sign language or any other means)' (s 3(1)(d)). This clearly covers people with physical disorders of the brain, for example head injuries or strokes, which prevent them communicating as well as people with disorders of the mind which have the same effect.

30. Section 30 of the 2003 Act, however, is only concerned with people who are 'unable to refuse because of or for a reason related to a mental disorder' (s 30(1)(c)). This inability may involve either the inability to choose (s 30(2)(a)) or the inability to communicate the choice made (s 30(2)(b)). 'Mental disorder' for this purpose has the same meaning as in section 1 of the Mental Health Act 1983 (s 79(1)). At the material time (before the amendments made by the Mental Health Act 2007 came into force) 'mental disorder' meant 'mental illness, arrested or incomplete development of mind, psychopathic disorder and any other disorder or disability of mind'; since the 2007 amendments, it means 'any disorder or disability of the mind' (s 1(2)). There are, of course, some physical disorders of the brain which lead to disorders of the mind. But it is quite clear that in the 2003 Act Parliament had in mind an inability to communicate which was the result of or associated with a disorder of the mind. There is no warrant at all for limiting it to a physical inability to communicate. It must include a person with such a degree of learning difficulty that they have never acquired the gift of speech, so that it is impossible to discover whether or not they can understand or make a choice. (For what it is worth, the Act deals with people who because of a physical disability are not able to communicate whether or not they have consented by placing an evidential burden on the defendant; see s 75(1), (2)(e).)

31. For these reasons, I would answer each of the certified questions in the affirmative and allow this appeal.

32. It may be worth observing that there were at least three offences which might have been charged on the evidence available. We are told that the defendants were originally charged with rape, but that charges under section 30 were substituted at a late stage. The view may have been taken that the offence under section 30 is somewhat easier to prove. The prosecution has only to prove the inability to refuse rather than that the complainant actually did not consent. This may not make much difference (although the Law Commission apparently thought that it did), given that both offences relate to a specific sexual act, and the Act provides that 'a person consents if he agrees by choice, and has the freedom and capacity to make that choice' (s 74). But the mens rea under section 30 is that the defendant knows or could reasonably be expected to know that the complainant has a mental disorder and that because of it or for a reason related to it she is likely to be unable to refuse (s 30(1)(d)). The mens rea for rape is that the defendant does not reasonably believe that the complainant consents (s 1(1)(c)). This puts a greater burden of restraint upon people who know or ought to know that a person's mental disorder is likely to affect her ability to choose. This may explain why the decision was made to charge the section 30 offence in this case. Less easy to understand is why the offence under section 34 was not charged in the alternative. This involves the same range of sexual acts as does the offence under section 30 and attracts the same levels of punishment. It covers intentional sexual touching with the agreement of the person touched (s 34(1)(a), (b)), where the defendant has obtained that agreement by means of an inducement offered or given, a threat made or a deception practised for that purpose (s 34(1)(c)), and the defendant knows or could reasonably be expected to know that the complainant has a mental disorder (s 34(1)(d)(e)). Perhaps the view was taken that the evidence of lack of capacity was more

robust than the evidence of any inducement, threat or deception. This is pure speculation. But the alternative charges would have enabled the judge to explain the various concepts by distinguishing them from one another and relating them to the evidence: a lack of consent arising from the lack of either the freedom or the capacity to make that choice; a lack of capacity to make that choice arising from or related to a mental disorder; and a choice procured by threats, inducement or deception of a person with a mental disorder. One difficulty which the jury might have had with the judge's reference to 'irrational fear' is that some of this complainant's fears may have been all too rational. But on the evidence and on the judge's direction they were entitled to conclude that she lacked the capacity either to choose or to communicate within the meaning of the Act and the conviction must therefore stand.

The Relevance of Intoxication to the Issue of Consent

R v Bree
[2007] EWCA Crim 804 (26 March 2007)

PRESIDENT OF THE QUEEN'S BENCH DIVISION:

1. On 26 October 2006, in the Crown Court at Bournemouth, before HHJ Jarvis and a jury, Benjamin Bree, a 25 year old man of excellent previous character, was convicted of rape. There was no dispute that, after a very heavy evening drinking together, he had sexual intercourse with a young woman aged 19 years whom we shall identify as 'M'. This appeal required us to address the effect of voluntary heavy alcohol consumption as it applies to the law of rape. After the hearing on 13th March we quashed the conviction. These are our reasons.

As we have indicated, at the start of the trial the prosecution alleged that the appellant raped M when her level of intoxication was so great that she was effectively unconscious. She lacked the capacity to consent, and therefore did not consent. However, by the end of the evidence, the prosecution case against the appellant had changed. The jury were no longer invited to conclude that M had been unable to consent to intercourse because she was unconscious, rather, the prosecution accepted that the gaps in her recollection were probably the result of intoxication, and lack of memory, rather than unconsciousness. The prosecution case, therefore, was not that the complainant lacked the capacity to consent, but that she did not in fact consent to intercourse. Her ability to resist was hampered by the effects of alcohol, but her capacity to consent remained. She knew what was happening. She knew that she did not want to have sexual intercourse, and so far as she could, made that clear. The appellant's case, as we have indicated, was unchanged from start to finish, that notwithstanding, and perhaps because of drink, M was consenting. He reasonably believed that she was . . .

24. Section 75 and section 76 of the 2003 Act address the issue of consent in practical situations which arise from time to time in cases of alleged sexual offences including rape. They are not, however, exhaustive. The presumptions in section 75 are evidential and rebuttable, whereas those in section 76 are irrebuttable and conclusive. In this appeal we are not concerned with either of the conclusive presumptions relating to consent specified in section 76. The common characteristic of the particular situations covered by the evidential presumptions in section 75 is that they are concerned with situations in which the complainant is involuntarily at a disadvantage. Section 75(2)(f) is plainly adequate to deal with the situation when a drink is 'spiked', but unless productive of a state of near unconsciousness, or incapacity, this paragraph does not address seductive blandishments to have 'just one more' drink. Section 75(2)(d) repeats well established common law principles, and acknowledges plain good sense, that, if the complainant is unconscious as a result of her voluntary consumption of alcohol, the starting point is to presume that she is not consenting to intercourse. Beyond that, the Act is silent about the impact of excessive but voluntary alcohol consumption on the ability to give consent to intercourse, or indeed to consent generally.

25. It is perhaps helpful to identify a number of features of the law relating to consent which although obvious are sometimes overlooked. On any view, both parties to the act of sexual intercourse with which this case is concerned were the worse for drink. Both were adults. Neither acted unlawfully in drinking to excess. They were both free to choose how much to drink, and with whom.

Both were free, if they wished, to have intercourse with each other. There is nothing abnormal, surprising, or even unusual about men and women having consensual intercourse when one, or other, or both have voluntarily consumed a great deal of alcohol. Provided intercourse is indeed consensual, it is not rape.

26. In cases which are said to arise after voluntary consumption of alcohol the question is not whether the alcohol made either or both less inhibited than they would have been if sober, nor whether either or both might afterwards have regretted what had happened, and indeed wished that it had not. If the complainant consents, her consent cannot be revoked. Moreover it is not a question whether either or both may have had very poor recollection of precisely what had happened. That may be relevant the reliability of their evidence. Finally, and certainly, it is not a question whether either or both was behaving irresponsibly. As they were both autonomous adults, the essential question for decision is, as it always is, whether the evidence proved that the appellant had sexual intercourse with the complainant without her consent.

27. Before the 2003 Act, it was not difficult to identify the relevant legal principles, and for a judge to explain the law relating to the voluntary consumption of alcohol (or drugs) by a complainant. Thus, for example, in R v Malone [1998] 2 CAR 447 the Court of Appeal upheld the direction:

'She does not claim to have physically resisted nor to have verbally protested. She says the drink has disabled her from doing either . . . .she has told you she did not consent . . . .you must be sure that the act of sexual intercourse occurred without (her) consent. Submitting to an act of sexual intercourse, because through drink she was unable physically to resist though she wished to, is not consent. If she submits to intercourse because of the drink she cannot physically resist, that, of course, is not consent. No right thinking person would say that in those circumstances she was genuinely consenting to what occurred. What occurred . . . .not wishing to have intercourse but being physically unable to do anything about it . . . would plainly, as a matter of common sense be against her will. It would be without her consent'.

28. We record this direction as illustrative of what was regarded as an appropriate direction in the circumstances of an individual case to a particular jury, rather than a learned disquisition of the law of consent as applied to rape. We should however highlight R v Lang [1976] 62 CAR 50 which summarised the relevant principle. The jury sought guidance from the judge on the question of whether the complainant's alcohol consumption may have vitiated her consent to sexual intercourse. The court observed

'. . .there is no special rule applicable to drink and rape. If the issue be, as here, did the woman consent? the critical question is not how she came to take the drink, but whether she understood her situation and was capable of making up her mind. In Howard [1965] 50 CAR 56 the Court of Criminal Appeal had to consider the case of a girl under 16. Lord Parker CJ . . . .said: . . . "in the case of a girl under 16 the prosecution . . . must prove either that she physically resisted, or, if she did not, that her understanding and knowledge was such that she was not in a position to decide whether to consent or resist". In our view these words are of general application whenever there is present some factor, be it permanent or transient, suggesting the absence of such understanding or knowledge . . . . None of this was explained to the jury. Their attention was focussed by the judge upon how she came to take drink, not upon the state of her understanding and her capacity to exercise judgment in the circumstances.'

29. In the context of the statutory provision in section 74, it is noteworthy that Lang decided thirty years or so ago, directly focussed on the 'capacity' of the complainant to decide whether to consent to intercourse or not. These are the concepts with which the 2003 Act itself is concerned.

30. We are not aware of any reported decisions which deal with this aspect of the new legislation. We should however refer to the much publicised case of R v Dougal, heard in Swansea Crown Court, in November 2005. Having heard the evidence of the complainant, the Crown decided to offer no further evidence. Before the jury counsel for the Crown explained:

'the prosecution are conscious of the fact that a drunken consent is still a consent and that in the answer, in cross examination, she said, in terms, that she could not remember giving her consent and that is fatal to the prosecution's case. In those circumstances the prosecution will have no further evidence on the issue of consent. This is a case of the word of the defendant against that of the complainant on that feature. It is fatal to the prosecution's case...'

31. The judge (Roderick Evans J) directed the jury that as the prosecution was no longer seeking a guilty verdict, there was only one verdict which could be returned, and that was an acquittal. He added that he agreed with the course the prosecution had taken.

32. Without knowing all the details of the case, and focussing exclusively on the observations of counsel for the Crown in *Dougal*, it would be open to question whether the inability of the complainant to remember whether she gave her consent or not might on further reflection be approached rather differently. Prosecuting counsel may wish he had expressed himself more felicitously. That said, one of the most familiar directions of law provided to juries who are being asked to conclude that the voluntary consumption of alcohol by a defendant should lead to the conclusion that he was too drunk to form the intention required for proof of the crime alleged against him, is that a drunken intent is still an intent (*R v Sheehan and Moore* [1975] 60 CAR 308 at 312). So it is, and that we suspect is the source of the phrase that a 'drunken consent is still consent'. In the context of consent to intercourse, the phrase lacks delicacy, but, properly understood, it provides a useful shorthand accurately encapsulating the legal position. We note in passing that it also acts as a reminder that a drunken man who intends to commit rape, and does so, is not excused by the fact that his intention is a drunken intention.

33. Some of the hugely critical discussion arising after *Dougal* missed the essential point. Neither counsel for the Crown, nor for that matter the judge, was saying or coming anywhere near saying, either that a complainant who through drink is incapable of consenting to intercourse must nevertheless be deemed to have consented to it, or that a man is at liberty to have sexual intercourse with a woman who happens to be drunk, on the basis that her drunkenness deprives her of her right to choose whether to have intercourse or not. Such ideas are wrong in law, and indeed, offensive. All that was being said in *Dougal* was that when someone who has had a lot to drink is in fact consenting to intercourse, then that is what she is doing, consenting: equally, if after taking drink, she is not consenting, then by definition intercourse is taking place without her consent. This is unexceptionable.

34. In our judgment, the proper construction of section 74 of the 2003 Act, as applied to the problem now under discussion, leads to clear conclusions. If, through drink (or for any other reason) the complainant has temporarily lost her capacity to choose whether to have intercourse on the relevant occasion, she is not consenting, and subject to questions about the defendant's state of mind, if intercourse takes place, this would be rape. However, where the complainant has voluntarily consumed even substantial quantities of alcohol, but nevertheless remains capable of choosing whether or not to have intercourse, and in drink agrees to do so, this would not be rape. We should perhaps underline that, as a matter of practical reality, capacity to consent may evaporate well before a complainant becomes unconscious. Whether this is so or not, however, is fact specific, or more accurately, depends on the actual state of mind of the individuals involved on the particular occasion.

35. Considerations like these underline the fact that it would be unrealistic to endeavour to create some kind of grid system which would enable the answer to these questions to be related to some prescribed level of alcohol consumption. Experience shows that different individuals have a greater or lesser capacity to cope with alcohol than others, and indeed the ability of a single individual to do so may vary from day to day. The practical reality is that there are some areas of human behaviour which are inapt for detailed legislative structures. In this context, provisions intended to protect women from sexual assaults might very well be conflated into a system which would provide patronising interference with the right of autonomous adults to make personal decisions for themselves.

36. For these reasons, notwithstanding criticisms of the statutory provisions, in our view the 2003 Act provides a clear definition of 'consent' for the purposes of the law of rape, and by defining it with reference to 'capacity to make that choice', sufficiently addresses the issue of consent in the context of voluntary consumption of alcohol by the complainant. The problems do not arise from the legal principles. They lie with infinite circumstances of human behaviour, usually taking place in private without independent evidence.

37. The striking feature of the summing up, which is criticised in a number of different ways, is that it does not directly address either the general problems to which this kind of case may give rise, nor their specific application to the present case.

38. The jury were rightly directed that an essential requirement before the appellant could be convicted was that M did not consent to intercourse. They were told that 'a person consents if he agrees by choice and has the freedom and capacity to make that choice'. The statutory definition having been read, no further elucidation was given. Our attention was drawn to *R v Olugboga* [1981] 73 CAR 344, decided after the enactment of the Sexual Offences (Amendment) Act 1976. As Professor Temkin and Professor Ashworth explain, the report *Setting the Boundaries: Reforming the Law on Sexual Offences* (2000) which echoed a much earlier report by an advisory group chaired by Heilbron J in November 1975, suggested that the broad approach to consent and submission adopted in *Olugboga* should be abandoned. In our view, even if these criticisms are justified, the judgment contains passages of continuing value. The court rejected the submission on behalf of the Crown that a trial judge was required 'merely to leave the issue of consent to a jury in a similar way to that in which the issue of dishonesty is left in trials for offences under the Theft Act'. Because of the myriad circumstances in which the issue of consent may arise, the judgment continued, 'We do not think that the issue of consent should be left to a jury without some further direction. What this should be will depend on the circumstances of each case.'

39. In this case the jury should have been given some assistance with the meaning of 'capacity' in circumstances where the complainant was affected by her own voluntarily induced intoxication, and also whether, and to what extent they could take that into account in deciding whether she had consented. Moreover, the judge did not address the changed way in which the prosecution put its case against the appellant. There is a significant difference between an allegation that the complainant was unconscious and for that reason not consenting to intercourse, and an allegation that, although she was capable of giving consent, despite her state, she was not in fact consenting to intercourse and was giving clear indications that she was rejecting the appellant. The potential for confusion was compounded by the fact that the complainant herself asserted, more than once, that she was unconscious at different stages of the encounter. At the same time the Crown conceded that what she believed to be and said were periods of unconsciousness should for the purposes of the trial be treated as moments of memory deficit caused by drink. Of course if the Crown was not contending that she was unconscious, that at least was consistent with the appellant's case that she was indeed conscious throughout.

40. The jury were not provided with any assistance about how properly to address these problems. Thus, when summing up, the judge referred more than once to the complainant's evidence of occasions when she had been unconscious without reminding them of the Crown's concessions. For example, he reminded the jury that M said 'she had no memory particularly of her hair being washed after the shampoo was asked for. She was unconscious. (Her) next memory is of her being on her bed . . . .' It is therefore at least possible that the jury proceeded on the basis that the complainant was indeed unconscious, contrary to the prosecution case in its developed form, but as she herself had asserted. If so, the conclusion that she was not consenting to intercourse would have followed without much difficulty. In a situation like this, the approach in *Olugboga*, that the issue of consent and capacity should be directly addressed, applied with yet greater force.

41. The problem was further compounded by the way in which the judge actually addressed the issue of voluntary intoxication. He rightly pointed out that 'drink has played a dominant feature in the evidence in this case', but that was said in the context that the appellant's 'self induced intoxication can never be a factor which can properly be taken into account when considering [sic] Mr Bree does not reasonably believe that M consented'. That attempted to address, whether adequately or not, the effect of drink on the appellant. So far as the complainant was concerned, the direction was even more limited. The judge pointed out that M accepted that 'she had drunk a great deal during the evening, and you must, of course, consider that and its potential impact upon her reliability . . . . It is something which I am sure you have in mind in any event, and it is fair that you bear that in mind when considering her evidence and the whole of the evidence in this case'.

42. In short, the only specific feature of the complainant's alcohol consumption identified by the judge was its possible relevance to her reliability as a witness. Beyond that, if the jury were able to

derive anything from what the judge said, it was vague in the extreme. The context, after all, was that although the appellant conceded that the complainant had been drunk, it was a fundamental part of his defence that she was conscious throughout and did in fact consent to sexual activities and intercourse with him. From the defence point of view, the drink she had consumed was a factor which may have led her to behave in a way which, if sober, she would not. She had drunk far more than she was accustomed to. This critical aspect of the case was not sufficiently addressed in the summing up, indeed it was not addressed at all. The questions whether she might have behaved differently drunk than she would have done sober, and whether, although and perhaps because drunk, she might have behaved as the appellant contended, and the way in which the jury should consider these important issues, were not mentioned at all.

43. A number of further features of the summing up were criticised, but it is unnecessary to deal with them. In a trial in which the issues of consent and voluntary intoxication were fundamental to the outcome, the jury were given no or no sufficient directions to enable the verdict which they reached to be regarded as safe. Accordingly the conviction was quashed.

■ NOTES AND QUESTIONS

1. Why, in the view of the Court of Appeal, might the jury have been misled by the trial judge's direction? What should he have told them? Is *Dougal*, referred to in the judgment, accurate in its assertion that a 'drunken consent is still consent'?

2. We saw in *R* v *G* a strong preference among the judges in the House of Lords for a 'subjective' as opposed to an 'objective' approach to *mens rea*. Does the requirement that A must 'reasonably' believe that B consented create an objective test that is tension with *R* v *G*?

3. Why has there been created both conclusive and non-conclusive (evidential) presumptions relating to absence of consent? Out of fairness to a defendant, should not all presumptions be subject to rebuttal? Otherwise, is not the defendant effectively denied possible defences relating to the absence of consent? Might this be a violation of Article 6 of the European Convention on Human Rights (ECHR)?

4. By placing the burden on the defendant of introducing evidence to rebut a presumption of non-consent once a prosecutor has established an evidential presumption, has Parliament in effect reversed the burden of proof. If so, is this violative of the presumption of innocence protected by ECHR, Article 6?

5. Is it possible to identify criteria that account for why some presumptions are conclusive and others evidential? Is it the egregiousness of B's conduct? If so, is obtaining consent by intentionally impersonating an individual known personally to the victim (which results in a conclusive presumption) more egregious than, say, obtaining consent through violence or threatened violence, or by administering a stupefying drug to the victim without her consent (all of which lead only to an evidential presumption)? If not, what other criteria might account for the categories?

6. Do you agee (see *Jheeta*) that *Linekar* would be decided in the same way today? Was the prostitute not deceived as to the nature and purpose of the act? She will surely wish to argue that although the purpose of the act **for the defendant** was the same (sexual satisfaction) whether or not he paid for it, the purpose of the act for **me (the prostitute)** was to gain money and not to satisfy any sexual desire.

7. In *Aydin* v *Turkey* (1997) 25 EHRR 251, the European Court of Human Rights indicated that rape by State police could in some instances constitute 'torture' prohibited by Article 3 of the ECHR.

(iii) Absence of a reasonable belief in the victim's consent

The *mens rea* of rape is the absence of a *reasonable* belief that A consented (see SOA 2003, s. (1)(c)). Under the previous leading decision of *DPP* v *Morgan* [1976] AC 182, the House of Lords had held that a defendant could not be convicted of rape if he *honestly* believed that the victim had consented, no matter how unreasonable his belief might be (reasonableness of the defendant's belief, however, could be relevant to whether the jury chose to disbelieve the defendant's testimony). In *Morgan*, the husband of the victim had spent the evening drinking with three friends. At one point he suggested that they should all return to his home and have sexual intercourse with his wife. According to the three friends, Morgan had told them not to be surprised if his wife struggled. He explained that she was 'kinky' and that this was the only way in which she could get 'turned on'. Thus Morgan's three companions claimed to believe that there was consent to their sexual acts despite the victim's screams and at times violent resistance. The House of Lords held that, assuming that the jurors believed the defendants, they were entitled to be acquitted. Lord Hailsham explained:

> Once one has accepted, what seems to me abundantly clear, that the prohibited act in rape is non-consensual sexual intercourse, and that the guilty state of mind is an intention to commit it, it seems to me to follow as a matter of inexorable logic that there is no room either for a 'defence' of honest belief or mistake, or of a defence of honest and reasonable belief or mistake. Either the prosecution proves that the accused had the requisite intent, or it does not. In the former case it succeeds, and in the latter it fails. Since honest belief clearly negatives intent, the reasonableness or otherwise of that belief can only be evidence for or against the view that the belief and therefore the intent was actually held.

The decision in *Morgan* was heavily criticised, with many maintaining that it would discourage victims from reporting sexual offences. The effect of the SOA 2003, s. (1)(c), is to reverse *Morgan*. Under this section, not only is the reasonableness of the defendant's belief not irrelevant, it is the central issue. Of course, a defendant must also honestly believe that the victim has consented, but an honest but incorrect belief in consent will not be sufficient to exonerate the defendant unless the belief is also reasonable.

The Sexual Offences Act 2003, s. 1(2), states that whether a defendant's belief is reasonable is to be determined 'having regard to all the circumstances, including any steps A has taken to ascertain whether or not B has consented.' The critical issue is likely to turn on the interpretation of the phrase 'all the circumstances'. What 'circumstances' are properly to be considered? What of A's provocative clothing – is this a relevant or irrelevant circumstance? What of the victim's sexual history and reputation? And what of a defendant's religious or cultural belief that the role of women is to submit to the sexual bidding of men? In response to a parliamentary question prior to passage of the Act, the Government stated that it would be for the jury to decide whether any of the attributes of the defendant were relevant, subject to the directions of the judge. This response is not helpful, and guideline directions to trial judges will be needed (but at the present time are yet to be issued).

(a) Implied consent

Can consent ever be implied? For centuries it was believed to be the law that, by virtue of marriage, a wife had consented to sexual intercourse with her husband. As a result, it was also presumed that a husband could not be prosecuted for rape. In 1991 this fiction was finally abandoned.

R v R – (rape: marital exemption)

[1992] AC 599, House of Lords

LORD KEITH OF KINKEL: My Lords, in this appeal to the House with leave of the Court of Appeal, Criminal Division that court has certified the following point of law of general public importance as being involved in its decision, namely: 'Is a husband criminally liable for raping his wife?'

...

The position then is that that part of Hale's proposition which asserts that a wife cannot retract the consent to sexual intercourse which she gives on marriage has been departed from in a series of decided cases. On grounds of principle there is no good reason why the whole proposition should not be held inapplicable in modern times. The only question is whether s 1(1) of the 1976 Act presents an insuperable obstacle to that sensible course. The argument is that 'unlawful' in the subsection means outside the bond of marriage. That is not the most natural meaning of the word, which normally describes something which is contrary to some law or enactment or is done without lawful justification or excuse. Certainly in modern times sexual intercourse outside marriage would not ordinarily be described as unlawful. If the subsection proceeds on the basis that a woman on marriage gives a general consent to sexual intercourse, there can never be any question of intercourse with her by her husband being without her consent. There would thus be no point in enacting that only intercourse without consent outside marriage is to constitute rape.

I am therefore of the opinion that s 1(1) of the 1976 Act presents no obstacle to this House declaring that in modern times the supposed marital exception in rape forms no part of the law of England. The Court of Appeal, Criminal Division took a similar view. Towards the end of the judgment of that court Lord Lane CJ said ([1991] 2 All ER 257 at 266, [1991] 2 WLR 1065 at 1074):

'The remaining and no less difficult question is whether, despite that view, this is an area where the court should step aside to leave the matter to the parliamentary process. This is not the creation of a new offence, it is the removal of a common law fiction which has become anachronistic and offensive and we consider that it is our duty having reached that conclusion to act upon it.'

I respectfully agree.

Appeal dismissed.

■ NOTES AND QUESTIONS

1. *R v R* abandons the fiction that wives consent to sexual intercourse does it leave, at least in theory, the status of any individual act of intercourse within marriage as potentially unlawful given the requirement that consent be freely given. Must a husband seek his wife's consent whenever he wishes to have sexual intercourse with her? One suspects that in some marriages individual acts of intercourse are actually submitted to under protest or under the belief that nothing can realistically be done to prevent it? Is this rape? Should it be?

2. The holding in *R v R* was put on a statutory footing in the Criminal Justice and Public Order Act 1994, s. 142. Is the result also required by the definition of consent in the SOA 2003?

3. Does a husband who is prosecuted for the alleged rape of his wife that occurred prior to the decision in *R v R* have a viable claim that the prosecution contravenes

Article 7(1) of the ECHR, which prohibits a conviction based on an act which did not constitute a criminal offence at the time it was committed? Does it matter how long before 1991 that the alleged rape took place? In 2002, C was convicted of a rape of his wife that occurred in 1970. His ECHR argument based on an Article 7 violation was subsequently rejected. See *R* v *C* [2004] EWCA Crim 192.

(b) Consent to what?

To what does a person who agrees to have sexual intercourse with another consent? The issue has arisen in cases where a person who is HIV positive has had unprotected sex with a partner who may or may not have been aware of the infected partner's condition.

R v Dica

[2004] EWCA Crim 1103, Court of Appeal

For facts and holding, see p. 311.

■ NOTES AND QUESTIONS

1. Why, if *Dica* tells us that consent to be effective must be informed, was Dica not charged with rape?

2. SOA 2003, s. 76(2), refers to intentionally deceiving the complainant as to the nature...of the relevant act. What is the relevant act when one is requested to have sex with a partner who is HIV positive but who does not disclose this fact? Has there been a deception?

3. Should an HIV positive individual have a duty to inform his or her sexual partners of the condition, or is it the responsibility of the partner to make inquiries? See *R* v *Konzani* [2005] EWCA 706. In *Konzani*, the court drew a distinction between running a risk and consenting to a risk, and held that the defendant's sexual partners, not having been informed of his known HIV status, could not consent to the risk. Can it be argued, however, that, in the modern age, virtually everybody is aware of the risks of sexual diseases from having unprotected sex?

4. Which is more critical – the fact of consent, the defendant's honest belief in consent, or whether a reasonable person would believe that consent had been given?

B: Assault by penetration

The Sexual Offences Act 2003, s. 2 establishes the offence of 'assault by penetration'. This offence is defined as follows:

2. Assault by penetration

   (1) A person (A) commits an offence if—

      (a) he intentionally penetrates the vagina or anus of another person (B) with a part of his body or anything else,

      (b) the penetration is sexual,

      (c) B does not consent to the penetration, and

      (d) A does not reasonably believe that B consents.

(2) Whether a belief is reasonable is to be determined having regard to all the circumstances, including any steps A has taken to ascertain whether B consents.

(3) Sections 75 and 76 apply to an offence under this section.

(4) A person guilty of an offence under this section is liable, on conviction on indictment, to imprisonment for life.

(i) Comparison with rape

A comparison of the offence of rape and the offence of assault by penetration reveals several elements that the two offences share in common. In both the prosecution must prove an intentional penetration, that the victim did not consent to the penetration, and that the defendant does not reasonably believe that the victim had consented. The conclusive presumptions in s. 76 and the evidential presumptions in s. 75 apply to both offences.

There are, on the other hand, several features which distinguish assault by penetration from rape. Assault by penetration is limited to penetrations of the vagina or anus of the victim; omitted is the reference to a penetration of the mouth. Secondly, the penetration is not limited to one by the defendant's penis as it is in rape. Section 2(1) refers to penetration by a 'part of [the defendant's] body' or 'anything else'. 'Anything else' would embrace, for example, a penetration by a finger, a bottle, a cane or even a vegetable. The significance of this expansion is that, unlike in respect of rape, which is restricted to male defendants (because of the penis requirement), assault by penetration may be committed by a woman. Finally, it must be proved that the penetration is 'sexual', raising the question of what is meant by this term.

(ii) A 'sexual' penetration

What does it mean to say that the penetration must be 'sexual'? The answer is provided in SOA 2003, s. 78:

78. 'Sexual'

For the purposes of this Part (except section 71), penetration, touching or any other activity is sexual if a reasonable person would consider that—

(a) whatever its circumstances or any person's purpose in relation to it, it is because of its nature sexual, or

(b) because of its nature it may be sexual and because of its circumstances or the purpose of any person in relation to it (or both) it is sexual.

Subsection (1)(a) tells the jurors that they can conclude that a penetration is 'sexual' if a reasonable person would believe that the *nature* of the act of penetration is sexual. Under this subsection the surrounding circumstances and the defendant's purpose are irrelevant. In contrast, subsection (b) refers to penetrations which may (or which may not) be sexual because of their nature, where a reasonable person might conclude that the penetration is sexual in light of the surrounding circumstances and/or the defendant's purpose. If the defendant's act is clearly not sexual by its nature, however, it cannot be brought within subsection (b) by the surrounding circumstances or the defendant's purpose.

Consider the following leading pre-Act case:

R v Court

[1989] AC 28, House of Lords

The appellant, an assistant in a shop, struck a 12-year-old girl visitor some 12 times, for no apparent reason as she thought, outside her shorts on her buttocks. In response to a question by the police as to why the appellant had done so he said 'I don't know – buttock fetish.' He was tried on a count charging indecent assault contrary to section 14(1) of the Sexual Offences Act 1956. He pleaded guilty to assault, denied that it was indecent and submitted that his statement about 'buttock fetish' should be excluded as being a secret uncommunicated motive and could not make indecent an assault not overtly indecent. The trial judge refused to exclude the statement, the appellant did not give evidence and he was convicted. The Court of Appeal (Criminal Division) dismissed the appellant's appeal against conviction.

LORD ACKNER: The judge in assisting the jury in his summing up as to the meaning of an *indecent* assault adopted, inter alia, a definition used by Professor Glanville Williams, *Textbook of Criminal Law*, 2nd ed. (1983), p. 231: '"indecent" may be defined as "overtly sexual."' This is a convenient shorthand expression, since most, but not necessarily all, indecent assaults will be clearly of a sexual nature although they, as in this case, may have only sexual undertones. A simpler way of putting the matter to the jury is to ask them to decide whether 'right-minded persons would consider the conduct indecent or not.' It is for the jury to decide whether what occurred was so offensive to contemporary standards of modesty and privacy as to be indecent.

It was common ground before your Lordships, as it was in the Court of Appeal, that if the circumstances of the assault are *incapable* of being regarded as indecent, then the undisclosed intention of the accused could not make the assault an indecent one ... Again it was common ground that if, as in this case, the assault involved touching the victim, it was not necessary to prove that she was aware of the circumstances of indecency or apprehended indecency. An indecent assault can clearly be committed by the touching of someone who is asleep or unconscious.

As to the facts of this case, it is important to bear in mind that at the trial, not only did the appellant admit that he was guilty of an assault, but on his behalf his counsel expressly conceded that what had happened *was capable* of amounting to an indecent assault. That concession was repeated in the Court of Appeal and accepted by the Court as being a correct concession. Sensibly no attempt was made before your Lordships to withdraw this concession, for the sound reason that the explanation of this unprovoked assault would reveal that the assault was an indecent one, as indeed the girl's father suspected and, as the jury so decided.

The assault which the prosecution seek to establish may be of a kind which is inherently indecent. The defendant removes against her will, a woman's clothing. Such a case, to my mind, raises no problem. Those very facts, *devoid of any explanation*, would give rise to the irresistible inference that the defendant intended to assault his victim in a manner which right-minded persons would clearly think was indecent. Whether he did so for his own personal sexual gratification or because, being a misogynist or for some other reason, he wished to embarrass or humiliate his victim, seems to me to be irrelevant. He has failed, ex-hypothesi, to show any lawful justification for his indecent conduct. This of course, was not such a case. The conduct of the appellant in assaulting the girl by spanking her was only *capable* of being an indecent assault. To decide whether or not right-minded persons might think that assault was indecent, the following factors were clearly relevant—the relationship of the defendant to his victim—were they relatives, friends or virtually complete strangers? How had the defendant come to embark on this conduct and *why* was he behaving in this way? Aided by such material, a jury would be helped to determine the quality of the act, the true nature of the assault and to answer the vital question—were they sure that the defendant not only intended to commit an assault upon the girl, but an assault which was indecent—was such an inference irresistible? For the defendant to be liable to be convicted of the offence of indecent assault, where the circumstances of the alleged offence can be given an innocent as well as an indecent interpretation, without the prosecution being obliged to establish that the defendant intended to commit both an assault and an indecent one, seems to me quite unacceptable and not what Parliament intended.

...

Kumar v *The Queen*
[2006] EWCA Crim 1946

LORD JUSTICE SCOTT BAKER:

1. These are the Court's reasons for dismissing the appellant's appeal against conviction.

2. In November 2002 in the Crown Court at Preston before Judge Blake the appellant was convicted of three counts of indecent assault. He was acquitted of two further counts of the same offence – one on the judge's direction. On 3 January 2003 he was sentenced to 9 months imprisonment concurrent on each offence.

3. He appeals against conviction with the leave of the Full Court but only in respect of one count – count four.

Facts

5. Miss K was 17 when she saw the appellant for the first time to go on the pill. He asked her questions which she was shocked by. She went straight home and told her mother. The questions were about how old she was when she first had sex, how many men she had been with and whether she charged for sex. This visit was in June 2000 and led to a complaint by Miss K's father to the Health Authority.

6. On 27 July 2001 she found a lump on her breast and went to the appellant's surgery. She undid her shirt and pointed to the lump above her bra. He told her to take her shirt and bra off which she did. He came round to the side of her and examined both breasts and under her arms. His head was very close, touching her. He pressed hard for about 5 minutes and then said it could be mastitis. She was upset and went home and told her mother...

12. It is important to have in mind that the Crown's case was that a breast examination for Miss K was clinically indicated but that the way the appellant carried it out was wholly improper and demonstrated an intention to use it as cover for indecently assaulting her. This was emphatically not a case of a doctor carrying out a clinically indicated procedure in a proper manner but having a sexually indecent intent.

13. The Full Court gave leave to appeal because of the answer that the judge had given to a question asked by the jury. The question which related to the count which is the subject of this appeal was as follows:

> 'Offence of indecently assaulting. If breast examination *is* required what constitutes the offence?'

14. The judge said the simple answer was whether they were certain the defendant intended to obtain sexual gratification from the examination. But he then expanded:

> 'In relation to Miss K, there is no issue that a breast examination was indicated clinically, there is no issue about that, and so there are various sets of circumstances as to the defendant's intention, because that is the important thing, as to whether the examination was a perfectly proper medical examination which would therefore not constitute an assault. Because of course a patient who agrees to an examination is consenting to just that, a medical examination. So therefore, if you are looking at the defendant's intention — and of course before you convict you must be sure about it — you might conclude that this intention was to obtain sexual gratification alone. No problem there, your conclusion in those circumstances would be "guilty". You may think that his intention might have been to obtain clinical information — straightforward

medical examination — but there again, no real difficulty, your verdict on that would be "not guilty". You may come to the conclusion and be satisfied that his intention was a dual intention, that he intended to carry out the examination because it was indicated clinically, but he also had an intention at the outset to obtain sexual gratification. In other words, he was using the legitimate breast examination, which was indicated clinically, as a cover to obtain sexual gratification and that was what his intention was at the outset. Then your verdict would be "guilty". It may be that you would say perhaps the situation is this, that he knew that a medical examination was indicated and that is what he intended to carry out, but in the course of the examination he, as a bi-product and not intending it, obtained sexual gratification. In those circumstances your verdict would be "not guilty".'

15. So the judge raised four different possibilities:

(1) Sole intention to gain sexual gratification — guilty;
(2) Sole intention to gain clinical information — not guilty;
(3) Dual intention — legitimate breast examination as cover, with that intention from the outset — guilty;
(4) Medical examination indicated and that was what he intended when carrying it out but in the course of examination and not intending it, he got sexual gratification — not guilty.

16. Mr William Coker Q.C., who has appeared on this appeal for the appellant submits that the judge's direction falls foul of the decision of the House of Lords in *R v Court* [1989] AC 28. Moses J. gave leave to appeal because, he said, it was strongly arguable in the light of *Court* that using a legitimate breast examination as cover for indecent assault when the doctor intended from the start to obtain sexual gratification did not make him guilty of indecent assault. He referred to Lord Ackner at 42C:

'It was also common ground before your Lordships, as it was in the court of appeal, that if the circumstances of the assault are *incapable* of being regarded as indecent, then the undisclosed intention of the accused could not make the assault an indecent one.'

He also referred to Lord Goff of Chieveley at 49G:

'A requirement that the defendant must have acted from a sexual motive, which I understand to be from the motive of obtaining sexual gratification from his act, would, as Professor Glanville Williams recognises, exclude from indecent assault cases where a man undressed a woman in public but did so not from the motive of obtaining sexual gratification, but because he was a misogynist, or because he wanted to cause the woman embarrassment, or out of sheer mischief. I cannot think that this is right. In their judgment, the Court of Appeal referred to the case of an examination of a 15 year old girl by a midwife or doctor for medical purposes, the point being that, by virtue of section 14(2) of the Act of 1956, a girl under the age of 16 cannot in law give any consent which would prevent an act being an assault for the purposes of the section. Professor Glanville Williams considers that such a case would not amount to indecent assault because the doctor or midwife acted from a non sexual motive. The Court of Appeal expressed their disagreement with this view, in the following passage from their judgment [1987] QB 156, 164:

"In our judgment it is not necessary to infer a requirement of proof a sexual purpose, or of an indecent intention, for proof that a person has made an indecent assault, in order to protect from the theoretical risk of conviction for indecent assault the midwife or doctor who intimately examines the girl under the age of 16 without effective consent. If consent has been given by the parent or guardian there is, of course, no assault. If no such consent has been given, an intimate examination carried out for genuine medical purposes is, in our view, not indecent. Neither the girl examined, nor the right thinking members of society, would regard such an examination as an affront to the modesty of the girl or conduct which contravened normal standards of decent behaviour. So long as the examination is carried out for genuine medical purposes in a manner and in circumstances consistent with those purposes, then in our view the fact that the doctor or midwife happens to have some secret indecent motive, or happens to obtain sexual gratification known only to himself from carrying out his legitimate work, cannot in our view render the circumstances indecent."

I entirely agree. As I see it, it is the fact that the assault is objectively indecent which constitutes the gravamen of the offence, which is to be found in the affront to modesty.'

17. It seems to us that the Court of Appeal makes an important qualification about the examination by the doctor or midwife in the clause:

'So long as the examination is carried out for genuine medical purposes *in a manner and in circumstances consistent with those purposes...*' (Our emphasis).

The issue in the present case was about how the examination was carried out.

18. The facts of *Court* were very different to those of the present case. The appellant, an assistant in a shop, struck a 12 year old girl visitor some 12 times, for no apparent reason as she thought, outside her shorts on her buttocks. In response to a question by the police as to why the appellant had done so he said 'I don't know—buttock fetish.' He pleaded guilty to assault but denied that it was indecent and submitted that his statement about 'buttock fetish' should be excluded as being a secret uncommunicated motive that could not make indecent an assault that was not overtly indecent. The trial judge refused to exclude the statement and the appellant, who did not give evidence, was convicted. The Court of Appeal (Criminal Division) dismissed his appeal against conviction. He appealed to the House of Lords. The House of Lords (Lord Goff dissenting) held that where a charge of indecent assault was founded on facts capable of being given an innocent as well as an indecent interpretation it was necessary for the prosecution to prove not only that the accused intentionally assaulted the victim but that in doing so he intended to commit an assault which right minded persons would think was indecent; and that evidence as to the accused motive tending to explain the course for his conduct was admissible to establish whether he intended to commit not only an assault but also an indecent assault; and that accordingly the evidence concerning the appellant's statement about buttock fetish had been properly admitted.

19. The defendant in *Court* was not a medical practitioner and the case was not about a medical examination at all. It is, we think, important to appreciate why it was that the Court of Appeal considered the position of a medical practitioner and why Lord Goff referred to it in his dissenting opinion. What happened was that the jury asked the judge a question expressing concern about the position of a doctor who carried out an intimate examination of a young girl. The trial judge, Mars-Jones J. answered the question in this way:

'In that situation what is vital is whether the examination was necessary or not. If it was not necessary, but indulged in by the medical practitioner it would be an indecent assault. But if it was necessary, even though he got sexual satisfaction out of it, that would not make it an indecent assault.'

20. As Lord Keith pointed at 33B, a wicked intention is an essential ingredient of the offence of indecent assault, as it is of most other crimes against the person. For the most part that intention can readily be inferred from the facts found proved as to the circumstances of the assault, and unless there are indications that those features of the circumstances which are capable of being considered indecent were not intended. He went on:

'In a narrow range of cases, however, the circumstances may not point unequivocally to the requisite wicked intention. The delivery of chastisement to the buttocks of child is capable of presenting a case of that nature, since chastisement is not necessarily indicative of intention to do something indecent. Where, however, there is direct evidence, as there was in the present case in the shape of the appellant's statement about buttock fetish, that it was the assailant's intention to use the victim for the purpose of gratifying a particular sexual instinct, and that his action did in fact amount to a using of her for that purpose, such evidence can, in my opinion, properly be taken into account so as to resolve any ambiguity about the nature of the act. The contrary view seems to me to fly in the face of all common sense.'

21. The judge in the present case does not appear to have had the case of *Court* drawn to his attention. There is, in our judgment, no reason why it should have been. Mr Killeen, for the Crown, submits that this was never a secret intent case. The Crown's case was that the appellant behaved

in a sexually overt fashion. It never was his case that he carried out an entirely appropriate examination that was properly carried out in all respects but that he obtained sexual satisfaction from it. The Crown called evidence that the appellant's conduct of the examination went way beyond best practice. The judge in his summing up put the issue fairly and squarely before the jury in the passage to which we have referred. Might the appellant have carried out a proper medical consultation and examination or did he do it for his own sexual gratification?

22. Assistance is gained from the exchange between counsel and the judge after receipt of the note from the jury. The judge said:

> 'I think perhaps what they are getting at really is if there was a breast examination required, how can it be an indecent assault, and the answer to the question is what did the defendant intend if it was simply his intention to carry out—and he did carry out—a simple breast examination, or that *may* be the position, then it would be appropriate to acquit. If on the other hand he used the opportunity to carry out a breast examination, took that opportunity to indulge in activities for his own sexual gratification and they are sure of that, then they could convict.'

Prosecuting counsel agreed with this and defence counsel was asked if he wished to say anything. His response was:

> 'The only addition, your Honour would be this, that in order to convict they would have to be sure that he did not have an intention to carry out a medical examination, particularly given the underlying assumption and the question.'

The judge said:

> 'He could, could he not, have intended to carry out a medical examination as well as using the opportunity for sexual gratification and that would be an offence.'

Defence counsel responded:

> 'Your Honour, forgive my hesitation, but if — and this of course was not canvassed with the doctor — but if it be the case that, for example, he intended to carry out a medical examination, and this is the way I put it to the jury, however inexpertly that was done, if, going through his mind at that time, was the idea and—I put this crudely, your Honour you will understand — that he was getting pleasure from it that would not be an indecent assault at all. What has to be proved is what he intended to do.'

23. It seems to us that what was there concerning defence counsel was the fourth possibility raised by the judge in answer to the jury's question namely obtaining sexual gratification from a medical examination without the intention to obtain such gratification.

24. As the judge put it at 24D, the Crown's case must be that he was carrying out the examination in appropriate circumstances in an inappropriate way *and* for his own sexual gratification.

25. The defence complaint is about the third possibility referred to by the judge, but nobody was suggesting that there was a legitimate breast examination properly carried out in all respects but that the appellant could nevertheless be guilty of indecent assault.

26. In our judgment it is crucial to keep in mind that the Crown's case was throughout that a breast examination, albeit properly required was conducted in an inappropriate manner and was used as a cloak for a sinister motive. In so far as *Court* is binding authority for the proposition that a doctor who obtains sexual satisfaction from a necessary medical examination properly conducted is not guilty of indecent assault, that was not the issue in the present case. It is we would add something that would only be likely to occur in the most unusual circumstances. The appellant never suggested he got secret satisfaction from appropriate medical examinations properly conducted on young girls on this or any of the other counts. It is not in our judgment necessary to give the jury a direction about every theoretical possibility that may arise in a case, however remote that possibility may be, where the defence have not raised it. In our judgment the conviction is safe and accordingly we dismissed the appeal.

■ NOTES AND QUESTIONS

1. Granted that the House of Lords in *Court* was concerned with the meaning of 'indecency' while the focus of s. 78 is on the meaning of 'sexual', is the approach taken in the statute basically the same as that taken by the House of Lords in *Court*?

2. What is the difference between a sadist who beats his victim because he derives sexual pleasure from the beating and a sadist who beats his victim because he likes to see his victims suffer? To the victim, is there any difference? Might not any act be sexual if motivated by a sexual purpose?

3. Under both subsections (a) and (b) of s. 78 the vantage point purports to be that of the 'reasonable person' and not that of the defendant or the victim. Nevertheless, the reference to the defendant's 'purpose' in subsection (b) would seem to bring into consideration his or her motives.

4. In light of the fact that 'penetration' by a part of the defendant's body may encompass penetration by the defendant's penis, why is there a need for a separate offence of rape, especially given that the maximum penalty for both rape and assault by penetration is life imprisonment?

5. If a doctor derives sexual satisfaction from conducting a cervical smear test (during which an instrument is inserted into a woman's vagina) would this act be caught by s. 78?

C: Sexual assault

The Sexual Offences Act 2003, s. 3 establishes the offence of sexual assault. This offence is defined as follows:

3. Sexual assault

    (1) A person (A) commits an offence if—
      (a) he intentionally touches another person (B),
      (b) the touching is sexual,
      (c) B does not consent to the touching, and
      (d) A does not reasonably believe that B consents.

    (2) Whether a belief is reasonable is to be determined having regard to all the circumstances, including any steps A has taken to ascertain whether B consents.

    (3) Sections 75 and 76 apply to an offence under this section.

    (4) A person guilty of an offence under this section is liable—
      (a) on summary conviction, to imprisonment for a term not exceeding 6 months or a fine not exceeding the statutory maximum or both;
      (b) on conviction on indictment, to imprisonment for a term not exceeding 10 years.

(i) Comparison with rape and assault by penetration

As in cases of rape and assault by penetration, 'sexual assault' requires proof of non-consent and that the defendant did not reasonably believe that the victim consented. Again, the conclusive presumptions in s. 76 and the evidential presumptions in s. 75 apply. Further, as is the case in respect of assault by penetration, sexual assault requires proof of a sexual *actus reus*, and s. 78 is relevant in determining whether a touching is 'sexual.'

What distinguishes the offence of sexual assault from assault by penetration is that any intentional 'touching' will satisfy the *actus reus* of a sexual assault, as long as the touching is sexual. This includes touchings that are non-penetrative. Section 79(8) states that the touching may be 'with any part of the defendant's body', with 'anything else', and 'through anything'.

---

79. Part 1: general interpretation

...

(8) Touching includes touching—
  (a) with any part of the body,
  (b) with anything else,
  (c) through anything,
and in particular includes touching amounting to penetration.

R v H

[2005] All ER (D) 16, Court of Appeal

The complainant had been approached by a man who had asked her 'Do you fancy a shag?', before grabbing her tracksuit bottoms in the area of her right hand pocket and attempting to place his hand over her mouth. She had then managed to break free before he had touched her mouth and she had escaped. In due course, the defendant had been identified as the offender and he had been tried for an offence of sexual assault, contrary to s 3 of the Sexual Offences Act 2003. At the close of the Crown's case, a submission of no case to answer had been made based on, inter alia: (i) that touching the complainant's tracksuit bottoms had not amounted to 'touching' within s 79(8) of the Act for the purposes of the offence; and (ii) that that touching had not been such that a reasonable person would consider it to be 'sexual' within the meaning of s 78 of the Act. The judge had rejected those submissions, ruling in relation to the second submission, that the circumstances in which the offence was alleged to have occurred, including the words used by the offender, had been such that the touching might properly be regarded as being sexual. In due course, the defendant had been convicted.

Complaint was made on appeal that the judge had erred by rejecting the submission of no case to answer and that he had misdirected the jury.

PANEL: LORD WOOLF CJ, DAVIS AND FIELD JJ:

DISPOSITION:

The appeal would be dismissed.

(1) Where a person was wearing clothing, touching of that clothing constituted 'touching' for the purposes of the offence contrary to s 3 of the Act.

Having regard to the fact that the matters referred to in s 78(8) were not exhaustive and the fact that s 78 was not a definition section, there was no doubt at all that Parliament had not intended that it was to be impossible for touching by touching what the victim was wearing to amount to a sexual assault.

(2) Where, as in the instant case, touching was not inevitably sexual because of its nature, s 78(b) of the Act applied. In such a case, a judge should identify two distinct questions for the jury (both of which had to be answered in the affirmative in order to find the defendant guilty), namely: (i) whether they, as 12 reasonable people, considered that the touching, in the particular circumstances before them, because of its nature, might be sexual; and (ii) whether they, as 12 reasonable people, considered that the touching, in view of its circumstances, or the purpose of any person in relation to it, or both, was in fact sexual. In relation to the first question, evidence as to the circumstances before and after the touching, and evidence of the purpose of any person in relation to that touching was irrelevant.

If that two-stage approach was not adopted, in a borderline case it would be possible to take into account a person's intent to show that the touching was sexual, even if that touching was not sexual. However, in most cases, the answer would be same whether the two-stage approach was adopted or whether the matter was looked at as a whole. In the circumstances of the instant case, the judge's failure to apply the two-stage approach in determining whether there was a case to leave to the jury and in the summing up did not have any effect on the safety of the conviction.

■ NOTES AND QUESTIONS

1. Does the concept of 'touching' extend to the case where a fully clothed woman, in a moment of exuberance, hugs a fully clothed man without first asking permission? Does it extend to the man in a crowded subway who allows himself to be bumped up against other passengers because he receives a sexual frisson from the contact?

2. Adam, a seller of lady's shoes, derives sexual pleasure whenever he puts shoes on the feet of his female customers. Has he violated s. 3? In a pre-SOA 2003 case, *R v George* [1956] Crim LR 52, the defendant admitted to deriving sexual pleasure from removing shoes from the feet of females. He was prosecuted for indecent assault, the prosecutor arguing that the defendant's acts were indecent because they were committed to gratify an indecent motive. The court ruled that an assault became indecent only if it was accompanied by circumstances of indecency towards the person alleged to have been assaulted, and that the removal or attempted removal of shoes could possibly amount to an indecent assault. Would the same result follow under s. 78?

3. In addition to its breadth, s. 3 can be criticised for its failure to use legal terminology accurately. We have seen previously that a battery is defined as a touching that is not consented to by the victim while an assault consists of putting the victim in fear of a battery. The definition of sexual assault, while requiring a 'touching' (i.e., a battery), characterises the touching as an 'assault'. If Adam orders Eve at gunpoint to take off her clothes and she complies, is Adam guilty of a 'sexual assault'? Has there been a 'touching'?

4. While both rape and assault by penetration carry potential life sentences following a conviction, the maximum penalty for conviction of a sexual assault is ten years' imprisonment. However, if the defendant is charged with the summary version of the offence and tried in a magistrates' court, the maximum sentence drops to six months. Given that a defendant who has technically committed either rape or assault by penetration (crimes punishable by life imprisonment) has also committed sexual assault, does s. 3 give the prosecutor too much discretion in charging?

D: Causing a person to engage in sexual activity without consent

The Sexual Offences Act 2003, s. 4 establishes the offence of causing a person to engage in sexual activity without consent. This offence is defined as follows:

4. Causing a person to engage in sexual activity without consent

  (1) A person (A) commits an offence if—

    (a) he intentionally causes another person (B) to engage in an activity,

    (b) the activity is sexual,

    (c) B does not consent to engaging in the activity, and

    (d) A does not reasonably believe that B consents.

(2) Whether a belief is reasonable is to be determined having regard to all the circumstances, including any steps A has taken to ascertain whether B consents.

(3) Sections 75 and 76 apply to an offence under this section.

(4) A person guilty of an offence under this section, if the activity caused involved—

    (a) penetration of B's anus or vagina,

    (b) penetration of B's mouth with a person's penis,

    (c) penetration of a person's anus or vagina with a part of B's body or by B with anything else, or

    (d) penetration of a person's mouth with B's penis, is liable, on conviction on indictment, to imprisonment for life.

(5) Unless subsection (4) applies, a person guilty of an offence under this section is liable—

    (a) on summary conviction, to imprisonment for a term not exceeding 6 months or to a fine not exceeding the statutory maximum or both;

    (b) on conviction on indictment, to imprisonment for a term not exceeding 10 years.

(i) Comparison with rape, assault by penetration and sexual touching

As was the case in the offences we have already examined, the offence of 'causing a person to engage in sexual activity without consent' shares the key elements that the victim did not consent to the sexual activity and the defendant did not reasonably believe that the victim consented. In respect of these elements, the conclusive presumptions in s. 76 and the evidential presumptions in s. 75 again may apply.

The offence of 'causing a person to engage in sexual activity without consent' is aimed at those who compel others to do sexual acts against their will. While the offences we have looked at previously envisaged two parties – the offender and the victim – the sexual acts involved in causing a person to engage in sexual activity without consent may be performed by or on a third party or even an animal. This would occur if, for example, A causes B to perform a sexual act on A's dog, or if A, a voyeur, forces a couple to have intercourse in order to observe the couple in the act. The third party in the latter example may be a friend or associate of A (as in *Morgan*) or may be a separate victim. While a s. 4 offence may involve multiple parties, the offence may also occur without the defendant taking part in the sexual activity. So, for example, if A by threats forces B to undress in front of her and masturbate, she may be guilty of 'causing a person to engage in sexual activity without consent'. As the latter example illustrates, this offence provides a vehicle for prosecuting a woman who forces a man to engage in sexual activity or to have sex with her.

Subsection (4) of s. 4 indicates that the types of sexual activity that may fall within this offence include acts that can give rise to the other three main offences – penetration of B's anus or vagina, penetration of B's mouth with another person's penis, penetration of a person's anus or vagina with a part of B's body or by B with anything else, and penetration of a person's mouth with B's penis. The offence is broader, however, as it also catches all activity classified as 'sexual' under s. 78. Recall that under s. 78(b) an act can be classified as 'sexual' because of its nature or, if the act only *may* be 'sexual', because of the defendant's purpose or the surrounding circumstances.

We noted in Chapter 2 the problems associated with the concept of causation. It can be expected that the same kinds of controversies are likely to arise in respect of the present offence, as one of its defining elements is the causing of sexual activity.

E: Summary

Having examined the four primary offences against adult victims, it may be useful to provide a summary. All four offences involve intentional conduct on the part of the defendant to which the victim does not consent. Non-consent will be conclusively presumed if either of the circumstances set out in s. 76 is proved (deception as to the nature or purpose of the relevant act; or impersonation of a person known personally to the victim). An evidential presumption of non-consent will arise if any of the circumstances set out in s. 75 is established, but this presumption, unlike that in s. 76, may be rebutted by the defendant. All of the primary offences relate to sexual activity. Assault by penetration, sexual assault, and causing a person to engage in sexual activity without consent all specifically use the term 'sexual' in their definition to describe the *actus reus*. While the offence of rape does not refer explicitly to 'sexual' activity, the very nature of the *actus reus* of rape – the defendant's penetrating the vagina, anus or mouth of the victim with his penis – is self-evidently sexual. Indeed, it is what most likely comes to mind when ordinary people contemplate serious sexual crimes.

A useful summary of the basic differences between the *actus reus* of the four offences is provided in the SOA 2003, s. 77:

Offence	Relevant Act
An offence under section 1 (rape).	The defendant intentionally penetrating, with his penis, the vagina, anus or mouth of another person ('the complainant').
An offence under section 2 (assault by penetration).	The defendant intentionally penetrating, with a part of his body or anything else, the vagina or anus of another person ('the complainant'), where the penetration is sexual.
An offence under section 3 (sexual assault).	The defendant intentionally touching another person ('the complainant'), where the touching is sexual.
An offence under section 4 (causing a person to engage in sexual activity without consent).	The defendant intentionally causing another person ('the complainant') to engage in an activity, where the activity is sexual.

SECTION 3: OFFENCES AGAINST CHILDREN

The Sexual Offences Act 2003 creates a number of specific offences designed to protect children from sexual exploitation. The category of child victims is subdivided by age. There are offences which apply to victims over 13 but under 16, and offences which apply only to victims under 13.

A: The age of consent

Critical to the creation of offences against children is the so-called 'age of consent'. This is the age at which a male or female may lawfully consent to sexual relations; or stated from a defendant's perspective, the age below which a victim's consent will not necessarily provide a defence to a charge of a sexual offence. The current age of consent is 16. While one may argue that this age is too high or too low, what is now clear is that, whatever the age of consent, it must be the same for both males and females.

Sutherland v United Kingdom

[1998] EHRLR 117, European Commission of Human Rights

...Complaints declared admissible

31. The Commission has declared admissible the applicant's complaints that the fixing of the minimum age for lawful homosexual activities at 18, rather than 16, is in violation of his right to respect for his private life, and is discriminatory.

...

32. Accordingly, the issue to be determined is whether there has been a violation of Article 8 alone or taken in conjunction with Article 14 of the Convention by reason of the prohibition of consensual homosexual acts between males over the age of 16 but under the age of 18 years.

...

33. Article 8 of the Convention provides so far as is material, as follows:

1. Everyone has the right to respect for his private...life...
2. There shall be no interference by a public authority with the exercise of this right except such as is in accordance with the law and is necessary in a democratic society...for the protection of health or morals, or for the protection of the rights and freedoms of others.

...[T]he Commission considers that the maintenance in force of the impugned legislation constituted an interference with the applicant's right to respect for his private life (which includes his sexual life) within the meaning of Article 8 para. 1 of the Convention. Even though the applicant has not in the event been prosecuted or threatened with prosecution, the very existence of the legislation directly affected his private life: either he respected the law and refrained from engaging in any prohibited sexual acts prior to the age of 18 or he committed such acts and thereby became liable to criminal prosecution. The Commission further finds no reason to doubt the general truth of the applicant's allegations as to the distress he felt in having to choose between engaging in a sexual relationship with a like-orientated person of around the same age and breaking the law.

38. The Commission recalls that the compatibility with Article 8 of the Convention of the setting of a minimum age below which male homosexual acts are prohibited has been considered in the case-law of the Court and of the Commission. It is well established by that case-law that there is a legitimate necessity in a democratic society for some restrictions over homosexual conduct, notably in order to provide safeguards against the exploitation and corruption of those who are specially vulnerable by reason of their youth...Article 14 of the Convention provides as follows:

> The enjoyment of the rights and freedoms set forth in this Convention shall be secured without discrimination on any ground such as sex, race, colour, language, religion, political or other opinion, national or social origin, association with a national minority, property, birth or other status.

...In the United Kingdom, prior to 3 November 1994, the minimum age for consensual male homosexual relations was 21 and, since that date, the minimum age has been 18. The age of consent for consensual heterosexual and lesbian relations has at all material times been 16. There were and are therefore at least two differences which are at issue: the difference in treatment of homosexual and heterosexual relationships, and the difference in treatment between male homosexual and lesbian relationships. The parties' submissions as to discrimination have concentrated principally on the difference of treatment between homosexuals and heterosexuals, and in the following discussion, the Commission will do likewise.

...

52. The Commission notes that it is not contested that the applicant, as a young man of 17 years of age who wished to enter into and maintain sexual relations with a male friend of the same age, was in a 'relevantly similar situation' to a young man of the same age who wished to enter into and maintain sexual relations with a female friend of the same age.

53. The Commission must accordingly next determine whether the difference in treatment of these categories pursued a legitimate aim.

54. The Commission accepts, as does the applicant, that the aim of protecting morals and the rights of others is legitimate. The Commission also accepts that legal measures which prescribe age limits for particular types of sexual behaviour are, in principle, a legitimate way of pursuing that aim. Whether, in the specific case, the aim of protection of morals can be sufficient to justify differing ages is a matter which the Commission will consider in connection with the proportionality of the means and the aim.

55. The third question for the Commission is whether there was a reasonable relationship of proportionality between the means employed and the aim sought to be realised, and it is in this connection that the Commission must bear in mind the margin of appreciation which the respondent enjoys in assessing whether and to what extent differences justify a different treatment.

56. The Government argue that it is well-established that Contracting States enjoy a very broad margin of appreciation concerning the assessment of the measures appropriate in relation to matters associated with questions of morality. It is true that, in the context of measures designed to protect the moral interests and welfare of the society, the Court has held that State authorities are in principle in a better position than the international judge to give an opinion on the exact content of those requirements. It is true too that, as noted above, the Court, in the context of Article 8 of the Convention, has acknowledged the legitimate necessity in a democratic society for some degree of control over homosexual conduct 'notably in order to provide safeguards against the exploitation of those who are specially vulnerable by reason, for example, of their youth' . . . On the other hand, the Court has underlined that in areas involving intimate aspects of private life, there must exist particularly serious reasons before interferences on the part of public authorities can be legitimate for the purposes of Article 8 para. 2 . . . Moreover, in matters concerning alleged discrimination on grounds of sex, very weighty reasons would have to be put forward before the Convention organs could regard a difference of treatment based exclusively on the ground of sex as compatible with the Convention (see Eur. Court HR, *Karlheinz Schmidt* v *Germany* judgment of 18 July 1994, Series A no. 291-B, p. 32, para. 24).

57. The Commission is of the opinion that, regardless of whether the difference in treatment of heterosexuals and homosexuals is based on 'sex' or 'other status', given that it impinges on a most intimate aspect of affected individuals' private lives, the margin of appreciation must be relatively narrow.

58. The Government draw attention to the consistent series of decisions by the Commission recognising that the criterion of social protection justifies not only the imposition of restrictions on male homosexual activity but the setting of a higher minimum age than in the case of heterosexuals. In particular, in *X* v *The United Kingdom* (No. 7212/75 . . .) the Commission found that an objective and reasonable justification existed for the different ages of consent, there being a realistic basis for the Government's opinion that, given the controversial and sensitive nature of the question involved, young men in the 18–21 bracket who were involved in homosexual relationships would be subject to substantial social pressures which could be harmful to their psychological development . . .

60. The Commission . . . considers it opportune to reconsider its earlier case-law in the light of . . . modern developments and, more especially, in the light of the weight of current medical opinion that to reduce the age of consent to 16 might have positively beneficial effects on the sexual health of young homosexual men without any corresponding harmful consequences.

61. In contending that there remains a reasonable and objective justification for maintaining different ages of consent for homosexual males and for heterosexuals, the Government place considerable reliance on the fact that the issue was recently and fully debated by a democratically elected Parliament which, on a free vote, decided to reduce the minimum age of consent to homosexual acts to 18 but rejected a proposal to assimilate the age of consent to that for heterosexuals.

62. The Commission agrees with the Government that some weight should be attached to the fact that the issue has been recently considered by the legislature and that the reduction of the minimum age to 16 was rejected. Nevertheless, this factor cannot of itself be decisive. Of more importance is the sufficiency of the reasons advanced to justify maintaining a different age of consent.

63. Two such principal arguments emerge from the speeches in Parliament and are adopted and repeated in the Government's submissions. In the first place it is argued that certain young men between the ages of 16 and 18 do not have a settled sexual orientation and that the aim of the law is to protect such vulnerable young men from activities which will result in considerable social pressures and isolation which their lack of maturity might cause them later to repent: it is claimed that the possibility of criminal sanctions against persons aged 16 or 17 is likely to have a deterrent effect and give the individual time to make up his mind. Secondly, it is argued that society is entitled to indicate its disapproval of homosexual conduct and its preference that children follow a hetero-sexual way of life.

64. The Commission does not consider that either argument offers a reasonable and objective justification for maintaining a different age of consent for homosexual and heterosexual acts or that maintaining such a differential age is proportionate to any legitimate aim served thereby. As to the former argument, as was conceded in the Parliamentary debates, current medical opinion is to the effect that sexual orientation is fixed in both sexes by the age of 16 and that men aged 16–21 are not in need of special protection because of the risk of their being 'recruited' into homosexuality. Moreover, as noted by the BMA, the risk posed by predatory older men would appear to be as seri-ous whether the victim is a man or woman and does not justify a differential age of consent. Even if, as claimed in the Parliamentary debate, there may be certain young men for whom homosexual experience after the age of 16 will have influential and potentially disturbing effects and who may require protection, the Commission is unable to accept that it is a proportionate response to the need for protection to expose to criminal sanctions not only the older man who engages in homo-sexual acts with a person under the age of 18 but the young man himself who is claimed to be in need of such protection.

65. As to the second ground relied on—society's claimed entitlement to indicate disapproval of homosexual conduct and its preference for a heterosexual lifestyle—the Commission cannot accept that this could in any event constitute an objective or reasonable justification for inequality of treatment under the criminal law. As the Court observed in its *Dudgeon* judgment in the context of Article 8 of the Convention:

> 'Decriminalisation' does not imply approval, and a fear that some sectors of the population might draw misguided conclusions in this respect from reform of the legislation does not afford a good ground for maintaining it in force with all its unjustifiable features.

...

66. Consequently, the Commission finds that no objective and reasonable justification exists for the maintenance of a higher minimum age of consent to male homosexual, than to heterosexual, acts and that the application discloses discriminatory treatment in the exercise of the applicant's right to respect for private life under Article 8 of the Convention.

CONCLUSION

67. The Commission concludes, by fourteen votes to four, that in the present case there has been a violation of Article 8 of the Convention, taken in conjunction with Article 14 of the Convention.

■ **NOTES AND QUESTIONS**

1. Following the decision in *Sutherland*, the age of consent was reduced to 16 for males, bringing it in line with that for females. See Sexual Offences (Amendment) Act 2000, s. 1.

2. Given that different children mature at different ages, does a fixed age of con-sent make sense? Why not ask in each case whether, as set out in the general definition of consent in s. 74, the alleged victim agreed 'by choice' and had the freedom and capacity to make that choice? The younger the child, the less likely

that consent could be established under s. 74 but this will not invariably be so. A case-by-case approach based on the child's maturity was adopted in respect of a child's access to contraceptives in *Gillick* v *West Norfolk and Wisbech Health Authority* [1986] AC 112.

B: Offences against a child under the age of 13

The Sexual Offences Act 2003, ss. 5–8, create four offences involving sexual crimes against children under the age of 13. These are rape of a child under 13, assault of a child under 13 by penetration, sexual assault of a child under 13, and causing or inciting a child under 13 to engage in sexual activity without consent:

5. Rape of a child under 13

(1) A person commits an offence if—
   (a) he intentionally penetrates the vagina, anus or mouth of another person with his penis, and
   (b) the other person is under 13.
(2) A person guilty of an offence under this section is liable, on conviction on indictment, to imprisonment for life.

6. Assault of a child under 13 by penetration

(1) A person commits an offence if—
   (a) he intentionally penetrates the vagina or anus of another person with a part of his body or anything else,
   (b) the penetration is sexual, and
   (c) the other person is under 13.
(2) A person guilty of an offence under this section is liable, on conviction on indictment, to imprisonment for life.

7. Sexual assault of a child under 13

(1) A person commits an offence if—
   (a) he intentionally touches another person,
   (b) the touching is sexual, and
   (c) the other person is under 13.
(2) A person guilty of an offence under this section is liable—
   (a) on summary conviction, to imprisonment for a term not exceeding 6 months or a fine not exceeding the statutory maximum or both;
   (b) on conviction on indictment, to imprisonment for a term not exceeding 14 years.

8. Causing or inciting a child under 13 to engage in sexual activity

(1) A person commits an offence if—
   (a) he intentionally causes or incites another person (B) to engage in an activity,
   (b) the activity is sexual, and
   (c) B is under 13.
(2) A person guilty of an offence under this section, if the activity caused or incited involved—
   (a) penetration of B's anus or vagina,
   (b) penetration of B's mouth with a person's penis,
   (c) penetration of a person's anus or vagina with a part of B's body or by B with anything else, or
   (d) penetration of a person's mouth with B's penis, is liable, on conviction on indictment, to imprisonment for life.

> (3) Unless subsection (2) applies, a person guilty of an offence under this section is liable—
>   (a) on summary conviction, to imprisonment for a term not exceeding 6 months or to a fine not exceeding the statutory maximum or both;
>   (b) on conviction on indictment, to imprisonment for a term not exceeding 14 years.

The above four offences correspond roughly to the comparable offences against adults contained in the SOA 2003, ss. 1–4, with two differences, one which is specific to s. 8 and the other which is more general. In s. 8, the counterpart to the s. 4 offence of 'causing a person to engage in sexual activity without consent', the *actus reus* of the offence has been expanded to include *inciting* a child under 13 to engage in sexual activity without consent. As we shall see in Chapter 10, incitement is an inchoate crime. What this means is that the substantive crime which it is the incitor's purpose to bring about need not be committed for the defendant to be guilty of incitement.

The more general – and more critical – distinction between the offences in ss. 5–8 and their counterparts in ss. 1–4 is that the victim's non-consent does not have to be proved by the prosecutor and the defendant's reasonable belief in the victim's consent will not exonerate the defendant. The term 'consent' does not appear in any of the sections relating to children under 13 and the logical inference is that a child under 13 is incapable of consenting to sexual activity (although nowhere in the Act is this explicitly stated). Thus, regardless of whether or not the child desires to enter into a sexual relationship, and regardless of whether or not the defendant honestly and reasonably believes that the child desires to enter into such a relationship, the defendant can be guilty of one of these offences. The defendant cannot rely on a belief in a victim's consent, however reasonable that belief may be.

What is less clear is whether the defendant's belief that the victim is over 13 may serve as a defence. The SOA 2003 is silent on this point but the House of Lords confirmed in *R* v *G* that for this offence liability is strict.

R v G (Appellant) (on Appeal from the Court of Appeal (Criminal Division))
[2008] UKHL 37

LORD HOFFMANN:
My Lords,
1. On 20 April 2005 the appellant pleaded guilty to the offence of rape of a child under 13, contrary to section 5 of the Sexual Offences Act 2003:

(1) A person commits an offence if—
  (a) he intentionally penetrates the vagina, anus or mouth of another person with his penis; and
  (b) the other person is under 13.
(2) A person guilty of an offence under this section is liable, on conviction on indictment, to imprisonment for life.

2. For the purpose of sentence, the prosecution accepted the appellant's version of the facts, namely that the accused was 15 at the time of the offence, the complainant had consented to intercourse and she had told him that she was 15. On 8 July 2005 Judge Hone sentenced him to a 12 month detention and training order. The appellant appealed on the grounds that (1) the

conviction violated his right to a fair trial and the presumption of innocence under article 6 of the Convention, because it was an offence of strict liability, and (2) it violated his right to privacy under article 8 because it was disproportionate to charge him with rape under section 5 when he could have been charged with a less serious offence under section 13, which deals with sex offences committed by persons under 18. The Court of Appeal dismissed the appeal against conviction but allowed an appeal against sentence and substituted a conditional discharge. It certified two questions as being of general public importance:

(1) May a criminal offence of strict liability violate article 6(1) and/or 6(2)...?

(2) Is it compatible with a child's rights under article 8...to convict him of rape contrary to section 5...in circumstances where the agreed basis of plea establishes that his offence fell properly within the ambit of section 13...?

(3) The mental element of the offence under section 5, as the language and structure of the section makes clear, is that penetration must be intentional but there is no requirement that the accused must have know that the other person was under 13. The policy of the legislation is to protect children. If you have sex with someone who is on any view a child or young person, you take your chance on exactly how old they are. To that extent the offence is one of strict liability and it is no defence that the accused believed the other person to be 13 or over.

(4) Article 6(1) provides that in the determination of his civil rights or any criminal charge, everyone is entitled to a 'fair and public hearing' and article 6(2) provides that everyone charged with a criminal offence "shall be presumed innocent until proved guilty according to the law". It is settled law that Article 6(1) guarantees fair procedure and the observance of the principle of the separation of powers but not that either the civil or criminal law will have any particular substantive content: see *Matthews v Ministry of Defence* [2003] UKHL 4; [2003] 1 AC 1163. Likewise, article 6(2) requires him to be presumed innocent of the offence but does not say anything about what mental or other elements of the offence should be. In the case of civil law, this was established (after a moment of aberration) by *Z v United Kingdom* (2001) 34 EHRR 97. There is no reason why the reasoning should not apply equally to the substantive content of the criminal law. In *R v Gemmell* [2002] EWCA Crim 1992; [2003] 1 Cr App R 343, 356, para 33 Dyson LJ said:

"The position is quite clear. So far as Article 6 is concerned, the fairness of the provisions of the substantive law of the Contracting States is not a matter for investigation. The content and interpretation of domestic substantive law is not engaged by Article 6."

(5) The only authority which is said to cast any doubt upon this proposition is the decision of the Strasbourg court in *Salabiaku v France* (1988) 13 EHRR 379 and in particular a statement in paragraph 28 (at p.388) that "presumptions of fact or of law" in criminal proceedings should be confined "within reasonable limits". No one has yet discovered what this paragraph means but your Lordships referred to a wealth of academic learning which tries to solve the riddle.

(6) My Lords, I think that judges and academic writers have picked over the carcass of this unfortunate case so many times in attempts to find some intelligible meat on its bones that the time has come to call a halt. The Strasbourg court, uninhibited by a doctrine of precedent or the need to find a ratio decidendi, seems to have ignored it. It is not mentioned in *Z v United Kingdom* (2001) 34 EHRR 97. I would recommend your Lordships to do likewise. For my part, I would simply endorse the remarks of Dyson LJ in *R v Gemmell* [2003] 1 Cr App R 343, 356.

(7) The other ground of appeal is that the conviction violated the appellant's proposition. This is, on the face of it, an astonishing proposition. Is it really being suggested that a human being under 18 has a human right to have undisturbed sexual intercourse with a child under 13? If anything is likely to bring human rights into disrepute, it is such a claim.

(8) When one examines the argument of Mr Owen QC for the appellant, however he is not saying any such thing. He does not claim that sexual intercourse with children under 13, even in privacy of the appellant's home, ought not to be prohibited. But he says that as he was only 15 at the time of the offence, the Crown acted unduly harshly by prosecuting him under section 5 rather than under section 13, which deals with sexual offences committed by persons under 18 and carries a maximum penalty of imprisonment for 5 years.

(9) Assuming this to be right, the case has in my opinion nothing to do with Article 8 or human rights. Article 8 confers a qualified right that the state shall not interfere with what you do in your private or family life. Any interference with your conduct by the state must be necessary and proportionate for one of the purposes mentioned in Article 8.2. But you either have such a right or you do not. If the state is justified in treating your conduct as unlawful, for example, because you are beating your wife or sexually abusing children, Article 8 does not generate an additional right that the state shall not be too hard on you for whatever reason you have done it because it happens to have been done at home.

(10) Prosecutorial policy and sentencing do not fall under Article 8. If the offence in question is a justifiable interference with private life, that is an end of the matter. If the prosecution has been unduly heavy handed, that may be unfair and unjust, but not an infringement of human rights. It is a matter for the ordinary system of criminal justice. It would be remarkable if Article 8 gave Strasbourg jurisdiction over sentencing for all offences which happen to have been committed at home. This case is another example of the regrettable tendency to try to convert the whole system of justice into questions of human rights.

(11) It is true that *Laskey, Jaggard and Brown v UK* (1997) 24 EHRR 39 (the sadomasochism case) the Strasbourg court, in deciding whether prosecution was a proportionate interference with indulgence in such practices in private, noted (at para 49) that "reduced sentences were imposed on appeal". And in *KA and AD v Belgium* (Application Nos 42758/98 and 45558/99) (unreported 17 February 2005), a similar case from Belgium, the court also noted that the sentences were disproportionate. But the issue in both cases was whether such activities should be criminalised at all. The judgments contain no explanation of why the sentences were thought to be relevant.

(12) In my opinion, therefore, the answers to the certified questions are no and yes respectively. That leaves only the question of whether in the particular circumstances of this case, it was an abuse of process for the Crown to prosecute under section 5. That is not a question which has been certified. For what it is worth, I agree with the Court of Appeal that the crown was not obliged to withdraw the charge under section 5 when they found themselves having to accept the appellant's version of events. "Rape of a child under 13" still accurately described what the appellant had done. Parliament decided to use this description because children under 13 cannot validly or even meaningfully consent to sexual intercourse. So far as the basis of plea provided mitigation, they were entitled to leave the judge to take it into account. I would dismiss the appeal.

■ NOTES AND QUESTIONS

1. Has Parliament indicated in the SOA 2003, either 'expressly or by implication', that it intends to preclude a defence based on a defendant's honest belief that the victim is over 16? What would be the arguments?

2. In *R v K* the House of Lords held that where the victim was over 13 but under 16 the presumption of *mens rea* applied.

3. Testifying against an adult defendant in court may be highly traumatic for a child. In recognition of this fact, there have been in recent years provisions created to allow receipt of the child's pre-recorded testimony, as well as to enable the child to testify via an electronic hook-up with the court.

4. What of the case where there has been consensual sexual activity (including, for instance, kissing, which may constitute sexual assault) between, say, two 12-year-olds? The only way for criminal charges to be avoided would be if the prosecution were to exercise its discretion and decline to charge. However, with often irate parents who have discovered their child in bed with a 'friend' pressing for a prosecution, this may prove to be a slender reed on which the 12-year-old potential defendant can rely.

C: Offences against a child over 13 but under 16

The Sexual Offences Act 2003 creates a number of offences that relate to victims between the age of 13 and 16. These include two offences that parallel those that can be committed against a child under 13 (see ss. 9–10) and several new offences which can also be committed against a child under 13 (but in which case carry a more severe penalty). The two offences we have already examined in respect of children under 13 are 'sexual activity with a child' and 'causing or inciting a child to engage in sexual activity':

9. Sexual activity with a child
(1) A person aged 18 or over (A) commits an offence if—
  (a) he intentionally touches another person (B),
  (b) the touching is sexual, and
  (c) either—
    (i) B is under 16 and A does not reasonably believe that B is 16 or over, or
    (ii) B is under 13.
(2) A person guilty of an offence under this section, if the touching involved—
  (a) penetration of B's anus or vagina with a part of A's body or anything else,
  (b) penetration of B's mouth with A's penis,
  (c) penetration of A's anus or vagina with a part of B's body, or
  (d) penetration of A's mouth with B's penis,
is liable, on conviction on indictment, to imprisonment for a term not exceeding 14 years.
(3) Unless subsection (2) applies, a person guilty of an offence under this section is liable—
  (a) on summary conviction, to imprisonment for a term not exceeding 6 months or to a fine not exceeding the statutory maximum or both;
  (b) on conviction on indictment, to imprisonment for a term not exceeding 14 years.

10. Causing or inciting a child to engage in sexual activity
(1) A person aged 18 or over (A) commits an offence if—
  (a) he intentionally causes or incites another person (B) to engage in an activity,
  (b) the activity is sexual, and
  (c) either—
    (i) B is under 16 and A does not reasonably believe that B is 16 or over, or
    (ii) B is under 13.
(2) A person guilty of an offence under this section, if the activity caused or incited involved—
  (a) penetration of B's anus or vagina,
  (b) penetration of B's mouth with a person's penis,
  (c) penetration of a person's anus or vagina with a part of B's body or by B with anything else, or
  (d) penetration of a person's mouth with B's penis,

is liable, on conviction on indictment, to imprisonment for a term not exceeding 14 years.

(3) Unless subsection (2) applies, a person guilty of an offence under this section is liable—

(a) on summary conviction, to imprisonment for a term not exceeding 6 months or to a fine not exceeding the statutory maximum or both;

(b) on conviction on indictment, to imprisonment for a term not exceeding 14 years.

Apart from the obvious differences in respect of the age of the victim, ss. 9–10 are similar to the provisions in ss. 7–8, which we examined in the previous section. The *actus reus* of s. 9 is an intentional sexual touching, as it is in s. 7, and the *actus reus* of s. 10 is intentionally causing or inciting a child to engage in sexual activity, as it is in s. 8. Both ss. 8 and 10 extend s. 4 by adding the *actus reus* of inciting. While there are no offences of 'rape' and 'assault by penetration' when the victim is over 13 but under 16, as there are when the victim is under 13, presumably these offences are covered by the general prohibitions of ss. 1–2.

However, the offences against children over 13 but under 16 differ from the comparable offences against children under 13 in several important respects. First, while the offences against a victim under 13 may be committed by 'any person', ss. 9–10 specify that the defendant must be 18 or over. But do not be misled: these crimes may be committed by a person under 18; the only difference lies in the penalty, which is less severe – see s. 13. More critically, while the defendant's honest belief as to the age of the child is not identified as a defence when the victim is under 13, under ss. 9–10 the defendant's belief that the victim is older than 16 may be a defence. Both of these latter sections provide that the defendant's reasonable belief that the victim is 16 or over may be a defence where the charge is an offence against a child over 13 but under 16. To succeed, the prosecution will have to prove either that A did not believe that B was over 16 or, if A did so believe, that A's belief was not reasonable.

B v DPP

[2000] 2 WLR 452, House of Lords

The defendant, aged 15, was convicted of inciting a girl under the age of 14 to commit an act of gross indecency with him. It was accepted that he honestly believed that the girl was over the age of 14.

LORD NICHOLLS OF BIRKENHEAD: My Lords, an indecent assault on a woman is a criminal offence. So is an indecent assault on a man. Neither a boy nor a girl under the age of 16 can, in law, give any consent which would prevent an act being an assault. These offences have existed for many years. Currently they are to be found in sections 14 and 15 of the Sexual Offences Act 1956. They have their origins in sections 52 and 62 of the Offences against the Person Act 1861 (24 & 25 Vict. c. 100).

In the early 1950s a lacuna in this legislation became apparent. A man was charged with indecent assault on a girl aged nine. At the man's invitation the girl had committed an indecent act on the man. The Court of Criminal Appeal held that an invitation to another person to touch the invitor could not amount to an assault on the invitee. As the man had done nothing to the girl which, if done against her will, would have amounted to an assault on her, the man's conduct did not constitute an indecent assault on the girl. That was *Fairclough* v *Whipp* [1951] 2 All ER 834. Two years later the same point arose and was similarly decided regarding a girl aged 11: see *Director of Public Prosecutions* v *Rogers* [1953] 1 WLR 1017. Following a report of the Criminal Law Revision Committee in August 1959 (First Report on Indecency with Children (Cmnd. 835)), Parliament enacted the

Indecency with Children Act 1960. Section 1(1) of this Act makes it a criminal offence to commit an act of gross indecency with or towards a child under the age of 14, or to incite a child under that age to such an act. The question raised by the appeal concerns the mental element in this offence so far as the age ingredient is concerned.

The answer to this question depends upon the proper interpretation of the section. There are, broadly, three possibilities. The first possible answer is that it matters not whether the accused honestly believed that the person with whom he was dealing was over 14. So far as the age element is concerned, the offence created by section 1 of the Act of 1960 is one of strict liability. The second possible answer is that a necessary element of this offence is the absence of a belief, held honestly and on reasonable grounds by the accused, that the person with whom he was dealing was over 14. The third possibility is that the existence or not of reasonable grounds for an honest belief is irrelevant. The necessary mental element is simply the absence of an honest belief by the accused that the other person was over 14.

The common law presumption

As habitually happens with statutory offences, when enacting this offence Parliament defined the prohibited conduct solely in terms of the proscribed physical acts. Section 1(1) says nothing about the mental element. In particular, the section says nothing about what shall be the position if the person who commits or incites the act of gross indecency honestly but mistakenly believed that the child was 14 or over.

In these circumstances the starting-point for a court is the established common law presumption that a mental element, traditionally labelled *mens rea*, is an essential ingredient unless Parliament has indicated a contrary intention either expressly or by necessary implication. The common law presumes that, unless Parliament indicated otherwise, the appropriate mental element is an unexpressed ingredient of every statutory offence. On this I need do no more than refer to Lord Reid's magisterial statement in the leading case of *Sweet* v *Parsley* [1970] AC 132, 148–149:

> there has for centuries been a presumption that Parliament did not intend to make criminals of persons who were in no way blameworthy in what they did. That means that whenever a section is silent as to *mens rea* there is a presumption that, in order to give effect to the will of Parliament, we must read in words appropriate to require *mens rea* ... it is firmly established by a host of authorities that *mens rea* is an essential ingredient of every offence unless some reason can be found for holding that that is not necessary.

...

The construction of section 1 of the Act of 1960

In section 1(1) of the Act of 1960 Parliament has not expressly negatived the need for a mental element in respect of the age element of the offence. The question, therefore, is whether, although not expressly negatived, the need for a mental element is negatived by necessary implication. 'Necessary implication' connotes an implication which is compellingly clear. Such an implication may be found in the language used, the nature of the offence, the mischief sought to be prevented and any other circumstances which may assist in determining what intention is properly to be attributed to Parliament when creating the offence.

I venture to think that, leaving aside the statutory context of section 1, there is no great difficulty in this case. The section created an entirely new criminal offence, in simple unadorned language. The offence so created is a serious offence. The more serious the offence, the greater is the weight to be attached to the presumption, because the more severe is the punishment and the graver the stigma which accompanies a conviction. Under section 1 conviction originally attracted a punishment of up to two years imprisonment. This has since been increased to a maximum of 10 years' imprisonment. The notification requirements under Part 1 of the Sex Offenders Act 1997 now apply, no matter what the age of the offender: see Schedule 1, paragraph 1(1)(b). Further, in addition to being a serious offence, the offence is drawn broadly ('an act of gross indecency'). It can embrace conduct ranging from predatory approaches by a much older paedophile to consensual sexual experimentation between precocious teenagers of whom the offender may be the younger of the two. The conduct may be depraved by any acceptable standard, or it may be relatively innocuous behaviour in private between two young people. These factors reinforce, rather than negative, the application of the presumption in this case.

The purpose of the section is, of course, to protect children. An age ingredient was therefore an essential ingredient of the offence. This factor in itself does not assist greatly. Without more, this does not lead to the conclusion that liability was intended to be strict so far as the age element is concerned, so that the offence is committed irrespective of the alleged offender's belief about the age of the 'victim' and irrespective of how the offender came to hold this belief.

Nor can I attach much weight to a fear that it may be difficult sometimes for the prosecution to prove that the defendant knew the child was under fourteen or was recklessly indifferent about the child's age. A well known passage from a judgment of that great jurist, Sir Owen Dixon, in *Thomas* v *The King* (1937) 59 CLR 279, 309, bears repetition:

> The truth appears to be that a reluctance on the part of courts has repeatedly appeared to allow a prisoner to avail himself of a defence depending simply on his own state of knowledge and belief. The reluctance is due in great measure, if not entirely, to a mistrust of the tribunal of fact—the jury. Through a feeling that, if the law allows such a defence to be submitted to the jury, prisoners may too readily escape by deposing to conditions of mind and describing sources of information, matters upon which their evidence cannot be adequately tested and contradicted, judges have been misled into a failure steadily to adhere to principle. It is not difficult to understand such tendencies, but a lack of confidence in the ability of a tribunal correctly to estimate evidence of states of mind and the like can never be sufficient ground for excluding from inquiry the most fundamental element in a rational and humane criminal code.

Similarly, it is far from clear that strict liability regarding the age ingredient of the offence would further the purpose of section 1 more effectively than would be the case if a mental element were read into this ingredient. There is no general agreement that strict liability is necessary to the enforcement of the law protecting children in sexual matters. For instance, the draft criminal code Bill prepared by the Law Commission in 1989 (Criminal Law, A Criminal Code for England and Wales (Law Com. No. 177)) proposed a compromise solution. Clauses 114 and 115 of the Bill provided for committing or inciting acts of gross indecency with children aged under 13 or under 16. Belief that the child is over 16 would be a defence in each case: see vol 1, Report and Draft Criminal Code Bill, p. 81.

Is there here a compellingly clear implication that Parliament should be taken to have intended that the ordinary common law requirement of a mental element should be excluded in respect of the age ingredient of this new offence? Thus far, having regard especially to the breadth of the offence and the gravity of the stigma and penal consequences which a conviction brings, I see no sufficient ground for so concluding.

Indeed, the Crown's argument before your Lordships did not place much reliance on any of the matters just mentioned. The thrust of the Crown's argument lay in a different direction: the statutory context. This is understandable, because the statutory background is undoubtedly the Crown's strongest point. The Crown submitted that the law in this field has been regarded as settled for well over 100 years, ever since the decision in *R* v *Prince* (1875) LR 2 CCR 154. That well known case concerned the unlawful abduction of a girl under the age of 16. The defendant honestly believed she was over 16, and he had reasonable grounds for believing this. No fewer than 15 judges held that this provided no defence. Subsequently, in *R* v *Maughan* (1934) 24 Cr App R 130 the Court of Criminal Appeal (Lord Hewart CJ, Avory and Roche JJ) held that a reasonable and honest belief that a girl was over 16 could never be a defence to a charge of indecent assault. The court held that this point had been decided in *R* v *Forde* [1923] 2 KB 400. The court also observed that in any event the answer was to be found in *Prince*'s case. Building on this foundation Mr Scrivener submitted that the Act of 1956 was not intended to change this established law, and that section 1 of the Act of 1960 was to be read with the Act of 1956. The preamble to the Act of 1960 stated that its purpose was to make 'further' provision for the punishment of indecent conduct towards young people. In this field, where Parliament intended belief as to age to be a defence, this was stated expressly: see, for instance, the 'young man's defence' in section 6(3) of the Act of 1956.

This is a formidable argument, but I cannot accept it. I leave on one side Mr O'Connor's sustained criticisms of the reasoning in *Prince*'s case and *Maughan*'s case. Where the Crown's argument breaks down is that the motley collection of offences, of diverse origins, gathered into the Act of 1956 displays no satisfactorily clear or coherent pattern. If the interpretation of section 1 of the Act of 1960 is to be gleaned from the contents of another statute, that other statute must give compelling guidance. The, Act of 1956 as a whole falls short of this standard. So do the two sections, sections 14 and 15, which were the genesis of section 1 of the Act of 1960.

Accordingly, I cannot find, either in the statutory context or otherwise, any indication of sufficient cogency to displace the application of the common law presumption. In my view the necessary mental element regarding the age ingredient in section 1 of the Act of 1960 is the absence of a genuine belief by the accused that the victim was 14 years of age or above. The burden of proof of this rests upon the prosecution in the usual way. If Parliament considers that the position should be otherwise regarding this serious social problem, Parliament must itself confront the difficulties and express its will in clear terms. I would allow this appeal.

I add a final observation. As just mentioned, in reaching my conclusion I have left on one side the criticisms made of *Prince*'s case and *Maughan*'s case. Those cases concerned different offences and different statutory provisions. The correctness of the decisions in those cases does not call for decision on the present appeal. But, without expressing a view on the correctness of the actual decisions in those cases, I must observe that some of the reasoning in *Prince*'s case is at variance with the common law presumption regarding *mens rea* as discussed above. To that extent, the reasoning must be regarded as unsound. For instance, Bramwell B, at p. 174, seems to have regarded the common law presumption as ousted because the act forbidden was 'wrong in itself'. Denman J, at p. 178, appears to have considered it was 'reasonably clear' that the Act of 1861 was an Act of strict liability so far as the age element was concerned. On its face this is a lesser standard than necessary implication. And in the majority judgment, Blackburn J reached his conclusion by inference from the intention Parliament must have had when enacting two other, ineptly drawn, sections of the Act. But clumsy parliamentary drafting is an insecure basis for finding a necessary implication elsewhere, even in the same statute. *Prince*'s case, and later decisions based on it, must now be read in the light of this decision of your Lordships' House on the nature and weight of the common law presumption.

■ NOTES AND QUESTIONS

1. If the age of consent is 16, is there any reason to treat a defendant's belief that a child over 13 but under 16 was in fact over 16 any differently from a defendant's belief that a child under 13 was in fact over 16? The defendant's testimony of an honest belief may be less credible in the case of the child under 13, but should the issue nonetheless be left to the jury?

2. Under the pre-SOA 2003 law, it was a criminal offence to have sexual intercourse with a girl under the age of 16 (who was legally incapable of giving consent), but there was a defence available (the 'young man's defence') where the defendant was under 24 years of age, had not previously been charged with a relevant sexual offence or an attempt to commit such an offence, and believed or had

reasonable belief that the victim was 16 or over. Why should such a defence have been limited to defendants under 24?

3. Has the decision in *B* v *DPP* been implicitly overruled by the SOA 2003?

The Sexual Offences Act 2003 also creates several new offences relating to children over 13 but under 16. These include 'engaging in sexual activity in the presence of a child' (s. 11), causing a child to watch a sexual act' (s. 12), 'arranging or facilitating commission of a child sexual offence' (s. 14) and meeting a child following sexual grooming' (s. 15):

11. Engaging in sexual activity in the presence of a child

(1) A person aged 18 or over (A) commits an offence if—
   (a) he intentionally engages in an activity,
   (b) the activity is sexual,
   (c) for the purpose of obtaining sexual gratification, he engages in it—
      (i)   when another person (B) is present or is in a place from which A can be observed, and
      (ii) knowing or believing that B is aware, or intending that B should be aware, that he is engaging in it, and
   (d) either—
      (i)   B is under 16 and A does not reasonably believe that B is 16 or over, or
      (ii) B is under 13.
(2) A person guilty of an offence under this section is liable—
   (a) on summary conviction, to imprisonment for a term not exceeding 6 months or a fine not exceeding the statutory maximum or both;
   (b) on conviction on indictment, to imprisonment for a term not exceeding 10 years.

12. Causing a child to watch a sexual act

(1) A person aged 18 or over (A) commits an offence if—
   (a) for the purpose of obtaining sexual gratification, he intentionally causes another person (B) to watch a third person engaging in an activity, or to look at an image of any person engaging in an activity,
   (b) the activity is sexual, and
   (c) either—
      (i)   B is under 16 and A does not reasonably believe that B is 16 or over, or
      (ii) B is under 13.
(2) A person guilty of an offence under this section is liable—
   (a) on summary conviction, to imprisonment for a term not exceeding 6 months or a fine not exceeding the statutory maximum or both;
   (b) on conviction on indictment, to imprisonment for a term not exceeding 10 years.

...

14. Arranging or facilitating commission of a child sex offence

(1) A person commits an offence if—
   (a) he intentionally arranges or facilitates something that he intends to do, intends another person to do, or believes that another person will do, in any part of the world, and
   (b) doing it will involve the commission of an offence under any of sections 9 to 13.
(2) A person does not commit an offence under this section if—
   (a) he arranges or facilitates something that he believes another person will do, but that he does not intend to do or intend another person to do, and
   (b) any offence within subsection (1)(b) would be an offence against a child for whose protection he acts.

(3) For the purposes of subsection (2), a person acts for the protection of a child if he acts for the purpose of—

    (a) protecting the child from sexually transmitted infection,

    (b) protecting the physical safety of the child,

    (c) preventing the child from becoming pregnant, or

    (d) promoting the child's emotional well-being by the giving of advice, and not for the purpose of obtaining sexual gratification or for the purpose of causing or encouraging the activity constituting the offence within subsection (1)(b) or the child's participation in it.

(4) A person guilty of an offence under this section is liable—

    (a) on summary conviction, to imprisonment for a term not exceeding 6 months or a fine not exceeding the statutory maximum or both;

    (b) on conviction on indictment, to imprisonment for a term not exceeding 14 years.

15. Meeting a child following sexual grooming etc.

(1) A person aged 18 or over (A) commits an offence if—

    (a) having met or communicated with another person (B) on at least two earlier occasions, he—

        (i) intentionally meets B, or

        (ii) travels with the intention of meeting B in any part of the world,

    (b) at the time, he intends to do anything to or in respect of B, during or after the meeting and in any part of the world, which if done will involve the commission by A of a relevant offence,

    (c) B is under 16, and

    (d) A does not reasonably believe that B is 16 or over.

(2) In subsection (1)—

    (a) the reference to A having met or communicated with B is a reference to A having met B in any part of the world or having communicated with B by any means from, to or in any part of the world;

    (b) 'relevant offence' means—

        (i) an offence under this Part,

        (ii) an offence within any of paragraphs 61 to 92 of Schedule 3, or

        (iii) anything done outside England and Wales and Northern Ireland which is not an offence within sub-paragraph (i) or (ii) but would be an offence within sub-paragraph (i) if done in England and Wales.

(3) In this section as it applies to Northern Ireland—

    (a) subsection (1) has effect with the substitution of '17' for '16' in both places;

    (b) subsection (2)(b)(iii) has effect with the substitution of 'sub-paragraph (ii) if done in Northern Ireland' for 'sub-paragraph (i) if done in England and Wales'.

(4) A person guilty of an offence under this section is liable—

    (a) on summary conviction, to imprisonment for a term not exceeding 6 months or a fine not exceeding the statutory maximum or both;

    (b) on conviction on indictment, to imprisonment for a term not exceeding 10 years.

The distinguishing features of s. 11 are:

(1) The defendant has the purpose of obtaining sexual gratification;

(2) In pursuit of that purpose, the defendant engages in sexual activity while B is present or in a place from which B can observe the activity; and

(3) The defendant knows or believes that B is aware, or intends that B should be aware, that he is so engaged.

Note that under s. 11 the victim need not actually witness the sexual activity. It is sufficient that the defendant believes or intends that the victim will witness it. The purpose of the section is to prevent adults over 18 from corrupting children under 16 by exposing them to sexual activity.

The offence in s. 12 is similarly directed at persons whose aim is to corrupt children but here the offence is broadened to include 'causing' the child to watch the sexual activity. The sexual activity need not take place 'live' but may be conveyed through a photograph, a moving picture or even an animated cartoon. For both the s. 11 and s. 12 offences, establishing that the defendant acted for the purpose of obtaining sexual gratification (as opposed, for instance, for the purpose of embarrassing or humiliating the victim) may prove problematic.

Section 14 creates the offence of intentionally 'arranging or facilitating commission of a child sex offence'. This offence is aimed at the growing problem of child sex trafficking. Often such trafficking will have international dimensions, which explains the reference in s. 14(1)(a) to 'any part of the world.' *Mens rea* is again critical under this section as there is no offence if the defendant does not intend the child to do the sexual acts in question or does not believe that it would be an offence against a child for whose protection the defendant acts. The latter provision would protect, for instance, police seeking to use a child as 'bait' in order to apprehend sex traffickers or medical personnel who provide the child with advice on contraception (see *Gillick* v *West Norfolk and Wisbech Health Authority* [1986] AC 112).

Sexual grooming of child victims over the Internet also has become a major problem in recent years. The Sexual Offences Act 2003, s. 15, is specifically aimed at combating the challenge posed by adults (often sexual paedophiles), who use Internet chat rooms to arrange meetings with gullible children. Often the adults will lie about their age. This offence is in tension with the law of attempt, which, as we shall see in Chapter 12, does not include acts that are 'merely preparatory' to the intended offence. Under s. 15, the arranged meeting with the child may be 'merely preparatory' to some other intended sexual offence. Note also the jurisdictional issues. The offender under s. 15 need not intend that the ultimate offence take place in England; the intended venue for the offence may be anywhere in the world. This constitutes a recognition of the worldwide threat to children posed by the grooming of child victims over the Internet. Also, the intended victim need not be English. The protection of s. 15 expands to children of all nationalities, wherever they may live. Again, this is a recognition that child grooming is a global and not just a national problem. The effect, however, may be to impose a distinctly 'English' view of what should be a criminal offence on a country whose law and culture does not find sexual activity with children objectionable.

■ NOTES AND QUESTIONS

1. Why, in respect of ss. 9–10, should proof of the defendant's intent matter? If, say, a teacher were to engage in sexual intercourse in front of her biology class

of under 16s, why should not the teacher be guilty of causing a child to watch a sexual act, whether or not the teacher has the purpose of obtaining sexual gratification?

2. Do the provisions of the SOA 2003 relating to child victims between the ages of 13 and 16 criminalise the types of 'normal' sexual experimenting that is common among children of that age? The drafters appear not to have made a serious attempt to discover or to take cognisance of what constitutes accepted sexual behaviour among the young. See Spencer, 'The Sexual Offences Act 2003: Child and Family Offences' [2004] Crim LR 347. But should the views of the potential victims be relevant?

3. As noted in respect of offences against children under 13, Parliament may have left to prosecutors, through the exercise of their discretion, the responsibility to rectify questionable legislative provisions. Is this a sensible way of proceeding, or a shirking of Parliament's responsibilities? Will not different prosecutors inevitably have different views as to what constitutes acceptable sexual activity where young persons are concerned?

SECTION 4: ECHR CONSIDERATIONS

Part of the impetus behind the SOA 2003 was the sense that crimes of rape were not being taken sufficiently seriously by the authorities. The European Court of Human Rights also has addressed this issue.

MC v Bulgaria
[2003] Application 39272/98, European Court of Human Rights

...

3. The applicant alleged violations of her rights under Articles 3, 8, 13 and 14 of the Convention in that domestic law and practice in rape cases and the investigation into the rape of which she had been a victim did not secure the observance by the respondent State of its positive obligation to provide effective legal protection against rape and sexual abuse.

...

1. The applicant is a Bulgarian national who was born in 1980.

2. She alleged that she had been raped by two men on 31 July and 1 August 1995, when she was 14 years and 10 months old. The ensuing investigation came to the conclusion that there was insufficient proof of the applicant having been compelled to have sex.

...

3. The applicant complained that Bulgarian law and practice did not provide effective protection against rape and sexual abuse, as only cases where the victim had resisted actively were prosecuted, and that the authorities had not investigated the events of 31 July and 1 August 1995 effectively. In her view, the above amounted to a violation of the State's positive obligations to protect the individual's physical integrity and private life and to provide effective remedies in this respect.

4. The relevant Convention provisions read:

Article 3

'No one shall be subjected to torture or to inhuman or degrading treatment or punishment.'

Article 8 § 1

'Everyone has the right to respect for his private ... life ...'

Article 13

'Everyone whose rights and freedoms as set forth in [the] Convention are violated shall have an effective remedy before a national authority notwithstanding that the violation has been committed by persons acting in an official capacity.'

5. The applicant considered that domestic law and practice in rape cases should determine the existence, or lack, of consent to sexual intercourse on the basis of all relevant factors. In her view, a legal framework and practice that required proof of physical resistance by the victim, and thus left unpunished certain acts of rape, were inadequate.

...

6. The Government submitted that the investigation had been thorough and effective. All possible steps had been taken: seventeen persons had been questioned, some of them repeatedly, experts in psychiatry and psychology had been appointed and all aspects of the case had been explored. The Government therefore considered that the conclusion of the national authorities that P. and A. must have acted on the assumption of the applicant's consent had been well-founded. In particular, the authorities had relied on all evidence about the events of 31 July to 1 August 1995, including information about the behaviour of the applicant. Furthermore, the applicant had gone out with P. after the events and there had been allegations by witnesses that her mother had attempted to extort money from P. and A. in return for dropping the rape allegations.

The Court's assessment

7. Having regard to the nature and the substance of the applicant's complaints in this particular case, the Court finds that they fall to be examined primarily under Articles 3 and 8 of the Convention.

...

8. Positive obligations on the State are inherent in the right to effective respect for private life under Article 8; these obligations may involve the adoption of measures even in the sphere of the relations of individuals between themselves. While the choice of the means to secure compliance with Article 8 in the sphere of protection against acts of individuals is in principle within the State's margin of appreciation, effective deterrence against grave acts such as rape, where fundamental values and essential aspects of private life are at stake, requires efficient criminal-law provisions. Children and other vulnerable individuals, in particular, are entitled to effective protection ...

9. In a number of cases, Article 3 of the Convention gives rise to a positive obligation to conduct an official investigation (see *Assenov and Others* v. *Bulgaria*, judgment of 28 October 1998, *Reports* 1998-VIII, p. 3290, § 102). Such a positive obligation cannot be considered in principle to be limited solely to cases of ill-treatment by State agents (see, *mutatis mutandis, Calvelli and Ciglio v. Italy* [GC], no. 32967/96, ECHR 2002-I).

10. Further, the Court has not excluded the possibility that the State's positive obligation under Article 8 to safeguard the individual's physical integrity may extend to questions relating to the effectiveness of a criminal investigation (see *Osman v. the United Kingdom*, judgment of 28 October 1998, *Reports* 1998-VIII, p. 3164, § 128).

11. On that basis, the Court considers that States have a positive obligation inherent in Articles 3 and 8 of the Convention to enact criminal law provisions effectively punishing rape and to apply them in practice through effective investigation and prosecution.

...

12. Turning to the particular facts of the applicant's case, the Court notes that, in the course of the investigation, many witnesses were heard and an expert report by a psychologist and a psychiatrist was ordered. The case was investigated and the prosecutors gave reasoned decisions, explaining their position in some detail...

13. The Court recognises that the Bulgarian authorities faced a difficult task, as they were confronted with two conflicting versions of the events and little 'direct' evidence. The Court does not underestimate the efforts made by the investigator and the prosecutors in their work on the case.

14. It notes, nonetheless, that the presence of two irreconcilable versions of the facts obviously called for a context-sensitive assessment of the credibility of the statements made and for verification of all the surrounding circumstances. Little was done, however, to test the credibility of the version of the events proposed by P. and A. [the accused rapists] and the witnesses called by them. In particular, the witnesses whose statements contradicted each other... were not confronted. No attempt was made to establish with more precision the timing of the events. The applicant and her representative were not given the opportunity to put questions to the witnesses whom she accused of perjury. In their decisions, the prosecutors did not devote any attention to the question whether the story proposed by P. and A. was credible, although some of their statements called for caution, such as the assertion that the applicant, 14 years old at the time, had started caressing A. minutes after having sex for the first time in her life with another man...

15. The Court thus considers that the authorities failed to explore the available possibilities for establishing all the surrounding circumstances and did not assess sufficiently the credibility of the conflicting statements made.

16. It is highly significant that the reason for that failure was, apparently, the investigator's and the prosecutors' opinion that, since what was alleged to have occurred was a 'date rape', in the absence of 'direct' proof of rape such as traces of violence and resistance or calls for help, they could not infer proof of lack of consent and, therefore, of rape from an assessment of all the surrounding circumstances. That approach transpires clearly from the position of the investigator and, in particular, from the regional prosecutor's decision of 13 May 1997 and the Chief Public Prosecutor's decision of 24 June 1997...

17. Furthermore, it appears that the prosecutors did not exclude the possibility that the applicant might not have consented, but adopted the view that in any event, in the absence of proof of resistance, it could not be concluded that the perpetrators had understood that the applicant had not consented.... The prosecutors forwent the possibility of proving the perpetrators' *mens rea* by assessing all the surrounding circumstances, such as evidence that they had deliberately misled the applicant in order to take her to a deserted area, thus creating an environment of coercion, and also by judging the credibility of the versions of the facts proposed by the three men and witnesses called by them.

18. The Court considers that, while in practice it may sometimes be difficult to prove lack of consent in the absence of 'direct' proof of rape, such as traces of violence or direct witnesses, the authorities must nevertheless explore all the facts and decide on the basis of an assessment of all the surrounding circumstances. The investigation and its conclusions must be centred on the issue of non-consent.

19. That was not done in the applicant's case. The Court finds that the failure of the authorities in the applicant's case to investigate sufficiently the surrounding circumstances was the result of their putting undue emphasis on 'direct' proof of rape. Their approach in the particular case was restrictive, practically elevating 'resistance' to the status of defining element of the offence.

20. In sum, the Court, without expressing an opinion on the guilt of P. and A., finds that the investigation of the applicant's case and, in particular, the approach taken by the investigator and the prosecutors in the case fell short of the requirements inherent in the States' positive obligations—viewed in the light of the relevant modern standards in comparative and international law— to establish and apply effectively a criminal law system punishing all forms of rape and sexual abuse.

...

21. The Court thus finds that in the present case there has been a violation of the respondent State's positive obligations under both Articles 3 and 8 of the Convention.

■ NOTES AND QUESTIONS

1. Has the European Court of Human Rights effectively appointed itself as the reviewer of police investigations in cases of rape? If so, is this appropriate? Will the Court's decision lead to its being flooded with claims from victims in all types of cases where the police have reached the conclusion that there is insufficient evidence to warrant recommendation of a prosecution; or is this consideration irrelevant?

2. After reviewing the law of other European States, as well as international law, the European Court of Human Rights in *MC* was also persuaded that any rigid approach to the prosecution of sexual offences, such as requiring proof of physical resistance in all circumstances, risked leaving certain types of rape unpunished and thus jeopardised the effective protection of the individual's sexual autonomy. In accordance with contemporary standards and trends in that area, the member States' positive obligations under Articles 3 and 8 of the Convention must be seen as requiring the penalisation and effective prosecution of any non-consensual sexual act, including in the absence of physical resistance by the victim.

While this admonition does not directly affect the UK, as physical resistance is not a prerequisite to a finding of rape under UK law, the pronouncement is important for it signals the willingness of the European Court of Human Rights to impose restrictions on State *substantive* law. Given the different historical and cultural traditions in the various European States, is this either appropriate or wise?

FURTHER READING

Wilson, *Criminal Law: Doctrine and Theory* (2011), Chapter 12

Davies, '*R v Dica*: Lessons in Practicing Unsafe Sex' (2004) 68 Journal of Criminal Law 498

Finch and Munro, 'Breaking Boundaries? Sexual Consent in the Jury Room' (2006) Legal Studies 303

Herring, 'Mistaken Sex' [2005] Crim LR 311; contra Hyman Gross [2005] Criminal Law Review 220

Power, 'Towards a Redefinition of the *Mens Rea* of Rape' (2003) 23 Oxford Journal of Legal Studies 379

Spencer, 'The Sexual Offences Act 2003: Child and Family Offences' [2004] Criminal Law Review 347

Stevenson, Davies and Gunn, *Blackstone's Guide to the Sexual Offences Act 2003* (2004)

Temkin, *Rape and the Legal Process* (2nd ed. 2002)

Temkin and Ashworth, 'Rape, Sexual Assaults and the Problems of Consent [2004] Criminal Law Review 328

Weait, 'Criminal Law and the Sexual Transmission of HIV: *R v Dica*' (2005) 68 Modern Law Review 121

7

Property Offences

The law of theft expresses the value society places on property rights. The biblical admonition that 'thou shalt not steal' perseveres in modern times. Although Parliament has decided to bring theft within the scope of the criminal law, most of the offences discussed in this chapter and the next on Fraud may also give rise to a civil action by the victim. Yet in a civil action an entirely different set of legal principles and analysis may be applied, which raises the question of whether the civil and criminal law on common issues should be harmonised.

A number of factors prompt the criminalisation of interference with property interests. One is the view (which may or may not be accurate) that making theft subject to criminal penalties is a more powerful deterrent than civil remedies. Indeed, a civil remedy may be worthless if the offender does not have the financial resources to pay damages and is unable to restore the goods taken. Leaving a victim to a civil suit may also not adequately convey how strongly society feels about persons who take another's property.

The laws promoting the security of property generally take little account of disparities in wealth: it is equally a crime for both a wealthy and a homeless person to steal a loaf of bread. The concentration on protection of the status quo as far as wealth is concerned reveals an inherent tension when such laws are applied in a capitalist society. It is extremely difficult to draw the line between aggressive and shady entrepreneurial activity and conduct that has traditionally been subject to criminal sanctions. The financial loss caused by 'white collar crimes' such as fraud, money laundering and insider dealing often dwarfs that caused by theft and burglary. Yet offenders who commit theft and burglary are more likely to be prosecuted and face a longer sentence if convicted than their white collar counterparts.

When the Theft Act 1968 (hereafter TA 1968) was drafted, the aim was to simplify and clarify the common law. Because the protection of property must to some extent depend on complicated rules concerning ownership of property, the TA 1968 is not always as simple as Parliament might have wished. Problems have arisen because the courts have imported into the criminal law civil law concepts relating to property while interpreting them differently. This problem of 'same terms, different meaning' is not unique to the law of theft but it probably is more pronounced here than elsewhere.

In some instances, too, the courts have had to deal with problems not of their own making. In some cases prosecutors have brought charges against a defendant which arguably did not fit the defendant's offence. In *DPP* v *Gomez* [1993] AC 442, below, for instance, the defendant was charged with theft rather than the seemingly more appropriate crime of obtaining property by deception (now fraud). This presented the House of Lords with a dilemma: they could quash the defendant's conviction because one of the elements of theft, an 'appropriation', had not been made out by the facts; or they could stretch the meaning of 'appropriation' in order to uphold the conviction of a clearly morally culpable individual. They chose the latter path, but in doing so may have distorted the scheme of liability intended by Parliament and diluted one of the foundation elements of the law of theft to the point of virtual meaninglessness.

Allen (*Textbook of Criminal Law*, 10th ed., 2009, p. 435) identifies three problems that the courts have created in interpreting the TA 1968: (1) leaving the definition of dishonesty to the jury has resulted in inconsistent decisions; (2) disregarding civil law concepts of property ownership has caused confusion in respect of such basic questions as to whom particular property belongs; and (3) defining the constituent elements of theft offences in isolation has led to incoherent and contradictory decisions. Even eminent judges in the House of Lords have struggled when analysing theft cases.

Analysing a theft offence

The TA 1968 can be usefully thought of as consisting of three 'tiers'. At the first tier lies the definition of the crime. The definition of 'theft' is set out in s. 1 of the Act. From this definition one can extract the basic elements of theft. At the second tier, to be found in subsequent sections of the Act, are more detailed explications or qualifications of one or more of the elements contained in the definition section. Thus, for example, s. 3 of the Act defines 'appropriation', s. 4 deals with the meaning of property and s. 5 outlines what it means for property to 'belong to another'. Despite this guidance, cases will inevitably arise that require the courts to interpret provisions of the statute. Our third tier of analysis therefore consists of the decisions of the courts interpreting and applying the statutory provisions.

THEFT ACT 1968

1.—(1) A person is guilty of theft if he dishonestly appropriates property belonging to another with the intention of permanently depriving the other of it; and 'thief' and 'steal' shall be construed accordingly.

Section 1 can be broken down into the following elements:

(a) an appropriation,

(b) of property,

(c) which belongs to another;

(d) dishonestly, and

(e) with an intent permanently to deprive the person to whom the property belongs of that property.

SECTION 2: *ACTUS REUS*

The *actus reus* of theft, set out in s. 1 of the Act, consists of three elements – (a) an appropriation (b) of property (c) which belongs to another. These elements are further explained in ss. 3, 4, and 5, respectively and in the case law.

A: Appropriation

What is an appropriation? It may range from an outright taking of property to a relatively trivial interference with property. Indeed, it may occur without any physical contact with the property on the part of the thief. Section 3 of TA 1968 defines appropriation as 'any assumption...of the rights of an owner'.

THEFT ACT 1968

3.—(1) Any assumption by a person of the rights of an owner amounts to an appropriation, and this includes, where he has come by the property (innocently or not) without stealing it, any later assumption of a right to it by keeping or dealing with it as an owner.

(a) Where not all the rights of the owner have been appropriated

Must a thief appropriate all of the rights of the owner or will the appropriation of any of the owner's rights suffice? To answer this question one must first identify what rights an owner has in property. These are remarkably extensive – an owner can sell (at whatever price she chooses to ask), lend, give away, bequeath, damage, destroy or discard property. An owner can even decide whether another will be permitted to touch the property. The person who appropriates *any* of these rights may, if the other elements of the offence are present, be guilty of theft.

R v Morris
[1984] AC 320, House of Lords

LORD ROSKILL: Mr Denison submitted that the phrase in section 3(1) 'any assumption by a person of *the rights*' (my emphasis) 'of an owner amounts to an appropriation' must mean any assumption of '*all* the rights of an owner.' Since neither respondent had at the time of the removal of the goods from the shelves and of the label switching assumed *all* the rights of the owner, there was no appropriation and therefore no theft. Mr Jeffreys for the prosecution, on the other hand, contended that *the* rights in this context only meant *any* of the rights. An owner of goods has many rights—they have been described as 'a bundle or package of rights.' Mr Jeffreys contended that on a fair reading of the subsection it cannot have been the intention that every one of an owner's rights had to be assumed by the alleged thief before an appropriation was proved and that essential ingredient of the offence of theft established.

My Lords, if one reads the words 'the rights' at the opening of section 3(1) literally and in isolation from the rest of the section, Mr Denison's submission undoubtedly has force. But the later words 'any later assumption of a right' in subsection (1) and the words in subsection (2) 'no later assumption by him of rights' seem to me to militate strongly against the correctness of the submission. Moreover the provisions of section 2(1)(a) also seem to point in the same direction. It follows therefore that it is enough for the prosecution if they have proved in these cases the assumption by the respondents of *any* of the rights of the owner of the goods in question, that is to say, the supermarket concerned....

(b) Assumption of the rights of an owner who is not in possession of his property

R v Pitham and Hehl
(1976) 65 Cr App R 45, Court of Appeal

One M, who knew an acquaintance X was in prison, decided to take advantage of X's incarceration to steal his furniture and sell it. M offered the furniture to the appellants for sale and they both went individually to X's house to look at the furniture and agreed to buy it, paying M a sum which they knew to be considerably under the true value. M and the appellants were later seen to enter X's house after arriving there in a furniture van. M was arrested, but the appellants escaped, but both were later interviewed by the police. They insisted that 'they had not screwed the place'. All three were charged on counts of burglary, the appellants additionally each on an individual count of handling stolen goods. M was convicted on two counts of burglary and the appellants only on the individual handling counts.

> LAWTON LJ: . . . What was the appropriation in this case? . . . what had [the defendant Millman] done? He had assumed the rights of the owner. He had done that when he took the two appellants to 20, Parry Road, showed them the property and invited them to buy what they wanted. He was then acting as the owner. He was then, in the words of the statute 'assuming the rights of the owner.' The moment he did that he appropriated McGregor's goods to himself. The appropriation was complete.

■ NOTES AND QUESTIONS

1. Would the decision in the case have been the same if the purchasers had offered to buy the goods before the defendants had offered to sell them?

2. Did the defendant steal *all* the contents of the house, or only those items which were sold? Those items offered for sale?

3. It is not uncommon for a person who works behind the bar in a pub to give free or discounted drinks to friends. Does this constitute an appropriation? Would it matter if the owner of the pub had told the bartender that he could give free drinks to 'high-rollers' to cultivate their business? In *Pilgram* v *Rice-Smith* [1977] 1 WLR 671 the defendant, a shop assistant, supplied a friend with meat at a reduced price. The Court of Appeal found the defendant had acted dishonestly and that the meat had been stolen despite the fact that before the defendant behaved dishonestly she was innocently in possession of all the articles at her counter.

(c) The relevance of consent of the owner?

The issue has been the subject of three well-known House of Lords decisions in *Lawrence*, *Gomez* and *Hinks* but the state of the law, once apparently settled by the preceding cases, has been thrown into confusion by the decision of the Court of Appeal in *Briggs*.

Lawrence v Metropolitan Police Commissioner
[1972] AC 626, House of Lords

The defendant was a taxi driver who picked up a foreign student, Mr Occhi, at Victoria Station. Mr Occhi spoke little English and was on his first trip to England.

He gave Lawrence a slip of paper indicating an address to which he wished to be taken. Lawrence said that it was very far and very expensive. Mr Occhi took £1 out of his wallet and gave it to Lawrence who proceeded to take a further £6 out of the wallet. The correct lawful fare for the journey was approximately 10s. 6d.

LORD DONOVAN: . . . I now turn to the third element 'property belonging to another.' Mr Back QC, for the appellant, contended that if Mr Occhi consented to the appellant taking the £6, he consented to the property in the money passing from him to the appellant and that the appellant had not, therefore, appropriated property belonging to another. He argued that the old distinction between the offence of false pretences and larceny had been preserved. I am unable to agree with this. The new offence of obtaining property by deception created by section 15(1) of the Theft Act also contains the words 'belonging to another'. 'A person who by any deception dishonestly obtains property belonging to another, with the intention of permanently depriving the other of it' commits that offence. 'Belonging to another' in section 1(1) and in section 15(1) in my view signifies no more than that, at the time of the appropriation or the obtaining, the property belonged to another, with the words 'belonging to another' having the extended meaning given by section 5. The short answer to this contention on behalf of the appellant is that the money in the wallet which he appropriated belonged to another, to Mr Occhi.

DPP v Gomez
[1993] AC 442, House of Lords

LORD KEITH OF KINKEL: . . . The facts of this case are that the defendant, Edwin Gomez, was employed as an assistant manager at a shop trading by retail in electrical goods. In September 1987 he was asked by an acquaintance called Jit Ballay to supply goods from the shop and to accept payment by two stolen building society cheques, one for £7,950 and the other for £9,250, which were undated and bore no payee's name. The defendant agreed, and prepared a list of goods to the value of £7,950 which he submitted to the manager, Mr Gilberd, saying that it represented a genuine order by one Johal and asking him to authorise the supply of the goods in return for a building society cheque in that sum. Mr Gilberd instructed the defendant to confirm with the bank that the cheque was acceptable, and the defendant later told him that he had done so and that such a cheque was 'as good as cash'. Mr Gilberd agreed to the transaction, the defendant paid the cheque into the bank, and a few days later Ballay took possession of the goods, the defendant helping him to load them into his vehicle. Shortly afterwards a further consignment of goods to the value of £9,250 was ordered and supplied in similar fashion (apart from one item valued at £1,002.99 which was not delivered), against the second stolen building society cheque. Mr Gilberd agreed to this transaction without further inquiry. Later the two cheques were returned by the bank marked 'Orders not to pay. Stolen cheque.'

The defendant, Ballay and another employee of the shop, named Rai, were arrested and later tried on an indictment the fourth and fifth counts in which charged all three with theft contrary to section 1(1) of the Theft Act 1968 in respect of the two transactions. After evidence had been led for the prosecution counsel for the defendant submitted that there was no case to answer on the theft charges because the manager of the shop had authorised the transactions, so that there had been no appropriation within the meaning of section 1(1) of the Act. . . .

In my opinion Lord Roskill was undoubtedly right when he said in [Morris [1983] QB 587] that the assumption by the defendant of any of the rights of an owner could amount to an appropriation within the meaning of section 3(1), and that the removal of an article from the shelf and the changing of the price label on it constituted the assumption of one of the rights of the owner and hence an appropriation within the meaning of the subsection. But there are observations in the passage which, with the greatest possible respect to my noble and learned friend Lord Roskill, I must regard as unnecessary for the decision of the case and as being incorrect. In the first place, it seems to me that the switching of price labels on the article is in itself an assumption of one of the rights of the owner, whether or not it is accompanied by some other act such as removing the article from the shelf and placing it in a basket or trolley. No one but the owner has the right to remove a price label from an article or to place a price label upon it. If anyone else does so, he does an act, as Lord Roskill puts it, by way of adverse interference with or usurpation of that right. This is no less so in the case of the practical joker figured by Lord Roskill than in the case of one who makes the switch with dishonest intent. The practical joker, of course, is not guilty of theft because he has not acted dishonestly and does not intend to deprive the owner permanently of the article. So the label switching in itself constitutes an appropriation and so to have held would have been sufficient for the dismissal of both appeals. On the facts of the two cases it was unnecessary to decide whether, as argued by Mr Jeffreys, the mere taking of the article from the shelf and putting it in a trolley or other receptacle amounted to the assumption of one of the rights of the owner, and hence an appropriation. There was much to be said in favour of the view that it did, in respect that doing so gave the shopper control of the article and the capacity to exclude any other shopper from taking it. However, Lord Roskill expressed the opinion, at p. 332, that it did not, on the ground that the concept of appropriation in the context of section 3(1) involves not an act expressly or impliedly authorised by the owner but an act by way of adverse interference with or usurpation of those rights.

While it is correct to say that appropriation for purposes of section 3(1) includes the latter sort of act, it does not necessarily follow that no other act can amount to an appropriation and in particular that no act expressly or impliedly authorised by the owner can in any circumstances do so. Indeed, *R v Lawrence* [1972] AC 626 is a clear decision to the contrary since it laid down unequivocally that an act may be an appropriation notwithstanding that it is done with the consent of the owner. It does not appear to me that any sensible distinction can be made in this context between consent and authorisation.

... *Lawrence* makes it clear that consent to or authorisation by the owner of the taking by the rogue is irrelevant. The taking amounted to an appropriation within the meaning of secton 1(1) of the Act of 1968. *Lawrence* also makes it clear that it is no less irrelevant that what happened may also have constituted the offence of obtaining property by deception under section 15(1) of the Act.

In my opinion it serves no useful purpose at the present time to seek to construe the relevant provisions of the Theft Act by reference to the report which preceded it, namely the Eighth Report of the Criminal Law Revision Committee on Theft and Related Offences (1966) (Cmnd. 2977). The decision in *Lawrence* was a clear decision of this House upon the construction of the word 'appropriate' in section 1(1) of the Act, which had stood for 12 years when doubt was thrown upon it by obiter dicta in *Morris*. *Lawrence* must be regarded as authoritative and correct, and there is no question of it now being right to depart from it.

...

R v Hinks
[2001] 2 AC 241, House of Lords

LORD STEYN: In 1996 the appellant was 38 years old. She was the mother of a young son. She was friendly with a 53-year-old man, John Dolphin. He was a man of limited intelligence. The appellant described herself as the main carer for John Dolphin. It is not in dispute that in the period April to November 1996 Mr Dolphin withdrew sums totalling around £60,000 from his building society account and that these sums were deposited in the appellant's account. During the summer of that year Mr Dolphin made withdrawals of the maximum permissible sum of £300 almost every day. Towards the end of this period Mr Dolphin had lost most of his savings and moneys inherited from his father. In 1997 the appellant was charged with six counts of theft, five counts covering moneys withdrawn and one count a television set transferred by Mr Dolphin to the appellant. In November 1997 the appellant stood trial on these counts in the Wolverhampton Crown Court before Judge Warner and a jury. It was the prosecution case that the appellant had influenced and coerced Mr Dolphin to withdraw the moneys from his building society account, which were then deposited in her account. A substantial volume of evidence was led during the trial which lasted five days. A police analyst produced documents summarising the flow of funds from Mr Dolphin's account to that of the appellant. Building society employees testified about the daily visits by the appellant and Mr Dolphin to effect withdrawals. The thrust of their evidence was that the appellant did most of the talking and would interrupt Mr Dolphin if he tried to say something. Dr Fuller, a consultant psychiatrist, assessed Mr Dolphin's IQ as in the range between 70 to 80 (the average being 90 to 110). He said that Mr Dolphin was able to live a normal if undemanding life. Mr Dolphin had worked as a packer in a dairy for some 30 years. Dr Fuller described him as naive and trusting and having no idea of the value of his assets or the ability to calculate their value. Dr Fuller accepted that Mr Dolphin would be capable of making a gift and understood the concept of ownership. He thought that Mr Dolphin was capable of making the decision to divest himself of money, but that it was unlikely that he could make the decision alone. Two police officers testified that after cautioning the appellant she denied 'having any money' from Mr Dolphin except for a single cheque which she said represented a loan. In a nutshell the prosecution case was that the appellant had taken Mr Dolphin for as much as she could get.

...

Counsel for the appellant submitted in the first place that the law as expounded in *Gomez* and *Lawrence* must be qualified to say that there can be no appropriation unless the other party (the owner) retains some proprietary interest, or the right to resume or recover some proprietary interest, in the property. Alternatively, counsel argued that 'appropriates' should be interpreted as if the word 'unlawfully' preceded it. Counsel said that the effect of the decisions in Lawrence and Gomez is to reduce the *actus reus* of theft to 'vanishing point' (see Smith & Hogan, Criminal Law, 9th ed (1999), p 505). He argued that the result is to bring the criminal law 'into conflict' with the civil law. Moreover, he argued that the decisions in *Lawrence* and *Gomez* may produce absurd and grotesque results. He argued that the mental requirements of dishonesty and intention of permanently depriving the owner of property are insufficient to filter out some cases of conduct which should not sensibly be regarded as theft. He did not suggest that the appellant's dishonest and repellent conduct came within such a category. Instead he deployed four examples for this purpose, namely:

(1) S makes a handsome gift to D because he believes that D has obtained a First. D has not and knows that S is acting under that misapprehension. He makes the gift. There is here a motivational mistake which, it is submitted, does not avoid the transaction. (Glanville Williams, Textbook of Criminal Law, 1st ed (1978), p 788.)

(2) P sees D's painting and, thinking he is getting a bargain, offers £100,000 for it. D realises that P thinks the painting is a Constable, but knows that it was painted by his sister and is worth no more than £100. He accepts P's offer. D has made an enforceable contract and is entitled to recover and retain the purchase price. (Smith & Hogan, Criminal Law, pp 507, 508.)

(3) A buys a roadside garage business from B, abutting on a public thoroughfare; unknown to A but known to B, it has already been decided to construct a bypass road which will divert substantially the whole of the traffic from passing A's garage. There is an enforceable contract and A is entitled to recover and retain the purchase price. The same would be true if B knew that A was unaware of the intended plan to construct a bypass road. (Compare Lord Atkin in *Bell v Lever Brothers Ltd* [1932] AC 161, 224.)

(4) An employee agrees to retire before the end of his contract of employment, receiving a sum of money by way of compensation from his employer. Unknown to the employer, the employee has committed serious breaches of contract which would have enabled the employer to dismiss him without compensation. Assuming that the employee's failure to reveal his defaults does not affect the validity of the contract, so that the employee is entitled to sue for the promised compensation, is the employee liable to be arrested for the theft the moment he receives the money? (Glanville Williams, 'Theft and Voidable Title' [1981] Crim LR 666, 672.)

My Lords, at first glance these are rather telling examples. They may conceivably have justified a more restricted meaning of section 3(1) than prevailed in *Lawrence* [1972] AC 626 and *Gomez* [1993] AC 442. The House ruled otherwise and I am quite unpersuaded that the House overlooked the consequences of its decision. On the facts set out in the examples a jury could possibly find that the acceptance of the transfer took place in the belief that the transferee had the right in law to deprive the other of it within the meaning of section 2(1)(a) of the Act. Moreover, in such cases a prosecution is hardly likely and if mounted, is likely to founder on the basis that the jury will not be persuaded that there was dishonesty in the required sense. And one must retain a sense of perspective. At the extremity of the application of legal rules there are sometimes results which may seem strange. A matter of judgment is then involved. The rule may have to be recast. Sir John Smith has eloquently argued that the rule in question ought to be recast. I am unpersuaded. If the law is restated by adopting a narrower definition of appropriation, the outcome is likely to place beyond the reach of the criminal law dishonest persons who should be found guilty of theft. The suggested revisions would unwarrantably restrict the scope of the law of theft and complicate the fair and effective prosecution of theft. In my view the law as settled in Lawrence and Gomez does not demand the suggested revision. Those decisions can be applied by judges and juries in a way which, absent human error, does not result in injustice.

Counsel for the appellant further pointed out that the law as stated in *Lawrence* [1972] AC 626 and *Gomez* [1993] AC 442 creates a tension between the civil and the criminal law. In other words, conduct which is not wrongful in a civil law sense may constitute the crime of theft. Undoubtedly, this is so. The question whether the civil claim to title by a convicted thief, who committed no civil wrong, may be defeated by the principle that nobody may benefit from his own civil or criminal wrong does not arise for decision. Nevertheless there is a more general point, namely that the inter-action between criminal law and civil law can cause problems: compare J Beatson and AP Simester, 'Stealing One's Own Property' (1999) 115 LQR 372. The purposes of the civil law and the criminal law are somewhat different. In theory the two systems should be in perfect harmony. In a practical world there will sometimes be some disharmony between the two systems. In any event, it would be wrong to assume on a priori grounds that the criminal law rather than the civil law is defective. Given the jury's conclusions, one is entitled to observe that the appellant's conduct should consti-tute theft, the only available charge. The tension between the civil and the criminal law is therefore not in my view a factor which justifies a departure from the law as stated in *Lawrence* and *Gomez*. Moreover, these decisions of the House have a marked beneficial consequence. While in some con-texts of the law of theft a judge cannot avoid explaining civil law concepts to a jury (eg in respect of section 2(1)(a)), the decisions of the House of Lords eliminate the need for such explanations in respect of appropriation. That is a great advantage in an overly complex corner of the law.

Appeal dismissed.

■ **NOTES AND QUESTIONS**

1. After *Lawrence* and *Gomez*, what was the difference between obtaining property by deception under s. 15 of the TA 1968 (now fraud under the Fraud Act 2006) and s. 1 theft? Could a prosecutor, on the same facts, charge either offence? If so, was such overlap in the law desirable or irrelevant?

2. Commenting on the House of Lord's approach to 'appropriation' in *Gomez*, Professor Smith wrote ([1993] CLR 306):

    Anyone doing anything whatever to property belonging to another, with or without the authority or consent of the owner, appropriates it: and, if he does so dishonestly and with intent, by that act or any subsequent act, permanently to deprive, he commits theft.

    Was Professor Smith correct?

3. After *Gomez*, should 'appropriation' be viewed as a neutral rather than a pejora-tive term? One effect would be to shift the focus even more than would other-wise be the case to the *mens rea* elements of theft. Might this be appropriate?

4. In contract law, ownership of property passes despite the buyer having been misled. The contract is voidable for fraud but otherwise valid. Were the victims in either *Lawrence* or *Hinks* likely to have sought to void the contract (albeit for different reasons)? If not, did they in effect have a license to steal? In any event, given the civil law, did they steal their own property?

5. In *Hinks* the defendant argued that the recipient of a valid gift could not be guilty of theft. Either there is a valid transfer of title or there is an appropriation; there cannot be both. Lord Steyn said that whether or not D had made a gift of the money, the appellant, by acquiring title, had appropriated it and was guilty of theft on proof of dishonesty. The acquisition of title, on this view, is simply the clearest case of 'assuming the rights of ownership'. The objection to this reasoning is that criminal liability requires a wrong as well as culpability. What wrong was committed in *Hinks*?

R v Briggs

[2004] 1 Cr App R, Court of Appeal

The defendant had deceived her elderly relatives, who were selling their house, into giving her a signed authority to receive the proceeds of the sale. Acting pursuant to that authority, the agents transferred the proceeds into an account which the defendant used to purchase another property in her name.

SILBER J: Mr Barry contends that there was an appropriation in this case as is illustrated by the decision of this court in *R v Hilton* [1997] 2 Cr App Rep 445, which was a case in which a defendant on a theft charge, who was one of the designated signatories to a bank account had caused monies to be transferred out of that account to other accounts. This court held that the instructions of the defendant had caused the bank to make the transfers and therefore the defendant had appropriated the charity's credit balance by assuming the charity's right to the balance. In that case, we consider that there was a clear act of appropriation because, in the words of the late Professor John Smith . . . 'There, [the defendant] had direct control of a bank account belonging to a charity. He caused payments to be made from that account to settle his personal debts. That was a completely straightforward case of theft of a chose in action belonging to another' . . . we consider that where a victim causes a payment to be made in reliance on deceptive conduct by the defendant, there is no 'appropriation' by the defendant. We are fortified in coming to that view by three further factors. First, no case has been cited to us where it has been held that an 'appropriation' occurs where the relevant act is committed by the victim albeit as a result of deception. Second, if Mr Barry was correct, there would be very little need for many deception offences as many acts of deceptive conduct would be covered by theft . . . Third, we have already referred to the explanation of the word 'appropriation' in s 3(1) of the Theft Act 1968 and it is a word which connotes a physical act rather than a more remote action triggering the payment which gives rise to the charge. The Oxford English Dictionary defines 'appropriation' as 'to take possession for one's own, to take to oneself'. It is not easy to see why an act of deceiving an owner to do something would fall within the meaning of 'appropriation'.

■ NOTES AND QUESTIONS

1. Amazingly, the decision in *Briggs* failed to refer to either *Gomez* or *Hinks*. Could the court (and counsel for the parties) have really been unaware of these decisions? Perhaps the Court of Appeal was attempting to 'row back' the state of the law from the chaos it believed had been created by the House of Lords.

2. Commenting on *Briggs*, Allen writes; 'Had this been a decision which pre-dated *Lawrence*, such reasoning may have had some merit; that the court can engage in it thirty-two years after that decision defies belief. The case law on appropriation over that period clearly indicates that "appropriation" is not confined to purely physical acts' (Allen, *Criminal Law*, (10th ed., 2009, p. 461)).

(d) The bona fide purchaser

The problem of the bona fide purchaser is specifically dealt with by s. 3(2) of the Theft Act 1968:

THEFT ACT 1968

3.—(2) Where property or a right or interest in property is or purports to be transferred for value to a person acting in good faith, no later assumption by him of rights which he believed himself to be acquiring shall, by reason of any defect in the transferor's title, amount to theft of the property.

The effect of this section is that a person who was not aware of the stolen character of the goods at the time of purchase and who pays fair value for goods is not guilty of theft. Nor does the purchaser become a thief if he subsequently discovers that the goods were stolen. Whether or not he can keep the goods if sued by the original owner is an altogether different question and a matter for the civil law. On the other hand, if, having discovered the stolen character of the goods, the original purchaser resells the goods, claiming or intimating he has good title, he will have committed fraud under the Fraud Act 2006.

B: Property

Section 4 of the 1968 Act excludes real property (land and rights to do with land) from the definition of property for the purposes of s. 1 of the Act unless the exceptions set out in the section are satisfied. Section 4 also makes clear that wild flowers are not property within s. 1 unless the defendant has a commercial purpose when picking them. Similarly, wild animals are not property unless another person has or is about to reduce the animal to possession.

THEFT ACT 1968

4.—(1) 'Property' includes money and all other property, real or personal, including things in action and other intangible property.

While some of the terms in s. 4 may seem straightforward, they may have been given a restricted definition for purposes of the law of theft. 'Money', for example, is limited to coins and banknotes, and does not include cheques. 'Real property' includes land but land can only be stolen in limited situations. 'Personal property' includes all moveable things which can be owned. Some terms in s. 4, on the other hand, are familiar only to lawyers. 'Things in action' (or *choses in action* as they are sometimes referred to) are personal rights in property which can be claimed or enforced by a legal action, and not by taking physical possession. 'Examples include copyrights, trademarks and contractual rights. 'Other intangible property' includes patents which, by the Patents Act 1977, s. 30, are not 'things in action' but are personal property. The generality of s. 4 has given rise to specific issues relating to what constitutes property.

(a) Information

Oxford v Moss
[1979] Crim LR 119, Queen's Bench Division

In 1976, M was an engineering student at Liverpool University. He acquired the proof of an examination paper for a Civil Engineering examination at the University: An information was preferred against him by O, alleging that he stole certain intangible property, i.e. confidential information, being property of the Senate of the University. It was agreed that he never intended to permanently deprive the owner of the piece of paper on which the questions were printed.

Held, by the stipendiary at Liverpool: on the facts of the case, confidential information is not a form of intangible property as opposed to property in the paper itself, and that confidence consisted in the right to control the publication of the proof paper and was a right over property other than a form of intangible property. The owner had not been permanently deprived of any intangible property. The charge was dismissed.

On appeal by the prosecutor, as to whether confidential information can amount to property within the meaning of section 4 of the Theft Act 1968.

Held: there was no property in the information capable of being the subject of a charge of theft, i.e. it was not intangible property within the meaning of section 4.

■ NOTES AND QUESTIONS

1. The court in *Oxford* v *Moss* was faced with a question to which the statute provided no clear answer. In civil law confidential information may be treated as the property of a company (see *Island Export Finance* v *Umunna* [1986] BCLC 460 and *Industrial Developments* v *Cooley* [1972] 2 All ER 162). Further, the Patents Act 1977 treats an invention for which no patent has been granted or applied for as intangible property. Is the situation in *Oxford* v *Moss* analogous?

2. In more modern guise the facts of *Oxford* v *Moss* probably arise in respect of information (such as an exam) stored on a computer, Many of the relevant issues have been addressed in the Computer Misuse Act 1990, as amended by the Police and Justice Act 2006, ss. 35–36.

3. Export quotas were held by the Privy Council to be intangible property in *Attorney-General of Hong Kong* v *Nai-Keung* (1987) 86 Cr App R 174.

(b) Body parts

R v Sharpe
(1857) Dears & B 160, Court of Criminal Appeal

The indictment in the first count charged that the defendant entered a certain burial ground belonging to a certain meeting house of a congregation of Protestants, dissenting from the Church of England, unlawfully and wilfully did break and enter; a certain grave there, in which the body of one Louisa Sharpe had before then been interred, with force and arms unlawfully, wilfully, and indecently did dig open, and the said body of the said Louisa Sharpe out of the same grave unlawfully, wilfully, and indecently did take and carry away.

ERLE J: We are of opinion that the conviction ought to be affirmed. The defendant was wrongfully in the burial ground, and wrongfully opened the grave, and took out several corpses, and carried away one. We say he did this wrongfully, that is to say, by trespass; for the licence which he obtained to enter and open, from the person who had the care of the place, was not given or intended for the purpose to which he applied it, and was, as to that purpose, no licence at all. Neither does our law recognise the right of any one child to the corpse of its parent as claimed by the defendant. Our law recognises no property in a corpse, and the protection of the grave at common law, as contradistinguished from ecclesiastical protection to consecrated ground, depends upon this form of indictment; and there is no authority for saying that relationship will justify the taking a corpse away from the grave where it has been buried.

■ NOTES AND QUESTIONS

1. In *R v Kelly* [1998] 3 All ER 741, Court of Appeal, a junior technician employed by the Royal College of surgeons had, at a sculptor's request, removed a number of body parts which were used for dissection by doctors training to be surgeons. Both the technician and the sculptor were convicted of theft. On appeal the court ruled that a corpse or parts thereof could be owned if subjected to some form of skill as in embalming or dissection. The court observed:

> Furthermore, the common law does not stand still. It may be that, if on some future occasion the question arises, the courts will hold that human body parts are capable of being property for the purposes of s 4, even without the acquisition of different attributes, if they have a use or significance beyond their mere existence.

What of the case where, after an individual's death, his or her body parts are removed for purposes of transplantation – e.g., the heart, eyes, kidneys, sperm (male), eggs (female), etc. or for scientific experimentation?

2. That fluids taken from a living body can be stolen was confirmed in *R v Rothery* [1976] RTR 550, Court of Appeal. In this case a motorist, having complied with the provisions of ss. 8 and 9 of the Road Traffic Act 1972 by providing a specimen of blood when requested to do so by a constable, later committed theft by taking the specimen.

(i) Real property

THEFT ACT 1968

4.—(2) A person cannot steal land, or things forming part of land and severed from it by him or by his directions, except in the following cases, that is to say—
  (a) when he is a trustee or personal representative, or is authorised by power of attorney, or as liquidator of a company, or otherwise, to sell or dispose of land belonging to another, and he appropriates the land or anything forming part of it by dealing with it in breach of the confidence reposed in him; or
  (b) when he is not in possession of the land and he appropriates anything forming part of the land by severing it or causing it to be severed, or after it has been severed; or
  (c) when, being in possession of the land under a tenancy, he appropriates the whole or part of any fixture or structure let to be used with the land.
    For purposes of this subsection 'land' does not include incorporeal hereditaments; 'tenancy' means a tenancy for years or any less period and includes an agreement for such a tenancy, but a person who after the end of a tenancy remains in possession under the tenancy, and 'let' shall be construed accordingly.

A distinction is made between property which is 'on' the land and property which 'forms part of the land'. The latter can be stolen only in the circumstances specified in s. 4(a), (b) and (c). What is the purpose of this distinction? Does the following case, interpreting a similar provision in the Larceny Act 1916, supply an answer?

Billing v Pill

[1954] 1 QB 70, Queen's Bench Division

An army hut, which was constructed in seven sections, rested on a concrete foundation, the floor of the hut being secured to the foundation by bolts let into the concrete. The hut was one of a number erected by the War Office during the war on land used as a gun emplacement. In 1946 the army vacated the huts, and in 1947 the local authority was instructed to demolish them. In 1951 the appellant, without lawful authority, dismantled the hut in question, removed it from the site and re-erected it on his own land. He was convicted by justices of stealing the hut....

LORD GODDARD CJ: Can anybody doubt that the hut in question was erected for a temporary purpose? It can be removed without doing any damage to the freehold at all. It rests upon a concrete bed which is let into the land. I should say that there is no question but that the concrete bed has become part of the land, but the hut which stands upon it has not become part of the land merely because some bolts have been put through the floor of the hut to stabilise or steady it. It was erected merely for a temporary purpose so that the Army personnel who were going to the site for a presumed temporary purpose, to man a gun emplacement during the war, would have somewhere to sleep.

In my opinion, it would be quite wrong to hold that this hut was attached to or formed part of the realty. It was not so attached any more than if one takes a garden seat out into one's garden and, because the seat may be in an exposed position and liable to be blown over, one drives a spike through it to hold it to the ground. In one sense that is an attachment, but it is not an attachment sufficient to make it part of the realty. It is simply a spike put in to hold the chattel firm. In my opinion, this hut was a chattel, remained a chattel and is capable of larceny....

■ NOTES AND QUESTIONS

1. The more difficult a 'thing' is to remove from the ground, the more likely it is that it will be regarded as 'land' or a 'thing forming part of the land'. Should the 'difficulty of removal' take into account the tools possessed by the would-be thief?

2. Section 4 sets out three instances when 'land' or 'things forming part of land' can be stolen.

    (a) If the defendant is in a position of trust then, according to s. 4(2)(a), he can steal land (or things forming part of it) to which his position of trust relates.

    (b) When the defendant is not in possession of land he can steal anything forming part of the land (but not the land itself) (s. 4(2)(b)).

    (c) When the defendant is in possession of the land under a tenancy he can steal a fixture or structure (e.g. a bath or a greenhouse – if a greenhouse is a structure – it is not a fixture: *Dean* v *Andrews and another, The Times*, 25 May 1985).

3. None of the subsections specifically covers a person who has permission to be on the land but has no lease. It is not clear whether such a person would be considered to be 'in possession' of the land. If he were, a curious situation would arise in that he would be in a better position than a person in possession of land under a tenancy.

4. Incorporeal hereditaments, such as rights of way and rent charges, can be stolen by dishonestly conveying the benefit of the right. 'Tenancy' includes a statutory

tenancy. A statutory tenancy arises when an ordinary lease comes to an end but the tenant remains in possession and continues to pay rent to the landlord.

(ii) Mushrooms, flowers, etc.

THEFT ACT 1968

4.—(3) A person who picks mushrooms growing wild on any land, or who picks flowers, fruit or foliage from a plant growing wild on any land, does not (although not in possession of the land) steal what he picks, unless he does it for reward or for sale or other commercial purpose.

For purposes of this subsection 'mushroom' includes any fungus, and 'plant' includes any shrub or tree.

■ NOTES AND QUESTIONS

1. What is the difference between 'severing' something forming a part of the land (s. 4(2)(b)), which can constitute theft, and 'picking' mushrooms, flowers, fruits, etc., which is not criminal under s. 4(3)? If Jill plucks a rose from a rose bush has she picked or severed it? Are 'picking' and 'severing' terms used by a court to justify the result the court wishes to reach?

2. If a plant is 'picked' 'for sale or other commercial purpose', the picker may be guilty of theft. When must the commercial purpose be formed? Dora picks wild blackberries, eats her fill, and then, not wishing to throw the remaining black-berries in the trash, decides to make blackberry jam to sell at the local church bazaar. Has she committed theft?

(iii) Wild creatures

THEFT ACT 1968

4.—(4) Wild creatures, tamed or untamed, shall be regarded as property; but a person cannot steal a wild creature not tamed nor ordinarily kept in captivity, or the carcase of any such creature, unless either it has been reduced into possession by or on behalf of another person and posses-sion of it has not since been lost or abandoned, or another person is in course of reducing it into possession.

R v Howlett

[1968] Crim LR 222, Court of Appeal

H was convicted of stealing, in 1965, mussels from a mussel bed on the foreshore. The foreshore was alleged to belong to S who had granted to L the exclusive right of taking shellfish from it. L had tended the bed in order to try to preserve and improve it but it remained subject to the action of the sea. H appealed on the grounds, *inter alia*, that the mussels were not capable of being stolen since they adhered to the realty, alternatively they were animals *ferae naturae* and not capable of being stolen until reduced into possession.

Held, allowing the appeal, it was not necessary to decide the first question because there was not sufficient evidence that the mussels had been reduced into possession. The most that could be said to have been done was that the bed was tended with a view to improving the growth and edible qualities of the mussels until they were removed from the bed. The mere act of raking over an exist-ing natural bed, and occasionally moving some mussels from a place where they were growing too thickly to a place where they were growing too thinly, and where they would again come to rest and adhere to the soil, did not amount to the reduction into possession of the mussels, particularly since in 1966 the majority of the mussels had disappeared as the result of the action of the sea.

■ NOTES AND QUESTIONS

1. The court in *Howlett* appears to assume that 'wild' refers to the way of life of the creature rather than its disposition. Although this was a decision under the Larceny Act 1916, there seems to be no reason why the position should be any different under the 1968 Act. Thus a wild creature can only be stolen if:
   (a) it is tamed or ordinarily kept in captivity;
   (b) it is in the course of being reduced into another's possession or has been reduced into and remains in another's possession.

2. When is a wild creature tamed? What if a monkey is confined to a cage in a zoo? Left free to roam in a boundaried 'safari park'?

3. If a fox is caught in a trap set by Ellen, has she committed a crime? If an animal rights activist sees the fox and releases it from the trap, has the activist committed a crime? What social and political values are reflected in the legal answers to these questions?

4. At what point in time has a bird which has been shot by a hunter from several hundred metres away been reduced into possession such that it can be stolen?

C: Belonging to another

Section 5 of the 1968 Act expands the scope of theft to protect not only those who own property, but also those who possess or control property. This section embraces even those who are illegally in possession of the property. Thus, it is possible to steal from a thief. For the purposes of the Theft Act 1968, property 'belongs to another' when that 'other' has ownership, possession or control of the property. Section 5(3) extends the concept of property to cover the situation where, although ownership of the property has passed to the defendant, the defendant is under an obligation to deal with that property in a particular way. Section 5(4) also extends the notion of property belonging to another to the situation where the defendant has received the relevant item only because of a mistake made by another person. Where the defendant is under an obligation to return the property, the law regards ownership as being retained by the person making the mistake.

THEFT ACT 1968

5.—(1) Property shall be regarded as belonging to any person having possession or control of it, or having in it any proprietary right or interest (not being an equitable interest arising only from an agreement to transfer or grant an interest).

Several issues arise under this provision of the statute:

(i) What is a proprietary right or interest?

The TA 1968 was drafted on the assumption that the property appropriated belonged to another at the time of appropriation. Following *Lawrence, Gomez* and *Hinks* (above), this is arguably no longer the case. However, the term 'belong to another' is not restricted to the owner of the property, but includes those in rightful possession or control of the property.

An owner of land owns anything that is on the land if he intends to exclude trespassers. This can extend to property the existence of which the owner is unaware.

R v Woodman
[1974] QB 754, Court of Appeal

The defendant was charged with the theft of scrap metal remnants from a disused factory site. The occupier of the site had no knowledge of the existence of the scrap, although a barbed-wire fence had been erected around the site to exclude trespassers. The defendant submitted that there was no case to answer on the ground that the scrap did not belong to another within the meaning of s. 5(1) of the Theft Act 1968. The recorder allowed the case to go to the jury on the question whether the occupier was in control of the scrap, and the defendant was convicted.

On appeal against conviction:—

Held, dismissing the appeal, that a person in control of a site, by excluding others from it, was prima facie also in control of articles on that site within the meaning of s. 5(1) of the Theft Act 1968, it being immaterial that he was unconcious [sic] of their existence; and accordingly the case had been rightly allowed to go to the jury.

Per curiam. If articles of serious criminal consequence, such as explosives or drugs, were placed within the barbed-wire fence by some third person in circumstances in which the occupier had no means of knowledge, it might produce a different result from that which arose under the general presumption....

■ NOTES AND QUESTIONS

1. Why does the court maintain that the victim's awareness of the existence of the items taken is irrelevant?

2. Abandoned property belongs to nobody and cannot be the subject of theft. However, in *Williams* v *Phillips* (1957) 41 Cr App R 5, the Court of Appeal held that property was not abandoned even after it had been put in a dustbin for the council to collect. But why is throwing property into a dust bin not a clear-cut indication of an intent to abandon? What more must an owner do?

3. Why did the Court adopt one test for the objects in *Woodman* and suggest the possibility of another test for objects of 'serious consequence'? Unlike in some countries there is not a distinction between grand and petty larceny (theft) in the UK. If it is a distinction worth making, what should the test be in the latter case?

Property can 'belong' to more than one person. In the case of a partnership, each partner has an interest in the partnership property. This is important for it means that one partner can steal partnership property as the thief would in effect be stealing the property of the other partners.

R v Bonner
[1970] 1 WLR 838, Court of Appeal

EDMUND DAVIES LJ: The facts which gave rise to this complicated trial were that on May 16, 1969, Bonner and the other three appellants called at the house of a Mr Webb. Putting it quite neutrally for the moment, Bonner and Webb were business associates. The defence was, in fact, that they were partners and, therefore, co-owners of all the property with which the trial was concerned.

Having called with a van at Webb's house in the afternoon at a time when Webb was out, they broke the lock of a garage and splintered the door and, having gained access that way, they loaded some metal from inside the garage on to the van and Anthony Town and Michael Town claimed that they were moving it for Bonner, who they thought had a right to do what he had asked them to do. Bonner's defence was that he honestly thought he had a right to take the lead as it was partnership property owned by himself and Webb, and, in any event, he did not intend to deprive Webb of it permanently.

Webb's case at first was that there was no partnership at all, and then that it was not what he called 'a true partnership'. During his evidence he specifically denied that he had ever applied for registration in the Business Names Register of himself and Bonner as partners. But this court has been furnished with a document, which unhappily was not before the lower court. It is a certified copy of an application made on March 8, 1966, for registration by a firm, and the business name is 'J. Webb, Excavation & Demolition Co.,' the partners are described as 'Joseph Webb' and 'George Andrew Bonner,' and it was signed by each of them.

I said a little earlier that the object of the Theft Act, 1968, was to get rid of the subtleties and, indeed, in many cases the absurd anomalies of the pre-existing law. The view of this court is that in relation to partnership property the provisions in the Theft Act, 1968, have the following result: provided there is the basic ingredient of dishonesty, provided there be no question of there being a claim of right made in good faith, provided there be an intent permanently to deprive, one partner can commit theft of partnership property just as much as one person can commit the theft of the property of another to whom he is a complete stranger.

Early though these days are, this matter has not gone without comment by learned writers. Professor Smith in his valuable work on the Theft Act, 1968, expresses his own view quite clearly in paragraph 80 under the heading 'Co-owners and partners' in this way:

> D and P are co-owners of a car. D sells the car without P's consent. Since P has a proprietary right in the car, it belongs to him under s. 5(1). The position is precisely the same where a partner appropriates the partnership property.

In the joint work of Professor Smith and Professor Hogan, the matter is thus dealt with (*Smith and Hogan's 'Criminal Law'*, 2nd ed. (1969), p. 361):

> ...D and P...may...be joint owners of property. Obviously, there is no reason in principle why D should not be treated as a thief if he dishonestly appropriates P's share, and he is so treated under the Theft Act.

We thus have no doubt that there may be an 'appropriation' by a partner within the meaning of the Act, and that in a proper case there is nothing in law to prevent his being convicted of the theft of partnership property.

(ii) Theft of one's own property

This may occur where another person has a right to possess or control the property which the owner violates. A typical case might involve a lease. Say that Gerald rents his car to Neil for a week. Mid-week he finds himself in desperate need of an automobile and, using his spare key, takes the car without asking Neil's permission. Gerald in fact is guilty of stealing his own car.

The situation where a second individual has an interest in an owner's property such that the owner can commit theft of his own property can arise in other situations as well:

R v Turner (No. 2)
[1971] 1 WLR 901, Court of Appeal

The defendant took the car of which he was the registered owner to a garage to have it repaired. Those repairs having been practically completed, the car was left in the road outside the garage. The defendant called at the garage and told the proprietor that he would return the following day, pay him and take the car: instead, he took the car away several hours later without paying for the repairs.

He was charged on indictment with theft of the car contrary to s. 1 of the Theft Act 1968. The defendant submitted that the car did not 'belong' to the proprietor within the meaning of s. 5(1) of the Theft Act 1968 and that the appropriation was not dishonest within the meaning of s. 2(1)(a) of the Act.

LORD PARKER CJ: This court is quite satisfied that there is no ground whatever for qualifying the words 'possession or control' in any way. It is sufficient if it is found that the person from whom the property is taken, or to use the words of the Act, appropriated, was at the time in fact in possession or control. At the trial there was a long argument as to whether that possession or control must be lawful, it being said that by reason of the fact that this car was subject to a hire purchase agreement, Mr Brown could never even as against the defendant obtain lawful possession or control. As I have said, this court is quite satisfied that the judge was quite correct in telling the jury they need not bother about lien, and that they need not bother about hire purchase agreements. The only question was whether Mr Brown was in fact in possession or control.

■ NOTES AND QUESTIONS

1. In *Turner* the garage almost certainly had a better right to possession of the car than the owner *at the time it was taken by him*. This is because the garage would have had a repairer's lien on the car – a right to keep the car until the bill was paid. However, the judge told the jury that they were not concerned with liens and the Court of Appeal upheld this direction. What if the bill for repairs was greater than originally agreed by the parties, the owner had paid the amount originally agreed and then taken the car – would this be theft?

2. Suppose a book is stolen from Mary, who later finds it among the possessions of the thief. If Mary believes it is against the law to take the book back, is she guilty of theft if she takes it?

3. Can a mother steal property belonging to her son of three months? Thirteen years? Thirty years? Can a husband steal the property of his wife, and vice versa (See TA 1968, s. 30)? Should the law abet domestic strife by allowing prosecutions for theft where one family member appropriates the property of another family member?

(iii) To whom does trust property belong?

THEFT ACT 1968

5.—(1) Property shall be regarded as belonging to any person having possession or control of it, or having in it any proprietary right or interest (not being an equitable interest arising only from an agreement to transfer or grant an interest).

An ordinary trust is created when one is appointed as a trustee to look after property on behalf of others. Parents, for example, may set up trusts for their children, and guardians may set up trusts for their wards. Both a trustee and the beneficiaries of a trust have interests in the property that are legally protected.

In contrast, a constructive trust is created when a court believes that the imposition of a trust-like framework will do justice in particular circumstances. In

Attorney-General's Reference (No. 1 of 1985) [1986] QB 491, the court excluded interests arising under constructive trusts from the ambit of the Theft Act. However, the seemingly opposite conclusion was reached in *Shadrokh-Cigari*, a decision which also has implications for the interpretation of s. 5(4) (see below).

R v Shadrokh-Cigari

[1988] Crim LR 465, Court of Appeal

The appellant was convicted of four counts of theft. He acted as guardian to his nephew whose father in Iran arranged for money to be paid to the child's bank account from the USA. Through an error by the United States bank $286,000 was credited to the account instead of $286. At the appellant's suggestion the child signed an authority for the issue of four banker's drafts drawn in favour of the appellant for sums of £51,300, £64,000, £53,000 and £29,000. The appellant paid two into his own bank account and used the others to open other accounts to his name. By the time of his arrest some three weeks later only £21,000 remained. He appealed against conviction on the ground that the judge should have directed the jury that they had to be satisfied that the drafts belonged to the Bank and that had he done so the jury would have been bound to have concluded that the drafts did not belong to the bank but were the property of the appellant and so there was no question of him appropriating property belonging to another.

Held, dismissing the appeal, the submission erred in assuming that the entire proprietary interest in the drafts existed and vested in the appellant leaving the bank with no rights at all. The mistake of the United States bank totally undermined the basic assumption upon which the English bank issued the drafts, namely that the funds which had been received could properly be dealt with as directed by the account holder. As between the English bank and the appellant, the transaction fell fairly and squarely within the principles of the law relating to the mistake—*Kelly* v *Solari* [1941] 9 M & W 547. The mistake must be fundamental or basic, one in respect of the underlying assumption of the contract or transaction—*Norwich Union* v *Price* [1934] AC 455. That was so here. If the mistake must be one of fact rather than law, that condition was satisfied in the present case. Thus the appellant was under an obligation to make restoration of the instruments on the basis that the English bank retained an equitable proprietary interest in the drafts as a result of the mistake. The fact that the choses in action created by the drafts could not be owned by the bank, since they were debts due from the bank was irrelevant. The bank created the drafts and before delivery they owned them, although as promissory notes they were inchoate and incomplete. Upon delivery under the mistake, the bank retained an equitable interest in those instruments. Such an equitable interest amounted to property within s. 5(1) of the Theft Act 1968. That conclusion was not only supported by s. 5(4) of the 1968 Act, but could be reached by another route through the application of that subsection. Even if it could not be said that the property belonged to another in the sense of that other having proprietary rights over the property itself, nevertheless (other things being equal) the property was to be regarded for the purposes of theft as belonging to that other even if the person getting it was only under an obligation to restore the proceeds of the property or its value as opposed to the property itself. The appellant was obliged to restore the proceeds or value of the instruments.

■ NOTES AND QUESTIONS

1. In *Shadrokh-Cigari* the Court held that an equitable proprietary interest arising from the imposition of a constructive trust *did* amount to property within s. 5(1). As we shall see, where there is an obligation to make restoration of property obtained because of a mistake, s. 5(4) creates fictional ownership in the original owner for the purpose of the statute. In the light of s. 5(4), why was it necessary for the Court to decide on an extended meaning of s. 5(1)?

2. May the court in *Shadrokh-Cigari* have been influenced by the amount of money taken by the defendant? By the defendant's evident dishonesty? Are these legitimate considerations for a court to take into account?

THEFT ACT 1968

5.—(2) Where property is subject to a trust, the persons to whom it belongs shall be regarded as including any person having a right to enforce the trust, and an intention to defeat the trust shall be regarded accordingly as an intention to deprive of the property any person having that right.

A beneficiary of a trust has a right to enforce the trust. A charitable trust, which may or may not have particular individuals as beneficiaries, is enforceable by the Attorney-General so that property which is the subject to such a trust will be regarded as belonging to the Attorney-General. Any non-charitable trust without human beneficiaries will be regarded as belonging to the person entitled to the residue. This subsection makes it impossible for anyone dishonestly taking trust funds to argue that the funds belonged to no one.

(v) When does an obligation arise to retain and deal with another's property?

THEFT ACT 1968

5.—(3) Where a person receives property from or on account of another, and is under an obligation to the other to retain and deal with that property or its proceeds in a particular way, the property or proceeds shall be regarded (as against him) as belonging to the other.

When does an obligation envisaged by the section arise, and to what property does it attach?

R v *Hall*
[1973] 1 QB 126, Court of Appeal

The defendant, who carried on the business of a travel agent, received money as deposits and payments for air trips to America. No flights were provided for the defendant's clients and no money was refunded. He was charged with seven counts of theft, contrary to s. 1 of the Theft Act 1968. The defendant claimed that the money received had become his property which he had applied in the conduct of the firm's business and that he had not been guilty of theft merely because the firm had failed and no money remained. He was convicted.

The defendant appealed on the ground, *inter alia*, that the moneys belonged to him and not to his clients as he was under no obligation, under s. 5(3) of the Theft Act 1968, to retain and deal with the money or its proceedings in a particular way.

EDMUND DAVIES LJ: Point (1) turns on the application of s. 5(3) of the Theft Act 1968, which provides that:

> Where a person receives property from or on account of another, and is under an obligation to the other to retain and deal with that property or its proceeds in a particular way, the property or proceeds shall be regarded (as against him) as belonging to the other.

Mr Jolly submitted that in the circumstances arising in [previous] cases there arose no such 'obligation' upon the defendant. He referred us to a passage in the eighth report of the Criminal Law Revision Committee (1966) (Cmnd. 2977), at p. 127, which reads:

> Subsection (3) provides for the special case where property is transferred to a person to retain and deal with for a particular person and he misapplies it or its proceeds. An example would be the treasurer of a holiday fund. The person in question is in law the owner of the property; but the subsection treats the property, as against him, as belonging to the persons to whom he owes the duty to retain and deal with the property as agreed. He will therefore be guilty of stealing from them if he misapplies the property or its proceeds.

Mr Jolly submitted that the example there given is, for all practical purposes, identical with the actual facts in *R* v *Pulham* (unreported) June 15, 1971, where, incidentally, s. 5(3) was not discussed, the convictions there being quashed, as we have already indicated, owing to the lack of a proper direction as to the accused's state of mind at the time he appropriated. But he submits that the position of a treasurer of a solitary fund is quite different from that of a person like the defendant, who was in general, and genuine, business as a travel agent, and to whom people pay money in order to achieve a certain object—in the present cases, to obtain charter flights to America. It is true, he concedes, that thereby the travel agent undertakes a contractual obligation in relation to arranging flights and at the proper time paying the air line and any other expenses. Indeed, the defendant throughout acknowledged that this was so, though contending that in some of the seven cases it was the other party who was in breach. But what Mr Jolly resists is that in such circumstances the travel agent 'is under an obligation' to the client 'to retain and deal with . . . in a particular way' sums paid to him in such circumstances.

What cannot of itself be decisive of the matter is the fact that the defendant paid the money into the firm's general trading account. As Widgery J said in *R* v *Yule* [1964] 1 QB 5, decided under s. 20(1)(iv) of the Larceny Act 1916, at p. 10:

> The fact that a particular sum is paid into a particular banking account . . . does not affect the right of persons interested in that sum or any duty of the solicitor either towards his client or towards third parties with regard to disposal of that sum.

Nevertheless, when a client goes to a firm carrying on the business of travel agents and pays them money, he expects that in return he will, in due course, receive the tickets and other documents necessary for him to accomplish the trip for which he is paying, and the firm are 'under an obligation' to perform their part to fulfil his expectation and are liable to pay him damages if they do not. But, in our judgment, what was not here established was that these clients expected them 'to retain and deal with that property or its proceeds in a particular way,' and that an 'obligation' to do this was undertaken by the defendant.

We must make clear, however, that each case turns on its own facts. Cases could, we suppose, conceivably arise where by some special arrangement (preferably evidenced by documents), the client could impose upon the travel agent an 'obligation' falling within s. 5(3). But no such special arrangement was made in any of the seven cases here being considered. It is true that in some of them documents were signed by the parties; thus, in respect of the counts 1 and 3 incidents there was a clause to the effect that the 'People to People' organisation did not guarantee to refund deposits if withdrawals were made later than a certain date; and in respect of counts 6, 7 and 8 the defendant wrote promising 'a full refund' after the flights paid for failed to materialise. But neither in those nor in the remaining two cases (in relation to which there was no documentary evidence of any kind) was there, in our judgment, such a special arrangement as would give rise to an 'obligation' within s. 5(3).

It follows from this that, despite what on any view must be condemned as scandalous conduct by the defendant, in our judgment upon this ground alone this appeal must be allowed and the conviction quashed.

R v Hayes

(1977) 64 Cr App Rep 82, Court of Appeal

The appellant started trading with another man as estate agents. He received money from clients as deposits on account of sales or purchase of houses. He was charged, *inter alia*, on 11 counts alleging theft contrary to s. 1 of the Theft Act 1968. In summing-up the judge, *inter alia*, failed to invite the jury to consider whether there was an obligation on the appellant to deal with the clients' money within s. 5(3) of the Act of 1968; nor did he direct them that there was an obligation on the prosecution to prove that at the time when the misappropriation took place there was already an intention to be dishonest. The appellant was convicted, *inter alia*, of theft.

...

THE LORD CHIEF JUSTICE: The case really revolved around s. 5(3) because, as will be understood from the brief extracts I have already given of the facts, the real issue which arose between the prosecution and the defence was whether the appellant was appropriating and therefore stealing property of another which would amount to an offence under the Theft Act 1968, or whether the true position was that he was apparently appropriating or stealing money which had become his because it had become his property according to this argument when the payment was made.

The circumstances which gave rise to count 1 form a useful illustration of the working of those principles. In the transaction on October 23, 1970 the appellant through Blake gave a receipt to a Mr Newman for £300, which was described as being a deposit and part-payment of a dwelling house at Sheppart Street, Stoke, the purchase price being £600. That money was paid over in cash. It was not paid into the bank, the bank at that time having only a credit balance of £13 in it. It was entered in a book kept by the appellant which was intended to disclose cash in hand, and it was entered in that book at a time in October 1970 when, according to the book, there was cash in hand to the tune of £6,480. The prosecution sought, not without some success, to show that this record of cash in hand was itself bogus and that the money referred to as being in hand never was in hand. But conclusions of that sort were not necessarily obtained on the directions which were given to the jury in this case, and I cite those facts merely to disclose the oddities of the transaction upon which count 1 is based, the other counts being based on similar oddities.

It is important, we think, to compare the situation in *Hall* [1973] 1 QB 126 with the situation in our present case. In *Hall* (*supra*) the argument on the one side was that the ticket agent receiving the money for the tickets was obliged to use that money in a particular way and to go and buy tickets with it. On the other side it was argued that he was not bound to use the particular money in a particular way. All that happened on his receiving the money was that he incurred a civil responsibility to carry out his side of the bargain. Edmund Davies LJ is taking the point there that in the absence of some special term in the contract the second view is the right one.

Convictions quashed.

Davidge v *Bunnett*

[1984] Crim LR 297, Queen's Bench Division

In July 1982 D shared a flat with two other young women, C and McF. In September 1982 they were joined by H. There was an oral agreement to share the costs of gas, electricity and telephone. The gas account was in C's name. In October 1982 C received a gas bill for £159.75. D, C and McF each agreed to pay £50, and H the balance of £9.75. D did not have a bank account. The others all did, and gave D cheques in the appropriate sums, made payable to P, D's employer. They thought that D would either encash the cheques with P, add her own £50 and pay the gas bill, or that P would write out a cheque for the Gas Board on receipt of funds totalling £159.75. They did not expect D to apply any actual banknotes received from P to the discharge of the bill. On November 18, 1982, £59.75 was paid to the Gas Board. The balance of £100 was carried over to the next account in December. In January 1983 C received a final demand. C asked D to look into the matter, to which D agreed. D then left the flat without giving notice or leaving a forwarding address. C and McF later discovered that their cheques for £50 had been cashed on November 1, 1982. When interviewed by the police, D admitted 'I spent the £100 on Christmas presents but intended to pay it back.' The magistrates convicted D of theft, finding that D was under a legal obligation to apply the proceeds of C and McF's cheques to the payment of the gas bill. They also found that the proceeds of the cheques were property belonging to another within the meaning of the Theft Act 1968, and that there was evidence of an appropriation of two sums of £50, notwithstanding the payment of £59.75.

Held, dismissing the appeal, that the position was simple. D was under an obligation to use the cheques or their proceeds in whatever way she saw fit to long as they were applied *pro tanto* to the discharge of the gas bill. This could have been achieved by one cheque from her employer, or a banker's draft, or her own cheque had so opened her own bank account, or by endorsing the other cheques. Hence the magistrates' finding that she was not obliged to use the actual banknotes. Using the proceeds of the cheques on presents amounted to a very negation of her obligation to discharge the bill. She was under an obligation to deal with the proceeds in a particular way. As against D, the proceeds of the cheques were property belonging to another within s. 5(3) of the Act.

R v Wain

[1995] 2 Cr App R 660, Court of Appeal

McCOWAN LJ : On January 9, 1992 in the Crown Court at York, before His Honour Judge Herrod QC, the appellant was convicted of theft and sentenced to six months' imprisonment. He appeals against that conviction, as of right, the trial judge having granted a certificate of fitness for appeal on the day of the conviction. The judge also granted the appellant bail on the same date.

It was the case for the Crown that the appellant had stolen £2,833.25 which he had helped to raise for charity over a nine month period in 1990/1991. The Yorkshire Television Company is the guiding hand behind a trust called 'The Telethon Trust'. This raises monies for various charities and distributes them amongst those it considers most deserving. The monies are raised by way of a bi-annual appeal, during which various people organise events and onlookers make donations to charity, which are collected by the organiser. The matter is well-publicised and selected events are screened on Yorkshire Television.

Each organiser running an event is required to complete a registration form and return it to the television company. Once the form is returned Telethon Trust, according to their usual practice, send out a whole package of documents which provide help in organising events, a recommendation that the money be paid into a separate bank account and information on where to obtain collecting boxes, balloons and such like. In this case the appellant said that he had never received such a package from Telethon Trust, but nonetheless he did in fact open a separate bank account in the name of the Scarborough Telethon Appeal.

The appellant organised a number of successful events on Whit Monday 1990, including two discotheques. The amount raised was £2,833.25. He was invited along to Yorkshire Television Headquarters where he presented a dummy cheque to a television celebrity. The monies remained in the bank account that he had opened until September 5, 1990.

In the meantime, the Deputy Chief Executive of Yorkshire Television contacted him requesting the monies which he had raised for Telethon. The appellant told him that the monies were still outstanding, and some of them, at any rate, had not yet been paid.

On September 5 one of the company representatives, Miss Wills, visited the appellant with a view to collecting the money on the spot. The appellant, on this occasion, had a different story. He told her that he was unable to hand over a cheque without some second signatory. He did, however, get authority from Miss Wills to transfer the money into his own account, which he did that day. That meant he was able to, and did, hand over to her a cheque drawn on his own business account. That seemed all right, but in fact the cheque was not honoured due to insufficient funds in his account.

He continued to make excuses on a number of occasions thereafter, even stating that he had broken his arms and was unable to sign cheques. He sent four cheques in all, none of which were honoured. In a period of about six days, following the transfer of the money into his own account, the appellant withdrew about £640 in cash (something which, the prosecution pointed out, he had never done before). He must have known, they said, that that cash was coming from the monies he had paid in, monies which belonged to The Telethon Trust.

The appellant was eventually arrested on February 21, 1991 and charged with the theft of the sum of £2,833.25....

It seems to us that the approach of the court in *Lethbridge* [1987] Crim LR 59 was a very narrow one based, apparently, on the finding by the justices that there was no requirement of the charity that the appellant hand over the same notes and coins. Neither was there in the present case. But what the Divisional Court does not appear to have considered in that case was the trust aspect. It was either not argued or the court felt, for some reason, that it could not be considered because of that finding of the justices. We are unable to agree with them about that. In our judgment, the criticisms of that case by Professor Smith are fully justified.

As we have already indicated, we feel that in deciding, as they did in the *Lethbridge* case, the Divisional Court was not following the decision in *Davidge* v *Bunnett*. In our judgment, those decisions conflict and we prefer the decision in *Davidge* v *Bunnett*. There the obligation on the defendant was 'to keep in existence a fund sufficient to pay the bill'. So also in the *Lethbridge* case, and so also in the present case.

Leaving aside all authorities, it seems to us that by virtue of section 5(3), the appellant was plainly under an obligation to retain, if not the actual notes and coins, at least their proceeds, that is to say the money credited in the bank account which he opened for the trust with the actual property. When he took the money credited to that account and moved it over to his own bank account, it was still the proceeds of the notes and coins donated which he proceeded to use for his own purposes, thereby appropriating them. There remained the question of dishonesty which Judge Herrod properly left to the jury.

We would add this. Whether a person in the position of the appellant is a trustee is to be judged on an objective basis. It is an obligation imposed on him by law. It is not essential that he should have realised that he was a trustee, but of course the question remains as to whether he was acting honestly or dishonestly in using the money for his own purposes. That is a matter of fact for the jury.

...

■ NOTES AND QUESTIONS

1. The above cases raise intriguing questions. Do the decisions turn on the obligation of the holder of the funds or the expectations of those whose moneys comprise the funds? Or does the key to understanding the decisions lie in the philosophical predilections of the court deciding the case? In *Hall* the court quashed the conviction of a defendant who it declared had engaged in scandalous and condemnable conduct; but why should such an evidently dishonest defendant escape his just desserts? In contrast, in *Wain*, the court said that it was prepared to 'leave aside all authorities', presumably to achieve what it regarded as the appropriate disposition in the case.

2. In *R* v *Klineberg and Marsden* [1999] Crim LR 417 the Court of Appeal applied s. 5(3) to a case where purchasers of timeshares had paid money on the basis that it would be held by a stakeholding trust company until the apartments were ready to be occupied. Only £233 of the £500,000 paid by the intending purchasers was transmitted to the trust company. The money was deemed to 'belong to the purchasers' because of s. 5(3).

3. Will s. 5(3) be of use only where the relationship between the victim and the defendant is contractual? See *R* v *Hallam and Blackburn* [1995] Crim LR 323. In civil law a defendant's liability will turn on the obligations of a person in a fiduciary position. At what point does a matter of family trust become a legal obligation? See *Attorney-General for Hong Kong* v *Reid* [1994] 1 AC 324. Should the criminal law embrace a similar approach?

4. Will the obligation in s. 5(3) arise only when a contractual relationship obliges the defendant to keep in existence for a reasonable time a fund sufficient to fulfil the purpose for which the money was given?

5. Carla is given money by Abdul, her uncle. He tells her that the money is to pay for pet food for his dog. As she leaves to go shopping, the window cleaner arrives, demanding payment, so she uses the money to pay him. Has Carla committed theft? Would it make a difference if the window cleaner was Carla's lover and the money was later used to buy Carla a present?

Must the 'obligation' be legally enforceable?

R v *Mainwaring*

(1982) 74 Cr App R 99, Court of Appeal

LAWTON LJ: The prosecution case was that when Mainwaring and Madders received money from prospective purchasers they did so knowing that it was in part payment of villas purchased from Frenchmen or Spaniards, that they were under an obligation to hand that money over to the developers in France or Spain, as the case might be, and that it would have been, and in fact was, dishonest of them to appropriate the money there and then for their own purposes.

...

Clearly there was some confusion in the mind of the learned judge about the operation of s. 5(3) of the Theft Act 1968.

We think that it may help judges if we make this comment about that section of the Act. Whether or not an obligation arises is a matter of law, because an obligation must be a legal obligation. But a legal obligation arises only in certain circumstances, and in many cases the circumstances cannot be known until the facts have been established. It is for the jury, not the judge, to establish the facts, if they are in dispute.

What, in our judgment, a judge ought to do is this: if the facts relied upon by the prosecution are in dispute he should direct the jury to make their findings on the facts, and then say to them: 'If you find the facts to be such-and-such, then I direct you as a matter of law that a legal obligation arose to which s. 5(3) applies.'

R v *Meech*

[1974] QB 549, Court of Appeal

ROSKILL LJ: . . . A man named McCord had obtained a cheque for £1,450 from a hire-purchase finance company by means of a forged instrument. The cheque itself was a perfectly valid document. McCord, who was an undischarged bankrupt, feared that were he to cash this cheque himself his crime would be more likely to be discovered than if he persuaded a friend to cash it for him. McCord, therefore, asked Meech (to whom McCord owed £40) to cash the cheque for him and Meech agreed so to do. At the time he agreed so to do Meech was wholly unaware of the dishonest means whereby McCord had become possessed of the cheque. Meech paid the cheque into his own account at a branch of Lloyds Bank Ltd. at High Wycombe on September 11, 1972. The bank was seemingly unwilling to allow him to cash the cheque until it had been cleared. On September 13, 1972, Meech drew his own cheque for £1,410 on his own account at that branch and that cheque was duly cashed by the bank on that day. The difference between the two sums was represented by McCord's £40 debt to Meech. By the time this cheque was cashed, the original cheque had been cleared. Between the paying in of the original cheque on September 11 and the obtaining of the cash on September 13, Meech became aware that McCord had acquired the original cheque dishonestly.

We were told by counsel that Meech, following legal argument at the end of the evidence, was allowed by the judge to be re-called. Meech then told the jury that not only did he find out about McCord's dishonesty but that he then honestly believed that if he cashed the cheque he would commit an offence. In view of the direction given by the judge to which we refer later, we think it clear that the jury must be taken to have rejected this story of honest belief on Meech's part.

Before the cheque was cashed but after Meech discovered its dishonest origin, Meech agreed with Parslow and Jolliffe that after the cheque was cashed Meech would take the money to a prearranged destination. The two other men were to join him there. A fake robbery, with Meech as the victim, was to be staged and indeed was staged, the purpose clearly being to provide some explanation to McCord of Meech's inability to hand over the money to McCord.

This was done; Parslow and Jolliffe between them removed the money after leaving Meech as the apparent victim. The bogus robbery was reported to the police, who being less credulous than the three men imagined McCord might be, investigated the matter and soon became convinced that the robbery story was bogus, as indeed it was soon shown to be. It is clear that Meech was influenced by the thought that even if the bogus nature of the robbery were suspected by McCord, McCord would never dare to go to the police and complain for that would involve revealing his own dishonesty.

...

Starting from this premise—that 'obligation' means 'legal obligation'—it was argued that even at the time when Meech was ignorant of the dishonest origin of the cheque, as he was at the time when he agreed to cash the cheque and hand the proceeds less the £40 to McCord, McCord could never have enforced that obligation because McCord had acquired the cheque illegally. In our view this submission is unsound in principle. The question has to be looked at from Meech's point of view, not McCord's.

Meech plainly assumed an 'obligation' to McCord which, on the facts then known to him, he remained obliged to fulfil and, on the facts as found, he must be taken at that time honestly to have intended to fulfil. The fact that on the true facts if known McCord might not and indeed would not subsequently have been permitted to enforce that obligation in a civil court does not prevent that 'obligation' on Meech having arisen. The argument confuses the creation of the obligation with the subsequent discharge of that obligation either by performance or otherwise. That the obligation might have become impossible of performance by Meech or of enforcement by McCord on grounds of illegality or for reasons of public policy is irrelevant. The opening words of s. 5(3) clearly look to the time of the creation of or the acceptance of the obligation by the bailee and not to the time of performance by him of the obligation so created and accepted by him.

■ **NOTES AND QUESTIONS**

1. Does Lord Roskill's judgment in *Meech* turn on whether the obligation was legally enforceable, or whether the defendant believed the obligation to be enforceable? In fact no legally enforceable obligation may ever have arisen between Meech and McCord. Section 5(3) refers to a situation where the defendant *is* 'under an obligation', not where he believes himself to be so. A possible way out of the difficulty would be to hold that a legal obligation did arise but it was not such as could be enforced by the dishonest McCord. But this would raise the question of whether there is in law a concept of an 'unenforceable obligation', which would presumably be useless to its possessor.

2. Whether s. 5(3) operates where no legally enforceable obligation has in fact arisen but the defendant believes himself to be under such an obligation must remain doubtful. Where the section does operate, ownership of the property concerned, by a fiction, remains with the person who has given the property to the defendant. The property therefore 'belongs to another' within the definition of theft. In view of *Gomez* and *Hinks* (above), may s. 5(3) no longer be necessary?

3. In deciding *Meech*, may the court have been influenced by the evident dishonesty of the defendants?

(vi) When does an obligation arise to restore property obtained as a result of another's mistake?

THEFT ACT 1968

5.—(4) Where a person gets property by another's mistake, and is under an obligation to make restoration (in whole or in part) of the property or its proceeds or of the value thereof, then to the extent of that obligation the property or proceeds shall be regarded (as against him) as belonging to the person entitled to restoration, and an intention not to make restoration shall be regarded accordingly as an intention to deprive that person of the property or proceeds.

Attorney-General's Reference (No. 1 of 1983)
[1985] QB 182, Court of Appeal

LORD LANE CJ: This is a reference under s. 36 of the Criminal Justice Act 1972 by the Attorney-General. It arises by virtue of the following facts. The respondent is a woman police officer and she received her pay from the Receiver of the Metropolitan Police. Owing to an error in the receiver's department she was credited, in a way which will have to be described in more detail in a moment, with the sum of £74.74 for wages and overtime in respect of a day when she was not at work at all. That amount, together with other sums which were properly due to her, was paid into her bank by direct debit by the receiver's bank. She knew nothing of the error until later, though it was not proved precisely when. There was some evidence before the jury that she had decided to say nothing about this unsolicited windfall which had come her way, and had decided to take no action about it after she discovered the error. No demand for payment of the sum was made by the Receiver of the Metropolitan Police or anyone else.

...

First of all, what is the legal position with regard to the payment of money by one bank to another for the credit of a customer's account? The position was described in clear language by Lord Goddard CJ in *R v Davenport* [1954] 1 WLR 569. He said [1954] 1 All ER 602, 603:

> although we talk about people having money in a bank, the only person who has money in a bank is a banker. If I pay money into my bank, either by paying cash or a cheque, that money at once becomes the money of the banker. The relationship between banker and customer is that of debtor and creditor. He does not hold my money as an agent or trustee. The leading case of *Foley* v *Hill* (1848) 2 HL Cas 28 exploded that idea. When the banker is paying out, whether in cash over the counter or whether by crediting the bank account of somebody else, he is paying out of his own money, not my money, but he is debiting me in my account with him. I have a chose in action, that is to say, I have a right to expect that the banker will honour my cheque, but he does it out of his own money.

From that exposition of the true relationship between bank and client, it follows that what the respondent in the present case got was simply the debt due to her from her own bank. That is so unless her account was overdrawn or overdrawn beyond any overdraft limit, in which case she did not even get that right to money. That point is made in a decision of this court in *R v Kohn* (1979) 69 Cr App R 395. There was no evidence in the present case as to whether the respondent's bank balance was in credit, overdrawn or anything about overdraft limits imposed by the manager of the bank. It was assumed on all hands that the account was in credit.

That brings us to the question of the basic definition of theft, which is to be found in s. 1(1) of the Theft Act 1968, which provides: 'A person is guilty of theft if he dishonestly appropriates property belonging to another with the intention of permanently depriving the other of it; and "thief" and "steal" shall be construed accordingly.'

The property in the present case was the debt owed by the bank to the respondent and in order to show that that can be property one turns to s. 4(1) of the Act of 1968 which reads: 'Property includes money and all other property, real or personal, including things in action and other intangible property.' The debt here was a thing in action, therefore the property was capable of being stolen.

It will be apparent that, at first blush, that debt did not belong to anyone except the respondent herself. She was the only person who had the right to go to her bank and demand the handing over of that £74.74. Had there been no statutory provision which altered that particular situation that would have been the end of the case, but if one turns to s. 5(4) of the Act, one finds these words:

> Where a person gets property by another's mistake, and is under an obligation to make restoration (in whole or in part) of the property or its proceeds or of the value thereof, then to the extent

of that obligation the property or proceeds shall be regarded (as against him) as belonging to the person entitled to restoration, and an intention not to make restoration shall be regarded accordingly as an intention to deprive that person of the property or proceeds.

In order to determine the effect of that subsection upon this case one has to take it piece by piece to see what the result is read against the circumstances of this particular prosecution. First of all: 'Did the respondent get property?' The word 'get' is about as wide a word as could possibly have been adopted by the draftsman of the Act. The answer is 'Yes,' the respondent in this case did get her chose in action, that is, her right to sue the bank for the debt which they owed her—money which they held in their hands to which she was entitled by virtue of the contract between bank and customer.

Secondly: 'Did she get it by another's mistake?' The answer to that is plainly: 'Yes.' The Receiver of the Metropolitan Police made the mistake of thinking she was entitled to £74.74 when she was not entitled to that at all.

'Was she under an obligation to make restoration of either the property or its proceeds or its value?' We take each of those in turn. 'Was she under an obligation to make restoration of the property?'—the chose in action. The answer to that is 'No.' It was something which could not be restored in the ordinary meaning of the word. 'Was she under an obligation to make restoration of its proceeds?' The answer to that is 'No.' There were no proceeds of the chose in action to restore. 'Was she under an obligation to make restoration of the value thereof?'—the value of the chose in action. The answer to that seems to us to be 'Yes.'

As a result of the provisions of s. 5(4) the debt of £74.74 due from the respondent's bank to the respondent notionally belonged to the Receiver of the Metropolitan Police; therefore the prosecution, up to this point, have succeeded in proving—remarkable though it may seem—that the 'property' in this case belonged to another within the meaning of s. 1 in the Theft Act 1968 from the moment when the respondent became aware that this mistake had been made and that her account had been credited with the £74.74 and she consequently became obliged to restore the value. Furthermore, by the final words of s. 5(4), once the prosecution succeed in proving that the respondent intended not to make restoration, that is notionally to be regarded as an intention to deprive the receiver of that property which notionally belongs to him.

...

Before parting with the case we would like to say that it should often be possible to resolve this type of situation without resorting to the criminal law. We do, however, accept that there may be occasions—of which this may have been one—where a prosecution is necessary. We do not feel it possible to answer the question posed to us in any more specific form than the form in which this opinion has been delivered and that is our answer to the question posed to us.

R v Davis

(1988) 88 Cr App R 347, Court of Appeal

The appellant was convicted of six counts of theft. The counts charged theft of specified amounts of money belonging to the London Borough of Richmond. The appellant was eligible for housing benefit from the local authority. By mistake the authority's computer generated duplicate issues of a number of payments, sending the appellant two cheques. When he ceased to be eligible for the benefit only one of the computer entries was deleted and the remaining entry continued to generate cheques. The appellant admitted to police that he had 'cashed' the cheques he had received. The evidence before the jury was that he had either endorsed the cheque over to a shopkeeper in return for cash or had endorsed it to his landlord for accommodation etc. He denied receiving some cheques and was acquitted of counts relating to those cheques. The appellant appealed against conviction.

Held, allowing the appeal in part and quashing two of the convictions, there was not sufficient evidence in relation to the cheques endorsed to the landlord that the appellant had received cash in exchange for the cheques. As to the remaining counts, the language of the first part of s. 5(4) of the Theft Act 1968 was framed to cater for the ordinary tangible article and to recognise that by the time the defendant comes to commit his dishonest appropriation, the article may be in one of three conditions: it may still exist, so that it can and should be returned: it may have been exchanged for money or goods, in which case the defendant may be under an obligation to account for the fruits of the exchange, at least if they are traceable; and it may have ceased to exist altogether or to have gone out of reach of recovery, in which event the defendant may be obliged to 'restore' the value. In those cases where the defendant is indeed under a duty to 'make restoration' the second part of the subsection will put him in peril of conviction for stealing the article or its proceeds, although not its value, since there is no reference to value in this part of the subsection. The deceptively plain words of s. 5(4) give rise to problems, e.g. when is the defendant obliged to 'make restoration'; where the property received by the defendant by mistake is exchanged for something else? The Court did not need to answer those questions in the circumstances of the present case. It was plain that if an article is sold for cash, the sum represents the 'proceeds' of the article; there is no reason why this should be any the less so where the transaction involves not simply the piece of paper but also the rights which it conveys. On the assumption that the appellant was paid cash for the cheque, the offences were made out subject to the proof of dishonesty.

■ NOTES AND QUESTIONS

1. When is a person under an obligation to make restoration of money to which the person has come into possession by virtue of another's mistake? Should this be determined by civil or criminal law?

2. If, as we have seen in Chapter 2, there is no general legal duty to help a person in distress, even when their life is at risk, why should there be a legal duty to help a person whose money one has acquired innocently?

3. Compare the overpayment in *A-G's Ref.* (approximately £75) with that in *Shadrokh-Cigari* (above)(in excess of £250,000). We asked at the time whether the amount of money at issue should matter (and if so, why), and that question should now be reconsidered in light of *A-G's Ref.*

4. In *A-G's Ref.* the court suggests that such situations might be resolved without resort to the criminal law. How? Should this be a relevant factor? Is the court implicitly criticising the prosecutor for filing criminal charges in the first place?

5. If a student receives an overpayment in her grant cheque, tells the relevant authorities of the overpayment and they do nothing, may she spend the money? Will she be guilty of theft if she does? Would the legal analysis of the situation change if the student failed to inform the authorities of the overpayment?

6. In *R v Gilks* [1972] 3 All ER 280, the court held that s. 5(4) was concerned with legal obligations and not those of a purely social or moral nature. Why should social or moral obligations not also be legally enforceable?

SECTION 3: *MENS REA*

THEFT ACT 1968

1.—(1) A person is guilty of theft if he dishonestly appropriates property belonging to another with the intention of permanently depriving the other of it: and 'thief' and 'steal' shall be construed accordingly.

The two elements in the *mens rea* of theft are:

(a) Dishonesty.
(b) Intent permanently to deprive.

A: Dishonesty

Dishonesty is probably the key concept in theft, and even more so in light of the decisions in *Lawrence*, *Gomez* and *Hinks*. Yet what constitutes dishonesty remains clouded. The term is not defined in the TA 1968 – or the Fraud Act 2006, where it is equally critical.

(i) The application of s. 2

While not providing a test of dishonesty, s. 2 of the TA 1968 identifies three situations where a defendant will not be deemed to have acted dishonestly.

THEFT ACT 1968

2.—(1) A person's appropriation of property belonging to another is not to be regarded as dishonest—
   (a) if he appropriates property in the belief that he has in law the right to deprive the other of it, on behalf of himself or of a third person; or
   (b) if he appropriates the property in the belief that he would have the other's consent if the other knew of the appropriation and the circumstances of it; or
   (c) (except where the property came to him as trustee or personal representative) if he appropriates the property in the belief that the person to whom the property belongs cannot be discovered by taking reasonable steps.
   In addition, s. 2 identifies a situation where a willingness to pay for property may not be inconsistent with a conviction for theft.
   (2) A person's appropriation of property belonging to another may be dishonest notwithstanding that he is willing to pay for the property.

■ NOTES AND QUESTIONS

1. The belief referred to in all three situations identified in s. 2(1) is an honest belief, i.e., one actually held by the defendant. There is no requirement that the belief should be reasonable. See, e.g., *R v Kell* [1985] Crim LR 239, *R v Holden* [1991] Crim LR 478. Why should the defendant's belief not have to be reasonable? Of course, if the defendant's belief is unreasonable, a jury may not credit the claim that it was honestly held.

2. Notice that under s. 2(2) a willingness to pay for the items taken will not prevent a finding that the defendant acted dishonestly.

3. Is Section 2(1) non-exclusive; that is, should it preclude other situations where an appropriation will not be deemed to be dishonest? In the Criminal Damage Act 1971 (discussed subsequently) the statute takes a similar approach to what constitutes a 'lawful excuse' (delineating situations where a 'lawful excuse' will be found) but then goes on to say that the illustrations given should not be construed to cast doubt on any other defence recognised in law. Should the contrary inference be drawn from s. 2(1) because of the absence of comparable language?

(ii) The test of dishonesty

In most cases the dishonesty of the defendant will be obvious if the facts alleged by the prosecution are proved. Normally, therefore, the jury need not be directed as to the legal meaning of 'dishonesty' (see *R v Squire* [1990] Crim LR 341). Where there is some doubt, the jury must be directed in accordance with the model direction set out in *R v Ghosh* (below). This case achieves a reconciliation between two conflicting lines of authority, one of which favoured a subjective test of dishonesty (i.e., did the defendant believe that he had been acting dishonestly?; see, e.g., *R v Gilks* [1972] 3 All ER 280) and the other of which favoured an objective test (i.e., would a reasonable person, as embodied by the jury, consider the defendant's behaviour dishonest?) (see, e.g., *R v Greenstein* [1976] 1 All ER 1).

R v Ghosh

[1982] 1 QB 1053, Court of Appeal

LORD LANE CJ: . . . Is 'dishonesty' in s. 1 of the Theft Act 1968 intended to characterise a course of conduct? Or is it intended to describe a state of mind? If the former, then we can well understand that it could be established independently of the knowledge or belief of the accused. But if, as we think, it is the latter, then the knowledge and belief of the accused are at the root of the problem.

Take for example a man who comes from a country where public transport is free. On his first day here he travels on a bus. He gets off without paying. He never had an intention of paying. His mind is clearly honest; but his conduct, judged objectively by what he has done, is dishonest. It seems to us that in using the word 'dishonestly' in the Theft Act 1968, Parliament cannot have intended to catch dishonest conduct in that sense, that is to say conduct to which no moral obloquy could possibly attach. This is sufficiently established by the partial definition in section 2 of the Theft Act itself. All the matters covered by section 2(1) relate to the belief of the accused. Section 2(2) relates to his willingness to pay. A man's belief and his willingness to pay are things which can only be established subjectively. It is difficult to see how a partially subjective definition can be made to work in harness with the test which in all other respects is wholly objective.

If we are right that dishonesty is something in the mind of the accused (what Professor Glanville Williams calls 'a special mental state'), then if the mind of the accused is honest, it cannot be deemed dishonest merely because members of the jury would have regarded it as dishonest to embark on that course of conduct.

So we would reject the simple uncomplicated approach that the test is purely objective, however attractive from the practical point of view that solution may be.

There remains the objection that to adopt a subjective test is to abandon all standards but that of the accused himself, and to bring about a state of affairs in which 'Robin Hood would be no robber': *R v Greenstein* [1975] 1 WLR 1353. This objection misunderstands the nature of the subjective test. It is no defence for a man to say 'I knew that what I was doing is generally regarded as dishonest; but I do not regard it as dishonest myself. Therefore I am not guilty.' What he is however entitled to say is 'I did not know that anybody would regard what I was doing as dishonest.' He may not be believed: just as he may not be believed if he sets up 'a claim of right' under section 2(1) of the Theft Act 1968, or asserts that he believed in the truth of a misrepresentation under section 15 of the Act of 1968. But if he *is* believed, or raises a real doubt about the matter, the jury cannot be sure that he was dishonest.

In determining whether the prosecution has proved that the defendant was acting dishonestly, a jury must first of all decide whether according to the ordinary standards of reasonable and honest people what was done was dishonest. If it was not dishonest by those standards, that is the end of the matter and the prosecution fails.

If it was dishonest by those standards, then the jury must consider whether the defendant himself must have realised that what he was doing was by those standards dishonest. In most cases, where the actions are obviously dishonest by ordinary standards, there will be no doubt about it. It will be obvious that the defendant himself knew that he was acting dishonestly. It is dishonest for a defendant to act in a way which he knows ordinary people consider to be dishonest, even if he asserts or genuinely believes that he is morally justified in acting as he did. For example, Robin Hood or those ardent anti-vivisectionists who remove animals from vivisection laboratories are acting dishonestly, even though they may consider themselves to be morally justified in doing what they do, because they know that ordinary people would consider these actions to be dishonest.

■ NOTES AND QUESTIONS

1. J. C. Smith, *Law of Theft* (8th ed., 1997) suggests that the test of dishonesty should be 'knowing that the appropriation will or may be detrimental to the interests of the owner in a significantly practical way'. Is this a more useful test than that of *Ghosh*?

2. It has been forcefully contended by critics of *Ghosh* that its test leaves every jury free to apply their own moral and social views of what is dishonest. As these will vary from jury to jury, inconsistent verdicts in factually similar cases would appear virtually inevitable. But is this an advantage or disadvantage? Are the same standards of dishonesty appropriate for a major city with a serious crime problem and a small hamlet where theft is rare and everybody knows everybody else? Is a local jury best suited to make this determination?

3. The *Ghosh* test may prove particularly troublesome in the context of business crimes, where the standards of the marketplace and the standards of ordinary people may clash. Most ordinary persons may have a distorted or unrealistic view of what constitutes honesty in the market place. Should this matter? Would recruiting a 'specialist' jury consisting of persons with a business background help to solve the problem – or create a new one?

4. The second part of the *Ghosh* test would appear to allow a defence to those whose sense of the community's standard of dishonesty is markedly distorted. Can this be squared with the generally correct proposition that ignorance of the law is no excuse (discussed in Chapter 10)?

B: Intent permanently to deprive

The intention of the defendant must be to deprive the victim of the whole of his interest in the property. If this is a limited interest, then, so long as an intention to deprive him of all of that interest can be shown, the requisite intent will be present. There is no requirement that the victim actually be permanently deprived of the property.

Three main issues arise in determining when there is an intent permanently to deprive:

(a) Is there an intent permanently to deprive if the defendant intends to return the goods?

(b) In what circumstances can an intended borrowing amount to an intention permanently to deprive?

(c) Can a 'conditional intention' be a sufficient *mens rea*?

(i) Intention to return goods

The courts have held that an intention to return money taken is not inconsistent with an intent permanently to deprive. They have reached this seemingly odd result by ruling that a defendant has to have the intent to return the identical coins and not their equivalent value (See *R v Velumyl* [1989] Crim LR 299). This would seem to create insurmountable problems, for example, where an employee appropriated money from an employer to deposit for a very short period in a fund offering extremely high and guaranteed interest, there being no question that the money originally appropriated would be returned.

Less troublesome are cases where the defendant may not be in a position to return the goods taken. This situation is specifically covered in the statute.

THEFT ACT 1968

6.—(2) Without prejudice to the generality of subsection (1) above, where a person, having possession or control (lawfully or not) of property belonging to another, parts with the property under a condition as to its return which he may not be able to perform, this (if done for purposes of his own and without the other's authority) amounts to treating the property as his own to dispose of regardless of the other's rights.

Section 6(2) was specifically designed to cover the case where the defendant pawns another's property without authority. The condition 'which he may not be able to perform' in those circumstances is the condition imposed by the pawnbroker that the property will not be returned unless repayment of the loan with interest is first forthcoming. However, the subsection is not confined to pawning situations and there may well be other cases falling within its ambit.

(ii) When can an intended borrowing amount to an intention permanently to deprive?

THEFT ACT 1968

6.—(1) A person appropriating property belonging to another without meaning the other permanently to lose the thing itself is nevertheless to be regarded as having the intention of permanently depriving the other of it if his intention is to treat the thing as his own to dispose of regardless of the other's rights; and a borrowing or lending of it may amount to so treating it if, but only if, the borrowing or lending is for a period and in circumstances making it equivalent to an outright taking or disposal.

Section 6(1) covers situations in which the defendant takes property intending to sell it back to the owner or to return it only upon payment of a ransom. There may be no permanent deprivation but the defendant is treating the property as her own to dispose of as she wishes. In *R v Fernandes* [1996] 1 Cr App R 175, the Court of Appeal stated: 'We consider that section 6 may apply to a person in possession or control of another's property who, dishonestly and for his own purpose, deals with that property in such a manner as he is risking its loss.'

Some confusion about the meaning of 'dispose of' in s. 6 has arisen, however:

R v Marshall
[1998] 2 Cr App R 282, Court of Appeal

MANTELL LJ: As part of an operation by London Underground Limited at Victoria Station the appellants were observed and videoed obtaining used travel tickets from passengers leaving the underground and selling them at a reduced rate to persons intending to travel. The tickets, which had been issued by London Underground Limited remained valid in the sense that their usefulness had not been exhausted. Thereby London Underground Limited was deprived of revenue which it might have expected to receive from those persons who had bought the tickets.

A number of submissions were made to the learned judge. The first was that the travel tickets were not the property of London Underground Limited within the meaning of section 1 of the Theft Act 1968. The judge rejected the submission ruling that although the tickets had passed into the possession and control of the customers, London Underground Limited retained a proprietary right or interest in the tickets which were to be regarded therefore as the property of London Underground Limited pursuant to section 5(1) of the Act. As a secondary reason for rejecting the submission he referred to the express term on the reverse of each ticket to the effect that it remained throughout the property of LRT, of which London Underground Limited is a part.

A second submission was made that in the circumstances there had been no appropriation so as to bring the case within the basic definition of theft. In rejecting the submission the judge referred to section 3(1) which reads:

> Any assumption by a person of the rights of an owner amounts to an appropriation, and this includes, where he has come by the property (innocently or not) without stealing it, any later assumption of a right to it by keeping or dealing with it as owner.

and to the decision of the House of Lords in *R* v *Morris* (1983) 77 Cr App R 309 in which it was held that it was not necessary to demonstrate an assumption by the accused of all the owners' rights, simply to show the assumption of some of the rights of the owner of the goods in question. The learned judge considered that the use of the ticket to the detriment of London Underground Limited was inconsistent with London Underground Limited's rights and consequently that the actions of the appellants amounted to an appropriation in law.

Thirdly, and lastly, it was submitted that on the agreed facts there was no evidence of an intention to permanently deprive. That submission also was rejected, the learned judge taking the view that the provisions of section 6(1) of the Theft Act covered the position. It will be necessary to refer to the terms of the subsection later in this judgment.

. . .

In our judgment and following *Fernandes* the subsection is not to be given the restricted interpretation for which the appellants contend.

The principal submission put forward on behalf of the appellants is that the issuing of the ticket is analogous to the drawing of a cheque in that in each instance a *chose in action* is created which in the first case belongs to the customer and in the second to the payee. So by parity of reasoning with that advanced by Lord Goff in *R* v *Preddy and Others* [1996] 2 Cr App R 524, the property acquired belonged to the customer and not London Underground Limited and there can have been no intention on the part of the appellant to deprive London Underground Limited of the ticket which would in due course be returned to the possession of London Underground Limited. Attractive though the submission appears at first blush we do not think that it can possibly be correct.

'A "*chose in action*" is a known legal expression used to describe all personal rights of property which can only be claimed or enforced by action, and not by taking physical possession.' (See *Talkington* v *Magee* (1902) 2 KB 427, *per* Channell J at p. 430.) On the issuing of an underground ticket a contract is created between London Underground Limited and the purchaser. Under that contract each party has rights and obligations. Theoretically those rights are enforceable by action. Therefore, it is arguable, we suppose, that by the transaction each party has acquired a *chose in action*. On the side of the purchaser it is represented by a right to use the ticket to the extent which it allows travel on the underground system. On the side of London Underground Limited it encompasses the right to insist that the ticket is used by no one other than the purchaser. It is that right which is disregarded when the ticket is acquired by the appellant and sold on. But here the charges were in relation to the tickets and travel cards themselves and a ticket form or travel card and, dare we say, a cheque form is not a *chose in action*. The fact that the ticket form or travel card may find its way back into the possession of London Underground Limited, albeit with its usefulness or 'virtue' exhausted, is nothing to the point. Section 6(1) prevails for the reasons we have given.

The appellants by their pleas having acknowledged that they were acting dishonestly it seems to us that there is no reason to consider the convictions unsafe and these appeals must be dismissed.

Appeals dismissed.

DPP v Lavender

[1994] Crim LR 297, Queen's Bench Division

An information was preferred against the respondent that he had stolen two doors. Justices dismissed the information but stated a case for the opinion of the High Court.

The respondent had taken the doors from a council property undergoing repair, and had used them to replace damaged doors at another council property of which his girlfriend was the tenant. He argued that he had not had the intention permanently to deprive the council of the doors.

Section 6(1) of the Theft Act 1968 provides that a person is to be regarded as having the intention to permanently deprive another of property if his intention is to treat the property as his own to dispose of regardless of the other's rights, and that borrowing property may amount to such an intention if for a period and in circumstances making it equivalent to an outright taking or disposal.

The question posed for the High Court was whether, on a proper construction of section 6(1), theft was made out.

Held, allowing the appeal and remitting the case to the justices to convict, the respondent had stolen the doors.

In *Lloyd and others* [1985] 2 All ER 661 the Court of Appeal had said that mere borrowing was never enough to constitute the necessary guilty mind, unless the intention was to return the thing in such a changed state that all its goodness or virtue was gone. It was difficult to describe the taking of the doors as borrowing but, even if it was, the doors would not change their character. The second limb of section 6(1) did not apply.

In regard to the first limb, the justices had applied a dictionary definition to the words 'to dispose of' and had decided they meant to get rid of, or to sell. That was too narrow a definition. A disposal could include disposal to the owner of the property (as contemplated in *Lloyd*) and could include dealing with the property (*Chan Man-Sin v A-G for Hong Kong* [1988] 1 All ER 1). The proper question was whether the respondent intended to treat the doors as his own, regardless of the council's rights. The answer was yes, the respondent had dealt with the doors regardless of the council's rights not to have them removed, and in so doing had manifested an intention to treat the doors as his own.

...

■ **NOTES AND QUESTIONS**

1. Were the defendants in *Marshall* criminals to be condemned – or entrepreneurs to be admired? Would it have made a difference if they had picked up and resold tickets still having a useful life but which had been thrown in a trash bin by the original purchaser? Does the fact that the defendants resold the tickets matter – what if Harry, while leaving the station, runs into Sally, an old friend, and simply 'gives' her his ticket?

2. Jane purchases a season ticket to watch Sheffield Wednesday football club. The ticket is valid for 13 matches. David takes the season ticket after Jane has been to three matches and returns it in time for her to attend the last match. Has David stolen Jane's ticket? See J.C. Smith, 'Current Topic; Stealing Tickets' [1998] Crim LR 723.

3. Should Parliament enact an offence of unauthorised borrowing? Or a crime of unlawful temporary deprivation of property belonging to another? See G. Williams 'Temporary Appropriation should be Theft' [1981] Crim LR 129.

4. The all too prevalent problem of joyriding (where there is usually no intent permanently to deprive the owner of her car) is specifically addressed in the Theft Act 1968, s. 12, and the Aggravated Vehicle Taking Act 1992.

(iii) Can a 'conditional intention' be sufficient mens rea?

This problem arises where the defendant only intends permanently to keep anything which he finds to be valuable after he has examined the property. In *Easom* [1971] 2 QB 315, where the defendant examined the contents of a handbag and decided nothing was worth taking, such an intention was held not to be sufficient for theft. Might the defendant be charged with attempted theft (see Chapter 12)?

SECTION 4: ROBBERY

Robbery is essentially an aggravated form of stealing which combines theft and assault, but which may lead to a greater potential penalty than if each of these offences had been charged separately.

THEFT ACT 1968

8.—(1) A person is guilty of robbery if he steals, and immediately before or at the time of doing so, and in order to do so, he uses force on any person or puts or seeks to put any person in fear of being then and there subjected to force.

(2) A person guilty of robbery, or of an assault with intent to rob, shall on conviction on indictment be liable to imprisonment for life.

A: Theft

As robbery is an aggravated form of stealing, it follows that if a defendant is not guilty of theft he cannot be guilty of robbery.

R v Robinson

[1977] Crim LR 173, Court of Appeal

R ran a clothing club. He was charged (with others) with robbing and assaulting I, who, with his wife, was a contributor to the club. I's wife owed £7. It was the prosecution case that R and two others had approached him in the street late at night, R brandishing a knife, and that a fight ensued during the course of which a £5 note fell from I's pocket. R had snatched the note and asked if I had any more money as he was still owed £2. R's defence to robbery, reduced by the jury to theft, was that I gave him the money and he had received it willingly as repayment of the debt and that it was not dishonestly appropriated. R appealed on the ground of misdirection to the jury that an honest belief by the defendant that he was entitled in law to get his money in a particular way was necessary before he could avail himself of the defence under s. 2(1)(a) of the Theft Act 1968.

Held, allowing the appeal, that the law as laid down in *Skivington* [1968] 1 QB 166 had not been altered by s. 2(1)(a) of the Theft Act 1968, and that it was unnecessary for a defendant to show that he had an honest belief not only that he was entitled to take the money but also that he was entitled to take it in the way that he did.

Corcoran v Anderton

[1980] Crim LR 385, Queen's Bench Division

Two youths, the defendant and his co-accused, saw a woman in the street, and agreed together to steal her handbag. The co-accused hit her in the back and tugged at her bag to release it, while the defendant participated. She released her bag, screamed, and fell to the ground. The two youths ran away empty-handed, and the woman recovered her bag, neither youth having had sole control of the bag at any time. The defendant was later convicted of robbery under s. 8 of the Theft Act 1968; which provided that a person was guilty of robbery if he stole, using force.

The defendant appealed against conviction on the ground that neither he nor the co-accused had sole control of the bag at any time.

Held, dismissing the appeal, that an appropriation took place at the moment when the youths, acting with an intention to deprive the woman of the bag, snatched it from her grasp so that she no longer had physical control of it. In doing so each accused was trying to exclude the woman from her exclusive claim to the bag, and was trying to treat the bag as his. Such an action was an unlawful assumption of the rights of the owner and accordingly the defendant was properly convicted by the justices.

■ NOTES AND QUESTIONS

1. Robinson was not guilty of robbery because theft could not be proved. Why not? Was the defendant nonetheless guilty of an assault? An aggravated assault?

2. Reconsider the approach to appropriation adopted by the House of Lords in *Gomez* and *Hinks*. Would applying it have simplified or complicated the analysis in *Corocan* v *Anderton*?

B: Force or threat of force

Section 8 is satisfied only if the defendant is found to have used 'force on any person' or to have sought 'to put any person in fear of being then and there subjected to force'. What amounts to force is a matter for the jury.

R v Dawson
[1976] Crim LR 692, Court of Appeal

D was convicted of robbery. He and two others approached a man in the street and two of them stood either side of him and the third behind him. One of them nudged the man so that he lost his balance and whilst he was thus unbalanced another stole his wallet. It was submitted that what D and his accomplices did could not amount to the use of force, relying on cases prior to the Theft Act 1968.

Held, dismissing the appeal, what counted now was the words of the Act, the object of which was to get rid of the old technicalities. The choice of the word force was not without interest because the Larceny Act 1916 used violence. Whether there was any difference between the words was not relevant to the case. Force was a word in ordinary use which juries understood. The judge left it to the jury to decide whether jostling to an extent which caused a person to have difficulty in keeping his balance amounted to the use of force. In deference to the submissions he said that the force must be substantial. It was not necessary to consider whether he was right to apply an adjective to the word of the Act. It was a matter for the jury and it could not be said that they were wrong. It had also been canvassed whether the force had been used for distracting the victim's attention or for overcoming resistance. That sort of refinement might have been relevant under the old law: the sole question under the new was whether force had been used in order to steal.

Appeal dismissed.

Must the force be used to overcome resistance to the theft, or is it sufficient that force is used to gain possession of the property?

R v Clouden

[1987] Crim LR 56, Court of Appeal

The appellant was seen to follow a woman who was carrying a shopping basket in her left hand. He approached her from behind and wrenched the basket down and out of her grasp with both hands and ran off with it. He was charged in two counts with robbery and theft respectively and convicted on the first count of robbery. He appealed on the grounds (i) that there was insufficient evidence of resistance to the snatching of the bag to constitute force on the person under s. 8 of the Theft Act 1968; and (ii) that the learned judge's direction to the jury on the requirement of force on the person was inadequate and confused.

Held, dismissing the appeal, the old cases distinguished between force on the actual person and force on the property which in fact causes force on the person but, following *Dawson and James* (1976) 64 Cr App R 170, the court should direct attention to the words of the statute without referring to the old authorities. The old distinctions have gone. Whether the defendant used force on any person in order to steal is an issue that should be left to the jury. The judge's direction to the jury was adequate. He told the jury quite clearly at the outset what the statutory definition was, though thereafter he merely used the word 'force' and did not use the expression 'on the person'.

■ NOTES AND QUESTIONS

1. The Criminal Law Revision Committee, which was responsible for drafting the Theft Act 1968, said (Cmnd. 2977, para. 65) that they 'would not regard mere snatching of property, such as a handbag, from an unresisting owner as using force for the purpose of the definition'. Does *Clouden* reflect this view?

2. In *Clouden*, would it have been more appropriate to have simply charged the defendant with theft? Or would this fail to capture the other dimensions of his offence?

C: Before or at the time of the theft

When must the force or threat of force occur? The statute speaks in terms of 'immediately before or at the time of [stealing]', but can an appropriation be deemed a continuing act for the purposes of robbery?

R v Hale

(1978) 68 Cr App R 415, Court of Appeal

The appellant was charged with robbery. The prosecution case was that he and one M, both wearing stocking masks, had forced their way into the house of a Mrs C who had answered the door to their knock. The appellant had then put his hand over Mrs C's mouth to stop her screaming while M went upstairs and returned carrying a jewellery box and had asked Mrs C 'where the rest was.' A neighbour who had heard Mrs C's scream had then rung up to ask if she was all right. Under threats from the appellant and M she replied that she was. They again asked Mrs C where she kept her money and before leaving the house tied her up and threatened what would happen to her young boy if she informed the police within five minutes of their leaving.

The trial judge read the definition of robbery in s. 8 of the Theft Act 1968 to the jury and the meaning of 'steal' in s. 1 of that Act. He directed them that the question they had to decide was whether they felt sure that the appellant by use of force or putting Mrs C in fear got hold of her property without her consent and without believing that he had her consent and intending to appropriate that property to himself without giving it back to her afterwards. The jury convicted. On appeal that the jury had been misdirected in that the judge's direction could indicate to the jury that if an accused used force in order to effect his escape with the stolen goods that would be sufficient to constitute robbery and that on the facts of the present case it was submitted that the theft was completed as soon as the jewellery box was seized.

EVELEIGH LJ: . . . In so far as the facts of the present case are concerned, counsel submitted that the theft was completed when the jewellery box was first seized and any force thereafter could not have been 'immediately before or at the time of stealing' and certainly not 'in order to steal.' The essence of the submission was that the theft was completed as soon as the jewellery box was seized.

Section 8 of the Theft Act 1968 begins: 'A person is guilty of robbery if he steals . . .' He steals when he acts in accordance with the basic definition of theft in s. 1 of the Theft Act; that is to say when he dishonestly appropriates property belonging to another with the intention of permanently depriving the other of it. It thus becomes necessary to consider what is 'appropriation' or, according to s. 3, 'any assumption by a person of the rights of an owner.' An assumption of the rights of an owner describes the conduct of a person towards a particular article. It is conduct which usurps the rights of the owner. To say that the conduct is over and done with as soon as he lays hands upon the property, or when he first manifests an intention to deal with it as his, is contrary to common-sense and to the natural meaning of words. A thief who steals a motor car first opens the door. Is it to be said that the act of starting up the motor is no more a part of the theft?

In the present case there can be little doubt that if the appellant had been interrupted after the seizure of the jewellery box the jury would have been entitled to find that the appellant and his accomplice were assuming the rights of an owner at the time when the jewellery box was seized. However, the act of appropriation does not suddenly cease. It is a continuous act and it is a matter for the jury to decide whether or not the act of appropriation has finished. Moreover, it is quite clear that the intention to deprive the owner permanently, which accompanied the assumption of the owner's rights was a continuing one at all material times. This Court therefore rejects the contention that the theft had ceased by the time the lady was tied up. As a matter of common-sense the appellant was in the course of committing theft; he was stealing.

There remains the question whether there was robbery. Quite clearly the jury were at liberty to find the appellant guilty of robbery relying upon the force used when he put his hand over Mrs Carrett's mouth to restrain her from calling for help. We also think that they were also entitled to rely upon the act of tying her up provided they were satisfied (and it is difficult to see how they could not be satisfied) that the force so used was to enable them to steal. If they were still engaged in the act of stealing the force was clearly used to enable them to continue to assume the rights of the owner and permanently to deprive Mrs Carrett of her box, which is what they began to do when they first seized it.

D: In order to steal

The force must be used 'in order to steal':

R v *Shendley*
[1970] Crim LR 49, Court of Appeal

S was convicted of robbery, contrary to s. 8 of the Theft Act 1968. The complainant said that S attacked him, took some of his property and forced him to sign receipts purporting to show that S had brought the property from him. S said that he had purchased the property. The judge directed the jury: 'robbery is stealing property in the presence of the owner . . . the allegation is that imme-diately before taking the property, or at the time of taking it, or immediately after, force was used towards [the complainant] to put him in fear . . . if you came to the conclusion that the violence was unconnected with the stealing but you were satisfied there was a stealing it does not mean that is an acquittal because it would be open to you to find [him] guilty of robbery, that is, robbery without violence.'

Held: the directions were wrong. The judge must have had in mind s. 23 of the Larceny Act 1916 and overlooked the fact that the definition of robbery in the Theft Act is different. There is no such thing as robbery without violence. What the judge no doubt intended to say was that if the jury were satisfied that S stole the property but not satisfied that he used violence for the purpose of stealing they should find him not guilty of robbery but guilty of theft (the court substituted a conviction for theft).

■ NOTES AND QUESTIONS

1. The reference to violence in *Shendley* should be read in light of *R* v *Dawson*, (above).

2. What is the purpose of the requirement that the force must be 'in order to steal'? George rapes Vera. He then runs off, taking her handbag. Has he committed robbery as well as rape? What if John and David are involved in a heated argu-ment, and a fight breaks out during which John hits David who is knocked unconscious. If John then decides to take David's wallet from him will John be guilty of robbery? Is the force involved in the above hypotheticals more of less deplorable than that in *Clouden* (above)?

SECTION 5: **BURGLARY**

Burglary historically was regarded as a most serious crime because it involved not only a threat to property but also a threat to the privacy of one's own home. The common law definition of burglary referred specifically to the 'dwelling house' of another as the locus of the crime. Arguably it is in one's home that one is most enti-tled to security (a man's [sic] home is his 'castle'). Further, the common law offence of burglary had to be committed 'at night', the period of maximum vulnerability.

After a hiatus following enactment of the TA 1968, the law now takes into account the sanctity of one's home. Section 26 of the Criminal Justice Act 1991 provides that if the building is a 'dwelling' the maximum penalty is 14 years' imprisonment; if it is any other building the maximum penalty is 10 years' imprisonment.

Nonetheless, nowadays the crime of burglary can be committed in any building (and indeed some non-buildings), whether or not occupied, and not necessarily committed at night. The modern incarnation of the offence can be found in the Theft Act 1968, s. 9. The section creates two quite distinct offences.

THEFT ACT 1968

9.—(1) A person is guilty of burglary if—
    (a) he enters any building or part of a building as a trespasser and with intent to commit any such offence as is mentioned in subsection (2) below; or

(b) having entered any building or part of a building as a trespasser he steals or attempts to steal anything in the building or that part of it or inflicts or attempts to inflict on any person therein any grievous bodily harm.

(2) The offences referred to in subsection (1)(a) above are offences of stealing anything in the building or part of a building in question, of inflicting on any person therein any grievous bodily harm, and of doing unlawful damage to the building or anything therein.

(3) A person guilty of burglary shall on conviction on indictment be liable to imprisonment for a term not exceeding fourteen years—

(4) References in subsections (1) and (2) above to a building, and the reference in subsection (3) above to a building which is a dwelling, shall also apply to an inhabited vehicle or vessel, and shall apply to any such vehicle or vessel at times when the person having a habitation in it is not there as well as at times when he is.

A: *Actus reus*

Both parts of s. 9(1) require proof that the defendant entered as a trespasser. If the requisite intent is present, a s. 9(1)(a) offence is committed at the moment of entry, whereas a s. 9(1)(b) offence is committed at the time that the ulterior offence is complete.

The *actus reus* of burglary presents a number of questions:

(a) What constitutes sufficient entry?

(b) When is a defendant trespassing?

(c) How are 'building' and 'part of a building' defined?

(d) For purposes of s. 9(1)(b), when will the ulterior offence be considered to have been committed?

(i) Entry

R v Ryan
[1996] Crim LR 320, Court of Appeal

At about 2.30 a.m. one morning an elderly householder found the defendant stuck in a downstairs window of his house. The defendant had his head and right arm inside the window and was trapped by the window itself which rested on his neck. The rest of his body remained outside the window. He was convicted of burglary. He appealed on the ground that, as a matter of law, his action was not capable of constituting an entry within the meaning of section 9 of the Theft Act 1968 since he could not have stolen anything from within the building because he was stuck firmly by his neck in the window.

Held, dismissing the appeal, that it was clear from *Brown* [1985] Crim LR 212 that for the purposes of section 9 of the 1968 Act a person could enter a building even if only part of his body was actually within the premises and it was totally irrelevant whether he was or was not capable of stealing anything because he was trapped halfway through the window.

■ NOTES AND QUESTIONS

1. The defendant's attempt to enter the householder's property was clearly not sufficient to put him in a position to achieve his ulterior purpose. Should this matter?

2. At what point does one commit an entry? Is it at the same moment that one commits the trespass? For example, suppose that a would-be burglar is standing on the householder's porch pondering whether it will be possible to gain entry? By 'trespassing' (?) on the householder's porch, has an entry already occurred?

3. What of instruments used to create an entry? Say that a defendant has inserted a crowbar under a window for the purpose of prising it open. Has he effected an entry?

(ii) Trespass

R v Collins
[1972] 2 All ER 1105, Court of Appeal

The defendant, desirous of having sexual intercourse with the victim stripped naked (except unaccountably for his socks) and climbed a ladder to the victim's bedroom. The victim, mistaking Collins for her boyfriend, signalled he should enter and they proceeded to have sex. At some point she discovered her mistake. Collins was subsequently convicted of burglary.

EDMUND DAVIES LJ:...The second ingredient of the offence—the entry must be as a trespasser—is one which has not, to the best of our knowledge, been previously canvassed in the courts. Views as to its ambit have naturally been canvassed by the textbook writers, and it is perhaps not wholly irrelevant to recall that those who were advising the Home Secretary before the Theft Bill was presented to Parliament had it in mind to get rid of some of the frequently absurd technical rules which had been built up in relation to the old requirement in burglary of a 'breaking and entering'. The cases are legion as to what this did or did not amount to, and happily it is not now necessary for us to consider them. But it was in order to get rid of those technical rules that a new test was introduced, namely that the entry must be as a 'trespasser'.

...In the judgment of this court, there cannot be a conviction for entering premises 'as a trespasser' within the meaning of s. 9 of the Theft Act 1968 unless the person entering does so knowing that he is a trespasser and nevertheless deliberately enters, or, at the very least, is reckless whether or not he is entering the premises of another without the other party's consent.

R v Smith and Jones
[1976] 3 All ER 54, Court of Appeal

JAMES LJ:...Christopher Smith's father, Alfred Smith, lived at 72 Chapel Lane, Farnborough. He was in the course of negotiating a move from the house to other premises. At the material time, in May 1975, in that house were two television sets; one owned by Mr Alfred Smith, the other owned by another person but lawfully in possession of Mr Alfred Smith. Christopher Smith lived with his own family at Aberfield. The appellant Jones lived in the opposite direction from Chapel Lane, Farnborough to Aberfield, namely in Lakeside Road, Ashvale.

In the early hours of 10 May, 1975, a police officer in Ashvale saw a motor car with the two appellants inside and a television set protruding from the boot of the car. Having regard to that which he saw and the time of the morning he followed the car which turned into a side road where eventually it was stopped by a gate being in its way. The officer called for further officers to attend and when another officer went to the car he saw the appellant Jones sitting on the back seat with a second television set behind him. In the front of the car was Smith. They were told that the police believed that the television sets were stolen and that they were being arrested. Smith responded with the questions: 'Are they bent?' and Jones made the observation: 'You cannot arrest me for just having a ride in a car.'

At the trial both of the appellants gave evidence. It was the case for Smith that he had permission from his father to go into the house of his father. With that permission was a general licence to go there at any time he wanted to. It was the case for Jones at the trial that, contrary to what he had said to the police, he had gone into the house, he had gone purely as a passenger with Smith and gone in in the belief, honestly held, that Smith had permission to take the television sets from his father and that in taking them Smith was not stealing them or acting in any dishonest way. He himself, in so far as he was concerned with the matter, was not acting in any dishonest way.

Mr Rose argues that a person who had a general permission to enter premises of another person cannot be a trespasser. His submission is as short and as simple as that. Related to this case he says that a son to whom a father has given permission generally to enter the father's house cannot be a trespasser if he enters it even though he had decided in his mind before making the entry to commit a criminal offence of theft against the father once he had got into the house and had entered the house solely for the purpose of committing that theft. It is a bold submission. Mr Rose frankly accepts that there has been no decision of the Court since this statute was passed which governs particularly this point. He has reminded us of the decision in *Byrne* v *Kinematograph Renters Society Ltd* [1958] 2 All ER 579, which he prays in aid of his argument. In that case persons had entered a cinema by producing tickets not for the purpose of seeing the show, but for an ulterior purpose. It was held in the action, which sought to show that they entered as trespassers pursuant to a conspiracy to trespass, that in fact they were not trespassers. The important words in the judgment of Harman J at p. 593D are 'They did nothing that they were not invited to do, . . .' That provides a distinction between that case and what we consider the position to be in this case.

We are also referred to *R* v *Collins* (1972) 56 Cr App R 554 and in particular to the long passage of Edmund Davies LJ, as he then was, commencing at pp. 559 and 104 of the respective reports where the learned Lord Justice commenced the consideration of what is involved by the words '. . . the entry must be "as a trespasser".' At p. 561 and pp. 104–105—again it is unnecessary to cite the long passage in full, suffice it to say that this Court on that occasion expressly approved the view expressed in Professor Smith's book on the *Law of Theft* (1968) (1st ed.) para. 462, and also the view of Professor Griew in his book on the *Theft Act* (1968) (1st ed.) para. 4–05 upon this aspect of what is involved in being a trespasser.

In our view the passage there referred to is consonant with the passage in the well known case of *Hillen and Pettigrew* v *I.C.I. (Alkali) Ltd* [1936] AC 65 where, in the speech of Lord Atkin these words appear at p. 69:

> My Lords, in my opinion this duty to an invitee only extends so long as and so far as the invitee is making what can reasonably be contemplated as an ordinary and reasonable use of the premises by the invitee for the purpose for which he has been invited. He is not invited to use any part of the premises for purposes which he knows are wrongfully dangerous and constitute an improper use. As Scrutton LJ has pointedly said [in *The Calgarth* [1926] P 93 at p. 110] 'When you invite a person into your house to use the staircase you do not invite him to slide down the banisters'.

That case of course was a civil case in which it was sought to make the defendant liable for a tort.

The decision in *Collins* (supra) in this Court, a decision upon the criminal law, added to the concept of trespass as a civil wrong only the mental element of *mens rea*, which is essential to the criminal offence. Taking the law as expressed in *Hillen and Pettigrew* v *I.C.I. Ltd* (supra) and in the case of *Collins* (supra) it is our view that a person is a trespasser for the purpose of section 9(1)(b) of the Theft Act 1968, if he enters premises of another knowing that he is entering in excess of the permission that has been given to him, or being reckless as to whether he is entering in excess of the permission that has been given to him to enter, providing the facts are known to the accused which enable him to realise that he is acting in excess of the permission given or that he is acting recklessly as to whether he exceeds that permission, then that is sufficient for the jury to decide that he is in fact a trespasser.

In this particular case it was a matter for the jury to consider whether, on all the facts, it was shown by the prosecution that the appellants entered with the knowledge that entry was being effected against the consent or in excess of the consent that had been given by Mr Smith senior to his son Christopher. The jury were, by their verdict satisfied of that....

■ NOTES AND QUESTIONS

1. Do *Collins* and *Smith and Jones* take the same approach to what constitutes a trespass? If not, are the positions reconcilable?

2. Is there a trespass when the defendant is invited into premises but, unknown to the person issuing the invitation, has a secret unlawful intent? If followed, would the rationale of *Smith and Jones* convert all instances of shoplifting into burglary?

3. We noted in respect of theft instances where prosecutors had created problems for the courts by charging theft in cases where property was in fact obtained by deception. In *Smith and Jones*, would it arguably have made more sense to charge the defendants with theft, a crime they clearly committed, rather than forcing the courts to strain the boundaries of burglary?

4. If Collins knew that the parents of the girl would not have approved of his presence, even if the girl did, would he have trespassed? Can a lodger invite guests into a party contrary to the wishes of a landlord? What if the guests stay for a week?

(iii) Building/part of a building

The TA 1968 s. 9 speaks in terms of a 'building' or 'part of a building'. 'Part of a building' includes any part into which the defendant has no authority to enter. There need be no physical barrier between the 'part' into which the defendant is invited and the 'part' in which she trespasses:

R v Walkington

(1979) 68 Cr App Rep 427, Court of Appeal

At 5.40 pm one evening the appellant entered a department store at a time when the assistants were 'cashing-up' their tills, the store closing at 6 pm. A store detective and two colleagues noticed that the appellant only appeared to be interested in the tills in the menswear department; but he was seen to ascend an escalator to the first floor to the dress display part where there was an unattached till in the centre of a three-sided counter, the till being left partially open and, unknown to the appellant but appreciated by the staff, empty. That drawer was located at least four yards inside the private area of the store restricted to the sales staff. The appellant moved into the opening of that counter, looked around him, and bent down and opened the drawer of the partially open till. After looking inside it, he slammed it shut and left the store when he was detained for questioning and later charged with burglary contrary to s. 9(1)(a) and (2) of the Theft Act 1968. The particulars of the offence alleged that he had entered the store in question as a trespasser with intent to steal therein. At the end of the prosecution case the appellant submitted that he had no case to answer in that there had been no trespass. The trial judge overruled that submission and directed that jury to consider first, so far as the store was concerned, whether the area where the half-opened till was situated was a prohibited area; secondly, if so, did the appellant realise when he crossed the limit that that area was prohibited; thirdly, at the time when he crossed that limit, the first two questions being decided against the appellant, did he have the intention to steal? The jury convicted. On appeal it was contended that the judge had erred in refusing to withdraw the case from the jury in that it was wrong to divide the store artificially and the appellant could not be said to have trespassed behind the counter...

GEOFFREY LANE LJ (approving the judge's summing-up which he quoted):

...The first question really arising out of this, which you have to consider is the use of the words 'part of a building'. The case for the prosecution is that the defendant formed an intent to steal while within this Debenhams, but before he entered the cash desk area, so that the prosecution are alleging that when he entered that area he was entering part of a building. Now, it is for you to decide whether on this section of the Theft Act that area was part of a building. Now, if you take the case of an ordinary shop, at the ordinary shop, which comprises a room with one part of it separated off by a counter, you might find little difficulty in deciding that the part of the room behind the counter was a separate part of the building from the shop area, and one which the public were not allowed to enter unless invited to do so. On the other hand, if you have the case of a large store, such as Debenhams, and there is a till placed on a table situated in the middle of the shop area, you might find it difficult, or even impossible, to say that any particular area, definable area, round that table was a separate part of the building. So that in approaching the problem you are entitled, of course, to use your own experience. You have been round shops, so you know the sort of layout you find in shops, so you may find it helpful to ask yourselves whether a shopper coming into a store and seeing the area with which you are concerned in this case would realise that that is an area to which the public were not entitled to go, and separate from the rest of the shopping area where they were entitled to go. It is a matter for you to decide. It is for you to decide whether that is the case. Coming back to the question of the definition of trespass, that is to say, of entering any part of a building as a trespasser, you now have to consider the next part of the definition, that is to say, 'with intent to steal.' Now in order to convict under this part of the section, section 9 of the Theft Act, the intent to steal must have been formed before the defendant entered that part of the area which was a separate part of the building....

When considering the definition of 'building', the extended definition in s. 9(4) should be noted:

THEFT ACT 1968

9.—(4) References in subsection (1) and (2) above to a building, and the reference in subsection (3) above to a building which is a dwelling, shall also apply to an inhabited vehicle or vessel, and shall apply to any such vehicle or vessel at times when the person having a habitation in it is not there as well as at times when he is.

■ NOTES AND QUESTIONS

1. When is a vehicle or vessel 'inhabited'? Is a caravan 'inhabited' during the week if it is kept ready to be used, but only used, at weekends? What about a yacht, fitted out but not yet launched?

2. While s. 9(1)(a) requires only an intent to commit an offence within the building, s. 9(1)(b) requires that the defendant steal or attempt to steal something that is in the building, or inflict or attempt to inflict grievous bodily harm on a person in the building. Thus in construing s. 9(1)(b) a court may need to refer to the substantive law of theft and GBH, as well as that of attempt.

3. Nigel enters Buckingham Palace to see how the 'other half' lives. He wanders around undetected for several hours before being discovered and apprehended by security guards. Has he committed burglary? If his artistic sensibilities are

affronted by a vase in the Palace which he picks up with the intention of smashing it on the pavement outside, will he have committed burglary? If so, when would the burglary have occurred?

B: *Mens rea*

There are different *mens rea* which may have to be proved, depending on which part of the statute is charged:

(a) An intention to commit one of the ulterior offences is required for a s. 9(1)(a) burglary.

(b) For a s. 9(1)(b) burglary, the *mens rea* of the ulterior offence must be proved.

The s. 9(1)(a) *mens rea* must be present at the time of entering the building; the s. 9(1)(b) *mens rea* need not be present at the time of entry, only at the time of the commission of the ulterior offence. Recall also that in respect to both s. 9(1)(a) and s. 9(1)(b), the defendant must *know* that he is entering as a trespasser.

The ulterior offences relevant to s. 9(1)(a) are specified in s. 9(2):

THEFT ACT 1968

9.—(2) The offences referred to in subsection (1)(a) above are offences of stealing anything in the building or part of a building in question, of inflicting on any person therein any grievous bodily harm, and of doing unlawful damage to the building or anything therein.

The ulterior offences relevant to s. 9(1)(b) are contained in the subsection itself. They are stealing or attempting to steal anything in the building or that part of it, or inflicting or attempting to inflict on any person therein any grievous bodily harm.

What if the defendant's intention is conditional?

Attorney-General's References (Nos. 1 & 2 of 1979)
[1980] QB 180, Court of Appeal

In the first reference a grocer who lived above his shop heard the backdoor open and close late one night and intercepted the defendant who was ascending the stairs. The police were called and arrested the defendant. They asked him why he had entered the house and he replied 'To rob £2,000' and on being asked why he thought there was £2,000 there he said 'I don't know, I was just going to take something.' The indictment before the Crown Court averred that he had entered the grocer's premises as a trespasser 'with intent to steal therein'. The trial judge withdrew the case from the jury at the close of the prosecution case and directed an acquittal. The Attorney-General referred to the court for opinion the question whether a man who had entered a house as a trespasser with the intention of stealing money therein was entitled to be acquitted of an offence against s. 9(1)(a) of the Theft Act 1968 on the ground that his intention to steal was conditional upon his finding money in the house.

In the second reference a householder heard a sound at the French windows at the rear of her house. She called the police who went to the rear of the house and found the defendant holding and turning the handle of the French windows and inserting a long thin stick between the door and the doorframe. Later at the police station the defendant made a written statement in which he said 'I wasn't going to do any damage in the house, only see if there was anything lying around.' The indictment averred that the defendant had attempted to enter the dwelling house concerned 'with intent to steal therein'. At the close of the prosecution case the judge directed the jury to return a verdict of not guilty upon the ground that the evidence did not disclose a present intention to steal but merely a conditional intention. The Attorney-General referred to the court for opinion the question whether a man who was attempting to enter a house as a trespasser with the intention of stealing anything of value which he might find therein was entitled to be acquitted of the offence of attempted burglary on the ground that at the time of the attempt his intention was insufficient to amount to 'the intention of stealing anything' necessary for conviction under s. 9 of the Theft Act 1968.

On the hearing of both references:—

Held: (1) that, under s. 9(1)(a) of the Theft Act 1968, the offence of burglary was committed if a person entered a building as a trespasser with an intention to steal; that, where a person was charged with burglary, it was no defence to show that he did not intend to steal any specific objects, and, accordingly, the fact that the intention to steal was conditional on finding money in the house did not entitle a person to be acquitted on a charge of entering premises as a trespasser with intent to steal therein; and that the question asked in the first reference was to be answered in the negative.

■ **NOTES AND QUESTIONS**

1. Is the issue of conditional intent in a sense a red herring if the defendant can be convicted of a crime of attempted burglary, where impossibility will not be a defence (see ch. 12)? This observation suggests a more basic question: Why is there a need for the offence of burglary at all? Why is it not sufficient to charge the defendant with either the ulterior offence committed, or, where the ulterior offence is not completed, an attempt to commit the ulterior offence?

2. As burglary under s. 9(1)(a) is a type of inchoate crime, in that it could have the effect of frustrating the ultimate offence that the offender contemplates when entering as a trespasser, is it too far removed to have a crime of attempted burglary?

SECTION 6: CRIMINAL DAMAGE

Like theft offences, the law of criminal damage aims to protect property interests; but whereas theft protects an owner or rightful possessor from having his property appropriated, an offence of criminal damage protects against damage to or destruction of property. The controlling statute is the Criminal Damage Act 1971. There are also aggravated forms of the offence.

A: Damaging or destroying property belonging to another

The basic offence is set out in s. 1 of the Criminal Damage Act 1971:

CRIMINAL DAMAGE ACT 1971

1.—(1) A person who without lawful excuse destroys or damages any property belonging to another intending to destroy or damage any such property or being reckless as to whether any such property would be destroyed or damaged shall be guilty of an offence.

...

(8) An offence committed under this section by destroying or damaging property by fire shall be charged as arson.

The maximum punishment for a violation of s. 1(1) following a trial on indictment is 10 years' imprisonment (s. 4(2)). Where the offence is committed by fire it will be charged as arson with a potential maximum sentence of life imprisonment. Why should arson be treated so seriously?

(i) *Actus reus*

Three main problems arise with respect to the basic offence:

(a) What is damage?

(b) What is property?

(c) When can property be regarded as belonging to another?

(a) *Damage*

Whether property is damaged is a question of fact. What constitutes damage is not defined in the Act, but it appears to involve a reduction in the value or usefulness of the property.

Cox v Riley

(1986) 83 Cr App R 54, Queen's Bench Division

STEPHEN BROWN LJ: This is an appeal by way of case stated from the decision of the justices for the petty sessional division of Tamworth in the county of Stafford on April 1, 1985. On that day the defendant was charged on 'an information which alleged that on July 30, 1984 at Tamworth without lawful excuse he damaged the plastic circuit card of a G.S.C. computerised saw to the value of £620, belonging to High-Tech Profiles Ltd., intending to damage such property or being reckless as to whether such property would be damaged, contrary to section 1(1) of the Criminal Damage Act, 1971.

The justices in the case state that they found the following facts: (i) the defendant was employed by Hi-Tech Profiles Limited to work on a computerised saw owned by that company; (ii) that the computerised saw relied for its operation on a printed circuit card being inserted into it, containing programs which enabled the saw to be operated so that it could cut window frame profiles of different designs; (iii) that the printed circuit card was of no use to the company unless it contained programs which enabled it to cause the saw to operate as (ii) above; (iv) that on July 30, 1984 the defendant blanked the computerised saw of all its 16 programs thereby erasing the said programs from the printed circuit card by operating the program cancellation facility, contained within the computerised saw, once for each individual program removed; (v) that the defendant's action rendered the computerised saw inoperable, save for limited manual operation, which would cause production to be slowed dramatically.

The damage alleged was the removing of the program and really, it seems to me, the only possible argument which Mr Orme could put forward is that there was no damage within the meaning of the Act.

The question of damage has been considered by the Court of Appeal, Criminal Division, on November 29, 1984 in the unreported case of *Henderson & Battley*. The Court was presided over by Lawton CJ and he was sitting with Cantley J and Sir John Thompson. Cantley J gave the judgment of the Court.

In that case the facts were different, but it is relevant on the meaning of damage. In that case the charge was one of damaging a development land site, intending to damage that property or being reckless as to whether it would be damaged. The facts concerned a development site in the Isle of Dogs which had been cleared for development. It was flat except for a pile of crushed concrete which was kept there intentionally so that it could be used eventually in the laying of temporary roads whilst the development was carried on.

On the occasion in question 30 lorry loads of soil and rubble and mud were tipped on to the site. The appellants in that case, pretending to act with authority, had been operating the site, as Cantley J said, impudently as a public tip and charging their customers for the rubbish which was tipped. There was a submission before the trial judge which was repeated before the Court of Appeal that what they had done could not be said to have damaged the land, bearing in mind that this was a site cleared for building development. The argument was that the land was not damaged because the land beneath the piles of rubbish which had been tipped upon it was in the same condition as it was before the rubbish was tipped upon it. It was argued that there must be a distinction between the cost of putting something right and actual damage.

Cantley J said in the course of his judgment at p. 3B of the transcript: There is of course such a distinction, but if as here there is evidence that the owner of the land reasonably found it necessary to spend about £2,000 to remove the results of the appellants' operations it is not irrelevant to the question of whether this land, as a building site, was damaged. Ultimately whether damage was done to this land was a question of fact and degree for the jury. Damage can be of various kinds. In the *Concise Oxford Dictionary* 'damage' is defined as 'injury impairing value or usefulness'. That is a definition which would fit in very well with doing something to a cleared building site which at any rate for the time being impairs its usefulness as such. In addition, as it necessitates work and the expenditure of a large sum of money to restore it to its former state, it reduces its present value as a building site. This land was a perfectly good building site which did not need £2,000 spending on it in order to sell or use it as such until the appellants began their operations.

Cantley J continued:

> It was held as long ago as 1865 in the case of *Fisher* (LR 1 CCR 7) that an obstruction temporarily rendering a machine useless for the purpose for which it was intended to be used can be damage. In that case the facts were briefly these. A disgruntled employee who had been employed to operate an agricultural steam-engine had parted from his employer and it had seemed to him to be a good idea to put the steam-engine out of action. He screwed it up fairly tightly and he put a piece of stick up the water feed, and did other things of that kind. It is not necessary to enumerate them all: it is sufficient if I say that it took two hours, but no more, and no materials, to restore the machine to proper working order.

Some 'ancestor' of counsel in that case said Cantley J

> argued that in all the cases decided on the statute charging his client with malicious damage a certain portion of the machinery had been removed, and some absolute damage had been done to prevent the machine from working, and that there must be some 'lesion', as he put it, to the machine. Pigott B said there was damage because labour was required to reinstate the machine; not money, be it noted, but just two hours labour. Delivering a very short judgment of the Court for Crown Cases Reserved Pollock CB said: 'We are all of opinion that the conviction is good. It is like the case of spiking a gun, where there is no actual damage done to the gun, although it is rendered useless.'

It seems to me that the principle as explained by Cantley J applies in full measure to the present case. Undoubtedly, as in the old case of *Fisher (supra)*, the defendant in this instance for some reason, perhaps a grudge, wished to put out of action, albeit temporarily, the computerised saw, and he was able to do that by operating the computer blanking mechanism in order to erase from the printed circuit card the relevant programs. That made it necessary for time and labour and money to be expended in order to replace the relevant programs on the printed circuit card.

■ **NOTES AND QUESTIONS**

1. The defendants in *Cox* v *Riley* would now likely be charged with violating the Computer Misuse Act 1990, as amended by the Police and Justice Act 2006.

2. What are the arguments for and against using the criminal law to protect property from damage? Are they the same as for protecting property from theft?

Is there a *'de minimis'* principle (*de minimis non curat lex* – the law is not concerned with trivial violations) in respect of damage? Compare the following two cases:

R v A

[1978] Crim LR 689, Kent Crown Court

A was convicted by the Brentford Juvenile Court of an offence of criminal damage and remitted to Folkestone Juvenile Court for sentence. He appealed against conviction. He was one of a number of football supporters who were being escorted to an 'away' football ground 'crocodile fashion' by several police officers. The evidence given for the prosecution was that a police constable walking beside the 'crocodile' saw the appellant spit once at the back of a uniformed police sergeant. The police constable saw spittle land upon the sergeant's raincoat which was already covered with similar spittle, and arrested A. The sergeant continued on duty unaware of what had happened. When later informed of the state of his raincoat, he attempted to remove the spittle with a paper tissue, so as to present a less embarrassing spectacle.

On his return to the police station, the sergeant heard of the arrest of the appellant for the offence of criminal damage to his coat and so no further attempts were made to clean the raincoat. At the hearing, the raincoat was produced and a faint mark could be seen upon it, in the general vicinity of where the constable said he saw the spittle land. The prosecution contended that the raincoat required dry-cleaning, and must, therefore, have been 'damaged'.

It was contended on behalf of A that there was no case to answer because the prosecution had failed to prove any damage. The court was referred to a definition of 'damage' as 'rendering imperfect or inoperative.'

Held, allowing the appeal, that when interpreting the word 'damage,' the court must consider the use of an ordinary English word. Spitting at a garment could be an act capable of causing damage. However, one must consider the specific garment which has been allegedly damaged. If someone spat upon a satin wedding dress, for example, any attempt to remove the spittle might in itself leave a mark or stain. The court would find no difficulty in saying that an article had been rendered 'imperfect' if, after a reasonable attempt at cleaning it, a stain remained. An article might also have been rendered 'inoperative' if, as a result of what happened, it had been taken to dry cleaners.

However, in the present case, no attempt had been made, even with soap and water, to clean the raincoat, which was a service raincoat designed to resist the elements. Consequently, there was no likelihood that if wiped with a damp cloth, the first obvious remedy, there would be any trace or mark remaining on the raincoat requiring further cleaning. Furthermore, the raincoat was not rendered 'inoperative' at the time; if it was 'inoperative,' it was solely on account of being kept as an exhibit.

Thus, in the view of the court, nothing occurred which could properly be described as damage. An offence of assault might well have been appropriate but this was not a point which the court had to decide.

Hardman and Others v The Chief Constable of Avon and Somerset Constabulary

[1986] Crim LR 330, Bristol Crown Court

The appellants were convicted by the Justices of causing criminal damage to a pavement. They appealed.

They were members of the Campaign for Nuclear Disarmament. On 6 August, 1985 (which was the fortieth anniversary of the Hiroshima bombing) they painted human silhouettes on an asphalt pavement to represent vaporised human remains. The 'paint' was a fat free unstable whitewash, which was soluble in water. It was specially mixed in the expectation that rainwater would wash away the markings. The evidence suggested that this was correct and that rainwater and pedestrian traffic would *eventually* eradicate the markings. However, the Local Authority had acted before this happened and a 'Graffiti Squad' was employed to clean the pavement using high pressure water jets. It was contended by the appellants that following *'A' (a Juvenile)* v *The Queen* (1978) Crim LR 689 there was no 'damage' within the meaning of s. 1 of the Criminal Damage Act 1971.

> *Held*: Notwithstanding the fact that the markings could be washed away there had nonetheless been damage, which had caused expense and inconvenience to the Local Authority. An unduly narrow definition of damage was not appropriate. The approach of Walters J in *Samuels* v *Stubbs*, 4 SASR 200 was approved when he said at p. 203:
>
> > It seems to me that it is difficult to lay down any very general and, at the same time, precise and absolute rule as to what constitutes 'damage'. One must be guided in a great degree by the circumstances of each case, the nature of the article, and the mode in which it is affected or treated. Moreover, the meaning of the word 'damage' must as I have already said, be controlled by its context. The word may be used in the sense of 'mischief done to property.' . . .

■ NOTES AND QUESTIONS

1. Are *Hardman* and *R* v *A* reconcilable? How much damage must be done to give rise to a charge of criminal damage? Is it critical whether the damage requires the expenditure of money to repair the damaged property?

2. Damage to a machine can be caused by dismantling it, even if the individual components are not themselves damaged. However, if damage by dismantling is alleged it must be charged as damage to the machine and not to the individual parts. In *Morphitis* v *Salmon* [1990] Crim LR 48, the defendant dismantled a barrier across the road. He was charged with damage to the bar component of the barrier and acquitted. If he had been charged with damage to the barrier as a whole he might have been convicted. The court also made the point that a scratch on the bar of the barrier would not have constituted sufficient damage for a conviction as it could not have impaired its value or usefulness as scaffolding components get scratched in the normal course of events.

3. Would a charge of battery have been successful in *R* v *A*?

4. The s. 1(1) offence speaks in terms of either damage to or destruction of property. Is the reference to destruction of property otiose? Can one destroy property without damaging it? Does the destruction of another's property also constitute theft?

(b) Property

CRIMINAL DAMAGE ACT 1971

10.—(1) In this Act 'property' means property of a tangible nature, whether real or personal, including money and—
  (a) including wild creatures which have been tamed or are ordinarily kept in captivity, and any other wild creatures or their carcases if, but only if, they have been reduced into possession which has not been lost or abandoned or are in the course of being reduced into possession; but
  (b) not including mushrooms growing wild on any land or flowers, fruit or foliage of a plant growing wild on any land.
  For the purposes of this subsection 'mushrooms' includes any fungus and 'plant' includes any shrub or tree.

(c) Belonging to another

CRIMINAL DAMAGE ACT 1971

10.—(2) Property shall be treated for the purposes of this act as belonging to any person—
  (a) having the custody or control of it;

> (b) having in it any proprietary right or interest (not being an equitable interest arising only from an agreement to transfer or grant an interest); or
>
> (c) having a charge on it.
>
> (3) Where property is subject to a trust, the persons to whom it belongs shall be so treated as including any person having a right to enforce the trust.
>
> (4) Property of a corporation sole shall be so treated as belonging to the corporation notwithstanding a vacancy in the corporation.

■ NOTES AND QUESTIONS

1. What are the differences between the definition of property in the Criminal Damage Act and that contained in s. 4 of the TA 1968? What might account for the differences?

2. The TA 1968, s. 5, uses the concepts of 'possession or control'. Is the Criminal Damage Act's reference to 'custody or control' clearer? See *Warner* v *MPC* [1969] 2 AC 256.

3. Is it possible to be guilty of criminal damage to property one owns? If an owner lends property to another and in a subsequent fit of rage destroys the property, is the owner guilty of criminal damage? If an owner destroys her own property in order to collect the insurance money, has she committed criminal damage?

(ii) *Mens rea*

The defendant must intend or be reckless in respect of causing the damage. The meaning of recklessness for purposes of the Criminal Damage Act was for many years a matter of controversy until the House of Lords decision in *R* v *G* [2003] UKHL 50.

R v *G*

[2003] UKHL 50, House of Lords

For facts and holding see p. 146.

■ NOTES AND QUESTIONS

1. Is the test of *R* v *G* likely to cause potential violators to think before they act? Or is it to their legal advantage to act first and think later?

2. The defendant in *Caldwell*, the decision in which the now discredited objective test of recklessness was first formulated, was drunk at the time of his offence. This drunkenness arguably provided an independent basis for upholding his conviction without need for their Lordships to have addressed the test of recklessness, as getting drunk may itself be a reckless act. But is it the type of reckless act that should satisfy the *mens rea* of criminal damage?

3. Should intent for the purposes of the Criminal Damage Act be given the same interpretation as in *Woollin*? (Ch. 3)?

4. The 'intent' required for the Criminal Damage Act is lacking if the defendant believes the property is his own. This latter requirement overlaps to some extent with the statutory defence set out in s. 5(2). See *R* v *Smith (David)* [1974] 1 QB 354.

(iii) 'Without lawful excuse'

The Criminal Damage Act 1971, s. 1(1) contains the phrase 'without lawful excuse'. This phrase is defined in s. 5:

CRIMINAL DAMAGE ACT 1971

5. 'Without lawful excuse'

(1) This section applies to any offence under section 1(1) above and any offence under section 2 or 3 above other than one involving a threat by the person charged to destroy or damage property in a way which he knows is likely to endanger the life of another or involving an intent by the person charged to use or cause or permit the use of something in his custody or under his control so to destroy or damage property.

(2) A person charged with an offence to which this section applies shall whether or not he would be treated for the purposes of this Act as having a lawful excuse apart from this subsection, be treated for those purposes as having a lawful excuse—

    (a) if at the time of the act or acts alleged to constitute the offence he believed that the person or persons whom he believed to be entitled to consent to the destruction of or damage to the property in question had so consented, or would have so consented to it if he or they had known of the destruction or damage and its circumstances; or

    (b) if he destroyed or damaged or threatened to destroy or damage the property in question or, in the cause of a charge of an offence under section 3 above, intended to use or cause or permit the use of something to destroy or damage it, in order to protect property belonging to himself or another or a right or interest in property which was or which he believed to be vested in himself or another, and at the time of the act or acts alleged to constitute the offence he believed—

        (i) that the property, right or interest was in immediate need of protection; and

        (ii) that the means of protection adopted or proposed to be adopted were or would be reasonable having regard to all the circumstances.

(3) For the purposes of this section it is immaterial whether a belief is justified or not if it is honestly held.

(4) For the purposes of subsection (2) above a right or interest in property includes any right or privilege in or over land, whether created by grant, licence or otherwise.

(5) This section shall not be construed as casting doubt on any defence recognised by law as a defence to criminal charges.

If the belief in permission to damage the property is honest, the reason for the action is not relevant, even if fraud is involved.

R v Denton

[1982] 1 All ER 65, Court of Appeal

LORD LANE CJ: . . . The facts of the case were somewhat unusual. There is no dispute that on 3 January 1980 the defendant set light to some machinery in the cotton mill. The machinery was very badly damaged, and as a result of that conflagration damage was also done, to a much lesser degree it is true, to the building itself. The total damage to stock and building was said to be some £40,000.

On Monday, 17 March 1980 the defendant presented himself at the police station and told the police that he had in fact started that fire. He described how he had done it, and he then made a statement under caution, in which he gave his reason for having started the fire: that it was for the benefit of the business, because the business was in difficulties, and, although he was going to get no direct benefit from it himself, he thought he would be doing a good turn to the financial status of the company if he were to set light to the premises and goods as he did. Hence the charge against him.

When it came to the trial he gave evidence that his employer, to whom we will refer to as 'T' for obvious reasons, had asked him to put the machines out of action and he had agreed to set light to it. The reason given to him by the employer for that request was because the company was in difficulties; the way that T put it was: 'There is nothing like a good fire for improving the financial circumstances of a business.'

...The fact that somebody may have had a dishonest intent which in the end he was going to carry out, namely to claim from the insurance company, cannot turn what was not originally a crime into a crime. There is no unlawfulness under the 1971 Act in burning a house. It does not become unlawful because there may be an inchoate attempt to commit fraud contained in it; that is to say it does not become a crime under the 1971 Act, whatever may be the situation outside of the Act.

Consequently it is apparent to us that the judge, in his ruling in this respect, was wrong. Indeed it seems to us, if it is necessary to go as far as this, that it was probably unnecessary for the defendant to invoke s. 5 of the 1971 Act at all, because he probably had a lawful excuse without it, in that T was lawfully entitled to burn the premises down. The defendant believed it. He believed that he was acting under the directions of T and that on its own, it seems to us, may well have provided him with a lawful excuse without having resort to s. 5.

■ NOTES AND QUESTIONS

1. In *Blake* v *DPP* [1993] Crim LR 587, the court held that God is not a person capable of giving consent to damage property and that the defendant's belief, no matter how powerful, genuine or honestly held, that he had God's authorisation to cause the damage in question was not a lawful excuse under English law. Is the decision in conflict with the freedom of religion guaranteed by Article 9 of the European Convention of Human Rights?

2. In *Chamberlain* v *Lindon* [1998] 1 WLR 1252, the defendant demolished a wall which had been built by his neighbour which he believed was obstructing his right of way. The Queen's Bench Division held that the defendant had a lawful excuse within s. 5(2)(b) in that he honestly believed that he had to destroy the wall in order to protect a right or interest in property that was in immediate need of protection and that the means adopted were reasonable in all the circumstances. Does the decision elevate the defendant's belief above the law – could he not have sued his neighbour?

3. Of what offence, if any, could Denton have been convicted? Has his employer committed an offence?

4. Under s. 5(2) the question of whether or not a particular act was done in order to protect property is answered by applying an objective test. See *R* v *Hunt* (1978) 66 Cr App R 105; *R* v *Hill* [1989] Crim LR 136; *Blake* v *DPP*, above; *Johnson* v *DPP* [1994] Crim LR 673. Is this inconsistent with *Denton*? With *R* v *G*?

B: Destroying or damaging property with intent to endanger life

CRIMINAL DAMAGE ACT 1971

1.—(2) A person who without lawful excuse destroys or damages any property, whether belonging to himself or another—

    (a) intending to destroy or damage any property or being reckless as to whether any property would be destroyed or damaged; and

> (b) intending by the destruction or damage to endanger the life of another or being reckless as to whether the life of another would be thereby endangered;
>
> shall be guilty of an offence.
>
> (3) An offence committed under this section by destroying or damaging property by fire shall be charged as arson.

The maximum punishment for this aggravated offence is life imprisonment (s. 4(1)). In many cases the defendant may also be subject to a charge of attempted murder. However, while the criminal damage offence requires proof of damage to property, it is wider than attempted murder because it is sufficient that the defendant is reckless as to whether life is endangered. Attempted murder will require proof of an intent to kill (see Chapter 12).

(i) *Actus reus*

The terms 'damage', 'destroy' and 'property' are defined as for s. 1(1), above. However, in the aggravated form of criminal damage note that the property need not belong to another; one can commit this crime by destroying one's own property. Why this difference?

(ii) *Mens rea*

The defendant must:

(a) intend or be reckless as to damaging or destroying property; and

(b) intend or be reckless that *by that damage* will endanger life.

R v Steer

[1987] 2 All ER 833, House of Lords

The defendant went to the house of his former business partner, against whom he had a grudge, and fired several shots at the house with an automatic rifle. No injuries were caused to the partner or his wife inside the house and there was no suggestions that any of the shots had been aimed at either of them. The defendant was charged with and convicted of, *inter alia*, damaging property being reckless whether the life of another would be endangered thereby, contrary to s. 1(2) of the Criminal Damage Act 1971. He appealed, contending that s. 1(2) only applied if property was damaged and the damage in turn caused danger to life, whereas any danger to the defendant's partner and his wife had been directly caused by the bullets fired by the defendant and not by the damaged property. The Crown contended that 'intending by the destruction or damage' in s. 1(2)(b) referred to the act which caused the destruction of or damage to property was the cause of the danger to life. The Court of Appeal allowed the defendant's appeal and quashed the conviction, holding that a person could only be convicted under s. 1(2) of recklessly endangering the life of another by damaging or destroying property if it was proved that the danger to life resulted from the destruction of or damage to property. The Crown appealed to the House of Lords.

Held: For a person to be guilty of the offence under s. 1(2) of the 1971 Act of destroying or damaging any property with intent to endanger the life of another by the destruction or damage or being reckless whether the life of another would be thereby endangered the prosecution had to prove that the danger to life resulted from the destruction of or damage to the property and it was not sufficient for the prosecution to prove that the danger to life resulted from the act which caused the destruction or damage. It followed therefore that the defendant was not guilty of the offence charged and the appeal would accordingly be dismissed...

R v Asquith, Webster and Seamans, R v Warwick
Joined Appeals House of Lords [1995] 1 Cr App R 492

In *Asquith, Webster and Seamans*

The appellants pushed a coping stone from a bridge on to a train passing below. It hit a carriage, showering the passengers with debris from the roof but did not fall into the carriage.

In *Warwick*

The appellant was the passenger in a stolen car who hurled bricks at a police car, smashing a window and showering the officers with glass. The stolen car also rammed the police car and another brick was thrown which hit an officer.

LORD TAYLOR CJ: If a defendant throws a brick at the windscreen of a moving vehicle, given that he causes *some* damage to the vehicle, whether he is guilty under s1(2) does not depend on whether the brick hits or misses the windscreen, but whether he intended that the damage therefrom should endanger life or whether he was reckless as to that outcome. As to the dropping of stones from bridges, the effect of the statute may be thought strange. If the defendant's intention is that the stone itself should crash through the roof of a train . . . and thereby directly injure a passenger or if he was reckless only as to that outcome, the section would not bite . . . If, however, the defendant intended or was reckless that the stone would smash the roof of the train or vehicle so that metal or wood struts from the roof would or . . . might descend upon a passenger, endangering life, he would surely be guilty. This may seem a dismal distinction.

Appeals dismissed. Convictions upheld.

The fact that lives are not endangered is not relevant if the requisite intention can be proved:

R v Dudley
[1989] Crim LR 57, Court of Appeal

D who had a grievance against the J family, consumed drink and drugs, went to their house and, using an accelerant, threw a fire bomb at the house, causing a high sheet of flame outside the glass door. The fire was extinguished by the J family and only trivial damage was caused. He was charged with arson under s. 1(1) and (2) of the Criminal Damage Act 1971; he pleaded guilty to simple arson and a trial proceeded on the counts laid under s. 1(2). At the close of the prosecution case D's counsel submitted that there was no case to answer because the jury could not properly find that the actual damage caused was intended to endanger life or was likely to do so, and he relied on *R v Steer* [1988] AC 111. The trial judge rejected the submission and D thereupon changed his plea to guilty to the count of arson being reckless as whether life would be endangered. He appealed against conviction, submitting that the judge's ruling was wrong in law.

Held, the appeal would be dismissed. The words 'destruction or damage' in s. 1(2)(b) of the Act (endangering life) referred back to destruction or damage intended, or as to which there was recklessness, in s. 1(2)(a) (damaging property). The words did not refer to the destruction or damage actually caused . . .

■ NOTES AND QUESTIONS

1. Note that the phrase 'without lawful excuse' does not have the same meaning in s. 1(2) as in s. 1(1). Section 5 specifically states that it does not apply to s. 1(2). Lawful excuse in the context of s. 1(2) is therefore confined to situations where the defendant acts in self-defence, defence of another, or in prevention of crime, or to apprehend an offender.

2. How does the 'dismal distinction' identified by Lord Taylor CJ in *Asquith* arise? How could the statute be re-worded to avoid it?

FURTHER READING

Wilson, *Criminal Law: Doctrine and Theory* (2011), Chapter 14

Ashworth, 'Robbery Re-assessed' [2002] Criminal Law Review 851

Beatson and Simester, 'Stealing One's Own Property' (1999) 115 Law Quarterly Review 372

Bogg and Stanton-Ife, 'Theft as Exploitation' (2003) 23 Legal Studies 402

Elliot, 'Endangering Life by Destroying or Damaging Property' [1997] Criminal Law Review 382

Griew, 'Dishonesty: The Objections to *Feely* and *Ghosh*' [1985] Criminal Law Review 341

Halpin, 'The Test for Dishonesty' [1996] Criminal Law Review 283

Hammond, 'Theft of Information' (1984) 100 Law Quarterly Review 252

Mellisaris, 'The Concept of Appropriation and the Offence of Theft' (2007) 70 Modern Law Review 581

Parsons, 'Dishonest Appropriation after *Gomez* and *Hinks*' (2004) 68 Journal of Criminal Law 520

Simester and Sullivan, 'The Nature and Rationale of Property Offences' in Duff and Green eds., *Defining Crimes* (2005) 172

Shute, 'Appropriation and the Law of Theft' [2002] Criminal Law Review 445

Shute and Horder, 'Thieving and Deceiving—What is the Difference?' (1993) 56 Modern Law Review 548

Smith's Law of Theft (2007) D. Ormerod and D. Williams

A.T.H. Smith, *Property Offences* (1994)

Steele, 'Permanently Borrowing and Lending: A New View of s. 6 Theft Act 1968' (2008) 17 Nottingham Law Review 3

8

Fraud and Making Off without Payment

SECTION 1: **INTRODUCTION**

The Fraud Act 2006 (FA 2006) abolishes a number of offences under the Theft Acts 1968 and 1978. The gist of the defences was the obtaining of some benefit, e.g. property, services, or the avoidance of a debt, by deception. These are replaced by a general offence of fraud, which can be committed in three ways. The major change made is that the offence is now constituted by the defendant's dishonest intention – to make a gain or cause a loss, rather than its result – the actual obtaining of the benefit. The FA 2006 also replaces the offence of obtaining services by deception with that of obtaining services dishonestly.

The change in emphasis – from result to intention – was thought necessary to address a number of problems under the old scheme of liability. One of the problems was its complexity. Avoiding payment of a debt by deception, for example, could be committed in one of three ways and it was not only law students who found it difficult to identify the right pigeon hole. Another problem was the question of proof. An abject villain could escape liability for her fraudulent deception if the prosecution were unable to prove that the victim was taken in by or was influenced by the deception. This was particularly problematic in the case of internet fraud such as 'phishing'. Very few people are taken in by internet scams. Fraudsters know this, but they also know that perhaps one in a million will be and have designed their scams accordingly. It was thought therefore that it should be the dishonesty of the scam rather than the obtaining of the benefit which triggers State intervention. The major offences are as follows:

By s. 1 of the Fraud Act 2006 a general offence of fraud is created which can be committed in one of three ways:

> (1) A person is guilty of fraud if he is in breach of any of the sections listed in subsection (2) (which provide for different ways of committing the offence).
> (2) The sections are—
>   (a) section 2 (fraud by false representation),
>   (b) section 3 (fraud by failing to disclose information), and
>   (c) section 4 (fraud by abuse of position).
> (3) A person who is guilty of fraud is liable—
>   (a) on summary conviction, to imprisonment for a term not exceeding 12 months or to a fine not exceeding the statutory maximum (or to both);
>   (b) on conviction on indictment, to imprisonment for a term not exceeding 10 years or to a fine (or to both).

A: Fraud by false representation

By section 2(1) fraud by false representation is committed where a person

> (a) dishonestly makes a false representation, and
> (b) intends, by making the representation—
>   (i) to make a gain for himself or another, or
>   (ii) to cause loss to another or to expose another to a risk of loss.
> (2) A representation is false if—
> (a) it is untrue or misleading, and
> (b) the person making it knows that it is, or might be, untrue or misleading.
> (3) 'Representation' means any representation as to fact or law, including a representation as to the state of mind of—
> (a) the person making the representation, or
> (b) any other person.
> (4) A representation may be express or implied.
> (5) For the purposes of this section a representation may be regarded as made if it (or anything implying it) is submitted in any form to any system or device designed to receive, convey or respond to communications (with or without human intervention).

(i) *Actus Reus*

The *actus reus* of the offence is making a false representation. Representation is not defined. The nearest synonym, where the representation is verbal, is 'statement'. Where the representation is not made expressly, a useful synonym is 'creating an impression'. So a person who hires a Rolls Royce in order to dupe the victim into giving him goods on credit is making a representation by creating an impression of credit worthiness. Fraud by representation cannot be committed in the absence of a representation. So a seller who fails to inform a purchaser that the car he is selling has a burnt out clutch is not guilty of fraud. The representation may be express, implied, or by conduct. Some examples follow:

1. **Express representations as to fact**: 'The cheque is in the post'; 'the car is a good little runner'; 'I have no convictions for any driving offence'; 'I intend to pay this bill with my next pay packet'; 'I think the bicycle is three years old'. These are verbal representations of fact, the latter two being representations as to the representor's state of mind. An express representation can also be made by conduct, for example wearing a golf club tie as a means of securing entrance to the course or changing the mileage reading on a car's odometer.

2. **Express representations as to law**: 'You have no right to claim a refund on the grounds of the refrigerator's lack of merchantable quality'; 'Bad luck. Your house purchase has fallen through. I'm afraid you cannot recover your deposit'.

3. **Implied representations as to fact**:
   A. Following a lapse in Dougal's membership of a gym he enters the gym, says hello to the receptionist and uses the facilities as usual. Here he is implying/creating the impression that he is still a member.
   B. Jane pays for a pair of trousers using a cheque and a cheque guarantee card. She is impliedly representing that (a) she has an account with the bank on which the cheque is drawn, (b) that she is the holder of the card,

(c) she has authority to use the cheque card, (d) the bank will honour the cheque,

C. Under the law prior to the FA 2006 a person who failed to disclose information would also, in two situations, be guilty of an offence of deception. The first situation was where there was a legal obligation of disclosure (see *Firth* below). This is now specifically covered by FA 2006, s. 1(2)(6) which provides that a person may be guilty of fraud by failing to disclose information he is under a duty to disclose. The second is where there had been a change of circumstances which change had not been communicated to the representee (*DPP* v *Ray*). This will continue to attract criminal liability under s. 2.

R v Firth

(1990) 91 Cr App R 217, Court of Appeal

The appellant, a consultant gynaecologist/obstetrician, was charged, *inter alia*, with four counts alleging an evasion of a liability by deception contrary to s. 2(1)(c) of the Theft Act 1978. The prosecution case was that he had avoided being billed for NHS hospital services by failing to inform a hospital of the private patient status of certain of his patients. He was convicted and appealed on the grounds, *inter alia*, that the recorder had erred in not acceding to a defence submission that the allegations to be proved required proof that the dishonest obtaining was achieved by acts of commission, whereas the evidence only showed acts of omission; further, the words 'legally enforceable' in s. 2(2) meant that the prosecution had to establish an existing liability at the time of the alleged deception.

THE LORD CHIEF JUSTICE: . . . we turn now to the perfected grounds of appeal. Ground 1 reads as follows:

'The learned recorder erred in not acceding to the submission made by the defence at the close of the Crown's case that counts 4, 5, 6 and 7 were wrongly laid in law in that the allegations to be proved required proof of acts of commission whereas the evidence disclosed only acts of omission.'

It is not altogether clear what that ground of appeal means. We take it to mean that the counts laid under section 2(1)(c) of the Theft Act cannot be brought home against the defendant unless the prosecution prove that the dishonest obtaining was achieved by acts of commission, that is to say the deception must be by commission, and not by omission.

One turns to the Act itself to see what the draftsman of the statute in fact says. Section 2 reads as follows:

"Evasion of liability by deception

(1) Subject to subsection (2) below, where a person by any deception . . . (c) dishonestly obtains any exemption from or abatement of liability to make a payment; he shall be guilty of an offence.

(2) For purposes of this section 'liability' means legally enforceable liability; and subsection (1) shall not apply in relation to a liability that has not been accepted or established to pay compensation for a wrongful act or omission . . . (4) For purposes of subsection (1)(c) 'obtains' includes obtaining for another or enabling another to obtain."

That would cover, for instance, if it were the case, this appellant obtaining an exemption on behalf of a patient whom he was treating.

The prosecution allegation in these various counts was that the appellant, by failing dishonestly to inform the hospital of the private patient status of the women, either Mrs. Quigley or Mrs. Haslam as the case may be, had caused either them or himself not to be billed for services which should have been charged against them.

If, as was alleged, it was incumbent upon him to give the information to the hospital and he deliberately and dishonestly refrained from doing so, with the result that no charge was levied either upon the patients or upon himself, in our judgment the wording of the section and subsection which I have just read is satisfied. It matters not whether it was an act of commission or an act of omission. Providing those matters were substantiated the prosecution had made out their case. That means, in brief, that the recorder was right to reject any submission to the contrary.

In *DPP* v *Ray* [1974] AC 370 (referred to in *R* v *Rai* below) the House of Lords ruled that by not informing B of a change of circumstances a person is impliedly (and falsely) representing them to be unchanged. This, it is presumed, will remain the result under the FA 2006.

R v Rai
(2000) 1 Cr App R 242, Court of Appeal

The appellant applied to the council for a grant to provide a bathroom downstairs in his house for the use of his elderly and infirm mother. Two days after the appellant was notified that the grant had been approved, his mother died. The appellant did not tell the council of his mother's death, and contractors did the building work on behalf of the council. The appellant's defence to a charge of obtaining services by deception, contrary to s. 1(1) of the Theft Act 1978, was that he had no legal or contractual duty to inform the council and that mere silence or inactivity could not constitute conduct amounting to deception within s. 15(4) of the Theft Act 1968 and thus there had been no deception under s. 1(1) of the Act of 1978. Before the jury was empanelled the trial judge ruled that the appellant's silence in the circumstances amounted to conduct sufficient to constitute a deception on the local authority, whereupon the appellant pleaded guilty on the specific factual basis that his only relevant conduct was his failure to inform the council of the death of his mother. He appealed against conviction on the ground that the judge's ruling was wrong.

The learned judge, in his reasoned ruling, based his decision principally on an analogy with the somewhat different facts of the House of Lords case of *Director of Public Prosecutions* v *Ray* (1974) 58 Cr App R 130, [1974] A.C. 370. He accurately summarised the facts of that case in the following terms:

> 'Five students went to a Chinese restaurant intending to have a meal and pay for it. After eating the main course, they decided not to pay for it but they remained where they were until the waiter went out of the room and then they ran from the restaurant and the defendant was convicted by the justices of dishonestly obtaining a pecuniary advantage by deception, and the charge was that the defendant obtained for himself a pecuniary advantage, namely a meal, and evaded the debt by running out of the restaurant without payment.'

He went on:

> 'It was submitted that as he did not change his mind until after the meal had been consumed, that he did nothing to evade the debt. By simply sitting there and then leaving the restaurant at a convenient moment, the House of Lords took the view that that was incorrect and that the transaction had to be regarded as a whole in that the defendant's conduct was a continuing representation of his present intention to pay.'

The relevant continuing conduct was staying in the restaurant; that was the basis for the finding by the majority in the House of Lords that there was sufficient conduct in that particular case to amount to a deception. The students had changed their minds about paying. They did so whilst sitting at the table in the restaurant. They continued to sit there for a time, and, in that sense, the conduct was continuing because they were then sitting there with their newly formed intention not to pay for their meals, thus falsifying their earlier implied representation that they would pay. This, in the opinion of the House of Lords, amounted to sufficient conduct to satisfy that essential element of the offence.

The basis in the present case of the learned judge's ruling was that this appellant's conduct was equivalent to that conduct on the part of those students, and the question for this Court is whether that was correct.

...the learned judge's ruling was, in our judgment, correct, and there is thus no basis for this Court to hold that the plea of guilty entered by the appellant is in any way wrong or that the conviction should be regarded as unsafe. For those reasons, the appeal against conviction is dismissed.

Fraud is only committed if the representation is false but under subsection (2) a representation is false if (a) it is untrue or misleading, and (b) the person making it knows that it is, or might be, untrue or misleading. This is a surprisingly wide definition. It includes the situation of someone who believes what he says to be true but knows it might not be true or knows it might be misleading.

Each representation in the following examples are potentially false; Adam, because he knows the statement is misleading due to the odometer reading; Claire because she knows the statement is misleading; Jane because, assuming the attribution to be incorrect, she knows the statement might not be true. Liability here depends simply upon proof of dishonesty.

1. Adam is a sales representative. He owns a BMW in which he has driven 111,000 miles since he bought it a year ago. The odometer, having 'gone round the clock', shows 11,000 miles. He puts a notice on his car windscreen in the following terms: 'BMW for sale. One year old. One careful owner. £30k'.

2. Claire is an art dealer. She describes a painting in the sales particulars as an 'early Constable'. The painting, as she knows, is painted not by John Constable, but by his son, John Charles Constable, a lesser artist.

3. Jane is an art dealer. She describes a painting in the sales particulars as an 'early Rembrandt'. She believes it to be a Rembrandt, and indeed bought it as such, but knows that in the case of this particular painter precise attribution is difficult due to the number of workshop versions of Rembrandt's work on the market. In fact it is not a Rembrandt.

Under the previous law it was of the essence of deception that the false representation was acted on by the victim. There is no longer any such requirement. So the *actus reus* of fraud is committed in all the above cases whether or not the sellers make a sale and whether or not anybody was deceived. There is not even a requirement that the representation be communicated to another. So Adam commits the *actus reus* of the offence the second he places the advert on his windscreen. He does so although, for example, he has not yet removed the car from the garage.

It was also not possible to make representation to a machine under the Theft Acts. The essence of the deception offences was the tricking of a human mind. The Fraud Act now makes it possible to commit fraud via a machine, since a representation is regarded as having been made 'if it (or anything implying it) is submitted in any form to any system or device designed to receive, convey or respond to communications, with or without human intervention'. This would include putting a foreign coin in a slot machine or putting false information on an online tax or insurance form.

(ii) *Mens Rea*

The core mens rea element is the defendant's intention by making the representation, to make a gain for himself or another, or to cause loss to another or to expose another to a risk of loss. Intention in this context, in line with its meaning in theft and unlike its meaning elsewhere, means purpose or knowledge of virtual certainty as a matter of law, rather than as a matter of evidence. If A knows that his representation will cause loss to V or expose V to the risk of loss he intends that consequence. Gain and loss, by s. 5 of the Act, *are restricted to* gains or loss in money or other property. Property in this context means 'any property whether real or personal including things in action and other intangible property'. So, making a false representation in order to gain a better place in a queue for a concert or misrepresenting one's golf handicap in order to join an exclusive club would not be covered. The gain or loss can be temporary or permanent so making a misrepresentation to induce a loan of a car or money or to gain time to pay a debt would be covered. In this latter example fraud is constituted as 'gain' includes a gain by keeping what one has, as well as a gain by getting what one does not have. 'Loss' includes a loss by not getting what one might get, as well as a loss by parting with what one has.

There are four possible cases of this *mens rea* requirement. The first, which will be the most usual, is the intention to make a gain for oneself by false representation. The second is the intention to make a gain for someone else, for example giving a false reference to secure someone a job or a loan.

The third case is where the representor intends to cause a loss to another. Usually this will go hand in hand with an intention to make a gain, either for oneself or for another but it will include cases where the representor's purpose is purely destructive as where his motive is to damage B.

The fourth case is where the representor intends not to cause a loss to the representee but to expose him to the risk of loss. An illustration occurs in a pre 2006 Act case.

R v Anthony Adward Allsop

(1977) 64 Cr App R 29, Court of Appeal

The appellant was a sub-broker for a hire-purchase company. His function as such was to introduce prospective purchasers of cars and to fill in application forms in respect of them. From time to time he put false particulars in the forms so as to induce the hire-purchase company to accept applications which they might otherwise have rejected. When doing this the appellant expected and believed that these transactions would be completed satisfactorily so that the hire-purchase company would profit from them. The appellant was charged with conspiracy to defraud. The judge directed the jury that they had to be sure that the appellant realised that the making of the false statements was likely to lead to the detriment or prejudice of the hire-purchase company in the sense of economic loss, but not necessarily the loss of money. The appellant was convicted and appealed on the ground, *inter alia*, that the judge's direction was too wide in that the jury should have been directed that they must be satisfied that the appellant intended to cause economic loss to the hire-purchase company.

SHAW LJ: This appeal raises a short but interesting question in relation to the nature of the intent requisite to constitute the offence of conspiracy to defraud. The argument advanced by Mr. Mervyn Heald on behalf of the appellant is that such an intent involves as an essential element the objective of causing actual economic loss to the person alleged to have been defrauded so that it is not sufficient if that person's economic interests are merely threatened incidentally. Miss Goddard, for the Crown, asserts that no more is necessary than the intent to bring about a situation in which the economic interests of the person deceived are threatened or prejudiced, or are likely to be threatened or prejudiced, albeit that such threat or prejudice is undesired or incidental so far as the person responsible for the deceit is concerned.

[The learned Lord Justice stated the facts and continued:]

... Generally the primary objective of fraudsmen is to advantage themselves. The detriment that results to their victims is secondary to that purpose and incidental. It is "intended" only in the sense that it is a contemplated outcome of the fraud that is perpetrated. If the deceit which is employed imperils the economic interest of the person deceived, this is sufficient to constitute fraud even though in the event no actual loss is suffered and notwithstanding that the deceiver did not desire to bring about an actual loss...

It matters not that in the end the hire-purchasers concerned paid to Prestige what was due to them. In the interim that corporation suffered economic loss in consequence of the misrepresentations made by the appellant. Mr. Heald argues that this is neither here nor there. The essential consideration so his argument ran is what the appellant intended at the outset; he averred that, it is not sufficient if the intention to put Prestige's interests at risk was merely incidental when the ultimate purpose was not to injure them. We do not agree. Interests which are imperilled are less valuable in terms of money than those same interests when they are secure and protected. Where a person intends by deceit to induce a course of conduct in another which puts that other's economic interests in jeopardy he is guilty of fraud even though he does not intend or desire that actual loss should ultimately be suffered by that other in this context.

We would adopt and apply the view expressed, also by Lord Diplock, in *Hyam v. D.P.P.* (1974) 59 Cr.App.R. 91, 110, [1975] A.C. 55, 86 where he said in crimes of this class: '...no distinction is to be drawn in English law between the state of mind of one who does an act because he desires it to produce a particular evil consequence, and the state of mind of one who does the act knowing full well that it is likely to produce that consequence although it may not be the object he was seeking to achieve by doing the act. What is common to both these states of mind is willingness to produce the particular evil consequence: and this, in my view is the *mens rea* need to satisfy a requirement, whether imposed by statute or existing at common law, that in order to constitute the offence with which the accused is charged he must have acted with "intent" to produce a particular evil consequence....'

We therefore reject the submissions made on behalf of the appellant and dismiss this appeal.

The final *mens rea* element is dishonesty. Dishonesty, in this context, is *Ghosh* dishonesty (see Ch. 7). There is no equivalent to s. 2 of the Theft Act 1968 in the Fraud Act. This means that a person who makes a false representation in order to gain what he believes (s. 2(1)(a)) he is in law entitled to is not automatically to be acquitted. It will be a matter for the jury. This was made clear in a pre-2006 Act case which, it seems likely, was not changed by the FA 2006.

R v Johnathan Robert Woolven
(1983) 77 Cr App R 231, Court of Appeal

The facts appear in the judgment.

LEONARD J: The question which arises for our decision in whether the learned judge's direction as to the element of dishonesty was adequate to do justice in the present case. At an early stage in the summing up he directed the jury in accordance with the judgment of this Court in *Ghosh* (1982) 75 Cr.App.R. 154; [1982] Q.B. 1053. In giving the judgment of the Court the Lord Chief Justice said at pp. 162–163 and p. 1064 respectively: 'In determining whether the prosecution has proved that the defendant was acting dishonestly, a jury must first of all decide whether according to the ordinary standards of reasonable and honest people what was done was dishonest. If it was not dishonest by those standards, that is the end of the matter and the prosecution fails. If it was dishonest by those standards, then the jury must consider whether the defendant himself must have realised that what he was doing was by those standards dishonest.'

The learned judge in the present case said to the jury at page 3F of the transcript: 'So the final...and the determining question...is whether on the evidence you are satisfied that [the appellant] was acting dishonestly.' He told them to ask themselves first what the appellant had done. Then they were to consider whether his actions were dishonest, measured by the standards of any ordinary honest man. Finally they had to decide whether they were satisfied that the appellant must have realised his conduct would be condemned as dishonest by any other ordinary person. He added the following words at p. 4D: 'If, having heard all the evidence in the case, your final conclusion is that notwithstanding what he did he may not have regarded it as dishonest, that is an answer to this charge.'

Towards the end of the summing up the learned judge again returned to the issue of dishonesty leaving it to the jury in these words: 'If you think in the face of those facts, members of the jury, that he may at the time have regarded his conduct as being perfectly honest, then he is entitled to be acquitted by your hand. If, having looked at the whole of the facts that he himself admits, if your conclusion is that he must have known at the time when he did these things that judged by ordinary standards of ordinary men he was acting dishonestly, then he is guilty of this offence. That is the issue for your consideration.'

In the judgment of this Court any direction based on the concept of claim of right as set out in section 2(1)(*a*). or otherwise, would have added nothing to what the learned judge in fact said. Indeed a direction based on *Ghosh* (*supra*) seems likely to us to cover all occasions when a section 2(1)(a) type direction might otherwise have been desirable.

Our attention was drawn to *Falconer-Atlee* (1973) 58 Cr.App.R. 348 —a case of theft to which section 2(1)(*a*) therefore applied. A claim of right was raised by the evidence. The learned judge directed the jury as to the elements which the prosecution had to prove in order to establish the offence. In dealing with the element of dishonesty he said: 'The all important word . . . in those four elements is 'dishonestly,' but of course, it may well be that you may not have much difficulty in deciding that if somebody in circumstances such as are alleged here appropriated property belonging to another with the intention of permanently depriving the other of it, then it was done dishonestly, but that is a matter for you. It is for you to decide whether whatever was done was done dishonestly. If you are not satisfied that it was, then you could not convict . . . .'

In delivering the judgment of this Court, Roskill L.J. (as he then was) said at p. 359: 'To give the jury the limited direction which the learned judge gave, impeccable so far as it went in relation to "dishonestly," but on the facts of this case not to go on to tell them what section 2(1)(*a*) expressly provided was *not* to be regarded as "dishonest" was to omit what was an extremely important direction.'

In contrast, the summing up in the present case clearly brought home to the jury that they must consider the appellant's own account of events and what he said about his state of knowledge and if, on that basis, they thought he might have regarded his actions as honest, they must acquit.

At pp. 32–33 the trial judge summarised the matters which were put forward by the appellant as part of his case. He had opened the bank account using a false name. He knew the account was going to have money transferred to it from an account belonging to Roberts. He understood that Roberts could not withdraw the money in the ordinary way because if he did so the bank would claim it so as to discharge or reduce the overdraft on the other account. It followed that Roberts's bank could not have known about his connection with the account from which the money was to be transferred. The appellant knew about the false letter which purported to establish his identity in order to induce the bank to part with the £16,200. He was carrying the letter when he went finally to the bank. He knew that the telephone number in the letter was that of a telephone box. We emphasise that these were the facts as propounded by the appellant. The jury, in all probability, considered them in the context of Roberts's version which imputed some knowledge of the true state of affairs to the appellant.

The jury in the present case had the facts before them. The appellant eventually conceded that ordinary people would, on the basis of his own version, have found his behaviour to be dishonest. He maintained that he himself had not thought it to be dishonest at the time. In the view of this Court it was inevitable that the jury would disbelieve the last proposition, even if they believed the appellant's account otherwise.

There is in our view nothing unsafe or unsatisfactory about this conviction. Accordingly, for the reasons stated, the appeal is dismissed.

■ NOTES AND QUESTIONS

1. The coverage of s. 2 is far broader than that under the Theft Act 1978, but sometimes, it is arguably excessive. For example, the absence of a requirement that D must intend permanent gain/loss means that the offence is committed where a debtor spins his creditor a false hard luck story in order to obtain for himself (or another) extra time to pay or to avoid payment entirely. Should it really be a criminal wrong to say something untrue, e.g. the cheque's in the post, my salary comes in in a week's time, for the purpose of gaining extra time to pay a debt?

2. The sometimes unnecessarily broad coverage of s. 2, together with the absence of any filtering mechanism, beyond the dishonesty requirement, for trivial acts of deception is likely to place far more of an onus on prosecutors to ensure prosecutions accord with common sense and are implemented fairly. As in the previous example, neither Adam's nor Eve's acts in the following scenarios deserve criminalisation but a greater injustice by far would be for the two scenarios to be treated differently.

> Adam is the vicar of All Hallows. In the course of his sermon on Charity he tells the congregation to give all the change that they have accumulated at the end of the week to the poor. He tells them that, having heard and acted upon his message, 'God will look favourably upon you if you do.'
>
> Adam is the owner of Hallows Entertainments, a gaming house. Desirous of providing some extra entertainment for those bored with the slot machines, and some harmless fun for his wife, Eve, who fancies trying her hand at fortune telling, he puts a booth in the middle of the gaming house and places next to it a sign which reads 'Visit Madame Morticia, the famed palm reader. Cross her palm with silver and she will tell you what the next 12 months has in store for you.'

3. V owes Adam £1000. V, who is very hard up, tells Adam he can have it at the end of the month when his salary is paid in. Adam replies that he needs it immediately because a creditor is threatening him with bankruptcy. In fact he needs it to pay a blackmailer who is threatening to expose him for fraud. Is Adam dishonest? Is it satisfactory, given that the money is owed him, that the question whether Adam is dishonest or not will be decided by the jury's view as to the honesty of securing payment under such circumstances? After all V does owe Adam the money.

B: Fraud by failing to disclose information

This provision is probably superfluous since it is clear that a failure to disclose information which one has a duty to disclose still counts as a representation for the purpose of s. 2. See *Firth* (above). Section 3 was included in order to simplify the proof of guilt. Section 3 allows a conviction simply upon proof of the duty to disclose and the failure to do so with the relevant intent. The important aspect of s. 3 is the requirement that the defendant be under a legal duty of disclosure. A moral duty is not enough.

The concept of 'legal duty' is explained in the Law Commission's Report on *Fraud*, which said: 'Such a duty may derive from statute (such as the provisions governing company prospectuses), from the fact that the transaction in question is one of the utmost good faith (such as a contract of insurance), from the express or implied terms of a contract, from the custom of a particular trade or market, or from the existence of a fiduciary relationship between the parties (such as that of agent and principal)'.

So an art dealer would not commit the offence if he bought a painting at a car boot sale knowing that the painting was worth a thousand times the asking price as he has only a moral duty of disclosure.

(i) *Mens Rea*

The *mens rea* for s. 3 is as for s. 2. There is no requirement that the defendant be aware that he is under a legal duty of disclosure although evidence of lack of awareness will, no doubt, influence the jury's assessment of dishonesty.

C: Fraud by abuse of position

LAW COMMISSION REPORT NO. 276 CM 5560 (2002)

(1) A person is in breach of this section if he—
  (a) occupies a position in which he is expected to safeguard, or not to act against, the financial interests of another person,
  (b) dishonestly abuses that position, and
  (c) intends, by means of the abuse of that position—
    (i) to make a gain for himself or another, or
    (ii) to cause loss to another or to expose another to a risk of loss.
(2) A person may be regarded as having abused his position even though his conduct consisted of an omission rather than an act.

The thinking behind this third form of fraud and relationships to which it might apply is summed up in the following statement of the Law Commission:

> The essence of the kind of relationship which in our view should be a prerequisite of this form of the offence is that the victim has voluntarily put the defendant in a privileged position, by virtue of which the defendant is expected to safeguard the victim's financial interests or given power to damage those interests. Such an expectation to safeguard or power to damage may arise, for example, because the defendant is given authority to exercise a discretion on the victim's behalf, or is given access to the victim's assets, premises, equipment or customers. In these cases the defendant does not need to enlist the victim's *further* co-operation in order to secure the desired result, because the necessary co-operation has been given in advance. The necessary relationship will be present between trustee and beneficiary, director and company, professional person and client, agent and principal, employee and employer, or between partners. It may arise otherwise, for example within a family, or in the context of voluntary work, or in any context where the parties are not at arm's length. In nearly all cases where it arises, it will be recognised by the civil law as importing fiduciary duties, and any relationship that is so recognised will suffice. We see no reason, however, why the existence of such duties should be essential. (Para 7.3)

The judge decides whether a person occupies a position in which he is expected to safeguard the interests of another. Usually this will be because the relationship, as in the case of trustee/beneficiary, contains or is constituted by explicit duties of acting in the others' interests or not acting against those interests. It may, however, simply be understood as where A is allowed to use a friend's house at weekends. It does not need spelling out that A would abuse his licence if he were to use it as a brothel or a bomb-making factory.

(ii) *Mens Rea*

The *mens rea* for s. 4 is as for s. 2. There is no requirement that the defendant be aware that he is under a duty to safeguard the other's financial interests although evidence of lack of awareness will, no doubt, influence the jury's assessment of dishonesty.

■ NOTES AND QUESTIONS

1. Consider whether Adam is guilty of fraud by abuse of position in the following examples, and whether his conduct is appropriate for criminalisation.

    Adam, who works for Eve, a computer retailer, advises Jim, a friend, not to purchase a computer on the spot but to come back next week when the prices are to be cut by 20 per cent.

    Adam, an employee of Eve, uses his PC to send friends e-mail invitations to his birthday party.

SECTION 2 **OBTAINING SERVICES DISHONESTLY**

A: Introduction

Section 11 replaces s. 2 of the Theft Act 1978. It covers any case where services, for which payment would be expected, are obtained as a result of dishonest conduct. The key difference from the offence it replaces is that it is not longer necessary for that conduct to take the form of a deception. So a person who takes a fairground ride without paying for it is guilty of this offence although no representation is made.

Section 11 differs from ss. 2, 3 and 4 of the Fraud Act in requiring the service actually to be obtained. However, where the relevant services are obtained as a result of a false representation rather than by some other form of dishonest act (e.g. gaining access to a cinema at half price by pretending to be a minor), it will be possible to proceed under either section since the would-be minor intends to make a gain (keeping part of the price of the ticket in his pocket) by his false representation as to his age.

Section 11 provides as follows:

(1) A person is guilty of an offence under this section if he obtains services for himself or another—
    (a) by a dishonest act, and
    (b) in breach of subsection (2).
(2) A person obtains services in breach of this subsection if—
    (a) they are made available on the basis that payment has been, is being or will be made for or in respect of them,
    (b) he obtains them without any payment having been made for or in respect of them or without payment having been made in full, and
    (c) when he obtains them, he knows—
        (i) that they are being made available on the basis described in paragraph (a), or
        (ii) that they might be,
but intends that payment will not be made, or will not be made in full.

(i) *Actus reus*

Only services made available on a payment basis are covered or where payment will be made. So the offence is committed where D's dishonest act enables him to avoid paying for a service but no offence is committed if the dishonest act results in V waiving payment for the service. So, if D, an impoverished golfer, sneaks onto a private school's nine-hole golf course, use of which is restricted to school boys on a non fee-paying basis, he is not guilty of an offence. If he does the same at his local pay and play course he is guilty of an offence.

(ii) *Mens rea*

The offence requires (*Ghosh*) dishonesty, knowledge that payment is required or might be required and an intention not to pay for the service or not to pay in full.

■ NOTES AND QUESTIONS

1. As we shall see, the House of Lords in *Allen* ruled that the offence of making off without payment is not committed unless, when the person makes off without paying, his intention is never to pay the required amount. So a person who parks his car in a pay and display car park and goes off without paying is only guilty of the offence if he has no intention to pay on his return. If his failure to pay and display is because he has no money and intends to pay later when he returns from his shopping he does not commit the offence. Might he be guilty of the s. 11 offence, however?

SECTION 3: **MAKING OFF WITHOUT PAYMENT**

Section 3 of the Theft Act 1978, which is still in force, provides:

> (1) Subject to subsection 3 below, a person who, knowing that payment on the spot for any goods supplied or service done is required or expected from him, dishonestly makes off without having paid as required or expected and with intent to avoid payment of the amount due shall be guilty of an offence.
> (2) For purposes of this section 'payment on the spot' includes payment at the time of collecting the goods on which work has been done or in respect of which service has been provided.
> (3) Subsection (1) above shall not apply where the supply of the goods or the doing of the service is contrary to law, or where the service done is such that payment is not legally enforceable.

This offence is designed to enable a prosecution where, although dishonest, it may be difficult to prove or prevent fraud or theft. It is easier to prove that a driver has dishonestly made off without paying for her petrol than to prove that she had an intention not to pay when first filling up the car.

A: *Actus reus*

A person can only be liable if he has made off from the spot where payment was due. Liability turns therefore on where that spot is and whether D has departed from it.

McDavitt
[1981] Crim LR 843, Court of Appeal

Following an argument about his bill M went towards the restaurant door having refused to pay for his meal. Upon being advised not to leave as the police were being called, M went to the toilet and waited there for the police. M admitted having intended to leave without paying.

A submission of no case to answer was accepted on a charge of making off without payment, contrary to the Theft Act 1978, s. 3 that 'making off' means making off from the spot where payment is required or expected. In this case the spot was the restaurant. The jury should have been directed that they could not convict of this offence but it was open to them to convict of an attempt.

A person commits the offence only if, when making off, payment on the spot is required or expected. If, therefore, the expectation is that D will be 'billed' for the goods or services he is not guilty even if it was his intention when making off that he would not pay. So also he will not commit the offence if there has been a breach of contract for the contract was otherwise unenforceable.

B: *Mens rea*

The *mens rea* for s. 3 is dishonesty and an intention to avoid payment of the amount due. In *Allen* the House of Lords considered the question whether the intention must be to make permanent default. The facts appear in the judgment.

LORD HAILSHAM OF ST. MARYLEBONE LC: The respondent appealed against a conviction for making off without payment. The Court of Appeal allowed the appeal and quashed the conviction. In refusing leave to appeal to your Lordships' House, the Court of Appeal certified the following point of law of general public importance:

'Upon a construction of the words 'with intent to avoid payment' in section 3(1) of the Theft Act 1978, namely, whether an intention to make permanent default on payment is required.'

The facts, which are not disputed, and which I draw from the case for the appellant, were as follows. The respondent, Christopher Allen, booked a room at an hotel for 10 nights from 15 January 1983. He stayed on thereafter and finally left on 11 February 1983 without paying his bill in the sum of £1,286.94. He telephoned two days later to explain that he was in financial difficulties because of some business transactions and arranged to return to the hotel on 18 February 1983 to remove his belongings and leave his Australian passport as security for the debt. He was arrested on his return and said that he genuinely hoped to be able to pay the bill and denied he was acting dishonestly. On 3 March 1983, he was still unable to pay the bill and provided an explanation to the police of his financial difficulties. The respondent's defence was that he had acted honestly and had genuinely expected to pay the bill from the proceeds of various business ventures.

After a fairly lengthy summing up by the trial judge to which, in the light of what happened, I need make no special reference, the jury retired at 1.00 p.m. and came back at 2.18 p.m. with a note containing the following specific question for guidance by the judge:

'Regarding count 2 of the indictment, the words "and with intent to avoid payment of the £1,286.94," do you refer to permanent intention or one applying only to the dates mentioned in the charge?'

To this question the judge gave the following explicit answer:

'The answer is: one applying only to 8 and 11 February 1983. You see it says in count 2, "knowing that payment on the spot for goods supplied and services done was required or expected from him . . ." "On the spot" means the day you leave. There was no payment on the spot when he should have paid. It contrasts sharply with count 1 where the intent there is permanent: that is not so in count 2 where he was required to pay on the spot; and there has been a failure to do that. Will you please, once more, retire to consider your verdict.'

Despite some (though not unanimous) text book opinions in an opposite sense (see Smith, *The Law of Theft*, 5th ed. (1984), para. 250, p. 130; Griew, *The Theft Acts 1968 and 1978*, 4th ed. (1982), para. 11–14, p. 155, and, less strongly, Glanville Williams, *Textbook of Criminal Law*, 2nd ed. (1983), p. 878), I consider this answer to be clearly erroneous.

Section 3(1) of the Act of 1978, under which count 2 was laid, reads as follows:

'Subject to subsection (3) below,' (which with subsection (4) is irrelevant for this purpose) 'a person who, knowing that payment on the spot for any goods supplied or service done is required or expected from him, dishonestly makes off without having paid as required or expected and with intent to avoid payment of the amount due shall be guilty of an offence.'

The offence thus created is triable on indictment and attracts a maximum penalty of two years.

The appellant's contention was that the effect of this section is to catch not only those who intend permanently to avoid payment of the amount due, but also those whose intention is to avoid payment on the spot, which, after all, is the time at which, ex hypothesi, payment has been 'expected or required,' and the time, therefore, when the 'amount' became 'due.'

The judgment of the Court of Appeal, with which I agree, was delivered by Boreham J. He said [1985] 1 W.L.R. 50, 57:

'To secure a conviction under section 3 the following must be proved: (1) that the defendant in fact made off without making payment on the spot; (2) the following mental elements – (a) knowledge that payment on the spot was required or expected of him; and (b) dishonesty; and (c) intent to avoid payment [sc. 'of the amount due'].'

I agree with this analysis. To it the judge adds the following comment:

'If (c) means, or is taken to include, no more than an intention to delay or defer payment of the amount due it is difficult to see what it adds to the other elements. Anyone who knows that payment on the spot is expected or required of him and who then dishonestly makes off without paying as required or expected must have at least the intention to delay or defer payment. It follows, therefore, that the conjoined phrase "and with intent to avoid payment of the amount due" adds a further ingredient – an intention to do more than delay or defer – an intention to evade payment altogether.'

My own view, for what it is worth, is that the section thus analysed is capable only of this meaning. But counsel for the appellant very properly conceded that, even if it were equivocal and capable of either meaning, in a penal section of this kind any ambiguity must be resolved in favour of the subject and against the Crown. Accordingly the appeal falls to be dismissed either if on its true construction it means unambiguously that the intention must be permanently to avoid payment, or if the clause is ambiguous and capable of either meaning. Even on the assumption that, in the context, the word 'avoid' without the addition of the word 'permanently' is capable of either meaning, which Boreham J. was inclined to concede, I find myself convinced by his final paragraph, which reads:

'Finally, we can see no reason why, if the intention of Parliament was to provide, in effect, that an intention to delay or defer payment might suffice, Parliament should not have said so in explicit terms. This *might* have been achieved by the insertion of the word "such" before payment in the phrase in question. It *would* have been achieved by a grammatical reconstruction of the material part of section 3(1) thus, "dishonestly makes off without having paid and with intent to avoid payment of the amount due as required or expected." To accede to the Crown's submission would be to read the section as if it were constructed in that way. That we cannot do. Had it been intended to relate the intention to avoid "payment" to "payment as required or expected" it would have been easy to say so. The section does not say so. At the very least it contains an equivocation which should be resolved in favour of the appellant.'

There is really no escape from this argument. There may well be something to be said for the creation of a criminal offence designed to protect, for instance, cab drivers and restaurant keepers against persons who dishonestly abscond without paying on the spot and without any need for the prosecution to exclude an intention to pay later, so long as the original act of 'making off' could be described as dishonest. Unlike that in the present section, such an offence might very well, as with the railway ticket offence, be triable summarily only, and counsel for the appellant was able to call in aid the remarks of Cumming-Bruce L.J. in *Corbyn* v *Saunders* [1978] 1 W.L.R. 400, 403 which go a long way to support such a view. But, as the Court of Appeal remarked, that decision was under a different statute and a differently worded section which did not contain both the reference to 'dishonestly' and the specific intention 'to avoid payment' as two separate elements in the mens rea of the offence. In order to give the section now under consideration the effect required the section would have to be remodelled in the way suggested by Boreham J. in the passage quoted above, or the word 'and' in the ultimate phrase would have to be read as if it meant 'that is to say' so that the required intent would be equated with 'dishonestly' in the early part of the subsection.

Apart from a minor matter not relevant to the judgment there is nothing really to be added to the judgment delivered by Boreham J.

■ NOTES AND QUESTIONS

1. Does a person who, on being asked for payment, dupes the supplier of goods and services into allowing him to pay at a later date intending never to pay make off without paying?
2. Does a person who tenders a worthless cheque make off without paying?
3. Why should a person be guilty of an offence for forming the intention not to pay before he leaves 'the spot' but is guilty of no offence if he forms that intention when he gets home?
4. Do you agree with the House of Lords decision in *Allen*? It seems to make proof of guilt rather difficult, doesn't it?

FURTHER READING

Wilson, *Criminal Law: Doctrine and Theory* (2011), Chapter 15

S. Green, *Lying, Cheating and Stealing* (2006)

Law Com No 276 Fraud (2002)

D. Ormerod, 'The Fraud Act 2006 – Criminalising Lying' [2007] Crim LR 193

D. Ormerod and D. Williams, *Smith's Law of Theft* (2007)

Simester and Sullivan, 'Nature and Rationale of Property Offences' in Duff and Green eds., *Defining Crimes* (2005)

PART III

Exculpatory Conditions and Defences

9

The Principle of Capacity

The twin assumptions upon which the criminal law rests are that human beings have the capacity to choose between good and evil and the capacity to control what they do. However, the courts also recognise that there are instances when these assumptions are less likely to hold true. There are certain classes of individuals – children and the mentally ill are the most common examples – who are not able to appreciate the consequences or wrongfulness of their acts. This may be attributable to a mental deficiency (in the case of the mentally ill) or to immaturity (in the case of a child). Children may also lack the training, experience or moral tuition needed to understand the hurtful consequences which may follow from certain actions.

In addition to those with cognitive incapacities, there are individuals who, while understanding intellectually the consequences of their acts and that their actions are wrongful, are unable to restrain themselves from acting. Theirs is what might be termed a physical incapacity. The courts generally refer to such individuals as 'automatons' and characterise their 'defence' as one of 'automatism'. Automatism is thereby linked to the concept of *actus reus*, and the requirement of a voluntary act. However, as the source of the defendant's incapacity may be mental, the defence of automatism commonly overlaps with that of insanity. The judges have had difficulty separating the two, and one often comes across decisions which speak of insane and non-insane automatism, which may serve only to generate confusion about the proper scope of each defence. Some automatons (for example, sleepwalkers or epileptics) seem intuitively – and medically – to fall outside the scope of the insane, yet the courts will insist on an insanity defence or nothing.

SECTION 1: THE AGE OF CRIMINAL RESPONSIBILITY (INFANCY)

As indicated above, the courts proceed on the assumption that those subject to the criminal law are able to understand its commands and to distinguish between what is permitted and what is forbidden. If an individual chooses to do what is forbidden, it is appropriate to punish that person for his or her acts. The assumption, however, is called into question when the actor is a child. It is generally accepted that children below a certain age may not truly understand the social significance of their acts. This may be due to an intellectual deficiency, or a gap in their moral and religious upbringing. Whatever the reason, the law is prepared to make allowances. As children grow older and mature, their moral and intellectual understanding also increases. But children mature at a different pace, so the question arises where to set the age of criminal responsibility. An age that takes account of the state of the child's individual development has appeal, but so does having a fixed age of responsibility (lest every trial involving a non-adult turn into a psychological inquiry into the defendant's state of maturation). The law has developed with these two themes in mind. Originally a distinction was drawn between children under 10, children between 10 and 14, and children above 14. In the late 1990s, the special treatment of 10 to 14-year-olds was abolished.

A: Children under 10

There is an irrebuttable presumption that a child under the age of 10 at the time of the alleged offence lacks the capacity to commit the offence (Children and Young Persons Act 1933, s. 50). In these circumstances no crime has been committed by the child.

Walters v Lunt
[1951] 2 All ER 645, King's Bench Division

LORD GODDARD CJ:This is a Case stated by justices for the city of Lincoln, before whom the respondents, a husband and wife, were charged under the Larceny Act 1916, s. 33(1), that

> ...they between Aug. 1 and 31, 1950, at the city of Lincoln, jointly feloniously did receive from Richard Norman Lunt (aged seven years) a child's tricycle of the value of £2, the property of Walter Cole, which had theretofore been feloniously stolen, knowing the same to have been so stolen.

There was a similar charge in respect of a child's fairy cycle alleged to have been received by them on Mar. 11, 1951, from Richard Norman Lunt, aged seven years, and we infer from the Case that Richard Norman Lunt is the child of the respondents. The justices refused to convict on the ground that, as the child was under eight years of age, under the Children and Young Persons Act 1933, s. 50, he was incapable of stealing and could not be convicted of the felonious act of larceny, and, therefore, the respondents could not be convicted, under s. 33(1) of the Act of 1916, of receiving stolen property because the property taken by the child was not property 'stolen or obtained...under circumstances which amount to felony or misdemeanour.'

...In the case now before us the child could not have been found guilty of larceny because he was under eight years of age, and, unless he is eight years old, he is not considered in law capable of forming the intention necessary to support a charge of larceny. Therefore, the justices came to a perfectly proper decision in point of law on the charge of receiving.

...

■ NOTES AND QUESTIONS

1. While no crime may have been committed by the child who executes the *actus reus*, others may be guilty of committing the offence through use of the child as an innocent agent. Were the parents in *Walters* v *Lunt* guilty of theft? See also *DPP* v *K and B* [1997] 1 Cr App R 36.

2. The United Nations Convention on the Rights of the Child, to which the UK is a signatory, requires states to establish a minimum age below which a child shall be presumed not to have the capacity to commit a crime. The problem lies in determining what that age should be. On what basis may it have been decided that ten was the appropriate age? In most other European countries, the age

of criminal responsibility is significantly higher (typically 14 or 16). However, these other countries may have other mechanisms, such as youth courts, for dealing with young offenders.

3. Until fairly recently, boys under the age of 14 were conclusively presumed to be incapable of sexual intercourse and thus could not be convicted of rape, even in cases where there was incontrovertible evidence that sexual intercourse had taken place. See, e.g., *R v Groombridge* (1835) C&P 582. This outdated and irrational presumption was abolished in the Sexual Offences Act 1993, s. 1.

4. All references to 'age' in the law refer to chronological and not mental age. But which does it make more sense to treat as an adult – a nine-year-old with the mental age and maturity of an 18-year-old, or an 18-year-old with the mental age and maturity of a nine-year-old?

The UK age of criminal responsibility has been challenged in the European Court of Human Rights:

V and T v UK (Application No. 24724/94)
30 EHRR 121 (1999), European Court of Human Rights

1. The offence
The applicant was born in August 1982.
On 12 February 1993, when he was ten years old, he and another ten-year-old boy, 'V', had played truant from school and abducted a two-year-old boy from a shopping precinct, taken him on a journey of over two miles and then battered him to death and left him on a railway line to be run over [the victim in the case was Jamie Bulger].

...

The Court has considered first whether the attribution to the applicant of criminal responsibility in respect of acts committed when he was ten years old could, in itself, give rise to a violation of Article 3. In doing so, it has regard to the principle, well established in its case-law that, since the Convention is a living instrument, it is legitimate when deciding whether a certain measure is acceptable under one of its provisions to take account of the standards prevailing amongst the member States of the Council of Europe...

In this connection, the Court observes that, at the present time there is not yet a commonly accepted minimum age for the imposition of criminal responsibility in Europe. While most of the Contracting States have adopted an age-limit which is higher than that in force in England and Wales, other States, such as Cyprus, Ireland, Liechtenstein and Switzerland, attribute criminal responsibility from a younger age. Moreover, no clear tendency can be ascertained from examination of the relevant international texts and instruments. Rule 4 of the Beijing Rules which, although not legally binding, might provide some indication of the existence of an international consensus, does not specify the age at which criminal responsibility should be fixed but merely invites States not to fix it too low, and Article 40(3)(a) of the UN Convention requires States Parties to establish a minimum age below which children shall be presumed not to have the capacity to infringe the criminal law, but contains no provision as to what that age should be.

The Court does not consider that there is at this stage any clear common standard amongst the member States of the Council of Europe as to the minimum age of criminal responsibility. Even if England and Wales is among the few European jurisdictions to retain a low age of criminal responsibility, the age of ten cannot be said to be so young as to differ disproportionately from the age-limit followed by other European States. The Court concludes that the attribution of criminal responsibility to the applicant does not in itself give rise to a breach of Article 3 of the Convention.

■ NOTES AND QUESTIONS

1. Although the European Court of Human Rights rejected the argument that setting the age of criminal responsibility at ten was contrary to Article 3 of the
Convention, it did find a violation of Article 6 (the right to a fair trial). The
Court stated that a public trial in an adult court was inappropriate for children
so young because they were not able to participate effectively. After the decision in *V and T*, a practice direction was issued outlining the procedures to be
followed in such cases in order to comply with Article 6. See *Practice Direction:
Crown Court Young Defendants* [2000] 1 WLR 659.

2. In *SC* v *United Kingdom* (Application No. 60958/00) 2004, the European Court of
Human Rights reiterated that the trial of an 11-year-old does not in and of itself
constitute a breach of Article 6 if the child is able to 'participate effectively' in
the proceedings. However, the defendant in that case had learning difficulties,
a mental age of 8 and obvious trouble understanding his situation (including
the role of the jury and the fact that he was facing a custodial sentence). In those
circumstances the European Court concluded that the 11-year-old had not been
able to participate effectively.

3. Another issue in *V and T* involved the fact that the Home Secretary had set
the 'tariff' (the minimum sentence to be served) for the defendants. The Court
ruled that the Home Secretary was not the 'independent and impartial tribunal'
envisaged by Article 6(1) of the Convention. The tariff also effectively precluded
the periodic review by a judicial body to which the defendants were entitled
under Article 5(4) of the Convention.

B: Children between the age of 10 and 14

Historically, there was a common law presumption – known as *doli incapax* – that a
child between ten and fourteen was presumed incapable of committing a criminal
offence. This presumption, however, could be rebutted by proof that the child knew
that the conduct in question was 'seriously wrong'. The presumption came into being
at a time when defendants found guilty of many crimes were routinely hanged.
With the virtual abolition of capital punishment, many questioned the continuing
role of the presumption and it was eventually abolished in s. 34 of the Crime and
Disorder Act 1998. One issue which remained at large was whether the defence had
been abolished as opposed to the presumption. In *CPS* v *P* [2007] EWHC 946 it was
stated obiter that only the presumption had been abolished, not the defence itself.
In other words in appropriate circumstances a child between 10 and 14 could avail
him/herself of it. This might be particularly important if the child lacked the normal mental facility for distinguishing between right and wrong. However, in *R* v *T*
(2009) UKHL 20, the House of Lords confirmed that the defence itself had been
abolished, leaving such young persons vulnerable to conviction.

■ NOTES AND QUESTIONS

1. Prior to enactment of s. 34 of the Crime and Disorder Act 1998, the House of
Lords in *C* (*a minor*) v *DPP* [1996] 1 AC 1, had observed:

> The distinction between the treatment and the punishment of child 'offenders' has popular and
> political overtones, a fact which shows that we have been discussing not so much a legal as a social

problem, with a dash of politics thrown in, and emphasises that it should be within the exclusive remit of Parliament. There is need to study other systems, including that which holds sway in Scotland, a task for which the courts are not equipped. Whatever change is made, it should come only after collating and considering the evidence and after taking account of the effect which a change would have on the whole law relating to children's anti-social behaviour. This is a classic case for parliamentary investigation, deliberation and legislation.

Was the Court being naïve – often Parliament has neither the time not the inclination to consider problematic legal issues, especially where the courts may have created the problems for themselves.

2. The vexing problem of what to do with young persons who cause serious harm but fall outside of the criminal law because of their age is one with which all jurisdictions have had to wrestle. Over the years various solutions have been proposed including restorative justice programmes, reparation orders, supervision orders, electronic tagging, weekend confinement, and – that favoured by the Labour government – ASBOs (anti-social behaviour orders). The success of these various initiatives is subject to debate. The only known cure for youth crime appears to consist of growing older.

SECTION 2: INSANITY

While the number of cases in which an insanity defence is raised has never been statistically significant, the defence is important because it raises some of the most profound issues in criminal law. Why should the insane offender who has caused harm to society (often, as in the case of a killer, quite grave harm) be excused from criminal liability? The individual is a danger to society, and clearly in need of restraint and rehabilitation.

One of the reasons why so few cases of insanity arise is that a defendant who is insane may also be 'unfit to plead.' A defendant does not understand the nature and purpose of a trial, is unable to assist counsel in selecting a jury, and/or cannot provide meaningful testimony may be found 'unfit to plead'. This finding will lead to postponement of the trial and confinement (usually in a mental institution) until the defendant's fitness is restored. However, there may be no known cure for certain types of mental illness, which may mean that defendant's fitness to plead will never be restored and that she will never be released from the institution.

This potentially indeterminate confinement could work a grave injustice in a case where the defendant was innocent of the crime charged. 'Partial' relief was created by the Criminal Procedure (Insanity and Unfitness to Plead) Act 1991, s. 4A, which allows for a provisional trial on whether the defendant committed the act or omission charged. If the jury concludes that the defendant did not commit the act charged, an acquittal will be entered. The reference to this section only providing *partial* relief is because defences that turn on the absence of *mens rea* – or for that matter insanity – cannot be raised at the provisional hearing. What justifies the difference in treatment?

Returning to the insanity defence, there are several considerations which are said to justify the defence. First, it is felt that an insane offender is not morally blameworthy. Offenders who, through no fault of their own, do not know what they are doing or that it is wrong do not have the rational capacity upon which the law is premised. There is the additional point that there is little deterrent purpose to be achieved in imposing criminal punishment, as those who are truly insane are unlikely to understand the commands of the law (indeed, this is implicit in the definition of insanity), or be deterred by criminal sanctions.

If one were to approach the issue *a priori* it could certainly be argued that insanity negatives *mens rea*. However, that is not the way the law has developed in practice. Rather, insanity is an independent defence unrelated to *mens rea*. If there is an advantage to the mentally ill in this approach it is that insanity can be pleaded as a defence to all crimes, including those which impose strict liability.

A: The *M'Naghten* rules

The legal test of insanity was enunciated in *M'Naghten's Case*. The defendant had been charged with killing Edward Drummond, secretary to the Prime Minister, Sir Robert Peel. His defence was that he was suffering from a morbid delusion that he was being persecuted which drove him to commit the shooting:

The medical evidence was in substance this: That persons of otherwise sound mind, might be affected by morbid delusions: that the prisoner was in that condition: that a person so labouring under a morbid delusion, might have a moral perception of right and wrong, but that in the case of the prisoner it was a delusion which carried him away beyond the power of his own control, and left him no such perception; and that he was not capable of exercising any control over acts which had connexion with his delusion: that it was of the nature of the disease with which the prisoner was affected, to go on gradually until it had reached a climax, when it burst forth with irresistible intensity: that a man might go on for years quietly, though at the same time under its influence, but would all at once break out into the most extravagant and violent paroxysms.

M'Naghten was found not guilty on the ground of insanity. This verdict, and the issues raised by it, were subsequently debated in the House of Lords, and it was decided to seek the opinion of the Judges on the governing law. This was the genesis of what has come to be known as the *M'Naghten* rules.

M'Naghten's Case
(1843) 10 Cl & F 200, House of Lords

LORD CHIEF JUSTICE TINDAL : . . . The first question proposed by your Lordships is this: 'What is the law respecting alleged crimes committed by persons afflicted with insane delusion in respect of one or more particular subjects or persons: as, for instance, where at the time of the commission of the alleged crime the accused knew he was acting contrary to law, but did the act complained of with a view, under the influence of insane delusion, of redressing or revenging some supposed grievance or injury, or of producing some supposed public benefit?'

In answer to which question, assuming that your Lordships' inquiries are confined to those persons who labour under such partial delusions only, and are not in other respects insane, we are of opinion that, notwithstanding the party accused did the act complained of with a view, under the influence of insane delusion, of redressing or revenging some supposed grievance or injury, or of producing some public benefit, he is nevertheless punishable according to the nature of the crime committed, if he knew at the time of committing such crime that he was acting contrary to law; by which expression we understand your Lordships to mean the law of the land.

Your Lordships are pleased to inquire of us, secondly, 'What are the proper questions to be submitted to the jury, where a person alleged to be afflicted with insane delusion respecting one or more particular subjects or persons, is charged with the commission of a crime (murder, for example), and insanity is set up as a defence?' And, thirdly, 'In what terms ought the question to be left to the jury as to the prisoner's state of mind at the time when the act was committed?' And as these two questions appear to us to be more conveniently answered together, we have to submit our opinion to be that the jurors ought to be told in all cases that every man is to be presumed to be sane, and to possess a sufficient degree of reason to be responsible for his crimes, until the contrary be proved to their satisfaction: and that to establish a defence on the ground of insanity, it must be clearly proved that, at the time of the committing of the act, the party accused was labouring under such a defect of reason from disease of the mind, as not to know the nature and quality of the act he was doing; or if he did know it, that he did not know he was doing what was wrong. The mode of putting the latter part of the question to the jury on these occasions has generally been, whether the accused at the time of doing the act knew the difference between right and wrong: which mode, though rarely, if ever leading to any mistake with the jury, is not, as we conceive, so accurate when put generally and in the abstract, as when put with reference to the party's knowledge of right and wrong in respect to the very act with which he is charged. If the question were to be put as to the knowledge of the accused solely and exclusively with reference to the law of the land, it might tend to confound the jury, by inducing them to believe that an actual knowledge of the law of the land was essential in order to lead to a conviction; whereas the law is administered upon the principle that every one must be taken conclusively to know it, without proof that he does know it. If the accused was conscious that the act was one which he ought not to do, and if that act was at the same time contrary to the law of the land, he is punishable; and the usual course therefore has been to leave the question to the jury, whether the party accused had a sufficient degree of reason to know that he was doing an act that was wrong: and this course we think is correct, accompanied with such observations and explanations as the circumstances of each particular case may require.

The fourth question which your Lordships have proposed to us is this:—'If a person under an insane delusion as to existing facts, commits an offence in consequence thereof, is he thereby excused?' To which question the answer must of course depend on the nature of the delusion: but, making the same assumption as we did before, namely, that he labours under such partial delusion only, and is not in other respects insane, we think he must be considered in the same situation as to responsibility as if the facts with respect to which the delusion exists were real. For example, if under the influence of his delusion he supposes another man to be in the act of attempting to take away his life, and he kills that man, as he supposes, in self-defence, he would be exempt from punishment. If his delusion was that the deceased had inflicted a serious injury to his character and fortune, and he killed him in revenge for such supposed injury, he would be liable to punishment.

■ NOTES AND QUESTIONS

1. A defendant is presumed to be sane. How does one go about rebutting this presumption? Under s. 1(1) of the Criminal Procedure (Insanity and Unfitness to Plead) Act 1991, a defendant may not be acquitted by reason of insanity except on the evidence of at least two registered medical practitioners, one of whom is a specialist approved by the Home Secretary.

2. Almost uniquely the burden of proof lies with the defence, unless the issue is raised by the prosecution, as it may be in response to a plea of diminished responsibility by the defence. This may be the subject of some future challenge under Article 6.2 of the ECHR ('Everyone charged with a criminal offence shall be presumed innocent until proved guilty according to law'.)

3. The court in *M'Naghten* said that the defence must be clearly proved – but by whom and to what standard? As articulated by the court, the defence must be proved by the defendant but only by a balance of probabilities rather than

by the more typical criminal law standard of proof beyond reasonable doubt. Nonetheless, the allocation to the defendant of any burden of persuasion reverses the prevailing practice in regard to most other defences, where the burden is on the prosecution to rebut the defence by proof beyond reasonable doubt. What is the justification for this departure from standard practice? Do reversed burdens of proof violate the European Convention of Human Rights? See *Salabiaku v France* (1988) 13 EHRR 37.

4. The insanity defence is concerned with the defendant's state of mind at the time of commission of the crime, not at the time of trial. One can be sane immediately prior to one's criminal act and immediately afterwards, but if insane at the time of the act, the defence is available. Conversely, if one is insane prior to the commission of the crime and insane thereafter, but commits the offence in a moment of lucidity, the defence is not available.

5. Note the difficulties facing a jury. The law is concerned with the defendant's mental state at the time of the crime; but a psychiatric examination of the defendant will probably not be conducted until after arrest. This may be some time – perhaps decades after the crime was committed. The jury will have to attempt to reconstruct what the defendant's state of mind was at the time of the crime, based on an after-the-fact psychiatric examination. Yet the jurors cannot rely on their observations of the defendant at trial, for the defendant's mental state at the time of the trial may not be the same as at the time of the crime.

6. In the normal case where the jury decides that the defendant has a defence to the crime charged, they return a verdict of 'not guilty'. If, on the other hand, the jury finds that the defendant was insane, they must return a verdict of 'not guilty by reason of insanity (NGRI)'. What justifies this departure from standard practice?

The *M'Naghten* test requires proof '*that ... the ... accused was labouring under such a defect of reason, from disease of the mind*'. The defect must be more than stupidity, absent-mindedness or confusion. See *R v Clarke* [1972] 1 All ER 219. Rather, there must be a total deprivation of the power to reason brought on by a disease of the mind. But what is meant by 'disease of the mind'?

R v Sullivan

[1984] 1 AC 156, House of Lords

LORD DIPLOCK: My Lords, the appellant, Mr Sullivan, a man of blameless reputation, has the misfortune to have been a lifelong sufferer from epilepsy. There was a period when he was subject to major seizures known as grand mal; but, as a result of treatment which he was receiving as an outpatient of the Maudsley Hospital from 1976 onwards, these major seizures had, by the use of drugs, been reduced by 1979 to seizures of less severity known as petit mal, or psychomotor epilepsy, though they continued to occur at a frequency of one or two per week.

One such seizure occurred on May 8, 1981, when Mr Sullivan, then aged 51, was visiting a neighbour, Mrs Killick, an old lady aged 86 for whom he was accustomed to perform regular acts of kindness. He was chatting there to a fellow visitor and friend of his, a Mr Payne aged 80, when the epileptic fit came on. It appears likely from the expert medical evidence about the way in which epileptics behave at the various stages of a petit mal seizure that Mr Payne got up from the chair to help Mr Sullivan. The only evidence of an eyewitness was that of Mrs Killick, who did not see what had happened before she saw Mr Payne lying on the floor and Mr Sullivan kicking him about the head and body, in consequence of which Mr Payne suffered injuries severe enough to require hospital treatment.

As a result of this occurrence Mr Sullivan was indicted upon two counts: the first was of causing grievous bodily harm with intent contrary to section 18 of the Offences against the Person Act 1861; the second of causing grievous bodily harm contrary to section 20 of that Act. At his trial, which took place at the Central Criminal Court before Judge Lymbery and a jury, Mr Sullivan pleaded not guilty to both counts. Mrs Killick's evidence that he had kicked Mr Payne violently about the head and body was undisputed and Mr Sullivan himself gave evidence of his history of epilepsy and his absence of all recollection of what had occurred at Mrs Killick's flat between the time that he was chatting peacefully to Mr Payne there and his returning to the flat from somewhere else to find that Mr Payne was injured and that an ambulance had been sent for. The prosecution accepted his evidence as true....

The evidence as to the pathology of a seizure due to psychomotor epilepsy can be sufficiently stated for the purposes of this appeal by saying that after the first stage, the prodram, which precedes the fit itself, there is a second stage, the ictus, lasting a few seconds, during which there are electrical discharges into the temporal lobes of the brain of the sufferer. The effect of these discharges is to cause him in the post-ictal stage to make movements which he is not conscious that he is making, including, and this was a characteristic of previous seizures which Mr Sullivan had suffered, automatic movements of resistance to anyone trying to come to his aid. These movements of resistance might, though in practice they very rarely would, involve violence.

...[I]t is submitted the medical evidence in the instant case shows that psychomotor epilepsy is not a disease of the mind, whereas in *Bratty* [1963] AC 386 it was accepted by all the doctors that it was. The only evidential basis for this submission is that Dr Fenwick said that in medical terms to constitute a 'disease of the mind' or 'mental illness,' which he appeared to regard as interchangeable descriptions, a disorder of brain functions (which undoubtedly occurs during a seizure in psychomotor epilepsy) must be prolonged for a period of time usually more than a day; while Dr Taylor would have it that the disorder must continue for a minimum of a month to qualify for the description 'a disease of the mind.'

The nomenclature adopted by the medical profession may change from time to time; Bratty was tried in 1961. But the meaning of the expression 'disease of the mind' as the cause of 'a defect of reason' remains unchanged for the purposes of the application of the M'Naghten Rules. I agree with what was said by Devlin J in *R v Kemp* [1957] 1 QB 399, 407, that 'mind' in the M'Naghten Rules is used in the ordinary sense of the mental faculties of reason, memory and understanding. If the effect of a disease is to impair these faculties so severely as to have either of the consequences referred to in the latter part of the rules, it matters not whether the aetiology of the impairment is organic, as in epilepsy, or functional, or whether the impairment itself is permanent or is transient and intermittent, provided that it subsisted at the time of commission of the act. The purpose of the legislation relating to the defence of insanity, ever since its origin in 1800, has been to protect society against recurrence of the dangerous conduct. The duration of a temporary suspension of the mental faculties of reason, memory and understanding, particularly if, as in Mr Sullivan's case, it is recurrent, cannot on any rational ground be relevant to the application by the courts of the M'Naghten Rules, though it may be relevant to the course adopted by the Secretary of State, to whom the responsibility for how the defendant is to be dealt with passes after the return of the special verdict of 'not guilty by reason of insanity.'

R v Hennessy
[1989] 1 WLR 287, Court of Appeal

LORD LANE CJ:...On Thursday, 28 May 1987, two police constables, Barnes and Grace, were on duty in St Leonards-on-Sea on the Sussex coast, among other things looking for a Ford Granada car which had been stolen. They found the car. It was unattended. They kept it under watch. As they watched they saw the appellant get into the car, switch on the headlights and ignition, start the car and drive off. The appellant at the wheel of the car correctly stopped the car at a set of traffic lights which were showing red against him. PC Grace then went over to the car as it was stationary, removed the ignition keys from the ignition-lock, but not before the appellant had tried to drive the motor car away and escape from the attention of the policeman. The appellant was put in the police car. On the way to the police station an informal conversation about motor vehicles took place between the appellant and the police officers, in particular about the respective merits of the new Rover motor car and the Ford Sierra. Indeed, the appellant appeared to PC Barnes not only to be fully in possession of his faculties but to be quite cheerful and intelligent. Indeed he went so far as to say to the police officer that if he had only got the car, which he was in the process of removing, onto the open road, he would have given the policemen a real run for their money.

However after having been at the police station for a time, the appellant was at a later stage escorted by PC Barnes to hospital. He seemed to be normal when he left the cell block at the police station, but when he arrived at the hospital he appeared to be dazed and confused. He complained to the sister in the casualty ward that he had failed to take his insulin and indeed had had no insulin since the previous Monday when he should have had regular self-injected doses. He was given insulin, with which he injected himself, and the hospital discharged him and he was taken back to the police station.

The appellant gave evidence to the effect that he had been a diabetic for about ten years. He needed, in order to stabilise his metabolism, two insulin injections on a daily basis, morning and afternoon. The amount required would depend on factors such as stress and eating habits. He was on a strict carbohydrate diet. At the time of the offence he said he had been having marital and employment problems. His wife had submitted a divorce petition some time shortly before, and he was very upset. He had not been eating and he had not been taking his insulin. He remembered very few details of the day. He could recall being handcuffed and taken to the charge room at the police station. He remembered being given insulin at the hospital and injecting himself and he remembers feeling better when he got back to the police station afterwards. He said he did not recall taking the car.

When cross-examined he agreed that he had understood proceedings at the police station and what had gone on there. Indeed he had given the name and address of his solicitor. That was a considerable time before he had had his insulin at the hospital.

His general practitioner, Dr Higginson, was called to give evidence. He spoke as to the appellant's medical condition. He described in broad outlines the effect of diabetes: it is a deficiency in the system of the production of hormones which should balance the sugar metabolism. The lacking hormone is of course insulin. In the absence of the hormone the blood sugar rises and that results in hyperglycaemia. If the patient does not take his insulin and does not stick to the proper diet, then hyperglycaemia will supervene. If unchecked, the liver will become affected and the increasingly high level of sugar makes the patient drowsy and he will ultimately go into a coma.

If on the other hand the balance tips the other way, if too much insulin is taken, then the blood sugar will fall and hypoglycaemia, that is to say too little sugar in the blood, will supervene.

According to the hospital notes, on the evening in question the appellant's blood sugar had been high at 22 plus millimolecules per litre, the normal being 8 or 9. According to Dr Higginson one would expect to see some physical manifestation of hyperglycaemia at that level. So the doctor was saying in short that eventually hyperglycaemia can result in drowsiness, loss of consciousness and coma, greater or less unresponsiveness to stimuli according to the degree of hyperglycaemia present. He added, I will read a passage from his evidence in a moment, that anxiety or depression can increase the blood sugar level, a person's ability and awareness of what is going on could be impaired if there were 'associated symptoms and he had other conditions and worries at the same time . . .'

. . .

The importance of the [M'Naghten] rules in the present context, namely the context of automatism, is this. If the defendant did not know the nature and quality of his act because of something which *did not* amount to defect of reason from disease of the mind then he will probably be entitled to be acquitted on the basis that the necessary criminal intent which the prosecution has to prove is not proved. But, if, on the other hand, his failure to realise the nature and quality of his act was due to a defect of reason from disease of the mind, then in the eyes of the law he is suffering from insanity, albeit M'Naghten insanity.

...

The question in many cases, and this is one such case, is whether the function of the mind was disturbed on the one hand by disease or on the other hand by some external factor....

The point was neatly raised in *R* v *Quick, R* v *Paddison* [1973] 3 All ER 347, [1973] QB 910, also referred to us by counsel for the appellant, in which Lawton LJ reviewed the authorities. It might perhaps help if I read a short passage from the headnote ([1973] QB 910):

> The defendants, Q and P, nurses at a mental hospital, were jointly and severally charged with assaulting a patient occasioning actual bodily harm. Both pleaded not guilty. Q, a diabetic, relied on the defence of automatism. He gave evidence that he had taken insulin as prescribed on the morning of the assault, had drunk a quantity of spirits and eaten little food thereafter and had no recollection of the assault. He called medical evidence to the effect that his condition at the material time was consistent with that of hypoglycaemia. The judge ruled that that evidence could only support a defence of insanity, not automatism. Q then pleaded guilty and P was convicted of aiding and abetting Q by encouragement. The defendants appealed against conviction.

I turn to the passage in the judgment where Lawton LJ said ([1973] 3 All ER 347 at 356, [1973] QB 910 at 922–923):

> A malfunctioning of the mind of transitory effect caused by the application to the body of some external factor such as violence, drugs, including anaesthetics, alcohol and hypnotic influences cannot fairly be said to be due to disease. Such malfunctioning, unlike that caused by a defect of reason from disease of the mind, will not always relieve an accused from criminal responsibility...In this case Quick's alleged mental condition, if it ever existed, was not caused by his diabetes but by his use of the insulin prescribed by his doctor. Such malfunctioning of his mind as there was, was caused by an external factor and not by a bodily disorder in the nature of a disease which disturbed the working of his mind. It follows in our judgment that Quick was entitled to have his defence of automatism left to the jury and that Bridge J's ruling as to the effect of the medical evidence called by him was wrong.

Thus in *R* v *Quick* the fact that his condition was, or may have been, due to the injections of insulin meant that the malfunction was due to an external factor and not to the disease. The drug it was that caused the hypoglycaemia, the low blood sugar. As suggested in another passage of the judgment of Lawton LJ, hyperglycaemia, high blood sugar, caused by an inherent defect and not corrected by insulin is a disease, and if, as the defendant was asserting here, it does cause a malfunction of the mind, then the case may fall within the M'Naghten rules.

The burden of the argument of counsel for the appellant to us is this. It is that the appellant's depression and marital troubles were a sufficiently potent external factor in his condition to override, so to speak, the effect of the diabetic shortage of insulin on him....

In our judgment, stress, anxiety and depression can no doubt be the result of the operation of external factors, but they are not, it seems to us, in themselves separately or together external factors of the kind capable in law of causing or contributing to a state of automatism....

■ **NOTES AND QUESTIONS**

1. In *Sullivan* and *Hennessy*, why did the courts treat a physical illness (epilepsy) as if it were a mental illness? In *Bratty* v *Attorney-General for Northern Ireland* [1963] AC 386, Lord Denning stated, 'It seems to me that any mental disorder which has manifested itself in violence and is prone to recur is a disease of the mind.' While this does not purport to be a medical opinion, it may explain the judicial reluctance to allow the epileptic a defence (automatism) that would result in his release back into the community while he still poses a danger to the public. At the time of the decision in *Bratty*, a defendant acquitted pursuant to an

NGRI (not guilty by reason of insanity) verdict was automatically committed to a mental hospital, where he could be kept under surveillance and provided treatment.

2. One might question whether the requirement of a 'disease of the mind' is really necessary. If a defendant does not know the nature and quality of her act or that it is wrong, and this is due to a defect of reason, why should it matter that the defect of reason is the product of a disease of the mind? In light of the reasons behind the insanity defence, does the source make any difference?

3. Mackay and Reuber, 'Epilepsy and the Insanity Defence – Time for Change?' [2007] CLR 782 point out that flashing lights and flash photography can trigger an epileptic seizure. If indeed this is true, could it be argued that the epileptic seizure is due to an external and not an internal event?

The defendant who is suffering from a defect of reason from a disease of the mind can come within the *M'Naghten* rules in either of two ways:

(a) the defendant can show that she did not know the nature and quality of the act she was doing; or
(b) the defendant can show that she did not know that what she was doing was wrong.

The issue that has arisen in respect to the second prong of the above test is whether the word 'wrong' refers to morally wrong or legally wrong.

R v Windle
[1952] 2 QB 826, Court of Criminal Appeal

The appellant, Francis Wilfred Windle, was convicted before Devlin J at Birmingham Assizes of the murder of his wife, and sentenced to death. He was a man, 40 years of age, of little resolution and weak character, and was married to a woman 18 years his senior. His married life was very unhappy; his wife was always speaking of committing suicide and the doctors who gave evidence at the trial were of opinion, from the history of the case, that she was certifiably insane. The appellant frequently discussed his home life with his workmates, until, as one of them said, they were sick and tired of hearing about it. Eventually a workmate said to the appellant, 'Give her a dozen aspirins,' and on the following day the appellant gave his wife 100 tablets. He sent for a doctor and told him that he had given his wife so many aspirins. She was taken to hospital, where she died. The appellant informed the police that he had given his wife 100 aspirins, and added: 'I suppose they will hang me for this?' At his trial a defence of insanity was put forward. A doctor was called for him who said that the appellant was suffering from a form of communicated insanity known as *folie à deux*. It was said that if a person was in constant attendance on another of unsound mind, in some way the insanity might be communicated to the attendant, so that, for a time at any rate, the attendant might develop a defect of reason or of mind. Rebutting medical evidence was allowed to be called for the prosecution, and the doctors called on either side expressed the opinion that the appellant, when administering the fatal dose of aspirin to his wife, knew that he was doing an act which the law forbade.

LORD GODDARD CJ:...The argument before us has really been on what is the meaning of the word 'wrong.' In this particular case, the only evidence given on the issue of insanity was that of the doctor called by the appellant and of the prison doctor who was allowed to be called by the prosecution to rebut, if indeed it was necessary, any evidence which had been given. It was probably right that the prison doctor should be called as he had had the appellant under constant observation. Both the doctors gave their evidence in a way that commended itself to the judge, and both, without hesitation, expressed the view that the appellant knew, when administering this poison, for such it was, to his wife, that he was doing an act which the law forbade. I need not put it higher than that.

It may well be that, in the misery in which he had been living, with this nagging and tiresome wife who constantly expressed the desire to commit suicide, he thought that she would be better out of this world than in it. He may have thought that it would be a kindly act to release her from what she was suffering from—or thought she was suffering from—but that the law does not permit. In the present case there was some exceedingly vague evidence that the appellant was suffering from a defect of reason. In the opinion of his own doctor, there was a defect of reason which he attributed to communicated insanity. In my opinion, if the only question in this case had been whether the appellant was suffering from a disease of the mind, I should say that that was a question which must have been left to the jury. That, however, is not the question.

...A man may be suffering from a defect of reason, but if he knows that what he is doing is 'wrong,' and by 'wrong' is meant contrary to law, he is responsible. Mr Shawcross, in the course of his very careful argument, suggested that the word 'wrong,' as it was used in the M'Naghten rules, did not mean contrary to law but had some kind of qualified meaning, such as morally wrong, and that if a person was in such a state of mind through a defect of reason that, although he knew that what he was doing was wrong in law, he thought that it was beneficial or kind or praiseworthy, that would excuse him.

Courts of law can only distinguish between that which is in accordance with law and that which is contrary to law....

In the opinion of the court there is no doubt that in the M'Naghten rules 'wrong' means contrary to law and not 'wrong' according to the opinion of one man or of a number of people on the question whether a particular act might or might not be justified. In the present case, it could not be challenged that the appellant knew that what he was doing was contrary to law, and that he realized what punishment the law provided for murder. That was the opinion of both the doctors who gave evidence.

■ NOTES AND QUESTIONS

1. Presumably the Court in *Windle* was attempting to narrow the meaning of the term 'wrong'. However, it could have the opposite effect in the case of an insane individual who appreciated that his act was morally wrong but, due to his mental illness, not that it was legally wrong.

2. Is granting a defence of insanity when the defendant is unaware that his act is legally wrong consistent with the general rule that 'ignorance of the law is no excuse.'?

3. Research tells us that in practice judges and juries give defendants who are unable, whatever their state of legal knowledge, to appreciate at the time they acted that they 'ought not to have acted' in this way appear to receive a more sympathetic hearing than the strict legal position might lead one to expect (R. Mackay, B. Mitchell L. Howe, 'Yet More Facts about the Insanity Defence Crim LR 399, at 406). Indeed, it is now the more popular of the two limbs. Commentators generally agree that the *Windle* test is too narrow. Nevertheless it has recently been approved by the Court of Appeal in *Johnson* [2007] EWCA Crim 1978.

4. There is a second branch of *M'Naghten* relating to partial delusions. The relevant question is set out in the *M'Naghten* extract (above). It is doubtful whether anything is added to the 'core' test by this passage, as a person under a delusion is presumably incapable of understanding the nature and quality of his act, or that it was wrong.

The *M'Naghten* rules are concerned with cognitive disabilities, where the defendant is unable to comprehend what he is doing or that what he is doing is wrong. What, however, of the defendant who is able to comprehend what he is doing, but is unable to stop himself from doing it?

R v Sodeman

[1936] 2 All ER 1138, Privy Council

The petitioner, who was a labourer, took a young girl for a ride on his bicycle, strangled her, tied her hands behind her back, stuffed some of her clothing into her mouth, and left her for dead. The cause of death was suffocation. The petitioner had committed three previous murders in very similar ways. The petitioner's defence was that he was insane at the time. At the trial two government prison doctors and a specialist in mental diseases gave evidence in support of that defence. No expert evidence on that issue was tendered by the Crown.

VISCOUNT HAILSHAM LC: ... [I]t is suggested by the petitioner that the rules in *M'Naghten's* case (1843) 10 Cl & F 200 are no longer to be treated as an exhaustive statement of the law with regard to insanity, and that there is to be engrafted upon those rules another rule that where a man knows that he is doing what is wrong, none the less he may be held to be insane if he is caused to do the act by an irresistible impulse produced by disease. It is admitted by Mr Pritt that, so far as this country is concerned, the more recent cases, ... excludes that addition to the law in *M'Naghten's* case, but it is argued that, since there have been earlier decisions which suggest that such a rule exists, this is a good opportunity for establishing the law beyond doubt. Their Lordships do not think that the argument is a sound one. If they are to take a different view of the law from that which prevailed the effect will be that different standards of law will prevail in England and in the Dominions. The adoption of such a view obviously cannot alter the authorities laid down by the English Court of Criminal Appeal, and their Lordships do not think that the ground suggested is one for granting special leave to appeal in a criminal case....

■ NOTES AND QUESTIONS

1. There seems to be strong judicial opposition to the concept of an irresistible impulse. Is this opposition consistent with the principle of capacity? Might it be attributable to the belief that an irresistible impulse defence would be too easy to feign? It has been observed, only partially in jest, that there is no such thing as an irresistible impulse when there is a constable at one's elbow.

2. It can be argued that the more difficult an impulse is to resist, the greater the legal sanction which is needed to counteract it. What are the merits of this argument?

3. In a case of homicide, a defendant who has acted pursuant to an irresistible impulse *may* be able to claim diminished responsibility (discussed in Chapter 4). The diminished responsibility defence was established in large measure to compensate for the perceived shortcomings in the defence of insanity.

4. Under s. 4.01(1) of the American Law Institute's Model Penal Code, a defendant is not responsible for criminal conduct 'if at the time of such conduct as a result of mental disease or defect he lacks substantial capacity either to appreciate the criminality of his conduct *or to conform his conduct to the requirements of the law* [emphasis added].' Is this a preferable approach to that taken in the UK with respect to irresistible impulses? Subsection 2 of s. 4.01 adds that 'the terms "mental disease or defect" do not include an abnormality manifested only by repeated criminal or otherwise anti-social conduct'. Does this make s. 4.01(1) more palatable?

B: Disposition of the defendant found not guilty by reason of insanity

We noted at the outset of the discussion that the insanity defence was not often raised by a defendant (the defence, however, could be raised by the Crown if the defendant placed his or her mental state in issue; see *Bratty* v *Attorney-General for Northern Ireland* [1963] AC 386). The reason for the infrequent invocation of the defence could be found in the effect of an NGRI verdict. Unlike in the case of other defences where, if the jury accepted the defence, the defendant was released, a free person, a defendant found not guilty by reason of insanity was automatically committed to a mental hospital, to remain at 'Her Majesty's Pleasure.' Such indefinite confinement could turn into permanent confinement if there were no known cure for the defendant's illness. Thus there was little incentive to plead insanity except when the charge was murder, where there existed the possibility of a sentence of life imprisonment. Furthermore, the less exacting (but only partial defence) of diminished responsibility (see Chapter 4) became available in 1957, further reducing the need to resort to a defence of insanity.

And so the defence lay relatively dormant – until enactment of the Criminal Procedure (Insanity and Unfitness to Plead) Act 1991. This Act addressed two troublesome aspects relating to the mentally ill offender. First was the problem of the defendant who may have had a valid defence to the charges but who was unable to obtain a trial because his mental state rendered him unfit to plead. We have noted previously that a defendant who is unfit to plead now may under the 1991 Act obtain a provisional trial, albeit limited to whether he committed the act charged.

The second issue addressed in the 1991 Act was that of the mandatory commitment of either a defendant found unfit to plead or found not guilty by reason of insanity. The Act provides as follows:

CRIMINAL PROCEDURE (INSANITY AND UNFITNESS TO PLEAD) ACT 1991

Powers to deal with persons not guilty by reason of insanity or unfit to plead etc.
5.—(1) This section applies where—
(a) a special verdict is returned that the accused is not guilty by reason of insanity; or
(b) findings are recorded that the accused is under a disability and that he did the act or made the omission charged against him.

(2) Subject to subsection (3) below, the court shall either—
  (a) make an order that the accused be admitted, in accordance with the provisions of Schedule 1 to the Criminal Procedure (Insanity and Unfitness to Plead) Act 1991, to such hospital as may be specified by the Secretary of State; or
  (b) where they have the power to do so by virtue of section 5 of that Act, make in respect of the accused such one of the following orders as they think most suitable in all the circumstances of the case, namely—
    (i) a guardianship order within the meaning of the Mental Health Act 1983;
    (ii) a supervision and treatment order within the meaning of Schedule 2 to the said Act of 1991; and
    (iii) an order for his absolute discharge.
(3) Paragraph (b) of subsection (2) above shall not apply where the offence to which the special verdict or findings relate is an offence the sentence for which is fixed by law.

C: Reform of the law

The defence of insanity propounded in *M'Naghten* has changed little since its initial articulation in 1843, a fact that one might find surprising in light of the advances in the understanding and treatment of mental illness. The explanation lies in the fact that insanity is measured by a *legal* rather than a *medical* test. The point is brought home by the judicial extension of the defence to those who suffer from physical illnesses that render them prone to episodes of recurring violence. Seen in the above light, it suggests that the courts may view the insanity defence as a means whereby the law can impose a form of preventive detention on dangerous individuals who for technical reasons could not be convicted of a crime or sectioned to a mental hospital. Whether the 1991 Act will bring about a change in this misuse of the defence is still unclear.

In any event, basic questions remain. What functions are served by the insanity defence? To whom should the defence be available? Is insanity a medical or legal concept? And are mentally ill offenders best dealt with within the criminal justice system or the mental health system? Over the years many of the alternatives to *M'Naghten* which have been proposed have sought to bring the test of insanity closer to a medical model of mental illness. The Draft Criminal Code's approach to the issue was based to a large extent on the recommendations of the Butler Committee (1975).

DRAFT CRIMINAL CODE BILL 1989

34. In this Act—
  'mental disorder' means—
    (a) severe mental illness; or
    (b) a state of arrested or incomplete development of mind; or
    (c) a state of automatism (not resulting only from intoxication) which is a feature of a disorder, whether organic or functional and whether continuing or recurring, that may cause a similar state on another occasion;
  'return a mental disorder verdict' means—
    (a) in relation to trial on indictment, return a verdict that the defendant is not guilty on evidence of mental disorder; and
    (b) in relation to summary trial, dismiss the information on evidence of mental disorder;

'severe mental illness' means a mental illness which has one or more of the following characteristics—

   (a) lasting impairment of intellectual functions shown by failure of memory, orientation, comprehension and learning capacity;

   (b) lasting alteration of mood of such degree as to give rise to delusional appraisal of the defendant's situation, his past or his future, or that of others, or lack of any appraisal;

   (c) delusional beliefs, persecutory, jealous or grandiose;

   (d) abnormal perceptions associated with delusional misinterpretation of events;

   (e) thinking so disordered as to prevent reasonable appraisal of the defendant's situation or reasonable communication with others;

'severe mental handicap' means a state of arrested or incomplete development of mind which includes severe impairment of intelligence and social functioning.

35.—(1) A mental disorder verdict shall be returned if the defendant is proved to have committed an offence but it is proved on the balance of probabilities (whether by the prosecution or by the defendant) that he was at the time suffering from severe mental illness or severe mental handicap.

   (2) Subsection (1) does not apply if the court or jury is satisfied beyond reasonable doubt that the offence was not attributable to the severe mental illness or severe mental handicap.

   (3) A court or jury shall not, for the purposes of a verdict under subsection (1), find that the defendant was suffering from severe mental illness or severe mental handicap unless two medical practitioners approved for the purposes of section 12 of the Mental Health Act 1983 as having special experience in the diagnosis or treatment of mental disorder have given evidence that he was so suffering.

   (4) Subsection (1), so far as it relates to severe mental handicap, does not apply to an offence under section 106(1), 107 or 108 (sexual relations with the mentally handicapped).

36. A mental disorder verdict shall be returned if—

   (a) the defendant is acquitted of an offence only because, by reason of evidence of mental disorder or a combination of mental disorder and intoxication, it is found that he acted or may have acted in a state of automatism, or without the fault required for the offence, or believing that an exempting circumstance existed; and

   (b) it is proved on the balance of probabilities (whether by the prosecution or by the defendant) that he was suffering from mental disorder at the time of the act.

37. A defendant may plead 'not guilty by reason of mental disorder'; and

   (a) if the court directs that the plea be entered the direction shall have the same effect as a mental disorder verdict; and

   (b) if the court does not so direct the defendant shall be treated as having pleaded not guilty.

38.—(1) Whether evidence is evidence of mental disorder or automatism is a question of law.

   (2) The prosecution shall not adduce evidence of mental disorder, or contend that a mental disorder verdict should be returned, unless the defendant has given or adduced evidence that he acted without the fault required for the offence, or believing that an exempting circumstance existed, or in a state of automatism, or (on a charge of murder) when suffering from mental abnormality as defined in section 57(2).

   (3) The court may give directions as to the stage of the proceedings at which the prosecution may adduce evidence of mental disorder.

   39. Schedule 2 has effect with respect to the orders that may be made upon the return of a mental disorder verdict, to the conditions governing the making of those orders, to the effects of those orders and to related matters.

   40. A defendant shall not, when a mental disorder verdict is returned in respect of an offence and while that verdict subsists, be found guilty of any other offence of which, but for this section, he might on the same occasion be found guilty—

   (a) on the indictment, count or information to which the verdict relates; or

   (b) on any other indictment, count or information founded on the same facts.

■ NOTES AND QUESTIONS

1. If the definition of insanity were to become more medically oriented, who should determine the defendant's sanity – a judge, a jury, a team of medical doctors, or a panel of mental health experts? One possibility would be to hold a bifurcated trial – in the first stage a jury would decide whether the defendant committed the crime charged, and in the second, assuming a verdict of guilty in the first stage, a panel of medical doctors or mental health experts would determine whether the defendant was insane at the time of the crime. A second question for the panel would be whether the defendant is still insane, and, if so, what should be the appropriate disposition. What are the advantages/disadvantages of such a bifurcated approach?

2. Another alternative (and perhaps the logical import of the suggestion in the preceding paragraph for a bifurcated trial) is to abolish the insanity defence altogether and consider insanity only at sentencing. A judge would be able, after receiving relevant evidence as to the defendant's mental state, to sentence the defendant (found 'guilty but insane' by a jury) to an institution in which he can receive appropriate treatment. The length of the sentence, however, would not be affected by the place of confinement. What are the advantages and disadvantages of such an approach?

3. If the insanity defence is to be retained and determined by the jury, perhaps it should be simplified. Consider the pros and cons of the formula proposed in 1953 by the Royal Commission on Capital Punishment:

> [A person is not responsible for his unlawful act if] at the time of the act the accused was suffering from disease of the mind (or mental deficiency) to such a degree that he ought not to be held responsible.

SECTION 3: AUTOMATISM

Not every act which on its face violates the law will result in criminal liability. The act has to be voluntary, i.e., an act of the will; or, stated perhaps more accurately, an act that one had, by the exercise of one's will, the power to refrain from doing. The justification for the voluntariness requirement is that an actor cannot be said to be responsible (in the moral sense of the term) for a truly involuntary act. Punishment is also pointless from a deterrence perspective, as involuntary acts cannot be deterred.

It may seem that characterising an act as involuntary is simply another way of saying that the defendant did not act with *mens rea*. In most instances the result of either line of analysis will be the same. However, in the case of strict liability crimes, where no *mens rea* need be proved and there is consequently no *mens rea* element which can be negated, only an involuntary act defence will be available to an accused.

A: Acts which are the product of an external force

Two types of 'involuntary act' cases can be distinguished. The first involves the situation where the defendant's act is the product of an external force. Say X pushes Y into Z, who falls into the path of an oncoming lorry and is killed. Y's act of pushing Z is not voluntary, and Y will not be held responsible for Z's death. Indeed, if anybody were to be charged, it would most likely be X, assuming his pushing of Y was deliberate. Y is nothing more than X's innocent agent, even though it was Y's acts that were the direct cause of the resulting harm.

The same principle may also apply where the defendant's acts, although not caused by an external force, are the product of external circumstances beyond the defendant's control.

Burns v Bidder
[1966] 3 All ER 29, Queen's Bench Division

The appellant was driving a motor car at a speed which was not high towards a pedestrian crossing. The road surface was good, although slightly wet. He passed the offside of a bus which had stopped at the crossing and which had been stationary there for several seconds. Several persons were using the crossing. The appellant failed to stop his car, at no time did he apply his hand-brake, and the car continued over the crossing and struck a pedestrian who was on the crossing some five or six feet from the centre of the road. The car came to a halt some distance beyond the crossing. Immediately afterwards the appellant complained that his footbrake had failed and, at the request of a police officer, took the car to a police station, where it was tested by an experienced traffic patrol officer who found that the footbrake worked correctly. On an information charging the appellant with unlawfully failing to accord precedence to a foot-passenger who was on the carriageway within the limits of an uncontrolled crossing, contrary to reg. 4 of the Pedestrian Crossings Regulations 1954, the stipendiary magistrate was not satisfied on a balance of probabilities that the brakes of the car had failed, nor was he satisfied that they had not failed and, as he considered that the offence was an absolute offence, he convicted the appellant.

JAMES J: . . . Counsel for the appellant contended that the learned stipendiary magistrate was wrong in his construction of that regulation as imposing an absolute obligation, and urges that to accord precedence involves a positive act such as 'a granting' or 'a bestowing' of something, and that, where the driver of a vehicle is precluded from doing a positive act, then he cannot be said to be failing to accord. Counsel for the appellant further points out that the magistrate was not satisfied that there was not a sudden failure of the brakes, and that there therefore remained a possibility that, due to a latent defect in the braking system, the appellant had been prevented through no fault of his own from according precedence to the pedestrian; this, he contends, being a regulation not imposing absolute obligations there was on that basis a complete defence to the information laid. . . . Some circumstances over which the driver had no reasonable or possible control brought about the collision. The basis is the same as that referred to by Nield J, in Levy v Hockey (1961) 105 SJ 157. Regulation 4 must be read 'subject to the principle of impossibility', as he put it in that case. In my judgment, the regulation does not impose an absolute duty come what may, and there is no breach of the obligation under the regulation in circumstances where the driver fails to afford precedence to a foot-passenger solely because his control of the vehicle is taken from him by the occurrence of an event which is outside his possible or reasonable control and in respect of which he is in no way at fault.

The cases of the driver suddenly stunned by a swarm of bees or suffering a sudden epileptiform disabling attack, or of a vehicle being propelled forward by reason of another vehicle hitting it from behind are illustrations of where no offence may be shown, because control over the vehicle is taken completely out of the hands of the driver, and his failure to accord precedence on that account would be no offence. Likewise, in my view, a sudden removal of control over the vehicle occasioned by a latent defect of which the driver did not know, and could not reasonably be expected to know, would render the resulting failure to accord precedence no offence, provided that he is in no way at fault himself. Beyond that limited sphere, however, the obligation of the driver under the regulations can properly be described, as it has been described, as an absolute one....

B: Automatism (and insanity revisited)

A different type of involuntary act is commonly referred to as automatism. There are two main subcategories. The first involves the situation where the defendant is conscious, but his acts are the product of a spasm, reflex, or convulsion. For example, a doctor hits a patient in the knee with a rubber hammer to test the patient's reflexes. The patient's reflexes are excellent and his leg flies forward, striking the doctor's assistant. If charged with assault, the patient would have a defence based on the fact that his act was a reflex action and involuntary.

The second subcategory of automatism involves the situation where the defendant commits an act in an unconscious or semi-conscious state, or in a state of impaired consciousness. This type of automatism case has proved quite resistant to reasoned analysis. While there is agreement that the automatism negates an element of the crime, there is disagreement as to whether the element negated is the *actus reus* or the *mens rea*, or possibly both.

When the automatism can be traced to a disease of the mind, the confusion seems to be compounded. Is the appropriate defence in such a case insanity or automatism? The difference can have significant ramifications. If insanity, the burden of proof will rest on the defendant, who must establish the defence on the balance of probabilities; if automatism, the burden of negating automatism will rest on the prosecution by proof beyond reasonable doubt. Of course, in either situation the Crown may be entitled to rely on the presumption that a defendant has the capacity to commit the crime until the defendant introduces evidence to the contrary.

The courts have further confused the issue by inventing a category of 'insane automatism'. It is arguable that this is simply an attempt to extend the category of defendants covered by the insanity defence. The temptation to do so may be great, especially where violence has not only occurred but may recur in the future. As we have seen, an NGRI verdict used to lead to the defendant's automatic confinement to a mental hospital, but it still will provide a court with the option of confining the defendant. In contrast, an acquittal on the grounds of automatism will lead to the defendant's release.

Bratty v Attorney-General for Northern Ireland
[1961] 3 All ER 523, House of Lords

The accused killed a girl, with whom he was driving in his car on an errand. He took off her stocking and strangled her with it. He gave evidence that a 'blackness' came over him and that 'I didn't know what I was doing. I didn't realise anything.' He also said that previously he had had 'feelings of blackness' and headaches, and there was evidence of his odd behaviour at times, of his mental backwardness and his religious leanings. There was medical evidence that the accused might have been suffering from an attack of psychomotor epilepsy, which was a disease of the mind affecting the reason and which could cause ignorance of the nature and quality of acts done. No other pathological cause for the accused's acts, or a state of automatism on his part was assigned by medical evidence at the trial. The defences of automatism (i.e., unconscious involuntary action) and of insanity within the M'Naghten rules were raised at the trial. The trial judge refused to leave the defence of automatism to the jury, but left to them the defence of insanity, which the jury rejected. The accused was convicted of murder.

VISCOUNT KILMUIR LC: My Lords, this is an appeal from the Court of Criminal Appeal in Northern Ireland.... The court certified that the decision involved two points of law of general public importance, namely:

(i) Whether, his plea of insanity having been rejected by the jury, it was open to the accused to rely on a defence of automatism; and

(ii) If the answer to (i) be in the affirmative, whether, on the evidence, the defence of automatism should have been left to the jury.

... The Court of Criminal Appeal [agreed] that the learned judge was right in not leaving to the jury the defence of automatism in so far as it purported to be founded on a defect of reason from disease of the mind within the M'Naghten rules. In this I think that they were right. To establish the defence of insanity within the M'Naghten rules the accused must prove on the preponderance of probabilities first a defect of reason from a disease of the mind, and, secondly, as a consequence of such a defect, ignorance of the nature and quality (or the wrongfulness) of the acts. We have to consider a case in which it is sought to do so by medical evidence to the effect that the conduct of the accused might be compatible with psychomotor epilepsy, which is a disease of the mind affecting the reason, and that psychomotor epilepsy could cause ignorance of the nature and quality of the acts done, but in which the medical witness can assign no other cause for that ignorance. Where the possibility of an unconscious act depends on, and only on, the existence of a defect of reason from disease of the mind within the M'Naghten rules, a rejection by the jury of this defence of insanity necessarily implies that they reject the possibility.

The Court of Criminal Appeal also took the view that where the alleged automatism is based solely on a disease of the mind within the M'Naghten rules, the same burden of proof rests on the defence whether the 'plea' is given the name of insanity or automatism. I do not think that statement goes further than saying that when one relies on insanity as defined by the M'Naghten rules one cannot by a difference of nomenclature avoid the road so often and authoritatively laid down by the courts.

What I have said does not mean that, if a defence of insanity is raised unsuccessfully, there can never, in any conceivable circumstances, be room for an alternative defence based on automatism. For example, it may be alleged that the accused had a blow on the head after which he acted without being conscious of what he was doing or was a sleep-walker. There might be a divergence of view whether there was a defect of reason from disease of the mind (compare the curious position which arose in *R* v *Kemp* [1957] 1 QB 399). The jury might not accept the evidence of a defect of reason from disease of the mind, but at the same time accept the evidence that the prisoner did not know what he was doing. If the jury should take that view of the facts they would find him not guilty. But it should be noted that the defence would only have succeeded because the necessary foundation had been laid by positive evidence which, properly considered, was evidence of something other than a defect of reason from disease of the mind. In my opinion, this analysis of the two defences (insanity and automatism) shows that where the only cause alleged for the unconsciousness is a defect of reason from disease of the mind, and that cause is rejected by the jury, there can be no room for the alternative defence of automatism. . . . It is necessary that a proper foundation be laid before a judge can leave 'automatism' to the jury. That foundation, in my view, is not forthcoming merely from unaccepted evidence of a defect of reason from disease of the mind . . . .

Nevertheless, one must not lose sight of the overriding principle, laid down by this House in *Woolmington's* case [1935] AC 462, that it is for the prosecution to prove every element of the offence charged. One of these elements is the accused's state of mind; normally the presumption of mental capacity is sufficient to prove that he acted consciously and voluntarily and the prosecution need go no further. But, if, after considering evidence properly left to them by the judge, the jury are left in real doubt whether or not the accused acted in a state of automatism, it seems to me that on principle they should acquit because the necessary mens rea—if indeed the actus reus—has not been proved beyond reasonable doubt . . . .

LORD DENNING: My Lords, in *Woolmington* v *Director of Public Prosecutions* [1935] AC 462 Viscount Sankey LC, said: 'When dealing with a murder case the Crown must prove (a) death as the result of a voluntary act of the accused and (b) malice of the accused.' The requirement that it should be a voluntary act is essential, not only in a murder case, but also in every criminal case. No act is punishable if it is done involuntarily: and an involuntary act in this context—some people nowadays prefer to speak of it as 'automatism'—means an act which is done by the muscles without any control by the mind such as a spasm, a reflex action or a convulsion; or an act done by a person who is not conscious of what he is doing such as an act done whilst suffering from concussion or whilst sleepwalking . . . . The term 'involuntary act' is, however, capable of wider connotations: and to prevent confusion it is to be observed that in the criminal law an act is not to be regarded as an involuntary act simply because the doer does not remember it. When a man is charged with dangerous driving, it is no defence for him to say 'I don't know what happened. I cannot remember a thing': see *Hill* v *Baxter* [1958] 1 All ER 193. Loss of memory afterwards is never a defence in itself, so long as he was conscious at the time; see *Russell* v *H. M. Advocate* [1946] SC (J) 37]; *R* v *Podola* [[1959] 3 All ER 418]. Nor is an act to be regarded as an involuntary act simply because the doer could not control his impulse to do it . . . .

My Lords, I think that Devlin J, was quite right in *R* v *Kemp* [1957] 1 QB 399 in putting the question of insanity to the jury, even though it had not been raised by the defence. When it is asserted that the accused did an involuntary act in a state of automatism, the defence necessarily puts in issue the state of mind of the accused man: and thereupon it is open to the prosecution to show what his true state of mind was. The old notion that only the defence can raise a defence of insanity is now gone. The prosecution are entitled to raise it and it is their duty to do so rather than allow a dangerous person to be at large . . . .

On the other point discussed by Devlin J, namely, what is a 'disease of the mind' within the M'Naghten rules, I would agree with him that this is a question for the judge. The major mental diseases, which the doctors call psychoses, such as schizophrenia, are clearly diseases of the mind. But in *R* v *Charlson* [1955] 1 WLR 317, Barry J, seems to have assumed that other diseases such as epilepsy or cerebral tumour are not diseases of the mind, even when they are such as to manifest themselves in violence. I do not agree with this. It seems to me that any mental disorder which has manifested itself in violence and is prone to recur is a disease of the mind. At any rate it is the sort of disease for which a person should be detained in hospital rather than be given an unqualified acquittal.

. . . [W]hilst the *ultimate* burden rests on the Crown of proving every element essential in the crime, nevertheless in order to prove that the act was a voluntary act, the Crown is entitled to rely on the *presumption* that every man has sufficient mental capacity to be responsible for his crimes: and that if the defence wish to displace that presumption they must give some evidence from which the contrary may reasonably be inferred . . . .

The presumption of mental capacity of which I have spoken is a provisional presumption only. It does not put the legal burden on the defence in the same way as the presumption of sanity does. It leaves the legal burden on the prosecution, but nevertheless, until it is displaced, it enables the prosecution to discharge the ultimate burden of proving that the act was voluntary. Not because the presumption is evidence itself, but because it takes the place of evidence. In order to displace the presumption of mental capacity, the defence must give sufficient evidence from which it may reasonably be inferred that the act was involuntary. The evidence of the man himself will rarely be sufficient unless it is supported by medical evidence which points to the cause of the mental incapacity.... When the only cause that is assigned for an involuntary act is drunkenness, then it is only necessary to leave drunkenness to the jury, with the consequential directions, and not to leave automatism at all. When the only cause that is assigned for it is a disease of the mind, then it is only necessary to leave insanity to the jury, and not automatism. When the cause assigned is concussion or sleepwalking, there should be some evidence from which it can reasonably be inferred before it should be left to the jury. If it is said to be due to concussion, there should be evidence of a severe blow shortly beforehand. If it is said to be sleepwalking, there should be some credible support for it. His mere assertion that he was asleep will not suffice. Once a proper foundation is thus laid for automatism, the matter becomes at large and must be left to the jury....

This brings me to the root question in the present case: Was a proper foundation laid here for the defence of automatism apart from the plea of insanity? There was the evidence of the appellant himself that he could not remember anything because 'this blackness was over me'. He said 'I did not realise exactly what I was doing', and added afterwards 'I didn't know what I was doing. I didn't realise anything'. He said he had four or five times previously had 'feelings of blackness' and frequently headaches. There was evidence, too, of his odd behaviour at times, his mental backwardness and his religious leanings. Added to this there was the medical evidence. Dr Sax, who was called on his behalf, said there was a possibility that he was suffering from psychomotor epilepsy. It was, he said, practically the only possibility that occurred to him. Dr Walker, his general practitioner, said you could not leave the possibility out of account. Dr Robinson, a specialist, who gave evidence on behalf of the Crown, said he thought it was extremely unlikely that it was an epileptic attack, but one could not rule it out. All the doctors agreed that psychomotor epilepsy, if it exists, is a defect of reason due to disease of the mind: and the judge accepted this view. No other cause was canvassed.

In those circumstances, I am clearly of opinion that, if the act of the appellant was an involuntary act, as the defence suggested, the evidence attributed it solely to a disease of the mind and the only defence open was the defence of insanity. There was no evidence of automatism apart from insanity. There was, therefore, no need for the judge to put it to the jury. And when the jury rejected the defence of insanity, they rejected the only defence disclosed by the evidence....

■ NOTES AND QUESTIONS

1. For an automatism claim to succeed, there must be a total loss of voluntary control. Proof of an impaired or reduced control is not enough. See *Attorney-General's Reference (No. 2 of 1992)* (1993) 97 Cr App R 429.

2. To return to a question raised previously, is it appropriate to characterise epilepsy as a mental disorder? Is this a medical opinion? The opinion of the ordinary person? Or a definition adopted by the judges solely for legal purposes? In any event, why should the defence of insanity take precedence over the defence of automatism?

3. When a defendant raises a defence of automatism, the prosecution is allowed to introduce evidence of insanity and to argue that the appropriate verdict should be not guilty by reason of insanity. Prior to enactment of the Criminal Procedure (Insanity and Unfitness to Plead) Act 1991 Act, the defendant who wished to raise a defence of automatism had to take the not inconsiderable risk that the prosecution would argue that the proper defence was insanity, and that the jury might agree, with the result that the defendant would be confined to a mental institution, possibly for life. Even after the 1991 Act, this remains a possibility. However, by virtue of the Domestic Violence, Crime and Victims Act 2007 an

order for hospitalisation must conform with the terms of the Mental Health Act 1983. This requires medical evidence that justifies detention on grounds of the defendant's medical state. The mere fact that the defendant has committed a serious offence would not justify detention if the condition did not necessitate hospitalisation. This point is discussed below in relation to sleepwalking.

The issues raised by *Bratty* were further explored in a case involving a diabetic:

R v Quick, R v Paddison
[1973] QB 910, Court of Appeal

LAWTON LJ: In its broadest aspects these appeals raise the question what is meant by the phrase 'a defect of reason from disease of the mind' within the meaning of the M'Naghten Rules. More particularly the question is whether a person who commits a criminal act whilst under the effects of hypoglycaemia can raise a defence of automatism, as the appellants submitted was possible, or whether such a person must rely on a defence of insanity if he wishes to relieve himself of responsibility for his acts, as Bridge J ruled.

The appellants were both employed at Farleigh Mental Hospital, Flax Bourton, Somerset. Quick was a charge nurse, Paddison a state enrolled nurse. At the trial it was not disputed that, at about 4 p.m. on 27th December 1971, one Green, a paraplegic spastic patient, unable to walk, was sitting in Rosemount Ward at the hospital, watching television. Quick was on duty; Paddison had gone off duty at 2 p.m. but was still present in the ward. Half an hour later, Green had sustained two black eyes, a fractured nose, a split lip which required three stitches, and bruising of his arm and shoulders. There was undisputed medical evidence that these injuries could not have been self-inflicted.

The Crown's case was that Quick had inflicted the injuries on Green and that Paddison had been present aiding and abetting him, not by actual physical participation, but by encouragement. On arraignment Quick pleaded not guilty. At the close of the evidence, following a ruling by the judge as to the effect in law of the evidence relied on by Quick to support a defence of automatism, he pleaded guilty to count 2 of the indictment. The judge's ruling was to the effect that this evidence could only be relied on to support a defence of insanity.

... Quick said that he could not remember assaulting Green. He admitted that he had been drinking and that his drinks had included whisky and a quarter of a bottle of rum. He also said that he was, and had been since the age of seven, a diabetic and that that morning he had taken insulin as prescribed by his doctor. After taking the insulin he had had a very small breakfast and no lunch. Dr Cates said that on 12 or more occasions Quick had been admitted to hospital either unconscious or semiconscious due to hypoglycaemia, which is a condition brought about when there is more insulin in the bloodstream than the amount of sugar there can cope with. When this imbalance occurs, the insulin has much the same effect as an excess of alcohol in the human body. At the onset of the imbalance the higher functions of the mind are affected. As the effects of the imbalance become more marked, more and more mental functions are upset; and unless an antidote is given (and a lump of sugar is an effective one) the sufferer can relapse into coma. In the later stages of mental impairment a sufferer may become aggressive and violent without being able to control himself or without knowing at the time what he was doing or having any recollection afterwards of what he had done....

At the trial and before this court it was accepted by the Crown that the evidence to which we have referred was enough to justify an issue being left to the jury whether Quick could be held responsible for what he had done to Green. If the jury were to accept the evidence relied on by Quick what should the verdict be? Quick's counsel submitted 'not guilty'; counsel for the Crown submitted that it should be 'not guilty by reason of insanity'. The judge ruled in favour of the Crown. As Quick did not want to put forward a defence of insanity, after consulting with his counsel, he pleaded guilty to count 2.

...In this case, if Quick's alleged condition could have been caused by hypoglycaemia and that condition, like psychomotor epilepsy, was a disease of the mind, then Bridge J's ruling was right.

The question remains, however, whether a mental condition arising from hypoglycaemia does amount to a disease of the mind....

...Quick was setting up a defence of insanity. He may have been at the material time in a condition of mental disorder manifesting itself in violence. Such manifestations had occurred before and might recur. The difficulty arises as soon as the question is asked whether he should be detained in a mental hospital? No mental hospital would admit a diabetic merely because he had a low blood sugar reaction; and common sense is affronted by the prospect of a diabetic being sent to such a hospital when in most cases the disordered mental condition can be rectified quickly by pushing a lump of sugar or a teaspoonful of glucose into the patient's mouth.

The 'affront to common sense' argument, however, has its own inherent weakness, as counsel for the Crown pointed out. If an accused is shown to have done a criminal act whilst suffering from a 'defect of reason from disease of the mind', it matters not 'whether the disease is curable or incurable...temporary or permanent' (see *R v Kemp* [1957] 1 QB 399, per Devlin J). If the condition is temporary, the Secretary of State may have a difficult problem of disposal; but what happens to those found not guilty by reason of insanity is not a matter for the courts.

In *Hill v Baxter* [1958] 1 All ER 193, Lord Goddard CJ did not equate unconsciousness due to a sudden illness, which must entail the malfunctioning of the mental processes of the sufferer, with disease of the mind, and in our judgment no one outside a court of law would...It seems to us that the law should not give the words 'defect of reason from disease of the mind' a meaning which would be regarded with incredulity outside a court...

In this quagmire of law seldom entered nowadays save by those in desperate need of some kind of a defence, *Bratty v Attorney-General for Northern Ireland* [1963] AC 386; [1961] 3 All ER 523 provides the only firm ground. Is there any discernible path? We think there is—judges should follow in a common sense way their sense of fairness.... In our judgment no help can be obtained by speculating (because that is what we would have to do) as to what the judges who answered the House of Lords' questions in 1843 meant by disease of the mind, still less what Sir Matthew Hale meant in the second half of the 17th century. A quick backward look at the state of medicine in 1843 will suffice to show how unreal it would be to apply the concepts of that age to the present time. Dr Simpson had not yet started his experiments with chloroform, the future Lord Lister was only 16 and laudanum was used and prescribed like aspirins are today. Our task had been to decide what the law means now by the words 'disease of the mind'. In our judgment the fundamental concept is of a malfunctioning of the mind caused by disease. A malfunctioning of the mind of transitory effect caused by the application to the body of some external factor such as violence, drugs, including anaesthetics, alcohol and hypnotic influences cannot fairly be said to be due to disease. Such malfunctioning, unlike an accused from criminal responsibility. A self-induced incapacity will not excuse...nor will one which could have been reasonably foreseen as a result of either doing, or omitting to do something, as, for example, taking alcohol against medical advice after using certain prescribed drugs, or failing to have regular meals whilst taking insulin. From to time to time difficult borderline cases are likely to arise. When they do, the test suggested by the New Zealand Court of Appeal...is likely to give the correct result, viz can this mental condition be fairly regarded as amounting to or producing a defect of reason from disease of the mind?

In this case Quick's alleged mental condition, if it ever existed, was not caused by his diabetes but by his use of the insulin prescribed by his doctor. Such malfunctioning of his mind as there was, was caused by an external factor and not by a bodily disorder in the nature of a disease which disturbed the working of his mind. It follows in our judgment that Quick was entitled to have his defence of automatism left to the jury and that Bridge J's ruling as to the effect of the medical evidence called by him was wrong. Had the defence of automatism been left to the jury, a number of questions of fact would have had to be answered. If he was in a confused mental condition, was it due to a hypoglycaemic episode or to too much alcohol? If the former, to what extent had he brought about his condition by not following his doctor's instructions about taking regular meals? Did he know that he was getting into a hypoglycaemic episode? If Yes, why did he not use the antidote of eating a lump of sugar as he had been advised to do? On the evidence which was before the jury Quick might have had difficulty in answering these questions in a manner which would have relieved him of responsibility for his acts. We cannot say, however, with the requisite degree of confidence, that the jury would have convicted him. It follows that his conviction must be quashed on the ground that the verdict was unsatisfactory.

Appeals allowed.

■ NOTES AND QUESTIONS

1. The Court of Appeal in *Quick* drew a distinction between the acts of a diabetic which may be attributable to insulin – an external source – and those which may be attributable to the diabetes itself – an internal source. What if a patient who is prescribed medication to control a mental illness suffers an adverse reaction from the medication which causes the patient to lose self-control? Are acts done in this state attributable to the disease or to the medication? Are not the two inextricably linked?

2. What if the external source is psychological rather than physical? In *R v Rabey* (1978) 79 DLR 3d 435 the Canadian court rejected an automatism defence where the defendant claimed his crime was committed while in a 'dissociative state' brought on by his rejection by a girl with whom he was infatuated. In *R v T* [1990] Crim LR 256 an automatism defence succeeded where the defendant was suffering from 'post-traumatic stress disorder' brought on as a result of having been raped. Are the cases distinguishable?

In *Quick* there was evidence that the defendant, contrary to his doctor's instructions, may have been drinking alcohol and not eating food. The Court indicated that such evidence may have defeated, rather than helped, his automatism claim. The issue of self-induced automatism was revisited in *R v Bailey*:

R v Bailey
[1983] 1 WLR 760, Court of Appeal

GRIFFITHS LJ: At the Crown Court at Bolton on October 14, 1982, the appellant was convicted of wounding with intent to cause grievous bodily harm, contrary to section 18 of the Offences against the Person Act 1861 (24 & 25 Vict. c. 100). The jury were not required to give a verdict on an alternative count of unlawful wounding contrary to section 20 of that Act. He now appeals against this conviction.

The appellant is a diabetic and has been so for some 30 years. He requires to take insulin to control his condition. His defence at the trial was that he was acting in a state of automatism caused by hypoglycaemia.

In early January 1982, the woman with whom the appellant had been living for the previous two years left him and formed an association with the victim, Mr Harrison. At about 7 p.m. on January 20, 1982, the appellant, seeming upset, visited Mr Harrison at his home. They had a cup of tea and discussed the matter. After 10 or 15 minutes the appellant said that he felt unwell and asked Mr Harrison to make him some sugar and water, which the appellant drank. About 10 minutes later the appellant started to leave. He then said that he had lost his glove and that it might be down the side of the chair on which he had been sitting. Mr Harrison bent down to look and the appellant struck him on the back of the head with an iron bar, which was a case opener about 18"long. The appellant remained there holding the iron bar. Mr Harrison ran from the house. His wound required 10 stitches.

The Crown's case was that although it was theoretically possible, from a medical point of view, for there to have been a temporary loss of awareness due to hypoglycaemia, as the appellant claimed, this was not what had happened. On the contrary, it was contended that the appellant, upset and jealous about Mr Harrison's relationship with his girlfriend, had armself with the iron bar and gone to Mr Harrison's house with the intention of injuring him . . . .

When he gave evidence, the appellant, who was a man of good character, maintained he had no intention of harming Mr Harrison and he had acted in a state of automatism. He said that he had to take two doses of insulin a day and was under his general practitioner and a special clinic. He had arrived home at 5.30 p.m. and had his insulin and a cup of tea. At 7 p.m. he decided to go and see Harrison and his account of what took place accorded with that of Mr Harrison up to the point where he asked Mr Harrison to look for his glove. The next thing he could remember was standing with the bar in his hand. He saw that Mr Harrison was injured and he said: 'What the hell am I doing?' He then described how he went home and later to the public house where he was arrested.

The appellant's general practitioner gave evidence. He confirmed that the appellant was a diabetic and received insulin treatment, after which he had to take food within a short period. If he failed to do so it could produce symptoms of weakness, palpitations, tremor and sweating. He might develop more aggressive tendencies than normal and this could be accompanied by loss of memory. After describing what the appellant had said he had had to eat he said that the appellant had not had sufficient to counteract and balance the dose of insulin. So far as he was aware the appellant in 30 years had never developed a condition of coma due to hypoglycaemia. He said that the effect of taking sugar and water in Mr Harrison's house would be to help bring back the sugar level within five or ten minutes. When he was cross-examined he said he thought it unlikely that there could have been the sudden switch-off effect alleged by the appellant and he regarded the likelihood of such a thing happening as being remote if sugar and water had been taken five minutes before it happened.

It was therefore the appellant's case that the attack had taken place during a period of loss of consciousness occurring due to hypoglycaemia caused by his failure to take sufficient food following his last dose of insulin. Accordingly it was submitted that he had neither the specific intent to cause grievous bodily harm for the purpose of section 18 nor the appropriate mens rea or basic intent for the purpose of the section 20 offence.

But the recorder, in effect, told the jury that this defence was not available to the appellant . . . . The recorder appears to have derived this proposition, which he applied to both counts of the indictment, from *R* v *Quick* [1973] QB 910 . . . .

But in that case, the offence, assault occasioning actual bodily harm, was an offence of basic intent. No specific intent was required. It is now quite clear that even if the incapacity of mind is self-induced by the voluntary taking of drugs or alcohol, the specific intent to kill or cause grievous bodily harm may be negatived: see *R* v *Majewski* [1977] AC 443. This being so, as it is conceded on behalf of the Crown, the direction to which we have referred cannot be correct so far as the offence under section 18 is concerned.

But it is also submitted that the direction is wrong or at least in too broad and general terms, so far as the section 20 offence is concerned. If . . . *R* v *Quick* correctly represents the law, then the direction given by the recorder was correct so far as the second count was concerned even though the appellant may have had no appreciation of the consequences of his failure to take food and even though such failure may not have been due to deliberate abstention but because of his generally distressed condition. In our judgment the passage from Lawton LJ's judgment was obiter and we are free to re-examine it.

Automatism resulting from intoxication as a result of a voluntary ingestion of alcohol or dangerous drugs does not negative the mens rea necessary for crimes of basic intent, because the conduct of the accused is reckless and recklessness is enough to constitute the necessary mens rea in assault cases where no specific intent forms part of the charge: see *R* v *Majewski* [1977] AC 443, 476 . . . But it seems to us that there may be material distinctions between a man who consumes alcohol or takes dangerous drugs and one who fails to take sufficient food after insulin to avert hypoglycaemia.

It is common knowledge that those who take alcohol to excess or certain sorts of drugs may become aggressive or do dangerous or unpredictable things, they may be able to foresee the risks of causing harm to others but nevertheless persist in their conduct. But the same cannot be said without more of a man who fails to take food after an insulin injection. If he does appreciate the risk that such a failure may lead to aggressive, unpredictable and uncontrollable conduct and he nevertheless deliberately runs the risk or otherwise disregards it, this will amount to reckless-ness. But we certainly do not think that it is common knowledge, even among diabetics, that such is a consequence of a failure to take food and there is no evidence that it was known to this appel-lant. Doubtless he knew that if he failed to take his insulin or proper food after it, he might lose consciousness, but as such he would only be a danger to himself unless he put himself in charge of some machine such as a motor car, which required his continued conscious control.

In our judgment, self-induced automatism, other than that due to intoxication from alcohol or drugs, may provide a defence to crimes of basic intent. The question in each case will be whether the prosecution have proved the necessary element of recklessness. In cases of assault, if the accused knows that his actions or inaction are likely to make him aggressive, unpredictable or uncontrolled with the result that he may cause some injury to others and he persists in the action or takes no remedial action when he knows it is required, it will be open to the jury to find that he was reckless....

But we have to consider whether, notwithstanding these misdirections, there has been any miscarriage of justice and whether the jury properly directed could have failed to come to the same conclusion. As Lawton LJ said in *Quick's* case at p. 922, referring to the defence of automa-tism, it is a 'quagmire of law seldom entered nowadays save by those in desperate need of some kind of a defence...' This case is no exception. We think it very doubtful whether the appellant laid a sufficient basis for the defence to be considered by the jury at all. But even if he did we are in no doubt that the jury properly directed must have rejected it. Although an episode of sudden transient loss of consciousness or awareness was theoretically possible it was quite inconsistent with the graphic description that the appellant gave to the police both orally and in his written statement. There was abundant evidence that he had armed himself with the iron bar and gone to Mr Harrison's house for the purpose of attacking him because he wanted to teach him a lesson and because he was in the way.

Moreover the doctor's evidence to which we have referred showed it was extremely unlikely that such an episode could follow some five minutes after taking sugar and water. For these reasons we are satisfied that no miscarriage of justice occurred and the appeal will be dismissed.

Appeal dismissed.

In *Bratty*, Lord Denning offered the sleepwalker as the paradigm example of an automaton. When this actual fact situation finally came before the courts, how-ever, it turned out to be more contentious.

R v Burgess

[1991] 2 QB 92, Court of Appeal

LORD LANE CJ: On 20 July 1989 in the Crown Court at Bristol before Judge Sir Ian Lewis and a jury, the appellant was found not guilty by reason of insanity on a charge of wounding with intent. He was ordered to be admitted and detained in such hospital as the Secretary of State should direct. He now appeals against that verdict by certificate of the trial judge under section 12 of the Criminal Appeal Act 1968.

The appellant did not dispute the fact that in the early hours of 2 June 1988 he had attacked Katrina Curtis by hitting her on the head first with a bottle when she was asleep, then with a video recorder and finally grasping her round the throat. She suffered a gaping three centimetre lacera-tion to her scalp requiring sutures.

His case was that he lacked the mens rea necessary to make him guilty of the offence, because he was 'sleepwalking' when he attacked Miss Curtis. He was, it was alleged, suffering from 'non-insane' automatism and he called medical evidence, in particular from Dr d'Orban and Dr Eames to support that contention.

Where the defence of automatism is raised by a defendant, two questions fall to be decided by the judge before the defence can be left to the jury. The first is whether a proper evidential foundation for the defence of automatism has been laid. The second is whether the evidence shows the case to be one of insane automatism, that is to say, a case which falls within the M'Naghten Rules, or one of non-insane automatism.

The judge in the present case undertook that task and on the second question came to the conclusion that—assuming the appellant was not conscious at the time of what he was doing—on any view of the medical evidence so far as automatism was concerned, it amounted to evidence of insanity within the M'Naghten Rules and not merely to evidence of non-insane automatism. The sole ground of appeal is that that ruling was wrong.

There can be no doubt but that the appellant, on the basis of the jury's verdict, was labouring under such a defect of reason as not to know what he was doing when he wounded Miss Curtis. The question is whether that was from 'disease of the mind'. The first point that has to be understood is that the phrase is 'disease of the mind' and not 'disease of the brain' . . . .

The appellant plainly suffered from a defect of reason from some sort of failure (for lack of a better term) of the mind causing him to act as he did without conscious motivation. His mind was to some extent controlling his actions which were purposive rather than the result simply of muscular spasm, but without his being consciously aware of what he was doing. Can it be said that that 'failure' was a *disease* of the mind rather than a defect or failure of the mind not due to disease? That is the distinction, by no means always easy to draw, upon which this case depends, as others have depended in the past.

What help does one derive from the authorities as to the meaning of 'disease' in this context? Lord Denning in *Bratty* v *Attorney-General for Northern Ireland* [1963] AC 386, 412 said:

> Upon the other point discussed by Devlin J, namely, what is a 'disease of the mind' within the M'Naghten Rules, I would agree with him that this is a question for the judge. The major mental diseases, which the doctors call psychoses, such as schizophrenia, are clearly diseases of the mind. But in *Charlson's* case [1955] 1 WLR 317, Barry J seems to have assumed that other diseases such as epilepsy or cerebral tumour are not diseases of the mind, even when they are such as to manifest themselves in violence. I do not agree with this. It seems to me that any mental disorder which has manifested itself in violence and is prone to recur is a disease of the mind. At any rate it is the sort of disease for which a person should be detained in hospital rather than be given an unqualified acquittal.

It seems to us that if there is a danger of recurrence that may be an added reason for categorising the condition as a disease of the mind. On the other hand, the absence of the danger of recurrence is not a reason for saying that it cannot be a disease of the mind. Subject to that possible qualification, we respectfully adopt Lord Denning's suggested definition.

It seems to us that on [the] evidence the judge was right to conclude that this was an abnormality or disorder, albeit transitory, due to an internal factor, whether functional or organic, which had manifested itself in violence. It was a disorder or abnormality which might recur, though the possibility of it recurring in the form of serious violence was unlikely. Therefore since this was a legal problem to be decided on legal principles, it seems to us that on those principles the answer was as the judge found it to be . . . .

This appeal must accordingly be dismissed.

Appeal dismissed.

R v Parks

[1992] 2 SCR 871

The respondent drove 23 km at night to his parents-in-law's house. There he killed one and seriously injured the other. Immediately after the incident, the respondent went to a nearby police station, again driving his own car, and told them what he had done. He claimed that he was sleepwalking throughout the incident.

The respondent was charged with first degree murder and attempted murder. At the trial the respondent presented a defence of automatism. The testimony of five expert witnesses called by the defence was not contradicted by the Crown. This evidence was that the respondent was sleepwalking and that sleepwalking is not a neurological, psychiatric or other illness. The trial judge put only the defence of automatism to the jury, which acquitted the respondent of first degree murder and then of second degree murder. The judge then acquitted the respondent of the charge of attempted murder. The Court of Appeal unanimously upheld the acquittal. On appeal by the prosecutor to the Supreme Court the issue was whether sleepwalking should be classified as non-insane automatism resulting in an acquittal or as a 'disease of the mind' (insane automatism), giving rise to the special verdict of not guilty by reason of insanity. The Supreme Court dismissed the appeal.

LAMER CJ and CORY J dissenting in part): The appeal should be dismissed.

LA FOREST, L'Heureurx-DUBE and Gonthier JJ: The trial judge correctly left only the defence of non-insane automatism with the jury. On this issue the findings of Lamer C.J. on the evidence were agreed with, but the distinction in law between insane and non-insane automatism, particularly as it relates to somnambulism, required further comment. In distinguishing between automatism and insanity the trial judge must consider not only the evidence but also overarching policy considerations.

Automatism, although spoken of as a 'defence', is conceptually a sub-set of the voluntariness requirement, which in turn is part of the *actus reus* component of criminal liability. An involuntary act, including one committed in an automatistic condition entitles an accused to an unqualified acquittal, unless the automatistic condition stems from a disease of the mind that has rendered the accused insane. In the latter case, the accused is not entitled to a full acquittal, but to a verdict of insanity.

When a defence of non-insane automatism is raised by the accused, the trial judge must determine whether the defence should be left with the trier of fact. This will involve two discrete tasks. First, he or she must determine whether there is some evidence on the record to support leaving the defence with the jury. An evidential burden rests with the accused; the mere assertion of the defence will not suffice.

Given the proper foundation, the trial judge must then consider whether the condition alleged by the accused is, in law, non-insane automatism. If the trial judge is satisfied that there is some evidence pointing to a condition that is in law non-insane automatism, then the defence can be left with the jury. The issue for the jury is one of fact: did the accused suffer from or experience the alleged condition at the relevant time? Because the Crown must always prove that an accused has acted voluntarily, the onus rests on the prosecution at this stage to prove the absence of automatism beyond a reasonable doubt.

The question of law at issue here, given that the accused laid the proper foundation for the defence of automatism, was whether sleepwalking should be classified as non-insane automatism or a disease of the mind, thereby leaving only the defence of insanity for the accused. Under the *Criminal Code* everyone is presumed to be and to have been sane until the contrary is proved. If the accused pleads automatism, the Crown is entitled to raise the issue of insanity, but must then bear the burden of proving that the condition in question stems from a disease of the mind.

'Disease of the mind' is a legal term and not a medical term of art but it contains a substantial medical component as well as a legal or policy component. The medical component of the term, generally, is medical opinion as to how the mental condition in question is viewed or characterized medically. The legal or policy component relates to (a) the scope of the exemption from criminal responsibility to be afforded by mental disorder or disturbance, and (b) the protection of the public by the control and treatment of persons who have caused serious harms while in a mentally disordered or disturbed state.

Because 'disease of the mind' is a legal concept, a trial judge cannot rely blindly on medical opinion. The judge must determine what mental conditions are included within the term 'disease of the mind', and whether there is any evidence that the accused suffered from an abnormal mental condition comprehended by that term.

Two distinct approaches to the policy component of insanity have emerged in automatism cases, the 'continuing danger' and 'internal cause' theories. The first theory holds that any condition likely to present recurring danger should be treated as insanity. The second holds that a condition stemming from the internal make-up of the accused, rather than external factors, should lead to a finding of insanity. Though seemingly divergent, both theories stem from a concern for the protection of the public.

Though the second theory has gained a certain ascendency, it is merely an analytical tool and is not universal. In particular, it is not helpful in assessing the nature of a somnambulistic condition. The distinction between internal and external causes is blurred during sleep, and certain causes that are discounted for a subject who is awake may have entirely different effects on a sleeping person. As for the 'continuing danger' test, it has been criticized as a general theory. However, the purpose of the insanity defence has always been the protection of the public against recurrent danger. As such, the possibility of recurrence, though not determinative, may be looked upon as a factor at the policy stage of the inquiry on the issue of insanity.

On the evidence there is no likelihood of recurrent violent somnambulism. Moreover, none of the other policy considerations relevant to the distinction between insanity and automatism, for example, the floodgates argument, or that automatism can be feigned, is of concern in this case.

Our system of justice is predicated on the notion that only those who act voluntarily should be punished under the criminal law. Here, no compelling policy factors preclude a finding that the accused's condition was one of non-insane automatism. As the Crown did not meet its burden of proving that somnambulism stems from a disease of the mind, committal under s. 614(2) of the *Criminal Code* is precluded, and the accused should be acquitted. However, because the medical evidence in each case impacts at several stages of the policy inquiry and is significant in its own right, sleepwalking in a different case on different evidence might be found to be a disease of the mind.

This matter should not be sent back to the trial judge for the possible imposition of an order to keep the peace. The judiciary is not practically equipped to administer such an order, and a number of practical reasons, in addition to those of Sopinka and McLachlin JJ., preclude its consideration. To be effective, any order to keep the peace would have to be permanent. This would violate established practice (if not the law) regarding peace orders, which requires a defined period for the order. It would also be unrealistic to expect respondent's family, who are the only persons able to monitor the order, to complain of any breach of the peace. Finally, it would be unreasonable to expect the respondent to bear the cost of a life-long surety necessary to enforce such an order.

McLACHLIN and IACOBUCCI JJ: The reasons of Lamer C.J., except on the question of referring the matter back to the trial judge for consideration as to whether an order to keep the peace should be imposed, and the reasons of La Forest and Sopinka JJ. were agreed with. Notwithstanding the justice of an acquittal here and the evidence that a recurrence is highly unlikely, great care should be taken to avoid the possibility of a similar episode in the future. An order restricting a person's liberty on account of an act for which he or she has been acquitted, however, raises difficult issues. It is inappropriate that the respondent, given his courageous efforts to re-establish his life over the past five years, should now be embroiled in a further set of proceedings concerned not with his guilt or innocence, but with the maintenance of his liberty. Generally, the courts do not grant remedies affecting the liberty of the subject unless asked to do so by the Crown. In the absence of an application by the Crown, the case should not be remitted for consideration of further measures against the accused.

SOPINKA J: The trial judge, for the reasons given by both Lamer C.J. and La Forest J., did not err in leaving the defence of automatism rather than that of insanity with the jury. This matter, however, should not be referred back to the trial judge to consider an order to keep the peace.

The common law preventative justice power has significant limits. It cannot be exercised on the basis of mere speculation but requires a proven factual foundation which raises a probable ground to suspect future misbehaviour. The uncontroverted expert evidence in this case is wholly inconsistent with such a conclusion.

The extent and continued validity of this common law power has yet to be considered in light of the *Charter*. The imposition of restrictive conditions following an acquittal on the basis of a remote possibility of recurrence may well be contrary to s. 7.

There is still the possibility of an information being laid pursuant to s. 810 of the *Criminal Code*, subject to the evidentiary basis 'that the informant has reasonable grounds for his fears' and to constitutional challenge. Such a proceeding, however, should not be initiated by this Court acting *proprio motu*.

If the respondent remains subject to the criminal justice system, the issue on cross-appeal of whether a stay should be entered by reason of a violation of s. 11(b) of the *Charter* would have to be considered.

LAMER C.J. and CORY J. (dissenting in part): The testimony revealed three very important points: (1) the respondent was sleepwalking at the time of the incident; (2) sleepwalking is not a neurological, psychiatric or other illness but rather is a sleep disorder very common in children and also found in adults; and, (3) there is no medical treatment as such, apart from good health practices, especially as regards sleep. This expert evidence was not in any way contradicted by the Crown, which had the advice of experts who were present during the testimony given by the defence experts and whom it chose not to call.

The defence of automatism – rather than that of insanity – was properly put to the jury. For a defence of insanity to have been put to the jury, together with or instead of a defence of automatism, as the case may be, there would have had to have been in the record evidence tending to show that sleepwalking was the cause of the respondent's state of mind. That was not the case here. This was not to say, however, that sleepwalking could never be a disease of the mind in another case on different evidence.

Notwithstanding the respondent's acquittal, some control could be exercised to prevent a possible recurrence in a situation like this through the common law power to make an order to keep the peace which is vested in any judge or magistrate. The rules of natural justice must be observed in any exercise of this power. Exploring, on notice, the possibility of some minimally intrusive conditions to assure the community's safety would not infringe s. 7 of the *Charter*. Any condition imposed must be rationally connected to the apprehended danger posed by the person and go no further than necessary to protect the public from this danger.

■ NOTES AND QUESTIONS

1. Not much is medically known about sleepwalking. Sleepwalkers seem to fall somewhere between a state of consciousness and unconsciousness. They are able to make their way about, opening doors and walking down steps, for example, without injuring themselves. Yet they seem to have no conscious awareness or subsequent recollection of their actions. Is it appropriate to characterise the sleepwalker as insane?

2. As *Parks* illustrates, the problem is what to do with sleepwalkers who commit serious violent acts in their sleep. Should they be sent to prison? To a mental institution? Or should they be allowed to return to the community? The pragmatic response of *Burgess* is that a special verdict will allow the courts to make an appropriate disposal order, possibly involving hospitalisation in serious cases. However, hospitalisation is now only possible where the condition demands it for medical as opposed to, say, public protection, grounds. (See discussion of

Domestic Violence, Crime and Victims Act 2004 above.) In two recent Crown Court cases offences committed while sleepwalking have resulted in the defendant 'walking free' from the court room. In one the defendant, Edward Leung, committed a sexual assault on a friend while she was asleep. He raised evidence of sleepwalking, and was acquitted by the jury on the ground of automatism. In another the defendant, Brian Thomas, a 'decent and devoted', husband strangled his wife while dreaming he was being attacked by intruders. Charged with murder the Crown Prosecution Service initially asked for a special verdict of not guilty due to insanity. Following evidence from a sleep psychiatrist, that he had not been in control of his actions and was not a danger to anyone else, it accepted that it would be inappropriate for the court to require hospitalisation. The Crown Prosecution Service decided, therefore, to offer no further evidence. The jury were directed to return a verdict of not guilty.

It is clear that the combined effect of the 1991 and 2004 Acts is to render a plea of not guilty by reason of insanity an extremely attractive option for those who are able to muster plausible evidence that they were suffering from a mental condition which rendered them susceptible to a 'one-off' act of violence/sexual assault. It may be time for a review of mental condition offences and powers of disposal. Further, the role of expert medical witnesses is likely to come under increasing scrutiny in areas, such as sleepwalking, where clinical diagnosis is hedged with uncertainty.

For discussion of this and other cases see W. Wilson, I. Ebrahim, et al., 'Violence Sleepwalking and the Criminal Law' [2005] Crim LR 601–623. (W. Wilson (2011) 9.8, 9.9)

3. Suppose that Arthur begins to drive home from work in a state of extreme drowsiness. He subsequently falls asleep at the wheel and is involved in a collision in which another driver is killed. If charged with causing death by dangerous driving, should Arthur be able to assert a defence of automatism? Is *Burgess* distinguishable?

4. In some instances the issue of automatism can be avoided by finding an antecedent act on which to premise criminal liability, such as the fact, in the example involving Arthur, that the defendant began driving knowing that he was sleepy or subject to blackouts. The decision to drive under such circumstances may itself be a reckless or dangerous act satisfying the *actus reus* (as well as the *mens rea*) elements of various criminal offences.

5. There are some experts who believe that what one does while sleepwalking reflects what one subconsciously wants to do but cannot bring oneself to do while in a conscious state. Assuming the validity of this hypothesis for the sake of argument, should it have any bearing on the sleepwalker's criminal liability?

FURTHER READING

Wilson, *Criminal Law: Doctrine and Theory* (2011), Chapter 8

Goldstein, *The Insanity Defense* (1967)

Goldstein and Katz, 'Abolish the "Insanity Defense"—Why Not?' (1963) 73 Yale Law Journal 853

Horder, 'Pleading Involuntary Lack of Capacity' (1993) 52 Cambridge Law Journal 298

Loughnan, ' "Manifest Madness" Towards a New Understanding of the Insanity defence' (2007) Modern Law Review 379

Mackay, 'Fact and fiction about the insanity defence' [1990] Criminal Law Review 247

Mackay, 'Righting the wrong? – some observations on the second limb of the McNaghten Rules' [2009] Criminal Law Review 80

Mackay and Kearns, 'More Fact(s) about the Insanity Defence' [1999] Criminal Law Review 714

Mackay and Mitchell, 'Sleepwalking, Automatism and Insanity' [2004] Criminal Law Review 901

Mackay, Mitchell and Howe, 'Yet More Facts about the Insanity Defence' [2006] Criminal Law Review 901

Mackay and Reuber, Epilepsy and the Insanity Defence—Time for Change?' [2007] Criminal Law Review 782

Sutherland and Gearty, 'Insanity and the European Court of Human Rights' [1992] Criminal Law Review 418

Walsh, 'Irrational Presumptions of Rationality and Comprehension' [1998] 3 Web JCLI

Wells, 'Whither Insanity?' [1983] Criminal Law Review 787

White, 'The Criminal Procedure (Insanity and Unfitness to Plead) Act' [1992] Criminal Law Review 4

Wilson, 'Violence, Sleepwalking and the Criminal Law: The Medical Aspects' [2005] Criminal Law Review 601

Wilson, 'Violence, Sleepwalking and the Criminal Law: The Legal Aspects' [2005] Criminal Law Review 614

10

Defences

In the previous chapter we examined issues of capacity. Lack of capacity can be viewed as a defence in that, if successful, it will lead to an acquittal. However, the term 'defence' is more commonly used in two other senses. The first occurs where the defendant denies an element of the crime. As it is the responsibility of the prosecution to establish each and every element of the offence by proof beyond reasonable doubt, a failure to establish any one of the elements will warrant an acquittal. Where an accused denies he acted with *mens rea*, or that his acts were the cause of the harmful result, or more simply that he was not the person who committed the offence, he in effect challenges the existence of one of the elements of the crime. If the accused raises a reasonable doubt about the element, one might say that the defence succeeded. More accurately, the prosecution's case will have failed for lack of proof. Defences such as mistake or intoxication challenge the existence of *mens rea*. If the jury acquits, it is because the prosecution has failed to prove *mens rea* beyond reasonable doubt.

The term 'defence' is also used in another sense. What might more accurately be called an *affirmative* defence occurs where the defendant does not contest the existence of the elements of an offence, but rather argues that he should be acquitted *despite* the existence of those elements. In effect, the defendant says: 'Yes, the Prosecution has proved all the elements of the offence, but there are other considerations for the jury (or judge) to consider that warrant my acquittal.' Duress, necessity, crime prevention, self-defence and defence of others are examples of affirmative defences that will be examined in this chapter.

The defendant bears the initial burden of introducing evidence to support an affirmative defence. While in theory there would be no objection to also placing on the defendant the burden of persuading the jury of the existence of the defence by proof beyond reasonable doubt, this is not the way the English law has developed. For most affirmative defences, the primary exception being insanity (which, as we suggested in the last chapter, can be looked at as an issue of capacity), the courts have held that, once the defendant has introduced some credible evidence to support the affirmative defence, the burden of negating the defence rests on the prosecution by proof beyond reasonable doubt (see *Woolmington* v *Director of Public Prosecutions* [1935] AC 462).

SECTION 2: DEFENCES WHICH NEGATE AN ELEMENT OF THE CRIME

A: Mistake

A 'mistake' by a defendant can negate an element of an offence. Typically, the element negated is that of *mens rea*. If Angela, when leaving a restaurant, takes an umbrella, mistakenly believing that the umbrella belongs to her when it in fact it belongs to some other person, she has not acted dishonestly and is not guilty of theft. A mistake may also cause a person to form a distorted view of the circumstances, as when one resists what one believes is an unlawful attack, whereas the alleged attacker is a plain clothes officer seeking to make a lawful arrest. In such circumstances the defendant has made a mistake which would provide a defence for his actions if the situation were as he believed it to be. (Note, however, that a different result may ensue if the defendant realises that he is being arrested but resists because he disputes the grounds for the arrest.) The question that needs to be addressed is when a mistake will lead to an acquittal.

(i) Irrelevant mistakes

We have seen previously that some mistakes, such as the identity of the victim (intent can be 'transferred'), or the victim's peculiar infirmities (one must take one's victim as one finds him), will be irrelevant. As a general proposition, only mistakes that serve to negate the *mens rea* element of the crime charged will provide a defence.

R v Ellis, Street and Smith
(1987) 84 Cr App R 235, Court of Appeal

O'CONNOR LJ: . . . All three appellants accepted that they participated in importing large quantities of cannabis into this country concealed in secret compartments in motor cars. They were indicted in the ordinary form for being knowingly concerned in the fraudulent evasion of the prohibition on the importation of a controlled drug contrary to section 170(2) of the Customs and Excise Management Act 1979. The particulars of offence were that on the relevant dates they were in relation to a class B controlled drug, namely in the case of Ellis and Street 29.3 kilograms and in the case of Smith 24.85 kilogrammes of cannabis, 'knowingly concerned in the fraudulent evasion of the prohibition on importation imposed by section 3(1) of the Misuse of Drugs Act 1971.'

In both cases the defendants as they then were pleaded not guilty and at once asked for a ruling as to whether they had a defence in law if the facts were that they knew that they were participating in the importation of prohibited goods but believed that the goods were pornographic goods which they knew to be subject to a prohibition and which were in fact subject to a prohibition.

. . . '"[K]nowingly" in the section in question is concerned with knowing that a fraudulent evasion of a prohibition in respect of goods is taking place.' It seems to us that it cannot make any difference whether a particular defendant says: 'I don't know what the goods were; I only know they were prohibited' or a defendant says: 'I didn't know what the goods in fact were. I thought that they were some other prohibited goods' . . .

■ NOTES AND QUESTIONS

1. There is a famous legal hypothetical involving Lady Eldon, who visits Paris and buys what she thinks is 'French' lace but is in fact English lace. When asked at customs whether she has any items to declare, Lady Eldon replies she has not. French lace must be declared; English lace need not be declared. Has Lady Eldon committed a crime? An attempt to commit a crime (see Chapter 12)? Would/ should it matter if she mistakenly believed that French lace did not have to be declared? What if she believed that failing to declare French lace was not a crime? We will re-visit the case of Lady Eldon when we discuss ignorance of law.

2. Might the Crown in *Ellis, Street and Smith* have been better advised to charge the defendants with an attempt to import pornographic goods? Would such a charge more accurately have captured the true nature of the defendants' fault (assuming that their story was to be believed)?

3. If a defendant receives stolen video tapes, believing them to be boxes of soap powder, will he be guilty of handling stolen goods? Is *Ellis, Street and Smith* distinguishable? See *R v McCullum* (1973) 57 Cr App R 645.

(ii) Must the defendant's mistake be reasonable?

An ongoing controversy has been whether a mistake must be 'reasonable' in order to constitute a defence. Or is it sufficient that the mistake is honestly believed?

R v Williams (Gladstone)
(1983) 78 Cr App R 276, Court of Appeal

LORD LANE CJ: The facts were somewhat unusual and were as follows. On the day in question the alleged victim, a man called Mason, saw a black youth seizing the handbag belonging to a woman who was shopping. He caught up with the youth and held him, he said with a view to taking him to a nearby police station, but the youth broke free from his grip. Mason caught the youth again and knocked him to the ground, and he then twisted one of the youth's arms behind his back in order to immobilise him and to enable him, Mason, so he said, once again to take the youth to a police station. The youth was struggling and calling for help at this time, and no one disputed that fact.

Upon the scene then came the appellant who had only seen the latter stages of this incident. According to Mason he told the appellant first of all that he was arresting the youth for mugging the lady and secondly, that he, Mason, was a police officer. That was not true. He was asked for his warrant card, which obviously was not forthcoming, and thereupon something of a struggle ensued between Mason on the one hand and the appellant and others on the other hand. In the course of these events Mason sustained injuries to his face, loosened teeth and bleeding gums.

The appellant put forward the following version of events. He said he was returning from work by bus, when he saw Mason dragging the youth along and striking him again and again. He was so concerned about the matter that he rapidly got off the bus and made his way to the scene and asked Mason what on earth he was doing. In short he said that he punched Mason because he thought if he did so he would save the youth from further beating and what he described as torture.

There was no doubt that none of these *dramatis personae* was known to each other beforehand.

. . .

One starts off with the meaning of the word 'assault.' 'Assault' in the context of this case, that is to say using the word as a convenient abbreviation for assault and battery, is an act by which the defendant, intentionally or recklessly, applies unlawful force to the complainant. There are circumstances in which force may be applied to another lawfully. Taking a few examples: first, where the victim consents, as in lawful sports, the application of force to another will, generally speaking, not be unlawful. Secondly, where the defendant is acting in self-defence: the exercise of any necessary and reasonable force to protect himself from unlawful violence is not unlawful. Thirdly, by virtue of section 3 of the Criminal Law Act 1967, a person may use such force as is reasonable in the circumstances in the prevention of crime or in effecting or assisting in the lawful arrest of an offender or suspected offender or persons unlawfully at large. In each of those cases the defendant will be guilty if the jury are sure that first of all he applied force to the person of another, and secondly that he had the necessary mental element to constitute guilt.

The mental element necessary to constitute guilt is the intent to apply unlawful force to the victim. We do not believe that the mental element can be substantiated by simply showing an intent to apply force and no more.

What then is the situation if the defendant is labouring under a mistake of fact as to the circumstances? What if he believes, but believes mistakenly, that the victim is consenting, or that it is necessary to defend himself, or that a crime is being committed which he intends to prevent? He must then be judged against the mistaken facts as he believes them to be. If judged against those facts or circumstances the prosecution fail to establish his guilt, then he is entitled to be acquitted.

The next question is, does it make any difference if the mistake of the defendant was one which, viewed objectively by a reasonable onlooker, was an unreasonable mistake? In other words should the jury be directed as follows: 'Even if the defendant may have genuinely believed that what he was doing to the victim was either with the victim's consent or in reasonable self-defence or to prevent the commission of crime, as the case may be, nevertheless if you, the jury, come to the conclusion that the mistaken belief was unreasonable, that is to say that the defendant as a reasonable man should have realised his mistake, then you should convict him.'

... The reasonableness or unreasonableness of the defendant's belief is material to the question of whether the belief was held by the defendant at all. If the belief was in fact held, its unreasonableness, so far as guilt or innocence is concerned, is neither here nor there. It is irrelevant. Were it otherwise, the defendant would be convicted because he was negligent in failing to recognise that the victim was not consenting or that a crime was not being committed and so on. In other words the jury should be directed first of all that the prosecution have the burden or duty of proving the unlawfulness of the defendant's actions; secondly, if the defendant may have been labouring under a mistake as to the facts, he must be judged according to his mistaken view of the facts; thirdly, that is so whether the mistake was, on an objective view, a reasonable mistake or not.

In a case of self-defence, where self-defence or the prevention of crime is concerned, if the jury came to the conclusion that the defendant believed, or may have believed, that he was being attacked or that a crime was being committed, and that force was necessary to protect himself or to prevent the crime, then the prosecution have not proved their case. If however the defendant's alleged belief was mistaken and if the mistake was an unreasonable one, that may be a powerful reason for coming to the conclusion that the belief was not honestly held and should be rejected.

Even if the jury come to the conclusion that the mistake was an unreasonable one, if the defendant may genuinely have been labouring under it, he is entitled to rely upon it.

Appeal allowed. Conviction quashed.

■ NOTES AND QUESTIONS

1. What are the arguments for and against requiring that a mistake be reasonable? Will a requirement of reasonableness force an individual to think more carefully before acting? Or do most offences, and particularly assaults, involve spur-of-the-moment actions without much forethought?

2. The more unreasonable the defendant's mistake, the less likely is the jury to be persuaded that the mistake was honestly entertained. But if the reasonableness of the defendant's belief will inevitably be considered by a jury, what is the harm in having reasonableness as a necessary component of the defence? Consider in this regard the law of rape. For the purposes of the law of rape a

genuine belief that the victim was consenting was, until 2003, an answer to a charge of rape. There was no requirement that the belief should be based on reasonable grounds although the more unreasonable the belief, the less likely was the jury to believe the defendant's story. The Sexual Offences Act 2003 has now removed the reasonableness of the defendant's belief from the definition. The defendant's belief must be reasonable as well as honestly entertained. See SOA, s. 1(1). See generally Chapter 6.

3. The decision in *Williams (Gladstone)* was affirmed by the Privy Council in *Beckford* v *R* [1988] AC 130.

(iii) Ignorance of law

There is a presumption that a citizen is aware of the requirements of the law. From this presumption flows the well-known (and generally correct) maxim that 'ignorance of the law is no excuse'.

R v Lee (Dennis Percival)

[2001] 1 Cr App R 19, Court of Appeal

ROSE LJ (Vice President): The relevant facts can be shortly stated. On September 24, 1999, the appellant was driving a motor car in Mace Lane, Ashford. He was stopped by police for a roadside safety check. His breath smelt of alcohol. He said he had only drunk a pint and a half. He was asked to provide a breath specimen. He did so in an alcolyser bag. It was common ground that the officers said the test was positive, in that the crystals had changed colour beyond the red line, but the appellant immediately, in subsequent interviews and in evidence, disputed this: he said there was a bubble in the crystals so that it was not clear that the line had been reached or crossed. According to the officers, after he had been told he was being arrested, the appellant punched both of them. The appellant admitted pushing one officer and punching the other. It is conceded on the appellant's behalf that there was evidence on which the jury could conclude that the officers were acting lawfully because the breathalyser test provided possible reasonable grounds to suspect the commission of a drink-driving offence.

The judge directed the jury as to the elements of the offence in a manner about which complaint is made by Mr Patterson, on behalf of the appellant, in only one presently relevant respect. The judge stressed that the offence could only be committed if the apprehension were lawful and that it would be lawful if the person arresting reasonably believed an arrestable offence had been committed. Mr Patterson submits that if the appellant genuinely, albeit wrongly, believed his arrest were unlawful he could not have intended to resist lawful apprehension: the judge should therefore have gone further and directed the jury that they must be sure that the defendant had no honest belief that he had not failed the breathalyser test. That is not a submission which Mr Patterson made to the trial judge when these matters were being discussed in the absence of the jury: but that would not be fatal to this appeal if the submission is well-founded.

. . .

In our judgment, the relevant authorities can be summarised in this way.

(1) *Fennell* and Lord Diplock's speech in *Sweet* v *Parsley* [1970] A.C. 132 at 163 are no longer authority for the proposition that, in order to afford a defence to offences involving *mens rea*, a defendant's belief as to facts must be reasonable, as well as genuine or honest. That approach, in relation to self-defence, was rejected in *Williams (Gladstone)* which was approved by the Privy Council in *Beckford* and by the House of Lords in *B*.

. . .

(4) But, to afford such a defence, the mistake must be one of fact. In *Blackburn* v *Bowering* at 1329C Sir Thomas Bingham, then Master of the Rolls, referred to *Fennell* and to 'the important qualification that the mistake must be one of fact (particularly as to the victim's capacity) and not a mistake of law as to the authority of a person acting in that capacity'. This approach accords

with the passage in Smith and Hogan on which Mr Fowler relies, with the passages in *Archbold* and *Blackstone* on which Mr Patterson relies and also with Sir John Smith's comment on *Brightling*, once it is understood that by 'circumstances' in that comment he was referring to facts this construction is supported by the passage in Smith and Hogan on which Mr Patterson relies, where circumstances are equated with facts.

(5) In *Bentley* (1850) 4 Cox C.C. 408, Talfourd J. put the point at page 410 in a way which in our judgment is still good law:

> 'I think that, to support a charge of resisting a lawful apprehension, it is enough that the prisoner is lawfully apprehended, and it is his determination to resist it. If the apprehension is in point of fact lawful, we are not permitted to consider the question, whether or not he believed it to be so, because that would lead to infinite niceties of discrimination. The rule is not, that a man is always presumed to know the law, but that no man shall be excused for an unlawful act from his ignorance of the law. It was the prisoner's duty, whatever might be his consciousness of innocence, to go to the station-house and hear the precise accusation against him. He is not to erect a tribunal in his own mind to decide whether he was legally arrested or not. He was taken into custody by an officer of the law, and it was his duty to obey the law.'

Applying these principles to the present case, it is clear that, even had the appellant given evidence (which it appears he did not) that he resisted arrest because his interpretation of the alcolyser lead him honestly to believe his arrest was unlawful, this would not have afforded a defence. Such a belief would have been not about any facts relating to the identity or conduct of the police officers at the time of the attempted arrest but about the legal consequences of believed antecedent facts. The appellant's position is, in our judgment, indistinguishable from that of a person sought to be arrested on grounds of reasonable suspicion for any arrestable offence which he knows or believes he has not committed. If, in such circumstances, that person assaults an officer whom he knows is acting as a police officer, we have never known it to be suggested that belief in innocence could afford a defence to assault, either with intent to resist arrest or on an officer in the execution of his duty.

In our judgment, once the lawfulness of the proposed arrest is established, the *mens rea* necessary for a section 38 offence is an intention by the defendant to resist arrest, accompanied by knowledge that the person he assaults (who may or may not be a police officer) is a person who is seeking to arrest him. Whether or not an offence has actually been committed or is believed by the defendant not to have been committed is irrelevant.

We reach this conclusion without regret. Neither public order nor the clarity of the criminal law would be improved if juries were required to consider in relation to section 38 offences the impact of a defendant's belief as to the lawfulness of his arrest in cases where a lawful arrest is being properly attempted on reasonable grounds.

Accordingly this appeal is dismissed.

Appeal dismissed.

R v Bailey

(1800) Russ & Ry 1, Crown Cases Reserved

It was then insisted that the prisoner could not be found guilty of the offence with which he was charged, because the Act of the 39 Geo. III. c. 37, upon which (together with the statute relating to maliciously shooting (9 Geo. I. c. 22; Black Act) the prisoner was indicted at this Admiralty Sessions, and which Act of the 39 Geo. III. is entitled, 'An Act for amending certain defects in the law respecting offences committed on the high seas,' only received the royal assent on the 10th of May, 1799, and the fact charged in the indictment happened on the 27th of June, in the same year, when the prisoner could not know that any such Act existed (his ship, the 'Langley', being at that time upon the coast of Africa).

Lord Eldon told the jury that he was of opinion that he was, in strict law, guilty within the statutes, taken together, if the facts laid were proved, though he could not then know that the Act of the 39 Geo. III. c. 37 had passed, and that his ignorance of that fact could in no otherwise affect the case, than that it might be the means of recommending him to a merciful consideration elsewhere should he be found guilty.

■ NOTES AND QUESTIONS

1. Even if Bailey had access to a law library, how likely is it that he (or any other ordinary citizen) will check the law before acting? Is this a relevant enquiry? Does the true basis of the court's decision in the case rest on its reluctance to create any exceptions to the general rule? Why might it have this reluctance?

2. Recall the hypothetical of Lady Eldon's French lace (above p. 461). What if the lace was indeed French lace but Lady Eldon honestly believed that it was not a crime not to declare the lace to Customs?

3. If a statutory instrument has not been published, ignorance of the law may excuse. See Statutory Instruments Act 1946, s. 3(2).

When ignorance of the law will be an excuse, the 'ignorance' will relate to some law other than the one which the accused is alleged to have violated.

R v Smith (David)
[1974] QB 354, Court of Appeal

JAMES LJ: ... The question of law in this appeal arises in this way. In 1970 the appellant became the tenant of a ground-floor flat at 209, Freemason's Road, E.16. The letting included a conservatory. In the conservatory the appellant and his brother, who lived with him, installed some electric wiring for use with stereo equipment. Also, with the landlord's permission, they put up roofing material and asbestos wall panels and laid floor boards. There is no dispute that the roofing, wall panels and floor boards became part of the house and, in law, the property of the landlord. Then in 1972 the appellant gave notice to quit and asked the landlord to allow the appellant's brother to remain as tenant of the flat. On September 18, 1972, the landlord informed the appellant that his brother could not remain. On the next day the appellant damaged the roofing, wall panels and floorboards he had installed in order—according to the appellant and his brother—to gain access to and remove the wiring. The extent of the damage was £130. When interviewed by the police, the appellant said: 'Look, how can I be done for smashing my own property. I put the flooring and that in, so if I want to pull it down it's a matter for me.'

... Section 1 of the Criminal Damage Act 1971 reads:

(1) A person who without lawful excuse destroys or damages any property belonging to another intending to destroy or damage any such property or being reckless as to whether any such property would be destroyed or damaged, shall be guilty of an offence.

... Construing the language of section 1(1) we have no doubt that the actus reus is 'destroying or damaging any property belonging to another.' It is not possible to exclude the words 'belonging to another' which describes the 'property.' Applying the ordinary principles of mens rea, the intention and recklessness and the absence of lawful excuse required to constitute the offence have reference to property belonging to another. It follows that in our judgment no offence is committed under this section if a person destroys or causes damage to property belonging to another if he does so in the honest though mistaken belief that the property is his own, and provided that the belief is honestly held it is irrelevant to consider whether or not it is a justifiable belief.

Secretary of State for Trade and Industry v *Hart*
[1982] 1 WLR 481, Queen's Bench Division

The defendant, who was a director and secretary of one company and a director of another, audited the annual accounts for the companies for the year ending March 31, 1979. Informations were preferred against him alleging that he had acted as an auditor when he knew that he was disqualified from so acting by reason of the offices that he held within the companies, contrary to section 161(2) of the Companies Act 1948 and section 13 of the Companies Act 1976. The magistrate accepted that the defendant was unaware of the offence and dismissed the informations on the ground that knowledge of the disqualification was a necessary ingredient of an offence under section 13(5).

On appeal by the prosecutor:—

Held, dismissing the appeal, that, giving the words of section 13(5) and (6) their ordinary meaning, 'knowledge' in subsection (5) had to be construed as knowledge not only of the relevant facts that constituted the offence but that in consequence of those facts a director was disqualified under the subsection from auditing the companies' accounts; that, accordingly, since the defendant had no knowledge of the statutory provisions, he had been properly acquitted of the offence....

■ NOTES AND QUESTIONS

1. Say that Lady Eldon (above p. 461) had consulted French and English solicitors, both of whom advised her that any lace she purchased in Paris did not have to be declared in England. If it should turn out that both solicitors were mistaken and criminal charges were brought against Lady Eldon, should her good faith reliance on the advice of her solicitors be a defence? The courts say not. See *Cooper* v *Simmons* (1862) 7 H and N 707. But what more can an ordinary citizen be expected to do to discover the law?

2. The criminal law is constantly expanding. Successive governments, eager to establish their anti-crime credentials, introduce new crime bills in virtually every session of Parliament. The result is that there are now tens of thousands (and counting) criminal offences on the statute books. Apart from the more serious offences such as murder, battery, rape, theft, burglary, etc, few persons – indeed, few lawyers – know the whole of the English criminal law. Given this reality, why is there a presumption that ordinary persons are aware of the law? Indeed, should not the presumption be the exact opposite?

3. Given the unsoundness of its premise, what accounts for the rule that that 'ignorance of the law is no excuse'?

B: Intoxication

Intoxication, whether the result of alcohol, drugs, medication or inhalation of a foreign substance such as glue or paint thinner (whatever turns one on), can impair a person's judgement and self-control. It can cause an individual to commit a crime which the individual would never have committed or even have considered committing if sober. In these situations, should the law take the defendant's intoxication into account? Should intoxication be a defence to a criminal offence? A factor in sentencing (aggravating or mitigating?)?

Over the years the courts have manifested almost a bipolar attitude to intoxication. On the one hand, judges recognise that, as a matter of theory, a defendant who lacks the *mens rea* of the crime charged should have a valid defence and that the reason why the defendant lacked *mens rea* should not necessarily be relevant. On the other, reducing oneself to an intoxicated state is not the type of behaviour that the legal system wishes to be seen to be either encouraging or condoning. In the opinion of many judges, drunkenness serves little socially useful purpose, and often leads to significant social harm. The challenge facing the courts is how to balance these competing considerations.

(i) Voluntary intoxication

The courts have distinguished between voluntary and involuntary intoxication. Voluntary intoxication, *per se*, is not a defence. It may, however, provide a basis on which the defendant may claim not to have had the requisite *mens rea* of the offence. The leading decision is that of the House of Lords in *Director of Public Prosecutions* v *Majewski*.

Director of Public Prosecutions v *Majewski*
[1977] AC 443, House of Lords

LORD ELWYN-JONES LC:...In view of the conclusion to which I have come that the appeal should be dismissed and of the questions of law which arise in the case, it is desirable that I should refer in some detail to the facts, which were largely undisputed. During the evening of February 19, 1973, the appellant and his friend, Leonard Stace, who had also taken drugs and drink, went to the Bull public house in Basildon. The appellant obtained a drink and sat down in the lounge bar at a table by the door. Stace became involved in a disturbance. Glasses were broken. The landlord asked Stace to leave and escorted him to the door. As he did so, Stace called to the appellant: 'He's putting me out.' The appellant got up and prevented the landlord from getting Stace out and abused him. The landlord told them both to go. They refused. The appellant butted the landlord in the face and bruised it, and punched a customer. The customers in the bar and the landlord forced the two out through the bar doors. They re-entered by forcing the outer door, a glass panel of which was broken by Stace. The appellant punched the landlord and pulled a piece of broken glass from the frame and started swinging it at the landlord and a customer, cutting the landlord slightly on his arm. The appellant then burst through the inner door of the bar with such force that he fell on the floor. The landlord held him there until the police arrived. The appellant was violent and abusive and spat in the landlord's face. When the police came, a fierce struggle took place to get him out. He shouted at the police: 'You pigs, I'll kill you all, you f...pigs, you bastards,' P.C. Barkway said the appellant looked at him and kicked him deliberately.

P.C. Bird was kicked on the shins. During the struggle to get the appellant into the police car he said to P.C. Barrett: 'You bastard, I'll get you' and then kicked him.

The appellant was placed in the cells of Basildon police station. The next morning Police Inspector Dickinson heard banging and saw the appellant in his cell trying to remove a metal flap under the bed platform. The inspector asked him, what he was doing. According to the inspector he said: 'Come in here and I will stripe you with this. I'll break your neck.' The inspector and other officers entered the cell. Before he was restrained, he struck the inspector with the handcuffs on his wrists. Dr Mitchell arrived and gave him an injection.

Cross-examined as to the appellant's condition that evening the publican said he seemed to have gone berserk, his eyes were a bit glazed and protruding. A customer said he was 'glary-eyed,' and went 'berserk' when the publican asked Stace to leave. He was screaming and shouting. A policeman said he was in a fearful temper.

The appellant gave evidence and said that on Saturday, February 17, 1973, he bought, not on prescription, about 40 Dexadrine tablets ('speeds') and early on Sunday morning consumed about half of them. That gave him plenty of energy until he 'started coming down.' He did not sleep throughout Sunday. On Monday evening at about 6 p.m. he acquired a bottle full of sodium nembutal tablets which he said were tranquillisers—'downers,' 'barbs' and took about eight of them at about 6.30.

He and his friends then went to the Bull. He said he could remember nothing of what took place there save for a flash of recollection of Stace kicking a window. All he recollected of the police cell was asking the police to remove his handcuffs and then being injected.

In cross-examination he admitted he had been taking amphetamines and barbiturates, not on prescription, for two years, in large quantities. On occasions he drank barley wine or Scotch. He had sometimes 'gone paranoid.' This was the first time he had 'completely blanked out.'

Dr Bird called for the defence, said that the appellant had been treated for drug addiction since November 1971. There was no history in his case of psychiatric disorder or diagnosable mental illness, but the appellant had a personality disorder. Dr Bird said that barbiturates and alcohol are known to potentiate each other and to produce rapid intoxication and affect a person's awareness of what was going on . . . .

What then is the mental element required in our law to be established in assault? This question has been most helpfully answered in the speech of Lord Simon of Glaisdale in *R v Morgan* [1976] AC 182, 216:

> By 'crimes of basic intent' I mean those crimes whose definition expresses (or, more often, implies) a *mens rea* which does not go beyond the *actus reus*. The *actus reus* generally consists of an act and some consequence. The consequence may be very closely connected with the act or more remotely connected with it: but with a crime of basic intent the *mens rea* does not extend beyond the act and its consequence, however, remote, as defined in the *actus reus*. I take assault as an example of a crime of basic intent where the consequence is very closely connected with the act. The *actus reus* of assault is an act which causes another person to apprehend immediate and unlawful violence. The *mens rea* corresponds exactly. The prosecution must prove that the accused foresaw that his act would probably cause another person to have apprehension of immediate and unlawful violence, or would possibly have that consequence, such being the purpose of the act, or that he was reckless as to whether or not his act caused such apprehension. This foresight (the term of art is 'intention') or recklessness is the *mens rea* in assault.

How does the fact of self-induced intoxication fit into that analysis? If a man consciously and deliberately takes alcohol and drugs not on medical prescription, but in order to escape from reality, to go 'on a trip', to become hallucinated, whatever the description may be and thereby disables himself from taking the care he might otherwise take and as a result by his subsequent actions causes injury to another—does our criminal law enable him to say that because he did not know what he was doing he lacked both intention and recklessness and accordingly is entitled to an acquittal?

. . . The authority which for the last half century has been relied upon in this context has been the speech of the Earl of Birkenhead LC in *Director of Public Prosecutions* v *Beard* [1920] AC 479, who stated, at p. 494:

> Under the law of England as it prevailed until early in the 19th century voluntary drunkenness was never an excuse for criminal misconduct; and indeed the classic authorities broadly assert that voluntary drunkenness must be considered rather an aggravation than a defence. This view was in terms based upon the principle that a man who by his own voluntary act debauches and destroys his will power shall be no better situated in regard to criminal acts than a sober man.

Lord Birkenhead LC made a historical survey of the way the common law from the 16th century on dealt with the effect of self-induced intoxication upon criminal responsibility. This indicates how, from 1819 on, the judges began to mitigate the severity of the attitude of the common law in such cases as murder and serious violent crime when the penalties of death or transportation applied or where there was likely to be sympathy for the accused, as in attempted suicide. Lord Birkenhead LC concluded, at p. 499, that (except in cases where insanity is pleaded) the decisions he cited

> establish that where a specific intent is an essential element in the offence, evidence of a state of drunkenness rendering the accused incapable of forming such an intent should be taken into consideration in order to determine whether he had in fact formed the intent necessary to constitute the particular crime. If he was so drunk that he was incapable of forming the intent required he could not be convicted of a crime which was committed only if the intent was proved . . . . In a charge of murder based upon intention to kill or to do grievous bodily harm,

if the jury are satisfied that the accused was, by reason of his drunken condition, incapable of forming the intent to kill or to do grievous bodily harm . . . he cannot be convicted of murder. But nevertheless unlawful homicide has been committed by the accused, and consequently he is guilty of unlawful homicide without malice aforethought, and that is manslaughter: *per* Stephen J in *R v Doherty* (1887) 16 Cox CC 306, 307.

He concludes the passage:

the law is plain beyond all question that in cases falling short of insanity a condition of drunkenness at the time of committing an offence causing death can only, when it is available at all, have the effect of reducing the crime from murder to manslaughter.

From this it seemed clear—and this is the interpretation which the judges have placed upon the decision during the ensuing half century—that it is only in the limited class of cases requiring proof of specific intent that drunkenness can exculpate. Otherwise in no case can it exempt completely from criminal liability.

. . .

I do not for my part regard that general principle as either unethical or contrary to the principles of natural justice. If a man of his own volition takes a substance which causes him to cast off the restraints of reason and conscience, no wrong is done to him by holding him answerable criminally for any injury he may do while in that condition. His course of conduct in reducing himself by drugs and drink to that condition in my view supplies the evidence of *mens rea*, of guilty mind certainly sufficient for crimes of basic intent. It is a reckless course of conduct and recklessness is enough to constitute the necessary *mens rea* in assault cases; see *R v Venna* [1975] 3 WLR 737 *per* James LJ at p. 743. The drunkenness is itself an intrinsic, an integral part of the crime, the other part being the evidence of the unlawful use of force against the victim. Together they add up to criminal recklessness . . . .

■ NOTES AND QUESTIONS

1. Why does the House of Lords draw a distinction between crimes of basic and specific intent? Is it because self-induced intoxication is itself a reckless act which will satisfy the recklessness requirement of a crime of basic intent? If so, a defendant would be ill-advised ever to raise intoxication as a defence when charged with a crime of basic intent, for by doing so he in effect concedes *mens rea*. Stated another way, does drunkenness inculpate or exculpate? See Simester, 'Intoxication is Never a Defence' [2009] Crim LR 3. Cf. Wilson (2011) 9.11.

2. In what sense is it accurate to say that the person who voluntarily becomes intoxicated is reckless? Is such an individual reckless in not foreseeing that she would become drunk, or not foreseeing that she would become drunk and commit an offence? Should it matter whether the individual had experienced such a reaction previously? Or is the point that a *reasonable person* would have appreciated before taking the first drink that there was a risk of becoming drunk and, that while drunk, engaging in antisocial activity of a criminal sort? If so, is there not a 'concurrence' issue buried within *Majewski*? You might wish to review the relevant sections of Ch. 3.

3. Might it make more sense to explain the disallowance of a defence of intoxication based on grounds of 'assumption of risk: that those who get drunk have to take the risk that the alcohol may impair their judgment, lead to a loss of self-control, and cause them to commit a crime which they might not have committed if sober? If that is the reasoning, as several of their Lordships in *Majewski* (and Lord Mustill in *R v Kingston*, below) intimate, then does the distinction between crimes of basic and specific intent make any sense? In the Draft Criminal Code Bill 1989, the distinction was abandoned.

4. The fact that intoxication *may* serve as a defence to a crime of specific intent does not mean that the defendant will escape all criminal liability. If, for example, the defendant is acquitted of murder (a specific intent crime) because of intoxication, he may nonetheless be convicted of involuntary manslaughter (a basic intent crime).

5. In a 1993 Consultation Paper, the Law Commission proposed an offence of causing harm while intoxicated. However, perhaps unduly influenced by judicial opposition, it subsequently retreated and recommended adherence to the law based on *Majewski* with some minor amendments. What considerations argue in favour of and against the original proposal? What about having a verdict of 'guilty but intoxicated'? Or an offence of 'dangerous drunkenness'?

The Law Commission has recently revisited the issue of intoxication. See Law Commission Report No. 314, 'Intoxication and Criminal Liability' (2009). Its principal recommendation is that **IF** a defendant is charged with having committed an offence as a perpetrator, **AND** the fault element of the offence is not an integral fault element (for example, because it merely requires proof of recklessness); **AND** the defendant was voluntarily intoxicated at the relevant time, **THEN** the defendant should be treated as having been aware at the material time of anything which he or she would have been aware of were it not for the intoxication. How does this proposal differ from the present law? Does it represent an improvement or a step backwards? The Commission's Report is explored in Child, 'Drink, Drugs and Law Reform: A Review of Commission Report No. 314' [2009] CLR 488.

6. Before a court decides the question, how can one know whether a crime is one of specific or basic intent? It has been suggested that a specific intent crime either involves purposive action (such as in intent to kill) or an ulterior intent (such as in theft the intent to permanently deprive the owner of his property). But does 'purposive' action add anything to the requirement of a voluntary *actus reus*? And is an 'ulterior intent' simply another way of stating that a statute has more than one *mens rea* element?

(ii) Involuntary intoxication

If the rationale for imposing criminal liability on persons who *voluntarily* become intoxicated is in part that they are responsible for their predicament, the same cannot be said of the person who is *involuntarily* intoxicated. Nor can it be maintained that such a person assumed the risks associated with becoming drunk. Involuntary intoxication can occur, for example, when someone is given a drink spiked with alcohol or drugs but is not told of that fact.

R v Kingston

[1994] 3 All ER 354, House of Lords

LORD MUSTILL : My Lords, this appeal concerns the effect on criminal liability of involuntary intoxication.

...The relevant facts are simple. The respondent was in dispute over business matters with a couple named Foreman, who employed Penn to obtain damaging information which they could use against the respondent, who is a homosexual with paedophiliac predilections. As part of this plan Penn invited the youth to his room. According to the evidence given by the youth at the trial he remembered nothing between the time when he was sitting on the bed and when he woke up, still in Penn's room, the following morning. It was the case for the prosecution, which the jury by their verdict on the second count must have accepted, that the boy fell asleep because Penn had secretly given him a soporific drug in a drink. On the same evening the respondent went to the room where the youth lay unconscious. He and Penn indulged in gross sexual acts with him. As part of the plan Penn made a recording of what was going on, and also took some photographs. Since an appeal against sentence is pending I will say nothing about these, although they obviously played an important part in the trial. Later, this material came into the hands of the police and charges were brought.

At the outset of the trial counsel for the respondent foreshadowed a defence on the lines that as part of the plan Penn had secretly administered drugs not only to the boy but also to the respondent. It was not said, and, in the light of the recordings and photographs, could not have been said, that the consequence was to make the respondent, like the boy, insensible; nevertheless his case was he had suffered effects which annulled the criminal liability which his acts would otherwise have involved. At rather short notice two questions were raised for decision:

> (i) If the jury find that Mr Kingston assaulted [the youth] pursuant to an intent induced by the influence of drugs administered secretly to him by Penn, is it open to them to find him not guilty?
> (ii) If the jury find that at the time of the alleged offence Mr Kingston was intoxicated by drugs secretly administered to him by Kevin Penn, is it open to them to find that this intoxication made negative intent/ *mens rea* so as to find Mr Kingston not guilty?

...

[T]he jury by a majority returned a verdict of Guilty against the respondent on the first count, and the learned judge imposed a sentence of five years' imprisonment. The respondent appealed against conviction and sentence. The Court of Appeal, Criminal Division allowed the appeal and quashed the convictions (see [1993] 4 All ER 373).

...

In due course the prosecutor obtained from the Court of Appeal a certificate that a point of law of general public importance was involved in the decision to allow the appeal, namely:

> (a) Whether, if it is proved that the necessary intent was present when the necessary act was done by him, a defendant has open to him a defence of involuntary intoxication;
> (b) if so, on whom does the burden of proof lie?

The starting point is the verdict of guilty coupled with the judge's direction on the necessity for intent. This implies that the majority either (a) were sure that the respondent had not involuntarily taken a drug or drugs at all or (b) were sure that whatever drug he may have taken had not had such an effect on his mind that he did not intend to do what he did. We are therefore not concerned with what is picturesquely called automatism; nor was it suggested that the effect of the drug was to produce a condition of temporary insanity. What then was said to have been the induced mental condition on which the respondent relies? Inevitably, since the judge's ruling meant that whatever medical evidence there may have been was not developed we cannot be sure. Still, the general nature of the case is clear enough. In ordinary circumstances the respondent's paedophiliac tendencies would have been kept under control, even in the presence of the sleeping or unconscious boy on the bed. The ingestion of the drug (whatever it was) brought about a temporary change in the mentality or personality of the respondent which lowered his ability to resist temptation so far that his desires overrode his ability to control them. Thus we are concerned here with a case of disinhibition. The drug is not alleged to have created the desire to which the respondent gave way, but rather to have enabled it to be released....

On these facts there are three grounds on which the respondent might be held free from criminal responsibility. First, that his immunity flows from general principles of the criminal law. Secondly, that this immunity is already established by a solid line of authority. Finally, that the court should, when faced with a new problem acknowledge the justice of the case and boldly create a new common law defence.

It is clear…that the Court of Appeal adopted the first approach. The decision was explicitly founded on general principle. There can be no doubt what principle the court relied upon, for at the outset the court recorded the submission of counsel for the respondent that 'the law recognises that, exceptionally, an accused person may be entitled to be acquitted if there is a possibility that, although his act was intentional, the intent itself arose out of circumstances for which he bears no blame'…

My Lords, with every respect I must suggest that no such principle exists or, until the present case, had ever in modern times been thought to exist. Each offence consists of a prohibited act or omission coupled with whatever state of mind is called for by the statute or rule of the common law which creates the offence. In those offences which are not absolute the state of mind which the prosecution must prove to have underlain the act or omission—the 'mental element'—will in the majority of cases be such as to attract disapproval. The mental element will then be the mark of what may properly be called a 'guilty mind'. The professional burglar is guilty in a moral as well as a legal sense; he intends to break into the house to steal, and most would confidently assert that this is wrong. But this will not always be so. In respect of some offences the mind of the defendant, and still less his moral judgment, may not be engaged at all. In others, although a mental activity must be the motive power for the prohibited act or omission the activity may be of such a kind or degree that society at large would not criticise the defendant's conduct severely or even criticise it at all. Such cases are not uncommon. Yet to assume that contemporary moral judgments affect the criminality of the act, as distinct from the punishment appropriate to the crime once proved, is to be misled by the expression *'mens rea'*, the ambiguity of which has been the subject of complaint for more than a century. Certainly, the 'mens' of the defendant must usually be involved in the offence; but the epithet 'rea' refers to the criminality of the act in which the mind is engaged, not to its moral character.

…

Accordingly, so far as general principles of criminality are concerned I would reject the respondent's argument. His second ground is more narrow, namely that involuntary intoxication is already recognised as a defence by authority which the House ought to follow.… [I]t is impossible to consider the exceptional case of involuntary intoxication without placing it in the context of intoxication as a whole. This area of the law is controversial, as regards the content of the rules, their intellectual foundations, and their capacity to furnish a practical and just solution. Since the law was not explored in depth during the arguments and since it is relevant only as part of the background it is better not to say any more about it than is strictly necessary. Some consideration of the law laid down in *DPP* v *Majewski* [1976] 2 All ER 142 is however inevitable. As I understand the position it is still the law that in the exceptional case where intoxication causes insanity the M'Naghten rules apply: see *DPP* v *Beard* [1920] AC 479 at 501 and *A-G for Northern Ireland* v *Gallagher* [1961] 3 All ER 299. Short of this, it is no answer for the defendant to say that he would not have done what he did had he been sober, provided always that whatever element of intent is required by the offence is proved to have been present. As was said in *R* v *Sheehan, R* v *Moore* [1975] 2 All ER 960 at 964, 'a drunken intent is still an intent'. As to proof of intent, it appears that at least in some instances self-induced intoxication can be taken into account as part of the evidence from which the jury draws its conclusions; but that in others it cannot. I express the matter in this guarded way because it has not yet been decisively established whether for this purpose there is a line to be drawn between offences of 'specific' and of 'basic' intent. That in at least some cases a defendant cannot say that he was so drunk that he could not form the required intent is however clear enough. Why is this so? The answer must, I believe, be the same as that given in other common law jurisdictions: namely that such evidence is excluded as a matter of policy. As Mason J put the matter in *R* v *O'Connor* (1979) 146 CLR 64 at 110:

> the view is taken that the act charged is voluntary notwithstanding that it might not be ordinarily considered so by reason of the condition of the perpetrator, because his condition proceeds from a voluntary choice made by him. These cases therefore constitute an exception to the general rule of criminal responsibility.

There remains the question by what reasoning the House put this policy into effect. As I understand it two different rationalisations were adopted. First that the absence of the necessary consent is cured by treating the intentional drunkenness (or more accurately, since it is only in the minority of cases that the drinker sets out to make himself drunk, the intentional taking of drink without regard to its possible effects) as a substitute for the mental element ordinarily required by the offence. The intent is transferred from the taking of drink to the commission of the prohibited act. The second rationalisation is that the defendant cannot be heard to rely on the absence of the mental element when it is absent because of his own voluntary acts. Borrowing an expression from a far distant field it may be said that the defendant is estopped from relying on his self-induced incapacity.

Your Lordships are not required to decide how these two explanations stand up to attack, for they are not attacked here. The task is only to place them in the context of an intoxication which is not voluntary. Taking first the concept of transferred intent, if the intoxication was not the result of an act done with an informed will there is no intent which can be transferred to the prohibited act, so as to fill the gap in the offence. As regards the 'estoppel' there is no reason why the law should preclude the defendant from relying on a mental condition which he had not deliberately brought about. Thus, once the involuntary nature of the intoxication is added the two theories of *Majewski* fall away, and the position reverts to what it would have been if *Majewski* had not been decided, namely that the offence is not made out if the defendant was so intoxicated that he could not form an intent. Thus, where the intoxication is involuntary *Majewski* does not *subtract* the defence of absence of intent; but there is nothing in *Majewski* to suggest that where intent is proved involuntary intoxication *adds* a further defence.

To recognise a new defence of this type would be a bold step. The common law defences of duress and necessity (if it exists) and the limited common law defence of provocation are all very old. Since counsel for the appellant was not disposed to emphasise this aspect of the appeal the subject was not explored in argument, but I suspect that the recognition of a new general defence at common law has not happened in modern times. Nevertheless, the criminal law must not stand still, and if it is both practical and just to take this step, and if judicial decision rather than legislation is the proper medium, then the courts should not be deterred simply by the novelty of it. So one must turn to consider just what defence is now to be created. The judgment under appeal implies five characteristics.

(1) The defence applies to all offences, except perhaps to absolute offences. It therefore differs from other defences such as provocation and diminished responsibility.

(2) The defence is a complete answer to a criminal charge. If not rebutted it leads to an outright acquittal, and unlike provocation and diminished responsibility leaves no room for conviction and punishment for a lesser offence. The underlying assumption must be that the defendant is entirely free from culpability.

(3) It may be that the defence applies only where the intoxication is due to the wrongful act of another and therefore affords no excuse when, in circumstances of no greater culpability, the defendant has intoxicated himself by mistake (such as by short-sightedly taking the wrong drug). I say that this may be so, because it is not clear whether, since the doctrine was founded in part on the dictum of Park J, the 'fraud or stratagem of another' is an essential element, or whether this was taken as an example of a wider principle.

(4) The burden of disproving the defence is on the prosecution.

(5) The defence is subjective in nature. Whereas provocation and self-defence are judged by the reactions of the reasonable person in the situation of the defendant, here the only question is whether this particular defendant's inhibitions were overcome by the effect of the drug. The more susceptible the defendant to the kind of temptation presented, the easier the defence is to establish.

My Lords, since the existence or otherwise of the defence has been treated in argument at all stages as a matter of existing law the Court of Appeal had no occasion to consider the practical and theoretical implications of recognising this new defence at common law, and we do not have the benefit of its views. In their absence, I can only say that the defence appears to run into difficulties at every turn. In point of theory, it would be necessary to reconcile a defence of irresistible impulse derived from a combination of innate drives and external disinhibition with the rule that irresistible impulse of a solely internal origin (not necessarily any more the fault of the offender) does not in itself excuse although it may be a symptom of a disease of the mind: see *A-G for the State of South*

Australia v *Brown* [1960] 1 All ER 734. Equally, the state of mind which founds the defence super-ficially resembles a state of diminished responsibility, whereas the effect in law is quite different. It may well be that the resemblance is misleading, but these and similar problems must be solved before the bounds of a new defence can be set.

On the practical side there are serious problems. Before the jury could form an opinion on whether the drug might have turned the scale witnesses would have to give a picture of the defendant's personality and susceptibilities, for without it the crucial effect of the drug could not be assessed; pharmacologists would be required to describe the potentially disinhibiting effect of a range of drugs whose identity would, if the present case is anything to go by, be unknown; psychologists and psychiatrists would express opinions, not on the matters of psychopathology familiar to those working within the framework of the Mental Health Acts but on altogether more elusive concepts. No doubt as time passed those concerned could work out techniques to deal with these questions. Much more significant would be the opportunities for a spurious defence. Even in the field of road traffic the 'spiked' drink as a special reason for not disqualifying from driving is a regular feature. Transferring this to the entire range of criminal offences is a disturbing prospect. The defendant would only have to assert, and support by the evidence of well-wishers, that he was not the sort of person to have done this kind of thing, and to suggest an occasion when by some means a drug might have been administered to him for the jury be sent straight to the question of a possible dis-inhibition. The judge would direct the jurors that if they felt any legitimate doubt on the matter—and by its nature the defence would be one which the prosecution would often have no means to rebut—they must acquit outright, all questions of intent, mental capacity and the like being at this stage irrelevant.

My Lords, the fact that a new doctrine may require adjustment of existing principles to accommo-date it, and may require those involved in criminal trials to learn new techniques, is not of course a ground for refusing to adopt it, if that is what the interests of justice require. Here, however, justice makes no such demands, for the interplay between the wrong done to the victim, the individual characteristics and frailties of the defendant, and the pharmacological effects of whatever drug may be potentially involved can be far better recognised by a tailored choice from the continuum of sentences available to the judge than by the application of a single yea-or-nay jury decision....

R v Hardie

[1984] 3 All ER 848, Court of Appeal

PARKER LJ: Shortly after 9.15 p.m. on 2 January 1982 fire broke out in a wardrobe in the bedroom of the ground-floor flat at 55 Bassingham Road, London SW 10. At that time there were in the flat the appellant, Mrs Jeanette Hardie, with whom the appellant had been living at the premises since May 1974 and who had changed her name to Hardie by deed poll in 1976, and her daughter Tonia. The upstairs flat was occupied by a Mrs Young.

Shortly before 2 January the appellant's relationship with Mrs Hardie had broken down and she had insisted that he must leave. He did not wish to do so, but on the morning of 2 January he packed a suitcase. At about lunchtime the appellant found two bottles of tablets in a cabinet. One con-tained valium which Mrs Hardie had had in 1974 and the other some tablets to assist urination.

The appellant's evidence in regard to this was that he had never taken valium before, that he took one at about 12 noon to calm him down, for he was in a distressed state, that it did not have much effect, that he and Mrs Hardie had then gone shopping, that he had taken two more in front of her and she had said, 'Take as many as you like, they are old stock and will do you no harm', that he had taken two more shortly afterwards, that he may have taken two of the other tablets also, and that shortly thereafter on return to the house he had fallen into a deep sleep and could thereafter remember only periods.

He was in fact collected from the flat by his mother and remained with her until returning to the flat again at 9.15 p.m. It was not disputed that he must have started the fire, for he was alone in the bedroom when it started. Having started it, he emerged, returned to the sitting room where were

Mrs Hardie and Tonia and stayed there. Shortly afterwards Mrs Hardie heard sounds from the bedroom, went there and found smoke and flames coming from the wardrobe. There was evidence that before, at the time of and after the fire the appellant was exhibiting signs of intoxication and that such signs might have resulted from the taking of valium some hours earlier.

The defence was that the appellant was so affected by the valium that he could remember nothing about the fire and had not the necessary *mens rea* to constitute either of the offences charged. On the basis no doubt of *DPP* v *Majewski* [1976] 2 All ER 142 and *R* v *Caldwell* [1981] 1 All ER 961, [1982] AC 341, the judge directed the jury in effect that, as the valium was voluntarily self-administered, it was irrelevant as a defence and its effects could not negative *mens rea*. The first point taken on appeal was that this was a misdirection.

...

In the present instance the defence was that the valium was taken for the purpose of calming the nerves only, that it was old stock and that the appellant was told it would do him no harm. There was no evidence that it was known to the appellant or even generally known that the taking of valium in the quantity taken would be liable to render a person aggressive or incapable of appreciating risks to others or have other side effects such that its self-administration would itself have an element of recklessness. It is true that valium is a drug and it is true that it was taken deliberately and not taken on medical prescription, but the drug is, in our view, wholly different in kind from drugs which are liable to cause unpredictability or aggressiveness. It may well be that the taking of a sedative or soporific drug will, in certain circumstances, be no answer, for example in a case of reckless driving, but if the effect of a drug is merely soporific or sedative the taking of it, even in some excessive quantity, cannot in the ordinary way raise a *conclusive* presumption against the admission of proof of intoxication for the purpose of disproving *mens rea* in ordinary crimes, such as would be the case with alcoholic intoxication or incapacity or automatism resulting from the self-administration of dangerous drugs.

In the present case the jury should not, in our judgment, have been directed to disregard any incapacity which resulted or might have resulted from the taking of valium. They should have been directed that if they came to the conclusion that, as a result of the valium, the appellant was, at the time, unable to appreciate the risks to property and persons from his actions they should then consider whether the taking of the valium was itself reckless. We are unable to say what would have been the appropriate direction with regard to the elements of recklessness in this case for we have not seen all the relevant evidence, nor are we able to suggest a model direction, for circumstances will vary infinitely and model directions can sometimes lead to more rather than less confusion. It is sufficient to say that the direction that the effects of valium were necessarily irrelevant was wrong.

■ NOTES AND QUESTIONS

1. Are the decisions in *Hardie* and *Kingston* reconcilable?

2. *Kingston* involved a situation where the defendant was unaware that drugs had been administered to him. What if the defendant was aware that he was taking drugs, but not the effect that the drugs would have on him? See *R* v *Allen* [1988] Crim LR 698.

3. In *Hardie* the Court of Appeal is not saying that the defendant should have been acquitted; only that the trial judge had erred in directing the jury that the effects of the valium were irrelevant. The jurors should have been directed that if they concluded that as a result of taking the valium the defendant could not have appreciated the risks to property from his action, they should then have considered whether the taking of the drug was itself a reckless act. Had the jury been properly directed, would they likely have convicted?

4. Compare *Hardie* with the case where a defendant is taking drugs pursuant to a medical prescription, and the drugs have an unanticipated, violent side effect. Is

this a stronger or a weaker case for allowing the defence? Would it matter if the defendant exceeded the prescribed dosage?

5. Adam's wife, Eve, has just left him for another man. In the comfort of his own home he gets drunk to blot out his misery. Eve unexpectedly returns. When she explains that she has only come back for her suitcase Adam goes berserk and smashes her several times over the head with the Scotch bottle. She suffers serious injuries. Adam is charged under s. 20 of the OAPA 1861, a crime of basic intent. Should this case be treated as *Hardie?* Put another way, was Adam reckless or otherwise at fault in getting drunk in these circumstances?

6. Section 6(5) of the Public Order Act 1986 provides:

> A person whose awareness is impaired by intoxication shall be taken to be aware of that of which he would be aware if not intoxicated, unless he shows either that his intoxication was not self-induced or that it was caused solely by the taking or administration of a substance in the course of medical treatment.

How does this section compare with *Kingston* and *Hardie*? With the Law Commission's various proposals previously set out?

(iii) Mistakes due to intoxication

We have seen that a mistake may negative the mens rea element of a crime and thereby lead to an acquittal. But what of the defendant makes a mistake while drunk that she would not have made if sober? If the facts as the defendant believed them to be would have warranted a defence of mistake, should that defence fail because of the intoxication? Should it matter whether the *mens rea* negated is one of specific or basic intent? The courts have not been consistent in dealing with this issue.

R v O'Grady
[1987] 3 WLR 321, Court of Appeal

The appellant, who was intoxicated, killed a man and stated to the police, 'If I had not hit him I would be dead myself.' He was tried on a count charging murder. The jury were directed that, if the appellant mistakenly believed he was under attack, he was entitled to defend himself but was not entitled to go beyond what was reasonable.

LORD LANE CJ: . . . How should the jury be invited to approach the problem? One starts with the decision of this court in *R v Williams (Gladstone)* (1983) 78 Cr App R 276, namely, that where the defendant might have been labouring under a mistake as to the facts he must be judged according to that mistaken view, whether the mistake was reasonable or not. It is then for the jury to decide whether the defendant's reaction to the threat, real or imaginary, was a reasonable one. The court was not in that case considering what the situation might be where the mistake was due to voluntary intoxication by alcohol or some other drug.

We have come to the conclusion that where the jury are satisfied that the defendant was mistaken in his belief that any force or the force which he in fact used was necessary to defend himself and are further satisfied that the mistake was caused by voluntarily induced intoxication, the defence must fail. We do not consider that any distinction should be drawn on this aspect of the matter between offences involving what is called specific intent, such as murder, and offences of so called basic intent, such as manslaughter. Quite apart from the problem of directing a jury in a case such as the present where manslaughter is an alternative verdict to murder, the question of mistake can and ought to be considered separately from the question of intent. A sober man who mistakenly believes he is in danger of immediate death at the hands of an attacker is entitled to be acquitted of both murder and manslaughter if his reaction in killing his supposed assailant was a reasonable one. What his intent may have been seems to us to be irrelevant to the problem of self-defence or no.

Jaggard v Dickinson
[1980] 3 All ER 716, Queen's Bench Division

MUSTILL J: . . . The facts set out in the case are short but striking. On the evening of 12th October 1978 the appellant had been drinking. At 10.45 pm she engaged a taxi to take her to 67 Carnach Green, South Ockendon, a house occupied by Mr R F Heyfron, a gentleman with whom she had a relationship such that, in the words of the magistrates, she had his consent at any time to treat his property as if it was her own. Alighting from the taxi, she entered the garden but was asked to leave by a Mrs Raven who was a stranger to her. Persisting, she broke the glass in the hallway of the house. She then went to the back door where she broke another window and gained entry to the house, damaging a net curtain in the process. At some time thereafter, in circumstances not described by the magistrates, it became clear that the house was not 67 Carnach Green but 35 Carnach Green, a house of identical outward appearance, occupied by Mrs Raven. The magistrates have found that the appellant did believe that she was breaking into the property of Mr Heyfron but that this mistake was induced by a state of self-induced intoxication.

. . . If the basis of the decision in *R v Majewski* [1976] 2 WLR 623 had been that drunkenness does not prevent a person from having an intent or being reckless, then there would be grounds for saying that it should equally be left out of account when deciding on his state of belief. But this is not in our view what *Majewski* decided. The House of Lords did not conclude that intoxication was irrelevant to the fact of the defendant's state of mind, but rather that, whatever might have been his actual state of mind, he should for reasons of policy be precluded from relying on any alteration in that state brought about by self-induced intoxication. The same considerations of policy apply to the intent or recklessness which is the mens rea of the offence created by s. 1(1) [Criminal Damage Act 1971] and that offence is accordingly regarded as one of basic intent (see *R v Stephenson* [1979] 1 QB 695). It is indeed essential that this should be so, for drink so often plays a part in offences of criminal damage, and to admit drunkenness as a potential means of escaping liability would provide much too ready a means of avoiding conviction. But these considerations do not apply to a case where Parliament has specifically required the court to consider the defendant's actual state of belief, not the state of belief which ought to have existed. This seems to us to show that the court is required by s. 5(3) to focus on the existence of the belief, not its intellectual soundness; and a belief can be just as much honestly held if it is induced by intoxication as if it stems from stupidity, forget-fulness or inattention.

It was, however, urged that we could not properly read s. 5(2) in isolation from s. 1(1), which forms the context of the words 'without lawful excuse' partially defined by s. 5(2). Once the words are put in context, so it is maintained, it can be seen that the law must treat drunkenness in the same way in relation to lawful excuse (and hence belief) as it does to intention and recklessness, for they are all part of the mens rea of the offence. To fragment the mens rea, so as to treat one part of it as affected by drunkenness in one way and the remainder as affected in a different way, would make the law impossibly complicated to enforce.

If it had been necessary to decide whether, for all purposes, the mens rea of an offence under s. 1(1) extends as far as an intent (or recklessness) as to the existence of a lawful excuse, I should have wished to consider the observations of James LJ, delivering the judgment of the Court of Appeal in *R v Smith* [1974] 1 All ER 632 at 636. I do not however find it necessary to reach a conclusion on this matter and will only say that I am not at present convinced that, when these observations are read in the context of the judgment as a whole, they have the meaning which the respondent has sought to put on them. In my view, however, the answer to the argument lies in the fact that any distinctions which have to be drawn as to the relevance of drunkenness to the two subsections arises from the scheme of the 1971 Act itself. No doubt the mens rea is in general indivisible, with no distinction being possible as regards the effect of drunkenness. But Parliament has specifically isolated one subjective element, in the shape of honest belief, and has given it separate treatment and its own special gloss in s. 5(3). This being so, there is nothing objectionable in giving it special treatment as regards drunkenness, in accordance with the natural meaning of its words.

In these circumstances, I would hold that the magistrates were in error when they decided that the defence furnished to the appellant by s. 5(2) was lost because she was drunk at the time. I would therefore allow the appeal.

■ NOTES AND QUESTIONS

1. In *O'Grady*, Lord Lane CJ said that mistake and intent ought to be considered separately. Is it realistic to expect a jury to be able to separate the two issues when the mistake so clearly affects the defendant's intent?

2. The Criminal Justice and Immigration Act 2008, s. 76(5) upholds the rule in *O'Grady*, followed by the Court of Appeal in *Hatton* (2006) 1 Cr App R 16, that a belief in the need for self defence (or the extent of force needed) caused by voluntary intoxication cannot be relied upon.

3. Derek, when drunk, shoots Percy and is charged with murder. Of what relevance is the fact that Derek mistakenly believes (a) that Percy is a bear, (b) that Percy is about to attack him, (c) that Percy is mad and bent on destroying the world?

4. Even if in *Jaggard* v *Dickinson* one were to accept the relevance of the defendant's drunken mistake as to whether the owner would have consented to destruction of his property (which seems doubtful despite his statement to 'treat the property as her own'), the defendant was also mistaken as to whose property she was damaging (despite the protestations of the true owner). Should these two issues have been treated separately?

(iv) 'Dutch courage'

What of the defendant who gets drunk in order to free his inhibitions and/or summon the courage to commit a crime?

Attorney-General for Northern Ireland v Gallagher
[1963] AC 349, House of Lords

LORD DENNING: My Lords, every direction which a judge gives to a jury in point of law must be considered against the background of facts which have been proved or admitted in the case. In this case the accused man did not give evidence himself. And the facts proved against him were:

He had a grievance against his wife. She had obtained a maintenance order against him and had been instrumental in getting him detained in a mental hospital.

He had made up his mind to kill his wife. He bought a knife for the purpose and a bottle of whisky—either to give himself Dutch courage to do the deed or to drown his conscience after it.

He did in fact carry out his intention. He killed his wife with the knife and drank much of the whisky before or after he killed her.

There were only two defences raised on his behalf: (1) Insanity; (2) Drunkenness. The Lord Chief Justice directed the jury that the *time* when they had to consider whether he was insane or not (within the M'Naughten Rules) was before he started on the bottle of whisky.' 'You should direct your attention,' he said to them, 'to the state of his mind before he opened the bottle of whisky.' If he was sane at that time, he could not make good the defence of insanity 'with the aid of that bottle of whisky.' Immediately after the jury retired, Mr Kelly took up this point of *time*. He suggested that it was inaccurate and inconsistent with the M'Naughten Rules. But the Lord Chief Justice adhered to his view. He declined to modify his charge to the jury on the matter. 'If I'm wrong,' he said, 'I can be put right.' It was on this view point of *time* that the Court of Criminal Appeal reversed him. His direction was, they said, 'inconsistent with the M'Naughten Rules,' which fix the crucial time as 'the time of the committing of the act,' that is, the time of the killing and not at an earlier time.

The question is whether the direction of the Lord Chief Justice as to the *time* was correct. At least that is how I read the question posed by the Court of Criminal Appeal. It is complicated by the fact that, according to the medical evidence, the accused man was a psychopath. That does not mean that he was insane. But it sharpens the point of the question. He had a disease of the mind. It was quiescent before he started on the whisky. So he was sane then. But the drink may have brought on an explosive outburst in the course of which he killed her. Can he rely on this self-induced defect of reason and put it forward as a defence of insanity?

My Lords, this case differs from all others in the books in that the accused man, whilst sane and sober, before he took to the drink, had already made up his mind to kill his wife. This seems to me to be far worse—and far more deserving of condemnation—than the case of a man who, before getting drunk, has no intention to kill, but afterwards in his cups, whilst drunk, kills another by an act which he would not dream of doing when sober. Yet by the law of England in this latter case his drunkenness is no defence even though it has distorted his reason and his will-power. So why should it be a defence in the present case? And is it made any better by saying that the man is a psychopath?

The answer to the question is, I think, that the case falls to be decided by the general principle of English law that, subject to very limited exceptions, drunkenness is no defence to a criminal charge, nor is a defect of reason produced by drunkenness....

My Lords, I think the law on this point should take a clear stand. If a man, whilst sane and sober, forms an intention to kill and makes preparation for it, knowing it is a wrong thing to do, and then gets himself drunk so as to give himself Dutch courage to do the killing, and whilst drunk carries out his intention, he cannot rely on this self-induced drunkenness as a defence to a charge of murder, nor even as reducing it to manslaughter. He cannot say that he got himself into such a stupid state that he was incapable of an intent to kill. So also when he is a psychopath, he cannot by drinking rely on his self-induced defect of reason as a defence of insanity. The wickedness of his mind before he got drunk is enough to condemn him, coupled with the act which he intended to do and did do. A psychopath who goes out intending to kill, knowing it is wrong, and does kill, cannot escape the consequences by making himself drunk before doing it. That is, I believe, the direction which the Lord Chief Justice gave to the jury and which the Court of Criminal Appeal found to be wrong. I think it was right and for this reason I would allow the appeal.

■ **NOTES AND QUESTIONS**

1. The theoretical issue raised in *Gallagher* was one of 'concurrence'. Assume that at the moment of committing the crime the defendant's drunkenness prevented him from forming the specific intent to kill. Of what relevance should it be that he had this intent before getting drunk?

2. The 'Dutch courage' cases may provide insight into why the judges generally take a sceptical attitude to voluntary intoxication as a defence. Many criminals fortify themselves with drink before embarking on their criminal enterprises, and then claim at trial a lack of *mens rea* based on intoxication. It is arguably not in society's interest to structure its legal rules to uphold such a defence.

(v) Intoxication and insanity

Prolonged use of alcohol or drugs can sometimes result in brain damage or severe mental impairment. In such cases, should the defendant's proper defence be intoxication or insanity?

R v Davis

(1881) 14 Cox CC 563, Newcastle Crown Court

On the 14th day of January, 1881, the prisoner (who had been previously drinking heavily, but was then sober) made an attack upon his sister-in-law, Mrs Davis, threw her down, and attempted to cut her throat with a knife. Ordinarily he was a very mild, quiet, peaceable, well-behaved man, and on friendly terms with her. At the police station he said, 'The man in the moon told me to do it. I will have to commit murder, as I must be hanged.' He was examined by two medical men, who found him suffering from *delirium tremens*, resulting from over-indulgence in drink. According to their evidence he would know what he was doing, but his actions would not be under his control. In their judgment neither fear of punishment nor legal nor moral considerations would have deterred him – nothing short of actual physical restraint would have prevented him acting as he did. He was disordered in his senses, and would not be able to distinguish between moral right and wrong at the time he committed the act. Under proper care and treatment he recovered in a week, and was then perfectly sensible.

For the defence it was submitted that he was of unsound mind at the time of the commission of the act, and was not responsible for his actions.

STEPHEN J to the jury: The prisoner at the bar is charged with having feloniously wounded his sister-in-law, Jane Davis, on the 14th day of January last with intent to murder her. You will have to consider whether he was in such a state of mind as to be thoroughly responsible for his actions. And with regard to that I must explain to you what is the kind or degree of insanity which relieves a man from responsibility. Nobody must suppose—and I hope no one will be led for one moment to suppose—that drunkenness is any kind of excuse for crime. If this man had been raging drunk, and had stabbed his sister-in-law and killed her, he would have stood at the bar guilty of murder beyond all doubt or question. But drunkenness is one thing and the diseases to which drunkenness leads are different things; and if a man by drunkenness brings on a state of disease which causes such a degree of madness, even for a time, which would have relieved him from responsibility if it had been caused in any other way, then he would not be criminally responsible. In my opinion, in such a case the man is a madman, and is to be treated as such, although his madness is only temporary. If you think he was so insane—that if his insanity had been produced by other causes he would not be responsible for his actions—then the mere fact that it was caused by drunkenness will not prevent it having the effect which otherwise it would have had, of excusing him from punishment. Drunkenness is no excuse, but *delirium tremens* caused by drunkenness may be an excuse if you think it produces such a state of mind as would otherwise relieve him from responsibility....

SECTION 3: AFFIRMATIVE DEFENCES

Unlike mistake and intoxication, which negative an element of the crime, an *affirmative* defence concedes the existence of all of the elements of the crime. The accused rather argues that he should be acquitted because his actions were in some way justified or excused. Duress and duress of circumstances are examples of defences that 'excuse'. The defendant admits that he has done something wrong but asserts that his actions should nonetheless be excused because of the circumstances. In contrast, when a defendant raises a claim of self-defence, defence of another or crime prevention, the defendant claims that under the circumstances he did the right thing, and that therefore his conduct was justified. Whether 'necessity' is an excuse or a justification is more a matter of debate.

Paul Robinson (*Structure and Function in Criminal Law* (1997) at p. 69) suggests that persons are 'excused' but conduct is 'justified'. In practical terms, whether a defence is characterised as an excuse or justification makes little difference; either will lead to an acquittal. There are some distinctions in theory, both for the accused (a mistake that is the basis for a defence which *excuses* may have to be reasonable while a mistake that *justifies* may only have to be honestly believed) and for third parties (a third party may be convicted of aiding and abetting a crime for which the principal has been acquitted due to an excuse, but not where the principal's acts have been found to be justified).

A: Necessity, duress and duress of circumstances – an introduction

The defences of necessity, duress, and duress of circumstances are close relatives. The situation that all three defences are concerned with is one in which the actor is faced with a choice of evils: either he has to commit a crime or suffer some unpleasant consequence.

If a robber were to hold a knife to a victim's throat and said: 'Your money or your life,' and the victim chose the former, nobody would be so crass as to suggest that the relinquishment of the money was a voluntary act. But if an individual were to hold a knife to another's throat and say 'Help me rob the bank or I will kill you', and the person chose to help rob the bank, can it be said that his participation in the bank robbery was any less involuntary? Arguably not, but these examples involve a different kind of involuntariness than that which we examined in respect of automatism. When we talked there about an involuntary *actus reus*, we were concerned with situations where the defendant was *physically* unable to resist doing the act in question. In duress and necessity cases, the defendant is physically capable of not committing the crime. The defendant has a choice, but an unpalatable one. She can choose not to commit the crime, but in so doing may be subjected to an extremely unpleasant consequence.

Yet this distinction between the *physical* inability to resist doing a criminal act and the *normative* inability to resist doing that act may account in no small measure to the hostility of judges to the defences of duress, necessity, and duress of circumstances. The judges are concerned that these defences will be invoked in circumstances where persons with a more robust moral fibre would not have yielded to the pressures to commit the offence. The judges may also want to provide a disincentive in the form of a potential criminal sanction to encourage persons to resist the pressure to commit the offence. Many judges will make reference to cases involving terrorists and recall that during the 'troubles' in Northern Ireland, those who aided and abetted terrorists frequently argued that they did so out of fear for their life (or that of their family members) if they had not cooperated. To many judges, perhaps jaded by experience, such defences seemed all too easy to fabricate.

While the defences cannot be justified on an involuntary act theory, or, for that matter, a theory that the defendant lacked mental capacity (for the defendant did have the ability to make a rational choice and arguably did make a rational choice), there are three arguments in support of their allowance.

(1) No individual should be punished for doing something that other reasonable persons in the same situation would have done. If criminal liability can be premised on a defendant's failure to act as would a reasonable person, should not acting as would a reasonable person serve as a defence?

(2) Courts should accept that the deterrent value of criminal sanctions will have little effect on the person faced with loss of life or grievous harm. Recall, however, that deterrence is only one of several rationales for punishment.

(3) As a matter of principle, in a choice-of-evils situation, the law should encourage a defendant to choose the lesser and avoid the greater evil, even if that means committing a crime. If the harm which will result from compliance with the law is greater than the harm which will result from violation of the law, it would be a strange set of priorities which required the defendant to choose the greater evil. This 'justification' for the defences draws support from the utilitarian philosophy of Jeremy Bentham and John Stuart Mill.

The burden of introducing some credible evidence relating to duress, necessity or duress of circumstances rests on the defendant. After that evidence is introduced, however, the burden shifts to the prosecution to negative the defence by proof beyond reasonable doubt.

B: Duress

In the typical case of duress the defendant concedes that he committed the crime charged but claims that he did so because he was subjected to a threat by another who said that he would inflict injury or death to the defendant or a member of his family if he did not commit the crime.

(i) The basic issues

Nine issues can arise in duress cases:

(1) Must the defendant *honestly* believe that s/he had to commit the crime to avoid more serious harm?

(2) Must the defendant's belief be *reasonable*?

(3) What types of threats will excuse the defendant's offence? Must the threat be one of *death or serious injury*?

(4) Must the threatened harm be *imminent*?

(5) Must the threat be directed at the defendant or may it be directed at a third party? Any third party?

(6) To what extent is the defendant expected to resist the threat?

(7) What *types of crimes* may the defendant commit in response to the threatened harm?

(8) Of what relevance are *alternative courses of action*?

(9) Does the defendant who has *voluntarily joined a criminal association* lose his right to claim duress?

Many of these questions were answered, albeit in obiter, in the decision of the House of Lords in *R* v *Hasan*. The case technically involved only the last question in our list, but Lord Bingham's opinion is wide-ranging and instructive.

R v *Hasan*
[2005] UKHL 22

LORD BINGHAM OF CORNHILL: . . . In brief summary, the relevant facts are these. The defendant had worked as a driver and minder for Claire Taeger, who ran an escort agency and was involved in prostitution. In about July or August 1999, according to the defendant, Sullivan became Taeger's boyfriend and also her minder in connection with her prostitution business. He had, the defendant said, the reputation of being a violent man and a drug dealer.

4. The prosecution alleged that on 29 August 1999 a man living in Croydon telephoned Taeger's agency asking for the services of a prostitute. The defendant went to the address with a prostitute. But the client had changed his mind and claimed that he had not made a telephone call. The defendant insisted that a £50 cancellation fee be paid, and forced his way into the house, producing a knife and demanding payment. The client went upstairs and opened a safe, whereupon the defendant took some £4000 from it and ran from the house. This incident founded the first count of aggravated burglary in the indictment later preferred against the defendant. But his account of the incident was quite different. He said that he had been given the £50 fee without any threat and had taken nothing from the safe. But he said that after this incident he had reported the existence of the safe and its contents to Taeger in the presence of Sullivan.

. . .

7. The second count of aggravated burglary in the indictment against the defendant related to an incident on 23 January 2000, involving the same house and the same victim as the earlier incident. The defendant admitted at trial that he had forced his way into the house on this occasion, armed with a knife, and had attempted to steal the contents of the safe, but claimed that he had acted under duress exerted by Sullivan, who had fortified his reputation for violence by talking of three murders he had recently committed. On the day in question, the defendant claimed, he had been ambushed outside his home by Sullivan and an unknown black man whom he described as a 'lunatic yardie'. Sullivan demanded that the defendant get the money from the safe mentioned on the earlier occasion, and told the defendant that the black man would go with him to see that this was done. Sullivan said that, if the defendant did not do it, he and his family would be harmed. The defendant claimed that he had no chance to escape and go to the police. The black man drove the defendant to the house and gave him a knife, saying that he himself had a gun. The defendant then broke into the house and tried unsuccessfully to open and then to remove the safe. The black man was in the vicinity throughout, and drove him away when the attempt failed.

. . .

12. The defendant's trial on two counts of aggravated burglary began on 30 January 2001 and ended on 9 February. The jury acquitted him on the first count but convicted him on the second. He was sentenced to 9 years' imprisonment.

13. . . . I shall . . . confine this opinion to the issue of duress.

14. On that issue the judge put four questions to the jury:

'Question 1: Was the defendant driven or forced to act as he did by threats which, rightly or wrongly, he genuinely believed that if he did not burgle [the] house, his family would be seriously harmed or killed? If you are sure that he was not forced by threats to act as he did, the defence fails and he is guilty. But if you are not sure go on to question 2. Would a reasonable person of the defendant's age and background have been driven or forced to act as the defendant did? If you are sure that a reasonable person would not have been forced to act as the defendant did, then the defence fails and he is guilty. If you are not sure, then go on to question 3. Could the defendant have avoided acting as he did without harm coming to his family? If you are sure he could, the defence fails and he is guilty. If you are not sure go on to question 4. Did the defendant voluntarily put himself in the position in which he knew he was likely to be subjected to threats?

If you are sure he did, the defence fails and he is guilty. If you are not sure, he is not guilty. Those four questions are really tests.'

...

17. The common sense starting point of the common law is that adults of sound mind are ordinarily to be held responsible for the crimes which they commit. To this general principle there has, since the 14th century, been a recognised but limited exception in favour of those who commit crimes because they are forced or compelled to do so against their will by the threats of another. Such persons are said, in the language of the criminal law, to act as they do because they are subject to duress.

18. Where duress is established, it does not ordinarily operate to negative any legal ingredient of the crime which the defendant has committed. Nor is it now regarded as justifying the conduct of the defendant, as has in the past been suggested...

19. Duress affords a defence which, if raised and not disproved, exonerates the defendant altogether. It does not, like the defence of provocation to a charge of murder, serve merely to reduce the seriousness of the crime which the defendant has committed. And the victim of a crime committed under duress is not, like a person against whom a defendant uses force to defend himself, a person who has threatened the defendant or been perceived by the defendant as doing so. The victim of a crime committed under duress may be assumed to be morally innocent, having shown no hostility or aggression towards the defendant. The only criminal defences which have any close affinity with duress are necessity, where the force or compulsion is exerted not by human threats but by extraneous circumstances, and, perhaps, marital coercion under section 47 of the Criminal Justice Act 1925.

20. Where the evidence in the proceedings is sufficient to raise an issue of duress, the burden is on the prosecution to establish to the criminal standard that the defendant did not commit the crime with which he is charged under duress: *R v Lynch*, above, p 668.... Professor Sir John Smith QC observed in his commentary on *R v Cole* [1994] Crim LR 582, 584, with reference to the Law Commission proposal,

> 'duress is a unique defence in that it is so much more likely than any other to depend on assertions which are peculiarly difficult for the prosecution to investigate or subsequently to disprove.'

The prosecution's difficulty is of course the greater when, as is all too often the case, little detail of the alleged compulsion is vouchsafed by the defence until the trial is under way.

21. Having regard to these features of duress, I find it unsurprising that the law in this and other jurisdictions should have been developed so as to confine the defence of duress within narrowly defined limits. Most of these are not in issue in this appeal, but it seems to me important that the issues the House is asked to resolve should be approached with understanding of how the defence has developed, and to that end I shall briefly identify the most important limitations:

(1) Duress does not afford a defence to charges of murder (*R v Howe* [1987] AC 417), attempted murder (*R v Gotts* [1992] 2 AC 412) and, perhaps, some forms of treason (Smith & Hogan, *Criminal Law*, 10th ed., 2002, p 254).

(2) To found a plea of duress the threat relied on must be to cause death or serious injury.

(3) The threat must be directed against the defendant or his immediate family or someone close to him: Smith & Hogan, above, p 258. In the light of recent Court of Appeal decisions such as *R v Conway* [1989] QB 290 and *R v Wright* [2000] Crim LR 510, the current (April 2003) specimen direction of the Judicial Studies Board suggests that the threat must be directed, if not to the defendant or a member of his immediate family, to a person for whose safety the defendant would reasonably regard himself as responsible. The correctness of such a direction was not, and on the facts could not be, in issue on this appeal, but it appears to me, if strictly applied, to be consistent with the rationale of the duress exception.

(4) The relevant tests pertaining to duress have been largely stated objectively, with reference to the reasonableness of the defendant's perceptions and conduct and not, as is usual in many other areas of the criminal law, with primary reference to his subjective perceptions.

(5) The defence of duress is available only where the criminal conduct which it is sought to excuse has been directly caused by the threats which are relied upon.

(6) The defendant may excuse his criminal conduct on grounds of duress only if, placed as he was, there was no evasive action he could reasonably have been expected to take. It is necessary to return to this aspect also, but this is an important limitation of the duress defence and in recent years it has, as I shall suggest, been unduly weakened.

(7) The defendant may not rely on duress to which he has voluntarily laid himself open....

...

I must acknowledge that the features of duress to which I have referred...incline me, where policy choices are to be made, towards tightening rather than relaxing the conditions to be met before duress may be successfully relied on. In doing so, I bear in mind in particular two observations of Lord Simon of Glaisdale in *R* v *Lynch* above (dissenting on the main ruling, which was reversed in *R* v *Howe*, above):

'....your Lordships should hesitate long lest you may be inscribing a charter for terrorists, gang-leaders and kidnappers.' (p 688).

'A sane system of criminal justice does not permit a subject to set up a countervailing system of sanctions or by terrorism to confer criminal immunity on his gang.' (p 696).

In *Perka* v *The Queen* [1984] 2 SCR 232, 250, Dickson J held that

'If the defence of necessity is to form a valid and consistent part of our criminal law it must, as has been universally recognised, be strictly controlled and scrupulously limited to situations that correspond to its underlying rationale.'

I agree. I also agree with the observation of the Supreme Court of Canada in *R* v *Ruzic* (2001)...

'Verification of a spurious claim of duress may prove difficult. Hence, courts should be alive to the need to apply reasonable, but strict standards for the application of the defence.'

If it appears at trial that a defendant acted in response to a degree of coercion but in circumstances where the strict requirements of duress were not satisfied, it is always open to the judge to adjust his sentence to reflect his assessment of the defendant's true culpability.

...

■ NOTES AND QUESTIONS

1. Why must the threat to the defendant be one of death or serious physical injury? Why can it not be one of exposure, in one of two senses? In *Singh* [1973] 1 All ER 122, the defendant was threatened with exposure of his sexual immorality, but this was held insufficient to permit a defence of duress. In *Southwark London Borough Council* v *Williams* [1971] 2 All ER 175 it was held that a homeless derelict who sought shelter from the cold in an unoccupied building would not be allowed a defence of necessity to a charge of criminal trespass.

2. Besides the defendant, at whom should the harm threatened have to be directed to afford a defence? Often in duress cases the threat is not to the defendant but to a member of the defendant's family. See *Ortiz* (1986) 83 Cr App R 173. Should this matter? What if the threat is directed at a good friend or work colleague? A casual acquaintance? Somebody one does not know?

3. Can duress be raised in a case where the alleged threat is to the population at large? See *R* v *Shayler* [2001] 1 WLR 2206, Court of Appeal (the decision was reviewed by the House of Lords, [2002] UKHL 11, but the duress issue was not discussed at length).

4. Why does Lord Bingham believe that courts should take a strict approach in limiting the conditions under which a defence of duress will be deemed appropriate?

The above and other issues relating to the scope of duress will be examined in the following sections.

(ii) May duress serve as a defence to a crime of homicide

To what crimes will duress be allowed as a defence? The obviously most troublesome case is where an innocent victim has been killed and the defendant is charged with murder. Often this issue arose in respect of defendants who committed or aided in the commission of homicide because terrorists had allegedly threatened to harm them or a member of their family if they did not commit the offence or provide the assistance.

A series of cases beginning with *Director of Public Prosecutions for Northern Ireland* v *Lynch* [1975] AC 653 examined the above issues. The defendant in *Lynch* was the driver on an IRA terrorist expedition in the course of which a police officer was killed. He was charged with aiding and abetting a murder. His defence was that he believed that he would be shot if he did not cooperate. In a three to two decision the House of Lords held that the defence of duress was available to one charged with aiding and abetting a murder. Two years later, however, in *Abbott* v *R* [1977] AC 755, it was held by the Judicial Committee of the Privy Council held that the defence of duress was not available to one charged as a principal to murder. While perhaps not in outright conflict, there was clearly a tension between *Lynch* and *Abbott* which needed to be resolved:

R v Howe and Others
[1987] 1 AC 417, House of Lords

LORD HAILSHAM OF ST MARYLEBONE:...*Count 1: murder of Elgar.* The first victim was a 17-year old youth called Elgar. He was offered a job as a driver by Murray. On the evening of 10 October 1983 all five men were driven by Murray up into the hills between Stockport and Buxton, eventually stopping at some public lavatories at a remote spot called Goytsclough. Murray at some stage told both appellants in effect that Elgar was a 'grass,' and that they were going to kill him. Bannister was threatened with violence if he did not give Elgar 'a bit of a battering.' From thenceforwards Elgar, who was naked, sobbing and begging for mercy, was tortured, compelled to undergo appalling sexual perversions and indignities, he was kicked and punched. Bannister and Howe were doing the kicking and punching. The coup de grace was executed by Bailey who strangled Elgar with a headlock. It is unnecessary to go into further details of the attack on Elgar which are positively nauseating. In brief the two appellants asserted that they had only acted as they did through fear of Murray, believing that they would be treated in the same way as Elgar had been treated if they did not comply with Murray's directions. The prosecution were content to assent to the proposition that death had been caused by Bailey strangling the victim, although the kicks and punches would have resulted in death moments later even in the absence of the strangulation. The body was hidden by the appellants and the other two men. On this basis the appellants were in the position of what would have earlier been principals in the second degree and duress was left to the jury as an issue on this count.

Count 2: murder of Pollitt. Very much the same course of conduct took place as with Elgar. On 11 October 1983 the men picked up Pollitt, a 19-year-old labourer, and took him to the same place where all four men kicked and punched the youth. Murray told Howe and Bannister to kill Pollitt, which they did by strangling him with Bannister's shoe lace. As the appellants were in the position of principals in the first degree, the judge did not leave duress to the jury on this count.

Count 3: conspiracy to murder Redfern. The third intended victim was a 21-year old man. The same procedure was followed, but Redfern suspected that something was afoot and managed with some skill to escape on his motorcycle from what would otherwise have inevitably been another horrible murder. The judge left the defence of duress to the jury on this charge of conspiracy to murder. The grounds of appeal, which are the same in respect of each of these appellants, are as follows. That the judge erred in directing the jury (1) in respect of count 2, that the defence of duress was not available to a principal in the first degree to the actual killing; (2) in respect of counts 1 and 3, that the test as to whether the appellants were acting under duress contains an 'objective' element; that is to say, if the prosecution prove that a reasonable man in the position of the defendant would not have felt himself forced to comply with the threats, the defence fails.

. . .

In general, I must say that I do not at all accept in relation to the defence of murder it is either good morals, good policy or good law to suggest, as did the majority in *Lynch* [1975] AC 653 and the minority in *Abbott* [1977] AC 755 that the ordinary man of reasonable fortitude is not to be supposed to be capable of heroism if he is asked to take an innocent life rather than sacrifice his own. Doubtless in actual practice many will succumb to temptation, as they did in *Dudley and Stephens*. But many will not, and I do not believe that as a 'concession to human frailty' the former should be exempt from liability to criminal sanctions if they do. I have known in my own lifetime of too many acts of heroism by ordinary human beings of no more than ordinary fortitude to regard a law as either 'just or humane' which withdraws the protection of the criminal law from the innocent victim and casts the cloak of its protection upon the coward and the poltroon in the name of a 'concession to human frailty.'

. . .

LORD GRIFFITHS: . . . [A]re there any present circumstances that should impel your Lordships to alter the law that has stood for so long and to extend the defence of duress to the actual killer? My Lords, I can think of none. It appears to me that all present indications point in the opposite direction. We face a rising tide of violence and terrorism against which the law must stand firm recognising that its highest duty is to protect the freedom and lives of those that live under it. The sanctity of human life lies at the root of this ideal and I would do nothing to undermine it, be it ever so slight.

. . . If the defence is not available to the killer what justification can there be for extending it to others who have played their part in the murder. I can, of course, see that as a matter of common-sense one participant in a murder may be considered less morally at fault than another. The youth who hero-worships the gangleader and acts as lookout man whilst the gang enter a jeweller's shop and kill the owner in order to steal is an obvious example. In the eyes of the law they are all guilty of murder, but justice will be served by requiring those who did the killing to serve a longer period in prison before being released on licence than the youth who acted as lookout. However, it is not difficult to give examples where more moral fault may be thought to attach to a participant in murder who was not the actual killer; I have already mentioned the example of a contract killing, when the murder would never have taken place if a contract had not been placed to take the life of the victim. Another example would be an intelligent man goading a weakminded individual into a killing he would not otherwise commit.

It is therefore neither rational nor fair to make the defence dependent upon whether the accused is the actual killer or took some other part in the murder.

■ NOTES AND QUESTIONS

1. Is the decision in *Howe* based on legal principle or social policy?
2. What if the defendant's efforts to kill prove unsuccessful, and the charge is attempted murder. Should duress then be a defence? In favour of allowing the defence is that no life has been taken. However, in *R v Gotts* [1992] 2 AC 412,

the House of Lords held that duress could not serve as a defence to attempted murder. Why not?

3. When considering the nature of the harm avoided and the nature of the harm caused, the courts seem to take a fairly dogmatic approach, placing strict limits on each of these elements. The harm avoided must be death or serious injury, and the harm caused must not be death. But why should the jury not be allowed to balance the harm avoided against the harm caused, allowing the defence when the former was greater than the latter?

4. In its consultation paper 'Legislating the Criminal Code: Offences against the Person and General Principles' (Law Comm No. 218) 177), the Law Commission originally recommended that duress should be a partial defence to reduce first degree murder to second degree murder (the two degrees of murder were also proposed by the Commission; they do not represent the current state of the law in England) . However, after a period of consultation, the Commission changed its view and recommended that duress should be a full defence to first degree murder, second degree murder and attempted murder. See Law Commission, 'Murder, Manslaughter and Infanticide' (Law Com No. 304, 2006), s. 1.56.

5. If necessity can be a defence to homicide, why not duress? See p. 504, *infra*.

(iii) From whose perspective is the threat to be judged?

In judging defence of duress, should the jury look at events through the defendant's eyes or those of the reasonable person? In other words should it apply a subjective or objective approach?

R v Hasan
[2005] UKHL 22

For facts, see p. 483.

> ...
> 23. The appellant did not challenge the judge's direction to the jury on questions 1 and 2. Save in one respect those directions substantially followed the formulation propounded by the Court of Appeal (Criminal Division) (Lord Lane CJ, Taylor and McCullough JJ) in *R v Graham* [1982] 1 WLR 294, 300, approved by the House of Lords in *R v Howe* at pp 436, 438, 446, 458–459. It is evident that the judge, very properly, based himself on the JSB's specimen direction as promulgated in August 2000. That specimen direction included the words, adopted by the judge, 'he genuinely believed'. But the words used in *R v Graham* and approved in *R v Howe* were 'he reasonably believed'. It is of course essential that the defendant should genuinely, ie. actually, believe in the efficacy of the threat by which he claims to have been compelled. But there is no warrant for relaxing the requirement that the belief must be reasonable as well as genuine....

R v Bowen
[1996] 2 Cr App R 157, Court of Appeal

> STUART-SMITH LJ: On August 2, 1995 in the Crown Court at Luton the appellant was convicted of five counts of obtaining services by deception. He was subsequently sentenced to 18 months' imprisonment, concurrent on each count. He now appeals against his convictions with leave of the single judge.

...

The appellant gave evidence; he accepted that he had obtained the goods on credit and had made few payments. He asserted that throughout the period he had acted under duress. He had been approached first by an acquaintance when buying a television for himself, and asked what was needed to obtain credit. Thereafter two men had accosted him in a public house, and he had been threatened by them that he and his family would be petrol-bombed if he did not obtain goods for them. On each occasion he was told what goods the men required. He was told that if he went to the police his family would be attacked. He said that he had not told the police this in interview because he was worried about the possible repercussions.

Two psychologists were called, Ms Kingswood for the appellant and Dr Gudjonsson for the Crown....

Before the jury, Ms Kingswood said that the appellant had an I.Q. of 68 and a reading age of a child of six years and eight months. His level of ability was in the lowest 2 per cent of the population. She found him abnormally suggestible. She said he was unlikely to have appreciated the significance of the questions put to him. She felt he was a 'vulnerable' individual.

Dr Gudjonsson did not accept these conclusions. He thought the appellant might be faking a poor result; he thought that the appellant's I.Q. was higher than 68.

The classic statement of the law is to be found in the judgment of the Court of Appeal in *Graham* (1982) 74 Cr App R 235. At pp. 240, 241 and p. 299 respectively, Lord Lane CJ, giving the judgment of the Court, quoted a passage from the Law Commission Report No. 83 on Defences of General Application at paragraph 2.28, which includes this passage:

> Whether the words 'in his situation' comprehend more than the surrounding circumstances, and extend to the characteristics of the defendant himself, it is difficult to say, and for that reason we would not recommend without qualification the adoption of that solution. We think that there should be an objective element in the requirements of the defence so that in the final event it will be for the jury to determine whether the threat was one which the defendant in question could not reasonably have been expected to resist. This will allow the jury to take into account the nature of the offence committed, its relationship to the threats which the defendant believed to exist, the threats themselves and the circumstances in which they were made and the personal characteristics of the defendant. The last consideration is, we feel, a most important one. Threats directed against the weak, immature or disabled person, may well be much more compelling than the same threats directed against a normal healthy person.
>
> As a matter of public policy, it seems to us essential to limit the defence of duress by means of an objective criterion formulated in terms of reasonableness. Consistency of approach in defences to criminal liability is obviously desirable. Provocation and duress are analogous. In provocation the words or actions of one person break the self-control of another. In duress the words or actions of one person break the will of another. The law requires a defendant to have the self-control reasonably to be expected of the ordinary citizen in his situation. It should likewise require him to have the steadfastness reasonably to be expected of the ordinary citizen in his situation. So too with self-defence, in which the law permits the use of no more force than is reasonable in the circumstances. And, in general, if a mistake is to excuse what would otherwise be criminal, the mistake must be a reasonable one.
>
> It follows that we accept Mr Sherrard's submission that the direction in this case was too favourable to the appellant. The Crown having conceded that the issue of duress was open to the appellant and was raised on the evidence, the correct approach on the facts of this case would have been as follows: (1) Was the defendant, or may he have been, impelled to act as he did because, as a result of what he reasonably believed King had said or done, he had good cause to fear that if he did not so act King would kill him or (if this is to be added) cause him serious physical injury? (2) If so, have the prosecution made the jury sure that a sober person of reasonable firmness, sharing the characteristics of the defendant, would not have responded to whatever he reasonably believed King said or did by taking part in the killing? The fact that a defendant's will to resist has been eroded by the voluntary consumption of drink or both is not relevant to this test.

This formulation was approved by the House of Lords in *R* v *Howe* (1987) 85 Cr App R 32 (see *per* Lord Mackay of Clashfern at pp. 65, 66).

But the question remains, what are the relevant characteristics of the accused to which the jury should have regard in considering the second objective test? This question had given rise to considerable difficulty in recent cases. It seems clear that age and sex are, and physical health or disability may be, relevant characteristics. But beyond that it is not altogether easy to determine from the authorities what others may be relevant.

...

What principles are to be derived from [the] authorities? We think they are as follows:

(1) The mere fact that the accused is more pliable, vulnerable, timid or susceptible to threats than a normal person are not characteristics with which it is legitimate to invest the reasonable/ ordinary person for the purpose of considering the objective test.

(2) The defendant may be in a category of persons who the jury may think less able to resist pressure than people not within that category. Obvious examples are age, where a young person may well not be so robust as a mature one; possibly sex, though many woman would doubtless consider they had as much moral courage to resist pressure as men; pregnancy, where there is added fear for the unborn child; serious physical disability, which may inhibit self protection; recognised mental illness or psychiatric condition, such as post traumatic stress disorder leading to learned helplessness.

(3) Characteristics which may be relevant in considering provocation, because they relate to the nature of the provocation, itself will not necessarily be relevant in cases of duress. Thus homosexuality may be relevant to provocation if the provocative words or conduct are related to this characteristic; it cannot be relevant in duress, since there is no reason to think that homosexuals are less robust in resisting threats of the kind that are relevant in duress cases.

(4) Characteristics due to self-induced abuse, such as alcohol, drugs or glue-sniffing, cannot be relevant.

(5) Psychiatric evidence may be admissible to show that the accused is suffering from some mental illness, mental impairment or recognised psychiatric condition provided persons generally suffering from such condition may be more susceptible to pressure and threats and thus to assist the jury in deciding whether a reasonable person suffering from such a condition might have been impelled to act as the defendant did. It is not admissible simply to show that in the doctor's opinion an accused, who is not suffering from such illness or condition, is especially timid, suggestible or vulnerable to pressure and threats. Nor is medical opinion admissible to bolster or support the credibility of the accused.

(6) Where counsel wishes to submit that the acccused has some characteristic which falls within (2) above, this must be made plain to the judge. The question may arise in relation to the admissibility of medical evidence of the nature set out in (5). If so, the judge will have to rule at that stage. There may, however, be no medical evidence or, as in this case, medical evidence may have been introduced for some other purpose, e.g. to challenge the admissibility or weight of a confession. In such a case counsel must raise the question before speeches in the absence of the jury, so that the judge can rule whether the alleged characteristic is capable of being relevant. If he rules that it is, then he must leave it to the jury.

(7) In the absence of some direction from the judge as to what characteristics are capable of being regarded as relevant, we think that the direction approved in *Graham* without more will not be as helpful as it might be, since the jury may be tempted, especially if there is evidence, as there was in this case, relating to suggestibility and vulnerability, to think that these are relevant. In most cases it is probably only the age and sex of the accused that is capable of being relevant. If so, the judge should, as he did in this case, confine the characteristics in question to these.

How are these principles to be applied in this case? Miss Levitt accepts, rightly in our opinion, that the evidence that the appellant was abnormally suggestible and a vulnerable individual is irrelevant. But she submits that the fact that he had, or may have had, a low I.Q. of 68 is relevant since it might inhibit his ability to seek the protection of the police. We do not agree. We do not see how low I.Q., short of mental impairment or mental defectiveness, can be said to be a characteristic that makes those who have it less courageous and less able to withstand threats and pressure. Moreover, we do not think that any such submission as is now made, based solely on the appellant's low I.Q., was ever advanced at the trial. Furthermore, it is to be noted that in two places—at pp. 14C-D and 42D-G—the judge told the jury that if they thought the appellant passed the subjective test they should acquit him. We are quite satisfied that in the circumstances of this case the judge's direction was sufficient. He directed the jury to consider the only two relevant characteristics, namely age and sex. It would not have assisted them and might well have confused them, if he had added, without qualification, that the person of reasonable firmness was one who shared the characteristics of the appellant.

■ NOTES AND QUESTIONS

1. Recall that in cases of mistake such as *R* v *Williams (Gladstone)* (above p. 461), mistake was measured from the subjective perspective of the defendant and did not have to be reasonable for mistake to be a defence. Why are duress cases different?

2. The Court of Appeal in *Bowen* accepted that certain of a defendant's characteristics (age, gender, physical disability) might be attributed to the reasonable person but that low intelligence was not one of these characteristics. Why not? Mental and psychiatric illness may, on the other hand, may be relevant characteristics, but does not this distinction put a premium on whether an expert witness couches her testimony in terms of the defendant being mentally ill or just not very smart? Likewise, should it matter whether an expert witness testifies that a mother who had been abused by the father of her child, and thus feared to prevent him from killing the child, suffered from excessive timidity or 'learned helplessness'? See *R* v *Emery (and Another)* (1993) 14 Cr App R (S) 394.

3. As the defences of duress, necessity and duress of circumstances are commonly said to be concessions to human frailty, why should the defendant's vulnerability or excessive timidity not be a proper consideration to be taken into account? In *Hasan*, Baroness Hale made the point this way:

   I accept that even the person with a knife at her back has a choice whether or not to do as the knifeman says. The question is whether she should have resisted the threat. But, perhaps because I am a reasonable but comparatively weak and fearful grandmother, I do not understand why the defendant's beliefs and personal characteristics are not morally relevant to whether she could reasonably have been expected to resist.

4. In *R* v *Flatt* [1996] Crim LR 576, the Court of Appeal held that drug addiction is not a relevant characteristic. Is this because drug addiction is self-induced, or because it does not affect an addict's ability to resist committing a crime?

(iv) Must the threat be imminent?

It is often said that the threat to the defendant must be immediate or imminent (is there a difference?). If the rationale for the defence is that the defendant's ability to resist committing the crime was overborne, then should the immediacy of the harm matter if the defendant's actions were the product of the threat?

R v Abdul-Husain and Others
[1999] Crim LR 570, Court of Appeal

The appellants were all Shiite Muslims from Southern Iraq. All save Hoshan had offended against the laws or regulations of the Saddam Hussein regime, from which they were fugitives. In 1996 they were living in Sudan and feared return to Iraq, where they believed they would face death. Hoshan had a valid permit to reside in the United Kingdom and would have become entitled to a right of permanent settlement. He helped Iraqis to obtain false papers and to bribe officials and believed that, because of his involvement in helping others, he was at risk of detection and deportation to Iraq where he would probably be executed. The appellants made several unsuccessful attempts to leave Sudan using false passports. By the end of August 1996 they were all overstayers in Sudan and feared deportation to Iraq. They decided to hijack an aeroplane. Accordingly, they boarded a Sudanese airbus bound for Amman in Jordan. They were equipped with plastic knives and plastic mustard bottles filled with salt, modified with black tape and plasticine to look like hand grenades. Once the flight was in Egyptian airspace they gained control of the aircraft by threatening the crew with the imitation knives and grenades. The aeroplane eventually landed at Stansted airport 12 hours later. After negotiations lasting some eight hours the passengers and crew were released and the appellants surrendered. At their trial they admitted the charge of hijacking but contended that they had done so as a last resort to escape death, either of themselves or of their families, at the hands of the Iraqi authorities. The trial judge ruled that the defence of necessity or duress of circumstances should not be left to the jury because the threat was insufficiently close and immediate to give rise to a virtually spontaneous reaction to the physical risk arising. They were all convicted and appealed against conviction on the grounds that the judge erred in withdrawing the defence of duress from the jury's consideration.

Held, allowing the appeals, that the defence of duress was available in relation to hijacking aircraft, although the terror induced in innocent passengers would generally raise issues of proportionality; that imminent peril of death or serious injury to the defendant or his dependants had to operate on the mind of the defendant at the time he committed the act so as to overbear his will, but the execution of the threat need not be immediately in prospect; that the period of time which elapsed between the inception of the peril and the defendant's act was a relevant but not determinative factor; that all the circumstances of the peril, including the number, identity and status of those creating it, and the opportunities (if any) to avoid it were relevant, initially for the judge and, in appropriate cases, for the jury, when assessing whether the defendant's mind was affected so as to overbear his will; and that, accordingly, the judge interpreted the law too strictly in seeking a virtually spontaneous reaction. He should have asked himself, in accordance with *R v Martin* (1989) 88 Cr App R 345 whether there was evidence of such fear operating on the minds of the appellants at the time of the hijacking as to impel them to act as they did and whether, if so, there was evidence that the danger they feared objectively existed and that hijacking was a reasonable and proportionate response to it. Had he done so he must have concluded that there was evidence for the jury to consider and that they should have been permitted to do so.

Per curiam. For the fourth time in five years the Court of Appeal emphasised the urgent need for legislation to define the defence of duress with precision.

R v Hasan

[2005] UKHL 22

For facts, see p. 483.

...

In the view of Lord Edmund-Davies (p 708) there had been

> 'for some years an unquestionable tendency towards progressive latitude in relation to the plea of duress.'

27. In making that observation Lord Edmund-Davies did not directly criticise the reasoning of the Court of Appeal in its then recent judgment in *R v Hudson and Taylor* [1971] 2 QB 202, but that was described by Professor Glanville Williams as 'an indulgent decision' (*Textbook of Criminal Law*, 2nd ed, 1983, p 636), and it has in my opinion had the unfortunate effect of weakening the requirement that execution of a threat must be reasonably believed to be imminent and immediate if it is to support a plea of duress. The appellants were two teenage girls who had committed perjury at

an earlier trial by failing to identify the defendant. When prosecuted for perjury they set up a plea of duress, on the basis that they had been warned by a group, including a man with a reputation for violence, that if they identified the defendant in court the group would get the girls and cut them up. They resolved to tell lies, and were strengthened in their resolve when they arrived at court and saw the author of the threat in the public gallery. The trial judge ruled that the threats were not sufficiently present and immediate to support the defence of duress but was held by the Court of Appeal to have erred, since although the threats could not be executed in the courtroom they could be carried out in the streets of Salford that same night. It was argued for the Crown that the appellants should have neutralised the threat by seeking police protection, but this argument was criticised as failing to distinguish between cases in which the police would be able to provide effective protection and those when they would not.

...

I can understand that the Court of Appeal in *R v Hudson and Taylor* had sympathy with the predicament of the young appellants but I cannot, consistently with principle, accept that a witness testifying in the Crown Court at Manchester has no opportunity to avoid complying with a threat incapable of execution then or there. When considering necessity in *R v Cole* [1994] Crim LR 582, 583, Simon Brown LJ, giving the judgment of the court, held that the peril relied on to support the plea of necessity lacked imminence and the degree of directness and immediacy required of the link between the suggested peril and the offence charged, but in *R v Abdul-Hussain*, above, the Court of Appeal declined to follow these observations to the extent that they were inconsistent with *R v Hudson and Taylor*, by which the court regarded itself as bound.

28. The judge's direction on question 3 was modelled on the JSB specimen direction current at the time, and is not in my opinion open to criticism. It should however be made clear to juries that if the retribution threatened against the defendant or his family or a person for whom he reasonably feels responsible is not such as he reasonably expects to follow immediately or almost immediately on his failure to comply with the threat, there may be little if any room for doubt that he could have taken evasive action, whether by going to the police or in some other way, to avoid committing the crime with which he is charged.

■ **NOTES AND QUESTIONS**

1. Why does Lord Bingham in *Hasan* reject the rationale of *Hudson and Taylor*? Does he confuse the immediacy of the threat operating on the defendant and the immediacy of the harm? Which is more relevant? Why?

2. Eve has been kidnapped. Her kidnappers telephone Adam, her husband, instructing him that he has one week to raise the ransom money if he wishes to see Eve alive again. Two days before the ransom is to be paid, Eve finds a pair of scissors, with which she attacks and kills her kidnappers. Will Eve's defence (of necessity?) to a charge of manslaughter fail because the threatened harm was not imminent? If Adam robs a bank one day after receiving the ransom demand, will his defence (of duress?) fail for similar reasons?

(v) The relevance of alternative courses of action

Related to the issue of the imminence of the threat is the question of alternative courses of action. If a defendant has alternative ways to avoid the threatened harm which do not involve committing a crime, must he take one of these? Should it matter how risky the alternative choices are?

R v Gill

[1963] 2 All ER 688, Court of Criminal Appeal

EDMUND DAVIES J: . . . The appellant was charged at Bedford County Sessions and convicted of (i) conspiring with James Lockett and other persons unknown to steal a lorry and its load, and (ii) with larceny pursuant to that conspiracy. Against those convictions he now appeals by leave of the full court. The appellant, who was employed as a lorry-driver by A. E. Meeks, Ltd., himself testified that he was approached by a group of men (of whom his co-accused Lockett was not one) who suggested that he should steal a valuable load from his employers and hand it over to them in return for a payment of £1,000, and that he agreed to do this. It was arranged that he would leave the loaded lorry in a car-park in Bristol, that during his absence it would be driven away, and that he would then falsely report to the police that it had been stolen without his knowledge. On this evidence, the learned deputy-chairman rightly told the jury that the conspiracy charge was clearly established on the appellant's own testimony, and (subject to two matters later to be mentioned) no question now arises as to the correctness of that direction or of the conviction on that count. According to the appellant, however, although the lorry and its load were in fact later stolen by his fellow-conspirators, this was done not pursuant to the conspiracy to which he had been a party, but wholly against his will. He testified that he repented of the conspiracy the day after he entered into it, and that, when 'Reg' (one of his fellow-conspirators) and three others arrived at his home by arrangement to collect him for the purpose of the theft being effected, he told them that he was not going through with it. They thereupon threatened physical violence both to him and to his wife, one of them flourishing a crowbar and another showing him a bottle of petrol, and, in great fear for the safety of his wife and himself, he obeyed their orders to accompany them to his employers' premises. They dropped him outside, he went into the yard and then, still in fear, collected his lorry and drove it to a point on the M.1 near St. Albans, where he was forced by threats to leave the lorry. It was then promptly driven away and has never since been recovered. When later seen by the police, however, the appellant signed two statements in which he confessed that he had been a party to the larceny and made no mention of having been subjected to duress.

. . .

The third and most interesting point taken relates only to the larceny count, it being submitted that the learned deputy-chairman wrongly directed the jury that it was for the appellant to establish that he was acting under duress. The account given by the appellant himself makes it very doubtful whether such a defence was strictly open to him, inasmuch as there was a time after the alleged threats when, having been left outside his employers' yard and having then entered it, he could presumably have raised the alarm and so wrecked the whole criminal enterprise. In *M'Growther's Case* (1746) Fost 13, Lee LCJ, directed the jury that, to establish a plea of duress, the defendant must have resisted or fled from the wrongdoer if that were possible. Seemingly, the position under American law is the same, as appears from the statement in *Professor Rollin Perkins Criminal Law* that, 'The excuse (of compulsion) is not available to someone who had an obviously safe avenue of escape before committing the prohibited act.'

The issue of duress was, nevertheless, left to the jury in the present case, and that may well have been the prudent course. Having been left, did the burden rest on the Crown conclusively to destroy this defence, in the same way as it is required to destroy such other defences as provocation or self-defence? Or was the appellant required to establish it, on the balance of probabilities? . . . The Crown are not called on to anticipate such a defence and destroy it in advance. The accused, either by the cross-examination of the prosecution witnesses or by evidence called on his behalf, or by a combination of the two, must place before the court such material as makes duress a live issue fit and proper to be left to the jury. But, once he has succeeded in doing this, it is then for the Crown to destroy that defence in such a manner as to leave in the jury's minds no reasonable doubt that the accused cannot be absolved on the grounds of the alleged compulsion . . . .

■ NOTES AND QUESTIONS

1. The alternative course of action most often suggested is for the defendant to notify the police. If one under duress fails to do so when presented with the opportunity, then the defence may be lost. The problem is that the police may not be prepared to intervene until a crime has actually been committed or is on the verge of being committed (see the discussion of attempt in Chapter 12).

2. Another problem with attempting to contact the police is that the defendant may not be prepared to take the risk that the police will be able to timely intervene and that the consequences may be the death of a loved one. If the defendant's concerns are honestly entertained, should it matter whether or not they would be shared by a reasonable person? Is this a situation where it is unrealistic to expect jurors to be able to put themselves in the defendant's shoes – where panic is more likely to prevail over rational thought processes.

(vi) Voluntary association with criminals

What of the situation where one associates with known criminals or joins a criminal organisation and is then threatened with death or serious harm if she does not help her colleagues commit an offence? Having voluntarily placed oneself in this position, does one lose the potential defence of duress?

R v Hasan

[2005] UKHL 22

For facts, see p. 483.

...

29. The judge's direction to the jury on question 4 is quoted in para 14 above and, as recorded in para 15, the Court of Appeal ruled that this was a misdirection because the judge had not directed the jury to consider whether the defendant knew that he was likely to be subjected to threats to commit a crime of the type of which he was charged. It is this ruling which gives rise to the certified question on this part of the case, which is:

'Whether the defence of duress is excluded when as a result of the accused's voluntary association with others:

(i) he foresaw (or possibly should have foreseen) the risk of being subjected to any compulsion by threats of violence, or

(ii) only when he foresaw (or should have foreseen) the risk of being subjected to compulsion to commit criminal offences, and, if the latter,

(iii) only if the offences foreseen (or which should have been foreseen) were of the same type (or possibly of the same type and gravity) as that ultimately committed.'

The Crown contend for answer (i) in its objective form. The defendant commends the third answer, omitting the first parenthesis.

...

34. In its Working Paper No 55 of 1974, the Law Commission in para 26 favoured

'a limitation upon the defence [of duress] which would exclude its availability where the defendant had joined an association or conspiracy which was of such a character that he was aware that he might be compelled to participate in offences of the type with which he is charged.'

This reference to 'offences of the type with which he is charged' was, in substance, repeated in the Law Commission's 'Report on Defences of General Application' (Law Com No 83) of 1977, paras 2.38 and 2.46(8), in clause 1(5) of the draft bill appended to that report, in clause 45(4) of the draft bill appended to the Law Commission's Report on 'Codification of the Criminal Law' (Law Com No 143) of 1985, as explained in para 13.19 of the Report, and in clause 42(5) of the Law Commission's draft 'Criminal Code Bill' (Law Com No 177) published in 1989. But there was no warrant for this gloss in any reported British authority until the Court of Appeal (Roch LJ, Richards J and Judge Colston QC) gave judgment in *R v Baker and Ward* [1999] 2 Cr App R 335 . . . The trial judge had directed the jury (p 341):

> 'A person cannot rely on the defence of duress if he has voluntarily and with full knowledge of its nature joined a criminal group which he was aware might bring pressure on him of a violent kind or require him if necessary to commit offences to obtain money where he himself had defaulted to the criminal group in payment to the criminal group.'

This was held to be a misdirection (p 344):

> 'What a defendant has to be aware of is the risk that the group might try to coerce him into committing criminal offences of the type for which he is being tried by the use of violence or threats of violence.'

. . .

37. The principal issue between the Crown on one side and the appellant and the Court of Appeal on the other is whether *R v Baker and Ward* correctly stated the law. To resolve that issue one must remind oneself of the considerations outlined in paras 18–22 above. The defendant is seeking to be wholly exonerated from the consequences of a crime deliberately committed. The prosecution must negative his defence of duress, if raised by the evidence, beyond reasonable doubt. The defendant is, *ex hypothesi*, a person who has voluntarily surrendered his will to the domination of another. Nothing should turn on foresight of the manner in which, in the event, the dominant party chooses to exploit the defendant's subservience. There need not be foresight of coercion to commit crimes, although it is not easy to envisage circumstances in which a party might be coerced to act lawfully. In holding that there must be foresight of coercion to commit crimes of the kind with which the defendant is charged, *R v Baker and Ward* mis-stated the law.

38. There remains the question, which the Court of Appeal left open in para 75 of their judgment, whether the defendant's foresight must be judged by a subjective or an objective test: i.e. does the defendant lose the benefit of a defence based on duress only if he actually foresaw the risk of coercion or does he lose it if he ought reasonably to have foreseen the risk of coercion, whether he actually foresaw the risk or not? I do not think any decided case has addressed this question, and I am conscious that application of an objective reasonableness test to other ingredients of duress has attracted criticism: see, for example, Elliott, '*Necessity, Duress and Self-Defence*' [1989] Crim LR 611, 614–615, and the commentary by Professor Ashworth on *R v Safi* [2003] Crim LR 721, 723. The practical importance of the distinction in this context may not be very great, since if a jury concluded that a person voluntarily associating with known criminals ought reasonably to have foreseen the risk of future coercion they would not, I think, be very likely to accept that he did not in fact do so. But since there is a choice to be made, policy in my view points towards an objective test of what the defendant, placed as he was and knowing what he did, ought reasonably to have foreseen. I am not persuaded otherwise by analogies based on self-defence or provocation for reasons I have already given. The policy of the law must be to discourage association with known criminals, and it should be slow to excuse the criminal conduct of those who do so. If a person voluntarily becomes or remains associated with others engaged in criminal activity in a situation where he knows or ought reasonably to know that he may be the subject of compulsion by them or their associates, he cannot rely on the defence of duress to excuse any act which he is thereafter compelled to do by them. It is not necessary in this case to decide whether or to what extent that principle applies if an undercover agent penetrates a criminal gang for bona fide law enforcement purposes and is compelled by the gang to commit criminal acts.

39. I would answer this certified question by saying that the defence of duress is excluded when as a result of the accused's voluntary association with others engaged in criminal activity he foresaw or ought reasonably to have foreseen the risk of being subjected to any compulsion by threats of violence.

■ NOTES AND QUESTIONS

1. Amy, a lover of all living creatures, joins an organisation opposed to cruelty to animals and accompanies its members on illegal protests involving trespass and minor acts of criminal damage. When scientists at the local university begin to conduct experiments on animals, the organisation decides to firebomb the laboratory. Amy wishes to draw a line and refuses to participate but is told that 'if she knows what's good for her', she will not abandon the cause. If she goes along with the firebombing, will Amy be liable? What if a night watchman is killed by the bomb?

C: Necessity

While the defence of duress is well established, there has always been some doubt as to whether a defence of necessity even existed; and, if so, to what crimes it applied. The issue was first addressed in what is one of the most famous criminal cases of all time.

R v Dudley and Stephens
(1884) 14 QBD 273, Queen's Bench Division

At the trial of an indictment for murder it appeared, upon a special verdict, that the prisoners D and S, seamen, and the deceased, a boy between seventeen and eighteen, were cast away in a storm on the high seas, and compelled to put into an open boat; that the boat was drifting on the ocean, and was probably more than 1,000 miles from land; that on the eighteenth day, when they had been seven days without food and five without water, D proposed to S that lots should be cast who should be put to death to save the rest, and that they afterwards thought it would be better to kill the boy that their lives should be saved; that on the twentieth day D, with the assent of S, killed the boy, and both D and S fed on his flesh for four days; that at the time of the act there was no sail in sight nor any reasonable prospect of relief; that under these circumstances there appeared to the prisoners every probability that unless they then or very soon fed upon the boy, or one of themselves, they would die of starvation.

LORD COLERIDGE CJ:...From these facts, stated with the cold precision of a special verdict, it appears sufficiently that the prisoners were subject to terrible temptation, to sufferings which might break down the bodily power of the strongest man, and try the conscience of the best. Other details yet more harrowing, facts still more loathsome and appalling, were presented to the jury, and are to be found recorded in my learned Brother's notes. But nevertheless this is clear, that the prisoners put to death a weak and unoffending boy upon the chance of preserving their own lives by feeding, upon his flesh and blood after he was killed, and with the certainty of depriving, *him* of any possible chance of survival. The verdict finds in terms that 'if the men had not fed upon the body of the boy they would *probably* not have survived,' and that 'the boy being in a much weaker condition was *likely* to have died before them.' They might possibly have been picked up next day by a passing ship; they might possibly not have been picked up at all; in either case it is obvious that the killing of the boy would have been an unnecessary and profitless act. It is found by the verdict that the boy was incapable of resistance, and, in fact, made none; and it is not even suggested that his death was due to any violence on his part attempted against, or even so much as feared by, those who killed him . . . .

Now, except for the purpose of testing how far the conservation of a man's own life is in all cases and under all circumstances, an absolute, unqualified, and paramount duty, we exclude from our consideration all the incidents of war. We are dealing with a case of private homicide, not one imposed upon men in the service of their Sovereign and in the defence of their country. Now it is admitted that the deliberate killing of this unoffending and unresisting boy was clearly murder, unless the killing can be justified by some well-recognised excuse admitted by the law. It is further admitted that there was in this case no such excuse, unless the killing was justified by what has been called 'necessity.' But the temptation to the act which existed here was not what the law has ever called necessity. Nor is this to be regretted. Though law and morality are not the same, and many things may be immoral which are not necessarily illegal, yet the absolute divorce of law from morality would be of fatal consequence; and divorce would follow if the temptation to murder in this case were to be held by law an absolute defence of it. It is not so. To preserve one's life is generally speaking a duty, but it may be the plainest and the highest duty to sacrifice it. War is full of instances in which it is a man's duty not to live, but to die. The duty in case of shipwreck, of a captain to his crew, of the crew to the passengers, of soldiers to women and children, as in the noble case of the *Birkenhead*; these duties impose on men the moral necessity, not of the preservation, but of the sacrifice of their lives for others, from which in no country, least of all, it is to be hoped, in England, will men ever shrink, as indeed, they have not shrunk. It is not correct, therefore, to say that there is any absolute or unqualified necessity to preserve one's life.

. . . It is not needful to point out the awful danger of admitting the principle which has been contended for. Who is to be the judge of this sort of necessity? By what measure is the comparative value of lives to be measured? Is it to be strength, or intellect, or what? It is plain that the principle leaves to him who is to profit by it to determine the necessity which will justify him in deliberately taking another's life to save his own. In this case the youngest, the most unresisting, was chosen. Was it more necessary to kill him than one of the grown men? The answer must be 'No'—

So spake the Fiend, and with necessity,

The tyrant's plea, excused his delivish deeds.

It is not suggested that in this particular case the deeds were 'devilish,' but it is quite plain that such a principle once admitted might be made the legal cloak for unbridled passion and atrocious crime. There is no safe path for judges to tread but to ascertain the law to the best of their ability and to declare it according to their judgment; and if in any case the law appears to be too severe on individuals, to leave it to the Sovereign to exercise that prerogative of mercy which the Constitution has intrusted to the hands fittest to dispense it.

It must not be supposed that in refusing to admit temptation to be an excuse for crime it is forgotten how terrible the temptation was; how awful the suffering; how hard in such trials to keep the judgment straight and the conduct pure. We are often compelled to set up standards we cannot reach ourselves, and to lay down rules which we could not ourselves satisfy. But a man has no right to declare temptation to be an excuse, though he might himself have yielded to it, nor allow compassion for the criminal to change or weaken in any manner the legal definition of the crime. It is therefore our duty to declare that the prisoners' act in this case was wilful murder, that the facts as stated in the verdict are no legal justification of the homicide; and to say that in our unanimous opinion the prisoners are upon this special verdict guilty of murder.

■ **NOTES AND QUESTIONS**

1. The court in *Dudley and Stephens* said: 'We are often compelled to set up standards we cannot reach ourselves, and to lay down rules which we could not ourselves satisfy.' Why? If no other person would be able to meet the court's

standards, why should the hapless defendant who found himself, through no fault of his own, in the predicament in question, be so required?

2. Might the court in *Dudley and Stephens* have been influenced by the method of selecting the victim? Might it have been more sympathetic if the victim had been chosen by lot, as occurred in the American counterpart to *Dudley and Stephens, United States* v *Holmes*, 26 F Cas 360 (No. 15,383) (CCED 1842)? If the randomness of the selection process in *Holmes* offends, is there a more rational method of choosing the victim?

3. Should numbers matter? As part of the 9/11 attacks, four hijackers forced their way into the cockpit of a flight from Newark to San Francisco, overpowered the pilots, and diverted the plane to Washington, D.C. Meanwhile several passengers had received mobile telephone calls from loved ones informing them of the attacks on the World Trade Center. The passengers rightly suspected that the hijackers had a similar plan in mind and decided to mount an assault and gain control of the aircraft. In the ensuing struggle the plane crashed and all 40 passengers, the crew and the hijackers were killed. But let us assume for a moment that the passenger who led the attack against the hijackers survived. If tried for murder could he claim duress on the grounds that thousands of victims would have been killed had he not foiled the terrorists' plan, even though his actions meant certain death for the passengers and crew. What if the President of the United States had ordered the plane to be shot down before it could reach Washington? Would either the President or the pilot who shot down the airplane be guilty of murder? (For discussion see Wilson (2011), Chapter 9, 10.5.)

4. Necessity, duress and duress of circumstances are all-or-nothing defences. Unlike provocation or diminished responsibility, they will not serve to reduce the seriousness of a crime (unless, as we have noted, the Law Commission's proposals were to be accepted). Under the present law, if successful, the defences will lead to a complete acquittal. However, even if unsuccessful, a court may take into account the defendant's predicament in sentencing. In *Dudley and Stephens*, the defendants, although convicted of murder, had their sentences commuted to six months' imprisonment. See also *R* v *Emery (and Another)* (1993) 14 Cr App R (S) 394.

Necessity crept into English law by the back door of the defence of duress of circumstances. In a number of cases in the 1980s it was accepted that a defendant was entitled to take action, otherwise unlawful, to allay the threat of death or serious injury to himself or another. These cases differed from *Dudley* v *Stephens* in one important particular, namely the action taken did not involve the victimisation of an innocent person. The crimes charged included reckless driving, driving without a licence and the possession of firearms. Recently necessity was raised as a defence to another 'crime without a victim'.

S & Anor, R v

[2009] EWCA Crim 85, Court of Appeal

LORD JUSTICE MOSES: On 22 December 2008 at the Crown Court at Southwark, the Honorary Recorder of Westminster, HHJ Rivlin QC, gave a preliminary ruling following a preparatory hearing pursuant to section 29(1) of the Criminal Procedure and Investigations Act 1996. He ruled that, as a matter of law, the defence of necessity was not available to the two defendants, S and L, and therefore could not be left to the jury…He did so on the basis of a preliminary ruling that the facts relied upon by the defence were too flimsy to entitle the jury to conclude that the defendants had no alternative to the action taken.

'The circumstances in which the judgment came to be made need not detain us for long. It is contended by the Security Industry Authority, SIA, that on certain days from March 2006 onwards at specific locations the defendants deployed unlicensed guards. ..The defendants have sought and persist in seeking to contend that the reason why unlicensed guards were deployed at those times in those places was because there was no alternative means (in the time available) for protecting those who might be passing by or those who were in those premises from death or serious injury other than by protection to be afforded by the guards. So grave was the risk of death or serious injury on the dates identified in those counts that these defendants had no choice but to deploy their employees, unlicensed as they were…'

26. We think that the judge was not in a position to rule out the possibility of the defence being able to use material, if it exists, to make good the points it now relies upon in so recent a note. If evidence was given that there was an immediate or imminent threat of a major terrorist attack on a retail store the safety for which these defendants were responsible, and there was no other way of avoiding the risk to those in the store or passing by, then it is conceivable that the defence would be available. But we, like the judge, are in no position to say one way or another without having far greater detail as to the evidence still less not having heard the evidence. Further, we cannot say whether there may or may not be material before the jury as to the impossibility of obtaining a licence, because we stress again, unless there is material that a licence could not be obtained, the whole defence fails long before any questions of belief or the reasonableness of that belief arises.

27. (However) we do not think that the judge was in a position to rule out the defence for all time, although we emphasise we quite understand the basis upon which he did make that ruling at that time and are far from saying he was wrong to do so. But, he could not, merely on his own factual conclusions, prevent the defence from seeking to establish the first point, namely an opportunity to obtain a licence, unless and until he could be satisfied that there was no possibility of adducing evidence as to the second and third element, namely as to the cause of the decision and there being no possibility of avoiding the danger asserted in any other way. It is now said that there will be such material.

28. Our conclusion, therefore, is that, at this stage, the defence ought not be shut out from advancing the defence of necessity.

In cases involving doctors and patients necessity has an application to ensure that treatment can be given to patients who lack the capacity to consent. The application was first limited to cases where the proposed treatment was in the patient's best interests.

F v *West Berkshire HA*
[1990] 2 A.C. 1, House of Lords

A 36 year-old mentally handicapped woman, F., who resided as a voluntary in-patient in a mental hospital and who had the mental age of a small child, had formed a sexual relationship with a male patient. The hospital staff considered that she would be unable to cope with the effects of pregnancy and giving birth, and that, since all other forms of contraception were unsuitable and it was considered undesirable to further curtail F.'s limited freedom of movement in order to prevent sexual activity, it would be in her best interests to be sterilised. F.'s mother, who for the same reasons also wished her to be sterilised, issued an originating summons seeking a declaration from the court under RSC, Ord. 15, r. 16 , that such an

operation would not amount to an unlawful act by reason only of the absence of
F.'s consent. The judge granted the declaration sought. On appeal by the Official
Solicitor, the Court of Appeal upheld the judge's order.

On appeal by the Official Solicitor:

LORD GOFF OF CHIEVELEY: It is well established that, as a general rule, the performance of a medical operation upon a person without his or her consent is unlawful, as constituting both the crime of battery and the tort of trespass to the person. Furthermore, before Scott Baker J. and the Court of Appeal, it was common ground between the parties that there was no power in the court to give consent on behalf of F. to the proposed operation of sterilisation, or to dispense with the need for such consent.

It follows that, as was recognised in the courts below, if the operation upon F. is to be justified, it can only be justified on the applicable principles of common law. The argument of counsel revealed the startling fact that there is no English authority on the question whether as a matter of common law (and if so in what circumstances) medical treatment can lawfully be given to a person who is disabled by mental incapacity from consenting to it. Indeed, the matter goes further; for a comparable problem can arise in relation to persons of sound mind who are, for example, rendered unconscious in an accident or rendered speechless by a catastrophic stroke. All such persons may require medical treatment and, in some cases, surgical operations. All may require nursing care. In the case of mentally disordered persons, they may require care of a more basic kind – dressing, feeding, and so on – to assist them in their daily life, as well as routine treatment by doctors and dentists. It follows that, in my opinion, it is not possible to consider in isolation the lawfulness of the proposed operation of sterilisation in the present case. It is necessary first to ascertain the applicable common law principles and then to consider the question of sterilisation against the background of those principles. ...

I start with the fundamental principle, now long established, that every person's body is inviolate. As to this, I do not wish to depart from what I myself said in the judgment of the Divisional Court in *Collins* v *Wilcock* [1984] 1 W.L.R. 1172 , and in particular from the statement, at p. 1177, that the effect of this principle is that everybody is protected not only against physical injury but against any form of physical molestation.

Of course, as a general rule physical interference with another person's body is lawful if he consents to it; though in certain limited circumstances the public interest may require that his consent is not capable of rendering the act lawful. There are also specific cases where physical interference without consent may not be unlawful – chastisement of children, lawful arrest, self-defence, the prevention of crime, and so on. As I pointed out in *Collins* v *Wilcock* [1984] 1 W.L.R. 1172 , 1177, a broader exception has been created to allow for the exigencies of everyday life – jostling in a street or some other crowded place, social contact at parties, and such like. This exception has been said to be founded on implied consent, since those who go about in public places, or go to parties, may be taken to have impliedly consented to bodily contact of this kind. Today this rationalisation can be regarded as artificial; and in particular, it is difficult to impute consent to those who, by reason of their youth or mental disorder, are unable to give their consent. For this reason, I consider it more appropriate to regard such cases as falling within a general exception embracing all physical contact which is generally acceptable in the ordinary conduct of everyday life.

In the old days it used to be said that, for a touching of another's person to amount to a battery, it had to be a touching 'in anger' (see *Cole* v *Turner* (1794) 6 Mod. 149 , *per* Holt C.J.); and it has recently been said that the touching must be 'hostile' to have that effect (see *Wilson* v *Pringle* [1987] Q.B. 237, 253). I respectfully doubt whether that is correct. A prank that gets out of hand; an over-friendly slap on the back; surgical treatment by a surgeon who mistakenly thinks that the patient has consented to it – all these things may transcend the bounds of lawfulness, without being characterised as hostile. Indeed the suggested qualification is difficult to reconcile with the principle that any touching of another's body is, in the absence of lawful excuse, capable of amounting to a battery and a trespass. Furthermore, in the case of medical treatment, we have to bear well in mind the libertarian principle of self-determination which, to adopt the words of Cardozo J. (in *Schloendorff* v *Society of New York Hospital* (1914) 105 N.E. 92 , 93) recognises that:

'Every human being of adult years and sound mind has a right to determine what shall be done with his own body; and a surgeon who performs an operation without his patient's consent commits an assault...'

This principle has been reiterated in more recent years by Lord Reid in *S. v. McC. (orse. S.) and M. (D.S. intervener); W.* v *W.* [1972] A.C. 24 , 43.

It is against this background that I turn to consider the question whether, and if so when, medical treatment or care of a mentally disordered person who is, by reason of his incapacity, incapable of giving his consent, can be regarded as lawful. As is recognised in Cardozo J.'s statement of principle, and elsewhere (see e.g. *Sidaway* v *Board of Governors of the Bethlem Royal Hospital and the Maudsley Hospital* [1985] A.C. 871 , 882, *per* Lord Scarman), some relaxation of the law is required to accommodate persons of unsound mind. In *Wilson* v *Pringle* [1987] Q.B. 237 , the Court of Appeal considered that treatment or care of such persons may be regarded as lawful, as falling within the exception relating to physical contact which is generally acceptable in the ordinary conduct of everyday life. Again, I am with respect unable to agree. That exception is concerned with the ordinary events of everyday life – jostling in public places and such like - and affects all persons, whether or not they are capable of giving their consent. Medical treatment - even treatment for minor ailments – does not fall within that category of events. The general rule is that consent is necessary to render such treatment lawful. If such treatment administered without consent is not to be unlawful, it has to be justified on some other principle.

Upon what principle can medical treatment be justified when given without consent? We are searching for a principle upon which, in limited circumstances, recognition may be given to a need, in the interests of the patient, that treatment should be given to him in circumstances where he is (temporarily or permanently) disabled from consenting to it. It is this criterion of a need which points to the principle of necessity as providing justification.

That there exists in the common law a principle of necessity which may justify action which would otherwise be unlawful is not in doubt. But historically the principle has been seen to be restricted to two groups of cases, which have been called cases of public necessity and cases of private necessity. The former occurred when a man interfered with another man's property in the public interest - for example (in the days before we could dial 999 for the fire brigade) the destruction of another man's house to prevent the spread of a catastrophic fire, as indeed occurred in the Great Fire of London in 1666. The latter cases occurred when a man interfered with another's property to save his own person or property from imminent danger – for example, when he entered upon his neighbour's land without his consent, in order to prevent the spread of fire onto his own land.

There is, however, a third group of cases, which is also properly described as founded upon the principle of necessity and which is more pertinent to the resolution of the problem in the present case. These cases are concerned with action taken as a matter of necessity to assist another person without his consent. To give a simple example, a man who seizes another and forcibly drags him from the path of an oncoming vehicle, thereby saving him from injury or even death, commits no wrong. But there are many emanations of this principle, to be found scattered through the books. These are concerned not only with the preservation of the life or health of the assisted person, but also with the preservation of his property (sometimes an animal, sometimes an ordinary chattel) and even to certain conduct on his behalf in the administration of his affairs. Where there is a pre-existing relationship between the parties, the intervenor is usually said to act as an agent of necessity on behalf of the principal in whose interests he acts, and his action can often, with not too much artificiality, be referred to the pre-existing relationship between them. Whether the intervenor may be entitled either to reimbursement or to remuneration raises separate questions which are not relevant in the present case.

We are concerned here with action taken to preserve the life, health or well-being of another who is unable to consent to it. Such action is sometimes said to be justified as arising from an emergency; in Prosser and Keeton, *Handbook on Torts*, 5th ed. (1984), p. 117, the action is said to be privileged by the emergency. Doubtless, in the case of a person of sound mind, there will ordinarily have to be an emergency before such action taken without consent can be lawful; for otherwise there would be an opportunity to communicate with the assisted person and to seek his consent. But this is not always so; and indeed the historical origins of the principle of necessity do not point to emergency as such as providing the criterion of lawful intervention without consent. The old Roman doctrine of negotiorum gestio presupposed not so much an emergency as a prolonged absence of the dominus from home as justifying intervention by the gestor to administer his affairs. The most ancient group of cases in the common law, concerned with action taken by the master of a ship in distant parts in the interests of the shipowner, likewise found its origin in the difficulty of communication with the owner over a prolonged period of time – a difficulty overcome today by modern means of communication. In those cases, it was said that there had to be an emergency before the master could act as agent of necessity; though the emergency could well be of some duration. But when a person is rendered incapable of communication either permanently or over a considerable period of time (through illness or accident or mental disorder), it would be an unusual use of language to describe the case as one of 'permanent emergency' – if indeed such a state of affairs can properly be said to exist. In truth, the relevance of an emergency is that it may give rise to a necessity to act in the interests of the assisted person, without first obtaining his consent. Emergency is however not the criterion or even a pre-requisite; it is simply a frequent origin of the necessity which impels intervention. The principle is one of necessity, not of emergency.

We can derive some guidance as to the nature of the principle of necessity from the cases on agency of necessity in mercantile law. When reading those cases, however, we have to bear in mind that it was there considered that (since there was a pre-existing relationship between the parties) there was a duty on the part of the agent to act on his principal's behalf in an emergency. From these cases it appears that the principle of necessity connotes that circumstances have arisen in which there is a necessity for the agent to act on his principal's behalf at a time when it is in practice not possible for him to obtain his principal's instructions so to do. In such cases, it has been said that the agent must act bona fide in the interests of his principal: see *Prager v Blatspiel Stamp & Heacock Ltd.* [1924] 1 K.B. 566 , 572 *per* McCardie J. A broader statement of the principle is to be found in the advice of the Privy Council delivered by Sir Montague Smith in *Australasian Steam Navigation Co.* v *Morse* (1872) L.R. 4 P.C. 222, 230, in which he said:

> 'when by the force of circumstances a man has the duty cast upon him of taking some action for another, and under that obligation, adopts the course which, to the judgment of a wise and prudent man, is apparently the best for the interest of the persons for whom he acts in a given emergency, it may properly be said of the course so taken, that it was, in a mercantile sense, necessary to take it.'

In a sense, these statements overlap. But from them can be derived the basic requirements, applicable in these cases of necessity, that, to fall within the principle, not only (1) must there be a necessity to act when it is not practicable to communicate with the assisted person, but also (2) the action taken must be such as a reasonable person would in all the circumstances take, acting in the best interests of the assisted person.

On this statement of principle, I wish to observe that officious intervention cannot be justified by the principle of necessity. So intervention cannot be justified when another more appropriate person is available and willing to act; nor can it be justified when it is contrary to the known wishes of the assisted person, to the extent that he is capable of rationally forming such a wish. On the second limb of the principle, the introduction of the standard of a reasonable man should not in the present context be regarded as materially different from that of Sir Montague Smith's 'wise and prudent man,' because a reasonable man would, in the time available to him, proceed with wisdom and prudence before taking action in relation to another man's person or property without his consent. I shall have more to say on this point later. Subject to that, I hesitate at present to indulge in any greater refinement of the principle, being well aware of many problems which may arise in its application – problems which it is not necessary, for present purposes, to examine. But as a general rule, if the above criteria are fulfilled, interference with the assisted person's person or property (as the case may be) will not be unlawful. Take the example of a railway accident, in which injured passengers are trapped in the wreckage. It is this principle which may render lawful the actions of other citizens – railway staff, passengers or outsiders – who rush to give aid and comfort to the victims:

the surgeon who amputates the limb of an unconscious passenger to free him from the wreckage; the ambulance man who conveys him to hospital; the doctors and nurses who treat him and care for him while he is still unconscious. Take the example of an elderly person who suffers a stroke which renders him incapable of speech or movement. It is by virtue of this principle that the doctor who treats him, the nurse who cares for him, even the relative or friend or neighbour who comes in to look after him, will commit no wrong when he or she touches his body.

The two examples I have given illustrate, in the one case, an emergency, and in the other, a permanent or semi-permanent state of affairs. Another example of the latter kind is that of a mentally disordered person who is disabled from giving consent. I can see no good reason why the principle of necessity should not be applicable in his case as it is in the case of the victim of a stroke. Furthermore, in the case of a mentally disordered person, as in the case of a stroke victim, the permanent state of affairs calls for a wider range of care than may be requisite in an emergency which arises from accidental injury. When the state of affairs is permanent, or semi-permanent, action properly taken to preserve the life, health or well-being of the assisted person may well transcend such measures as surgical operation or substantial medical treatment and may extend to include such humdrum matters as routine medical or dental treatment, even simple care such as dressing and undressing and putting to bed.

Whether 'necessity' can justify the victimisation of an innocent has now arisen. It seems that it can but only if the innocent suffers harm as a side effect of an otherwise lawful act. Necessity does not entitle individuals to be used as a means to an end, as in forced blood transfusions or organ transplants.

Re A (Conjoined Twins: Medical Treatment)
[2001] 1 FLR 1, Court of Appeal

LORD JUSTICE WARD: In the past decade an increasing number of cases have come before the courts where the decision whether or not to permit or to refuse medical treatment can be a matter of life and death for the patient....

In this case the right answer is not at all as easy to find. I freely confess to having found it truly difficult to decide—difficult because of the scale of the tragedy for the parents and the twins, difficult for the seemingly irreconcilable conflicts of moral and ethical values and difficult because the search for settled legal principle has been especially arduous and conducted under real pressure of time....

It truly is a unique case. In a nutshell the problem is this. Jodie and Mary are conjoined twins. They each have their own brain, heart and lungs and other vital organs and they each have arms and legs. They are joined at the lower abdomen. Whilst not underplaying the surgical complexities, they can be successfully separated. But the operation will kill the weaker twin, Mary. That is because her lungs and heart are too deficient to oxygenate and pump blood through her body. Had she been born a singleton, she would not have been viable and resuscitation would have been abandoned. She would have died shortly after her birth. She is alive only because a common artery enables her sister, who is stronger, to circulate life sustaining oxygenated blood for both of them. Separation would require the clamping and then the severing of that common artery. Within minutes of doing so Mary will die. Yet if the operation does not take place, both will die within three to six months, or perhaps a little longer, because Jodie's heart will eventually fail. The parents cannot bring themselves to consent to the operation. The twins are equal in their eyes and they cannot agree to kill one even to save the other. As devout Roman Catholics they sincerely believe that it is God's will that their children are afflicted as they are and they must be left in God's hands. The doctors are convinced they can carry out the operation so as to give Jodie a life which will be worthwhile. So the hospital sought a declaration that the operation may be lawfully carried out. Johnson J. granted it on 25th August 2000. The parents applied to us for permission to appeal against his order. We have given that permission and this is my judgment on their appeal.
...

3. The interface with the criminal law

It should not need stating that the court cannot approve of a course of action which may be unlaw-ful. The stark fact has to be faced in this case that to operate to separate the twins may be to murder Mary. It seems to me, however, that the question of what is in the best interests of the child is a dis-crete question from whether what is proposed to be done is unlawful. A patient in terminal decline, racked with pain which treatment may not be able fully to alleviate, may beg to die and it may be said—at least by some—that it is in his best interests that he should be allowed to do so, but that would not justify unlawfully killing him. In my judgment, although the nature of what is proposed to be done has a bearing on how one ascertains where the patient's best interests lie, the ascertain-ment of those interests is the first but a separate stage of the court's task. If the operation is in the best interests of a child patient, then the court can, as Stage 1 of the task which it has to undertake, give leave for the operation to be undertaken provided, and this will become Stage 2 of the court's task, it can be lawfully done.

. . .

WALKER LJ:

. . .

2. Is there some immunity for doctors?

Archbold 2000: Criminal Pleading Evidence & Practice, para. 19–38, states that:—

> 'Bona fide medical or surgical treatment is not "unlawful" and therefore death resulting there-from does not amount to murder, even though death or serious injury is foreseen as a probable consequence. Nor does it amount to manslaughter, unless the person giving the treatment has been guilty of "gross negligence"'.

No authority is given for this sweeping statement. It is true that in *Gillick* Lord Scarman said at p. 190:—

> 'The bona fide exercise by a doctor of his clinical judgment must be a complete negation of the guilty mind which is an essential ingredient of the criminal offence of aiding and abetting the commission of unlawful sexual intercourse.'

Lord Mustill speaks of it in *Bland*. Yet hanging over *Bland* is the spectre of murder. To have crossed the Rubicon would have been to murder. I, therefore, approach the question of lawfulness of the proposed separation on the basis that, whatever immunity doctors do enjoy, they have no com-plete immunity. I have to be satisfied that in this case they will not be guilty of unlawfully killing Mary by active intervention—and perhaps of unlawfully killing Jodie by omitting to act in her interests if there is a duty upon them to do so.

. . .

7.1 The search for settled principle

The search for settled principle is difficult where the law is as uncertain in this area as Brooke L.J.'s masterly analysis has shown it to be. Doing the best I can, I have come to these conclusions.

7.2 Necessity

Necessity in the *Dudley and Stephens* sense arises where A. kills B. to save his own life. The threat to A.'s life is posed by the circumstances, rather than an act of threat by B. on A. in conventional self-defence terms.

7.3 Duress

Similar considerations apply to duress. There is, of course, a difference between them but as Lord Hailsham of St. Marylebone L.C. said in *Reg.* v *Howe* [1987] 1 A.C. 417, 427:—

> 'This, however, is, in my view a distinction without a relevant difference, since on this view dur-ess is only that species of the genus of necessity which is caused by wrongful threat. I cannot see that there is any way in which a person of ordinary fortitude can be excused from one type of pressure on his will rather than the other.'

7.4   The policy of the law

The policy of the law is to prevent A. being judge in his own cause of the value of his life over B.'s life or his loved one C.'s life, and then being executioner as well. The policy of the law was expressed in similar terms in Hale's Pleas of the Crown (1736), Vol. 1, p. 51, and Blackstone, Commentaries on the Laws of England (1857 Ed.) Vol. 4, p. 28. Blackstone wrote that a man under duress 'ought rather to die himself than escape by the murder of an innocent'. The sanctity of life and the inherent equality of all life prevails. ..

It is . . . necessary to state two important features of this case.

The first important feature is that the doctors cannot be denied a right of choice if they are under a duty to choose. They are under a duty to Mary not to operate because it will kill Mary, but they are under a duty to Jodie to operate because not to do so will kill her. It is important to stress that it makes no difference whether the killing is by act or by omission. That is a distinction without a difference . . .

The second reason why the right of choice should be given to the doctors is that the proposed operation would not in any event offend the sanctity of life principle. That principle may be expressed in different ways but they all amount to the same thing. Some might say that it demands that each life is to be protected from unjust attack. . . . The reality here—harsh as it is to state it, and unnatural as it is that it should be happening—is that Mary is killing Jodie. That is the effect of the incontrovertible medical evidence and it is common ground in the case. Mary uses Jodie's heart and lungs to receive and use Jodie's oxygenated blood. This will cause Jodie's heart to fail and cause Jodie's death as surely as a slow drip of poison. How can it be just that Jodie should be required to tolerate that state of affairs? One does not need to label Mary with the American terminology which would paint her to be 'an unjust aggressor', which I feel is wholly inappropriate language for the sad and helpless position in which Mary finds herself. I have no difficulty in agreeing that this unique happening cannot be said to be unlawful. . . . I can see no difference in essence between . . . resort to legitimate self-defence and the doctors coming to Jodie's defence and removing the threat of fatal harm to her presented by Mary's draining her life-blood. The availability of such a plea of quasi self-defence, modified to meet the quite exceptional circumstances nature has inflicted on the twins, makes intervention by the doctors lawful.

8. Conclusion

I conclude that the operation which I would permit can be lawfully carried out.

LORD JUSTICE BROOKE: . . .

I have considered very carefully the policy reasons for the decision in *R* v *Dudley and Stephens*, supported as it was by the House of Lords in *R* v *Howe*. These are, in short, that there were two insuperable objections to the proposition that necessity might be available as a defence for the Mignonette sailors. The first objection was evident in the court's questions: Who is to be the judge of this sort of necessity? By what measure is the comparative value of lives to be measured? The second objection was that to permit such a defence would mark an absolute divorce of law from morality.

In my judgment, neither of these objections are dispositive of the present case. Mary is, sadly, self-designated for a very early death. Nobody can extend her life beyond a very short span. Because her heart, brain and lungs are for all practical purposes useless, nobody would have even tried to extend her life artificially if she had not, fortuitously, been deriving oxygenated blood from her sister's bloodstream.

It is true that there are those who believe most sincerely—and the Archbishop of Westminster is among them—that it would be an immoral act to save Jodie, if by saving Jodie one must end Mary's life before its brief allotted span is complete. For those who share this philosophy, the law, recently approved by Parliament, which permits abortion at any time up to the time of birth if the conditions set out in Section 1(1)(d) of the Abortion Act 1967 (as substituted) are satisfied, is equally repugnant. But there are also those who believe with equal sincerity that it would be immoral not to assist Jodie if there is a good prospect that she might live a happy and fulfilled life if this operation is performed. The court is not equipped to choose between these competing philosophies. All that a court can say is that it is not at all obvious that this is the sort of clear-cut case, marking an absolute divorce from law and morality, which was of such concern to Lord Coleridge and his fellow judges.

There are sound reasons for holding that the existence of an emergency in the normal sense of the word is not an essential prerequisite for the application of the doctrine of necessity. The principle is one of necessity, not emergency: see Lord Goff (in *In re F* at p 75D), the Law Commission in its recent report (Law Com No 218, paras 35.5 to 35.6), and Wilson J in *Perka* (at p 33).

There are also sound reasons for holding that the threat which constitutes the harm to be avoided does not have to be equated with 'unjust aggression', as Professor Glanville Williams has made clear in Section 26.3 of the 1983 edition of his book. None of the formulations of the doctrine of necessity which I have noted in this judgment make any such requirement: in this respect it is different from the doctrine of private defence.

If a sacrificial separation operation on conjoined twins were to be permitted in circumstances like these, there need be no room for the concern felt by Sir James Stephen that people would be too ready to avail themselves of exceptions to the law which they might suppose to apply to their cases (at the risk of other people's lives). Such an operation is, and is always likely to be, an exceptionally rare event, and because the medical literature shows that it is an operation to be avoided at all costs in the neonatal stage, there will be in practically every case the opportunity for the doctors to place the relevant facts before a court for approval (or otherwise) before the operation is attempted.

According to Sir James Stephen, there are three necessary requirements for the application of the doctrine of necessity:

(i) the act is needed to avoid inevitable and irreparable evil;
(ii) no more should be done than is reasonably necessary for the purpose to be achieved;
(iii) the evil inflicted must not be disproportionate to the evil avoided.

Given that the principles of modern family law point irresistibly to the conclusion that the interests of Jodie must be preferred to the conflicting interests of Mary, I consider that all three of these requirements are satisfied in this case.

Finally, the doctrine of the sanctity of life respects the integrity of the human body. The proposed operation would give these children's bodies the integrity which nature denied them.

For these reasons I, too, would dismiss this appeal.

Appeal dismissed.

■ NOTES AND QUESTIONS

1. *Re A* was an extremely difficult case not only because of its unusual and tragic facts but also because it raised thorny questions at the intersection of Medical Law, Family Law and Criminal Law. Further complicating the case was the fact that fundamental moral and religious issues also came into play. In respect of the latter, the court received submissions from the Roman Catholic Archbishop of Westminster. As summarised by Lord Justice Walker:

   Those submissions make five salient points based on Roman Catholic faith and morality. These are, first, that human life is sacred and inviolable. Secondly, a person's bodily integrity should not be invaded when that can confer no benefit. Thirdly, the duty to preserve one person's life cannot without grave injustice be effected by a lethal assault on another. Fourthly, there is no duty on doctors to resort to extraordinary means in order to preserve life. Fifthly, the rights of parents should be overridden only where they are clearly 'contrary to what is strictly owing to their children'.

   Did the Archbishop's submissions clarify – or further complicate – the resolution of the legal issues?

2. The parents of the twins refused to give their consent to the operation, maintaining that their children's fate should rest with God. What weight should have been given to their views?

3. In Family Law, the paramount consideration in a case involving a child is the child's best interest. Does this principle advance the analysis of the criminal law issues in the case? Were the interests of the twins in irreconcilable conflict? Was the Court ineluctably drawn into balancing the interests of Jodie and Mary?

508 Exculpatory Conditions and Defences

4. Consider the dilemma faced by the doctors who have an ethical and professional duty to preserve life. If they had failed to operate, Jodie would have died; if they operated, Mary would die. Legally, they could be liable for Jodie's death as a result of their failure to operate, or Mary's death if they performed the operation. What were they to do?

5. Is there a difference between the *sanctity* of life and the *quality* of life that is relevant to the analysis of the necessity issue in *Re A*? Was Mary 'designated for death' in any event? Should this matter?

6. Doctors who seek to do what is in the best interest of their patients do not fit within the ordinary person's image of a cold-blooded murderer, even if their actions have the effect of shortening a patient's life or causing the patient's death. Whether or not one agrees with the doctor's decision, most would accept that the doctor has acted from an honourable rather than a dishonourable motive. Few doctors are prosecuted for homicide although off-the-record many will admit to having helped terminal patients to die. The search to solve the 'doctor's dilemma' seems to have led to an increasing willingness to recognise a defence of 'medical necessity.' The process may have begun with *R v Bourne* [1939] 1 KB 687, where the court recognised necessity as a defence where a doctor had committed an illegal abortion to preserve the life of a rape victim. Other more recent cases which indicate a willingness of the courts to accept such a defence include *Gillick* v *West Norfolk and Wisbech AHA* [1986] AC 112, House of Lords (provision of contraceptives to minor); *F* v *West Berkshire Health Authority* [1990] 2 AC 1, House of Lords (sterilisation of a mental patient because of risk of pregnancy that might be traumatic for the patient); *R* v *Bournewood Community and Mental Heath NHS Trust* [1998] 3 All ER 289, House of Lords (detention and treatment of mentally incompetent person). While none of the above cases involved causing a patient's death, the same could not be said of *Airedale NHS Trust* v *Bland*, p. 69 and *Re A (conjoined twins)*. These may represent the latest chapters in the development of the 'medical necessity' defence. Is the defence of 'medical necessity' an excuse or a justification?

7. Is the defence of necessity in *S & Anor, R v* (499 supra) really not a defence of duress of circumstances?

While the necessity defence traces its origins to the common law, many contemporary statutes, such as the Control of Pollution Act 1974, specifically recognise a necessity defence. Other statutes, such as the Criminal Damage Act 1971, are said to recognise the defence by implication.

CRIMINAL DAMAGE ACT 1971

1.—(1) person who without lawful excuse destroys or damages any property belonging to another intending to destroy or damage any such property or being reckless as to whether any such property would be destroyed or damaged shall be guilty of an offence.

■ NOTES AND QUESTIONS

1. The key phrase in the Criminal Damage Act 1971 is 'without lawful excuse'. The question is whether if one destroys property in a situation of necessity,

the destruction is with 'lawful excuse.' Section (5) of the Act, which provides examples of situations where a lawful excuse will be found, concludes by stating that 'this section shall not be construed as casting doubt on any defence recognised by law as a defence to criminal charges.' Does this provide for the existence of a necessity defence to a charge of criminal damage? Or does it simply re-raise the question of whether a necessity defence exists in law?

2. Some crimes contain the word 'unlawful' in describing the *actus reus* of the offence. It might at first blush seem that the term is unnecessary and otiose, since an *actus reus* would seem by definition to be 'unlawful'. The argument that may give content to 'unlawful' is that the term should be interpreted to mean 'without lawful excuse or justification'.

D: Duress of circumstances

For many years there was debate as to whether the defence of necessity actually existed. That issue has for practical purposes now become moot. Beginning in the mid–1980s, the courts began to develop the independent defence of duress of circumstances. This defence differs from duress in several respects. In the classic case of duress the defendant is ordered to commit a crime by a third party, who threatens him with death or serious injury if he does not comply. In contrast, a defence of duress of circumstances is not dependent upon the defendant being ordered to commit a crime. The defendant chooses what crime to commit based on the 'circumstances'.

As in necessity, the defendant claims duress of circumstances based on the pressure of external conditions. In contrast to necessity, however, the pressure comes not from natural events, but from a human source. Most of the initial cases, interestingly, involved motor vehicle offences.

R v Willer
[1987] RTR 22, Court of Appeal

WATKINS LJ: The appellant is 19 years of age. He is of excellent character. He appeals against his conviction for reckless driving.

What happened to bring him to conviction was that at about 9.30 p.m. on 24 April 1984 he and two school friends, Martin and Richard Jordan, were driving around the town of Hemel Hempstead in the appellant's Vauxhall Cavalier car. They heard a broadcast on the car's, what is known as, Citizen Band radio. From what they heard, the appellant was persuaded to drive to a shopping precinct at Leverstock Green. There they expected to meet another enthusiast of Citizen Band radio. At one stage of the journey the appellant had to drive up a very narrow turning off a road called Green Lane in order to keep his assignment with the other enthusiast mentioned. As he made his way up what is called Leaside, which is, as we see from the photographs, an alleyway, he was suddenly confronted with a gang of shouting and bawling youths, 20 to 30 strong. He heard one of them shouting: 'I'll kill you Willer'—and—'I'll kill you Jordan'.

He stopped and tried to turn the car round. These youths surrounded him. They banged on the car. A youth called Smallpiece opened the rear door of the car and dived upon Richard Jordan who was sitting in the back of it. Martin Jordan, his brother, got out of the front seat to help. The appellant realised that the only conceivable way he could somehow escape from this formidable gang of youths, who were obviously bent upon doing further violence, was to mount the pavement on the right-hand side of Leaside and on the pavement to drive through a small gap into the front of the shopping precinct. That he did quite slowly, it was accepted, at about 10 mph.

Having gained the security, if that was what it could be called, of the front of the shopping precinct and moved somewhere in the vicinity of a car park which was there, he realised that he had lost one of his companions. So he turned the car round and drove very slowly, at five mph, back towards the gap and through it. He had to make a couple of turns in his search for his missing companion. All this time Smallpiece was in the back of the car fighting with Richard Jordan. With that going on the appellant drove to the local police station and reported the matter. For his pains he was prosecuted—a very surprising turn of events indeed.

He was charged with reckless driving. Very properly, so it seems to us, he chose trial by jury. He appeared at the Crown Court of St Albans on 16 April 1985. The trial was presided over by Mr Curwen, an assistant recorder. During the course of the trial an argument developed between the assistant recorder and counsel over the question whether or not the defence of necessity was available to the appellant. The assistant recorder ruled that it was not. . . .

. . . The appellant in fact said: 'I could do no other in the face of this hostility than to take the right turn as I did, to mount the pavement and to drive through the gap out of further harm's way—harm to person and harm to my property'. Thus the defence of duress, it seems to us, arose but was not pursued. What ought to have happened here, therefore, was that the assistant recorder on those facts should have directed that he would leave to the jury the question whether or not on the outward or the return journey, or both, the appellant was wholly driven by force of circumstances into doing what he did and did not drive the car otherwise than under that form of compulsion.

R v Martin
[1989] 1 All ER 652, Court of Appeal

SIMON BROWN LJ: . . . The circumstances which the appellant desired to advance by way of defence of necessity were essentially these. His wife has suicidal tendencies. On a number of occasions before the day in question she had attempted to take her own life. On the day in question her son, the appellant's stepson, had overslept. He had done so to the extent that he was bound to be late for work and at risk of losing his job unless, so it was asserted, the appellant drove him to work. The appellant's wife was distraught. She was shouting, screaming, banging her head against a wall. More particularly, it is said she was threatening suicide unless the appellant drove the boy to work.

The defence had a statement from a doctor which expressed the opinion that 'in view of her mental condition it is likely that Mrs Martin would have attempted suicide if her husband did not drive her son to work'.

The appellant's case on the facts was that he genuinely, and he would suggest reasonably, believed that his wife would carry out that threat unless he did as she demanded. Despite his disqualification he therefore drove the boy. He was in fact apprehended by the police within about a quarter of a mile of the house.

Sceptically though one may regard that defence on the facts (and there were, we would observe, striking difficulties about the detailed evidence when it came finally to be given before the judge in mitigation), the sole question before this court is whether those facts, had the jury accepted they were or might be true, amounted in law to a defence. If they did, then the appellant was entitled to a trial of the issue before the jury. The jury would of course have had to be directed properly on the precise scope and nature of the defence, but the decision on the facts would have been for them. As it was, such a defence was pre-empted by the ruling. Should it have been?

In our judgment the answer is plainly not. The authorities are now clear. Their effect is perhaps most conveniently to be found in the judgment of this court in *R v Conway* [1988] 3 All ER 1025. The decision reviews earlier relevant authorities.

The principles may be summarised thus: first, English law does, in extreme circumstances, recognise a defence of necessity. Most commonly this defence arises as duress, that is pressure on the accused's will from the wrongful threats or violence of another. Equally however it can arise from other objective dangers threatening the accused or others. Arising thus it is conveniently called 'duress of circumstances'.

Second, the defence is available only if, from an objective standpoint, the accused can be said to be acting reasonably and proportionately in order to avoid a threat of death or serious injury.

Third, assuming the defence to be open to the accused on his account of the facts, the issue should be left to the jury, who should be directed to determine these two questions: first, was the accused, or may he have been, impelled to act as he did because as a result of what he reasonably believed to be the situation he had good cause to fear that otherwise death or serious physical injury would result; second, if so, would a sober person of reasonable firmness, sharing the characteristics of the accused, have responded to that situation by acting as the accused acted? If the answer to both those questions was Yes, then the jury would acquit; the defence of necessity would have been established.

That the defence is available in cases of reckless driving is established by *R* v *Conway* itself and indeed by an earlier decision of the court in *R* v *Willer* (1986) 83 Cr App R 225. *R* v *Conway* is authority also for the proposition that the scope of the defence is no wider for reckless driving than for other serious offences. As was pointed out in the judgment, 'reckless driving can kill' (see [1988] 3 All ER 1025 at 1029).

We see no material distinction between offences of reckless driving and driving whilst disqualified so far as the application and scope of this defence is concerned. Equally we can see no distinction in principle between various threats of death; it matters not whether the risk of death is by murder or by suicide or indeed by accident. One can illustrate the latter by considering a disqualified driver being driven by his wife, she suffering a heart attack in remote countryside and he needing instantly to get her to hospital.

It follows from this that the judge quite clearly did come to a wrong decision on the question of law, and the appellant should have been permitted to raise this defence for what it was worth before the jury.

It is in our judgment a great pity that that course was not taken. It is difficult to believe that any jury would have swallowed the improbable story which this appellant desired to advance. There was, it emerged when evidence was given in mitigation, in the house at the time a brother of the boy who was late for work, who was licensed to drive, and available to do so; the suggestion was that he would not take his brother because of 'a lot of aggravation in the house between them'. It is a further striking fact that when apprehended by the police this appellant was wholly silent as to why on this occasion he had felt constrained to drive. But those considerations, in our judgment, were essentially for the jury, and we have concluded, although not without hesitation, that it would be inappropriate here to apply the proviso to s. 2(1) of the 1968 Act.

In the result this appeal must be allowed and the conviction quashed.

Director of Public Prosecutions v Lorraine Tomkinson (2001)
[2001] EWHC Admin 182, DC (Latham LJ, Potts J) 16/2/2001

The Director of Public Prosecutions ('DPP') appealed by the way of case stated against a decision by magistrates to dismiss an information laid against the respondent ('D'), which alleged an offence of driving a motor vehicle having consumed excess alcohol contrary to s.5 Road Traffic Act 1988. D had been physically attacked by her husband in the marital home, who then left her alone, injured. Before leaving, D's husband destroyed the telephones in the house, warning her not to be at home when he returned. D did not know anyone in the area. Since she was frightened for her life a distance of 72 miles to her former home town. The magistrates accepted D's plea of necessity by way of duress of circumstances. The DPP submitted that: (i) there was no credible evidence to support the defence of duress; and (ii) had such evidence existed, it was no longer available by the time of D's arrest.

HELD: This case was distinguished from *Director of Public Prosecutions* v *Bell* (1992) RTR 334, where the defendant had escaped his terror of serious physical harm by driving, despite having been drinking all the evening. However, there was no evidence that he had driven further than necessary. In the present case, D had driven further than had been necessary to escape the danger she had sought to avoid. The facts of this case had more in common with those of *Director of Public Prosecutions* v *Jones* (1990) RTR 33, where the defendant drove further than was necessary and the Court of Appeal held that the defendant could not rely on the defence of duress. Therefore, the magistrates had not been correct in concluding that the defence of duress was available to D.

Appeal allowed.

R v Pommell

(1995) 2 Cr App R 607, Court of Appeal

KENNEDY LJ: . . . On October 27, 1993 the appellant appeared before the Crown Court at Woolwich charged on two indictments. The first indictment alleged in Count 1 that on June 4, 1993 he had, without authority, in his possession a firearm, namely a sub-machine gun, contrary to section 5(1)(a) of the Firearms Act 1968. The second count alleged that on the same date he had possession of 55 rounds of ammunition without a firearm certificate, contrary to section 1(1)(b) of the same Act. In the second indictment there was one count. It alleged that on the same date he had possession of counterfeit currency notes. To that second indictment he pleaded guilty, and no issue now arises in relation to it. However, so far as the first indictment is concerned, the trial judge indicated at the outset of the proceedings his view that the defence which it was proposed to advance would not amount to a defence in law. Having heard submissions he so ruled, and the appellant then, on re-arraignment, entered pleas of guilty to both counts. As to those counts he now appeals against conviction by leave of the full court.

. . . [T]he prosecution case was that at about 8 a.m. on June 4, 1993 police officers entered the appellant's home to execute a search warrant. He was found lying in bed with a loaded gun in his right hand. He was asked if the gun was his and he replied, 'I took it off a geezer who was going to do some people some damage with it'. In the same bedroom police officers found a brown holdall containing ammunition. The appellant was arrested and interviewed. When interviewed he was asked to explain his possession of the gun, and he said:

> Last night someone come round to see me, this guy by the name of Erroll, and he had it with him with the intention to go and shoot some people because they had killed his friend and he wanted to kill their girlfriends and relatives and kids, and I persuaded him, I took it off him and told him that it's not right to do that.

The appellant went on to say that Erroll had called between 12.30 a.m. and 1 a.m. and, after he left, the appellant took the gun upstairs and kept it from his girlfriend and took the bullets out of it. He appears to have achieved this by removing a loaded magazine containing 23 rounds. He then decided to wait until morning and decided to put the bullets back into it. To do this he must have inserted the loaded magazine back into the gun. He agreed that at the time of his arrest he was lying in bed with the gun against his leg because, he said, he did not want his girlfriend to see it. He said that he was going to hand the gun to his brother so that he could hand it to the police because his brother gets on with the police and had handed in guns in the past. For present purposes, it is unnecessary to look at the interview in any greater detail.

We turn now to the events of October 27, 1993. In the course of an *ex parte* application as to discovery, prosecuting counsel advised the judge that the defence was going to be that the defendant had the weapon in his possession, holding it for another, so that the defence might be described as a defence of necessity. . . .

That brings us to the central question of whether on the facts, as they emerged from the prosecution papers, the judge was entitled to conclude that as a matter of law the defence of necessity could not be established.

The two provisions of the Firearms Act 1968 with which we are concerned in this case, so far as they are material, read as follows:

Section 1(1) . . . it is an offence for a person—. . .

(b) to have in his possession . . . any ammunition to which this section applies without holding a firearm certificate in force at the time, . . .

Section 5(1) A person commits an offence if, without the authority of the Defence Council, he has in his possession, . . .

(a) any firearm which is so designed or adapted that two or more missiles can be successively discharged without repeated pressure on the trigger, . . .

We accept that the provisions of the Firearms Act are intended to be strictly enforced . . . .

. . . There is an obvious attraction in the argument that if A finds B in possession of a gun which he is about to use to commit a crime, and if A is then able to persuade B to hand over the gun so that A may hand it to the police, A should not immediately upon taking possession of the gun become guilty of a criminal offence . . . .

The strength of the argument that a person ought to be permitted to breach the letter of the criminal law in order to prevent a greater evil befalling himself or others has long been recognised (see, for example, *Stephen's Digest of Criminal Law*), but it has, in English law, not given rise to a recognised general defence of necessity . . . As Dickson J said in the Supreme Court of Canada in *Perka et al v R* (1985) 13 DLR (4th) 1, at p. 14:

'. . . no system of positive law can recognise any principle which would entitle a person to violate the law because on his view the law conflicted with some higher social value'. The Criminal Code has specified a number of identifiable situations in which an actor is justified in committing what would otherwise be a criminal offence. To go beyond that and hold that ostensibly illegal acts can be validated on the basis of their expediency, would import an undue subjectivity into the criminal law. It would invite the courts to second-guess the legislature and to assess the relative merits of social policies underlying criminal prohibitions.

However, that does not really deal with the situation where someone commendably infringes a regulation in order to prevent another person from committing what everyone would accept as being a greater evil with a gun. In that situation it cannot be satisfactory to leave it to the prosecuting authority not to prosecute, or to individual courts to grant an absolute discharge. The authority may, as in the present case, prosecute because it is not satisfied that the defendant is telling the truth, and then, even if he is vindicated and given an absolute discharge, he is left with a criminal conviction which, for some purposes, would be recognised as such.

It was, as it seems to us, to meet this difficulty that the limited defence of duress of circumstances has been developed in English law in relation to road traffic offences. It was first recognised in *R v Willer* (1986) 83 Cr App R 225, where the accused drove onto a pavement and in and out of a shopping centre in order to escape a gang of youths seeking to attack him and his passenger. *Willer* was followed and applied in *R v Conway* (1989) 88 Cr App R 159, in which the Court of Appeal quashed a conviction on a charge of reckless driving. Having considered existing authorities, textbooks and the proposals of the Law Commission, the Court in that case said at p. 164:

. . . it is still not clear whether there is a general defence of necessity or, if there is, what are the circumstances in which it is available.

In our judgment, that is still the position, but the Court in *Conway* went on to say that necessity can be a defence to a charge of reckless driving where the facts establish duress of circumstances, that is to say when the defendant is constrained to drive as he did to avoid death or serious bodily harm to himself or some other person.

Then came *Martin*, a decision to which we referred earlier in this judgment, and *DPP v Bell* [1992] RTR 335, where the defendant, whose alcohol level was over the prescribed limit, was pursued to his car and, fearing serious injury, drove some distance down the road. The Crown Court allowed his appeal on the basis of duress of circumstances, and an appeal by way of case stated was dismissed. The Divisional Court particularly noted the finding of fact that the appellant drove only some distance down the road and not, for example, all the way home, so that the defence of duress of circumstances continued to avail him. In *DPP* v *Jones* [1990] RTR 33, it was held that any defence of necessity available to a driver would cease to be available if he drove for a longer period than necessary. Commenting on the case of *Bell*, Professor Sir John Smith has written:

> All the cases so far have concerned road traffic offences but there are no grounds for suppos-ing that the defence is limited to that kind of case. On the contrary, the defence, being closely related to the defence of duress by threats, appears to be general, applying to all crimes except murder, attempted murder and some forms of treason, ...': see [1992] Crim LR 176.

We agree.

7. Conclusion

That leads to the conclusion that in the present case the defence was open to the appellant in respect of his acquisition of the gun. The jury would have to be directed to determine the two ques-tions identified in the passage which we have cited from the judgment in *Martin*. That leaves the question as to his continued possession of the gun thereafter. In our judgment, the test laid down in *Martin* is not necessarily the appropriate test for determining whether a person continues to have a defence available to him. For example, a person takes a gun off another in the circumstances in which this appellant says he did and then locks it away in a safe with a view to safeguarding it while the police are informed. When the gun is in the safe, the test laid down in *Martin* may not be satis-fied: there would then be no immediate fear of death or serious injury. In our judgment, a person who has taken possession of a gun in circumstances where he has the defence of duress by circum-stances must 'desist from committing the crime as soon as he reasonably can' ...

... Can it be said, in this case, that there was no evidence upon which a jury could have reached the conclusion that the appellant did desist, or may have desisted, as soon as he reasonably could? In answering this question, the jury would have to have regard to the delay that had occurred between, on the appellant's account, his acquisition of the gun and ammunition at 12.30 to 1 a.m., and the arrival of the police some hours later. The appellant has offered an explanation for that delay, but, as it seems to us, the defence of duress of circumstances could not avail him once a rea-sonable person in his position would have known that the duress, in this case the need to obtain and retain the firearm, had ceased. In the present case the judge said that the failure of the appellant to go immediately to the police 'robs him of a defence'. We accept that in some cases a delay, espe-cially if unexplained, may be such as to make it clear that any duress must have ceased to operate, in which case the judge would be entitled to conclude that even on the defendant's own account of the facts, the defence was not open to him. There would then be no reason to leave the issue to the jury. However, the situation does not seem to us to have been sufficiently clear cut to make that an appropriate step in the present case. In the first place, the delay of a few hours overnight might not be regarded as being unduly long and, secondly, the defendant did offer an explanation for it, therefore, in our judgment, the proposed defence should have been left to the jury.

We have considered whether the reloading of the gun and the fact that the appellant had the gun in his bed deprived him of the defence. Must a person who has acquired a gun in circumstances in which he has the defence of duress of circumstances not only desist from committing the offence as soon as he reasonably can but, in the meanwhile, act in a reasonable manner with the gun? The answer is that if he does not do so, it will be difficult for the court to accept that he desisted from committing the offence as soon as he reasonably could. Therefore, in our judgment, the acts of reloading and putting the gun in the bed do not of themselves deprive him of the defence, but are matters which may be taken into account by the jury in deciding the issues to which we have already made reference.

■ NOTES AND QUESTIONS

1. The defendant in *Willer* took it upon himself to violate the law because of his perceived fear that to do otherwise would have resulted in serious bodily harm. Should it matter whether his judgment was correct? Reasonable?

2. Duress of circumstances can arise from innocent circumstances. For example, while driving along a street within the speed limit, a child suddenly darts into the road. To avoid hitting the child, you veer to the right and into the house on the side of the street, causing damage. If charged with criminal damage, should you not be able to plead duress of circumstances?

3. May the defence of duress although originally available, be lost if the threat evaporates? What does *Pommell* have to say on this issue?

4. Is one justified in speeding on a deserted road to take the victim of an accident to the hospital? What if the driver caused the accident? Can one speed in order not to be late for an important appointment? In order not to miss one's criminal law lecture? Should the reasons for 'being late' matter?

E: Self-defence, defence of others and crime prevention

As a practical matter, one who is attacked will instinctively take self-defensive actions. The law gives recognition to this quasi-automatic response by allowing a defence to criminal charges.

So too if one acts not from selfish but from altruistic motives and goes to the aid of a victim who is the subject of an attack. Indeed, there are many who would argue that the law should encourage citizens to help one another, and to deny a defence in this situation would be to discourage such assistance. Nonetheless, the law has proceeded cautiously in this area, not wanting to give too great a license to vigilantes who are prepared to act first and discover the facts later.

Self-defence and defence of another are similar to duress, necessity and duress of circumstances in some respects but different in others. All involve choice-of-evils situation. All are affirmative defences which do not come into play until the elements of the crime have been established by the prosecutor. None of the defences seeks to negate *mens rea* or any other element of the crime (although there are some academics who have maintained that the absence of excuse or justification is part of the *actus reus*). The defences are of the all-or-nothing variety in that they either succeed or fail, but will not serve as a basis for reducing the seriousness of the crime, as do provocation and diminished responsibility.

On the other hand, self-defence and defence of another are distinguishable from duress, necessity and duress of circumstances. The latter are defences of excuse. The actions of one who is attacked or who goes to the defence of another who has been attacked, are said to be 'justified'. This important distinction explains why many of the limitations which have arisen in respect of duress, necessity and duress of circumstances have not been extended to the defences of self-defence and defence of another. So, for example, one can raise self-defence or defence of another to a charge of murder. Nor does one have to be defending against death or serious bodily harm to invoke these defences.

(i) Common provisions

The law on self-defence and defence of others, while of common law origin, has now been codified in the Criminal Justice and Immigration Act 2008, s. 76 (hereafter CJIA). The overlapping and quite similar law relating to crime prevention, which had previously been codified in the Criminal Law Act 1967, has now also been incorporated into the CJIA.

CRIMINAL JUSTICE AND IMMIGRATION ACT 2008

76. Reasonable force for purposes of self-defence etc.

(1) This section applies where in proceedings for an offence—
   (a) an issue arises as to whether a person charged with the offence ("D") is entitled to rely on a defence within subsection (2), and
   (b) the question arises whether the degree of force used by D against a person ("V") was reasonable in the circumstances.

(2) The defences are—
   (a) the common law defence of self-defence; and
   (b) the defences provided by section 3(1) of the Criminal Law Act 1967 (c. 58) or section 3(1) of the Criminal Law Act (Northern Ireland) 1967 (c. 18 (N.I.)) (use of force in prevention of crime or making arrest).

(3) The question whether the degree of force used by D was reasonable in the circumstances is to be decided by reference to the circumstances as D believed them to be, and subsections (4) to (8) also apply in connection with deciding that question.

(4) If D claims to have held a particular belief as regards the existence of any circumstances—
   (a) the reasonableness or otherwise of that belief is relevant to the question whether D genuinely held it; but
   (b) if it is determined that D did genuinely hold it, D is entitled to rely on it for the purposes of subsection (3), whether or not—
      (i) it was mistaken, or
      (ii) (if it was mistaken) the mistake was a reasonable one to have made.

(5) But subsection (4)(b) does not enable D to rely on any mistaken belief attributable to intoxication that was voluntarily induced.

(6) The degree of force used by D is not to be regarded as having been reasonable in the circumstances as D believed them to be if it was disproportionate in those circumstances.

(7) In deciding the question mentioned in subsection (3) the following considerations are to be taken into account (so far as relevant in the circumstances of the case)—
   (a) that a person acting for a legitimate purpose may not be able to weigh to a nicety the exact measure of any necessary action; and
   (b) that evidence of a person's having only done what the person honestly and instinctively thought was necessary for a legitimate purpose constitutes strong evidence that only reasonable action was taken by that person for that purpose.

(8) Subsection (7) is not to be read as preventing other matters from being taken into account where they are relevant to deciding the question mentioned in subsection (3).

(9) This section is intended to clarify the operation of the existing defences mentioned in subsection (2).

(10) In this section—
   (a) "legitimate purpose" means—
      (i) the purpose of self-defence under the common law, or
      (ii) the prevention of crime or effecting or assisting in the lawful arrest of persons mentioned in the provisions referred to in subsection (2)(b);
   (b) references to self-defence include acting in defence of another person; and
   (c) references to the degree of force used are to the type and amount of force used.

■ **NOTES AND QUESTIONS**

1. While several commentators have expressed the view that the CJIA was unnecessary, it arguably serves the purpose both of providing a definitive statement of the law in this area and in bringing the disparate provisions of the law together in one place. Prior to passage of the CJIA, one often needed to refer to a number of

discrete decisions, each of which may have addressed only one dimension of the relevant law. Furthermore, the practice of judges to use their own words in expressing even a well-settled legal doctrine gave rise to uncertainty, and left room for legal argumentation about the precise limits of the defences. While no doubt in future cases lawyers will likewise find much in the new legislation to argue about, the statutory language provides a more fixed and certain starting point.

2. The three major issues raised in the CJIA are:

   (1) whether the need for force is to be measured from a subjective or objective perspective;

   (2) the relevance of voluntary intoxication in determining a defendant's perception of the need for force;

   (3) the degree of force permissible and the principles relevant to this determination.

3. Prior to the CJIA, there was a question of whether a defendant could plead both crime prevention and self-defence (or defence of another). See *R v Cousins* [1982] QB 526. That should no longer be an issue as all three defences are assimilated within s. 76.

4. The defendant who raises one of the s.76 defences has the initial evidential burden of introducing some evidence in support of the claimed defence, but the ultimate burden of proof rests on the prosecution to disprove the defence by proof beyond reasonable doubt. See *Beckford* v *R* [1988] AC 130, 144.

(ii) The need for force – The 'necessity' prong

The entitlement to use force in self-defence, defence of another or crime prevention depends on the necessity of using such force. The critical issue in determining the necessity of using force has been the perspective (that of the defendant or that of a reasonable person) from which this issue is to be judged.

R v Drane

[2008] EWCA Crim 1746, Court of Appeal

In October 2007, the defendant and the complainant were involved in an altercation which culminated in the former punching the latter in the face. The complainant suffered a significant injury. The defendant was subsequently arrested and charged with an offence of inflicting grievous bodily harm contrary to s. 20 of the Offences Against the Person Act 1861. At trial, the principal issue was self-defence. Before the jury retired to consider its verdict, the judge stated that it fell upon the prosecution to disprove the defence of self-defence; that the force used by the defendant had to have been necessary; and further, that defensive action would be permitted in circumstances where an attack was imminent. The judge then directed the jury to consider two questions: first, 'was it necessary to do what he [the defendant] in fact did?; and secondly, 'is what he [the defendant] did in striking... [the complainant] a reasonable response to what had happened?'. In the event, the jury returned a guilty verdict. The defendant appealed against conviction.

Held – The appeal would be allowed. In the circumstances, no complaint could be made of the beginning parts of the judge's directions; however, the questions which had been posed thereafter were inadequate. The jury should have been directed that they had to be satisfied, beyond reasonable doubt, that the defendant had not acted in a way which was justified on the basis of what he had believed was the case.

Accordingly, the conviction was unsafe and would be quashed.

■ NOTES AND QUESTIONS

1. Whether the need for force should be determined from a subjective or objective perspective has now been authoritatively settled by CJIA s. 76(3) and (4) which adopts the subjective perspective of the defendant.

2. In *Re A (Conjoined Twins: Medical Treatment)* (for facts and holding, see p. 504) Ward LJ described Mary as an 'innocent' aggressor who threatened the life of her conjoined twin, Jodie. If true, who was to be the judge of the need for force under the circumstances?

If the need for force is to be measured subjectively and the reasonable person's view disregarded, what of the converse case where a reasonable person in full knowledge of the facts would have deemed force to be necessary, but the actual defendant was lacking in some critical piece of information?

R v Dadson

(1881) 3 Car & Kerr 148, Kent Assizes

ERLE J: It appeared that the prisoner, being a constable, was employed to guard a copse from which wood had been stolen, and for this purpose carried a loaded gun. From this copse he saw the prosecutor come out, carrying wood, which he was stealing, and called him to stop. The prosecutor ran away, and the prisoner having no other means of bringing him to justice fired, and wounded him in the leg. These were the facts on which the prisoner acted, but it was alleged in addition that Waters was actually committing a felony, he having been before convicted repeatedly of stealing wood; but these convictions were unknown to the prisoner, nor was there any reason for supposing that he knew the difference between the rules of law relating to felony and those relating to less offences.

I told the jury that this shooting by the prisoner with intent to do grievous bodily harm amounted to the felony charged, unless from other facts there was a justification, and that neither the belief of the prisoner that it was his duty to fire if he could not otherwise apprehend the prosecutor, nor the alleged felony, it being unknown to him, constituted such justification.

The jury found the prisoner guilty of the felony.

■ NOTES AND QUESTIONS

1. Should the law allow a defence where the accused has been shown to be incorrect in his assumptions about the need for force? Will this encourage intervention without adequate investigation? In both *Dadson* and *Williams (Gladstone)*, the views of the reasonable person were seemingly disregarded. Why?

2. The *Dadson* decision has been critically discussed in the legal literature (see Hogan, 'The *Dadson* Principle'[1989] Crim LR 679) but was affirmed in *Chapman* v *DPP* [1988] Crim LR 843. For discussion, see Wilson (2011) 4.3.

(iii) Must the need to employ force be imminent?

We have seen that, in respect of duress, necessity and duress of circumstances, the courts require that the threat must be imminent. It is sometimes similarly asserted that one who acts in self-defence or defence of another must be faced with an immediate or imminent threat of harm. If an attack is not threatened until some future point in time, how can it be said that any force is necessary in defence? The use of a pre-emptive strike may be more difficult still to justify. However, perhaps surprisingly, the courts have shown greater flexibility in this area than in respect of duress, etc.

Devlin v *Armstrong*
[1971] NILR 13, Court of Appeal

After serious disturbances in the City of Londonderry the appellant was charged with and convicted of four offences of riotous behaviour and incitement to riotous behaviour in Londonderry on 13 August 1969, and she was sentenced to six months' imprisonment. The facts found by the resident magistrate showed that on different occasions on 13 August the appellant had exhorted a crowd of people who had been stoning the police to build a barricade to keep the police out of an area known as the Bogside, to man the barricades and to fight the police with petrol bombs, and that the appellant had herself thrown a stone towards the police. The defence was one of justification, it being submitted that the appellant did the acts complained of because she honestly and reasonably believed that the police were about to behave unlawfully in assaulting people and damaging property in the Bogside, though it was not suggested that there had in fact been any unlawful conduct on the part of any of the police.

Held by the Court of Appeal that, if it be assumed that the appellant did honestly and reasonably believe that the police were about to behave unlawfully in the ways mentioned, such belief did not afford a defence to the charges against her in that: (i) it was one of the common purposes of the appellant and the persons incited to exclude the police from the Bogside by force; (ii) the danger which the appellant was alleged to have anticipated was not sufficiently specific or imminent to justify her actions; and since the police were at the time engaged in containing a riot in the course of their duty, the interventions of the appellant were too aggressive and premature to rank as justifiable efforts to prevent the prospective danger of the police getting out of hand and behaving unlawfully; (iii) the force used by the appellant, assuming it to have been in the exercise of a right of self-defence or of a statutory right to prevent crime, was so excessive as to be unwarrantable; (iv) as regards the charges of incitement, there was no evidence or finding to show that those who were exhorted by the appellant to riot were actuated by an honest and reasonable apprehension of unlawful violence on behalf of the police such as the appellant is assumed to have had. Her incitements were therefore directed to encourage others to do what for them was prima facie unlawful; (v) while it might be that in a case of extreme necessity where the forces of law are absent or have ceased to act as such, individuals could be justified in doing acts which would otherwise be unlawful, the right to do such acts could not justify action directed against a lawfully constituted constabulary while acting as such in the exercise of its proper functions; (vi) there was no sufficient relationship between the appellant and the people of the Bogside to justify her acting in their defence or exercising a right of self-defence on their behalf; (vii) the common law duty imposed on all citizens to help in the suppression of riots and assist the constabulary in so doing made it impossible for the appellant to justify her conduct in encouraging the rioters as she did.

■ NOTES AND QUESTIONS

1. In *Beckford* v *R* [1988] 1 AC 130, Lord Griffiths wrote (at p. 144): '[A] man about to be attacked does not have to wait for his assailant to strike the first blow or fire the first shot; circumstances may justify a pre-emptive strike.' What this quotation does not tell us is how close an attack should be before one should be allowed to engage in a pre-emptive strike? A matter of minutes? Hours? Weeks?

2. The argument against pre-emptive action is that when an attack is not threatened until the future, there is time to take other action, such as

notifying the police. The police, however, may not be able to provide effective protection.

3. If a pre-emptive strike is permitted, does it follow that one can take reasonable preparatory actions, such as arming oneself in anticipation of the expected attack, if the preparatory actions would otherwise themselves be illegal? See *Attorney-General's Reference (No. 2 of 1983)* [1984] QB 456.

Another troublesome issue relating to the necessity prong is whether any force is necessary when one who is attacked can, by retreating, avoid the need for force. Should there be a duty to retreat, when retreat can be safely accomplished, before resorting to force?

R v Bird

[1985] 1 WLR 816, Court of Appeal

LORD LANE CJ: . . . On 24 January 1985 in the Crown Court at Chelmsford, the appellant, as she now is, this court having given her leave to appeal against conviction, was convicted after a re-trial of unlawful wounding under section 20 of the Offences against the Person Act 1861, and she was sentenced to nine months' youth custody.

The facts of the case are these. On 10 March 1984 the appellant, Debbie Bird, was celebrating her seventeenth birthday. There was a party at a house in Harlow. Unhappily it was at that party that the events occurred which ended with her being sent to youth custody. There was a guest at the party called Darren Marder, who was to be the victim of the events which occurred thereafter. He and the appellant had been friendly and had been going out together between about January and the middle of 1983. That close friendship had come to an end, but Marder arrived at the party with his new girlfriend and, for reasons which it is not necessary to explore, an argument broke out. After a great deal of bad language and shouting, the appellant told Marder to leave, and leave he did. A little later he unwisely came back and a second argument took place together with a second exchange of obscenities between the two of them. What happened thereafter was the subject of dispute between the parties, though not so much dispute as often arises in these sudden events. The appellant poured a glassful of Pernod over Marder, and he retaliated by slapping her around the face. Further incidents of physical force took place between them. The appellant said that the time came when she was being held and held up against a wall, at which point she lunged at Marder with her hand, which was the hand, unhappily, which held the Pernod glass. The glass hit him in the face, broke, and his eye as a result was lost. It was a horrible event in the upshot, but of course she would not realise the extent to which she was going to cause injury to this young man.

The prosecution case was this, that Marder only slapped the appellant once and that was in order to calm her down, the commonly believed remedy for hysterics. The jury were accordingly invited to infer from that that she could not possibly have been acting in reasonable self-defence when she retaliated against that slap with a weapon as grave as a glass. Secondly, there was evidence of Marder, and also a Miss Bryant, who was his new girlfriend, that so far from showing remorse after the event, the appellant said that she would do it again if the same situation arose. Thirdly, there was the evidence of Mrs Sharpe, who was the owner of the house where the party was taking place, who said that after the incident the appellant had admitted to her, Mrs Sharpe, that she had slashed Marder in the face with a glass after he had punched her.

The appellant herself was interviewed by the police. She said that it was only afterwards that she realised that a glass was in her hand, the hand with which she struck the appellant. The appellant gave evidence. She insisted that she had been acting in self-defence. She was being pushed. Marder had said to her that he would hit her if she did not shut up. He slapped her in the face, she was being held by him and thought the only thing for her to do was to strike back to defend herself. In the agony of the moment, so to speak, she did not realise that she was holding the glass. These are the comparatively simple facts of the case.

The grounds of appeal are these. First of all, the judge was in error in directing the jury that before the appellant could rely upon a plea of self-defence, it was necessary that she should have demonstrated by her action that she did not want to fight. That really is the essence of the appellant's case put forward by Mr Pavry to this court in what, if we may say so, was a most helpful argument.

The relevant passages in the summing up are these—first, towards the beginning of the direction to the jury:

> You cannot wrap up an attack in the cloak of self-defence and it is necessary that a person claiming to exercise a right of self-defence should demonstrate by her action that she does not want to fight. At one time it was thought that in order to demonstrate that, that the person seeking to raise a question of self-defence had to retreat. That is not so any longer at all, but there is an obligation to see whether the person claiming to exercise the right of self-defence should have demonstrated that she does not want to fight at all.

Towards the end of the summing up the judge used these words:

> You will have to consider whether in the circumstances of this case self-defence has any application at all. Does it look to you that this lady, who was behaving in this fashion, had demonstrated that she did not want to fight, was the use of the glass with a hard blow which broke it, reasonable in the circumstances? All these are matters for you and not for me.

The court in *R v Julien* [1969] 1 WLR 839 was anxious to make it clear that there was no duty, despite earlier authorities to the contrary, actually to turn round or walk away from the scene. But reading the words which were used in that judgment, it now seems to us that they placed too great an obligation upon a defendant in circumstances such as those in the instant case, an obligation which is not reflected in the speeches in *Palmer v The Queen* [1971] AC 814.

The matter is dealt with accurately and helpfully in *Smith and Hogan Criminal Law*, 5th ed. (1983), p. 327:

> There were formerly technical rules about the duty to retreat before using force, or at least fatal force. This is now simply a factor to be taken into account in deciding whether it was necessary to use force, and whether the force was reasonable. If the only reasonable course is to retreat, then it would appear that to stand and fight must be to use unreasonable force. There is, however, no rule of law that a person attacked is bound to run away if he can but it has been said that—'. . . what is necessary is that he should demonstrate by his actions that he does not want to fight. He must demonstrate that he is prepared to temporise and disengage and perhaps to make some physical withdrawal.' [*R v Julien* [1969] 1 WLR 839, 842]. It is submitted that it goes too far to say that action of this kind is *necessary*. It is scarcely consistent with the rule that it is permissible to use force, not merely to counter an actual attack, but to ward off an attack honestly and reasonably believed to be imminent. A demonstration by [the defendant] at the time that he did not want to fight is, no doubt, the best evidence that he was acting reasonably and in good faith in self-defence; but it is no more than that. A person may in some circumstances so act without temporising, disengaging or withdrawing; and he should have a good defence.

We respectfully agree with that passage. If the defendant is proved to have been attacking or retaliating or revenging himself, then he was not truly acting in self-defence. Evidence that the defendant tried to retreat or tried to call off the fight may be a cast-iron method of casting doubt on the suggestion that he was the attacker or retaliator or the person trying to revenge himself. But it is not by any means the only method of doing that.

It seems to us therefore that in this case the judge—we hasten to add through no fault of his own—by using the word 'necessary' as he did in the passages in the summing up to which we have referred, put too high an obligation upon the appellant.

■ **NOTES AND QUESTIONS**

1. What are the pros and cons of a retreat rule? Does the law make cowards of us all, or simply demand that we respond in a prudent rather than a belligerent manner to an attack?

2. Is part of the reluctance to insist on a duty to retreat the difficulty of making a snap decision in the heat of the moment when faced with an attack? Or, as United States Supreme Court Justice Oliver Wendell Holmes put it: 'Detached reflection cannot be demanded in the face of an uplifted knife.' This principle is now enshrined in CJIA, s. 7(a).

3. Even if there is no formal duty to retreat, it may behove one contemplating using force in self-defence to make clear that he is willing to cease and desist, if for no other reason than to lay the groundwork for a subsequent defence.

4. To the extent that the announcement of a willingness to desist is a relevant evidential consideration, then arguably its importance increases with the amount of force that is contemplated being used. If deadly force is contemplated, it is arguable that a fairly clear indication of willingness to desist should be made before resort to such force. Presumably, however, a communication to this effect is unnecessary when it would clearly be useless, as when one's assailant is holding a gun; even more so when it would be dangerous to take the time to make such a communication.

5. Is an offer to retreat, as maintained by the court in *Bird*, in fact the best evidence that the defendant was acting in a reasonable manner? See *R v Shannon* (1980) 71 Cr App R 192.

(iv) What if the defendant's belief in the need for force is mistaken?

R v Williams (Gladstone)
(1983) 78 Cr App R 276, Court of Appeal
For facts and holding, see p. 461.

■ NOTES AND QUESTIONS

1. The views embodied in *Williams (Gladstone)* are now codified in CJIA, s. 4(b). Of course, the more unreasonable the defendant's mistake, the less likely is a jury to believe the defendant's claim that he was mistaken.

2. Should a defendant's individual characteristics (and if so, which ones?) be taken into account in determining whether the defendant made a mistake as to the need for force. In *Martin (Anthony)* [2001] EWCA Crim 2245, Court of Appeal, Lord Woolf observed that:

> [S]elf-defence is raised in a great many cases resulting from minor assaults and it would be wholly disproportionate to encourage medical disputes in cases of that sort.

Even conceding the correctness of Lord Woolf's general observation, why should medical evidence not be admitted when it is clearly relevant in a given case? Martin, on trial for murder, claimed that he suffered from a personality disorder that would have caused him to be more susceptible to and to exaggerate more than would an ordinary person the danger he was facing (not that what an ordinary person would have perceived is relevant under either *Williams* or the CJIA). See *Shaw (Norman) v The Queen* [2001] UKPC26.

(v) The amount of permissible force – The 'proportionality' prong

Only reasonable force is permitted in self-defence, defence of another or crime prevention. But how is a jury to measure reasonableness? The generally stated position

is that the force used in defence must be proportional to the attack. If it is disproportionate , then it is unreasonable.

Palmer v R
[1971] AC 814, Privy Council

LORD MORRIS OF BORTH-Y-GEST: . . . In their Lordships' view the defence of self-defence is one which can be and will be readily understood by any jury. It is a straightforward conception. It involves no abstruse legal thought. It requires no set words by way of explanation. No formula need be employed in reference to it. Only common sense is needed for its understanding. It is both good law and good sense that a man who is attacked may defend himself. It is both good law and good sense that he may do, but may only do, what is reasonably necessary. But everything will depend upon the particular facts and circumstances. Of these a jury can decide. It may in some cases be only sensible and clearly possible to take some simple avoiding action. Some attacks may be serious and dangerous. Others may not be. If there is some relatively minor attack it would not be common sense to permit some action of retaliation which was wholly out of proportion to the necessities of the situation. If an attack is serious so that it puts someone in immediate peril then immediate defensive action may be necessary. If the moment is one of crisis for someone in imminent danger he may have to avert the danger by some instant reaction. If the attack is all over and no sort of peril remains then the employment of force may be by way of revenge or punishment or by way of pay-ing off an old score or may be pure aggression. There may no longer be any link with a necessity of defence. Of all these matters the good sense of a jury will be the arbiter. There are no prescribed words which must be employed in or adopted in a summing up. All that is needed is a clear expos-ition, in relation to the particular facts of the case, of the conception of necessary self-defence. If there has been no attack then clearly there will have been no need for defence. If there has been attack so that defence is reasonably necessary it will be recognised that a person defending himself cannot weigh to a nicety the exact measure of his necessary defensive action. If a jury thought that in a moment of unexpected anguish a person attacked had only done what he honestly and instinct-ively thought was necessary that would be most potent evidence that only reasonable defensive action had been taken. A jury will be told that the defence of self-defence, where the evidence makes its raising possible, will only fail if the prosecution show beyond doubt that what the accused did was not by way of self-defence. But their Lordships consider that if the prosecution have shown that what was done was not done in self-defence then that issue is eliminated from the case. If the jury consider that an accused acted in self-defence or if the jury are in doubt as to this then they will acquit. The defence of self-defence either succeeds so as to result in an acquittal or it is disproved in which case as a defence it is rejected . . . .

■ NOTES AND QUESTIONS

1. Lord Morris states in *Palmer* that what an attacked individual 'honestly and instinctively thought was necessary . . . would be most potent evidence that only reasonable defensive action had been taken'. A similar position is taken in s. 7(b). If a lecturer believes that deadly force is necessary to prevent a student from stealing her notes and kills the student, is the lecturer's belief as to the appropriate amount of force warranted by the circumstances relevant let alone 'most potent evidence that only reasonable defensive action has been taken'?

2. A distinction is sometimes drawn between the force used and the threat to use force. One may be able to threaten to use more force than one in fact would be legally entitled to use. Why?

The most difficult question and the one with the most far-reaching consequences is 'When may one use deadly force?'

Attorney-General for Northern Ireland Reference (No. 1 of 1975)
[1977] AC 105, House of Lords

The accused was a soldier serving with the armed forces of the Crown. His unit was engaged in the suppression of terrorist activities in Northern Ireland. The accused was a member of an army patrol on foot in an area where terrorists were believed to be active. During the course of the patrol the accused saw the deceased, who was on his own, and ordered him to halt. The deceased ran off and thereupon the accused shot and killed him. The accused was charged with murder and was tried by a judge sitting alone under s. 2 of the Northern Ireland (Emergency Provisions) Act 1972. The accused was acquitted. The judge gave a judgment stating his reasons for finding the accused not guilty and set out his findings of fact in considerable detail. In particular the judge stated that he was not satisfied that it had been the accused's intention to kill or seriously wound the deceased. Following the acquittal the Attorney-General, acting under s. 48A of the Criminal Appeal (Northern Ireland) 1968 and the Criminal Appeal (References of Points of Law) (Northern Ireland) Rules 1973, referred, inter alia, the following point of law to the Court of Criminal Appeal in Northern Ireland: 'Whether a soldier commits a crime when, in the circumstances set out in [the reference], he fires to kill or seriously wound an unarmed person because he honestly and reasonably believes that that person is a member of a proscribed organisation (in this case the Provisional IRA) who is seeking to run away, and the soldier's shot kills that person.' Paragraph 2 of the reference, in accordance with r. 3(1) of the 1973 rules, set out the 'facts of the case [which were] necessary for the proper consideration of the point of law'. Those facts, which were taken from the judgment of the trial judge, included expressions of opinion as to the likelihood of attack on the patrol and as to the accused's state of mind at the time when he fired the shot. The Court of Criminal Appeal gave its opinion on the point of law and, on the application of the Attorney-General, referred the point to the House of Lords under s. 48A(3) of the 1968 Act.

LORD DIPLOCK : ...My Lords, to kill or seriously wound another person by shooting is prima facie unlawful. There may be circumstances, however, which render the act of shooting and any killing which results from it lawful; and an honest and reasonable belief by the accused in the existence of facts which if true would have rendered his act lawful is a defence to any charge based on the shooting. So for the purposes of the present reference one must ignore the fact that the deceased was an entirely innocent person and must deal with the case as if he were a member of the Provisional IRA and a potentially dangerous terrorist, as the accused honestly and reasonably believed him to be.

The facts to be assumed for the purposes of the reference are not capable in law of giving rise to a possible defence of 'self-defence'. The deceased was in fact, and appeared to the accused to be, unarmed. He was not attacking the accused; he was running away. So if the act of the accused in shooting the deceased was lawful it must have been on the ground that it was done in the performance of his duty to prevent crime or in the exercise of his right to stop and question the deceased under s. 16 or to arrest him under s. 12 of the Northern Ireland (Emergency Provisions) Act 1973.

There is little authority in English law concerning the rights and duties of a member of the armed forces of the Crown when acting in aid of the civil power; and what little authority there is relates almost entirely to the duties of soldiers when troops are called on to assist in controlling a riotous assembly. Where used for such temporary purposes it may not be inaccurate to describe the legal rights and duties of a soldier as being no more than those of an ordinary citizen in uniform. But such a description is in my view misleading in the circumstances in which the army is currently employed in aid of the civil power in Northern Ireland. In some parts of the province there has existed for some years now a state of armed and clandestinely organised insurrection against the lawful government of Her Majesty by persons seeking to gain political ends by violent means, that is by committing murder and other crimes of violence against persons and property. Due to the efforts of the army and police to suppress it the insurrection has been sporadic in its manifestations but, as events have repeatedly shown, if vigilance is relaxed the violence erupts again. In theory it may be the duty of every citizen when an arrestable offence is about to be committed in his presence to take whatever reasonable measures are available to him to prevent the commission of the crime; but the duty is one of imperfect obligation and does not place him under any obligation to do anything by which he would expose himself to risk of personal injury, nor is he under any duty to search for criminals or seek out crime. In contrast to this a soldier who is employed in aid of the civil power in Northern Ireland is under a duty, enforceable under military law, to search for criminals if so ordered by his superior officer and to risk his own life should this be necessary in preventing terrorist acts. For the performance of this duty he is armed with a firearm, a self-loading rifle, from which a bullet, if it hits the human body, is almost certain to cause serious injury if not death.

The use of force in the prevention of crime or in effecting the lawful arrest of suspected offenders is now regulated by s. 3 of the Criminal Law (Northern Ireland) Act 1967 as follows:

(1) A person may use such force as is reasonable in the circumstances in the prevention of crime, or in effecting or assisting in the lawful arrest of offenders or suspected offenders or of persons unlawfully at large.

(2) Subsection (1) shall replace the rules of the common law as to the matters dealt with by that subsection.

That section states the law applicable to the defence raised by the accused at the trial of his case.

In the instant reference the relevant purpose for which it is to be assumed that force was used by the accused is the prevention of crime. That is the purpose for which the power to stop and question is conferred on soldiers by s. 16 of the Northern Ireland (Emergency Provisions) Act 1973; and it has not been suggested that shooting to kill or seriously wound would be justified in attempting to effect the arrest under s. 12 of a person who, though he was suspected of belonging to a proscribed organisation (which constitutes an offence under s. 19), was not also believed on reasonable grounds to be likely to commit actual crimes of violence, if he succeeded in avoiding arrest.

What amount of force is 'reasonable in the circumstances' for the purpose of preventing crime is, in my view, always a question for the jury in a jury trial, never a 'point of law' for the judge.

The form in which the jury would have to ask themselves the question in a trial for an offence against the person in which this defence was raised by the accused, would be: are we satisfied that no reasonable man (a) with knowledge of such facts as were known to the accused or reasonably believed by him to exist (b) in the circumstances and time available to him for reflection (c) could be of opinion that the prevention of the risk of harm to which others might be exposed if the suspect were allowed to escape, justified exposing the suspect to the risk of harm to him that might result from the kind of force that the accused contemplated using?

To answer this the jury would have first to decide what were the facts that did exist and were known to the accused to do so and what were mistakenly believed by the accused to be facts. In respect of the latter the jury would have had to decide whether any reasonable man on the material available to the accused could have shared that belief. To select, as is done in para. 2(13) of the reference, two specific inferences of fact as to which it is said that the accused had no belief is merely to exclude them from the jury's consideration as being facts mistakenly believed by the accused to exist; but this does not preclude the jury from considering what inferences of fact a reasonable man would draw from the primary facts known to the accused.

The jury would have also to consider how the circumstances in which the accused had to make his decision whether or not to use force, and the shortness of the time available to him for reflection, might affect the judgment of a reasonable man. In the facts that are to be assumed for the purposes of the reference there is material on which a jury might take the view that the accused had reasonable grounds for apprehension of imminent danger to himself and other members of the patrol if the deceased were allowed to get away and join armed fellow members of the Provisional IRA who might be lurking in the neighbourhood, and that the time available to the accused to make up his mind what to do was so short that even a reasonable man could only act intuitively. This being so, the jury in approaching the final part of the question should remind themselves that the postu-lated balancing of risk against risk, harm against harm, by the reasonable man is not undertaken in the calm analytical atmosphere of the court room after counsel with the benefit of hindsight have expounded at length the reasons for and against the kind and degree of force that was used by the accused; but in the brief second or two which the accused had to decide whether to shoot or not and under all the stresses to which he was exposed.

In many cases where force is used in the prevention of crime or in effecting an arrest there is a choice as to the degree of force to use. On the facts that are to be assumed for the purposes of the reference the only options open to the accused were either to let the deceased escape or to shoot at him with a service rifle. A reasonable man would know that a bullet from a self-loading rifle if it hit a human being, at any rate at the range at which the accused fired, would be likely to kill him or to injure him seriously. So in one scale of the balance the harm to which the deceased would be exposed if the accused aimed to hit him was predictable and grave and the risk of its occurrence high. In the other scale of the balance it would be open to the jury to take the view that it would not be unreasonable to assess the kind of harm to be averted by preventing the deceased's escape was even graver—the killing or wounding of members of the patrol by terrorists in ambush, and the effect of this success by members of the Provisional IRA in encouraging the continuance of the armed insurrection and all the misery and destruction of life and property that terrorist activity in Northern Ireland has entailed. The jury would have to consider too what was the highest degree at which a reasonable man could have assessed the likelihood that such consequences might follow the escape of the deceased if the facts had been as the accused knew or believed them reasonably to be.

My Lords, the facts as they have been stated for the purpose of the reference are much less detailed than those that were proved at the trial of the accused before MacDermott J without a jury. As stated they are so scanty and couched in such general terms (e.g. there was 'a real threat') that for my part I should not find it possible as a judge of fact to say that in the circumstances as stated the force used by the accused was not reasonable.

In the result I do not think that this House can give to the first question in the reference any more specific answer than that which was given by the majority of the Court of Criminal Appeal in Northern Ireland:

> Point (i) The facts and circumstances set out in the reference are sufficient to raise an issue for the tribunal of fact as to whether the Crown had established beyond reasonable doubt that the respondent's act of shooting constituted, in the circumstances, unreasonable force.

■ **NOTES AND QUESTIONS**

1. In *A-G's Ref*, was the defendant himself under threat of immediate attack? Was anybody? Was the threat, if it did exist, real or hypothetical?

2. If the defendant believed that at some future point in time the escaped individual would pose a threat to others, would that have been sufficient to justify the use of deadly force under Lord Diplock's test? Would it matter if that point in time was the following week? The following month? The following year? Ten years in the future?

3. The burden of persuading the jury that deadly force was not reasonable in the circumstances rests on the prosecution. Once the defendant has introduced some relevant evidence, the prosecution must negate the claim by proof beyond reasonable doubt.

4. The issue of the permissibility of using deadly force in defence of property has frequently arisen and is exceedingly controversial. Often the issue is subsumed on whether the defendant was entitled to rely on a defence of self-defence (see *Martin (Anthony)* [2001] EWCA Crim 2245, Court of Appeal) or crime prevention.

What if a woman living alone hears an intruder making his way towards her bedroom at night, may/should she assume that the burglar poses a threat of (a) theft, (b) rape, or (c) murder? May she hide behind the door to the bedroom and, when the intruder enters, (a) hit him over the head with a cricket bat (potentially GBH), (b) shoot him with a gun (potentially murder), or (c) do nothing until she learns of the intruder's true intentions?

In the case of *Munir Hussain*, Lord Judge, the most senior judge in England and Wales, reduced the sentence of an Asian businessman who used a cricket bat to pummel into a state of potentially permanent brain damage a criminal who had invaded his home and had, tied up and threatened his family. Within weeks of Lord Judge's decision, a jury acquitted a householder who killed a burglar. Is the present law which disapproves the use of potentially lethal force in defence of property out of step with the views of both the public and the judiciary? In *R (On the application of Abbott)* v *Colchester Magistrates Court* [2001] Crim LR 564, the defendants were charged with criminal damage for damaging a crop of genetically modified maize in an environmental protest. A jury acquitted after hearing their defence that they were defending nearby organic crops from damage by the spread of pollen from the GM crops.

Given that the need to use any force is to be judged from the defendant's perspective, should the amount of force necessary in the circumstances also be judged from this perspective?

R v Owino

[1996] 2 Cr App R 128, Court of Appeal

COLLINS J: On October 17, 1994 the appellant, a senior registrar in microbiology, appeared before the Crown Court at Wood Green on an indictment charging him with four offences of violence against his wife, Marie. The first alleged the causing of grievous bodily harm with intent; the other three, assault occasioning actual bodily harm...

It is clear that in relation to counts 3 and 4, self-defence was being raised, the appellant's case being that any bruising suffered by his wife for which he was responsible was caused only by reasonable force used in restraining her and in preventing her from assaulting him. In those circumstances it was obviously incumbent upon the learned judge to give a full and proper direction as to the elements of self-defence and also to draw the jury's attention to the distinction between provocation by words or by conduct, which would not, and threats or actual attack which could raise an issue of self-defence. If there is material which raises this issue, the burden is of course on the prosecution to prove that the violence used was excessive and was not used in self-defence.

Unfortunately, the learned judge did not refer to self-defence at all in his summing-up and the jury retired shortly after 1 p.m. without any such direction being given to them. It was perfectly plain that such a direction ought to have been given.

Then about an hour and a half after their retirement, the jury sent a note to the judge. It read as follows:

Question on law:

We have come to an impasse on the issue of the definition of assault. If a person reacts to being assaulted themselves by grabbing or pushing, is that assault? What might be regarded as unreasonable force, i.e. is lifting someone out of a room against their will (struggling) regarded as an assault? Also, one or two of us wish to take into account provocation, others of us do not believe we should do. Can you direct us, is it a question of fairness?

With the greatest of respect to the learned judge, if, as indeed was clear, the issue of self-defence had been raised on the evidence, he had a duty to put it to the jury and to direct the jury upon it. The fact, if it be a fact, that counsel had not specifically referred to self-defence in the course of their speeches was no reason for the learned judge not to deal with it in his summing-up.

...The essential elements of self-defence are clear enough. The jury have to decide whether a defendant honestly believed that the circumstances were such as required him to use force to defend himself from an attack or a threatened attack. In this respect a defendant must be judged in accordance with his honest belief, even though that belief may have been mistaken. But the jury must then decide whether the force used was reasonable in the circumstances as he believed them to be.

R v Scarlett (1994) 98 Cr App R 290 was a case where a landlord of a public house had been ejecting, and perfectly lawfully and properly ejecting, a drunken customer from his public house. The allegation was that he had used excessive force in the course of ejecting him so that the customer fell down the steps of the entrance to the pub and unfortunately hit his head and was killed. What Mr Mendelle relies upon in the case of *Scarlett* is a passage at pp. 295, 296 and p. 636 of the respective reports, where Beldam LJ, giving the judgment of the Court, said this:

> Where, as in the present case, an accused is justified in using some force and can only be guilty of an assault if the force used is excessive, the jury ought to be directed that he cannot be guilty of an assault unless the prosecution prove that he acted with the mental element necessary to constitute his action in assault, that is 'that the defendant intentionally or recklessly applied force to the person of another'. Further, they should be directed that the accused is not to be found guilty merely because he intentionally or recklessly used force which they consider to have been excessive. They ought not to convict him unless they are satisfied that the degree of force used was plainly more than was called for by the circumstances as he believed them to be and, provided he believed the circumstances called for the degree of force used, he is not to be convicted even if his belief was unreasonable.
>
> In this case the learned judge gave no direction to the jury that the prosecution, to establish an assault, had to prove that the appellant intentionally or recklessly applied excessive force in seeking to evict the deceased.

...[W]hat, in the context, the learned Lord Justice was really saying was, in our view, this: he was indicating that the elements of an assault involved the unlawful application of force. In the context of an issue of self-defence or reasonable restraint, which was what *Scarlett* was essentially about, then clearly a person would not be guilty of an assault unless the force used was excessive, and in judging whether the force used was excessive, the jury had to take account of the circumstances as he believed them to be. That is what is made clear in the first part of the sentence, which we will isolate and read again:

> They ought not to convict him unless they are satisfied that the degree of force used was plainly more than was called for by the circumstances as he believed them to be and, provided he believed the circumstances called for the degree of force used, he is not to be convicted even if his belief was unreasonable.

So far as the second half of the sentence is concerned, what we understand the learned Lord Justice to have been saying was that, in judging what he believed the circumstances to be, the jury are not to decide on the basis of what was objectively reasonable; and that even if he, the defendant, was unreasonable in his belief, if it was an honest belief and honestly held, that he is not to be judged by reference to the true circumstances. It is in that context that the learned Lord Justice talks about '[belief] that the circumstances called for the degree of force used', because clearly you cannot divorce completely the concept of degree of force and the concept of the circumstances as you believe them to be. In our judgment, that is effectively all that the learned Lord Justice was saying.

What he was not saying, in our view (and indeed if he had said it, it would be contrary to authority) was that the belief, however ill-founded, of the defendant that the degree of force he was using was reasonable, will enable him to do what he did. As Kay J, indicated in argument, if that argument was correct, then it would justify, for example, the shooting of someone who was merely threatening to throw a punch, on the basis that the defendant honestly believed, although unreasonably and mistakenly, that it was justifiable for him to use that degree of force. That clearly is not and cannot be, the law.

■ NOTES AND QUESTIONS

1. Why should the need for any force be judged from the perspective of the defendant while the appropriate amount of force is judged from the perspective of a reasonable person?

2. If the defendant's force is deemed excessive, a claim of self-defence will fail. But should a flawed or imperfect claim of self-defence serve to reduce the seriousness of the defendant's crime? The House of Lords in *R* v *Clegg* [1995] 1 AC 482 expressed some sympathy for this position, but answered in the negative, stating that it was Parliament's responsibility to clarify the law, which it has now done in the CJIA. Or has it?

3. Does the reasonableness requirement reflect a judicial desire to obviate revenge attacks or something else?

4. *Owino* is enshrined in s. 76(6) CJI Act 2008.

5. People who use disproportionate force in self defence may be able to avail themselves of the partial defence of loss of self control under the Coroners and Justice Act 2009, but only where the use of force results in death. See p. 211 above.

(vi) Deadly force and the European Convention of Human Rights

The use of deadly force, and the State's responsibility for the decision to authorise its use, have been considered by the European Court of Human Rights:

McCann v *United Kingdom*
(1996) 21 EHRR 97, European Court of Human Rights

Following intelligence information that the Provisional IRA were planning a terrorist attack on Gibraltar, SAS soldiers were sent to assist the Gibraltar authorities to arrest the IRA active service unit. The three suspects were subsequently shot and killed by members of the SAS. The applicants complained that the killings violated Article 2 of the Convention and claimed just satisfaction under Article 50.

In its report of 4 March 1994, the Commission made the following findings on questions of fact:

— that the suspects were effectively allowed to enter Gibraltar to be picked up by the surveillance operatives in place in strategic locations for that purpose;

— that there was no evidence to support the applicants' contention of a premeditated design to kill Mr McCann, Ms Farrell and Mr Savage;

— that there was no convincing support for any allegation that the soldiers shot Mr McCann and Ms Farrell when they were attempting to surrender or when they were lying on the ground. However the soldiers carried out the shooting from close proximity. The forensic evidence indicated a distance of as little as three feet in the case of Ms Farrell;

— Ms Farrell and Mr McCann were shot by Soldiers A and B at close range after the two suspects had made what appeared to the soldiers to be threatening movements. They were shot as they fell to the ground but not when they were lying on the ground;—it was probably either the sound of the police siren or the sound of the shooting of Mr McCann and Ms Farrell at the Shell garage, or indeed both, which caused Mr Savage to turn round to face the soldiers who were behind him. It was not likely that Soldiers C and D witnessed the shooting of Mr McCann and Ms Farrell before proceeding in pursuit of Savage;

— there was insufficient material to rebut the version of the shooting given by Soldiers C and D. Mr Savage was shot at close range until he hit the ground and probably in the instant as or after he hit the ground. This conclusion was supported by the pathologists' evidence at the subsequent inquest;

— Soldiers A to D opened fire with the purpose of preventing the threat of detonation of a car bomb in the centre of Gibraltar by suspects who were known to them to be terrorists with a history of previous involvement with explosives;

— a timer must in all probability have been mentioned at the Commissioner's operational briefing. For whatever reason, however, it was not a factor which was taken into account in the soldiers' view of the operation.

The Government submitted that the deprivations of life to which the applications relate was justified under Article 2(2)(a) as resulting from the use of force which was no more than absolutely necessary in defence of the people of Gibraltar from unlawful violence and the Court was invited to find that the facts disclosed no breach of Article 2 of the Convention in respect of any of the three deceased.

The applicants submitted that the Government have not shown beyond reasonable doubt that the planning and execution of the operation was in accordance with Article 2 H 2 of the Convention. Accordingly, the killings were not absolutely necessary within the meaning of this provision.

As to the law

I. Alleged violation of Article 2 of the Convention The applicants alleged that the killing of Mr McCann, Ms Farrell and Mr Savage by members of the security forces constituted a violation of Article 2 of the Convention which reads:

1. Everyone's right to life shall be protected by law. No one shall be deprived of his life intentionally save in the execution of a sentence of a court following his conviction of a crime for which this penalty is provided by law.

2. Deprivation of life shall not be regarded as inflicted in contravention of this Article when it results from the use of force which is no more than absolutely necessary:

   (a) in defence of any person from unlawful violence;
   (b) in order to effect a lawful arrest or to prevent the escape of a person lawfully detained;
   (c) in action lawfully taken for the purpose of quelling a riot or insurrection.

The Court considers that the exceptions delineated in paragraph 2 indicate that this provision extends to, but is not concerned exclusively with, intentional killing. As the Commission has pointed out, the text of Article 2, read as a whole, demonstrates that paragraph 2 does not primarily define instances where it is permitted intentionally to kill an individual, but describes the situations where it is permitted to 'use force' which may result, as an unintended outcome, in the deprivation of life. The use of force, however, must be no more than absolutely necessary for the achievement of one of the purposes set out in sub-paragraphs (a), (b) or (c) (see *Stewart* v *The United Kingdom* (appl. no. 10444/ 82), 10 July 1984, Decisions and Reports, volume 39, pp. 169–171).

In this respect the use of the term 'absolutely necessary' in Article 2(2) indicates that a stricter and more compelling test of necessity must be employed from that normally applicable when determining whether State action is 'necessary in a democratic society' under paragraph 2 of Articles 8 to 11 of the Convention. In particular, the force used must be strictly proportionate to the achievement of the aims set out in sub-paragraphs (2)(a), (b) and (c) of Article 2.

In keeping with the importance of this provision in a democratic society, the Court must, in making its assessment, subject deprivations of life to the most careful scrutiny, particularly where deliberate lethal force is used, taking into consideration not only the actions of the agents of the State who actually administer the force but also all the surrounding circumstances including such matters as the planning and control of the actions under examination.

In carrying out its examination under Article 2 of the Convention, the Court must bear in mind that the information that the United Kingdom authorities received that there would be a terrorist attack in Gibraltar presented them with a fundamental dilemma. On the one hand, they were required to have regard to their duty to protect the lives of the people in Gibraltar including their own military personnel and, on the other, to have minimum resort to the use of lethal force against those suspected of posing this threat in the light of the obligations flowing from both domestic and international law.

Several other factors must also be taken into consideration. In the first place, the authorities were confronted by an active service unit of the IRA composed of persons who had been convicted of bombing offences and a known explosives expert. The IRA, judged by its actions in the past, had demonstrated a disregard for human life, including that of its own members.

Secondly, the authorities had had prior warning of the impending terrorist action and thus had ample opportunity to plan their reaction and, in co-ordination with the local Gibraltar authorities, to take measures to foil the attack and arrest the suspects. Inevitably, however, the security authorities could not have been in possession of the full facts and were obliged to formulate their policies on the basis of incomplete hypotheses.

Against this background, in determining whether the force used was compatible with Article 2, the Court must carefully scrutinise, as noted above, not only whether the force used by the soldiers was strictly proportionate to the aim of protecting persons against unlawful violence but also whether the anti-terrorist operation was planned and controlled by the authorities so as to minimise, to the greatest extent possible, recourse to lethal force. The Court will consider each of these points in turn.

It is recalled that the soldiers who carried out the shooting (A, B, C and D) were informed by their superiors, in essence, that there was a car-bomb in place which could be detonated by any of the three suspects by means of a radio-control device which might have been concealed on their persons; that the device could be activated by pressing a button; that they would be likely to detonate the bomb if challenged, thereby causing heavy loss of life and serious injuries, and were also likely to be armed and to resist arrest.

As regards the shooting of Mr McCann and Ms Farrell, the Court recalls the Commission's finding that they were shot at close range after making what appeared to Soldiers A and B to be threatening movements with their hands as if they were going to detonate the bomb.

...

It was subsequently discovered that the suspects were unarmed, that they did not have a detonator device on their persons and that there was no bomb in the car.

All four soldiers admitted that they shot to kill. They considered that it was necessary to continue to fire at the suspects until they were rendered physically incapable of detonating a device. According to the pathologists' evidence Ms Farrell was hit by eight bullets, Mr McCann by five and Mr Savage by sixteen.

The Court accepts that the soldiers honestly believed, in the light of the information that they had been given, as set out above, that it was necessary to shoot the suspects in order to prevent them from detonating a bomb and causing serious loss of life. The actions which they took, in obedience to superior orders, were thus perceived by them as absolutely necessary in order to safeguard innocent lives.

It considers that the use of force by agents of the State in pursuit of one of the aims delineated in paragraph 2 of Article 2 of the Convention may be justified under this provision where it is based on an honest belief which is perceived, for good reasons, to be valid at the time but which subsequently turns out to be mistaken. To hold otherwise would be to impose an unrealistic burden on the State and its law enforcement personnel in the execution of their duty, perhaps to the detriment of their lives and those of others.

It follows that, having regard to the dilemma confronting the authorities in the circumstances of the case, the actions of the soldiers do not, in themselves, give rise to a violation of this provision.

The question arises, however, whether the anti-terrorist operation as a whole was controlled and organised in a manner which respected the requirements of Article 2 and whether the information and instructions given to the soldiers which, in effect, rendered inevitable the use of lethal force, took adequately into consideration the right to life of the three suspects.

...

The decision not to stop the three terrorists from entering Gibraltar is a relevant factor to take into account under this head.

The Court notes that at the briefing on 5 March attended by Soldiers A, B, C, and D it was considered likely that the attack would be by way of a large car-bomb. A number of key assessments were made. In particular, it was thought that the terrorists would not use a blocking car; that the bomb would be detonated by a radio-control device; that the detonation could be effected by the pressing of a button; that it was likely that the suspects would detonate the bomb if challenged; that they would be armed and would be likely to use their arms if confronted.

In the event, all of these crucial assumptions, apart from the terrorists' intentions to carry out an attack, turned out to be erroneous. Nevertheless, as has been demonstrated by the Government, on the basis of their experience in dealing with the IRA, they were all possible hypotheses in a situation where the true facts were unknown and where the authorities operated on the basis of limited intelligence information.

In fact, insufficient allowances appear to have been made for other assumptions. For example, since the bombing was not expected until 8 March when the changing of the guard ceremony was to take place, there was equally the possibility that the three terrorists were on a reconnaissance mission. While this was a factor which was briefly considered, it does not appear to have been regarded as a serious possibility.

In addition, at the briefings or after the suspects had been spotted, it might have been thought unlikely that they would have been prepared to explode the bomb, thereby killing many civilians, as Mr McCann and Ms Farrell strolled towards the border area since this would have increased the risk of detection and capture. It might also have been thought improbable that at that point they would have set up the transmitter in anticipation to enable them to detonate the supposed bomb immediately if confronted.

Moreover, even if allowances are made for the technological skills of the IRA, the description of the detonation device as a 'button job' without the qualifications subsequently described by the experts at the Inquest, of which the competent authorities must have been aware, over-simplifies the true nature of these devices.

It is further disquieting in this context that the assessment made by Soldier G, after a cursory external examination of the car, that there was a 'suspect car-bomb' was conveyed to the soldiers, according to their own testimony, as a definite identification that there was such a bomb. It is recalled that while Soldier G had experience in car-bombs, it transpired that he was not an expert in radio communications or explosives; and that his assessment that there was a suspect car bomb, based on his observation that the car aerial was out of place, was more in the nature of a report that a bomb could not be ruled out.

In the absence of sufficient allowances being made for alternative possibilities, and the definite reporting of the existence of a car-bomb which, according to the assessments that had been made, could be detonated at the press of a button, a series of working hypotheses were conveyed to Soldiers A, B, C and D as certainties, thereby making the use of lethal force almost unavoidable.

However, the failure to make provision for a margin of error must also be considered in combination with the training of the soldiers to continue shooting once they opened fire until the suspect was dead. As noted by the Coroner in his summing up to the jury at the Inquest, all four soldiers shot to kill the suspects. Soldier E testified that it had been discussed with the soldiers that there was an increased chance that they would have to shoot to kill since there would be less time where there was a 'button' device. Against this background, the authorities were bound by their obligation to respect the right to life of the suspects to exercise the greatest of care in evaluating the information at their disposal before transmitting it to soldiers whose use of firearms automatically involved shooting to kill.

Although detailed investigation at the Inquest into the training received by the soldiers was prevented by the public interest certificates which had been issued, it is not clear whether they had been trained or instructed to assess whether the use of firearms to wound their targets may have been warranted by the specific circumstances that confronted them at the moment of arrest.

Their reflex action in this vital respect lacks the degree of caution in the use of firearms to be expected from law enforcement personnel in a democratic society, even when dealing with dangerous terrorist suspects, and stands in marked contrast to the standard of care reflected in the instructions in the use of firearms by the police which had been drawn to their attention and which emphasised the legal responsibilities of the individual officer in the light of conditions prevailing at the moment of engagement.

This failure by the authorities also suggests a lack of appropriate care in the control and organisation of the arrest operation.

In sum, having regard to the decision not to prevent the suspects from travelling into Gibraltar, to the failure of the authorities to make sufficient allowances for the possibility that their intelligence assessments might, in some respects at least, be erroneous and to the automatic recourse to lethal force when the soldiers opened fire, the Court is not persuaded that the killing of the three terrorists constituted the use of force which was no more than absolutely necessary in defence of persons from unlawful violence within the meaning of Article 2(2)(a) of the Convention.

Accordingly, it finds that there has been a breach of Article 2 of the Convention.

■ NOTES AND QUESTIONS

1. The European Court of Human Rights notes that the suspects were not arrested at the time that they entered Gibraltar. Might limitations in the law of attempt (namely, that to be convicted of an attempt a defendant must have done something more than an act of 'mere preparation'; see Chapter 10) have affected the decision not to arrest?

2. Is the test for when deadly force is permissible set out by the European Court more or less stringent than that articulated in *Attorney-General for Northern Ireland Reference (No. 1 of 1975)* (above)? Should the answer turn on what the actor considers to be reasonable, or on what an ordinary person would consider reasonable?

3. In *Andronicou and Constantinou v Cyprus* (1998) 25 EHRR 491, the European Court of Human Rights again had occasion to examine the use of deadly force by State authorities. C was being held hostage by A, who was known by police to be armed and unstable. In response to being shot at by A, the special police unit discharged several rounds of automatic fire. A was killed instantly; C was wounded and died shortly thereafter. While regretting the use of so much fire power, the Court nonetheless found that it did not exceed what was 'absolutely necessary' under the circumstances. What are the differences between *Andronicou* and *McCann*? Both cases were decided by the narrowest of margins (ten votes to nine in *McCann*; five votes to four in *Andronicou*), suggesting strong divisions within the Court.

FURTHER READING

Wilson, *Criminal Law: Doctrine and Theory* (2011), Chapters 10

Colvin, 'Exculpatory Defences in Criminal Law' (1990) 10 Oxford Journal of Legal Studies 381

Elliot, 'Necessity, Duress and Self-defence' [1989] Criminal Law Review 611

Fuller, 'The Case of the Speluncean Explorers' (1949) 62 Harvard Law Review 616

Gardner, 'Direct Action and the Defence of Necessity' [2005] Criminal Law Review 371

Gardner, 'The Gift of Excuses' (1998) Buffalo Crim LR 575

Horder, *Excusing Crime* (2004)

Horder, 'Redrawing the Boundaries of Self-Defence' (1995) 58 Modern Law Review 431

Lanham, 'Offensive Weapons and Self-defence' [2005] Criminal Law Review 85

Leverick, *Killing in Self Defence* (2007)

Leverick, 'Is English Self-defence Law Incompatible with Article 2 of the EHCR' [2002] Criminal Law Review 347

Michalowski, 'Sanctity of life—Are Some Lives More Sacred than Others?' (2002) 22 Legal Studies 377

Simester, 'Mistakes in Defence' (1992) 12 Oxford Journal of Legal Studies 295

Simester, 'Intoxication is Never a Defence' [2009] Criminal Law Review 3

J.C. Smith, *Justification and Excuse in the Criminal Law* (1989)

K. Smith, 'Duress and Steadfastness: In Pursuit of the Unintelligible' [1999] Criminal Law Review 363

Tadros, *Criminal Responsibility* (2005)

Tadros, 'The Characters of Excuse' (2001) Oxford Journal of Legal Studies 495

Uniacke, *Permissible Killing* (1994)

Williams, 'The Theory of Excuses' [1982] Criminal Law Review 732

Wilson, 'The Filtering Role of Crisis in the Constitution of Criminal Defences' [2004] Canadian Journal of Law and Jurisprudence 387

Wilson, 'The Structure of Criminal Defences' [2005] Criminal Law Review 108

11

European Criminal Law

A: EU criminal law, the constitutional issues

European criminal law is hotly contested because of issues of sovereignty. The Member States of the EU do not like their domestic criminal law interfered with by the EU because each government feels that their criminal law should be local because it is socially bound to the way that the population is governed. In the past the UK Government and Parliament enjoyed what was largely an unfettered discretion to decide what conduct should be made criminal and what conduct should be left unregulated. This changed when the UK joined the European Union on 1 January 1973. By virtue of the European Communities Act 1972, s. 9(2), the UK accepted the supremacy of EC law. It thus opened the door to a defendant charged with an offence under UK law to challenge the validity of the law as being in conflict with EU law. This defence is available whether or not the creation of the UK offence pre-dated the relevant European law (*Marleasing SA* v *La Commercial Internacional de Alimentacion SA* (Case C-106/89) [1990] ECR 1-4135). Thus, as a member of the EU, the UK has to take account of its European Union obligations in shaping its criminal law and criminal justice system. Further the EU has now created a proliferation of new offences. We cannot write about all of these, but the most important of them will be mentioned. One of the most controversial new changes, is the European Arrest Warrant. This is considered below.

Because of the hostility of the Member States to the EU's burgeoning political power, the EU identified a so-called 'third pillar' which denotes a looser cooperation in criminal law compared to commercial law. This structure is already in a boiling pot with many cases pending with the ability to change the EU's constitution, as we will see, but the latest changes will not be implemented during this book's published lifetime. The latest EU Treaty is the Lisbon Treaty which will bind the members to more cooperation and a tighter control concerning criminal law, partly because of issues of terrorism which concern the whole of the EU and, in fact, the whole of the world. The Lisbon Treaty will make a number of changes, but it is too early in the process to know how the legislation will eventually look. At the moment the ECJ is not allowed to institute proceedings which infringe the third pillar if;

> "[reviewing] the proportionality of operations carried out by the police or other law enforcement services of a Member State or the exercise of the responsibilities incumbent upon

Member States with regard to the maintenance of the law and order and the safeguarding of internal security. (Article 35(5) of the Maastricht Treaty.")

The cases reveal the underlying issues of sovereignty which vex European criminal law many are concerned not with the substance in the cases but; rather with the tug of war that the EU is waging with the Member States. We will see this in a number of sectors but it is always in the background. One recent very controversial case is Case-C-176/03, *Commission v Council* [2005] ECR [2005] 1-7879 (below) where the ECJ settled some of the constitutional problems about competence and harmonisation. All the cases show a mish mash of issues, the competence and the constitutional problems in the EU, and of course the importance of human rights and fundamental rights which are paramount. Here the European Court of Human Rights and the European Court of Justice are at one, the ECJ willing to follow judgments of the European Court of Human Rights.

One decision of the ECJ which made a significant splash on these important constitutional topics; this was Case C-105/03, *Maria Pupino* ECR [2–5] 1-5285. This vital case showed that the ECJ was able to judge actions about criminal legislation. Though the particular dispute was about procedure, after the judgment the ECJ has a clear mandate and jurisdiction to judge substantive actions and offences. And the impact of the judgment was huge, in effect the whole of the Italian Criminal Code had to be rewritten. So it will be possible for the ECJ to overturn domestic jurisdictions. This is clearly very significant for English and Welsh criminal law.

Maria Pupino

Case C-105/03 ECR [2–5] 1-5285

Judgment

1. The reference for a preliminary ruling concerns the interpretation of Articles 2, 3 and 8 of Council Framework Decision 2001/220/JHA of 15 March 2001 on the standing of victims in criminal proceedings (OJ 2001 L 82, p. 1; 'the Framework Decision').

2. The reference has been made in the context of criminal proceedings against Mrs Pupino, a nursery school teacher charged with inflicting injuries on pupils aged less than five years at the time of the facts.

3. Under Article 34(2) EU, in the version resulting from the Treaty of Amsterdam, which forms part of Title VI of the Treaty on European Union, headed 'Provisions on police and judicial cooperation in criminal matters':

'The Council shall take measures and promote cooperation, using the appropriate form and procedures as set out in this Title, contributing to the pursuit of the objectives of the Union. To that end, acting unanimously on the initiative of any Member State or of the Commission, the Council may:

...

b) adopt framework decisions for the purpose of approximation of the laws and regulations of the Member States. Framework decisions shall be binding upon the Member States as to the result to be achieved but shall leave to the national authorities the choice of form and methods. They shall not entail direct effect;

...'

4. Article 35 EU provides:

'1. The Court of Justice shall have jurisdiction, subject to the conditions laid down in this Article, to give preliminary rulings on the validity and interpretation of framework decisions, and decisions on the interpretation of conventions established under this Title and on the validity and interpretation of the measures implementing them.

2. By a declaration made at the time of signature of the Treaty of Amsterdam or at any time thereafter, any Member State shall be able to accept the jurisdiction of the Court of Justice to give preliminary rulings as specified in paragraph 1.

3. A Member State making a declaration pursuant to paragraph 2 shall specify that either:

a) any court or tribunal of that State against whose decisions there is no judicial remedy under national law may request the Court of Justice to give a preliminary ruling on a question raised in a case pending before it and concerning the validity or interpretation of an act referred to in paragraph 1 if that court or tribunal considers that a decision on the question is necessary to enable it to give judgment; or

b) any court or tribunal of that State may request the Court of Justice to give a preliminary ruling on a question raised in a case pending before it and concerning the validity or interpretation of an act referred to in paragraph 1 if that court or tribunal considers that a decision on the question is necessary to enable it to give judgment.

...'

6. Under Article 2 of the Framework Decision, headed 'Respect and recognition':

'1. Each Member State shall ensure that victims have a real and appropriate role in its criminal legal system. It shall continue to make every effort to ensure that victims are treated with due respect for the dignity of the individual during proceedings and shall recognise the rights and legitimate interests of victims with particular reference to criminal proceedings.

2. Each Member State shall ensure that victims who are particularly vulnerable can benefit from specific treatment best suited to their circumstances.'

7. Article 3 of the Framework Decision, headed 'Hearings and provision of evidence' provides:

'Each Member State shall safeguard the possibility for victims to be heard during proceedings and to supply evidence.

Each Member State shall take appropriate measures to ensure that its authorities question victims only insofar as necessary for the purpose of criminal proceedings.'

8. Article 8 of the Framework Decision, headed 'Right to protection', provides in paragraph 4:

'Each Member State shall ensure that, where there is a need to protect victims – particularly those most vulnerable – from the effects of giving evidence in open court, victims may, by decision taken by the court, be entitled to testify in a manner which will enable this objective to be achieved, by any appropriate means compatible with its basic legal principles.'

9. Under Article 17 of the Framework Decision, each Member State is required to bring into force the laws, regulations and administrative provisions necessary to comply.

...

Factual background and the question referred

12. The order for reference shows that, in the criminal proceedings against Mrs Pupino, it is alleged that, in January and February 2001, she committed several offences of 'misuse of disciplinary measures' within the meaning of Article 571 of the Italian Criminal Code ('the CP') against a number of her pupils aged less than five years at the time, by such acts as regularly striking them, threatening to give them tranquillisers and to put sticking plasters over their mouths, and forbidding them from going to the toilet. She is further charged that, in February 2001, she inflicted 'serious injuries', as referred to in Articles 582, 585 and 576 of the CP, in conjunction with Article 61(2) and (11) thereof, by hitting a pupil in such a way as to cause a slight swelling of the forehead. The proceedings before the Tribunale di Firenze are at the preliminary enquiry stage.

13. The referring court states in that respect that, under Italian law, criminal procedure comprises two distinct stages. During the first stage, namely that of the preliminary enquiry, the Public Prosecutor's Office makes enquiries and, under the supervision of the judge in charge of preliminary enquiries, gathers the evidence on the basis of which it will assess whether the prosecution should be abandoned or the matter should proceed to trial. The final decision on whether to allow

the prosecution to proceed or to dismiss the matter is taken by the judge in charge of preliminary enquiries at the conclusion of an informal hearing.

14. A decision to send the examined person for trial opens the second stage of the proceedings, namely the adversarial stage, in which the judge in charge of preliminary enquiries does not take part. The proceedings proper begin with this stage. It is only at that stage that, as a rule, evidence must be taken at the initiative of the parties and in compliance with the adversarial principle. The referring court states that it is during the trial that the parties' submissions may be accepted as evidence within the technical sense of the term. In those circumstances, the evidence gathered by the Public Prosecutor's Office during the preliminary enquiry stage, in order to enable the Office to decide whether to institute criminal proceedings by proposing committal for trial or to ask for the matter to be closed, must be subjected to cross-examination during the trial proper in order to acquire the value of 'evidence' in the full sense.

15. The national court states, however, that there are exceptions to that rule, laid down by Article 392 of the CP, which allow evidence to be established early, during the preliminary enquiry period, on a decision of the judge in charge of preliminary enquiries and in compliance with the adversarial principle, by means of the Special Inquiry procedure. Evidence gathered in that way has the same probative value as that gathered during the second stage of the proceedings. Article 392(1a) of the CPP has introduced the possibility of using that special procedure when taking evidence from victims of certain restrictively listed offences (sexual offences or offences with a sexual background) aged less than 16 years, even outside the cases envisaged in paragraph 1 of that article. Article 398(5a) of the CP also allows the same judge to order evidence to be taken, in the case of enquiries concerning offences referred to in Article 392(1a) of the CP, under special arrangements allowing the protection of the minors concerned. According to the national court, those additional derogations are designed to protect, first, the dignity, modesty and character of a minor witness, and, secondly, the authenticity of the evidence.

16. In this case, the Public Prosecutor's Office asked the judge in charge of preliminary enquiries in August 2001 to take the testimony of eight children, witnesses and victims of the offences for which Mrs Pupino is being examined, by the special procedure for taking evidence early, pursuant to Article 392(1a) of the CP, on the ground that such evidence could not be deferred until the trial on account of the witnesses' extreme youth, inevitable alterations in their psychological state, and a possible process of repression. The Public Prosecutor's Office also requested that evidence be gathered under the special arrangements referred to in Article 398(5a) of the CP, whereby the hearing should take place in specially designed facilities, with arrangements to protect the dignity, privacy and tranquillity of the minors concerned, possibly involving an expert in child psychology by reason of the delicate and serious nature of the facts and the difficulties caused by the victims' young age. Mrs Pupino opposed that application, arguing that it did not fall within any of the cases envisaged by Article 392(1) and (1a) of the CP.

17. The referring court states that, under the national provisions in question, the application of the Public Prosecutor's Office would have to be dismissed. Those provisions do not provide for the use of the Special Inquiry procedure, or for the use of special arrangements for gathering evidence, where the facts are such as those alleged against the defendant, even if there is no reason to preclude those provisions also covering cases other than those referred to in Article 392(1) of the CP in which the victim is a minor. A number of offences excluded from the scope of Article 392(1) of the CP might well prove more serious for the victim than those referred to in that provision. That, in the view of the national court, is the case here, where, according to the Public Prosecutor's Office, Mrs Pupino maltreated several children aged less than five years, causing them psychological trauma.

18. Considering that, 'apart from the question of the existence or otherwise of a direct effect of Community law', the national court must 'interpret its national law in the light of the letter and the spirit of Community provisions', and having doubts as to the compatibility of Articles 392(1a) and 398(5a) of the CP with Articles 2, 3 and 8 of the Framework Decision, inasmuch as the provisions of that code limit the ability of the judge in charge of preliminary enquiries to apply the Special Inquiry procedure for the early gathering of evidence, and the special arrangements for its gathering, to sexual offences or offences with a sexual background, the judge in charge of preliminary enquires

at the Tribunale di Firenze has decided to stay the proceedings and ask the Court of Justice to rule on the scope of Articles 2, 3 and 8 of the Framework Decision.

...

31. Having regard to the arguments of the French, Italian, Swedish, Netherlands and United Kingdom Governments, it has to be examined whether, as the national court presupposes and as the French, Greek and Portuguese Governments and the Commission maintain, the obligation on the national authorities to interpret their national law as far as possible in the light of the wording and purpose of Community directives applies with the same effects and within the same limits where the act concerned is a framework decision taken on the basis of Title VI of the Treaty on European Union.

32. If so, it has to be determined whether, as the French, Italian, Swedish and United Kingdom Governments have observed, it is obvious that a reply to the question referred cannot have a concrete impact on the solution of the dispute in the main proceedings, given the inherent limits on the obligation of conforming interpretation.

33. It should be noted at the outset that the wording of Article 34(2)(b) EU is very closely inspired by that of the third paragraph of Article 249 EC. Article 34(2)(b) EU confers a binding character on framework decisions in the sense that they 'bind' the Member States 'as to the result to be achieved but shall leave to the national authorities the choice of form and methods'.

34. The binding character of framework decisions, formulated in terms identical to those of the third paragraph of Article 249 EC, places on national authorities, and particularly national courts, an obligation to interpret national law in conformity.

35. The fact that, by virtue of Article 35 EU, the jurisdiction of the Court of Justice is less extensive under Title VI of the Treaty on European Union than it is under the EC Treaty, and the fact that there is no complete system of actions and procedures designed to ensure the legality of the acts of the institutions in the context of Title VI, does nothing to invalidate that conclusion.

36. Irrespective of the degree of integration envisaged by the Treaty of Amsterdam in the process of creating an ever closer union among the peoples of Europe within the meaning of the second paragraph of Article 1 EU, it is perfectly comprehensible that the authors of the Treaty on European Union should have considered it useful to make provision, in the context of Title VI of that treaty, for recourse to legal instruments with effects similar to those provided for by the EC Treaty, in order to contribute effectively to the pursuit of the Union's objectives.

37. The importance of the Court's jurisdiction to give preliminary rulings under Article 35 EU is confirmed by the fact that, under Article 35(4), any Member State, whether or not it has made a declaration pursuant to Article 35(2), is entitled to submit statements of case or written observations to the Court in cases which arise under Article 35(1).

38. That jurisdiction would be deprived of most of its useful effect if individuals were not entitled to invoke framework decisions in order to obtain a conforming interpretation of national law before the courts of the Member States.

39. In support of their position, the Italian and United Kingdom Governments argue that, unlike the EC Treaty, the Treaty on European Union contains no obligation similar to that laid down in Article 10 EC, on which the case-law of the Court of Justice partially relied in order to justify the obligation to interpret national law in conformity with Community law.

40. That argument must be rejected.

41. The second and third paragraphs of Article 1 of the Treaty on European Union provide that that treaty marks a new stage in the process of creating an ever closer union among the peoples of Europe and that the task of the Union, which is founded on the European Communities, supplemented by the policies and forms of cooperation established by that treaty, shall be to organise, in a manner demonstrating consistency and solidarity, relations between the Member States and between their peoples.

42. It would be difficult for the Union to carry out its task effectively if the principle of loyal cooperation, requiring in particular that Member States take all appropriate measures, whether general or particular, to ensure fulfilment of their obligations under European Union law, were not also binding in the area of police and judicial cooperation in criminal matters, which is moreover entirely

based on cooperation between the Member States and the institutions, as the Advocate General has rightly pointed out in paragraph 26 of her Opinion.

43. In the light of all the above considerations, the Court concludes that the principle of conforming interpretation is binding in relation to framework decisions adopted in the context of Title VI of the Treaty on European Union. When applying national law, the national court that is called upon to interpret it must do so as far as possible in the light of the wording and purpose of the framework decision in order to attain the result which it pursues and thus comply with Article 34(2)(b) EU.

The judgment of *Pupino* signals that the EU, traditionally cautious in entering into the field of criminal law, is likely to become more active in the future. On 23 November 2005 the European Commission published details of seven offences that it intended to require member states to punish as contravening the criminal law of member states. Meanwhile, the European Court of Justice (ECJ) in Case C-176/03 *Commission of the European Community* v *Council of the European Union*, 13 September 2005 (discussed below) ruled that the European Community has the power to require member states to lay down criminal penalties for the purpose of protecting the environment. The new offences to be created relate to:

- counterfeiting euro notes and coins;
- credit card and cheque fraud;
- money laundering;
- people-trafficking;
- computer hacking and virus attacks;
- private sector corruption;
- marine pollution.

The ECJ has signalled its intention to set the level of penalties for these offences. This is a controversial move which transfers an area of previously fiercely guarded sovereignty from Member States to the EU. In the UK, for example, most of the substantive offences identified above already are on the statute books, but the penalties for their violation have been set by Parliament and the UK courts.

In Case C-176/03 *Commission of the European Community* v *Council of the European Union*, 13 September 2005, the ECJ ruled that the European Community has the power to require Member States to lay down criminal penalties for the purpose of protecting the environment. The case concerned a dispute over the relative powers of the Council and the Commission to pass legislation in respect of environmental matters. The ECJ held that the protection of the environment is one of the essential objectives of the Community and that therefore 'environmental protection requirements must be integrated into the definition and implementation of the Community's policies and activities.' The Council, supported by 11 Member States including the UK, argued that there were no grounds for accepting that the power to require criminal sanctions had been implicitly transferred from the Member States to the EU and that such a transfer was difficult to imply because of the importance to the sovereignty of the Member States of the power to impose criminal sanctions. The ECJ disagreed:

Commission of the European Community v *Council of the European Union*
Case C-176/03 13 September 2005

...

Judgment

1. By its application the Commission of the European Communities is seeking annulment of Council Framework Decision 2003/80/JHA of 27 January 2003 on the protection of the environment through criminal law (OJ 2003 L 29, p. 55; 'the framework decision').

Legal framework and background

2. On 27 January 2003, on the initiative of the Kingdom of Denmark, the Council of the European Union adopted the framework decision.

3. Based on Title VI of the Treaty on European Union, in particular Articles 29 EU, 31(e) EU and 34(2)(b) EU, as worded prior to the entry into force of the Treaty of Nice, the framework decision constitutes, as is clear from the first three recitals in its preamble, the instrument by which the European Union intends to respond with concerted action to the disturbing increase in offences posing a threat to the environment.

4. The framework decision lays down a number of environmental offences, in respect of which the Member States are required to prescribe criminal penalties.

5. Thus, Article 2 of the framework decision, entitled 'Intentional offences', provides:

'Each Member State shall take the necessary measures to establish as criminal offences under its domestic law

  (a) the discharge, emission or introduction of a quantity of substances or ionising radiation into air, soil or water which causes death or serious injury to any person;

  (b) the unlawful discharge, emission or introduction of a quantity of substances or ionising radiation into air, soil or water which causes or is likely to cause their lasting or substantial deterioration or death or serious injury to any person or substantial damage to protected monuments, other protected objects, property, animals or plants;

  (c) the unlawful disposal, treatment, storage, transport, export or import of waste, including hazardous waste, which causes or is likely to cause death or serious injury to any person or substantial damage to the quality of air, soil, water, animals or plants;

  (d) the unlawful operation of a plant in which a dangerous activity is carried out and which, outside the plant, causes or is likely to cause death or serious injury to any person or substantial damage to the quality of air, soil, water, animals or plants;

  (e) the unlawful manufacture, treatment, storage, use, transport, export or import of nuclear materials or other hazardous radioactive substances which causes or is likely to cause death or serious injury to any person or substantial damage to the quality of air, soil, water, animals or plants;

  (f) the unlawful possession, taking, damaging, killing or trading of or in protected wild fauna and flora species or parts thereof, at least where they are threatened with extinction as defined under national law;

  (g) the unlawful trade in ozone-depleting substances,

when committed intentionally.'

6. Article 3 of the framework decision, entitled 'Negligent offences', provides:

'Each Member State shall take the necessary measures to establish as criminal offences under its domestic law, when committed with negligence, or at least serious negligence, the offences enumerated in Article 2.'

7. Article 4 of the framework decision states that each Member State is to take the necessary measures to ensure that participating in or instigating the conduct referred to in Article 2 is punishable.

8. Article 5(1) of the framework decision provides that the penalties thus laid down must be 'effective, proportionate and dissuasive' including, 'at least in serious cases, penalties involving deprivation of liberty which can give rise to extradition'. Article 5(2) adds that the criminal penalties 'may be accompanied by other penalties or measures'.

9. Article 6 of the framework decision governs the liability, as the result of an act or omission, of legal persons and Article 7 sets out the sanctions to which they are to be subject, which 'include criminal or non-criminal fines and may include other sanctions'.

10. Finally, Article 8 of the framework decision concerns jurisdiction and Article 9 deals with prosecutions brought by a Member State which does not extradite its own nationals.

11. The Commission objected in the various Council bodies to the legal basis relied on by the Council to require the Member States to impose criminal penalties on persons committing environmental offences. In its submission, the correct legal basis in that respect was Article 175(1) EC and it had indeed put forward, on 15 March 2001, a proposal for a Directive of the European Parliament and of the Council on the protection of the environment through criminal law (OJ 2001 C 180 E, p. 238, 'the proposed directive'), based on Article 175 EC, the annex to which listed the Community law measures to which the offences set out in Article 3 of the proposal relate.

12. On 9 April 2002, the European Parliament expressed its view on both the proposed directive, at first reading, and on the draft framework decision.

13. It concurred with the Commission's view of the scope of the Community's competence, whilst calling on the Council (i) to use the framework decision as a measure complementing the directive that would take effect in relation to the protection of the environment through criminal law solely in respect of judicial cooperation and (ii) to refrain from adopting the framework decision before adoption of the proposed directive (see texts adopted by the Parliament on 9 April 2002 bearing references A5-0099/2002 (first reading) and A5-0080/2002).

14. The Council did not adopt the proposed directive, but the fifth and seventh recitals to the framework decision are worded as follows:

'(5) The Council considered it appropriate to incorporate into the present Framework decision a number of substantive provisions contained in the proposed Directive, in particular those defining the conduct which Member States have to establish as criminal offences under their domestic law.

...

(7) The Council has considered this proposal but has come to the conclusion that the majority required for its adoption by the Council cannot be obtained. The said majority considered that the proposal went beyond the powers attributed to the Community by the Treaty establishing the European Community and that the objectives could be reached by adopting a Framework-Decision on the basis of Title VI of the Treaty on European Union. The Council also considered that the present Framework Decision, based on Article 34 of the Treaty on European Union, is a correct instrument to impose on the member States the obligation to provide for criminal sanctions. The amended proposal submitted by the Commission was not of a nature to allow the Council to change its position in this respect.'

15. The Commission appended the following statement to the minutes of the Council meeting at which the framework decision was adopted:

'The Commission takes the view that the Framework Decision is not the appropriate legal instrument by which to require Member States to introduce sanctions of a criminal nature at national level in the case of offences detrimental to the environment.

As the Commission pointed out on several occasions within Council bodies, it considers that in the context of the competences conferred on it for the purpose of attaining the objectives stated in Article 2 of the Treaty establishing the European Community, the Community is competent to require the Member States to impose sanctions at national level – including criminal sanctions if appropriate – where that proves necessary in order to attain a Community objective.

This is the case for environmental matters which are the subject of Title XIX of the Treaty establishing the European Community.

Furthermore, the Commission points out that its proposal for a Directive on the protection of the environment through criminal law has not been appropriately examined under the codecision procedure.

If the Council adopts the Framework Decision despite this Community competence, the Commission reserves all the rights conferred on it by the Treaty.'

...

Arguments of the parties

[the Commission argues]

19. Although it does not claim that the Community legislature has a general competence in criminal matters, the Commission submits that the legislature is competent, under Article 175 EC, to require the Member States to prescribe criminal penalties for infringements of Community environmental-protection legislation if it takes the view that that is a necessary means of ensuring that the legislation is effective. The harmonisation of national criminal laws, in particular of the constituent elements of environmental offences to which criminal penalties attach, is designed to be an aid to the Community policy in question.

20. The Commission recognises that there is no precedent in this area. It relies, however, in support of its argument, on the case-law of the Court concerning the duty of loyal cooperation and the principles of effectiveness and equivalence (see, inter alia, Case 50/76 Amsterdam Bulb [1977] ECR 137, paragraph 33, Case C-186/98 Nunes and de Matos [1999] ECR I-4883, paragraphs 12 and 14, and the order of 13 July 1990 in Case C-2/88 IMM Zwartveld and Others [1990] ECR I-3365, paragraph 17

...

...[The Council argued]

30. None of the judgments or secondary legislation to which the Commission refers lends support to its argument.

31. First, the Court has never obliged the Member States to adopt criminal penalties. According to its case-law, it is certainly the responsibility of the Member States to ensure that infringements of Community law are penalised under conditions, both procedural and substantive, which are analogous to those applicable to infringements of national law of a similar nature and importance, and the penalty must, moreover, be effective, dissuasive and proportionate to the infringement; furthermore, the national authorities must proceed with respect to infringements of Community law with the same diligence as that which they bring to bear in implementing corresponding national laws (see, in particular, Case 68/88 Commission v Greece [1989] ECR 2965, paragraphs 24 and 25). However, the Court has not held, either expressly or by implication, that the Community is competent to harmonise the criminal laws applicable in the Member States. It has rather held that the choice of penalties is a matter for the Member States.

Findings of the Court

...

40. It is therefore necessary to ascertain whether Articles 1 to 7 of the framework decision affect the powers of the Community under Article 175 EC inasmuch as those articles could, as the Commission maintains, have been adopted on the basis of the last-mentioned provision.

41. On that point, it is common ground that protection of the environment constitutes one of the essential objectives of the Community (see Case 240/83 ADBHU [1985] ECR 531, paragraph 13, Case 302/86 Commission v Denmark [1988] ECR 4607, paragraph 8, Case C-213/96 Outokumpu [1998] ECR I-1777, paragraph 32). In that regard, Article 2 EC states that the Community has as its task to promote 'a high level of protection and improvement of the quality of the environment' and, to that end, Article 3(1)(l) EC provides for the establishment of a 'policy in the sphere of the environment'.

42. Furthermore, in the words of Article 6 EC '[e]nvironmental protection requirements must be integrated into the definition and implementation of the Community policies and activities', a provision which emphasises the fundamental nature of that objective and its extension across the range of those policies and activities.

...

46. As regards the aim of the framework decision, it is clear both from its title and from its first three recitals that its objective is the protection of the environment. The Council was concerned 'at the rise in environmental offences and their effects which are increasingly extending beyond the borders of the States in which the offences are committed', and, having found that those offences constitute 'a threat to the environment' and 'a problem jointly faced by the Member States', concluded that 'a tough response' and 'concerted action to protect the environment under criminal law' were called for.

47. As to the content of the framework decision, Article 2 establishes a list of particularly serious environmental offences, in respect of which the Member States must impose criminal penalties. Articles 2 to 7 of the decision do indeed entail partial harmonisation of the criminal laws of the Member States, in particular as regards the constituent elements of various criminal offences committed to the detriment of the environment. As a general rule, neither criminal law nor the rules of criminal procedure fall within the Community's competence (see, to that effect, Case 203/80 Casati [1981] ECR 2595, paragraph 27, and Case C-226/97 Lemmens [1998] ECR I-3711, paragraph 19).

48. However, the last-mentioned finding does not prevent the Community legislature, when the application of effective, proportionate and dissuasive criminal penalties by the competent national authorities is an essential measure for combating serious environmental offences, from taking measures which relate to the criminal law of the Member States which it considers necessary in order to ensure that the rules which it lays down on environmental protection are fully effective.

49. It should also be added that in this instance, although Articles 1 to 7 of the framework decision determine that certain conduct which is particularly detrimental to the environment is to be criminal, they leave to the Member States the choice of the criminal penalties to apply, although, in accordance with Article 5(1) of the decision, the penalties must be effective, proportionate and dissuasive.

50. The Council does not dispute that the acts listed in Article 2 of the framework decision include infringements of a considerable number of Community measures, which were listed in the annex to the proposed directive. Moreover, it is apparent from the first three recitals to the framework decision that the Council took the view that criminal penalties were essential for combating serious offences against the environment.

51. It follows from the foregoing that, on account of both their aim and their content, Articles 1 to 7 of the framework decision have as their main purpose the protection of the environment and they could have been properly adopted on the basis of Article 175 EC.

52. That finding is not called into question by the fact that Articles 135 EC and 280(4) EC reserve to the Member States, in the spheres of customs cooperation and the protection of the Community's financial interests respectively, the application of national criminal law and the administration of justice. It is not possible to infer from those provisions that, for the purposes of the implementation of environmental policy, any harmonisation of criminal law, even as limited as that resulting from the framework decision, must be ruled out even where it is necessary in order to ensure the effectiveness of Community law.

53. In those circumstances, the entire framework decision, being indivisible, infringes Article 47 EU as it encroaches on the powers which Article 175 EC confers on the Community.

54. There is therefore no need to examine the Commission's argument that the framework decision should in any event be annulled in part in so far as Articles 5(2), 6 and 7 leave the Member States free also to provide for penalties other than criminal penalties, even to choose between criminal penalties and other penalties, matters allegedly falling undeniably within the Community's competence.

In the light of all the foregoing, the framework decision must be annulled.

The reaction to the 'Environment Case' became a point of contention between the Member States and the EU. There were also an institutional argument between the Commission and the Council, but this is not the most important issue for our purposes. The case highlighted the way that the EU was implementing more and more offences and because of this there was a furore which has not been resolved yet. The focus is no longer limited to terrorism offences and similar crimes, but the EU been extended offences such as those which criminalise intellectual property rights, immigration offences and crimes concerning labour and employment issues. Many of the Member States think that the EU should not have power to impose criminal sanctions and that the issue of criminalisation has been over-emphasised. Despite the worries of the Member States' and the arguments and fierce contention, the ECJ continues to think that EU criminal law should be extended. In Case-440/05, *Commission* v *Council* [2007] 1-9097 that the ECJ annulled a Framework Directive, this time concerning marine pollution.

As well as the constitutional issues, the EU is devising many European substantive offences, often about terrorism but also about organised crime including trafficking in human beings, sexual exploitation and criminal and child pornography, drug trafficking, corruption in the private sector, attacks against information systems, counterfeiting of the Euro, and non-cash means of payment. There are several Framework Directives which are expected, including those on racism and xenophobia. The EU Commission has published a Green Paper which concedes that there are great difficulties with regard to the criminal law in each state because of the way that the law is made historically and culturally.

> The differences between members states' legislation on penalties are still quite acute. There are historical, cultural and legal reasons for this, deep-rooted in their legal systems, which have evolved over time as well as the way in which member states have faced and answered fundamental questions about criminal law. These systems have their own internal coherence and amending individual rules without regard to the overall picture would risk creating distortion. (Green Paper, COM (2007) 334 final, Brussels, 30 April 2004, pg. The Lisbon Treaty which is now being implemented will change the way that the third pillar of the EU will be considered and we can see that the third pillar has already been altered and diluted. It was supposed to be a cooperation measure but the ECJ has moved the goal posts by making all of the other measures, including the market measures, wide open to interpretation. The Lisbon Treaty will further align this idea, it is too early to know exactly what will happen but it seems that a further integration of EU criminal law is almost certain.

B: The way that EU market provisions impact UK criminal law

Complying with EU obligations in the sphere of criminal law may work either positively or negatively. In some instances the UK is precluded from criminalising certain conduct because to do so would infringe on a European recognised right. In other instances, the UK is required to criminalise certain conduct in order to give effect to a European mandate.

If the law of a Member State of the EU is in conflict with EU law, it is not valid. In *Costa v ENEL* (case 6/64) [1964] ECR 585, the ECJ stated:

> By contrast with ordinary national treaties, [the Treaty founding the European Community] has created its own legal systems which, on the entry into force of the Treaty, became an integral part of the legal systems of the Member States and which their courts are bound to apply.

By creating a Community of unlimited duration, having its own institutions, its own personality, its own legal capacity…the Member States have limited their sovereign rights, albeit within limited fields, and have thus created a body of law which binds their nationals and themselves.

Note that this case was decided before Parliament enacted the European Communities Act 1972, by which the UK implemented its decision to join the Community and accepted the supremacy of EC law (see s. 9(2) of the Act).

A defendant seeking to challenge the validity of a UK law as being incompatible with EU law has to persuade the UK court that a relevant EU rule is involved and that it is in conflict with the UK law creating the offence. If there is any doubt about this the UK court should refer the case to the ECJ for its interpretation. The reference will take place under Article 236 of the EC Treaty. The ECJ will consider the referred question and return the case to the Member State court which will then give judgment, taking note of the guidance issued by the ECJ.

In cases involving European law it is necessary to take account of the purposive interpretation of the EC Treaty adopted by the ECJ. A literal interpretation of the text is not a proper approach.

R v Henn and Darby

(Case 34/79) [1979] ECR 3795, European Court of Justice

I—FACTS AND PROCEDURE

1. The national legislation applicable

Section 42 of the Customs Consolidation Act, 1876, prohibits the importation into the United Kingdom of 'indecent or obscene' articles, and provides that articles imported contrary to the prohibition shall be forfeited and may be destroyed or otherwise disposed of as the Commissioners of Customs may direct. The seventh schedule to the Customs and Excise Act, 1952, provides a procedure for testing the liability of goods to forfeiture under section 42 either in the High Court of Justice or in a court of summary jurisdiction.

...

Section 304 of the Customs and Excise Act, 1952, makes it a criminal offence for any person to be in any way knowingly concerned in the fraudulent evasion or attempted evasion of the prohibition on importation. Infringement is made punishable by the imposition of a financial penalty of three times the value of the goods involved or £100, whichever is the greater, and/or imprisonment for a term not exceeding two years.

On 17 May 1977 at Ipswich Crown Court the appellants were indicted, inter alia, with being knowingly concerned in the fraudulent evasion of the prohibition of the importation of indecent or obscene articles contrary to section 42 of the Customs Consolidation Act, 1876, and section 304 of the Customs and Excise Act, 1952.

Both the films (which were of a size ordinarily used in domestic projectors) and the magazines depict detailed and explicit sexual activities, including aberrant sexual behaviour. The films include a number of scenes of violence and two of the magazines contain only photographs of naked girls between about five and fourteen years old engaging in or having engaged in sexual activity with an adult man. Five of the magazines contain advertisements inviting readers to apply to a 'Model Contact', and one magazine advertises for models for another magazine which depicts acts of buggery. All the films and magazines included in the charge were made by a firm called 'Color Climax' and originated in Denmark.

The films and magazines depict the commission of acts which are contrary to the criminal law of the United Kingdom in a variety of ways.

At the outset of the trial application was made to the trial judge by counsel acting for both appellants to quash the count which is the subject of this reference on the grounds that since the accession of the United Kingdom to the European Communities by reason of section 2(1) and Schedule I part 1 paragraph 2 of the European Communities Act, 1972, Article 30 (now Article 28) of the EEC Treaty operated so as to invalidate section 42 of the Customs Consolidation Act, 1876, in so far as it related to goods coming from a Member State and defined by Article 9 of the Treaty. This application was rejected. The appellants pleaded 'Not Guilty' to the charge. The application was renewed at the end of the case for the prosecution. It was again rejected.

Both appellants were convicted. On 15 July they were sentenced: Henn to eighteen months' imprisonment, Darby to two years' imprisonment. They were further ordered to pay a financial penalty.

Both appellants appealed against their convictions. The appeals were heard by the Court of Appeal (Criminal Division) on 4 to 7 July 1978. The court refused to refer any questions to the Court of Justice under Article 177 of the Treaty and dismissed the appeals. The court certified in accordance with section 33 of the Criminal Appeal Act, 1968, that a point of law, of general public importance was involved in the appeals, namely:

> Whether section 42 of the Customs Consolidation Act, 1876, is effective to prevent the importation of pornographic articles from Holland notwithstanding Articles 30 and 36 of the European Economic Community Treaty.

JUDGMENT OF THE COURT

...

Under the terms of Article 36 (now Article 30) of the Treaty the provisions relating to the free movement of goods within the Community are not to preclude prohibitions on imports which are justified inter alia 'on grounds of public morality'. In principle, it is for each Member State to determine in accordance with its own scale of values and in the form selected by it the requirements of public morality in its territory. In any event, it cannot be disputed that the statutory provisions applied by the United Kingdom in regard to the importation of articles having an indecent or obscene character come within the powers reserved to the Member States by the first sentence of Article 36.

Each Member State is entitled to impose prohibitions on imports justified on grounds of public morality for the whole of its territory, as defined in Article 227 (now Art 229) of the Treaty, whatever the structure of its constitution may be and however the powers of legislating in regard to the subject in question may be distributed. The fact that certain differences exist between the laws enforced in the different constituent parts of a Member State does not thereby prevent that State from applying a unitary concept in regard to prohibitions on imports imposed, on grounds of public morality, on trade with other Member States.

... According to the second sentence of Article 36 the restrictions on imports referred to in the first sentence may not 'constitute a means of arbitrary discrimination or a disguised restriction on trade between Member States'.

In order to answer the questions which have been referred to the Court it is appropriate to have regard to the function of this provision, which is designed to prevent restrictions on trade based on the grounds mentioned in the first sentence of Article 36 from being diverted from their proper purpose and used in such a way as either to create discrimination in respect of goods originating in other Member States or indirectly to protect certain national products. That is not the purport of a prohibition, such as that in force in the United Kingdom, on the importation of articles which are of an indecent or obscene character. Whatever may be the differences between the laws on this subject in force in the different constituent parts of the United Kingdom, and notwithstanding the fact that they contain certain exceptions of limited scope, these laws, taken as a whole, have as their purpose the prohibition, or at least, the restraining, of the manufacture and marketing of publications or articles of an indecent or obscene character. In these circumstances it is permissible to conclude, on a comprehensive view, that there is no lawful trade in such goods in the United Kingdom. A prohibition on imports which may in certain respects be more strict than some of the laws applied within the United Kingdom cannot therefore be regarded as amounting to a measure designed to give indirect protection to some national product or aimed at creating arbitrary discrimination between goods of this type depending on whether they are produced within the national territory or another Member State.

The answer to the fourth question must therefore be that if a prohibition on the importation of goods is justifiable on grounds of public morality and if it is imposed with that purpose the enforcement of that prohibition cannot, in the absence within the Member State concerned of a lawful trade in the same goods, constitute a means of arbitrary discrimination or a disguised restriction on trade contrary to Article 36.

THE COURT, in answer to the questions referred to it by the House of Lords by order of 22 February 1979, hereby rules:

(1) A law of a Member State prohibiting any importation of pornographic articles into that State constitutes a quantitative restriction on imports within the meaning of Article 30 of the Treaty.

(2) The first sentence of Article 36 upon its true construction means that a Member State may, in principle, lawfully impose prohibitions on the importation from any other Member State of articles which are of an indecent or obscene character as understood by its domestic laws and that such prohibitions may lawfully be applied to the whole of its national territory even if, in regard to the field in question, variations exist between the laws in force in the different constituent parts of the Member State concerned.

(3) If a prohibition on the importation of goods is justifiable on grounds of public morality and if it is imposed with that purpose the enforcement of that prohibition cannot, in the absence within the Member State concerned of a lawful trade in the same goods, constitute a means of arbitrary discrimination or a disguised restriction on trade contrary to Article 36.

C: Which provisions of EU law may be relevant?

All of them! Treaty Articles, Regulations and Directives all may nullify or modify Member State criminal provisions. In view of the purposive interpretations adopted by the ECJ, considerable expertise in EU law is required in order to understand the potentially far-reaching effect of some European provisions.

(i) Treaty articles

See *R* v *Henn and Darby* (above) and consider also:

R v Robert Tymen

(Case 269/80) [1981] CMLR 493, European Court of Justice

Decision

By order of 14 November 1980, which was received at the Court on 5 December 1980, the Court of Appeal, Criminal Division, London, referred to the Court for a preliminary ruling under Article 177 (now Art 234) of the EEC Treaty five questions as to the interpretation of Article 102 of the Act of 22 January 1972 concerning Conditions of Accession and the Adjustments to the Treaties and certain other provisions of Community law in relation to a United Kingdom measure concerning fisheries.

These questions were raised in the context of criminal proceedings against the master of a French trawler, Mr Tymen, for the infringement of the Fishing Nets (North-East Atlantic) (Variation) Order 1979 (SI 1979 No 744). That order, which entered into force on 1 July 1979 and which amended the Fishing Nets (North-East Atlantic) Order 1977 (SI 1977 No 440), prohibits in a specified zone of the Atlantic and Arctic Oceans and the seas adjacent to those oceans the presence on board fishing boats of nets having a mesh-size less than certain prescribed minimum sizes.

In the case in point Mr Tymen was found guilty by Cardiff Crown Court of offences contrary to the above-mentioned orders, having been found in possession on 16 October 1979 on board his ship

within the United Kingdom fishing zone of nets having an average mesh-size less than the minimum permitted mesh-size. He appealed against that judgment to the Court of Appeal, Criminal Division.
...

First question

The first question inquires whether the Member States still retained power after 31 December 1978 to adopt conservation measures of the kind contained in the United Kingdom order in question.

As the Court has already held in its above-mentioned judgment of 5 May 1981, the power to adopt, as part of the common fisheries policy, measures relating to the conservation of the resources of the sea has belonged fully and definitively to the Communities since the expiration on 1 January 1979 of the transitional period laid down by Article 102 of the Act of Accession so that after that date the Member States are no longer entitled to exercise any power of their own in this matter and may henceforth only act as trustees of the common interest, in the absence of appropriate action on the part of the Council.

Second question

The second question inquires in substance whether individuals may be prosecuted under a measure which is found to be contrary to Community law.

The same question has already formed the subject-matter of the judgment 16 February 1978 (Schonenberg (case 88/77) [1978] ECR 473). In that judgment, which, like the present case, concerned a breach of national fishery provisions, the Court found that where criminal proceedings were brought by virtue of a national measure which is held to be contrary to Community law a conviction in those proceedings is also incompatible with that law.

The reply to the second question must accordingly be that where criminal proceedings are brought by virtue of a national measure which is held to be contrary to Community law a conviction in those proceedings is also incompatible with that law.

(ii) Sanctions

As we have seen, some offences are in direct conflict with EU rules. On other occasions it is the relevant sanction that can fall foul of EU rules. Sanctions, as the ECJ has stated on more than one occasion, should be effective, proportional and dissuasive.

R v Stanislaus Pieck
(Case 157/79) [1980] 3 CMLR 220, European Court of Justice

Mr Pieck is a Dutch national. As may be seen from his passport he first entered the United Kingdom on 3 August 1973 and subsequently has resided there on several occasions. His passport was renewed at the Netherlands Consulate in London on 12 April 1976; on that occasion his address on the passport was changed from 'Wellington, New Zealand' to 'Cardiff, G.B.'. Since entering the United Kingdom on 3 December 1977, Mr Pieck has been and is still employed as a printer at an undertaking known as 'Graphics Prints' at Taffs Well near Cardiff.

Mr Pieck left the United Kingdom on 22 July 1978 and returned one week later, on 29 July. On each occasion on which he entered the United Kingdom the immigration authorities entered on his passport the date and place of entry together with the words 'given leave to enter the United Kingdom for six months' in compliance with Rule 51 of the Statement of Immigration Rules for Control on Entry (EEC and other Non-Commonwealth Nationals) (HP 81), adopted by the Home Secretary in pursuance of section 3(2) of the Immigration Act 1971.

Rule 51 reads:

When an EEC national is given leave to enter, no condition is to be imposed restricting his employment or occupation in the United Kingdom. Admission should normally be for a period of six months, except in the case of a returning resident or the holder of a valid residence permit.

The six months' leave of entry into the United Kingdom granted to Mr Pieck on 29 July 1978 expired on 21 January 1979. In March 1979 Mr Pieck voluntarily went to the South Wales Constabulary, explained that he had overstayed his leave and asked for advice. He was advised to send his passport to the Home Office together with an application for a further stay. Mr Pieck did nothing. On 3 May 1979 he was required by a police officer to produce his passport. He replied: 'I was going to send it off but I forgot.' On that date Mr Pieck was charged with an offence contrary to the Immigration Act 1971, section 24(1)(b)(i), which reads:

> (24)(1): A person who is not a patrial shall be guilty of an offence punishable on summary conviction with a fine of not more than £200 or with imprisonment for not more than six months or with both, in any of the following cases . . .
>> (b) if, having only a limited leave to enter or remain in the United Kingdom he knowingly . . .
>>> (i) remains beyond the time limited by the leave.

The charge against Mr Pieck reads as follows:

> For that you being a person who is not patrial and only having a limited leave to remain in the United Kingdom knowingly remained in the United Kingdom beyond 29 January 1979, the time limited by the leave.

At the same time a notice was served on Mr Pieck in pursuance of section 6(2) of the Immigration Act 1971 to the effect that if he was convicted of the above offence the court would have power to recommend his deportation under section 3(6) of the Immigration Act 1971.

On 12 July 1979 Mr Pieck appeared before the Pontypridd Magistrates' Court and, whilst not contesting the evidence adduced by the prosecution, pleaded not guilty to the charge. He relied on Article 48(3)(b) and (c) of the EEC Treaty and the provisions of Directive 68/360 to show that the initial grant of six months' leave to enter the United Kingdom and the requirement to extend it were incompatible with Community law.

By order of 5 September 1979 the Magistrates' Court asked the Court of Justice to give a preliminary ruling on the three following questions:

1. What is the meaning of 'entry visa or equivalent document' in Article 3(2) of Council Directive 68/360/EEC of 15 October 1968?
2. Upon entry into a member-State by a EEC national, is the granting by that member-State of an initial leave to remain for a period limited to six months consistent with the rights secured to such a national by Articles 7 and 48 of the Treaty establishing the EEC and the provisions of Council Directives 64/221/EEC of 25 February 1964 and 68/360/EEC of 15 October 1968?
3. (Only applicable if the answer to Question 2 is affirmative) Where such a national is given a six months' limited leave to remain in a member-State and being employed as a worker but having failed to apply for a resident's permit he overstays that leave, can such a breach of law be punished in that member-State by measures which include imprisonment and/or a recommendation for deportation?

THE COURT RULED THAT:

(1) Article 3(2) of Council Directive 68/360 of 15 October 1958 prohibiting member-States from demanding an entry visa or equivalent requirement from Community workers moving within the Community must be interpreted as meaning that the phrase 'entry visa or equivalent requirement' covers any formality for the purpose of granting leave to enter the territory of a member-State which is coupled with a passport or identity card check at the frontier, whatever may be the place or time at which that leave is granted and in whatever form it may be granted.

(2) (a) The issue of a special residence document provided for in Article 4 of Council Directive 68/360 of 15 October 1968 has only a declaratory effect and for aliens to whom Article 48 of the Treaty or parallel provisions give rights, it cannot be assimilated to a residence permit such as is prescribed for aliens in general, in connection with the issue of which the national authorities have a discretion.

(b) A member-State may not require from a person enjoying the protection of Community law that he should possess a general residence permit instead of the document provided for in Article 4(2) of Directive 68/360 in conjunction with the Annex thereto.

(3) The failure on the part of a national of a member-State of the Community, to whom the rules on freedom of movement for workers apply, to obtain the special residence permit prescribed in Article 4 of Directive 68/360 may not be punished by a recommendation for deportation or by measures which go as far as imprisonment.

(iii) European law as a brake on national law

European law guarantees various rights, including, most notably, the free movement of persons, goods, services and capital. These rights take priority over any national legislation purporting to restrict them (see *Costa* v *ENEL* [1964] ECR 585 above). In case of conflict, national legislation must yield to the European right.

Aldo Bordessa and Others
(Cases C-358/93 and C-416/93), [1995] ECR I-361, European Court of Justice

Those questions were raised in two sets of criminal proceedings. On 10 November 1992 Aldo Bordessa (Case C-358/93), an Italian national residing in Italy, arrived at the customs post of La Junquera, Gerona (Spain) travelling towards France. When his car was inspected, banknotes worth approximately PTA 50 million were discovered in it, concealed in different places. Since Mr Bordessa did not possess the authorization required under Spanish law for the export of such a sum, he was arrested and the money confiscated. On 19 November 1992, Mari Mellado and Barbero Maestre (Case C-416/93), a married couple of Spanish nationality residing in Spain, crossed the frontier at the same customs post. In the course of an inspection carried out inside France, the French authorities subsequently discovered banknotes worth a total of PTA 38 million in their car. Since no application had been made to the Spanish authorities for authorisation to export that amount, criminal proceedings were initiated before the Spanish courts.

Under Article 4(1) of Royal Decree 1816 of 20 December 1991 on economic transactions with other countries, the export of such items as coins, banknotes and bank cheques payable to the bearer, made out in pesetas or in foreign currencies, is subject to a prior declaration when the amount is in excess of PTA 1 million per person and per journey and subject to prior administrative authorisation when the amount is in excess of PTA 5 million per person and per journey.

That decree was amended by Royal Decree 42 of 15 January 1993 which, according to the national court, constitutes no more than a technical improvement.

The national court considers that it is necessary to determine the validity and effect of that provision in the light of Community law before making a finding on a criminal offence under Law No. 40 of 10 December 1979 on the regulations governing exchange control, as amended by Organic Law No. 10 of 16 August 1983. Accordingly it stayed proceedings and submitted the following questions to the Court for a preliminary ruling:

(1) Does Article 30 [now Art 28] of the EEC Treaty preclude rules of a Member State which require a person leaving national territory bearing coins, banknotes or bearer cheques to make a prior declaration if the amount is in excess of PTA 1 million and to obtain prior administrative authorisation if the amount exceeds PTA 5 million, where non-compliance with those requirements entails criminal penalties which may include detention?
(2) Does Article 59 [now Art 49] of the EEC Treaty preclude rules such as those described in Question 1?
(3) Are rules such as those described in the previous questions compatible with Articles 1 and 4 of Directive 88/361/EEC?
(4) If Question 3 is answered in the negative, do the rules in Article 1 in conjunction with Article 4 of Directive 88/361/EEC meet the necessary conditions in order for them to be relied on as against the Spanish State before national courts and to render inapplicable national rules which conflict with them?

By order of the President of 13 June 1994 the two cases were joined, in accordance with Article 43 of the Rules of Procedure, for the purposes of the oral procedure and the final judgment.

...

By its third question, the national court is essentially asking whether Articles 1 and 4 of the Directive preclude national legislation from making the export of coins, banknotes or bearer cheques conditional on a prior declaration or authorisation.

It should first be noted that the Directive brought about the full liberalization of capital movements, for which purpose Article 1 required Member States to abolish restrictions on movements of capital taking place between persons resident in Member States.

Under the first paragraph of Article 4 of the Directive, Member States may 'take all requisite measures to prevent infringements of their laws and regulations, inter alia in the field of taxation and prudential supervision of financial institutions, or to lay down procedures for the declaration of capital movements for purposes of administrative or statistical information'.

The effectiveness of tax controls and the fight against illegal activities, such as tax evasion, money laundering, drug trafficking and terrorism, have been invoked as aims justifying the rules at issue.

It must therefore be examined whether Member States, in pursuing those aims, are taking measures which fall under the first paragraph of Article 4 of the Directive and consequently concern interests which those States are entitled to protect.

The first paragraph of Article 4 of the Directive expressly refers to the requisite measures to prevent infringements of the laws and regulations of Member States, 'inter alia' in the field of taxation and the prudential supervision of financial institutions. It follows that other measures are also permitted in so far as they are designed to prevent illegal activities of comparable seriousness, such as money laundering, drug trafficking or terrorism.

That interpretation is confirmed moreover by the insertion in the Treaty establishing the European Community of Article 73d, paragraph (1)(b) of which essentially reproduces the first paragraph of Article 4 of the Directive but also provides that Member States have the right to take measures which are justified on grounds of public policy or public security.

It is in the light of those considerations that it should be determined whether the requirement laid down by the authorities of a Member State of a prior declaration or authorization for the transfer of coins, banknotes or bearer cheques is to be regarded as a requisite measure within the meaning of the first paragraph of Article 4 of the Directive.

As the Advocate General pointed out at point 17 of his Opinion, authorisation has the effect of suspending currency exports and makes them conditional in each case upon the consent of the administrative authorities, which must be sought by means of a special application.

A requirement of that nature would cause the exercise of the free movement of capital to be subject to the discretion of the administrative authorities and thus be such as to render that freedom illusory (see Luisi and Carbone v Ministero del Tesoro (cases 286/82 and 26/83) [1984] ECR 377, paragraph 34). It might have the effect of impeding capital movements carried out in accordance with Community law, contrary to the second paragraph of Article 4 of the Directive.

However, the Spanish Government defended the need for prior authorisation, claiming that it was only by virtue of such a system that non-compliance could be classified as criminal and hence criminal penalties imposed. Failure to meet that requirement could also lead to confiscation of the capital sums involved in the crime.

That view must, however, be rejected.

The Spanish Government has failed to provide sufficient proof that it is impossible to attach criminal penalties to the failure to make a prior declaration.

Consequently, it should be stated in reply to the third question that Articles 1 and 4 of the Directive preclude the export of coins, banknotes or bearer cheques being made conditional on prior authorisation but do not by contrast preclude transactions of that nature being made conditional on a prior declaration.

By its fourth question, the national court is asking whether the provisions of Article 1 in conjunction with Article 4 of the Directive have direct effect.

The requirement under Article 1 of the Directive for Member States to abolish all restrictions on movements of capital is precise and unconditional and does not require a specific implementing measure.

Application of the proviso in Article 4 of the Directive is amenable to review by the courts, and hence the fact that a Member State may avail itself of that possibility does not prevent Article 1 of the Directive, which enshrines the principle of the free movement of capital, from conferring rights on individuals which they may rely on before the courts and which the national courts must uphold.

Consequently, the reply to the national court's fourth question should be that Article 1 in conjunction with Article 4 of the Directive may be relied on before national courts and render inapplicable national rules which conflict with those provisions.

■ NOTES AND QUESTIONS

1. For an example of a case where a State national law was found to infringe the free movement of persons, see *Royer* (case 48/75) [1976] ECR 497.

2. Often policies of the EU will be in potential conflict. What then? For example, which policy should take priority, the free flow of money and people or the need of Member States to rein in fraud against the Union? Will the attempts by the European Commission to criminalise some conduct (see above) fall foul of this clash of aims?

3. The Commission of the European Union is a body of civil servants who have not been elected. Is it acceptable for these unelected officials to be able to dictate the content of national criminal law?

4. Is the real problem about criminalising EU offences the way that national governments want to retain their traditional powers, or does the EU have sensible substantive reasons for criminalising some offences. Often legal procedure in different States is very different, but are the substantive crimes very different, for murder, manslaughter and assault, surely the law is the same?

(iii) The European Arrest Warrant

The European arrest warrant is a judicial decision issued by a Member State with a view to the arrest and surrender by another Member State of a person being sought for a criminal prosecution or a custodial sentence. It was intended to be designed to strengthen cooperation between the judicial authorities of the Member States by eliminating the use of extradition. It is based on the principle of mutual recognition of decisions in criminal matters. The European Arrest Warrant is based on a Framework Decision adopted by the Council on 13 June 2002 and has ben applied from 1 January 2004. Again the European Arrest Warrant is contentious, particularly because the Member States' constitutional law might be in conflict with the EU's. Germany has been one of the most important States in this argument because of its history, including the holocaust. Because of this history, Human Rights are extremely important in German constitutional law.

A crucial case involved a European Arrest Warrant issued by Spain requesting the surrender of one Mamoun Darkazanli. Darkazanli had both German and Syrian citizenship and was prosecuted in Spain for being involved in terrorism and having links to the activities of Al-Qaeda. The first instance court in Germany allowed the extradition but the defendant appealed to the German Constitutional Court. The grounds included the belief that the European Arrest Warrant was insufficiently grounded in implementing legislation which lacked democratic legitimacy. However, although the Court accepted the complaint, the Court said that the reason was not that the Framework Directive and the implementing legislation was defective, but rather that it was the Constitution which was at fault and the Constitution in itself was in breach of the Framework Directive. This is extremely interesting since it seems to change the focus of the EU's intentions to harmonise the criminal law. Human Rights became the focus rather than the challenge to the legitimacy of the EU's criminal law as against a Member State's criminal law. The reasons that the German Constitutional Court gave for the judgment had to do with fundamental constitutional human rights, especially the right to protect German nationals when they might find themselves at risk of extradition. The Court emphasised the link between the German constitution and the citizen and also the uncertainty that might arise if a European Arrest Warrant was served. The appellant's complaint was allowed and the complainant was not surrendered. Similar court cases in Poland, Cyprus and the Czech Republic have challenged the European Arrest Warrant although the court's reasons were different in each case and country-specific. However, all of the cases challenged the European Arrest Warrant because of the constitutional arrangements for their citizen's security. The cases show that the constitutional arrangements of the Member States cannot easily trump Human Rights and vital constitutional rights. The first case where the ECJ considered the European Arrest Warrant was a Belgian case:

Advocaten voor de Wereld VZW v Leden van de Ministerraad

...

Judgment

1. The reference for a preliminary ruling concerns the assessment as to the validity of Council Framework Decision 2002/584/JHA of 13 June 2002 on the European arrest warrant and the surrender procedures between Member States (OJ 2002 L 190, p. 1) ('the Framework Decision').

2. This reference has been submitted in the course of an action brought by Advocaten voor de Wereld VZW ('Advocaten voor de Wereld') before the Belgian Arbitragehof (Court of Arbitration) and seeking the annulment of the Belgian Law of 19 December 2003 on the European arrest warrant (Belgisch Staatsblad of 22 December 2003, p. 60075) ('the Law of 19 December 2003'), in particular Articles 3, 5(1) and (2) and 7 thereof.

Legal context

3. Recital (5) in the preamble to the Framework Decision provides:

'The objective set for the Union to become an area of freedom, security and justice leads to abolishing extradition between Member States and replacing it by a system of surrender between judicial authorities. Further, the introduction of a new simplified system of surrender of sentenced or suspected persons for the purposes of execution or prosecution of criminal sentences makes it possible to remove the complexity and potential for delay inherent in the present extradition procedures. Traditional cooperation relations which have prevailed up till now between Member States should be replaced by a system of free movement of judicial decisions in criminal matters, covering both pre-sentence and final decisions, within an area of freedom, security and justice.'

4. Recital (6) in the preamble to the Framework Decision is worded as follows:

'The European arrest warrant provided for in this Framework Decision is the first concrete measure in the field of criminal law implementing the principle of mutual recognition which the European Council referred to as the "cornerstone" of judicial cooperation.'

5. Recital (7) in the preamble to the Framework Decision provides:

'Since the aim of replacing the system of multilateral extradition built upon the European Convention on Extradition of 13 December 1957 cannot be sufficiently achieved by the

Member States acting unilaterally and can therefore, by reason of its scale and effects, be better achieved at Union level, the Council may adopt measures in accordance with the principle of subsidiarity as referred to in Article 2 of the Treaty on European Union and Article 5 of the Treaty establishing the European Community. In accordance with the principle of proportionality, as set out in the latter Article, this Framework Decision does not go beyond what is necessary in order to achieve that objective.'

...

8. Article 2 of the Framework Decision provides:

'1. A European arrest warrant may be issued for acts punishable by the law of the issuing Member State by a custodial sentence or a detention order for a maximum period of at least 12 months or, where a sentence has been passed or a detention order has been made, for sentences of at least four months.

2. The following offences, if they are punishable in the issuing Member State by a custodial sentence or a detention order for a maximum period of at least three years and as they are defined by the law of the issuing Member State, shall, under the terms of this Framework Decision and without verification of the double criminality of the act, give rise to surrender pursuant to a European arrest warrant:
- participation in a criminal organisation,
- terrorism,
- trafficking in human beings,
- sexual exploitation of children and child pornography,
- illicit trafficking in narcotic drugs and psychotropic substances,
- illicit trafficking in weapons, munitions and explosives,
- corruption,
- fraud, including that affecting the financial interests of the European Communities within the meaning of the Convention of 26 July 1995 on the protection of the European Communities' financial interests,
- laundering of the proceeds of crime,
- counterfeiting currency, including of the euro,
- computer-related crime,
- environmental crime, including illicit trafficking in endangered animal species and in endangered plant species and varieties,
- facilitation of unauthorised entry and residence,
- murder, grievous bodily injury,
- illicit trade in human organs and tissue,
- kidnapping, illegal restraint and hostage-taking,
- racism and xenophobia,
- organised or armed robbery,
- illicit trafficking in cultural goods, including antiques and works of art,
- swindling,
- racketeering and extortion,
- counterfeiting and piracy of products,
- forgery of administrative documents and trafficking therein,
- forgery of means of payment,
- illicit trafficking in hormonal substances and other growth promoters,
- illicit trafficking in nuclear or radioactive materials,
- trafficking in stolen vehicles,
- rape,
- arson,
- crimes within the jurisdiction of the International Criminal Court,
- unlawful seizure of aircraft/ships,
- sabotage.'

...

28. As is clear in particular from Article 1(1) and (2) of the Framework Decision and recitals (5), (6), (7) and (11) in its preamble, the purpose of the Framework Decision is to replace the multilateral system of extradition between Member States with a system of surrender, as between judicial authorities, of convicted persons or suspects for the purpose of enforcing judgments or of criminal proceedings based on the principle of mutual recognition.

29. The mutual recognition of the arrest warrants issued in the different Member States in accordance with the law of the issuing State concerned requires the approximation of the laws and regulations of the Member States with regard to judicial cooperation in criminal matters and, more specifically, of the rules relating to the conditions, procedures and effects of surrender as between national authorities.

30. That is precisely the purpose of the Framework Decision in regard, inter alia, to the rules relating to the categories of listed offences in respect of which there is no verification of double criminality (Article 2(2)), to the grounds for mandatory or optional non-execution of the European arrest warrant (Articles 3 and 4), to the content and form of that warrant (Article 8), to the transmission of such a warrant and the detailed procedures governing such transmission (Articles 9 and 10), to the minimum guarantees which must be granted to a requested or arrested person (Articles 11 to 14), to the time-limits and procedures for the decision to execute that warrant (Article 17) and to the time-limits for surrender of the person sought (Article 23).

31. The Framework Decision is based on Article 31(1)(a) and (b) EU, which provides that common action on judicial cooperation in criminal matters is, respectively, to facilitate and accelerate judicial cooperation in relation to proceedings and the enforcement of decisions and to facilitate extradition between Member States.

...

44. Advocaten voor de Wereld contends, in contrast to all of the other parties which have submitted observations in these proceedings, that, to the extent to which it dispenses with verification of the requirement of the double criminality of the offences mentioned in it, Article 2(2) of the Framework Decision is contrary to the principle of equality and non-discrimination and to the principle of legality in criminal matters.

45. It must be noted at the outset that, by virtue of Article 6 EU, the Union is founded on the principle of the rule of law and it respects fundamental rights, as guaranteed by the European Convention for the Protection of Human Rights and Fundamental Freedoms, signed in Rome on 4 November 1950, and as they result from the constitutional provisions common to the Member States, as general principles of Community law. It follows that the institutions are subject to review of the conformity of their acts with the Treaties and the general principles of law, just like the Member States when they implement the law of the Union (see, inter alia, Case C-354/04 P Gestoras Pro Amnistía and Others v Council [2007] ECR I-0000, paragraph 51, and Case C-355/04 P Segi and Others v Council [2007] ECR I-0000, paragraph 51).

46. It is common ground that those principles include the principle of the legality of criminal offences and penalties and the principle of equality and non-discrimination, which are also reaffirmed respectively in Articles 49, 20 and 21 of the Charter of Fundamental Rights of the European Union, proclaimed in Nice on 7 December 2000 (OJ 2000 C 364, p. 1).

47. It is accordingly a matter for the Court to examine the validity of the Framework Decision in the light of those principles.

The principle of the legality of criminal offences and penalties

48. According to Advocaten voor de Wereld, the list of more than 30 offences in respect of which the traditional condition of double criminality is henceforth abandoned if those offences are punishable in the issuing Member State by a custodial sentence or detention order for a maximum period of at least three years is so vague and imprecise that it breaches, or at the very least is capable of breaching, the principle of legality in criminal matters. The offences set out in that list are not accompanied by their legal definition but constitute very vaguely defined categories of undesirable conduct. A person deprived of his liberty on foot of a European arrest warrant without verification of double criminality does not benefit from the guarantee that criminal legislation must satisfy conditions as to precision, clarity and predictability allowing each person to know, at the time when an

act is committed, whether that act does or does not constitute an offence, by contrast to those who are deprived of their liberty otherwise than pursuant to a European arrest warrant.

49. The principle of the legality of criminal offences and penalties (nullum crimen, nulla poena sine lege), which is one of the general legal principles underlying the constitutional traditions common to the Member States, has also been enshrined in various international treaties, in particular in Article 7(1) of the European Convention for the Protection of Human Rights and Fundamental Freedoms (see in this regard, inter alia, Joined Cases C-74/95 and C-129/95 X [1996] ECR I-6609, paragraph 25, and Joined Cases C-189/02 P, C-202/02 P, C-205/02 P to C-208/02 P and C-213/02 P Dansk Rørindustri and Others v Commission [2005] ECR I-5425, paragraphs 215 to 219).

50. This principle implies that legislation must define clearly offences and the penalties which they attract. That condition is met in the case where the individual concerned is in a position, on the basis of the wording of the relevant provision and with the help of the interpretative assistance given by the courts, to know which acts or omissions will make him criminally liable (see, inter alia, European Court of Human Rights judgment of 22 June 2000 in Coëme and Others v Belgium, Reports 2000-VII, § 145).

51. In accordance with Article 2(2) of the Framework Decision, the offences listed in that provision give rise to surrender pursuant to a European arrest warrant, without verification of the double criminality of the act, 'if they are punishable in the issuing Member State by a custodial sentence or a detention order for a maximum period of at least three years and as they are defined by the law of the issuing Member State'.

52. Consequently, even if the Member States reproduce word-for-word the list of the categories of offences set out in Article 2(2) of the Framework Decision for the purposes of its implementation, the actual definition of those offences and the penalties applicable are those which follow from the law of 'the issuing Member State'. The Framework Decision does not seek to harmonise the criminal offences in question in respect of their constituent elements or of the penalties which they attract.

53. Accordingly, while Article 2(2) of the Framework Decision dispenses with verification of double criminality for the categories of offences mentioned therein, the definition of those offences and of the penalties applicable continue to be matters determined by the law of the issuing Member State, which, as is, moreover, stated in Article 1(3) of the Framework Decision, must respect fundamental rights and fundamental legal principles as enshrined in Article 6 EU, and, consequently, the principle of the legality of criminal offences and penalties.

54. It follows that, in so far as it dispenses with verification of the requirement of double criminality in respect of the offences listed in that provision, Article 2(2) of the Framework Decision is not invalid on the ground that it infringes the principle of the legality of criminal offences and penalties.

The principle of equality and non-discrimination

55. According to Advocaten voor de Wereld, the principle of equality and non-discrimination is infringed by the Framework Decision inasmuch as, for offences other than those covered by Article 2(2) thereof, surrender may be made subject to the condition that the facts in respect of which the European arrest warrant was issued constitute an offence under the law of the Member State of execution. That distinction, it argues, is not objectively justified. The removal of verification of double criminality is all the more open to question as no detailed definition of the facts in respect of which surrender is requested features in the Framework Decision. The system established by the latter gives rise to an unjustified difference in treatment as between individuals depending on whether the facts alleged to constitute the offence occurred in the Member State of execution or outside that State. Those individuals will thus be judged differently with regard to the deprivation of their liberty without any justification for that difference.

56. The principle of equality and non-discrimination requires that comparable situations must not be treated differently and that different situations must not be treated in the same way unless such treatment is objectively justified (see, in particular, Case C-248/04 Koninklijke Coöperatie Cosun ECR I-0000, paragraph 72 and the case-law there cited).

57. With regard, first, to the choice of the 32 categories of offences listed in Article 2(2) of the Framework Decision, the Council was able to form the view, on the basis of the principle of mutual recognition and in the light of the high degree of trust and solidarity between the Member States, that, whether by reason of their inherent nature or by reason of the punishment incurred of a maximum of at least three years, the categories of offences in question feature among those the seriousness of which in terms of adversely affecting public order and public safety justifies dispensing with the verification of double criminality.

58. Consequently, even if one were to assume that the situation of persons suspected of having committed offences featuring on the list set out in Article 2(2) of the Framework Decision or convicted of having committed such offences is comparable to the situation of persons suspected of having committed, or convicted of having committed, offences other than those listed in that provision, the distinction is, in any event, objectively justified.

59. With regard, second, to the fact that the lack of precision in the definition of the categories of offences in question risks giving rise to disparate implementation of the Framework Decision within the various national legal orders, suffice it to point out that it is not the objective of the Framework Decision to harmonise the substantive criminal law of the Member States and that nothing in Title VI of the EU Treaty, Articles 34 and 31 of which were indicated as forming the legal basis of the Framework Decision, makes the application of the European arrest warrant conditional on harmonisation of the criminal laws of the Member States within the area of the offences in question (see by way of analogy, inter alia, Joined Cases C-187/01 and C-385/01 Gözütok and Brügge [2003] ECR I-1345, paragraph 32, and Case C-467/04 Gasparini and Others ECR I-0000, paragraph 29).

60. It follows that, in so far as it dispenses with verification of double criminality in respect of the offences listed therein, Article 2(2) of the Framework Decision is not invalid inasmuch as it does not breach Article 6(2) EU or, more specifically, the principle of legality of criminal offences and penalties and the principle of equality and non-discrimination.

61. In the light of all of the foregoing, the answer must be that examination of the questions submitted has revealed no factor capable of affecting the validity of the Framework Decision.

SECTION 4: THE RELEVANCE OF THE EUROPEAN CONVENTION FOR THE PROTECTION OF HUMAN RIGHTS AND FUNDAMENTAL FREEDOMS

Following World War II, the Council of Europe promulgated the 'European Convention for the Protection of Human Rights and Fundamental Freedoms' (often referred to, more simply, as the European Convention on Human Rights or by the acronym ECHR). The UK played a key role in the drafting of the Convention and was the first country to ratify it (March 1951). The Convention sets out the basic human rights to which all persons are entitled. It also created a European Commission (since abolished) and a European Court of Human Rights to enforce these rights.

While the UK ratified the European Convention early, it did not incorporate it into its domestic law, as did most other European States. The most significant ramification of the UK approach was that the rights set out in the Convention could not be enforced in a court in England or Wales. Thus, in order to vindicate their rights, aggrieved individuals had to take their case against the Government to Strasbourg (the home of the Commission and Court). Unfortunately, this was often an expensive and time-consuming process.

(i) The Human Rights Act 1998

In 1998 Parliament enacted the HRA 1998. The Act came into force on 2 October 2000. It has implications for Parliament's authority to create crimes, and may alter the historic balance between the judiciary and Parliament. Most significantly, the Act allows individuals who believe that their human rights have been violated by the Government to have their claims heard in a domestic court.

Section 1 of the Act specifies the Articles and Protocols of the Convention which are to be incorporated into domestic law (see below for specific provisions). Section 2 instructs courts and tribunals that they must, in determining issues which raise questions of rights under the Convention, take into account the relevant judgments, decisions, declarations and advisory opinions of the European Commission, the European Court of Human Rights and the Committee of Ministers of the Council of Europe. In this regard it should be noted that the UK does not have to have been a party to the original decision for its courts to have to take account of it. Section 3 provides that all primary and subordinate legislation must, as far as possible, be interpreted in a way that is compatible with the Convention. Section 4 permits the courts to make a 'declaration of incompatibility' when the law in question fails to comply with the requirements of the Convention. The effect of a 'declaration of incompatibility' is not to invalidate primary legislation (the courts will, however, be able to strike down secondary legislation) but to alert Parliament of the need to amend the law so that it will be compatible. The White Paper accompanying the Bill confidently predicted that prompt Parliamentary action to redress any incompatibility would be forthcoming but to heighten the likelihood of this prediction coming true, the Act provides for a 'fast-track' procedure which allows a Government Minister to take immediate steps to change the law with prompt subsequent submission of the Minister's order to Parliament for approval (s. 10). Judicial proceedings to enforce the Convention may be brought by any individual whose rights under the Convention have been, or threaten to be, violated by a public authority (s. 7) and reliance on Convention rights may be had in any legal proceeding.

Among the more important, from a criminal law perspective, of the Articles of the European Convention which have been incorporated into the HRA 1998 are the following:

SECTION 5: CONVENTION FOR THE PROTECTION OF HUMAN RIGHTS AND FUNDAMENTAL FREEDOMS

Article 2

1. Everyone's right to life shall be protected by law. No one shall be deprived of his life intentionally save in the execution of a sentence of a court following his conviction of a crime for which this penalty is provided by law.

2. Deprivation of life shall not be regarded as inflicted in contravention of this Article when it results from the use of force which is no more than absolutely necessary:

    (a) in defence of any person from unlawful violence;

    (b) in order to effect a lawful arrest or to prevent the escape of a person lawfully detained;

    (c) in action lawfully taken for the purpose of quelling a riot or insurrection.

Article 3

No one shall be subjected to torture or to inhuman or degrading treatment or punishment.

Article 4

...

Article 5

1. Everyone has the right to liberty and security of person. No one shall be deprived of his liberty save in the following cases and in accordance with a procedure prescribed by law:

    (a) the lawful detention of a person after conviction by a competent court;

    (b) the lawful arrest or detention of a person for non-compliance with the lawful order of a court or in order to secure the fulfilment of any obligation prescribed by law;

    (c) the lawful arrest or detention of a person effected for the purpose of bringing him before the competent legal authority on reasonable suspicion of having committed an offence or when it is reasonably considered necessary to prevent his committing an offence or fleeing after having done so;

    (d) the detention of a minor by lawful order for the purpose of educational supervision or his lawful detention for the purpose of bringing him before the competent legal authority;

    (e) the lawful detention of persons for the prevention of the spreading of infectious diseases, of persons of unsound mind, alcoholics or drug addicts or vagrants;

    (f) the lawful arrest or detention of a person to prevent his effecting an unauthorised entry into the country or of a person against whom action is being taken with a view to deportation or extradition.

2. Everyone who is arrested shall be informed promptly, in a language which he understands, of the reasons for his arrest and of any charge against him.

3. Everyone arrested or detained in accordance with the provisions of paragraph 1c of this Article shall be brought promptly before a judge or other officer authorised by law to exercise judicial power and shall be entitled to trial within a reasonable time or to release pending trial. Release may be conditioned by guarantees to appear for trial.

4. Everyone who is deprived of his liberty by arrest or detention shall be entitled to take proceedings by which the lawfulness of his detention shall be decided speedily by a court and his release ordered if the detention is not lawful.

5. Everyone who has been the victim of arrest or detention in contravention of the provisions of this Article shall have an enforceable right to compensation.

Article 6

1. In the determination of his civil rights and obligations or of any criminal charge against him, everyone is entitled to a fair and public hearing within a reasonable time by an independent and impartial tribunal established by law. Judgment shall be pronounced publicly but the press and public may be excluded from all or part of the trial in the interest of morals, public order or national security in a democratic society, where the interests of juveniles or the protection of the private life of the parties so require, or to the extent strictly necessary in the opinion of the court in special circumstances where publicity would prejudice the interests of justice.

2. Everyone charged with a criminal offence shall be presumed innocent until proved guilty according to law.

3. Everyone charged with a criminal offence has the following minimum rights:

    (a) to be informed promptly, in a language which he understands and in detail, of the nature and cause of the accusation against him;

    (b) to have adequate time and facilities for the preparation of his defence;

    (c) to defend himself in person or through legal assistance of his own choosing or, if he has not sufficient means to pay for legal assistance, to be given it free when the interests of justice so require;

(d) to examine or have examined witnesses against him and to obtain the attendance and examination of witnesses on his behalf under the same conditions as witnesses against him;

(e) to have the free assistance of an interpreter if he cannot understand or speak the language used in court.

Article 7

1. No one shall be held guilty of any criminal offence on account of any act or omission which did not constitute a criminal offence under national or international law at the time when it was committed. Nor shall a heavier penalty be imposed than the one that was applicable at the time the criminal offence was committed.

2. This Article shall not prejudice the trial and punishment of any person for any act or omission which, at the time when it was committed, was criminal according to the general principles of law recognised by civilised nations.

Article 8

1. Everyone has the right to respect for his private and family life, his home and his correspondence.

2. There shall be no interference by a public authority with the exercise of this right except such as is in accordance with the law and is necessary in a democratic society in the interests of national security, public safety or the economic well-being of the country, for the prevention of disorder or crime, for the protection of health or morals, or for the protection of the rights and freedoms of others.

Article 9

1. Everyone has the right to freedom of thought, conscience and religion; this right includes freedom to change his religion or belief and freedom, either alone or in community with others and in public or private, to manifest his religion or belief, in worship, teaching, practice and observance.

2. Freedom to manifest one's religion or beliefs shall be subject only to such limitations as are prescribed by law and are necessary in a democratic society in the interests of public safety, for the protection of public order, health or morals, or for the protection of the rights and freedoms of others.

Article 10

1. Everyone has the right to freedom of expression. This right shall include freedom to hold opinions and to receive and impart information and ideas without interference by public authority and regardless of frontiers. This Article shall not prevent States from requiring the licensing of broadcasting, television or cinema enterprises.

2. The exercise of these freedoms, since it carries with it duties and responsibilities, may be subject to such formalities, conditions, restrictions or penalties as are prescribed by law and are necessary in a democratic society, in the interests of national security, territorial integrity or public safety, for the prevention of disorder or crime, for the protection of health or morals, for the protection of the reputation or rights of others, for preventing the disclosure of information received in confidence, or for maintaining the authority and impartiality of the judiciary.

Article 11

1. Everyone has the right to freedom of peaceful assembly and to freedom of association with others, including the right to form and to join trade unions for the protection of his interests.

2. No restrictions shall be placed on the exercise of these rights other than such as are prescribed by law and are necessary in a democratic society in the interests of national security or public safety, for the prevention of disorder or crime, for the protection of health or morals or for the protection of the rights and freedoms of others. This Article shall not prevent the imposition of lawful restrictions on the exercise of these rights by members of the armed forces, of the police or of the administration of the State.

...

> **Article 14**
>
> The enjoyment of the rights and freedoms set forth in this Convention shall be secured without discrimination on any ground such as sex, race, colour, language, religion, political or other opinion, national or social origin, association with a national minority, property, birth or other status.

■ NOTES AND QUESTIONS

1. Some of the Articles of the Convention create rights which appear absolute while others create rights that are qualified in some way. Which rights fall into which category? What qualifications apply when a right is qualified? Should not all human rights by definition be absolute?

2. Professor Ashworth has sought to identify the areas where the Convention is likely to have the most impact on domestic criminal law (Ashworth, 'The European Convention and Criminal Law' in The Human Rights Act and the Criminal and Regulatory Process (1999)):

   Article 2 (right to life): self-defence and justifiable force in the prevention of crime, etc.; abortion;

   Article 3 (right not to be subjected to torture or inhuman or degrading treatment): the defence of parental chastisement;

   Article 5 (right to liberty and security of person): the defence of insanity;

   Article 6.2 (presumption of innocence): burden of proof; offences of strict liability;

   Article 8 (right to respect for private life): homosexual offences (both generally and in respect of private premises, and the age of consent as compared with heterosexual offences); child abduction; failing to leave, or re-entering, land after the issuance of a notice to gypsies or other travellers (ss. 77–80 of the Criminal Justice and Public Order Act 1994);

   Article 9 (freedom of religion): blasphemy (also Article 10);

   Article 10 (freedom of expression): obscenity; racial hatred offences; contempt of court; criminal libel; incitement to disaffection;

   Article 11 (freedom of assembly): breach of the peace (also Articles 5 and 10); various offences under the Public Order Act 1986 and Criminal Justice and Public Order Act 1994 concerned with processions and demonstrations.

3. What happens when rights collide? Say that the police torture X, a terrorist – in pursuit of the Government's obligation under Article 2 to protect life but in arguable violation of Article 3's proscription of torture – in order to force him to disclose the location of a bomb that, if it were to explode, might kill thousands of innocent persons. Have X's human rights been violated?

(ii) Application of the HRA 1998

It is important to bear in mind that the HRA 1998 does not give the courts the power to hold legislation invalid. Most Articles in the Convention are concerned with procedural issues and may not be able to be successfully invoked to strike down substantive criminal law provisions. See, e.g., *R v Concannon* [2002] Crim LR 213. Nonetheless, imaginative lawyers may be able to use the Convention to fashion creative arguments in favour of rights not previously recognised in English law, the effect of which would be to bring about reform in the substantive law. The following case, although ultimately unsuccessful, illustrates this potential.

R (on the application of Pretty) v *Director of Public Prosecutions*
[2002] 1 All ER 1, House of Lords

LORD BINGHAM OF CORNHILL: . . . My Lords, no one of ordinary sensitivity could be unmoved by the frightening ordeal which faces Mrs Dianne Pretty, the appellant. She suffers from motor neurone disease, a progressive degenerative illness from which she has no hope of recovery. She has only a short time to live and faces the prospect of a humiliating and distressing death. She is mentally alert and would like to be able to take steps to bring her life to a peaceful end at a time of her choosing. But her physical incapacity is now such that she can no longer, without help, take her own life. With the support of her family, she wishes to enlist the help of her husband to that end. He himself is willing to give such help, but only if he can be sure that he will not be prosecuted under s 2(1) of the Suicide Act 1961 for aiding and abetting her suicide. Asked to undertake that he would not under s 2(4) of that Act consent to the prosecution of Mr Pretty under s 2(1) if Mr Pretty were to assist his wife to commit suicide, the Director of Public Prosecutions (the Director) has refused to give such an undertaking. On Mrs Pretty's application for judicial review of that refusal, the Queen's Bench Divisional Court ([2001] EWHC Admin 788, [2001] All ER (D) 251 (Oct)) upheld the Director's decision and refused relief. Mrs Pretty claims that she has a right to her husband's assistance in committing suicide and that s 2 of the 1961 Act, if it prohibits his helping and prevents the Director undertaking not to prosecute if he does, is incompatible with the European Convention for the Protection of Human Rights and Fundamental Freedoms (Rome, 4 November 1950; TS 71 (1953): Cmd 8969) (as set out in Sch 1 to the Human Rights Act 1998). It is on the convention, brought into force in this country by the 1998 Act, that Mrs Pretty's claim to relief depends. It is accepted by her counsel on her behalf that under the common law of England she could not have hoped to succeed.

. . .

Article 2 of the convention
Article 2 of the convention provides:

'*Right to life*

1. Everyone's right to life shall be protected by law. No one shall be deprived of his life intentionally save in the execution of a sentence of a court following his conviction of a crime for which this penalty is provided by law.
2. Deprivation of life shall not be regarded as inflicted in contravention of this Article when it results from the use of force which is no more than absolutely necessary: (a) in defence of any person from unlawful violence; (b) in order to effect a lawful arrest or to prevent the escape of a person lawfully detained; (c) in action lawfully taken for the purpose of quelling a riot or insurrection.'

The article is to be read in conjunction with arts 1 and 2 of the Sixth Protocol, which are among the convention rights protected by the 1998 Act (see s 1(1)(c)) and which abolished the death penalty in time of peace.

On behalf of Mrs Pretty it is submitted that art 2 of the convention protects not life itself but the right to life. The purpose of the article is to protect individuals from third parties (the state and public authorities). But the article recognises that it is for the individual to choose whether or not to live and so protects the individual's right to self-determination in relation to issues of life and death. Thus a person may refuse life-saving or life-prolonging medical treatment, and may lawfully choose to commit suicide. The article acknowledges that right of the individual. While most people want to live, some want to die, and the article protects both rights. The right to die is not the antithesis of the right to life but the corollary of it, and the state has a positive obligation to protect both.

The Secretary of State has advanced a number of unanswerable objections to this argument which were rightly upheld by the Divisional Court. The starting point must be the language of the article. The thrust of this is to reflect the sanctity which, particularly in Western eyes, attaches to life. The article protects the right to life and prevents the deliberate taking of life save in very narrowly defined circumstances. An article with that effect cannot be interpreted as conferring a right to die or to enlist the aid of another in bringing about one's own death. In his argument for Mrs Pretty, Mr Havers QC was at pains to limit his argument to assisted suicide, accepting that the right claimed could not extend to cover an intentional consensual killing (usually described in this context as 'voluntary euthanasia', but regarded in English law as murder). The right claimed would be sufficient to cover Mrs Pretty's case and counsel's unwillingness to go further is understandable. But there is in logic no justification for drawing a line at this point. If art 2 does confer a right to self-determination in relation to life and death, and if a person were so gravely disabled as to be unable to perform any act whatever to cause his or her own death, it would necessarily follow in logic that such a person would have a right to be killed at the hands of a third party without giving any help to the third party and the state would be in breach of the convention if it were to interfere with the exercise of that right. No such right can possibly be derived from an article having the object already defined.

It is true that some of the guaranteed convention rights have been interpreted as conferring rights not to do that which is the antithesis of what there is an express right to do. Article 11, for example, confers a right not to join an association (Young v UK (1981) 4 EHRR 38), art 9 embraces a right to freedom from any compulsion to express thoughts or change an opinion or divulge convictions (Clayton and Tomlinson, The Law of Human Rights (2000) p 974 (para 14.49)) and I would for my part be inclined to infer that art 12 confers a right not to marry (but see Clayton and Tomlinson p 913 (para 13.76)). It cannot, however, be suggested (to take some obvious examples) that arts 3, 4, 5 and 6 confer an implied right to do or experience the opposite of that which the articles guarantee. Whatever the benefits which, in the view of many, attach to voluntary euthanasia, suicide, physician-assisted suicide and suicide assisted without the intervention of a physician, these are not benefits which derive protection from an article framed to protect the sanctity of life.

...

Article 3 of the convention

Article 3 of the convention provides:

'*Prohibition of torture*

No one shall be subjected to torture or to inhuman or degrading treatment or punishment.'

This is one of the articles from which a member state may not derogate even in time of war or other public emergency threatening the life of the nation (see art 15). I shall for convenience use the expression 'proscribed treatment' to mean 'inhuman or degrading treatment' as that expression is used in the convention.

In brief summary the argument for Mrs Pretty proceeded by these steps. (1) Member states have an absolute and unqualified obligation not to inflict the proscribed treatment and also to take positive action to prevent the subjection of individuals to such treatment (see A v UK (1998) 5 BHRC 137, Z v UK [2001] 2 FCR 246 at 265 (para 73)). (2) Suffering attributable to the progression of a disease may amount to such treatment if the state can prevent or ameliorate such suffering and does not do so (see D v UK (1997) 2 BHRC 273 at 283–285 (paras 46–54)). (3) In denying Mrs Pretty the opportunity to bring her suffering to an end the United Kingdom (by the Director) will subject her to the proscribed treatment. The state can spare Mrs Pretty the suffering which she will otherwise endure since, if the Director undertakes not to give his consent to prosecution, Mr Pretty will assist his wife to commit suicide and so she will be spared much suffering. (4) Since, as the Divisional Court held, it is open to the United Kingdom under the convention to refrain from prohibiting assisted suicide, the Director can give the undertaking sought without breaking the United Kingdom's obligations under the convention. (5) If the Director may not give the undertaking, s 2 of the 1961 Act is incompatible with the convention.

...

Article 3 enshrines one of the fundamental values of democratic societies and its prohibition of the proscribed treatment is absolute (D v UK (1997) 2 BHRC 273 at 283 (para 47)). Article 3 is, as I think, complementary to art 2. As art 2 requires states to respect and safeguard the lives of individuals within their jurisdiction, so art 3 obliges them to respect the physical and human integrity of such individuals. There is in my opinion nothing in art 3 which bears on an individual's right to live or to choose not to live. That is not its sphere of application: indeed, as is clear from X v Germany, a state may on occasion be justified in inflicting treatment which would otherwise be in breach of art 3 in order to serve the ends of art 2. Moreover, the absolute and unqualified prohibition on a member state inflicting the proscribed treatment requires that 'treatment' should not be given an unrestricted or extravagant meaning. It cannot, in my opinion, be plausibly suggested that the Director or any other agent of the United Kingdom is inflicting the proscribed treatment on Mrs Pretty, whose suffering derives from her cruel disease.

...

Article 8 of the convention

Article 8 of the convention provides:

'Right to respect for private and family life

1. Everyone has the right to respect for his private and family life, his home and his correspondence.
2. There shall be no interference by a public authority with the exercise of this right except such as is in accordance with the law and is necessary in a democratic society in the interests of national security, public safety or the economic well-being of the country, for the prevention of disorder or crime, for the protection of health or morals, or for the protection of the rights and freedoms of others.'

Counsel for Mrs Pretty submitted that this article conferred a right to self-determination (see X v Netherlands (1985) 8 EHRR 235, Rodriguez v A-G of Canada [1994] 2 LRC 136, Re A (children) (conjoined twins: surgical separation) [2000] 4 All ER 961, [2001] Fam 147). This right embraces a right to choose when and how to die so that suffering and indignity can be avoided. Section 2(1) of the 1961 Act interferes with this right of self-determination: it is therefore for the United Kingdom to show that the interference meets the convention tests of legality, necessity, responsiveness to pressing social need and proportionality (see R v A (No 2) [2001] UKHL 25, [2001] 3 All ER 1, [2001] 2 WLR 1546, Johansen v Norway (1996) 23 EHRR 33, R (P) v Secretary of State for the Home Dept, R (Q) v Secretary of State for the Home Dept [2001] EWCA Civ 1151, [2001] 1 WLR 2002). Where the interference is with an intimate part of an individual's private life, there must be particularly serious reasons to justify the interference (Smith v UK (2000) 29 EHRR 493 at 530 (para 89)). The court must in this case rule whether it could be other than disproportionate for the Director to refuse to give the undertaking sought and, in the case of the Secretary of State, whether the interference with Mrs Pretty's right to self-determination is proportionate to whatever legitimate aim the prohibition on assisted suicide pursues. Counsel placed particular reliance on certain features of Mrs Pretty's case: her mental competence, the frightening prospect which faces her, her willingness to commit suicide if she were able, the imminence of death, the absence of harm to anyone else, the absence of far-reaching implications if her application were granted. Counsel suggested that the blanket prohibition in s 2(1), applied without taking account of particular cases, is wholly disproportionate, and the materials relied on do not justify it. Reference was made to R v UK (1983) 33 DR 270 and Sanles v Spain [2001] EHRLR 348.

The Secretary of State questioned whether Mrs Pretty's rights under art 8 were engaged at all, and gave a negative answer. He submitted that the right to private life under art 8 relates to the manner in which a person conducts his life, not the manner in which he departs from it. Any attempt to base a right to die on art 8 founders on exactly the same objection as the attempt based on art 2, namely, that the alleged right would extinguish the very benefit on which it is supposedly based. Article 8 protects the physical, moral and psychological integrity of the individual, including rights over the individual's own body, but there is nothing to suggest that it confers a right to decide when or how to die.

...

I would for my part accept the Secretary of State's submission that Mrs Pretty's rights under art 8 are not engaged at all. If, however, that conclusion is wrong, and the prohibition of assisted suicide in s 2 of the 1961 Act infringes her convention right under art 8, it is necessary to consider whether the infringement is shown by the Secretary of State to be justifiable under the terms of art 8(2).

In considering that question I would adopt the test advocated by counsel for Mrs Pretty, which is clearly laid down in the authorities cited.

Since suicide ceased to be a crime in 1961, the question whether assisted suicide also should be decriminalised has been reviewed on more than one occasion. The Criminal Law Revision Committee in its fourteenth report Offences against the Person (Cmnd 7844 (1980)) reported some divergence of opinion among its distinguished legal membership, and recognised a distinction between assisting a person who had formed a settled intention to kill himself and the more heinous case where one person persuaded another to commit suicide, but a majority was of the clear opinion that aiding and abetting suicide should remain an offence (pp 60–61 (para 135)).

Following the decision in Bland's case a much more broadly-constituted House of Lords Select Committee on Medical Ethics received extensive evidence and reported. The committee in its report (HL Paper (1993–94) 21–b drew a distinction between assisted suicide and physician-assisted suicide (p 11 (para 26)) but its conclusion was unambiguous (p 54 (para 262)):

> 'As far as assisted suicide is concerned, we see no reason to recommend any change in the law. We identify no circumstances in which assisted suicide should be permitted, nor do we see any reason to distinguish between the act of a doctor or of any other person in this connection.'

...

If, as I have concluded, none of the articles on which Mrs Pretty relies gives her the right which she has claimed, it follows that art 14 would not avail her even if she could establish that the operation of s 2(1) is discriminatory. A claim under this article must fail on this ground.

R (on the application of Purdy) (Appellant) v Director of Public Prosecutions
[2009] UKHL 45

LORD HOPE OF CRAIGHEAD:
My Lords,
17. The position in which Ms Purdy finds herself can be stated very simply. She suffers from primary progressive multiple sclerosis for which there is no known cure. It was diagnosed in 1995, and it is progressing. By 2001 she was permanently using a self-propelling wheelchair. Since then her condition has deteriorated still further. She now needs an electric wheelchair, and she has lost the ability to carry out many basic tasks for herself. She has problems in swallowing and has choking fits when she drinks. Further deterioration in her condition is inevitable. She expects that there will come a time when her continuing existence will become unbearable. When that happens she will wish to end her life while she is still physically able to do so. But by that stage she will be unable to do this without assistance. So she will want to travel to a country where assisted suicide is lawful, probably Switzerland. Her husband, Mr Omar Puente, is willing to help her to make this journey.

The risk of prosecution

Assisting a person to commit suicide is a crime in this country. Section 2(1) of the Suicide Act 1961 provides:

> 'A person who aids, abets, counsels or procures the suicide of another, or an attempt by another to commit suicide, shall be liable on conviction on indictment to imprisonment for a term not exceeding fourteen years.'

As Lord Judge CJ said in the Court of Appeal, this provision is clear and unequivocal: [2009] EWCA Civ 92, para 2. The offence which it describes is an offence in itself. It is not ancillary to anything else. Its language suggests that it applies to any acts of the kind it describes that are performed within this jurisdiction, irrespective of where the final act of suicide is to be committed. So acts which help another person to make a journey to another country, in the knowledge that its purpose is to enable the person to end her own life there, are within its reach. Its application cannot be avoided by arranging for the final act of suicide to be performed on the high seas, for example, or in Scotland. Otherwise it would be all too easy to exclude the vulnerable or the easily led from its protection. Furthermore it does not permit of any exceptions.

...

25. All that having been said it is plain, to put the point at its lowest, that there is a substantial risk that the acts which Ms Purdy wishes her husband to perform to help her to travel to Switzerland will give rise to a prosecution in this country. My noble and learned friend Lord Phillips of Worth Matravers has suggested that the offence that he would be committing by assisting her to commit suicide abroad might be that of murder which, of course, carries a sentence of life imprisonment. That would be the inevitable conclusion if section 2(1) of the 1961 Act does not apply. I think that it needs to be stressed however that this case has been conducted throughout, as was *R (Pretty) v Director of Public Prosecutions (Secretary of State for the Home Department Intervening)* [2001] UKHL 61, [2002] 1 AC 800 (where the place where Mrs Pretty was intending to commit suicide was never identified), on the basis that the common law offence has been displaced by the offence that was created in 1961 by Parliament. At no point has any law officer even hinted that in a case such as this a prosecution for murder is in contemplation. It is, of course, not possible to decide this issue in these proceedings, nor is it necessary. It is the risk that the Director of Public Prosecutions will consent to her husband's prosecution under section 2(1) of the 1961 Act that deters Ms Purdy from taking the course that she wishes to take. That is sufficient in itself to give rise to the issue which she now asks your Lordships to resolve.

The issue

26. It must be emphasised at the outset that it is no part of our function to change the law in order to decriminalise assisted suicide. If changes are to be made, as to which I express no opinion, this must be a matter for Parliament. No-one who listened to the recent debate in the House of Lords on Lord Falconer of Thoroton's amendment to the Coroners and Justice Bill, in which he sought to define in law acts which were not capable of encouraging or assisting suicide, or has read the report of the debate in Hansard (HL Debates, vol 712, 7 July 2009, cols 595–634) can be in any doubt as to the strength of feeling on either side or the difficulties that such a change in the law might give rise to. We do not venture into that arena, nor would it be right for us to do so. Our function as judges is to say what the law is and, if it is uncertain, to do what we can to clarify it.

27. On one view the law, as it stands, could not be clearer. It is an offence to assist someone to travel to Switzerland or anywhere else where assisted suicide is lawful. Anyone who does that is liable to be prosecuted. He is in the same position as anyone else who offends against section 2(1) of the 1961 Act. As with any other crime, the test that will be applied is that which the Crown Prosecution Service code lays down. He may be prosecuted if there is enough evidence to sustain a prosecution and it is in the public interest that this step should be taken. But the practice that will be followed in cases where compassionate assistance of the kind that Ms Purdy seeks from her husband is far less certain. The judges have a role to play where clarity and consistency is lacking in an area of such sensitivity.

28. Lord Pannick QC for Ms Purdy directed his argument to section 2(4) of the 1961 Act, which provides that no proceedings shall be instituted for an offence under that section except by or with the consent of the Director of Public Prosecutions, and to her right to respect for her private life under article 8(1) of the European Convention on Human Rights. He submits, first, that the prohibition in section 2(1) of the 1961 Act constitutes an interference with Ms Purdy's right to respect for her private life under article 8(1) of the European Convention on Human Rights; and, second, that this interference is not 'in accordance with the law' as required by article 8(2), in the absence of an offence-specific policy by the Director of Public Prosecutions ('the Director') which sets out the factors that will be taken into account by him and Crown Prosecutors acting on his behalf in deciding under section 2(4) of the 1961 Act whether or not it is in the public interest to bring a prosecution under that section.

29. As is well known, article 8 of the European Convention provides as follows:

'1. Everyone has the right to respect for his private and family life, his home and his correspondence.

2. There shall be no interference by a public authority with the exercise of this right except such as is in accordance with the law and is necessary in a democratic society in the interests of national security, public safety or the economic well-being of the country, for the prevention of disorder or crime, for the protection of health or morals, or for the protection of the rights and freedoms of others.'

The words which are under scrutiny in this case are the words 'respect for his private life' in article 8(1) and 'in accordance with the law' in article 8(2). The Director accepts that he is a public authority within the meaning of article 8(2). He is also a public authority for the purposes of section 6(1) of the Human Rights Act 1998. It is unlawful for him to act in a way which is incompatible with a Convention right.

30. Ms Purdy does not ask that her husband be given a guarantee of immunity from prosecution. An exception of that kind, as Lord Pannick accepts, would be a matter for Parliament. What she seeks is information. It is information that she says she needs so that she can take a decision that affects her private life. A number of other people have already made the journey to countries where assisted suicide is lawful, and those who have assisted them have not been prosecuted. Your Lordships were told that by the time of the hearing there had been 115 such cases. Of those cases only eight had been referred to the Director for a decision as to whether or not the assistants should be prosecuted. In all but two of them the decision not to prosecute had been taken on the ground that there was insufficient evidence. But on 9 December 2008 the Director decided not to prosecute the parents and a family friend of Daniel James, who had sustained a serious spinal injury in a rugby accident and had travelled with his parents to Switzerland to end his life, on the ground that a prosecution was not needed in the public interest. He took this decision personally, he gave his reasons in writing for having done so and he made those reasons available to the public. This was an exception, as the public have not been told what the reasons were in the other cases that have so far been referred to the Director which include one other case which on public interest grounds was not prosecuted. Other cases appear to have been discontinued by the police on public interest grounds. Here too no reasons for the decisions that have been taken are available.

31. Ms Purdy's request for information is to be seen in the light of that background. As has been said, she does not seek an immunity. Instead she wants to be able to make an informed decision as to whether or not to ask for her husband's assistance. She is not willing to expose him to the risk of being prosecuted if he assists her. But the Director has declined to say what factors he will take into consideration in deciding whether or not it is in the public interest to prosecute those who assist people to end their lives in countries where assisted suicide is lawful. This presents her with a dilemma. If the risk of prosecution is sufficiently low, she can wait until the very last moment before she makes the journey. If the risk is too high she will have to make the journey unaided to end her life before she would otherwise wish to do so. Moreover she is not alone in finding herself in this predicament. Statements have been produced showing that others in her situation have chosen to travel without close family members to avoid the risk of their being prosecuted. Others have given up the idea of an assisted suicide altogether and have been left to die what has been described as a distressing and undignified death. It is patently obvious that the issue is not going to go away.

32. The Court of Appeal expressed very considerable sympathy for the predicament in which Ms Purdy and Mr Puente now find themselves. But it held that it was unable to find in Ms Purdy's favour on either branch of her argument. In *R (Pretty) v Director of Public Prosecutions (Secretary of State for the Home Department Intervening)* [2002] 1 AC 800, the House held that article 8 was directed to the protection of personal autonomy while the person was alive but did not confer a right to decide when or how to die. The European Court of Human Rights disagreed. In *Pretty v United Kingdom* (2002) 35 EHRR 1, para 67, the court said:

> 'The applicant in this case is prevented by law from exercising her choice to avoid what she considers will be an undignified and distressing end to her life. The Court is not prepared to exclude that this constitutes an interference with her right to respect for private life as guaranteed under article 8(1) of the Convention. It considers below whether this interference conforms with the requirements of the second paragraph of article 8.'

Nevertheless the Court of Appeal held that it was bound to follow the decision of this House and was not at liberty to apply the ruling of the Strasbourg court. No other course was open to it: see *Kay v Lambeth London Borough Council* UKHL 10, 2 AC 465, paras 28, 42–45, per Lord Bingham of Cornhill; *R (RJM) v Secretary of State for Work and Pensions* [2008] UKHL 63, [2009] 1 AC 311, para 64, per Lord Neuberger of Abbotsbury.

33. As for the question whether the requirements of article 8(2) were satisfied, the Court of Appeal said that the absence of a crime-specific policy relating to assisted suicide did not make

the effect of section 2(1) of the 1961 Act unlawful or mean that it was not in accordance with the law: para 79. The statute itself was sufficiently clear to satisfy the requirements of article 8(2) as to certainty. What Ms Purdy was seeking was in reality a guarantee that her husband would not be prosecuted. She could not achieve that objective without his being given what amounted to an immunity from prosecution or the promulgation of a case-specific policy which recognised exceptional defences to the offence which had not been enacted by Parliament. The Director was not in dereliction of his statutory duty in declining to do this.

Article 8(1): respect for private life

34. The House is, of course, free to depart from its earlier decision and to follow that of the Strasbourg court. As Lord Bingham said in *R (Ullah)* v *Special Adjudicator* [2004] UKHL 26, [2004] 2 AC 323, para 20, it is ordinarily the clear duty of our domestic courts to give practical recognition to the principles laid down by the Strasbourg court as governing the Convention rights as the effectiveness of the Convention as an international instrument depends on the loyal acceptance by member states of the principles that, as the highest authority on the interpretation of those rights, it lays down. Practice Statement (Judicial Precedent) which was issued on 26 July 1966 states that, while the House will still treat its former decisions as normally binding, it would depart from a previous decision when it appeared right to do so:

...

35. The difference between the House and the Strasbourg court on the application of article 8(1) to Mrs Pretty's case was on a narrow but very important point. Lord Steyn expressed the view of the majority most clearly when he said that the guarantee under article 8 prohibits interference with the way in which an individual leads his life and it does not relate to the manner in which he wishes to die: [2002] 1 AC 800, para 61. It is clear from Lord Bingham's opinion, paras 19 to 23 that he was strongly influenced by the fact that the right to liberty and security in section 7 of the Canadian Charter of Rights and Freedoms which was held by the majority in the Supreme Court of Canada in *Rodriguez* v *Attorney General of Canada* [1994] 2 LRC 136 to confer a right to personal autonomy extending even to decisions on life and death had no close analogy in the European Convention, and by the absence of Strasbourg jurisprudence on this point, when he said in para 23 that there was nothing in article 8 to suggest that it had reference to the choice to live no longer.

36. I describe this as the view of the majority because, although I did not expressly dissent from it, the view which I expressed on this point in para 100 of my own opinion was directly to the contrary:

> 'Respect for a person's "private life", which is the only part of article 8(1) which is in play here, relates to the way a person lives. The way she chooses to pass the closing moments of her life is part of the act of living, and she has the right to ask that this too must be respected. In that respect Mrs Pretty has a right of self-determination. In that sense, her private life is engaged even where in the face of a terminal illness she chooses death rather than life.'

The Strasbourg court referred to this passage in my opinion in para 64 of its judgment with approval, and the rest of its reasoning is consistent with it. In para 65 the court said:

> 'The very essence of the Convention is respect for human dignity and human freedom. Without in any way negating the principle of sanctity of life protected under the Convention, the Court considers that it is under article 8 that notions of the quality of life take on significance. In an era of growing medical sophistication combined with longer life expectancies, many people are concerned that they should not be forced to linger on in old age or in states of advanced physical or mental decrepitude which conflict with strongly held ideas of self and personal identity.'

37. Mr Foster for the Society for the Protection of Unborn Children, intervening, pointed to the Strasbourg court's observation in para 67 that it was not prepared to exclude that the fact that Mrs Pretty was prevented by law from exercising her choice to avoid what she considered to be an undignified and distressing end to her life constituted an interference with her right to respect for private life as guaranteed by article 8. He said these words showed that it had refrained from committing itself to a decision on this point. As the Court of Appeal noted in para 49 of its judgment, the Divisional Court found the choice of language by the Strasbourg court in para 67 to be 'curious'

and 'elliptical'. He also drew attention to the importance that the Strasbourg court had attached in para 40 of its judgment to the right to life which is protected absolutely by article 2. He said that, as the Strasbourg court's position on the question whether article 8 was engaged was unclear, the House should follow its own decision in Pretty and that it should not be deflected from doing so by what had been said about this in Strasbourg.

38. I would reject Mr Foster's submission, for two reasons. The first is that it is plain, when its judgment is read as a whole, that the Strasbourg court did find that Mrs Pretty's rights under article 8(1) were engaged. It said so in terms in the first sentence of para 87, where it referred in a footnote to its discussion of the issue in paras 61 to 67. That sentence removes any doubt that the words used in para 67 might give rise to. The second is that, even if there was a doubt as to whether article 8(1) was engaged in Mrs Pretty's case, the same cannot be said in the case of Ms Purdy. It seems to me that her situation is addressed directly by what the Strasbourg court said in para 65 of its judgment.

Mrs Pretty, who could no longer do anything for herself, was seeking an undertaking that her husband would be immune from prosecution if he assisted her in the very act of committing suicide. Unlike Ms Purdy, she was not contemplating travelling to another country for this purpose. Nor was there any question, in Mrs Pretty's case, of her being forced by lack of information about prosecution policy to choose between ending her life earlier than she would otherwise have wished while she was still able to do this without her husband's assistance. The difference is a subtle one. But, if there was any room for doubt as to what the position was in Mrs Pretty's case, I would not find any room for doubt in the case of Ms Purdy.

39. I would therefore depart from the decision in *R (Pretty) v Director of Public Prosecutions (Secretary of State for the Home Department Intervening)* [2002] 1 AC 800 and hold that the right to respect for private life in article 8(1) is engaged in this case.

Article 8(2): in accordance with the law

40. The Convention principle of legality requires the court to address itself to three distinct questions. The first is whether there is a legal basis in domestic law for the restriction. The second is whether the law or rule in question is sufficiently accessible to the individual who is affected by the restriction, and sufficiently precise to enable him to understand its scope and foresee the consequences of his actions so that he can regulate his conduct without breaking the law. The third is whether, assuming that these two requirements are satisfied, it is nevertheless open to the criticism that it is being applied in a way that is arbitrary because, for example, it has been resorted to in bad faith or in a way that is not proportionate.

. . .

42. The issue that Ms Purdy raises however is directed not to section 2(1) of the Act, but to section 2(4) and to the way in which the Director can be expected to exercise the discretion which he is given by that subsection whether or not to consent to her husband's prosecution if he assists her.

43. This is where the requirement that the law should be formulated with sufficient precision to enable the individual, if need be with appropriate advice, to regulate his conduct is brought into focus in this case. In *Hasan and Chaush v Bulgaria* (2000) 34 EHRR 1339, para 84, the court said:

> 'For domestic law to meet these requirements [that is, of accessibility and foreseeability] it must afford a measure of legal protection against arbitrary interferences by public authorities with the rights safeguarded by the Convention. In matters affecting fundamental rights it would be contrary to the rule of law, one of the basic principles of a democratic society enshrined in the Convention, for a legal discretion granted to the executive to be expressed in terms of an unfettered power. Consequently, the law must indicate with sufficient clarity the scope of any such discretion conferred on the competent authorities and the manner of its exercise.
>
> The level of precision required of domestic legislation – which cannot in any case provide for every eventuality – depends to a considerable degree on the content of the instrument in question, the field it is designed to cover and the number and status of those to whom it is addressed.'

That was a case where the complaint was that there had been an unlawful and arbitrary interference with the applicants' religious liberties where decisions were taken about the organisation and leadership of their religious community for which no reasons had been given. But there is here a clear statement of principle. The question is to what extent it is applicable to this case.

The Director's discretion

44. It has long been recognised that a prosecution does not follow automatically whenever an offence is believed to have been committed. In *Smedleys Ltd* v *Breed* [1974] AC 839, 856, Viscount Dilhorne made these comments on the propriety of instituting a prosecution under the food and drugs legislation in that case:

> 'In 1951 the question was raised whether it was not a basic principle of the rule of law that the operation of the law is automatic where an offence is known or suspected. The then Attorney-General, Sir Hartley Shawcross, said: "It has never been the rule in this country – I hope it never will be – that criminal offences must automatically be the subject of prosecution." He pointed out that the Attorney- General and the Director of Public Prosecutions only intervene to direct a prosecution when they consider it in the public interest to do so and he cited a statement made by Lord Simon in 1925 when he said:
>
>> "... there is no greater nonsense talked about the Attorney-General's duty than the suggestion that in all cases the Attorney-General ought to decide to prosecute merely because he thinks there is what the lawyers call a case. It is not true and no one who has held the office of Attorney-General supposes it is."
>
> Sir Hartley Shawcross's statement was indorsed, I think, by more than one of his successors.'

45. The purpose of section 2(4) of the 1961 Act must be understood in the light of this background. It was submitted for Ms Purdy that it was clear that Parliament did not intend that all those who might be guilty of an offence under section 2(1) should be punished or even prosecuted for the offence. In *Dunbar* v *Plant* [1998] Ch 412, 437, Phillips LJ said that this was the logical conclusion to be drawn from the provision in section 2(4). But I would accept the view of the Court of Appeal that this observation does not fully reflect the purpose of the requirement for his consent. As it said in para 67, the better approach is to be discerned in the Law Commission's Report, Consents to Prosecution (No 255), para 3.33, where it quoted from the Home Office Memorandum to the Departmental Committee on section 2 of the Official Secrets Act 1911 (The Franks Report, 1972, Cmnd 5104, vol 2, p 125, para 7), in which the point was made that the basic reason for including in a statute a restriction on the bringing of prosecutions was that otherwise there would be a risk of prosecutions being brought in inappropriate circumstances.

46. Among the five reasons that were given by the Franks Committee were to secure consistency of practice, to prevent abuse of the kind that might otherwise result in a vexatious private prosecution, to enable account to be taken of mitigating factors and to provide some central control of the use of the criminal law where it has to intrude into areas which are particularly sensitive or controversial. All these factors are in play where consideration is being given to the question whether someone who is suspected of having committed an offence against section 2(1) should be prosecuted. Consistency of practice is especially important here. The issue is without doubt both sensitive and controversial. Many people view legally assisted suicide as an appalling concept which undermines the fundamental human right to life itself. On the other hand there are those, like Ms Purdy, who firmly believe that the right to life includes the right to end one's own life when one can still do so with dignity. Crown Prosecutors to whom the decision-taking function is delegated need to be given the clearest possible instructions as to the factors which they must have regard to when they are performing it.

...

48. The current version of the Code was published in November 2004. It applies to all criminal offences and makes no distinction between different offences. It sets out two tests for a decision whether to prosecute. These are the 'Full Code Test' and the 'Threshold Test'. The latter test is applied only at an early stage in the investigation, so for present purposes it is only the Full Code Test that is relevant. Para 5.1 of the Code states that the Full Code Test has two stages. The first is consideration of the evidence. If the case passes the tests that are to be applied at the evidential stage, Crown Prosecutors must then consider whether a prosecution is needed in the public

interest. Para 5.7 states that a prosecution will usually take place unless there are public interest factors tending against prosecution which clearly outweigh those tending in favour, or it appears more appropriate to divert the person from prosecution. Para 5.8 tells Crown Prosecutors that they must balance factors for and against prosecution carefully and fairly and that the factors that apply will depend on the facts in each case. Para 5.9 then sets out what it describes as some common public interest factors in favour of prosecution. There are seventeen factors in this list, subparas (a) to (q). Para 5.10 sets out what it describes as some common public interest factors against prosecution. There are nine factors in this list, subparas (a) to (i). I shall not set them out. The details are given in the Court of Appeal's judgment, para 16, where paras 5.9 and 5.10 are quoted in full.

49. As the Court of Appeal observed in para 17, it is perfectly obvious that many of the factors in these lists can have no relevance in a case of assisted suicide. This point is reinforced by the Director's decision in the case of Daniel James. In para 28 of that decision he reminded himself that para 5.7 of the Code states that a prosecution will usually take place unless there are public interest factors tending against prosecution which clearly outweigh those tending in favour, adding that the more serious the offence the more likely it is that a prosecution will be needed in the public interest. He then said this:

> '29. I consider that the offence of aiding and abetting the suicide of another under section 2(1) Suicide Act 1961 is unique in that the critical act – suicide – is not itself unlawful, unlike any other aiding and abetting offence. For that reason, I have decided that many of the factors identified in the Code in favour or against a prosecution do not really apply in this case (I include within this the factors identified in paras 5.9(b), (c), (d), (e), (j), (k), (m), (n) and (p) and 5.10(b), (c), (d), (e), (f), (g), (h) and (i) of the Code).'

50. In para 30 of the decision the Director said that, although para 5.9(a) – whether a conviction was likely to result in a significant sentence – was relevant, it was not a factor in favour of prosecution in Daniel James's case. In para 31 he said that although Daniel James's parents played some part in the co-ordination of the arrangements, they were not 'ring-leaders' or 'organisers' in the sense meant by para 5.9(f). Nor was the offence pre-meditated in the sense meant by para 5.9(g) or a 'group' offence in the sense meant by para 5.9(h). That left paras 5.9(e), (i), (l) and (q): that the defendant was in a position of authority or trust, that the victim of the offence was vulnerable, that there was a marked difference between the actual or mental ages of the defendant and the victim and that a prosecution would have a significant positive impact on maintaining community confidence. On the facts of that case, paras 5.9(e), (i) and (l) did not apply, and he did not think that a prosecution would be likely to have a significant positive impact on community confidence. As for the facts against prosecution, para 5.10(a) was relevant as the penalty in that case was likely to be nominal. But he did not think that much weight could be attached to the remaining factor, para 5.10(c), that the offence was the result of a mistake or a misunderstanding. The result of this careful and commendably frank analysis was that very few, if any, of the factors listed in the Code were of any real assistance.

51. The Director then reminded himself that the factors listed in the Code were not exhaustive of the public interest factors that may be relevant in any given case. Focussing on the particular facts of the case, he noted (a) that an offence under section 2(1) of the 1961 Act is serious, (b) that neither his parents nor his family friend influenced Daniel James to commit suicide – on the contrary his parents tried relentlessly to persuade him not to do so, (c) the conduct of his parents and the family friend was towards the less culpable end of the spectrum, and (d) that neither his parents nor the family friend stood to gain any advantage, financial or otherwise by his death – on the contrary, for his parents, it caused them profound distress. Taking those factors into account he decided that a prosecution was not needed in the public interest.

52. Events have moved on since the current version of the Code was published. The Director has created a Special Crimes Division staffed by a small number of specially trained officers whose function is to supervise prosecutions of exceptional sensitivity or difficulty. I would accept that this change in prosecution practice has gone one step further towards meeting the challenge of arbitrariness. Furthermore, as Ms Dinah Rose QC for the Director said, in addition to the Code Ms Purdy now has the guidance that can be obtained from the Director's decision in the case of Daniel James.

She submitted that sufficient guidance was now available as to how in practice decisions were likely to be taken in cases of that kind. It was undesirable for the Director to go any further in setting out his policy. Very serious ethical issues were involved, especially as there were many examples of people who were severely disabled leading full and fulfilling lives. A finding that the Code did not provide sufficient guidance would have serious implications as this could inhibit the width of the Director's discretion.

53. But it seems to me that, for anyone seeking to identify the factors that are likely to be taken into account in the case of a person with a severe and incurable disability who is likely to need assistance in travelling to a country where assisted suicide is lawful, these developments fall short of what is needed to satisfy the Convention tests of accessibility and foreseeability. The Director's own analysis shows that, in a highly unusual and extremely sensitive case of this kind, the Code offers almost no guidance at all. The question whether a prosecution is in the public interest can only be answered by bringing into account factors that are not mentioned there. Furthermore, the further factors that were taken into account in the case of Daniel James were designed to fit the facts of that case. There could be others just as unsuitable for prosecution where, for example, it could be said that those who offered assistance stood to gain an advantage, financial or otherwise, by the death. An assistant who was not a relative or a family friend might have to be paid, for example, and a relative might derive some benefit under the deceased's will or on intestacy. The issue whether the acts of assistance were undertaken for an improper motive will, of course, be highly relevant. But the mere fact that some benefit might accrue is unlikely, on its own, to be significant.

Conclusion

54. The Code will normally provide sufficient guidance to Crown Prosecutors and to the public as to how decisions should or are likely to be taken whether or not, in a given case, it will be in the public interest to prosecute. This is a valuable safeguard for the vulnerable, as it enables the prosecutor to take into account the whole background of the case. In most cases its application will ensure predictability and consistency of decision-taking, and people will know where they stand. But that cannot be said of cases where the offence in contemplation is aiding or abetting the suicide of a person who is terminally ill or severely and incurably disabled, who wishes to be helped to travel to a country where assisted suicide is lawful and who, having the capacity to take such a decision, does so freely and with a full understanding of the consequences. There is already an obvious gulf between what section 2(1) says and the way that the subsection is being applied in practice in compassionate cases of that kind.

55. The cases that have been referred to the Director are few, but they will undoubtedly grow in number. Decisions in this area of the law are, of course, highly sensitive to the facts of each case. They are also likely to be controversial. But I would not regard these as reasons for excusing the Director from the obligation to clarify what his position is as to the factors that he regards as relevant for and against prosecution in this very special and carefully defined class of case. How he goes about this task must be a matter for him, as also must be the ultimate decision as to whether or not to prosecute. But, as the definition which I have given may show, it ought to be possible to confine the class that requires special treatment to a very narrow band of cases with the result that the Code will continue to apply to all those cases that fall outside it.

56. I would therefore allow the appeal and require the Director to promulgate an offence-specific policy identifying the facts and circumstances which he will take into account in deciding, in a case such as that which Ms Purdy's case exemplifies, whether or not to consent to a prosecution under section 2(1) of the 1961 Act.

■ NOTES AND QUESTIONS

1. Although the European Court of Human Rights in *Pretty* said that the UK Government had not violated her rights, it said that her rights under Article 8 were engaged. What does this mean?

2. If suicide is no longer a crime, why should the act of assisting a suicide be treated differently from that of committing suicide? Even if there are valid reasons for

treating the two differently, should an exception have been made in a case such as that of *Pretty*, where her condition prevented her from being able to commit suicide?

3. Should the law on assisted suicide in England and Wales be amended, as assisting a suicide is currently a criminal offence? Effectively in *Purdy*, that issue has been left on the table, but the law should be certain and the way that the House of Lords dealt with the issue leaves a constitutional mess.

4. The HL in *Purdy* strongly advocated the fact that the DPP should promulgate guidelines about assisting people who wanted to kill themselves in different jurisdictions. These have now been issued. But are guidelines simply a way for the court to sidestep its responsibility to decide the underlying issues?

5. What was the contention between the Human Rights Court and the Lords about the right of private life, particularly the different concept of a right of living and dying?

6. We can see in *Purdy* that the Lords allowed that, in addition to giving the courts more far-reaching powers, the HRA 1998 may lead to judges taking a more 'European' approach to decision-making. Historically, UK courts have tended to give great weight to precedent (the practice of adhering to past judicial decisions which have addressed the same or similar issues). The ECtHR, on the other hand, regards the Convention as a 'living instrument' and is therefore not averse to departing from precedent when changing social conditions and attitudes support doing so.

7. When cases involving national law are considered by the ECtHR, the Court allows the state some leeway, what is referred to as a 'margin of appreciation'. What purposes are served by allowing a 'margin of appreciation'? Should this 'margin of appreciation' also be extended when a UK court considers a domestic statute pursuant to the HRA 1998? What is the difference?

8. How should a UK court proceed when it decides that a statute is incompatible with the Convention? The court is not permitted to rewrite the statute, but if it interprets it in a way not intended by Parliament, is the effect not the same?

9. The potential for legislative–judicial conflicts may lead to caution on the part of both Parliament and the judiciary: Parliament in enacting legislation (indeed, in the future the Government will have to make a statement that any proposed Bill is compatible with the Convention); and the judiciary in making a declaration of incompatibility. Does *Purdy* suggest a compromise between the judiciary and Parliament?

The ultimate effect of the HRA 1998 will depend in part on how 'activist' judges are prepared to be in interpreting and implementing its provisions. Traditionally, UK courts have given great deference to 'Parliamentary sovereignty' (the principle that the courts may not question laws properly enacted by Parliament). The justification for this doctrine is that members of Parliament (or, more accurately, members of the House of Commons) derive their authority from a democratic mandate, while judges are appointed and do not have to stand for re-election. Under the HRA 1998, although courts cannot invalidate legislation enacted by Parliament, they can declare that a statute is incompatible with the Convention. But how robust will (should) courts be in making such a 'declaration of incompatibility'? Compare the decisions (below) of a distinguished panel of the Queen's Bench Division and the House of Lords (now the Supreme Court) in a case which raised the question of whether a reverse burden of proof (the burden of proof in respect of an element of the crime being placed on the defendant rather than the prosecution) conflicted with Article 6 of the Convention.

R v Director of Public Prosecutions, ex parte Kebeline and others
[1999] 4 All ER 801, Queen's Bench Division

LORD BINGHAM OF CORNHILL CJ: The four applicants before the court are defendants to criminal proceedings brought against them under the Prevention of Terrorism (Temporary Provisions) Act 1989 as amended. They seek to challenge the continuing decision of the Director of Public Prosecutions to consent to the institution of proceedings against them. Their challenge, although put in several different ways, is based on the European Convention for the Protection of Human Rights and Fundamental Freedoms (Rome, 4 November 1950, TS 71 (1953); Cmd 8969) and the enactment of the Human Rights Act 1998. The crucial issues between the parties concern the impact (if any) of the 1998 Act on the exercise of the Director's discretion to prosecute during this interim period between enactment of the 1998 Act and the bringing into force of the main provisions of that Act; and the role and jurisdiction (if any) of this court in reviewing that exercise of discretion.

In May 1997 the applicants Kebeline and Boukemiche were arrested and charged with an offence of possession of items for the purposes of committing terrorism abroad, contrary to s 16A of the 1989 Act. In July 1997 the applicant Souidi was arrested and charged with the same offence. Consent was given by the Director to the institution of proceedings against Kebeline and Boukemiche on 13 August 1997 and they were committed for trial the next day. Consent to the prosecution of Souidi was given on 3 October 1997 and he was committed for trial on 16 October. Following plea and directions hearings in October and December 1997, a trial was fixed for 9 March 1998. On that date there was an abuse of process application which lasted five days and led to the postponement of the trial, which began before Judge Pownall QC at the Central Criminal Court on 12 October 1998. Following argument on and rejection of a further application for a stay, a jury was empanelled on 27 October, the case was opened and prosecution evidence called. At the conclusion of the evidence counsel for the applicants submitted that s 16A, under which these applicants had been prosecuted, was in conflict with art 6(2) of the convention. Having heard argument the judge ruled in favour of the applicants, giving his reasons on 23 November. The solicitor for the applicants wrote to the Director asking him in the light of this ruling to reconsider his consent to the proceedings. Counsel for the Crown sought an adjournment so that the Director could consider the matter, which had been raised for the first time. The Director sought advice from Mr Rabinder Singh, counsel of acknowledged authority in this field. He submitted a skeleton argument, reflecting (as we understand) the advice given to the Director, and appeared in court with the judge's consent to submit that the judge's earlier ruling had been wrong and should be revised. The judge, having heard argument on both sides, adhered to his earlier ruling. The Director for his part remained of opinion that there was no inconsistency between s 16A of the 1989 Act and art 6(2) of the convention. A further argument was addressed to the judge on abuse of process, partly relying on the convention, but the judge rejected it. On 14 December 1998 the jury was, however, discharged, for reasons unconnected with the issues before us.

...

The compatibility of ss 16A and 16B with art 6(2) of the convention
The applicants' argument depends, in very brief summary, on four contentions. They argue, first, that the right to a fair trial is a fundamental constitutional right recognised by the common law and guaranteed by the convention and other international human rights instruments. This proposition is not, and cannot be, disputed. It calls for no citation of authority.

The applicants submit, secondly, that an essential ingredient of a fair trial is the rule that every-one charged with a criminal offence shall be presumed innocent until proved guilty according to law. This rule also is recognised by the common law. It is expressed in these terms in art 6(2) of the convention. It is also to be found in art 14(2) of the International Covenant on Civil and Political Rights (New York, 16 December 1966; TS 6 (1977); Cmnd 6702) and it has its equivalents in other human rights instruments around the world. This proposition also is not, and could not be, challenged.

The applicants submit, thirdly, that the presumption of innocence is undermined if a legal burden is placed on a defendant to disprove any substantial ingredient of the offence of which he is accused.

...

The task of the court is, as the applicants fourthly submit, to study the substantial effect of a legislative provision said to infringe the presumption of innocence in order to decide whether in practical terms it does so or not. The gravamen of the offence charged by s 16A is the possession of articles, in themselves innocent, for terrorist purposes. The crucial ingredients of the offence are in reality possession (the actus reus) and the terrorist purpose (the mens rea). But neither of these crucial ingredients need be proved by the prosecution to the criminal standard to secure a conviction. Subsection (4) relieves the Crown of the need to prove possession in the ordinary way and places a reverse burden on the defendant. Subsection (1) allows the prosecution to establish the terrorist purpose by showing something short of proof (see Hussien v Chong Fook Kam [1969] 3 All ER 1626 at 1630, [1970] AC 942 at 948) and again places a reverse burden on the defendant in sub-s (3). A defendant who chooses not to give or call evidence may be convicted by virtue of presumptions against him and on reasonable suspicion falling short of proof.

The gravamen of the offence charged in s 16B is the collection or possession of information, in itself innocent, for purposes of terrorism. In this instance the actus reus is the collection or possession, and this must be proved to the criminal standard. But the mens rea is the purpose for which the information is collected or possessed. This need not be proved by the prosecution at all. Instead, a reverse burden is placed on the defendant to prove lawful authority or reasonable excuse for collecting or possessing the information. A defendant who chooses not to give or call evidence may be convicted without the mens rea of the offence being proved against him.

It seems to me that on their face both sections undermine, in a blatant and obvious way, the presumption of innocence.

...

Under s 16A a defendant could be convicted even if the jury entertained a reasonable doubt whether he knew that the items were in his premises and whether he had the items for a terrorist purpose. Under s 16B a defendant could be convicted even if the jury entertained a reasonable doubt whether the information had been collected or was possessed for any terrorist purpose. In both sections the presumption of innocence is violated.

Mr Pannick strongly contests this conclusion. He relies on the clear Parliamentary intention expressed in ss 16A and 16B; on evidence from a senior Home Office official describing the practical need for provisions such as these; on the recent recommendation by Lord Lloyd of Berwick that these provisions be retained; on the urgent need to take effective action against international terrorism; and on the reasonableness of requiring a defendant to adduce evidence of matters better known to him than anyone else. These are all considerations which deserve careful attention. But they do not, singly or cumulatively, dissuade me from the conclusion already expressed.

R v Director of Public Prosecutions, ex parte Kebeline and Others (On Appeal From a Divisional Court of The Queen's Bench Division)

[2000] 2 AC 326, House of Lords

LORD COOKE OF THORNDON:

...

I am constrained to part company with the Divisional Court on their putting aside of s 3(1) of the 1998 Act. In my respectful view, it is not altogether logical, nor is it necessary, to consider the likely impact of the other main provisions of that Act on United Kingdom law without taking into account also s 3(1), which is a key element in the 1998 Act.

When the whole 1998 Act comes into force, the new canon of interpretation will be that, so far as it is possible to do so, primary legislation and subordinate legislation must be read and given effect in a way which is compatible with the convention rights. This is a strong adjuration. It seems distinctly possible that it may require s 16A of the 1989 Act to be interpreted as imposing on the defendant an evidential, but not a persuasive (or ultimate), burden of proof.

LORD HOPE OF CRAIGHEAD:

. . .

Classification

The first stage in any inquiry as to whether a statutory provision is vulnerable to challenge on the ground that it is incompatible with art 6(2) of the convention is to identify the nature of the provision which is said to transfer the burden of proof from the prosecution to the accused. Various techniques have been adopted. Some provisions are more objectionable than others. The extent to which they encroach upon the presumption of innocence depends upon the legislative technique which has been used. The field can be narrowed considerably by means of this preliminary analysis.

It is necessary in the first place to distinguish between the shifting from the prosecution to the accused of what Glanville Williams pp 185–186 described as the 'evidential burden', or the burden of introducing evidence in support of his case, on the one hand and the 'persuasive burden', or the burden of persuading the jury as to his guilt or innocence, on the other. A 'persuasive' burden of proof requires the accused to prove, on a balance of probabilities, a fact which is essential to the determination of his guilt or innocence. It reverses the burden of proof by removing it from the prosecution and transferring it to the accused. An 'evidential' burden requires only that the accused must adduce sufficient evidence to raise an issue before it has to be determined as one of the facts in the case. The prosecution does not need to lead any evidence about it, so the accused needs to do this if he wishes to put the point in issue. But if it is put in issue, the burden of proof remains with the prosecution. The accused need only raise a reasonable doubt about his guilt.

Statutory presumptions which place an 'evidential' burden on the accused, requiring the accused to do no more than raise a reasonable doubt on the matter with which they deal, do not breach the presumption of innocence. They are not incompatible with art 6(2) of the convention. They take their place alongside the common law evidential presumptions which have been built up in the light of experience. They are a necessary part of preserving the balance of fairness between the accused and the prosecutor in matters of evidence. It is quite common in summary prosecutions for routine matters which may be inconvenient or time-consuming for the prosecutor to have to prove but which may reasonably be supposed to be within the accused's own knowledge to be dealt with in this way. It is not suggested that statutory provisions of this kind are objectionable.

Statutory presumptions which transfer the 'persuasive' burden to the accused require further examination. Three kinds were identified by the respondents in their written case. I am content to adopt their analysis, which Mr Pannick QC for the Director did not dispute. First, there is the 'mandatory' presumption of guilt as to an essential element of the offence. As the presumption is one which must be applied if the basis of fact on which it rests is established, it is inconsistent with the presumption of innocence. This is a matter which can be determined as a preliminary issue without reference to the facts of the case. Secondly, there is a presumption of guilt as to an essential element which is 'discretionary'.

The tribunal of fact may or may not rely on the presumption, depending upon its view as to the cogency or weight of the evidence. If the presumption is of this kind it may be necessary for the facts of the case to be considered before a conclusion can be reached as to whether the presumption of innocence has been breached. In that event the matters cannot be resolved until after trial.

The third category of provisions which fall within the general description of reverse onus clauses consists of provisions which relate to an exemption or proviso which the accused must establish if he wishes to avoid conviction but is not an essential element of the offence.

. . .

According to the classification which I have outlined, sub-s (3) of s 16A imposes a persuasive burden of proof on the accused, on a balance of probabilities, that the article was not in his possession for a purpose connected with terrorism. If that burden is not discharged, or the accused elects not to undertake it, sub-s (1) contains a mandatory presumption that the article was in his possession for a purpose connected with terrorism which is applied if the prosecutor proves that it was in his possession in circumstances giving rise to a reasonable suspicion that it was in his possession for that purpose. Subsection (4) imposes a persuasive burden of proof on the accused that he did not know that the article was in the premises or, if he did, that he had no control over it. If that burden is not discharged, or the accused elects not to undertake it, the subsection contains a discretionary presumption that he was in possession of the article.

...

Section 16A(3) sets out the defence. The onus is on the accused, but at least it can be said that the matter is not left to inference or to the discretion of the trial court. This is a defence which is provided for expressly by the statute. It has to be seen in the context of sub-s (4). If the accused can show that he did not know that the article was in the premises or that he had no control over it, he can by giving evidence to that effect deprive the prosecution of the presumption that he was in possession of the article. He will only need to rely on sub-s (3) if he was in possession of the article and the circumstances are such as to give rise to the reasonable suspicion mentioned in sub-s (1). A sound judgment as to whether the burden which he has to discharge is an unreasonable one is unlikely to be possible until the facts are known. It is not immediately obvious that it would be imposing an unreasonable burden on an accused who was in possession of articles from which an inference of involvement in terrorism could be drawn to provide an explanation for his possession of them which would displace that inference. Account would have to be taken of the nature of the incriminating circumstances and the facilities which were available to the accused to obtain the necessary evidence. It would be one thing if there was good reason to think that the accused had easy access to the facts, quite another if access to them was very difficult.

Then there is the nature of the threat which terrorism poses to a free and democratic society. It seeks to achieve its ends by violence and intimidation. It is often indiscriminate in its effects, and sophisticated methods are used to avoid detection both before and after the event. Society has a strong interest in preventing acts of terrorism before they are perpetrated—to spare the lives of innocent people and to avoid the massive damage and dislocation to ordinary life which may follow from explosions which destroy or damage property. Section 16A is designed to achieve that end. It would not be appropriate for us in this case to attempt to resolve the difficult question whether the balance between the needs of society and the presumption of innocence has been struck in the right place. But it seems to me that this is a question which is still open to argument.

LORD HOBHOUSE OF WOODBOROUGH:

...

The scheme of the 1998 Act is that no decision of the courts can invalidate an Act of Parliament. Under s 4(2) a court (being one of those specified in s 4(5)) may, if satisfied that a provision of an Act of Parliament is incompatible with a convention right, make a 'declaration of that incompatibility'. But, by s 4(6), such a declaration: '... (a) does not affect the validity, continuing operation or enforcement of the provision in respect of which it is given; and (b) is not binding on the parties to the proceedings in which it is made.' Section 3(2)(b) contains a similar reservation of validity. Thus, incompatibility does not found any right under the 1998 Act. The procedure to be followed after a declaration of invalidity is laid down in ss 10 and 20 of the 1998 Act and Sch 2. Whether the incompatible legislation should be amended so as to confer the relevant convention right is a matter for the minister and Parliament. Unless and until such an amendment is made, the existing law remains in force notwithstanding the incompatibility and things done in accordance with that law remain lawful (see also s 6(6)). Whether any amendment had retrospective effect would also depend upon the terms of the amendment (Sch 2, para 1).

...

If s 16A is, on the existing principles of statutory construction compatible with the convention, the defendants' ground for applying for judicial review falls away. The point is fully arguable within the criminal trial and any resultant appeal and the Crown Court or the Court of Appeal will give effect to s 16A so construed. If, on the other hand, s 16A is irretrievably incompatible, as the Divisional Court held that it was, the defendants' application again cannot succeed. Whether the 1998 Act has come into force or not the position remains the same. The incompatibility does not deprive s 16A of its force and validity nor does it affect the criminal trial or any convictions resulting from the application of s 16A. The defendants' guilt or innocence has to be determined in accordance with s 16A. All this Lord Lester had to and did accept.

. . .

This case and other similar cases decided under the convention show that it is necessary to examine each case on its merits. There may be a justification for the terms in which the legislation is drafted even though on its face it would appear to be contrary to the convention. Similarly, it is necessary to examine whether the relevant provision has in fact resulted in an injustice to the complainant. This last point ties in with the use in s 7(1) of the 1998 Act of the term 'victim'. Criminal statutes which in certain circumstances partially reverse the burden of proof are not uncommon nor are they confined to the United Kingdom. The judgments and decisions of the European Court of Human Rights and the Commission (account of which must be taken under s 2 of the 1998 Act) show that they are not necessarily incompatible with the convention.

These are not matters which it is necessary or proper to enter upon on the present appeal. If they need at some later stage, in the Crown Court or elsewhere, to be decided in relation to these defendants or any of them under s 16A, that is the time at which they should be decided. The position is not as clear cut as the Divisional Court seem to have thought nor is it right that these proceedings by way of the attempted judicial review of the Director's conduct should be used as a vehicle for their decision now.

I agree that the appeal should be allowed as proposed by your Lordships.

Appeal allowed.

■ NOTES AND QUESTIONS

1. There have been other challenges to so-called 'reverse burdens of proof', the majority of which have failed. See, e.g., *R v E* [2004] EWCA Crim 1025. On the whole, courts are more willing to uphold a reverse burden of proof that relates to an evidential burden (who has the burden of introducing evidence on an issue) than one that relates to a persuasive burden (who has the burden of persuading the jury on the issue). See *R v Lambert* [2001] UKHL 37.

2. In the ECtHR, challenges to reverse burdens of proof have also been rejected. See, e.g., *Salabiaku v France* (1988) 13 EHRR 37.

3. A common method of creating a reverse burden of proof is for Parliament to enact a strict liability offence (that is, one where the prosecution does not have to prove the defendant's wrongful state of mind) and then allow a 'due diligence' defence which the accused must establish. What considerations might prompt Parliament to draft a statute in this form? While most reverse burdens of proof relate to statutory crimes, the one major common law exception is that defendants bear the burden of proof when they raise a defence of insanity. See Chapter 9.

4. When a reverse burden of proof is placed on the accused, he or she will only have to establish the defence by a balance of probabilities, and not by proof beyond reasonable doubt.

SECTION 6: WHAT IS A CRIME?

A: Relevant considerations

How can one tell whether or not one is dealing with a 'crime'? This is a critical question because it will determine not only the potential consequences of failing to abide by the relevant law, but also the procedures which will be followed if there is to be a trial. Indeed, the latter point was given prominence by Glanville Williams in his conception of a crime as an act capable of being followed by criminal proceedings (Williams, 'The Definition of Crime' [1955] Current Legal Problems 107). The problem with Williams' definition is that it puts the cart before the horse. Under the jurisprudence of the European Court of Human Rights (ECtHR) (whose decisions must be taken into account by national courts under the HRA 1998), one must determine whether an offence or charge is criminal in order to determine what procedures will be applied. In making this determination, a court is not bound by the label or characterisation placed on the misconduct by Parliament:

Benham v United Kingdom

(1996) 22 EHRR 293, European Court of Human Rights

On 1 April 1990 Mr Benham became liable to pay a community charge of £325. Since he did not pay it, on 21 August 1990 the Poole Magistrates' Court ordered the issue of a liability order, entitling Poole Borough Council ('the charging authority') to commence enforcement proceedings against him.

Mr Benham did not pay the amount owed, and bailiffs visited his parents' house (where he was living), but were told that he had no goods of any value there or elsewhere which could be seized by them and sold in order to pay the debt.

Under Regulation 41 of the Community Charge (Administration and Enforcement) Regulations 1989 if a person is found to have insufficient goods on which to levy outstanding community charge the charging authority may apply to a magistrates' court for an order committing him to prison. On such an application being made, the court must inquire in the presence of the debtor as to his present means and also whether his failure to pay which led to the liability order being made was due to wilful refusal or culpable neglect.

The charging authority applied for such an order, and on 25 March 1991 Mr Benham appeared at the Poole Magistrates' Court for the inquiry required by the Regulations.

He was not assisted or represented by a lawyer, although he was eligible for 'Green Form' legal advice and assistance before the hearing, and the magistrates could have made an order for Assistance by Way of Representation ('ABWOR') if they had thought it necessary.

The magistrates found that Mr Benham, who had 9 'O' level General Certificates of Secondary Education, had started a Government Employment Training Scheme in September 1989, but had left it in March 1990 and had not worked since. He had applied for income support, but had been turned down because it is not payable to those who are voluntarily unemployed, and he had no personal assets or income.

On the basis of this evidence, the magistrates concluded that his failure to pay the community charge was due to his culpable neglect, 'as he clearly had the potential to earn money to discharge his obligation to pay'. Accordingly, they decided that he ought to be sent to prison for thirty days unless he paid what was owing.

Mr Benham was taken to Dorchester prison on the same day.

. . .

The applicant, with whom the Commission agreed, argued that the proceedings before the magistrates involved the determination of a criminal charge for the purposes of Article 6(3)(c). He referred to the facts that what was in issue was not a dispute between individuals but rather liability to pay a tax to a public authority, and that the proceedings had many 'criminal' features, such as the safeguards available to defendants aged under 21, the severity of the applicable penalty and the requirement of a finding of culpability before a term of imprisonment could be imposed. Furthermore, it was by no means clear that the proceedings were classified as civil rather than criminal under the domestic law.

The Government argued that Article 6(3)(c) did not apply because the proceedings before the magistrates were civil rather than criminal in nature, as was borne out by the weight of the English case-law. The purpose of the detention was to coerce the applicant into paying the tax owed, rather than to punish him for not having paid it.

The case-law of the Court establishes that there are three criteria to be taken into account when deciding whether a person was 'charged with a criminal offence' for the purposes of Article 6. These are the classification of the proceedings under national law, the nature of the proceedings and the nature and degree of severity of the penalty.

As to the first of these criteria, the Court agrees with the Government that the weight of the domestic authority indicates that, under English law, the proceedings in question are regarded as civil rather than criminal in nature. However, this factor is of relative weight and serves only as a starting-point.

The second criterion, the nature of the proceedings, carries more weight. In this connection, the Court notes that the law concerning liability to pay the community charge and the procedure upon non-payment was of general application to all citizens, and that the proceedings in question were brought by a public authority under statutory powers of enforcement. In addition, the proceedings had some punitive elements. For example, the magistrates could only exercise their power of committal to prison on a finding of wilful refusal to pay or of culpable neglect.

Finally, it is to be recalled that the applicant faced a relatively severe maximum penalty of three months' imprisonment and was in fact ordered to be detained for thirty days.

Having regard to these factors, the Court concludes that Mr Benham was 'charged with a criminal offence' for the purposes of Article 6(1) and (3). Accordingly, these two paragraphs of Article 6 are applicable . . . .

■ NOTES AND QUESTIONS

1. Of the three criteria identified in *Benham* as bearing on whether there is a criminal offence at issue, why is the characterisation of the offence by Parliament not given more weight? Why is the penalty accorded so much weight? In respect of the penalty, should the critical factor be the potential penalty to which the defendant could have been subjected or the actual penalty imposed in the case?

2. The importance that attaches from a determination that a defendant has been charged with a criminal offence is that the fair trial provisions of Article 6 of the ECHR must be observed. The criminal defendant is entitled to the presumption of innocence, prompt notice of the charges, adequate time and facilities for the preparation of a defence, legal assistance and the right to an interpreter if needed, the right to compel the attendance of witnesses and to cross-examine witnesses, and the right to be tried by an independent and impartial tribunal at a public hearing held within a reasonable time of the offence. Included in the right to legal assistance is the right to a free lawyer if required by the defendant's financial circumstances and the interests of justice.

3. Article 7 of the ECHR provides that no one shall be convicted of a criminal offence which was not an offence at the time of its commission. Do common law crimes violate Article 7?

Gay News Ltd and Lemon v United Kingdom
(1982) 5 EHRR 123, European Court of Human Rights

The applicants, who are respectively the publisher and the responsible editor of a journal for homosexuals, were found guilty of the common law offence of blasphemous libel in connection with the publication of a certain poem. They complain that this conviction amounted to an unjustified interference with their freedom of expression as guaranteed by Article 10 of the Convention. They further claim that the publication of the poem amounted to an exercise of their right to freedom of thought and religion within the meaning of Article 9 of the Convention, and that the interference with this right was likewise unjustified. Apart from the argument that the restriction imposed on them was not necessary in a democratic society for any of the legitimate purposes enumerated in the above two Convention Articles, the applicants submit in particular that their conviction was based on legal principles which had not existed, or at least had not been defined with sufficient clarity, at the time of the commission of the offence. In this respect they claim that the restriction was not 'prescribed by law' as required under paragraph (2) of Articles 9 and 10, and they allege in addition a violation of Article 7 of the Convention. The applicants finally complain that they have been discriminated against, contrary to Article 14 of the Convention, in the exercise of their freedom under Articles 9 and 10 of the Convention.

...

In the present case, the parties are first of all in disagreement as to whether the criminal offence of blasphemous libel was defined with sufficient certainty in the common law principles which were applied by the courts. The existence of the offence, i.e. the fact that it has not fallen in desuetudo, is apparently no longer challenged even by the applicants themselves. But they contend that essential elements of the offence, in particular the principle of strict liability (i.e. the necessity to prove only the intent to publish but not the intent to blaspheme), had not been laid down in pre-existing rules of law but were developed by the courts only in the course of the proceedings in their own case. In this connection it is alleged that even the majority of the House of Lords itself recognised the law-making function of its decision when it took up this particular issue. The Government, on the other hand, denies that the courts, including the House of Lords, created new law in this case when they applied a standard of strict liability. They merely clarified the existing law and in doing so based themselves on established case law without departing from the views expressed in recent leading textbooks.

The Commission first observes that not only written statutes but also rules of common or other customary law may provide a sufficient legal basis both for restrictions of fundamental rights subject to exception clauses such as the one contained in Article 10(2) of the Convention, and for the criminal convictions envisaged in Article 7 of the Convention. The problem in the present case therefore does not reside in the fact that the offence of blasphemous libel was not a statutory, but a common law offence.

The crucial point is rather one of the certainty of the law, and the functions of the courts in clarifying or developing vague legal provisions or concepts. This problem was also considered in the Sunday Times case both by the Commission and the Court (see European Court of Human Rights A30 (1979)). In paragraph 49 of its judgment, the Court said the following:

In the Court's opinion, the following are two of the requirements that flow from the expression 'prescribed by law'. Firstly, the law must be adequately accessible: the citizen must be able to have an indication that is adequate in the circumstances of the legal rules applicable to a given case. Secondly, a norm cannot be regarded as a 'law' unless it is formulated with sufficient precision to enable the citizen to regulate his conduct: he must be able—if need be with appropriate advice—to foresee, to a degree that is reasonable in the circumstances, the consequences which a given action may entail. Those consequences need not be foreseeable with absolute certainty:

experience shows this to be unattainable. Again, whilst certainty is highly desirable, it may bring in its train excessive rigidity and the law must be able to keep pace with changing circumstances. Accordingly, many laws are inevitably couched in terms which, to a greater or lesser extent, are vague and whose interpretation and application are questions of practice.

...

The Commission considers that the same principles also apply to the interpretation and application of the common law. While this branch of the law presents certain particularities for the very reason that it is by definition law developed by the courts, it is nevertheless subject to the rule that the law-making function of the courts must remain within reasonable limits. In particular in the area of the criminal law it is excluded, by virtue of Article 7(1) of the Convention, that any acts not previously punishable should be held by the courts to entail criminal liability, or that existing offences should be extended to cover facts which previously clearly did not constitute a criminal offence. This implies that constituent elements of an offence such as, e.g. the particular form of culpability required for its completion may not be essentially changed, at least not to the detriment of the accused, by the case law of the courts. On the other hand it is not objectionable that the existing elements of the offence are clarified and adapted to new circumstances which can reasonably be brought under the original concept of the offence.

The Commission notes that the Law Commission has criticised the state of the law of blasphemous libel in particular with regard to its lacking clarity, but it nevertheless considers that the courts in the present case in fact did not go beyond the limits of a reasonable interpretation of the existing law. The House of Lords in particular was aware of the limits of its law-making functions in the area of the criminal law which had been circumscribed in the practice statement of 1966 and put into operation in the case of Knuller v DPP [1973] AC 435. The courts of all degrees confirmed the continued existence of the offence of blasphemous libel. There was only one point which was not clear, namely the particular requirements as to the mens rea of a person who commits this offence. This question was answered in the same way by each of the courts. Despite the admission by the Court of Appeal and the majority of the House of Lords that a point of principle was involved in the determination of this question which required clarification, it is equally clear that the application of a test of strict liability and the exclusion of evidence as to the publisher's and editor's intention to blaspheme did not amount to the creation of new law in the sense that earlier case law clearly denying such strict liability and admitting evidence as to the blasphemous intentions was overruled. By stating that the mens rea in this offence did only relate to the intention to publish, the courts therefore did not overstep the limits of what can still be regarded as an acceptable clarification of the law. The Commission further considers that the law was also accessible to the applicants and that its interpretation in this way was reasonably foreseeable for them with the assistance of appropriate legal advice. In conclusion therefore the Commission finds that there is no appearance of a violation of Article 7(1) of the Convention in this case, and the applicants' complaint in this respect must accordingly be rejected as being manifestly ill-founded within the meaning of Article 27(2) of the Convention. From that it follows that the requirement under Article 10(2) of the Convention that any restriction on the freedom of expression must be 'prescribed by law' has also been complied with.

■ NOTES AND QUESTIONS

1. In *R* v *Goldstein* [2003] EWCA Crim 3450, the Court of Appeal recognised the common law offence of public nuisance, rejecting an Article 7 challenge.

2. In most European countries there are neither common law crimes nor statutes but written codes. Unlike statutes, which are adopted piecemeal over time, a code constitutes a comprehensive and integrated expression of the whole of a country's law. Greater consistency in terminology can be achieved than in statutes passed by different Parliaments at different times. Often the code will go beyond providing a simple catalogue of crimes and defences and include a statement of general criminal law principles. Examples and commentary may also be included.

In 1989 the Law Commission (the official body created by Parliament for promoting the reform of the law in England and Wales in the Law Commissions Act 1965) proposed a draft criminal code for the UK. This draft criminal code has never been enacted. Nonetheless, its provisions will, where appropriate, be referred to in this book because they represent the well-formed views of persons who have given the issues under consideration serious thought and deliberation. The Law Commission has recently revived this project.

3. The Hon. Mrs. Justice Arden has argued that the passage of the HRA 1998 strengthens the case for a criminal code (Arden, 'Criminal Law at the Crossroads: The Impact of Human Rights from the Law Commission's Perspective and the Need for a Code' [1999] Crim LR 439). Why should this be so? You may wish to reconsider this question after reading the section 3 of this chapter on the HRA 1998.

4. To say that the common law has largely been replaced by statute is not to say that judges no longer have a role in the development of the law. It remains the responsibility of courts:

   (a) to interpret the meaning of the terms of the statute;

   (b) to determine what conduct falls within the ambit of the statute and what defences may be raised by way of excuse, justification or mitigation;

   (c) to provide guidance to juries, and, in the case of appellate courts, to trial judges; and

   (d) to determine the appropriate sentence, within limits set by Parliament, for those convicted of violating the statute.

PART IV

Inchoate Offences and Parties to Crime

12

Encouragement, Assistance, Conspiracy and Attempt

The offences of encouraging or assisting a crime (formerly incitement), conspiracy and attempt are designed to permit law enforcement personnel to intervene at a stage of criminal activity before actual harm occurs. These offences are commonly referred to as 'inchoate'. An inchoate offence occurs when steps have been taken towards commission of a crime but the crime has not been carried through to its intended conclusion. Inchoate crimes are not defined in terms of result, and therefore, when an inchoate crime is charged, it is not necessary for the prosecution to identify a victim or prove that actual harm has occurred.

Although the goal is to prevent harm, the prosecution must nonetheless provide evidence of the defendant's willingness to break the law; evil thoughts alone do not constitute a criminal offence.

R v Higgins

(1801) 2 East 5, King's Bench Division

LE BLANC J: It is contended that the offence charged in the second count, of which the defendant has been convicted, is no misdemeanor, because it amounts only to a bare wish or desire of the mind to do an illegal act. If that were so, I agree that it would not be indictable. But this is charge of an act done; namely, an actual solicitation of a servant to rob his master, and not merely a wish or desire that he should do so. A solicitation or inciting of another, by whatever means it is attempted, is an act done; and that such an act done with a criminal intent is punishable by indictment has been clearly established by the several cases referred to . . . .

SECTION 1: ENCOURAGING OR ASSISTING A CRIME

The common law crime of incitement has now been abolished (Serious Crime Act 2007, s. 59) and replaced by the statutory offence of encouraging or assisting a crime.

A. The offence

SERIOUS CRIME ACT 2007

PART 2 ENCOURAGING OR ASSISTING CRIME

Inchoate offences

44 Intentionally encouraging or assisting an offence

(1) A person commits an offence if—

(a) he does an act **capable** of encouraging or assisting the commission of an offence; and

(b) he intends to encourage or assist its commission.

(2) But he is not to be taken to have intended to encourage or assist the commission of an offence merely because such encouragement or assistance was a foreseeable consequence of his act.

45   Encouraging or assisting an offence believing it will be committed

A person commits an offence if—
  (a) he does an act capable of encouraging or assisting the commission of an offence; and
  (b) he believes—
      (i) that the offence will be committed; and
      (ii) that his act will encourage or assist its commission.

■ NOTES AND QUESTIONS

1. There are many way of encouraging an offence. One might encourage by a threat, an exhortation, promise of reward or bribe, or by putting pressure on someone to commit an offence by threatening to expose a crime that the individual has committed. What is not necessary is for the prosecution to prove that the encouragement has the intended effect on the person encouraged. Why not; where is the harm if the encouragement is ignored?

2. Prior to the Serious Crime Act a fairly clear line separated the offence of incitement and that of aiding and abetting (although an incitor could be charged as an accessory if the crime incited were to be committed by the incitee). By combining encouragement and assistance in the same statutory provisions, does the 2007 Act unnecessarily blur this distinction?

3. When is an act 'capable' of encouraging an offence? When a sporting goods proprietor sells a cricket bat, is not the bat capable of being used to commit GBH? And may not a kitchen knife be capable of killing somebody? How does the law protect the seller in these situations?

4. Can one satisfy the 'act' requirement by failing to act? Consider the case of the night watchman who informs a known thief when he goes on extended coffee breaks. Must the thief be aware that the night watchman intended to encourage the offence? Must the night watchman have such an intention? See Serious Crime Act 2007, s. 47(8)(a).

5. The *mens rea* of s. 44 s. is an *intention* to encourage or assist the offence. In contrast, the mens rea of s. 45 is a *belief* that an offence will be committed and that the defendant's act will encourage or assist its commission. While foresight of an offence being committed is not to be equated with 'intent' under s. 44(2), might it qualify as a belief under s. 45? In respect to belief, is what a reasonable person would believe relevant?

6. Is s. 45 satisfied when a defendant only 'suspects' that an offence might be committed as a result of his act? In the following scenarios, does the owner of a store that sells guns violate s. 45 if he complies with his customer's request? Assume that the owner has no 'intent' other than to make a sale.

   (1) The customer asks the owner to sell her a gun capable of killing a large animal.

   (2) The customer makes the same request but prefaces it by saying 'You know, I really cannot stand my husband.'

   (3) The customer, more specifically, asks the owner to sell her a gun capable of killing a 100 kilo bear. The owner knows that the customer's husband

weighs approximately 100 kilos and that no bears have been seen in the vicinity for over a decade.

The Serious Crime Act s. 59 purports to abolish the *common law* offence of incitement, but *statutory* forms of the offence may have survived; for example:

— Incitement to murder (Offences against the Person Act 1861, s. 4)
— Incitement to Disaffection Act 1934
— Causing or inciting a child to engage in sexual activity (Sexual Offences Act 2003, sec. 10)
— Incitement to racial hatred (Public Order Act 1986, Pt. III)
— Stirring up racial or religious hatred (Religious Offences Act 2005)

Sometimes a person who encourages or assists a crime does not know what crime the person encouraged will in fact commit. Section 46 of the Serious Crime Act 2007 addresses this situation.

46 Encouraging or assisting offences believing one or more will be committed

(1) A person commits an offence if—
    (a) he does an act capable of encouraging or assisting the commission of one or more of a number of offences; and
    (b) he believes—
        (i) that one or more of those offences will be committed (but has no belief as to which); and
        (ii) that his act will encourage or assist the commission of one or more of them.
(2) It is immaterial for the purposes of subsection (1)(b)(ii) whether the person has any belief as to which offence will be encouraged or assisted.
(3) If a person is charged with an offence under subsection (1)—
    (a) the indictment must specify the offences alleged to be the "number of offences" mentioned in paragraph (a) of that subsection; but
    (b) nothing in paragraph (a) requires all the offences potentially comprised in that number to be specified.

■ NOTES AND QUESTIONS

1. Jane volunteers to drive two friends to a pub, knowing that her friends have a long standing feud with the owner of the pub. Assuming Jane believes (suspects?) that her friends plan either to rob the owner, assault the owner, kill the owner, or burn down the pub, has she violated s. 46? What if her friends simply have a drink at the pub (their intention from the outset) and then leave without committing any crime?

2. Stan sells Vincent, whom he suspects to be a professional burglar, a crowbar of the type that can be used to pry open windows. Does Stan 'assist' every burglary that Vincent commits using the crowbar?

3. The same issue of 'known offender, unknown offence' arises when one is charged with being an accessory to a criminal offence without knowing what offence is to be committed. See Chapter 13.

The offence of encouragement, when the encouragement is verbal, may be in tension with the concept of free expression embodied in the European Convention of Human Rights, Art. 10. The following cases, all decided prior to enactment of the Serious Crime Act, raise troublesome issues relating to free speech, even if one disapproves of the defendant's actions.

Race Relations Board v *Applin*
[1973] 1 QB 815, Court of Appeal

LORD DENNING MR : Mr and Mrs Watson have for 23 years fostered children in need of a temporary home. They do it from sincere and unselfish motives. They see it as a practical expression of their Christian faith. Normally they take four or five children at a time, but it may rise to seven on occasion. The children only stay for two or three weeks. Quite a number of the children are coloured. Just over half, about 60 per cent.

In January 1970 Mr and Mrs Watson moved to 61 Oakroyd Avenue, Potters Bar, Hertfordshire. There they hoped to extend their good work. At first some of the neighbours objected. They said that the house was under covenant to be used for residential purposes only. But those objections were overcome. Soon afterwards, however, objections were made on another score. An organisation calling itself the National Front complained that most of the children fostered by Mr and Mrs Watson were coloured children. The National Front acted through its branch organiser, Mr Applin, and its area organiser, Mr Taylor, the defendants. These two gentlemen brought pressure on Mr and Mrs Watson to get them to take white children only. These were some of the things they did: on August 5, 1971, Mr Applin sent a circular to the residents of Oakroyd Avenue. It referred to 'the enlargement of premises in Oakroyd Avenue for use as a foster home for largely non-British children.' It accused Mr and Mrs Watson of making 'malicious and disgraceful attacks' on their neighbours. It stated as a fact: 'that immigrant parents, because of their different standards and attitudes are quite prepared to let others take responsibility for their excess offspring.'

In a letter to Mr Watson of August 16, 1971, Mr Taylor said:

> In answer to your question asking me if I am urging you to tell the local authorities that you will only except (sic) white children. Yes I am, as stated in my letter: 'Charity should begin at home.' The number of immigrant parents who are only too ready to dump their unwanted children on to the local ratepayers is a national scandal. Every week one sees advertisements in local papers and in shop windows concerning immigrants who wish to foster out their children. In my opinion, if we the indigenous population did likewise, there would be hell to pay.

On August 26, 1971, the National Front organised a public meeting at Potters Bar. Mr Applin read extracts from the circular. Mr Taylor said:

> While you have people such as Mr Watson who delight in putting immigrants' welfare before their own people's, this process of turning more and more of British towns and cities into coloured ghettoes will continue.

On February 9, 1972, the Race Relations Board issued proceedings in the county court claiming that the acts done by Mr Applin and Mr Taylor were unlawful and seeking an injunction.

It is not easy to apply the Act to the situation before us, but I will try and explain it. It is quite clear that Mr and Mrs Watson were acting perfectly lawfully. They were fostering children without making any difference between them on the ground of colour. Mr Applin and Mr Taylor were bringing pressure to bear on Mr and Mrs Watson to get them to take white children only, and not coloured ones. That pressure did not succeed. Mr and Mrs Watson have resisted it. They have continued to take white and coloured children without making any difference. They continue so to take them. But, the point is this: suppose the pressure had succeeded. Suppose that Mr and Mrs Watson had stipulated 'We will only take white children.' Would that conduct of Mr and Mrs Watson have been unlawful? If it would have been unlawful, then it was unlawful of Mr Applin and Mr Taylor to bring pressure to bear on Mr and Mrs Watson to do an unlawful act. This follows from section 12 of the Act of 1968, which says:

> Any person who deliberately aids, induces or incites another person to do an act which is unlawful by virtue of any provision of this Part of this Act shall be treated for the purposes of this Act as doing that act.

If therefore, Mr Applin and Mr Taylor 'incited' Mr and Mrs Watson to do an unlawful act, i.e., to take white children only, they are to be treated as themselves doing that act, even though the incitement did not succeed. Here I may mention a small point. Mr Vinelott suggested that to 'incite' means to urge or spur on by advice, encouragement, and persuasion, and not otherwise. I do not think the word is so limited, at any rate in this context. A person may 'incite' another to do an act by threatening or by pressure, as well as by persuasion. Mr Applin and Mr Taylor undoubtedly brought pressure to bear on Mr and Mrs Watson to take white children only, and thus 'incited' them to do so.

R v Most
(1881) 7 QBD 244, Queen's Bench Division

M was indicted under 24 & 25 Vict. c. 100, s. 4. The encouragement and endeavour to persuade to murder, proved at the trial, was the publication and circulation by him of an article, written in German in a newspaper published in that language in London, exulting in the recent murder of the Emperor of Russia, and commending it as an example to revolutionists throughout the world.

LORD COLERIDGE CJ: ... We have to deal here with a publication proved by the evidence at the trial to have been written by the defendant, to have been printed by the defendant, that is, he ordered and paid for the printing of it, sold by the defendant, called by the defendant his article, and intended, as the jury have found, and most reasonably found, to be read by the twelve hundred or more persons who were the subscribers to, or the purchasers of, the *Freiheit* newspaper; and, further, one which the jury have found, and I am of opinion have quite rightly found, to be naturally and reasonably intended to incite and encourage, or to endeavour to persuade persons who should read that article to the murder either of the Emperor Alexander, or the Emperor William, or, in the alternative, the crowned and uncrowned heads of states, as it is expressed in one part of the article, from Constantinople to Washington....

...An endeavour to persuade or an encouragement is none the less an endeavour to persuade or an encouragement, because the person who so encourages or endeavours to persuade does not in the particular act of encouragement or persuasion personally address the number of people, the one or more persons, whom the address which contains the encouragement or the endeavour to persuade reaches. The argument has been well put, that an orator who makes a speech to two thousand people, does not address it to any one individual amongst those two thousand; it is addressed to the number. It is endeavouring to persuade the whole number, or large portions of that number, and if a particular individual amongst that number addressed by the orator is persuaded, or listens to it and is encouraged, it is plain that the words of this statute are complied with; because according to well-known principles of law the person who addresses those words to a number of persons must be taken to address them to the persons who, he knows, hear them, who he knows will understand them in a particular way, do understand them in that particular way, and do act upon them....

Invicta Plastics v Clare
[1976] RTR 251, Queen's Bench Division

The defendant company manufactured a device called 'Radatec', which emitted a high-pitched whine when within 800 yards of wireless telegraphy transmissions including those used for police radar speed traps. The company advertised the device in a motoring magazine, the advertisement reading: 'You ought to know more about Radatec. Ask at your accessory shop or write for name of nearest stockist to' the company; the advertisement also depicted a view of a road and a speed limit sign through a car windscreen with the device attached.

PARK J: ... The first question which the justices had to decide was whether a person who used the Radatec in his motor car without a licence from the Secretary of State would be using apparatus for wireless telegraphy contrary to section 1 of the Act of 1949. On the evidence before them they decided that such a person would be committing such an offence. There is no submission to this court that the justices were wrong in coming to that conclusion. So, on the first summons, which concerned the company, the question was whether the company by the advertisement in the magazine incited its readers to commit an offence under the Act.

When summing up to the jury on a case of incitement, judges sometimes use such words as 'incitement involves the suggestion to commit the offence' or 'a proposal to commit the offence' or 'persuasion or inducement to commit the offence' which the defendant is alleged to have incited. But Lord Denning MR considered the meaning of 'incitement' in *Race Relations Board* v *Applin* [1973] QB 815, 825 G, where he said:

> Mr Vinelott suggested that to 'incite' means to urge or spur on by advice encouragement, and persuasion, and not otherwise. I do not think the word is so limited, at any rate in this context. A person may 'incite' another to do an act by threatening or by pressure, as well as persuasion.

Accordingly, the justices had to decide whether, in the context, the advertisement amounted to an incitement to the readers of the magazine to commit the offence.

It is submitted on behalf of the company that, before the offence of incitement could be committed by means of the advertisement, there had to be in it an incitement to use the device which was advertised; that, if not, any matter in the advertisement would not constitute incitement, as it would not be sufficiently proximate to the offence alleged to have been incited; and that, as the advertisement merely encouraged readers to find out more about the device, it did not amount to incitement in fact or in law.

I think that it is necessary to look at the advertisement as a whole. Approaching it in this way, I have come to the conclusion that the company did incite a breach of the Act by means of the advertisement. I think, therefore, that the justices were right to convict the company of this offence.

■ NOTES AND QUESTIONS

1. By urging the foster parents to foster 'white-only' children did the defendants in *Applin* do anything more than exercise their right of free speech? Would foster parents commit a criminal offence by telling the fostering agency that they will only accept white children for fostering? If not, what crime was incited/encouraged in *Applin*? What if an MP advocates curtailing immigration of all non-whites into the country?

2. *Most* and *Invicta Plastics* raised issues of 'commercial' speech. Assuming they incited/encouraged a crime, who has committed the offence – the person who writes the newspaper article/advertisement or the publisher? Or both?

3. Note that in neither *Most* and *Invicta Plastics* did the defendants have any idea of who, if anybody might have been encouraged by their article/advertisements? What if nobody saw either? Should this matter?

4. In modern times a person may be encouraged by information that appears on a website or blog. If instructions on how to make a firebomb can be found on the blog, will the blogger be guilty of violating the Serious Crime Act if a reader constructs a firebomb using the blogger's instructions and blows up a pub?

5. What if illegal pornography is offered at a discount price on a website. Has encouragement occurred? If so, who has encouraged whom? See *R (on the application of O)* v *Coventry Magistrates Court* [2004] EWHC 905 (admin).

B. Defences

There are some defences specified under the Act:

50. Defence of acting reasonably

(1) A person is not guilty of an offence under this Part if he proves—
  (a) that he knew certain circumstances existed; and
  (b) that it was reasonable for him to act as he did in those circumstances.

(2) A person is not guilty of an offence under this Part if he proves—
  (a) that he believed certain circumstances to exist;
  (b) that his belief was reasonable; and
  (c) that it was reasonable for him to act as he did in the circumstances as he believed them to be.

(3) Factors to be considered in determining whether it was reasonable for a person to act as he did include—
  (a) the seriousness of the anticipated offence (or, in the case of an offence under section 46, the offences specified in the indictment);
  (b) any purpose for which he claims to have been acting;
  (c) any authority by which he claims to have been acting.

51. Protective offences: victims not liable

(1) In the case of protective offences, a person does not commit an offence under this Part by reference to such an offence if—
  (a) he falls within the protected category; and
  (b) he is the person in respect of whom the protective offence was committed or would have been if it had been committed.

(2) "Protective offence" means an offence that exists (wholly or in part) for the protection of a particular category of persons ("the protected category").

■ NOTES AND QUESTIONS

1. 'Intent' (s. 44) and 'belief' (s. 45) are measured by what the defendant actually intended or believed. Are these subjective standards undercut by the requirement of reasonableness in s. 50(1)(b) and 50(2)(b)?

2. The factors which will be evidence of reasonableness are listed in s. 50(3). Presumably these are not intended to be exclusive.

3. The defence in s. 51 finds its roots in the common law case of *R* v *Tyrell* (1894) 1 QB 710 discussed in Chapter 13, p. 678. **What is the rationale of this defence?**

What if the act that the defendant encourages would not be a criminal offence? This could occur in three situations:

(a) Where the act encouraged, if committed, would not be a crime.

(b) Where the person encouraged would have a personal defence.

(c) Where the person encouraged would be (in law) the victim of the offence in question.

The third situation is covered by section 51, but the other two are less clear.

R v Whitehouse

[1977] QB 868, Court of Appeal

SCARMAN LJ: ... The indictment which the defendant faced in 1976 was an indictment charging him with incitement to commit incest, and the particulars of the offence charged were that he, on a date unknown between December 1, 1975, and February 10, 1976, unlawfully incited a girl then aged 15, who was to his and her knowledge his daughter, to have sexual intercourse with him. To that count he pleaded guilty, as also to a second count charging incitement to commit incest, but on a different occasion, and he pleaded guilty to that as well.

When the court saw those two counts framed in the way I have just described, we queried whether it was an offence known to law and we doubted whether it was because a girl aged 15 is incapable of committing the crime of incest. Later in this judgment it will be necessary to look at the terms of section 11 of the Sexual Offences Act 1956 but that shortly is the effect of the section so far as material to the issue in this case.

... It is of course accepted by the Crown that at common law the crime of incitement consists of inciting another person to commit a crime. When one looks at this indictment in the light of the particulars of the offence pleaded, one sees that it is charging the defendant, with inciting a girl to commit a crime which in fact by statute she is incapable of committing. If therefore the girl was incapable of committing the crime alleged, how can the defendant be guilty of the common law crime of incitement? The Crown accepts the logic of that position and does not seek in this court to rely on section 11 of the Act of 1956 or to suggest that this man could be guilty of inciting his daughter to commit incest, to use the old phrase, as a principal in the first degree. But the Crown says that it is open to them upon this indictment to submit that it covers the offence of inciting the girl to aid and abet the man to commit the crime of incest upon her. Section 10 of the Act of 1956 makes it an offence for a man to have sexual intercourse with a woman whom he knows to be his daughter, and the Crown says that upon this indictment it is possible to say that the defendant has committed an offence known to the law, the offence being that of inciting his daughter under the age of 16 to aid and abet him to have sexual intercourse with her.

There is no doubt of the general principle, namely, that a person, provided always he or she is of the age of criminal responsibility, can be guilty of aiding or abetting a crime even though it be a crime which he or she cannot commit as a principal in the first degree. There are two famous illustrations in the books of this principle. A woman can aid and abet a rape so as herself to be guilty of rape, and a boy at an age where he is presumed impotent can nevertheless aid and abet a rape ....

The important matters in our judgment are these. First this girl, aged 15, belongs to a class which is protected, but not punished, by sections 10 and 11 of the Sexual Offences Act 1956, and secondly the girl is alleged to be the victim of this notional crime. The whole question has an air of artificiality because nobody is suggesting either that the father has committed incest with her or that she has aided and abetted him to commit incest upon her. What is suggested is that the father has committed the crime of incitement because by his words and conduct he has incited her to do that which, of course, she never has done.

... Clearly the relevant provisions of the Sexual Offences Act 1956 are intended to protect women and girls. Most certainly, section 11 is intended to protect girls under the age of 16 from criminal liability, and the Act as a whole exists, in so far as it deals with women and girls exposed to sexual threat, to protect them. The very fact that girls under the age of 16 are protected from criminal liability for what would otherwise be incest demonstrates that this girl who is said to have been the subject of incitement was being incited to do something which, if she did it, could not be a crime by her.

...

We have therefore come to the conclusion, with regret, that the indictment does not disclose an offence known to the law because it cannot be a crime on the part of this girl aged 15 to have sexual intercourse with her father, though it is of course a crime, and a very serious crime, on the part of the father. There is here incitement to a course of conduct, but that course of conduct cannot be treated as a crime by the girl. Plainly a gap or lacuna in the protection of girls under the age of 16 is exposed by this decision. It is regrettable indeed that a man who importunes his daughter under the age of 16 to have sexual intercourse with him but does not go beyond incitement cannot be found guilty of a crime ....

■ NOTES AND QUESTIONS

1. *Whitehouse* was decided as it was because of a gap in the law. The defendant in *Whitehouse* might now be guilty of an offence under Criminal Law Act 1977, s. 54.

2. If the individual encouraged to commit a crime lacks the capacity to commit a crime, such as in the case of a child below the age of criminal responsibility, the defendant may not be guilty of encouragement. However, the person who does the encouraging may be liable as a principal acting through an innocent agent if the child commits the offence. If the child refuses, why should the encourager not be guilty of the inchoate offence?

C. Impossibility

The law generally distinguishes between legal and factual impossibility. If the acts encouraged would not, if committed, constitute a crime, then the defendant is not guilty of encouragement. This is a case of legal impossibility. Thus if A urges B to drive at 50 mph thinking that the speed limit on the road is 40 mph when it is in fact 70 mph, he is not guilty of encouragement. Similarly, if a woman attempts to persuade a married man to commit adultery in the belief that adultery is a criminal offence (which it is not), no offence will have been committed.

Factual impossibility is another matter. Here there may be encouragement to commit what would be a crime except that, due to factual circumstances unknown to the incitor, the crime is incapable of being committed. As we shall see, by statute factual impossibility is not a defence to a charge of either attempt or conspiracy. However, in *R v Fitzmaurice* [1983] QB 1083, the Court of Appeal stated in *obiter* that if an offence was factually impossible, the defendant could not be liable for inciting the offence. An example would be where A incited B to kill a victim who was already dead. Difficulties may arise where the encouragement to kill C 'next Thursday' takes place on Monday when C is alive, but C dies on Wednesday – is the defendant guilty of encouragement?

R v Shephard
[1919] 2 KB 125, Court of Appeal

On 20 September, 1917, the appellant wrote to one Cicely Maria Shephard, who was then about six weeks gone with child, a letter in which he said: 'When the kiddie is born you must lie on it in the night. Do not let it live.' The child was born alive on 31 May 1918. In March, 1919, the appellant was convicted at the Central Criminal Court on an indictment which charged him with having 'on September 20, 1917, solicited and endeavoured to persuade Cicely Maria Shephard thereafter to murder a newly born child lately before then born of her body.' The indictment was framed under s. 4 of the Offences against the Person Act 1861.

BRAY J: . . . All that is essential to bring a case within the section is that there should be a person capable of being murdered at the time when the act of murder is to be committed. If there is such a person then in existence it is quite immaterial that that person was not in existence at the date of the incitement . . . .

■ NOTES AND QUESTIONS

1. Eve encourages Adam to steal a diamond ring, telling him that there will be an opportunity to take the ring in three days' time. Will Eve be guilty of encouragement in each of the following circumstances?

(a) Adam already owns the ring, having bought it as a surprise gift for Eve;

(b) before Adam has an opportunity to take the ring, the owner loses it ;

(c) the owner decides to give the ring to Adam not knowing of the encouragement to steal it;

(d) the opportunity to steal the ring never arises.

2. In theory, is there any reason why the law in respect to factual impossibility in regard to encouragement should be different than it is in respect to conspiracy and attempt? The Law Commission in its Draft Criminal Code recommended bringing the law in this area into line with attempt and conspiracy. See Draft Criminal Code 1989, s. 50.

SECTION 2: CONSPIRACY

The law of conspiracy is aimed at the special dangers posed by criminal groups. These groups range from those formed for the purpose of committing a single offence, after which the members disband, to ongoing organisations and syndicates who are in the 'business' of committing crime. The latter usually are comprised of professional criminals, and, among the typical offences committed by them are drug trafficking, money laundering, extortion, and trafficking in women and children. Crimes of violence, including murder for hire, are also not uncommon. In some instances there are statutes which address specific forms of conspiracy separate from the general offence of conspiracy:

OFFENCES AGAINST THE PERSON ACT 1861

4. Conspiring or soliciting to commit murder

All persons who shall conspire, confederate, and agree to murder any person, whether he be a Subject of Her Majesty or not, and whether he be within the Queen's Dominions or not, and whosoever shall solicit, encourage, persuade, or endeavour to persuade, or shall propose to any person, to murder any other person, whether he be a Subject of Her Majesty or not, and whether he be within the Queen's Dominions or not, shall be guilty of a misdemeanor, and being convicted thereof shall be liable, at the discretion of the court, to be kept in penal servitude for any term not more than ten and not less than three years,—or to be imprisoned for any term not exceeding two years, with or without hard labour.

A: Common law and statutory conspiracies

At common law the offence of conspiracy was defined as an agreement between two or more persons to do 'an unlawful act or a lawful act by unlawful means'. The ambit of the offence included agreements to commit acts which would not of themselves be crimes. The justification was that a group engaged in a socially harmful albeit not criminal enterprise was threatening to society, and that once such a group was formed, it might well progress to criminal activity. See *R* v *Mulcahy* (1868) LR 3 HL 306, *R* v *Kamara* [1974] AC 104.

Why are criminal groups considered so much more dangerous than crimes committed by a single individual? More ambitious, sophisticated and complex crimes become possible when a group is involved. Further, the likelihood of success increases as more people apply their minds to the planning. Peer group pressure may also militate against abandonment of the criminal enterprise. (Against this is the fact that the more people who are involved, the greater the chance of a slip-up or a damaging revelation that alerts the authorities to the criminal plan.)

While at common law the parties to the conspiracy need not have agreed to commit what was a crime, the law has now changed. The current law is embodied in the Criminal Law Act 1977.

CRIMINAL LAW ACT 1977

(as amended by the Criminal Attempts Act 1981)

1.—(1) Subject to the following provisions of this Part of this Act, if a person agrees with any other person or persons that a course of conduct shall be pursued which, if the agreement is carried out in accordance with their intentions, either—

(a) will necessarily amount to or involve the commission of any offence or offences by one or more of the parties to the agreement, or

(b) would do so but for the existence of facts which render the commission of the offence or any of the offences impossible,

he is guilty of conspiracy to commit the offence or offences in question.

(2) Where liability for any offence may be incurred without knowledge on the part of the person committing it of any particular fact or circumstance necessary for the commission of an offence, a person shall nevertheless not be guilty of conspiracy to commit that offence by virtue of subsection (1) unless he and at least one other party to the agreement intend or know that that fact or circumstance shall or will exist at the time when the conduct constituting the offence is to take place.

As we shall see, some common law conspiracies remain in force. In *R v Ayres* [1984] AC 447, however, the House of Lords stated that where the carrying out of the conspirators' agreement would necessarily involve a crime, the indictment must charge a statutory and not a common law conspiracy.

B: Common elements in statutory and common law conspiracies

Common law and statutory conspiracies share many of the same elements. At the heart of each is the requirement of an agreement. The agreement need never be put into effect. The offence is complete when the agreement is made and the conspiracy continues as long as the agreement continues in effect.

Director of Public Prosecutions v Doot

[1973] AC 807, House of Lords

The respondents, American citizens, formed a plan abroad to import cannabis into the United States by way of England. In pursuance of the plan, two vans with cannabis concealed in them were shipped from Morocco to Southampton. The cannabis in one of the vans was discovered at Southampton; the other van was traced to Liverpool, from where the vans were to have been shipped to America, and the cannabis in it was found. The respondents were charged with, *inter alia*, conspiracy to import dangerous drugs. At the trial, they contended that the court had no jurisdiction to try them on that count since the conspiracy had been entered into abroad. Lawson J overruled that submission, but the Court of Appeal quashed the respondents' convictions, holding that the offence of conspiracy was completed when the agreement was made.

On appeal by the Director of Public Prosecutions:

LORD WILBERFORCE: . . . In my opinion, the key to a decision for or against the offence charged can be found in an answer to the question why the common law treats certain actions as crimes. And one answer must certainly be because the actions in question are a threat to the Queen's peace, or, as we would now perhaps say, to society. Judged by this test, there is every reason for, and none that I can see against, the prosecution. Conspiracies are intended to be carried into effect, and one reason why, in addition to individual prosecution of each participant, conspiracy charges are brought is because criminal action organised, and executed, in concert is more dangerous than an individual breach of the law. Why, then, refrain from prosecution where the relevant concert was, initially, formed outside the United Kingdom?

Often in conspiracy cases the implementing action is itself the only evidence of the conspiracy—this is the doctrine of overt acts. Could it be said, with any plausibility, that if the conclusion or a possible conclusion to be drawn from overt acts in England was that there was a conspiracy, entered into abroad, a charge of conspiracy would not lie? Surely not: yet, if it could, what difference should it make if the conspiracy is directly proved or is admitted to have been made abroad? The truth is that, in the normal case of a conspiracy carried out, or partly carried out, in this country, the location of the formation of the agreement is irrelevant: the attack upon the laws of this country is identical wherever the conspirators happened to meet; the 'conspiracy' is a complex, formed indeed, but not separately completed, at the first meeting of the plotters.
. . .

VISCOUNT DILHORNE: . . . The conclusion to which I have come after consideration of these authorities and of many others to which the House was referred but to which I do not think it is necessary to refer is that though the offence of conspiracy is complete when the agreement to do the unlawful act is made and it is not necessary for the prosecution to do more than prove the making of such an agreement, a conspiracy does not end with the making of the agreement. It continues so long as the parties to the agreement intend to carry it out. It may be joined by others, some may leave it. Proof of acts done by the accused in this country may suffice to prove that there was at the time of those acts a conspiracy in existence in this country to which they were parties and, if that is proved, then the charge of conspiracy is within the jurisdiction of the English courts, even though the initial agreement was made outside the jurisdiction.

■ **NOTES AND QUESTIONS**

1. Should the result in *DPP* v *Doot* be affected by whether or not the conspirators would be subject to prosecution in the country in which the conspiracy was formed? Might those who conspire to engage in illegal international trade be subject to prosecution in multiple jurisdictions? Is this fair?

2. Note the jurisdictional issue decided in *DPP* v *Doot*: a conspiracy formed outside of the jurisdiction can be prosecuted in the UK if the parties committed acts within the jurisdiction. In *Somchai Liangsiriprasert* v *United States* [1990] AC 607, the Privy Council specifically stated that no overt act need be committed within the jurisdiction. See also *R* v *Sansom* [1991] 92 Cr App R 115; *R* v *Naini (Jamshid Hashami)* [1999] 2 Cr App R 398.

Conspiracy is a continuing offence, and from time to time new members may join an existing conspiracy. They too become liable for conspiracy, although not for crimes committed prior to their joining. Thus it often becomes critical to determine the period during which a defendant is a member of the conspiracy.

R v Scott

(1979) 68 Cr App R 164, Court of Appeal

GEOFFREY LANE LJ: . . . The prosecution put their case in two ways. They suggested that the appellant must have known from the beginning what Jensby and Donovan were up to; having acquired that knowledge she continued to help them, and was therefore proved to have conspired. Had the prosecution left the matter there, no difficulty would have arisen. There was a formidable body of evidence to support the argument; the appellant herself admitted that she knew that Jensby and Donovan were involved in a scheme which was illegal and added 'the only conclusion I could draw since Jan (Jensby) was in Kenya was that I suspected it was drugs. I suppose I closed my mind.'

However, the prosecution, in an endeavour to make assurance double sure, contended that the appellant's admitted knowledge acquired on February 28, 1976, even if that was the first time she had the guilty knowledge, was enough to prove her guilty of conspiracy, despite the fact that thereafter she did no overt act in pursuance of the illegal scheme. She admitted that if she had been asked after that date to help by paying in cheques received from Donovan, she would have done so, but it was plain that she had not been so asked, and that she had not informed either Jensby or Donovan whether or not she was willing to help.

The judge, in directing the jury on the second limb of the prosecution case, used the following words:

> If up to that point she had been an innocent party in doing what she did, she then ceased to be an innocent party [say the prosecution] and became a conspirator so as to render herself liable to conviction in respect of this offence. That is what it comes to, and you have to decide what was meant by it when it was said, if it was . . . that if the cheques had arrived she would have paid them in. Is that, members of the jury, from your point of view, evidence which convinces you that at that stage she was prepared to act in furtherance of her agreement? Is it evidence that the agreement which she was saying that she then had was, whether she liked it or not, to assist in the supplying of drugs by being a person who would, if the cheques had arrived, no doubt as a result of the supply and sale of drugs, she would have then paid them into such accounts as she had been asked to—and thereby assist in the workings of this conspiracy?

What the learned judge was doing there was to put forward to the jury the prosecution's proposition, namely, that even if she was not aware of the illegality of Jensby's activities until February 28, 1976, yet nevertheless she was guilty of conspiracy at that moment by reason of her secret and uncommunicated intention to deal in the way Jensby had requested with any cheques which might arrive from Donovan.

It may be that the jury came to the conclusion (not entirely disavowed by the prosecution) that the appellant was until February 28, 1976, unaware of the true nature of Jensby's activities. On that date she learnt for the first time for certain that he was smuggling drugs. She then determines that she would nevertheless continue to help him in what she then realised for the first time were illegal activities relating to the importation of cannabis. That determination she never communicated to anyone else. It was submitted for the respondent that this was sufficient to make her party to an agreement to assist in the supply of controlled drugs and therefore a conspirator. We do not think it was. It is evidence that she had secretly determined to assist Jensby in his importation and supply of cannabis, should the opportunity arise. It is evidence of what doubtless she would have done, given the chance. But an intent, should the occasion arise, to join in an illegal enterprise, an intent which is never communicated in any way whatsoever to any other person, remains only an intent and cannot at any rate in these circumstances amount to an indictable conspiracy.

The further suggestion put forward is equally untenable, namely that the appellant, by failing to notify Jensby or Donovan after February 28, 1976, that she was no longer prepared to help, notionally or constructively became a party to the illegal enterprise. An intention to enter into an agreement must, to become effective as an agreement, be communicated to the other party by some means or other. It is difficult to see how non-communication can amount to communication. The long and short of this matter is that after February 28 the appellant never went beyond the intention or wish to act illegally. However reprehensible that may be, it was not proof of the conspiracy alleged. To that extent the prosecution's second contention and the judge's direction based upon it were wrong.

. . .

■ NOTES AND QUESTIONS

1. At lunch Ian proposes to Elaine and Eleanor that they spray-paint the university's administrative building that evening at midnight. Neither responds one way or the other. At midnight Elaine, but not Eleanor, shows up outside the administration building, where Ian is waiting. Is there a conspiracy to commit criminal damage? Who are its members? When was it formed? Did Eleanor need to inform either Ian or Elaine that she did not wish to participate in order to avoid liability?

2. If there is an agreement in principle but details remain to be worked out, the parties can still be convicted of conspiracy.

With whom can one conspire? For purposes of the criminal law, a company is often treated as if it were a person (see Interpretation Act 1889). In *R v ICR Haulage Ltd* [1944] 1 All ER 691 it was held that a company could be guilty of conspiracy. But, how then, to explain the following case?

R v McDonnell

[1966] 1 QB 233, Queen's Bench Division

At all material times the defendant was a director and the sole person in each of two companies responsible for the acts of the company. He was charged on an indictment containing ten counts: two of the counts (one in respect of each company) charged him with conspiring with the company to defraud, one with conspiring with one of the companies to induce persons to acquire a right or interest in land, four counts charged him with fraudulent conversion of the property of the companies.

> NIELD J: . . . [T]hese charges of conspiracy cannot be sustained, upon the footing that in the particular circumstances here, where the sole responsible person in the company is the defendant himself, it would not be right to say that there were two persons or two minds. If it were otherwise, I feel that it would offend against the basic concept of a conspiracy, namely, an agreement of two or more to do an unlawful act, and I think it would be artificial to take the view that the company, although it is clearly a separate legal entity, can be regarded here as a separate person or a separate mind, in view of the admitted fact that this defendant acts alone so far as these companies are concerned.

■ NOTES AND QUESTIONS

1. A husband and wife cannot conspire by themselves, although they can commit conspiracy with a third party. This rule traces its origins to the common law, where husband and wife were treated as a unity. In modern times, where both husband and wife often have separate and independent legal identities, is there any justification for preserving the rule relating to conspiracy?

2. Where the only other party to the conspiracy is a child under 10 or the intended victim of the offence (Criminal Law Act 1977, s. 2 (2)) there can be no conspiracy. Why should this be so? The Draft Criminal Code Bill would have removed both this exemption and that relating to spouses, leaving the cases to be governed by the general law of conspiracy.

3. One need not be (and often is not) aware of the identity of the other parties to the conspiracy to be guilty of the offence. See *R v Phillips* (1987) 86 Cr App R 18. Why should this be so?

May a person who is not capable of committing the substantive offence which is the object of the conspiracy nonetheless be guilty of conspiracy?

Rv Burns (and others)

(1984) 79 Cr App R 173, Court of Appeal

By s. 56 of the Offences Against the Person Act 1861: 'Whosoever shall unlawfully...by force...take away...any child under the age of 14 years, with intent to deprive any parent...of the possession of such child...shall be...liable, at the discretion of the court, to imprisonment for any term not exceeding seven years...Provided that no person who shall have claimed any right to the possession of such child, or shall be the mother or shall have claimed to be the father of an illegitimate child, shall be liable to be prosecuted by virtue hereof on account of the getting possession of such child, or taking such child out of the possession of any person having lawful charge thereof.'

The appellant J B married a second time in 1975 and had two children. Between the births of those children he had another child by his second wife's sister who was also living with them. That child became a ward of court and J B divorced his second wife. The children were committed to the care of their mothers, both of whom had returned to their parents' home to live. J B was not allowed access to the children. He decided to seize the children and recruited the three applicants, R, J and S B, for that purpose. One night all four men drove to the house where the women and children were living, forced an entry and took the children, then aged between three and six and a half years, out of the house and into the waiting car. J B then took the children to accommodation he had prepared for them and the three applicants returned to their respective homes. All four men were charged with conspiracy to take the children and substantive counts, again against all four, of child stealing contrary to s. 56 of the Offences Against the Person Act 1861. When put to his election, prosecution counsel decided to proceed on the conspiracy count only against J B, and on the child stealing count only against the three applicants. All four were convicted. J B appealed against his conviction on the ground that the judge should not have exercised his discretion in a way that allowed him to be put in jeopardy of being convicted of conspiracy to commit an offence when he could not have been charged with the substantive offence (which he had in fact committed) because of the immunity from prosecution provided by s. 56 of the 1861 Act.

WATKINS LJ:...The dangers of permitting a father of children to collect a posse of men and suddenly to launch a siege of the home of his erstwhile wife, to break in and then snatch away sleeping children are surely self-evident. The criminal law does not in our view permit that sort of conduct. When a father who is exempt under section 56 behaves in that way, it is, in our judgment, not only lawful but right and just that the prosecution should be free to bring a charge of conspiracy against him.

■ NOTES AND QUESTIONS

1. The Court in *Burns* states that the dangers of a father's breaking into his wife's home and snatching the children are 'surely self-evident'. But equally surely, these dangers were self-evident to the Parliament which granted the husband exemption from the substantive crime. Why should a court be able to undermine this policy decision and impose liability through the back door of conspiracy?

2. Section 56 of the Offences Against the Person Act 1861 was repealed by the Child Abduction Act 1984.

What if some of the parties to a conspiracy are acquitted? Must alleged co-conspirators also be acquitted? The issue is addressed in ss. 5(8) and (9) of the Criminal Law Act 1977:

CRIMINAL LAW ACT 1977

5.—(8) The fact that the person or persons who, so far as appears from the indictment on which any person has been convicted of conspiracy, were the only other parties to the agreement on which his conviction was based have been acquitted of conspiracy by reference to that agreement (whether after being tried with the person convicted or separately) shall not be a ground for quashing his conviction unless under all the circumstances of the case his conviction is inconsistent with the acquittal of the other person or persons in question.

(9) Any rule of law or practice inconsistent with the provisions of subsection (8) above is hereby abolished.

R v Longman and Cribben
(1980) 72 Cr App R 121, Court of Appeal

THE LORD CHIEF JUSTICE: The facts of the case were these. Longman was the proprietor of a garage and car-sales business. Cribben worked for him as a salesman. The prosecution allegation was that they had conspired to defraud an insurance company of £3,323 by making a false claim in respect of the theft of a car; that the purported purchase of the car by Longman from a man called Pentow and the purported sale by Longman to Cribben were shams; that the car was never stolen; that the whole pretended transaction was designed by the two men with a view to perpetrating a fraud on the insurance company.

The evidence adduced by the prosecution was mostly circumstantial evidence of suspicious or highly suspicious actions by the two men. Longman was seen by the police and throughout hotly denied all the allegations made against him. He asserted that the man Pentow had brought the car to his garage, it was apparently in good repair; he bought it and later sold it to Cribben in the ordinary course of business. He denied any fraud.

The case against Cribben was much stronger. In addition to the circumstantial evidence, he made what amounted to a full confession to the police, stating in terms that he had, in fact, conspired with Longman to defraud the insurance company and that the car had never been delivered to the garage at all and had certainly never been bought by him. In short, that confession, if the jury were satisfied as to its truth, was conclusive evidence against Cribben that he had conspired with Longman in the way that the prosecution alleged. Longman gave evidence at the trial. Cribben did not.

... [T]he situation has been changed by the provisions of the Criminal Law Act 1977, s. 5(8) and (9) ...

In our judgment the effect of those two subsections is to ... [abolish] the rule of common law that if two persons are accused of conspiring together and one is acquitted and the other convicted, the conviction must be quashed. They also mean that the trial judge is no longer obliged to direct juries that they must convict both conspirators or acquit both conspirators ....

We also respectfully adopt the conclusion reached by the Court in that case that the provisions of the Criminal Law Act 1977, s. 5 (8) and (9) do not mean that such a direction may never be given if the circumstances warrant it. When a trial judge is faced with the task of directing a jury in a case of this sort, where the charge is that A and B conspired together but with no one else to commit crime, he will, as in other cases involving two defendants, as a general rule have to tell the jury that they must consider the evidence against each defendant separately. Where the strength of the evidence against each is markedly different, usually (as in the instant case) because A has confessed and B has not, he should then go on to explain that because there is that difference in the evidence against each, the jury may come to the conclusion that the prosecution have proved beyond doubt against A that A conspired with B, but have not proved against B that any such conspiracy existed.

That may appear to be illogical, but it is the necessary result of the rules of evidence which are designed to ensure fairness. If, therefore, the jury are satisfied that A conspired with B but are not satisfied that there is adequate evidence of B's guilt, they should convict A and acquit B. We can see no reason why the jury should not understand such a direction.

Where at the close of the prosecution case the evidence against one of the defendants is such that it would be unsafe to ask any jury to convict, then it goes without saying that the judge should so rule, and the case can then continue against the other defendant.

There will, however, be cases where the evidence against A and B is of equal weight or nearly so. In such a case there may be a risk of inconsistent verdicts, and the judge should direct the jury that because of the similarity of the evidence against each, the only just result would be the same verdict in respect of each: that is to say, both guilty or both not guilty. He must be careful to add, however, that if they are unsure about the guilt of one, then both must be found not guilty.

Whether he gives such a direction will, of course, depend on the way the evidence has emerged. The test is this. Is the evidence such that a verdict of guilty in respect of A and not guilty in respect of B would be, to all intents and purposes, inexplicable and therefore inconsistent? If so, it would be an occasion for the 'both guilty or both not guilty' direction. If not, then the separate verdict direction is required.

C: Statutory conspiracy

The definition of a statutory conspiracy is contained in the Criminal Law Act 1977, s. 1(1) (above).

(i) Agreement that a course of conduct shall be pursued

At common law the prosecution had to prove that each conspirator intended the commission of the offence envisaged. Otherwise there could exist the possibility that a conspiracy could exist even though no conspirator actually intended an offence to be committed.

The phrase 'course of conduct' within the statute is not limited to physical acts and extends to intended consequences. Arguably, then, the *mens rea* implicit in the requirement of an agreement is an intention that the offence will be committed, even if the offence itself may be committed with a lesser *mens rea* than intent. An example is a conspiracy to murder, which requires an intention to kill on the part of the conspirators. Murder itself can be committed by a defendant who intends only grievous bodily harm, but such an intent is not sufficient to establish a conspiracy to murder. Similarly, even though strict liability or negligence may suffice as to a circumstance of a crime, a conspiracy to commit the crime cannot be established without proof that the conspirators 'intend or know' that the relevant circumstance will exist at the time the offence is to take place. The courts, however, have struggled with this issue.

R v Anderson
[1986] AC 27, House of Lords

LORD BRIDGE OF HARWICH: . . . In June 1981 the appellant and Ahmed Andaloussi were both in custody on remand in Lewes prison. Andaloussi was awaiting trial on charges of very serious drug offences and was rightly believed by the appellant to have large sums of money at his disposal. The appellant was on remand in connection with some entirely different matter. He spent one night in the same cell as Andaloussi. The appellant was then confidently expecting that in a short time he would be, as in the event he was, released on bail. During the night they spent together the appellant agreed with Andaloussi to participate in a scheme to effect Andaloussi's escape from prison. Other participants in the scheme were to be Ahmed Andaloussi's brother Mohammed and Mohammed Assou. They were to maintain contact with Ahmed in prison after the appellant's release. The appellant was to be paid £20,000 for his part in the escape scheme. It is not clear, nor is it significant for the purpose of any issue arising in the appeal, how far the details of the escape plan were worked out at the initial meeting in prison between the appellant and Ahmed Andaloussi. What is clear is that either at that meeting or after the appellant's release from prison and after one or more meetings between the appellant and Assou, it was agreed that the appellant would purchase and supply diamond wire, a cutting agent capable of cutting through metal bars, to be smuggled into the prison by Assou or Mohammed Andaloussi to enable Ahmed Andaloussi to escape from his cell. Further steps in the escape plan were to include the provision of rope and a ladder to enable Ahmed Andaloussi to climb on to the roof of an industrial building in the prison and thence over the main wall, transport to drive him away from the prison and safe accommodation where he could hide.

What happened in the event was that the appellant received from Assou a payment of £2,000 on account of the agreed fee of £20,000. Shortly after this the appellant was injured in a road accident and thereafter took no further step in pursuance of the escape plan. His admitted intention, however, was to acquire the diamond wire and give it to Assou. His further intention, according to the version of the facts which we must for present purposes accept, was then to insist that before he would proceed further he should be paid a further £10,000 on account, on receipt of which he would have left the country and gone to live in Spain, taking no further part in the scheme to effect Andaloussi's escape.

On those facts the submission for the appellant which was rejected both by the trial judge and the Court of Appeal was that the appellant lacked the mental element essential to sustain his conviction of a conspiracy to effect Andaloussi's escape, since he never intended that the escape plan, in which, according to what had been agreed, he was to play a major part, should be carried into effect nor, according to some of his statements to the police, which again we must for present purposes accept as indicating his true state of mind, did he believe that, in the circumstances, the plan to enable Andaloussi to escape could possibly succeed.

The Court of Appeal, having dismissed his appeal, certified that their decision involved a point of law of general public importance in terms which can conveniently be divided into two parts, since, in truth, there are two separate questions involved:

(1) Is a person who 'agrees' with two or more others, who themselves intend to pursue a course of conduct which will necessarily involve the commission of an offence, and who has a secret intention himself to participate in part only of that course of conduct, guilty himself of conspiracy to commit that offence under section 1(1) of the Criminal Law Act 1977?

(2) If not, is he liable to be indicted as a principal offender under section 8 of the Accessories and Abettors Act 1861?

... I am clearly driven by consideration of the diversity of roles which parties may agree to play in criminal conspiracies to reject any construction of the statutory language which would require the prosecution to prove an intention on the part of each conspirator that the criminal offence or offences which will necessarily be committed by one or more of the conspirators if the agreed course of conduct is fully carried out should in fact be committed. A simple example will illustrate the absurdity to which this construction would lead. The proprietor of a car hire firm agrees for a substantial payment to make available a hire car to a gang for use in a robbery and to make false entries in his books relating to the hiring to which he can point if the number of the car is traced back to him in connection with the robbery. Being fully aware of the circumstances of the robbery in which the car is proposed to be used he is plainly a party to the conspiracy to rob. Making his car available for use in the robbery is as much a part of the relevant agreed course of conduct as the robbery itself. Yet, once he has been paid, it will be a matter of complete indifference to him whether the robbery is in fact committed or not. In these days of highly organised crime the most serious statutory conspiracies will frequently involve an elaborate and complex agreed course of conduct in which many will consent to play necessary but subordinate roles, not involving them in any direct participation in the commission of the offence or offences at the centre of the conspiracy. Parliament cannot have intended that such parties should escape conviction of conspiracy on the basis that it cannot be proved against them that they intended that the relevant offence or offences should be committed.

There remains the important question whether a person who has agreed that a course of conduct will be pursued which, if pursued as agreed, will necessarily amount to or involve the commission of an offence is guilty of statutory conspiracy irrespective of his intention, and, if not, what is the *mens rea* of the offence. I have no hesitation in answering the first part of the question in the negative. There may be many situations in which perfectly respectable citizens, more particularly those concerned with law enforcement, may enter into agreements that a course of conduct shall be pursued which will involve commission of a crime without the least intention of playing any part in furtherance of the ostensibly agreed criminal objective, but rather with the purpose of exposing and frustrating the criminal purpose of the other parties to the agreement. To say this is in no way to encourage schemes by which police act, directly or through the agency of informers, as agents provocateurs for the purpose of entrapment. That is conduct of which the courts have always strongly disapproved. But it may sometimes happen, as most of us with experience in criminal trials well know, that a criminal enterprise is well advanced in the course of preparation when it comes to the notice either of the police or of some honest citizen in such circumstances that the only prospect of exposing and frustrating the criminals is that some innocent person should play the part of an intending collaborator in the course of criminal conduct proposed to be pursued. The mens rea implicit in the offence of statutory conspiracy must clearly be such as to recognise the innocence of such a person, notwithstanding that he will, in literal terms, be obliged to agree that a course of conduct be pursued involving the commission of an offence.

I have said already, but I repeat to emphasise its importance, that an essential ingredient in the crime of conspiring to commit a specific offence or offences under section 1(1) of the Act of 1977 is that the accused should agree that a course of conduct be pursued which he knows must involve the commission by one or more of the parties to the agreement of that offence or those offences. But, beyond the mere fact of agreement, the necessary mens rea of the crime is, in my opinion, established if, and only if, it is shown that the accused, when he entered into the agreement, intended to play some part in the agreed course of conduct in furtherance of the criminal purpose which the agreed course of conduct was intended to achieve. Nothing less will suffice; nothing more is required.

Applying this test to the facts which, for the purposes of the appeal, we must assume, the appellant, in agreeing that a course of conduct be pursued that would, if successful, necessarily involve the offence of effecting Andaloussi's escape from lawful custody, clearly intended, by providing diamond wire to be smuggled into the prison, to play a part in the agreed course of conduct in furtherance of that criminal objective. Neither the fact that he intended to play no further part in attempting to effect the escape, nor that he believed the escape to be impossible, would, if the jury had supposed they might be true, have afforded him any defence.

In the result, I would answer the first part of the certified question in the affirmative and dismiss the appeal. Your Lordships did not find it necessary to hear argument directed to the second part of the certified question and it must, therefore, be left unanswered.

■ NOTES AND QUESTIONS

1. Of what offence could Anderson have been convicted without arguably distorting the law of conspiracy? For example, could the examples given by Lord Bridge be adequately dealt with by charging aiding and abetting a conspiracy? Is there such a crime? See *R* v *Kenning* [2008] EWCA Crim 1534.

2. As a result of Lord Bridge's opinion, what is the position of the police officer who feigns agreement with persons already party to a conspiracy and, further, carries out minor acts towards completion of the offence? Is the officer guilty of conspiracy? See *Yip Chiu-Cheng* (below).

The decision in *Anderson* was the object of much criticism, and in *Siracusa* the Court of Appeal sought to clarify the law.

R v Siracusa (and others)
(1990) 90 Cr App R 340, Court of Appeal

O'CONNOR LJ:...The case arises out of the operations of an organisation of smugglers engaged in moving massive quantities of heroin from Thailand and cannabis from Kashmir to Canada via England. The scheme was simple. The drugs were to be housed in secret compartments in selected items of locally produced furniture, which would be included in substantial shipments of furniture. The object of passing the consignments through England was to support the manifests to be presented to the Canadian customs declaring the country of origin of the goods as England.

...

The importation of controlled drugs into this country is prohibited by section 3(1)(a) of the Misuse of Drugs Act 1971. That section does not create any offence. The offence is created by section 170(2)(b) of the Customs and Excise Management Act 1979 which provides:

(2) ...if any person is, in relation to any goods, in any way knowingly concerned in any fraudulent evasion or attempt at evasion:... (b) of any prohibition or restriction for the time being in force with respect to the goods under or by virtue of any enactment...he shall be guilty of an offence....

At the relevant time, the effect of section 170(4) and Schedule 1 of the Act was that importation of drugs of Class A or Class B was punishable with up to 14 years' imprisonment.

In cases where controlled drugs are imported into this country and a substantive offence is charged as a contravention of section 170(2)(b), the particulars of the offence identify the drug and the class to which it belongs so that the appropriate penalty is not in doubt. Case law has established that although separate offences are created as a result of the different penalties authorised, the *mens rea* is the same. The prosecution must prove that the defendant knew that the goods were prohibited goods. They do not have to prove that he knew what the goods in fact were. Thus it is no defence for a man charged with importing a Class A drug to say he believed he was bringing in a Class C drug or indeed any other prohibited goods: *R v Hussain* (1969) 53 Cr App R 448; *R v Shivpuri* (1986) 83 Cr App R 178; *R v Ellis* (1987) 84 Cr App R 235.

The appellants contend that where conspiracy to contravene section 170(2)(b) is charged, the position is different so that in this case the prosecution had to prove against each defendant that he knew that the Kashmir operation involved cannabis and that the Thailand operation involved heroin. If this submission is well-founded, then it is said that the learned judge's direction on conspiracy is flawed and strength is added to the contentions of those appellants who submit that in respect of one, other or both counts, there was no case to go to the jury at the end of the prosecution case.

[In *R v Anderson* [1986] AC 27, Lord Bridge said:...]

I have said already, but I repeat to emphasise its importance, that an essential ingredient in the crime of conspiring to commit a specific offence or offences under section 1(1) of the Act of 1977 is that the accused should agree that a course of conduct be pursued which he knows must involve the commission by one or more of the parties to the agreement of that offence or those offences. But, beyond the mere fact of agreement, the necessary *mens rea* of the crime is, in my opinion, established if, and only if, it is shown that the accused, when he entered into the agreement, intended to play some part in the agreed course of conduct in furtherance of the criminal purpose which the agreed course of conduct was intended to achieve. Nothing less will suffice; nothing more is required.

The last paragraph above cited must be read in the context of that case. We think it obvious that Lord Bridge cannot have been intending that the organiser of a crime who recruited others to carry it out would not himself be guilty of conspiracy unless it could be proved that he intended to play some active part himself thereafter. Lord Bridge had pointed out at p. 259 and p. 38 respectively that

in these days of highly organised crime the most serious statutory conspiracies will frequently involve an elaborate and complex agreed course of conduct in which many will consent to play necessary but subordinate roles, not involving them in any direct participation in the commission of the offence or offences at the centre of the conspiracy.

The present case is a classic example of such a conspiracy. It is the hallmark of such crimes that the organisers try to remain in the background and more often than not are not apprehended. Secondly, the origins of all conspiracies are concealed and it is usually quite impossible to establish when or where the initial agreement was made, or when or where other conspirators were recruited. The very existence of the agreement can only be inferred from overt acts. Participation in a conspiracy is infinitely variable: it can be active or passive. If the majority shareholder and director of a company consents to the company being used for drug smuggling carried out in the com-pany's name by a fellow director and minority shareholder, he is guilty of conspiracy. Consent, that is the agreement or adherence to the agreement, can be inferred if it is proved that he knew what was going on and the intention to participate in the furtherance of the criminal purpose is also established by his failure to stop the unlawful activity. Lord Bridge's *dictum* does not require anything more.

We return to the first sentence of this paragraph in Lord Bridge's speech. He starts by saying: 'I have said already, but I repeat to emphasise its importance. . . .' We have cited what he had already said when dealing with his clause 2. It is clear that he was not intending to say anything different. So when he goes on to say:

> an essential ingredient in the crime of conspiring to commit a specific offence or offences under section 1(1) of the Act of 1977 is that the accused should agree that a course of conduct be pursued which he knows must involve the commission by one or more of the parties to the agreement of that offence or those offences,

he plainly does not mean that the prosecution have to prove that persons who agree to import prohibited drugs into this country know that the offence which will be committed will be a contravention of section 170(2) of the Customs and Excise Act. He is not to be taken as saying that the prosecution must prove that the accused knew the name of the crime. We are satisfied that Lord Bridge was doing no more than applying the words of section 1 of the Criminal Law Act 1977, namely, that when the accused agreed to the course of conduct, he knew that it involved the commission of an offence.

The *mens rea* sufficient to support the commission of a substantive offence will not necessarily be sufficient to support a charge of conspiracy to commit that offence. An intent to cause grievous bodily harm is sufficient to support the charge of murder, but is not sufficient to support a charge of conspiracy to murder or of attempt to murder.

. . .

Yip Chiu-Cheung v *R*
[1994] 3 WLR 514, Privy Council

LORD GRIFFITHS: On 27 March 1991 the defendant was convicted of conspiracy to traffic in heroin and on 28 March sentenced to 15 years' imprisonment. His appeal was dismissed by the Court of Appeal of Hong Kong on 15 May 1992 and he now appeals from that decision.

The indictment charged the defendant as follows:

> *Statement of offence*. Conspiracy to traffic in a dangerous drug, contrary to common law and section 4 of the Dangerous Drugs Ordinance, c. 134.

Particulars of offence. Yip Chiu-Cheung, between 19 August 1989 and 15 November 1989 in Thailand and Hong Kong, conspired with Philip Needham and another person unknown to traffic in a dangerous drug, namely salts of esters of morphine commonly known as heroin.

. . .

The prosecution case was based primarily on the evidence of Philip Needham who was an undercover drug enforcement officer of the United States of America and named in the indictment as a co-conspirator. The other conspirator, referred to in the indictment as a person unknown, was introduced to Needham by the defendant under the name of Hom.

In outline Needham's evidence was that he had a series of meetings in Thailand with the defendant, at one of which Hom also took part, at which it was arranged that Needham would act as a courier to carry five kilos of heroin from Hong Kong to Australia, travelling by air.

The arrangement was that Needham would fly to Hong Kong on 22 October 1989 under the name of Larsen, where he would be met by the defendant. He would then stay at the Nathan Hotel in Kowloon for a few days and then fly on to Australia with five kilos of heroin supplied by the defendant. For this service he would be paid U.S.$16,000. In fact Needham did not fly to Hong Kong on 22 October because the flight was delayed and he missed the rescheduled flight. Needham said he had no way of contacting the defendant in Hong Kong and had been advised by the Hong Kong authorities that the Nathan Hotel would be a dangerous place for him to stay. Needham therefore proceeded no further with the plan, and did not go to Hong Kong.

The defendant raised a number of grounds of appeal before the Court of Appeal all of which failed, and only one of which is now pursued before the Board, which is that Needham, the drug enforcement officer, cannot in law be a co-conspirator because he lacked the necessary *mens rea* for the offence.

...

On the principal ground of appeal it was submitted that the trial judge and the Court of Appeal were wrong to hold that Needham, the undercover agent, could be a conspirator because he lacked the necessary *mens rea* or guilty mind required for the offence of conspiracy. It was urged upon their Lordships that no moral guilt attached to the undercover agent who was at all times acting courageously and with the best of motives in attempting to infiltrate and bring to justice a gang of criminal drug dealers. In these circumstances it was argued that it would be wrong to treat the agent as having any criminal intent, and reliance was placed upon a passage in the speech of Lord Bridge of Harwich in *R v Anderson (William Ronald)* [1986] AC 27, 38–39; but in that case Lord Bridge was dealing with a different situation from that which exists in the present case. There may be many cases in which undercover police officers or other law enforcement agents pretend to join a conspiracy in order to gain information about the plans of the criminals, with no intention of taking any part in the planned crime but rather with the intention of providing information that will frustrate it. It was to this situation that Lord Bridge was referring in *Reg v Anderson*. The crime of conspiracy requires an agreement between two or more persons to commit an unlawful act with the intention of carrying it out. It is the intention to carry out the crime that constitutes the necessary *mens rea* for the offence. As Lord Bridge pointed out, an undercover agent who has no intention of committing the crime lacks the necessary *mens rea* to be a conspirator.

The facts of the present case are quite different. Nobody can doubt that Needham was acting courageously and with the best of motives; he was trying to break a drug ring. But equally there can be no doubt that the method he chose and in which the police in Hong Kong acquiesced involved the commission of the criminal offence of trafficking in drugs by exporting heroin from Hong Kong without a licence. Needham intended to commit that offence by carrying the heroin through the customs and on to the aeroplane bound for Australia.

Neither the police, nor customs, nor any other member of the executive have any power to alter the terms of the Ordinance forbidding the export of heroin, and the fact that they may turn a blind eye when the heroin is exported does not prevent it from being a criminal offence.

...

Naturally, Needham never expected to be prosecuted if he carried out the plan as intended. But the fact that in such circumstances the authorities would not prosecute the undercover agent does not mean that he did not commit the crime albeit as part of a wider scheme to combat drug dealing.

Knowledge of Facts and Circumstances

D cannot be guilty of conspiracy unless he and at least one person intend or know of any facts or circumstances necessary for the substantive offence.

■ NOTES AND QUESTIONS

1. Does Yip Chiu-Cheung provide a more satisfactory approach to the undercover officer than that suggested in *Anderson*?
2. Would it make more sense to take a 'unilateral' view of agreement, whereby X may agree with Y even though Y did not agree with X? Y would only have to

give 'nominal' agreement, excluding any hidden reservations on Y's part (e.g., stemming from the fact that he is working for the police).

3. The Law Commission would require that at least two persons share an intent that the crime be committed in order for there to be a conspiracy. In light of cases such as *Yip Chiu-Cheung*, is this advisable?

4. A and B add alcohol to C's lemonade, intending that he drive with a higher alcohol level than permitted by law. What must the prosecution show before A and B can be convicted of a conspiracy to commit an offence? What if A but not B believed that the alcohol added was insufficient to cause C to be guilty of an offence?

5. The Law Commission recommend that suspicion should be enough where reck- lessness is sufficient for the substantive offence.

(ii) Necessarily involve a crime

Under the Criminal Law Act 1977, s. 1(1), the agreement that a course of conduct shall be pursued must be such that if carried out in accordance with the conspira- tors' intention, it would amount to or involve the commission of an offence or offences by one or more parties to the agreement (or would have done so except for facts which made the commission of the offence impossible). Sometimes an agree- ment may involve a number of alternative courses of action which will be pursued by the conspirators depending on other events. If one course of action is criminal and the other not, is this an agreement to pursue a course of conduct which will necessarily involve a crime? Similarly, if two different crimes are envisaged, which crime have the defendants agreed to?

R v Reed
[1982] Crim LR 819, Court of Appeal

The fourth submission was that the summing up had not adequately conveyed the requirements of the Criminal Law Act 1977, s. 1 (1). These, it was said, clearly indicate that a course of conduct agreed upon must necessarily amount to or involve the commission of an offence if the agreement is carried out in accordance with the parties' intentions. The agreement on the relevant course of conduct must therefore not be capable of a successful conclusion without a crime being committed (*cf.* Smith and Hogan, *Criminal Law* (4th ed.), pp. 226–227). It was argued that the most that could be inferred about the nature of the agreement between L and R was that L would visit individuals and either give them faith healing, consolation and comfort while discouraging suicide or he would actively help them to commit suicide, depending on his assessment of the appropriate course of action. Such an agreement was capable of execution without the law being broken, and therefore should not have attracted the charge of conspiracy. It was argued that the jury should have at least been made aware of such a possible defence in the directions given.

The Court held against the applicant on this point. Donaldson LJ considered two examples:

In the first, A and B agree to drive from London to Edinburgh in a time which can be achieved with- out exceeding the speed limits, but only if the traffic which they encounter is exceptionally light. Their agreement will not necessarily involve the commission of any offence, even if it is carried out in accordance with their intentions, and they do arrive from London to Edinburgh within the agreed time. Accordingly the agreement does not constitute the offence of statutory conspiracy or indeed of any offence. In the second example, A and B agree to rob a bank, if when they arrive at the bank it seems safe to do so. Their agreement will necessarily involve the commission of the offence of robbery if it is carried out in accordance with their intentions. Accordingly, they are guilty of the statutory offence of conspiracy. The instant case is an example of the latter type of agreement. If circumstances had permitted and the agreement of R and L had been carried out in accordance with their intentions L would have aided, abetted, counselled, and procured a suicide....

. . .

R v Jackson
[1985] Crim LR 442, Court of Appeal

The appellants were convicted of conspiracy to pervert the course of public justice. Their code-fendant, Whitlock, pleaded guilty to inciting a person to have a firearm with criminal intent. All four had discussed Whitlock's plan to have himself shot so as to provide mitigation in the event of being convicted of the burglary offence for which he was being tried. Before the end of that trial Whitlock was shot in the leg and was permanently disabled. The appellants had spent part of the evening in question with Whitlock but lied to the police about their whereabouts. They eventually admitted knowing of the plan. In their defence the appellants denied having any part in the plan and claimed not to have taken Whitlock seriously. The particulars of the offence, charged that the appellants made false statements as to their and Whitlock's whereabouts; that they concealed the identity of the person responsible for the shooting and that they concealed the fact that Whitlock had arranged to be shot to mislead his court of trial. The appellants appealed against conviction on the ground that no offence had been committed since it depended upon a contingency which might not have taken place—the conviction of Whitlock for burglary. Counsel relied upon examples cited in *Reed* (CACD: March 26, 1982) and submitted that the agreement did not 'necessarily' involve the commission of an offence.

Held, dismissing the appeals, planning was taking place for a contingency and if that contingency occurred the conspiracy would necessarily involve the commission of an offence. 'Necessarily' is not to be held to mean that there must inevitably be the carrying out of an offence, it means, if the agreement is carried out in accordance with the plan, there must be the commission of the offence referred to in the conspiracy count....

■ NOTES AND QUESTIONS

1. In the driving example given in *Reed*, why did the Court believe there was no conspiracy? Was there not an agreement to commit a crime in the event of heavy traffic being encountered?
2. What would be the result in the following situations?
   (a) An agreement to burgle a house, using violence if the occupier returns.
   (b) An agreement to steal a car unless police officers are patrolling the street.
   (c) An agreement to have intercourse with a woman whether or not she consents.
3. In *R v O'Hadhmaill* [1996] Crim LR 509, the defendant (a member of the IRA) was convicted of conspiracy to carry out explosions. On appeal he argued that he did not plan to cause explosions so long as the cease-fire then in force held. Should this argument have been successful?

(iii) Conspiring to do the impossible

The differences between factual and legal impossibility were outlined previously in the section on encouragement. The issue of 'impossible' conspiracies is specifically addressed in s. 1(1)(b) of the Criminal Law Act 1977:

1.—(1) Subject to the following provisions of this Part of this Act, if a person agrees with any other person or persons that a course of conduct shall be pursued which, if the agreement is carried out in accordance with their intentions, either—
   (a) will necessarily amount to or involve the commission of any offence or offences by one or more of the parties to the agreement, or

(b) *would do so but for the existence of facts which render the commission of the offence or any of the offences impossible,*

he is guilty of conspiracy to commit the offence or offences in question. (emphasis added)

It would seem that whatever ambiguity there may have been in the law before the Act, it is now clear that factual impossibility is not a defence to a charge of *statutory* conspiracy (impossibility as a defence to common law conspiracies will be addressed when that topic is considered). There is still, however, the qualifying and confusing language of s. 1(2) to consider:

1.—(2) Where liability for any offence may be incurred without knowledge on the part of the person committing it of any particular fact or circumstance necessary for the commission of an offence, a person shall nevertheless not be guilty of conspiracy to commit that offence by virtue of subsection (1) unless he and at least one other party to the agreement intend or know that that fact or circumstance shall or will exist at the time when the conduct constituting the offence is to take place.

R v Saik

[2007] 1 A.C. 18, House of Lords

LORD NICHOLLS OF BIRKENHEAD:

My Lords,

1. This appeal raises questions about the ingredients of the statutory offence of conspiracy and their application in the circumstances of this case. Shorn of its complexities the context is a charge of conspiracy to launder money brought against the appellant, Mr Abdulrahman Saik. He operated a bureau de change in London, near Marble Arch. At his trial he pleaded guilty, subject to the quali-fication that he did not know the money was the proceeds of crime. He only suspected this was so. This qualified plea was accepted. The issue before your Lordships is whether the offence to which the appellant pleaded guilty in this qualified way is an offence known to law. Reasonable grounds for suspicion are enough for the substantive offence of laundering money. But are they enough for a conspiracy to commit that offence?

3. The Criminal Law Act 1977 redefined conspiracy and put it on a statutory footing. The offence-creating provision is section 1(1):

'... if a person agrees with any other person or persons that a course of conduct shall be pur-sued which, if the agreement is carried out in accordance with their intentions ... (a) will nec-essarily amount to or involve the commission of any offence or offences by one or more of the parties to the agreement ... he is guilty of conspiracy to commit the offence or offences in question.'

The offence therefore lies in making an agreement. Implicitly, the subsection requires also that the parties intend to carry out their agreement. The offence is complete at that stage ... even if the par-ties do not carry out their agreement.

4. Thus under this subsection the mental element of the offence, apart from the mental element involved in making an agreement, comprises the intention to pursue a course of conduct which will necessarily involve commission of the crime in question by one or more of the conspirators. The conspirators must intend to do the act prohibited by the substantive offence. The conspirators' state of mind must also satisfy the mental ingredients of the substantive offence. If one of the ingre-dients of the substantive offence is that the act is done with a specific intent, the conspirators must intend to do the prohibited act ... with the prescribed intent.

5. An intention to do a prohibited act is within the scope of section 1(1) even if the intention is expressed to be conditional on the happening, or non-happening, of some particular event. The

question always is whether the agreed course of conduct, if carried out in accordance with the parties' intentions, would necessarily involve an offence. In the nature of things, every agreement to do something in the future is hedged about with conditions, implicit if not explicit. In theory if not in practice, the condition could be so far-fetched that it would cast doubt on the genuineness of a conspirator's expressed intention to do an unlawful act.

6. Section 1(2) qualifies the scope of the offence created by section 1(1). Its essential purpose is to ensure that strict liability and recklessness have no place in the offence of conspiracy:

> 'Where liability for any offence may be incurred without knowledge on the part of the person committing it of any particular fact or circumstance necessary for the commission of the offence, a person shall nevertheless not be guilty of conspiracy to commit that offence by virtue of subsection (1) above unless he and at least one other party to the agreement intend or know that that fact or circumstance shall or will exist at the time when the conduct constituting the offence is to take place.'

7. Under this subsection conspiracy involves a third mental element: intention or knowledge that a fact or circumstances necessary for the commission of the substantive offence will exist.

8. It follows from this requirement of intention or knowledge that proof of the mental element needed for the commission of a substantive offence will not always suffice on a charge of conspiracy to commit that offence. In respect of a material fact or circumstance conspiracy has its own mental element. In conspiracy this mental element is set as high as 'intend or know'. This subsumes any lesser mental element, such as suspicion, required by the substantive offence in respect of a material fact or circumstances. In this respect the mental element of conspiracy is distinct from and supersedes the mental element in the substantive offence. When this is so, the lesser mental element in the substantive offence becomes otiose.To include it in the particulars of the offence of conspiracy is potentially confusing and should be avoided.

9. The phrase 'fact or circumstance necessary for the commission of the offence' is opaque. Difficulties have sometimes arisen in its application. The key seems to lie in the distinction apparent in the subsection between 'intend or know' on the one hand and any particular 'fact or circumstance necessary for the commission of the offence' on the other hand. The latter is directed at an element of the actus reus of the offence. A mental element of the offence is not itself a 'fact or circumstance' for the purposes of the subsection.

13. The rationale underlying this approach is that conspiracy imposes criminal liability on the basis of a person's intention. This is a different harm from the commission of the substantive offence. So it is right that the intention which is being criminalised in the offence of conspiracy should itself be blameworthy. This should be so, irrespective of the provisions of the substantive offence in that regard.

14. Against that background I turn to some issues concerning the scope and effect of section 1(2). The starting point is to note that this relieving provision is not confined to substantive offences attracting strict liability. The subsection does not so provide. Nor would such an interpretation of the subsection make sense. It would make no sense for section 1(2) to apply, and require proof of intention or knowledge, where liability for the substantive offence is absolute but not where the substantive offence has built into it a mental ingredient less than knowledge, such as suspicion.

15. A more difficult question arises where an ingredient of the substantive offence is that the defendant must *know* of a material fact or circumstance. On its face section 1(2) does not apply in this case.

16. Plainly Parliament did not intend that a person would be liable for conspiracy where he lacks the knowledge required to commit the substantive offence. Parliament could not have intended such an absurd result. Rather, the assumption underlying section 1(2) is that, where knowledge of a material fact is an ingredient of a substantive offence, knowledge of that fact is also an ingredient of the crime of conspiring to commit the substantive offence.

17. There are two ways this result might be achieved. One is simply to treat section 1(2) as inapplicable in this type of case.... The other route is to adopt the interpretation of section 1(2) suggested by Sir John Smith that section 1(2) applies in such a case despite the opening words of

the subsection. Section 1(2) is to be read as applicable *even* 'where liability for an offence may be incurred without knowledge [etc]'. It is difficult to see what other function the word 'nevertheless' has in the subsection.

19. The first route accords more easily with the language of section 1(2), but I prefer the second route. A conspiracy is an agreement about future conduct. When the agreement is made the 'particular fact or circumstance necessary for the commission' of the substantive offence may not have happened. So the conspirator cannot be said to *know* of that fact or circumstance at that time. Nor, if the happening of the fact or circumstance is beyond his control, can it be said that the conspirator *will* know of that fact or circumstance.

20. Section 1(2) expressly caters for this situation. The conspirator must 'intend or know' that this fact or circumstance 'shall or will exist' when the conspiracy is carried into effect. Although not the happiest choice of language, 'intend' is descriptive of a state of mind which is looking to the future. This is to be contrasted with the language of substantive offences. Generally, references to 'knowingly' or the like in substantive offences are references to a past state of affairs. No doubt this language could be moulded appropriately where the offence charged is conspiracy. But the more direct and satisfactory route is to regard section 1(2) as performing in relation to a conspiracy the function which words such as 'knowingly' perform in relation to the substantive offence. That approach accords better with what must be taken to have been the parliamentary intention on how the phrase 'intend or know' in section 1(2) would operate in this type of case.

24. In this type of case, namely, where the conspiracy related to unidentified property, there is no question of having to prove that the property *was* the proceeds of criminal conduct. In this type of case that is not possible. It is not possible because the property which was the subject of the conspiracy had not been identified when the conspiracy was entered into. Despite this, the crime of conspiracy will be committed.

25. What, however, if the property to which the conspiracy relates *was* specifically identified when the conspirators made their agreement? In that event the prosecution must prove the conspirators 'knew' the property was the proceeds of crime. This is the next point of difficulty in the interpretation of section 1(2). Does 'know' in this context have the meaning attributed to it in the *Montila* case when considering the substantive offence? If it does, the identified property to which the conspiracy related must actually be or represent the proceeds of crime, and the conspirator must be aware of this. Or does 'know' in this context mean 'believe', as seems to be suggested in *R v Ali* [2006] 2 WLR 316, 335, para 98? On the ordinary use of language a person cannot 'know' whether property is the proceeds of crime unless he participated in the crime. He can only believe this is so, on the basis of what he has been told. Adopting this approach would mean that, so far as section 93C is concerned, equating knowledge with belief in the case of identified property would achieve a measure of symmetry with the requirement of intention in the case of unidentified property. It would mean that in both cases what matters is the conspirator's state of mind: the actual provenance of the property would not be material.

26. I do not think the latter approach can be accepted. The phrase under consideration ('intend or know') in section 1(2) is a provision of general application to all conspiracies. In this context the word 'know' should be interpreted strictly and not watered down. In this context knowledge means true belief. As applied to section 93C(2) it means that, in the case of identified property, a conspirator must be aware the property was in fact the proceeds of crime.

The appellant's plea

27. The offence with which this appellant was charged was 'conspiracy to convert the proceeds of drug trafficking and/or criminal conduct contrary to section 1(1) of the Criminal Law Act 1977'. The essence of the particulars of the offence was that the appellant and others 'conspired together … to convert … banknotes, for the purpose of assisting another to avoid prosecution for … a criminal offence …, knowing or having reasonable grounds to suspect that such property … represented another person's proceeds of … criminal conduct.'

29. This formulation of the particulars may well have contributed to the qualified form in which the appellant entered his plea of guilty. He pleaded guilty 'on the basis of laundering money which he suspected was the proceeds of crime'.

30. From what has been said above, it is evident that this conviction for conspiracy cannot stand. Suspicion is not sufficient in respect of a fact to which section 1(2) applies. Knowledge or intention regarding the provenance of the property must be proved or admitted.

LORD HOPE OF CRAIGHEAD:

44. The appellant operated a currency exchange office. The prosecution case was that in the course of that business and between the dates referred to he converted a substantial quantity of pounds sterling provided by other defendants in the form of cash into foreign currency, and that the cash was or represented the proceeds of drug trafficking or other criminal activity.

45. When the appellant pleaded guilty to count 3 he did so in accordance with a written basis of plea which was drawn on his behalf by leading counsel, signed by him and accepted by the prosecution. So far as material to his appeal against conviction it was in these terms: "(1)The defendant Saik pleads guilty on the basis of laundering money which he suspected was the proceeds of crime. (2) He only became suspicious from about December 2001, when the number of transactions became more voluminous."

46. In the Court of Appeal the appeal against conviction was argued on two distinct grounds. The first was that the conviction was unsafe as a matter of law. The second was that the plea of guilty was the result of erroneous advice that the appellant had received from his legal advisers. The Court of Appeal, having rejected both arguments, certified that the following points of law of general public importance were involved in the first ground only:

"(1) Can a defendant be convicted of a statutory conspiracy to contravene section 93C(2) of the Criminal Justice Act 1988 if he enters into an agreement to convert property in respect of which he had reasonable grounds to suspect and did in fact suspect but did not actually know was the proceeds of crime? (2) Is the objective requirement that a defendant can be convicted of an offence under section 93C(2) of the Criminal Justice Act 1988 if he had reasonable grounds to suspect that the property converted etc was the proceeds of crime (without having actual knowledge or suspicion) incompatible with the subjective requirement that the activity of the defendant must be for the specified purpose of assisting another to avoid prosecution for a criminal offence or avoiding the making or enforcement of a confiscation order?"

The statutory provisions

47. To put flesh on the bones of what is set out in the preceding paragraphs I must now set out the statutory provisions on which count 3 of the indictment was based. They are to be found in section 1 of the 1977 Act and in section 93C(2) of the 1988 Act. Section 93C(2) was repealed when the Drug Trafficking Act 1994, the 1988 Act and the corresponding legislation in Scotland and Northern Ireland were replaced by the Proceeds of Crime Act 2002.

75. It seems to me that the best way to discover the meaning of the words used in section 1 to define the statutory offence of conspiracy is to assume that one is dealing, as the Law Commission intended, with an allegation of an inchoate crime. A conspiracy is complete when the agreement to enter into is formed, even if nothing is done to implement it. Implementation gives effect to the conspiracy, but it does not alter its essential elements. The statutory language adopts this approach. It assumes that implementation of the agreement lies in the future. The question whether its requirements are fulfilled is directed to the stage when the agreement is formed, not to the stage when it is implemented.

76. First there is section 1(1). It refers to (i) an agreement, (ii) a course of conduct to be pursued under that agreement and (iii) the fact that, if the agreement is carried out as intended, it "will necessarily" amount to or involve the commission of an offence by one or more of the parties to the agreement. Let us assume that there are two parties to the agreement: parties X and Y. X is

in possession of cash which he knows is the proceeds of crime (A). Y does not know the cash is A, which it is. But he suspects that it is A, and he has reasonable grounds for his suspicion. The agreement is that X will hand over the cash to Y, and that Y will immediately convert it into a different currency. If the agreement is carried out as they intend, the cash will be converted. The conversion of cash which is A by someone who knows that it is A is an offence contrary to section 93C(2). X knows that the cash is A. So the carrying out of the agreement between X and Y in accordance with their intentions will necessarily amount to the commission of an offence by X. This is enough to satisfy section 1(1)(a). But the carrying out of the agreement will also necessarily amount to the commission of an offence by Y. The cash will be A, because that is the fact known to X. And the conversion of cash which is in fact A by someone who has reasonable grounds to suspect that it is A is an offence under section 93C(2).

78. But there remains section 1(2). It is necessary to address this question too, because Y can incur liability for an offence under section 93C(2) without knowledge of a fact necessary for the commission of the offence-that the cash is A. Section 1(2) tells us that a person shall not be guilty of the conspiracy to commit that offence by virtue of subsection (1) unless he and at least one other party to the agreement "intend or know" that the fact necessary for the commission of the offence-that the cash is A-"shall or will exist" at the time when the cash is converted into a different currency. There is no problem about X, of course. He knows that the cash which he will hand over to Y is A. He knows that it will be A when the conduct takes place-when it is converted into a different currency. But what about Y? He suspects that the cash is A. But he does not know that it is, or that it will be when it is handed over to him and he converts it. Can it be said that he intends that it should be A, when he does not know what he will be dealing with? Solving this problem is not easy because the word "intend" in section 1(2) refers to the existence of a fact or a circumstance, not to the consequences of giving effect to the agreement. But the words "shall or will" indicate that nothing short of intention or knowledge as to its existence will do.

79. I think that the answer to this question will depend on the facts. It could be said of Y that he knows enough about the purpose of the transaction because of the grounds for his suspicion for it not to matter whether he will be able to tell by looking at the cash that it is in fact the proceeds of crime. It may be open to the Crown to prove that Y knew very well what the purpose of the agreement was-that he knew that the cash was to be converted to assist someone to avoid prosecution for an offence or the making or enforcement of a confiscation order, which is what section 93C(2) refers to. It might be going too far to say that he knew that the cash would be A when he came to deal with it. But it could be inferred that he intended that the cash would be A, because he knew that that was the only purpose of the transaction.

80. But in this case all we know is that the appellant suspected that the money "was" the proceeds of crime. The appellant must be dealt with according to the terms of his plea. We cannot say that he was wilfully blind as to the purpose of the agreement, because that is not what he admits to. He suspected that he was being asked to convert the proceeds of criminal conduct. But he did not know that this was the origin of the money that was actually being given to him. He was prepared to go ahead and convert the money without knowing that it was in fact the proceeds of crime. It would not be quite right to say that he was reckless. All he was to do was simply to convert money from one currency into another-an everyday transaction which involves no risk to anyone. But he was willing to go ahead with this without troubling to find out whether or not what he was proposing to do was criminal. A person who is in that state of mind cannot be said to intend that the fact or circumstance that makes his act criminal should exist. That being the position I would hold that, although he was suspicious, the appellant cannot be said to have intended that the money should be the proceeds of crime when he came to deal with it.

Conclusion

81. Given the terms of his plea, I see no escape from the conclusion that the appellant's case is caught by section 1(2) of the 1977 Act. He cannot be said to be guilty of the conspiracy to commit the

substantive offence under section 93C(2) because he did not know, and therefore did not intend, that the money which he agreed to convert would be the proceeds of crime when at some future date he came to perform his part of the agreement. I would allow the appeal and set aside the conviction.

■ NOTES AND QUESTIONS

1. Would it have been preferable if s. 1(2) had been phrased in terms of 'belief' rather than intention or knowledge?
2. Why not charge a defendant like Saik simply with money laundering? What lies behind a prosecutor's decision to charge conspiracy instead of, or in addition to, the substantive offence?

D: Common law conspiracies

(i) Conspiracy to defraud

The common law offence of conspiracy to defraud was expressly preserved by s. 5(2) of the Criminal Law Act 1977, pending a review of the law relating to fraud by the Law Commission which has now been completed and has led to enactment of the Fraud Act 2006. Since a statutory conspiracy can now be charged in cases involving fraud, the continuing status of s. 12 of the Criminal Justice Act 1987 must remain in doubt:

CRIMINAL JUSTICE ACT 1987

> **12.**—(1) If—
> (a) a person agrees with any other person or persons that a course of conduct shall be pursued; and
> (b) that course of conduct will necessarily amount to or involve the commission of any offence or offences by one or more of the parties to the agreement if the agreement is carried out in accordance with their intentions,
> the fact that it will do so shall not preclude a charge of conspiracy to defraud being brought against any of them in respect of the agreement.

The common law crime of conspiracy to defraud will usually take one of three forms:

(a) Where loss is suffered.
(b) Where the victim is deceived into taking an economic risk.
(c) Where a public official is induced by deception to act contrary to his public duty.

(a) Where loss is suffered

Where actual loss is suffered by the victim, no deceit on the part of the defendant needs to be shown.

Scott v Metropolitan Police Commissioner

[1975] AC 819, House of Lords

VISCOUNT DILHORNE: . . . During the course of the opening of the case for the prosecution Mr Blom-Cooper, who represented the appellant, said that the appellant was prepared to admit, and the appellant did admit, the following facts, namely, that he

> Agreed with employees of cinema owners temporarily to abstract, without permission of such cinema owners, and in return for payments to such employees, cinematograph films, without the knowledge or consent of the owners of the copyright and/or of distribution rights in such films, for the purpose of making infringing copies and distributing the same of a commercial basis.

On these admitted facts Mr Blom-Cooper submitted the appellant could not be convicted on the first count. His contention that there could not be a conspiracy to defraud unless there was deceit was rejected by Judge Hines and the appellant then pleaded guilty to the first and seventh counts and was sentenced to two years' imprisonment on count one and one year's imprisonment on count two.

. . .

The Court of Appeal certified that a point of law of general public importance was involved in the decision to dismiss the appeal against conviction on count one, namely,

> Whether, on a charge of conspiracy to defraud, the Crown must establish an agreement to deprive the owners of their property by deception; or whether it is sufficient to prove an agreement to prejudice the rights of another or others without lawful justification and in circumstances of dishonesty.

. . .

In the course of the argument many cases were cited. It is not necessary to refer to all of them. Many were cases in which the conspiracy alleged was to defraud by deceit. Those cases do not establish that there can only be a conspiracy to defraud if deceit is involved and there are a number of cases where that was not the case.

. . .

One must not confuse the object of a conspiracy with the means by which it is intended to be carried out. In the light of the cases to which I have referred, I have come to the conclusion that Mr Blom-Cooper's main contention must be rejected. I have not the temerity to attempt an exhaustive definition of the meaning of 'defraud.'

As I have said, words take colour from the context in which they are used, but the words 'fraudulently' and 'defraud' must ordinarily have a very similar meaning. If, as I think, and as the Criminal Law Revision Committee appears to have thought, 'fraudulently' means 'dishonestly,' then 'to defraud' ordinarily means, in my opinion, to deprive a person dishonestly of something which is his or of something to which he is or would or might but for the perpetration of the fraud be entitled.

In *Welham* v *Director of Public Prosecutions* [1961] AC 103, 124 Lord Radcliffe referred to a special line of cases where the person deceived is a person holding public office or a public authority and where the person deceived was not caused any pecuniary or economic loss. Forgery whereby the deceit has been accomplished, had, he pointed out, been in a number of cases treated as having been done with intent to defraud despite the absence of pecuniary or economic loss.

In this case it is not necessary to decide that a conspiracy to defraud may exist even though its object was not to secure a financial advantage by inflicting an economic loss on the person at whom the conspiracy was directed. But for myself I see no reason why what was said by Lord Radcliffe in relation to forgery should not equally apply in relation to conspiracy to defraud.

In this case the accused bribed servants of the cinema owners to secure possession of films in order to copy them and in order to enable them to let the copies out on hire. By so doing Mr Blom-Cooper conceded they inflicted more than nominal damage to the goodwill of the owners of the copyright and distribution rights of the films. By so doing they secured for themselves profits which but for their actions might have been secured by those owners just as in *R* v *Button*, 3 Cox CC 229 the defendants obtained profits which might have been secured by their employer. In the circumstances it is, I think, clear that they inflicted pecuniary loss on those owners.

(b) Where the victim is deceived into taking an economic risk

R v Allsop
(1976) 64 Cr App R 29, Court of Appeal

The appellant was a sub-broker for a hire-purchase company. His function as such was to introduce prospective purchasers of cars and to fill in application forms in respect of them. From time to time he put false particulars in the forms so as to induce the hire-purchase company to accept applications which they might otherwise have rejected. When doing this the appellant expected and believed that these transactions would be completed satisfactorily so that the hire-purchase company would profit from them. The appellant was charged with conspiracy to defraud.

SHAW LJ: This appeal raises a short but interesting question in relation to the nature of the intent requisite to constitute the offence of conspiracy to defraud. The argument advanced by Mr Mervyn Heald on behalf of the appellant is that such an intent involves as an essential element the objective of causing actual economic loss to the person alleged to have been defrauded so that it is not sufficient if that person's economic interests are merely threatened incidentally. Miss Goddard, for the Crown, asserts that no more is necessary than the intent to bring about a situation in which the economic interests of the person deceived are threatened or prejudiced, or are likely to be threatened or prejudiced, albeit that such threat or prejudice is undesired or incidental so far as the person responsible for the deceit is concerned.

...

It seemed to this Court that Mr Heald's argument traversed the shadowy region between intent and motive. Generally the primary objective of fraudsmen is to advantage themselves. The detriment that results to their victims is secondary to that purpose and incidental. It is 'intended' only in the sense that it is a contemplated outcome of the fraud that is perpetrated. If the deceit which is employed imperils the economic interest of the person deceived, this is sufficient to constitute fraud even though in the event no actual loss is suffered and notwithstanding that the deceiver did not desire to bring about an actual loss.

...'Economic loss' may be ephemeral and not lasting, or potential and not actual; but even a threat of financial prejudice while it exists it may be measured in terms of money.

...

...In the present case, the part of the history which is common ground reveals that in this sense Prestige did suffer actual loss for they paid too much for cars worth less than their pretended value; and they relied upon the creditworthiness of hire-purchasers as measured by the deposit stated to have been paid when none had been paid.

It matters not that in the end the hire-purchasers concerned paid to Prestige what was due to them. In the interim that corporation suffered economic loss in consequence of the misrepresentation made by the appellant. Mr Heald argues that this is neither here nor there. The essential consideration so his argument ran is what the appellant intended at the outset; he averred that, it is not sufficient if the intention to put Prestige's interests at risk was merely incidental when the ultimate purpose was not to injure them. We do not agree. Interests which are imperilled are less valuable in terms of money than those same interests when they are secure and protected. Where a person intends by deceit to induce a course of conduct in another which puts that other's economic interests in jeopardy he is guilty of fraud even though he does not intend or desire that actual loss should ultimately be suffered by that other in this context.

(c) Where a public official is induced by deception to act contrary to his public duty

Welham v Director of Public Prosecutions
[1961] AC 103, House of Lords

The appellant was tried on an indictment which included two counts which charged him with uttering forged documents, contrary to s. 6 of the Forgery Act 1913. The appellant, as sales manager of Motors (Brighton) Ltd, had witnessed forged hire-purchase agreements on the strength of which certain finance companies had advanced large sums of money to Motors (Brighton) Ltd. The appellants' defence was that he had believed that the agreements were brought into being to enable the finance companies to lend money which they could not ordinarily do because of credit restrictions, and because by their memorandum and articles of association they could not act as moneylenders. He claimed that the purpose of the hire-purchase agreements was to make it appear that the finance companies were advancing money in the way of their business as finance companies, and he accordingly contended that he had had no intention to defraud the finance companies but was merely uttering the documents to mislead the relevant authority who might inspect the records to see that the credit restrictions were being observed and whose duty it was to prevent their contravention. The jury were directed that this was a sufficient intention to defraud and the appellant was convicted. He appealed on the ground that his intention was merely an intention to deceive and not an intention to defraud, which involved causing some economic loss to the person deceived.

LORD DENNING: ... Much valuable guidance is to be obtained from the dictum of Buckley J in the *Whittaker Wright* case, *In re London and Globe Finance Corporation* [1903] 1 Ch 728, but this has been criticised by modern scholars. It has even been hinted that it conceals within it the fallacy of the illegitimate antistrophe, which sounds, I must say, extremely serious. These scholars seem to think they have found the solution. 'To defraud,' they say, involves the idea of economic loss. I cannot agree with them on this. If a drug addict forges a doctor's prescription so as to enable him to get drugs from a chemist, he has, I should have thought, an intent to defraud, even though he intends to pay the chemist the full price and no one is a penny the worse off.

Seeing, therefore, that the words of the statute are of doubtful import, it is, I think, legitimate to turn for guidance to the previous state of the law before the Act. And here I would say at once that the phrase 'with intent to defraud' has been the standard usage of lawyers in defining forgery for over 160 years. In 1796 all the judges of England laid down the definition of forgery as 'the false making of a note or other instrument *with intent to defraud*' (see *R v Parkes and Brown* (1797) 2 Leach 775, 785); and ever since that time it has been held that the very essence of forgery is an *intent to defraud*, and it must be laid in the indictment (see East, Pleas of the Crown (1803), vol. 2, p. 988; Chitty, Criminal Law (1826), vol. 3, pp. 1039, 1042). I cannot help thinking that when Parliament in section 4(1) of the Act of 1913 used a phrase so hallowed by usage, it used it in the sense in which it had been used by generations of lawyers. It was never by them confined to the causing of economic loss. Let me prove this by taking some examples: Take the case where a man forges a reference as to character, intending to get employment by means of it. It is clear forgery: see *R v Sharman* (1854) 1 Dears CC 285; *R v Moah* (1858) 7 Cox CC 503, 504. But there may well be no economic loss intended. The man may intend, if he gets the job, to render full service in return for his wages. Or the post which he seeks may be unpaid, such as a justice of the peace. But he has the intent to defraud all the same.

Take next the case where a servant steals his master's money and afterwards forges a receipt or other document so as to cover up his defalcations. This, too, is forgery: see *R v Martin* (1836) 1

Mood CC 483. He does not intend to deprive his master of anything: for he has already done that. He may not even do it so as to keep his job, because he may be under notice. What he really intends to do is to cover up his tracks so that he should not be found out. But he has the intent to defraud none the less.

Then there are the cases concerned with the release of prisoners. If a man forges an order or letter to the sheriff or to the governor of a prison, intending thereby to secure the release of a prisoner, he is guilty of forgery at common law: see *Fawcett's* case (1793) 2 East PL 862 and *R* v *Harris* 1 Mood CC 393. There is no idea of economic loss here. He has no intent to deprive the gaoler of any money or valuable thing. But at common law he is held to have an intent to defraud. Mr Gardiner rather suggested that the reason for those decisions was that the documents were documents of a public nature. But I do not so read them. Even if they were public documents it was still essential that there should be an intent to defraud. Ever since *Ward's* case 2 LD Ryam 1461, 3 LD Ryam 358; 2 Str 787 in 1726 public and private documents were at common law on the same footing in this respect: see East's Pleas of the Crown, pp. 859–861. The forgery of any of them was a misdemeanour if done with intent to defraud, but not otherwise: see *R* v *Hodgson* Dedrs. B. 3, 8 by Jervis CJ.

There remains the case of *R* v *Toshack* 4 Cox CC 38, 41, which is to my mind decisive. Toshack, a seaman, forged a certificate of good conduct so as to be admitted to sit for an examination for his master's certificate. He had no intention to deprive the examiners or Trinity House of any money or valuable thing. The piece of paper, value one penny, was not mentioned in the counts on which he was convicted. But he was held guilty of forgery. Alderson B said: 'It does amount to a very serious offence if persons do forge certificates of this sort and are found to utter them for the purpose of deceiving the Trinity House.'

What is the common element in all these cases? It is, I think, best expressed in the definition given by East in his Pleas of the Crown, vol. 2, p. 852. He treats the subject, I think, better than any writer before or since:

> *To forge*, (a metaphorical expression borrowed from the occupation of the smith), means, properly speaking, no more than to *make* or *form*: but in our law it is always taken in an evil sense; and therefore Forgery at common law denotes a *false* making (which includes every alteration of or addition to a true instrument), a making malo animo, of any written instrument for the purpose of fraud and deceit. This definition results from all the authorities ancient and modern taken together.

That was written in 1803, but it has been always accepted as authoritative. It seems to me to provide the key to the cases decided since it was written, as well as those before. The important thing about this definition is that it is not limited to the idea of economic loss, nor to the idea of depriving someone of something of value. It extends generally to *the purpose of fraud and deceit*. Put shortly, 'with intent to defraud' means 'with intent to practise a fraud' on someone or other. It need not be anyone in particular. Someone in general will suffice....

At this point it becomes possible to point the contrast in the statute between an 'intent to deceive' and an 'intent to defraud.' 'To deceive' here conveys the element of deceit, which induces a state of mind, without the element of fraud, which induces a course of action or inaction. Take the case of a private document. For instance, where a man fabricates a letter so as to puff himself up in the opinion of others. Bramwell B put the instance: 'If I were to produce a letter purporting to be from the Duke of Wellington inviting me to dine, and say, "See what a respectable person I am"': *R* v *Moah*. There would then be an intent to deceive but it would not be punishable at common law or under the statute, because then it would not be done with intent to defraud. Take next the case of a public document. For instance, a parish register. If a man should falsify it so as to make himself appear to be descended of noble family, for the sake of his own glorification, he would not be guilty of an intent to defraud and would therefore not be punishable at common law (see *R* v *Hodgson*), but he would have an intent to deceive and he would be punishable under the present statute, as indeed he was under its predecessors, such as the Forgery Act 1861, s. 36.

So much for the principal point under discussion. Mr Gerald Gardiner did make a further point. He said that the intent must be to defraud the particular person to whom the document is first presented or his agent, and that it was insufficient if he intended to defraud somebody else. This is not correct. It has long been ruled that it is no answer to a charge of forgery to say that there was no intent to defraud any particular person, because a general intent to defraud is sufficient to constitute the crime. So also it is no answer to say that there was no intent to defraud the recipient, if there was intent to defraud somebody else: see *R* v *Taylor* (1779) 1 Leach 214.

■ NOTES AND QUESTIONS

1. *Welham* was not a case concerning conspiracy to defraud but the court seemed to accept that similar principles were applicable.

2. Note that in the third category of conspiracy to defraud, the possibility or actuality of economic loss is irrelevant. Why should this be so?

3. The 1987 statute could be viewed as a stopgap measure permitting prosecutions of those who conspired to fraud. Now that the Fraud Act 2006 has been enacted, has s. 12 of the CJA 1987 become otiose?

(d) Mens rea

For conspiracy to defraud, the prosecution must prove dishonesty according to the test set out in *Ghosh*, p. 380. Although *Ghosh* dealt with the *mens rea* of theft, the test of dishonesty which it established has been applied in other contexts, including fraud. The test has two prongs:

(i) was the defendant dishonest as judged by the standards of reasonable and honest people; and

(ii) did the defendant realise that his acts were dishonest under that standard?

Can a defendant have the requisite intent for conspiracy to defraud where there is no intent to cause economic loss? This issue was addressed by the Privy Council in *Wai Yu-tsang* v *R*.

Wai Yu-tsang v R
[1991] 4 All ER 664, Privy Council

LORD GOFF OF CHIEVELEY: . . . The appellant was the chief accountant of the Hang Lung Bank (the bank). He was charged that, between 7 September and 13 November 1982, he conspired together with Cheng Eng-kuan, Lee Hoi-kwong and others to defraud the bank and its existing and potential shareholders, creditors and depositors, by dishonestly concealing in the accounts of the bank the dishonouring of US dollar cheques in the sum of $US124m, drawn on the account of Overseas Maritime Co. Ltd SA with Citibank International, Chicago, such cheques having been purchased by the bank. Of the other members of the alleged conspiracy, Cheng was the managing director of the bank and Lee was the general manager. Cheng fled the jurisdiction, as did another associate of his, John Mao. Lee originally stood trial with the appellant but, following preliminary argument on the admissibility of certain evidence, the Crown abandoned its case against him. In the result, the appellant stood trial alone.

The events giving rise to the charge against the appellant were as follows. For some years a cheque-kiting cycle, known as the Capri cycle, had been run by John Mao, using a number of companies as its principal vehicle. In May 1982, in order to bring the Capri cycle to an end, a new cheque-kiting cycle (known as the OMC cycle) was set up to create funds for Overseas Maritime Co. Ltd SA (OMC). The object was to transfer the funds into the Capri cycle so that the final cheques in circulation in that cycle could be met. The bank purchased cheques in US currency via a company called Southseas Finance Co. Ltd (SSF). The cheques, drawn on the OMC account, were purchased by the bank from SSF. The proceeds were credited to the account of SSF with the bank, and the cheques were cleared through the bank's foreign exchange with Chemical Bank. Those purchases required the approval of Cheng as the managing director of the bank. However, on 7 September 1982 a rumour started by a taxi-driver caused a run on the bank, and in consequence Cheng gave instructions that no further US dollar cheques or drafts were to be purchased. This had the effect that the second cheque-kiting cycle was brought to a premature end, and that cheques then in circulation could not be met. On 14 September Chemical Bank advised the bank that two or three of the OMC cheques had been returned, and on 18 September another seven. The total face value of those cheques (which had been purchased by the bank from SSF) was $US124m (the equivalent of $HK755m), an amount which exceeded the assets of the bank at that time.

There was no suggestion that the appellant was in any way involved in either of the two cheque-kiting cycles. It was however alleged that he conspired with Cheng and others to defraud the bank and its existing and potential shareholders, creditors and depositors, by dishonestly concealing in the bank's accounts the dishonouring of the US dollar cheques in the sum of $US124m which had been purchased by the bank. During the run on the bank, it had been supported by the Standard Chartered Bank, to which the appellant was under a duty to report, as he was to the Commissioner of Banking. He did not however report the dishonour of the cheques, nor did he cause the dishonour to be recorded in the bank's computerised ledgers. The details of the transactions were recorded only in private ledgers, called 'K' vouchers. Instead there were recorded in the bank's accounts entries purporting to show that the bank had drawn 16 US dollar drafts on Chemical Bank in amounts equivalent to the total amount of the dishonoured cheques, and had sold them to SSF, that short-term loans had been granted to two companies called Thring Trading Ltd (Thring) and Texas Finance Ltd (Texas), and that SSF had paid for the drafts with cheques drawn on its own account and on the accounts of Thring and Texas. The drafts were never presented for payment, although the accounts were debited with the amounts of the cheques. This gave the false picture of balances in the Chemical Bank account and in the SSF account which were approximately the same as they would have been if the dishonoured cheques had been recorded as debits in the SSF account and credits in the Chemical Bank account.

...

Before the Court of Appeal, a number of issues were raised by the appellant founded upon criticisms of the summing up of the learned judge. All of those criticisms were rejected by the Court of Appeal. Before their Lordships, however, the appellant's case was directed solely to the judge's direction on the mental element required for a conspiracy to defraud. The judge explained to the jury that the appellant must have been party to an agreement with one or more of the other named conspirators which had a common intention to defraud one or more of the persons or categories of persons named in the indictment. He explained that such an intention must involve dishonesty on the part of the conspirators, and continued as follows:

> It is fraud if it is proved that there was the dishonest taking of a risk which there was no right to take, which—to Mr Wai's knowledge at least—would cause detriment or prejudice to another, detriment or prejudice to the economic or proprietary rights of another. That detriment or prejudice to somebody else is very often incidental to the purpose of the fraudsman himself. The prime objective of fraudsmen is usually to gain some advantage for themselves, any detriment or prejudice to somebody else is often secondary to that objective but nonetheless is a contemplated or predictable outcome of what they do. If the interests of some other person—the economic or proprietary interests of some other person are imperilled, that is sufficient to constitute fraud even though no loss is actually suffered and even though the fraudsman himself did not desire to bring about any loss.

It is plain that that direction was founded upon the judgment of the Court of Appeal in *R v Allsop* (1976) 64 Cr App R 29. It was the contention of the appellant that the direction was erroneous in so far as it stated that, for this purpose, the imperilling of an economic interest or the threat of financial prejudice was sufficient to establish fraud, whatever the motive of the accused may have been; and that in so far as *Allsop's* case so decided, it was wrong and should not be followed.

[In *Scott v Metropolitan Police Commissioner* [1975] AC 819, Lord Diplock said:]

... (2) Where the intended victim of a 'conspiracy to defraud' is a private individual the purpose of the conspirators must be to cause the victim economic loss by depriving him of some property or right, corporeal or incorporeal, to which he is or would or might become entitled ... (3) Where the intended victim of a 'conspiracy to defraud' is a person performing public duties as distinct from a private individual it is sufficient if the purpose is to cause him to act contrary to his public duty …

With the greatest respect to Lord Diplock, their Lordships consider this categorisation to be too narrow. In their opinion, in agreement with the approach of Lord Radcliffe in *Welham's* case, the cases concerned with persons performing public duties are not to be regarded as a special category in the manner described by Lord Diplock, but rather as exemplifying the general principle that conspiracies to defraud are not restricted to cases of intention to cause the victim economic loss. On the contrary, they are to be understood in the broad sense described by Lord Radcliffe and Lord Denning in *Welham's* case—the view which Viscount Dilhorne favoured in *Scott's* case, as apparently did the other members of the Appellate Committee who agreed with him in that case (apart, it seems, from Lord Diplock).

… The question whether particular facts reveal a conspiracy to defraud depends upon what the conspirators have dishonestly agreed to do, and in particular whether they have agreed to practise a fraud on somebody. For this purpose it is enough for example that, as in R v *Allsop* and in the present case, the conspirators have dishonestly agreed to bring about a state of affairs which they realise will or may deceive the victim into so acting, or failing to act, that he will suffer economic loss or his economic interests will be put at risk. It is however important in such a case, as the Court of Appeal stressed in *Allsop's* case, to distinguish a conspirator's intention (or immediate purpose) dishonestly to bring about such a state of affairs from his motive (or underlying purpose). The latter may be benign to the extent that he does not wish the victim or potential victim to suffer harm; but the mere fact that it is benign will not of itself prevent the agreement from constituting a conspiracy to defraud. Of course, if the conspirators were not acting dishonestly, there will have been no conspiracy to defraud; and in any event their benign purpose (if it be such) is a matter which, if they prove to be guilty, can be taken into account at the stage of sentence.

■ NOTES AND QUESTIONS

1. What was the defendant's motive in *Wai Yu-tsang* v *R*? Is motive relevant? Does its relevance depend on which category of conspiracy to defraud is at issue? Or does the Privy Council reject the idea of categories completely?

2. If no intention to cause economic loss is required in the case of deceit of private persons, is it a crime to pretend to be of noble descent (see Lord Denning in *Welham*)? To pretend to be wealthy when one is poor or vice versa?

3. If a victim suffers no economic loss, there is no substantive crime. Should it follow that there is no liability for conspiracy?

(ii) Conspiracy to corrupt public morals or outrage public decency

Section 5(3) of the Criminal Law Act 1977, specifically preserved the common law offence of conspiracy to corrupt public morals or outrage public decency.

CRIMINAL LAW ACT 1977

5.—(1) Subject to the following provisions of this section, the offence of conspiracy at common law is hereby abolished.

(2) …

(3) Subsection (1) above shall not affect the offence of conspiracy at common law if and in so far as it may be committed by entering into an agreement to engage in conduct which—

(a) tends to corrupt public morals or outrages public decency; but

(b) would not amount to or involve the commission of an offence if carried out by a single person otherwise than in pursuance of an agreement.

Knuller v Director of Public Prosecutions

[1973] AC 435, House of Lords

The appellants were directors of a company which published a fortnightly magazine. On an inside page under a column headed 'Males' advertisements were inserted inviting readers to meet the advertisers for the purpose of homosexual practices. The appellants were convicted on counts of conspiracy to corrupt public morals and conspiracy to outrage public decency.

LORD SIMON OF GLAISDALE:...In my view, counsel for the appellants was right to concede that there is a common law offence of conspiring to outrage public decency.

(3) As for whether such an offence is applicable to books and newspapers, the argument based on section 2(4) of the Obscene Publications Act 1959 is concluded against the appellants by the construction put upon that subsection in *Shaw* v *Director of Public Prosecutions* [1962] AC 220. The passage I have cited from *Mirehouse* v *Rennell* (1833) 1 Cl & F 527, 546 indicates that the fact that the authorities show no example of the application of the rule of law in circumstances such as the instant does not mean that it is not applicable, provided that there are circumstances, however novel, which fall fairly within the rule. Counsel for the appellants could not suggest any demarcation in principle. To attempt delimitation would produce absurd anomalies. The newspaper placard would presumably fall within the offence: it would be odd if similar material on the exposed front page of the newspaper did not do so. A picture fly-posted in a small village would fall within the offence; but, on the argument for the appellants, not the same picture contained in a newspaper or book of mass circulation. Safeguards are to be found in the requirement of publicity for the offence to be established, and in the parliamentary undertaking to which my noble and learned friend, Lord Reid, has referred—this must be taken to apply to conspiracy to outrage public decency as much as to conspiracy to corrupt public morals.

(4) I turn, then, to the requirement of publicity. *R* v *Mayling* [1963] 2 QB 717 shows that the substantive offence (and therefore the conduct the subject of the conspiracy) must be committed in public, in the sense that the circumstances must be such that the alleged outrageously indecent matter could have been seen by more than one person, even though in fact no more than one did see it. If it is capable of being seen by one person only, no offence is committed.

It was at one time argued for the appellants that the matter must have been visible to two or more people simultaneously; and that an article in a newspaper did not fulfil this requirement. But this point was rightly abandoned, and I need not examine it further.

...

It was argued for the Crown that it was immaterial whether or not the alleged outrage to decency took place in public, provided that the sense of decency of the public or a substantial section of the public was outraged. But this seems to me to be contrary to many of the authorities which the Crown itself relied on to establish the generic offence. The authorities establish that the word 'public' has a different connotation in the respective offences of conspiracy to corrupt public morals and conduct calculated to, or conspiracy to, outrage public decency. In the first it refers to certain fundamental rules regarded as essential social control which yet lack the force of law: when applicable to individuals, in other words, 'public' refers to persons in society. In the latter offences, however, 'public' refers to the place in which the offence is committed. This is borne out by the way the rule was framed by my noble and learned friend, Lord Reid, in *Shaw* v *Director of Public Prosecutions* [1962] AC 220 in the passage which I have just cited. It is also borne out by what is presumably the purpose of the legal rule—namely, that reasonable people may venture out in public without the risk of outrage to certain minimum accepted standards of decency.

On the other hand, I do not think that it would necessarily negative the offence that the act or exhibit is superficially hid from view, if the public is expressly or impliedly invited to penetrate the cover. Thus, the public touting for an outrageously indecent exhibition in private would not escape: see *R* v *Saunders* (1875) 1 QBD 15. Another obvious example is an outrageously indecent exhibit with a cover entitled 'Lift in order to see....' This sort of instance could be applied to a book or newspaper; and I think that a jury should be invited to consider the matter in this way. The conduct must at least in some way be so projected as to have an impact in public: cf. *Smith* v *Hughes* [1960] 1 WLR 830.

(5) There are other features of the offence which should, in my view, be brought to the notice of the jury. It should be emphasised that 'outrage,' like 'corrupt,' is a very strong word. 'Outraging public decency' goes considerably beyond offending the susceptibilities of, or even shocking, reasonable people. Moreover the offence is, in my view, concerned with recognised minimum standards of decency, which are likely to vary from time to time. Finally, notwithstanding that 'public' in the offence is used in a locative sense, public decency must be viewed as a whole; and I think the jury should be invited, where appropriate, to remember that they live in a plural society, with a tradition of tolerance towards minorities, and that this atmosphere of toleration is itself part of public decency.

(6) The Court of Appeal said of the direction on count 2 that it might be that it was not wholly satisfactory. I would myself go further. I regard it as essential that the jury should be carefully directed, on the lines that I have ventured to suggest, on the proper approach to the meaning of 'decency' and 'outrage' and the element of publicity required to constitute the offence. The summing up was generally a careful and fair one, but I think it was defective in these regards; and I therefore do not think it would be safe to allow the conviction on count 2 to stand.

■ NOTES AND QUESTIONS

1. Is it possible to know from a reading of the cases what types of behaviour will be caught by these common law offences? If not, how can those who desire to be law-abiding citizens regulate their conduct to avoid prosecution?

2. In *Knuller* the House of Lords stated that the courts had no residual discretion to create new criminal offences. Does this signal an awareness of the potential abuses inherent in common law conspiracies? Common law crimes generally?

3. The Criminal Law Act 1977, s. 5(3), stipulates that a charge of conspiracy will lie only where there would be an offence if carried out by a single person. While *R* v *Gibson* [1991] 1 All ER 439 confirmed the existence of a substantive offence of *outraging public decency*, it remains unclear whether there is behaviour which would not amount to the substantive offence if committed by an individual acting alone, but would constitute conspiracy if done by several.

4. It is also not clear if there is a substantive offence of corrupting public morals. The House of Lords did not determine the issue in *Shaw* v *DPP* [1962] AC 220 although the Court of Appeal held that there was such a substantive offence.

5. The Law Commission has recommended the abolition of the common law conspiracies to corrupt public morals or outrage public decency, but neither the courts nor Parliament seem inclined to do so. Might the answer lie in the observation in *Shaw* that it is valuable for the law to have a means of protecting society against those who devise novel and harmful, even if not necessarily criminal schemes.

If a common law conspiracy, impossibility remains a possible defence.

Director of Public Prosecutions v Nock

[1978] AC 979, House of Lords

LORD RUSSELL OF KILLOWEN: My Lords, I have had the advantage of reading in draft the speech in these consolidated appeals of my noble and learned friend, Lord Scarman. I agree with his conclusion that these appeals should be allowed and with the reasons to which he attributes that conclusion.

The important point to note is that the agreement that is said to have been an unlawful conspiracy was not an agreement in general terms to produce cocaine, but an agreement in specific terms to produce cocaine from a particular powder which in fact, however treated, would never yield cocaine. In order to see whether there is a criminal conspiracy it is necessary to consider the whole agreement. The specific limits of the agreement cannot be discarded, leaving a general agreement to produce cocaine, for that would be to find an agreement other than that which was made: and that is not a permissible approach to any agreement, conspiracy or other.

It is, I apprehend, clear on authority that neither appellant, discovered in the act of vainly and optimistically applying sulphuric acid (or any other treatment) to this particular powder, would be guilty of an attempt to produce cocaine. It would appear to me strange that the two should be guilty of a crime if together they bent over the same test tube, having agreed on the joint vain attempt. These appellants thought that they would succeed in their endeavour. But what if they had doubted success, and their agreement had been to 'try it'? That would be an agreement to attempt, and since the attempt would not be unlawful the agreement could not be a criminal conspiracy. But if the conclusion against which these appeals are made were correct, it would mean that those erroneously confident of success would be guilty of the crime of conspiracy, but not those who, unconvinced, agreed to try. The gullible would be guilty, the suspicious stainless. That could not be right.

■ NOTES AND QUESTIONS

1. Does the decision in *Nock* turn on principle or the particular facts of the case?

2. Given the clear trend to eliminate impossibility as a defence to inchoate crimes, is there any justification for treating common law conspiracies differently?

SECTION 3: ATTEMPT

The difference between the person who tries to commit a crime and fails and his counterpart who is more successful may be nothing more than a gun which misfires, a victim who ducks, or poor aim. From a criminological perspective, both offenders may be equally dangerous and equally in need of rehabilitation and restraint. Therein lies the rationale behind a crime of attempt.

Attempting to commit a crime is now a statutory offence defined by the Criminal Attempts Act 1981. The basic definition is contained in s. 1:

CRIMINAL ATTEMPTS ACT 1981

1.—(1) If, with intent to commit an offence to which this section applies, a person does an act which is more than merely preparatory to the commission of the offence, he is guilty of attempting to commit the offence.

(2) A person may be guilty of attempting to commit an offence to which this section applies even though the facts are such that the commission of the offence is impossible.

(3) In any case where—

(a) apart from this subsection a person's intention would not be regarded as having amounted to an intent to commit an offence; but

(b) if the facts of the case had been as he believed them to be, his intention would be so regarded, then, for the purposes of subsection (1) above, he shall be regarded as having had an intent to commit that offence.

(4) This section applies to any offence which, if it were completed, would be triable in England and Wales as an indictable offence, other than—

(a) conspiracy (at common law or under section 1 of the Criminal Law Act 1977 or any other enactment);

(b) aiding, abetting, counselling, procuring or suborning the commission of an offence;

(c) offences under section 4(1) (assisting offenders) or 5(1) (accepting or agreeing to accept consideration for not disclosing information about an arrestable offence) of the Criminal Law Act 1967.

■ NOTES AND QUESTIONS

1. Look carefully at the language of s. 1 of the Criminal Attempts Act 1981. Can there be an offence of attempting to commit a summary offence? An offence of attempting to commit an offence by failing to act? A crime of attempted voluntary manslaughter?

2. It may be useful to distinguish between 'complete' attempts (where the defendant has done everything she intended but has not achieved her criminal objective) and 'incomplete' attempts (where the defendant is apprehended while there is still more to be done). Should the two types of attempt be treated differently by the courts? Why? There is a third category of 'impossible' attempts, which will be examined subsequently.

3. Under s. 1(4)(b) of the Act it is no longer an offence to attempt to aid and abet the commission of an offence. However, in some instances aiding and abetting is, by statute, itself an offence. Where this is so, there can be a conviction for attempting to commit the statutory crime. An example might be assisting suicide contrary to the Suicide Act 1961, s. 2(1).

A: Mens rea

For an attempt, it must be proved that the defendant intended to commit the offence, whether or not intention is the *mens rea* for the completed offence.

R v Whybrow
(1951) 35 Cr App R 141, Court of Appeal

LORD GODDARD: . . . The facts of the case, so far as it is necessary to state them, are these: the appellant was living on bad terms with his wife and it was shown that at the time he, a married man with a family, was carrying on a liaison with another young woman. That, of course, was put forward as the motive, and, indeed, it is the oldest motive in the world that is brought up in cases of murder or attempted murder of a wife. It was proved to exist and a letter was produced from the appellant to that young woman's father which could leave no doubt in anybody's mind that the appellant's affections had been transferred to that young woman.

The appellant had had some, but no very great, experience of electrical installations. He had been a labourer in the employ of the electrical department of the Southend Corporation Electricity Works and had no doubt, on occassions, gone round with electricians. He also had had a wireless apparatus and so forth in this house and probably had what may be described as an amateur's knowledge of electricity. On the night of the alleged crime the wife was taking a bath and the appellant was in an adjoining room. He said that he was in the lavatory, but he might equally well have been in the bedroom. The wife was heard to call out, and she complained of having received an electric shock while in the bath. The next day it came to light that an apparatus had been connected with the soap dish, the bath being a porcelain bath and either the soap dish itself or its support being made of metal. An apparatus was found connected with this soap dish which, if prepared intentionally, showed a deliberate, cold-blooded resolve to administer a shock of 230 volts of electricity to a woman in her bath. It is common knowledge, and the appellant admitted that he knew it, that to administer an electric shock to a person in a bath is the most dangerous thing that can be done in that way.

The case lasted two days and the learned Judge's summing-up, so far as the facts were concerned, was meticulouly careful and meticulously accurate, but unfortunately he did, in charging the jury, confuse in his mind for a moment the direction given to a jury in a case of murder with the direction given to a jury in a case of attempted murder. In murder the jury is told—and it has always been the law—that if a person wounds another or attacks another either intending to kill or intending to do grievous bodily harm, and the person attacked dies, that is murder, the reason being that the requisite malice aforethought, which is a term of art, is satisfied if the attacker intends to do grievous bodily harm.... But, if the charge is one of attempted murder, the intent becomes the principal ingredient of the crime. It may be said that the law, which is not always logical, is somewhat illogical in saying that, if one attacks a person intending to do grievous bodily harm and death results, that is murder, but that if one attacks a person and only intends to do grievous bodily harm, and death does not result, it is not attempted murder, but wounding with intent to do grievous bodily harm. It is not really illogical because, in that particular case, the intent is the essence of the crime while, where the death of another is caused, the necessity is to prove malice aforethought, which is supplied in law by proving intent to do grievous bodily harm.

R v O'Toole

[1987] Crim LR 759, Court of Appeal

On July 31, 1986 the appellant who was a regular customer of a public house in North London was 'barred' from that public house. At closing time, the appellant returned with a can of petrol and splashed it around a vestibule at the entrance of the public house. When he was taxed by the barmaid, he stated that he did not care whether she be burned alive. He had earlier been heard to say that he would smash the public house. When arrested, he told the police that if he did not smash the public house up that night he would do it the following night. In interview he said 'I'll burn the lot of them and you (the police) as well.' The defence case was that the applicant was drunk. He had the can of petrol with him because he was filling the petrol reservoir of his motor car. Whilst doing so he had heard a noise from the public house. He decided to speak with the landlord. Whilst trying to look through a window, he had accidentally spilled petrol into the vestibule.

The appellant was charged with two counts, the first alleging that he attempted to damage by fire the public house intending to damage the same or being reckless as to whether it would be damaged and intending to endanger the life of the barmaid. Count 2 alleged as follows:

> On 31st day of July 1986 without lawful excuse attempted to damage by fire the Star Public House, Charlbert Street NW8 belonging to another, intending to damage the said property or being reckless as to whether property would be damaged and being reckless as to whether the life of [the barmaid] would thereby be endangered.

The defendant was convicted by the jury of count 2. In summing up the case to the jury, the learned trial judge defined 'attempt' and 'intent' and 'reckless' in relation to the question of damaging property. The jury having retired to consider their verdicts, sent a note in which they said that they were unanimous in their decision that the defendant was 'not guilty of intent (on both counts)' and asking how significant was 'being reckless.'

The learned trial judge directed them that their note seemed to have disposed of count 1. In relation to count 2 he defined 'attempt' yet again saying that if they were not sure that the appellant intended to damage by fire at all then they should acquit. However he went on to say that if they were satisfied that he attempted to damage, then they must go on to consider whether he intended to damage the property or was reckless as to whether it be damaged by fire.

The Court of Appeal in allowing the appeal and quashing the conviction held that intent is an element inherent in the definition of attempt and is the same at least if not greater than the intent necessary to constitute the full offence. The learned trial judge was in error in relating back to the question of recklessness and intent to damage. There was no room for a reckless damage to property when the offence itself is an attempt because the attempt must have the necessary intent.

It was further held that the difficulty in this case arose from the Indictment. When the offence is an attempt under section 1(1) of the Criminal Attempts Act 1981 it is unnecessary and wrong to include the words 'or being reckless as to whether property would be damaged.' When the substantive offence is charged as opposed to an attempt, the words used are correct. It is only when an attempt to damage property is charged that the words 'being reckless as to whether such property would be damaged' are otiose and wrong.

■ NOTES AND QUESTIONS

1. The requirement that the defendant must intend to commit the offence attempted implicitly requires that the defendant must also have any intent required for the underlying offence. For example, if charged with attempted theft it must be proved that the defendant intended permanently to deprive the victim of her property.

2. The requirement that the defendant must intend to commit the offence also means that if the offence is defined in terms of result (e.g., murder), it must be proved that the defendant intended to bring about the proscribed result. An intent to inflict GBH may be insufficient, even if sufficient for the completed offence. What if, however, the defendant does not desire the result but knows that it is virtually certain to follow from his acts? As we have seen previously (*R v Woollin*, 131) such knowledge may satisfy the *mens rea* for murder; but should it satisfy the *mens rea* for attempted murder?

R v Walker and Hayles
(1990) 90 Cr App R 226, Court of Appeal

LLOYD LJ: On September 9, 1988, these two appellants, Walker and Hayles, were convicted of attempted murder at the Central Criminal Court before the recorder and a jury. They were sentenced to seven years' and five years' imprisonment respectively.

They now appeal against their convictions. The facts were that Walker's sister, Christine, was having an affair with a man called Royston John, the victim. A week or so before September 20, 1987, there had been a violent quarrel between Christine and John. Christine received two black eyes and a torn fingernail.

On the evening in question (September 20), the two appellants visited Christine's flat. The appellant Hayles was living with another of Walker's sisters. Christine's flat was on the third floor of a block of flats in Battersea Park Road. Royston John was there. He had a key to Christine's flat. He was asked to hand over the key to Christine. He refused. There was then a fight. John ran out onto the balcony, which lead towards the central staircase. The appellants followed him.

According to the prosecution case, the appellants caught him up, lifted him over the balcony, and dropped him horizontally to the ground. Somehow or the other he survived, perhaps because he landed on some grass. In the course of the fight the appellants had banged the victim's head against the wall, saying that they were going to kill him. There were bloodstains found on the wall. One of the appellants produced a knife and threatened the victim's throat. Just before they threw the victim over the balcony, he said: 'You deserve to die. I am going to kill you. We don't like you.'

...

We turn to the main ground of appeal, namely the direction on intention. Since the charge was attempted murder, the prosecution had to prove an intention to kill. Intention to cause really serious harm would not have been enough. We were told that this is the first case in which this Court has had to consider the correct direction in a case of attempted murder since *R v Moloney* (1985) 81 Cr App R 93, *R v Hancock and Shankland* (1986) 82 Cr App R 264 and *R v Nedrick* (1986) 83 Cr App R 267.

We have already said that there could be no criticism of the initial direction at the start of the summing-up, and repeated at the conclusion. The recorder was right to keep it short. 'Trying to kill' was the expression he used as a paraphrase. That was easy for the jury to understand, and could not on any view of the law be regarded as too favourable to the prosecution. 'Trying to kill' is synonymous with purpose. It has never been suggested that a man does not intend what he is trying to achieve. The difficulty only arises when he brings about a result which he is not trying to achieve.

But when the jury returned, the recorder, as we have seen, went further....

We can...understand why the recorder went further, since he had only just given a direction in simple terms, which was as clear as could be. Moreover the position is not quite the same in a case of attempted murder as it is in murder. In the great majority of murder cases, as the Court pointed out in *Nedrick* (*supra*), the defendant's desire goes hand in hand with his intention. If he desires serious harm, and death results from his action, he is guilty of murder. A simple direction suffices in such cases. The rare and exceptional case is where the defendant does not desire serious harm, or indeed any harm at all. But where a defendant is charged with attempted murder, he may well have desired serious harm, without desiring death. So the desire of serious harm does not provide the answer. It does not go hand in hand with the relevant intention, as it does in the great majority of murder cases, since in attempted murder the relevant intention must be an intention to kill.

Considerations such as these may have led the recorder to give the expanded direction in terms of foresight. But, as we have said, it would have been better if he had not done so. The mere fact that a jury calls for a further direction on intention does not of itself make it a rare and exceptional case requiring a foresight direction. In most cases they will only need to be reminded of the simple direction which they will already have been given, namely that the relevant intention is an intention to kill, and that nothing less will suffice.

[The recorder] may have confused the jury. He may have led them to equate the probability of death and the foresight of death with an intention to kill. That was the very error exposed in *R* v *Moloney* (*supra*) and *Nedrick* (1986) 83 Cr App R 267.

[But it] is important to note that the recorder said that the jury would be *entitled* to draw the inference: he was not saying that they must draw the inference. By the use of the word 'entitled,' he was making it sufficiently clear to the jury that the question whether they drew the inference or not was a question for them. This is borne out by the passage which immediately followed in which the recorder said that the jury would be entitled to bear in mind the speed of events on the one hand and the speed at which a man can make up his mind on the other.

So we reject the submission that the recorder was equating foresight with intent, or that he may have given that impression to the jury. He was perfectly properly saying that foresight was something from which the jury could infer intent. He was treating the question as part of the law of evidence, not as part of the substantive law of attempted murder.

Where a lesser *mens rea* is required in respect of the circumstances of the offence, is the lesser *mens rea* sufficient for an offence of attempt?

R v Khan

[1990] 2 All ER 783, Court of Appeal

RUSSELL LJ: These appeals raise the short but important point of whether the offence of attempted rape is committed when the defendant is reckless as to the woman's consent to sexual intercourse. The appellants submit that no such offence is known to the law.

Before examining the submissions, we deal briefly with the facts. On 24 June 1987 at the Central Criminal Court before his Honour Judge Rant QC and a jury the appellants Mohammed Iqbal Khan, Mahesh Dhokia, Jaswinder Singh Banga and Navaid Faiz were convicted of the attempted rape of a 16-year-old girl. The case for the Crown was that on 19 March 1986 the girl met and danced with the appellant Dhokia at a daytime discotheque in Uxbridge. Thereafter she accompanied Dhokia and four other youths in a motor car which was driven to an address in Waltham Road, Uxbridge, where the occupants of the car, who included Faiz and Khan as well as Dhokia, were joined by others, including Banga.

Inside the house Dhokia, without success, attempted to have sexual intercourse with the girl. He was followed by others. Three youths succeeded in having sexual intercourse; three others, the remaining appellants, attempted to have sexual intercourse but failed. The girl did not consent to any sexual activity in the house. After her ordeal, she left and travelled to a friend's house, where she made a complaint.

The judge dealt with the offence of rape as follows:

... [W]e have had regard to the observations of Mustill LJ giving the judgment of the Court of Appeal, Criminal Division in *R v Millard and Vernon* [1987] Crim LR 393. That was a case involving a charge of attempting to damage property the particulars of offence reading:

> Gary Mann Millard and Michael Elliot Vernon, on 11th May 1985, without lawful excuse, attempted to damage a wooden wall at the Leeds Road Football Stand belonging to Huddersfield Town Association Football Club, intending to damage the said wall or being reckless as to whether the said wall would be damaged.

Mustill LJ said (and we read from the transcript):

> The appellants' case is simple. They submit that in ordinary speech the essence of an attempt is a desire to bring about a particular result, coupled with steps towards that end. The essence of recklessness is either indifference to a known risk or (in some circumstances) failure to advert to an obvious risk. The two states of mind cannot co-exist. Section 1(1) of the Criminal Attempts Act 1981 expressly demands that a person shall have an intent to commit an offence if he is to be guilty of an attempt to commit that offence. The word 'intent' may, it is true, have a special-ised meaning in some contexts. But even if this can properly be attributed to the word where it is used in s. 1(1) there is no warrant for reading it as embracing recklessness, nor for reading into it whatever lesser degree of *mens rea* will suffice for the particular substantive offence in question. For an attempt nothing but conscious volition will do. Accordingly, that part of the particulars of offence which referred to recklessness was meaningless, and the parts of the direction which involved a definition of recklessness, and an implied invitation to convict if the jury found the appellants to have acted recklessly, were misleading. There was thus, so it was contended, a risk that the jury convicted on the wrong basis and the verdict cannot safely be allowed to stand. At the conclusion of the argument it appeared to us that this argument was logically sound and that it was borne out by the authorities cited to us, especially *R v Whybrow* (1951) 35 Cr App R 141, *Cunliffe v Goodman* [1950] 1 All ER 720 at 724 and *R v Mohan* [1975] 2 All ER 193, and that it was not inconsistent with anything in *Hyam v DPP* [1974] 2 All ER 41. Our attention had, however, been drawn to a difference of opinion between commentators about the relationship between the *mens rea* in an attempt and the ingredients of the substantive offence, and we therefore reserved judgment so as to consider whether the question was not perhaps more difficult than it seemed. In the event we have come to the conclusion that there does exist a problem in this field, and that it is by no means easy to solve, but also that it need not be solved for the purpose of deciding the present appeal. In our judgment two different situations must be distinguished. The first exists where the substantive offence consists simply of the act which constitutes the actus reus (which for present purposes we shall call the 'result') coupled with some element of volition, which may or may not amount to a full intent. Here the only question is whether the 'intent' to bring about the result called for by s. 1(1) is to be watered down to such a degree, if any, as to make it correspond with the mens rea of the substantive offence. The second situation is more complicated. It exists where the substantive offence does not consist of one result and one mens rea, but rather involves not only the underlying intention to produce the result, but another state of mind directed to some circumstance or act which the prosecution must also establish in addition to providing the result. The problem may be illustrated by reference to the offence of attempted rape. As regards the substantive offence the 'result' takes the shape of sexual intercourse with a woman. But the offence is not established without proof of an additional circumstance (namely that the woman did not con-sent), and a state of mind relative to that circumstance (namely that the defendant knew she did not consent, or was reckless as to whether she consented). When one turns to the offence of attempted rape, one thing is obvious, that the result, namely the act of sexual intercourse,

must be intended in the full sense. Also obvious is the fact that proof of an intention to have intercourse with a woman, together with an act towards that end, is not enough: the offence must involve proof of something about the woman's consent, and something about the defendant's state of mind in relation to that consent. The problem is to decide precisely what that something is. Must the prosecution prove not only that the defendant intended the act, but also that he intended it to be non-consensual? Or should the jury be directed to consider two different states of mind, intent as to the act and recklessness as to the circumstances? Here the commentators differ: contrast Smith and Hogan *Criminal Law* (5th edn, 1983) p 255 ff with a note on the Act by Professor Griew in *Current Law Statutes 1981*.

We must now grapple with the very problem that Mustill LJ identifies in the last paragraph of the passage cited.

In our judgment an acceptable analysis of the offence of rape is as follows: (1) the intention of the offender is to have sexual intercourse with a woman; (2) the offence is committed if, but only if, the circumstances are that (a) the woman does not consent *and* (b) the defendant knows that she is not consenting or is reckless as to whether she consents.

Precisely the same analysis can be made of the offence of attempted rape: (1) the intention of the offender is to have sexual intercourse with a woman; (2) the offence is committed if, but only if, the circumstances are that (a) the woman does not consent *and* (b) the defendant knows that she is not consenting or is reckless as to whether she consents.

The only difference between the two offences is that in rape sexual intercourse takes place whereas in attempted rape it does not, although there has to be some act which is more than preparatory to sexual intercourse. Considered in that way, the intent of the defendant is precisely the same in rape and in attempted rape and the *mens rea* is identical, namely an intention to have intercourse plus a knowledge of or recklessness as to the woman's absence of consent. No question of attempting to achieve a reckless state of mind arises; the attempt relates to the physical activity; the mental state of the defendant is the same. A man does not recklessly have sexual intercourse, nor does he recklessly attempt it. Recklessness in rape and attempted rape arises not in relation to the physical act of the accused but only in his state of mind when engaged in the activity of having or attempting to have sexual intercourse.

If this is the true analysis, as we believe it is, the attempt does not require any different intention on the part of the accused from that for the full offence of rape. We believe this to be a desirable result which in the instant case did not require the jury to be burdened with different directions as to the accused's state of mind, dependent on whether the individual achieved or failed to achieve sexual intercourse.

We recognise, of course, that our reasoning cannot apply to all offences and all attempts. Where, for example as in causing death by reckless driving or reckless arson, no state of mind other than recklessness is involved in the offence, there can be no attempt to commit it.

In our judgment, however, the words 'with intent to commit an offence' to be found in s. 1 of the 1981 Act mean, when applied to rape, 'with intent to have sexual intercourse with a woman in circumstances where she does not consent and the defendant knows or could not care less about her absence of consent'. The only 'intent', giving that word its natural and ordinary meaning, of the rapist is to have sexual intercourse. He commits the offence because of the circumstances in which he manifests that intent, i.e. when the woman is not consenting and he either knows it or could not care less about the absence of consent.

Attorney-General's Reference (No. 3 of 1992)
[1994] 2 All ER 121, Court of Appeal

SCHIEMANN J: The court has heard a reference made under s. 36(1) of the Criminal Justice Act 1972. The point of law which has been referred to us was formulated as follows:

> Whether on a charge of attempted arson in the aggravated form contemplated by Section 1(2) of the Criminal Damage Act 1971, in addition to establishing a specific intent to cause damage by fire, it is sufficient to prove that the defendant was reckless as to whether life would thereby be endangered.

Summary of the relevant facts

The acquittals which have given rise to this reference had the following background according to the prosecution evidence. Following previous attacks upon their property the complainants maintained a night-time watch over their premises from a motor car (a Ford Granada). In the early hours of the morning the defendants came upon the scene in a vehicle. Inside this car (a Sierra) was a milk crate containing a number of petrol bombs, matches, a petrol can and some rags. As the Sierra approached the complainants (four inside their car and two persons on the pavement talking to them) a lighted petrol bomb was thrown towards them from the Sierra. The Crown's case was that it was thrown at the Granada and its occupants. The petrol bomb in fact passed over the top of the Granada and smashed against the garden wall of a house a pavement's width away from the car. The Sierra accelerated away but crashed, and the defendants were arrested.

At the trial count 1 of the indictment alleged attempted aggravated arson, specifying in the particulars of offence, inter alia, an intent to endanger life. Count 2 alleged attempted aggravated arson, specifying in the particulars of offence, inter alia, recklessness as to whether life would be endangered. At the conclusion of the Crown's case the learned judge ruled that there was no evidence upon which the jury could find the necessary intent to endanger life required in count 1, and accordingly directed the jury to return 'not guilty' verdicts in respect of that count. This reference is not concerned with that ruling, but with her directing an acquittal in relation to count 2. In essence her reasoning was that (1) there can be no conviction of an attempt to commit an offence unless the defendant intends to commit that offence; (2) the evidence could not support an allegation that the defendants intended by the destruction of the car to endanger the life of its occupants, or the bystanders; (3) it is impossible to intend to be reckless as to whether the life of another would be endangered by damage to property; and therefore (4) it is impossible in law to convict of an attempt to commit aggravated arson if all that can be proved is that the defendant intended to damage property being reckless as to whether the life of another would be endangered by such damage.

...

So far as the completed simple offence is concerned, the prosecution needs to prove (1) property belonging to another was damaged by the defendant and (2) the state of mind of the defendant was one of the following: (a) he intended to damage such property or (b) he was reckless as to whether any such property would be damaged.

In the case of the completed aggravated offence the prosecution needs to prove (1) the defendant in fact damaged property, whether belonging to himself or another; and (2) that the state of mind of the defendant was one of the following, (a) he intended to damage property, and intended by the damage to endanger the life of another or (b) he intended to damage property and was reckless as to whether the life of another would be thereby endangered or (c) he was reckless as to whether any property would be damaged and was reckless as to whether the life of another would be thereby endangered.

It is to be noted that the property referred to under (1) (to which we shall hereafter refer as 'the first-named property') is not necessarily the same property as that referred to in (2) (to which we shall refer as 'the second-named property'), although it normally will be. Thus a man who (1) owns a crane from which is suspended a heavy object and (2) cuts the rope (the first-named property) which holds the object with the result that (3) the object falls and hits the roof of a passing car (the second-named property) which roof (4) collapses killing the driver would be guilty if it could be shown that he damaged the rope, was reckless as to whether this would damage the car, and was reckless as to whether the life of the driver of the car would be endangered by the damage to the car.

All the foregoing is common ground. The problem which has given rise to this reference relates to an attempt to commit the aggravated offence in circumstances where the first-named property is the same as the second-named property—in the instant case a car. It amounts to this: whether, if the state of mind of the defendant was that postulated in (2)(b) above, namely that he intended to damage property and was reckless as to whether the life of another would thereby be endangered, and whilst in that state of mind he did an act which was more than merely preparatory to the offence, he is guilty of attempting to commit that offence.

...

We turn...to the attempt to commit the aggravated offence. In the present case, what was missing to prevent a conviction for the completed offence was damage to the property referred to in the opening lines of s. 1(2) of the 1981 Act...Such damage is essential for the completed offence. If a defendant does not intend to cause such damage he cannot intend to commit the completed offence. At worst he is reckless as to whether the offence is committed. The law of attempt is concerned with those who are intending to commit crimes. If that intent cannot be shown, then there can be no conviction.

However, the crime here consisted of doing certain acts in a certain state of mind in circumstances where the first-named property and the second-named property were the same, in short where the danger to life arose from the damage to the property which the defendant intended to damage. The substantive crime is committed if the defendant damaged property in a state of mind where he was reckless as to whether the life of another would thereby be endangered. We see no reason why there should not be a conviction for attempt if the prosecution can show that he, in that state of mind, intended to damage the property by throwing a bomb at it. One analysis of this situation is to say that although the defendant was in an appropriate state of mind to render him guilty of the completed offence the prosecution had not proved the physical element of the completed offence, and therefore he is not guilty of the completed offence. If, on a charge of attempting to commit the offence, the prosecution can show not only the state of mind required for the completed offence but also that the defendant intended to supply the missing physical element of the completed offence, that suffices for a conviction. That can not be done merely by the prosecution showing him to be reckless. The defendant must intend to damage property, but there is no need for a graver mental state than is required for the full offence.

The learned trial judge in the present case, however, went further than this and held that not merely must the defendant intend to supply all that was missing from the completed offence—namely damage to the first-named property—but also that recklessness as to the consequences of such damage for the lives of others was not enough to secure a conviction for attempt, although it was sufficient for the completed offence. She held that before a defendant could be convicted of attempting to commit the offence it had to be shown that he intended that the lives of others should be endangered by the damage which he intended.

She gave no policy reasons for so holding, and there is no case which bound her so to hold...

An attempt was made in argument to suggest that *R v Khan* was wrongly decided. No policy reasons were advanced for that view and we do not share it. The result is one which accords with common sense, and does no violence to the words of the statute.

What was missing in *R v Khan* was the act of sexual intercourse, without which the offence was not complete. What was missing in the present case was damage to the first-named property, without which the offence was not complete. The mental state of the defendant in each case contained everything which was required to render him guilty of the full offence. In order to succeed in a prosecution for attempt, it must be shown that the defendant intended to achieve that which was missing from the full offence. Unless that is shown the prosecution have not proved that the defendant intended to commit the offence. Thus in *R v Khan* the prosecution had to show an intention to have sexual intercourse, and the remaining state of mind required for the offence of rape. In the present case, the prosecution had to show an intention to damage the first-named property, and the remaining state of mind required for the offence of aggravated arson.

While the learned judge in the instant case opined that *R v Khan* was distinguishable she did not indicate any policy reasons for distinguishing it. We see none, and none have been submitted to us directly.

We now remind ourselves of the precise question posed by the reference:

> Whether on a charge of attempted arson in the aggravated form contemplated by Section 1(2) of the Criminal Damage Act 1971, in addition to establishing a specific intent to cause damage by fire, it is sufficient to prove that the defendant was reckless as to whether life would thereby be endangered.

We answer it in the affirmative. We add that, in circumstances where the first-named property is not the same as the second-named property, in addition to establishing a specific intent to cause damage by fire to the first-named property, it is sufficient to prove that the defendant was reckless as to whether any second-named property was damaged and reckless as to whether the life of another would be endangered by the damage to the second-named property.

■ NOTES AND QUESTIONS

1. Is the analogy to *Khan* made by the court in *A-G's Ref.* persuasive?

2. Is the allowance of proof of recklessness as to a circumstance of the crime consistent with the requirement of proof of intention as to the crime itself? After *R v G*, will *Cunningham* recklessness have to be proved in these situations?

3. If the defendant has a 'conditional intent', i.e., an intention to commit the offence only if certain circumstances exist, will the defendant be guilty of attempt if acts which are more than merely preparatory are committed but the conditions are then found not to exist? The Criminal Attempts Act 1981 specifically excludes the defence of impossibility. Accordingly, if a defendant were to be charged, for instance, with an attempt to steal a handbag and it was shown that he had an intention to steal the handbag *only* if it contained certain items, he could be convicted of attempt even if the handbag were empty. (See below, impossibility.)

B: Actus reus

The *actus reus* of attempt, as set out in the Criminal Attempts Act 1981, s. 1(1), consists of doing an act 'which is more than merely preparatory to the commission of the offence'. While a judge may decide that the threshold requirement of an act beyond mere preparation has not been met and direct the jury to acquit, in the converse case where a judge reaches the conclusion that the threshold requirement is met, the judge must leave it to the jury to decide whether the defendant's acts were more than merely preparatory.

CRIMINAL ATTEMPTS ACT 1981

4.—(3) Where, in proceedings against a person for an offence under section 1 above, there is evidence sufficient in law to support a finding that he did an act falling within subsection (1) of that section, the question whether or not his act fell within that subsection is a question of fact.

The line between 'mere preparation' and attempt is not always clear and in practice has proved difficult to draw.

R v Gullefer
[1987] Crim LR 195, Court of Appeal

The appellant was convicted of attempted theft. During a race at a greyhound racing stadium the appellant had climbed on to the track in front of the dogs and in an attempt to distract them had waved his arms. His efforts were only marginally successful and the stewards decided it was unnecessary to declare 'no race.' Had they done so the bookmakers would have had to repay the amount of his stake to any punter, but would not have been liable to pay any winnings to those punters who would have been successful had the race been valid. The appellant told the police he had attempted to stop the race because the dog on which he had staked £18 was losing. He had hoped for a 'no race' declaration and the recovery of his stake. The appellant's main ground of appeal was that the acts proved to have been carried out by the appellant were not 'sufficiently proximate to the completed offence of theft to be capable of comprising an attempt to commit theft.'

Held, allowing the appeal and quashing the conviction, the appellant was not guilty of attempted theft. The judge's task was to decide whether there was evidence on which a jury could reasonably conclude that the defendant had gone beyond mere preparation and had embarked on the actual commission of the offence. If not, the judge had to withdraw the case from the jury. If there was such evidence, it was then for the jury to decide whether the defendant did in fact go beyond mere preparation. That was how the judge had approached the case and he had ruled there was sufficient evidence. Counsel for the appellant submitted his ruling had been wrong. The Court's first task was to apply the words of the Criminal Attempts Act 1981, s. 1, to the facts. Was the appellant still in the stage of preparation to commit the substantive offence, or was there a basis of fact which would have entitled the jury to say that he had embarked on the theft itself? Might it properly be said that when he jumped onto the track he was trying to steal £18? In the view of the Court it could not be said that at that stage he was in the process of committing theft. What he was doing was jumping onto the track in an effort to distract the dogs, which in its turn, he hoped, would force the stewards to declare 'no race,' which would in its turn give him the opportunity to demand his £18 stake from the bookmaker. There was insufficient evidence that the appellant had, when he jumped on the track, gone beyond mere preparation.

R v Jones

[1990] 1 WLR 1057, Court of Appeal

TAYLOR LJ: . . . The appellant, a married man, started an affair with a woman named Lynn Gresley in 1985. She lived with him in Australia during 1986. In September 1987, back in England, she began a relationship with the victim, Michael Foreman. She continued, however, to see the appellant to whom she was still very attached. In November 1987 she decided to break off the relationship with the appellant, but he continued to write to her, begging her to come back to him.

On 12 January 1988 the appellant applied for a shotgun certificate, and three days later bought two guns in company with two companions. He bought two more guns a few days later on his own. On 23 January he shortened the barrel of one of them and test fired it twice the following day.

The appellant told a colleague at work that he would be away on Tuesday, 26 January. On 24 January he phoned Lynn Gresley in a distraught state. The next day he apologised, but she again refused his invitation to resume their relationship. The appellant then told his wife he had packed a bag as he was going to Spain to do some work on their chalet. On 26 January he left home dressed normally for work, saying he would telephone his wife as to whether he was leaving for Spain that evening.

That same morning, the victim, Michael Foreman, took his daughter to school by car as usual. After the child left the car, the appellant appeared, opened the door and jumped into the rear seat. He was wearing overalls, a crash helmet with the visor down, and was carrying a bag. He and the victim had never previously met. He introduced himself, said he wanted to sort things out and asked the victim to drive on. When they stopped on a grass verge, the appellant handed over a letter he had received from Lynn. Whilst the victim read it, the appellant took the sawn-off shotgun from the bag. It was loaded. He pointed it at the victim at a range of some 10 to 12 inches. He said, 'You are not going to like this' or similar words. The victim grabbed the end of the gun and pushed it sideways and upwards. There was a struggle during which the victim managed to throw the gun out of the window. As he tried to get out, he felt a cord over his head pulling him back. He managed to break free and run away, taking the gun with him. From a nearby garage he telephoned the police.

Meanwhile, the appellant drove off in the victim's car. He was arrested jogging away from it carrying his holdall. He said he had done nothing and only wanted to kill himself. His bag contained a hatchet, some cartridges and a length of cord. He also had a sharp kitchen knife which he threw away. In the appellant's car parked near the school was £1,500 sterling together with a quantity of French and Spanish money. The evidence showed that the safety catch of the shotgun had been in the on position. The victim was unclear as to whether the appellant's finger was ever on the trigger. When interviewed, the appellant declined to make any comment.

At the end of the prosecution case, after the above facts had been given in evidence, a submission was made to the judge that the charge of attempted murder should be withdrawn from the jury. It was argued that since the appellant would have had to perform at least three more acts before the full offence could have been completed, i.e., remove the safety catch, put his finger on the trigger and pull it, the evidence was insufficient to support the charge. There was a discussion as to the proper construction of section 1(1) of the Criminal Attempts Act 1981. After hearing full argument, the judge ruled against the submission and allowed the case to proceed on count 1. Thereafter, the appellant gave evidence. In the result, the jury convicted him unanimously of attempted murder. It follows that they found he intended to kill the victim.

The sole ground of appeal is that the judge erred in law in his construction of section 1(1) and ought to have withdrawn the case....

Counsel's second proposition is that section 1(1) of the Act of 1981 has not resolved the question as to which is the appropriate test. Thirdly, he submits that the test deriving from *R v Eagleton* (1855) 6 Cox CC 559 should be adopted.

This amounts to an invitation to construe the statutory words by reference to previous conflicting case law. We believe this to be misconceived. The Act of 1981 is a codifying statute. It amends and sets out completely the law relating to attempts and conspiracies. In those circumstances the correct approach is to look first at the natural meaning of the statutory words, not to turn back to earlier case law and seek to fit some previous test to the words of the section..

We do not accept Mr Farrer's contention that section 1(1) of the Act of 1981 in effect embodies the 'last act' test derived from *R v Eagleton* [(1855) 6 Cox CC 559]. Had Parliament intended to adopt that test, a quite different form of words could and would have been used.

It is of interest to note that the Act of 1981 followed a report from the Law Commission on Attempt, and Impossibility in Relation to Attempt, Conspiracy and Incitement (1980) (Law Com. No. 102). At paragraph 2.47 the report states:

> The definition of sufficient proximity must be wide enough to cover two varieties of cases; first, those in which a person has taken all the steps towards the commission of a crime which he believes to be necessary as far as he is concerned for that crime to result, such as firing a gun at another and missing. Normally such cases cause no difficulty. Secondly, however, the definition must cover those instances where a person has to take some further step to complete the crime, assuming that there is evidence of the necessary mental element on his part to commit it; for example, when the defendant has raised the gun to take aim at another but has not yet squeezed the trigger. We have reached the conclusion that, in regard to these cases, it is undesirable to recommend anything more complex than a rationalization of the present law.

In paragraph 2.48 the report states:

> The literal meaning of 'proximate' is 'nearest, next before or after (in place, order, time, connection of thought, causation etc.).' Thus, were this term part of a statutory description of the actus reus of attempt, it would clearly be capable of being interpreted to exclude all but the 'final act'; this would not be in accordance with the policy outlined above.

Clearly, the draftsman of section 1(1) must be taken to have been aware of the two lines of earlier authority and of the Law Commission's report. The words 'an act which is more than merely preparatory to the commission of the offence' would be inapt if they were intended to mean 'the last act which lay in his power towards the commission of the offence.'

[T]he question for the judge in the present case was whether there was evidence from which a reasonable jury, properly directed, could conclude that the appellant had done acts which were more than merely preparatory. Clearly his actions in obtaining the gun, in shortening it, in loading it, in putting on his disguise, and in going to the school could only be regarded as preparatory acts. But, in our judgment, once he had got into the car, taken out the loaded gun and pointed it at the victim with the intention of killing him, there was sufficient evidence for the consideration of the jury on the charge of attempted murder. It was a matter for them to decide whether they were sure those acts were more than merely preparatory. In our judgment, therefore, the judge was right to allow the case to go to the jury, and the appeal against conviction must be dismissed.

R v Geddes

[1996] Crim LR 894, Court of Appeal

The appellant was convicted of attempted false imprisonment contrary to section 1(1) of the Criminal Attempts Act 1981. He had been seen by a teacher in the boys' lavatory block of a school. He had no connection with the school and no right to be there. He had a rucksack with him. A woman police officer who was, by chance, on the premises saw him and shouted at him, but he left. In a cubicle in the lavatory block there was a cider can which had belonged to the appellant. His rucksack was later found in some bushes. Its contents included a large kitchen knife, some lengths of rope and a roll of masking tape. The appellant was arrested and identified by the teacher and some pupils. The prosecution alleged that the presence of the cider can showed that the appellant had been inside a lavatory cubicle, and that the contents of the rucksack could have been used to catch and restrain a boy entering the lavatory. The defence was that the prosecution case was based on speculation. At the start of the trial the Crown had intended to rely on the evidence of a local authority housing officer who had a series of conversations with the appellant in which he had revealed that he harboured designs against young boys and wished to kidnap a child for sexual purposes. The judge ruled that that evidence was inadmissible, and the trial continued with very limited evidence called for the prosecution, a series of written admissions as to the factual basis of the Crown case having been agreed by counsel on both sides. At the close of the prosecution case the defence submitted that there was insufficient evidence to leave to the jury to support the allegation that the appellant was guilty of attempted false imprisonment. The judge rejected that submission, and the appellant called no evidence. The appellant appealed on the ground that the evidence, almost entirely contained in the factual admissions made on his behalf, did not permit the jury to conclude that he had done any act which was more than merely preparatory to the commission of a crime.

Held, allowing the appeal, that the authorities showed that the line of demarcation between acts which were merely preparatory and acts which might amount to an attempt was not always clear or easy to recognise. There was no rule of thumb test, and there must always be an exercise of judgment based on the particular facts of the case. It was an accurate paraphrase of the statutory test to ask whether the available evidence, if accepted, could show that a defendant had done an act showed that he had actually tried to commit the offence in question, or whether he had only got ready or put himself in a position or equipped himself to do so. In the present case there was not much room for doubt about the appellant's intention, and the evidence was clearly capable of showing that he had made preparations, had equipped himself, had got ready, had put himself in a position to commit the offence charged. It was true that he had entered the school, but he had never had any contact or communication with, nor had confronted, any pupil at the school. The whole story was one which filled the court with the gravest unease, but on the facts of the case the court felt bound to conclude that the evidence was not sufficient in law to support a finding that the appellant had done an act which was more than merely preparatory to wrongfully imprisoning a person unknown.

■ NOTES AND QUESTIONS

1. What more would Gullefer have had to have done to be guilty of attempt? While it might not make sense to insist on proof that the defendant did 'the last act necessary', does it follow that where the defendant has done the last act which he intended to do (a 'completed' attempt), he should not be convicted of attempt, assuming the other elements of attempt are satisfied? Is this a fair description of what happened in *Gullefer*?

2. The Court in *Jones* said that the defendant's acts in obtaining the gun, shortening it, loading it, putting on his disguise and going to the school 'could only be regarded as preparatory acts'. How much closer to the commission of the crime did Jones have to come? Is the court trying to draw too fine a line? Had not Jones clearly demonstrated his intent to kill, and why should this not be sufficient?

3. In *Geddes* the Court of Appeal stated 'there was not much room for doubt about the appellant's intention'. If so, and given that the appellant did more than just fantasise about committing the crime, did he escape conviction because he was lucky enough to have been stopped before he could find a victim ? See also *R v Nash* [1999] Crim LR 308, where a letter requesting a specimen of urine was held not to be proximate enough to amount to an attempt to procure an act of gross indecency.

4. In *R v Campbell* [1991] Crim LR 268, the defendant had been arrested outside a post office carrying an imitation firearm and a threatening note. In reversing his conviction, the Court, classified these as mere acts of preparation. Were the police in effect penalised for their efficient detective work? Would they have been better advised to wait until Campbell had proceeded further?

5. If part of the rationale for criminalising attempts is to protect society by allowing the conviction of those who have manifested their dangerousness, do the above decisions achieve – or frustrate – this end? Does the law as interpreted by the courts encourage a dangerous game of brinkmanship where the police must risk the commission of the crime and its concomitant social harm or else jeopardize a conviction, letting the defendant free possibly to try again?

6. Might the police be sued in the civil courts for failing to timely intervene in the face of information that a crime is about to be committed when the crime is committed and serious harm follows? See *Osman v UK* [1999] 1 FLR 193, European Court of Human Rights.

C: Impossibility

CRIMINAL ATTEMPTS ACT 1981

(2) A person may be guilty of attempting to commit an offence to which this section applies even though the facts are such that the commission of the offence is impossible.

(3) In any case where—

(a) apart from this subsection a person's intention would not be regarded as having amounted to an intent to commit an offence: but

(b) if the facts of the case had been as he believed them to be, his intention would be so regarded,

then, for the purposes of subsection (1) above, he shall be regarded as having had an intent to commit that offence.

Although the statute seems to make clear that factual impossibility is not a defence to a charge of attempt, the House of Lords rejected that interpretation in *Anderton v Ryan* [1985] AC 560. However, that decision was quickly reversed.

R v Shivpuri
[1987] AC 1, House of Lords

LORD BRIDGE OF HARWICH: . . . The facts plainly to be inferred from the evidence, interpreted in the light of the jury's guilty verdicts, may be shortly summarised. The appellant, on a visit to India, was approached by a man named Desai, who offered to pay him £1,000 if, on his return to England, he would receive a suitcase which a courier would deliver to him containing packages of drugs which the appellant was then to distribute according to instructions he would receive. The suitcase was duly delivered to him in Cambridge. On 30 November 1982, acting on instructions, the appellant went to Southall station to deliver a package of drugs to a third party. Outside the station he and the man he had met by appointment were arrested. A package containing a powdered substance was found in the appellant's shoulder bag. At the appellant's flat in Cambridge, he produced to customs officers the suitcase from which the lining had been ripped out and the remaining packages of the same powdered substance. In answer to questions by customs officers and in a long written statement the appellant made what amounted to a full confession of having played his part, as described, as recipient and distributor of illegally imported drugs. The appellant believed the drugs to be either heroin or cannabis. In due course the powdered substance in the several packages was scientifically analysed and found not to be a controlled drug but snuff or some similar harmless vegetable matter.

...

[T]he first question to be asked is whether the appellant intended to commit the offences of being knowingly concerned in dealing with and harbouring drugs of Class A or Class B with intent to evade the prohibition on their importation. Translated into more homely language the question may be rephrased, without in any way altering its legal significance, in the following terms: did the appellant intend to receive and store (harbour) and in due course pass on to third parties (deal with) packages of heroin or cannabis which he knew had been smuggled into England from India? The answer is plainly yes, he did. Next, did he in relation to each offence, do an act which was more than merely preparatory to the commission of the offence? The act relied on in relation to harbouring was the receipt and retention of the packages found in the lining of the suitcase. The act relied on in relation to dealing was the meeting at Southall station with the intended recipient of one of the packages. In each case the act was clearly more than preparatory to the commission of the *intended* offence; it was not and could not be more than merely preparatory to the commission of the *actual* offence, because the facts were such that the commission of the actual offence was impossible. Here then is the nub of the matter. Does the 'act which is more than merely preparatory to the commission of the offence' in section 1(1) of the Act of 1981 (the actus reus of the statutory offence of attempt) require any more than an act which is more than merely preparatory to the commission of the offence which the defendant intended to commit? Section 1(2) must surely indicate a negative answer; if it were otherwise, whenever the facts were such that the commission of the actual offence was impossible, it would be impossible to prove an act more than merely preparatory to the commission of that offence and subsections (1) and (2) would contradict each other.

This very simple, perhaps over simple, analysis leads me to the provisional conclusion that the appellant was rightly convicted of the two offences of attempt with which he was charged. But can this conclusion stand with *Anderton v Ryan* [1985] AC 560? The appellant in that case was charged with an attempt to handle stolen goods. She bought a video recorder believing it to be stolen. On the facts as they were to be assumed it was not stolen. By a majority the House decided that she was entitled to be acquitted. I have re-examined the case with care. If I could extract from the speech of Lord Roskill or from my own speech a clear and coherent principle distinguishing those cases of attempting the impossible which amount to offences under the statute from those which do not. I should have to consider carefully on which side of the line the instant case fell. But I have to confess that I can find no such principle.

If we fell into error, it is clear that our concern was to avoid convictions in situations which most people, as a matter of common sense, would not regard as involving criminality. In this connection it is to be regretted that we did not take due note of paragraph 2.97 of the Law Commission's report (Criminal Law: Attempt, and Impossibility in Relation to Attempt, Conspiracy and Incitement (1980) (Law Commission No. 102)) which preceded the enactment of the Act of 1981, which reads:

> If it is right in principle that an attempt should be chargeable even though the crime which it is sought to commit could not possibly be committed, we do not think that we should be deterred by the consideration that such a change in our law would also cover some extreme and exceptional cases in which a prosecution would be theoretically possible. An example would be where a person is offered goods at such a low price that he believes that they are stolen, when

in fact they are not; if he actually purchases them, upon the principles which we have discussed he would be liable for an attempt to handle stolen goods. Another case which has been much debated is that raised in argument by Bramwell B. in *R* v *Collins* (1864) 9 Cox CC 497. If A takes his own umbrella, mistaking it for one belonging to B and intending to steal B's umbrella, is he guilty of attempted theft? Again, on the principles which we have discussed he would in theory be guilty, but in neither case would it be realistic to suppose that a complaint would be made or that a prosecution would ensue.

The prosecution in *Anderton* v *Ryan* itself falsified the Commission's prognosis in one of the 'extreme and exceptional cases.' It nevertheless probably holds good for other such cases, particularly that of the young man having sexual intercourse with a girl over 16, mistakenly believing her to be under that age, by which both Lord Roskill and I were much troubled.

However that may be, the distinction between acts which are 'objectively innocent' and those which are not is an essential element in the reasoning in *Anderton* v *Ryan* and the decision, unless it can be supported on some other ground, must stand or fall by the validity of this distinction. I am satisfied on further consideration that the concept of 'objective innocence' is incapable of sensible application in relation to the law of criminal attempts. The reason for this is that any attempt to commit an offence which involves 'an act which is more than merely preparatory to the commission of the offence' but for any reason fails, so that in the event no offence is committed, must ex hypothesi, from the point of view of the criminal law, be 'objectively innocent.' What turns what would otherwise, from the point of view of the criminal law, be an innocent act into a crime is the intent of the actor to commit an offence. I say 'from the point of view of the criminal law' because the law of tort must surely here be quite irrelevant. A puts his hand into B's pocket. Whether or not there is anything in the pocket capable of being stolen, if A intends to steal, his act is a criminal attempt; if he does not so intend, his act is innocent. A plunges a knife into a bolster in a bed. To avoid the complication of an offence of criminal damage, assume it to be A's bolster. If A believes the bolster to be his enemy B and intends to kill him, his act is an attempt to murder B; if he knows the bolster is only a bolster, his act is innocent. These considerations lead me to the conclusion that the distinction sought to be drawn in *Anderton* v *Ryan* between innocent and guilty acts considered 'objectively' and independently of the state of mind of the actor cannot be sensibly maintained. .

■ NOTES AND QUESTIONS

1. Factual impossibility might be compared to the defence of mistake of fact, examined previously. If a defendant's conduct would not be illegal if the facts were as he believed them to be, why should he not be able to escape liability when the facts turn out to be other than he expected?

2. Juan intends to rape Eva. Unknown to him, however, Eva secretly desires to have sex with him and would have consented if asked. Juan, however, never asks. Is he guilty of attempted rape if he carries out his intention?

3. Legal impossibility, where the offence the defendant intends to commit is not a crime, is a valid defence. Thus, if Ivan tries to break the speed limit by driving at 50 mph but the speed limit is 70 mph, he has committed no crime of attempt. Why should this be so, given this manifestation of his willingness to ignore the requirements of the law?

D: Abandonment

What if, after a defendant has gone beyond the preparatory stage but before the substantive offence has been completed, the defendant decides to abandon the criminal enterprise? Has the crime of attempt been committed? At common law the answer was 'yes', and that answer does not seem to have changed.

R v Becerra

(1975) 62 Cr App R 212, Court of Appeal.

For facts and holding, see Chapter 13, p. 680.

■ NOTES AND QUESTIONS

1. Why should voluntary abandonment not be a defence? Is a defendant who abandons his crime dangerous or in need of rehabilitation? Does the answer depend on whether there was a genuine change of heart, or the discovery of circumstances which rendered the completion of the crime more difficult, such as the fact that the bank to be robbed was surrounded by armed guards? Is it possible for the law to discriminate in practice between these types of cases?

2. Does the reluctance of the law to recognise abandonment as a defence provide a disincentive to abandonment of a criminal project? Even if not a defence, abandonment might be taken into account as a mitigating factor in sentencing.

3. Similar policy issues arise in respect of a conspirator who attempts to withdraw from the conspiracy. Technically such withdrawal will be ineffective, for the crime of conspiracy is already complete. On a policy level, however, a case can be made to allow withdrawal as a defence to encourage conspirators to withdraw.

SECTION 4: OTHER INCHOATE OFFENCES

While it has become traditional to think of encouragement, conspiracy, and attempt as comprising the totality of inchoate crimes, in fact there are many more offences which could be seen in a similar light. The common theme inchoate crimes is that of punishing behaviour which is a prelude to criminal behaviour. Viewed in this light, it can be seen that, for example, assault (strictly defined as causing another to apprehend the application of immediate unlawful force), is designed to be an inchoate form of battery, which is the actual application of unlawful force. So too traffic offences, ranging from speeding to driving dangerously, are aimed in part at preventing more serious harms such as causing death by dangerous driving. Likewise, crimes like the unlawful possession of firearms are designed to prevent firearm offences, and public drunkenness may be aimed at deterring the offences likely to follow when one becomes drunk.

And consider the offence of burglary under s. 9(1)(a) of the Theft Act 1968. The defendant only has to enter a building with the intent to commit a crime therein. There is no requirement that crime actually be committed. Again, this species of burglary can be conceptualised as an attempt to commit the offence intended to be committed within the building.

One advantage of focusing on inchoate forms of crime is that it removes the 'fortuity of consequences' (see Chapter 2, section 3c). Why should a defendant whose gun misfires be guilty of attempted murder, while another whose weapon proves more reliable is convicted of the substantive offence? In recognition of this point the maximum punishment for the inchoate offence is usually the same as or comparable to that for the completed crime. However, the actual sentence imposed in practice may well be less. The practical point is underscored in respect to homicide, where the imposition of a life sentence for murder is mandatory, but only discretionary in the case of an attempted murder,.

■ NOTES AND QUESTIONS

1. Should all crimes be written in inchoate form to avoid the 'fortuity of consequences' (review the materials in Chapter 2 on causation)? What are the arguments for and against?

2. Should all inchoate crimes be abolished on the theory that society is not harmed until the crime is completed? What are the arguments for and against?

3. In respect to crimes written in inchoate form, does it make sense to allow a conviction for an attempt to commit such a crime? For example, should there be such an offence as attempted burglary? Some would argue that this is pushing the point of criminality too far back in time. Should this matter if the defendant's intent to commit an offence has clearly been demonstrated?

FURTHER READING

Wilson, *Criminal Law: Doctrine and Theory* (2010), chapters 1–3

Ashworth, 'Defining Criminal Offences without Harm' in P. Smith (ed.) *Criminal Law: Essays in Honour of J.C. Smith* (1987)

Dennis, 'The Rationale of Criminal Conspiracy' (1977) 93 Law Quarterly Review 39

Dennis, 'The Elements of Attempt' [1980] Criminal Law Review 758

Duff, *Criminal Attempts* (1996)

Glazebrook, 'Should we have a Law of Attempted Crime' (1969) 85 Law Quarterly Review 28

Hogan, 'The Criminal Attempts Act and Attempting the Impossible' [1984] Criminal Law Review 584

Horder, 'Varieties of Intention, Criminal Attempts and Endangerment' (1994) 14 Legal Studies 335

Orchard, 'Agreement in Criminal Conspiracy' [1974] Criminal Law Review 297

Ormerod and Fortson, 'Serious Crime Act 2007: The Part 2 Offences [2009] Criminal Law Review 389

Rogers, 'The Codification of Attempts and the Case for "Preparation"' [2008] Criminal Law Review 937

Wasik, 'Abandoning Criminal Attempt' [1980] Criminal Law Review 785

Williams, 'The Lords and Impossible Attempts, or *quis cusodiet ipsos custodes*' (1986) Cambridge Law Journal 33

13

Parties to Crime

Often more than one person is involved in the commission of a criminal offence. The perpetrator of the offence – the person who is the most immediate cause of the *actus reus* is known in law as the *principal*. If two or more persons are involved in committing the same crime, as for example, when members of a gang fatally stab the victim, all may be principals. If the *actus reus* is performed by someone who lacks the capacity to commit a crime (e.g., a child) or has a legally accepted defence (e.g., self-defence), the person who commits the *actus reus* that may be seen as 'an innocent agent' and the person who counseled or procured the *actus reus* will be held liable for the crime.

Everyone else who is involved in the commission of the offence and is criminally liable is referred to as an *accessory* or *secondary party*. The law is somewhat confusing as the consequence for being convicted as an accessory or secondary party can be exactly the same as for being convicted as a principal. The Accessories and Abettors Act 1861, s. 8, provides that one can be charged as an accessory and convicted as a principal. Accessories and principals, moreover, are subject to the same maximum penalty. On the other hand, the *actus reus* and *mens rea* elements which must be proved may differ significantly depending on whether one is charged as a principal or an accessory; and some defences may be available to an accessory that are not available to a principal, and vice versa. One can also be convicted as an accessory to a crime for which the principal himself cannot be convicted, as illustrated in the following case:

R v Austin and Others
[1981] 1 All ER 374, Court of Appeal

A husband, who was living apart from his wife, employed a firm of enquiry agents, of which W was a member, to find his wife and their three-year-old child. After the firm had done so, the husband instructed W to recover the child, who was in the lawful possession of the wife. W enlisted the services of A, T and F, and the four of them lay in wait, with the husband, for the wife and child. The husband forcibly snatched the child from the wife and then he and the others made off. W, A, T and F were charged with, and convicted of, child stealing, contrary to s. 56 of the Offences against the Person Act 1861. They appealed, contending that although they had deliberately aided and abetted the husband, they were not guilty of the offence charged because the husband had not been acting 'unlawfully' within the meaning of s. 56 and had committed no offence, or, alternatively, even if he had been acting unlawfully, they were entitled to immunity from prosecution under the proviso to s. 56 since they were the agents of a 'person who...claimed [a] right to the possession of such child'.

WATKINS LJ: . . . At the close of the case for the Crown in the Crown Court at Winchester counsel for the appellants, to whom we are extremely indebted for his restrained, able and frank submissions to us, made a number of concessions on behalf of the appellants. He has repeated them to this court. They are: (1) that each of these appellants aided and abetted King in taking Lara away from the possession of her mother; and (2) that the child was taken by King by the use of force on the mother and on the child. It was also conceded that they all knew the child was in the lawful possession of the mother, since there was no order in this country which affected her right to that at the material time and the order of the American court could not affect it in any practical way. It was also admitted that they had the intention to deprive the mother of possession of the child.

Having regard to those admissions and the background of this affair, one looks at s. 56 of the 1861 Act which provides:

> Whosoever shall unlawfully . . . by force . . . take away . . . any child under the age of fourteen years, with intent to deprive any parent . . . of the possession of such child . . . shall be liable, at the discretion of the court . . . to be imprisoned: Provided, that no person who shall have claimed any right to the possession of such child, or shall be the mother or shall have claimed to be the father of an illegitimate child, shall be liable to be prosecuted by virtue hereof on account of the getting possession of such child . . .

It is submitted that there are two questions relevant to the issue of whether the appellants were rightly convicted: (1) did King commit an offence under s. 56, bearing in mind that he assaulted his wife and when taking the child away the child too, and (2) if King committed an offence under s. 56, does it follow that the appellants are also guilty of that offence? Furthermore, suppose King had been indicted and found not guilty by reason only of being able to take advantage of the proviso, could the appellants have escaped conviction in that way too?

. . .

Undoubtedly King could properly have claimed a right of possession to the child and so have gained the protection of the proviso. What would have been the effect of that? The effect would have been that, although he had committed the offence of child stealing, because he was the child's father and could claim a right to possession of the child he would not have been prosecuted. It is submitted on the appellants' behalf that the proviso also protects a class of persons wide enough to include those who aid a person such as the father of the child in gaining possession of his child by force. They become his agents for the purpose. Many persons have from time to time the temporary possession of a child as agents of parents. Why are they not protected to the same extent as parents when regaining possession as agents of parents?

In our view the only sensible construction of the proviso allows of its protection being granted to a small class of persons only, which includes the father and the mother of the child, whether the child be legitimate or illegitimate, or a guardian appointed by a testamentary document, or by an order conferring the status of guardianship, or a person to whom is granted an order conferring some form of care, control, custody or access. We can think of no other who could claim exemption from prosecution by reason of the proviso.

What of these appellants? They had no good reason for doing what they did. They had no right to assert, and no interest in, the possession of the child. They were the paid hirelings of King to aid him in the commission of a criminal offence, namely stealing a child, and with him they committed it as aiders and abettors. While King may shelter behind the proviso, there is no room there for them. Parliament in its wisdom undoubtedly decided that the mischiefs of matrimonial discord which are unhappily so widespread should not give rise to wholesale criminal prosecutions arising out of disputes about children, about who should have possession and control of them. That and that alone is the reason for the existence of the proviso to s. 56. Thus, as we have said, its application is confined to the select class of persons we have endeavoured to define.

It should be clearly understood that those such as these appellants who aid a father or a mother to take possession of a child from the other parent, and who do so by the use of force as aiders and abettors to it, commit the offence of child stealing, and that they are not immune from prosecution.

This was a wicked example of aiding and abetting the commission of the offence, child stealing. In the judgment of this court, the appellants are extremely fortunate that the trial judge treated them so mercifully by the sentences he imposed. This kind of activity must be condemned and those who are tempted to engage in it should be deterred from doing so.

Appeals dismissed.

■ NOTES AND QUESTIONS

1. Why is it that the defendants in *Austin* could be guilty of an offence for helping another person to do something which would not have been an offence if that other person had acted alone? Has the court created a crime where none was intended by Parliament?

2. Sometimes Parliament addresses the issue more directly. For example, although it is no longer criminal to commit suicide, it is an offence to be an accessory to a suicide. See Suicide Act 1961.

3. The courts have sometimes seemed to apply a 'derivative' theory of accessorial liability; that is, a theory that views the accessory's liability as deriving from that of the principal. The strict logic of this theory would lead one to the conclusion that there could not be a guilty accessory unless there was a guilty principal. However, there are numerous cases, many of which will be examined in this chapter, that suggest that the courts' adherence to this theory is not as rigorous as it is sometimes represented to be. Confronting the basic thesis head-on, however, why should an accessory's liability depend on whether the principal is either guilty of or can be convicted of (the two are not necessarily the same) an independent crime? Why should not the accessory be judged on the basis of his or her own acts, and the mental state with which those acts were performed?

4. There is another group of persons who provide assistance, but after the crime has been committed by the principal. These post-crime assisters are not generally treated within the law of complicity; that is, they are not liable for the substantive offence, but may be guilty of separate statutory offences (see Criminal Law Act 1967, s. 4). This is a recognition of the fact that their crime is more appropriately characterised as one of obstructing the course of justice, rather than one of furthering the substantive offence which has already occurred.

5. The Serious Crime Act 2007, s. 62 affirms the principle established in the Corporate Manslaughter and Corporate Homicide Act 2007, s. 18 that an individual cannot be liable as an accessory to an offence of corporate manslaughter committed by a company.

SECTION 1: LIABILITY AS A PRINCIPAL

The person who acts with the requisite intent and whose acts cause the prohibited harm is in law deemed to be the principal. It is not necessary, however, that the principal personally commits the act which causes the harmful result. A principal may act through an 'innocent agent', as in the case where a person sends a letter bomb through the post – the principal is the sender of the letter and not the postal employee who delivers it. There can be more than one principal to a crime:

Mohan v R
[1967] 2 AC 187, Privy Council

The appellants, father and son, were convicted at Port of Spain Assizes of the murder of M., who received several wounds in an encounter with the appellants and died from his injuries. He had received, together with minor wounds, a very severe wound on the right leg and a very severe wound in the back. On the evidence there was a possibility that the death might have been caused solely by the leg wound, and the case was considered on that hypothesis.

LORD PEARSON: ... The question ... arises whether each of the appellants can be held responsible for the leg wound, when it may have been inflicted by the other of them. There is conflicting evidence as to which of them struck the blow on Mootoo's leg, the evidence for the prosecution tending to show that the appellant Deonath struck it and the evidence for the defence tending to show that the appellant Ramnath struck it. There is uncertainty on that point.

Also it cannot be inferred with any certainty from the evidence that the appellants had a pre-arranged plan for their attack on Mootoo.

It is, however, clear from the evidence for the defence, as well as from the evidence for the prosecution, that at the material time both the appellants were armed with cutlasses, both were attacking Mootoo, and both struck him. It is impossible on the facts of this case to contend that the fatal blow was outside the scope of the common intention. The two appellants were attacking the same man at the same time with similar weapons and with the common intention that he should suffer grievous bodily harm. Each of the appellants was present, and aiding and abetting the other of them in the wounding of Mootoo.

That is the feature which distinguishes this case from cases in which one of the accused was not present or not participating in the attack or not using any dangerous weapon, but may be held liable as a conspirator or an accessory before the fact or by virtue of a common design if it can be shown that he was party to a pre-arranged plan in pursuance of which the fatal blow was struck. In this case one of the appellants struck the fatal blow, and the other of them was present aiding and abetting him. In such a case the prosecution do not have to prove that the accused were acting in pursuance of a pre-arranged plan.

■ **NOTES AND QUESTIONS**

1. Why is the court in *Mohan* not more concerned with which of the defendants struck the fatal blow? With both defendants attacking the victim, was it little more than chance whose blow would prove fatal? The case would presumably have been analysed differently if one defendant had attacked the victim with his fists and the other with a knife, the victim dying from a knife wound – or would it?

2. In *R v Peters and Parfitt* [1995] Crim LR 501, the Court of Appeal held that in a similar situation to that in *Mohan*, 'the common purpose or intention had to be more than merely them both separately intending to do some harm to J'. In this case, both defendants had punched the victim, and one (although it was not clear which) had delivered a fatal kick. The Court of Appeal quashed the conviction for manslaughter because the trial judge had not adequately

directed the jury as to whether the defendants had acted pursuant to a 'common purpose'.

There is a somewhat similar situation to that of the co-principals that needs to be distinguished, where the two defendants cannot be shown to be acting in concert. Say that the leaders of the Conservative, Labour and Liberal Democrat parties closet themselves in a locked room to settle their political differences. Only two walk out alive. The third has been strangled to death. Both of the survivors claim that the other was the strangler. If the prosecution are unable to prove which of the two survivors was the murderer, even though they know for certain it was one of them, there cannot be a criminal conviction in the absence of a showing, as in *Mohan*, of a joint enterprise or concert of action. It may seem strange that one of the politicians will have gotten away with murder but the burden of proof is upon the prosecution to establish guilt beyond a reasonable doubt, and all that exists under the stated facts is a fifty-fifty probability that each of the potential defendants is guilty. The philosophy embodied in the requirement of proof beyond reasonable doubt is that it is preferable that a guilty person go free, which is what will happen, than that an innocent person go to jail, which is what would happen if both were to be convicted.

Sometimes this result can be avoided if one of the two parties is under a duty to prevent the harm which occurred:

R v Russell and Russell

(1987) 85 Cr App R 388, Court of Appeal

The appellants A and M were registered drug addicts, in receipt of daily prescriptions of methadone, which they obtained in liquid form. They were living with their 15-month-old daughter. One day the child died from a massive overdose of methadone. When interviewed separately by the police the appellants both denied giving methadone to the child save that they had on occasion dipped her dummy into the liquid methadone to placate her while she was teething. The appellants were charged with the child's manslaughter (count 1) and with cruelty to a person under 16, contrary to s. 1(1) of the Children and Young Persons Act 1933 (count 2). The evidence at their trial was that, as to count 1, the amount of the drug in the child's body was such that it could not have been ingested solely by the dipping of the dummy into the mixture. Forensic evidence was given on the likely effect upon a baby of the administration of methadone on a dummy. At the close of the prosecution case a submission of no case to answer on behalf of A was overruled by the trial judge. The jury convicted A and M on both counts, as to count 1, indicating that they did so on the basis of deliberate administration.

THE LORD CHIEF JUSTICE: . . . Generally speaking, parents of a child are in no different position from any other defendants jointly charged with a crime. To establish guilt against either, the Crown must prove at the least that that defendant aided, abetted, counselled or procured the commission of the crime by the other. The only difference in the position of parents, as opposed to others jointly indicted, is that one parent may have a duty to intervene in the ill-treatment of their child by the other where a stranger would have no such duty . . . .

Appeals against conviction dismissed.

■ NOTES AND QUESTIONS

1. The result in *Russell* is now embodied in statute. The Domestic Violence, Crime and Victims Act 2004, s. 5 provides that where (a) a child or vulnerable adult dies as a result of the unlawful act of a person who was a member of the same household as the victim and had frequent contact with him; (b) the defendant was such a person at the time of the act; (c) there was a significant risk of serious physical harm being caused to the victim by the unlawful act of such a person; and (d) either the defendant was the person whose act caused the victim's death, or the defendant was, or ought to have been aware of the risk mentioned in (c), failed to take such steps as he could reasonably have been expected to take to protect the victim from the risk, and the act occurred in circumstances of the kind that the defendant foresaw or ought to have foreseen.

2. A related situation where one person may be criminally liable for the acts of another is when the law imposes **vicarious liability.** This form of liability usually arises in the context of an employer–employee relationship, the employer being held vicariously liable for the crimes of the employee who has acted within the scope or authority of his employment. Liability is most often imposed by statute. The employer can be vicariously liable not only for acts which he did not authorise (if he did authorise the acts, he would be liable on normal principal/ accessory principles), but even for acts which he may have expressly forbidden. Interestingly, where an employer is vicariously liable for the acts of an employee, it has been held that the employee may be liable as an accessory. See *Griffiths* v *Studebakers* [1924] 1 KB 102.

SECTION 2: LIABILITY AS AN ACCESSORY

An accessory is one who aids, abets, counsels or procures the commission of a crime but who is not the principal. The controlling statute is the Accessories and Abettors Act 1861, as amended by the Criminal Law Act 1977:

ACCESSORIES AND ABETTORS ACT 1861

8. Whosoever shall aid, abet, counsel, or procure the commission of any indictable offence, whether the same be an offence at common law, or by virtue of any Act passed or to be passed, shall be liable to be tried, indicted, and punished as a principal offender.

A: Elements of the offence

In order to convict a defendant as an accessory, the prosecution must prove that:

(a) an offence (or at least the *actus reus* of an offence) was committed;

(b) the defendant aided, abetted, counselled or procured the offence (the *actus reus* of accessorial liability); and

(c) the defendant had the intent to further the commission of the offence or knew that his assistance would have this effect (the *mens rea*). This intent must be proven even though the offence aided may be one of strict liability.

(i) An offence was committed

The prosecution must prove that an offence (or at least the *actus reus* of an offence) has been committed.

Thornton v Mitchell
[1940] 1 All ER 339, King's Bench

Appeal by the conductor by way of case stated from a decision of a court of summary jurisdiction sitting at Rochdale, whereby the conductor of an omnibus was convicted of having aided and abetted the driver of the omnibus in driving without due care and attention and without using reasonable consideration for others using the road. The charges against the driver were dismissed. On the hearing of the information, the following facts were proved or admitted. On 18 March 1939, the omnibus arrived at a road junction where all the passengers disembarked. Before the omnibus reversed, the conductor looked out of the back to see if the road was clear. Then he rang the bell three times as a signal to the driver to reverse. At the time when he gave the signal, the conductor, following his usual practice, was standing on the platform at the back of the omnibus. The time was about 7.45 p.m., and the visibility was poor. After giving the signal, the conductor jumped off the omnibus, which was reversed slowly. Two persons who had just disembarked were knocked down by the back of the omnibus as it was reversing, and one of them received fatal injuries. The driver could not see any person immediately behind the omnibus while he was reversing, owing to the obstruction caused by the steps to the upper deck, and owing to the height of the window at the back, and he had, therefore, to rely upon the conductor's signal.

LORD HEWART LCJ: In my opinion, it is quite clear that this appeal must be allowed.... [t]his case is *a fortiori* upon *Morris* v *Tolman* [1923] 1 KB 166, to which our attention has been directed. I will read one sentence from the judgment of Avory J, at p. 171:

> ...in order to convict, it would be necessary to show that the respondent was aiding the principal, but a person cannot aid another in doing something which that other has not done.

That, I think, is the very thing which these justices have decided that this bus conductor did. In one breath they say that the principal did nothing which he should not have done, and in the next breath they hold that the bus conductor aided and abetted the driver in doing something which had not been done or in not doing something which he ought to have done. I really think that, with all respect to the ingenuity of counsel for the respondent, the case is too plain for argument, and this appeal must be allowed and the conviction quashed.

■ NOTES AND QUESTIONS

1. Why, once the case against the driver was dismissed, should the conductor have escaped all liability? After all, harm did occur and arguably would not have occurred were it not for his reckless conduct. Are there other possible bases on which to premise a case against the conductor? Should accessorial liability be dependent on principal liability? Is *Thornton* v *Mitchell* reconcilable with *Austin*?

2. In *R v Millward* [1994] Crim LR 527, the defendant was aware that the hitch between a tractor and trailer was defective but nonetheless allowed his employee, to drive the tractor. The hitch detached while the employee was driving the vehicle and an innocent victim was killed. The employee was acquitted of causing death by reckless driving, but Millward's conviction for procuring was upheld. Compare *R v Loukes* [1996] Crim LR 341; *R v Roberts and George* [1997] Crim LR 209 (drivers of trucks were acquitted of causing death by dangerous driving because the dangerous condition of their vehicles would not have been 'obvious to a competent and careful driver', the employers' convictions for procuring were quashed).

One must be careful to distinguish between the case where no crime has occurred and the case where a crime has occurred but the principal cannot be convicted. *Austin* (above) provides an example where the principal is exempt from prosecution, but what if the principal has a defence?

R v Bourne

(1952) 36 Cr App R 125, Court of Appeal

The appellant was convicted at Worcestershire Assizes on 21 May 1952, on two counts of an indictment charging him with aiding and abetting his wife to commit buggery with a dog, and was sentenced by Hallett J to eight years' imprisonment. He was also convicted on two counts charging incitement to commit buggery, and on two counts charging indecent assault on his wife, and in respect of these he received concurrent sentences.

The indictment alleged an offence to have been committed on two separate occasions. The evidence showed that the appellant had on each occasion sexually excited the animal, and then caused his wife to submit to its having connection with her *per vaginam*. The wife stated in her evidence that she had been terrorised into submission and that the acts were entirely against her will. The judge left questions to the jury as follows:–(1) 'Did the prisoner on a day in or about the month of September 1949, in the county of Stafford cause his wife, Adelaide Bourne, to have carnal knowledge of a dog?' to which the jury replied: 'Yes.' (2) 'Are you satisfied that she did not consent to having such carnal knowledge?' to which the jury replied: 'Yes, we are satisfied she did not consent,' and he also left two similar questions with regard to the second offence, and the jury returned similar answers.

THE LORD CHIEF JUSTICE: The case against the appellant was that he was a principal in the second degree to the crime of buggery which was committed by his wife, because if a woman has connection with a dog, or allows a dog to have connection with her, that is the full offence of buggery. She may be able to show that she was forced to commit the offence. I will assume that the plea of duress could have been set up by her on the evidence, and in fact we have allowed Mr Green to argue this case on the footing that the wife would have been entitled to be acquitted on the ground of duress. The learned judge left no question to the jury on duress, but the jury have found that she did not consent. Assuming that she could have set up duress, what does that mean? It means that she admits that she has committed the crime but prays to be excused from punishment for the consequences of the crime by reason of the duress, and no doubt in those circumstances the law would allow a verdict of Not Guilty to be entered....

There may be certain doctrines with regard to murder which do not apply to other cases, but I am willing to assume for the purpose of this case, and I think my brethren are too, that if this woman had been charged herself with committing the offence, she could have set up the plea of duress, not as showing that no offence had been committed, but as showing that she had no *mens rea* because her will was overborne by threats of imprisonment or violence so that she would be excused from punishment. But the offence of buggery whether with man or beast does not depend upon consent; it depends on the act, and if an act of buggery is committed, the felony is committed.

...

In the opinion of the court, there is no doubt that the appellant was properly indicted for being a principal in the second degree to the commission of the crime of buggery. That is all that it is necessary to show. The evidence was, and the jury by their verdict have shown they accepted it, that he caused his wife to have connection with a dog, and if he caused his wife to have connection with a dog he is guilty, whether you call him an aider and abettor or an accessory, as a principal in the second degree. For that reason, this appeal fails and is dismissed.

Appeal dismissed.

■ **NOTES AND QUESTIONS**

1. Note the critical distinction between an affirmative defence and a defence which negates an element of the crime. Duress, as we have seen previously, is an affirmative defence. If the defence were one that negated an element of the crime there would be no crime to which the defendant could have been an accessory. What if the wife in *Bourne* could not have been convicted because of insanity? Would the result have been the same? Do Bourne's acts become any less reprehensible because of the reason why his wife could not be convicted of the substantive offence (or is this the wrong question to be asking)?

2. While the requirement of an offence having been committed seems to be logically inherent in the definition of accessorial liability, the courts at times seem prepared to hold a defendant liable as an accessory as long as the principal has committed the *actus reus* of the offence, even if the alleged principal cannot be convicted of the offence because he did not have the requisite *mens rea*. In these situations, ironically, it is *the accessory* who has the requisite *mens rea* for the substantive offence.

R v *Cogan and Leak*
[1976] 1 QB 217, Court of Appeal

The defendant L took the defendant C back to his home and told his wife that C wanted to have sexual intercourse with her and that he was going to see that she did. L's wife was not willing to have intercourse with C but she was frightened of L who made her go to the bedroom where C had sexual intercourse with her. The wife was sobbing throughout the intercourse. She did not struggle with C but she did try to turn away from him. C was charged with rape and L was charged with 'being aider and abettor to' that rape: the particulars of the offence being that he 'at the same time and place did abet counsel and procure [C] to commit the said offence.' At the trial, C's defence was that he believed that L's wife had consented to the intercourse. In a written statement he made to the police, L, who did not give evidence at the trial, confessed that he had procured C to have sexual intercourse with his wife, that she had not consented to that intercourse and that he had intended her to be raped by C. The jury found both defendants guilty and returned a special verdict that C had believed the wife was consenting but that he had no reasonable grounds for such belief. Both defendants appealed against conviction and C's appeal was allowed.

LAWTON LJ: . . . At the trial Cogan gave evidence that he thought Mrs Leak had consented. The basis for his belief was what he had heard from her husband about her. The drink he had had seems to have been a reason, if not the only one, for mistaking her sobs and distress for consent.

The trial started on October 23, 1974. A few days before, namely, on October 14, press publicity had been given to the fact that the Court of Appeal in *R v Morgan* [1976] AC 182 had certified a point of law of general public importance as to whether in rape the defendant can properly be convicted notwithstanding that he in fact believed that the woman consented if such belief was not based on reasonable grounds and had given leave to appeal to the House of Lords. In the course of his summing up the trial judge stressed the need for the jury to be sure before convicting either of the defendants that the wife had not consented to sexual intercourse. He then went on to direct them in relation to Cogan's case in accordance with the decision of the Court of Appeal in *R v Morgan*. He prudently decided to ask the jury to make a finding as to whether any belief in consent which Cogan may have had was based upon reasonable grounds. The jury returned a verdict of guilty against Cogan thereby showing that they were sure the wife had not consented. They went on to say that Cogan had believed she was consenting but that he had had no reasonable grounds for such belief.

As to Leak he directed the jury that even if Cogan believed that the wife was consenting and had reasonable grounds for such a belief they would still be entitled to find Leak guilty as charged.

Cogan's appeal against conviction was based on the ground that the decision of the House of Lords in *R v Morgan* [1976] AC 182 applied. It did. There is nothing more to be said. It was for this reason that we allowed the appeal and quashed his conviction.

Leak's appeal against conviction was based on the proposition that he could not be found guilty of aiding and abetting Cogan to rape his wife if Cogan was acquitted of that offence as he was deemed in law to have been when his conviction was quashed.

. . . [O]ne fact is clear—the wife had been raped. Cogan had had sexual intercourse with her without her consent. The fact that Cogan was innocent of rape because he believed that she was consenting does not affect the position that she was raped.

Her ravishment had come about because Leak had wanted it to happen and had taken action to see that it did by persuading Cogan to use his body as the instrument for the necessary physical act. In the language of the law the act of sexual intercourse without the wife's consent was the *actus reus*: it had been procured by Leak who had the appropriate *mens rea*, namely, his intention that Cogan should have sexual intercourse with her without her consent. In our judgment it is irrelevant that the man whom Leak had procured to do the physical act himself did not intend to have sexual intercourse with the wife without her consent. Leak was using him as a means to procure a criminal purpose.

Before 1861 a case such as this, pleaded as it was in the indictment, might have presented a court with problems arising from the old distinctions between principals and accessories in felony. Most of the old law was swept away by section 8 of the Accessories and Abettors Act 1861 and what remained by section 1 of the Criminal Law Act 1967. The modern law allowed Leak to be tried and punished as a principal offender. In our judgment he could have been indicted as a principal offender. It would have been no defence for him to submit that if Cogan was an 'innocent' agent, he was necessarily in the old terminology of the law a principal in the first degree, which was a legal impossibility as a man cannot rape his own wife during cohabitation. The law no longer concerns itself with niceties of degrees in participation in crime; but even if it did Leak would still be guilty. The reason a man cannot by his own physical act rape his wife during cohabitation is because the law presumes consent from the marriage ceremony: see *Hale, Pleas of the Crown* (1778), vol. 1, p. 629. There is no such presumption when a man procures a drunken friend to do the physical act for him. Hale CJ put this case in one sentence, at p. 629:

. . . tho in marriage she hath given up her body to her husband, she is not to be by him prostituted to another: see loc. cit.

Had Leak been indicted as a principal offender, the case against him would have been clear beyond argument. Should he be allowed to go free because he was charged with 'being aider and abettor to the same offence'? If we are right in our opinion that the wife had been raped (and no one outside a court of law would say that she had not been), then the particulars of offence accurately stated what Leak had done, namely, he had procured Cogan to commit the offence. This would suffice to uphold the conviction. We would prefer, however, to uphold it on a wider basis. In our judgment convictions should not be upset because of mere technicalities of pleading in an indictment. Leak knew what the case against him was and the facts in support of that case were proved. But for the fact that the jury thought that Cogan in his intoxicated condition might have mistaken the wife's sobs and distress for expressions of her consent, no question of any kind would have arisen about the form of pleading. By his written statement Leak virtually admitted what he had done. As Judge Chapman said in *R v Humphreys* [1965] 3 All ER 689, 692:

> It would be anomalous if a person who admitted to a substantial part in the perpetration of a misdemeanour as aider and abettor could not be convicted on his own admission merely because the person alleged to have been aided and abetted was not or could not be convicted.

In the circumstances of this case it would be more than anomalous: it would be an affront to justice and to the common sense of ordinary folk. It was for these reasons that we dismissed the appeal against conviction.

■ NOTES AND QUESTIONS

1. If an accessory can be convicted of a crime committed by a principal even though the principal himself cannot be convicted of the crime, it would seem to follow that an accessory can be convicted of a more serious crime than the principal. For example, in the presence of both parties, Alice informs Ben that his wife is having an affair with Charles. Ben loses his self-control and kills Charles, as Alice intended. Even if Ben's offence were to be reduced to manslaughter, Alice may be convicted of being an accessory to murder. See *R v Howe* [1987] 1 AC 417.

2. Sometimes the alleged principal is acquitted for lack of evidence. She may, for example, have an alibi. In this situation the jury have not found that no offence has occurred, only that there was insufficient evidence to convict the alleged principal. One who aids, abets, counsels or procures the offence may still be convicted of being an accessory. See, e.g., *R v Hughes* (1860) Bell CC 242.

(ii) *Actus reus*

In order to secure a conviction as an accessory, the prosecutor must show that the defendant either aided, abetted, counselled or procured the offence. In theory each of these terms describes conceptually distinct behaviour. 'Aid' means to help or assist, 'abet' involves instigation or encouragement, 'counsel' implies advising or urging, and 'procure' has been defined as 'causing to be committed'. The line between the categories is often blurred, however, and the Crown is permitted to list all of these acts in the same charge. This is in part no doubt to avoid the absurdity of a defendant, charged with aiding, arguing that he is not guilty because he procured the offence, and then on a subsequent charge of procuring that he really was guilty of abetting, and then on a charge of abetting....

The range of activity which will render one liable as an accessory is as diverse as the human imagination. While aiding, abetting, and counselling are fairly straightforward concepts, this is not true of procuring.

ATTORNEY-GENERAL'S REFERENCE (NO. 1 OF 1975)
[1975] QB 773, Court of Appeal

LORD WIDGERY CJ: This case comes before the court on a reference from the Attorney-General under s. 36 of the Criminal Justice Act 1972, and by his reference he asks the following question:

> Whether an accused who surreptitiously laced a friend's drinks with double measures of spirits when he knew that his friend would shortly be driving his car home, and in consequence his friend drove with an excess quantity of alcohol in his body and was convicted of the offence under the Road Traffic Act 1972, s. 6(1) is entitled to a ruling of no case to answer on being later charged as an aider and abetter, counsellor and procurer, on the ground that there was no shared intention between the two, that the accused did not by accompanying him or otherwise positively encourage the friend to drive, or on any other ground . . . .

The present question has no doubt arisen because in recent years there have been a number of instances where men charged with driving their motor cars with an excess quantity of alcohol in the blood have sought to excuse their conduct by saying that their drinks were 'laced', as the jargon has it; that is to say some strong spirit was put into an otherwise innocuous drink and as a result the driver consumed more alcohol than he had either intended to consume or had the desire to consume. The relevance of all that is not that it entitles the driver to an acquittal, because such driving is an absolute offence, but that it can be relied on as a special reason for not disqualifying the driver from driving. Hence no doubt the importance which has been attached in recent months to the possibility of this argument being raised in a normal charge of driving with excess alcohol.

The question requires us to say whether on the facts posed there is a case to answer, and needless to say in the trial from which this reference is derived the judge was of the opinion that there was no case to answer and so ruled. We have to say in effect whether he is right.

The language in the section which determines whether a 'secondary party', as he is sometimes called, is guilty of a criminal offence committed by another embraces the four words 'aid, abet, counsel or procure'. The origin of those words is to be found in s. 8 of the Accessories and Abettors Act 1861 which provides:

> Whosoever shall aid, abet, counsel, or procure the commission of any misdemeanor, whether the same be a misdemeanor at common law or by virtue of any Act passed or to be passed, shall be liable to be tried, indicted, and punished as a principal offender.

Thus, in the past, when the distinction was still drawn between felony and misdemeanor, it was sufficient to make a person guilty of a misdemeanor if he aided, abetted, counselled or procured the offence of another. When the difference between felonies and misdemeanors was abolished in 1967, s. 1 of the Criminal Law Act 1967 in effect provided that the same test should apply to make a secondary party guilty either of treason or felony.

Of course it is the fact that in the great majority of instances where a secondary party is sought to be convicted of an offence there has been a contact between the principal offender and the secondary party. Aiding and abetting almost inevitably involves a situation in which the secondary party and the main offender are together at some stage discussing the plans which they may be making in respect of the alleged offence, and are in contact so that each knows what is passing through the mind of the other.

In the same way it seems to us that a person who counsels the commission of a crime by another, almost inevitably comes to a moment when he is in contact with that other, when he is discussing the offence with that other and when, to use the words of the statute, he counsels the other to commit the offence.

The fact that so often the relationship between the secondary party and the principal will be such that there is a meeting of minds between them caused the trial judge in the case from which this reference is derived to think that this was really an essential feature of proving or establishing the guilt of the secondary party and, as we understand his judgment, he took the view that in the absence of some sort of meeting of minds, some sort of mental link between the secondary party and the principal, there could be no aiding, abetting or counselling of the offence within the meaning of the section.

So far as aiding, abetting and counselling is concerned we would go a long way with that conclusion. It may very well be, as I said a moment ago, difficult to think of a case of aiding, abetting or counselling when the parties have not met and have not discussed in some respects the terms of the offence which they have in mind. But we do not see why a similar principle should apply to procuring. We approach s. 8 of the 1861 Act on the basis that the words should be given their ordinary meaning, if possible. We approach the section on the basis also that if four words are employed here, 'aid, abet, counsel or procure', the probability is that there is a difference between each of those four words and the other three, because, if there were no such difference, then Parliament would be wasting time in using four words where two or three would do. Thus, in deciding whether that which is assumed to be done under our reference was a criminal offence we approach the section on the footing that each word must be given its ordinary meaning.

To procure means to produce by endeavour. You procure a thing by setting out to see that it happens and taking the appropriate steps to produce that happening. We think that there are plenty of instances in which a person may be said to procure the commission of a crime by another even though there is no sort of conspiracy between the two, even though there is no attempt at agreement or discussion as to the form which the offence should take. In our judgment the offence described in this reference is such a case.

If one looks back at the facts of the reference: the accused surreptitiously laced his friend's drink. This is an important element and, although we are not going to decide today anything other than the problem posed to us, it may well be that in similar cases where the lacing of the drink or the introduction of the extra alcohol is known to the driver quite different considerations may apply. We say that because where the driver has no knowledge of what is happening, in most instances he would have no means of preventing the offence from being committed. If the driver is unaware of what has happened, he will not be taking precautions. He will get into his car seat, switch on the ignition and drive home and, consequently, the conception of another procuring the commission of the offence by the driver is very much stronger where the driver is innocent of all knowledge of what is happening, as in the present case where the lacing of the drink was surreptitious.

The second thing which is important in the facts set out in our reference is that following and in consequence of the introduction of the extra alcohol, the friend drove with an excess quantity of alcohol in his blood. Causation here is important. You cannot procure an offence unless there is a causal link between what you do and the commission of the offence, and here we are told that in consequence of the addition of this alcohol the driver, when he drove home, drove with an excess quantity of alcohol in his body.

Giving the words their ordinary meaning in English, and asking oneself whether in those circumstances the offence has been procured, we are in no doubt that the answer is that it has. It has been procured because, unknown to the driver and without his collaboration, he has been put in a position in which in fact he has committed an offence which he never would have committed otherwise. We think that there was a case to answer and that the trial judge should have directed the jury that an offence is committed if it is shown beyond reasonable doubt that the accused knew that his friend was going to drive, and also knew that the ordinary and natural result of the additional alcohol added to the friend's drink would be to bring him above the recognised limit of 80 milligrammes per 100 millilitres of blood.

■ NOTES AND QUESTIONS

1. Consider the case of the social host who encourages his guests to imbibe of a punch liberally laced with alcohol. The guests know that the punch contains alcohol but not the percentage amount. Is the host liable as an accessory to drunk driving in the case of guests who drive home while over the legal limit? If the guest were to run over a child while driving under the influence, would the host be an accessory to the homicide?

2. Under the approach of the court in *Attorney-General's Reference (No. 1 of 1975)* there need be no agreement between principal and accessory, the two do not

ever have to have met, and the principal does not have to know of the accessory's assistance or existence. If there is an agreement, on the other hand, the two may also be guilty of conspiracy.

(a) Presence, activity and inactivity
Can one become an accessory by doing nothing?

R v Clarkson and Others
[1971] 3 All ER 344, Courts-Martial Appeal Court

MEGAW LJ: . . . The relevant facts will be recited as briefly as possible. The victim of the offences was an 18 year old girl named Elke von Groen. On 9th May 1970 she, having recently come out of hospital where she had undergone an operation to her womb, went to a party at the barracks at Menden. At about midnight she left the party to go to see a soldier with whom she had in the past been familiar. She went to his room. He was not there but other soldiers were there. Eventually she went to another room, room 64, where the rapes occurred. There she was raped at least by Newton, by Holloway and by Marshall at one time or another between midnight and about 3.15 a.m. She was physically injured and her clothes were torn to shreds. To say that those who attacked her behaved like animals would be unjust to animals. At some time after the raping began and when she had been screaming and moaning, there were clustered outside the door of room 64 a number of men, including the three appellants, no doubt listening to what was going on inside. The only thing to be said in their favour is that they may have been in a drunken condition when their moral sense and sense of the requirements of human decency had left them. The door of room 64 opened and they, including the three appellants, in the words of a witness 'piled in' to the room. There is no doubt that they remained there for a considerable time and there is no doubt that during that time the unfortunate girl was raped. . . . there was no evidence on which the prosecution sought to rely that either the appellant Clarkson or the appellant Carroll had done any physical act or uttered any word which involved direct physical participation or verbal encouragement. There was no evidence that they had touched the girl, helped to hold her down, done anything to her, done anything to prevent others from assisting her or to prevent her from escaping, or from trying to ward off her attackers, or that they had said anything which gave encouragement to the others to commit crime or to participate in committing crime. Therefore, if there was here aiding and abetting by the appellants Clarkson or Carroll it could only have been on the basis of inferences to be drawn that by their very presence they, each of them separately as concerns himself, encouraged those who were committing rape. Let it be accepted, and there was evidence to justify this assumption, that the presence of those two appellants in the room where the offence was taking place was not accidental in any sense and that it was not by chance, unconnected with the crime, that they were there. Let it be accepted that they entered the room when the crime was committed because of what they had heard, which indicated that a woman was being raped, and they remained there.

R v Coney (1882) 8 QBD 534 decided that non-accidental presence at the scene of the crime is not conclusive of aiding and abetting. The jury has to be told by the judge, or as in this case the court-martial has to be told by the judge-advocate, in clear terms what it is that has to be proved before they can convict of aiding and abetting; what it is of which the jury or the court-martial, as the case may be, must be sure as matters of inference before they can convict of aiding and abetting in such a case where the evidence adduced by the prosecution is limited to non-accidental presence. What has to be proved is stated by Hawkins J in a well-known passage in his judgment in R v Coney where he said:

> In my opinion, to constitute an aider and abettor some active steps must be taken by word, or action, with the intent to instigate the principal, or principals. Encouragement does not of necessity amount to aiding and abetting, it may be intentional or unintentional, a man may unwittingly encourage another in fact by his presence, by misinterpreted words, or gestures, or by his silence, or non-interference, or he may encourage intentionally by expressions, gestures,

or actions intended to signify approval. In the latter case he aids and abets, in the former he does not. It is no criminal offence to stand by, a mere passive spectator of a crime, even of a murder. Non-interference to prevent a crime is not itself a crime. But the fact that a person was voluntarily and purposely present witnessing the commission of a crime, and offered no opposition to it, though he might reasonably be expected to prevent and had the power so to do, or at least to express his dissent, might under some circumstances, afford cogent evidence upon which a jury would be justified in finding that he wilfully encouraged and so aided and abetted. But it would be purely a question for the jury whether he did so or not.

...

It is not enough, then, that the presence of the accused has, in fact, given encouragement. It must be proved that the accused intended to give encouragement; that he *wilfully* encouraged. In a case such as the present, more than in many other cases where aiding and abetting is alleged, it was essential that that element should be stressed; for there was here at least the possibility that a drunken man with his self-discipline loosened by drink, being aware that a woman was being raped, might be attracted to the scene and might stay on the scene in the capacity of what is known as a voyeur; and, while his presence and the presence of others might in fact encourage the rapers or discourage the victim, he himself, enjoying the scene or at least standing by assenting, might not intend that his presence should offer encouragement to rapers and would-be rapers or discouragement to the victim; he might not realise that he was giving encouragement; so that, while encouragement there might be, it would not be a case in which, to use the words of Hawkins J, the accused person 'wilfully encouraged'.

■ NOTES AND QUESTIONS

1. What more would the defendants in *Clarkson* have had to have done to be deemed accessories? What if they had shouted encouragement to the rapists? Would (or should) it matter whether the rapists heard their shouts? Whether they were spurred on by them?

2. Should the defendants in *Clarkson* have been liable for failing to summon the police? Should failure to report a crime itself be a crime, perhaps on the theory that one has a social responsibility and duty as a citizen to do so? At one point in English history, such an offence (misprision of felony) existed (see *Sykes* v *Director of Public Prosecutions* [1961] 3 All ER 33), but it was abolished by the Criminal Law Act 1967. Now it is only a crime to accept consideration for not disclosing an arrestable offence (Criminal Law Act 1967, s. 5(1)). Should the law have gone in the opposite direction? If assistance to a victim of a crime can be provided at no risk to the actor, why should such assistance not be legally required, and why should one not be criminally liable for failing to provide such assistance?

3. To be guilty as an accessory, must the principal be aware of the accessory's presence? Can a principal ever draw support from an uncommunicated resolve to help? See *R* v *Allan* [1965] 1 QB 130, Court of Criminal Appeal.

4. Assume that the spectators in *Clarkson* had made a mental resolve to prevent the police from interrupting of the rape, without communicating their resolve to the rapists. Would this be sufficient to hold them liable as accessories, even if it should turn out that their assistance was not required? How does this hypothetical situation differ from that where a defendant has agreed to serve as lookout for a principal but no third parties intervene, and therefore no need arises for a warning to the principal?

Compare *Clarkson* with *Wilcox* v *Jeffery*.

Wilcox v Jeffery

[1951] 1 All ER 464, King's Bench Division

LORD GODDARD CJ: This is a Case stated by the metropolitan magistrate at Bow Street Magistrate's Court before whom the appellant, Herbert William Wilcox, the proprietor of a periodical called 'Jazz Illustrated,' was charged on an information that 'on Dec. 11, 1949, he did unlawfully aid and abet one Coleman Hawkins in contravening art. 1(4) of the Aliens Order, 1920, by failing to comply with a condition attached to a grant of leave to land, to wit, that the said Coleman Hawkins should take no employment paid or unpaid while in the United Kingdom, contrary to art. 18(2) of the Aliens Order, 1920.' Under the Aliens Order, art. 1(1), it is provided that

> …an alien coming…by sea to a place in the United Kingdom—(a) shall not land in the United Kingdom without the leave of an immigration officer…'

It is provided by art. 1(4) that:

> An immigration officer, in accordance with general or special direction of the Secretary of State, may, by general order or notice or otherwise, attach such conditions as he may think fit to the grant of leave to land, and the Secretary of State may at any time vary such conditions in such manner as he thinks fit, and the alien shall comply with the conditions so attached or varied…

If the alien fails to comply, he is to be in the same position as if he has landed without permission, i.e., he commits an offence.

The case is concerned with the visit of a celebrated professor of the saxophone, a gentleman by the name of Hawkins who was a citizen of the United States. He came here at the invitation of two gentlemen of the name of Curtis and Hughes, connected with a jazz club which enlivens the neighbourhood of Willesden. They, apparently, had applied for permission for Mr Hawkins to land and it was refused, but, nevertheless, this professor of the saxophone arrived with four French musicians. When they came to the airport, among the people who were there to greet them was the appellant. He had not arranged their visit, but he knew they were coming and he was there to report the arrival of these important musicians for his magazine. So, evidently, he was regarding the visit of Mr Hawkins as a matter which would be of interest to himself and the magazine which he was editing and selling for profit. Messrs Curtis and Hughes arranged a concert at the Princes Theatre, London. The appellant attended that concert as a spectator. He paid for his ticket. Mr Hawkins went on the stage and delighted the audience by playing the saxophone. The appellant did not get up and protest in the name of the musicians of England that Mr Hawkins ought not to be here competing with them and taking the bread out of their mouths or the wind out of their instruments. It is not found that he actually applauded, but he was there having paid to go in, and, no doubt, enjoying the performance, and then, lo and behold, out comes his magazine with a most laudatory description, fully illustrated, of this concert. On those facts the magistrate has found that he aided and abetted.

…

There was not accidental presence in this case. The appellant paid to go to the concert and he went there because he wanted to report it. He must, therefore, be held to have been present, taking part, concurring, or encouraging, whichever word you like to use for expressing this conception. It was an illegal act on the part of Hawkins to play the saxophone or any other instrument at this concert. The appellant clearly knew that it was an unlawful act for him to play. He had gone there to hear him, and his presence and his payment to go there was an encouragement. He went there to make use of the performance, because he went there, as the magistrate finds was justified in finding, to get 'copy' for his newspaper. It might have been entirely different, as I say, if he had gone there and protested, saying: 'The musicians' union do not like you foreigners coming here and playing and you ought to get off the stage.' If he had booed, it might have been some evidence that he was not aiding and abetting. If he had gone as a member of a *claque* to try to drown the noise of the saxophone, he might very likely be found not guilty of aiding and abetting. In this case it seems clear that he was there, not only to approve and encourage what was done, but to take advantage of it by getting 'copy' for his paper. In those circumstances there was evidence on which the magistrate could find that the appellant aided and abetted, and for these reasons I am of opinion that the appeal fails.

■ NOTES AND QUESTIONS

1. Would the defendant have been liable if he had written an unfavourable review? What about the members of the audience – did they also commit an offence? Did it matter whether or not they protested? Whether or not they applauded? Whether or not they had paid admission to the concert? The purpose in asking these questions is to identify what constituted the aiding and abetting and at what point in time the requisite assistance occurred.

2. What is the difference between *Wilcox* v *Jeffrey* and *Clarkson*? Is it the fact that in *Clarkson* the rape was already underway when the alleged aiding occurred, while in *Wilcox* v *Jeffrey* there would have been no crime if there had been no audience? Did the audience in *Wilcox* v *Jeffrey* provide more in the way of positive encouragement than the audience in *Clarkson*? See also *R* v *Coney* (1882) 8 QBD 534.

3. Must a causal relationship between the acts of the accessory and the offence of the principal be proved? Sometimes, while the accessory's assistance may have facilitated the commission of an offence, the principal would in any event have committed it. Does it depend on the form that the accessory's participation is alleged to have taken? In *R* v *Luffman* [2008] EWCA Crim 1752, it was held that where the prosecution claimed that the defendant had *counseled* the offence committed, it did not have to prove causation. Might there be a different result in respect of proving causation when *procuring* is alleged? What does *Attorney-General's Reference (No. 1 of 1975)* (p. 655) have to say on this issue?.

In the context of liability for inaction you may recall (see Chapter 2) that one may be under a legal duty to act such that the failure to act can give rise to criminal liability. Often that liability will take the form of a conviction as an accessory.

Rubie v Faulkner

[1940] 1 KB 571, King's Bench Division

The appellant, while in a motor vehicle driven by the holder of a provisional licence (a 'learner-driver') who was driving under his supervision in accordance with reg. 16(3)(a) of the Motor Vehicles (Driving Licences) Regulations 1937, was in a position to see that the driver was about to overtake another vehicle by pulling considerably to the offside at a pronounced bend of the road, but he neither said nor did anything to prevent it. An accident having occurred and the driver having been convicted of driving without due care and attention:–

Held, that the appellant was rightly convicted of aiding and abetting the driver in the commission of the offence.

LORD HEWART CJ: ... [T]he condition on which the holder of a provisional licence is allowed to drive a motor-vehicle on a highway is that he is under the supervision of an experienced driver. The very essence of the matter is that there should be a supervisor competent to supervise. The duty being clear on the face of the regulation, it was a pure question of fact for the justices to decide whether that duty had been performed.

It seems to me that it was open to the justices to find that the appellant, by his passive conduct in circumstances which required him to be active, if only by exclaiming: 'Keep in!', failed to discharge the duty which he had undertaken, and thus was guilty of the offence with which he was charged. In my opinion, therefore, this appeal should be dismissed.

HILBERY J: I agree. The regulation is framed to make some provision for the protection of the public against the dangers to which they are exposed through a car being driven on the road by a driver who is still a learner and therefore assumed to be not fully competent. It is, I can only suppose, because a learner-driver is assumed to be not fully competent that the regulation provides that a supervisor shall accompany him. This being so, the supervisor must be intended by the regulation to have the duty, by supervision, of making up as far as possible for the driver's incompetence. In other words, it is the supervisor's duty, when necessary, to do whatever can reasonably be expected to be done by a person supervising the acts of another to prevent that other from acting unskilfully or carelessly or in a manner likely to cause danger to others, and to this extent to participate in the driving.

In this case it was found that the supervisor could see the driver was about to do the unlawful act of which he was convicted and the magistrates found that the supervisor remained passive. There is no hint in the case that the supervisor in evidence ever asserted that he did anything. For him to refrain from doing anything when he could see that an unlawful act was about to be done, and his duty was to prevent an unlawful act if he could, was for him to aid and abet.

(iii) *Mens rea*

Proof of *mens rea* is essential to liability as an accessory. This is true even when the offence of the principal is one of strict liability. There are, however, two schools of thought as to what constitutes the *mens rea* of accessorial liability.

All would agree that one who aids, abets, counsels or procures a crime with the **intent** that the crime be committed is guilty as an accessory if the crime is committed. We have seen in the previous chapter that, if the substantive offence is not committed, such a person may be convicted under s. 44 of the Serious Crime Act 2007 (encouragement or assistance).

The more controversial issue relates to the role of knowledge. One cannot be convicted of being an accessory **unless** one knows (or perhaps is wilfully blind or reckless to the fact) that a crime will be committed as a result of one's assistance. But what if one **knows** that the effect of his assistance will be to bring about a crime? Is that enough to warrant a conviction? There is both judicial and scholarly support for the position that such a person – one who **knows** that a crime will be committed because of his assistance – may be convicted of being an accessory, regardless of whether or not the defendant intends that the crime be committed, is ambivalent as to whether the crime is committed, or actively prefers that the crime not be committed.

National Coal Board v *Gamble*
[1959] 1 QB 11, Queen's Bench Division

On 3 October 1957, M, the servant of a firm of hauliers, took his lorry to a colliery of the National Coal Board where it was filled with coal from a hopper and was then taken to a weighbridge, where the weighbridge operator H, who was employed by the board, weighed the lorry and its load and told M that the load was nearly 4 tons overweight. M., saying that he would risk taking the over-load, took the weigh-bridge ticket from H and left the colliery premises. He was subsequently stopped by the police and his firm were later convicted of contravening the Motor Vehicles (Construction and Use) Regulations 1955. It appeared that the hauliers were collecting the coal for carriage to a power station of an electricity authority, to whom the Coal Board were bound by contract to supply a bulk quantity of coal. The board were charged with aiding and abetting the firm in the commission of an offence.

DEVLIN J:...It was contended on behalf of the board that Haslam had no option after weighing but to issue the ticket for the amount then in the lorry. I think that this contention is unsound. In the circumstances of this case the loading must be taken as subject to adjustment; otherwise, if the contract were for a limited amount, the seller might make an over-delivery or an under-delivery which could not thereafter be rectified and the carrier might be contractually compelled to carry away a load in excess of that legally permitted. I think that the delivery of the coal was not completed until after the ascertained weight had been assented to and some act was done signifying assent and passing the property. The property passed when Haslam asked Mallender whether he intended to take the load and Mallender said he would risk it and when the mutual assent was, as it were, sealed by the delivery and acceptance of the weighbridge ticket. Haslam could therefore after he knew of the overload have refused to transfer the property in the coal.

...[A] man is presumed to intend the natural and probable consequences of his acts, and the consequence of supplying essential material is that assistance is given to the criminal. It is always open to the defendant, as in *R v Steane* [1947] KB 997, to give evidence of his real intention. But in this case the defence called no evidence. The prima facie presumption is therefore enough to justify the verdict, unless it is the law that some other mental element besides intent is necessary to the offence.

This is what Mr Thompson argues, and he describes the additional element as the purpose or motive of encouraging the crime. No doubt evidence of an interest in the crime or of an express purpose to assist it will greatly strengthen the case for the prosecution. But an indifference to the result of the crime does not of itself negative abetting. If one man deliberately sells to another a gun to be used for murdering a third, he may be indifferent about whether the third man lives or dies and interested only in the cash profit to be made out of the sale, but he can still be an aider and abettor. To hold otherwise would be to negative the rule that mens rea is a matter of intent only and does not depend on desire or motive.

...[T]he facts show an act of assent made by Haslam after knowledge of the proposed illegality and without which the property would not have passed. If some positive act to complete delivery is committed after knowledge of the illegality, the position in law must, I think, be just the same as if the knowledge had been obtained before the delivery had been begun. Of course, it is quite likely that Haslam was confused about the legal position and thought that he was not entitled to withhold the weighbridge ticket. There is no mens rea if the defendant is shown to have a genuine belief in the existence of circumstances which, if true, would negative an intention to aid.... But this argument, which might have been the most cogent available to the defence, cannot now be relied upon, because Haslam was not called to give evidence about what he thought or believed....

Gillick v West Norfolk and Wisbech Area Health Authority
[1984] 1 QB 581, Queen's Bench Division

WOOLF J:...*Does the prescribing of contraceptives to a girl under 16 amount to criminal conduct on the part of a doctor?*

Section 28(1) of the Sexual Offences Act 1956 makes it

an offence for a person to cause or encourage...the commission of unlawful sexual intercourse with...a girl under the age of 16 for whom he is responsible.

Subsection (3) provides:

The persons who are to be treated for the purposes of this section as responsible for a girl are ...(c) any other person who has the custody, charge or care of her.

Putting aside the question of whether or not the doctor's conduct could be said to amount to encouraging unlawful sexual intercourse, I cannot accept Mr Wright's submission that when a girl goes to a clinic for advice and/or treatment, she is in the ad hoc care of the doctor or the clinic. The words should not be narrowly construed but, in my view, they are inappropriate to cover a situation where a girl attends a clinic to seek help.

So far as the offence against section 6 of the Sexual Offences Act 1956, is concerned, I accept that a doctor who is misguided enough to provide a girl who is under the age of 16, or a man, with advice and assistance with regard to contraceptive measures with the intention thereby of encouraging them to have sexual intercourse, is an accessory before the fact to an offence contrary to section 6. I stress the words 'with the intention thereby of encouraging them to have sexual intercourse.' However, this, I assume, will not usually be the attitude of a doctor.

There will certainly be some cases, and I hope the majority of cases, where the doctor decides to give the advice and prescribe contraceptives despite the fact he was firmly against unlawful sexual intercourse taking place but felt, nevertheless, that he had to prescribe the contraceptives because, whether or not he did so, intercourse would in fact take place and the provision of contraceptives would, in his view, be in the best interests of the girl in protecting her from an unwanted pregnancy and the risk of a sexually transmitted disease. It is as to whether or not in such a situation the doctor is to be treated as being an accessory, that I have found the greatest difficulty in applying the law.

Mr Wright submits, and I accept that he is right in this submission, that it is necessary to distinguish between motive and intent. Even if your motives are unimpeachable, if you in fact assist in the commission of an offence, Mr Wright submits you are an accessory. He relies on the judgment of Devlin J in *National Coal Board* v *Gamble* [1959] 1 QB 11. In that case, Devlin J said, at p. 20:

> A person who supplies the instrument for a crime or anything essential to its commission aids in the commission of it; and if he does so knowingly and with intent to aid, he abets it as well and is therefore guilty of aiding and abetting.... Another way of putting the point is to say that aiding and abetting is a crime that requires proof of *mens rea*, that is to say, of intention to aid as well as of knowledge of the circumstances, and that proof of the intent involves proof of a positive act of assistance voluntarily done.

Devlin J's judgment in that case was considered by Lord Simon of Glaisdale in *Director of Public Prosecutions for Northern Ireland* v *Lynch* [1975] AC 653, 698–699:

> As regards the *actus reus*, 'aiding' and 'abetting' are, as *Smith and Hogan* notes (p. 93), synonymous. But the phrase is not a pleonasm; because 'abet' clearly imports mens rea, which 'aid' might not. As Devlin J said in *National Coal Board* v *Gamble*...—and he quotes the passage I have just quoted—The *actus reus* is the supplying of an instrument for a crime or anything essential for its commission. On Devlin J's analysis the *mens rea* does not go beyond this. The act of supply must be voluntary (in the sense I tried to define earlier in this speech), and it must be foreseen that the instrument or other object or service supplied will probably (or possibly and desiredly) be used for the commission of a crime. The definition of the crime does not in itself suggest any ulterior intent; and whether anything further in the way of mens rea was required was precisely the point at issue in *Gamble's* case. Slade J thought the very concept of aiding and abetting imported the concept of motive. But Lord Goddard CJ and Devlin J disagreed with this. So do I. Slade J thought that abetting involved assistance or encouragement, and that both implied motive. So far as assistance is concerned, this is clearly not so. One may lend assistance without any motive, or even with the motive of bringing about a result directly contrary to that in fact assisted by one's effort.

However, in applying those statements of the law, three matters have to be borne in mind. First of all, contraceptives do not in themselves directly assist in the commission of the crime of unlawful sexual intercourse. The analogy of providing the motor car for a burglary or providing poison to the murderer, relied on in argument, are not true comparisons. While if the man wears a sheath, there may be said to be a physical difference as to the quality of intercourse, the distinction that I am seeking to draw is clearer where the woman takes the pill or is fitted with an internal device, when the unlawful act will not be affected in any way. The only effect of the provision of the means of contraception is that in some cases it is likely to increase the likelihood of a crime being committed by reducing the inhibitions of the persons concerned to having sexual intercourse because of their fear of conception or the contraction of disease. I therefore see a distinction between the assistance or aiding referred to by Lord Simon of Glaisdale and Devlin J and the act of the doctor in prescribing contraceptives. I would regard the pill prescribed to the woman as not so much 'the instrument for a crime or anything essential to its commission' but a palliative against the consequences of the crime.

The second factor that has to be borne in mind is that the girl herself commits no offence under section 6 since the section is designed to protect her from herself: see *R* v *Tyrrell* [1894] 1 QB 710. This creates problems with regard to relying upon any encouragement by the doctor as making him the accessory to the offence where the girl alone attends the clinic. The well-known case, *R* v *Bourne* (1952) 36 Cr App R 125, has to be distinguished because there, the woman can be said to have committed the offence although she was not criminally responsible because of duress. The doctor, if he is to be an accessory where the woman alone consults him, will only be an accessory if it can be shown that he acted through the innocent agency of the woman, the situation dealt with in *R* v *Cooper* (1833) 5 C & P 535.

The final point that has to be borne in mind is that there will be situations where long-term contraceptive measures are taken to protect girls who, sadly, will strike up promiscuous relationships whatever the supervision of those who are responsible for their well-being, the sort of situation that Butler-Sloss J had to deal with in *In re P (A Minor)* (1981) 80 LGR 301. In such a situation the doctor will prescribe the measures to be taken purely as a safeguard against the risk that at some time in the future, the girl will form a casual relationship with a man when sexual intercourse will take place. In order to be an accessory, you normally have to know the material circumstances. In such a situation the doctor would know no more than that there was a risk of sexual intercourse taking place at an unidentified place with an unidentified man on an unidentified date—hardly the state of knowledge which is normally associated with an accessory before the fact.

Under this limb of the argument, the conclusion which I have therefore come to is, that while a doctor could, in following the guidance, so encourage unlawful sexual intercourse as to render this conduct criminal, in the majority of situations the probabilities are that a doctor will be able to follow the advice without rendering himself liable to criminal proceedings. Before leaving this limb of the argument, I should make it absolutely clear that the absence of consent of the parents makes no difference to the criminal responsibility of the doctor. If his conduct would be criminal without the parents' consent, it would be equally criminal with their consent.

■ **NOTES AND QUESTIONS**

1. Are *Gillick* (which one should note was a civil and not a criminal case) and *Gamble* reconcilable? For all intents and purposes, did not the doctor in *Gillick* know as surely as the weighbridge operator in *Gamble* that the assistance provided would lead to the commission of a crime?

2. In *Gamble*, the defendants stood to gain neither financially nor in any other way when the lorry driver proceeded with his overweight load. In *Gillick*, the doctor's goal was to prevent an unwanted pregnancy and the risk of a sexually transmitted disease. Should the doctor's ulterior purpose matter?

3. Is the effect of the decision in *Gamble* to create a private police force – must citizens prevent crimes from being committed or risk being deemed accessories? Or is *Gamble* distinguished by the fact that the weighbridge operator *knew* that with the ticket he provided the lorry driver would commit a crime? Where should the law draw the line of liability as we move away from 'knowledge' to some lesser state of awareness? What about criminal consequences which are foreseen to a high degree of probability? Foreseen as more probable than not? Foreseen as a possibility but not a probability? See also *Carter* v *Richardson* [1974] RTR 314.

4. Should the nature of the aid provided be relevant? What if the aid consists of an item of ordinary commerce, purchasable anywhere? Arlene walks into Sherlock's

cutlery shop and asks for a knife sharp enough to kill a person. Sherlock, suspecting a crime may be afoot, refuses to sell Arlene the knife. Will not Arlene now simply purchase the knife at another store, being less indiscreet about her intentions? Should Sherlock have to report his suspicions to the police? Should he be under a duty to do so? Was this the position that the weighbridge operator in *Gamble* found himself?

5. In his opinion in *Gillick* in the House of Lords, Lord Scarman spoke of cases where '[t]he bona fide exercise by a doctor of his clinical judgment must be a complete negation of the guilty mind which is an essential ingredient of the criminal offence of aiding and abetting the commission of unlawful sexual intercourse'. Is this correct as a matter of law or simply reflective of a desirable public policy? The Sexual Offences Act 2003 s. 73 provides:

Exceptions to aiding, abetting and counselling

(1) A person is not guilty of aiding, abetting or counselling the commission against a child of an offence to which this section applies if he acts for the purpose of—

(a) protecting the child from sexually transmitted infection,

(b) protecting the physical safety of the child,

(c) preventing the child from becoming pregnant, or

(d) promoting the child's emotional well-being by the giving of advice,

and not for the purpose of obtaining sexual gratification or for the purpose of causing or encouraging the activity constituting the offence or the child's participation in it.

. . .

(3) This section does not affect any other enactment or any rule of law restricting the circumstances in which a person is guilty of aiding, abetting or counselling an offence under this Part.

B: Scope of liability

Sometimes one who provides assistance to a criminal enterprise knows that a crime will be committed but does not know what that crime will be. Is the accessory then liable for whatever crime is committed?

R v Bainbridge

[1960] 1 QB 129, Court of Criminal Appeal

On the night of 30 October 1958, the Stoke Newington branch of the Midland Bank was broken into by cutting the bars of a window, the doors of the strong room and of a safe inside the strong room. They were opened by means of oxygen cutting equipment and nearly £18,000 was stolen. The cutting equipment was left behind and it was later found that that cutting equipment so left behind by the thieves had been purchased by the appellant, Alan Bainbridge, some six weeks earlier. He appealed against his conviction of being accessory before the fact to office-breaking.

LORD PARKER CJ: . . . The case against him [the appellant] was that he had bought this cutting equipment on behalf of one or more of the thieves with the full knowledge that it was going to be used, if not against the Stoke Newington branch of the Midland Bank, at any rate for the purposes of breaking and entering premises.

The appellant's case, as given in his evidence, was this:

True, I had bought this equipment from two different firms. I had gone there with a man called Shakeshaft to buy it for him. As a result of conversation which I had with him I was suspicious that he wanted it for something illegal, I thought it was for breaking up stolen goods which Shakeshaft had received, and as the result in those purchases I gave false names and addresses, but I had no knowledge that the equipment was going to be used for any such purpose as it was used.

...

Mr Simpson, who has argued this case very well, contends that...in order that a man should be convicted of being accessory before the fact, it must be shown that at the time he bought the equipment in a case such as this he knew that a particular crime was going to be committed, and by a particular crime Mr Simpson means that the premises in this case which were going to be broken into were known to the appellant and contemplated by him, and not only the premises in question but the date when the breaking in was going to occur; in other words, that he must know that on a particular date the Stoke Newington branch of the Midland Bank is intended to be broken into.

The court fully appreciates that it is not enough that it should be shown that a man knows that some illegal venture is intended. To take this case, it would not be enough if he knew—he says he only suspected—that the equipment was going to be used to dispose of stolen property. That would not be enough. Equally, this court is quite satisfied that it is unnecessssry that knowledge of the particular crime which was in fact committed should be shown to his knowledge to have been intended, and by 'particular crime' I am using the words in the same way in which Mr Simpson used them, namely, on a particular date and particular premises.

It is not altogether easy to lay down a precise form of words which will cover every case that can be contemplated but, having considered the cases and the law this court is quite clear that the direction of Judge Aarvold in this case cannot be criticised.

Judge Aarvold in this case...makes it clear that there must be not merely suspicion but knowledge that a crime of the type in question was intended, and that the equipment was bought with that in view. In his reference to the felony of the type intended it was, as he stated, the felony of breaking and entering premises and the stealing of property from those premises. The court can see nothing wrong in that direction.

Director of Public Prosecutions for Northern Ireland v Maxwell
[1978] 3 All ER 1140, House of Lords

The appellant was a member of an illegal organisation in Northern Ireland which had been responsible for sectarian murders and bombings. On the night of 3 January 1976 the appellant was told by a member of the organisation to guide a car at night to a public house in a remote country area. The appellant knew that he was being sent on a terrorist attack but did not know what form it would take. Driving his own car he led another car containing three or four men to the public house. When he arrived there the appellant drove slowly past and then drove home. The other car stopped opposite the public house, one of the occupants got out, ran across to the public house and threw a pipe bomb containing 5 lbs of explosive into the hallway. The attack failed due to action taken by the licensee's son. The appellant was charged with doing an act with intent to cause an explosion by a bomb, contrary to s. 3(a) of the Explosive Substances Act 1883 and with possession of a bomb contrary to s. 3(b) of that Act. The appellant was convicted of both offences as principal in the second degree (i.e. as an accomplice). He appealed contending that since he did not know what form the attack would take or of the presence of the bomb in the other car he could not properly be convicted of aiding and abetting in the commission of crimes of which he was ignorant. The Court of Criminal

Appeal in Northern Ireland dismissed his appeal. The appellant appealed to the House of Lords.

VISCOUNT DILHORNE: ... At the trial, counsel for the appellant submitted that there was no evidence that the appellant knew the nature of the job that was to be done or that he knew of the presence of the bomb in the Cortina and that he could not be convicted of aiding and abetting in the commission of crimes of which he was ignorant. In the course of a careful and thorough judgment this submission was rejected by MacDermott J. It was repeated before the Court of Criminal Appeal in Northern Ireland and rejected by them. They, however, certified that the following point of law of general public importance was involved, namely:

> If the crime committed by the principal, and actually assisted by the accused, was one of a number of offences, one of which the accused knew the principal would probably commit, is the guilty mind which must be proved against an accomplice thereby proved against the accused?

... When the appellant was told at Dunadry what he was required to do, he must have known that he was required to take part in a UVF 'military' operation. He cannot have thought that at that time of the evening welfare was involved. MacDermott J inferred that the preparation for timing and route of the journey indicated that the job was to be an attack on the Crosskeys bar. Even if the appellant did not appreciate that, which is most unlikely, he must have known that the 'military' operation was to take place at or near the Crosskeys Inn. Knowing that, he led the way and so played an important part in the operation. Counsel for the appellant however contended that he could not properly be convicted unless he knew either as a moral certainty or possibly beyond reasonable doubt or arguably on a balance of probabilities that a bomb was to be placed in the bar (count 1) and that the Cortina was carrying it (count 2).

I do not agree. In *R v Bainbridge* [1959] 1 QB 129 Bainbridge was convicted of being an accessory before the fact to office breaking. A bank had been broken into and oxygen cutting equipment left there. It was found to have been bought by Bainbridge some six weeks earlier. On appeal it was contended that he should not have been convicted unless it was shown that when he bought the equipment he knew it was to be used for breaking into that bank. Lord Parker CJ, delivering the judgment of the Court of Criminal Appeal, while recognising that it was not enough to show that a man knows that some illegal venture is intended, said that it was unnecessary that 'knowledge of the particular crime which was in fact committed should be shown to his knowledge to have been intended'. He approved of the direction given by Judge Aarvold who had told the jury that it must be proved that Bainbridge knew the type of crime which was in fact committed was intended.

That case establishes that a person can be convicted of aiding and abetting the commission of an offence without his having knowledge of the actual crime intended. I do not think that any useful purpose will be served by considering whether the offences committed by the UVF can or cannot be regarded as the same type of crime. Liability of an aider and abettor should not depend on categorisation. The question to be decided appears to me to be what conduct on the part of those in the Cortina was the appellant aiding and abetting when he led them to the Crosskeys Inn. He knew that a 'military' operation was to take place. With his knowledge of the UVF's activities, he must have known that it would involve the use of a bomb or shooting or the use of incendiary devices. Knowing that he led them there and so he aided and abetted whichever of these forms the attack took. It took the form of placing a bomb. To my mind the conclusion is inescapable that he was rightly convicted on count 1.

I would dismiss the appeal.

LORD HAILSHAM OF ST MARYLEBONE: My Lords, in my opinion this appeal should be dismissed. The appellant was the owner and driver of the guide car in what subsequently turned out to be a terrorist attack by members of the criminal and illegal organisation known as the Ulster Volunteer Force ('UVF') on a public house owned by a Roman Catholic licensee at 40 Grange Road, Toomebridge, and known as the Crosskeys Inn. The attack was carried out on the night of 3rd January 1976 by the occupants of a Cortina car and took the form of throwing a pipe bomb containing about five pounds of explosive into the hallway of the public house. The attack failed because the son of the proprietor had the presence of mind to pull out the burning fuse and detonator and throw it outside the premises where the detonator exploded either because the fuse had reached the detonator or on contact with the ground....

The only substantial matter to be discussed in the appeal is the degree of knowledge required before an accused can be found guilty of aiding, abetting, counselling or procuring. To what extent must the accused be proved to have particular knowledge of the crime in contemplation at the time of his participation and which was ultimately committed by its principal perpetrators? For myself I am content for this purpose to adopt the words of Lord Parker CJ in *R v Bainbridge* [1959] 1 QB 129 when, after saying that it is not easy to lay down a precise form of words which will cover every case, he observed that 'there must not be merely suspicion but knowledge that a crime of the type in question was intended', and the words of Lord Goddard CJ in *Johnson v Youden* [1950] 1 KB 544, endorsed by this House in *Churchill v Walton* [1967] 1 All ER 497 at 502–503, that 'Before a person can be convicted of aiding and abetting the commission of an offence he must at least know the essential matters which constitute that offence'. The only question in debate in the present appeal is whether the degree of knowledge possessed by the appellant was of the 'essential matters constituting' the offence in fact committed, or, to put what in the context of the instant case is exactly the same question in another form, whether the appellant knew that the offence in which he participated was 'a crime of the type' described in the charge.

For that purpose I turn to two passages in the findings of fact of the learned judge. The first is as follows:

> In my judgment, the facts of this case make it clear to me that the accused knew the men in the Cortina car were going to attack the inn and had the means of attacking the inn with them in their car. The accused may not, as he says, have known what form the attack was going to take, but in my judgment he knew the means of the attack, be they bomb, bullet or incendiary device, were present in that car.

In the second passage MacDermott J said:

> In my judgment, the accused knew that he was participating in an attack on the inn. He performed an important role in the execution of that attack. He knew that the attack was one which would involve the use of means which would result in danger to life or damage to property. In such circumstances, where an admitted terrorist participates actively in a terrorist attack, having knowledge of the type of attack intended, if not of the weapon chosen by his colleagues, he can in my view be properly charged with possession of the weapon with which it is intended that life should be endangered or premises seriously damaged.

The learned judge also found, *inter alia*, that the word 'job' (as used in the appellant's statements) is 'synonymous with military action which raises, having regard to the proven activities of the UVF, the irresistible inference [that] the attack would be one of violence in which people would be endangered or premises seriously damaged'.

R v Gilmour (Thomas Robert Garfield)
[2000] 2 Cr App R 407 Court of Appeal

CARSWELL LCJ: On July 12, 1998 in the early hours of the morning a large petrol bomb was thrown through the living room window of a house in Carnany Park, Ballymoney, in which six people were in bed asleep. A fierce fire quickly developed, and thick smoke filled the house, following which flames burst out of the ground floor windows. The three adults in the house escaped, not without difficulty and injury, but three young boys, children of Christine Quinn, were trapped by the fire and died from the effects of carbon monoxide poisoning, notwithstanding strenuous efforts by fire officers to rescue them.

The appellant was charged with the murder of the three boys, the attempted murder of the three adults and arson of the dwelling house. On October 29, 1999, following a trial at Belfast Crown Court before McCollum L.J. sitting without a jury, he was convicted on the three charges of murder. On the charges of attempted murder of Christine Quinn and Christina Archibald the judge found the appellant not guilty of attempted murder but guilty of attempting to cause them grievous bodily harm, and on the charge of attempted murder of Raymond Frank Craig he found him not guilty of that charge but guilty of causing him grievous bodily harm. The count of arson was ordered to lie on the file. On the three counts of murder the judge sentenced the appellant to imprisonment for life and on each of the three other counts on which he returned a verdict he sentenced him to 12 years imprisonment, to run concurrently. The appellant appealed to this Court against conviction and sentence on a number of grounds. The issue on which the appeal turned was the intention to be attributed to the appellant and whether the judge's conclusion that he realised that the petrol bomb was to be used in order to cause grievous bodily harm to the persons in the house could be sustained.

...

Throwing petrol bombs at dwelling houses is regrettably common and always contains an element of potential danger to the occupants. It is right to say, however, that it has fortunately been only a rare consequence that occupants have been injured in such attacks, and the majority of them appear, so far as judicial notice can take us, to cause only minor fires. There is not in our view sufficient evidence to conclude that the appellant was aware that the petrol was contained in an unusually large bottle, which might be expected to cause a larger conflagration and result in greater danger to the occupants. On the evidence he realised at a late stage that a petrol bomb attack was about to take place, and his intention was formed in that short period before he co-operated in driving the principals away from the scene. It would be difficult to attribute to him with any degree of certainty an intention that the attack should result in more than a blaze which might do some damage, put the occupants in fear and intimidate them into moving from the house. The principals and the appellant did have a grudge against Colm Quinn, but there is not sufficient evidence to establish that they expected him to be sleeping in the house that night. Nor do we think that the talk that Colm Quinn was 'going to be used as a Guy Fawkes' is enough to establish beyond reasonable doubt that the appellant intended that those who were in occupation should suffer injuries in the fire. We therefore do not consider that the judge's finding that the principals intended to inflict grievous bodily harm can be supported as a safe conclusion of fact.

We conclude accordingly that the appellant's conviction for murder cannot be sustained. Nor can his conviction on counts 4, 5 and 6, each of which involves an intention to commit grievous bodily harm. The issue then is whether he can be found guilty of manslaughter on the first three counts, on the basis that if the principals had thrown the petrol bomb into the house without the intention of killing or inflicting grievous bodily harm on any person they would have properly been convicted of that offence. It was argued on behalf of the appellant that if he did not share the intention of the principals he should not be found guilty of either murder or manslaughter, in the same way as if the principals go outside the contemplated acts involved in the joint enterprise the accessory cannot be convicted of either offence: see our recent decision in *Crooks* [1999] N.I. 226, following the principles laid down in *R. v. Powell and English* [1998] 1 Cr.App.R. 261, [1999] A.C. 1.

The issue is discussed in Blackstone's *Criminal Practice*, 2000 ed., para. A5.5 at p. 75, in which the example is posed where the principal and accessory agree that the principal will post an incendiary device to the victim, the accessory contemplating only superficial injuries but the principal foreseeing and hoping that the injuries will be serious or fatal. The principal will be guilty of murder and the accessory will not. The editors conclude that the accessory should in such a case be convicted of manslaughter, because the act done by the principal is precisely what was envisaged.

In our opinion this is the correct principle to apply in the present case. The appellant foresaw that the principals would carry out the act of throwing a petrol bomb into the house, but did not realise that in so doing they intended to kill or do grievous bodily harm to the occupants. To establish that a person charged as an accessory to a crime of specific intent is guilty as an accessory it is necessary to prove that he realised the principal's intention: see *Hyde* (1991) 92 Cr.App.R. 131, 135, [1991] Q.B. 134, 139, *per* Lord Lane C.J., approved by Lord Hutton in *R. v. Powell and English* [1998] 1 Cr.App.R. 261, 283, [1999] A.C. 1, 27–28. The line of authority represented by such cases as *Anderson and Morris* (1966) 50 Cr.App.R. 216, [1966] 2 Q.B. 110, approved in *R. v. Powell and English*, deals with situations where the principal departs from the contemplated joint enterprise and perpetrates a more serious act of a different kind unforeseen by the accessory. In such cases it is established that the accessory is not liable at all for such unforeseen acts. It does not follow that the same result should follow where the principal carries out the very act contemplated by the accessory, though the latter does not realise that the principal intends a more serious consequence from the act.

We do not consider that we are obliged by authority to hold that the accessory in such a case must be acquitted of manslaughter as well as murder. The cases in which an accessory has been found not guilty both of murder and manslaughter all concern a departure by the principal from the *actus reus* contemplated by the accessory, not a difference between the parties in respect of the *mens rea* of each. In such cases the view has prevailed that it would be wrong to hold the accessory liable when the principal committed an act which the accessory did not contemplate or authorise. We do not, however, see any convincing policy reason why a person acting as an accessory to a principal who carries out the very deed contemplated by both should not be guilty of the degree of offence appropriate to the intent with which he so acted. It is of course conceivable, as is suggested in *Blackstone, loc. cit.*, that in some cases the nature of the principal's *mens rea* may change the nature of the act committed by him and take it outside the type of act contemplated by the accessory, but it does not seem to us that the existence of such a possibility affects the validity of the basic principle which we have propounded. A verdict of guilty of manslaughter on this basis was upheld by the Court of Appeal in *Stewart and Schofield* [1995] 1 Cr.App.R. 441, [1995] 3 All E.R. 159. The judgment has been strongly criticised by Sir John Smith in [1995] Crim.L.R. 296 and [1995] Crim.L.R. 422 and in Smith & Hogan, *Criminal Law*, 9th ed., 1999 p. 145. Even if there may be ground for criticism of some of the propositions enunciated in the Court's judgment, the principle accepted as its basis is in our view sustainable.

We accordingly allow the appeal, substitute a verdict of not guilty of murder but guilty of manslaughter on counts 1 to 3 and set aside the verdicts of guilty on counts 4 to 6.

Appeals allowed.

■ **NOTES AND QUESTIONS**

1. Are *Maxwell* and *Gilmour* distinguishable? On what basis?

2. Daniels, a gun dealer, sells a gun to a person who is widely reputed to be a hit man for the mob. Does Daniel thereby become an accessory to every murder which the 'hit man' commits with the gun? Would Bainbridge have been liable for all offences committed using the equipment he supplied?

3. Alan enters Margaret's house using a key which he bought from the gardener. The gardener knows that Alan intends to commit a crime within the house, but does not know and does not care what crime he commits. Is the gardener liable as an accessory to rape if Alan sexually assaults Margaret? To theft if Alan steals a painting from the house? To burglary under the Theft Act 1968, s. 9(1)(a) if Alan entered with the intention of stealing a painting but found no painting worth stealing? How relevant is Lord Scarman's observation in *Maxwell* that 'An accessory who leaves it to his principal to choose is liable, provided always the choice is made from the range of offences from which the accessory contemplates the choice will be made.'

(i) 'Joint enterprises'

Accessoryship involves different forms of relationship. At one extreme there is the relationship between a principal and someone who happens to give help or encouragement without any commitment to the criminal project of the principal. *Gamble* is an example. At the other extreme are cases of joint enterprise where two or more parties come together for the purpose of committing an offence. Gang crime is the obvious example. When one of the parties to a joint enterprise acts beyond the scope of their agreement, are the others liable for the crime committed by their comrade?

R v Powell and another, R v English
[1997] 4 All ER 545, House of Lords

LORD HUTTON: My Lords, the appeals before your Lordships' House relate to the liability of a participant in a joint criminal enterprise when another participant in that enterprise is guilty of a crime, the commission of which was not the purpose of the enterprise.

...

In the case of Powell and Daniels the purpose of the joint enterprise was to purchase drugs from a drug dealer. Three men, including the two appellants, Powell and Daniels, went to purchase drugs from a drug dealer, but having gone to his house for that purpose, the drug dealer was shot dead when he came to the door. The Crown was unable to prove which of the three men fired the gun which killed the drug dealer, but it was the Crown case that if the third man fired the gun, the two appellants were guilty of murder because they knew that the third man was armed with a gun and realised that he might use it to kill or cause really serious injury to the drug dealer.

In the course of summing up to the jury at the trial, the Recorder of London said:

... if B or C realised, without agreeing to such conduct being used, that A may kill or intentionally inflict serious injury and they nevertheless continue to participate with A in the venture, that will amount to a sufficient mental element for B or C to be guilty of murder if A with the requisite intent kills in the course of the venture. In those circumstances B and C have lent themselves to the enterprise and by so doing have given assistance and encouragement to A in carrying out an enterprise which they realised may involve murder. These are general principles which must be applied to the facts of this case.

Powell and Daniels were convicted of murder and their appeals were rejected by the Court of Appeal, and the question certified for the opinion of your Lordships' House is:

Is it sufficient to found a conviction for murder for a secondary party to a killing to have realised that the primary party might kill with intent to do so or must the secondary party have held such intention himself?

In the case of English the purpose of the joint enterprise in which he and another young man, Weddle, took part was to attack and cause injury with wooden posts to a police officer, Sergeant Forth, and in the course of the attack Weddle used a knife with which he stabbed Sergeant Forth to death.

It was a reasonable possibility that English had no knowledge that Weddle was carrying a knife, and on this basis the learned trial judge, Owen J, stated in his summing up to the jury:

If he did not know of the knife then you have to consider whether nevertheless he knew that there was a substantial risk that Weddle might cause some really serious injury with the wooden post which was used in the manner which you find it to have been used. So there is the question; 'Has the prosecution proved'—and this is an alternative, of course—'that English joined in an unlawful attack on the sergeant realising at that time that there was a substantial risk that in that attack Weddle might kill or at least cause some really serious injury to the sergeant. If no, not guilty' ...

The judge then, in effect, directed the jury that if they answered that question in the affirmative they should find English guilty of murder.

Weddle and English were convicted of murder and their appeals were rejected by the Court of Appeal. English now appeals to your Lordships' House and the two questions certified for the opinion of the House are as follows:

(i) Is it sufficient to found a conviction for murder for a secondary party to a killing to have realised that the primary party might kill with intent to do so or with intent to cause grievous bodily harm or must the secondary party have held such an intention himself?

(ii) Is it sufficient for murder that the secondary party intends or foresees that the primary party would or may act with intent to cause grievous bodily harm, if the lethal act carried out by the primary party is fundamentally different from the acts foreseen or intended by the secondary party?

The question certified in the appeals of Powell and Daniels and the first question certified in the appeal of English raise the issue whether foresight of a criminal act which was not the purpose of the joint enterprise (in the case of Powell and Daniels the use of a gun, and in the case of English the use of a knife) is sufficient to impose criminal liability for murder on the secondary party in the event that the jury find that the primary party used the weapon with intent to kill or cause really serious harm.

In the case of Powell and Daniels, the Crown case was that the two appellants knew that the third man was armed with a gun, and the Crown accepted that if the jury did not find this knowledge the appellants would not be guilty of murder. But in the case of English the Crown case was that, even if he did not know that Weddle had a knife, English foresaw that Weddle would cause really serious injury to the police officer, and that this foresight was sufficient to impose criminal liability upon him for the murder. Accordingly the second question arises in the case of English and that question is, in essence, whether the secondary party is guilty of murder if he foresaw that the other person taking part in the enterprise would use violence that would cause really serious injury, but did not foresee the use of the weapon that was used to carry out the killing.

My Lords, the first question gives rise, in my opinion, to two issues. The first issue is whether there is a principle established in the authorities that where there is a joint enterprise to commit a crime, foresight or contemplation by one party to the enterprise that another party to the enterprise may in the course of it commit another crime, is sufficient to impose criminal liability for that crime if committed by the other party even if the first party did not intend that criminal act to be carried out. (I shall consider in a later part of this judgment whether the foresight is of a possibility or of a probability.) The second issue is whether, if there be such an established principle, it can stand as good law in the light of the decisions of this House that foresight is not sufficient to constitute the *mens rea* for murder in the case of the person who actually causes the death and that guilt only arises if that person intends to kill or cause really serious injury.

My Lords, I consider that there is a strong line of authority that where two parties embark on a joint enterprise to commit a crime, and one party foresees that in the course of the enterprise the other party may carry out, with the requisite *mens rea*, an act constituting another crime, the former is liable for that crime if committed by the latter in the course of the enterprise. This was decided by the Court of Appeal, constituted by five judges, in *R v Smith (Wesley)* [1963] 3 All ER 597.

...

My Lords, I recognise that as a matter of logic there is force in the argument advanced on behalf of the appellants, and that on one view it is anomalous that if foreseeability of death or really serious harm is not sufficient to constitute *mens rea* for murder in the party who actually carries out the killing, it is sufficient to constitute *mens rea* in a secondary party. But the rules of the common law are not based solely on logic but relate to practical concerns and, in relation to crimes committed in the course of joint enterprises, to the need to give effective protection to the public against criminals operating in gangs. As Lord Salmon stated in *DPP v Majewski* [1976] 2 All ER 142 at 157, in rejecting criticism based on strict logic of a rule of the common law, 'this is the view that has been adopted by the common law of England, which is founded on common sense and experience rather than strict logic'.

In my opinion, there are practical considerations of weight and importance related to considerations of public policy which justify the principle stated in *Chan Wing-siu* v *R* and which prevail over considerations of strict logic. One consideration is that referred to by Lord Lane CJ in *R v Hyde* [1990] 3 All ER 892 at 896, where he cited with approval the observation of Professor Smith in his comment on *R v Wakely*:

> If B realises (without agreeing to such conduct being used) that A may kill or intentionally inflict serious injury, but nevertheless continues to participate with A in the venture, that will amount to a sufficient mental element for B to be guilty of murder if A, with the requisite intent, kills in the course of the venture. As Professor Smith points out, B has in those circumstances lent

himself to the enterprise and by so doing he has given assistance and encouragement to A in carrying out an enterprise which B realises may involve murder.

A further consideration is that, unlike the principal party who carries out the killing with a deadly weapon, the secondary party will not be placed in the situation in which he suddenly has to decide whether to shoot or stab the third person with intent to kill or cause really serious harm. There is, in my opinion, an argument of considerable force that the secondary party who takes part in a criminal enterprise (for example the robbery of a bank) with foresight that a deadly weapon may be used, should not escape liability for murder because he, unlike the principal party, is not suddenly confronted by the security officer so that he has to decide whether to use the gun or knife or have the enterprise thwarted and face arrest. This point has been referred to in cases where the question has been discussed whether in order for criminal liability to attach the secondary party must foresee an act as more likely than not or whether it suffices if the secondary party foresees the act only as a possibility.

In *Chan Wing-siu* v *R* [1985] AC 168 at 172 counsel for the Crown submitted:

> Regard must be had to public policy considerations. Public policy requires that when a man lends himself to a criminal enterprise knowing it involves the possession of potentially murderous weapons which in fact are used by his partners with murderous intent, he should not escape the consequences to him of their conduct by reliance upon the nuances of prior assessment of the likelihood that such conduct will take place. In these circumstances an accomplice who knowingly takes the risk that such conduct might, or might well, take place in the course of that joint enterprise should bear the same responsibility for that conduct as those who use the weapons with the murderous intent.

Sir Robin Cooke stated ([1984] 3 All ER 877 at 882):

> What public policy requires was rightly identified in the submissions of the Crown. Where a man lends himself to a criminal enterprise knowing that potentially murderous weapons are to be carried, and in the event they are in fact used by his partner with an intent sufficient for murder, he should not escape the consequences by reliance on a nuance of prior assessment, only too likely to have been optimistic.

. . .

Therefore, for the reasons which I have given I would answer the certified question of law in the appeals of Powell and Daniels and the first certified question in the appeal of English by stating that (subject to the observations which I make in relation to the second certified question in the case of English) it is sufficient to found a conviction for murder for a secondary party to have realised that in the course of the joint enterprise the primary party might kill with intent to do so or with intent to cause grievous bodily harm. Accordingly, I would dismiss the appeals of Powell and Daniels.

The second certified question in the appeal of English arises because of the last sentence in the following passage in the trial judge's summing up to the jury to which I have previously referred:

> If he had the knife and English knew that Weddle had the knife, what would have been—must have been—in the mind of English, bearing in mind whatever condition you find that he was in as a result of drink? So you have to ask that question. If he did not know of the knife then you have to consider whether nevertheless he knew that there was a substantial risk that Weddle might cause some really serious injury with the wooden post which was used in the manner which you find it to have been used.

In *R* v *Hyde* [1990] 3 All ER 892 at 896 as already set out, Lord Lane CJ stated:

> If B realises (without agreeing to such conduct being used) that A may kill or intentionally inflict serious injury, but nevertheless continues to participate with A in the venture, that will amount to a sufficient mental element for B to be guilty of murder if A, with the requisite intent, kills in the course of the venture.

. . .

[If] the weapon used by the primary party is different to, but as dangerous as, the weapon which the secondary party contemplated he might use, the secondary party should not escape liability for murder because of the difference in the weapon, for example, if he foresaw that the primary party might use a gun to kill and the latter used a knife to kill, or vice versa . . . .

In *R* v *Rahman* the House of Lords expanded on the 'fundamental difference' theme and when it might warrant acquitting an accessory of murder in a case of a joint enterprise.

R v *Rahman*
[2008] UKHL 45, House of Lords

LORD BINGHAM OF CORNHILL: My Lords,
On 4 March 2005 the four appellants were convicted in the Crown Court at Leeds before Wakerley J and a jury of murdering Tyrone Clarke on 22 April 2004.... It was not alleged or proved that any of the appellants had personally struck the fatal blow or blows and they were convicted as accessories or secondary parties to the joint enterprise which culminated in the death of the deceased. The Criminal Division of the Court of Appeal (Hooper LJ, Gibbs and Roderick Evans JJ) dismissed their appeals against conviction on 23 February 2007, for reasons given by Hooper LJ: [2007] EWCA Crim 342, [2007] 1 WLR 2191. Their appeals to the House raise a narrow but significant question on the direction to be given to the jury concerning the liability of an accessory on facts such as arose in the present case.

The facts

There was, it seems, a history of confrontation between the deceased and some of his friends on one side and a group of young Asians including two of the appellants on the other. In a chance encounter involving minor violence on 20 April 2004 some members of the latter group were worsted. There was talk of revenge, and on the afternoon of 22 April the deceased and some of his friends were sighted by the opposing group. A number of young Asians gathered. They were carrying a variety of weapons including baseball bats, a cricket bat, a scaffolding pole, a metal bar, a table leg and pieces of wood. Their numbers increased, and as they walked through the streets there were two groups, one of 10 to 12 with a group of about 5 to 7 shortly behind. The deceased and his friend armed themselves with pieces of wood taken from a fence and fighting broke out between the two groups. A further group of Asian men arrived and the deceased and his friend were pursued as they sought to escape through lanes and a ginnel (the Rock ginnel), until they reached a grassy area at the back of some houses in Brett Gardens, Beeston in Leeds. The deceased tried to enter the rear gate of one of the houses, but was caught there and attacked by a group of between 7 and 15 persons. After he collapsed to the ground some members of the group were seen to assault him with blunt instrument weapons and kicks.

On post mortem examination of the body of the deceased it was found that he had sustained three knife wounds. One of these, on the left side of the back between the shoulder blade and the midline, just to the right of the left shoulder blade, was made by a knife which entered the body relatively straight and penetrated to a depth of 8 centimetres, causing massive haemorrhage, rapid collapse, rapid unconsciousness and death.

There was no evidence that any of the appellants inflicted the fatal injuries. The participant who did was probably not apprehended. The prosecution alleged that the role of each appellant in the attack involved either the deliberate and intentional infliction of serious physical harm to the deceased or, by their conduct, the intentional encouragement of others to do likewise; that each appellant shared a common intention that serious bodily harm should be inflicted; and that the circumstances of the attack were such that each of them knew that weapons such as baseball bats, a scaffolding pole and a knife or knives might be used to inflict serious bodily harm.

The evidence of each appellant was that he had joined the enterprise with at most an intention to cause serious harm, without knowledge or foresight that anyone else involved in the assault intended to kill, that he did not have a knife and did not know or foresee that anyone else had a knife and that, accordingly, the acts of the primary offender were outside the scope of any joint enterprise to inflict serious bodily harm.

It is accepted that the jury must have found that each appellant participated in the attack either (i) by using violence to the victim, or (ii) by surrounding him to enable others to use such violence, or (iii) by being present intending that his presence should encourage others to attack the victim.

The criminal liability of accessories

In the ordinary way a defendant is criminally liable for offences which he personally is shown to have committed. But, even leaving aside crimes such as riot, violent disorder or conspiracy where the involvement of multiple actors is an ingredient of the offence, it is notorious that many, perhaps most, crimes are not committed single-handed. Others may be involved, directly or indirectly, in the commission of a crime although they are not the primary offenders. Any coherent criminal law must develop a theory of accessory liability which will embrace those whose responsibility merits conviction and punishment even though they are not the primary offenders.

English law has developed a small number of rules to address this problem, usually grouped under the general heading of 'joint enterprise'. These rules, as Lord Steyn pointed out in *R v Powell (Anthony)*, *R v English* [1999] 1 AC 1, 12, are not applicable only to cases of murder but apply to most criminal offences. Their application does, however, give rise to special difficulties in cases of murder. This is because, as established in *R v Cunningham* [1982] AC 566, the mens rea of murder may consist of either an intention to kill or an intention to cause really serious injury. Thus if P (the primary offender) unlawfully assaults V (the victim) with the intention of causing really serious injury, but not death, and death is thereby caused, P is guilty of murder.

As the Privy Council (per Lord Hoffmann) said in *Brown and Isaac v The State* [2003] UKPC 10, para 8,

> 'The simplest form of joint enterprise, in the context of murder, is when two or more people plan to murder someone and do so. If both participated in carrying out the plan, both are liable. It does not matter who actually inflicted the fatal injury. This might be called the paradigm case of joint enterprise liability'.

...

Countless juries have over the years been directed along these lines, the example of a bank robbery in which the masked robbers, the look-out man and the get-away driver play different parts but are all liable being often used as an illustration. In this situation the touchstone of liability is the intention of those who participate.

But there is what Sir Robin Cooke in *Chan Wing-Siu v The Queen*, p 175, called a 'wider principle'. In *R v Powell (Anthony)*, *R v English*, above, as Lord Hutton made plain in the opening sentence of his leading opinion (p 16), the House had to consider a more difficult question: the liability of a participant in a joint criminal enterprise when another participant in that enterprise is guilty of a crime, the commission of which was not the purpose of the enterprise...

[T]he House held (p 21) that 'participation in a joint criminal enterprise with foresight or contemplation of an act as a possible incident of that enterprise is sufficient to impose criminal liability for that act carried out by another participant in the enterprise'. Thus the House answered the certified question in the appeal of Powell and Daniels and the first certified question in the appeal of English by stating that (subject to the ruling on the second certified question in English) 'it is sufficient to found a conviction for murder for a secondary party to have realised that in the course of the joint enterprise the primary party might kill with intent to do so or with intent to cause grievous bodily harm'. Thus in this context the touchstone is one of foresight.

In *R v Smith (Wesley)*, above, pp 1206-1207, it had been recognised that a radical departure by the primary killer from the foreseen purpose of an enterprise might relieve a secondary party of liability.

In *R v Powell (Anthony)*; *R v English*, above, p 29, the House held ... that to be guilty under the principle in *Chan Wing-Siu v The Queen*, above, the secondary party must foresee an act of the type which the principal party committed, and that in English's case the use of a knife was fundamentally different to the use of a wooden post.

The decision of the House in *R v English* did not lay down a new rule of accessory liability or exoneration. Its significance lies in the emphasis it laid (a) on the overriding importance in this context of what the particular defendant subjectively foresaw, and (b) on the nature of the acts or behaviour said to be a radical departure from what was intended or foreseen. The greater the difference between the acts or behaviour in question and the purpose of the enterprise, the more ready a jury may be to infer that the particular defendant did not foresee what the other participant would do.

...

The main argument for the appellants, persuasively advanced by Mr Michael Harrison QC, took as its starting point the pathological findings .... Those, it was said, showed that the stab wound which caused the death of the deceased was inflicted with the intention to kill and not merely to cause really serious injury. The location and direction of the wound, and the force with which it was delivered, showed that to be so, or at least raised a strong possibility that it was so. But the appellants intended and foresaw no more than the infliction of really serious injury. In consequence, it was strongly arguable that the principal's intention to kill, if found by the jury, took his (the principal's) action outside the scope of the common design and rendered it fundamentally different from anything the appellants had foreseen or contemplated. These were not inferences which the jury would necessarily draw, but inferences which, properly directed, they might draw. The trial judge had, however, declined to direct the jury along these lines, and this non-direction was a misdirection which deprived the appellants of a chance of acquittal they should have enjoyed.

It was, inevitably, common ground between the parties that an accessory may only be criminally liable for a crime which the principal has committed, in murder unlawful killing with intent to kill or cause really serious injury. It was also common ground that the test of an accessory's liability under the wider principle explored in *R v English* is one of foresight. The crucial divide between the parties was: foresight of what? The appellants' answer would include foresight of the principal's intention. The respondent's answer, clearly given by Mr Robert Smith QC for the Crown, was: foresight of what the principal might do. On the Crown's analysis the principal's undisclosed intention is beside the point. It is his acts which matter.

The appellants' argument derives little assistance, in my opinion, from authority ....

Authority apart, there are in my view two strong reasons, one practical, the other theoretical, for preferring the respondent's contention. The first is that the law of joint enterprise in a situation such as this is already very complex, as evidenced by the trial judge's direction and the Court of Appeal's judgment on these appeals, and the appellants' submission, if accepted, would introduce a new and highly undesirable level of complexity. Given the fluid, fast-moving course of events in incidents such as that which culminated in the killing of the deceased, incidents which are unhappily not rare, it must often be very hard for jurors to make a reliable assessment of what a particular defendant foresaw as likely or possible acts on the part of his associates. It would be even harder, and would border on speculation, to judge what a particular defendant foresaw as the intention with which his associates might perform such acts. It is safer to focus on the defendant's foresight of what an associate might do, an issue to which knowledge of the associate's possession of an obviously lethal weapon such as a gun or a knife would usually be very relevant.

Secondly, the appellants' submission, as it seems to me, undermines the principle on which, for better or worse, our law of murder is based. In the prosecution of a principal offender for murder, it is not necessary for the prosecution to prove or the jury to consider whether the defendant intended on the one hand to kill or on the other to cause really serious injury. That is legally irrelevant to guilt. The rationale of that principle plainly is that if a person unlawfully assaults another with intent to cause him really serious injury, and death results, he should be held criminally responsible for that fatality, even though he did not intend it. If he had not embarked on a course of deliberate violence, the fatality would not have occurred. This rationale may lack logical purity, but it is underpinned by a quality of earthy realism. To rule that an undisclosed and unforeseen intention to kill on the part of the primary offender may take a killing outside the scope of a common purpose to cause really serious injury, calling for a distinction irrelevant in the case of the primary offender, is in my view to subvert the rationale which underlies our law of murder.

I would accordingly reject the appellants' submission on this point. I would also reject a subsidiary submission that the judge should have explained to the jury what was meant by 'fundamentally different'. This is not a term of art. It may, or may not, be regarded as a helpful turn of phrase, but its meaning is plain and cannot be misunderstood by a jury to whom the governing principle has been explained, as it was here.

The Court of Appeal certified the following point of law of general public importance as involved in its decision:

> If in the course of a joint enterprise to inflict unlawful violence the principal party kills with an intention to kill which is unknown to and unforeseen by a secondary party, is the principal's intention relevant,
>
> (i) to whether the killing was within the scope of a common purpose to which the secondary party was an accessory?
>
> (ii) to whether the principal's act was fundamentally different from the act or acts which the secondary party foresaw as part of the joint enterprise?

I would answer both parts of the question in the negative, and would accordingly dismiss these appeals.

■ NOTES AND QUESTIONS

1. If the same result as intended occurred but by an unforeseen manner, can the result ever be deemed fundamentally different? Suppose that Xavier counsels Yates to beat the victim to death with a cricket bat. Desiring a quicker solution, Yates instead shoots the victim. In *Rahman*, Lord Brown, referring to the 'fundamental difference' principle, spoke of situations where the perpetrator uses a 'more lethal weapon' which the accessory was not aware of and was not within the contemplation of the parties. Assuming that a gun is more lethal than a cricket bat and its use was not foreseen by Xavier, will the latter be acquitted of being an accessory to murder?

2. Francis supplies Gary with a gun to kill her husband but the gun malfunctions. Unwilling to accept defeat, Gary strangles the husband to death. Is Francis liable as an accessory?

3. Peter and Penelope agree to commit a robbery. Penelope stands lookout while Peter approaches the victim in a dark alley. Peter, however, not only robs the victim but shoots her when she offers resistance. This was not part of their agreed plan, but Penelope knew that Peter always carried with him a weapon when he carried out a robbery.

4. In *Gilmour* the court distinguished *Powell and English* although the crime of throwing the petrol bomb was the very crime contemplated by the accessory defendant and in fact carried out. Nevertheless, Gilmour was acquitted of murder on the grounds that the *consequence* of the principal's action was more serious. Can the cases be reconciled?

5. Does the identity of the victim matter to the accessory's liability? Ann supplies Barry with a gun to kill her husband Carl. Barry instead shoots his wife Diane with Ann's gun. Is Ann an accessory to Diane's murder? Is this a proper case for the application of the doctrine of 'transferred intent'? See *Saunders and Archer* (1573) 2 Plowden 473.

6. The 'fundamentally different' rule is causing problems of application. See for example *R v Mendez* (2010) EWCA Crim 516. V died of a stab wound to the heart in the course of a violent attack in which M took part. Toulson LJ: 'In cases where the common purpose was not to kill but to cause serious harm, D was not liable for the murder of V if the direct cause of death was a deliberate act by P that was of a kind unforeseen by D and likely to be altogether more life-threatening that acts of the kind intended or foreseen by D.'

C: Defences

(i) Protected individuals

Where the law exists to protect a category of potential victims, it makes little sense to charge the victim as an accessory.

R v Tyrrell

[1894] 1 QB 710, Court for Crown Cases Reserved

The defendant, Jane Tyrrell, was on 15 September 1893, tried and convicted at the Central Criminal Court on an indictment charging her, in the first count, with having unlawfully aided and abetted, counselled, and procured the commission by one Thomas Ford of the misdemeanor of having unlawful carnal knowledge of her whilst she was between the ages of thirteen and sixteen, against the form of the statute, etc.; and, in the second count, with having falsely, wickedly, and unlawfully solicited and incited Thomas Ford to commit the same offence.

It was proved at the trial that the defendant did aid, abet, solicit and incite Thomas Ford to commit the misdemeanor made punishable by s. 5 of the Criminal Law Amendment Act 1885. The question for the opinion of the Court was, 'Whether it is an offence for a girl between the ages of thirteen and sixteen to aid and abet a male person in the commission of the misdemeanor of having unlawful carnal connection with her, or to solicit and incite a male person to commit that misdemeanor.'

LORD COLERIDGE CJ: The Criminal Law Amendment Act 1885, was passed for the purpose of protecting women and girls against themselves. At the time it was passed there was a discussion as to what point should be fixed as the age of consent. That discussion ended in a compromise, and the age of consent was fixed at sixteen. With the object of protecting women and girls against themselves the Act of Parliament has made illicit connection with a girl under that age unlawful; if a man wishes to have such illicit connection he must wait until the girl is sixteen, otherwise he breaks the law; but it is impossible to say that the Act, which is absolutely silent about aiding or abetting, or soliciting or inciting, can have intended that the girls for whose protection it was passed should be punishable under it for the offences committed upon themselves. I am of opinion that this conviction ought to be quashed.

MATHEW J: I am of the same opinion. I do not see how it would be possible to obtain convictions under the statute if the contention for the Crown were adopted, because nearly every section which deals with offences in respect of women and girls would create an offence in the woman or girl. Such a result cannot have been intended by the legislature. There is no trace in the statute of any intention to treat the woman or girl as criminal.

Conviction quashed.

■ **NOTES AND QUESTIONS**

1. Is the result in *Tyrrell* justified on the theoretical basis that, since the purpose of the statute was in part to protect emotionally immature girls from themselves, it would be perverse to punish them for that same immaturity; or on the practical basis that it would be counterproductive to prosecute the victim, for it would discourage victims from reporting crimes?

2. Of what relevance is Parliamentary intent? Is it possible in *Tyrrell* to determine what Parliament intended?

3. What if another girl of the victim's age assisted Tyrrell by arranging the rendez-vous – could she be convicted as an accessory? Is the decision of the court helpful in answering this question?

4. Does the reasoning of *Tyrrell* apply to:

    (a) the woman who voluntarily subjects herself to an illegal abortion;

    (b) the previously unmarried partner in a bigamous marriage?

    (c) a person who asks another to assist her in committing suicide. Note that while suicide is not longer a criminal offence (Suicide Act 1961, s.1) one can be liable as an accessory to suicide. Suicide Act 1961, s. 2(1) provides:

        (1) A person who aids, abets, counsels or procures the suicide of another, or an attempt by another to commit suicide, shall be liable on conviction on indictment to imprisonment for a term not exceeding fourteen years.

If one who wishes to commit suicide is unable to do so (perhaps because she is in a complete state of paralysis), should a loved one who helps end her life be liable for a crime that the victim cannot commit? The human rights implications are explored in Chapter 11.

When the nature of a crime is such that two persons will inevitably be involved (e.g., dueling), must both or neither be liable for the offence?

Sayce v Coupe

[1953] 1 QB 1, Queen's Bench Division

Two informations were preferred by the appellant, George Sayce, an officer of the Customs and Excise, against the respondent, Wilson Coupe, the licensee of the Plough Inn, Manchester Street, Oldham, alleging (1) that on 4 December 1951, he knowingly kept uncustomed goods, namely, 3,580 American cigarettes, with intent to defraud His Majesty of the duty thereon contrary to s. 186 of the Customs Consolidation Act 1876, and (2) that on 24 November 1951, he did aid, abet, counsel and procure a person unknown to sell certain tobacco, to wit 5,600 cigarettes, otherwise than as a licensed manufacturer of or dealer in or retailer of tobacco selling tobacco in his entered premises or on premises wherein he carried on the business of a licensed dealer in or retailer of tobacco contrary to s. 13 of the Tobacco Act 1842, as amended by s. 8 of the Revenue Act 1867.

LORD GODDARD CJ: [In the first part of its opinion the court found that the respondent had committed the offence of keeping uncustomed goods with intent to defraud the Revenue of the duties thereon.]

The second summons charged the respondent with aiding and abetting Wood—it says a person unknown but it must have been Wood—to commit an offence under section 13 of the Tobacco Act, 1842, by buying the cigarettes from a person who to his knowledge was not a licensed dealer in tobacco, and it is quite clear that the offence charged in the second information was committed.

Mr Hinchliffe has argued that because the statute does not make it an offence to buy, but only makes it an offence to sell, we ought to hold that the offence of aiding and abetting the sale ought not to be preferred or could not be preferred. It is obvious that it can be preferred. The statute does not make it an offence to buy, but obviously, on ordinary general principles of criminal law, if in such a case a person knows the circumstances and knows, therefore, that an offence is being committed and takes part in, or facilitates the commission of the offence, he is guilty as a principal in the second degree, for it is impossible to say that a person who buys does not aid and abet a sale.

For these reasons the justices ought also to have convicted on the second information.

■ **NOTES AND QUESTIONS**

1. Is *Sayce* v *Coupe* distinguishable from *Tyrrell*?

2. Is the decision in *Sayce* v *Coupe* consistent with Parliamentary intent? Presumably Parliament must have appreciated that in every sale there would be both a buyer and a seller, and, in making only the seller liable, made a conscious decision not to penalise the buyer.

3. A child is kidnapped. The parents, without informing the police, pay the ransom. Are they accessories to kidnapping?

(ii) Withdrawal

Is it – or should it be – the rule that once an accomplice, always an accomplice? A thief who steals another's property cannot escape liability if she has a subsequent change of heart and returns the stolen goods; the crime is already complete. Should the same be true in cases of an accessory?

R v Becerra
(1975) 62 Cr App R 212, Court of Appeal

The appellant, B, broke into the house with two other men C and one G. Their intention was to steal from the householder. While in the house, the tenant of a flat on the first floor surprised them and B calling 'let's go' climbed out of a window followed by G and ran away. C, meanwhile, who had been handed a knife by B, stabbed and killed the tenant. B and C were charged, *inter alia*, with the tenant's murder, and at their trial the prosecution case was that B and C were acting in concert in pursuance of a common agreement to kill or inflict bodily harm should the need arise. B contended that he had withdrawn from the joint adventure before the attack on the tenant and, therefore, was not liable to be convicted of murder. The jury were directed that the words 'let's go' and the appellant B's departure through the window were insufficient to constitute a withdrawal. Both B and C were convicted of murder.

ROSKILL LJ: ... The basic prosecution case against Becerra and Cooper was that they had entered into a common agreement to use such force as was necessary against anyone in the house to get the money or to avoid identification or arrest. It was urged that this common agreement included the use, if necessary, of the knife to inflict serious bodily injury, if not death, and it was alleged that Cooper, in furtherance of that common agreement, murdered Lewis with the knife in his left hand while he pinioned Lewis from behind with his right arm around Lewis's shoulder.

... It was argued ... on behalf ... of Becerra, that even if there were this common design, ... whatever Cooper did immediately before and at the time of the killing of Lewis, Becerra had by then withdrawn from that common design and so should not be convicted of the murder of Lewis ....

It is necessary, before dealing with that argument in more detail, to say a word or two about the relevant law. It is a curious fact, considering the number of times in which this point arises where two or more people are charged with criminal offences, particularly murder or manslaughter, how relatively little authority there is in this country upon the point. But the principle is undoubtedly of long standing.

Perhaps it is best first stated in *R* v *Saunders and Archer* (1577) 2 Plowden 473 (in the eighteenth year of the first Queen Elizabeth) at p. 476, in a note by *Plowden*, thus:

> …for if I command one to kill J. S. and before the Fact done I go to him and tell him that I have repented, and expressly charge him not to kill J. S. and he afterwards kills him, there I shall not be Accessory to this Murder, because I have countermanded my first Command, which in all Reason shall discharge me, for the malicious Mind of the Accessory ought to continue to do ill until the Time of the Act done, or else he shall not be charged; but if he had killed J. S. before the Time of my Discharge or Countermand given, I should have been Accessory to the Death, notwithstanding my private Repentance.

The next case to which I may usefully refer is some 250 years later, but over 150 years ago: *R* v *Edmeads and Others* (1828) 3 C & P 390, where there is a ruling of Vaughan B at a trial at Berkshire Assizes, upon an indictment charging Edmeads and others with unlawfully shooting at game keepers. At the end of his ruling the learned Baron said on the question of common intent, at p. 392,

> that is rather a question for the jury; but still, on this evidence, it is quite clear what the common purpose was. They all draw up in lines, and point their guns at the game-keepers, and they are all giving their countenance and assistance to the one of them who actually fires the gun. If it could be shewn that either of them separated himself from the rest, and showed distinctly that he would have no hand in what they were doing, the objection would have much weight in it.

I can go forward over 100 years. Mr Owen (to whose juniors we are indebted for their research into the relevant Canadian and United States cases) referred us to several Canadian cases, to only one of which is it necessary to refer in detail, a decision of the Court of Appeal of British Columbia in *Whitehouse (alias Savage)* (1941) 1 WWR 112. I need not read the headnote. The Court of Appeal held that the trial judge concerned in that case, which was one of murder, had been guilty of misdirection in his direction to the jury on this question of 'withdrawal.' The matter is, if I may most respectfully say so, so well put in the leading judgment of Sloan J.A., that I read the whole of the passage at pp. 115 and 116:

> Can it be said on the facts of this case that a mere change of mental intention and a quitting of the scene of the crime just immediately prior to the striking of the fatal blow will absolve those who participate in the commission of the crime by overt acts up to that moment from all the consequences of its accomplishment by the one who strikes in ignorance of his companions' change of heart? I think not. After a crime has been committed and before a prior abandonment of the common enterprise may be found by a jury there must be, in my view, in the absence of exceptional circumstances, something more than a mere mental change of intention and physical change of place by those associates who wish to dissociate themselves from the consequences attendant upon their willing assistance up to the moment of the actual commission of that crime. I would not attempt to define too closely what must be done in criminal matters involving participation in a common unlawful purpose to break the chain of causation and responsibility. That must depend upon the circumstances of each case but it seems to me that one essential element ought to be established in a case of this kind: Where practicable and reasonable there must be timely communication of the intention to abandon the common purpose from those who wish to dissociate themselves from the contemplated crime to those who desire to continue in it. What is 'timely communication' must be determined by the facts of each case but where practicable and reasonable it ought to be such communication, verbal or otherwise, that will serve unequivocal notice upon the other party to the common unlawful cause that if he proceeds upon it he does so without the further aid and assistance of those who withdraw. The unlawful purpose of him who continues alone is then his own and not one in common with those who are no longer parties to it nor liable to its full and final consequences.

The learned judge then went on to cite a passage from 1 Hale's *Pleas of the Crown* 618 and the passage from *Saunders and Archer* (*supra*) to which I have already referred.

In the view of each member of this Court, that passage, if we may respectfully say so, could not be improved upon and we venture to adopt it in its entirety as a correct statement of the law which is to be applied in this case.

...

We therefore turn back to consider the direction which the learned judge gave in the present case to the jury and what was the suggested evidence that Becerra had withdrawn from the common agreement. The suggested evidence is the use by Becerra of the words 'Come on let's go,' coupled, as I said a few moments ago, with his act in going out through the window. The evidence, as the judge pointed out, was that Cooper never heard that nor did the third man. But let it be supposed that that was said and the jury took the view that it was said.

On the facts of this case, in the circumstances then prevailing, the knife having already been used and being contemplated for further use when it was handed over by Becerra to Cooper for the purpose of avoiding (if necessary) by violent means the hazards of identification, if Becerra wanted to withdraw at that stage, he would have to 'countermand,' to use the word that is used in some of the cases or 'repent' to use another word so used, in some manner vastly different and vastly more effective than merely to say 'Come on, let's go' and go out through the window.

It is not necessary, on this application, to decide whether the point of time had arrived at which the only way in which he could effectively withdraw, so as to free himself from joint responsibility for any act Cooper thereafter did in furtherance of the common design, would be physically to intervene so as to stop Cooper attacking Lewis, as the judge suggested, by interposing his own body between them or somehow getting in between them or whether some other action might suffice. That does not arise for decision here. Nor is it necessary to decide whether or not the learned judge was right or wrong, on the facts of this case, in that passage which appears at the bottom of p. 206, which Mr Owen criticised: 'and at least take all reasonable steps to prevent the commission of the crime which he had agreed the others should commit.' It is enough for the purposes of deciding this application to say that under the law of this country as it stands, and on the facts (taking them at their highest in favour of Becerra), that which was urged as amounting to withdrawal from the common design was not capable of amounting to such withdrawal. Accordingly Becerra remains responsible, in the eyes of the law, for everything that Cooper did and continued to do after Becerra's disappearance through the window as much as if he had done them himself.

Cooper being unquestionably guilty of murder, Becerra is equally guilty of murder. Mr Owen's careful argument must therefore be rejected and the application by Becerra for leave to appeal against conviction fails.

(a) Where there is 'spontaneous violence'

In *Beccera* the burglary was planned and the defendant had supplied the murder weapon (the knife). If violence breaks out spontaneously, on the other hand, should it be easier or more difficult to effect a withdrawal? In *R* v *Mitchell* [1999] Crim LR 496 the defendant and two others fought with the owner of a restaurant and two of his sons. The victim was left on the ground after being attacked by all three men who beat him with a stick, kicked him and stamped on his head. The defendant then left but there was evidence that one of the three men (X) had returned to continue beating the victim with a stick. The Court of Appeal quashed the defendant's conviction for murder and ordered a retrial on the basis that the judge's direction had not clearly left to the jury the possibility that the beating by X had caused the death and at that time the defendant had desisted from the attack. Communication of withdrawal was deemed not to be necessary. Commentators generally were of the opinion that this holding was too favourable to accessories and the issue has been reconsidered:

R v Robinson

Case No. 9903443Y3, 3 February 2000, Court of Appeal

The defendant and a group of youths followed the victim, taunting him. The group called on the defendant to hit the victim. He did so and the rest of the group then joined in the attack. During the attack, the defendant stood back but intervened when the attack was becoming more serious than he intended and the attack ceased.

Held, following *Becerra* that where violence was not spontaneous, communication of withdrawal was necessary.

OTTON LJ: There is a clear line of authority that where a party has given encouragement to others to commit an offence it cannot be withdrawn once the offence has commenced . . . it can only be in exceptional circumstances that a person can withdraw from a crime he has initiated. Similarly in those rare circumstances communication of withdrawal must be given in order to give the principal offenders the opportunity to desist rather than complete the crime. This must be so even in situations of spontaneous violence unless it is not practicable or reasonable so to communicate as in the exceptional circumstances pertaining in *Mitchell* where the accused threw down his weapon and moved away before the final and fatal blows were inflicted.

Appeal dismissed.

R v O'Flaherty
[2004] EWCA Crim 526, Court of Appeal

A course of spontaneous violence occurred between two groups. At place A there was an exchange of blows between the victim and the three appellants F, R and T, each of whom were respectively armed with a cricket bat, a bottle and a claw hammer. The victim was then pursued by other individuals. F followed to place B, where the deceased was on the ground surrounded and being attacked by a number of men. F advanced to within a few feet of the victim still armed with the cricket bat, which he did not use again and was the first to move away from the scene. R and T were not present at place B. The victim died, having sustained a head injury and stab wounds. The medical evidence at trial indicated that the head injury had not itself been fatal but was inconclusive as to whether the head injury could have been a contributory cause of death. The Crown therefore could not prove what had been the cause of death or where the fatal injury had been inflicted. The judge directed the jury to consider whether there had been one evolving incident or two; if two they had to be satisfied that the fatal injuries had been sustained when the joint enterprise was continuing and that each applicant had still been acting within the joint enterprise.

  Held:

  (i) that whilst a strict view of what in fact constituted withdrawal could be taken, the preclusion of withdrawal in any circumstances was not correct either in principle or as a matter of policy; that there was a distinction to be drawn between cases of grievous bodily harm, where it was the totality of the injuries which determined whether they were really serious, and murder, where an injury was, or was not, causative of death; that the question whether a person had done enough to demonstrate that he or she was withdrawing from the joint enterprise was ultimately a question of fact and degree for the jury (in that regard it was not necessary for reasonable steps to have been taken to prevent the crime); and that the question whether or not the violence formed one evolving incident or two was separate and discrete incidents was relevant in deciding whether a particular defendant had disengaged before the fatal injury or injuries were caused or had joined in after they had been caused. Accordingly, in the present case, the jury should have been directed that they had to be satisfied that the fatal injuries were sustained whilst the joint enterprise was continuing and that an appellant was still acting within that joint enterprise; the distinction between whether there had been one evolving event or two meant that the jury had not been directed in that way if they concluded that the incident was one evolving continuing event and, in that regard, the direction had been inappropriate.

  (ii) the fact that F had followed the group to place B, still armed with the cricket bat, provided an evidential foundation for the jury to conclude, if properly directed, that he was still within the joint enterprise; and that, notwithstanding the inadequacy of the direction, any reasonable jury would conclude from the fact that he was holding the cricket bat as the group attacked the victim that he was present and, at the very least, providing encouragement or prepared to lend support. Accordingly F's appeal would be dismissed.

(iii) In a case of spontaneous violence where there had been no prior agreement, a jury had to infer the scope of the agreement from the knowledge and actions of the individual participants; that there had been no evidence from which it could be inferred that the pursuit was part of any joint enterprise by R and T; and that there was no evidence that an injury causative of death was inflicted at place A. Accordingly, there had been no evidence concerning R and T to go before the jury and their appeals would be allowed.

■ NOTES AND QUESTIONS

1. As a matter of social policy, should the law allow a defence of withdrawal? What are the arguments for and against? Should a distinction be drawn between cases involving planned enterprises and 'spontaneous violence'? In *O'Flaherty* would it have made a difference if the gang thought that R and T were still with them, continuing to support them?

2. Should the reason for the withdrawal be relevant? Compare the case of the accessory who experiences a genuine change of heart because he appreciates the moral wrongfulness of his conduct with that of the accessory who experiences a change of mind because he observes police at the scene of the crime.

3. What more would Beccara have had to have done for his defence to succeed? Does there come a point where it is too late to withdraw? Had Beccara reached that point? Consider the case where G provides information to burglars regarding the premises to be burgled, including the location of alarms and what must be done to neutralise them. Before the burglary G has a change of heart, and announces that he no longer wishes to be involved. Is this sufficient to constitute a withdrawal? The rub is that by this point G is irrelevant as he has already provided all the help that the burglars need to succeed. See *Grundy* [1977] Crim LR 543.

4. If the law is to recognise a defence of withdrawal, what must an accessory do in order to be able to lay claim to it? Is it enough for the accessory to refrain from any further involvement in the criminal enterprise, or should he have to report the principal to the police or otherwise frustrate the accomplishment of the crime? The answer may depend on how far the criminal enterprise has progressed:

   (a) If all that the accessory has done is to encourage a crime, a verbal countermand of the former encouragement or instructions, or otherwise making clear that there has been a change of mind may be enough, but in *R v Rook* [1993] 1 WLR 1005 the Court of Appeal left this question open. Note, however, that the accessory may still be guilty of incitement.

   (b) If the crime is already well under way, then arguably the accessory should have to take steps, such as notifying the victim, or perhaps even the police, to prevent the crime's commission. However, in *R v Mitchell (Frank)* [1999] Crim LR 496 the Court of Appeal held that communication of withdrawal from a joint enterprise was necessary where the offence was one of premeditated violence but not where the violence was spontaneous. Is this ruling too favourable to the defendant?

5. Withdrawal, while it may affect one's liability as an accessory, will not affect one's liability for conspiracy or attempt (if the enterprise has gone beyond the stage of mere preparation). See Chapter 12.

(iii) Entrapment

What of the person who inveigles another into committing a crime for the purpose of seeing that other person arrested? A 'friend' tells you that there is a valuable painting inside a home and that the owners are away. The friend offers to stand guard while you enter the home and take the painting, if you will agree to split the proceeds of the sale with him. As soon as you are inside the home, however, the friend telephones the police, who arrive and arrest you. Under these circumstances, should you be entitled to a defence of entrapment?

R v Birtles

(1969) 53 Cr App R 469, Court of Appeal

The appellant pleaded guilty at West Riding Quarter Sessions in March 1969 to burglary and to carrying an imitation firearm with intent to commit burglary and was sentenced by the Chairman to consecutive terms of three years' and two years' imprisonment.

THE LORD CHIEF JUSTICE: . . . As I have said, no one will perhaps ever know the exact truth, but it certainly seems to this Court, doing the best that they can in the matter, that there is a real possibility here that the appellant was encouraged by the informer and indeed by the police officer concerned to carry out this raid on the post office. Whether or not he would have done it without that, again no one can say, but there is, as it seems to this Court, a real likelihood that he was encouraged to commit an offence which otherwise he would not have committed.

It is in those circumstances that this Court is asked to review this sentence. On that assumption, that he was so encouraged, the Court is quite satisfied that some reduction in sentence is required. Doing the best they can, bearing in mind not only this possible encouragement but at the same time the fact that the appellant had been minded to use a real firearm, this Court feels that the greatest reduction that they can make is to make these two sentences concurrent instead of consecutive, in other words, that the appellant in the circumstances shall serve three years' imprisonment.

Before leaving this case, the Court would like to say a word about the use which, as the cases coming before the Court reveal, is being made of informers. The Court of course recognises that, disagreeable as it may seem to some people, the police must be able in certain cases to make use of informers, and further—and this is really a corollary—that within certain limits such informers should be protected. At the same time, unless the use made of informers is kept within strict limits, grave injustice may result. In the first place, it is important that the Court of trial should not be misled. A good example of that occurred in the case of *R v Macro and Others*, again a raid on a sub-post office, which came before this Court on February 10 ([1969] Crim LR 205; *The Times*, February 11, 1969). There the charge was one of robbery with aggravation, with a man 'unknown.' In fact, the man 'unknown' was an informer who, together with the police, had warned the victim of what was going to take place, and had in fact gone through the pretence of tying up the victim while the police were concealed upon the premises. Now there the effect was that the appellant in that case pleaded Guilty to an offence which had never been committed. If the facts had been known, there could not have been a robbery at all, and accordingly it was for that reason that the Court substituted the only verdict apt on the facts which was open to it, namely, a verdict of larceny. There is, of course, no harm in not revealing the fact that there is an informer, but it is quite another thing to conceal facts which go to the quality of the offence.

Secondly, it is vitally important to ensure so far as possible that the informer does not create an offence, that is to say, incite others to commit an offence which those others would not otherwise have committed. It is one thing for the police to make use of information concerning an offence that is already laid on. In such a case the police are clearly entitled, indeed it is their duty, to mitigate the consequences of the proposed offence, for example, to protect the proposed victim, and to that end it may be perfectly proper for them to encourage the informer to take part in the offence or indeed for a police officer himself to do so. But it is quite another thing, and something of which this Court thoroughly disapproves, to use an informer to encourage another to commit an offence or indeed an offence of a more serious character, which he would not otherwise commit, still more so if the police themselves take part in carrying it out.

In the result, this appeal is allowed and the sentence reduced to one of three years.

Sentence reduced.

■ NOTES AND QUESTIONS

1. Should it matter whether the entrapper is a 'friend' or a police officer? Why? From the entrapped individual's perspective, is it not a matter of fortuity? See *R v Hardwicke* [2001] Crim LR 220 (entrapment by journalists).

2. The right to a fair trial under Article 6 of the European Convention on Human Rights may be implicated by the use of evidence obtained as a result of police entrapment. In *Teixeira de Castro* v *Portugal* (1999) 28 EHRR 101, the defendant had been induced by two undercover police officers to purchase illegal drugs on their behalf. The European Court of Human Rights found a violation of Article 6. The Court distinguished its prior decision in *Ludi* v *Switzerland* (1993) 15 EHRR 173, also involving a police officer posing as a purchaser of drugs, because the drugs deal was already under way.

3. Should it matter whether the entrapper plants the idea for the crime in the principal's head, or whether the principal conceives of the plan on his own, with the entrapper simply providing the principal with the means to carry through with it? Where the police create, rather than simply encourage, the commission of the offence, is there a stronger case for allowing a defence? Why? What purpose is served by freeing a defendant who has demonstrated a disposition to break the law when given the opportunity? Allen, *Textbook on Criminal Law*, 8th ed. (2005), pp. 221, suggests a distinction between:

   (a) those who merely observe the crime but play no part in the instigation of the offence, namely spies;

   (b) those decoys who accede to the accused's suggestions and thereby help provide the opportunity for the commission of the offence, namely collaborators;

   (c) those decoys who expose the accused to temptation and thereby facilitate the commission of the offence, namely temptors; and

   (d) those decoys who actively entice, encourage or persuade the accused to commit an offence which he would not otherwise commit, for the purpose of entrapping him, namely *agents provocateurs*.

Should the law attempt to discriminate between these categories? How so?

What of the entrapper? Is he guilty as an accessory?

R v Clarke
(1984) 80 Cr App R 344, Court of Appeal

MACPHERSON J: . . . On November 22, 1983, before Judge Gerber, Dennis Geoffrey Clarke was convicted by a jury of an offence of aiding and abetting burglary. He was absolutely discharged. He appeals against conviction by certificate of the trial judge who certified the case as fit for appeal on the ground that: 'I directed the jury with regard to count 2 as follows. The prosecution have to prove that: (a) Clarke knew the burglary was to be committed. (b) With that knowledge he volunteered and deliberately assisted Larch and Emery to carry it out. I further directed the jury that the fact that Clarke had prior to the date of the burglary given full information about it to a police officer was no defence to the charge set out in count 2.'

As we can see from the judgment upon counsels' submissions and the summing-up, the learned judge did in fact direct the jury to convict upon count 2 should they acquit (as they did) on count 1 of the indictment which the appellant faced . . .

Before the trial began it was known to all, because of what the appellant had said to the policeman who arrested him on June 3, 1984, that he, Clarke, would accept that he did indeed participate in the burglary. But he asserted that he took part solely in order to give information to a police sergeant named Eastwood with whom he had made contact, and with whom he had been involved since 1982 both as an accused man in another matter and as an informer. The appellant said that he had told Sergeant Eastwood about the proposed Muswell Hill burglary two or three weeks before it took place, and he said that not only had he kept Eastwood informed but that Eastwood knew that the appellant was going to take part in the burglary, and told the appellant to try to find out the full identity of Ross, the inside man. The appellant said that he had arranged a place for the storage of the stolen goods, but that this also was done so that he could tell Sergeant Eastwood where the goods were so that they would be recovered almost at once. The appellant was saying that he did not act 'in a criminal sense' (as the judge put it in his summing-up) but was involved solely to assist the police and to give Eastwood information. And he was saying that his intention was that the others should not get away with their crime, and that the stolen goods would be recovered so that their owner would not be deprived permanently of them.

. . . [T]he judge directed the jury to convict on count 2 even if they accepted the appellant's evidence that he was acting honestly and solely in order to betray his associates and ensure the recovery of the goods.

In the result the jury acquitted the appellant on count 1 [burglary] and convicted on count 2. The basis upon which the jury acquitted him on count 1 must have been that they were not sure that the appellant was acting dishonestly (because he intended to bring his confederates to justice), and/or that they were not sure that he intended permanently to deprive the owner of his goods.

Counsel for the Crown accepted in argument in this Court that it is a necessary consequence of his submissions that any person acting as the appellant did, whether he was a police officer or someone acting as an informer or on his behalf, is necessarily and in all circumstances guilty of aiding and abetting provided only that (a) the offence is complete (as of course the burglary was upon the instant facts) before steps are taken to bring those involved to justice, and (b) the accused aider and abettor in some way positively assisted in the carrying out of the offence, knowing all the circumstances . . . .

When a man says (as did the appellant) that he joined the team solely to betray the others involved and to defeat the long term retention by the team of the owner's goods, the question whether he did so and joined thus honestly into a 'laid on' offence or crime ought in our judgment to be at least a matter for the jury's decision in a case where it is appropriate for an aiding and abetting allegation or count to be considered at all.

Normally in an entrapment case the encouraging or entrapping policeman or informer will not have a defence, since they counsel or procure the commission of the offence by their encouragement. 'The fact that the counsellor and procurer is a policeman or police informer, although it may be of relevance in mitigation of penalty for the offence, cannot affect the guilt of the principal offender; both the physical element (*actus reus*) and the mental element (*mens rea*) of the offence with which he is charged are present in his case' (*R v Sang* (1979) 69 Cr App R 282, 286). Such cases, it should be noted, are properly cases of incitement or procurement to offend, and would properly be charged as such or as cases of counselling or procuring rather than aiding and abetting in any event.

The present case falls in our judgment within the compass of the *dicta* of Lord Parker CJ in the case of *R* v *Birtles* (1969) 53 Cr App R 469, 472–473....

In using the expression 'it may be perfectly proper' the Lord Chief Justice was, in our judgment, contemplating that in such exceptional cases where an informer (and/or a policeman) took part in a 'laid on' case there should be no finding that it was unlawful so to do. It would indeed be a rare case in which the facts would allow such a defence and in which a jury would say that a man might have been thus acting lawfully. But that there are such cases and that the jury should decide whether or not a case is within that exceptional and rare category is in our judgment both right and just. The learned judge should (if this had been a case in which the count of aiding and abetting remained alive at all) at least have left the matter to the jury....

Further, however, we are convinced that this was a case in which the alternative count should not have been added or finally pursued. As a matter of exact analysis the appellant could of course have been said to have aided and abetted the others involved, but in reality he was either a burglar and guilty as such as a primary offender or, in our judgment, he was to be acquitted. Doubtless the appellant Clarke was exceedingly fortunate to be acquitted on count 1 upon the evidence.... But the jury did acquit him, and it must have been upon the basis that his evidence may have been true. It would in our judgment be illogical that the appellant should be not guilty of count 1 (in which he accepted that he was fully involved but said that he acted honestly and lawfully within the confines of the Lord Chief Justice's statement in *Birtles*' case), but guilty upon count 2 of aiding and abetting. In our judgment he should be guilty or not guilty of count 1, the full offence, and should not have been made guilty by the artificial addition of count 2.

■ **NOTES AND QUESTIONS**

1. Does the entrapper have the *mens rea* of an accessory? On the one hand, the entrapper's objective is not to see a crime successfully committed but precisely the opposite. But in *Yip Chiu-Cheung* v *R* [1994] 3 WLR 514 (for facts and holding, see p. 566) the Privy Council held that the motive of a defendant who intended to traffic in heroin was irrelevant even where that motive was the detection of crime. On the other hand, the entrapper has encouraged or counselled, and in some cases aided, the commission of a crime that might not otherwise have taken place. Has the entrapper performed a public service, or is he a public nuisance?

2. Is the court in *Clarke* correct that it is illogical to acquit an entrapper of the substantive offence while convicting him of aiding and abetting? Do not the crimes require proof of different *mens rea*?

3. Should motive be relevant? What if the entrapper's motive is not to expose a would-be criminal but to gain private revenge? See *Wilson* v *People*, 103 Colo 441, 87 P 2d 5 (1939).

4. The Draft Criminal Code Bill 1989 would allow a defence for *agents provocateurs* who actually prevent the commission of a crime.

FURTHER READING

Wilson, *Criminal Law: Doctrine and Theory* (2010), Chapters 1–3

Ashworth, 'Redrawing the Boundaries of Entrapment' [2002] Criminal Law Review 161

Buxton, 'Joint Enterprise' [2009] Criminal Law Review 389

Clarkson, 'Complicity, *Powell* and Manslaughter' [1998] Criminal Law Review 556

Dennis, 'The Mental Element for Accessories' in P. Smith (ed.), *Criminal Law Essays in Honour of J.C. Smith* (1987)

Heydon, 'The Problems of Entrapment' [1973] Cambridge Law Journal 268

J.C. Smith, 'Criminal Liability of Accessories' (1997) 113 Law Quarterly Review 453

K.J.M. Smith, *A Modern Treatise on Complicity* (1991)

Spencer, 'Trying to Help Another Person Commit a Crime' in P. Smith (ed) *Criminal Law Essays in Honour of J.C. Smith* (1987)

Sullivan, 'The Law Commission Consultation Paper on Complicity: Fault Elements and Joint Enterprise' [1994] Criminal Law Review 252

Taylor, 'Complicity, Legal Scholarship and the Law of Unintended Consequences' (2009) Legal Studies 1

Wilson, *Central Issues in Criminal Theory* (2002) chapter 7

INDEX